Government by the People

22nd EDITION

DAVID B. MAGLEBY
Brigham Young University

DAVID M. O'BRIEN
University of Virginia

PAUL C. LIGHT
New York University

J.W. PELTASON
University of California

THOMAS E. CRONIN
Colorado College

PEARSON

Prentice
Hall

Upper Saddle River, New Jersey 07458

PRESIDENT: *Yolanda de Rooy*
EDITORIAL DIRECTOR: *Charlyce Jones Owen*
EXECUTIVE EDITOR: *Dickson Musslewhite*
DIRECTOR OF MARKETING: *Brandy Dawson*
MARKETING MANAGER: *Kate Mitchell*
VP, DIRECTOR OF PRODUCTION AND MANUFACTURING:
  Barbara Kittle
SENIOR MANAGING EDITOR: *Lisa Iarkowski*
PREPRESS AND MANUFACTURING MANAGER:
  Nick Sklitsis
PREPRESS AND MANUFACTURING BUYER:
  Mary Ann Gloriande
CREATIVE DESIGN DIRECTOR: *Leslie Osher*
ART DIRECTOR: *Nancy Wells*
INTERIOR AND COVER DESIGNER: *Michelle Wiggins*
IDIRECTOR, IMAGE RESOURCE CENTER:
  Melinda Patelli

MANAGER, VISUAL RESEARCH: *Beth Brenzel*
MANAGER, COVER VISUAL RESEARCH AND PERMISSIONS:
  Karen Sanatar
IMAGE PERMISSIONS COORDINATOR:
  Michelina Viscusi
PHOTO RESEARCHER: *Francelle Carapetyan,*
  Image Research Editorial Services
PRODUCTION EDITOR: *Dennis Troutman/*
  Stratford Publishing Services
PRODUCTION LIAISON: *Joe Scordato*
COMPOSITION: *Stratford Publishing Services*
PRINTER/BINDER: *R. R. Donnelley & Sons, Inc.*
COVER PRINTER: *Phoenix Color Corp.*
Cover Photo: NASA

Credits and acknowledgments borrowed from other sources and reproduced, with permission, in this textbook appear on appropriate page within text or, in the case of photographs, on p. C-1.

Pearson Education LTD.
Pearson Education Singapore, Pte. Ltd
Pearson Education, Canada, Ltd
Pearson Education—Japan

Pearson Education Australia PTY, Limited
Pearson Education North Asia Ltd
Pearson Educación de Mexico, S.A. de C.V.
Pearson Education Malaysia, Pte. Ltd

10 9 8 7 6 5 4
ISBN-13: 978-0-13-134682-6
ISBN-10: 0-13-134682-2

Brief Contents

Contents

A Message from the Authors

Government and politics matter. The decisions to go to war in Afghanistan and Iraq are but two examples. How we deal with other countries like North Korea and Iran are additional examples of government decisions and policies that have broad implications. Americans understand that the world is a more dangerous place because of terrorism, and that global perceptions towards the United States have been adversely impacted by our response to terrorism.

The attacks of September 11, 2001, changed the agenda of American politics. Homeland security became a much higher priority as did bringing to justice those who were in any way involved in the 9-11 attacks. President Bush and his political team skillfully exploited the security issues in the 2002 and 2004 elections, and in the months before the 2006 election promised to do so again. In 2006, however, Bush and the Republicans faced a different environment because of doubts about the Iraq and Afghanistan wars, the failure of the United States to capture or kill Osama bin Laden, and more generally the standing of the United States in the world. And security concerns continue to arise whether because of bombings on buses or subways in London, or threats directed against trans-Atlantic air travel and trains in European countries.

The law matters. One of the points we make in this book is that citizenship is often taken for granted by some Americans, in part because it comes with birth for many. The debate on illegal immigration again underscores the importance of government because it is within the powers of government to define the requirements for citizenship or legal status for aliens. Under some proposed legislation, illegal immigrants would have to leave the country and possibly would not be able to return. Other proposals call for enhanced border security and enforcement. An inter-

esting alliance of the business community, some Democrats, President Bush, and some Republicans favors policies that would allow most immigrants now here to stay and work legally.

Elections matter. A lot was at stake in the 2006 election. Beyond the one-third of all U.S. Senate seats, all 435 House seats, and most governorships, there were hundreds of other choices voters made in candidate contests and ballot referendums. Most of the focus in 2006 was on congressional contests, where the Republicans held a narrow majority in the House and a somewhat safer majority in the Senate. But mid-term elections like 2006 can be referendums on the sitting president, a theme the Democrats tried to encourage given President Bush's very low job approval ratings. Republicans emphasized candidate choice in the individual races, and in some key races the candidates distanced themselves from President Bush and his administration. Evidence that elections matter was shown in the intensity of the campaign from candidates, party committees, and outside interest groups. The change in party control in both houses of congress brought with it a very different political environment for President Bush in the last two years of his administration. Not only does he face Democratic committee chairs, but those committees will likely launch multiple congressional investigations of his administration. Congressional investigations of the Bush administration have been a rarity between 2001 and 2007.

As we show in this text, government matters in such areas as the economy, educational opportunity, and public health. One of the lessons from the government's poor response to Hurricane Katrina in 2005 is that in such times we all depend to a great degree on government to provide safety and security. Without that security, we face a world of anarchy. While government can fail, as it did in its response to Katrina, it can

also succeed. One of government's greatest achievements was the NASA space program and our placing of astronauts on the moon. We selected a photo from this historic space mission for our cover to underscore that government can achieve much that is important. We repeat this theme in every chapter with less visible but still consequential examples of achievements government has made. Many of these achievements have come through the efforts of individuals, a fact that underscores the important role citizens play in a constitutional democracy. In every chapter we also highlight such history makers as role models for future history makers.

We title this book *Government by the People* because we want to emphasize the important role people play in our constitutional democracy. Understanding American politics and government must include an appreciation of the people, their similarities and differences, their beliefs and attitudes, and their behaviors. A foundation of that understanding of the people is our chapter on the American political landscape in which we examine such aspects of our population as race, ethnicity, gender, age, religion, income, and region. Our country is diverse and that diversity is important politically. We repeat this theme in every chapter by highlighting in a box the changing face of American politics and what these changes mean for us today.

The study of American government should be engaging, relevant, and rigorous. As authors of this book, we see politics and government as topics worthy of careful study. Constitutional democracy—the kind we have in the United States—is exceedingly hard to achieve, equally hard to sustain, and often hard to understand. Our political history has been an evolution toward an enlarged role for citizens and voters. Citizens have more rights and political opportunities in 2007 and 2008 than they had in 1800 or 1900. The framers of our

Constitution warned that we must be vigilant in safeguarding our rights, liberties, and political institutions. But to do this, we must first understand these institutions and the forces that have shaped them.

We want you to come away from reading this book with a richer understanding of American politics, government, and the job of politicians. We hope you will participate actively in making this constitutional democracy more vital and responsive to the urgent problems of the twenty-first century.

Reviewers

The writing of this book has profited from the informed, professional, and often critical suggestions of our colleagues around the country. This and previous editions have been considerably improved as a result of reviews by the following individuals, for which we thank them all:

Scott Adler, *University of Colorado*
Wayne Ault, *Southwestern Illinois College–Belleville*
Paul Babbitt, *Southern Arkansas University*
Thomas Baldino, *Wilkes University*
Barry Balleck, *Georgia Southern University*
Robert Ballinger, *South Texas College*
Jodi Balma, *Fullerton College*
Jeff Berry, *South Texas College*
Cynthia Carter, *Florida Community College–Jacksonville, North Campus*
Leonard Champney, *University of Scranton*
Mark Cichock, *University of Texas at Arlington*
Ann Clemmer, *University of Arkansas, Little Rock*
Alison Dagnes, *Shippensburg University*
Paul Davis, *Truckee Meadows Community College*
Ron Deaton, *Prince George's Community College*
Robert DeLuna, *St. Philips College*
Anthony Di Giacomo, *Wilmington College*
Richardson Dilworth, *Drexel University*
Rick Donohoe, *Napa Valley College*
Art English, *University of Arkansas, Little Rock*
Alan Fisher, *CSU–Dominguez Hills*
Bruce Franklin, *Cossatot Community College of the University of Arkansas*
Eileen Gage, *Central Florida Community College*
Richard Glenn, *Millersville University*
David Goldberg, *College of DuPage*
Nicholas Gonzalez, *Yuen DeAnza College*
Charles Grapski, *University of Florida*
Billy Hathorn, *Laredo Community College*
Dr. Max Hilaire, *Morgan State University*
James Hoefler, *Dickinson College*
Justin Hoggard, *Three Rivers Community College*
Gilbert Kahn, *Kean University*
Rogan Kersh, *Syracuse University*
Todd Kunioka, *CSU–Los Angeles*
La Della Levy, *Foothill College*
Jim Lennertz, *Lafayette College*
John Liscano, *Napa Valley College*
Amy Lovecraft, *University of Alaska–Fairbanks*
Howard Lubert, *James Madison University*

Michael McConachie, *Collin County Community College*
Lowell Markey, *Allegany College of MD*
Larry Martinez, *CSU–Long Beach*
Toni Marzotto, *Towson University*
Brian Newman, *Pepperdine University*
Adam Newmark, *Appalachian State University*
Randall Newnham, *Penn State University–Berks*
Keith Nicholls, *University of South Alabama*
Sean Nicholson-Crotty, *University of Missouri–Columbia*
Richard Pacelle, *Georgia Southern University*
William Parente, *University of Scranton*
Ryan Peterson, *College of the Redwoods*
Robert Rigney, *Valencia Community College–Osceola Campus*
Bren Romney, *Vernon College*
Jack Ruebensaal, *West Los Angeles College*
Bhim Sandhu, *West Chester University*
Gib Sansing, *Drexel University*
Colleen Shogan, *George Mason University*
Tom Simpson, *Missouri Southern*
Linda Simmons, *Northern Virginia Community College–Manassas Campus*
Dan Smith, *Northwest Missouri State University*
Jay Stevens, *CSU–Long Beach*
Lawrence Sullivan, *Adelphi University*
Halper Thomas, *CUNY–Baruch*
Jose Vadi, *CSU–Pomona*
Avery Ward, *Harford Community College*
Shirley Warshaw, *Gettysburg University*
Ife Williams, *Delaware County Community College*
Margie Williams, *James Madison University*
Christy Woodward-Kaupert, *San Antonio College*
Chris Wright, *University of Arkansas–Monticello*

Acknowledgments

This book builds on a long tradition of clear and accessible writing, good scholarship, and currency. James MacGregor Burns and Jack Peltason, the founding authors of the book, and Tom Cronin, who later joined them, set a high standard in these areas. As additional authors have joined the book we have worked hard to maintain this legacy while at the same time extensively revising each new edition. Writing the book requires teamwork—first among the coauthors who converse often about the broad themes, features, and focus of the book and who read and rewrite each others drafts; then with our research assistants, who track down loose ends and give us the perspective of current students; and finally with the editors and other professionals at Prentice Hall. Important to each revision are the detailed reviews by teachers and researchers, who provide concrete suggestions on how to improve the book. Our revision of the chapters on state and local government especially benefited from the input of Thomas Gais and Nick Jenny, both of the State University of New York. We are grateful to all who helped with this edition.

Research assistants for the current edition of *Government by the People* are Aaron M. Anderson, David Lassen, Virginia Maynes, Emily McClintock, Lindsay Nielson, David Trichler, Paul V. Russell, and Brandon Wilson at Brigham Young University.

Books for major college courses like this feature state-of-the-art teaching and learning tools. Web-based items for students and instructors are some examples of these ancillaries. We welcome your feedback on the book and any of the ancillaries.

We gratefully acknowledge the professionalism, energy, and commitment of Political Science Editor Dickson Musslewhite. Jennifer Murphy, Dickson's assistant was also attentive and helpful. Others at Prentice Hall we wish to thank for their continued support are Yolanda de Rooy and Charlyce Jones Owen.

Many skilled professionals were important to the publication of this book. They include Dennis Troutman for production, Jessee Carter for page layout, Francelle Carapetyan for photo research, Mirella Signoretto for line art creation, Michelle Wiggins and Nancy Wells for cover design and design supervision, and Betty Gatewood and Gerald Lombardi for text development.

We also want to thank you, the professors and students who use our book, and who send us letters and email messages with suggestions for improving *Government by the People*. Please write us in care of the Political Science Editor at Prentice Hall, 1 Lake Street, Upper Saddle River, New Jersey 07458, or contact us directly:

David B. Magleby Distinguished Professor of Political Science and Dean of FHSS, Brigham Young University, Provo, UT 84602 david_magleby@byu.edu

David M. O'Brien Leone Reaves and George W. Spicer Professor, Department of Government and Foreign Affairs, University of Virginia, Charlottesville, VA 22903 dmo2y@virginia.edu

Paul C. Light Paulette Goddard Professor of Public Service at New York University and Douglas Dillon Senior Fellow at the Brookings Institution pcl226@nyu.edu

J. W. Peltason School of Social Sciences, University of California, Irvine, CA 92717-5700 jwpeltas@uci.edu

Thomas E. Cronin McHugh Professor of American Institutions and Leadership, Colorado College, Department of Political Science, 14 E. Cache La Poudre, Colorado Springs, CO 80903

Read by
over a **million students,**
informed by the latest
research...

Grounded in the most authoritative scholarship available, ***Government by the People*** is a complete introduction to American politics and the discipline of political science. It is built around a simple goal—to make students effective and enthusiastic participants in our political culture.

Government's Greatest Endeavors
Reducing Workplace Discrimination

The United States has one of the most diverse workforces in the world. As diversity has grown, so have calls for protection against workplace discrimination. Most of these calls have been answered by the federal judiciary, where women, older Americans, and the disabled have won a series of victories assuring their basic rights.

Many of these victories involved the 1964 Civil Rights Act, the 1967 Age Discrimination Act, and the 1990 Americans with Disabilities Act. Together, these three acts have created protections that have made reducing workplace discrimination one of the federal government's greatest achievements.

The 1964 Civil Rights Act was particularly important for guaranteeing equal rights for women. Under the original bill, women were not included in the law. Ironically, it was a conserva-

tive Democrat who added the word "sex" to the prohibition against discrimination on the basis of "race, color, religion, or national origin" in the act. He did so in the belief that Congress would not pass a bill guaranteeing equality of the sexes. However, the bill did pass, and women had the legislation that would provide the opportunity to take employers to court for sex discrimination.

Disabled Americans won similar protection under the 1990 Americans with Disabilities Act. The fight for passage was led by Senator Bob Dole (R-Kans.), who had lost the use of his right arm in World War II. In 1998, the Supreme Court ruled that people with HIV/AIDS were protected against discrimination under the law, demonstrating the important link between such laws and eventual judicial action in assuring basic rights.

MARTA (Metropolitan Atlanta Rapid Transit Authority) allows disabled citizens access to Atlanta's mass transit system.

QUESTIONS
Have you ever experienced workplace discrimination, and, if so, how was it resolved?

What new forms of workplace discrimination need action?

minorities, they cannot find well-paying jobs. Without such jobs, they often cannot afford to live in nicer neighborhoods with decent housing. And because of their location in less desirable communities, good educational systems are less likely to be available.[61]

In 1948, the Supreme Court made racial or religious **restrictive covenants** (a provision in a deed to real property that restricts to whom it can be sold) legally unenforceable.[62] The 1968 Fair Housing Act forbids discrimination in housing, excluding from its protection what it called "Mrs. Murphy boardinghouses," housing owned by private individuals who own no more than three houses; dwellings that have no more than four separate living units in which the owner maintains a residence; and religious organizations and private clubs housing their own members on a noncommercial basis. The act forbids owners of all other housing to refuse to sell or rent to any person because of race, color, religion, national origin, sex, or physical handicap or because a person has children. Discrimination in housing also covers efforts to deny loans to minorities.

The Department of Justice has filed hundreds of cases, especially those involving large apartment complexes, yet African Americans and Hispanics still face discrimination in housing. Some real estate agents steer African Americans and Hispanics toward neighborhoods that are not predominantly white and require minority renters to pay larger deposits than white renters. Yet those affected complain about less than 1 percent of these actions because the discrimination is so subtle that victims are often

restrictive covenant
A provision in a deed to real property prohibiting its sale to a person of a particular race or religion. Judicial enforcement of such deeds is unconstitutional.

ABCNEWS Video Case Study
Part One – Constitutional Principles

KATRINA RANKS AS THE COUNTRY'S MOST EXPENSIVE NATURAL disaster and one of the

**Moment of Crisis—
System Failure**

ORIGINALLY AIRED: 9/15/05
PROGRAM: Primetime
RUNNING TIME: 29:12

deadliest in U.S. history. It has killed more than 700 people, uprooted tens of thousands of families, destroyed countless homes, and forced the evacuating of a major American city. Two and a half weeks after the hurricane roared ashore, just east of New Orleans, the country is trying to make sense of the resulting failures of local, state, and federal government. On this program, ABC News will piece together what we know and where the breakdowns occurred.

Born as a garden-variety tropical depression, Katrina grew into a tropical storm and officially earned hurricane status on August 24, 2005. It initially made landfall north of Miami, causing serious flooding and eleven deaths. But only when it marched across the Florida peninsula and hit the warm waters of the Gulf of Mexico did Katrina rapidly intensify and unleash its full fury. And as it evolved into a monster storm, The National Hurricane Center issued pointed warnings to the target communities along the Gulf Coast. The director made phone calls to key officials, including the mayor of New Orleans, saying Katrina could be "the big one" officials had long feared. Simultaneously, weather service bulletins were issued with unusually apocalyptic language. One predicted a storm of "unprecedented strength," "the area will be uninhabitable for weeks," and went on to predict human suffering "incredible by modern standards."

Given the dire warnings, should the deaths and suffering throughout the Gulf region have been as great? Were the recommendations issued by the 9/11 Commission put into practice?

Ted Koppel hosts a Primetime special edition, "Moment of Crisis: System Failure," a moment-by-moment chronology of what went so terribly wrong in the horrific days following Katrina's strike on the Gulf Coast. This was America's first major test of emergency response since 9/11; a test that has received failing grades.

Critical Thinking Questions

After viewing "MOMENT OF CRISIS—SYSTEM FAILURE" on your ABCNEWS DVD answer the following questions.

STATE AND LOCAL OFFICIALS blame federal officials for the grossly inadequate response to the natural disaster, and federal officials blame state and local officials. What are the responsibilities of the federal government, particularly agencies such as FEMA and the Department of Homeland Security, in regard to both natural and man-made disasters? What are the responsibilities of state and local governments?

HOW MUCH OF A ROLE DID POVERTY play in the aftermath of Hurricane Katrina? Do you have the impression from viewing the program that race had any impact on the way the federal government responded to the crisis?

3. COULD THIS DISASTER BEEN AVERTED simply by reinforcing New Orleans' levee system years ago as a preventive measure? Does the federal government have an obligation to maintain and update the infrastructure in places such as New Orleans, or is this the responsibility of state and local governments?

4. DOES THE CONSTITUTION PROVIDE ANY guidance on whether the response to disasters such as Hurricane Katrina should be orchestrated at the federal level or at the state and local levels?

5. IN LIGHT OF THE RESPONSE TO Hurricane Katrina, what can be said about American federalism both in theory and in practice? Would a stronger federal government have been better equipped to deal with the crisis, or was the

inadequate response an isolated case of mismanagement that does not reflect upon the basic structure of the U.S. government?

xvi

With unique features like the **ABC VIDEO case studies** that open every part, *Government by the People* intellectually engages students in the institutions, actors, and processes of American politics by exploring its real world implications.

Invites critical thinking and connects to real world issues...

NEW! ABC NEWS Video Case Studies Fully integrated into *Government by the People*. Students are raised in a media-rich world, but until now their American Government books have not provided the means, the methods, or the vocabulary for understanding the information about government that nightly fills their television screens. Featuring the latest news clips from ABC News programs and a rich set of critical thinking questions, ABC News will get your students excited and informed about our political culture.

Government's Greatest Endeavors

Increasing Access to Education

QUESTIONS

How has the federal government helped you go to college?

Have federal loans had any impact on your tuition?

In 1944, the GI Bill began assisting veterans to attend college.

The framers believed an educated public was essential to a strong government. As Thomas Jefferson wrote late in his life, "I know no safe depository of the ultimate powers of the society but the people themselves; and if we think them not enlightened enough to exercise their control with a wholesome discretion, the remedy is not to take it from them, but to inform their discretion by education."

For most of American history, however, the federal government left college education to individuals and the states. Although federal officials understood that an educated public was essential to economic growth, the federal government did not become involved in providing access to college until World War II. With more than 15 million soldiers about to return home in search of jobs and opportunity, Congress passed the Servicemen's Readjustment Act of 1944, popularly known as the "GI Bill." This bill provided grants for college and other benefits to war veterans.

The federal government did not become involved in helping students from low-income families go to college until the late 1950s, however. Convinced that the nation desperately needed more scientists and engineers to fight the cold war with the Soviet Union, Congress passed the National Defense Education Act of 1958. The act provided government funding for students pursuing degrees in technical fields or the modern languages, which were considered essential for building weapons and collecting intelligence.

In 1992, Congress approved the Higher Education Act, which allows students at any income level to obtain a federally guaranteed college loan. The following year, Congress passed the Budget Reconciliation Act, an omnibus bill that included provisions for the Federal Direct Student Loan program. The new plan allowed students to borrow money for college directly from the government rather than from banks. Under these and other programs, millions of college students have been able to finance their college education. ∎

NEW! Government's Greatest Endeavors. Highlights government's attempts to solve big problems such as poverty among the elderly, discrimination, and nuclear arms control, and its successes.

Compelling features engage and ignite student interest in learning…

Agents of Change

Elizabeth Martin and WomensLaw

Elizabeth Martin

WomensLaw was founded in 2000 by a group of lawyers, teachers, activists, and Web designers to use the power of the Internet to help survivors of domestic violence. Convinced that women do not have enough information to protect their civil rights, WomensLaw provides basic information and resources to women living with or trying to escape domestic violence. The organization provides state-by-state information on laws against domestic violence for advocates of change, and it helps victims of abuse by guiding them to help in their own communities.

WomensLaw was created by Elizabeth Martin, who graduated from Duke University and received her law degree from the University of North Carolina. Before starting WomensLaw, she worked as a legal services attorney in Asheville, North Carolina, and as a volunteer attorney in domestic violence cases. She also serves on a number of boards of domestic violence organizations, and has worked to build coalitions within the domestic violence community. She has been instrumental in building the organization, and recently moved to New York City to work with the Blue Ridge Foundation, which provides basic support to young organizations.

WomensLaw has already helped thousands of women find help even though, as the WomensLaw Web site says, "We cannot give you legal advice." However, with more than 20,000 visits to its Web site each month, the information the site provides appears to be getting through. ∎

Learn more about WomensLaw at www.womenslaw.org.

QUESTIONS

Why is WomensLaw an important addition to the many organizations that work to reduce domestic violence?

Why do women need its help?

NEW! Agents of Change. Features young Americans who are trying to change their communities, country, and even world through social action.

History Makers

Martin Luther King Jr.

Martin Luther King Jr. was born January 25, 1929, in Atlanta, Georgia. After graduating from high school, he entered Morehouse College in 1944 and majored in sociology, but in his junior year, he decided to enter the ministry. After Morehouse, King entered the Crozer Theological Seminary in Pennsylvania. There he became a follower of the Indian pacifist Mohandas Gandhi. Following graduation, King earned a doctorate from Boston University in 1955. He then became pastor of the Dexter Avenue Baptist Church in Montgomery, Alabama.

In 1957, King and another Baptist minister, Ralph Abernathy, founded the Southern Christian Leadership Conference to advance the cause of civil rights. In that year, King's home and church were bombed and violence against black protesters began to escalate. In March 1963, King was jailed in Birmingham, Alabama, for leading a protest parade without a permit. Subsequently, he led the March on Washington, on August 28, 1963, at which hundreds of thousands of civil rights activists focused national attention on the racial problems in the country. The march built support for the passage of the Civil Rights Act of 1964.

Speaking at the march from the steps of the Lincoln Memorial, King delivered his famous "I Have A Dream" speech, in which he said he dreamed of the day when "my four little children . . . will not be judged by the color of their skin but by the content of their character," and concluded with the memorable line, "Free at last! Thank God Almighty, we are free at last!"

In 1963, King became *Time* magazine's Man of the Year, and in 1964, he was awarded the Nobel Peace Prize for his leadership in the civil rights movement and advocacy of nonviolent protest. In 1968, King was assassinated, and riots erupted in more than 100 cities. ∎

Martin Luther King Jr.

NEW! History Makers. Biographical sketches that spotlight specific individuals who have contributed to American politics in enduring ways and provides recognizable and tangible examples of the influence of the many principles and theories discussed in the text.

How Other Nations Govern. How Other Nations Govern examines foreign political structures and processes, and how these similar and/or differing approaches can affect—and be affected by—American politics.

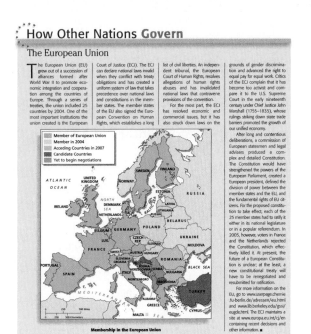

How Other Nations Govern

The European Union

The European Union (EU) grew out of a succession of alliances formed after World War II to promote economic integration and cooperation among the countries of Europe. Through a series of treaties, the union included 25 countries by 2004. One of the most important institutions the union created is the European Court of Justice (ECJ). The ECJ can declare national laws invalid when they conflict with treaty obligations and has created a uniform system of law that takes precedence over national laws and constitutions in the member states. The member states of the EU also signed the European Convention on Human Rights, which establishes a long list of civil liberties. An independent tribunal, the European Court of Human Rights, resolves allegations of human rights abuses and has invalidated national laws that contravene provisions of the convention.

For the most part, the ECJ has resolved economic and commercial issues, but it has also struck down laws on the grounds of gender discrimination and advanced the right to equal pay for equal work. Critics of the ECJ complain that it has become too activist and compare it to the U.S. Supreme Court in the early nineteenth century under Chief Justice John Marshall (1755–1835), whose rulings striking down state trade barriers promoted the growth of our unified economy.

After long and contentious deliberations, a commission of European statesmen and legal advisers produced a complex and detailed Constitution. The Constitution would have strengthened the powers of the European Parliament, created a European president, defined the division of power between the member states and the EU, and the fundamental rights of EU citizens. For the proposed constitution to take effect, each of the 25 member states had to ratify it either in its national legislature or in a popular referendum. In 2005, however, voters in France and the Netherlands rejected the Constitution, which effectively killed it. At present, the future of a European Constitution is unclear; at the least, a new constitutional treaty will have to be renegotiated and resubmitted for ratification.

For more information on the EU, go to www.userpage.chemie.fu-berlin.for/adressen/eu.html and www.lib.berkeley.edu/gssi/eugde.html. The ECJ maintains a site at www.europa.eu.int/cj/en containing recent decisions and other information. ■

Membership in the European Union

Member of European Union
Member in 2004
Acceding Countries in 2007
Candidate Countries
Yet to begin negotiations

---

496 | **PART FOUR** Rights and Liberties

CHAPTER 17 Equal Rights Under the Law | 497

The Changing Face of American Politics

Racial and Ethnic Identification

1860	1870	1880	1890	1900	1910	1920	1930	1940	1950
White	White	White	White	White	White	White	White	White	White
Black	Black	Black	Black	Black	Black	Black	Black	Black	**Negro**
Mulatto	Mulatto	Mulatto	Mulatto	Mulatto	Mulatto	Mulatto			
		Chinese	Chinese	Chinese	Chinese	Chinese	Chinese	Chinese	Chinese
		Indian	Indian	Indian	Indian	Indian	Indian	Indian	American Indian
			Quadroon						
			Octoroon						
			Japanese	Japanese	Japanese	Japanese	Japanese	Japanese	Japanese
					Filipino	Filipino	Filipino	Filipino	Filipino
					Hindu	Hindu	Hindu		
					Korean	Korean	Korean		
							Mexican		
					Other	Other	Other	Other	Other

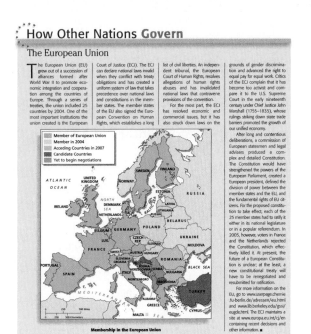

Since 1860, the U.S. census has changed its classifications of race and ethnicity several times to reflect the nation's growing diversity and political developments. The classifications continue to provoke controversy. For example, in 1975, an ad hoc government committee picked the classification "Hispanic" over "Latino" to identify Spanish-speaking individuals. It chose the term because "Hispanic" connotes the cultural diaspora of centuries-old conquests by Spain in Mexico, Central America, and South America. In recent years "Latino" has become a more popular term because it refers to the Latin-based Romance languages of Spain, France, Italy, and Portugal, as well as to Portuguese-speaking Brazilians. But many still prefer "Hispanic" because it connotes a history of colonialism and does not include the French and Italians.*

Below are the categories used in the decennial counts from 1860 to 2000. Each new category is boldfaced at its first inclusion. ■

Tiger Woods, the prize-winning golfer, is proud of his diverse heritage. He is both African American and Asian (Thai). He feels that ethnic background should not make a difference. It doesn't to him. As Woods says, "I am an American and proud of it."

*Darly Fears, "The Roots of 'Hispanic,'" The Washington Post, October 15, 2003, p. A21.

1960	1970	1980	1990	2000
White	White	White	White	White
Negro	Negro/Black	Black/Negro	Black/Negro	Black/**African American**/Negro
Chinese	Chinese	Chinese	Chinese	Chinese
American Indian	American Indian	Indian	Indian	**American Indian or Alaska Native**
Japanese	Japanese	Japanese	Japanese	Japanese
Filipino	Filipino	Filipino	Filipino	Filipino
		Asian Indian	Asian Indian	Asian Indian
	Korean	Korean	Korean	Korean
Aleut		Aleut	Aleut	
Eskimo		Eskimo	Eskimo	
Hawaiian	Hawaiian	Hawaiian	Hawaiian	**Native Hawaiian**
Part Hawaiian				
		Vietnamese	Vietnamese	Vietnamese
		Guamanian	Guamanian	Guamanian or **Chamorro**
		Samoan	Samoan	Samoan
			Other Asian	Other Asian
			Pacific Islander	Pacific Islander
Other	Other	Other	**Other race**	**Some other race**
Ethnicity	Mexican	**Mexican American**	Mexican/Mexican American	Mexican/Mexican American
		Chicano	Chicano	Chicano
Puerto Rican	Puerto Rican	Puerto Rican	Puerto Rican	Puerto Rican
Central/South American				
Cuban	Cuban	Cuban	Cuban	Cuban
Other Spanish	Other Spanish/Hispanic	Other Spanish/Hispanic	Other Spanish/Hispanic	Other Spanish/Hispanic/**Latino**
(None of these)	**Not Spanish**/Hispanic	Not Spanish/Hispanic	Not Spanish/Hispanic	Not Spanish/Hispanic/Latino

---

own internal affairs, subject to congressional supervision. States cannot regulate or tax the tribes or extend the jurisdiction of their courts over them unless Congress authorizes the states to do so.[22] In recent years, Congress has stepped in to mediate growing tensions between Indian tribes who have used their sovereignty over reservations to operate gambling casinos and the states in which these reservations are located.

By acts of Congress, Native Americans are citizens of the United States and of the states in which they live. They have the right to vote. Native Americans living off reservations and working in the general community pay taxes just like everyone else; off reservations they have the same rights as any other Americans. If they are enrolled members of a recognized tribe, they are entitled to certain benefits created by law and by treaty. The Bureau of Indian Affairs of the Department of the Interior administers these benefits.

During the period of assimilation that began in 1887 and lasted until 1934, tribal governments were weak, some reservations were dissolved, and the federal government severed its governing relationship with more than 100 tribes.[23] The civil rights movement of the 1960s created a more favorable climate for Native Americans. Their goals were to reassert treaty rights and secure greater autonomy for the tribes. Under the leadership of the Native American Rights Fund (NARF), more Indian law cases were brought in the past several decades than at any time in our history.[24]

As a result of these efforts and of a greater national consciousness to minorities, most Americans are now aware that many Native Americans live in poverty. Native Americans "are in far worse health than the rest of the population, dying earlier and suffering disproportionately from alcoholism, accidents, diabetes, and pneumonia."[25] Although in recent years the rest of the United States has enjoyed about 4 percent unemployment, many reservations continue to experience 50 to 60 percent unemployment. Some reservations lack adequate health care facilities, schools, decent housing, and jobs. Congress has started to compensate Native Americans for past injustices and to provide more opportunities to develop tribal economic independence, and judges are showing greater vigilance in enforcing Indian treaty rights.

In 1986, Ben Nighthorse Campbell, a Colorado Democrat, became the first Native American to be elected to Congress. He later became a Republican after being elected to the Senate in 1992; he retired in 2005.

Changing Face of American Politics. Explores the impact of the ever-increasing level of diversity in the American political landscape, including how race and gender are changing the way the American government works. These unique boxes are designed to reflect the concerns and experiences of ethnic and minority groups in American politics.

NEW!
MyPoliSciLab

PRENTICE HALL
mypoliscilab™
Where participation leads to action!

An easy-to-use online resource that enables students to diagnose their progress by completing an online self-assessment test. Based on the results of this test, each student is provided with a customized study plan, including a variety of tools to help them fully master the material. MyPoliSciLab offers the major resources, including Make It Real online resources and ABC NEWS video clips, in one convenient location. www.mypoliscilab.com

High School adopters should receive registration information with their text purchase. For directions go to PHSchool.com/advanced or contact your local representative.

Your instructor resources...

Government by the People is accompanied by an extensive supplements package that delivers classroom support in a variety of media.

A comprehensive Instructor's Resource Manual offers recent news and pop culture examples, discussion topics, activities, and assignments, and a list of related Internet activities for students all correlated to related content in each chapter.

The Faculty Resource CD-ROM contains PowerPoint presentations including a Lecture presentation that covers each chapter in detail, a Special Topic presentation for each chapter, and a Graphics presentation that includes all of the chapter's graphs, charts, and illustrations. It also includes the Test Item File and Instructor's Manual.

First Amendment Rights

In what way can First Amendment rights be considered "preferred freedoms"?

First Amendment Rights: Freedom of Speech

Free speech laws must balance individual liberties and societal interests

KATRINA RANKS AS THE COUNTRY'S MOST EXPENSIVE NATURAL

Moment of Crisis— System Failure

—————

ORIGINALLY AIRED: 9/15/05

PROGRAM: **Primetime**

RUNNING TIME: 29:12

—————

disaster and one of the deadliest in U.S. history. It has killed more than 700 people, uprooted tens of thousands of families, destroyed countless homes, and forced the evacuating of a major American city. Two and a half weeks after the hurricane roared ashore, just east of New Orleans, the country is trying to make sense of the resulting failures of local, state, and federal government. On this program, ABC News will piece together what we know and where the breakdowns occurred.

Born as a garden-variety tropical depression, Katrina grew into a tropical storm and officially earned hurricane status on August 24, 2005. It initially made landfall north of Miami, causing serious flooding and eleven deaths. But only when it marched across the Florida peninsula and hit the warm waters of the Gulf of Mexico did Katrina rapidly intensify and unleash its full fury. And as it evolved into a monster storm, The National Hurricane Center issued pointed warnings to the target communities along the Gulf Coast. The director made phone calls to key officials, including the mayor of New Orleans, saying Katrina could be "the big one" officials had long feared. Simultaneously, weather service bulletins were issued with unusually apocalyptic language. One predicted a storm of "unprecedented strength," "the area will be uninhabitable for weeks," and went on to predict human suffering "incredible by modern standards."

Given the dire warnings, should the deaths and suffering throughout the Gulf region have been as great? Were the recommendations issued by the 9/11 Commission put into practice?

Ted Koppel hosts a Primetime special edition, "Moment of Crisis: System Failure," a moment-by-moment chronology of what went so terribly wrong in the horrific days following Katrina's strike on the Gulf Coast. This was America's first major test of emergency response since 9/11; a test that has received failing grades.

Critical Thinking Questions

After viewing "MOMENT OF CRISIS—SYSTEM FAILURE" *on your* ABCNEWS DVD *answer the following questions.*

1. STATE AND LOCAL OFFICIALS blame federal officials for the grossly inadequate response to this natural disaster, and federal officials blame state and local officials. What are the responsibilities of the federal government, particularly agencies such as FEMA and the Department of Homeland Security, in regard to both natural and man-made disasters? What are the responsibilities of state and local governments?

2. HOW MUCH OF A ROLE DID POVERTY play in the tragic aftermath of Hurricane Katrina? Do you get the impression from viewing the program that race had any impact on the way the federal government responded to the crisis?

3. COULD THIS DISASTER BEEN AVERTED simply by reinforcing New Orleans' levee system years ago as a preventive measure? Does the federal government have an obligation to maintain and update the infrastructure in places such as New Orleans, or is this the responsibility of state and local governments?

4. DOES THE CONSTITUTION PROVIDE ANY guidance on whether the response to disasters such as Hurricane Katrina should be orchestrated at the federal level or at the state and local levels?

5. IN LIGHT OF THE RESPONSE TO Hurricane Katrina, what can be said about American federalism both in theory and in practice? Would a stronger federal government have been better equipped to deal with the crisis, or was the

inadequate response an isolated case of mismanagement that does not reflect upon the basic structure of the U.S. government?

Chapter 1

Constitutional Democracy

★

THE OLDEST CONSTITUTIONAL DEMOCRACY IN THE WORLD, THE UNITED STATES OF AMERICA, HAS SURVIVED FOR MORE THAN TWO CENTURIES, YET IT IS STILL AN EXPERIMENT AND A WORK IN PROGRESS. WE THINK OF IT AS AN ENDURING, STRONG GOVERNMENT, BUT OUR CONSTITUTIONAL POLITICAL SYSTEM IS BUILT ON A FRAGILE FOUNDATION. THE U.S. CONSTITUTION AND BILL OF RIGHTS SURVIVE NOT BECAUSE WE STILL HAVE THE PARCHMENT THEY WERE WRITTEN ON, BUT BECAUSE EACH GENERATION OF AMERICANS has respected, renewed, and worked to understand the principles and values found in these documents. Different generations have faced different challenges in preserving, protecting, and defending our way of government. Some have faced depressions, others world wars. More recently, Americans have confronted foreign attacks like those on the World Trade Center and Pentagon on September 11, 2001; terrorism around the world; protracted wars in Iraq and Afghanistan; and rebuilding of communities after natural disasters such as Hurricane Katrina, which devastated New Orleans and the neighboring Gulf Coast in August 2005.

The debate about how to respond to terrorism, especially after the terrorist attacks of September 11, 2001, has come to dominate American politics. The U.S. response to terrorism has implications for civil liberties, the powers of Congress, the courts, the presidency, and the economy. Republicans in Congress, and especially President Bush and his advisors, have sought to characterize themselves and their party as best able to "wage the war on terror." This strategy was used effectively in the midterm elections of 2002 and the presidential election of 2004. The effort to define George Bush as strong in dealing with terrorism and John Kerry as weak was a major focus of some of the most memorable ads in the 2004 presidential election, including some from Swift Boat Veterans for Truth, a group not connected to Bush or the Republicans, which attacked John Kerry's character and leadership ability. Karl Rove, President Bush's chief political advisor, sought to define the 2006 midterm election in similar terms when he said, "At the core, we are dealing with two parties that have fundamentally different views on national security. . . . Republicans have a post-9/11 worldview and many Democrats have a pre-9/11 worldview. That does not make them unpatriotic—not at all. But it does make them wrong—deeply and profoundly and consistently wrong."[1] What actually defined the 2006 election was concern with the Iraq war, with scandal and government mismanagement, and with the economy. Voters signaled a desire for change.

President Bush, in responding to terrorism, expanded presidential powers by ordering wiretapping of suspected terrorists without a court warrant. In so doing he disregarded a 1978 act of Congress which established the Foreign Intelligence Surveillance Court that

"Such democracies [as the Greek and Roman] have ever been found incompatible with personal security, or the rights of property; and have in general been as short in their lives, as they have been violent in their deaths."

JAMES MADISON, *THE FEDERALIST*, No. 10

grants warrants for wiretaps when the government presents evidence of engagement in spying or international terrorism against the United States on behalf of a foreign power.[2] Critics of this asserted presidential power claim that it violates fundamental civil liberties, including those found in the Fourth Amendment, which protects against unreasonable searches and seizures. The president and his defenders point to his constitutional role as commander in chief and his duty to "protect and defend" the American people. Attorney General Alberto Gonzales claimed that seeking court permission "doesn't provide the speed and the agility that we need in all circumstances to deal with this new kind of threat."[3]

Economically, waging wars in Iraq and Afghanistan has forced debates about whether to raise taxes to pay for these wars. The cost of oil, and the United States' heavy dependence on oil from the Middle East, are also important economically and politically. One respected writer about the Middle East, Thomas Friedman, has claimed U.S. citizens are "financing both sides in the war on terrorism: the U.S. Army with our tax dollars, and Islamist charities, madrasas and terrorist organizations through our oil purchases."[4] The cost of the wars in Afghanistan and Iraq has also contributed to higher federal budget deficits. Defenders of the Bush administration point to a strong domestic economy tax increases could have weakened.

How to wage and finance the war on terrorism is not the only pressing issue for American government today. The Supreme Court's docket is full of significant issues, and the question of who serves on that court is highly controversial. Health care, education, jobs, and such matters as defining marriage are important to many people, and they want their local, state, and national government to respond. Clearly, government is important in setting priorities and making policies. It is also clear that whoever holds power makes a substantial difference in what government does or does not do, and sharp divisions in partisanship and ideology intensify conflict and make compromise more difficult. Even with these challenges, American government is resilient, and is a subject that deserves careful study.

American Government and Politicians in Context

The American constitutional democracy, founded on enduring values, has shown resiliency and adaptability. We have held 110 presidential and midterm elections (including the 2006 election), and we have witnessed the peaceful transfer of power from one party to another on dozens of occasions. The United States has succeeded largely because Americans love their country, revere the Constitution, and respect the free enterprise system. We also believe that debate, compromise, and free elections are the best ways to reconcile our differences. From an early age, we practice democracy in elementary school elections, and even though we may be critical of elected leaders, we recognize the need for political leadership. We also know that there are deep divisions and unsolved problems in the United States. Many people are concerned about the persistence of racism, about religious bigotry, about the gap in economic opportunities between rich and poor, and about how to control the violence that disproportionately afflicts children and minorities. And we want our government, in addition to defending us against terrorism and foreign enemies, to provide us with basic health care and education, and to address other domestic problems.

But what is this government of which we expect so much? The reality is that "government" is merely a shorthand term to refer to hundreds of thousands of our fellow Americans: the people we elect and the people they appoint to promote the general welfare, provide for domestic tranquility, and secure the blessings of liberty for us.

Let us define some of the basic terms we'll be using throughout this book. *Government* refers to the procedures and institutions (such as elections, courts, and legislatures) by which a people govern and rule themselves. *Politics* is the process by which people decide, at least in our system of government, who shall govern and what policies shall be adopted. Such processes invariably involve discussions, debates, and compromises about tactics and goals. *Politicians* are the people who fulfill the tasks of an operating government. Some politicians—legislators, mayors, and presidents—come to office through an election. Nonelected politicians may be political party officials or aides, advisers, or consultants to elected officials. *Political science* is the study of the principles, procedures, and structures of government and the analysis of political ideas, institutions, behavior, and practices.

More than any other form of government, the kind of democracy that has emerged under the U.S. Constitution requires active participation and a balance between faith and skepticism. Government by the people, however, does not require that *everyone* be involved in politics and policy making. It does require persons to run for office seeking to represent the voters in government; however, many citizens will always be too busy doing other things, and some people will always be apathetic about government and politics. But government by the people does require that the public be attentive, interested, involved, informed, and willing, when necessary, to criticize and change the direction of government.

Thomas Jefferson, author of the Declaration of Independence and one of our best-known champions of constitutional democracy, believed in the common sense of the people and in the possibilities of the human spirit. Jefferson warned that every government degenerates when it is left solely in the hands of the rulers. The people themselves, Jefferson wrote, are the only safe repositories of government. He believed in popular control, representative processes, and accountable leadership. But he was no believer in the simple participatory democracy of ancient Greece or revolutionary France. The power of the people, too, must be restrained from time to time.

Government by the people requires faith in our common human enterprise, a belief that if the people are informed and care, they can be trusted with their own self-government and an optimism that when things begin to go wrong, the people can be relied on to set them right. But we also need a healthy skepticism. Democracy requires us to question our leaders and never entrust a group or institution with too much power. And even though constitutional advocates prize majority rule, they must remain skeptical about whether the majority is always right.

Constitutional democracy requires constant attention to protecting the rights and opinions of others, to ensure that our democratic processes serve principles of liberty, equality, and justice. Thus a peculiar blend of faith and skepticism is warranted when dealing with the will of the people.

Constitutional democracy means government by representative politicians. A central feature of democracy is that those who hold power do so only by winning a free election. In our political system, the fragmentation of powers requires elected officials to mediate among factions, build coalitions, and work out compromises among and within the branches of our government to produce policy and action. We expect our politicians to operate within the rules of democracy, and to be honest, humble, patriotic, compassionate, sensitive to the needs of others, well informed, competent, fair-minded, self-confident, and inspirational. They must represent all the people, not just the ones with money. We want politicians, in other words, to be perfect, to have all the answers, and to have all the "correct" values (as we perceive them). We want them to solve our problems, yet we also make them scapegoats for the things we dislike about government: taxes, regulations, hard times, and limits on our freedom. Many of these ideals are unrealistic, and no one could live up to all of them. Like all people, politicians live in a world in which perfection may be the goal, but compromise, ambition, fund raising, and self-promotion are necessary.

Americans will never be satisfied with their political candidates and politicians. The ideal politician is probably a myth because the perfect official would be able to please everyone, make conflict disappear, and not ask us to make sacrifices. Politicians become "ideal" only when they are dead.

But the love of liberty invites disagreements over ideology and values. Politicians and candidates, as well as the people they represent, have different ideas about what is best for the nation. That's why we have politics, candidates, opposition parties, heated political debates, and elections.

Thomas Jefferson—Author of the Declaration of Independence, third President of the United States, and founder of the University of Virginia.

"The Athenians are here, Sire, with an offer to back us with ships, money, arms, and men—and, of course, their usual lectures about democracy."

Defining Democracy

The word **"democracy"** is nowhere to be found in the Declaration of Independence or in the U.S. Constitution, nor was it a term the founders used. It is both an ancient term and a modern one. When this nation was founded, democracy was used to describe undesirable groups and conditions: mobs, lack of standards, and a system that encouraged leaders to gain power by appealing to the emotions and prejudices of the rabble.

The distinguishing feature of democracy is that government derives its authority from its citizens. In fact, the word comes from two Greek words: *demos* (the people) and *kratos* (authority or power). Thus **democracy** means *government by the people*, not government by one person (a monarch, dictator, or priest) or government by the few (an oligarchy or aristocracy).

Ancient Athens and a few other Greek city-states and the Roman Republic had a **direct democracy** in which citizens assembled to discuss and pass laws and select their officials. Most of these Greek city-states and the Roman Republic degenerated into mob rule and then resorted to dictators or rule by aristocrats. When the word "democracy" came into use in English in the seventeenth century, it denoted this kind of direct democracy. It was a term of derision, a negative word, a reference to power wielded by an unruly mob.

In 1787, James Madison, in *The Federalist*, No. 10, reflected the view of many of the framers of the U.S. Constitution when he wrote, "Such democracies [as the Greek and Roman] . . . have ever been found incompatible with personal security, or the rights of property; and have in general been as short in their lives, as they have been violent in their deaths" (*The Federalist*, No. 10, is reprinted in the Appendix at the back of this book). Madison feared that empowering citizens to decide policy directly would be dangerous to freedom, minorities, and property, and would result in violence of one group against another.

Over time our democracy has increasingly combined representative and direct democracy. The most important examples of direct democracy were added roughly a century ago and include the direct primary, which selects who may run for office; the initiative and referendum, which allow citizens to vote on state laws or constitutional amendments; and the recall, which lets voters remove state and local elected officials from office between elections. Initiative and referenda have been used frequently, and 2003 saw the first governor recalled in 82 years when California voters replaced Gray Davis with Arnold Schwarzenegger. Taking policy disputes directly to the voters became a mode of attempting to govern for Governor Schwarzenegger, who pressed for a special election in 2005 to decide four ballot initiatives. The voters roundly defeated all four measures, and Schwarzenegger later stated that he "would rely far less on campaigns and ballot fights as a governing strategy."[5] He also said, "If I were to do another *Terminator* movie, I would have the Terminator travel back in time to tell Arnold not to have a special election."[6]

Today it is no longer possible, even if desirable, to assemble the citizens of any but the smallest towns to make their laws or to select their officials. Rather, we have invented a system of representation. Democracy today means **representative democracy**, or a *republic,* in which those who have governmental authority get and retain authority directly or indirectly by winning free elections in which all adult citizens are allowed to participate. The framers used the term "republic" to avoid any confusion between direct democracy, which they disliked, and representative democracy, which they liked and thought secured all the advantages of a direct democracy while curing its weaknesses.

Many of the ideas that came to be part of the Constitution can be traced to philosophers' writing—in some cases centuries before the American Revolution and constitutional convention. Among those the framers would have read and been influenced by were Aristotle, Hobbes, Locke, and Montesquieu. Aristotle, a Greek philosopher, writing in the fourth century BC, had provided important ideas on a political unit called a state, but also on the idea of a constitution, and on various forms of

democracy
Government by the people, both directly or indirectly, with free and frequent elections.

direct democracy
Government in which citizens vote on laws and select officials directly.

representative democracy
Government in which the people elect those who govern and pass laws; also called a *republic*.

governing.[7] John Locke, an English philosopher, also profoundly influenced the authors of the Declaration of Independence and Constitution. Locke rejected the idea that kings had a divine right to rule, advocated a constitutional democracy, and provided a philosophic justification for revolution.[8] Locke, like his fellow Englishman Thomas Hobbes, asserted that there was a social contract whereby men formed governments for security and to avoid what he called the state of nature where chaos existed and where "everyone was against everyone."[9]

In defining democracy, we need to clarify other terms. **Constitutional democracy** refers to a government in which the individuals exercise governmental powers as the result of winning free and relatively frequent elections. *It is a government in which there are recognized, enforced limits on the powers of all governmental officials.* It also generally involves a written set of governmental rules and procedures—a constitution. The idea that constitutional provisions can limit power by having another part of the government balance or check it is another good example of how the founders applied ideas from earlier thinkers; in this case, the idea was from the French philosopher Charles de Montesquieu.[10]

Constitutionalism is a term we apply to arrangements—checks and balances, federalism, separation of powers, rule of law, due process, a bill of rights—that require our leaders to listen, think, bargain, and explain before they make laws, in order to prevent them from abusing power. We then hold them politically and legally accountable for how they exercise their powers.

Like most political concepts, democracy encompasses many ideas and has many meanings. It is a way of life, a form of government, a way of governing, and a type of nation, a state of mind, and a variety of processes. We can divide these many meanings of democracy into three broad categories: a system of interacting values, a system of interrelated political processes, and a system of interdependent political structures. Before we begin our discussion of these three categories, we will outline the conditions that are necessary to foster constitutional democracy.

Conditions Conducive to Constitutional Democracy

Democracy is often difficult to establish and does not always flourish. Although it is hard to specify the precise conditions that are essential for establishing and preserving a democracy, we have learned a few things.

EDUCATIONAL CONDITIONS   The exercise of voting privileges requires an educated citizenry. But a high level of education (measured by the number of high school diplomas and university degrees) does not guarantee democratic government, as the examples of Nazi Germany and the Soviet Union (where many had these credentials) illustrate. And in some democracies, such as India, many people are illiterate. Still, voting makes little sense unless many of the voters can read and write and express their interests and opinions. The poorly educated and illiterate often get left out in a democracy. Direct democracy puts a further premium on education. Better-educated persons are more able to understand and participate in policy making through initiatives and referenda.[11]

ECONOMIC CONDITIONS   A relatively prosperous nation, with an equitable distribution of wealth, provides the best context for democracy. Starving people are more interested in food than in voting. Where economic power is concentrated, political power is also likely to be concentrated. Well-to-do nations have a better chance of sustaining democratic governments than do those with widespread poverty. Extremes of wealth and poverty undermine the possibilities for a healthy constitutional democracy. Thus the prospects for an enduring democracy are greater in Canada or France than in Zimbabwe or Egypt, for example.

Private ownership of property and a relatively favorable role for the market economy are also related to the creation and maintenance of democratic institutions. Democracies can range from heavily regulated economies with public ownership of many enterprises, such as Sweden, to those in which there is little government regulation of the marketplace, such as the United States. But there are no democracies with a

constitutional democracy
A government that enforces recognized limits on those who govern and allows the voice of the people to be heard through free, fair, and relatively frequent elections.

constitutionalism
The set of arrangements, including checks and balances, federalism, separation of powers, rule of law, due process, and a bill of rights, that requires our leaders to listen, think, bargain, and explain before they act or make laws. We then hold them politically and legally accountable for how they exercise their powers.

highly centralized government-run economy and little private ownership of property, although many authoritarian nations like Oman or Saudi Arabia have a market economy. There are no truly democratic communist states, nor have there ever been any.

SOCIAL CONDITIONS   Economic development generally makes democracy possible, yet proper social conditions are necessary to make it real.[12] In a society fragmented into warring groups that fiercely disagree on fundamental issues, government by discussion and compromise is difficult, as we have seen in Afghanistan and Iraq. When ideologically separated groups consider the issues at stake to be vital, they may prefer to fight rather than accept the verdict of the ballot box, as happened in the United States in 1861 with the outbreak of the Civil War.

In a society that consists of many overlapping associations and groupings, however, individuals are less likely to identify completely with a single group and give their allegiance to it. For example, Joe Smith is a Baptist, an African American, a southerner, a Democrat, an electrician, a member of the National Rifle Association, and he makes $50,000 a year. On some issues, Joe thinks as a Baptist, on others as a southerner, and on still others as an African American. Sue Jones is a Catholic, a white Republican, an auto dealer, and a member of the National Organization for Women (NOW); she comes from a Polish background, and she makes $150,000 a year. Sometimes she acts as a Republican, sometimes as an American of Polish descent, and sometimes as a member of NOW. Jones and Smith differ on some issues and agree on others. In general, the differences between them are not likely to be greater than their common interest in maintaining a democracy.[13]

IDEOLOGICAL CONDITIONS   Americans have basic beliefs about power, government, and political practices—beliefs that arise out of the educational, economic, and social conditions of an individual's experience. Out of these conditions must also develop a general acceptance of the ideals of democracy and a willingness of a substantial part of the people to agree to proceed democratically. This acceptance is sometimes called the *democratic consensus*. Widely accepted ideals of democracy include one-person-one-vote, majority rule, freedom of speech, and freedom of assembly.

Democracy as a System of Interacting Values

Belief in representative democracy may be as near a universal faith as the world has today. Respect for human dignity, freedom, liberty, individual rights, and other democratic values are widespread. Personal liberty, respect for the individual, equality of opportunity, and popular consent are at the core of democratic values. As the Taliban regime in Afghanistan demonstrated, some governments not only suppress democratic values but terrorize other governments that do embrace them.

PERSONAL LIBERTY   Liberty has been the single most important value in American history. It was for "life, liberty, and the pursuit of happiness" that independence was declared; it was to "secure the Blessings of Liberty" that the Constitution was drawn up and adopted. Even our patriotic songs extol the "sweet land of liberty." The essence of liberty is *self-determination*, meaning that all individuals must have the opportunity to realize their own goals. Liberty is not simply the absence of external restraint on a person (freedom *from*); it is also a person's freedom and capacity to reach his or her goals (freedom *to*). Moreover, both history and reason suggest that individual liberty is the key to social progress. The greater the people's freedom, the greater is the chance of discovering better ways of life.

RESPECT FOR THE INDIVIDUAL   Popular rule in a democracy flows from a belief that every person has the potential for common sense, rationality, and fairness. Individuals have important rights; collectively, those rights are the source of all legitimate governmental authority and power. These concepts pervade democratic thought. They are woven into the writings of Thomas Jefferson, especially in the Declaration of Independence: "All men . . . are endowed by their Creator with certain unalienable rights." (The Declaration of Independence is reprinted in the Appendix.) Constitutional democracies make the *person*—rich or poor, black or white, male or female—the central measure of value.

Agents of Change

Karen Young, Jenny Sazama, and Youth on Board

Questions

How might Youth on Board affect the future of the Constitution?

Should young Americans have a voice on national issues such as immigration reform, global warming, and terrorism?

Youth on Board was founded in 1994 to prepare young Americans to be active in their communities. Designed to give young people the skills to engage in the life of their churches, communities, and schools, Youth on Board believes that young Americans have important opinions to share with the rest of the nation. Although most young Americans cannot vote, they can be heard, whether by speaking up in their classrooms around issues of fairness and social justice, or working with other organizations that are trying to improve their communities.

Youth on Board was created out of Karen Young's and Jenny Sazama's vision that young Americans live in what Young calls "a society that really does not respect young people's ideas, opinions, and experiences." Founded only years after Young and Sazama graduated from Humbolt State University in California and Clark University in Worcester, Massachusetts, respectively, the organization reflects their belief that young Americans need to participate in decisions that affect their lives. "We needed to find ways to support their involvement: to train adults to listen, and young people to learn," says Young.

Having worked as a community organizer on a range of social issues in college, Young often felt unprepared and intimidated when she had to speak before adults about her work. She and Sazama developed Youth on Board to develop training programs so that younger people could have a stronger voice in democratic life and con-

Karen Young and Jenny Sazama

front what she calls "adultism," which are the negative stereotypes and discrimination against young people based on their age.

Over the years, Youth on Board has trained more than 12,000 young Americans to participate, sold thousands of manuals to help adults understand how to listen, and provided training to schools and government agencies. By 2005, its reach had expanded to 45 states and 11 countries. ∎

Learn more about Youth on Board at www.youthonboard.org.

Not all political systems put the individual first. Some promote **statism**, a form of government based on centralized authority and control, especially over the economy. China, Vietnam, and Cuba, for example, take this approach. In a modern democracy, the nation, or even the community, is less important than the individuals who compose it.

EQUALITY OF OPPORTUNITY   The democratic value of *equality* enhances the importance of the individual: "All men are created equal and from that equal creation they derive rights inherent and unalienable, among which are the preservation of liberty and the pursuit of happiness." So reads Jefferson's first draft of the Declaration of Independence, and the words indicate the primacy of the concept. The nineteenth-century French statesman Alexis de Tocqueville and other foreign students of American democracy were all struck by the strength of egalitarian thought and practice in our political and social lives.

But what does equality mean? And equality for whom? For African Americans as well as white people? For women as well as men? For Native Americans, descendants of the Pilgrims, and recent immigrants? And what kind of equality—economic, political, legal, social, or some other kind? Does equality of opportunity mean that everyone should have the same place at the starting line? Or does it mean that society should try to equalize the factors that determine a person's economic or social well-being? These enduring issues arise often in American politics.

statism
The idea that the rights of the nation are supreme over the rights of the individuals who make up the nation.

The concrete expression of the principle of popular consent can be seen in action as these Maryland voters cast their ballots. This scene is repeated across the country on the federal, state, and local levels.

POPULAR CONSENT   The animating principle of the American Revolution, the Declaration of Independence, and the resulting new nation was **popular consent**, the idea that a just government must derive its powers from the *consent of the people it governs*. A commitment to democracy thus means that a community must be willing to participate and make decisions in government. These principles sound unobjectionable, but in practice they mean that certain individuals or groups may not get their way. A commitment to popular consent means that people must be willing to lose when more people vote the other way.

DEMOCRATIC VALUES IN CONFLICT   The basic values of democracy do not always coexist happily. Individualism may conflict with the collective welfare or the public good. Self-determination may conflict with equal opportunity. For example, the freedom of the press of a media outlet to publish classified documents about foreign or defense policy may conflict with the government's constitutional requirement to "provide for the common defense."

Much of our political combat revolves around how to strike a balance among democratic values, how to protect the Declaration of Independence's unalienable rights of life, liberty, and the pursuit of happiness while trying to "form," as the Constitution announces, "a more perfect Union, establish Justice, insure domestic Tranquility, provide for the common defense, promote the general Welfare, and secure the Blessings of Liberty to ourselves and our Posterity." (See the Preamble to the Constitution on page 48.) Over the years, the American political system has moved, despite occasional setbacks, toward greater freedom for individuals and more democracy.

Expansion of democracy in the United States and elsewhere in the world was in many ways a twentieth-century phenomenon. Although on dozens of occasions in the past century, democracies around the world gave way to authoritarian regimes, even more democracies triumphed. Indeed, "the global range and influence of democratic ideas, institutions, and practices has made [the last century] far and away the most flourishing period for democracy."[14]

Democracy as a System of Interrelated Political Processes

To be successful, democratic government requires a well-defined political process as well as a stable governmental structure. To make democratic values a reality, a nation must incorporate them into its political process, most importantly in the form of free and fair elections, majority rule, freedom of expression, and the right for its citizens to peaceably assemble and protest.

popular consent
The idea that a just government must derive its powers from the consent of the people it governs.

FREE AND FAIR ELECTIONS   Democratic government is based on free and fair elections held at intervals frequent enough to make them relevant to policy choices. Elections are one of the most important devices for keeping officials and representatives accountable.

We previously described representative democracy as a government in which those who have the authority to make decisions with the force of law acquire and retain this authority either directly or indirectly by winning free elections in which adult citizens are allowed to participate. Crucial to modern-day definitions of democracy is the idea that opposition political parties can exist, can run candidates in elections, and have a chance to replace those who currently hold public office. Thus *political competition and choice* are crucial to the existence of democracy.

Although all citizens should have equal voting power, free and fair elections do not imply that everyone must or will have equal political influence. Some people, because of wealth, talent, or position, inevitably have more influence than others. How much extra influence should key figures be allowed to exercise is frequently debated. But in an election, each citizen—president or plumber, corporate CEO or ditch digger—casts only one vote.

MAJORITY AND PLURALITY RULE   Majority rule—governance according to the expressed preferences of the majority—is a basic rule of democracy. The **majority** candidate or party is the one that receives *more than half* the votes and so wins the election and takes charge of the government until the next election. In practice, however, majority rule is often **plurality** rule, in which the candidate or party with the *most* votes wins the election, even though it may not have received more than half the votes because votes were divided among three or more candidates or parties. About a third of our presidents have won with pluralities in the popular vote rather than majorities.[15] Once elected, officials do not have a right to curtail the attempts of political minorities to use all peaceful means to become the new majority. Even as the winners take power, the losers are at work to try to get it back at the next election.[16]

Should the side with the most votes always prevail? Americans answer this question in various ways. Some insist that majority views should be enacted into laws and regulations. However, an effective representative democracy involves far more than simply ascertaining and applying the statistical will of most of the people. In a constitutional democracy, the will of a majority of the people may not contradict the rights of individuals. For example, the Supreme Court struck down a 1964 California initiative that would have allowed discrimination against minorities in the sale of residential housing.[17] Legislating in a representative democracy is a complicated and often untidy process in which the people and their agents debate, compromise, and arrive at a decision only after thoughtful deliberation.

The framers of the U.S. Constitution wanted to guard society against any one faction of the people oppressing any other faction of the people. The Constitution reflects their fear of tyranny by majorities, especially momentary majorities that spring from temporary passions. They insulated certain rights (such as freedom of speech) and institutions (such as the Supreme Court and, until the Constitution was changed in 1913, even the Senate) from popular choice. Effective representation of the people, the framers insisted, should not be based solely on parochial interests or shifting breezes of opinion.

FREEDOM OF EXPRESSION   Free and fair elections depend on access to information relevant to voting choices. Voters must have access to facts, competing ideas, and the views of candidates. Free and fair elections require a climate in which competing, nongovernment-owned newspapers, radio stations, and television stations can flourish. If the government controls what is said and how it is said, there is no democracy. Without free speech, elections cannot be free and fair. We examine free expression in greater detail in Chapter 15.

THE RIGHT TO ASSEMBLE AND PROTEST   Citizens must be free to organize for political purposes. Obviously, individuals can be more effective if they join with others in a party, a pressure group, a protest movement, or a demonstration. The right to oppose

majority rule
Governance according to the expressed preferences of the majority.

majority
The candidate or party that wins more than half the votes cast in an election.

plurality
Candidate or party with the most votes cast in an election, not necessarily more than half.

the government, to form opposition parties, and to have a chance to defeat incumbents is a defining characteristic of a democracy.

Democracy as a System of Interdependent Political Structures

Democracy is, of course, more than values and processes. It also entails political structures that safeguard these values and processes. The Constitution and its first ten amendments (the Bill of Rights) set up an ingenious structure—one that both grants and checks government power. A system of political parties, interest groups, media, and other institutions that intercede between the electorate and those who govern and thus help maintain democratic stability reinforces this constitutional structure.

The U.S. constitutional system has five distinctive elements: *federalism*, the division of powers between the national and state governments; *separation of powers* among the executive, judicial, and legislative branches; *bicameralism*, the division of legislative power between the House of Representatives and the Senate; *checks and balances* in which each branch is given the constitutional means, the political independence, and the motives to check the powers of the other branches; and a judicially enforceable, written, explicit *Bill of Rights* that provides a guarantee of individual liberties and due process before the law.

The Constitutional Roots of the American Experiment

Americans often take democracy for granted. Most of us probably consider it inevitable. We take pride in our ability to make it work, yet we have essentially inherited a functioning system. Its establishment was the work of others, nine or ten generations ago. Our job is not just to keep it going but to improve it and adapt it to the challenges of our times. To do so, however, we must first understand it, and this requires us to discuss our democratic and constitutional roots.

The Colonial Beginnings

Our democratic experiment might have failed for many reasons. The 13 original states (formerly colonies) were independent and could have gone their separate ways. Sectional differences based on social and economic conditions, especially the southern states' dependence on slavery, were an obvious problem. Religious, ethnic, and racial diversity, which challenges so many governments around the world today, also existed in the early United States.

Given these potential problems, how did democracy survive? How did this nation establish democratic principles for its government? How did it limit potential abuses? These questions are important not only to Americans but also to everyone who values freedom and democracy. The United States has been a world leader in promoting the use of democratic institutions, in effect universalizing its successful experiment.

The framers of the U.S. Constitution had experience to guide them. For almost two centuries, Europeans had been sailing to the New World in search of liberty—especially religious liberty—as well as land and work. While still aboard the *Mayflower,* the Pilgrims drew up a compact in 1620 to protect their religious freedom and to make possible "just and equal laws." The experience of settling a new land, overcoming obstacles, and enjoying the fruits of their labors was also important to the spirit of independence in the colonies.[18]

But the picture of freedom in the colonies was mixed. The Puritans in Massachusetts established a **theocracy**, a system of government in which religious leaders claimed divine guidance and in which other religious sects were denied religious liberty. Later, as that system was challenged, the Puritans continued to worry "about what would maintain order in a society lacking an established church, an attachment to place, and the uncontested leadership of men of merit."[19] Nine of the 13 colonies eventually set up a state church. Throughout the 1700s, Puritans in Massachusetts

theocracy
Government by religious leaders, who claim divine guidance.

barred certain men from voting on the basis of church membership. To the Anglican establishment in Virginia, campaigns for toleration were in themselves subversive. Women, slaves, and Native Americans could not vote at all.

By the 1700s in the American colonies, editors found they could speak freely in their newspapers, dissenters could distribute leaflets, and agitators could protest in taverns or in the streets. And yet, dissenters were occasionally exiled, imprisoned, and even executed, and some printers were beaten and had their shops closed. In short, the colonists struggled with the balance between unity and diversity, stability and dissent, order and liberty.

The Rise of Revolutionary Fervor

As resentment against British rule mounted during the 1770s and revolutionary fervor rose, Americans became determined to fight the British to win their rights and liberties. In 1776, a year after the fighting broke out in Massachusetts, the Declaration of Independence proclaimed in ringing tones that all men are created equal, endowed by their Creator with certain unalienable rights; that among them are "life, liberty, and the pursuit of happiness"; that to secure those rights, governments are instituted among men; and that whenever a government becomes destructive of those ends, it is the right of the people to alter or abolish it. (Read the full text of the Declaration of Independence in the Appendix.)

We have heard these great ideals so often that we take them for granted. Revolutionary leaders did not. They were deadly serious about these rights and willing to fight and pledge their lives, fortunes, and sacred honor for them. Indeed, by signing the Declaration of Independence they were effectively signing their own death warrants if the Revolution failed.[20] Bills of rights in the new state constitutions guaranteed free speech, freedom of religion, and the natural rights to life, liberty, and property. All their constitutions spelled out the rights of persons accused of crime, such as knowing the nature of the accusation, confronting their accusers, and receiving a timely and public trial by jury.[21] Moreover, these guarantees were set out *in writing*, in sharp contrast to the unwritten British constitution.

Toward Unity and Order

As the war against the British widened to include all 13 colonies, the need arose for a stronger central government. Sensing the need for more unity, in 1777 Congress established a new national government under a written document called the **Articles of Confederation**. While established in 1777, the Articles were not approved by all the state legislatures until 1781, after Washington's troops had been fighting for six years.

The Confederation was more like a fragile league of friendship than a national government. There was no national executive, judiciary, or coinage. Congress had to work through the states. It had no direct authority over citizens. It could not levy taxes, regulate trade between the states or with other nations, or prevent the states from taxing each other's goods or issuing their own currencies. The lack of a judicial system meant that the national government had to rely on state courts to enforce national laws and settle disputes between the states. In practice, state courts could overturn national laws. Moreover, with the end of the Revolutionary War in 1783, the sense of urgency that had produced unity among the states began to fade. Conflicts between states and between creditors and debtors within the various states grew intense. Foreign threats continued; territories ruled by England and Spain surrounded the weak new nation. As pressures on the Confederation mounted, many leaders became convinced that a stronger central government was needed to create a union strong enough to deal with internal diversity and factionalism and to resist external threats.

In September 1786, under the leadership of Alexander Hamilton, supporters of a truly national government took advantage of the **Annapolis Convention**—a meeting in Annapolis, Maryland, on problems of trade and navigation attended by delegates from five states—to issue a call for a convention to consider basic amendments to the Articles of Confederation. The delegates were to meet in Philadelphia on the

Articles of Confederation
The first governing document of the confederated states, drafted in 1777, ratified in 1781, and replaced by the present Constitution in 1789.

Annapolis Convention
A convention held in September 1786 to consider problems of trade and navigation, attended by five states and important because it issued the call to Congress and the states for what became the Constitutional Convention.

Government's Greatest Endeavors

Tax Reform

The "Boston Tea Party"

Questions

What taxes do you pay?

Why do you think the federal tax system is so complex?

A
lthough no single event sparked the American Revolution, "taxation without representation" was a rallying cry. Indeed, most of the "insults and injuries" that Thomas Jefferson listed in the Declaration of Independence involved British efforts to raise more money from the 13 colonies. The most famous was the Tea Act of 1773, which raised the price of tea dramatically and prompted 150 colonists to dump tea from three cargo holds into Boston Harbor.

More than 200 years later, Americans still think taxes are too high and the system too complex. However, the federal government has made several recent efforts to make the system easier to use and understand. First, it now allows taxpayers to file their tax returns electronically, which makes refunds faster. Second, it has streamlined the tax forms, especially the 1040EZ, which single taxpayers without children can use to report their income. Third, it has created a much more taxpayer-friendly Web site that is easier to navigate. The Web site has a fast and accurate frequently-asked-questions page, and it even gives taxpayers advice on how to pay their taxes if they do not have enough money on April 15th when taxes are due.

The federal government also implemented sweeping tax reform under legislation passed by Congress and signed into law by President Ronald Reagan in 1986. This act reduced the amount of taxes paid by individuals and corporations and simplified the tax system to make it more understandable. Although Congress has passed several tax laws since, the 1986 reforms were particularly important in creating a simpler, fairer system, although it is still too complex for many Americans to understand. ∎

> *"I like a little rebellion now and then . . . the tree of liberty must be refreshed from time to time with the blood of patriots and tyrants."*
>
> THOMAS JEFFERSON, 1786

Constitutional Convention
The convention in Philadelphia, May 25 to September 17, 1787, that debated and agreed upon the Constitution of the United States.

Shays's Rebellion
Rebellion led by Daniel Shays of farmers in western Massachusetts in 1786–1787, protesting mortgage foreclosures. It highlighted the need for a strong national government just as the call for the Constitutional Convention went out.

second Monday of May 1787, "to devise such further provisions as shall appear to them necessary to render the Constitution of the Federal Government adequate to the exigencies of the Union." This meeting became the **Constitutional Convention**.

For a short time, all was quiet. Then, late in 1786, messengers rode into George Washington's plantation at Mount Vernon in Virginia with the kind of news he and other leaders had dreaded. Farmers in western Massachusetts, crushed by debts and taxes, were rebelling against foreclosures, forcing judges out of their courtrooms, and freeing debtors from jails. As a patriot and a wealthy landowner, Washington was appalled. "What, gracious God, is man?" he exclaimed.

Not all Americans reacted as Washington did to what became known as **Shays's Rebellion** (named for Daniel Shays, its leader). When Abigail Adams, the politically knowledgeable wife of John Adams, the Revolutionary statesman from Massachusetts, sent news of the rebellion to Thomas Jefferson, the Virginian replied, "I like a little rebellion now and then," noting also that the "tree of liberty must be refreshed from time to time with the blood of patriots and tyrants. It is its natural manure."[22] But the rebellion highlighted the danger to private property that the absence of a strong government posed. Some, like historian Charles A. Beard, have argued that the primary motive for the authors of the U.S. Constitution was the protection of their economic interests.[23] Beard's views have been challenged.[24] Most agree that while the early leaders of the United States were protecting their own economic interests, that was not their only motive.

Shays's Rebellion petered out after the farmers attacked an arsenal and were cut down by cannon fire. Shays's rebellion threatened prosperity, established order, and the rule of law, and reinforced the view that a stronger national government was needed. Congress issued a cautiously worded call to all the state legislatures to appoint delegates for the "sole and express purpose of revising the Articles of Confederation." The suspicious congressional legislators specified that no recommendation would be effective unless approved by Congress and confirmed by all the state legislatures, as provided by the Articles.

The Constitutional Convention of 1787

The delegates who assembled in Philadelphia that May had to establish a national government powerful enough to prevent the young nation from dissolving but not so powerful that it would crush individual liberty. What these men did continues to have a major impact on how we are governed. It also provides an outstanding lesson in political science for the world.

The Delegates

The various states appointed 74 delegates, but only 55 arrived in Philadelphia. Of these, approximately 40 actually took part in the work of the convention. It was a distinguished gathering. Many of the most important men of the nation were there: successful merchants, planters, bankers, lawyers, and former and present governors and congressional representatives (39 of the delegates had served in Congress). Most had read the classics of political thought. Most had experience constructing local and state governments. Many had also worked hard to create and direct the national confederation of the states. And the Constitutional Convention also included eight of the 56 signers of the Declaration of Independence.

The convention was as representative as most political gatherings were at the time: The participants were all white male landowners. These well-read, well-fed, well-bred, and often well-wed delegates were mainly state or national leaders, for in the 1780s, ordinary people were not likely to participate in politics. (Even today, farm laborers, factory workers, and truck drivers are seldom found in Congress, although a haberdasher, a peanut farmer, and a movie actor have made their way to the White House.)

Although active in the movement to revise the Articles of Confederation, George Washington had been reluctant to attend the convention. He accepted only when persuaded that his prestige was needed for its success. He was selected unanimously to preside over the meetings. According to the records, he spoke only twice during the deliberations, yet his influence was felt in the informal gatherings as well as during the sessions. Everyone understood that Washington favored a more powerful central

The Changing Face of American Politics

Constitutional Convention

If a constitutional convention were convened today, how would the delegates compare to the all-white, all-male, property-owning delegates who drafted the Constitution in Philadelphia in 1787? One likely similarity in the delegates then and now is that they would be successful and generally well-educated individuals. Another similarity would be a willingness to engage in public service.

Many of those who drafted the Constitution had served in state legislatures. One way to speculate about the changing face of this constitutional convention if called today is to look at the composition of state legislatures and Congress today. While not directly representative of the U.S. population, U.S. Senators and Representatives today are much more diverse than those who wrote the Constitu-

tion. Federal lawmakers are 15 percent female, and in some state legislatures the proportion of female legislators has exceeded 50 percent. Congress today is nearly 90 percent white, with the remainder being black, Hispanic, and Asian American.

Today's delegates would likely come disproportionately from the legal profession or have been successful business

managers. If the delegates to today's constitutional convention were drawn from these groups, the proportion of women participating would be between 35 and 40 percent, and 15 percent of the delegates would not be white.* While these proportions show a growing diversity in likely constitutional convention delegates, they do not yet reflect the diversity of the population at large. ■

*SOURCE: U.S. Equal Employment Opportunity Commission, "Diversity in Law Firms" at www.eeoc.gov/stats/reports/diversitylaw/index.html.

History Makers

Alexander Hamilton and James Madison

Alexander Hamilton

James Madison

Like most of the other framers, Hamilton and Madison were superbly educated.

In the Constitution of the United States, the framers offered perhaps the most brilliant example of collective intellectual genius (combining theory and practice) in the history of the Western world. How could such a sparsely populated country by today's standards produce several dozen men of genius who met in Philadelphia and probably another hundred or so equally talented political thinkers who did not attend? The lives of two prominent delegates, Alexander Hamilton and James Madison, help explain the origins of this collective genius.

Alexander Hamilton (1757–1804) had come to the United States from the West Indies and while still a college student had won national attention for his brilliant pamphlets in defense of the Revolutionary cause. During the war, he served as General Washington's aide, and his experiences confirmed his distaste for a Congress so weak it could not even supply the Revolution's troops with enough food or arms. He had been the engineer of the Annapolis Convention, and as early as 1778, he had been urging that the national government be made stronger.

James Madison (1751–1836) had helped frame Virginia's first constitution in 1780 and had served both in the Virginia Assembly and in the Continental Congress. Madison was also a leader of those who favored a stronger national government.

Like most of the other framers, Hamilton and Madison were superbly educated. Both had extensive private tutoring—a one-to-one teacher–student ratio. Like scores of other thinkers of the day, both also had wide practical experience in religion, politics, and government.

Both men were also "moral philosophers." They had strong views on the supreme value of liberty as well as on current issues. Instead of simply sermonizing about liberty, they analyzed it; they debated what liberty meant, how to protect it, and how to expand it. ∎

government led by a president. The general expectation that Washington would be the first president played a crucial role in the creation of the presidency. "No one feared that he would misuse power. . . . His genuine hesitancy, his reluctance to assume the position, only served to reinforce the almost universal desire that he do so."[25]

The proceedings of the convention were kept secret. To encourage everyone to speak freely, delegates were forbidden to discuss the debates with outsiders. It was feared that if a delegate publicly took a firm stand on an issue, it would be harder for him to change his mind after debate and discussion. The delegates also knew that if word of the inevitable disagreements got out, it would provide ammunition for the many enemies of the convention. There were critics of this secrecy rule, but without it, agreement might not have been possible.

Consensus

The Constitutional Convention is usually discussed in terms of its three famous compromises: the compromise between large and small states over representation in

Congress, the compromise between North and South over the regulation and taxation of foreign commerce, and the compromise between North and South over the counting of slaves for the purposes of taxation and representation. There were other important compromises. Yet on many significant issues, most of the delegates were in agreement.

Although a few delegates might have privately favored a limited monarchy, all publicly supported a republican form of government based on elected representatives of the people. This was the only form the convention seriously considered and the only form acceptable to the nation. Equally important, all the delegates opposed arbitrary and unrestrained government.

Most of the delegates were in favor of *balanced government*. They wanted to construct a national government in which no single interest would dominate, and the national government would be strong enough to protect property and business from outbreaks like Shays's Rebellion.

Representing different constituencies and different ideologies, the Constitutional Convention devised a totally new form of government that provided for a central government strong enough to rule but still responsible to its citizens and to the member states.

Benjamin Franklin, the 81-year-old delegate from Pennsylvania, favored extending the right to vote to all white males, but most of the delegates believed that landowners were the best guardians of liberty. James Madison feared that those without property, if given the right to vote, might combine to deprive property owners of their rights. Delegates agreed in principle on limited voting rights but differed over the kind and amount of property one must own in order to vote. Because most states were relaxing qualifications for the vote, the framers recognized that they would jeopardize approval of the constitution if they made the qualifications to vote in federal elections more restrictive than those of the states. As a result, each state was left to determine the qualifications for electing members of the House of Representatives, the only branch of the national government that was to be elected directly by the voters.

Within five days of its opening, the convention—with only the Connecticut delegates dissenting—voted that "a national government ought to be established consisting of a supreme legislative, executive, and judiciary." This decision to establish a supreme national government profoundly altered the nature of the union from a loose confederation of states to a true nation.

"Remember, gentlemen, we aren't here just to draft a constitution. We're here to draft the best damn constitution in the world."

Few dissented from proposals to give the new Congress all the powers of the old Congress plus all other powers necessary to ensure that state legislation would not challenge the integrity of the United States. After the delegates agreed on the extensive powers of the legislative and the close connection between its lower house and the people, they also agreed that a strong executive, which the Articles of Confederation had lacked, was necessary to provide energy, direction, and a check on the legislature. They also accepted an independent judiciary without much debate. Other issues, however, sparked conflict.

Conflict and Compromise

There were serious differences among the various delegates, especially between those from the large and small states, which predated the Constitutional Convention. With the success of the War of Independence, the United States gained the formerly British land west of the colonial borders. States with large western borders like Virginia claimed that their borders should simply be extended further west, as depicted in the accompanying map. Landlocked colonies like New Jersey and Connecticut took exception to these claims, reinforcing the tension between the colonies. (See Figure 1–1.) The matter was resolved in the Land Ordinance of 1785 and the Northwest Ordinance

FIGURE 1-1 **Western Expansion, 1791.**

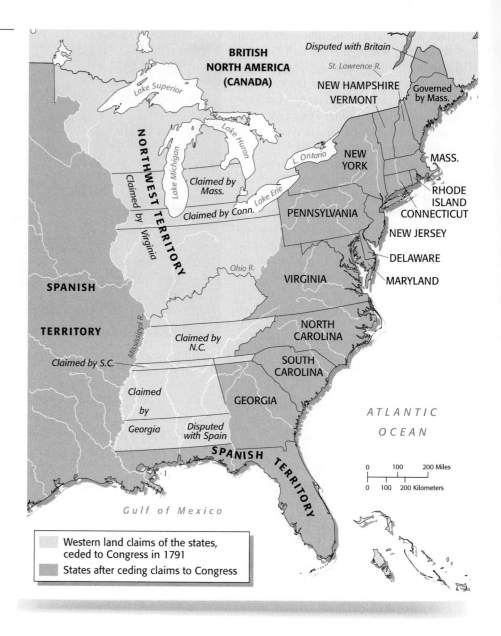

Western land claims of the states, ceded to Congress in 1791

States after ceding claims to Congress

bicameralism
The principle of a two-house legislature.

Virginia Plan
Initial proposal at the Constitutional Convention made by the Virginia delegation for a strong central government with a bicameral legislature dominated by the big states.

of 1787, when all states agreed to cede the Western lands to the national government and permit the newly acquired land eventually to become part of new states rather than expand the border of existing states. But the rivalries between the former colonies remained sharp at the convention in Philadelphia in 1787. For example, the large states also favored a strong national government (which they expected to dominate), while delegates from small states were anxious to avoid being dominated.

This tension surfaced in the first discussions of representation in Congress. Franklin favored a single-house national legislature, but most states had had two-chamber legislatures since colonial times, and the delegates were used to this system. **Bicameralism**—the principle of the two-house legislature—reflected delegates' belief in the need for balanced government. The Senate, the smaller chamber, would represent the states, and to some extent the wealthier classes, and offset the larger, more democratic House of Representatives.

THE VIRGINIA PLAN The Virginia delegation took the initiative. They presented 15 resolutions known as the **Virginia Plan**. This called for a strong central government with a legislature composed of two chambers. The voters were to elect the members of the more representative chamber, which would choose the members of the smaller chamber from nominees submitted by the state legislatures. Representation in both houses would be based on either wealth or numbers, which would give the wealthier and more populous states—Massachusetts, Pennsylvania, and Virginia—a majority in the national legislature.

The Congress thus created was to have all the legislative power of its predecessor under the Articles of Confederation, as well as the power "to legislate in all cases in which the separate States are incompetent," to veto state legislation that conflicted with the proposed constitution, and to choose a national executive with extensive jurisdiction. A national Supreme Court, along with the executive, would have a qualified veto over acts of Congress. In sum, the Virginia Plan would have created a strong national government with disproportionate power to the more populous states and with the smaller states much less powerful.

THE NEW JERSEY PLAN   The Virginia Plan dominated the discussion for the first few weeks. But by June 15, delegates from the small states began a counterattack. William Paterson of New Jersey presented a series of resolutions known as the **New Jersey Plan**. Paterson did not question the need for a strengthened central government, but he was concerned about how this strength might be used. The New Jersey Plan would give Congress the right to tax and regulate commerce and to coerce states, and it would retain the single-house (unicameral) legislature (as under the Articles of Confederation) in which each state, regardless of size, would have the same vote.

The New Jersey Plan contained the germ of what eventually came to be a key provision of our Constitution: the *supremacy clause*. The national Supreme Court was to hear appeals from state judges, and the supremacy clause would require all judges—state and national—to treat laws of the national government and the treaties of the United States as superior to the constitutions and laws of each of the states. (Table 1–1 outlines the key features of the Virginia and New Jersey Plans.)

For a time the convention was deadlocked. The small states believed that all states should be represented equally in Congress, especially in the smaller "upper house" if there were to be two chambers. The large states insisted that representation in both houses be based on population or wealth and that voters, not state legislatures, should elect national legislators. Finally, the so-called Committee of Eleven was elected to devise a compromise. On July 5, it presented its proposals.

THE CONNECTICUT COMPROMISE   Another important compromise, known as the **Connecticut Compromise** (because of the prominent role the Connecticut delegation played in constructing this plan), called for one house in which each state would have an equal vote and a second house in which representation would be based on population and in which all bills for raising or appropriating money—a key function of government—would originate. This proposal was a setback for the large states, which agreed to it only when the smaller states made it clear this was their price for union. After the delegates accepted equality of state representation in the Senate, most objections to a strong national government dissolved.

NORTH-SOUTH COMPROMISES   Other issues split the delegates from the North and South. Southerners were afraid that a northern majority in Congress might discriminate against southern trade. They had some basis for this concern. John Jay, a New Yorker who was secretary of foreign affairs for the Confederation, had proposed a treaty with Great Britain that would have given advantages to northern merchants at the expense of southern exporters of agricultural products like tobacco and cotton. To protect themselves, the southern delegates insisted that a two-thirds majority in the Senate was required to ratify a treaty.

One subject that appears to have been not open for resolution was slavery. The widely shared view is that the states with a greater reliance on slaves would have left the convention if the document had reduced or eliminated the practice. The issue did arise over whether to count slaves for the purpose of apportioning seats in the House of Representatives. To gain more representatives, the South wanted to count slaves; the North resisted. After heated debate, the delegates agreed on the **three-fifths compromise**. Each slave would be counted as three-fifths of a free person for the purposes of

New Jersey Plan
Proposal at the Constitutional Convention made by William Paterson of New Jersey for a central government with a single-house legislature in which each state would be represented equally.

Connecticut Compromise
Compromise agreement by states at the Constitutional Convention for a bicameral legislature with a lower house in which representation would be based on population and an upper house in which each state would have two senators.

three-fifths compromise
Compromise between northern and southern states at the Constitutional Convention that three-fifths of the slave population would be counted for determining direct taxation and representation in the House of Representatives.

TABLE 1–1   The Virginia and New Jersey Plans

Virginia Plan	New Jersey Plan
Legitimacy derived from citizens, based on popular representation	Derived from states, based on equal votes for each state
Bicameral legislature	Unicameral legislature
Executive size undetermined, elected and removable by Congress	More than one person, removable by state majority
Judicial life-tenure, able to veto state legislation	No power over states
Legislature can override state laws	Government can compel obedience to national laws
Ratification by citizens	Ratification by states

apportionment in the House and of direct taxation. This fraction was chosen because it maintained a balance of power between North and South. The issue of balance between North and South would recur in the early history of our nation as territorial governments were established and territories that applied for statehood decided whether to permit or ban slavery. The compromise also included a provision to eliminate the importation of slaves within 20 years, and Congress did so in 1808.

How Other Nations Govern

The New Constitutions in Afghanistan and Iraq: Balancing Islam and Democracy

In December 2001, following the overthrow of the Taliban regime in Afghanistan, several Afghan groups met under United Nations guidance to begin planning for democracy in Afghanistan. Their agreement set in motion the election of a transitional government, a nine-member Constitutional Drafting Commission and a larger Constitutional Commission of 35 members that revised the draft constitution and conducted hearings in the provinces and among refugees.

The new constitution ratified in 2004 by a national assembly or grand council called the Loya Jirga combines Islamic and democratic values, and guarantees basic liberties, with elections to follow. It declares Afghanistan an Islamic Republic, makes Islam the official religion of the country, and requires that all laws conform to Islamic law. School curriculums must be "based on the provisions of the sacred religion of Islam, national culture, and in accordance with academic principles."* However, non-Muslims may freely practice their own religions. The constitution also guarantees fundamental rights to women as well as men, and promises government "based on the people's will and democracy." It notes that Afghanistan is committed to the United Nations Charter and to the Universal Declaration of Human Rights. Women must make up at least 16.5 percent of the membership of the upper legislative house. Neither the U.S. House nor the U.S. Senate presently meet this threshold.

In October 2005, after a protracted process, the voters of Iraq ratified a constitution. Like Afghanistan, the constitution in Iraq blends Islam and democracy. It is unclear how this blending will work in practice. Iraq's constitution allows for a semi-autonomous region for the Kurds who may also have their own constitution. Iraq, unlike Afghanistan, ratified its constitution by referendum. Iraq's constitutional language about human rights is less well defined than Afghanistan's.

This blending of Islam and democracy in Iraq and Afghanistan breaks new ground in the Middle East. Turkey, which has a largely Muslim population, has had a secular government since the 1920s. If Afghanistan succeeds in living up to its constitution, it may join Turkey in providing models for other nations in the region. ∎

*Afghan Government, n.d., "Afghan Draft Constitution: 2004," *www.afghan government.com/2004constitution.htm*, December 30, 2003.
†Edmund Sanders, "The Conflict in Iraq: Islamic Slant in Charter Decried," *Los Angeles Times*, August 25, 2005.

OTHER ISSUES   Delegates also argued about other issues. Should the national government have lower courts, or would one federal Supreme Court be enough? This issue was left to Congress to resolve. The Constitution states that there shall be one Supreme Court and that Congress may establish lower courts.

How should the president be selected? For a long time, the convention favored allowing Congress to pick the president, but the delegates feared that Congress would dominate the president, or vice versa. It also rejected election by the state legislatures because the delegates distrusted the state legislatures. Finally, the delegates settled on election of the president by the electoral college, a group of individuals equal in number to the number of U.S. senators and representatives, who elect the president. Originally it was thought electors would exercise their own judgment in selecting the president, but the College quickly came to reflect partisanship, and today for most states, electors cast ballots for the candidate who won the popular vote of that state. We discuss the Electoral College in greater detail in Chapter 9. This was perhaps the delegates' most novel and contrived contribution and has long been one of the most criticized provisions in the Constitution.[26] (See Article II, Section 1, of the Constitution, which is reprinted between Chapters 2 and 3.)

After three months, the delegates stopped debating. On September 17, 1787, all but three of those still present signed the document they were recommending to the nation. Others who opposed the general drift of the convention had already left. Their work well done, delegates adjourned to the nearby City Tavern to celebrate.

According to an old story, a woman confronted Benjamin Franklin as he left the last session of the convention.

"What kind of government have you given us, Dr. Franklin?" she asked. "A republic or a monarchy?"

"A republic, Madam," he answered, "if you can keep it."

To Adopt or Not to Adopt?

The delegates had gone far. Indeed, they had disregarded Congress's instruction to do no more than revise the Articles of Confederation. In particular, they had ignored Article XIII, which declared the Union to be perpetual and prohibited any alteration of the Articles unless Congress and *every one of the state legislatures* agreed—a provision that had made it impossible to amend the Articles. The convention delegates, however, boldly declared that their newly proposed Constitution should go into effect when ratified by popularly elected conventions in nine states.

They turned to this method of ratification for practical considerations as well as to secure legitimacy for their proposed government. Not only were the delegates aware that there was little chance of winning approval of the new Constitution in all state legislatures, many also believed that a constitution approved *by the people* would have higher legal and moral status than one approved only by a legislature. The Articles of Confederation had been a compact of state governments, but the Constitution was based on the people (recall its opening words: "We the People . . ."). Still, even this method of ratification would not be easy. The nation was not ready to adopt the Constitution without a thorough debate.

Federalists Versus Antifederalists

Supporters of the new government, by cleverly appropriating the name **Federalists**, took some of the sting out of charges they were trying to destroy the states and establish an all-powerful central government. By calling their opponents **Antifederalists**, they pointed up the negative character of the arguments of those who opposed ratification.

The split was in part geographic. Seaboard and city regions tended to be Federalist strongholds; backcountry regions from Maine (then part of Massachusetts) through Georgia, inhabited by farmers and other relatively poor people, were generally Antifederalist. But as in most political contests, no single factor completely accounted for

Federalists
Supporters of ratification of the Constitution and of a strong central government.

Antifederalists
Opponents of ratification of the Constitution and of a strong central government generally.

"Liberty, the greatest of earthly possessions... that precious jewel!"

PATRICK HENRY, 1788

The Federalist
Essays promoting ratification of the Constitution, published anonymously by Alexander Hamilton, John Jay, and James Madison in 1787 and 1788.

the division between Federalists and Antifederalists. Thus in Virginia, the leaders of both sides came from the same general social and economic class. New York City and Philadelphia strongly supported the Constitution, yet so did predominantly rural New Jersey and Connecticut.

The great debate was conducted through pamphlets, newspapers, letters to editors, and speeches. The issues were important, but with few exceptions, the argument about the merits of the Constitution was carried on in a quiet and calm manner. The great debate is an outstanding example of a free people publicly discussing the nature of their fundamental laws. Out of the debate came a series of essays known as *The Federalist*, written (using the pseudonym Publius) by Alexander Hamilton, James Madison, and John Jay to persuade the voters of New York to ratify the Constitution. *The Federalist* is still "widely regarded as the most profound single treatise on the Constitution ever written and as among the few masterly works in political science produced in all the centuries of history."[27] (Three of the most important *Federalist* essays, Nos. 10, 51, and 78, are reprinted in the Appendix of this book. We urge you to read them.)

The Antifederalists' most telling criticism of the proposed Constitution was its failure to include a bill of rights.[28] They opposed the creation of a strong central government, preferring state governments to retain more power because they believed state and local governments would remain more responsive to local needs and concerns. They worried that under the Constitution Congress would "impose barriers against commerce," and they were concerned that the Constitution did not do enough to ensure "frequent rotation of office," meaning elected officials could not be recalled through elections and over time would become less concerned with their constituents.[29] The Federalists believed a bill of rights was unnecessary because the proposed national government had *only* the specific powers that the states and the people delegated to it. Thus there was no need to specify that Congress could not, for example, abridge freedom of the press because the states and the people had not given it power to regulate the press. Moreover, the Federalists argued, to guarantee some rights might be dangerous, because rights not listed could be denied. The Constitution already protected some important rights—trial by jury in federal criminal cases, for example. Hamilton and others also insisted that paper guarantees were feeble protection against governmental tyranny.

The Antifederalists were unconvinced. If some rights were protected, what could be the objection to providing constitutional protection for others? Without a bill of rights,

Patrick Henry's famous cry of "Give Me Liberty or Give Me Death!" symbolizes the underlying spirit of optimism in the United States. This spirit has endured throughout this country's history, despite the many problems the country has experienced.

what was to prevent Congress from using one of its delegated powers to abridge free speech? If bills of rights were needed in state constitutions to limit state governments, why did the national constitution not include a bill of rights to limit the national government? This was a government farther from the people, they contended, with a greater tendency to subvert natural rights than was true of state governments.

The Politics of Ratification

The absence of a bill of rights in the proposed constitution dominated the struggle over its adoption. In taverns, churches, and newspaper offices, people were muttering, "No bill of rights—no constitution!" This feeling was so strong that some Antifederalists, who were far more concerned with states' rights than individual rights, joined forces with those wanting a bill of rights to defeat the proposed Constitution.

The Federalists began the debate over the Constitution as soon as the delegates left Philadelphia in mid-September 1787. Their tactic was to secure ratification in as many states as possible before the opposition had time to organize. The Antifederalists were handicapped because most newspapers supported ratification. Moreover, Antifederalist strength was concentrated in rural areas, which were underrepresented in some state legislatures and difficult to arouse to political action. The Antifederalists needed time to organize, while the Federalists moved in a hurry.

Most of the small states, now satisfied by equal Senate representation, ratified the Constitution without difficulty. Delaware was the first state to ratify, and by early 1788, Pennsylvania, New Jersey, Georgia, and Connecticut had also ratified (see Table 1–2). In Massachusetts, however, opposition was growing. Key leaders, such as John Hancock and Samuel Adams, were doubtful or opposed. The debate in Boston raged for most of January 1788 into February. But in the end, the Massachusetts Convention narrowly ratified the Constitution in Massachusetts, 187 to 168.

By June 21, 1788, Maryland, South Carolina, and New Hampshire had also ratified, giving the Constitution the nine states required for it to go into effect. But two big hurdles remained: Virginia and New York. It would be impossible to begin the new government without the consent of these two major states. Virginia was crucial. As the most populous state, the home of Washington, Jefferson, and Madison, it was a link between North and South. The Virginia ratifying convention rivaled the Constitutional Convention in the caliber of its delegates. Madison, who had only recently switched to favoring a bill of rights after saying earlier that it was unnecessary, captained the Federalist forces. The fiery Patrick Henry led the opposition. In an epic debate, Henry cried that liberty was the issue: "Liberty, the greatest of earthly possessions... that precious jewel!" But Madison promised that a bill of rights embracing the freedoms of religion, speech, and assembly would be added to the Constitution as soon as the new government was established. Washington tipped the balance with a letter urging ratification. News of the Virginia vote, 89 for the Constitution and 79 opposed, was rushed to New York.[30]

TABLE 1–2 Ratification of the U.S. Constitution

State	Date
Delaware	December 7, 1787
Pennsylvania	December 12, 1787
New Jersey	December 18, 1787
Georgia	January 2, 1788
Connecticut	January 9, 1788
Massachusetts	February 6, 1788
Maryland	April 28, 1788
South Carolina	May 23, 1788
New Hampshire	June 21, 1788
Virginia	June 25, 1788
New York	July 26, 1788
North Carolina	November 21, 1789
Rhode Island	May 29, 1790

The great landowners along New York's Hudson River, unlike the southern planters, opposed the Constitution. They feared federal taxation of their holdings, and they did not want to abolish the profitable tax New York had been levying on trade and commerce with other states. When the convention assembled, the Federalists were greatly outnumbered, but they were aided by Alexander Hamilton's strategy and skill, and by word of Virginia's ratification. New York approved by a margin of three votes. Although North Carolina and Rhode Island still remained outside the Union (the former ratified in November 1789, the latter six months later), the new nation was created. In New York, a few members of the old Congress assembled to issue the call for elections under the new Constitution. Then they adjourned without setting a date for reconvening.

Summary

1. As the United States has waged the war on terrorism, the Bush administration has asserted presidential powers in such areas as wiretapping, bypassing a court established to review such cases. This is an example of how the application of the Constitution is worked out in each generation and in the context of new challenges and problems. Proponents of the use of the wiretaps point to the need to provide security for the country while opponents worry about the loss of civil liberties. These issues have been central to recent politics.

2. Americans have long been skeptical of politicians and politics. Yet politics is necessary and politicians are indispensable to making our system of separated institutions and checks and balances work.

3. "Democracy" and "republic" are often-misused terms that have many different meanings. We use them here to refer to a system of interacting values, interrelated political processes, and interdependent political structures. The vital principle of democracy is that a just government must derive its powers from the consent of the people and that this consent must be regularly renewed in free and fair elections. In many respects the Constitution established a Republic, with only the U.S. House of Representatives directly elected. In a Republic, elected officials decide policy on behalf of those who vote for them. Over time the United States has moved more toward direct democracy with such reforms as the direct election of U.S. senators, and voters deciding who will run for office in primary elections. The initiative and referendum are other examples of direct democracy.

4. The essential democratic values are a belief in personal liberty, respect for the individual, equality of opportunity, and popular consent. Essential elements of the democratic process are free and fair elections, majority rule, freedom of expression, and the right to assemble and protest.

5. Stable constitutional democracy is encouraged by various conditions, such as an educated citizenry, a healthy economy, and overlapping associations and groups within a society in which major institutions interact to achieve a certain degree of consensus.

6. Constitutionalism is a general label we apply to arrangements such as checks and balances, federalism, separation of powers, rule of law, due process, and the Bill of Rights that force our leaders and representatives to listen, think, bargain, and explain before they act and make laws. A constitutional government recognizes and limits the powers of those who govern.

7. Democracy developed gradually. It took several years after the Revolution before a national constitution could be written and almost another year for it to be ratified.

Further Reading

BERNARD BAILYN, ED., *The Debate on the Constitution: Federalist and Antifederalist Speeches, Articles, and Letters During the Struggle over Ratification,* 2 vols. (Library of America, 1993).

LANCE BANNING, *The Sacred Fire of Liberty: James Madison and the Founding of the Federal Republic* (Cornell University Press, 1995).

WILLIAM J. CROTTY, ED., *The State of Democracy in America* (Georgetown University Press, 2001).

ROBERT A. DAHL, *How Democratic Is the American Constitution,* 2d ed. (Yale University Press, 2003).

ROBERT A. DAHL, *On Democracy* (Yale University Press, 1998).

S. N. EISENSTADT, *Paradoxes of Democracy: Fragility, Continuity and Change* (Johns Hopkins University Press, 1999).

ALEXANDER HAMILTON, JAMES MADISON, AND JOHN JAY, *The Federalist Papers,* ed. Clinton Rossiter (New American Library, 1961). Also in several other editions.

SAMUEL P. HUNTINGTON, *The Third Wave: Democratization in the Late Twentieth Century* (University of Oklahoma Press, 1991).

DANIEL LESSARD LEVIN, *Representing Popular Sovereignty: The Constitution in American Political Culture* (State University of New York Press, 1999).

AREND LIJPHART, *Patterns of Democracy: Government Forms and Performance in Thirty-Six Countries* (Yale University Press, 1999).

DREW R. MCCOY, *The Last of the Fathers: James Madison and the Republican Legacy* (Columbia University Press, 1989).

DAVID MCCULLOUGH, *1776* (Simon & Schuster, 2005).

RICHARD B. MORRIS, *Witnesses at the Creation: Hamilton, Madison, and Jay and the Constitution* (Holt, Rinehart and Winston, 1985).

PIPPA NORRIS, ED., *Critical Citizens: Global Support for Democratic Institutions* (Oxford University Press, 1999).

JACK N. RAKOVE, *Original Meanings: Politics and Ideas in the Making of the Constitution* (Vintage Books, 1997).

MICHAEL J. SANDEL, *Democracy's Discontent: America in Search of a Public Philosophy* (Belknap Press, 1996).

MICHAEL SCHUDSON, *The Good Citizen: A History of American Civic Life* (Harvard University Press, 1998).

THEDA SKOCPOL AND **MORRIS P. FIORINA,** EDS., *Civic Engagement in American Democracy* (Brookings/Russell Sage, 1999).

CASS R. SUNSTEIN, *Designing Democracy: What Constitutions Do* (Oxford University Press, 2001).

ALEXIS DE TOCQUEVILLE, *Democracy in America,* 2 vols. (1835).

GARRY WILLS, *A Necessary Evil: A History of American Distrust of Government* (Simon & Schuster, 1999).

GORDON S. WOOD, *The Creation of the American Republic, 1776–1787* (University of North Carolina Press, 1969).

See also the *Journal of Democracy* (Johns Hopkins University Press).

Key Terms

democracy, p. 6

direct democracy, p. 6

representative democracy, p. 6

constitutional democracy, p. 7

constitutionalism, p. 7

statism, p. 9

popular consent, p. 10

majority rule, p. 11

majority, p. 11

plurality, p. 11

theocracy, p. 12

Articles of Confederation, p. 13

Annapolis Convention, p. 13

Constitutional Convention, p. 14

Shays's Rebellion, p. 14

bicameralism, p. 18

Virginia Plan, p. 18

New Jersey Plan, p. 19

Connecticut Compromise, p. 19

three-fifths compromise, p. 19

Federalists, p. 21

Antifederalists, p. 21

The Federalist, p. 22

Make It Real

CONSTITUTIONAL DEMOCRACY

This module includes a look at the *Federalist Papers* and the Articles of Confederation.

Chapter 2

The Living Constitution

★

THERE HAVE BEEN MORE THAN 10,000 EFFORTS TO CHANGE THE CONSTITUTION THROUGH AMENDMENTS OVER THE PAST 200 YEARS, BUT ONLY 27 AMENDMENTS HAVE BEEN RATIFIED, OR APPROVED BY THE STATES. THE FRAMERS KNEW THE CONSTITUTION MIGHT HAVE TO CHANGE WITH THE TIMES, BUT THEY DELIBERATELY MADE THE AMENDING PROCESS DIFFICULT.

ONE OF THE 27 AMENDMENTS THAT WAS EVENTUALLY ADOPTED WAS INTRODUCED IN 1789, SENT TO THE STATES BY CONGRESS, AND ABANDONED SEVERAL YEARS LATER WHEN seven of the 13 states refused to act on it. Under this amendment, members of Congress would have been banned from raising their salaries until after the next election, thereby giving voters a chance to express their opinions about the salary increase before it took effect.

In 1982, Gregory Watson, a University of Texas undergraduate, discovered the long-forgotten amendment while writing a term paper in a political science course. Although Watson only got a C on his term paper, he spent the next ten years convincing enough states to ratify the amendment. When Michigan joined the list in 1992, the proposal became the Twenty-Seventh Amendment to the Constitution.

Most proposed amendments are easily defeated, however, usually because they cannot win the two-thirds vote in both houses of Congress needed to send a proposal to the states for ratification. In recent years, for example, Congress has rejected amendments to require a balanced federal budget, to define marriage as a union between a man and a woman, and to ban abortion.

The most popular amendment currently being debated would ban burning the American flag. Because the Supreme Court declared that the First Amendment to the Constitution protects burning the flag as a form of political speech, only a constitutional amendment can make flag burning illegal. Under a proposal that passed the House of Representatives in 2005 by a 286-130 vote, Congress would have the power to prohibit the "physical desecration of the flag of the United States," meaning any effort to deliberately destroy or damage the American flag.

Even though the House has now voted seven times since the early 1990s to send this amendment forward, the Senate has been unable to muster the two-thirds vote needed to send it to the states. Although most senators criticize flag burning as anti-American, at least 34 of them appear to agree with the Supreme Court's view that flag burning is a form of political speech, which is why the amendment has never been sent to the states for possible ratification.

By late 2005, however, 64 senators appeared ready to vote for the amendment—just three votes short of the number needed to send it to the states. Advocates of the amendment received a boost in December 2005 when Senator Hillary Clinton (D-NY), announced her support for a law against flag burning. Although such a law would be unconstitutional under the Supreme Court's

> *"In questions of power, then, let no more be heard of confidence in man, but bind him down from mischief by the chains of the Constitution."*

THOMAS JEFFERSON

earlier decision, Clinton's announcement signaled that she might support the amendment. Even with her support, however, the amendment would still be two votes short in the Senate, which would guarantee its failure despite continued support in the House.

The flag-burning amendment illustrates the ongoing debate over what the Constitution means in America today. Having fought the Revolutionary War, the framers almost certainly could not have imagined that citizens might burn the American flag as a form of protest. But they did understand that citizens might decide to challenge the new government and call for changes in the Constitution. As this chapter will show, the framers decided to create a living Constitution that could be changed, but that would also check power with power, and guard against abuse by giving each institution of government the tools to protect liberty. Change would be possible, but difficult, which is exactly what the debate about flag burning illustrates.

Views of the Constitution

The Constitution of the United States is the world's oldest written constitution. Some 224 countries have written constitutions, but more than half (122) have been adopted or significantly revised since 1990, with 17 new ones ratified since 2000. Seven other countries have no written constitution, including Oman, New Zealand, and the United Kingdom.[1]

The Constitution is also one of the shortest. The original, unamended Constitution, which went into effect in 1789, contains just 4,543 words. Its basic structure is straightforward. Article I establishes a bicameral Congress, with a House of Representatives and a Senate, and empowers it to enact legislation; for example, governing foreign and interstate commerce (as discussed further in Chapter 11). Article II vests the executive power in the president (as discussed in Chapter 12), and Article III vests the judicial power in the Supreme Court and other federal courts that Congress may establish (as discussed in Chapter 14). Article IV guarantees the privileges and immunities of citizens and specifies the conditions for admitting new states. Article V provides for the methods of amending the Constitution, and Article VI specifies that the Constitution and all laws made under it are the supreme law of the land. Finally, Article VII provides that the Constitution had to be ratified by nine of the original 13 states to go into effect. In 1791 the first ten amendments, the Bill of Rights, were added, and subsequently another 17 amendments have been added. The entire Constitution and amendments appear at the end of this chapter.

The Constitution, nonetheless, established the framers' experiment in free-government-in-the-making that each generation reinterprets and renews. That is why after more than 220 years we have not had another written constitution—let alone two, three, or more, like other countries around the world. Part of the reason is the widespread acceptance of the Constitution by optimists and pessimists alike. But the Constitution has also endured because it is a brilliant structure for limited government and one that the framers designed to be adaptable and flexible.

As the Constitution won the support of citizens in the early years of the Republic, it took on the aura of **natural law**—law that defines right from wrong, law that is higher than human law. "The [Founding] Fathers grew ever larger in stature as they receded from view; the era in which they lived and fought became a Golden Age; in that age there had been a fresh dawn for the world, and its men were giants against the sky."[2] This early Constitution worship helped bring unity to the diverse new nation. Like the crown in Great Britain, the Constitution became a symbol of national loyalty, evoking both emotional and intellectual support from Americans, regardless of their differences. The framers' work became part of the American creed and culture.[3] The Constitution stands for liberty, equality before the law, limited or expanded government—indeed, for just about anything anyone wanted to read into it.

Even today, Americans generally revere the Constitution, though many do not know what is in it. A poll by the National Constitution Center found that nine out of ten Americans are proud of the Constitution and feel it is important to them. However, a

"You must first enable the government to control the governed; and in the next place oblige it to control itself."

JAMES MADISON, *THE FEDERALIST,* No. 51

natural law
God's or nature's law that defines right from wrong and is higher than human law.

third think the Constitution establishes English as the country's official language. One in six believes the Constitution establishes America as a Christian nation. Only one out of four could name a single First Amendment right. Although two out of three knew that the Constitution creates three branches of the national government, only one in three could name all three branches.[4]

The Constitution is more than a symbol, however. It is the supreme and binding law that both grants and limits powers. "In framing a government which is to be administered by men over men," wrote James Madison in *The Federalist*, No. 51, "the great difficulty lies in this: you must first enable the government to control the governed; and in the next place oblige it to control itself." (See *The Federalist*, No. 51, in the Appendix of this book, or go on the Web to www.law.ou.edu/hist/federalist/.) The Constitution is both a positive instrument of government, which enables the governors to control the governed, and a restraint on government, which enables the ruled to check the rulers. How does the Constitution limit the power of the government? How does it create governmental power? How has it managed to serve as a great symbol of national unity and at the same time as an adaptable instrument of government? The secret is an ingenious separation of powers and a system of checks and balances that limits power with power.

Checking Power with Power

It may seem strange to begin by stressing how the Constitution *limits* governmental power, but remember the dilemma the framers faced. They wanted a stronger and more effective national government than they had under the Articles of Confederation. But they were keenly aware that the people would not accept too much central control. Efficiency and order were important concerns, but liberty was more important. The framers wanted to ensure domestic tranquility and prevent future rebellions, but they also wanted to forestall the emergence of a homegrown King George III. Accordingly, they allotted certain powers to the national government and reserved the rest for the states, thus establishing a system of *federalism* (whose nature and problems we discuss in Chapter 3). Even this was not enough. They believed additional restraints were needed to limit the national government.

The most important way they devised to make public officials observe the constitutional limits on their powers was through *free and fair elections;* voters could throw those who abuse power out of office. Yet the framers were not willing to depend solely on political controls, because they did not fully trust the people's judgment. "Free government is founded on jealousy, and not in confidence," said Thomas Jefferson. "In questions of power, then, let no more be heard of confidence in man, but bind him down from mischief by the chains of the Constitution."[5]

No less important, the framers feared that a majority might deprive minorities of their rights. "A dependence on the people is, no doubt, the primary control on the government," Madison argued in *The Federalist*, No. 51, "but experience has taught mankind the necessity of auxiliary precautions." What were these "auxiliary precautions" against popular tyranny?

Separation of Powers

The first step was the **separation of powers**, the distribution of constitutional authority among the three branches of the national government. In *The Federalist*, No. 47, Madison wrote, "No political truth is certainly of greater intrinsic value, or is stamped with the authority of more enlightened patrons of liberty, than that . . . the accumulation of all powers, legislative, executive, and judiciary, in the same hands . . . may justly be pronounced the very definition of tyranny."[6] Chief among the "enlightened patrons of liberty" to whose authority Madison was appealing were the eighteenth-century philosophers John Locke and Montesquieu, whose works most educated Americans knew well.

"Free government is founded on jealousy, and not in confidence."

THOMAS JEFFERSON

7-4

"And there are three branches of government, so that each branch has the other two to blame everything on."

separation of powers
Constitutional division of powers among the legislative, executive, and judicial branches, with the legislative branch making law, the executive applying and enforcing the law, and the judiciary interpreting the law.

TABLE 2–1 The Exercise of Checks and Balances, 1789–2007

vetoes Presidents have vetoed more than 2,500 acts of Congress. Congress has overridden presidential vetoes more than 100 times.

judicial review The Supreme Court has ruled some 174 congressional acts or parts thereof unconstitutional. Its 1983 decision striking down legislative vetoes (*INS* v. *Chadha*) affects another 200 provisions.

impeachment The House of Representatives has impeached two presidents, one senator, one secretary of law, and 11 federal judges; the Senate has convicted seven of the judges but neither president.

confirmation The Senate has refused to confirm nine cabinet nominations. Many other cabinet and subcabinet appointments were withdrawn because the Senate seemed likely to reject them.

For additional resources on the Constitution, go to www.prenhall.com/burns.

The intrinsic value of the dispersion of power, however, does not by itself account for its inclusion in the Constitution. Dispersion of power, at least between colonial governors and legislatures, had been the general practice in the colonies for more than 100 years. Only during the Revolutionary period did some of the states concentrate authority in the hands of the legislature, and that unhappy experience confirmed the framers' belief in the merits of the separation of powers. Many attributed the evils of state government and the lack of energy in the central government under the Articles of Confederation to the lack of a strong executive to check legislative abuses and to give energy and direction to administration.

Still, separating power was not enough. The framers feared that different officials with different powers might pool their authority and act together. Separation of powers by itself might not prevent the branches of the government and officials from responding to the same pressures—from the demand of an overwhelming majority of the voters to suppress an offensive book or newspaper, for example, or to impose confiscatory taxes on the rich. If separating power was not enough, what else could be done?

Checks and Balances: Ambition to Counteract Ambition

The framers' answer was a system of **checks and balances**. "The great security against a gradual concentration of the several powers in the same department," wrote Madison in *The Federalist*, No. 51, "consists in giving to those who administer each department the necessary constitutional means and personal motives to resist encroachments of the others: . . . Ambition must be made to counteract ambition." Each branch therefore has a role in the actions of the others (see Figure 2–1). Congress enacts legislation, which the president must sign into law, or veto. The Supreme Court can declare laws passed by Congress and signed by the president unconstitutional, but the president appoints the justices and all the other federal judges, with the Senate's approval. The president administers the laws, but Congress provides the money to run the government. Moreover, the Senate and the House of Representatives have an absolute veto over each other, because both houses must approve bills before they can become law.

Not only does each branch have some authority over the others, but each is politically independent of the others. Voters in each local district choose members of the House; voters in each state choose senators; the president is elected by the voters in all the states. With the consent of the Senate, the president appoints federal judges, who remain in office until they retire or are impeached.

The framers also ensured that a majority of the voters could win control over only part of the government at one time. Although in an off-year (nonpresidential) election a new majority might take control of the House of Representatives, the president still has at least two more years, and senators hold office for six years. Finally, there are independent federal courts, which exercise their own powerful checks.

Constitutional Silences and Changes

Distrustful of both the elites and the masses, the framers deliberately built into our political system mechanisms to make change difficult. They designed the decision-making process so that the national government can act decisively only when there is a consensus among most groups and after all sides have had their say. "The doctrine of separation of powers was adopted by the convention of 1787," in the words of Justice Louis D. Brandeis, "not to promote efficiency but to preclude the exercise of arbitrary power. The purpose was not to avoid friction, but, by means of the inevitable friction

checks and balances
Constitutional grant of powers that enables each of the three branches of government to check some acts of the others and therefore ensure that no branch can dominate.

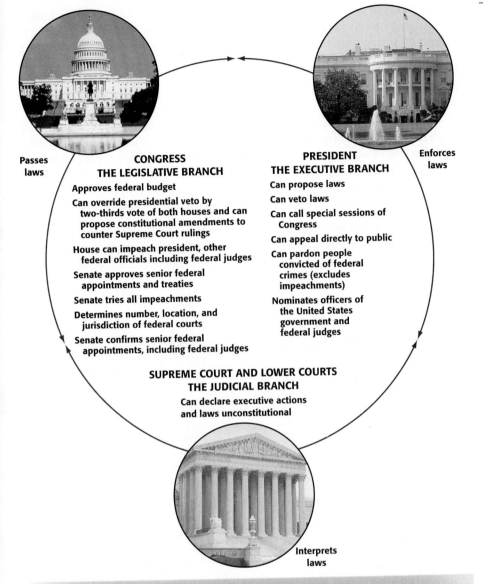

FIGURE 2–1 **The Separation of Powers and Checks and Balances.**

Passes laws

CONGRESS
THE LEGISLATIVE BRANCH

Approves federal budget

Can override presidential veto by two-thirds vote of both houses and can propose constitutional amendments to counter Supreme Court rulings

House can impeach president, other federal officials including federal judges

Senate approves senior federal appointments and treaties

Senate tries all impeachments

Determines number, location, and jurisdiction of federal courts

Senate confirms senior federal appointments, including federal judges

PRESIDENT
THE EXECUTIVE BRANCH

Can propose laws

Can veto laws

Can call special sessions of Congress

Can appeal directly to public

Can pardon people convicted of federal crimes (excludes impeachments)

Nominates officers of the United States government and federal judges

Enforces laws

SUPREME COURT AND LOWER COURTS
THE JUDICIAL BRANCH

Can declare executive actions and laws unconstitutional

Interprets laws

incident to the distribution of the governmental powers among three departments, to save the people from autocracy."[7] Still, even though the fragmentation of political power written into the Constitution remains, constitutional silences and subsequent developments have modified how the system of checks and balances works.

THE RISE OF NATIONAL POLITICAL PARTIES AND INTEREST GROUPS Political parties can serve as unifying factors, at times drawing together the president, senators, representatives, and sometimes even judges behind common programs. When parties do this, they help bridge the separation of powers. Yet parties can be splintered and weakened by having to work through a system of fragmented governmental power and by the increasing influence of special interest groups (discussed further in Chapter 6), so they never become too strong or cohesive. When one party controls Congress or one of its chambers and the other party controls the White House (**divided government**) partisanship is intensified, and Congress is more inclined to exercise oversight. Because his party controlled Congress during most of his presidency, President Bush has been remarkably free from congressional investigations of his administration. However, even when one party controls both branches, the pressures of competing interest groups may make cooperation difficult.

Because of the institutional competition between the legislative and executive branches, we find "each institution protecting and promoting itself through a broad

divided government
Governance divided between the parties, especially when one holds the presidency and the other controls one or both houses of Congress.

interpretation of its constitutional and political status, even usurping the other's power when the opportunity presents itself."[8] Thus we have had battles over the budget and angry confirmation hearings for the appointment of justices of the Supreme Court and even lower federal courts and members of the executive branch. The division of powers also makes it difficult for the voters to hold anyone or any party accountable. "Presidents blame Congress . . . while members of Congress attack the president. . . . Citizens genuinely cannot tell who is to blame."[9]

Yet, when all the shouting dies down, political scientist David Mayhew concludes, there have been just as many congressional investigations and just as much important legislation passed when one party controls Congress and another controls the presidency as when the same party controls both branches.[10] And Charles Jones, a noted authority on Congress and the presidency, adds that divided government is precisely what the voters appear to have wanted through much of our history.[11]

"I know no safe depositary of ultimate powers of the society but by the people themselves."

THOMAS JEFFERSON

EXPANSION OF THE ELECTORATE AND THE MOVE TOWARD MORE DIRECT DEMOCRACY The framers wanted the electoral college—wise, independent citizens free from popular passions and hero worship—rather than ordinary citizens to choose the president.

Government's Greatest Endeavors

Increasing Access to Education

QUESTIONS

How has the federal government helped you go to college?

Have federal loans had any impact on your tuition?

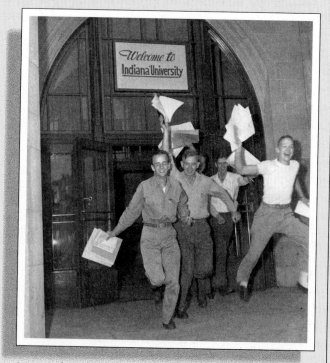

In 1944, the GI Bill began assisting veterans to attend college.

The framers believed an educated public was essential to a strong government. As Thomas Jefferson wrote late in his life, "I know no safe depositary of the ultimate powers of the society but the people themselves; and if we think them not enlightened enough to exercise their control with a wholesome discretion, the remedy is not to take it from them, but to inform their discretion by education."

For most of American history, however, the federal government left college education to individuals and the states. Although federal officials understood that an educated public was essential to economic growth, the federal government did not become involved in providing access to college until World War II. With more than 15 million soldiers about to return home in search of jobs and opportunity, Congress passed the Servicemen's Readjustment Act of 1944, popularly known as the "GI Bill." This bill provided grants for college and other benefits to war veterans.

The federal government did not become involved in helping students from low-income families go to college until the late 1950s, however. Convinced that the nation desperately needed more scientists and engineers to fight the cold war with the Soviet Union, Congress passed the National Defense Education Act of 1958. The act provided government funding for students pursuing degrees in technical fields or the modern languages, which were considered essential for building weapons and collecting intelligence.

In 1992, Congress approved the Higher Education Act, which allows students from families at any income level to obtain a federally guaranteed college loan. The following year, Congress passed the Budget Reconciliation Act, an omnibus bill that included provisions for the Federal Direct Student Loan program. The new plan allowed students to borrow money for college directly from the government rather than from banks. Under these and other programs, millions of college students have been able to finance their college education. ■

Almost from the beginning, though, the electoral college did not work this way.[12] Rather, voters actually do select the president, because the presidential electors the voters choose pledge in advance to cast their electoral votes for their party's candidates for president and vice president. Nevertheless, presidential candidates may occasionally win the national popular vote but lose the vote in the electoral college, as happened when Al Gore won the popular vote in the 2000 presidential election but lost the electoral college with 266 votes to George W. Bush's 271.

The kind of people allowed to vote has expanded from free, white, property-owning males to include all citizens over 18 years of age. In addition, during the past century, American states have expanded the role of the electorate by adopting **direct primaries**, in which the voters elect party nominees for the House and Senate and even for president; by permitting the voters in about half the states to propose and vote on laws (**initiatives**); by allowing voters to reconsider actions of the legislature (**referendums**); and even to remove elected state and local officials from office (**recall**). And since the ratification of the Seventeenth Amendment in 1913, senators are no longer elected by state legislatures but are chosen directly by the people.

ESTABLISHMENT OF AGENCIES DESIGNED TO EXERCISE LEGISLATIVE, EXECUTIVE, AND JUDICIAL FUNCTIONS When the national government began to regulate the economy in the late nineteenth and twentieth centuries, it found that it was impossible to legislate precise and detailed rules on complex matters such as railroad safety, mass communications, the health and safety of working conditions, and environmental protection. Consequently, in assigning these regulatory responsibilities, Congress has provided administrative agencies with the power to make and apply rules and to decide disputes. Beginning in 1887, Congress created *independent regulatory commissions* such as the Interstate Commerce Commission (which went out of business in 1995, although many of its functions were transferred to the Surface Transportation Board within the Department of Transportation) and later the Federal Communications Commission. More recently, it has established *independent executive agencies* such as the Environmental Protection Agency.

CHANGES IN TECHNOLOGY The system of checks and balances operates differently today from the way it did in 1789. Back then, there were no televised congressional committee hearings; no electronic communications; no *Larry King Live* talk shows; no *New York Times, USA Today*, CNN, Fox News, or C-SPAN; no Internet; no nightly news programs with national audiences; no presidential press conferences; and no live coverage of wars and of Americans fighting in foreign lands. Nuclear bombs, television, computers, cellular telephones, and the Internet—these and other innovations create conditions today that are unimaginably different from those of two centuries ago. We also live in a time of instant communication and polls that tell us what people are thinking almost from one day to the next about public issues.

In some ways, these new technologies have added to the powers of presidents by permitting them to appeal directly to millions of people and giving them immediate access to public opinion. And these new technologies have also enabled organized interests to target thousands of letters and calls at members of Congress, to orchestrate campaigns to write letters to editors, and to organize and mobilize on the Internet. New technologies have also given greater independence and influence to nongovernmental institutions such as the press and special interest groups. They have made it possible for rich people like former U.S. senator and now New Jersey governor Jon Corzine, who spent his own money to win elections, and for religious leaders like Pat Robertson, who have access to ample financial resources of followers in their interest groups and organizations, to bypass political parties and carry their message directly to the electorate.

THE GROWTH OF PRESIDENTIAL POWER Today problems elsewhere in the world—Afghanistan, Israel, Pakistan, Iran, North Korea, Iraq—often create crises for the United States. The need to deal with perpetual emergencies has concentrated power in the hands of the chief executive and the presidential staff. The president of the United States has emerged as the most significant player on the world stage, and media coverage of summit conferences with foreign leaders enhances his status. Headline-

direct primary
Election in which voters choose party nominees.

initiative
Procedure whereby a certain number of voters may, by petition, propose a law or constitutional amendment and have it submitted to the voters.

referendum
Procedure for submitting to popular vote measures passed by the legislature or proposed amendments to a state constitution.

recall
Procedure for submitting to popular vote the removal of officials from office before the end of their term.

How Other Nations **Govern**

The European Union

The European Union (EU) grew out of a succession of alliances formed after World War II to promote economic integration and cooperation among the countries of Europe. Through a series of treaties, the union included 25 countries by 2004. One of the most important institutions the union created is the European Court of Justice (ECJ). The ECJ can declare national laws invalid when they conflict with treaty obligations and has created a uniform system of law that takes precedence over national laws and constitutions in the member states. The member states of the EU also signed the European Convention on Human Rights, which establishes a long list of civil liberties. An independent tribunal, the European Court of Human Rights, resolves allegations of human rights abuses and has invalidated national laws that contravene provisions of the convention.

For the most part, the ECJ has resolved economic and commercial issues, but it has also struck down laws on the grounds of gender discrimination and advanced the right to equal pay for equal work. Critics of the ECJ complain that it has become too activist and compare it to the U.S. Supreme Court in the early nineteenth century under Chief Justice John Marshall (1755–1835), whose rulings striking down state trade barriers promoted the growth of our unified economy.

After long and contentious deliberations, a commission of European statesmen and legal advisers produced a complex and detailed Constitution. The Constitution would have strengthened the powers of the European Parliament, created a European president, defined the division of power between the member states and the EU, and the fundamental rights of EU citizens. For the proposed constitution to take effect, each of the 25 member states had to ratify it either in its national legislature or in a popular referendum. In 2005, however, voters in France and the Netherlands rejected the Constitution, which effectively killed it. At present, the future of a European Constitution is unclear; at the least, a new constitutional treaty will have to be renegotiated and resubmitted for ratification.

For more information on the EU, go to www.userpage.chemie.fu-berlin.de/adressen/eu.html and www.lib.berkeley.edu/gssi/eugde.html. The ECJ maintains a site at www.europa.eu.int/cj/en containing recent decisions and other information. ■

	Member of European Union
	Member in 2004
	Acceding Countries in 2007
	Candidate Countries
	Yet to begin negotiations

Membership in the European Union

generating events give the president a visibility no congressional leader can achieve. The office of the president has on occasion modified the system of checks and balances, especially between the executive branch and Congress, and provided a measure of national unity. Drawing on constitutional, political, and emergency powers, the president can sometimes overcome the restraints the Constitution imposes on the exercise of governmental power—to the applause of some Americans and the alarm of others.

Judicial Review and the "Guardians of the Constitution"

The judiciary has become so important in our system of checks and balances that it deserves special attention. Judges did not claim the power of **judicial review**—the power of a court to strike down a law or a government regulation that in the opinion of the judges conflicts with the Constitution—until some years after the Constitution was adopted. From the beginning, however, judges were expected to restrain legislative majorities. "The independence of judges," wrote Alexander Hamilton in *The Federalist*, No. 78 (which appears in the Appendix), "may be an essential safeguard against the effects of occasional ill humors in the society."

Judicial review is a major contribution of the United States to the art of government, a contribution that many other nations have adopted. In Canada, Germany, France, Italy, and Spain, constitutional courts review laws referred to them to ensure that the laws comply with their constitutions, including with the charter of rights that is now part of those constitutions.[13] (See also the box on the growth of judicial power in the European Union.)

> *"The independence of judges may be an essential safeguard against the effects of occasional ill humors in the society."*
>
> ALEXANDER HAMILTON, *THE FEDERALIST*, NO. 78

Origins of Judicial Review

The Constitution says nothing about who should have the final word in disputes that might arise over its meaning. Whether the delegates to the Constitutional Convention of 1787 intended to give the courts the power of judicial review has long been debated. The framers clearly intended that the Supreme Court have the power to declare state legislation unconstitutional, but whether they intended to give it the same power over *congressional* legislation and the president is not clear. Why didn't the framers specifically provide for judicial review? Probably because they believed the power could be inferred from certain general provisions and the necessity of interpreting and applying a written constitution.

The Federalists—who urged ratification of the Constitution and controlled the national government until 1801—generally supported a strong role for federal courts and favored judicial review. Their opponents, the Jeffersonian Republicans (called Democrats after 1832), were less enthusiastic. In the Kentucky and Virginia Resolutions of 1798 and 1799, respectively, Jefferson and Madison (who by this time had left the Federalist camp) came close to arguing that state legislatures—and not the Supreme Court—had the ultimate power to interpret the Constitution. These resolutions seemed to question whether the Supreme Court even had final authority to review state legislation, something about which there had been little doubt.

When the Jeffersonians defeated the Federalists in the election of 1800, it was still undecided whether the Supreme Court would actually exercise the power of judicial review. There were logical reasons—and even some precedents—to support such a doctrine; nevertheless, judicial review was not an established power. Then in 1803 came *Marbury* v. *Madison*, the most pathbreaking Supreme Court decision of all time.[14]

Marbury Versus *Madison*

President John Adams and fellow Federalists did not take their defeat in 1800 easily. Indeed, they were alarmed at what they considered to be the "enthronement of the rabble." Yet there was nothing much they could do about it before leaving office—or was there? The Constitution gives the president, with the consent of the Senate, the power to appoint federal judges to hold office during "good Behaviour"—basically, lifetime tenure, subject to removal only by impeachment. With the judiciary in the hands of Federalists, thought Adams and his associates, they could stave off the worst consequences of Jefferson's victory.

The outgoing Federalist Congress consequently created dozens of new federal judgeships. By March 3, 1801, the day before Jefferson was due to become president, Adams had appointed and the Senate had confirmed loyal Federalists to all these new

judicial review
The power of a court to refuse to enforce a law or a government regulation that in the opinion of the judges conflicts with the U.S. Constitution or, in a state court, the state constitution.

History Makers

Thurgood Marshall and the Civil Rights Movement

As a leader in the civil rights movement in the 1940s and 1950s, Thurgood Marshall was a crusading lawyer for the National Association for the Advancement of Colored People's Legal and Educational Defense Fund. He argued before the Supreme Court and won a companion case with the landmark ruling in *Brown* v. *Board of Education of Topeka* (1954), which held that segregated public schools were unconstitutional. President John Kennedy appointed him to the federal appellate bench in 1961. President Lyndon Johnson then persuaded Marshall to become solicitor general of the United States (the solicitor general argues the government's cases before the Supreme Court), and President Lyndon Johnson appointed him to the Supreme Court in 1967. As the first African American on the Supreme Court, Justice Marshall served until 1991 and continued to champion the cause of civil rights throughout his career.

On the anniversary of the Bicentennial of the Constitution in 1987, he spoke out in dissent and defended his view of our "living Constitution":

I do not believe that the meaning of the Constitution was forever "fixed" at the Philadelphia Convention. Nor do I find the wisdom, foresight, and sense of justice exhibited by the framers particularly profound. To the contrary, the government they devised was defective from the start, requiring several amendments, a civil war, and momentous social transformation to attain the system of constitutional government, and its respect for the individual freedoms and human rights, that we hold as fundamental today. When contemporary Americans cite "The Constitution," they invoke a concept that is vastly different from what the framers barely began to construct two centuries ago.

For a sense of the evolving nature of the Constitution we need look no further than the first three words of the document's preamble: "We the People." When the Founding Fathers used this phrase in 1787, they did not have in mind the majority of America's citizens. "We the People" included, in the words of the framers, "the whole Number of free Persons." On a matter so basic as the right to vote, for example, Negro slaves were excluded, although they were counted for representational purposes—at three-fifths each. Women did not gain the right to vote for over a hundred and thirty years. . . .

And so we must be careful, when focusing on the events which took place in Philadelphia two centuries ago, that we not overlook the momentous events which fol-

Justice Thurgood Marshall

lowed, and thereby lose our proper sense of perspective. . . . If we seek, instead, a sensitive understanding of the Constitution's inherent defects, and its promising evolution through 200 years of history, the celebration of the "Miracle at Philadelphia" will, in my view, be a far more meaningful and humbling experience. We will see that the true miracle was not the birth of the Constitution, but its life, a life nurtured through two turbulent centuries of our own making, and a life embodying much good fortune that was not.* ∎

*Remarks at the annual seminar of the San Francisco Patent and Trademark Law Association, Maui, Hawaii, May 16, 1987. In David M. O'Brien, ed., *Judges on Judging*, 2d ed. (C.Q. Press, 2004).

positions. Adams signed the commissions and turned them over to John Marshall, his secretary of state, to be sealed and delivered. Marshall had just received his own commission as chief justice of the United States, but he continued to serve as secretary of state until Adams's term as president expired. Working right up until nine o'clock on the evening of March 3, Marshall sealed, but was unable to deliver, all the commissions. The only ones left were for the justices of the peace for the District of Columbia. The newly appointed chief justice left the delivery of these commissions for his successor as secretary of state, James Madison.

This "packing" of the judiciary angered Jefferson, now inaugurated as president. When he discovered that some of the commissions were still lying on a table in the Department of State, he instructed a clerk not to deliver them. Jefferson could see no reason why the District needed so many justices of the peace, especially Federalist justices.[15]

Among the commissions not delivered was one for William Marbury. After waiting in vain, Marbury decided to seek action from the courts. Searching through the statute books, he came across Section 13 of the Judiciary Act of 1789, which authorized the Supreme Court "to issue writs of mandamus." A **writ of mandamus** is a court order directing an official, such as the secretary of state, to perform a duty about which the official has no discretion, such as delivering a commission. So, thought Marbury, why not ask the Supreme Court to issue a writ of mandamus to force James Madison,

writ of mandamus
Court order directing an official to perform an official duty.

the new secretary of state, to deliver the commission? Marbury and his companions went directly to the Supreme Court and, citing Section 13, they made the request.

What could Marshall do? On the one hand, if the Court issued the writ, Jefferson and Madison would probably ignore it. The Court would be powerless, and its prestige, already low, might suffer a fatal blow. On the other hand, by refusing to issue the writ, the judges would appear to support the Jeffersonian Republicans' claim that the Court had no authority to interfere with the executive. Would Marshall issue the writ? Most people thought he would; angry Republicans even threatened impeachment if he did so.

On February 24, 1803, the Supreme Court delivered its opinion. The first part was as expected. Marbury was entitled to his commission, said Marshall, and Madison should have delivered it to him. Moreover, the proper court could issue a writ of mandamus, even against so high an officer as the secretary of state.

Then came a surprise. Section 13 of the Judiciary Act appears to give the Supreme Court the power to issue a writ of mandamus in cases of original jurisdiction, such as this one in question. But Section 13, said Marshall, is contrary to Article III of the Constitution, which gives the Supreme Court original jurisdiction only when an ambassador or other foreign minister is affected or when a state is a party. Even though this is a case of original jurisdiction, Marbury is neither a state nor a foreign minister. Under the Constitution, wrote Marshall, the Court had no power to issue a writ of mandamus in cases on original jurisdiction.

Marshall then posed the question in a more pointed way: Should the Supreme Court enforce an unconstitutional law? Of course not, he concluded. *The Constitution is the supreme and binding law,* and the courts cannot enforce any action of Congress that conflicts with it, even if it expands the power of the Court. Thus by limiting the Court's power to what is granted in the Constitution, Marshall gained the much more important power to declare laws passed by Congress unconstitutional. It was a brilliant move.

Subsequent generations might have interpreted *Marbury* v. *Madison* in a limited way. It could have been interpreted to mean that the Supreme Court had the right to determine the scope of its own powers under Article III, but Congress and the president had the authority to interpret their powers under Articles I and II. But over the decades, building on Marshall's precedent, the Court has taken the commanding position as the authoritative interpreter of the Constitution.

Several important consequences follow from the acceptance of Marshall's argument that judges are the official interpreters of the Constitution. The most important is that people can challenge laws enacted by Congress and approved by the president. Simply by bringing a lawsuit, those who lack the clout to get a bill through Congress can often secure a judicial hearing. And organized interest groups often find that they can achieve goals through litigation that they could not attain through legislation. Litigation thus supplements, and at times even takes precedence over, legislation as a way to make public policy.[16]

Chief Justice John Marshall (1755–1835), our most influential Supreme Court justice. Appointed in 1801, Marshall served until 1835. Earlier he had been a staunch defender of the U.S. Constitution at the Virginia ratifying convention, a member of Congress, and a secretary of state. He was one of those rare people who served in all three branches of government.

The Constitution as an Instrument of Government

As careful as the Constitution's framers were to limit the powers they gave the national government, the main reason they assembled in Philadelphia was to create a stronger national government. Having learned that a weak central government was a danger to liberty, they wished to establish a national government within the framework of a federal system with enough authority to meet the needs of all time. They made general grants of power, leaving it to succeeding generations to fill in the details and organize the structure of government in accordance with experience.

Hence our formal, written Constitution is only the skeleton of our system. It is filled out in numerous ways that must be considered part of our constitutional system in a larger sense. In fact, our system is kept up to date primarily through changes in the informal, unwritten Constitution. These changes are found in certain basic statutes and historical practices of Congress, presidential actions, and Supreme Court decisions.

The Unwritten Constitution

CONGRESSIONAL ELABORATION   Because the framers gave Congress authority to provide for the structural details of the national government, it is not necessary to amend the Constitution every time a change is needed. Rather, Congress can create legislation to meet the need. Examples of congressional elaboration appear in such legislation as the Judiciary Act of 1789, which laid the foundations for our national judicial system; in the laws establishing the organization and functions of all federal executive officials subordinate to the president; and in the rules of procedure, internal organization, and practices of Congress.

A dramatic example of congressional elaboration of our constitutional system is the use of the impeachment and removal power. An **impeachment** is a formal accusation against a public official and the first step in removing him or her from office. Constitutional language defining the grounds for impeachment is sparse. Look at the Constitution (reprinted between this chapter and the next) and note that Article II (the Executive Article) calls for removal of the president, vice president, and all civil officers of the United States on impeachment for, and conviction of, "Treason, Bribery, or other High Crimes and Misdemeanors." Still, Congress has to give meaning to that language.

Article I (the Legislative Article) gives the House of Representatives the sole power to initiate impeachments and the Senate the sole power to try them. If the president is tried, the chief justice of the United States presides, as Chief Justice William H. Rehnquist did in the impeachment of President Bill Clinton in 1999. Article I also requires conviction on impeachment charges to have the agreement of two-thirds of the senators present. Judgments shall extend no further than removal from office and disqualification from holding any office under the United States, but a person convicted by the Senate may also be liable to indictment, trial, judgment, and punishment according to the law. Article I also exempts cases of impeachment from the president's pardoning power. Article III (the Judicial Article) exempts cases of impeachment from the jury trial requirement. That is all the relevant constitutional language about impeachment. We must look to history to answer most questions about the proper exercise of these and other powers.[17]

Fortunately, experience has triggered few acute constitutional disputes about the interpretation of impeachment procedures, so there is little history to go on. The House of Representatives has investigated 67 individuals for possible impeachment and has impeached 16 (including two presidents—Andrew Johnson in 1868, and Bill Clinton in 1999).

Presidential Practices

Although the formal constitutional powers of the president have not changed, the office is dramatically more important and more central today than it was in 1789. Vigorous presidents—George Washington, Thomas Jefferson, Andrew Jackson, Abraham Lincoln, Theodore Roosevelt, Woodrow Wilson, Franklin Roosevelt, Harry Truman, Lyndon Johnson, Bill Clinton, and George W. Bush—have boldly exercised their political and constitutional powers, especially during times of national crisis like the current war against international terrorism. Their presidential practices have established important precedents, building the power and influence of the office.

A major practice involves **executive orders**, which carry the full force of law. They may make major policy changes, such as withholding federal contracts from businesses engaging in racial discrimination, or they may simply be formalities, such as the presidential proclamation of Earth Day.

Other practices include **executive privilege** (the right to confidentiality of executive communications, especially those that relate to national security); **impoundment** by a president of funds previously appropriated by Congress; the power to send our armed forces into hostilities; and most important, the authority to propose legislation and work actively to secure its passage by Congress.

impeachment
Formal accusation by the lower house of a legislature against a public official, the first step in removal from office.

executive order
Directive issued by a president or governor that has the force of law.

executive privilege
The power to keep executive communications confidential, especially if they relate to national security.

impoundment
Presidential refusal to allow an agency to spend funds that Congress authorized and appropriated.

Foreign and economic crises as well as nuclear-age realities and the war against international terrorism have expanded the president's role: "When it comes to action risking nuclear war, technology has modified the Constitution: the President, perforce, becomes the only such man in the system capable of exercising judgment under the extraordinary limits now imposed by secrecy, complexity, and time."[18] The presidency has also become the pivotal office for regulating the economy and promoting the general welfare through an expanded federal bureaucracy (as discussed in Chapter 13). In addition, the president has become a leader in sponsoring legislation as well as the nation's chief executive.

Custom and Usage

Custom and usage also play a role in our governmental system. The development of structures outside the formal Constitution—such as national political parties, the proliferation of interest groups, and the expansion of suffrage in the states—has democratized our Constitution. Other examples of custom and usage are in televised press conferences and presidential and vice presidential debates. Through such developments, the president has become responsive to the people and has a political base different from that of Congress. Consequently, the constitutional relationship between the branches today is considerably different from what the framers envisioned.

Judicial Interpretation

As discussed earlier, judicial interpretation of the Constitution, especially by the Supreme Court, plays an important role in keeping the constitutional system up to date. As social and economic conditions change and new national demands develop, the Supreme Court has changed how it interprets the Constitution.

Although we have the oldest written constitution in the world, we do not have an agreed-on theory of how it should be interpreted, nor does the document itself say how it should be read. Justices, no less than politicians and citizens, differ over how to interpret it. Some, such as Justices Antonin Scalia and Clarence Thomas, contend that judges should adhere to the "original intent" of the Constitution, while others, such as Justices William J. Brennan Jr. and David H. Souter, view the Constitution as a "living document" that requires contemporary ratification.

Justice Scalia, a staunch conservative, contends that departing from the original intent of the Constitution undermines the legitimacy of the Court and leads to judicial legislation. In his words:

> A democratic society does not, by and large, need constitutional guarantees to insure that its laws will reflect "current values." Elections take care of that quite well. The purpose of constitutional guarantees—and in particular those constitutional guarantees of individual rights that are at the center of this controversy—is precisely to prevent the law from reflecting certain changes in original values that the society adopting the Constitution thinks fundamentally undesirable.[19]

By contrast, Justice Brennan, a leading liberal on the Court from 1956 to 1990, emphasized the problems with appealing to original intent: "It is arrogant to pretend that from our vantage [point] we can gauge accurately the intent of the framers on application of principle to specific, contemporary questions. Typically, all that can be gleaned is that the framers themselves did not agree about the application or meaning of particular constitutional provisions and hid their differences in cloaks of generality." Moreover, Justice Brennan maintained:

> Current justices read the Constitution in the only way that we can: as [contemporary] Americans. . . . [T]he ultimate question must be: What do the words of the text mean in our time? For the genius of the Constitution rests not in any static meaning it might have had in a world that is dead and gone, but in the adaptability of its great principles to cope with current problems and current needs.[20]

Still others, including Justices Ruth Bader Ginsburg and Stephen Breyer, contend that constitutional interpretation should be incremental and pragmatic, with particular

Two U.S. presidents, Andrew Johnson and Bill Clinton, have been impeached by the U.S. House of Representatives. In both cases the U.S. Senate did not muster a two-thirds majority vote, which would have been needed to convict these two presidents. President Richard Nixon almost surely would also have been impeached by the House of Representatives in 1974 but he resigned and left the presidency, and this decision preempted the House's action.

attention paid to the Court's institutional role and to the consequences and impact of its rulings.[21]

Because the Constitution requires interpretation and has been adapted to changing times, it has not often been formally amended. To appreciate the advantages of this flexibility, compare the national Constitution with the rigid and often overly specific state constitutions. Many state constitutions, like that of California, are so detailed that they tie the hands of public officials and must be amended or replaced frequently.

Changing the Letter of the Constitution

The idea of a constantly changing system disturbs many people. How, they contend, can you have a constitutional government when the Constitution is constantly being twisted by interpretation and changed by informal methods? This view fails to distinguish between two aspects of the Constitution. As an expression of *basic and timeless personal liberties,* the Constitution does not, and should not, change. For example, a government cannot destroy free speech and still remain a constitutional government. In this sense, the Constitution is unchanging. But when we consider the Constitution as an *instrument of government* and a positive grant of power, we realize that if it does not grow with the nation it serves, it would soon be irrelevant and ignored.

The framers could never have conceived of the problems facing the government of a large, powerful, and wealthy nation of about 300 million people at the beginning of the twenty-first century. Although the general purposes of government remain the same—to establish liberty, promote justice, ensure domestic tranquillity, and provide for the common defense—the powers of government that were adequate to accomplish these purposes in 1787 are simply insufficient more than 220 years later. Through its remarkable adaptability, our Constitution has survived democratic and industrial revolutions, civil war, major economic depressions, world wars, and international terrorism.

The framers knew that future experiences would call for changes in the text of the Constitution and that it would need to be formally amended. In Article V, they gave responsibility for amending the Constitution to Congress and to the states. The president has no formal authority over constitutional amendments; presidential veto power does not extend to them, although presidential influence is often crucial in getting amendments proposed and ratified.

Proposing Amendments

The first method for proposing amendments—and the only one used so far—is by *a two-thirds vote of both houses of Congress.* Dozens of resolutions proposing amendments are introduced in every session, but Congress has proposed only 31 amendments, of which 27 have been ratified (see Figure 2–2).

Why is proposing amendments to the Constitution so popular? In part because interest groups unhappy with Supreme Court decisions seek to overturn them. In part because groups frustrated by their inability to get things done in Congress hope to bypass it. And in part because scholars or interest groups (not necessarily mutually exclusive categories) seek to change the procedures and processes of government to make the system more responsive.

The second method for proposing amendments—*a convention called by Congress* at the request of the legislatures in two-thirds of the states—has never been used. Under Article V of the Constitution, Congress could call for such a convention without the concurrence of the president. This method presents difficult questions.[22] First, can state legislatures apply for a convention to propose specific amendments on one topic, or must they request a convention with full powers to revise the entire Constitution? How long do state petitions remain alive? How should delegates to a convention be chosen? How should such a convention be run? Congress has considered bills to answer some of these questions but has not passed any, in part because most

Agents of Change

Earl Phalen and Building Educated Leaders for Life

In 1992, a group of African American and Hispanic students at Harvard University's law school founded Building Educated Leaders for Life (BELL). Designed to teach students to read, write, and do basic math, BELL was created to ensure that all students get an equal chance to complete high school and go on to college. Having started in just one school in Cambridge, Massachusetts, BELL now serves 7,000 young scholars in four cities.

BELL was founded by Earl Phalen, a young law-school graduate who brought his own life experiences to the organization. Abandoned at birth in 1967, he seemed destined for a life of poverty until a couple adopted him as part of their family. "We had always been so involved in the civil rights struggle that we thought that if nothing else, we could adopt a male child," Phalen's mother later said. "We had a happy home, so we decided to do that."

Having learned about social justice from his parents, Phalen eventually attended Yale University, where he earned varsity letters in basketball and track. After graduating from Yale in 1989, he spent the year before he entered law school volunteering at a homeless shelter with the Lutheran Church in Washington, D.C. That is where he first saw the problems young children were having. He recognized that they would need to learn enough in school to have a fighting chance at success.

Phalen then went to Jamaica to work on human rights issues involving police abuses. During law school, he worked as a teaching assistant at an orphanage and eventually started mentoring young children. BELL was born from that experience, and now has a graduation rate of more than 80 percent among its students, compared with the 30 percent rate among African American and Hispanic students nationwide. ■

Learn more about BELL at www.bellnational.org.

Earl Phalen, founder of BELL

Questions

How does BELL make a difference in the future of the Constitution?

Why does helping students succeed make the Constitution more effective in promoting civic engagement?

members do not wish to encourage a constitutional convention for fear that once in session it might propose amendments on any and all topics. See Table 2–2 on how the amending power has been used.

Under most proposals, each state would have as many delegates to the convention as it has representatives and senators in Congress. Finally and crucially, a constitutional convention would be limited to considering only the subject specified in the state legislative petitions and described in the congressional call for the convention. Scholars are divided, however, on whether Congress has the authority to limit what a constitutional convention might propose.[23]

Ratifying Amendments

After an amendment has been proposed, it must be ratified by the states before it takes effect. Again, the Constitution provides two methods: approval by the legislatures in three-fourths of the states, or approval by special ratifying conventions in three-fourths of the states. Congress determines which method is used. Congress has

FIGURE 2–2 **Four Methods of Amending the Constitution.**

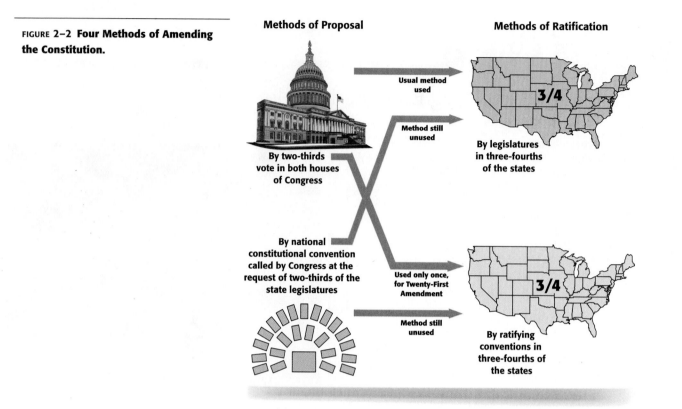

submitted all amendments except one—the Twenty-First (to repeal the Eighteenth, the Prohibition Amendment)—to the state legislatures for ratification.

Seven state constitutions specify that their state legislatures must ratify a proposed amendment to the U.S. Constitution by majorities of three-fifths or two-thirds of each chamber. Although a state legislature may change its mind and ratify an amendment after it has voted against ratification, the weight of opinion is that once a state has ratified an amendment, it cannot "unratify" it.[24]

The Supreme Court has said that ratification must take place within a "reasonable time." When Congress proclaims an amendment to be part of the Constitution, it must decide whether the amendment has been ratified within a reasonable time, so that it is "sufficiently contemporaneous to reflect the will of the people."[25] However, Congress approved ratification of the Twenty-Seventh Amendment, which had been before the nation for almost 203 years, so there seems to be no limit on what it considers a "reasonable time." Because of the experience with the Twenty-Seventh Amendment, Congress will probably continue the current practice of stipulating in the text of a proposed amendment that the necessary number of states must ratify it within seven years from the date of submission by Congress. In fact ratification ordinarily takes place rather quickly (see Figure 2–3).

Ratification Politics

The failure of the Equal Rights Amendment (ERA) to be ratified provides a vivid example of the pitfalls of ratification. First introduced in 1923, the ERA did not get much support until the 1960s. An influential book by Betty Friedan, *The Feminine Mystique* (1963), challenged stereotypes about the role of women. The National Organization for Women (NOW), formed in 1966, made passage of the ERA its central mission. By the 1970s, the ERA had overwhelming support in both houses of Congress and in both national party platforms. Every president from Harry Truman to Ronald Reagan, and many of their wives, endorsed the amendment. More than 450 organizations with

TABLE 2–2   The Amending Power and How It Has Been Used

Leaving aside the first ten amendments (the Bill of Rights), the power of constitutional amendment has served a number of purposes:

To Increase or Decrease the Power of the National Government

The Eleventh took some jurisdiction away from the national courts.

The Thirteenth abolished slavery and authorized Congress to legislate against it.

The Sixteenth enabled Congress to levy an income tax.

The Eighteenth authorized Congress to prohibit the manufacture, sale, or transportation of liquor.

The Twenty-First repealed the Eighteenth and gave states the authority to regulate liquor sales.

The Twenty-Seventh limited the power of Congress to set members' salaries.

To Expand the Electorate and Its Power

The Fifteenth extended suffrage to all male African Americans over the age of 21.

The Seventeenth took the right to elect United States senators away from state legislatures and gave it to the voters in each state.

The Nineteenth extended suffrage to women over the age of 21.

The Twenty-Third gave voters of the District of Columbia the right to vote for president and vice president.

The Twenty-Fourth outlawed the poll tax, thereby prohibiting states from taxing the right to vote.

The Twenty-Sixth extended suffrage to otherwise qualified persons 18 years of age or older.

To Reduce the Electorate's Power

The Twenty-Second took away from the electorate the right to elect a person to the office of president for more than two full terms.

To Limit State Government Power

The Thirteenth abolished slavery.

The Fourteenth granted national citizenship and prohibited states from abridging privileges of national citizenship; from denying persons life, liberty, and property without due process; and from denying persons equal protection of the laws. This amendment has come to be interpreted as imposing restraints on state powers in every area of public life.

To Make Structural Changes in Government

The Twelfth corrected deficiencies in the operation of the electoral college that the development of a two-party national system had revealed.

The Twentieth altered the calendar for congressional sessions and shortened the time between the election of presidents and their assumption of office.

The Twenty-Fifth provided procedures for filling vacancies in the vice presidency and for determining whether presidents are unable to perform their duties.

a total membership of more than 50 million were on record in support of the ERA.[26] The ERA provided:

Section 1.   Equality of rights under the law shall not be denied or abridged by the United States or by any State on account of sex.

Section 2.   The Congress shall have power to enforce, by appropriate legislation, the provisions of this article.

Section 3.   This amendment shall take effect two years after the date of ratification.

Soon after Congress passed the amendment and submitted it to the states in 1972, many legislatures ratified it—sometimes without hearings—and by overwhelming majorities. By the end of that year, 22 states had ratified the amendment, and it appeared that the ERA would soon become part of the Constitution. But due to opposition organized under the leadership of Phyllis Schlafly, a prominent spokesperson for conservative causes, the ERA became controversial.

Opponents argued that "women would not only be subject to the military draft but also assigned to combat duty. Full-time housewives and mothers would be forced to join the labor force. Further, women would no longer enjoy existing advantages under

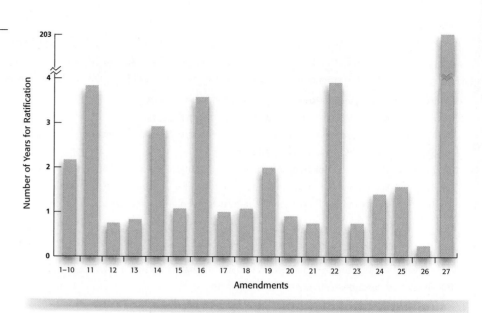

FIGURE **2–3 The Time for Ratification of the 27 Amendments to the Constitution.**

state domestic relations codes and under labor law."[27] The ERA also became embroiled in the controversy over abortion. Many opponents contended that its ratification would jeopardize the power of states and Congress to regulate abortion and would compel public funding of abortions.[28]

After the ERA became controversial, state legislatures held lengthy hearings, and floor debates became heated. Legislators hid behind parliamentary procedures and avoided making a decision for as long as possible. Opposition to ratification arose chiefly in the same cluster of southern states that had opposed ratification of the Nineteenth Amendment, which gave women the right to vote. As the opposition grew more active, proponents redoubled their efforts.

In the autumn of 1978, it appeared that the ERA would fall three short of the necessary number of ratifying states before the expiration of the seven-year limit on March 22, 1979. After an extended debate, and after voting down provisions that would have authorized state legislatures to change their minds and rescind ratifi-

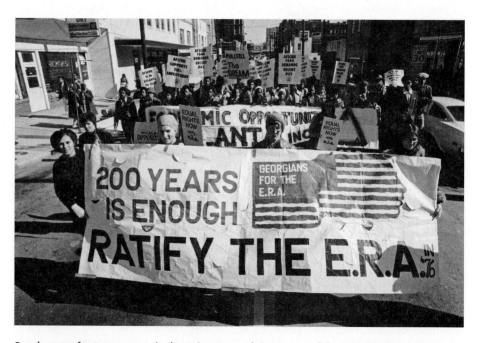

People came from every state in the union to march in support of the passage of the Equal Rights Amendment.

The Changing Face of American Politics

America's Racial Heritage

During his rise as one of golf's greatest players, Tiger Woods has repeatedly refused to identify himself as a member of any one race, be it white, African American, Asian American, or Hispanic. Instead, Woods says that he decided as a child that he was a "Cablinasian," a reference to being *Ca*ucasian (white), *Bl*ack, American *In*dian, and *Asian*. However, before the 2000 census, which is conducted every ten years as mandated by the Constitution, he was not allowed to declare himself as a member of more than one race. He could check only one of five boxes for race—Caucasian, African American, Asian, or Native American. Hispanics or Latinos were identified separately.

Starting in 2000, Woods and millions of other multiracial Americans were able to identify themselves more accurately in the census. Under federal rules adopted in 1998, he was allowed to check off one or all

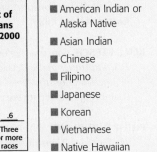

of seven boxes, including new categories for Native Hawaiian and other Pacific Islanders, which used to be included in "Asian." Once Woods identified himself as any race other than white, he was also free to identify with one or more of the following races, or with another race entirely:

- American Indian or Alaska Native
- Asian Indian
- Chinese
- Filipino
- Japanese
- Korean
- Vietnamese
- Native Hawaiian
- Guamanian or Chamorro
- Samoan
- Other Pacific Islander

The new rules reflect the new reality that America is becoming more diverse. Its population includes more Americans of mixed-racial heritage. The census, which is used to divide the states into congressional districts, is working to keep up with the changing face of America, which means that citizens like Tiger Woods will be able to find a home in the portraits of the citizenry. Although the percentage of multiracial Americans is low, it still represents more than 7 million of the nation's 281 million citizens. ■

cation, Congress, by a simple majority vote, extended the time limit until June 30, 1982. Nonetheless, by the final deadline, the amendment was still three states short of the 38 needed for ratification.

The framers intended that amending the Constitution should be difficult, and the ERA ratification battle demonstrates how well they planned. Still, through interpretation, practices, usages, and judicial decisions, the Constitution has proved a remarkably enduring and adaptable governing document.

Summary

1. The U.S. Constitution, adopted in 1789, is the world's oldest. It has lasted because it is adaptable and flexible. It both grants and limits governmental power. The Constitution's separation of powers distributes authority among three branches of government: the legislative, executive, and judicial. Checks and balances limit the power of each branch.

2. Political parties may sometimes overcome the separation of powers, especially if the same party controls both houses of Congress and the presidency. Typically, this is not the case, however, and a divided government intensifies checks and balances. Presidential power, which has increased over time, has sometimes overcome restraints the Constitution imposes on it.

3. Judicial review is the power of the courts to strike down acts of Congress, the executive branch, and the states as unconstitutional. The Supreme Court's power of judicial review was established in the 1803 case of *Marbury* v. *Madison*.

4. The Constitution is the framework of our governmental system. The constitutional system has been modified over time, adapting to new conditions through congressional elaboration, presidential practices, custom and usage, and judicial interpretation.

5. Although adaptable, the Constitution itself needs to be altered from time to time, and the framers provided a procedure for its amendment. An amendment must be both proposed and ratified: proposed by either a two-thirds vote in each chamber of Congress or by a national convention called by Congress on

petition of the legislatures in two-thirds of the states; ratified either by the legislatures in three-fourths of the states or by special ratifying conventions in three-fourths of the states.

6. The Constitution has been formally amended 27 times. The usual method has been proposal by a two-thirds vote in both houses of Congress and ratification by the legislatures in three-fourths of the states.

Further Reading

AKHILL REED AMAR, *America's Constitution: A Biography* (Random House, 2005).

LANCE BANNING, *The Sacred Fire of Liberty: James Madison and the Founding of the Federal Republic* (Cornell University Press, 1995).

CAROL BERKIN, *A Brilliant Solution: Inventing the American Constitution* (Harcourt, 2002).

STEPHEN BREYER, *Active Liberty: Interpreting Our Democratic Constitution* (Knopf, 2005).

JAMES MACGREGOR BURNS, *The Vineyard of Liberty* (Knopf, 1982).

NEIL H. COGAN, *The Complete Bill of Rights: The Drafts, Debates, Sources, and Origins* (Oxford University Press, 1997).

MICHAEL KAMMEN, *A Machine That Would Go of Itself: The Constitution in American Culture* (Knopf, 1986).

KEN I. KERSCH, *Constructing Civil Liberties: Discontinuities in the Development of American Constitutional Law* (Cambridge University Press, 2004).

PHILIP B. KURLAND AND **RALPH LERNER,** *The Founders' Constitution*, 5 vols. (University of Chicago Press, 1987).

LIBRARY OF CONGRESS, CONGRESSIONAL RESEARCH SERVICE, JONNY KILLIAN, ED., *The Constitution of the United States of America: Analysis and Interpretation,* (U.S. Government Printing Office, 2006).

ANTONIN SCALIA, *A Matter of Interpretation: Federal Courts and the Law* (Princeton University Press, 1997).

CASS SUNSTEIN, *Designing Democracy: What Constitutions Do* (Oxford University Press, 2001).

JOHN R. VILE, ED. *Encyclopedia of Constitutional Amendments, Proposed Amendments, and Amending Issues, 1789–2002* (ABC-Clio, 2003).

Key Terms

natural law, p. 28	initiative, p. 33	impeachment, p. 38
separation of powers, p. 29	referendum, p. 33	executive order, p. 38
checks and balances, p. 30	recall, p. 33	executive privilege, p. 38
divided government, p. 31	judicial review, p. 34	impoundment, p. 38
direct primary, p. 33	writ of mandamus, p. 36	

Make It Real

CONSTITUTIONAL DEMOCRACY

This module includes a look at the *Federalist Papers* and the Articles of Confederation.

On Reading the Constitution

★

More than 218 years after its ratification, our Constitution remains the operating charter of our republic. It is neither self-explanatory nor a comprehensive description of our constitiutional rules. Still, it remains the starting point. Many Americans who swear by the Constitution have never read it seriously, although copies can be found in most American government and American history textbooks.

Justice Hugo Black, who served on the Supreme Court for 34 years, kept a copy of the Constitution with him at all times. He read it often. Reading the Constitution would be a good way for you to begin (and then reread again to end) your study of the government of the United States. We have therefore included a copy of it at this point in the book. Please read it carefully.

The Constitution of the United States

⋆

The Preamble

𝖂𝖊 𝖙𝖍𝖊 𝕻𝖊𝖔𝖕𝖑𝖊 of the United States, in Order to form a more perfect Union, establish Justice, insure domestic Tranquility, provide for the common defense, promote the general Welfare, and secure the Blessings of Liberty to ourselves and our Posterity, do ordain and establish this Constitution for the United States of America.

Article I—The Legislative Article

Legislative Power

SECTION 1   All legislative Powers herein granted shall be vested in a Congress of the United States, which shall consist of a Senate and House of Representatives.

House of Representatives: Composition; Qualifications; Apportionment; Impeachment Power

SECTION 2

Clause 1   The House of Representatives shall be composed of Members chosen every second Year by the People of the several States, and the Electors in each State shall have the Qualifications requisite for Electors of the most numerous Branch of the State Legislature.

Clause 2   No Person shall be a Representative who shall not have attained to the Age of twenty five Years, and been seven Years a Citizen of the United States, and who shall not, when elected, be an inhabitant of that State in which he shall be chosen.

Clause 3   Representatives and direct Taxes[1] shall be apportioned among the several States which may be included within this Union, according to their respective Numbers, which shall be determined by adding to the whole Number of free Persons, including those bound to Service for a Term of Years, and excluding Indians not taxed, three fifths of all other Persons.[2] The actual Enumeration shall be made within three Years after the first Meeting of the Congress of the United States, and within every subsequent Term of ten Years, in such Manner as they shall by Law direct. The Number of Representatives shall not exceed one for every thirty Thousand, but each State shall have at Least one Representative; and until such enumeration shall be made, the State of New Hampshire shall be entitled to chuse three, Massachusetts eight, Rhode-Island and Providence Plantations one, Connecticut five, New-York six, New Jersey four, Pennsylvania eight, Delaware one, Maryland six, Virginia ten, North Carolina five, South Carolina five, and Georgia three.

Clause 4   When vacancies happen in the Representation from any State, the Executive Authority thereof shall issue Writs of Election to fill such Vacancies.

Clause 5   The House of Representatives shall chuse their Speaker and other Officers; and shall have the sole Power of Impeachment.

Senate Composition: Qualifications, Impeachment Trials

SECTION 3

Clause 1   The Senate of the United States shall be composed of two Senators from each State, chosen by the Legislature thereof,[3] for six Years; and each Senator shall have one Vote.

Clause 2   Immediately after they shall be assembled in Consequence of the first Election, they shall be divided as equally as may be into three Classes. The Seats of the Senators of the first Class shall be vacated at the Expiration of the second Year, of the second Class at the Expiration of the fourth Year, and of the third Class at the Expiration of the sixth Year, so that one third may be chosen every second Year; and if Vacancies happen by Resignation, or otherwise, during the Recess of the Legislature of any State, the Executive thereof may make temporary Appointments until the next Meeting of the Legislature, which shall then fill such Vacancies.[4]

Clause 3   No person shall be a Senator who shall not have attained to the Age of thirty Years, and been nine Years a Citizen of the United States, and who shall not, when elected, be an Inhabitant of that State for which he shall be chosen.

Clause 4   The Vice President of the United States shall be President of the Senate, but shall have no Vote, unless they be equally divided.

Clause 5   The Senate shall chuse their other Officers, and also a President pro tempore, in the Absence of the Vice

---

[1]Modified by the 16th Amendment
[2]Replaced by Section 2, 14th Amendment

[3]Repealed by the 17th Amendment
[4]Modified by the 17th Amendment

President, or when he shall exercise the Office of President of the United States.

Clause 6   The Senate shall have the sole Power to try all Impeachments. When sitting for that Purpose, they shall be on Oath or Affirmation. When the President of the United States is tried, the Chief Justice shall preside: And no Person shall be convicted without the Concurrence of two thirds of the Members present.

Judgment in Cases of Impeachment shall not extend further than to removal from Office, and disqualification to hold and enjoy any Office of honor, Trust or Profit under the United States; but the Party convicted shall nevertheless be liable and subject to Indictment, Trial, Judgment and Punishment, according to Law.

Congressional Elections: Times, Places, Manner

SECTION 4   The Times, Places and Manner of holding Elections for Senators and Representatives, shall be prescribed in each State by the Legislature thereof; but the Congress may at any time by Law make or alter such Regulations, except as to the Places of chusing Senators.

The Congress shall assemble at least once in every Year, and such Meeting shall be on the first Monday in December, unless they shall by Law appoint a different Day.[5]

Powers and Duties of the Houses

SECTION 5

Clause 1   Each House shall be the Judge of the Elections, Returns and Qualifications of its own Members, and a Majority of each shall constitute a Quorum to do Business; but a smaller Number may adjourn from day to day, and may be authorized to compel the Attendance of absent Members, in such Manner, and under the Penalties as each House may provide.

Clause 2   Each House may determine the Rules of its Proceedings, punish its Members for disorderly Behaviour, and, with the Concurrence of two thirds, expel a Member.

Clause 3   Each House shall keep a Journal of its Proceedings, and from time to time publish the same, excepting such Parts as may in their Judgment require Secrecy; and the Yeas and Nays of the Members of either House on any question shall, at the Desire of one fifth of those Present, be entered on the Journal.

Clause 4   Neither House, during the Session of Congress, shall, without the Consent of the other, adjourn for more than three days, nor to any other place than that in which the two Houses shall be sitting.

Rights of Members

SECTION 6

Clause I   The Senators and Representatives shall receive a Compensation for their Services, to be ascertained by Law,

and paid out of the Treasury of the United States. They shall in all Cases, except Treason, Felony and Breach of the Peace, be privileged from Arrest during their Attendance at the Session of their respective Houses, and in going to and returning from the same; and for any Speech or Debate in either House, they shall not be questioned in any other Place.

Clause 2   No Senator or Representative, shall, during the time for which he was elected, be appointed to any civil Office under the Authority of the United States, which shall have been created, or the Emoluments whereof shall have been increased during such time; and no Person holding any Office under the United States, shall be a Member of either House during his Continuance in Office.

Legislative Powers: Bills and Resolutions

SECTION 7

Clause 1   All Bills for raising Revenue shall originate in the House of Representatives; but the Senate may propose or concur with Amendments as on other Bills.

Clause 2   Every Bill which shall have passed the House of Representatives and the Senate, shall, before it becomes a Law, be presented to the President of the United States; if he approve he shall sign it, but if not he shall return it, with his Objections to that House in which it shall have originated, who shall enter the Objections at large on their Journal, and proceed to reconsider it. If after such Reconsideration two thirds of that House shall agree to pass the Bill, it shall be sent, together with the Objections, to the other House, by which it shall likewise be reconsidered, and if approved by two thirds of that House, it shall become a Law. But in all such Cases the Votes of both Houses shall be determined by yeas and Nays, and the Names of the Persons voting for and against the Bill shall be entered on the Journal of each House respectively. If any Bill shall not be returned by the President within ten Days (Sundays excepted) after it shall have been presented to him, the Same shall be a Law, in like Manner as if he had signed it, unless the Congress by their Adjournment prevent its Return, in which Case it shall not be a Law.

Clause 3   Every Order, Resolution, or Vote to which the Concurrence of the Senate and House of Representatives may be necessary (except on a question of Adjournment) shall be presented to the President of the United States; and before the Same shall take Effect, shall be approved by him, or being disapproved by him, shall be repassed by two thirds of the Senate and House of Representatives, according to the Rules and Limitations prescribed in the Case of a Bill.

Powers of Congress

SECTION 8

Clause 1   The Congress shall have Power To lay and collect Taxes, Duties, Imposts and Excises, to pay the Debts and provide for the common Defence and general Welfare of the

---

[5]Changed by the 20th Amendment

United States; but all Duties, Imposts and Excises shall be uniform throughout the United States.

To borrow Money on the credit of the United States;

To regulate Commerce with foreign Nations, and among the several States, and with the Indian Tribes;

To establish an uniform Rule of Naturalization, and uniform Laws on the subject of Bankruptcies throughout the United States;

To coin Money, regulate the Value thereof, and of foreign Coin, and fix the Standard of Weights and Measures;

To provide for the Punishment of counterfeiting the Securities and current Coin of the United States;

To establish Post Offices and post Roads;

To promote the Progress of Science and useful Arts, by securing for limited Times to Authors and Inventors the exclusive Right to their respective Writings and Discoveries;

To constitute Tribunals inferior to the supreme Court;

To define and punish Piracies and Felonies committed on the high Seas, and Offences against the Law of Nations;

To declare War, grant Letters of Marque and Reprisal, and make Rules concerning Captures on Land and Water;

To raise and support Armies, but no Appropriation of Money to that Use shall be for a longer Term than two Years;

To provide and maintain a Navy;

To make Rules for the Government and Regulation of the land and naval Forces;

To provide for calling for the Militia to execute the Laws of the Union, suppress Insurrections and repel Invasions;

To provide for organizing, arming, and disciplining the Militia, and for governing such Part of them as may be employed in the Service of the United States, reserving to the States respectively, the Appointment of the Officers, and the Authority of training the Militia according to the discipline prescribed by Congress;

Clause 2 To exercise exclusive Legislation in all Cases whatsoever, over such District (not exceeding ten Miles square) as may, by Cession of particular States, and the Acceptance of Congress, become the Seat of the Government of the United States, and to exercise like Authority over all Places purchased by the Consent of the Legislature of the State in which the Same shall be, for the Erection of Forts, Magazines, Arsenals, dock-Yards; and other needful Buildings;—And

Clause 3 To make all Laws which shall be necessary and proper for carrying into Execution the foregoing Powers, and all other Powers vested by this Constitution in the Government of the United States, or in any Department or Officer thereof.

Powers Denied to Congress

SECTION 9

Clause 1 The Migration or Importation of such Persons as any of the States now existing shall think proper to admit, shall not be prohibited by the Congress prior to the Year one thousand eight hundred and eight, but a Tax or duty may be imposed on such Importation, not exceeding ten dollars for each Person.

Clause 2 The privilege of the Writ of Habeas Corpus shall not be suspended, unless when in Cases of Rebellion or Invasion the public Safety may require it.

Clause 3 No Bill of Attainder or ex post facto Laws shall be passed.

Clause 4 No Capitation, or other direct, Tax shall be laid, unless in Proportion to the Census or Enumeration herein before directed to be taken.[6]

Clause 5 No Tax or Duty shall be laid on Articles exported from any State.

Clause 6 No Preference shall be given by any Regulation of Commerce or Revenue to the Ports of one State over those of another; nor shall Vessels bound to, or from, one State, be obliged to enter, clear, or pay Duties in another.

Clause 7 No Money shall be drawn from the Treasury, but in Consequence of Appropriations made by Law; and a regular Statement and Account of the Receipts and Expenditures of all public Money shall be published from time to time.

Clause 8 No Title of Nobility shall be granted by the United States; And no Person holding any Office of Profit or Trust under them, shall, without the Consent of Congress, accept of any present, Emolument, Office, or Title, of any kind whatever, from any King, Prince, or foreign State.

Powers Denied to the States

SECTION 10

Clause 1 No State shall enter into any Treaty, Alliance, or Confederation; grant Letters of Marque and Reprisal; coin Money; emit Bills of Credit; make any Thing but gold and silver Coin a Tender in Payment of Debts; pass any Bill of Attainder, ex post facto Law, or Law impairing the Obligation of Contracts of grant any Title of Nobility.

Clause 2 No State shall, without the Consent of the Congress, lay any Imposts or Duties on Imports or Exports, except what may be absolutely necessary for executing its inspection Laws: and the net Produce of all Duties and Imposts, laid by any State on Imports or Exports, shall be for the Use of the Treasury of the United States; and all such Laws shall be subject to the Revision and Controul of the Congress.

Clause 3 No State shall, without the Consent of Congress, lay any Duty of Tonnage, keep Troops, or Ships of War in time of Peace, enter into any Agreement or Compact with another State, or with a foreign Power, or engage in War, unless actually invaded, or in such imminent Danger as will not admit of Delay.

---

[6]Modified by the 16th Amendment

Article II—The Executive Article

Nature and Scope of Presidential Power

SECTION 1

Clause 1 The executive Power shall be vested in a President of the United States of America. He shall hold his Office during the Term of four Years and, together with the Vice President, chosen for the same Term, be elected as follows:

Clause 2 Each State shall appoint, in such Manner as the Legislature thereof may direct, a Number of Electors, equal to the whole Number of Senators and Representatives to which the State may be entitled in the Congress: but no Senator or Representative, or Person holding an Office of Trust or Profit under the United States, shall be appointed an Elector.

Clause 3 The Electors shall meet in their respective States, and vote by Ballot for two Persons, of whom one at least shall not be an Inhabitant of the same State with themselves. And they shall make a List of all the Persons voted for, and of the Number of Votes for each; which List they shall sign and certify, and transmit sealed to the Seat of the Government of the United States, directed to the President of the Senate. The President of the Senate shall, in the Presence of the Senate and House of Representatives, open all the Certificates, and the Votes shall then be counted. The Person having the greatest Number of Votes shall be the President, if such Number be a Majority of the whole Number of Electors appointed; and if there be more than one who have such Majority and have an equal Number of Votes, then the House of Representatives shall immediately chuse by Ballot one of them for President; and if no Person have a Majority, then from the five highest on the List the said House shall in like Manner chuse the President. But in chusing the President, the Votes shall be taken by States, the Representation from each State having one Vote; A quorum for this Purpose shall consist of a Member or Members from two thirds of the States, and a Majority of all the States shall be necessary to a Choice. In every Case, after the Choice of the President, the person having the greatest Number of Votes of the Electors shall be the Vice President. But if there should remain two or more who have equal Vote, the Senate shall chuse from them by Ballot the Vice President.[7]

Clause 4 The Congress may determine the Time of chusing the Electors, and the Day on which they shall give their Votes; which Day shall be the same throughout the United States.

Clause 5 No Person except a natural born Citizen, or a Citizen of the United States, at the time of the Adoption of this Constitution, shall be eligible to the Office of President; neither shall any Person be eligible to that Office who shall not have attained to the Age of thirty five Years, and been fourteen Years a Resident within the United States.

Clause 6 In Case of the Removal of the President from Office, or of his Death, Resignation, or Inability to discharge the Powers and Duties of the said Office, the same shall devolve on the Vice President, and the Congress may by Law provide for the Case of Removal, Death, Resignation, or Inability, both of the President and Vice President, declaring what Officer shall then act as President, and such Officer shall act accordingly, until the Disability be removed, or a President shall be elected.[8]

Clause 7 The President shall, at stated Times, receive for his Services, a Compensation, which shall neither be increased nor diminished during the Period of which he shall have been elected, and he shall not receive within that Period any other Emolument from the United States, or any of them.

Clause 8 Before he enter on the Execution of his Office, he shall take the following Oath or Affirmation:—"I do solemnly swear (or affirm) that I will faithfully execute the Office of President of the United States, and will to the best of my Ability, preserve, protect and defend the Constitution of the United States."

Powers and Duties of the President

SECTION 2

Clause 1 The President shall be the Commander in Chief of the Army and Navy of the United States, and of the Militia of the several States, when called into the actual Service of the United States, he may require the Opinion, in writing, of the principal Officer in each of the executive Departments, upon any Subject relating to the Duties of their respective Offices, and he shall have the Power to grant Reprieves and Pardons for Offences against the United States, except in Cases of Impeachment.

Clause 2 He shall have Power, by and with the Advice and Consent of the Senate to make Treaties, provided two thirds of the Senators present concur; and he shall nominate, and by and with the Advice and Consent of the Senate, shall appoint Ambassadors, other public Ministers and Consuls, Judges of the supreme Court, and all other Officers of the United States, whose Appointments are not herein otherwise provided for, and which shall be established by Law: but the Congress may by Law vest the Appointment of such inferior Officers, as they think proper in the President alone, in the Courts of Law, or in the Heads of Departments.

Clause 3 The President shall have Power to fill up all Vacancies that may happen during the Recess of the Senate, by granting Commissions which shall expire at the End of their next Session.

SECTION 3 He shall from time to time give to the Congress Information of the State of the Union, and recommend to their Consideration such Measures as he shall judge necessary and expedient; he may, on extraordinary Occasions, convene both Houses, or either of them and in Case of Disagreement between them, with Respect to the Time of Adjournment, he may adjourn them to such Time as he shall think proper; he shall receive Ambassadors and other public Ministers; he shall

---

[7]Changed by the 12th and 20th Amendments

[8]Modified by the 25th Amendment

take Care that the Laws be faithfully executed, and shall Commission all the Officers of the United States.

SECTION 4   The President, Vice President and all civil Officers of the United States, shall be removed from Office on Impeachment for, and Conviction of, Treason, Bribery, or other High Crimes and Misdemeanors.

Article III—The Judicial Article

Judicial Power, Courts, Judges

SECTION 1   The judicial Power of the United States, shall be vested in one supreme Court, and in such inferior Courts as the Congress may from time to time ordain and establish. The Judges, both the supreme and inferior Courts, shall hold their Offices during good Behaviour, and shall, at stated Times, receive for their Services, a Compensation, which shall not be diminished during their Continuance in Office.

Jurisdiction

SECTION 2   The judicial Power shall extend to all Cases, in Law and Equity, arising under this Constitution, the Laws of the United States, and Treaties made, or which shall be made, under their Authority;—to all Cases affecting Ambassadors, other public Ministers and Consuls;—to all Cases of admiralty and maritime Jurisdiction;—to Controversies to which the United States shall be a Party;—to Controversies between two or more States; between a State and Citizens of another State;[9]—between Citizens of different States;—between Citizens of the same State claiming Lands under Grants of different States, and between a State, or the Citizens thereof, and foreign States, Citizens, or Subjects.

In all Cases affecting Ambassadors, other public Ministers and Consuls, and those in which a State shall be Party, the supreme Court shall have original Jurisdiction. In all the other Cases before mentioned, the supreme Court shall have appellate Jurisdiction, both as to Law and Fact, with such Exceptions, and under such Regulations as Congress shall make.

The Trial of all Crimes, except in Cases of Impeachment, shall be by Jury; and such Trial shall be held in the State where the said Crimes shall have been committed; but when not committed within any State, the Trial shall be at such Place or Places as the Congress may by Law have directed.

Treason

SECTION 3   Treason against the United States, shall consist only in levying War against them, or in adhering to their Enemies, giving them Aid and Comfort. No Person shall be convicted of Treason unless on the Testimony of two Witnesses to the same overt Act, or on Confession in open Court.

The Congress shall have Power to declare the Punishment of Treason, but no Attainder of Treason shall work Corruption of Blood, or Forfeiture except during the Life of the Person attainted.

Article IV—Interstate Relations

Full Faith and Credit Clause

SECTION 1   Full Faith and Credit shall be given in each State to the public Acts, Records, and judicial Proceedings of every other State. And the Congress may by general Laws prescribe the Manner in which such Acts, Records and Proceedings shall be proved, and the Effect thereof.

Privileges and Immunities; Interstate Extradition

SECTION 2

Clause 1   The Citizens of each State shall be entitled to all Privileges and Immunities of Citizens in the several States.

Clause 2   A person charged in any State with Treason, Felony or other Crime, who shall flee from Justice, and be found in another State, shall on Demand of the executive Authority of the State from which he fled, be delivered up, to be removed to the State having Jurisdiction of the Crime.

Clause 3   No person held to Service or Labour in one State, under the Laws thereof, escaping into another, shall, in Consequence of any Law or Regulation therein, be discharged from such Service or Labour, but shall be delivered up on Claim of the Party to whom such Service or Labour may be due.[10]

Admission of States

SECTION 3   New States may be admitted by the Congress into this Union; but no new State shall be formed or erected within the Jurisdiction of any other State; nor any State to be formed by the Junction of two or more States, or Parts of States, without the Consent of the Legislatures of the States concerned as well as of the Congress.

The Congress shall have Power to dispose of and make all needful Rules and Regulations respecting the Territory or other Property belonging to the United States; and nothing in this Constitution shall be so construed as to Prejudice any Claims of the United States, or of any particular State.

Republican Form of Government

SECTION 4   The United States shall guarantee to every State in this Union a Republican Form of Government, and shall protect each of them against Invasion; and on Application of the Legislature, or of the Executive (when the Legislature cannot be convened) against domestic Violence.

Article V—The Amending Power

The Congress, whenever two thirds of both Houses shall deem it necessary, shall propose Amendments to this Constitution, or, on the Application of the Legislatures of two thirds of several States, shall call a Convention for proposing Amendments, which, in either Case, shall be valid to all Intents and Purposes, as Part of this Constitution, when ratified by the Legislatures of

---

[9]Modified by the 11th Amendment

[10]Repealed by the 13th Amendment

three fourths of the several States, or by Conventions in three fourths thereof, as the one or the other Mode of Ratification may be proposed by the Congress; Provided that no Amendment which may be made prior to the Year One thousand eight hundred and eight shall in any Manner affect the first and fourth Clauses in the Ninth Section of the first Article; and that no State, without its Consent, shall be deprived of its equal Suffrage in the Senate.

Article VI—The Supremacy Act

Clause 1

All Debts contracted and Engagements entered into, before the Adoption of this Constitution, shall be as valid against the United States under the Constitution, as under the Confederation.

Clause 2

This Constitution, and the Laws of the United States which shall be made in Pursuance thereof; and all Treaties made, or which shall be made, under the Authority of the United States, shall be the supreme Law of the Land; and the Judges in every State shall be bound thereby, any Thing in the Constitution or Laws of any State to the Contrary notwithstanding.

Clause 3

The Senators and Representatives before mentioned, and the Members of the several State Legislatures, and all executive and judicial Officers, both of the United States and of the several States, shall be bound by Oath or Affirmation, to support this Constitution; but no religious Test shall ever be required as a Qualification to any Office or public Trust under the United States.

Article VII—Ratification

The Ratification of the Conventions of nine States, shall be sufficient for the Establishment of this Constitution between the States so ratifying the Same.

Done in Convention by the Unanimous Consent of the States present the Seventeenth Day of September in the Year of our Lord one thousand seven hundred and Eighty seven and of the Independence of the United States of America the Twelfth In Witness whereof We have hereunto subscribed our Names.

Amendments
The Bill of Rights

[The first ten amendments were ratified on December 15, 1791, and form what is known as the "Bill of Rights."]

Amendment 1—
Religion, Speech, Assembly, and Politics

Congress shall make no law respecting an establishment of religion, or prohibiting the free exercise thereof; or abridging the freedom of speech, or of the press; or the right of the people peaceably to assemble, and to petition the government for a redress of grievances.

Amendment 2—
Militia and the Right to Bear Arms

A well-regulated Militia, being necessary to the security of a free State, the right of the people to keep and bear Arms, shall not be infringed.

Amendment 3—
Quartering of Soldiers

No Soldier shall, in time of peace be quartered in any house, without the consent of the Owner, nor in time of war, but in manner to be prescribed by law.

Amendment 4—
Searches and Seizures

The right of the people to be secure in their persons, houses, papers, and effects, against unreasonable searches and seizures, shall not be violated, and no Warrants shall issue, but upon probable cause, supported by Oath or affirmation, and particularly describing the place to be searched, and the persons or things to be seized.

Amendment 5—
Grand Juries, Self-Incrimination, Double Jeopardy, Due Process, and Eminent Domain

No person shall be held to answer for a capital, or otherwise infamous crime, unless on a presentment or indictment of a Grand jury, except in cases arising in the land or naval forces, or in the Militia, when in actual service in time of War or public danger; nor shall any person be subject for the same offence to be twice put in jeopardy of life or limb; nor shall be compelled in any criminal case to be a witness against himself, nor be deprived of life, liberty, or property, without due process of law; nor shall private property be taken for public use, without just compensation.

Amendment 6—
Criminal Court Procedures

In all criminal prosecutions, the accused shall enjoy the right to a speedy and public trial, by an impartial jury of the State and district wherein the crime shall have been committed, which district shall have been previously ascertained by law, and to be informed of the nature and cause of the accusation; to be confronted with the witnesses against him; to have compulsory process for obtaining Witnesses in his favor, and to have the Assistance of Counsel for his defence.

Amendment 7—
Trial by Jury in Common Law Cases

In Suits at common law, where the value in controversy shall exceed twenty dollars, the right of trial by jury shall be preserved, and no fact tried by a jury shall be otherwise re-examined in any Court of the United States, than according to the rules of the common law.

Amendment 8— Bail, Cruel and Unusual Punishment

Excessive bail shall not be required, nor excessive fines imposed, nor cruel and unusual punishments inflicted.

Amendment 9— Rights Retained by the People

The enumeration in the Constitution, of certain rights, shall not be construed to deny or disparage others retained by the people.

Amendment 10— Reserved Powers of the States

The powers not delegated to the United States by the Constitution, nor prohibited by it to the States, are reserved to the States respectively, or to the people.

Amendment 11—Suits Against the States

[Ratified February 7, 1795]

The Judicial power of the United States shall not be construed to extend to any suit in law or equity, commenced or prosecuted against one of the United States by Citizens of another State, or by Citizens or Subjects of any Foreign State.

Amendment 12—Election of the President

[Ratified June 15, 1804]

The Electors shall meet in their respective states, and vote by ballot for President and Vice-President, one of whom, at least, shall not be an inhabitant of the same state with themselves; they shall name in their ballots the person voted for as President, and in distinct ballots the person voted for as Vice-President, and they shall make distinct lists of all persons voted for as President, and of all persons voted for as Vice-President, and of the number of votes for each, which lists they shall sign and certify, and transmit sealed to the seat of the government of the United States, directed to the President of the Senate;—The President of the Senate shall, in presence of the Senate and House of Representatives, open all the certificates and the votes shall then be counted;—The person having the greatest number of votes for President, shall be the President, if such number be a majority of the whole number of Electors appointed; and if no person have such majority, then from the persons having the highest numbers not exceeding three on the list of those voted for as President, the House of Representatives shall choose immediately, by ballot, the President. But in choosing the President, the votes shall be taken by states, the representation from each state having one vote; a quorum for this purpose shall consist of a member or members from two-thirds of the states, and a majority of all states shall be necessary to a choice. And if the House of Representatives shall not choose a President whenever the right of choice shall devolve upon them, before the fourth day of March next following, then the Vice-President shall act as President, as in the case of the death or other constitutional disability of the President.[11] The person having the greatest

number of votes as Vice-President, shall be the Vice-President, if such a number be a majority of the whole numbers of Electors appointed, and if no person have a majority, then from the two highest numbers on the list, the Senate shall choose the Vice-President; a quorum for the purpose shall consist of two-thirds of the whole number of Senators, and a majority of the whole number shall be necessary to a choice. But no person constitutionally ineligible to the office of President shall be eligible to that of Vice-President of the United States.

Amendment 13—Prohibition of Slavery

[Ratified December 6, 1865]

SECTION 1 Neither slavery nor involuntary servitude, except as a punishment for crime whereof the party shall have been duly convicted, shall exist within the United States, or any place subject to their jurisdiction.

SECTION 2 Congress shall have power to enforce this article by appropriate legislation.

Amendment 14—Citizenship, Due Process, and Equal Protection of the Laws

[Ratified July 9, 1868]

SECTION 1 All persons born or naturalized in the United States, and subject to the jurisdiction thereof, are citizens of the United States and of the State wherein they reside. No State shall make or enforce any law which shall abridge the privileges or immunities of citizens of the United States; nor shall any State deprive any person of life, liberty, or property, without due process of law; nor deny to any person within its jurisdiction the equal protection of the laws.

SECTION 2 Representatives shall be apportioned among the several States according to their respective numbers, counting the whole number of persons in each State, excluding Indians not taxed. But when the right to vote at any election for the choice of electors for President and Vice President of the United States, Representatives in Congress, the Executive and Judicial officers of a State, or the members of the Legislature thereof, is denied to any of the male inhabitants of such State, being twenty-one[12] years of age, and citizens of the United States, or in any way abridged, except for participation in rebellion, or other crime, the basis of representation therein shall be reduced in the proportion which the number of such male citizens shall bear to the whole number of male citizens twenty-one years of age in such State.

SECTION 3 No person shall be a Senator or Representative in Congress, or elector of President and Vice President, or hold any office, civil or military, under the United States, or under any State, who, having previously taken an oath, as a member of Congress, or as an officer of the United States, or as a member of any State legislature, or as an executive or judicial officer of any State, to support the Constitution of the United States, shall have engaged in insurrection or rebellion against the

---

[11]Changed by the 20th Amendment

[12]Changed by the 26th Amendment

same, or given aid or comfort to the enemies thereof. But Congress may by a vote of two-thirds of each House, remove such disability.

SECTION 4 The validity of the public debt of the United States, authorized by law, including debts incurred for payment of pensions and bounties for services in suppressing insurrection or rebellion, shall not be questioned. But neither the United States nor any State shall assume or pay any debt or obligation incurred in aid of insurrection or rebellion against the United States, or any claim for the loss or emancipation of any slave; but all such debts, obligations and claims shall be held illegal and void.

SECTION 5 The Congress shall have power to enforce, by appropriate legislation, the provisions of this article.

Amendment 15—The Right to Vote

[Ratified February 3, 1870]

SECTION 1 The right of citizens of the United States to vote shall not be denied or abridged by the United States or by any State on account of race, color, or previous condition of servitude.

SECTION 2 The Congress shall have power to enforce this article by appropriate legislation.

Amendment 16—Income Taxes

[Ratified February 3, 1913]

The Congress shall have power to lay and collect taxes on incomes, from whatever source derived, without apportionment among the several States, and without regard to any census or enumeration.

Amendment 17—Direct Election of Senators

[Ratified April 8, 1913]

The Senate of the United States shall be composed of two Senators from each State, elected by the people thereof, for six years; and each Senator shall have one vote. The electors in each State shall have the qualifications requisite for electors of the most numerous branch of the State legislatures.

When vacancies happen in the representation of any State in the Senate, the executive authority of such State shall issue writs of election to fill such vacancies: Provided, That the legislature of any State may empower the executive thereof to make temporary appointment until the people fill the vacancies by election as the legislature may direct. This amendment shall not be so construed as to affect the election or term of any Senator chosen before it becomes valid as part of the Constitution.

Amendment 18—Prohibition

[Ratified January 16, 1919. Repealed December 5, 1933 by Amendment 21]

SECTION 1 After one year from the ratification of this article the manufacture, sale, or transportation of intoxicating liquors within, the importation thereof into, or the exportation thereof from the United States and all territory subject to the jurisdiction thereof for beverage purposes is hereby prohibited.

SECTION 2 The Congress and the several states shall have concurrent power to enforce this article by appropriate legislation.

SECTION 3 This article shall be inoperative unless it shall have been ratified as an amendment to the Constitution by the legislatures of the several states, as provided in the Constitution, within seven years from the date of the submission hereof to the States by the Congress.[13]

Amendment 19—For Women's Suffrage

[Ratified August 18, 1920]

The right of the citizens of the United States to vote shall not be denied or abridged by the United States or by any State on account of sex.

Congress shall have power, by appropriate legislation, to enforce the provision of this article.

Amendment 20—The Lame Duck Amendment

[Ratified January 23, 1933]

SECTION 1 The terms of the President and Vice President shall end at noon on the 20th day of January, and the terms of the Senators and Representatives at noon on the 3rd day of January, of the years in which such terms would have ended if this article had not been ratified, and the terms of their successors shall then begin.

SECTION 2 The Congress shall assemble at least once in every year, and such meeting shall begin at noon on the 3rd day of January, unless they shall by law appoint a different day.

SECTION 3 If, at the time fixed for the beginning of the term of the President, the President elect shall have died, the Vice President elect shall become President. If a President shall not have been chosen before the time fixed for the beginning of his term, or if the President elect shall have failed to qualify, then the Vice President elect shall act as President until a President shall have qualified; and the Congress may by law provide for the case wherein neither a President elect nor a Vice President elect shall have qualified, declaring who shall then act as President, or the manner in which one who is to act shall be selected, and such person shall act accordingly until a President or Vice President shall have qualified.

SECTION 4 The Congress may by law provide for the case of the death of any of the persons from whom the House of Representatives may choose a President whenever the right of choice shall have devolved upon them, and for the case of the death of any of the persons from whom the Senate may choose a Vice President whenever the right of choice shall have devolved upon them.

[13]Repealed by the 21st Amendment

SECTION 5 Sections 1 and 2 shall take effect on the 15th day of October following the ratification of this article.

SECTION 6 This article shall be inoperative unless it shall have been ratified as an amendment to the Constitution by the legislatures of three-fourths of the several States within seven years from the date of its submission.

Amendment 21—
Repeal of Prohibition

[Ratified December 5, 1933]

SECTION 1 The eighteenth article of amendment to the Constitution of the United States is hereby repealed.

SECTION 2 The transportation or importation into any State, Territory, or Possession of the United States for delivery or use therein of intoxicating liquors, in violation of the laws thereof, is hereby prohibited.

SECTION 3 This article shall be inoperative unless it shall have been ratified as an amendment to the Constitution by conventions in the several States, as provided in the Constitution, within seven years from the date of the submission hereof to the States by the Congress.

Amendment 22—
Number of Presidential Terms

[Ratified February 27, 1951]

SECTION 1 No person shall be elected to the office of the President more than twice, and no person who has held the office of President, or acted as President, for more than two years of a term to which some other person was elected President shall be elected to the office of the President more than once. But this Article shall not apply to any person holding the office of President when this article was proposed by the Congress, and shall not prevent any person who may be holding the office of President, or acting as President, during the term within which this Article becomes operative from holding the office of President or acting as President during the remainder of such term.

SECTION 2 This Article shall be inoperative unless it shall have been ratified as an amendment to the Constitution by the legislatures of three-fourths of the several states within seven years from the date of its submission to the States by the Congress.

Amendment 23—
Presidential Electors for the District of Columbia

[Ratified March 29, 1961]

SECTION 1 The District constituting the seat of government of the United States shall appoint in such manner as the Congress may direct:

A number of electors of President and Vice President equal to the whole number of Senators and Representatives in Congress to which the District would be entitled if it were a State, but in no event more than the least populous State; they shall be in addition to those appointed by the States, but they shall be considered for the purposes of the election of President and Vice President, to be electors appointed by a State; and they shall meet in the District and perform such duties as provided by the twelfth article of amendment.

SECTION 2 The Congress shall have power to enforce this article by appropriate legislation

Amendment 24—
The Anti-Poll Tax Amendment

[Ratified January 23, 1964]

SECTION 1 The right of citizens of the United States to vote in any primary or other election for President or Vice President, for electors for President or Vice President, or for Senator or Representative in Congress, shall not be denied or abridged by the United States or any state by reason of failure to pay any poll tax or other tax.

SECTION 2 The Congress shall have power to enforce this article by appropriate legislation.

Amendment 25—
Presidential Disability,
Vice Presidential Vacancies

[Ratified February 10, 1967]

SECTION 1 In case of the removal of the President from office or his death or resignation, the Vice President shall become President.

SECTION 2 Whenever there is a vacancy in the office of the Vice President, the President shall nominate a Vice President who shall take the office upon confirmation by a majority vote of both Houses of Congress.

SECTION 3 Whenever the President transmits to the President pro tempore of the Senate and the Speaker of the House of Representatives his written declaration that he is unable to discharge the powers and duties of his office, and until he transmits to them a written declaration to the contrary, such powers and duties shall be discharged by the Vice President as Acting President.

SECTION 4 Whenever the Vice President and a majority of either the principal officers of the executive departments, or of such other body as Congress may by law provide, transmit to the President pro tempore of the Senate and the Speaker of the House of Representatives their written declaration that the President is unable to discharge the powers and duties of his office, the Vice President shall immediately assume the powers and duties of the office as Acting President.

Thereafter, when the President transmits to the President pro tempore of the Senate and the Speaker of the House of Representatives his written declaration that no inability exists, he shall resume the powers and duties of his office unless the Vice President and a majority of either the principal officers of the executive departments, or of such other body as Congress may by law provide, transmit within four days to the President pro tempore of the Senate and the Speaker of the House of Representatives their written declaration that the President is unable to discharge the powers and duties of his office. Thereupon Congress shall decide the issue, assembling within forty-eight hours for that purpose if not in session. If the Congress, within twenty-one days after receipt of the latter written declaration, or, if Congress is not in session, within twenty-one days after Congress is required to assemble, determines by two-thirds vote of both houses that the President is unable to discharge the powers and duties of his office, the Vice President shall continue to discharge the same as Acting President; otherwise, the President shall resume the powers and duties of his office.

Amendment 26—Eighteen-Year-Old Vote

[Ratified July 1, 1971]

SECTION 1   The right of citizens of the United States, who are 18 years of age, or older, to vote shall not be denied or abridged by the United States or by any state on account of age.

SECTION 2   The Congress shall have power to enforce this article by appropriate legislation.

Amendment 27—Congressional Salaries

[Ratified May 7, 1992]

No law, varying the compensation for the services of the Senators and Representatives, shall take effect, until an election of Representatives shall be intervened.

Chapter 3

American Federalism

★

HURRICANE KATRINA, FOLLOWED BY HURRICANE RITA, DEVASTATED NEW ORLEANS AND MUCH OF SOUTHERN LOUISIANA, MISSISSIPPI, AND PARTS OF ARKANSAS DURING THE 2005 HURRICANE SEASON. IN NEW ORLEANS, AFTER THE LEVEES BROKE AND THE CITY FLOODED, 80 PERCENT OF THE CITY'S POPULATION OF 470,000 WAS EVACUATED. BUT 100,000 PEOPLE, MOSTLY LOW-INCOME AND AFRICAN AMERICAN RESIDENTS, WERE LEFT STRANDED WITH NO WAY TO GET OUT OF THE CITY. SOME 25,000 PEOPLE WERE temporarily housed in the New Orleans Superdome and Convention Center before they and thousands of others were relocated to Atlanta, Houston, and elsewhere. More than 100,000 homes were destroyed and more than 1,000 people died in New Orleans alone; about 1.5 million residents along the Gulf Coast were displaced.

In the days and weeks that followed, New Orleans Mayor Ray Nagin and Louisiana's Democratic Governor Kathleen Blanco sharply criticized the delays and disorganized response of the Federal Emergency Management Agency (FEMA), which had been made part of the Department of Homeland Security, and the Bush administration. Within weeks, FEMA's director, Michael Brown, was forced to resign. Mayor Nagin and Governor Blanco in turn confronted charges that they were too slow to call for evacuations and to arrange to evacuate more people from the city. They and other state and local officials were also criticized for other failures as "first responders" to emergencies.

The failure of rapid and coordinated responses to the disaster highlighted the complexity, fragmentation, and what has been termed the "mild chaos" of intergovernmental relations in federal systems.[1] The failures of timely governmental responses turned this "mild chaos" into a national catastrophe. Recovery will take years, perhaps decades. Yet, the rebuilding of New Orleans and other parts of the Gulf Coast will require the cooperation and coordination of local, state, and federal governments. The federal government will spend an estimated $200 billion on the reconstruction. State and local funds and tax incentives will contribute billions more.

The controversy over the response to Hurricane Katrina and who is responsible and how to respond to such national emergencies underscores the continuing debate over federalism. That debate also includes other issues like addressing some states' recognition of civil unions and same-sex marriages, and the respective roles of the national government and the states in combating illegal immigration, in maintaining homeland security, and in improving social services. How do and how should states interact with each other and with the national government? What is the proper balance of power between the national government and the states in controlling illegal immigration and providing homeland security, for example, as well as in improving education and fighting corporate corruption or environment pollution?

Since the founding of the Republic, Americans have debated the relationship of the national government to the states.[2] In 1787, the Federalists defended

*"Cities are not
sovereign entities."*

U.S. SUPREME COURT

59

the creation of a strong national government, whereas the Antifederalists warned that a strong national government would overshadow the states. The great debate over which level of government performs best continues to rage. In the 1850s, the Republican party started its history as the party of the National Union, while for most of its history the Democratic party was the champion of states' rights, but over the course of the twentieth century these roles changed. Under Franklin Roosevelt, and in the 1960s Lyndon Johnson, the Democrats pushed an agenda in education, health care, and social security that nationalized social policy. Later, under Richard Nixon and then again in the 1990s, Republicans led the charge against Washington. They urged the return of many functions to the states—a **devolution revolution**[3]—and they have had some success, such as when President Bill Clinton agreed in 1996 to turn over more responsibilities for welfare to the states. Still, Democrats have been reluctant to remove all federal standards, especially for regulating the environment and the workplace. Moreover, President George W. Bush and Republican leaders in Congress have pushed for expanded federal powers to counter threats to national security, to improve educational standards, and to expand Medicare coverage to include some of the costs of prescription drugs. Democrats in turn have countered that some homeland security programs do not go far enough and others go too far, that funding for education remains inadequate, and that the prescription drug coverage is both inadequate and overly complex.

Federalism has recently emerged as a hot topic in other countries as well. Western European countries have formed the European Union (EU), with member nations giving up considerable authority over the regulation of businesses and labor. The EU has adopted a common monetary policy and currency (the euro). More recently with the addition of ten Central and Eastern European countries, and a stalled attempt to ratify a Treaty Establishing a Constitution for Europe, the EU faces continuing challenges.[4] (See the box on p. 34 in Chapter 2.)

Heightened interest in federalism also comes from demands for greater autonomy for ethnic nationalities. The Canadian federal system, for example, which gives much more authority to the Canadian provinces than American states enjoy, strains under the demands of the French-speaking province of Quebec for special status and even independence. In the United Kingdom, devolution has occurred with Scotland, Northern Ireland, and Wales gaining their own parliaments or assemblies with considerable authority and even, in Scotland, limited power to tax. Belgium, Italy, and Spain have also been devolving powers from their central governments to regional governments. The new Iraqi constitution also establishes a federal system, setting up regional governments with extensive powers and authority over revenue.

In contrast to some countries, the United States, except during the Civil War (1861–1865), has had a relatively peaceful experience with the shifting balances of power under federalism. Since the New Deal in the 1930s, power and responsibility have drifted from the states to the national government. Although presidents from Richard Nixon to Bill Clinton slowed the growth of the national government, it was not until the late 1990s that the Republican-controlled Congress sought major changes that heated the debate over federalism. As with welfare reform in 1996, Congress promoted decentralization in education with the Educational Flexibility Partnership Demonstration Act of 1999, which authorized the secretary of education to grant states waivers from federal rules setting educational goals. Still, despite such moves toward decentralization, Congress continues to expand federal law by making such offenses as the burning of churches, carjacking, and acts of terrorism federal crimes, even though they are already state and local crimes.

After more than half a century of privileging federal authority, the Supreme Court has placed constraints on congressional powers in the name of federalism.[5] Like Congress, however, the Court's recent record on federalism is mixed. Despite recent rulings holding that Congress exceeded its powers and may not authorize individuals to sue states to enforce federal laws,[6] the Court nevertheless ruled that state welfare programs may not restrict benefits to new residents to what they would have received in the states from which they moved[7] and that Congress may restrict states from selling drivers' personal information.[8]

devolution revolution
The effort to slow the growth of the federal government by returning many functions to the states.

Debates over federalism resemble those over whether "the glass is half-empty or half-full."[9] People who think they can get more of what they want from the national government usually advocate national action. Those who view states as more responsive and accountable argue for decentralization. Although Republicans today generally favor action at the state level and Democrats tend to support action by the national government, neither party is consistent in its positions on the balance of power between the national government and the states. Their positions often depend on the issue at stake.

In this chapter, we first define federalism and its advantages. We then look at the constitutional basis for our federal system and how court decisions and political developments have shaped, and continue to shape, federalism in the United States.

Defining Federalism

Scholars argue and wars (including our own Civil War) have been fought over what federalism means. One scholar counted 267 definitions.[10] Canadian political scientist Ronald L. Watts, for one, emphasizes that "'Federalism' is basically not a descriptive but a normative term and refers to the advocacy of multi-tiered government combining elements of shared-rule and regional self-rule."[11]

Federalism, as we define it, is a form of government in which a constitution distributes authority and powers between a central government and subdivisional governments—usually called states, provinces, or republics—giving to both the national government and states or regional governments substantial responsibilities and powers, including the power to collect taxes and to pass and enforce laws regulating the conduct of individuals.

The mere existence of both national and state governments does not make a system federal. What is important is that a *constitution divides governmental powers between the national government and the subdivisional governments,* giving clearly defined functions to each. Neither the central nor the subdivisional government receives its powers from the other; both derive them from a common source—the Constitution. No ordinary act of legislation at either the national or the state level can change this constitutional distribution of powers. Both levels of government operate through their own agents and exercise power directly over individuals.

Our definition of federalism is broad enough to include competing ideas of it and the range of federal systems around the world. The following are some of the leading ideas of federalism.

- *Dual federalism* views the Constitution as giving a limited list of powers—primarily foreign policy and national defense—to the national government, leaving the rest to sovereign states. Each level of government is dominant within its own sphere. The Supreme Court serves as the umpire between the national government and the states in disputes over which level of government has responsibility for a particular activity. During our first hundred years, dual federalism was the favored interpretation given by the Supreme Court.

- *Cooperative federalism* stresses federalism as a system of intergovernmental relations in delivering governmental goods and services to the people and calls for cooperation among various levels of government.

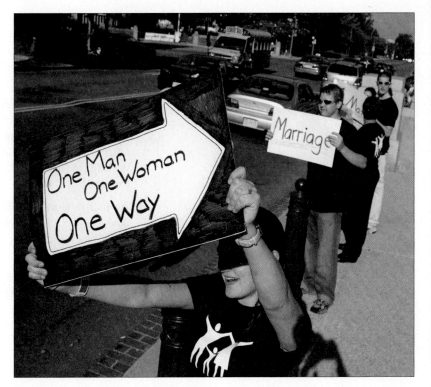

Members of Teen Pact in Washington, DC urge passage of a constitutional amendment banning same-sex marriage. Constitutional amendments typically originate with Congress at the federal level, but they must be ratified at the state level.

federalism
Constitutional arrangement in which power is distributed between a central government and subdivisional governments, called states in the United States. The national and the subdivisional governments both exercise direct authority over individuals.

- *Marble cake federalism,* a term coined by political scientist Morton Grodzins, conceives of federalism as a marble cake in which all levels of government are involved in a variety of issues and programs, rather than a layer cake, or dual federalism, with fixed divisions between layers or levels of government.[12]

- *Competitive federalism,* a term first used by political scientist Thomas R. Dye, views the national government, 50 states, and thousands of local governments as competing with each other over ways to put together packages of services and taxes. Applying the analogy of the marketplace, Dye emphasizes that at the state and local levels, we have some choice about which state and city we want to "use," just as we have choices about what kind of telephone service we use.[13]

- *Permissive federalism* implies that although federalism provides "a sharing of power and authority between the national and state government, the states' share rests upon the permission and permissiveness of the national government."[14]

- *"Our federalism,"* championed by Ronald Reagan, Justices Antonin Scalia and Clarence Thomas, along with former Chief Justice William Rehnquist and Justice Sandra Day O'Connor, presumes that the power of the federal government is limited in favor of the broad powers reserved to the states.

Federal nations are diverse and include Argentina, Australia, Brazil, Canada, Germany, India, Mexico, Nigeria, Russia, South Africa, Spain, and Switzerland. Although their number is not large, they "cover more than half of the land surface of the globe and include almost half of the world's population."[15] Federalism thus appears well suited for large countries with large populations, even though only about 25 of the world's approximately 224 countries claim to be federal.

Constitutionally, the federal system of the United States consists of only the national government and the 50 states. "Cities are not," the Supreme Court reminded us, "sovereign entities." But in a practical sense, we are a nation of almost 88,000 governmental units, from the national government to the school board district. This does not make for a tidy, efficient, easy-to-understand system; yet, as we shall see, it has its virtues.

Alternatives to Federalism

Among the alternatives to federalism are **unitary systems** of government, in which a constitution vests all governmental power in the central government. The central government, if it so chooses, may delegate authority to constituent units, but what it delegates, it may take away. China, France, the Scandinavian countries, and Israel have unitary governments. In the United States, state constitutions usually create this kind of relationship between the state and its local governments.

At the other extreme from unitary governments are **confederations**, in which sovereign nations, through a constitutional compact, create a central government but carefully limit its authority and do not give it the power to regulate the conduct of individuals directly. The central government makes regulations for the constituent governments, but it exists and operates only at their direction. The 13 states under the Articles of Confederation operated in this manner (see Figure 3–1), as did the southern Confederacy during the Civil War. The European Union is another example, though debates over its integration continue.[16]

Why Federalism?

In 1787, federalism was a compromise between centrists, who supported a strong national government, and those who favored decentralization. Confederation had proved unsuccessful. A unitary system was out of the question because most people were too deeply attached to their state governments to permit subordination to central

unitary system
Constitutional arrangement that concentrates power in a central government.

confederation
Constitutional arrangement in which sovereign nations or states, by compact, create a central government but carefully limit its power and do not give it direct authority over individuals.

Government Under the Articles of Confederation, 1781–1788

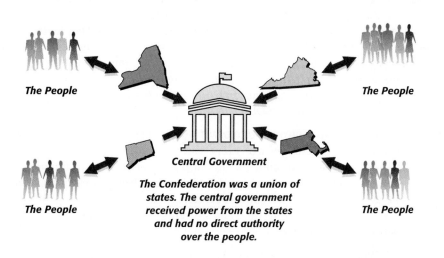

The People

The People

The People

The People

Central Government

The Confederation was a union of states. The central government received power from the states and had no direct authority over the people.

FIGURE 3–1 **A Comparison of Federalism and Confederation.**

Government Under the U.S. Constitution (Federation) Since 1789

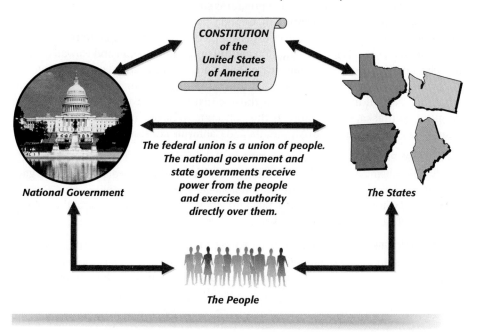

CONSTITUTION of the United States of America

National Government

The federal union is a union of people. The national government and state governments receive power from the people and exercise authority directly over them.

The States

The People

rule. Many scholars think that federalism is ideally suited to the needs of a heterogeneous people spread over a large continent, suspicious of concentrated power, and desiring unity but not uniformity. Federalism offered, and still offers, many advantages for such a people.

FEDERALISM CHECKS THE GROWTH OF TYRANNY Although in the rest of the world, federal forms have not always prevented tyranny (Germany's federal constitution did not, for example, prevent Hitler from seizing power in the 1930s), and many unitary governments are democratic, Americans tend to associate freedom with federalism.[17] As James Madison pointed out in *The Federalist*, No. 10: If "factious leaders . . . kindle a flame within their particular states," national leaders can check the spread of the "conflagration through the other states" (*The Federalist*, No. 10, appears in the Appendix of this book). Moreover, when one political party loses control of the national government, it is still likely to hold office in a number of states. It can then regroup, develop new policies and new leaders, and continue to challenge the party in power at the national level.

Such diffusion of power creates its own problems. It makes it difficult for a national majority to carry out a program of action, and it permits those who control state governments to frustrate the policies enacted by Congress and administered by federal agencies. To the framers, these obstacles were an advantage. They feared that a single interest group might capture the national government and suppress the interests of others. Of course, the size of the nation and the many interests within it are the greatest obstacles to the formation of a single-interest majority—a point often overlooked today but emphasized by Madison in *The Federalist*, No. 10. If such a majority were to occur, having to work through a federal system would check its power.

FEDERALISM ALLOWS UNITY WITHOUT UNIFORMITY   National politicians and parties do not have to iron out every difference on every issue that divides us, whether it be abortion, same-sex marriage, gun control, capital punishment, welfare financing, or assisted suicide. Instead, these issues are debated in state legislatures, county courthouses, and city halls. But this advantage of federalism is becoming less significant as many local issues become national ones and as events in one state immediately affect policy debates at the national level.

FEDERALISM ENCOURAGES EXPERIMENTATION   Supreme Court Justice Louis Brandeis pointed out that state governments provide great "laboratories" for public policy experimentation; states may serve as proving grounds. If they adopt programs that fail, the negative effects are limited; if programs succeed, they can be adopted by other states and by the national government. Georgia, for example, was the first state to permit 18-year-olds to vote; Wisconsin experimented with putting welfare recipients to work; California pioneered air pollution control programs; Oregon and Hawaii created new systems for providing health care. Nevada is the only state, so far, to legalize statewide gambling, but more than half the states now permit some form of casino gambling. Not all innovations, even those considered successful, become widely adopted. Nebraska, for example, is the only state to have a unicameral legislature, although in recent years both Minnesota and California considered adopting one.

FEDERALISM PROVIDES TRAINING GROUNDS   While encouraging experiments in public policy, federalism also provides a training ground for state and local politicians to gain experience before moving to the national stage. Presidents Jimmy Carter, Ronald Reagan, Bill Clinton, and George W. Bush previously served as governor of the respective states of Georgia, California, Arkansas, and Texas.

FEDERALISM KEEPS GOVERNMENT CLOSER TO THE PEOPLE   By providing numerous arenas for decision making, federalism involves many people in government and helps keep government closer to the people. Every day, thousands of Americans are busy serving on city councils, school boards, neighborhood associations, and planning commissions. Since they are close to the issues and have firsthand knowledge of what

TABLE 3–1   Number of Governments in the United States

National	1
States	50
Counties	3,034
Municipalities	19,431
Townships or towns	16,506
School districts	13,522
Special districts	35,356
Total	87,900

SOURCE: U.S. Bureau of the Census, *Statistical Abstract of the United States*, available at www.census.gov/prod/2003pubs/02statab/stlocgov.pdf.

The Changing Face of American Politics

Immigrants and Federal, State, and Local Responses

For most of the past century, the highest percentage of immigrants to the United States came from Europe. Beginning in the 1960s, more Latin Americans than Europeans have immigrated to the United States. Immigrants from Asia also now exceed immigrants from Europe.

In recent years, the number of immigrants arriving in the United States has been growing. Many of them enter the country illegally and join the workforce. The Census Bureau reported in 2005 that the United States had 34.2 million foreign-born residents, about 12 percent of the population. But that statistic may underreport the number of illegal immigrants. The Pew Hispanic Center estimates that there are more than 10 million undocumented immigrants, with more arriving each year.

As a result, illegal immigrants and "broken borders" have become very controversial issues. Many object to undocumented workers taking jobs away from American citizens. But some studies find that even if all citizens and legal immigrants were employed, there would still be a labor shortage in low-income jobs such as house cleaners, and agricultural, maintenance, restaurant, and construction workers. Broken borders are associated with gang violence and drug and human trafficking, as well as with increased costs of providing social services.

The controversy is complex, and there is no consensus about how to resolve it. President George W. Bush has called for reform of the immigration system and proposed giving undocumented workers a temporary visa for three years that would be renewable once. More than 50 immigration bills have been introduced in Congress. They address many issues: extending more worker visas, establishing new procedures for legalizing undocumented workers, and increasing border security, among others.

State legislatures considered almost 300 bills related to immigration and passed 47 in 2005. Some, like Colorado and Florida, extended medical and child welfare benefits to immigrants. Fifteen other states considered bills restricting benefits; however, Virginia's prohibition of any state or local benefits for undocumented immigrants was the only one signed into law. Other states are considering either extending or restricting education and employment benefits, as well as requiring all immigrants to have identification cards as proof of their legal status.

Likewise, local governments have enacted conflicting laws and policies. Costa Mesa, California, for example, directed its police to enforce federal immigration laws, but elsewhere there has been strong opposition to that policy, both because of the cost and concerns about community relations where there are large Hispanic populations. ∎

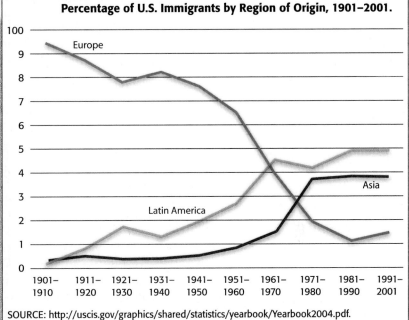

Percentage of U.S. Immigrants by Region of Origin, 1901–2001.

SOURCE: http://uscis.gov/graphics/shared/statistics/yearbook/Yearbook2004.pdf.

needs to be done, they may be more responsive to problems than the experts in Washington.

We should be cautious, however, about generalizing that state and local governments are necessarily closer to the people than the national government. True, more people are involved in local and state politics than in national affairs, and confidence in state governments has increased while respect for national agencies has diminished. A majority of the public often appears dissatisfied with the federal government. Yet national and international affairs are on people's minds more often than state or local politics. And fewer voters participate in state and local elections than in congressional and presidential elections.

The Constitutional Structure of American Federalism

Dividing powers and responsibilities between the national and state governments has resulted in thousands of court decisions, hundreds of books, and endless speeches to explain them—and even then the division lacks precise definition. Nonetheless, a basic understanding of how the Constitution divides these powers and responsibilities and of what obligations it imposes on each level of government is helpful (see Table 3–2).

The formal constitutional framework of our federal system may be stated relatively simply:

1. The national government has only those powers delegated to it by the Constitution (with the important exception of the inherent power over foreign affairs).

2. Within the scope of its operations, the national government is supreme.

3. The state governments have the powers not delegated to the central government, except those denied to them by the Constitution and their state constitutions.

4. Some powers are specifically denied to both the national and state governments; others are specifically denied only to the states or to the national government.

Powers of the National Government

The Constitution, chiefly in the first three articles, delegates legislative, executive, and judicial powers to the national government. In addition to these enumerated or **express powers**, such as the power to regulate interstate commerce and to appropriate funds, Congress has assumed constitutionally **implied powers**, such as the power to create banks, which are inferred from the express powers. The constitutional basis for the implied powers of Congress is the **necessary and proper clause** (Article I, Section 8, Clause 3). This clause gives Congress the right "to make all Laws which shall be necessary and proper for carrying into Execution the foregoing Powers, and all other Powers vested . . . in the Government of the United States."

In foreign affairs, the national government has **inherent powers**. The national government has the same authority to deal with other nations as if it were the central government in a unitary system. Such inherent powers do not depend on specific con-

express powers
Powers the Constitution specifically grants to one of the branches of the national government.

implied powers
Powers inferred from the express powers that allow Congress to carry out its functions.

necessary and proper clause
Clause of the Constitution (Article I, Section 8, Clause 3) setting forth the implied powers of Congress. It states that Congress, in addition to its express powers, has the right to make all laws necessary and proper to carry out all powers the Constitution vests in the national government.

inherent powers
The powers of the national government in foreign affairs that the Supreme Court has declared do not depend on constitutional grants but rather grow out of the very existence of the national government.

TABLE 3–2 The Federal Division of Powers

Powers Delegated to the National Government	Some Powers Reserved for the States	Some Concurrent Powers Shared by the National and State Governments
■ Express powers stated in the Constitution	■ To create a republican form of government	■ To tax citizens and businesses
■ Implied powers that may be inferred from the express powers	■ To charter local governments	■ To borrow and spend money
	■ To conduct elections	■ To establish courts
■ Inherent powers that allow the nation to present a united front to foreign powers	■ To exercise all powers not delegated to the national government or denied to the states by the Constitution	■ To pass and enforce laws
		■ To protect civil rights

stitutional provisions. For example, the government of the United States may acquire territory by purchase or by discovery and occupation, though no specific clause in the Constitution allows such acquisition. (The federal government may not, however, cede the territory of a state to a foreign power or to another state without its consent.) Even if the Constitution were silent about foreign affairs—which it is not—the national government would still have the power to declare war, make treaties, and appoint and receive ambassadors.

Together, these express, implied, and inherent powers create a flexible system that allows the Supreme Court, Congress, the president, and the people to expand the central government's powers to meet the needs of a modern nation in a global economy and confront threats of international terrorism. This expansion of central government functions rests on four constitutional pillars.

These constitutional pillars—the *national supremacy article,* the *war power,* the *commerce clause,* and especially, the *power to tax and spend* for the general welfare—have permitted a tremendous expansion of the functions of the national government, so much so that despite the Supreme Court's recent declaration that some national laws exceed Congress's constitutional powers, the national government has, in effect, almost full power to enact any legislation that Congress deems necessary, so long as it does not conflict with the provisions of the Constitution designed to protect individual rights and the powers of the states. In addition, Section 5 of the Fourteenth Amendment, ratified in 1868 and discussed further in Chapter 17, gives Congress the power to enact legislation to remedy constitutional violations and the denial of due process and the equal protection of the laws.

THE NATIONAL SUPREMACY ARTICLE   One of the most important pillars is found in Article VI of the Constitution: "This Constitution, and the Laws of the United States which shall be made in Pursuance thereof; and all Treaties made . . . under the Authority of the United States, shall be the supreme Law of the Land; and the Judges in every State shall be bound thereby; any Thing in the Constitution or Laws of any State to the Contrary notwithstanding." All officials, state as well as national, swear an oath to support the Constitution of the United States. States may not override national policies; this restriction also applies to local units of government, since they are agents of the states. National laws and regulations of federal agencies *preempt* the field, so that conflicting state and local regulations are unenforceable.

THE WAR POWER   The national government is responsible for protecting the nation from external aggression, whether from other nations or international terrorism. The government's power to protect national security includes the power to wage war. In today's world, military strength depends not only on troops in the field but also on the ability to mobilize the nation's industrial might as well as to apply scientific and technological knowledge to the tasks of defense. As Charles Evans Hughes, before becoming chief justice in 1930, observed: "The power to wage war is the power to wage war successfully."[18] In short, the national government has the power to do almost anything not in direct conflict with constitutional guarantees.

THE POWER TO REGULATE INTERSTATE AND FOREIGN COMMERCE   Congressional authority extends to all commerce that affects more than one state. Commerce includes the production, buying, selling, renting, and transporting of goods, services, and properties. The **commerce clause** (Article I, Section 8, Clause 1) packs a tremendous constitutional punch; it gives Congress the power "to regulate Commerce with foreign Nations, and among the several States, and with the Indian Tribes." In these few words, the national government has found constitutional justification for regulating a wide range of human activity, because few aspects of our economy today affect commerce in only one state and are thus outside the scope of the national government's constitutional authority.

The landmark ruling of *Gibbons* v. *Ogden* in 1824 affirmed the broad authority of Congress over interstate commerce. There, in interpreting the commerce clause, Chief

commerce clause
The clause in the Constitution (Article I, Section 8, Clause 1) that gives Congress the power to regulate all business activities that cross state lines or affect more than one state or other nations.

TABLE 3–3 An Expanding Nation

A great advantage of federalism—and part of the genius and flexibility of our constitutional system—has been the way in which we acquired territory and extended rights and guarantees by means of statehood, commonwealth, or territorial status, and thus grew from 13 to 50 states, plus territories.

Louisiana Purchase	1803
Florida	1819
Texas	1845
Oregon	1846
Mexican Cession	1848
Gadsden Purchase	1853
Alaska	1867
Hawaii	1898
Philippines	1898–1946
Puerto Rico	1899
Guam	1899
American Samoa	1900
Canal Zone	1904–2000
U.S. Virgin Islands	1917
Pacific Islands Trust Territory	1947

Justice John Marshall asserted national interests over those of the states and laid the basis for the subsequent growth in congressional power over commerce and activities that affect interstate commerce.

Gibbons v. *Ogden* arose from a dispute over a monopoly to operate steamboats in New York waters that the state of New York had granted to Robert Livingston and Robert Fulton. They in turn licensed Aaron Ogden to have the exclusive right to operate steamboats between New York and New Jersey. Ogden sued to stop Thomas Gibbons from running a competing ferry. Gibbons countered that his boats were licensed under a 1793 act of Congress governing vessels "in the coasting trade and fisheries." New York courts sided with Ogden in holding that both Congress and the states may regulate commerce, just as each has the power to tax. Congress, therefore, had not preempted New York from granting the monopoly. Gibbons appealed to the Supreme Court.

The stakes were high in *Gibbons* v. *Ogden,* for at issue was the very concept of "interstate commerce." May both Congress and the states regulate interstate commerce? And when conflicts arise between national and state regulations, which prevails?

Chief Justice Marshall asserted that national interests prevail and astutely defined "interstate commerce" as "intercourse that affects more states than one." Unlike the power of taxation, Congress's power over interstate commerce is complete and overrides conflicting state laws.[19]

Gibbons v. *Ogden* was immediately heralded for promoting a national economic common market in holding that states may not discriminate against interstate transportation and out-of-state commerce. Marshall's brilliant definition of "commerce" as *intercourse among the states* provided the basis clause for national regulation of "things in commerce"[20] and an expanding range of economic activities, from the sale of lottery tickets[21] to prostitution[22] to radio and television broadcasts,[23] and telecommunications and the Internet.

The commerce clause has also been used to sustain legislation that goes beyond commercial matters, if those activities have a "substantial effect on commerce." When the Supreme Court upheld the Civil Rights Act of 1964, forbidding discrimination because of race, religion, gender, or national origin in places of public accommodation, it said: "Congress's action in removing the disruptive effect which it found racial discrimination has on interstate travel is not invalidated because Congress was also legislating against what it considers to be moral wrongs."[24] Discrimination restricts the flow of interstate commerce; therefore, Congress could legislate against discrimination. Moreover, the law applies even to local places of public accommodation because local incidents of discrimination have a substantial and harmful impact on interstate commerce.

More recently, the Court has limited congressional power to address similar harms because it did not find a substantial connection with interstate commerce. In *United States* v. *Lopez*,[25] for example, a bare majority struck down the Gun-Free School Zones Act, which made it a federal crime to possess a firearm within 1,000 feet of a school, because it did not find a substantial connection between violence in schools and the national economy. However, in *Gonzales* v. *Raich* (2005), the Court upheld Congress's power to criminalize the use of marijuana, even for medicinal purposes by seriously ill people, as ten states had permitted.[26] The Court ruled that the aggregative impact of such individual marijuana usage had a substantial connection to, and would undercut the regulation of, marijuana in interstate commerce.

THE POWER TO TAX AND SPEND Congress lacks constitutional authority to pass laws solely on the grounds that they will promote the general welfare, but it may raise taxes and spend money for this purpose. For example, Congress lacks the power to regulate education or agriculture directly, yet it does have the power to appropriate money to support education or to pay farm subsidies. By attaching conditions to its grants of money, Congress may thus regulate what it cannot directly control by law.

When Congress puts up the money, it determines how the money will be spent. By withholding or threatening to withhold funds, the national government can influence or control state operations and regulate individual conduct. For example, Congress has stipulated that federal funds should be withdrawn from any program in which any person is denied benefits because of race, color, national origin, sex, or physical handicap. Congress also used its power of the purse to force states to raise the drinking age to 21 by tying such a condition to federal dollars for highways.

Congress frequently requires states to do certain things—for example, provide services to indigent mothers and clean up the air and water. These requirements are called **federal mandates**. Often Congress does not supply the funds required to carry out these "unfunded mandates" (discussed further later in the chapter). Its failure to do so has become an important issue as states face growing expenditures with limited resources. The Supreme Court has also ruled that Congress may not compel states through "unfunded mandates" to enact particular laws or require state officials to enforce federal laws, such as requiring checks on the backgrounds of handgun purchasers, which the Court struck down as an unfunded federal mandate in *Printz* v. *United States*.[27]

Powers of the States

The Constitution *reserves for the states all powers not granted to the national government,* subject only to the limitations of the Constitution. The states may exercise powers not given exclusively to the national government by the Constitution or judicial interpretation, as long as the exercise of those powers does not conflict with national law. Such **concurrent powers** with the national government include the power to levy taxes and regulate commerce internal to each state.

In general, states may levy taxes on the same items the national government taxes, such as incomes, alcohol, and gasoline, but a state cannot, by a tax, "unduly burden" commerce among the states, interfere with a function of the national government, complicate the operation of a national law, or abridge the terms of a treaty of the United States. Where Congress has not preempted the field, states may regulate

federal mandate
A requirement the federal government imposes as a condition for receiving federal funds.

concurrent powers
Powers that the Constitution gives to both the national and state governments, such as the power to levy taxes.

interstate businesses, provided that these regulations do not cover matters requiring uniform national treatment or unduly burden interstate commerce.

Who decides what matters require "uniform national treatment" or what actions might place an "undue burden" on interstate commerce? Congress does, subject to final review by the Supreme Court. When Congress is silent or does not clearly state its intent, the courts—ultimately, the Supreme Court—decide if there is a conflict with the national Constitution or if a state law or regulation has preempted federal authority.

Constitutional Limits and Obligations

To ensure that federalism works, the Constitution imposes restraints on both the national and the state governments. States are prohibited from:

1. Making treaties with foreign governments

2. Authorizing private persons to prey on the shipping and commerce of other nations

3. Coining money, issuing bills of credit, or making anything but gold and silver coin legal tender in payment of debts

4. Taxing imports or exports

5. Taxing foreign ships

6. Keeping troops or ships of war in time of peace (except the state militia, now called the National Guard)

7. Engaging in war, unless invaded or in such imminent danger as will not admit of delay

In turn, the Constitution requires the national government to refrain from exercising its powers, especially its powers to tax and to regulate interstate commerce, in such a way as to interfere substantially with the states' abilities to perform their responsibilities. But, politicians, judges, and scholars disagree about whether the national political process—specifically Congress and the president—or the courts should ultimately define the boundaries between the powers of the national government and the states. Some argue that the protection states have from intrusions by the national government comes primarily from the political process because senators and representatives elected from the states participate in the decisions of Congress.[28] Others maintain that the Supreme Court should limit the national government and defend the states.[29]

The Court has held that Congress may not command states to enact laws to comply with or order state employees to enforce unfunded federal mandates; for example, as noted earlier, *Printz* v. *United States* held that Congress may not require local law enforcement officials to make background checks prior to handgun sales.[30] It has also ruled that the Eleventh Amendment's guarantee of states' sovereign immunity from lawsuits forbids state employees from suing states in federal and state courts to force state compliance with federal employment laws.[31] Although Congress may not use those sticks, it may still offer the carrot of federal funding if states comply with national policies, such as establishing a minimum drinking age.

The Constitution also requires the national government to guarantee to each state a "republican form of government." The framers used this term to distinguish a republic from a monarchy, on the one side, and from a pure, direct democracy, on the other. Congress, not the courts, enforces this guarantee and determines what is or is not a republican form of government. By permitting the congressional delegation of a state to be seated in Congress, Congress acknowledges that the state has the republican form of government the Constitution guarantees.

The Constitution also obliges the national government to protect states against *domestic insurrection*. Congress has delegated to the president the authority to dispatch troops to put down such insurrections when the proper state authorities request them. If there are contesting state authorities, the president decides which is the proper one. The president does not have to wait, however, for a request from state authorities to send federal troops into a state to enforce federal laws.

Interstate Relations

Three clauses in the Constitution, taken from the Articles of Confederation, require states to give full faith and credit to each other's public acts, records, and judicial proceedings; to extend to each other's citizens the privileges and immunities of their own citizens; and to return persons who are fleeing from justice.

FULL FAITH AND CREDIT   The **full faith and credit clause** (Article IV, Section 1), one of the more technical provisions of the Constitution, requires state courts to enforce the civil judgments of the courts of other states and accept their public records and acts as valid.[32] It does not require states to enforce the criminal laws or legislation and administrative acts of other states; in most cases, for one state to enforce the criminal laws of another would raise constitutional issues. The clause applies primarily to enforcing judicial settlements and court awards.

Recently the clause has become controversial. The Massachusetts State Supreme Judicial court ruling that same-sex couples may not be discriminated against, which may be overridden by a state constitutional amendment, renewed a national debate over the full faith and credit clause. In 1996, Congress passed and President Clinton signed the Defense of Marriage Act (DOMA), which relieves states of any obligation to recognize same-sex marriages even if other states recognize them and stipulates that the national government only recognizes heterosexual marriages for federal benefits such as Social Security.[33] Supporters of the law argue that the Constitution gives Congress the responsibility to prescribe how states are to comply with the full faith and credit clause. But the DOMA is likely to be challenged in the courts for exceeding the power of Congress to provide states with an exemption from their constitutional obligation under the full faith and credit clause. Similar DOMA laws in 38 states are likely to be challenged as well, in light of the Supreme Court's ruling in *Lawrence* v. *Texas*[34] invalidating state laws criminalizing homosexual sodomy.

INTERSTATE PRIVILEGES AND IMMUNITIES   Under Article IV, Section 2, states must extend to citizens of other states the privileges and immunities they grant to their own citizens, including the protection of the laws, the right to engage in peaceful occupations, access to the courts, and freedom from discriminatory taxes. Because of this clause, states may not impose unreasonable residency requirements; that is, withhold rights to American citizens who have recently moved to the state and thereby have become citizens of that state. For example, a state may not set unreasonable time limits to withhold state-funded medical benefits from new citizens or to keep them from voting. How long a residency requirement may a state impose? A day seems about as long as the Supreme Court will tolerate to withhold welfare payments or medical care, 50 days or so for voting privileges, and one year for eligibility for in-state tuition for state-supported colleges and universities.

Financially independent adults who move into a state just before enrolling in a state-supported university or college may be required to prove that they have become citizens of that state and intend to remain after finishing their schooling by supplying such evidence of citizenship as tax payments, a driver's license, car registration, voter registration, and a continuous, year-round off-campus residence. Students who are financially dependent on their parents remain citizens of their parents' state.

EXTRADITION   In Article IV, Section 2, the Constitution asserts that when individuals charged with crimes have fled from one state to another, the state to which they have fled is to deliver them to the proper officials upon the demand of the executive authority of the state from which they fled. This process is called **extradition**. "The obvious objective of the Extradition Clause," the courts have claimed, "is that no State should become a safe haven for the fugitives from a sister State's criminal justice system."[35]

full faith and credit clause
Clause in the Constitution (Article IV, Section 1) requiring each state to recognize the civil judgments rendered by the courts of the other states and to accept their public records and acts as valid.

extradition
Legal process whereby an alleged criminal offender is surrendered by the officials of one state to officials of the state in which the crime is alleged to have been committed.

Congress has supplemented this constitutional provision by making the governor of the state to which fugitives have fled responsible for returning them. Yet despite their constitutional obligation, governors of asylum states have refused to honor a request for extradition.

INTERSTATE COMPACTS The Constitution also requires states to settle disputes with one another without the use of force. States may carry their legal disputes to the Supreme Court, or they may negotiate **interstate compacts**. Interstate compacts often establish interstate agencies to handle problems affecting an entire region. Before most interstate compacts become effective, Congress has to approve them. After a compact has been signed and approved by Congress, it becomes binding on all signatory states, and the federal judiciary can enforce its terms. A typical state may belong to 20 compacts dealing with such subjects as environmental protection, crime control, water rights, and higher education exchanges.[36]

interstate compact

An agreement among two or more states. Congress must approve most such agreements.

How Other Nations Govern

Different Visions of Federalism

Canada combines a federal system with a parliamentary form of government that has authority to legislate on all matters pertaining to "peace, order, and good government." The system was established in 1867, in part to prevent conflicts similar to those between the states that led to the American Civil War. In each of the ten Canadian provinces, the lieutenant governor who represents the crown is appointed on the advice of the prime minister of the province and must approve any provincial law before it goes into effect. The legislative powers of the provinces are thus checked and limited. However, the provinces retain residual powers, and unlike the U.S. Supreme Court, the Canadian judiciary has generally encouraged decentralization in recognition of its multicultural society. Thus Canadian provinces exercise greater power and the national government is weaker than in the United States. In addition, the special status claimed by French-speaking Quebec has led to intergovernmental relations that alternate between periods of centralization and decentraliza-

tion. Moreover, every province must consent to any changes in the Canadian constitution, a requirement that gives individual provinces an absolute veto over amending the constitution.

The Federal Republic of Germany, whose Basic Laws of 1949 became the constitution of a united Germany when East and West Germany were reunified in 1990, is often referred to as an example of cooperative federalism. Like the Canadian provinces, its 16 states, or Länder, exercise far more power than states do in the United States. The central government has a president and a bicameral parliament composed of an upper house (the Federal Council) and a lower house (the Federal Assembly), as well as an independent judiciary. The central government has exclusive authority over foreign affairs, money, immigration, and telecommunications. But the Länder retain residual powers over all other matters and have concurrent powers over civil and criminal law, along with matters related to education, health, and the public welfare. Moreover, national legislation does not become law unless approved by

There is no single model for dividing authority between national and state governments or for power sharing in intergovernmental relations. The federal systems in Canada, Germany, and Switzerland are illustrative.

a majority of the Federal Council, whose members are selected by legislatures in the Länder, not by popular elections.

Switzerland established a confederation centuries ago on the basis of regional governments (cantons). The cantons reflect the ethnic, linguistic, and sometimes religious differences of their German-, French-, and Italian-speaking populations. The central government officially recognizes all three languages. But of the 22 cantons, there are 18 that are unilingual, three that are bilingual, and one that is trilingual. They exercise most lawmaking powers and are represented in a bicameral legislature, which consists of the National Council and the Council of States. Recent constitutional reforms further entrenched a tripartite federalism by expressly recognizing the autonomy of

cities and municipalities, along with that of cantons and the federal government. As a result, cities and municipalities, unlike in the United States where these bodies are agents of the states, have constitutional status. In 2008, constitutional reforms will promote fiscal equalization among rich and poor cantons for the cost of social welfare, as well as greater cantonal collaboration in education, transportation, and waste management.

For more on comparative federalism, go to the Web site of the International Political Science Association's Section on Comparative Federalism at www.iu.edu/~soeaweb/IPSA and to the Forum on Federations at www.forumfed.org. See also Ann L. Griffiths, ed., *Handbook of Federal Countries, 2005* (McGill-Queen's University Press, 2005). ■

The Role of the Federal Courts: Umpires of Federalism

Although the political process ultimately decides how power will be divided between the national and the state governments, the federal courts—and especially the Supreme Court—are often called on to umpire the ongoing debate about which level of government should do what, for whom, and to whom. This role for the courts was claimed in the celebrated case of *McCulloch* v. *Maryland.*

McCulloch Versus *Maryland*

In *McCulloch* v. *Maryland* (1819), the Supreme Court had the first of many chances to define the division of power between the national and state governments.[37] Congress had established the Bank of the United States, but Maryland opposed any national bank and levied a $10,000 tax on any bank not incorporated within the state. James William McCulloch, the cashier of the bank, refused to pay on the grounds that a state could not tax an instrument of the national government.

Maryland was represented before the Court by some of the country's most distinguished lawyers, including Luther Martin, who had been a delegate to the Constitutional Convention. Martin said that the Constitution did not expressly delegate the power to incorporate a bank to the national government. He maintained that the necessary and proper clause gives Congress only the power to choose those means and to pass those laws absolutely essential to the execution of its expressly granted powers. Because a bank is not absolutely necessary to the exercise of its delegated powers, he argued, Congress had no authority to establish it. As for Maryland's right to tax the bank, the power to tax is one of the powers reserved to the states; they may use it as they see fit.

Equally distinguished counsel, including Daniel Webster, represented the national government. Webster conceded that the power to create a bank is not one of the express powers of the national government. However, the power to pass laws necessary and proper to carry out Congress's express powers is specifically delegated to

There have been times throughout U.S. history when federal law has superseded state and local law. One example of this in recent history is the Voting Rights Act of 1965, which enforced the voting rights of African Americans in the South. In this photo, African American citizens in Montgomery, Alabama, are registering to vote for the very first time following a march that took place during one of the many voter registration drives of 1964 and 1965.

> *"The power to tax involves the power to destroy."*
>
> CHIEF JUSTICE JOHN MARSHALL

Congress. Therefore, Congress may incorporate a bank as an appropriate, convenient, and useful means of exercising the granted powers of collecting taxes, borrowing money, and caring for the property of the United States. Although the power to tax is reserved to the states, Webster argued that states cannot interfere with the operations of the national government. The Constitution leaves no room for doubt; when the national and state governments conflict, the national government is supreme.

Speaking for a unanimous Court, Chief Justice John Marshall rejected every one of Maryland's contentions. He summarized his views on the powers of the national government in these now-famous words: "Let the end be legitimate, let it be within the scope of the Constitution, and all means which are appropriate, which are plainly adapted to that end, which are not prohibited, but consist with the letter and spirit of the constitution, are constitutional." Having thus established the doctrine of *implied national powers*, Marshall set forth the doctrine of **national supremacy**. No state, he said, can use its taxing powers to tax a national instrument. "The power to tax involves the power to destroy. . . . If the right of the States to tax the means employed by the general government be conceded, the declaration that the Constitution, and the laws made in pursuance thereof, shall be the supreme law of the land, is empty and unmeaning declamation."

The long-range significance of *McCulloch* v. *Maryland* in providing support for the developing forces of nationalism and a unified economy cannot be overstated. If the contrary arguments in favor of the states had been accepted, they would have strapped the national government in a constitutional straitjacket and denied it powers needed to deal with the problems of an expanding nation.

Federal Courts and the Role of the States

The authority of federal judges to review the activities of state and local governments has expanded dramatically in recent decades because of modern judicial interpretations of the Fourteenth Amendment, which forbids states from depriving any person of life, liberty, or property without *due process of the law*. States may not deny any person the *equal protection of the laws,* including congressional legislation enacted to implement the Fourteenth Amendment. Almost every action by state and local officials is now subject to challenge before a federal judge as a violation of the Constitution or of federal law.

Preemption occurs when a federal law or regulation takes precedence over enforcing a state or local law or regulation. State and local laws are preempted not only when they conflict directly with federal laws and regulations but also if they touch a field in which the "federal interest is so dominant that the federal system will be assumed to preclude enforcement of state laws on the same subject."[38] Examples of federal preemption include laws regulating hazardous substances, water quality, clean air standards, and many civil rights acts, especially the Civil Rights Act of 1964 and the Voting Rights Act of 1965.

Over the years, federal judges, under the leadership of the Supreme Court, have generally favored the powers of the federal government over the states. Despite the Supreme Court's recent bias in favor of state over national authority, few would deny the Supreme Court the power to review and set aside state actions. As Justice Oliver Wendell Holmes of the Supreme Court once remarked: "I do not think the United States would come to an end if we lost our power to declare an Act of Congress void. I do think the Union would be imperiled if we could not make that declaration as to the laws of the several States."[39]

national supremacy
Constitutional doctrine that whenever conflict occurs between the constitutionally authorized actions of the national government and those of a state or local government, the actions of the federal government prevail.

preemption
The right of a federal law or regulation to preclude enforcement of a state or local law or regulation.

The Great Debate: Centralists Versus Decentralists

From the beginning of the Republic, there has been an ongoing debate about the "proper" distribution of powers, functions, and responsibilities between the national government and the states. Did the national government have the authority to outlaw slavery in the territories? Did the states have the authority to operate racially segregated schools? Could Congress regulate labor relations? Does Congress have the power to regulate the sale and use of firearms? Does Congress have the right to tell states how to clean up air and water pollution? Even today, as in the past, such debates are frequently phrased in constitutional language, with appeals to the great principles of federalism. But they are also arguments over who gets what, where, when, and how.

During the Great Depression of the 1930s, the nation debated whether Congress had the constitutional authority to enact legislation on agriculture, labor, education, housing, and welfare. Only 40 years ago, legislators and public officials—as well as scholars—questioned the constitutional authority of Congress to legislate against racial discrimination. The debate continues between **centralists**, who favor national action, and **decentralists**, who defend the powers of the states and favor action at the state and local levels.

THE DECENTRALIST POSITION Among Americans favoring the decentralist or **states' rights** interpretation were the Antifederalists, Thomas Jefferson, the pre-Civil War statesman from South Carolina John C. Calhoun, the Supreme Court from the 1920s to 1937, and more recently, Presidents Ronald Reagan and George H. W. Bush, the Republican leaders of Congress, former Chief Justice William H. Rehnquist, and Justices Antonin Scalia and Clarence Thomas.

Most decentralists contend that the Constitution is basically a compact among sovereign states that created the central government and gave it limited authority. Thus the national government is little more than an agent of the states, and every one of its powers should be narrowly defined. Any question about whether the states have given a particular function to the central government or have reserved it for themselves should be resolved in favor of the states.

Decentralists hold that the national government should not interfere with activities reserved for the states. The Tenth Amendment, they claim, makes this clear. It states: "The powers not delegated to the United States by the Constitution, nor prohibited by it to the States, are reserved to the States respectively, or to the people." Decentralists insist that state governments are closer to the people and reflect the people's wishes more accurately than the national government does. The national government, they add, is inherently heavy-handed and bureaucratic; to preserve our federal system and our liberties, central authority must be kept under control.

Decentralists also argue that increased urbanization has made states more responsive to the needs of communities, and they have become as sensitive to the needs of the poor and minorities as the national government. In recent years, many state and local governments have been more willing to raise taxes than the national government has, and they have reformed and modernized to become more effective.

THE CENTRALIST POSITION The centralist position has been supported by Chief Justice John Marshall; Presidents Abraham Lincoln, Theodore Roosevelt, and Franklin Roosevelt; and throughout most of our history, the Supreme Court.

Centralists reject the whole idea of the Constitution as an interstate compact. They view the Constitution as a supreme law established by the people. The national government is an agent of the people, not of the states, because it was the people who drew up the Constitution and created the national government. They intended that the national political process should define the central government's powers and that the national government is denied authority only when the Constitution clearly prohibits it from acting.

Centralists argue that the national government is a government of all the people, whereas each state speaks only for some of the people. Although the Tenth Amendment clearly reserves powers for the states, it does not deny the national government the authority to exercise, to the fullest extent, all of its powers. Moreover, the supremacy of the national government restricts the states, because governments representing part of the people cannot be allowed to interfere with a government representing all of them.

centralists
People who favor national action over action at the state and local levels.

decentralists
People who favor state or local action rather than national action.

states' rights
Powers expressly or implicitly reserved to the states.

Some centralists also argue that state and local officials are often less competent than national officials and tend to be concerned only with the narrow interests of their constituents. State and local governments are more apt to reflect local racial and ethnic biases as well as the interests of dominant local industries.

The Supreme Court and the Role of Congress

From 1937 until the 1990s, the Supreme Court essentially removed federal courts from what had been their role of protecting states from acts of Congress. The Supreme Court broadly interpreted the commerce clause to allow Congress to do whatever Congress thought necessary and proper to promote the common good, even if federal laws and regulations infringed on the activities of state and local governments. The Court even told the states that they should look to the political process to protect their interests, not to the federal courts.

In the past decade, however, a bare majority of the Supreme Court has signaled that federal courts should no longer remain passive in resolving federalism issues.[40] The Court declared that a state could not impose term limits on its members of Congress, but it did so only by a 5 to 4 vote. Justice John Paul Stevens, writing for the majority, built his argument on the concept of the federal union as espoused by the great Chief Justice John Marshall, as a compact among the people, with the national government serving as the people's agent. By contrast, Justice Clarence Thomas, writing for the dissenters, espoused a view of federalism not heard from a justice of the Supreme Court since before the New Deal. He interpreted the Tenth Amendment as requiring the national government to justify its actions in terms of an enumerated power and granting to the states all other powers not expressly given to the national government. "The ultimate source of the Constitution's authority is the consent of the people of each individual State, not the undifferentiated consent of the Nation as a whole."[41]

The Court also declared that the clause in the Constitution empowering Congress to regulate commerce with the Indian tribes did not give Congress the power to authorize federal courts to hear suits against a state brought by Indian tribes.[42] Unless states consent to such suits, they enjoy "sovereign immunity" under the Eleventh Amendment. The effect of this decision goes beyond Indian tribes. As a result, except to enforce rights stemming from the Fourteenth Amendment, which the Court explicitly acknowledged to be within Congress's power, Congress may no longer authorize individuals to bring legal actions against states to force their compliance with federal law in either federal or state courts.[43]

Building on those rulings, the Court continues to press ahead with its "constitutional counterrevolution"[44] in returning to an older vision of federalism not embraced since the constitutional crisis over the New Deal in the 1930s. Among other recent rulings, in *United States* v. *Morrison* the Court struck down the Violence Against Women Act, which had given women who are victims of violence the right to sue their attackers for damages.[45] Congress had found that violence against women annually costs the national economy $3 billion, but a bare majority of the Court held that gender-motivated crimes did not have a substantial impact on interstate commerce and, hence, Congress exceeded its powers in enacting the law and intruded on the powers of the states.

These Supreme Court decisions—most of which split the Court 5 to 4 along ideological lines, with the conservative justices favoring states' rights—have signaled a shift in the Court's interpretation of the constitutional nature of our federal system. Chief Justice Rehnquist, joined by Justices Scalia, Thomas, O'Connor, and frequently Justice Anthony M. Kennedy, have pushed the Court toward a decentralist position. President Clinton's two appointees, Justices Ruth Bader Ginsburg and Stephen Breyer, joined by Justices David Souter and John Paul Stevens, have resisted this movement back to a states' rights interpretation of our federal system. Not surprisingly, federalism issues came up during the confirmation hearings for Chief Justice John Roberts in 2005 and Justice Samuel Alito, Jr., in 2006, and will likely continue to be debated.

"The ultimate source of the Constitution's authority is the consent of the people of each individual State, not the undifferentiated consent of the Nation as a whole."

JUSTICE CLARENCE THOMAS

Regulatory Federalism: Grants, Mandates, and New Techniques of Control

Congress authorizes programs, establishes general rules for how the programs will operate, and decides whether and how much room should be left for state or local discretion. Most important, Congress appropriates the funds for these programs and generally has deeper pockets than even the richest states. Federal grants are one of Congress's most potent tools for influencing policy at the state and local levels.

Federal grants serve four purposes, the most important of which is the fourth:

1. To supply state and local governments with revenue.

2. To establish minimum national standards for such things as highways and clean air.

3. To equalize resources among the states by taking money from people with high incomes through federal taxes and spending it, through grants, in states where the poor live.

4. To attack national problems yet minimize the growth of federal agencies.

History Makers

Chief Justice William H. Rehnquist

When asked his career plans by his elementary school teacher, William H. Rehnquist once recalled saying, "I am going to change the government."* After serving in the army during World War II, he majored in political science at Stanford University and later graduated first in his class from Stanford Law School. He then clerked for a Supreme Court justice and went into private legal practice, while becoming active in Republican politics.

As an assistant attorney general in the administration of President Richard M. Nixon, he was appointed associate justice of the Supreme Court in 1972. In his early years on the Court he emerged as a champion of federalism, limiting the power of the national government and re-

turning power to the states. However, he could not persuade a majority to go along with his views and earned the nickname "Lone Ranger" for writing more dissenting opinions than any other justice at the time. In 1986, President Ronald Reagan elevated him to chief justice, and he presided over the Court until his death in 2005.

A major legacy of the Rehnquist Court is how it curbed Congress in defense of the states. Besides resurrecting the rhetoric of states' rights and the Tenth Amendment, Chief Justice Rehnquist commanded a majority for holding that:

■ Congress must make a "plain statement" of its intent to pre-empt state laws; otherwise the Court will defer to the states.[†]

■ Congress's power over interstate commerce has inherent limits, and it may not compel states to enact laws in compliance with federal standards or compel them to enforce federal laws.[‡]

■ Congress's power under the commerce clause permits it to regulate noneconomic activities but only if they "substantially affect interstate commerce."[§]

■ Congress's power to enforce the Fourteenth Amendment's guarantee of equal protection of the law is limited to remedying violations that the Court recognizes and does not extend to creating rights.[||]

■ States' immunity from lawsuits, under the Eleventh Amendment, bars lawsuits against them, without their consent, in federal and state courts and by citizens of

William H. Renquist

other states as well as of their own state who seek state compliance with federal laws forbidding, for example, discrimination on the basis of age or disability.[¶]

In short, Chief Justice Rehnquist presided over a Court that curbed the expansion of congressional powers and federal regulations in a renewed defense of the boundaries of federalism. ■

*Quoted in Craig Bradley, "William H. Rehnquist," in Clare Cushman, ed., *The Supreme Court Justices* (C.Q. Press, 1993), p. 496.
[†]*Gregory* v. *Ashcroft,* 501 U.S. 452 (1991).
[‡]*New York* v. *United States,* 505 U.S. 144 (1992), and *Printz* v. *United States,* 521 U.S. 898 (1997).
[§]*United States* v. *Lopez,* 514 U.S. 549 (1995), and *United States* v. *Morrison,* 529 U.S. 598 (2000); but see *Nevada* v. *Hibbs,* 538 U.S. 721 (2003).
[||]*City of Bourne* v. *Lopez,* 521 U.S. 507 (1997), and *United States* v. *Morrison,* 529 U.S. 598 (2000).
[¶]See, e.g., *Alden* v. *Maine,* 527 U.S. 706 (1998).

Types of Federal Grants

Three types of federal grants are currently being administered: *categorical-formula grants, project grants,* and *block grants* (sometimes called *flexible grants*). From 1972 to 1987, there was also *revenue sharing*—federal grants to state and local governments to be used at their discretion and subject only to general conditions. But when budget deficits soared in the second Reagan administration (1985–1989) and there was no revenue to share, revenue sharing was terminated—to the states in 1986 and to local governments in 1987.

CATEGORICAL-FORMULA GRANTS   Congress appropriates funds for specific purposes, such as school lunches or for building airports and highways. These funds are allocated by formula and are subject to detailed federal conditions, often on a matching basis; that is, the local government receiving the federal funds must put up some of its own dollars. Categorical grants, in addition, provide federal supervision to ensure that the federal dollars are spent as Congress wants. There are hundreds of grant programs, but two dozen, including Medicaid, account for more than half of total spending for categoricals.

PROJECT GRANTS   Congress appropriates a certain sum, which is allocated to state and local units and sometimes to nongovernmental agencies, based on applications from those who wish to participate. Examples are grants by the National Science Foundation to universities and research institutes to support the work of scientists or grants to states and localities to support training and employment programs.

BLOCK GRANTS   These are broad grants to states for prescribed activities—welfare, child care, education, social services, preventive health care, and health services—with only a few strings attached. States have great flexibility in deciding how to spend block grant dollars, but when the federal funds for any fiscal year are gone, there are no more matching federal dollars.

The Politics of Federal Grants

Republicans "have consistently favored fewer strings, less federal supervision, and the delegation of spending discretion to the state and local governments."[46] Democrats have generally been less supportive of broad discretionary block grants, favoring instead more detailed, federally supervised spending. The Republican-controlled Congress in the 1990s gave high priority to creating block grants, but it ran into trouble by trying to lump together welfare, school lunch and breakfast programs, prenatal nutrition programs, and child protection programs in one block grant.

Republicans, however, with President Clinton's support, made a major change in federal–state relations—a devolution of responsibility for welfare from the national government to the states. The Personal Responsibility and Work Opportunity Reconciliation Act of 1996 put an end to the 61-year-old program of Aid to Families with Dependent Children (AFDC), a federal guarantee of welfare checks for all eligible mothers and children. The 1996 act substituted for AFDC a welfare block grant to each state, with caps on the amount of federal dollars that the state will receive. It also put another big federal child care program into another block grant—the Child Care and Development Block Grant (CCDBG).

Welfare block grants give states flexibility in how they provide for welfare, but no federal funds can be used to cover recipients who do not go to work within two years, and no one can receive federally supported benefits for more than five years. To slow down the "race to the bottom," in which states may try to make themselves "the least attractive state in which to be poor,"[47] Congress also stipulated that to receive their full share of federal dollars, states must continue to spend at least 75 percent of what they had been spending on welfare.

The battle over the appropriate level of government to control funding and to exercise principal responsibility for social programs tends to be cyclical. As one scholar of federalism explains, "Complaints about excessive federal control tend to be followed by proposals to shift more power to state and local governments. Then, when problems arise in state and local administration—and problems inevitably arise when any organization tries to administer anything—demands for closer federal supervision and tighter federal controls follow."[48]

Federal Mandates

Fewer federal dollars do not necessarily mean fewer federal controls. On the contrary, the federal government has imposed mandates on states and local governments, often without providing federal funds. State and local officials complained about this, and their protests were effective. The Unfunded Mandates Reform Act of 1995 was championed by then House Republican Speaker Newt Gingrich as part of the GOP's Contract with America. The law requires the Congressional Budget Office (CBO) and federal agencies to issue reports about the impact of unfunded mandates. The act also imposed mild constraints on Congress itself. A congressional committee that approves any legislation containing a federal mandate must draw attention to the mandate in its report and describe its cost to state and local governments. If the committee intends any mandate to be partially unfunded, it must explain why it is appropriate for state and local governments to pay for it.

Whether the Unfunded Mandates Reform Act will significantly slow down federal mandates appears doubtful. So far, it has had little effect. The Americans with Disabilities Act (1990), for example, called on state and local governments to build ramps and alter curbs—renovations that cost millions of dollars—to make public buildings accessible to the blind and persons in wheelchairs or on crutches. Environmental Protection Agency regulations require states to build automobile pollution-testing stations and take other actions to reduce pollution, but without corresponding federal dollars. However, states often view unfunded mandates more broadly than the act, because recent legislation has reduced federal funding for programs without reducing requirements for the states, and has created underfunded national expectations for improvements in education and homeland security.[49] Still, state officials praise the Unfunded Mandates Reform Act for increasing congressional awareness of unfunded mandates. It has forced members of Congress to take into account how a bill would affect state and local governments.[50]

New Techniques of Federal Control

In recent decades, Congress has used other techniques to establish federal regulations, including *direct orders, cross-cutting requirements, crossover sanctions,* and *total and partial preemption.*

DIRECT ORDERS In a few instances, federal regulation takes the form of direct orders that must be complied with under threat of criminal or civil sanction. An example is the Equal Employment Opportunity Act of 1972, barring job discrimination by state and local governments on the basis of race, color, religion, sex, and national origin.

CROSS-CUTTING REQUIREMENTS Federal grants may establish certain conditions that extend to all activities supported by federal funds, regardless of their source. The first and most famous of these is Title VI of the 1964 Civil Rights Act, which holds that in the use of federal funds, no person may be discriminated against on the basis of race, color, or national origin. Other laws extend these protections to persons because of gender or disability status. More than 60 cross-cutting requirements concern such matters as the environment, historic preservation, contract wage rates, access to government information, the care of experimental animals, and the treatment of human subjects in research projects.

CROSSOVER SANCTIONS These sanctions permit the use of federal money in one program to influence state and local policy in another. For example, a 1984 act reduced federal highway aid by up to 15 percent for any state that failed to adopt a minimum drinking age of 21.

TOTAL AND PARTIAL PREEMPTION Total preemption rests on the national government's power under the supremacy and commerce clauses to preempt conflicting state and local activities. Building on this constitutional authority, federal law in certain areas entirely preempts state and local governments from the field.[51] Sometimes federal law provides for partial preemption in establishing basic policies but requires states to administer them. Some programs give states an option not to participate, but if a state chooses not to do so, the national government steps in and runs the program. Even worse from the states' point of view is *mandatory partial preemption,* in which the national government requires states to act on peril of losing other funds but provides no funds to support state action. The Clean Air Act of 1990 is an example of mandatory partial preemption; the federal government set national air quality standards and required states to devise plans and pay for their implementation.[52] Homeland security legislation is another example of the national government providing some funds but requiring states to provide services as "first responders" that cost more than federal funds cover.

The Politics of Federalism

The formal structures of our federal system have not changed much since 1787, but the political realities, especially during the past half-century, have greatly altered how federalism works. To understand these changes, we need to look at some of the trends that continue to fuel the debate about the meaning of federalism.

The Growth of Big Government

Over the past two centuries, power has accrued to the national government. As the Advisory Commission on Intergovernmental Relations observed in a 1981 report, "No one planned the growth, but everyone played a part in it."[53] This shift occurred for a variety of reasons. One is that many of our problems have become national in scope. Much that was local in 1789, in 1860, or in 1930 is now national, even global. State governments could supervise the relations between small merchants and their few employees, but only the national government can supervise relations between multinational corporations and their thousands of employees, many of which are organized in national unions.

As industrialization proceeded, powerful interests made demands on the national government. Business groups called on the government for aid in the form of tariffs, a national banking system, subsidies to railroads and the merchant marine, and uniform rules on the environment. Farmers learned that the national government could give more aid than the states, and they too began to demand help. By the beginning of the twentieth century, urban groups in general and organized labor in particular pressed their claims. Big business, big agriculture, and big labor all added up to big government.

The growth of the national economy and the creation of national transportation and communications networks altered people's attitudes toward the national government. Before the Civil War, the national government was viewed as a distant, even foreign, government. Today, in part because of television and the Internet, most people know more about Washington than they know about their state capitals. People are apt to know more about the president than about their governor and more about their national senators and representatives than about their state legislators or even about the local officials who run their cities and schools.

The Great Depression of the 1930s stimulated extensive national action on welfare, unemployment, and farm surpluses. World War II brought federal regulation of wages, prices, and employment, as well as national efforts to allocate resources, train personnel, and support engineering and inventions. After the war, the national government helped veterans obtain college degrees and inaugurated a vast system of support for university research. The United States became the most powerful leader of the free world, maintaining substantial military forces even in times of peace. The Great Society programs of the 1960s poured out grants-in-aid to states and localities. City dwellers who had migrated from the rural South to northern cities began to seek federal funds for—at the very least—housing, education, and mass transportation.

Although economic and social conditions created many of the pressures for expanding the national government, so did political claims. Until federal budget deficits became a hot issue in the 1980s and early 1990s, members of Congress, presidents, federal judges, and federal administrators actively promoted federal initiatives.

Even with the return of deficit spending in the 2000s, Congress appears willing to actively promote some federal programs, at least in homeland security and prescription drug coverage. True, when there is widespread conflict about what to do—how to reduce the federal deficit, adopt a national energy policy, reform Social Security, provide health care for the indigent—Congress waits for a national consensus. But when an organized constituency wants something and there is no counterpressure, Congress "responds often to everyone, and with great vigor."[54] Once established, federal programs generate groups with vested interests in promoting, defending, and expanding them. Associations are formed and alliances are made. "In a word, the growth of government has created a constituency of, by, and for government."[55]

The politics of federalism are changing, however, and Congress is being pressured to reduce the size and scope of national programs, but at the same time to deal with the demands for homeland security. Meanwhile, the cost of entitlement programs such as Social Security and Medicare are rising because there are more older people and they are living longer. These programs have widespread public support, and to cut them is politically risky. "With all other options disappearing, it is politically tempting to finance tax cuts by turning over to the states many of the social programs . . . that have become the responsibility of the national government."[56]

The Devolution Revolution: Rhetoric Versus Reality

Recent Congresses, like their predecessors, have increased the authority of the national government in many areas. To be sure, the Republican-controlled Congress in the 1990s returned some functions, especially welfare, to the states. President Clinton also proclaimed, "The era of big government is over," though he tempered his comments by saying, "But we cannot go back to the time when our citizens were left to fend for themselves." Congress and the president came together to overhaul welfare and, to a lesser degree, education. Congress also freed the states to set their own highway speed limits, changed the Safe Drinking Water Act to allow states to operate certain programs, and gave states a greater role over how to use federal rural development funds.

In the aftermath of the attacks of September 11, 2001, and in confronting the continuing threats of terrorism, however, the role of the federal government in defending homeland security has expanded, and some states, like New York, have objected to inadequate federal funding and to the increased cost of using state agencies as "first responders." Congress also established national criteria for state-issued drivers' licenses, forbade states from selling drivers' personal information, ended state regulation of mutual funds, nullified state laws restricting telecommunications competition, and made a host of offenses federal crimes, including carjacking and acts of terrorism. Appropriation bills pressured states to keep criminals behind bars by threatening to take grants away from states that fail to meet federal standards.

Moreover, while President George W. Bush has devolved some social programs, he pushed into law his No Child Left Behind education bill, which mandates annual standardized testing of elementary school children. School districts in Michigan, Texas, and Vermont have sued, claiming that the program is underfunded and the Utah legislature allowed school districts to ignore the law if its mandates require spending state money to comply with them.[57] As a result, in 2005, the administration eased some of its regulations on rating schools' progress in meeting student performance standards.[58]

In sum, the only two major achievements of the devolution revolution remain the 1996 reform of welfare and the repeal of a national speed limit.[59] As one reporter concluded, "The 'devolution' promised by Congressional Republicans . . . has mostly fizzled. Instead of handing over authority to state and local governments, they're taking it away."[60]

The Future of Federalism

During the Great Depression in the 1930s, with state governments helpless, one writer stated, "I do not predict that the states will go, but affirm that they have gone."[61] Such prophets were wrong; the states are stronger than ever. During

> *"In a word, the growth of government has created a constituency of, by, and for government."*
>
> **AARON WILDAVSKY**

Government's Greatest Endeavors

Giving Responsibilities Back to the States

A 1996 overhaul of the welfare system shifted more control to the states.

QUESTIONS

Why do states want more responsibilities returned to them?

How would you decide whether a responsibility such as education or health care belongs to the federal or state government?

As the federal government has grown, states have complained that it is taking over responsibilities such as education that properly belong to the states. The federal government has responded with a number of programs to help states act on the public's behalf.

In 1972, for example, Congress gave the states $30 billion over five years in what was called "revenue sharing," which distributed dollars to the states based on their populations. This was widely applauded as a way to help states administer new federal programs designed to aid the poor and protect the environment. Indeed, the bill required states and localities to put the new revenue into "priority expenditures," which meant police and fire departments, environmental protection, public transportation, health, libraries, social services, and recreation. The bill also required that two-thirds of the $30 billion go to local governments. Revenue sharing ran out in the 1980s, however, and was not renewed.

Congress has also helped states through several efforts to "devolve," or pass federal responsibilities back to the states. Although these efforts have often been limited, they reflect at least some awareness that the federal government may be reaching too far in asking states to implement federal mandates, which are requirements that rarely come with the federal dollars needed to act on them. In 1995, Congress passed a law to discourage such "unfunded mandates" by requiring members to consider the actual cost of asking states to implement federal legislation without funding.

Congress also passed a bill in 1996 that overhauled the welfare system by giving states much greater freedom to determine the future of welfare recipients. The bill gave the states much greater control over federal welfare dollars. ∎

recent decades, state governments have undergone a major transformation. Most have improved their governmental structures, taken on greater roles in funding education and welfare, launched programs to help distressed cities, expanded their tax bases, and are assuming greater roles in maintaining homeland security and fighting corporate corruption. Able men and women have been attracted to governorships. "Today, states, in formal representational, policy making, and implementation terms at least, are more representative, more responsive, more activist, and more professional in their operations than they ever have been. They face their expanded roles better equipped to assume and fulfill them."[62]

After the civil rights revolution of the 1960s, segregationists feared that national officials would work for racial integration. Thus they praised local government, emphasized the dangers of centralization, and argued that the protection of civil rights was not a proper function of the national government. As one political scientist observed, "Federalism has a dark history to overcome. For nearly two hundred years, states' rights have been asserted to protect slavery, segregation, and discrimination."[63]

Today the politics of federalism, even with respect to civil rights, is more complicated than in the past. The national government is not necessarily more favorable to the claims of minorities than state or city governments are. Rulings on same-sex marriages and "civil unions" by state courts interpreting their state constitutions have extended more protection for these rights than has the Supreme Court's interpretation of the U.S. Constitution. Other states, however, are passing legislation that would eliminate such protections, and opponents are pressing for a constitutional amendment to bar same-sex marriages.

States are also increasingly aggressive in addressing economic and environmental matters. State attorneys general are prosecuting anticompetitive business practices, as they did in joining the suit against Microsoft and, more recently, as New York attorney general Eliot Spitzer did in suing the mutual fund industry and spammers. After the Bush administration abandoned 50 investigations into violations of the Clean Air Act and changed policy on regulating power plants, Spitzer and other state attorneys general sued the Bush administration and power plant companies to force them to improve pollution controls.[64] Business interests have argued that conflicting state regulations unduly burden interstate commerce and have sought broader preemptive federal regulation to save them not only from stringent state regulations but also from the uncertainties of complying with 50 different state laws. As a lawyer representing trade groups in the food and medical devices industries observed: "One national dumb rule is better than 50 inconsistent rules of any kind."[65]

The national government is not likely to retreat to a pre-1930 or even a pre-1960 posture. Indeed, international terrorism, the wars in Afghanistan and Iraq, and rising deficits have substantially altered the underlying economic and social conditions that generated the demand for federal action. In addition to such traditional issues as helping people find jobs and preventing inflation and depressions—which still require national action—the growth of a global economy based on the information explosion, e-commerce, advancing technologies, and combating international terrorism have added countless new issues to the national agenda.

Agents of Change

Wendy Kopp and Teach For America

QUESTIONS

How can 3,500 Teach for America volunteers hope to improve public education in a system governed by federal, state, and local laws?

Why has Teach for America become such a popular program for recent graduates?

Teach for America has become one of the nation's largest and best-known organizations for helping low-income children. Last year, 3,500 Teach for America recruits served more than 1,000 schools in 22 regions of the United States. Teach for America recruits do not need an undergraduate degree to apply, but they do need to commit to two years of service at the same starting salaries that other teachers receive.

Wendy Kopp designed Teach for America as an undergraduate at Princeton University. After reading her undergraduate thesis and considering her plan to launch the new organization right after graduation, her thesis advisor said, "Listen, kid, this is obviously deranged." Kopp was not deterred, however. "I believe so strongly in this idea, it just had to happen. And I was blessed with naiveté. Inexperience was my greatest asset at the time, because I just did not know why it couldn't be done,

and why I couldn't be the one to make it happen." With donated office space and less than $26,000 in starting support, Kopp went ahead with her plan. Within 10 years, Teach for America had a $55 million budget.

Since 1990, when the first class of Teach for America volunteers began work, more than 14,000 individuals have reached 2 million students. Although Teach for America volunteers cannot replace the 7 million teachers who work in the public schools, they often bring needed energy to teaching jobs that other teachers reject. Last year, nearly 20,000 college graduates applied for a Teach for America job. ∎

Wendy Kopp

Learn more about Teach for America at www.teachforamerica.org.

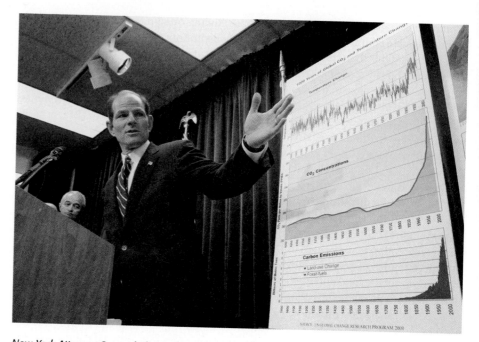

New York Attorney General Eliot Spitzer was one of several state attorneys general to sue the Bush administration and power plant companies over pollution control.

Most Americans have strong attachments to our federal system—in the abstract. They remain loyal to their states and show a growing skepticism about the national government. Yet evidence suggests the anti-Washington sentiment "is 3,000 miles wide but only a few miles deep."[66] The fact is that Americans are pragmatists: We appear to prefer federal–state–local power sharing[67] and are prepared to use whatever levels of government are necessary to meet our needs and new challenges.

Summary

1. A federal system is one in which the constitution divides powers between the central government and subdivisional governments—states or provinces. Alternatives to federalism are unitary systems, in which all constitutional power is vested in the central government, and confederations, which are loose compacts among sovereign states.

2. Federal systems can check the growth of tyranny, allow unity without uniformity, encourage state experimentation, permit power sharing between the national government and the states, and keep government closer to the people.

3. The national government has the constitutional authority, stemming primarily from the national supremacy clause, the war powers, and its powers

to regulate commerce among the states to tax and spend, to do what Congress thinks is necessary and proper to promote the general welfare and to provide for the common defense. These constitutional pillars have permitted tremendous expansion of the functions of the federal government.

4. States must give full faith and credit to each other's public acts, records, and judicial proceedings; extend to each others' citizens the privileges and immunities they give their own; and return fugitives from justice to states that claim them.

5. The federal courts umpire the division of power between the national and state governments. The Marshall Court, in decisions such as *Gibbons* v. *Ogden* and *McCulloch* v. *Maryland*,

asserted the power of the national government over the states and promoted a national economic common market. These decisions also reinforced the supremacy of the national government over the states.

6. Today, debates about federalism are less often about its constitutional structure than about whether action should come from the national or state and local levels. Recent Supreme Court decisions favor a decentralist position and signal shifts in the Court's interpretation of the constitutional nature of our federal system.

7. The major instruments of federal intervention in state programs have been various kinds of financial grants-in-aid, of which the most prominent are categorical-formula

grants, project grants, and block grants. The national government also imposes federal mandates and controls activities of state and local governments by other means.

8. Over the past 229 years, power has accrued to the national government, but recently Congress has been pressured to reduce the size and scope of national programs and to shift some existing programs back to the states. Although responsibility for welfare has been turned over to the states, the authority of the national government has increased in many other areas.

Further Reading

SAMUEL H. BEER, *To Make a Nation: The Rediscovery of American Federalism* (Harvard University Press, 1993).

CENTER FOR THE STUDY OF FEDERALISM, *The Federalism Report* (published quarterly by Temple University; this publication notes research, books and articles, and scholarly conferences).

CENTER FOR THE STUDY OF FEDERALISM, *Publius: The Journal of Federalism* (published quarterly by Temple University; one issue each year is an "Annual Review of the State of American Federalism"; and has a Web site at www.lafayette.edu/~publius).

TIMOTHY J. CONLAN, *From New Federalism to Devolution: Twenty-Five Years of Intergovernmental Reforms* (Brookings Institution, 1998).

DANIEL J. ELAZER AND **JOHN KINCAID,** *The Covenant Connection: From Federal Theology to Modern Federalism* (Lexington Books, 2000).

JOHN FEREJOHN AND **BARRY WEINGAST,** *The New Federalism: Can the States Be Trusted?* (Hoover Institute Press, 1998).

JOHN KINCAID AND **G. ALLEN TARR,** EDS., *Constitutional Origins, Structure, and Change in Federal Countries* (McGill-Queens University Press, 2005).

NEIL C. MCCABE, ED., *Comparative Federalism in the Devolution Era* (Rowman & Littlefield, 2002).

FORREST MCDONALD, *States' Rights and the Union: Imperim in Imperio, 1776–1876* (University Press of Kansas, 2000).

KALYPSO NICOLAIDIS AND **ROBERT HOWSE,** EDS., *The Federal Vision: Legitimacy and Levels of Governance in the United States and the European Union* (Oxford University Press, 2001).

JOHN T. NOONAN, *Narrowing the Nation's Power: The Supreme Court Sides with the States* (University of California Press, 2002).

DAVID M. O'BRIEN, *Constitutional Law and Politics: Struggles for Power and Governmental Accountability,* 6th ed. (Norton, 2005).

WILLIAM H. RIKER, *The Development of American Federalism* (Academic, 1987).

KEVIN SMITH, ED., *State and Local Government, 2005–2006* (CQ Press, 2005).

CARL VAN HORN, ED., *The State of the States* (CQ Press, 2005).

KeyTerms

devolution revolution, p. 60	inherent powers, p. 66	national supremacy, p. 74
federalism, p. 61	commerce clause, p. 67	preemption, p. 74
unitary system, p. 62	federal mandate, p. 69	centralists, p. 75
confederation, p. 62	concurrent powers, p. 69	decentralists, p. 75
express powers, p. 66	full faith and credit clause, p. 71	states' rights, p. 75
implied powers, p. 66	extradition, p. 71	
necessary and proper clause, p. 66	interstate compact, p. 72	

Make It Real

FEDERALISM

This unit delves into *McCulloch* v *Maryland* and Katrina.

OVER THE LAST COUPLE OF YEARS, WHAT HAS COME TO BE called the Christian Right has

become more and more active in supporting the Sharon government in its war with the Palestinians and their political clout with the Bush administration is considerable. They are opposed to giving the Palestinians any land, taking a much harder line than many Americans. The reason? Prophecy. Many believe that what is playing out now in the Middle East is all part of the process leading toward the Second Coming. The existence of the state of Israel is crucial to that process and many believe that Israel must cover all of the land, including the occupied territories, in order for this process to move forward. So they send money, take trips to Israel, meet regularly with Israeli officials, including Sharon, and at the same time, seem to be breaking what was a strong alliance between American Jews and the Democratic Party. That would certainly change the political landscape in this country as well. Israel needs friends now, facing serious criticism from much of the world over its tactics in the current conflict.

God and Country

ORIGINALLY AIRED: 11/26/02

PROGRAM: **Nightline**

RUNNING TIME: 12:41

And so both sides are sort of glossing over a theological issue. According to the prophecies that many Christians believe, as part of the Second Coming, Jews will have the opportunity to either convert to Christianity, or perish. In other words, they will disappear as a people, or religion, one way or the other. You might think that this would be a point of contention between the two religions, but it doesn't appear to be. Ted Koppel interviews Pat Robertson, founder and chairman of the Christian Broadcasting Network. He is a former presidential candidate and arguably one of the most recognized leaders of the evangelical Christian community.

Critical Thinking Questions

*After viewing "*God and Country*" on your* ABCNEWS DVD *answer the following questions.*

1. CONSERVATIVE CHRISTIANS EXPLAIN their strong support for Israel, especially their support of Jewish occupation of the West Bank. Briefly discuss the reasons they give for this support.

2. NOT ALL JEWS WELCOME THE SUPPORT of conservative American Christians. What implications of that support concern them?

3. AS A GENERAL RULE, INTEREST GROUPS rarely have a decisive role in the formulation of foreign policy. How might conservative Christian support for Israel be an exception to that rule?

87

Chapter 4

Political Culture and Ideology

IN THE DAYS AND WEEKS AFTER RECENT CATASTROPHES LIKE THE TSUNAMI THAT HIT SOUTHEAST ASIA, HURRICANE KATRINA THAT DEVASTATED THE GULF COAST, AND THE TERRORIST STRIKES ON THE WORLD TRADE CENTER AND THE PENTAGON, MANY AMERICANS RESPONDED BY CONTRIBUTING MONEY TO RELIEF EFFORTS, DONATING BLOOD, OR VOLUNTEERING.[1] FOR EXAMPLE, CHARITABLE CONTRIBUTIONS IN RESPONSE TO THE ATTACKS OF SEPTEMBER 11, 2001 TOTALED $2.2 BILLION[2] WITH AN ESTIMATED $1.25 BILLION MADE by individuals[3] and the remainder coming from corporations or groups. Americans gave $1.3 billion toward tsunami relief, and contributions to victims of Hurricanes Katrina, Rita, and Wilma totaled $2.2 billion.[4]

Overall, charitable donations doubled in real dollar terms in the decade from 1992 to 2002.[5] The number of people giving blood increased dramatically after the terrorist attacks of 2001 and the hurricanes of 2005.[6] Another remarkable response to these events is the extent to which individuals volunteered their time to relief efforts. An estimated 300,000 volunteers from the Red Cross and other organizations provided assistance to victims of Hurricane Katrina.[7]

The propensity of Americans to want to help in times of emergency is not new. Indeed, the citizens of the United States have long been unusual in their willingness to make charitable contributions to churches, the Red Cross, and other organizations. When private charities are included, the United States is among the most generous donor countries in the world.[8] In addition, as former Prime Minister Margaret Thatcher once observed, "Who has the greatest voluntary effort in the world? Your country [the United States]."[9]

Does this public spiritedness in times of crisis have broader political implications? There is evidence, at least from the response to September 11, 2001, that Americans came to trust one another more and also to trust government and the police more after the terrorist attacks.[10] Whether the effects of these events on trust and confidence will endure is debatable, but what is clear is that the tradition of volunteering and contributing money to relief efforts remains a strong component of the American political culture.

Defining the American Political Culture

Many Americans' first experience with democracy is a school election, sometimes as early as in elementary school. What are the expectations of these young voters, and what do their expectations teach us about our political culture? Were we to observe such an election, we would see recurrent patterns. For example, it would be considered unfair if some students' votes counted for more than others', or if some

"Who has the greatest voluntary effort in the world? Your country [the United States]."

PRIME MINISTER MARGARET THATCHER

students were not allowed to vote at all. The candidates would probably be asked to speak, and may even make campaign promises. When the votes are counted, the young participants expect the person with the most votes to be elected.

Other elements of our political culture are learned in the family, or from peers. Many important elements of our political culture are widely shared by Americans, others are evolving, and some are no longer widely shared. This chapter examines our assumptions, beliefs, and values about politics, government, participation, freedom, and liberty.

Political scientists use the term **political culture** to refer to the widely shared beliefs, values, and norms concerning the relationship of citizens to government and to one another. We can discover the specifics of a nation's political culture not only by studying what its people believe and say but also by observing how they behave. A nation's political culture is composed of the underlying beliefs, assumptions, attitudes, and patterns of behavior that its people have toward government and politics. Political culture involves such fundamental issues as who may participate in political decisions, what rights and liberties citizens have, how political decisions are made, and what people think about politicians and government generally. Some elements of our political culture—like our fear of concentrated power and our reverence for individual liberty—have remained constant over time. In other respects, our political culture has changed from a belief that only property-owning white men should be allowed to vote to a conviction that all adults, excluding felons in some states, should have the right to vote. Political participation does not consist only of voting—it includes protesting, volunteering for a campaign, donating money, displaying a campaign sign, and many other activities. Thus, citizens now vote in party primaries to select nominees for office, whereas for much of our history, party leaders determined who would run for office. The surge in political activity on the Internet in the 2004 election may be a harbinger of a new political culture in which citizens interact more with candidates, contribute money to campaigns, and mobilize each other.

The idea of people coming together, listening to each other, exchanging ideas, learning to appreciate each other's differences, and defending their opinions is sometimes called "deliberation" and builds what has been called **social capital**. Such interaction is thought to foster and strengthen community and relationships in ways that do not happen when citizens only cast ballots. Political scientist Robert Putnam has defined social capital as "features of social organization such as networks, norms, and social trust that facilitate coordination and cooperation for mutual benefit."[11] Because of a decline in public participation in town council meetings, community groups, the PTA, labor unions, business associations, and other civic groups, Putnam believes that we as a people are losing the skills and learning that people can develop in such settings. Not all political scientists agree with Putnam's assessment that social capital is in decline.[12] More recently, Putnam found that civic engagement—but not volunteering—had grown in the weeks after the terrorist attacks of September 11, 2001.[13]

The social capital debate has rekindled an interest in the nature and viability of the American political culture and has spurred an examination of how it is changing. Americans have conflicting ideas and beliefs about the proper role of government and where and how political power should be exercised. As we saw in Chapter 1, these attitudes and beliefs, when coherent and consistent, are what political scientists call *ideology*. In this chapter, we look at our political culture and ideology.

American political culture centers on democratic values like liberty, equality, individualism, justice, the rule of law, patriotism, optimism, and idealism. There is no "official" list of American political values; however, and as we noted in Chapter 1, these widely shared democratic values overlap and sometimes conflict with each other.

Shared Values

Before the American and French Revolutions of the late eighteenth century, discussions about individual liberty, freedom, equality, private property, limited government, and popular consent were rare. Europe had been dominated by aristocracies, had experienced centuries of political and social inequality, and had been ruled by governments that often exercised power arbitrarily. Liberal political philosophers rebelled

political culture
The widely shared beliefs, values, and norms about how citizens relate to government and to one another.

social capital
Democratic and civic habits of discussion, compromise, and respect for differences, which grow out of participation in voluntary organizations.

against these traditions and proclaimed the principles of classical liberalism. They claimed that individuals have certain **natural rights**—the rights of all people to dignity and worth—and that government must be limited and controlled because it was a threat to those rights. During this same period, the economic system was changing from a mercantile system under which countries sought to strengthen the role of the state, establish colonies, and develop industry by encouraging exports and discouraging imports, to a free market system with the government taking a more "hands off" approach to the economy, including encouraging fewer trade barriers. (Remnants of mercantilism persist today in policies like farm subsidies.[14]) People began to think they could improve their lot in life and enhance their political and social status. Radical new ideas like these influenced the thinking of the founders of our nation and influenced the values that are essential to the United States' political culture today.

LIBERTY No value in the American political culture is more revered than liberty. "We have always been a nation obsessed with liberty. Liberty over authority, freedom over responsibility, rights over duties—these are our historic preferences," wrote the late Clinton Rossiter, a noted political scientist. "Not the good man but the free man has been the measure of all things in this sweet 'land of liberty'; not national glory but individual liberty has been the object of political authority and the test of its worth."[15] Not all students of American thought accept this emphasis on freedom and individualism over virtue and the public good, and in reality both sets of values are important.[16]

EQUALITY Jefferson's famous words in the Declaration of Independence express the importance of our views of equality: "We hold these truths to be self-evident, that all men are created equal, that they are endowed by their Creator with certain unalienable rights, that among these are life, liberty, and the pursuit of happiness." In contrast to Europeans, our nation shunned aristocracy, and our Constitution explicitly prohibits governments from granting titles of nobility. While our rhetoric about equality was not always matched by our policy—slavery, racial segregation in schools, etc.—the value of social equality is now deeply rooted.

In addition to social equality, Americans believe in *political equality,* the idea that every individual has a right to equal protection under the law and equal voting power. Although political equality has always been a goal, it has not always been a reality. In the past, African Americans, Native Americans, Asian Americans, and women were denied the right to vote and otherwise participate in the nation's political life.

natural rights
The rights of all people to dignity and worth; also called *human rights.*

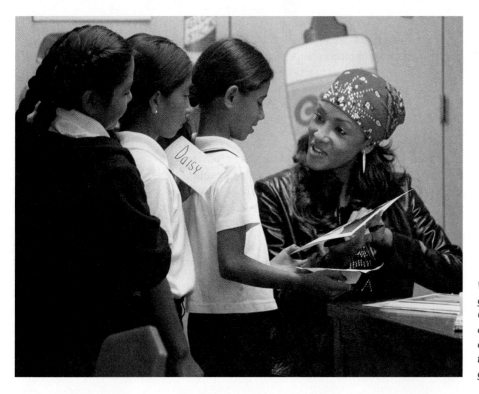

Vivica Fox autographs photographs for fifth-grade elementary school students in Lynwood, California, as part of Teach For America Week, an annual event in which successful Americans discuss their career with schoolchildren with the hope of inspiring them to realize their own goals and ambitions.

The Changing Face of American Politics

Assimilation and the American Political Culture

As a nation of immigrants, the United States has assimilated individuals from many countries into the American political culture. This process takes time as new immigrants learn the language, pursue education, and begin to understand the institutions and process of government, including elections. The scholar Samuel Huntington has recently argued that Mexican immigrants are not following the traditional pattern of assimilation. Huntington finds that over time, immigrants from Mexico are less likely to support core American values and learn English than are first- and second-generation immigrants from other Latin American countries.*

Huntington quotes others who have also found that Mexican immigrants have "a strong resistance to acculturation ... [and] persistence of their communal bonds."† Given the rela-

tively large number of immigrants coming to the United States from Mexico in recent years, Huntington's findings suggest that for this immigrant group at least, the long-standing acculturation process is not working and there is the potential for problems of separatism to arise in the future.

Huntington also finds that Muslims have been slower to assimilate into American society than other groups. Muslims, for example, express stronger loyalty to Islamic countries than to the United States. For both Mexican and Muslim immigrants, some of this tendency not to assimilate may be the result of discrimination or the fact that many Mexican immigrants entered the United States illegally. ■

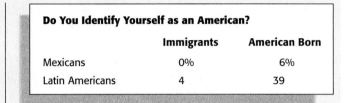

Do You Identify Yourself as an American?		
	Immigrants	American Born
Mexicans	0%	6%
Latin Americans	4	39

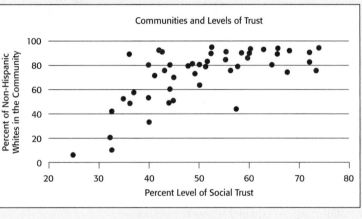

*Morris Janowitz, *The Reconstruction of Patriotism: Education for Civic Consciousness* (University of Chicago Press, 1974), 128–137.
†Samuel P. Huntington, *Who Are We? The Challenges to America's National Identity* (Simon & Schuster, 2004), pp. 189–190.

Equality encompasses the idea of *equal opportunity*, especially with regard to improving our economic status. Americans believe that social background should not limit our opportunity to achieve to the best of our ability, nor should race, gender, or religion. The nation's commitment to public education programs like Head Start for underprivileged preschool children, state support for public colleges and universities, and federal financial aid for higher education reflects this belief in equal opportunity.

INDIVIDUALISM The United States is characterized by a persistent commitment to the individual. Under our system of government, citizens have both rights and responsibilities. Policies that limit individual choice generate intense political conflict. The debate over legalized abortion is often framed in these terms. Although Americans agree with individual rights and freedoms, they also understand that their rights can conflict with another person's rights or with the government's need to maintain order.

RESPECT FOR THE COMMON PERSON Most Americans have faith in the common sense and collective wisdom of ordinary people. Most prefer action to reflection. We are often anti-expert and sometimes anti-intellectual. The emphasis on practicality and common sense has become part of our national image. Poets like Walt Whitman and Carl Sandburg and storytellers like Mark Twain, Will Rogers, Eudora Welty, and Garrison Keillor have helped shape this tradition. This reverence for the common people helps explain our ambivalence toward power, politics, and government authority. To relate to most constituents, politicians often downplay the advantages of their privileged backgrounds.

DEMOCRATIC CONSENSUS A **democratic consensus**, a fairly widespread agreement on fundamental principles of governance and the values that undergird them, binds most of us together. We are a people from many different cultural and ethnic backgrounds, histories, and religions. Despite these differences, our political culture includes widely shared attitudes and beliefs about government, procedures, documents, and institutions. Americans have strong opinions about who has power to do what, how people acquire power, and how they are removed from power. There is a consensus about these fundamental "rules of the game." But this shared commitment does not necessarily mean that people vote, keep up with public affairs, or believe that government is always fair or just.

Majority rule and popular sovereignty are parts of the democratic consensus. We believe in **majority rule**—governance according to the expressed preferences of the majority as expressed through regular elections. Yet we also believe that people in the minority should be free to try to win majority support for their opinions. Even though many Americans lack strong party attachments, we favor a two-party system and the idea of competition between the parties. Our institutions are based on the principles of representation and consent of the governed. We believe in **popular sovereignty**—that ultimate power resides in the people. Government exists to serve the people rather than the other way around. The government learns the will of the people through *elections,* perhaps the most important expression of popular consent. But sometimes, other fundamental rights limit popular sovereignty and majority rule.[17] Examples include California's 1964 vote in a referendum that the courts later overturned to permit people to discriminate in the sale of residential housing and the same state's 1996 vote to prohibit affirmative action in state governmental bodies, including universities and colleges.

The Constitution, especially the first ten amendments (the Bill of Rights) and the Thirteenth, Fourteenth, Fifteenth, and Nineteenth amendments, spells out many of the limits on what governments can do. The Constitution is revered as a national symbol, yet we often differ about what it means. We honor many of these constitutional rights more in the abstract than in the particular. About half of us, for instance, think that books with dangerous ideas should be banned from public school libraries (see Table 4–1). Intolerance of dissenting or offensive views is amply demonstrated in public opinion polls and is observed on college and university campuses. Still, most Americans support democratic and constitutional values.

Police help a man into a rescue boat as he leaves his flooded home in New Orleans after Hurricane Katrina pounded parts of Louisiana and Mississippi in 2005. Americans contributed $2.2 billion toward hurricane relief efforts that year.

democratic consensus
Widespread agreement on fundamental principles of democratic governance and the values that undergird them.

majority rule
Governance according to the expressed preferences of the majority.

popular sovereignty
A belief that ultimate power resides in the people.

TABLE 4–1 What Do You Mean by Rights and Freedoms? It Depends . . .

	Agree	Disagree	Don't Know
Freedom of speech should apply to groups that are sympathetic to terrorists.	45%	50%	5%
There has been real improvement in the position of African Americans.	57	35	8
Books that contain dangerous ideas should be banned from public school libraries.	50	47	3
Protection rights should apply to the unborn.	72	24	4
The police should be allowed to search the houses of known drug dealers without a court order.	44	54	2
School boards ought to have the right to fire teachers who are known homosexuals.	33	62	5

SOURCE: The Pew Research Center for the People and the Press, *Evenly Divided and Increasingly Polarized: 2004 Political.* Data collected in August 2003.

> *"We are a different country than we were on September 10th: sadder and less innocent; stronger and more united; and in the face of ongoing threats, determined and courageous."*
>
> PRESIDENT GEORGE W. BUSH

TABLE 4–2 Satisfaction With Democracy

	Like	Dislike
Kenya	87%	6%
Vietnam	68	24
Venezuela	67	30
Japan	62	27
South Africa	53	32
Ukraine	53	35
Canada	50	40
Germany	47	45
Tanzania	43	31
United Kingdom	43	42
France	42	53
Mexico	41	41
India	36	27
Brazil	35	51
Turkey	33	50
Bangladesh	31	31
Russia	28	46

SOURCE: World Values Survey, 2004.

JUSTICE AND THE RULE OF LAW Inscribed over the entrance to the U.S. Supreme Court are the words "Equal Justice Under Law." The rule of law means that government is based on a body of law applied equally and by just procedures, as opposed to arbitrary rule by an elite whose whims decide policy or resolve disputes. In 1803, Chief Justice John Marshall summarized this principle: "The government of the United States has been emphatically termed a government of laws, not of men."[18] Americans believe strongly in fairness: Everyone is entitled to the same legal rights and protections.

To adhere to the rule of law, government should follow these five rules:

1. *Generality:* Laws should be stated generally and not single out any group or individual.

2. *Prospectivity:* Laws should apply to the present and the future, not punish something someone did in the past.

3. *Publicity:* Laws cannot be kept secret and then enforced.

4. *Authority:* Valid laws are made by those with legitimate power, and the people legitimate that power through some form of popular consent.

5. *Due process:* Laws must be enforced impartially with fair processes.

PATRIOTISM, OPTIMISM, AND IDEALISM Americans are highly nationalistic, sharing a sense of values and identity. The terrorist attacks of 2001 united the nation and reinforced this nationalism. As President George W. Bush said, "We are a different country than we were on September 10th: sadder and less innocent; stronger and more united; and in the face of ongoing threats, determined and courageous."[19] We are proud of our past and our role in the world today. We are optimistic, though far more about people than about government.

We believe in opportunity, choice, individualism, and, most of all, in the freedom to improve ourselves and to achieve success with as little interference as possible from others or from government. As Table 4–2 indicates, U.S. citizens are more satisfied with their democratic government than are the citizens of many other countries.

We know that our system is imperfect, yet we still believe in government by the people. We often grumble that elected officials have lost touch with us, we are disgusted by scandals, and we are impatient with how long the system takes to solve problems like health care, crime, drug abuse, and terrorism. Despite the dissatisfactions, we believe that America is better, stronger, and more virtuous than other nations. Like every country, the United States has interests and motives that are selfish as well as generous, cynical as well as idealistic. Still, our support of human needs and rights throughout the world is evidence of an enduring idealism.

Where We Learn the American Political Culture

One important source of political culture in the United States, as in other nations, is the family. Young children are taught what it means to be an American. They are curious about why people vote, what the president does, and whether Grandpa fought in Korea or Vietnam. The questions may vary from family to family, yet the themes of authority, freedom, equality, liberty, and partisanship are common. Families are the most important reference group, with parents and siblings orienting each other to politics, the media, and the community more generally. Compared to families in other cultures, American families are much more egalitarian, with children having more input in family decisions than in other cultures.[20]

Public schools are another source of the American political culture. Children and teachers often begin the school day by saluting the flag, reciting the Pledge of Allegiance, or singing the national anthem. American political and economic values are part of the curriculum. Not only are values taught in American history classes, but they are put into practice in school elections and newspapers and in encouraging students to participate in small-scale economic ventures.[21]

Colleges and universities also help foster the American political culture. Students who attend college are often more confident than other persons in dealing with bureaucracy and politics generally, more likely to participate in politics and to vote, and know more about government.[22] Many states require students at state colleges and universities to take courses in American or state government, in part to instill a sense of civic duty.

Religious freedom and diversity have played a part in forming and maintaining the American political culture. American churches, synagogues, and mosques have long fostered a common understanding of right and wrong and of freedom, including freedom of religion, individualism, pluralism, and civic duty. Churches do not all take the same positions on political issues, but they have played important roles in such major social and political movements as the abolition of slavery, the expansion of civil rights, and opposition to war. Civic organizations like the Boy Scouts, 4-H Clubs, League of Women Voters, Rotary Club, and Chambers of Commerce encourage citizen participation and pride in community and nation.[23]

In modern times, the mass media have taken over some functions that the family used to perform. By the time children leave high school, they will have spent more time watching television than talking to their parents. They may have learned more about politics from MTV than from their parents, schools, or other media.[24] Finally, Americans educate each other about political values at work, at PTA meetings, or in more expressly political activities.

The American Dream

Many of our political values come together in the **American dream**, a complex set of ideas that holds that the United States is a land of opportunity and that individual initiative and hard work can bring economic success. Whether fulfilled or not, this American dream speaks to our most deeply held hopes and goals. The essence of the American dream is expressed in our enthusiasm for **capitalism**, an economic system based on private property, competitive markets, economic incentives, and limited government involvement in the production, pricing, and distribution of goods and services.[25]

The concept of *private property* enjoys extraordinary popularity in the United States. In many European democracies, the state owns and operates transportation systems and other businesses that are privately owned and operated in the United States, although there has been some privatization of communications systems like telephone companies and broadcast media in Europe. Americans cherish the dream of acquiring property. Moreover, most Americans believe that the owners of property have the right to decide how to use it.

The right to private property is just one of the economic incentives that cement our support for capitalism and fuel the American dream. While comparison in social mobility across countries is difficult, the American dream is more attainable for middle-income persons in the United States than in Europe while the bottom fifth of the economic distribution in the United States appears to be more trapped than in Europe.[26]

What explains these differences? We assume that people who have more ability or who work hard will get ahead, earn more, and enjoy economic rewards. We also believe that people should be able to pass most of the wealth they have accumulated along to their children and relatives. Even the poorest Americans generally oppose high inheritance taxes or limits on how much someone can earn. Americans believe that the free market system gives almost everyone a fair chance, that capitalism is necessary, and that freedom depends on it. We reject communism and socialism—a rejection fortified in recent decades as most communist nations shifted toward capitalism. In the United States, individuals and corporations have acquired wealth

Coming from humble beginnings, Oprah Winfrey—television host, movie actress, and one of the highest-paid people in the country—epitomizes the American dream.

American dream
The widespread belief that the United States is a land of opportunity and that individual initiative and hard work can bring economic success.

capitalism
An economic system characterized by private property, competitive markets, economic incentives, and limited government involvement in the production, distribution, and pricing of goods and services.

Government's Greatest Endeavors

Financial Security in Retirement

February 1, 1940 marked the first day that Americans were eligible to receive Social Security checks.

Before 1935, when the Social Security program was enacted, older Americans were mostly on their own in providing for their needs after retirement. Low-income Americans could apply for federal and state assistance, but they often found it embarrassing to receive welfare. As a result, older Americans had the highest rates of poverty in the country.

Social Security soon became one of the most popular programs in America, and is one of the few federal endeavors about which both Democrats and Republicans agree should be expanded. This is what Congress did when it increased the size of monthly Social Security checks in 1950, 1952, 1954, 1956, 1958, 1961, 1967, 1969, 1971, and 1972. Many of these bills providing increases also funded grants to the states for additional aid to blind, disabled, and older Americans.

In an effort to control their own tendency to increase Social Security payments to enhance their popularity back home, members of Congress decided to "index" Social Security benefits in 1972 to rise automatically with price increases. This cost-of-living adjustment, or COLA, tied Social Security benefits to the Consumer Price Index (CPI) to ensure that benefits would increase with prices.

Although Social Security is now in financial trouble as the number of older Americans continues to rise, it has become one of the federal government's most popular programs and has reduced poverty rates among older Americans to record lows. Younger Americans wonder whether the program will exist when they retire, but nonetheless support the program for today's beneficiaries. ∎

QUESTIONS

What makes the Social Security program so popular with the public?

Do you think you will receive Social Security benefits when you retire?

---

and, at the same time, exercised political clout. Their power has in turn been widely criticized. The Enron Corporation, for example, made more than $2 million in political contributions in the 2000 elections, and between 1995 and 2001, Enron was one of the 15 largest donors of "soft" money to political parties. Soft money, now banned, could go in unlimited amounts to political parties from corporate general funds.[27] Enron later filed for bankruptcy and became a notorious example of corporate mismanagement and dishonest accounting.[28] Wealthy individuals have used their assets to fund their campaigns for public office (Jon Corzine spent $60 million on his successful New Jersey Senate race in 2000 and another $43 million on his successful gubernatorial race in 2005),[29] or to influence elections or public policy (George Soros gave $27 million to organizations like America Coming Together, the Media Fund, MoveOn.org, Joint Victory Campaign, Young Democrats for America, and a few other groups working to defeat George W. Bush).[30]

The conflict in values between a *competitive economy*, in which individuals reap large rewards for their initiative and hard work, and an *egalitarian society*, in which everyone earns a decent living, carries over into politics. How the public resolves this tension changes over time and from issue to issue.

How Other Nations Govern

Political Culture in Mexico

In 2000, Mexico experienced the first transfer of power from one party to another in 71 years when Vicente Fox of the National Action Party (PAN) won the 2000 presidential election defeating the Institutional Revolutionary Party (PRI) that had held unbroken power since the 1920s. Fox's party, however, did not control Congress, frustrating his ability to enact his legislative program. Fox was in turn succeeded by Felepe Calderon in 2006 in the closest election in Mexican history. The election was clouded by charges of fraud and the outcome was contested by the losing candidate, Andréas Manuel López Obrador, who threatened to organize his own government.[*]

Given Mexico's new experience with party competition, how do Mexicans view their democracy? Has their view changed with the peaceful transfer of power between parties? Alejandro Moreno and Patricia Mendez, drawing from data from the World Values Surveys from 1995–1997 and 2000–2001, attempt to answer these questions.[†] The political culture of Mexico remains less supportive of democracy than in more experienced democracies. Those surveyed in Mexico were roughly twice as likely to say that having a strong leader is very good or fairly good (41 percent), compared to 22 percent in more mature democracies like Germany, Australia, Canada, and the United States. Moreover, one in four Mexicans say that having the army rule is very good or fairly good, compared to 6 percent in advanced democracies. Just under two-thirds of Mexicans say democracy is the best system (65 percent) compared to 86 percent in advanced democracies. Finally, in terms of social trust, 24 percent of Mexicans surveyed felt most people could be trusted, compared to 41 percent in Germany, Australia, Canada, and the United States.

This research on Mexico reminds us how popular support for democracy and democratic values like trust and tolerance takes time to develop and how lingering tendencies to authoritarianism, like a preference for military rule, take time to dissipate. Moreno and Mendez conclude that Mexicans "aspire to live in a better, high-quality democracy. As they learn about it we should expect changes in democratic values and attitudes in the next years."[†] ∎

---

[*]James C. McKinley, Jr., "Election Ruling in Mexico Goes to Conservative," *New York Times*, September 6, 2006.
[†]Alejandro Moreno and Patricia Mendez, "Attitudes Toward Democracy: Mexico in Comparative Perspective." This article and information on the World Values Survey can be found at www.worldvaluessurveyorg/library/index.html.
[†]Moreno and Mendez, p. 24.

As important as the American dream is to the national consciousness, Americans know it remains unfulfilled. The gap between rich and poor has grown in recent years, and a sharp difference between white and black income remains tenacious.[31] For more people than we want to admit, chances for success still depend on the family they were born into, the neighborhood they grew up in, or the college they attended. An underclass persists in the form of impoverished families, malnourished and poorly educated children, and the homeless.[32] Many cities are actually two cities, where some residents live in luxury while others live in squalor. This reality was starkly reinforced in the aftermath of Hurricane Katrina as the world observed that poor people were much more likely to lack the transportation or resources to flee the hurricane-stricken city. National public opinion polls showed stark differences along racial lines in perceptions of whether the government's response would have been different if most of the victims had been white and not black. Two-thirds of African Americans held this view, compared to fewer than one in five whites.[33]

Political and Economic Change

Historical developments and economic and technological growth affect political values. The Declaration of Independence and the Constitution identified such important political values as individual liberty, property rights, and limited government.[34] Early in our history, we emphasized separation of powers, checks and balances, states' rights, and the Bill of Rights. It took multiple generations before we also began to seriously expand **suffrage** and have competitive nominations and elections. Notions of political equality and effective participation emerged during the presidency of Andrew Jackson (1829–1837) and matured during the nineteenth century. By 1900, populists and suffragists were putting ideals into action and had formed large-scale

suffrage
The right to vote.

movements to achieve more democratic forms of participation and more responsive forms of governance.

THE INDUSTRIAL TRANSFORMATION   By 1900, industrial capitalism and the growth of giant corporations had largely replaced the agrarian society of small farmers and plantations that the framers had known. These changes irreversibly transformed our political and social ideology. Large privately owned corporations changed not only the economic order, but the role of government and how people viewed each other. No one captures the implications of this shift better than political scientist Robert A. Dahl:

> One of the consequences of the new order has been a high degree of inequality in the distribution of wealth and income, and far greater inequality than had ever been thought likely or desirable under an agrarian order by Democratic Republicans like Jefferson and Madison, or had ever been thought consistent with democratic or republican government in the historic writings on the subject from Aristotle to Locke, Montesquieu, and Rousseau. Previous theorists and advocates had, like many of the framers of our own Constitution, insisted that a republic could exist only if the citizen body continued neither rich nor poor. Citizens, it was argued, must enjoy a rough equality of conditions.[35]

The success of the American economy led to the concentration of great wealth in the hands of a few—the "robber barons" or tycoons. Many had taken great risks or earned their fortunes through inventions and efficient production practices. But as disparities of income grew, so did disparities in political resources. Economic resources can be converted into political resources by investing time, energy, and money in political campaigns, parties, and candidates.[36] At the beginning of the twentieth century, the rise of corporations and the concentration of individual wealth in the United States created class divisions and resentment. Muckraking journalists charged that the huge corporations had become **monopolies**, using their dominance of an industry to exploit workers and limit competition. Unsafe working conditions led to some regulation of the workplace by the states, but it seemed that only the national government had the power to ensure fair treatment in the marketplace. This sentiment not only gave rise to the nation's first **antitrust legislation**—federal laws that try to prevent monopolies from dominating an industry, stifling competition, and restraining trade—but also reinforced the idea that the national government could—and should— as the Constitution asserts, "promote the general Welfare" by regulating working conditions, product safety, and labor-management disputes.

monopoly
Domination of an industry by a single company that fixes prices and discourages competition; also, the company that dominates the industry by these means.

antitrust legislation
Federal laws (starting with the Sherman Act of 1890) that try to prevent a monopoly from dominating an industry and restraining trade.

Breadlines like this provided handouts of food to thousands of unemployed and destitute people during the Great Depression.

THE GREAT DEPRESSION AND THE NEW DEAL
The Great Depression of the 1930s and the near collapse of the capitalistic system that followed it shaped much of our thinking about the role of government in a capitalistic system. The depression was largely blamed on unrestrained capitalism and an unregulated market. The collapse of the stock market, massive unemployment, and a failed banking system caused widespread suffering. Americans had no unemployment compensation, no guarantee for the money they put in banks, no federal regulation of the stock market, and no Social Security. People turned to the government to improve the lot of millions of jobless and homeless citizens. Beginning with President Franklin D. Roosevelt's New Deal in the 1930s, most Americans came to accept that governments, at both the national and state levels, should use their powers and resources to ensure some measure of equal opportunity and social justice.

Roosevelt's State of the Union Address in 1944 outlined a "Second Bill of Rights" for all citizens in which he declared that this nation must make a firm commitment to "economic security and independence." Included in his Second Bill of Rights were the following:

- The right to a useful and remunerative job in the industries, shops, farms, or mines of the nation
- The right to earn enough to provide adequate food and clothing and recreation
- The right of every farmer to raise and sell his products at a return that would give him and his family a decent living
- The right of every businessman, large and small, to trade in an atmosphere of freedom from unfair competition and domination by monopolies at home or abroad
- The right of every family to a decent home
- The right to adequate medical care and the opportunity to achieve and enjoy good health
- The right to adequate protection from the economic fears of old age, sickness, accident, and unemployment
- The right to a good education[37]

Roosevelt's policies and later efforts by Presidents John F. Kennedy and Lyndon B. Johnson in the 1960s to pass civil rights and voting rights legislation and launch a "war on poverty" defined the ideological and political fights of the second half of the twentieth century. Modern-day liberalism and conservatism turn, in large measure, on how much one believes in Roosevelt's Second Bill of Rights and how much one believes that governments should help minorities, women, and others who have suffered discrimination or have been left behind by the industrial or technological revolutions of the twentieth century. Today, free enterprise is no longer unbridled. Government regulations, antitrust laws, job safety regulations, environmental standards, and minimum wage laws try to balance freedom of enterprise against the rights of individuals. Most people today support a semi-regulated or mixed free enterprise system that checks the worst tendencies of capitalism, but they reject excessive government intervention (see Table 4–3). Much of American politics centers on how to achieve this balance. Currently, most liberals and conservatives agree that some governmental intervention is necessary to assist Americans who fall short in the competition for education and economic prosperity.

TABLE 4–3 Attitudes on Business and Labor

The strength of this country is mostly based on the success of American business.	75%
Government regulation of business usually does more harm than good.	53
Business corporations generally strike a fair balance between making profits and serving the public interest.	38
There is too much power concentrated in the hands of a few big companies.	77
Labor unions are necessary to protect the working person.	74

SOURCE: The Pew Research Center for the People and the Press, *Evenly Divided and Increasingly Polarized: 2004 Political Landscape*. Data collected in August 2003.

Political Ideology and Attitudes Toward Government

Political ideology refers to a consistent pattern of ideas or beliefs about political values and the role of government. It includes the views people have about how government should work and how it actually works. Ideology links our basic values to the day-to-day operations or policies of government.

political ideology
A consistent pattern of beliefs about political values and the role of government.

TABLE 4–4 Differences in Political Ideology

	Conservative	Moderate	Liberal	Don't Know/ Haven't Thought About It
Sex				
Male	38%	25%	20%	17%
Female	26	27	24	24
Race				
White	36	25	24	15
Black	15	34	12	42
Asian	34	24	24	19
Hispanic	21	25	29	25
Age				
18–34	24	29	29	17
35–45	36	25	16	23
46–55	37	12	25	15
56–64	38	22	21	19
Religion				
Protestant	35	24	15	25
Catholic	30	28	24	18
Jewish	23	21	56	0
Education				
Less than high school	18	17	15	49
High school diploma	27	34	12	27
Some college	36	26	23	15
Bachelor's degree	43	22	31	3
Advanced degree	34	17	46	3
Party				
Democrat	38	27	9	26
Independent	23	31	26	20
Republican	66	19	3	11

SOURCE: Center for Political Studies, University of Michigan, *2004 American National Election Study Guide to Public Opinion and Electoral Behavior.*

Two major schools of political ideology dominate American politics: *liberalism* and *conservatism.* Two less popular schools of thought—*socialism* and *libertarianism*—also help define the spectrum of ideology in the United States. (See Table 4–4.)

Liberalism

In the eighteenth and nineteenth centuries, classical liberals fought to minimize the role of government. They stressed individual rights and perceived government as the primary threat to rights and liberties. Classical liberals favored *limited government* and sought to protect people from governmental harassment in their political and economic lives. Over time, the liberal emphasis on individualism remained constant, but the perception of the need for government changed.

CONTEMPORARY LIBERALS In its current American usage, **liberalism** refers to a belief that government can bring about justice and equality of opportunity. Modern-day liberals wish to preserve the rights of the individual and the right to own private property, yet they believe that some government intervention in the economy is necessary to remedy the defects of capitalism. Liberals advocate equal access to health care, housing, and education for all citizens. They generally believe in affirmative action programs, protections for workers' health and safety, tax rates that rise with a person's income, and unions' rights to organize and strike.

On a more philosophical level, liberals generally believe in the probability of progress. They believe that the future will be better than the past or the present—that obstacles can be overcome. This positive set of beliefs may explain liberals' willingness to trust government programs. Modern liberals contend that modern technology and industrialization cry out for government programs to offset the loss of liberties that the poor and the weak suffer. Liberals such as Senators Edward Kennedy and Hillary Rodham Clinton frequently stress the need for an involved and affirmative government.

Liberals charge that conservatives usually act out of self-interest and follow the maxim that "a rising tide will lift all boats," or economic growth benefits all. In contrast, liberals would agree with President Harry Truman who said in 1949, "We have rejected the discredited theory that the fortunes of the nation should be in the hands of a privileged few. Instead, we believe that our economic system should rest on a democratic foundation and that wealth should be created for the benefit of all. . . . Every segment of our population and every individual has a right to expect from his government a fair deal."[38]

Liberals consider equality of opportunity essential, and to achieve it, they believe that government must eliminate discrimination. Some liberals favor reducing the great inequalities of wealth that make equality of opportunity impossible. Most favor a certain minimum level of income for all Americans. Rather than placing a cap on wealth, they want to build a floor beneath the poor. In short, liberals seek to extend opportunities to all, regardless of how poor they may be. If necessary they favor raising taxes to achieve these goals. To learn more about liberal ideology, go to www.prospect.org.

Liberals are generally seen as more inclined to favor environmental protection over

liberalism
A belief that government can and should achieve justice and equality of opportunity.

commercial development in such areas as logging or oil drilling off shore or in the Arctic. A concern for the environment has fostered the formation of Green Parties and in countries like Finland, Germany, Switzerland, Sweden, Luxembourg, Austria, France, and the Netherlands. Green Party legislators have been elected, and until 2006 the Green Party was part of the liberal-left coalition that governed Germany. In the United States the Green presidential candidate in 2000, Ralph Nader, enhanced the visibility of the party but still won less than 3 percent of the vote in the general election. In 2004, David Cobb, who lacked Nader's stature, received less than one-tenth of one percent of the vote. The state in which the Green party has had the most visible presence is New Mexico, but no Green Party candidate has been elected to Congress or a state legislature.

CRITICISMS OF LIBERALISM   Critics say that liberals rely too much on government, higher taxes, and bureaucracy to solve the nation's problems. These opponents argue that liberals have forgotten that government has to be limited if it is to serve our best interests. Power tends to corrupt, and too much dependence on government can corrupt the spirit, undermine self-reliance, and make people forget those cherished personal freedoms and property rights our Republic was founded to secure and protect. Too many governmental regulations, too much government bureaucracy, and too much taxation tend to undermine the self-help ethic that "made America great." In short, critics of modern liberalism contend that the welfare and regulatory state that liberals advocate will ultimately destroy individual initiative, the entrepreneurial spirit, and the very engine of economic growth that might lead to true equality of economic opportunity.

In recent elections, Republicans have made liberalism a villain while claiming that their own presidential candidates represent the mainstream. In 1988, George H. W. Bush consistently referred to Michael Dukakis as from the "liberal Democratic party." Bill Clinton was careful not to label his programs as liberal, focusing on the need for economic growth, jobs, and a balanced budget. He insisted he was a "New Democrat." In 2000, Al Gore also positioned himself as a centrist, not a liberal, but George W. Bush charged that Gore was an advocate of big government. Their Republican opponents and their allies often level the same charge against congressional Democratic candidates.

The movement to the center by some Democrats and the conventional wisdom that liberal or progressive approaches are in decline are disputed by political commentator E. J. Dionne Jr., whose book on how progressives can regain power is aptly titled *They Only Look Dead.* Dionne contends that the current political mood reflects less as a revolt against *big* government than a rebellion against *bad* government—government that has proved ineffectual in grappling with the political, economic, and moral crises that have shaken the country. Dionne challenges the claims that big government is bad or even over. Pointing to past progressive or liberal successes, Dionne contends that Americans want a government that eases economic transitions, helps "preserve a broad middle class," and "expands the choices available to individuals."[39]

The popularity of liberalism and conservatism and the importance of particular issues change with world events. For a time, we were preoccupied with budget deficits. With the end of the cold war, we became more concerned about domestic policy than about foreign policy. Policy concerns changed again with the terrorist attacks of September 11, 2001, and the war on terrorism that followed. Budget deficits replaced projected surpluses, and Americans became focused on places like Iraq, Afghanistan, Iran, and North Korea.

The reelection of George W. Bush in 2004, along with a net loss of four U.S. Senate seats by the Democrats that year, was due in part to the importance of the national security issue, but it also reflected public concerns with moral values. Referendums in thirteen states that defined marriage as between a man and a woman forced moral values questions into the presidential election. Efforts by liberals to define the same-sex marriage issue as primarily about rights failed, and all the referendums passed. In 2006 eight states had referendums on the ballot to limit same-sex marriage. Seven states passed their referendums; the exception was Arizona, where it narrowly failed.

Senator Ted Kennedy (D-Mass.) has been a champion of liberal programs and legislation for many years. He is shown here at a press conference called by the consumer advocacy group Families USA to address the rising cost of the top fifty prescription drugs sold to senior citizens.

"We have rejected the discredited theory that the fortunes of the nation should be in the hands of a privileged few."

PRESIDENT HARRY TRUMAN

Grover Norquist, head of Americans for Tax Reform, is a major proponent of lowering federal, state, and local taxes. Conservatives believe that by lowering taxes, people will have more money to invest in the economy and to donate to charitable organizations.

Conservatism

Belief in private property rights and free enterprise are cardinal attributes of contemporary **conservatism**. In contrast to liberals, conservatives want to enhance individual liberty by keeping government small, especially the national government, although they support a strong national defense. Conservatives take a more pessimistic view of human nature than liberals do. They maintain that people need strong leadership, firm laws, and strict moral codes. The primary task of government is to ensure order. Conservatives also believe that people are the architects of their own fortune and must solve their own problems and create their own successes.

TRADITIONAL CONSERVATIVES Conservatives are emphatically pro-business. They favor tax cuts and resist all but the minimum antitrust, trade, and environmental regulations on corporations. They believe that the sole functions of government should be to protect the nation from foreign enemies, preserve law and order, enforce private contracts, foster competitive markets, encourage free and fair trade, and promote family values. Traditional conservatives favor dispersing power throughout the political and social systems to avoid an overly powerful national government; the market, not the government, should provide services. Conservatives believe that globalization, free markets, and limited government provide the right incentives for economic growth, thereby making everyone better off.

Until recent decades, conservatives opposed the New Deal programs of the 1930s, the War on Poverty in the 1960s, and many civil rights and affirmative action programs. Families and private charities, they say, can and should take care of human needs and social and economic problems. Conservatives are more inclined to trust the private sector and dislike turning to government, especially the national government, to solve social problems. Government social activism, they say, has been expensive and counterproductive. State and local government should address those social problems that do need a government response. An example would be policies on abortion, which conservatives have long held should be a matter for state and local governments to decide. Another example is education, long seen as a matter for state and local governments. President Bush's federal program known as "No Child Left Behind" encountered opposition from some of the most conservative and Republican states because they saw the policy as interfering with the ability of states to manage education.

Conservatives, especially when in office, do, however, selectively advocate government activism, often expressing a desire for a more effective and efficient government. For example: early in the 2000 presidential campaign, George W. Bush said, "Too often, my party has confused the need for a limited government with a disdain for government itself." Love of country, he said, "is undermined by sprawling, arrogant, aimless government. It is restored by focused and effective and energetic government."[40] To learn more about conservative beliefs, go to www.aei.org or www.heritage.org.

SOCIAL CONSERVATIVES Some conservatives focus less on economics and more on morality and lifestyle. Social conservatives favor strong governmental action to protect children from pornography and drugs. Conservatives want to overturn or repeal judicial rulings and laws that permit abortion, same-sex marriage, and affirmative action programs. In disputes between workers and employers they are more likely to side with employers. This brand of conservatism—sometimes called the New Right, ultraconservatism, or even the Radical Right—emerged in the 1980s. The New Right shares traditional conservatism's love of freedom and backs an aggressive effort to defend America's interests abroad. It favors the return of organized prayer in public schools and opposes policies like job quotas, busing, and tolerance of homosexuality. In sum, a defining characteristic of the New Right is a strong desire to impose *social controls*.

An example of a group that supports social conservatism includes Focus on the Family, a Christian organization devoted to preserving traditional values and protecting the institution of the family. These religious conservatives were not only active in supporting the reelection of President Bush in 2004 but also in criticizing President Bush's nomination of Harriet Miers for the U.S. Supreme Court. When Bush withdrew Ms. Miers's nomination, Focus on the Family became a strong advocate of Judge Samuel Alito.

conservatism
A belief that limited government ensures order, competitive markets, and personal opportunity.

Groups like Focus on the Family wax and wane in importance. In the 1980s and early 1990s, the Christian Coalition, an organization founded by Reverend Pat Robertson, was an important political force. The Coalition has become much less important in recent years.[41] During its more prominent period the Coalition was active in informing and mobilizing voters. Evidence of the decline of the Coalition is the fact that the Republican Party created its own large-scale effort to mobilize conservative religious voters in 2004.[42]

Some conservatives are uncomfortable with the close association between the Republican Party and the Christian Right. Former U.S. Senator Warren Rudman of New Hampshire has observed, "Politically speaking, the Republican Party is making a terrible mistake if it appears to ally itself with the Christian right. There are some fine, sincere people in its ranks, but there are also enough anti-abortion zealots, would-be censors, homophobes, bigots, and latter-day Elmer Gantrys to discredit any party that is unwise enough to embrace such a group."[43] Rudman's statement was later used to justify phone calls by Robertson to Christian Coalition members urging them to vote for George W. Bush in the 2000 South Carolina and Michigan primaries instead of for John McCain, whose campaign Rudman co-chaired.[44]

CRITICISMS OF CONSERVATISM Not everyone agreed with Ronald Reagan's statement that "government is the problem." Indeed, critics point out that conservatives themselves urge more government when it serves their needs—regulating pornography and abortion, for example—but are opposed to government when it serves somebody else's. Conservatives may also have fewer objections to big government when individuals have a choice in determining how government will affect them. Vouchers for schools, choices in prescription drug benefit plans, and options to manage Social Security savings are examples of such choices that President George W. Bush has supported.[45] Critics of these proposals see conservatives as selective in their criticism of big government or supportive of it only when it fits their assumptions about what government should do.

Conservatives place great faith in the market economy—critics say too much faith. This often puts conservatives at odds with labor unions and consumer activists and in close alliance with businesspeople, particularly large corporations. Hostility to regulation and a belief in competition lead conservatives to push for deregulation. This approach has not always had positive results, as the collapse of many savings and loan companies in the 1980s,[46] the energy crisis in California in the early 2000s,[47] and the business and accounting failures at Enron and other major corporations in 2002 have shown.[48] Conservatives counter that it is still best to rely on the free market.

The policy of lowering taxes during the Reagan and George W. Bush administrations was consistent with the conservative hostility to big government. Many conservatives embraced the idea that if the rich pay fewer taxes, they will spend and invest more, and the benefits of this increased economic activity will "trickle down" to the poor. But Democrats argued that the growth in income and wealth was largely concentrated among the well-to-do and that that reduced taxes and increased government spending, especially for defense, tripled the deficit during the 1980s, when conservatives were in control.[49] President George W. Bush pushed through tax cuts during his first term and pressed to make them permanent after his reelection in 2004. Democrats and some conservative Republicans criticized Bush for lowering taxes at the same time the budget deficit was growing.

Liberals charge that some conservatives repeatedly fail to acknowledge and endorse policies that deal with racism and sexism. They cite conservative opposition to civil rights laws in the 1960s and to affirmative action more recently. They also blame conservatives for trying to weaken the enforcement of these laws by the executive branch and the courts.

Both liberals and social conservatives have been inconsistent in their approach to government. Liberals favor vigorous governmental programs to help the poor but oppose governmental intrusion into people's private lives in the name of national security, while some social conservatives preach less government except when they consider it necessary to counter what they consider to be social evils like drugs and pornography.

"Politically speaking, the Republican Party is making a terrible mistake if it appears to ally itself with the Christian right. There are some fine, sincere people in its ranks, but there are also enough anti-abortion zealots, would-be censors, homophobes, bigots, and latter-day Elmer Gantrys to discredit any party that is unwise enough to embrace such a group."

FORMER U.S. SENATOR WARREN RUDMAN

Bernard Sanders, a self-described Socialist, represents Vermont in the U.S. Senate as an Independent.

Socialism

Socialism is an economic and governmental system based on public ownership of the means of production and exchange. The nineteenth-century German philosopher Karl Marx once described socialism as a transitional stage of society between capitalism and communism. In a capitalist system, the means of production and most property are privately owned; in a communist system, the state owns property in common for all the people, and a single political party that represents the working classes controls the government. In communist countries like Cuba and China, the Communist party allows no opposition. Some countries, like Sweden, have combined limited government ownership and operation of business with democracy. Most Western European countries and Canada have various forms of socialized or government-run medical systems and sometimes telecommunications networks, while keeping most economic sectors private.

In one of the most dramatic transformations in recent times, Russia, its sister republics, and its former eastern European satellites abandoned communism in the early 1990s and have been attempting to establish free markets. These countries previously had a system of rigid state ownership and centralized government planning of the economy. This required the government to arbitrarily set prices and production levels, which ultimately led to a very unstable economic system. But political and economic failure in the Soviet Union demoralized its communist leadership and weakened its hold over its satellite states. With the collapse of Soviet power, a tide of political and economic reform left communism intact in only a few countries, such as Cuba, China, and Vietnam.

American socialists—of whom there are only a few prominent examples—favor a greatly expanded role for the government but argue that such a system is compatible with democracy. They would nationalize certain industries, institute a public jobs program so that all who want to work could work, tax the wealthy much more heavily, and drastically cut defense spending.[50] Canada and most of the democracies of Western Europe are more influenced by socialist ideas than we are in the United States, but they remain, like the United States, largely market economies. Debate will continue about the proper role of government and what the market can do better than government can.[51]

Libertarianism

Libertarianism is a political ideology that cherishes individual liberty and insists on sharply limited government. It carries some overtones of anarchism, of the classical English liberalism of the nineteenth century (defined earlier in this chapter), and of a 1930s-style conservatism. The Libertarian party has gained a small following among people who believe that both liberals and conservatives are inconsistent in their attitude toward the power of the national government.

Libertarians oppose almost all government programs. They favor massive cuts in government spending and an end to the Federal Bureau of Investigation, the Central Intelligence Agency, the Internal Revenue Service, and most regulatory commissions. They oppose U.S. participation in the United Nations and favor armed forces that would defend the United States only if directly attacked. They oppose *all* government regulation, including, for example, mandatory seat-belt and helmet laws. They are opposed to these regulations because they believe that individuals will all be better off from the benefits of an undistorted free market. Unlike conservatives, libertarians would repeal laws that regulate personal morality, including abortion, pornography, prostitution, and illicit drugs.

A Libertarian party candidate for president has been on the ballot in all 50 states in recent presidential elections, although the party has never obtained more than 1 percent of the vote. The 2000 Libertarian platform called for immediate and complete removal of the federal government from education, energy, regulation, crime control, welfare, housing, transportation, health care, and agriculture; repeal of the income tax and all other

socialism

An economic and governmental system based on public ownership of the means of production and exchange.

libertarianism

An ideology that cherishes individual liberty and insists on minimal government, promoting a free market economy, a noninterventionist foreign policy, and an absence of regulation in moral, economic, and social life.

History Makers

Rachel Carson and the Environmental Movement

"There was once a town in the heart of America where all life seemed to live in harmony with its surroundings. . . . Then a strange blight crept over the area and everything began to change. . . . There was a strange stillness. . . . The few birds seen anywhere were moribund; they trembled violently and could not fly. It was a spring without voices."* These words of Rachel Carson, found at the beginning of her most famous book, *Silent Spring,* published in 1962, elicited a response that was anything but silent.

A gifted marine biologist and writer, Carson had been only one of two women employed on a professional level by the U.S. Bureau of Fisheries (later the U.S. Fish and Wildlife Service). Her first book, *Under the Sea Wind,* demonstrated her ability to describe the natural world. During her years in government service, from 1936 to 1949, she became alarmed by the harmful effects of pesticides on the environment. She contacted *Reader's Digest* to write an article on the subject, but was met with a lack of concern.[†] Eventually, the alarming death rates among wildlife in areas sprayed by pesticides drove her to write and publish *Silent Spring* despite the deaths of a niece and her mother and a diagnosis that she had terminal cancer.[‡] In response to attacks by the chemical industry, the Department of Agriculture, and many in the media, she said, "I have felt bound by a solemn obligation to do what I could."[§] Carson's book had an enormous popular impact abroad and in the United States, where it virtually created the modern environmental movement. It led to legislation banning the use of DDT and to the establishment of the Environmental Protection Agency.[‖] ∎

Rachel Carson

*Peter Matthiessen, "Rachel Carson," *Time Magazine,* March 29, 1999, www.time.com/time/time100/scientist/profile/carson02.html.
[†]www.pbs.org/wgbh/aso/databank/entries/btcars.html.
[‡]Matthiessen, www.time.com/time/time100/scientist/profile/carson03.html.
[§]For a more detailed biography of Rachel Carson see www.fws.gov/northeast/ rachelcarson/carsonbio.html.
[‖]Rachel Carson, *Silent Spring* (Houghton Mifflin, 1962), pp. 1, 2.

---

direct taxes; decriminalization of drugs and pardons for prisoners convicted of nonviolent drug offenses; and withdrawal of overseas military forces. Libertarian positions are rarely timid; at the least, they prompt intriguing political debate.[52] The Libertarian party's 2004 candidate, Michael Badnarik, received 380,000 votes—the most votes of all official candidates for the minor parties.[53] In 2004, the Libertarian party endorsed same-sex marriage, legalizing drugs, repealing the Patriot Act, withdrawing from Iraq, eliminating all gun control laws, repealing business regulations, and eliminating the Food and Drug Administration. To learn more about libertarianism, go to www.lp.org.

A Word of Caution

Political labels have different meanings across national boundaries as well as over time. To be a liberal in most European nations and Australia is to be on the right; to be a liberal in the United States and Canada is to be on the left. In recent elections, the term "liberal"—which while Franklin Roosevelt was president in the 1930s and 1940s had been popular—became "the L-word," a label most politicians sought to avoid. But liberalism is more than a label. On big questions—such as the role of government in the economy, in promoting equality of opportunity, and in regulating the behavior of individuals or businesses—real differences separate conservative and liberal groups. This does not mean, however, that people who are conservative in one area are necessarily conservative in another or that all liberals always agree with each other.

It is important to appreciate that ideology both causes events and is affected by them. Just as the Great Depression resulted in a tidal wave of ideological change, so did

Libertarian Party

Michael Badnarik, Libertarian candidate for president in 2004. Badnarik received 380,000 votes in the 2004 election—just 20,000 less than Ralph Nader and the most of all official candidates for the minor parties.

our involvement in World War II. The attacks on the World Trade Center and the Pentagon on September 11, 2001, may also have a lasting impact. For example, World War II, which showed how government can work to defend freedom, increased support for the role of the national government. The Vietnam War probably had the opposite effect, producing disillusionment with government. The antigovernment sentiment in recent presidential elections is undoubtedly related to Vietnam, the Watergate scandal of the early 1970s, and allegations of sexual and financial misconduct by political leaders in recent years. The surge in patriotism and sense of national unity in the war against terrorism after September 11 stands in sharp contrast to the national mood during the mid-1970s in the final years of the Vietnam War. It also reflects, at least in the short term, a view that government has an important role to play in responding to a crisis.

Political Ideology and the American People

For some people, ideological controversy today centers on the role of the government in improving schools, encouraging a stronger work ethic, and stopping the flow of drugs into the country. For others, ideology is centered on whether to permit openly gay people into the military or sanction same-sex marriages, and on the best ways to instill moral values, build character, and encourage cohesive and lasting families.

Despite the twists and turns of American politics, the distribution of ideology in the nation has been remarkably consistent (see Figure 4–1). Conservatives outnumber liberals, but the proportion of conservatives did not increase substantially with the decisive Republican presidential victories of the 1980s or congressional victories of the 1990s.

Moreover, in the United States most people are moderates or report not knowing whether they are liberal or conservative. In 2000, 2002, and 2004, only 2 percent of the population saw themselves as extreme liberals, while extreme conservatives ranged from 2–4 percent (see Figure 4–2). These percentages have changed little over time. Despite claims by ideological extremes in both parties to move to the right or to the left, there are simply more voters in the middle who are moderate or do not have a preferred ideology.[54]

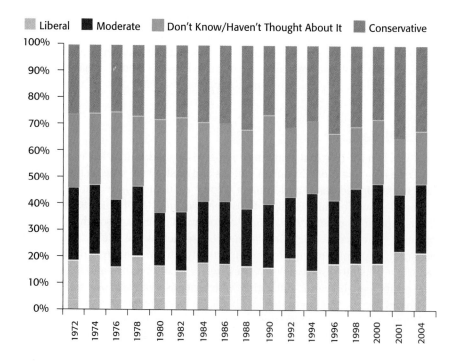

FIGURE 4–1 Ideology over Time.

SOURCE: Center for Political Studies, University of Michigan, *2004 American National Election Study Guide to Public Opinion and Electoral Behavior.*

FIGURE 4-2 **Ideology Curve.**

SOURCE: Center for Political Studies, University of Michigan, *2004 American National Election Study Guide to Public Opinion and Electoral Behavior*.

NOTE: We have combined with the "moderate" persons with those who do not know their ideology or had not thought much about it. Rows may not add up to 100 percent due to rounding.

Both major parties targeted moderate or centrist voters in the 2000 presidential election, as reflected in the stands of the candidates on key issues, including their efforts to minimize ideological battles at the conventions. Governor Tommy Thompson of Wisconsin, who chaired the Republican Platform Committee, stated that their more conservative partisans did not push their issues because "they want to win."[55] In 2004, both presidential candidates again courted the "swing" or undecided voters in states where the race was close. But both parties also worked hard to activate more ideological voters, sometimes called the "base" vote. Kerry stressed jobs and a middle-class tax cut to secure support from working people. Bush sought to reach conservative Christian voters and Republicans who had moved into outlying suburbs, sometimes called exurbs.

For those who have a liberal or conservative preference, ideology provides a lens through which to view candidates and public policies. It helps simplify the complexities of politics, policies, personalities, and programs. However, most Americans are selective or even inconsistent in their political views. A voter may support increased spending for defense but vote for the party that is for reducing defense spending because he or she has always voted for that party or prefers its stand on the environment. Or a person may favor tax cuts and a balanced budget while opposing substantial reductions in government programs.

The degree to which people have ideologically consistent attitudes and opinions varies but is often relatively low. Much of the time, people look at political issues individually and do not evaluate parties or candidates systematically or according to an ideological litmus test. Indeed, many citizens find it difficult to connect a government policy area to a government policy in a different area. This problem becomes more complex as government gets involved in more and more policy areas. Hence many people, not surprisingly, have difficulty finding candidates who reflect their ideological preferences across a wide range of issues.

The absence of widespread and solidified liberal and conservative positions in the United States makes for politics and policy-making processes that are markedly different from those in most nations. Policy making in this country is characterized more by ad hoc coalitions than by fixed alignments that pit one set of ideologies against another. Our politics is marked more by moderation, pragmatism, and accommodation than by a prolonged battle between competing philosophies of government. Elsewhere, especially in countries where a strong Socialist, Green, or Christian Democratic party exists, like in Sweden or Germany, things are different. This does not, however, mean that policies or ideas are not important in American politics. There has been, for instance, a shift since 1995 to more partisan and ideological voting in the House of Representatives.[56] Part of the explanation for the increasing importance of ideology in Congress is that the Republicans have become more conservative and the Democrats more liberal. Conservative Republicans have made large gains in the South, where the remaining Democrats have become more liberal[57]; in other parts of the country, such as New England and parts of the Midwest, liberal Democrats have replaced moderate Republicans. Perhaps even more important, congressional districts are now being drawn to make more of them safe for one party or the other, so Republican members of Congress tend to appeal to the more conservative wing of their party, while Democratic members of Congress tend to appeal to the more liberal wing of their party.

Ideology and Tolerance

Is there a connection between the ideologies of liberalism and conservatism and support for civil liberties and tolerance for racial minorities? Some political scientists assert that conservatives are generally less tolerant than liberals.[58] This view is stoutly contested by conservatives, who have charged liberals with trying to impose a "politically correct" position on faculty and students in universities, colleges, and the media. Liberals are usually more tolerant than conservatives of dissent from some quarters and the expression of unorthodox opinions. However, liberals, too, can be intolerant—of abortion foes, for example, or of the National Rifle Association or of the views of people like conservative talk show host Sean Hannity. On the other side, some conservatives have tried to get faculty members and clergy who have been critical of the war against terrorism fired.

Most liberals are strongly opposed to crime and lawbreaking, yet they are also concerned about the causes of crime and about trying to eliminate them. Perhaps for this reason, liberals exhibit more concern than conservatives for the rights of the accused and are more willing to expand the rights of due process. Conservatives usually take a harder line and, in recent years, have won popular support for their greater concern for the victims of crime than for the rights of the accused.

Such differences are most evident in the responses of liberals and conservatives to questions of civil rights and civil liberties. Conservatives are usually seen as less willing to permit speech that is out of the political or cultural mainstream. Perhaps conservatives are less tolerant because those who claim to be exercising the right of free speech often attack established values. Liberals favor limiting speech in areas like cigarette advertising or campaign spending but favor fewer restrictions than conservatives do on countercultural individuals or groups.[59]

Conservatives believe that the United States has become too morally permissive. Many conservatives, especially in the New or Religious Right, are highly critical of homosexuals, drug users, prostitutes, unwed mothers, and pornographers. They worry about what they claim has been a decline in moral standards and, interestingly, call on government to help reverse these trends. Most liberals, by contrast, generally accept nonconformity in conduct and opinion as an inescapable by-product of freedom.[60] In this regard, liberals are like libertarians.

Ideologies have consequences. These sharp cleavages in political thinking stir opposing interest groups into action. A wide variety of groups promote their views of what is politically desirable. It is also these differences in ideological perspectives that reinforce party loyalties and divide us at election time. Policy fights in Congress, between Congress and the White House, and during judicial confirmation hearings also have their roots in our uneasily coexisting ideological values.

Our hard-earned rights and liberties are never entirely safeguarded; they are fragile and shaped by the political, economic, and social climate of the day. In later

"It's been hell! The breakfast bagels aren't toasted, I can't sleep with a nightlight, there's no "dry hair" formula shampoo in the showers, and the guard won't get close enough for me to stab him with a spoon!"

By Steve Stack, Minneapolis *Star-Tribune*. Reprinted with permission of *Star Tribune*.

Agents of Change

John Wood and Room to Read

John Wood, a former Microsoft executive, founded Room to Read in 2000 to build schools in small villages around the world. By providing grants that challenge villages to provide at least some of their own resources, Room to Read creates an environment in which local communities become much more involved in making sure their new school succeeds. These schools are changing the landscape of democracy in poor nations in Southeast Asia. Over its first five years, Room to Read has helped build 180 new schools, opened 2,000 libraries, donated more than 1 million books, and improved education for 800,000 Asian children.

During a trek through Nepal, which took him to small villages with no schools at all, Wood noticed more than just the lack of schools. As Microsoft's second-highest official in China, he toured dozens of schools that needed more than computers to succeed. They also needed chairs and tables, better class-rooms, and decent libraries. "Microsoft didn't need me," he remembers, "the children of Nepal did." But he did bring his business training to the effort, especially in requiring that communities provide a share of the money needed to improve their own schools. "When they feel a little bit of pain," he says, "they feel more involved, a bigger sense of ownership of the project."

Room to Read is located in San Francisco, where Wood does most of the work raising money from other charities to support the effort. As he says, Microsoft "taught me not to rest on my laurels. I want to be the Microsoft of the charity world, a trusted global brand." With Room to Read growing rapidly, he may yet achieve his goal. ■

Learn more about Room to Read at www.roomtoread.org.

QUESTIONS

How do schools alter the political landscape of a democracy?

Should such programs be funded by the U.S. government as a form of foreign aid, and if so, why?

John Wood, founder of Room to Read

chapters, we examine the interest groups and political parties that are battling to advance their values and compete in the American political culture. But before turning to those topics, we examine the social and economic diversity of the American political landscape in Chapter 5 and see why agreement on shared democratic values is all the more remarkable.

Summary

1. The United States, like every other nation or society, has a distinctive political culture. It consists of a widely held set of fundamental political values and accepted processes and institutions that help us manage conflict and resolve problems. In the United States, at least in the abstract, people respect the Constitution, the Bill of Rights, the two-party system, and the right to elect officials on the basis of majority rule. Our belief in social equality has fostered acceptance of the notion that government should guarantee equality of opportunity through programs like education and job training.

2. Americans share a widespread commitment to classical liberalism, which embraces the importance of individual liberty, equality, individualism, power to the people, private property, limited government, national-ism, optimism, idealism, the democratic consensus, and justice and the rule of law. They also believe that the American dream should be something we can all pursue.

3. American political values have been and continue to be affected by historical and economic developments. Among these developments have been the industrial revolution, the growth of large corporations and other large institutions, the Great Depression, and a global economy.

4. The sources of the American political culture include the family, schools, religious and civic organizations, the mass media, and political activities.

5. Two broad schools of thought are important in American politics today: liberalism, a belief that government can and should help achieve justice and equality of opportunity; and conservatism, a belief in limited government to ensure order, competitive markets, and personal opportunity while relying on free markets and individual initiative to solve social and economic problems. Socialism and libertarianism also attract modest followings.

6. Most Americans are nonideological, moderate pragmatists. Few Americans are extremists.

7. Ideological orientation affects how tolerant we are of the views and conduct of others. Liberals tend to be more tolerant, whereas conservatives generally favor tradition, stability, and more social control. These differences influence elections and policies.

Further Reading

H. W. BRANDS, *The Strange Death of American Liberalism* (Yale University Press, 2001).

JIMMY CARTER, *Our Endangered Values: America's Moral Crisis* (Simon and Schuster, 2005).

JAMES W. CEASER, *Reconstructing America: The Symbol of America in Modern Thought* (Yale University Press, 1997).

E. J. DIONNE JR., *They Only Look Dead: Why Progressives Will Dominate the Next Political Era* (Simon & Schuster, 1996).

JEAN BETHKE ELSHTAIN, *Democracy on Trial* (Basic Books, 1995).

E. H. H. GREEN, *Ideologies of Conservatism: Conservative Political Ideas in the Twentieth Century* (Oxford University Press, 2004).

AMY GUTMANN AND **DENNIS THOMPSON,** *Democracy and Disagreement: Why Moral Conflict Cannot Be Avoided in Politics, and What Should Be Done About It* (Harvard University Press, 1996).

SAMUEL P. HARRINGTON, ED., *Who Are We?* (Simon and Schuster, 2004).

LOUIS HARTZ, *The Liberal Tradition in America* (Harcourt, 1955).

CAROL A. HORTON, *Race and the Making of American Liberalism* (Oxford University Press, 2005).

GEORGE KLOSKO, *Democratic Procedures and Liberal Consensus* (Oxford University Press, 2000).

IRVING KRISTOL, *Neoconservatism: The Autobiography of an Idea* (Free Press, 1995).

DAVID C. LEEGE, KENNETH D. WALD, BRIAN S. KRUEGER, AND **PAUL D. MUELLER,** *The Politics of Cultural Differences* (Princeton University Press, 2002).

HERBERT MCCLOSKY AND **JOHN ZALLER,** *The American Ethos: Public Attitudes Toward Capitalism and Democracy* (Harvard University Press, 1984).

LISA McGIRR, *Suburban Warriors: The Origins of the New American Right* (Princeton University Press, 2001).

CHARLES MURRAY, *What It Means to Be a Libertarian: A Personal Interpretation* (Broadway Books, 1997).

MICHAEL NEWMA, *Socialism: A Very Short Introduction* (Oxford University Press, 2005).

MARCUS G. RASKIN, *Liberalism: The Genius of American Ideals* (Rowman and Littlefield, 2004).

JOHN RENSENBRINK, *Against All Odds: The Green Transformation of American Politics* (Leopold Press, 1999).

JEREMY RIFKIN, *The European Dream* (Penguin Group, 2005).

ALEXIS DE TOCQUEVILLE, *Democracy in America,* 2 vols. (1835).

JOHN KENNETH WHITE, *The Values Divide* (Seven Bridges Press, 2003).

GARRY WILLS, *A Necessary Evil: A History of American Distrust of Government* (Simon & Schuster, 1999).

KeyTerms

political culture, p. 90

social capital, p. 90

natural rights, p. 91

democratic consensus, p. 93

majority rule, p. 93

popular sovereignty, p. 93

American dream, p. 95

capitalism, p. 95

suffrage, p. 97

monopoly, p. 98

antitrust legislation, p. 98

political ideology, p. 99

liberalism, p. 100

conservatism, p. 102

socialism, p. 104

libertarianism, p. 104

Make It Real

POLITICAL IDEOLOGY

In this simulation, students map their ideological beliefs.

Chapter 5

The American Political Landscape

⭐

IMMIGRATION REFORM BECAME A FRONT-PAGE STORY IN SPRING 2006 AS THOUSANDS OF PROTESTERS TOOK TO THE STREETS TO OPPOSE THE REPUBLICAN-SPONSORED IMMIGRATON LEGISLATION ENACTED BY THE HOUSE OF REPRESENTATIVES IN LATE 2005. THE LEGISLATION PROPOSED MAKING ILLEGAL PRESENCE IN THE UNITED STATES A CRIME, INCREASED THE PENALTIES FOR EMPLOYERS OF UNDOCUMENTED ALIENS AND OTHERS WHO ASSIST THEM, AND CALLED FOR THE CONSTRUCTION OF A 700-MILE-LONG FENCE

between Mexico and the United States.[1] In March 2006, more than one million people across the country and in every major city gathered to protest the House bills, with the biggest rallies in cities like Washington D.C., Los Angeles, Dallas, and Phoenix.[2] In May 2006, in a protest called "A Day Without Immigrants," immigrants and their supporters attempted to show the important role immigrants play in the economy by not working that day, and by participating in rallies that drew more than 600,000 protesters in Los Angeles and 400,000 in Chicago.[3]

President Bush and a bipartisan group in the United States Senate proposed less restrictive laws on immigration. These proposals called for "guest worker" privileges for the estimated 12 million undocumented migrant workers. Some proposals allowed for eventual citizenship; others limited the time a guest worker could be in the United States. The Republican party is especially divided on the question of how to deal with immigration. Those Republicans most concerned with border security and upholding the law favor deportation. Traditional allies of the Republicans, like many employers who depend on undocumented workers, support some form of guest worker program, including the possibility of eventual U.S. citizenship. In October 2006, Congress shelved immigration reform in favor of building a 700-mile fence along the U.S.–Mexico border. As both parties look to the 2008 election they want to gain support of Hispanic voters, many of whom care deeply about this issue.

Not lost in the current debate over immigration is the fact that the United States is a nation of immigrants, which is a source of national pride. Franklin D. Roosevelt once began a speech to the Daughters of the American Revolution by saying, "You and I, especially, are descended from immigrants and revolutionists."[4] The hope for prosperity and freedom has long drawn immigrants to America. However, while the first generation to come to America rarely achieves the American dream, there are notable

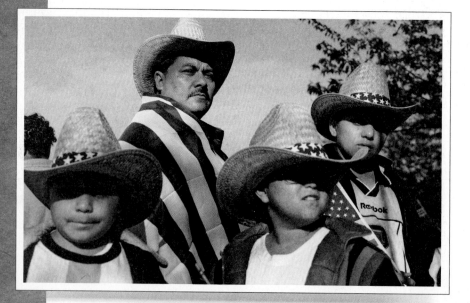

"You and I, especially, are descended from immigrants and revolutionists."

PRESIDENT FRANKLIN D. ROOSEVELT

113

exceptions. Take, for example, George Soros, an international financier who is among the most successful businesspeople in the United States. Soros was born in Hungary, educated in England, and then moved to the United States. Today, Soros is the founder of the Open Society Institute and is a noted philanthropist. Arte Moreno, a fourth-generation Mexican American and the owner of the Los Angeles Angels of Anaheim, is the first Hispanic to own a major U.S. sports franchise. Moreno started a billboard business with a partner during college. Over time the business expanded into a huge conglomerate that Moreno sold in 1999 for $8.3 billion.[5] Our system of government not only permits fortunate and hardworking immigrants to accumulate wealth, it also allows them to translate that wealth into political influence. Soros, an outspoken critic of President George W. Bush, gave $27 million in 2003–2004 to groups opposing Bush's reelection. Arte Moreno has contributed on a much smaller scale to predominantly Republican candidates and the Republican party.

We have conflicting ideas about immigration. We celebrate our immigrant past and proudly recite the words of Emma Lazarus inscribed at the base of the Statue of Liberty: "Give me your tired, your poor, your huddled masses yearning to breathe free." And yet our borders are not open to all who wish to come here. We allow only specific numbers of immigrants to enter from each country each year. Hundreds of thousands avoid these limitations by crossing our borders illegally. Opponents of the "guest worker" idea see it as rewarding those who broke the law to enter the United States by granting them legal guest worker status. They argue this will not stop the flow of people entering the country and encourages contempt for the law. Representative Tom Tancredo (R-Colo.) stated that a proposal in the Senate to create a guest worker program "makes a mockery of our laws and crushes our already strained legal immigration system."[6]

The current debate about immigration also demonstrates widespread misperceptions about the number of illegal immigrants in the country and their contribution to the economy. Albert Einstein, who himself immigrated to the United States from Germany in the 1930s, once said that most people are incapable of expressing opinions that differ much from the prejudices of their social upbringing.[7] This **ethnocentrism**—selective perception based on one's background, attitudes, and biases—is not uncommon. People often assume that others share their economic opportunities, social attitudes, sense of civic responsibility, and self-confidence. In this chapter, we consider how our social environment explains, or at least shapes, our opinions and prejudices. We also look at our diversity as Americans and at how geographic, social, and economic divisions can affect politics and government. Specifically, this chapter explores the effects of regional or state identity on political perspectives; how differences in race, ethnicity, gender, family structure, religion, wealth and income, occupation, and social class influence opinions and voting choices; and the relationship between age and education and political participation. Because people's personal characteristics or attributes are important to political interest groups (Chapter 6), we examine attitudes and behavior before discussing political parties (Chapter 7); public opinion, participation, and voting (Chapter 8); and campaigns and elections (Chapter 9). This chapter lays the foundation of how different aspects of who we are as people influences how we behave politically.

A Land of Diversity

Most nations consist of groups of people who have lived together for centuries and who speak the same language, embrace the same religious beliefs, and share a common history. Most Japanese citizens are Japanese in the fullest sense of the word, and this sense of identity and oneness is generally the same in Sweden, Saudi Arabia, and China. The United States is different. We have attracted the poor and oppressed, the adventurous, and the talented from all over the world, and we have been more open to accepting these people than many other nations.

Many people want to come to the United States because it holds a promise of religious, political, and economic freedom. It is also a place of opportunity for the

ethnocentrism

Belief in the superiority of one's nation or ethnic group.

enterprising. Our economic system has provided widespread (but not universal) opportunity for individuals to improve their economic standing. The American dream—that anyone can find success in the United States—is widely shared. Perceptions about the American way of life in popular culture—movies, music videos, TV shows—also attract some to our shores.

Several elements of our diversity have political significance. Many Americans retain an identity with the land of their ancestors, even after three or four generations. Families, churches, and other close-knit ethnic groups foster these ties.

Political socialization is the process by which parents and others teach children about political values, beliefs, and attitudes. This teaching occurs in the home, in school, on the playground, and in the neighborhood. In addition to fostering group identities, political socialization also strongly influences how individuals see politics and which political party they prefer. Where we live and who we are in terms of age, education, religion, and occupation affect how we vote. Social scientists call such characteristics of populations **demographics**. Persons in certain demographic categories tend to vote alike and to share certain **political predispositions**, which can predict political behavior, although there are often individual differences within socioeconomic and demographic categories.

When social and economic differences reinforce each other, they make the differences between groups more important. Social scientists call these differences **reinforcing cleavages**; where these differences are reinforcing, political conflict becomes more intense and society becomes more polarized. In Italy, for example, the tendency of parts of the industrialized north to lean toward the Socialist or Communist parties and of the poorer and more agrarian south to be politically conservative and Catholic in orientation reinforces the historical divide between north and south that has existed for centuries.

Nations can also have **cross-cutting cleavages**, instances where differences among people do not reinforce each other but rather pull people in different directions. To illustrate, if all the rich people in a nation belong to one religion and the poor to another, the nation would have reinforcing cleavages that would intensify political conflict between the groups. But if there are both rich and poor in all religions and if people sometimes vote on the basis of their religion and sometimes on the basis of their wealth, the divisions would be cross-cutting. American diversity has generally been more of the cross-cutting type than the reinforcing type, lessening political conflict because individuals have multiple allegiances.

In some societies, politics centers largely on passions over economic and religious differences. Although socioeconomic differences are important to understanding American government and politics, they are not as central to our politics as religion is in Bosnia or class distinctions are in Brazil. In Northern Ireland, the religious differences between Catholics and Protestants have produced centuries of violent strife that is yet to be resolved.

Even though America has been and remains a nation of immigrants from around the world, we Americans often prefer to associate only with people "like us" and are suspicious of people "like them." From hostility toward different religions in the early colonies to the "nativist" and anti-Asian movements of the 1800s to the anti-immigration and anti-civil rights ballot initiatives of the last two decades, Americans have exhibited ethnocentrism. Indeed, for much of our history, minorities have been excluded from full participation in American political and economic life.

political socialization
The process by which we develop our political attitudes, values, and beliefs.

demographics
The study of the characteristics of populations.

political predisposition
A characteristic of individuals that is predictive of political behavior.

reinforcing cleavages
Divisions within society that reinforce one another, making groups more homogeneous or similar.

cross-cutting cleavages
Divisions within society that cut across demographic categories to produce groups that are more heterogeneous or different.

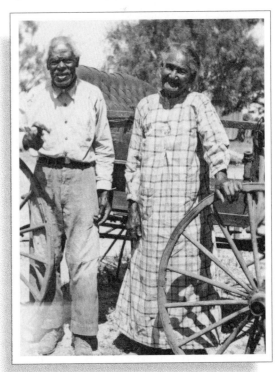

Slavery epitomizes the dark side of this country's national identity. During Reconstruction, some former slaves were able to purchase and work their own land while others moved north to take part in the industrial revolution of the late nineteenth century.

Geography and National Identity

The United States is a geographically large and historically isolated country. In the 1830s, French commentator Alexis de Tocqueville studied the early development of the United States and observed that the country had no major political or economic powers on its borders "and consequently no great wars, financial crises, invasions, or conquests to fear."[8] Geographic isolation from the major powers of the world during our government's formative period helps explain American politics. The Atlantic Ocean served as a barrier to foreign meddling, giving us time to establish our political tradition and develop our economy. The western frontier provided room to grow and avoid some of the social and political tensions that Europe experienced. Two great oceans also reinforced our sense of isolation from Europe and foreign alliances. American reluctance to become involved in foreign wars and controversies still emerges in debates over foreign policy.

Before the terrorist attacks of September 2001, only one foreign enemy had struck the continental United States—England in the War of 1812. (The war against Mexico of 1846–1848 was fought almost entirely in what was then Mexico, large parts of which the United States later annexed after winning the war. The only other war fought on our soil was, of course, the Civil War.) By contrast, Poland has been invaded repeatedly and was partitioned by Austria, Prussia, and Russia in the eighteenth century and by Nazi Germany and the Soviet Union in 1939. The difference is explained largely by location: Poland was surrounded by great powers. Had the United States been closer to Europe and not isolated by two oceans, it might have been overrun like Poland was several times and our Constitution and institutions repeatedly changed or eliminated to suit the invaders. The presence of powerful and aggressive neighbors can impede the development of democracy in relatively weak nations.

The ability of terrorists to harm the United States and other countries, especially if willing to die along with their victims, as was the case with the attacks in 2001, means that national defense and homeland security need to be rethought. The two oceans that protected the United States for so long cannot deter a small band of determined terrorists. Our newly recognized vulnerability to terrorist attacks on our own soil has changed the context in which we debate the balance between liberty and security and has led some to advocate the idea of preemptive war.

Size also confers an advantage. The landmass of the United States exceeds that of all but three nations in the world—Russia, Canada, and Brazil. In contrast, India has a population more than three and a half times that of the United States on a landmass one-third the size. Geographic space gave the expanding population of the United States room to spread out. This defused some of the political conflicts arising from religion, social class, and national origin because groups could isolate themselves from one another. Moreover, the large and accessible landmass helped foster the perspective that the United States had a **manifest destiny** to be a continental nation reaching from the Atlantic to the Pacific Oceans. Early settlers used this notion to justify taking land from Native Americans, Canadians, and Mexicans, especially the huge territory acquired following victory in the Mexican-American War.

The United States is also a land of abundant natural resources. We have rich farmland, which not only feeds our population but also makes us the largest exporter of food in the world.[9] We are rich in such natural resources as coal, iron, uranium, oil, and precious metals. All these resources enhance economic growth, provide jobs, and stabilize government. As de Tocqueville observed, "Yet what takes place in the United States is much less attributable to the institutions of the country than to the country itself."[10]

Our isolation, relative wealth and prosperity, and sense of destiny have fostered a view that the United States is different from the world. This *American exceptionalism*, a term first used by de Tocqueville in 1831, has historically been defined as "the perception that the United States differs qualitatively from other developed nations, because of its unique origins, national credo, historical evolution, and distinctive political and religious institutions."[11] The term has long been used to describe not only the distinctive elements of the United States, but the sense that the United States is a just and moral country. Exceptionalism can thus convey a sense of moral superiority or power that is not well received outside the United States, especially when the United States is seen to be acting in ways that other nations find objectionable or hypocritical. For this reason one observer subtitled his book on exceptionalism "A Double-Edged Sword."[12] For some, at least, the Bush doctrine of preventive war—the idea that American power can and should be used preemptively against other nations who pose a danger or potential danger to the United States—is an extension of American exceptionalism.

manifest destiny
A notion held by nineteenth-century Americans that the United States was destined to rule the continent, from the Atlantic to the Pacific.

Geography also helps explain our diversity. Parts of the United States are wonderfully suited to agriculture, others to mining or ranching, and still others to shipping and manufacturing. These differences produce diverse regional economic concerns, which in turn influence politics. For instance, a person from the agricultural heartland may see foreign trade differently from the way an automobile worker in Detroit sees it. But if that automobile worker is African American, her race may be more important to her politics than what she does or where she lives. To understand American politics, we must appreciate these differences and their relative importance.

Sectional Differences

Unlike many other countries, geography in the United States does *not* define an ethnic or religious division. All the Serbs in the United States do not live in one place, all French-speaking Catholics in another, and all Hispanic immigrants in another. Sectional differences in the United States are primarily geographic, not ethnic or religious.

The most distinct section of the United States remains the South, although its differences from other parts of the country are diminishing. From the beginning of the Republic, the agricultural South differed from the North, where commerce and later manufacturing were more significant. But the most important difference between the regions was the institution of slavery. Northern opposition to slavery, which grew increasingly intense by the 1850s, reinforced sectional economic interests. The 11 Confederate states, by virtue of their decision to secede from the Union, reinforced a common political identity. After the Civil War, Reconstruction and the problems of race relations reinforced sectional differences.

The South is becoming less distinct from the rest of the United States. In addition to undergoing tremendous economic change, a large in-migration has diminished the sense of regional identity. The civil rights revolution of the 1960s eliminated legal and social barriers that prevented African Americans from voting, ended legal segregation, opened up new educational opportunities, and helped integrate the South into the national economy. African Americans still lag behind Southern white people in voter registration, but the gap is now no wider in the South than elsewhere and is explained more by differences in education than by race.[13] In economic terms, the South still falls below the rest of the country in per capita income and education, but much less so than 50 years ago. The traditional religious and moral conservatism of the South, however, remains notable.

Until the 1970s, political observers spoke of the "solid South"—a region that voted for Democrats at all levels. "The Civil War made the Democratic party the party of the South, and the Republican party, the party of the North."[14] The Democratic "solid South" remained a fixture of American politics for more than a century. Since 1968 that has changed dramatically, first at the presidential level and increasingly at the state and local levels. As two respected observers of the region comment, "The fall of the South as an assured stronghold of the Democratic Party in presidential elections is one of the most significant developments in modern American politics."[15] "The decline of the South in the Democratic party would fundamentally reorder the American party system and realign the electorate."[16] The political alignment has shifted as African Americans have been enfranchised and become overwhelmingly Democrats and many white Southerners have become Republicans. In 1992 and 1996, even with two southerners (Bill Clinton and Al Gore) on the ticket, Democrats won only four of the 11 former Confederate states. In 2000, George W. Bush carried all 11 southern states, including Al Gore's home state of Tennessee. Once again in 2004, George W. Bush carried all 11 former Confederate states, including vice presidential candidate John Edwards's home state of North Carolina.

What explains this dramatic reversal? Part of the explanation is that the Democrats' advocacy of aggressive action on civil rights in the 1960s alienated some southern white people. In addition, the debate within the Democratic party over the Vietnam War in the late 1960s and 1970s was "perceived by many southern voters as unpatriotic."[17] Democrats are aware of divisive or "wedge" issues; Howard Dean in 2004 expressed this concern: "We have got to stop having the campaigns run in this

"We have got to stop having the campaigns run in this country based on abortion, guns, God and gays."

2004 PRESIDENTIAL CANDIDATE HOWARD DEAN

country based on abortion, guns, God and gays."[18] Republican presidential candidates continue to emphasize family values, opposition to taxes and to same-sex marriage, and law-and-order issues that appeal to conservative southern voters. They also have emphasized their strong response to terrorism. As Karl Rove stated months before the 2006 election, "At the core, we are dealing with two parties that have fundamentally different views on national security . . . Republicans have a post-9/11 worldview and many Democrats have a pre-9/11 worldview. That does not make them unpatriotic—not at all. But it does make them wrong—deeply and profoundly and consistently wrong."[19] Republican success at the presidential level was slow to affect contests for Congress and state legislatures. Yet in recent years, Republicans had more than half of southern votes for the U.S. House of Representatives (see Table 5–1), and in 2007 they controlled 6 of the 11 governorships in the former Confederate states. Only two of these states elected governors in the 2006 election. In Arkansas the Democrats took back the statehouse from Republicans, and in Florida Republicans retained control.[20] In the state legislatures, remnants of the old "solid South" remain, but Republicans have made major inroads, and politics in the region is now predictably Republican, at least at the presidential level.

Both parties could point to successes in the South since 2002. The Democrats picked up or retained the governorships in Tennessee, Louisiana, North Carolina, and Virginia, and the Republicans did the same in Georgia, Alabama, South Carolina, and Mississippi. In Georgia, this was the first Republican governor since Reconstruction. Overall, Republicans have regularly come to control more governorships than Democrats in the South, but in 2007 Democrats again controlled a majority of southern governorships. In the U.S. Senate Republicans have a much more commanding advantage, with 18 of the 22 U.S. Senate seats from the former Confederate states. Democratic U.S. Senate victories in Florida and Virginia in 2006 were both critical to the Democrats taking control of the Senate from Republicans.

Another sectional division is the Sun Belt—the 11 former Confederate states plus New Mexico, Arizona, Nevada, and the southern half of California. Sun Belt states are growing much more rapidly than the rest of the country. Arizona, California, Florida, Georgia, Nevada, North Carolina, and Texas gained 12 seats in the House of Representatives after the 2000 census.[21] Moreover, population growth in the South and West is occurring in different age groups. In the South, growth is largest among those over 65; in the West, younger persons provide the growth. Sun Belt states have also experienced greater economic growth as industries have headed south and southwest, where land and labor are cheaper and more abundant (see Figure 5–1). The shift of seats to the Sun Belt has helped Republicans, as the states picking up additional seats have tended to be more Republican. That tendency was reinforced in 2003–2004 in Texas where the state legislature, after a protracted political battle, replaced the 2002 Texas boundaries for the U.S. House of Representatives drawn by the courts with new districts aimed at defeating Democratic incumbents in the 2004 election.[22] The Supreme Court upheld the constitutionality of most elements of the redistricting plan in a June 2006 ruling.[23]

State and Local Identity

Different states have rather distinctive political traditions. Mention Utah, Mississippi, Oregon, New York, or Kansas, and a certain type of politics comes to mind. The same is true for many other states. Like most stereotypes, these images are often misleading, yet they reflect the fact that states have a sense of identity as political units that goes beyond demographic characteristics and is supported by recent empirical evidence. States have distinctive political cultures that affect public opinion and policies.[24] Part of the reason for the enduring state identities is that we elect members of Congress and the president at the state level. States like Iowa and New Hampshire also play important roles in narrowing the field of presidential candidates seeking their party's nomination. Differences in state laws relating to driving, drinking, gambling, and taxes also reinforce the relevance of state identity. Colleges and universities may have the same effect while reinforcing competition between different states.

TABLE 5–1   Voting Patterns in the 11 Former Confederate States

Republican Vote for President

1960	46%	1984	62%
1964	49	1988	59
1968	35	1992	43
1972	70	1996	46
1976	45	2000	54
1980	50	2004	57

Republican Vote for U.S. Representatives

1960	22%	1990	43%
1964	37	1992	48
1968	35	1994	58
1972	42	1996	53*
1976	36	1998	58
1980	40	2000	53
1982	39	2002	56
1984	42	2004	55
1986	41	2006	53
1988	42		

Republican Share of State Legislators	House	Senate
1960	5%	4%
1964	7	11
1968	13	13
1972	17	15
1976	12	10
1980	18	17
1982	22	14
1984	23	17
1986	24	20
1988	27	24
1990	28	26
1992	31	31
1994	37	37
1996	44	44
1998	42	40
2000	44	42
2002	47	46
2004	50	49
2006	48	49

*The 1996 Texas runoff elections are not included.

SOURCE: For 1960–1964, U.S. Bureau of Census, at www2.census.gov/prod2/statcomp/documents/ 1965-04.pdf; for 1968–1972, U.S. Bureau of Census, at www2.census.gov/prod2/statcomp/documents/ 1974-07.pdf; for 1976, U.S. Bureau of the Census, at www2.census.gov/prod2/statcomp/documents/ 1980-06.pdf; for 1980–2000, U.S. Bureau of the Census, *Statistical Abstract of the United States,* 1993–2000; for 2004, CNN at www.cnn.com/ELECTION/2004; and *Congressional Quarterly Weekly Report,* November 11, 2000, pp. 2694–2703; and Todd Edwards, Council of State Governments, Southern Office, personal communication, December 22, 2000, and Doris Smith, Council of State Governments, Southern Office, November 10, 2004.

FIGURE 5–1 Percent Change in Resident Population, 2000–2005.

SOURCE: U.S. Bureau of the Census, www.census .gov/popest/gallery/maps/Per_Num_Chg_2004_ 2005.pdf.

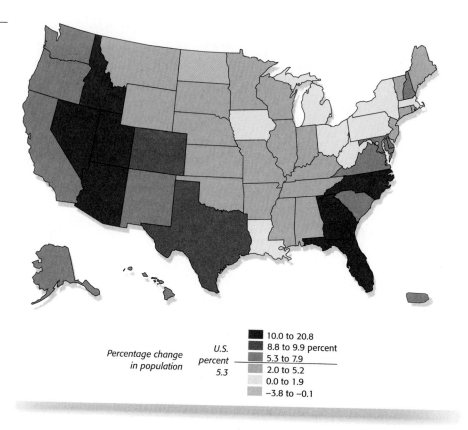

Percentage change in population

U.S. percent 5.3

- 10.0 to 20.8
- 8.8 to 9.9 percent
- 5.3 to 7.9
- 2.0 to 5.2
- 0.0 to 1.9
- −3.8 to −0.1

In American politics today, one state—California—stands out. Nearly one out of eight Americans is a Californian.[25] In terms of economic and political importance, California is in a league by itself; its 53 members of the House of Representatives exceed the total number of representatives from the smallest 20 states. California's 55 electoral votes are key for any presidential candidate.[26] California's reputation for distinctive politics was reinforced in 2003 when voters replaced Governor Gray Davis with movie star Arnold Schwarzenegger in the first recall of a governor since North Dakota voters recalled Governor Lynn G. Frazier in 1921.[27]

Where We Live

Four out of five Americans now live in urban areas.[28] During the early twentieth century, the movement of population was from rural areas to central cities, but the movement since the 1950s has been from the central cities to their suburbs. Today the most urban state is California (over 94 percent of its population lives in cities or suburbs). Vermont is the least urban, with only 38 percent living in cities or suburbs.[29] Regionally, the West and Northeast are the most urban, the South and Midwest the most rural.

People move from cities to the suburbs for many reasons—better housing, new transportation systems that make it easier to get to work, the desire for cleaner air and safer streets. Another reason is white flight, the movement of white people away from the central cities so that children can avoid being bused for racial balance and attend generally better schools. White, middle-class migration to the suburbs has made American cities increasingly poor, African American, and Democratic. More than half of all African Americans now live in central cities, as opposed to only about one-fifth of white people, and the poverty level among black people living in central cities is higher than among white people living in the same cities.[30] The proportions are nearly reversed for the suburbs, where more than half of all white Americans reside. Approximately one-third of African Americans live in the suburbs, up from one-fifth in 1980.[31]

TABLE 5–2 Cities with Populations of 100,000 or More
That Are at Least 50 Percent African American, 2000

City	Population	Percent African American
Atlanta, Ga.	416,474	61.4%
Baltimore, Md.	651,154	64.3
Birmingham, Ala.	242,820	73.5
Detroit, Mich.	951,270	81.6
Gary, Ind.	102,746	84.0
Jackson, Miss.	184,256	70.6
Memphis, Tenn.	650,100	61.4
Newark, N.J.	273,546	53.5
New Orleans, La.	484,674	67.3
Richmond, Va.	197,790	57.2
Savannah, Ga.	131,510	57.1
Washington, D.C.	572,059	60.0

SOURCE: U.S. Bureau of the Census, www.census.gov/population/cen2000/phc-t6/tab05.pdf.
NOTE: The population of New Orleans was significantly reduced due to the destruction of Hurricane Katrina.

In large cities such as Washington, D.C., Detroit, Baltimore, and Atlanta, the city population is now well over 50 percent African American (see Table 5–2). Hispanics constitute roughly three-fourths of the population of El Paso, Texas, and Santa Ana, California, and nearly two-thirds the population of Miami, Florida.[32]

As the economically better off have left many of the cities, the cities' problems have become more acute, and their tax base has not increased proportionate to their problems. Older suburban areas now face the same problems as the inner cities, as they too suffer from out-migration to newer cities and towns, so-called exurbs. High-tech and professional service companies frequently relocate to the suburbs to avoid traffic congestion and to be closer to the bedroom communities of their workers. Political boundaries, which define local governments and delineate responsibility for services, create understandable tensions among cities, suburbs, and rural areas. Tax revenues, legislative representation, zoning laws, and governmental priorities are hotly contested issues in most metropolitan areas.

Who We Are

Sectional distinctions are less prominent today than they were a century or even a half-century ago. Today Americans are more likely to define themselves by a number of characteristics, each of which may influence how they vote or think about candidates, issues, or policies.

Race and Ethnicity

Racial and ethnic differences have always had political significance. **Race** can be defined as a grouping of human beings with distinctive physical characteristics determined by genetic inheritance. Some scholars define race as more culturally determined than genetic.[33] **Ethnicity** is a social division based on national origin, religion, and language, often within the same race, and includes a sense of attachment to that group. Examples of ethnic groups with enduring relevance to American politics

race
A grouping of human beings with distinctive characteristics determined by genetic inheritance.

ethnicity
A social division based on national origin, religion, language, and often race.

Government's Greatest Endeavors

Building the Interstate Highway System

The interstate highway system has cost more than $350 billion to build.

The federal government has been building roads and bridges since the founding of the Republic. Indeed, the framers believed that a network of postal roads was essential for holding the nation together, while building support for a truly national government. Road building was also seen as a way to strengthen the national economy by encouraging interstate commerce.

More than 200 years later, the federal government continues to build roads and bridges linking the states together, adding steadily to the 43,000 miles of interstate highway system. This system was authorized under the Interstate Highway Act of 1956, and has cost the nation more than $350 billion to build, of which 90 percent has come from the federal government. The original system called for a set of simple highways that would crisscross the nation linking major cities together, but it has steadily expanded to include new cities and more highway lanes to accommodate increased traffic. As such, it will never be fully complete.

The federal government also spends billions per year on lesser state and local roads and bridges. Such spending is often promoted by individual members of Congress who publicize their role in creating improved highways and construction jobs in their campaigns.

Nevertheless, the nation's system of interconnected highways is one of its greatest modern achievements. It has reduced auto accidents by regulating speeds and eliminating intersections, while saving Americans billions of dollars in shipping costs. Although it has great benefits, however, some experts argue that the system has created more highway congestion, while reducing the amount of money available for more environmentally friendly mass transportation such as buses and subways. ■

QUESTIONS

How does the federal government affect your own transportation?

Does the United States spend too much money on highways and not enough on mass transportation?

include Italian Americans, Irish Americans, Polish Americans, and Korean Americans. In the United States, race and ethnicity issues focus primarily on African Americans, Asian Americans, Native Americans, and Hispanics.

There are more than 37 million African Americans in the United States, nearly 13 percent of the population. Asian Americans constitute about 4 percent of the population, and Native Americans, about 1 percent.[34] Most American Hispanics classify themselves as white, although Hispanics can be of any race. Hispanics are the fastest-growing ethnic group; there are roughly 41 million American Hispanics, constituting more than 14 percent of the population.[35] Because of differences in immigration and birthrates, white Americans will have declined to less than three-quarters of the population by the year 2050. The percentage of non-Hispanic whites will be about 50 percent by 2050.[36]

NATIVE AMERICANS The original inhabitants of what became the United States have played an important role in American history and continue to be important to the

The Changing Face of American Politics

A More Diverse Population

	1950	1990	2004	2025	2050
White	89.4%	83.9%	80.4%	76.8%	72.1%
Non-Hispanic White	—	75.7	67.7	59.5	50.1
African American	10.0	12.2	12.8	13.7	14.6
Native American, Inuit, Aleut	0.2	0.8	1.0	1.0	1.1
Asian and Pacific Islander	0.2	3.0	4.4	6.5	9.3
Hispanic	—	8.9	14.1	18.9	24.4

SOURCE: 1950 figures from the U.S. Bureau of the Census, *Census of Population: 1950 Volume II Part I*, p. 106. 1990 figures from U.S. Bureau of the Census, *Statistical Abstract of the United States, 2001* (Government Printing Office, 2001), pp. 16–17. 2004 figures from U.S. Bureau of the Census, *Statistical Abstract of the United States, 2006* (Government Printing Office, 2006), p. 16. All other figures from U.S. Bureau of the Census, *Statistical Abstract of the United States, 2003* (Government Printing Office, 2003), pp. 15, 18.

NOTE: Percentages do not equal 100 because Hispanics can be of any race. Figures for 2025 and 2050 are projections. Categories from the 1950 census are different from those used in the last several decades. For example, the 1950 census did not provide a classification for Hispanic, Native Americans were classifed as "Indian," and Asians were separated into Japanese and Chinese.

politics of states like South Dakota, New Mexico, and Oklahoma. More than half of the names of states and hundreds of the names of cities, rivers, and mountains in the United States have Indian names. During much of our history, the policy of the United States government was removal of Native Americans from their tribal lands and relocation to reservations. The establishment of reservations isolated Native Americans and for decades reinforced poverty and related social problems. More recently, with the advent of Indian casinos, some Native Americans have experienced wealth and political influence but also increases in violent crime.[37] In recent U.S. Senate elections in South Dakota, the Native American vote has been important.[38] Ben Nighthorse Campbell from Colorado, who served in the U.S. Senate from 1993 to 2005, was a Native American.

AFRICAN AMERICANS   Most immigrants chose to come to this country in search of freedom and opportunity. In contrast, until recently, most African Americans came against their will, as slaves. Although the Emancipation Proclamation and Thirteenth Amendment ended slavery in the 1860s, racial divisions still affect American politics. Until 1900, more than 90 percent of all African Americans lived in the South; a century later, that figure was 55 percent.[39] Many African Americans left the South hoping to improve their lives by settling in the large cities of the Northeast, Midwest, and West. But what many of them found was urban poverty. More recently, African Americans have been returning to the South, especially to its urban areas.

Most African Americans are economically worse off than most white Americans. African American median family income is around $34,000, compared to about $56,000 for white Americans.[40] About 22 percent of African American families live below the poverty level, compared to about 8 percent of white American families.[41] Poverty rates among Native Americans and Alaskan Natives have averaged 26 percent in recent years, a proportion slightly higher than for African Americans and Hispanics.[42] However, African Americans have been doing

In 2006, Duval Patrick was elected governor of Massachusetts. He became the first African American governor in that state's history.

FIGURE 5–2 Median Net Worth of Households in the United States by Race.

SOURCE: U.S. Bureau of the Census, www.census.gov/prod/2003pubs/p70-88.pdf.

Barack Obama, elected to the U.S. Senate from Illinois in 2004, is only the third African American senator in a century. Obama enjoyed the support of many Republicans as well as Democrats in his 2004 campaign, in part because his initial GOP opponent dropped out of the race. Obama delivered a passionate keynote address at the 2004 Democratic National Convention and is a rising star in the party.

better in recent years; one-third of African American households earn more than $50,000 (compared to 54 percent of white households).[43] Some African Americans, like Shaquille O'Neal, the Miami Heat basketball player, and Oprah Winfrey, the syndicated talk show host, have risen to top of their professions in terms of earnings.

Another way to measure economic well-being is in terms of assets or wealth. *Wealth* is the economic value of the things you own (savings, stocks, property), compared to *income*, which is how much money you make from your job or investments. One way to measure wealth is called net worth, which is the sum of assets a person has in savings, property, and stocks. As a group, the median net worth of African Americans is less than one-tenth that of white Americans, and the median net worth of Hispanics is only slightly more than that of African Americans (see Figure 5–2).[44] As a result, most African Americans and Hispanics have fewer resources to fall back on in hard times, and they are less likely to have the savings to help a child pay for college.

Middle-class African Americans, of whom there are a growing number, are role models for the young of all races, yet their still comparatively small number is a reminder that most African Americans remain behind white Americans in an economy that relies more and more on education and job skills. About 28 percent of white Americans graduate from college, whereas only about 18 percent of African Americans do.[45] Among recent high school graduates, 66 percent of white Americans go on to college, but only 58 percent of African Americans do.[46]

Finally, the African American population is much younger than the white population; the median age for white Americans in 2004 was 37.5 years, compared to 30.8 for African Americans.[47] The combination of a younger African American population, a lower level of education, and their concentration in economically depressed urban areas has resulted in a much higher unemployment rate for young African Americans. Unemployment can in turn lead to social problems like crime, drug and alcohol abuse, and family dissolution.

African Americans had little political power until after World War II. Owing their freedom from slavery to the "party of Lincoln," most African Americans initially identified with the Republicans, but this loyalty started to change in the 1930s and 1940s under President Franklin D. Roosevelt, who insisted on equal treatment for African Americans in his New Deal programs.[48] After World War II, African Americans came to see the Democrats as the party of civil rights. The 1964 Republican platform position on civil rights espoused *states' rights*—at the time, the creed of southern segregationists—in what appeared to be an effort to win the support of southern white voters.

Virtually all African Americans voted for Lyndon Johnson in 1964, and in presidential elections between 1984 and 2004, their Democratic vote averaged over 86 percent.[49] In the 2004 election, 88 percent of African American voters voted for John Kerry.[50]

Recently, African Americans have become much more important politically because more of them are voting and because they are concentrated in certain geographical areas. African Americans constitute only 0.3 percent of the population in Montana and 0.6 percent in Idaho, but 37 percent in Mississippi, 30 percent in Georgia, and 29 percent in South Carolina.[51] Southern senators and representatives can no longer afford to ignore the African American vote.[52] Evidence of growing African American political power is the dramatic increase in the number of African American state legislators, which rose from 168 in 1970 to 599 in 2004.[53] Georgia has 49 African American state legislators, the most of any state. Alabama, Louisiana, Maryland, Mississippi, New York, and South Carolina all have over 30.[54] In what was one of the most intensely fought U.S. Senate contests in 2006, African American Democrat Harold Ford, Jr. very nearly defeated Republican Bob Corker. A controversial ad run by the Republican party raised charges of racism in the contest.

HISPANICS (LATINOS) Hispanic Americans, who generally prefer to be called Latinos, are not a monolithic group, and while they share a common linguistic heritage in Spanish, they often differ from one another depending on which country they or their forebears emigrated from. Cuban Americans, for instance, tend to be Republicans, while Mexican Americans and Puerto Ricans living on the mainland are disproportionately Democrats.[55] Latinos are politically important in a growing number of states. Nearly two-thirds of Cuban Americans live in Florida, especially in greater Miami. Mainland Puerto Ricans are concentrated in and around New York City; and many Mexican Americans live in the Southwest and California. More than 12 million Hispanics live in California.[56]

A somewhat higher proportion of Cuban Americans earn $50,000 or more than do Mainland Puerto Ricans and Mexican Americans.[57] A recent study found differences among Latinos of Mexican, Puerto Rican, and Cuban descent in partisanship, ideology, and rates of political participation, but widespread support for a liberal domestic agenda, including increased spending on health care, crime and drug control, education, the environment, child services, and bilingual education.[58] But because Hispanics are not politically homogeneous, they are not a united voting bloc.

In the 1990s, America's Hispanic population grew by 58 percent.[59] However, a similar surge in political participation or representation has not accompanied this surge in growth. Researchers cite many reasons for this, including redistricting, low rates of citizenship and motivations for voting, and a lack of common party commitment.

Hispanics have fared worse in redistricting than other groups. The many noncitizens and large younger population among Hispanics diminishes their political power. For example, 9.5 million foreign-born Hispanics are not citizens, and more than half—5.4 million—are in this country illegally. This group of Hispanics cannot vote, nor can those under 18, who make up a greater percentage of the Hispanic population than is found in other ethnic groups. Language problems also reduce Hispanic citizens' voter registration and turnout. Despite their huge increase in population, the redrawing of legislative district boundaries after the 2000 census disappointed Hispanic groups.[60] This has spurred lawsuits as Hispanic activists seek to eliminate gerrymandering (the drawing of district boundaries to benefit a group or party).

Given the overall growth of the Latino population, both major parties are aggressively cultivating Latino candidates. Several Hispanics have been cabinet members. Mel Martinez resigned as secretary of Housing and Urban Development (HUD) to run successfully for the U.S. Senate from Florida in 2004. Ken Salazar, a Latino Democrat, was also elected to the Senate in 2004 from Colorado. Bob Mendez was appointed to the Senate from New Jersey, and then elected in a contested race in 2006. Alberto R. Gonzales left the Texas Supreme Court to join the Bush administration as White House counsel. After John Ashcroft's resignation in November 2004, President George W. Bush nominated Gonzales as his new attorney general.

Ken Salazar, elected to the U.S. Senate from Colorado in 2004, is the fourth U.S. senator of Latino descent in U.S. history. Salazar replaced Ben Nighthorse Campbell, a Native American and Republican, who did not seek reelection. Salazar previously served two terms as Colorado attorney general.

Alberto Gonzales, who served as White House general counsel during George W. Bush's first term, has been a prominent advisor to the president. Bush picked Gonzales to serve as attorney general for his second term in office.

Neither party has developed an effective strategy to mobilize the Hispanic vote. The Democrats, who have historically been the party of new immigrant groups, have done somewhat better among Hispanics than Republicans. Gore carried approximately 65 percent of the Latino vote in 2000, while Kerry only carried 56 percent in 2004. This was largely attributed to Latinos' high level of religiosity and Bush's appeal among highly religious people.

ASIAN AMERICANS   The Census Bureau classifies Asian Americans together for statistical purposes, but, like Latinos, there are significant differences among them in culture, language, and political experience in the United States. Asian Americans include, among others, persons of Chinese, Japanese, Indian, Korean, Vietnamese, Filipino, and Thai origin, as well as persons from the Pacific Islands. As with Latinos, there are

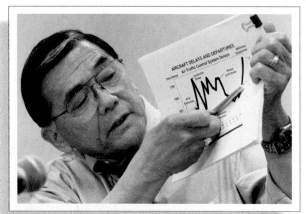

Former Secretary of Transportation Norman Mineta is an Asian American, former Congressman, and was the only Democrat in President George W. Bush's cabinet until he resigned on July 7, 2006.

differences among these subgroups.[61] For example, Japanese Americans were more likely to register as Democrats than Korean Americans or other Asian Americans. Japanese Americans also were somewhat more likely to vote than other Asian ethnic groups.[62]

The United States is home to nearly 13 million Asian Americans and Pacific Islanders, residing primarily in the western states, especially California, Hawaii, and Washington.[63] The number of Asian Americans grew during the 1970s and 1980s, largely as a result of immigration from Southeast Asia. Immigrants from China, India, Korea, the Philippines, and Vietnam account for five of the top ten countries of foreign-born persons living in this country.[64]

Many Asian Americans have done well economically and educationally. Their income is well above the national median. Forty-nine percent of Asian Americans have graduated from college, compared to 28 percent of white Americans and 18 percent of African Americans.[65] Asian Americans are becoming more politically important and more visible in politics. Gary Locke, the first Chinese American governor of a state in the continental United States, served two terms in Washington. Elaine Chao, who emigrated from China at the age of eight, has served as Secretary of Labor in the Bush administration.

THE TIES OF ETHNICITY   Except for Native Americans and the descendants of slaves, all Americans have immigrant ancestors who chose to come to the American continent. Except in the Southwest and Louisiana, most early settlers were English-speaking Protestants; even today, people of English, Scottish, and Welsh background are the largest "ethnic" group in the United States. Irish immigrants, who were largely Catholics, started coming to the United States before the potato famine in Ireland in the 1840s and came in much larger numbers after it. When they arrived, they experienced economic exploitation and religious bigotry. Irish Americans responded by retreating among themselves, forming a strong ethnic consciousness. Other ethnic groups that followed—Germans, Italians, Greeks, Slavs, Jews, and Chinese—each experienced a similar cycle: departure from their homeland and happy arrival here, then discrimination, exploitation, residential clustering, and the formation of a strong group identity.

The largest number of immigrants came between 1900 and 1924, when 17.3 million people relocated to the United States—by far the biggest mass migration to one country in any quarter-century in human history. From 1991 to 2004, the United States welcomed nearly 13 million immigrants,[66] primarily from the Caribbean, Mexico, and Asian countries such as the Philippines, Vietnam, and China. The foreign-born population in the United States has increased from 14 million in 1980 to more than 33 million in 2003. Today there are more foreign-born people in the United States than ever before,[67] although at 10 percent, they represent a smaller proportion of the population than the 14.8 percent of the U.S. population that was foreign born in 1890.[68]

Large numbers of immigrants can pose challenges to any political and social system. Immigrants are often a source of social conflict as they compete with more established groups for jobs, rights, political power, and influence.

How Other Nations Govern

Immigration Politics in Canada

On a proporational basis, Canada has more immigrants each year than does the United States. Canada also allows more skilled immigrants that does the United States, and has a special status for potential immigrants who are willing to invest money in a Canadian business and hire Canadian workers. Unlike American states, the Canadian provinces have some say in whom they will allow as "independent immigrants" (not coming for family reunification or other purposes). The province of Quebec has taken advantage of this policy because it wants to ensure that immigrants either already speak French or are willing to learn it.* Canadians also view immigrants more favorably than the people of any other nation do.

The historic patterns of immigration to Canada and the United States also provide an interesting contrast. Both countries are world leaders in welcoming immigrants, and both countries until 1900 "absorbed large inflows from the British Isles."[†] But Irish Catholics were more likely to go to the United States, while Irish Protestants were more likely to immigrate to Canada. In the last half-century, Canada experienced a "massive demographic shift as hundreds of thousands of non-British, non-French—including many Asians—came in."[‡]

Following the terrorist attacks of September 11, 2001, Canada's immigration policies were criticized for providing a "haven to terrorists."[§] The United States significantly tightened its immigration policies as part of the war on terrorism, but Canada rarely detains refugees who cannot provide identification.[||] The State Department criticized Canada in 2004 as having "lax immigration laws," with implications not only for terrorism but for human trafficking and prostitution. Canadian diplomats responded "that the United States should worry more about the undocumented masses flowing in through its Southern border."[¶] ∎

*Information provided by Earl Fry, Political Science Department, Brigham Young University, February 27, 2004, and May 9, 2006.

†Seymour Martin Lipset, *Continental Divide*, (Routledge, Chapman, and Hall, Inc., 1991), p. 182.

‡Ibid., p. 185

§James Neff, "Few Resources Spent Guarding Canada Border," *Seattle Times*, September 23, 2001, p. A1; see also Bob McDonald, "Bush Showing His Toughness," *Toronto Sun*, September 26, 2001, p. 6.

||Allan Thompson, "Is Canada Really the Weak Link?" *Toronto Star*, October 6, 2001, p. A1.

¶Sheldon Alberts, "U.S. Raps Canadian Immigration," *Ottawa Citizen*, February 26, 2004, p. A9.

Gender

For most of U.S. history, politics and government were men's business. Women first gained the right to vote primarily in the western territories, beginning with Wyoming in 1869 and Utah in 1870, and then in Colorado and Idaho before 1900.[69] The right was not extended nationally to women until 1920 with passage of the Nineteenth Amendment. The fears of some opponents of *women's suffrage* (the right to vote)—that women would form their own party and vote largely for women or fundamentally alter our political system—have not been realized. During Susan B. Anthony's suffrage campaign in the late nineteenth and early twentieth centuries, Jonas H. Upton, editor of the *Democratic Salem Monitor* in Salem, Oregon, contended that women, if given the right to vote, would combine to vote for war because they were exempt from the draft.[70] Others feared that women would unite to vote for Prohibition.[71]

For a half-century after gaining the right to vote, American women voted at a lower rate than women in other Western democracies.[72] But in the past 12 years, slightly more women than men have voted in presidential elections, and there is no significant difference between the genders in rates of voting in midterm elections.[73] In the 2004 election, women comprised 54 percent of all voters and had a turnout rate 3 percent higher than men.[74] Because women outnumber men, there are more potential female than male voters. Women have chosen to work within the existing political parties and do not overwhelmingly support female candidates, especially if they must cross party lines to do so.[75]

Since 1917, less than 6 percent of representatives in the U.S. House have been women. In the past, women often entered the Senate through appointment after their husband's death. The number of women in Congress reached new highs in the 1990s. Following the 2006 elections, there were nine female governors, sixteen women serving in the Senate, and 71 women in the House with one race still undecided. There

History Makers

Lucretia Mott and Elizabeth Cady Stanton

The movement for voting rights for women, emancipation of the slaves, and Prohibition found early and strong leadership from Lucretia Coffin Mott. She demonstrated her commitment to the abolition of slavery by making her home a station on the Underground Railroad.[*] Women like Mott were key leaders in efforts to prohibit the sale of alcohol, which they believed hurt families and the poor.

But it was overcoming inequality for women that brought Mott together with Elizabeth Cady Stanton. In 1848, they organized the Women's Rights Convention in Seneca Falls, New York.[†] In a document titled the "Declaration of Sentiments of 1848," they called for equal rights and the vote for women.[‡] Another important leader of this movement was Susan B. Anthony. Mott, Stanton, and others had hoped that the Reconstruction Era amendments, which granted voting rights to former slaves, would extend the same rights to women. Although neither Mott nor Stanton lived to see ratificaton of the Nineteenth Amendment in 1920, their leadership helped persuade several states to grant suffrage to women well before that day.

As M. Margaret Conway, a leading scholar on gender and politics, has said, "Initially, women's rate of voter turnout was lower than expected and continued to be lower than that of men until 1980."[§] Since then, the proportion of women voting in presidential elections has consistently exceeded the proportion of men voting.[||] But voting is only one form of political participation. As we explore in this book, women remain underrepresented in elective office, judgeships, and other appointed offices. Mott's and Stanton's hopes have not yet been realized. ∎

[*]William J. Switala, *The Underground Railroad in Pennsylvania* (Stackpole Books, 2001).
[†]E.C. Stanton, S. B. Anthony, and M. J. Gage, eds., *History of Women's Suffrage*, Vol. 1 (1887), p. 70.
[‡]USIA, *Basic Readings in U.S. Democracy: Seneca Falls Declaration, 1848*, at http://usinfo.state.gov/usa/infousa/facts/democrac/17.htm, September 1, 2006.
[§]M. Margaret Conway, Gertrude A. Steuernagel, and David W. Ahern, *Women and Political Participation: Cultural Change in the Political Arena* (CQ Press, 1997), p. 79
[||]Harold W. Stanley and Richard G. Niemi, *Vital Statistics on American Politics, 2005–2006* (CQ Press, 2006), p. 16.

were ten female major-party gubernatorial candidates in 2006, and on election day, six of them were elected. Three of the six successful candidates were Democrats. The proportion of women serving in the House of Representatives is about the same as in the Senate: a little more than 15 percent. In contrast, some state legislative chambers are nearly 40 percent female. The number of female officeholders is rising in part because women are increasingly running in contests in which there is no incumbent.[76]

One group that has aggressively promoted female candidates is EMILY's List, which funds pro-choice Democrats. EMILY is an acronym for "Early Money Is Like Yeast," meaning that campaign contributions given to candidates early in their campaigns can help raise more money, just as yeast helps dough rise. EMILY's List supporters are proud of the fact that there are more women in the U.S. House than ever before. EMILY's List has also helped fund racial and ethnic minority female candidates. Roughly one-third of the candidates it has supported are African American or Latina. Republicans have duplicated EMILY's List with their own political action committee, Wish List, which gives to Republican female candidates who are pro-choice.

Is there a **gender gap**, or a persistent difference between men and women in voting and in attitudes on important issues? Women have typically divided their vote between the two major political parties. However, in recent elections, women have been more likely than men to vote for Democratic presidential candidates (see Figure 5–3). In 2000, Al Gore's share of the vote among women was 12 percent higher than among men.[77] In 2004, women preferred Kerry over Bush by 53 percent to 47 percent.[78]

The women's movement in American politics encompasses a comprehensive agenda, including voting and political rights as well as extending the basic liberties of the Bill of Rights and the Fourteenth Amendment. Women also seek equal opportunity, education, jobs, skills, and respect in what has been a male-dominated system.[79] Women are more likely than men to oppose violence in any form—the death penalty,

gender gap
The difference between the political opinions or political behavior of men and of women.

new weapon systems, or the possession of handguns. Women, as a group, are more compassionate than men in that they are more likely to favor government that provides health insurance and family services. They also identify work and family issues such as day care, maternity leave, and equal treatment in the workplace as important.[80] Other gender issues, some of them focal points in recent elections, include reproductive rights, restrictions on pornography, gun control, and sexual harassment.[81]

There are serious income inequalities between men and women. Nearly twice as many women than men have an annual income of less than $15,000.[82] Because an increasing number of women today are the sole breadwinners for their families, the implications of this low income level are significant. Women earn on average less than men for the same work. Even among college graduates aged 25 to 34, women earn an average of 84 cents for every dollar earned by men of the same age and education level.[83] After controlling for characteristics such as job experience, education, occupation, and other measures of productivity, a U.S. Census Bureau study shows that wage discrimination between the genders is 77 cents on every dollar.[84] As age increases, the earnings gap widens.

In law schools, women now constitute about half of entering classes[85] and of those who land summer jobs at law firms, but only about 17 percent of partners in law firms are women.[86] In business schools women constitute about a third of entering classes,[87] and while they share approximately half of the total decision-making power in management, their earnings are significantly less than that of their male counterparts.[88]

Sexual Orientation

Differences in sexual orientation have become important politically in recent years. The modern movement for expanded rights for gays and lesbians traces its roots to 1969, when New York City police raided the Stonewall Inn, a bar in Greenwich Village, and a riot ensued.[89]

Precise data on the number of homosexuals in the United States are in dispute. The gay and lesbian communities mention a figure of 10 percent; other estimates come in much lower.[90] One source estimates that 2.8 percent of men and 1.4 percent of women identify themselves as homosexual or bisexual.[91] Regardless of its overall size, the homosexual community has become important politically in several cities, notably San Francisco. Both political parties have openly professed gay members of Congress.

In 2000, Vermont became the first state to enact legislation granting gay and lesbian couples "civil union" status, which confers many of the benefits of marriage. Before this law took effect, the Vermont Supreme Court ruled that denying gay couples the same rights and benefits as heterosexual couples was unconstitutional. In 2003, the Massachusetts Supreme Judicial Court ruled that not allowing gay couples to marry was discriminatory, and that the only remedy was full marriage rights for both heterosexual and homosexual couples.[92] This decision pushed gay marriage onto the national agenda. Social conservatives argued that traditional marriage, defined as marriage between a man and a woman, needed constitutional protection, a cause that President Bush endorsed. In the wake of the Massachusetts ruling, mayors in San Francisco and New Paltz, New York authorized their cities to issue marriage licenses and perform same-sex marriages. San Francisco mayor Gavin Newsom said his policy was constitutional because it removed a form of discrimination.[93] However, the state governments of California and New York did not recognize these marriages and successfully sued in court to stop the mayors from issuing licenses.[94] The Massachusetts Supreme Judicial Court ruled in 2006 that its earlier decision applied only to residents of Massachusetts, upholding an old, longstanding law forbidding the state to marry out-of-state individuals who would not be allowed to marry in their home states. The issue of gay marriage has also been debated on the national level, and in June 2006 the Senate rejected a constitutional ban on gay marriage by a margin of 49-48, falling 18 votes short of the two-thirds majority needed to pass a constitutional amendment.[95]

FIGURE 5–3 Gender and the Vote for President, 2004.

SOURCE: Edison Media Research and Mitofsky International's Exit Poll Shows Most Unmarried Women Voted for Kerry http://www.edisonresearch.com/home/archives/WashingtonTimes-1-15-05.pdf, September 5, 2006.

Rosie O'Donnell, a gay parent, is a vocal advocate for gays who want to adopt children. O'Donnell and her partner were among many gay couples that traveled to San Francisco in early 2004 to obtain a marriage license.

The political agenda for gay and lesbian advocacy groups includes fighting discrimination, including the military's "Don't ask, don't tell" policy. On some fronts, the groups have been successful. Many local governments and and private employers now grant health care and other benefits for same-sex domestic partners. Cities, counties, and states have passed antidiscrimination statutes protecting people from discrimination in housing and employment on the basis of sexual orientation. Groups like the Human Rights Campaign advocate eliminating restrictions based on sexual orientation. Hate crimes against gays and lesbians have led some to propose including sexual orientation in federal hate crimes legislation.[96]

To some extent, these efforts have produced a backlash. Congress passed the Defense of Marriage Act in 1996, which excludes same-sex spouses from federal benefits. Conservative groups with support from conservative Protestants, Catholics, and Mormons were successful in enacting initiatives in 13 states in 2004 defining marriage as a union between a man and a woman. Congress considered but did not enact a proposed constitutional amendment along the same lines. Democrats accused Republicans of trying to exploit the marriage issue for partisan advantage.

The courts have also been drawn into the battle over sexual orientation. In 2000, the Supreme Court ruled 5 to 4 that requiring the Boy Scouts of America to allow homosexuals to occupy local leadership positions violated their First Amendment right to freedom of association.[97] However, just three years later, the Supreme Court's decision in *Lawrence* v. *Texas* overturned state laws against sodomy.[98] This decision could provide a basis for a more expansive set of court decisions on same-sex marriage.

Family Structure

Over the past half-century, the typical American family has been transformed from a "traditional family" (mother and father married, with children in the home) to a variety of living arrangements and family structures. Americans are much more likely to approve of premarital sex than they did in the early 1970s. From 1996 to 2002, the number of Americans who cohabit (live with someone of the opposite sex without being married) increased by 50 percent.[99] Cohabitation raises public policy questions, such as whether the live-in partner is eligible for employment benefits and welfare payments. Contraception is widely used and accepted, and yet over one-third of all births now occur to unmarried women.[100] Because unmarried women tend to have lower incomes, these children will often need social services and financial assistance.

People now marry later in life: The average age for first marriage for men is 27; for women it is 26.[101] Yet marrying later has not reduced the divorce rates. On the contrary, the divorce rate nearly doubled between 1950 and 1996. Today it is estimated that about half of all marriages will end in divorce.[102]

Since the 1960s, birthrates have steadily declined in the United States. In the early 1960s, a woman statistically averaged about 3.5 children. By 2001, that number dropped to 2.1 children, barely meeting the 2.1 needed to replace the population. In other words, if the current trend continues, the American native-born population will actually decrease over time.[103] Some other countries have even lower average fertility rates per woman: Japan 1.3, Italy 1.3, Spain 1.3, and Sweden 1.6.[104]

Divorce is one reason why the number of households headed by women has risen. Attitudes about the role of women in marriage and the family have also changed. In 1972, one-third of Americans thought that a woman belonged in the home and should not work outside it, but in 1998, only one-sixth of all Americans felt this way.[105]

Religion

In many parts of the world, religious differences, especially when combined with disputes over territory or sovereignty, are a source of violence. The conflict between Israelis and Palestinians has involved suicide bombers who kill Israeli civilians along with themselves, and Israeli attacks on Palestinian settlements and leaders. The war between India and Pakistan over Kashmir is largely a religious battle between Muslims and Hindus, as are the conflicts between Muslims and Christians in Indonesia

The risk of having children later in life has recently been the subject of cover stories in news magazines.

and Nigeria. Other countries like Afghanistan, Lebanon, Sri Lanka, and Sudan have also experienced intense religious conflicts in recent years. The Shi'ite–Sunni conflict among different branches of Islam threatens the stability of the new government in Iraq.

Jews have often been the target of religious discrimination and persecution (anti-Semitism), which reached its greatest intensity in the Holocaust of the 1940s, during which the Nazis murdered an estimated 6 million Jews.[106] The United States has not been immune from such hatred, despite its principle of religious freedom. In 1838, Governor Lilburn W. Boggs of Missouri issued an extermination order against the Mormons.[107]

Our government is founded on the premise that religious liberty flourishes when there is no predominant or official faith, which is why the framers of the Constitution did not sanction a national church. In fact, James Madison wrote in *The Federalist*, No. 51, "In a free government the security for civil rights must be the same as that for religious rights. It consists in the one case in the multiplicity of interests, and in the other in the multiplicity of sects" (see the Appendix).

The absence of an official American church does not mean that religion is unimportant in American politics; indeed, there were established churches in individual states in this country until the 1830s. Some observers contend that "the root of American political and social values . . . is the distinctive Puritanism of the early New England settlers."[108] Politicians frequently refer to God in their speeches or demonstrate their piety in other ways. In 2000, Democratic vice presidential candidate Joseph Lieberman, an observant Jew, frequently mentioned God and religion in his speeches. George W. Bush concluded his 2004 State of the Union Address, in many ways the kick-off for his reelection campaign, by saying "We can trust in that greater power who guides the unfolding of the years. And in all that is to come, we can know that His purposes are just and true. May God bless the United States of America. Thank you."[109] The title he selected for his political memoir, *A Charge to Keep*, made a more subtle reference to religion. It comes from a hymn that many Protestants will recognize and presumably approve of. The second verse of the hymn reads, "To serve the present age—My calling to fulfill—O may it all my powers engage—To do my Master's will."[110]

At one time, it was thought that a Catholic could not be elected president. The election of 1960 resolved that issue. John F. Kennedy directly confronted the question of whether a Catholic would put aside religious teachings if they conflicted with constitutional obligations. He said, "I am not the Catholic candidate for President. I am the Democratic party's candidate for President who happens also to be Catholic. I do not speak for my church on public matters, and the church does not speak for me."[111] Nevertheless, a candidate's religion may still become an issue today if the candidate's religious convictions on sensitive issues such as abortion threaten to conflict with public obligations.

During the 2004 Democratic party battle for the presidential nomination, Howard Dean initially contended that candidates should not interject religion into politics. In a town hall meeting in New Hampshire, Dean criticized President Bush for his opposition to stem-cell research saying, "I think we ought to make scientific decisions, not theological and theoretical decisions."[112] When challenged on this comment, especially in light of the importance of religion in the South, he retreated to his original position, that religion plays a role in his decision making, citing religion as important to his support of civil unions as governor. Dean's flip-flop on religion in 2004 is an example of the continuing importance of religion, at least in many parts of the country.

Religion has also been an important catalyst for political change. The Catholic church helped overthrow communism in parts of eastern Europe. Black churches provided many of the leaders in the American civil rights movement. As Taylor Branch explains in his history of the civil rights movement, the black church "served not only as a place of worship but also as a bulletin board to a people who owned no organs of communication, a credit union to those without banks, and even a kind of people's court."[113] African American ministers, like the Reverend Martin Luther King, Jr., became leaders of the civil rights movement; others, like Jesse Jackson and more

"In a free government the security for civil rights must be the same as that for religious rights. It consists in the one case in the multiplicity of interests, and in the other in the multiplicity of sects."

JAMES MADISON, *THE FEDERALIST*, NO. 51

"We can trust in the greater power who guides the unfolding of the years. And in all that is to come, we can know that His purposes are just and true. May God bless the United States of America. Thank you."

PRESIDENT GEORGE W. BUSH,
2004 STATE OF THE UNION ADDRESS

fundamentalists
Conservative Christians who as a group have become more active in politics in the last two decades and were especially influential in the 2000 presidential election.

recently Al Sharpton, have run for national office. Hence, religion can be not only a source of personal values but also a foundation for political activity.

More recently, political activity among fundamentalist Christians has increased. Led by ministers like Jerry Falwell and Pat Robertson, evangelicals (sometimes called **fundamentalists**) have supported political organizations such as the Moral Majority and the Christian Coalition. For two decades, they have sought to influence the national agenda, and Robertson taped telephone endorsements for George W. Bush in 2000. Christian conservatives have also been active at the local level—school boards, city councils, mayorships, and local GOP leadership.[114] Their agenda includes the return of school prayer, the outlawing of abortion, restrictions on homosexuals, and opposition to gun control and to the teaching of evolution in public schools. (To learn more about the Christian Coalition, go to www.cc.org.)

Many Americans take their religious beliefs seriously, more so than people of other democracies.[115] Approximately a quarter of Americans seldom attend houses of worship, 15 percent at least once a month, 11 percent almost every week, and 35 percent at least once a week.[116] Religion, like ethnicity, is a *shared identity*. People identify themselves as Baptist, Catholic, Jewish, or Buddhist. Sometimes religious attendance or nonattendance rather than belonging to a particular religion or denomination determines attitudes toward issues. "Among both Catholics and Protestants, opposition to abortion increases with frequency of church attendance, but the percentages expressing pro-choice and pro-life sentiments are quite similar for the Catholic and Protestant groups."[117]

The United States has a tremendous variety of religious denominations. About half the people in the United States describe themselves as Protestant (see Figure 5–4). The largest Protestant denomination is Baptist, followed by Methodists, Lutherans, Presbyterians, Pentecostals, and Episcopalians. Because Protestants are divided among so many different churches, Catholics have the largest single membership in the United States, constituting nearly a quarter of the population.[118] Jews represent 2 percent of the population.[119] Muslims number more than 1,100,000.[120]

Religion is important in American politics in part because people of particular religions are concentrated in a few states. Catholics, as noted, make up nearly a quarter of the U.S. population, yet they number over half of the population of Rhode Island.[121] Baptists represent 16 percent of the U.S. population, yet they account for roughly a third of the population of Mississippi and Alabama.[122] Mormons represent less than 2 percent of the U.S. population but constitute two-thirds of the population of Utah.[123] The state of New York has the highest percentage of Jews with 9 percent; the New York City metro area is 11 percent Jewish.[124]

In recent presidential elections, most Protestants voted Republican, while most Catholics and Jews voted Democratic.[125] However, in 2004, Bush received a majority of the Catholic vote and increased his majority among Protestants to 59 percent. Kerry received 75 percent of the Jewish vote. The perception among many Catholics and Jews

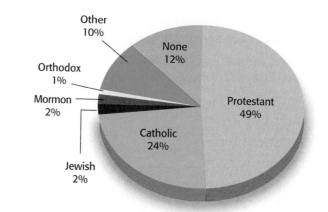

FIGURE 5–4 Religious Groups in America.

SOURCE: The Gallup Organization, www.gallup.com/poll/focus/sr040302.asp.

that the Democratic party is more open to them helps explain the strength of their Democratic identification. Democrats won the loyalty of many Catholics by their willingness to nominate Al Smith for the presidency in 1928 and John Kennedy in 1960. Jewish voters' long-standing identification with the Democratic party may have been reinforced by Al Gore's selection of Joseph Lieberman to be his running mate in 2000. Southern Protestants have been Democrats for different reasons, having largely to do with the sectional issues discussed earlier.

Religious groups vary in their rates of participation. In recent elections Jews have the highest rate of reported voter turnout, over 90 percent in 2000 and 2004, while those who claim no religious affiliation have the lowest, an average of 60 percent in 2000 and 2004.[126]

Religion can be related to other politically important characteristics. For instance, Jews are the most prosperous and best educated of any ethnic or religious group. Nearly 54 percent of Jewish adults are college graduates, compared to 29 percent of non-Hispanic white Protestants and 27 percent of non-Hispanic Catholics.[127] More than one in four Jews in the United States has a postgraduate education.[128] In this example, as in others, religion is a cross-cutting cleavage in American politics; the differences do not reinforce one another. On the basis of income and education, we might expect Jews to be Republicans, but 79 percent of American Jews voted for Al Gore in 2000.[129] Catholics had cross-pressures in 2004 because John Kerry is Catholic. This did not stop a majority of Catholics from voting for Bush, and Catholics who attend church weekly gave him 56 percent of their votes. Southern white Protestants who were 64 percent Democratic in 1960 are now 52 percent Republican.[130]

Wealth and Income

The United States is a wealthy nation. Indeed, to some knowledgeable observers, "the most striking thing about the United States has been its phenomenal wealth."[131] Most Americans lead comfortable lives. They eat and live well and have first-class medical care. But the unequal distribution of wealth and income results in political divisions and conflicts.

Wealth (total value of possessions) is more concentrated than income (annual earnings). The wealthiest families hold most of the property and other forms of wealth like stocks and savings. Historically, concentrated wealth fosters an aristocracy. Thomas Jefferson sought to break up the "aristocracy of wealth" by changing from laws based on *primogeniture* (the eldest son's exclusive right to inherit his father's estate) to laws that encouraged or compelled people to divide their estates equally among all their children. Jefferson sought to encourage an "aristocracy of virtue and talent" through a public school system open to all for the primary grades and for the best students through the university level.[132]

Most college students come from the top quarter of American families in income—those earning $50,000 a year or more. Education is in turn one of the most important means to achieve upward economic and social mobility. People who go to college earn more than those who have not, and those from wealthier families are more inclined to get an education at nearly twice the rate as those positioned lower on the socioeconomic ladder.[133]

College tuition and other costs have climbed substantially in recent years. Tuition, for example, rose 144 percent, on average, at public colleges and universities and 113 percent at private institutions since 1990.[134] Rising costs affect low-income students more than others. These students come from families that are less likely to be able to help pay these costs. "College costs eat up 71% of earnings for low-income families but only 6% of the income of the top 25% of earners."[135] Some colleges' shift away from a need-based system of scholarships has also hurt low-income students. Part of the problem for low-income students is also a success story. Because more of them now qualify for admission, the competition for support has become more intense.

The framers of the Constitution recognized the dangers of an unequal concentration of wealth. "The most common and durable source of factions has been the various

"Those who hold, and those who are without property, have ever formed distinct interests in society."

JAMES MADISON, *THE FEDERALIST*, NO. 10

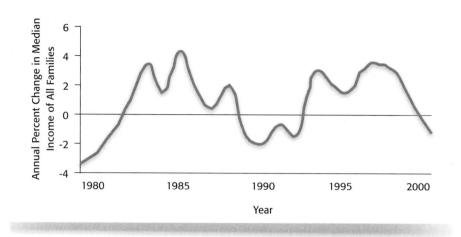

FIGURE 5–5 Median Family Income, 1980–2003.

SOURCE: Harold W. Stanley and Richard G. Niemi, *Vital Statistics on American Politics, 2005–2006* (CQ Press, 2006), pp. 366–367.

and unequal distribution of property," wrote James Madison in *The Federalist*, No. 10 (reprinted in the Appendix). "Those who hold, and those who are without property, have ever formed distinct interests in society." Madison was right. Economic differences often lead to conflict, and Americans remain divided politically along economic lines. Aside from race, income may be the single most important factor in explaining views on issues, partisanship, and ideology. Most rich people are Republicans, and most poor people are Democrats, and this has been true since at least the Great Depression of the 1930s.

Between the 1950s and the 1970s inflation-adjusted income doubled. More recently, as Figure 5–5 shows, inflation-adjusted income has gone up and down.[136] Why has the pattern changed? Some economists cite higher energy costs, low levels of personal savings, and the worldwide slowdown in productivity.[137] More recent data, however, point to increased productivity, in part due to the rising use of computers and information technology.[138] While the long-term trend has been for income to rise, the income of the bottom 10 percent of the population has actually declined. At the same time, the income of the top 10 percent has grown substantially. Economists refer to this as *dispersion*, or the difference in growth patterns among income levels.

The bottom 12.7 percent in income is also the segment of the population that falls below the poverty line.[139] In 2005, the official poverty level for a family of four with two children was an income below $19,806.[140] Families headed by a single female are more than two times as likely to fall below the poverty line than families headed by a single male, with 28 percent of all households headed by females falling below the poverty line.[141] Over 36 percent of the poor are children under 18 years of age, and many appear to be trapped in a cycle of poverty (see Figure 5–6).[142] African American and Hispanic children are more than twice as likely to be poor as white children.[143]

The definition of poverty is itself political, and a change in the definition of poverty can make it appear that there are more or fewer poor people than before. Defining

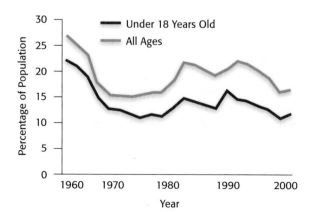

FIGURE 5–6 Percentage of Americans Living in Poverty, by Age, 1959–2000.

Agents of Change

Neil Cantor, Timothy Prestero, and Design that Matters

Design that Matters was founded at the Massachusetts Institute of Technology in 2001 to direct the resources of higher education toward social innovation for the purpose of alleviating poverty in under-resourced communities. The nonprofit has worked with students in four continents to develop technologies such as the "Kinkajou" Microfilm Projector, which improves teaching conditions for nighttime literacy classes in Mali, Africa, and an improved IV drip device, which improves clinical treatment of diseases such as cholera in the developing world.

"The goal isn't to create more problems for a community," Timothy Prestero explains. "We don't want our products to make waste, or burden communities with expense, because then they simply aren't going to use it." Having graduated from MIT with two master's degrees in Mechanical and Oceanographic Engineering, the 33-year-old Prestero felt himself driven toward a career in social change. "Service is a family tradition," he says. "I wanted to do something useful with my career." He served as a Peace Corps volunteer in the Ivory Coast, Africa, right after college, where he discovered that most poor communities want to improve their situation but often lack the tools to take advantage of their own resources.

Design that Matters focuses on bringing intellectual capital to social enterprises in the developing world, creating new products and services that allow social entrepreneurs to overcome barriers to better serving their beneficiaries. Through DtM's collaborative design process, over 700 students and students and professional volunteer from around the world have contributed to the development of DtM products—for many their first exposure to problems faced daily by people in underserved communities. DtM volunteers are embracing their role as citizens of the world, and many have realigned their life trajectories to include work in the social sector. ∎

Read more about Design that Matters at www.designthatmatters.org.

QUESTIONS

How does Design that Matters alter the political landscape of university campuses and, perhaps, the U.S. as a whole?

Does your university have any programs that try to help the poor gain the basic economic rights that improve political participation?

Neil Cantor

Timothy Prestero

poverty at a lower or higher level of income also has implications for eligibility for some government programs. The poverty classification is intended to identify persons who cannot meet a minimum standard in such basics as housing, food, and medical care. Regardless of how one defines poverty, however, the poor are a minority who lack political power. They vote less than wealthier people and are less confident and organized in dealing with politics and government. Over the past two decades, inequality between rich and poor has been increasing, unlike in the 1960s, when the gap between rich and poor narrowed.[144] Although the gap began to decrease under the first Bush administration (1989–1993), inequality between rich and poor has risen again since then.[145]

The distribution of income in a society can have important consequences for democratic stability. If enough people believe that only the few at the top of the economic ladder can hope to earn enough for an adequate standard of living, domestic unrest and even revolution may follow. Income is related to participation in politics. People who need the most help from government are the least likely to participate. They are also the most likely to favor social welfare programs.

Occupation

Americans at the time of Jefferson and for several generations thereafter worked primarily on farms, but by 1900, the United States had become the world's leading industrial nation. As workers moved from farms to cities to find better-paying jobs, American cities rapidly grew. Labor conditions, including child labor, the length of the work week, and safety conditions in mines and factories, became important political issues. New technology, combined with abundant natural and human resources, meant that the U.S. **gross domestic product (GDP)** rose, after adjusting for inflation, by more than 333 percent from 1960 to 2004.[146]

The United States has recently entered what Daniel Bell, a noted sociologist, labeled the "postindustrial" phase of its development. "A post-industrial society, being primarily a technical society, awards less on the basis of inheritance or property . . . than on education and skill."[147] *Knowledge* is the organizing device of the postindustrial era. Postindustrial societies have greater affluence and a class structure less defined along traditional labor-versus-management lines.

Figure 5–7, which shows the percentage of U.S. workers in various occupations, demonstrates the changing dynamics of the American labor force. The white-collar sector of our economy has grown tremendously. This sector includes managers, accountants, and lawyers, as well as professionals and technicians in such rapid-growth areas as computers, communications, finance, insurance, and research. A dramatic decline in the number of people engaged in agriculture and a more modest decline in the number of people in manufacturing (which together make up the blue-collar sector) has accompanied this shift. Today agriculture employs only 1.6 percent of working Americans, and manufacturing employs only 11.8 percent.[148] Governments are among the biggest employers in this country. Federal, state, and local governments account for more than 18 percent of our gross domestic product.[149]

Women and racial minorities have distinct occupational patterns. Men hold most blue-collar jobs.[150] As noted earlier, women generally earn less than men of the same age and education. Occupations in which women predominate, like teaching and clerical work, are generally lower-paying than industrial or management jobs. And as women try to advance in their careers, especially in management, they encounter a barrier that has been referred to as the "glass ceiling."

gross domestic product (GDP)
The total output of all economic activity in the nation, including goods and services.

socioeconomic status (SES)
A division of population based on occupation, income, and education.

SOCIAL CLASS   Why do Americans not divide themselves into social classes as Europeans do? American workers have not formed their own political party, nor does class seem to dominate our political life. Marxist categories of *proletariat* (those who sell their labor) and *bourgeoisie* (those who own or control the means of production) are far less important here than they have been in Europe. Still, we do have social classes and what social scientists call **socioeconomic status (SES)**—a division of the population based on occupation, income, and education.

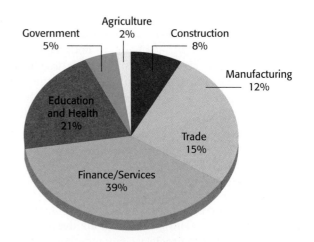

FIGURE 5–7 Occupational Groups, 2002.

SOURCE: U.S. Bureau of the Census, *Statistical Abstract of the United States, 2006* (Government Printing Office, 2006), p. 404.

Most Americans say they are "middle class." Few admit to seeing themselves as lower class or upper class. In many other industrial democracies, large proportions of the population think of themselves as "working class" rather than middle class.[151] In England, nearly three out of five persons identify themselves as working class.[152] But Americans rarely use that designation.

What constitutes the "middle class" in the United States is highly subjective. For instance, some individuals perform working-class tasks (such as plumbing), but their income places them in the middle class or even the upper-middle class. A school-teacher's income is below that of many working-class jobs, but in terms of status, teaching ranks among middle-class jobs.

Americans may define themselves as middle class because the American dream involves upward mobility. Or their responses may reflect the hostility many feel toward organized labor. In any case, compared to many countries, class divisions in the United States are less defined and less important to politics. As political scientist Seymour Martin Lipset has written, "The American social structure and values foster an emphasis on competitive individualism, an orientation that is not congruent with class consciousness, support for socialist or social democratic parties, or a strong union movement."[153]

"It's like this. If the rich have money, they invest. If the poor have money, they eat."

Age

Americans are living longer, a phenomenon that has been dubbed the "graying of America" (Figure 5–8). This demographic change has increased the proportion of the population over age 65 and increased the demand for medical care, retirement benefits, and a host of other age-related services. Persons over the age of 65 constitute less than 13 percent of the population yet account for more than 26 percent of the total medical expenditures.[154] With the decreasing birthrate discussed earlier, the graying of America has given rise to concern about maintaining an adequate workforce in the future. Other industrialized countries are also experiencing this demographic shift.[155]

Older Americans are more politically aware and vote more often than younger Americans, making them a potent political force. Their vote is especially important in western states and in Florida, the state with the largest proportion of people over age 65. The "gray lobby" not only votes in large numbers but also has four other political assets not found in other age groups that make it politically powerful: disposable income, discretionary time, a clear focus on issues, and effective organization. When older Americans compete for their share of the budget pie, the young, minorities, and the poor often lose out.[156]

Legislative victories have changed the lives of older citizens. For instance, the poverty rate among the elderly dropped from 15.7 percent in 1980 to 10.2 percent in

FIGURE 5–8 Percentage of Population over Age 65, 1900–2000.

SOURCE: U.S. Bureau of the Census, www.census.gov/statab/hist/HS-03.pdf.

2003, a change partly due to improved medical benefits—Medicare and Medicaid—enacted during the 1960s.[157] As a group, older Americans fight to protect Social Security; they value Medicare and favor prescription drug coverage. They are effectively represented by lobbying groups like the American Association of Retired Persons (AARP). Despite their desire for services that benefit themselves, seniors also favor tax cuts.

Congress passed a limited prescription drug benefit in 2003. The measure was not popular with some conservative Republicans who felt it was too expensive, or with some Democrats who felt the plan did not go far enough. Early indications are that the costs of the program will exceed projected costs at the time the legislation passed. Other concerns with the new program centered on its complexity.[158] Defenders of the plan see it as giving access to prescriptions to some seniors who previously could not afford them.[159]

Age is important to politics in two additional ways: life cycle and generational effects. *Life-cycle effects* have shown that as people become middle-aged, they become more politically conservative, less mobile, and more likely to participate in politics. As they age further and rely more on the government for services, they tend to grow more liberal.[160] Young people, in contrast, are more mobile and less concerned about the delivery of government services.

Several groups made registering younger voters and getting them to the polls a high priority in 2004. Exit polls from the 2004 election found that turnout among those 18 to 29 years old rose from 42 percent in 2000 to 51 percent in 2004. An estimated 4.6 million more 18- to 29-year-olds voted in 2004. But because overall turnout was higher in 2004, the proportion of the voters aged 18 to 29 remained constant at 17 percent.[161]

Generational effects in politics arise when a particular generation has had experiences that make it politically distinct. For example, for those who lived through it, the Great Depression of the 1930s shaped their lifelong views of political parties, issues, and political leaders. Some members of this generation saw Franklin D. Roosevelt as the leader who saved the country by pulling it out of the depression; others felt he sold the country down the river by launching too many government programs. More recently and to a lesser extent, the baby boomers shared a common and distinctive political experience. These Americans came of age politically in the 1960s and 1970s during the civil rights movement and the Vietnam War.

Education

Differences in education affect not only economic well-being but political participation and involvement as well. Thomas Jefferson wrote of education, "Enlighten the people generally, and tyranny and oppressions of body and mind will vanish like evil spirits at the dawn of day."[162] Most Americans are educated in public schools. Nine out of every ten students in kindergarten through high school attend public schools, and more than three out of four college students are in public institutions.[163]

Only recently has the number of college graduates in America surpassed the number of persons who did not graduate from high school.[164] Just over half of all Americans have not gone to college, though many college students assume that almost everyone goes to college. Around 28 percent of whites are college graduates, compared to 17 percent of African Americans and 12 percent of Hispanics; roughly 19 percent of African Americans and 41 percent of all Hispanics left school before completing high school (see Table 5–3).[165]

Education is one of the most important variables in predicting political participation, confidence in dealing with government, and awareness of issues. Education is also related to the acquisition of democratic values. People who have failed to learn the prevailing norms of American society are far more likely to express opposition to democratic and capitalist ideals than those who are well educated and politically knowledgeable.[166]

"Enlighten the people generally, and tyranny and oppressions of body and mind will vanish like evil spirits at the dawn of day."

THOMAS JEFFERSON

TABLE 5–3 Educational Attainment in the United States

Percent of Population—Highest Educational Level Attained

	Population (1,000)	Not a High School Graduate	High School Graduate	Bachelor's Degree	Advanced Degree
Age					
18 to 24 years old	27,824	29	65	6	–
25 to 34 years old	39,201	13	56	30	7
35 to 44 years old	43,573	12	60	20	9
45 to 54 years old	41,069	10	60	18	12
55 to 64 years old	28,375	14	57	16	12
65 to 74 years old	18,238	24	56	13	7
75 years old or over	16,421	31	52	11	6
Sex (Persons 25 years old and over)					
Male	86,558	15	54	19	10
Female	97,319	15	59	18	8
Race (Persons 25 years old and over)					
White	155,557	14	58	19	9
Black	20,812	19	63	13	5
Hispanic	21,596	42	46	9	3
Asian/Pacific Islander	8,312	13	38	32	17

SOURCE: U.S. Census Bureau, *Educational Attainment in the United States: 2004*, www.census.gov/population/www/socdemo/education/cps2004.html, May 6, 2006.
NOTE: Percentages may not add up to 100 percent due to rounding error. "High school graduate" percentages and "some college" percentages are combined.

Unity in a Land of Diversity

As remarkable as American diversity is, the existence of a strong and widely shared sense of national unity and identity may be even more remarkable. Writing about the United States some years ago, a famous reporter, John Gunther, summarized the insights he gained from traveling around the country:

> Whoever invented the motto *E Pluribus Unum* [out of many, one] has given the best three-word description of the United States ever written. The triumph of America is the triumph of a coalescing federal system. Complex as the nation is almost to the point of insufferability, it interlocks. Homogeneity and diversity—these are the stupendous rival magnets. . . . Think of the United States as an immense blanket or patchwork quilt solid with different designs and highlights. But, no matter what colors burn and flash in what corners, the warp and woof, the basic texture and fabric, is the same from corner to corner, from end to end.[167]

Social scientists sometimes speak of the "melting pot," meaning that as various ethnic groups associate with other groups, they are assimilated into American society and come to share democratic values like majority rule, individualism, and the ideal of America as a land of opportunity. Critics have argued that the melting pot idea assumes that there is something wrong with differences between groups, and that these distinctions should be discouraged. In its place, they propose the concept of the "salad bowl," in which "though the salad is an entity, the lettuce can still be distinguished from the chicory, the tomatoes from the cabbage."[168]

As this chapter has demonstrated, regional, social and economic differences have important political consequences. They influence public opinion, participation, voting, interest groups, and political parties. At the same time, our country has achieved a sense of unity despite our remarkable diversity.

Summary

1. The character of a political society and its social environment are important to understanding its politics and government.
2. America is a nation of immigrants. Different family structures and religions reflect our diversity of race and culture. Americans also differ in wealth and income, occupation, social class, age, and education. Gender and sexual orientation have recently become politically and socially more important. Most divisions in the United States cut across demographic categories rather than reinforce them.
3. Geography, room to grow, abundant natural resources, wealth, and relative isolation from foreign entanglements help explain American politics and traditions, including the notions of manifest destiny, ethnocentrism, and isolationism.
4. Until recently, the South was a distinct region in the United States, in large part because of its agricultural base and its history of slavery and troubled race relations. With migration from other parts of the country and the impact of the civil rights movement, it is becoming more Republican. Recently, the most significant migration in the United States has been from cities to suburbs. Today many large American cities are increasingly poor, African American, and Democratic, surrounded by suburbs that are primarily middle class, white, and Republican.

5. Race has been and remains among the most important of the differences in our political landscape. Although we fought a civil war over freedom for African Americans, racial equality was largely postponed until the latter half of the twentieth century. Ethnicity, including the rising numbers of Hispanics, continues to be a factor in politics.
6. Gender is important in American politics. Women now play important roles in our government, and they differ from men in their attitudes on some issues. Sexual orientation policies, especially relating to same-sex marriage, are among the most contentious in our society.
7. Since World War II, attitudes toward sexuality, marriage, and family have changed in important ways. More people cohabit, and those who marry are older. Divorce has also become much more commonplace. Changing family structures and attitudes affect our tax policies, child care, parental leave, and gender equality. They are also important political issues.
8. The United States has many religious denominations, and these differences help explain public opinion and political behavior. Important differences also exist between Americans who are religious and those who are not.
9. Although the United States is a land of wealth with a large middle class,

not everyone has an adequate share in the American economic success. Poverty has grown over the past two decades, and it is most concentrated among African Americans, Native Americans, Hispanics, and single-parent households. Women as a group continue to earn less than men, even in the same occupations. Differences in income and wealth remain important.
10. The United States has shifted from an agricultural to an industrial and now to a postindustrial society, with consequences for occupations and politics. Governments are a major source of employment. Social class is less important in America than in other industrialized democracies.
11. Age and education are important to understanding American politics. Older citizens participate much more than young voters and are a potent political force. Education not only opens up economic opportunities in America but also explains many important aspects of political participation.
12. Despite our diversity, Americans share an important unity. We are united by our shared commitment to democratic values, economic opportunity, work ethic, and the American dream.

Further Reading

DOUGLAS L. ANDERSON, RICHARD BARTNETT, AND **DONALD BOGUE,** *The Population of the United States*, 3d ed. (Free Press, 1996).

DAVID H. BENNETT, *The Party of Fear* (University of North Carolina Press, 1990).

EARL BLACK AND **MERLE BLACK,** *The Rise of Southern Republicans* (Belknap Press, 2002).

DAVID T. CANON, *Race, Redistricting, and Representation: The Unintended Consequences of Black Majority Districts* (University of Chicago Press, 1999).

MAUREEN DEZELL, *Irish America: Coming Into Clover* (Anchor Books, 2000).

JULIE ANNE DOLAN, MELISSA M. DECKMAN, AND **MICHELLE L. SWERS,** *Women in Politics* (Prentice Hall, 2006).

LOIS LOVELACE DUKE, ED., *Women in Politics: Outsiders or Insiders?* 4th ed. (Prentice Hall, 2005).

SARAH H. EVANS, *Born for Liberty: A History of Women in America* (Free Press, 1989).

GEOFFREY FOX, *Hispanic Nation: Culture, Politics and the Constructing of Identity* (Birch Lane Press, 1996).

RODOLFO O. DE LA GARZA, LOUIS DE SIPIO, F. CHRIS GARCIA, JOHN GARCIA, AND **ANGELO FALCON,** *Latino Voices: Mexican, Puerto Rican, and Cuban Perspectives on American Politics* (Westview Press, 1992).

JOHN C. GREEN, MARK J. ROZELL, AND **CLYDE WILCOX,** EDS., *The Christian Right in American Politics: Marching to the Millenium* (Georgetown University Press, 2003).

DONALD R. KINDER AND **LYNN M. SANDERS,** *Divided by Color: Racial Politics and Democratic Ideals* (University of Chicago Press, 1996).

MATTHEW D. LASSITER, *The Silent Majority: Suburban Politics in the Sunbelt South* (Princeton University Press, 2005).

TAEKU LEE, S. KARTHICK RAMAKRISHNAN, AND **RICARDO RAMIREZ,** *Transforming Politics, Transforming America: The Political and Civic Incorporation of Immigrants in the United States (Race, Ethnicity, and Politics)* (University Press of Virginia, 2006).

JAN E. LEIGHLEY, *Strength in Numbers? The Political Mobilization of Racial and Ethnic Minorities* (Princeton University Press, 2001).

PEL-TE LIEN, M. MARGARET CONWAY, AND **JANELLE WONG,** *The Politics of Asian Americans* (Routledge, 2004).

JEREMY D. MAYER, *Running On Race: Racial Politics in Presidential Campaign, 1960–2000* (Random House, 2002).

NANCY E. MCGLEN, KAREN O'CONNOR, LAURA VAN ASSENDELFT, AND **WENDY GUNTHER-CANADA,** *Women, Politics, and American Society,* 4th ed. (Longman, 2004).

S. KARTHICK RAMAKRISHNAN, *Democracy in Immigrant America: Changing Demographics and Political Participation* (Stanford University Press, 2005).

MARK ROBERT RANK, *One Nation, Underprivileged: Why American Poverty Affects Us All* (Oxford University Press, 2004).

STANLEY A. RENSHON, ED., *One America? Political Leadership, National Identity, and the Dilemmas of Diversity* (Georgetown University Press, 2001).

RUBEN G. RUMBAUT AND **ALEJANDRO PORTES,** *Ethnicities: Children of Immigrants in America* (University of California Press, 2001).

ARTHUR M. SCHLESINGER JR., *The Disuniting of America* (Norton, 1992).

PETER H. SCHUCK, *Diversity In America* (Belknap Press, 2003).

JEFFREY M. STONECASH, *Class and Party in American Politics* (Westview Press, 2000).

ALEXIS DE TOCQUEVILLE, *Democracy in America,* ed. J. P. Mayer, trans. George Lawrence (Doubleday, 1969). Originally published 1835.

KENNETH D. WALD, *Religion and Politics in the United States,* 4th ed. (Rowman & Littlefield, 2003).

JANELLE WONG, *Democracy's Promise: Immigrants and American Civic Institutions (The Politics of Race and Ethnicity)* (University of Michigan Press, 2006).

KeyTerms

Chapter 6

Interest Groups

THE POLITICS OF INFLUENCE

★

T IS RARE FOR A POLITICAL LOBBYIST TO BE ON THE COVER OF *TIME* MAGAZINE AS JACK ABRAMOFF WAS IN 2006 WITH THE HEADLINE "THE MAN WHO BOUGHT WASHINGTON: JACK ABRAMOFF TOOK INFLUENCE PEDDLING TO NEW HEIGHTS—AND DEPTHS."[1] JACK ABRAMOFF WAS A WASHINGTON, D.C. LOBBYIST WHO CHARGED CLIENTS MILLIONS OF DOLLARS FOR THE ACCESS HE COULD GIVE THEM TO GOVERNMENT OFFICIALS AND FOR THE RESULTS HE DELIVERED IN FAVORABLE LEGISLATION OR POLICY RULINGS. ABRAMOFF

offered legislators free meals at his restaurant and hosted fundraisers at the four skyboxes he leased at major sports venues in Washington, D.C.[2] Three Republican congressmen also went on golf trips to Scotland funded by Abramoff. He personally was a major donor to Republican candidates and party committees, and several groups he represented as a lobbyist also gave millions of dollars to Republicans.

Some of Abramoff's major clients included seven Indian tribes. Abramoff and his associate Michael Scanlon are accused of defrauding these tribes of many millions of dollars.[3] The tribes ostensibly paid

Abramoff and Scanlon to secure policy rulings or legislation at the state or federal level that was favorable to the gambling casinos the tribes ran. In early 2006, Abramoff pled guilty to three felony counts involving some of these activities.[4] Scanlon also pled guilty and cooperated with the government's ongoing investigation.

Abramoff got his start in partisan politics when he was elected National Chairman of the College Republican National Committee. His campaign manager was Grover Norquist, who later became a prominent antitax leader. Norquist's group, Americans for Tax Reform, received money from the Choctaw Indian tribe before passing funds along to Ralph Reed, another friend of Abramoff. Reed's involvement with Abramoff became a major negative in his unsuccessful 2006 campaign for Georgia lieutenant governor.[5]

Abramoff pled guilty in January 2006 to multiple felony charges and was sentenced to serve time in federal prison and pay more than $21 million in restitution.[6] His sentence was part of a plea bargain between the government and Abramoff in which Abramoff agreed to cooperate with the government's investigation of congressional corruption.[7] Abramoff's associates also face prison time. As a result of Abramoff's criminal behavior, Republican officeholders and congressional and White House staffers have been the subject of intense media scrutiny. Many who had received contributions from Abramoff have now donated those campaign contributions to charity.[8] The Abramoff scandal has increased pressure on Congress to enact lobbying reform.

"You can't swim in the ocean without getting wet; you can't be part of this system without getting dirty."

FORMER SENATOR WARREN RUDMAN

OUTLINE

★

Interest Groups Past and Present: The "Mischiefs of Faction"

★

Types of Interest Groups

★

Characteristics and Power of Interest Groups

★

The Influence of Lobbyists

★

Money and Politics

★

How Much Do Interest Groups Influence Elections and Legislation?

★

Curing the Mischiefs of Faction—Two Centuries Later

Americans have long been concerned about the power of what some call "special interests" and the tendency of groups to pursue self-interest at the expense of less-organized groups or the general public. Restraining the negative tendencies of interest groups while protecting liberty is not easy. Efforts to reform campaign finance and limit the potential for interest groups to corrupt that process while also safeguarding electoral competition are examples of this balancing. In this chapter we examine the full range of interest group activities as well as efforts to limit their potentially negative influences.

faction

A term the founders used to refer to political parties and special interests or interest groups.

pluralism

A theory of government that holds that open, multiple, and competing groups can check the asserted power by any one group.

interest group

A collection of people who share a common interest or attitude and seek to influence government for specific ends. Interest groups usually work within the framework of government and try to achieve their goals through tactics such as lobbying.

Interest Groups Past and Present: The "Mischiefs of Faction"

What we call **interest groups**, the founders of the Republic called **factions**. (They also thought of political parties as factions.) For the framers of the Constitution, the daunting problem was how to establish a stable and orderly constitutional system that would also respect the liberty of free citizens and prevent the tyranny of the majority or of a single dominant interest. As a good practical politician and a brilliant theorist, James Madison offered both a diagnosis and a solution in *The Federalist*, No. 10 (reprinted in the Appendix). He began with a basic proposition: "The latent causes of faction are thus sown in the nature of man." All individuals pursue their self-interest, seeking advantage or power over others. Acknowledging that Americans live in a maze of group interests, Madison argued that the "most common and durable source of factions has been the various and unequal distribution of property." Madison wrote that a faction is "a number of citizens, whether amounting to a majority or minority of the whole, who are united and actuated by some common impulse of passion, or of interest, adversed to the rights of other citizens, or to the permanent and aggregate interests of the community." For Madison, "the *causes* of faction cannot be removed, and . . . relief is only to be sought in the means of controlling its *effects*."[9]

James Madison played a critical role in drafting and enacting the Constitution, and many of the Constitution's provisions have become important in impeding the "mischiefs of faction." Separation of powers and checks and balances make it hard for a faction to dominate government. Staggered terms of office make it necessary for a faction to endure to prevail. But rather than try to greatly limit factions, the Constitution encourages and protects them. Individuals and groups have a right to petition the government and they have freedom of speech. The Constitution envisions a plurality of groups competing with each other, an idea that has been called **pluralism**. How well pluralism has worked in practice is debated.[10] As we will discuss in this chapter, over time government has sought to regulate factions as a response to the power some groups like corporations, unions, and wealthy individuals have had in American government. The debate over interest group power and how to check it without damaging liberty is an enduring one.

Interest groups often use advertising to promote issues that they consider important. This advertisement, created by the National Rifle Association, is a caricature of John Kerry as a dog that "don't hunt." Judging from the animal's appearance, this dog was obviously not bred to be a hunting dog. This mailer attacks Kerry's positions on gun-related issues.

A Nation of Interests

As we noted in Chapter 5, some Americans identify with groups distinguished by race, gender, ethnic background, age, occupation, or sexual orientation. Others form voluntary groups based on issues like gun control or tax reduction. When such associations seek to influence government, they are called **interest groups**.

Interest groups are sometimes called "special interests." Politicians and the media often use this term in a pejorative way. What makes an interest group a "special" one?

The answer is highly subjective. One person's special interest is another's public interest. Some interest groups claim to speak for the "public interest." Yet so-called public interest groups like Common Cause or the League of Women Voters support policies that not everyone agrees with. Politics is best seen as a clash among interests with differing concepts of what is in the public interest rather than a battle between the special interests on one side and "the people" or the public interest on the other.

When political scientists call something an "interest group" or a "special interest," they are not denigrating it. These are general terms to describe a group that speaks for some, but not all, of us. Much of our politics focuses on arguments about what is in the national interest. In a democracy, there are many interests and many organized interest groups. The democratic process exists to decide among those competing interests. Part of the politics of interest groups is to persuade the general public that your group's interest is better, broader, more beneficial, and more general than other groups' and at the same time label groups that oppose yours as "special interests." The term "special interest" conveys a selfish or narrow view, one that may lack credibility. For this reason, in this chapter we use the neutral term "interest groups."

"The latent causes of faction are thus sown in the nature of man."

JAMES MADISON, *THE FEDERALIST,* No. 10

Social Movements

Interest groups sometimes begin as movements. A **movement** consists of many people who are interested in a significant issue, idea, or concern and who are willing to take action to support or oppose it. Examples include the abolitionist, temperance, civil rights, environmental, antitax, animal rights, and women's rights movements. Each movement represents groups that have felt unrepresented by government. Such groups often arise at the grassroots level and spread across the nation. Movements tend to see their causes as morally right and their opponents as morally wrong.

Our Constitution protects the liberties and independence of movements. The Bill of Rights protects movements, whether popular or unpopular, by supporting free assembly, free speech, and due process. Consequently, those who disagree with government policies do not have to engage in violence or other extreme activities in the United States, as they do in some countries, and they need not fear persecution for demonstrating peacefully. In a democratic system that restricts the power of government, movements have considerable room to operate *within* the constitutional system.

Types of Interest Groups

Interest groups vary widely. Some are formal associations or organizations like the National Rifle Association; others have no formal organization. Some are organized primarily to persuade public officials on issues of concern to the group such as restrictions on gun ownership; others conduct research, or influence public opinion by publishing reports and mass mailings.

Interest groups can be categorized into several broad types: (1) economic, including both business and labor; (2) ideological or single-issue; (3) public interest; (4) foreign policy; and (5) government itself. Obviously, these categories are not mutually exclusive. The varied and overlapping nature of interest groups in the United States has been described as *interest group pluralism*, meaning that competition among open, responsive, and diverse groups helps preserve democratic values and limits the concentration of power in any single group.

Most Americans are represented by a number of interest groups, some of which they are aware of and others of which they may not be and with which they may often differ. For instance, citizens over 50 may not be aware that the AARP (which began as the American Association of Retired Persons) claims to represent their interests, and now is open to anyone over age 50, whether retired or not. Others may not know that when they join the American Automobile Association (AAA), they are not only

movement
A large body of people interested in a common issue, idea, or concern that is of continuing significance and who are willing to take action. Movements seek to change attitudes or institutions, not just policies.

purchasing travel assistance and automobile towing when they need it but are also joining a group that lobbies Congress and the Federal Highway Administration on behalf of motorists.

Economic Interest Groups

There are thousands of economic interests: agriculture, consumers, plumbers, the airplane industry, landlords, truckers, bondholders, property owners, and on and on. Economic interests pursue what benefits them, both financially and politically.

BUSINESS   The most familiar business institution is probably the large corporation. Corporations range from one-person enterprises to vast multinational entities. Large corporations—General Motors, AT&T, Microsoft, Coca-Cola, McDonald's, Phillip Morris, Wal-Mart and other large companies—exercise considerable political influence, as do hundreds of smaller corporations (see Table 6–1). Corporate power and a changing domestic and global economy make business practices important political issues. As Microsoft and Wal-Mart have come under heightened government and public scrutiny, their political contributions have grown substantially. Wal-Mart contributed $2,159,290 in 2003–2004 to federal candidates or parties, compared with $75,000 in 1999–2000.[11] Microsoft also donated more than four times the amount in the 2004 cycle than it did in the 1998 cycle.[12]

Small business can have an important voice in public policy. Within the Commerce Department, there is a Small Business Administration. Small businesses are also organized into groups. An example is the National Federation of Independent Business, which is involved in electing pro-business candidates and lobbies the national government on behalf of this constituency.

TRADE AND OTHER ASSOCIATIONS   Businesses with similar interests in government regulations and other issues join together as *trade associations*, which are as diverse as the products and services they provide. Businesses of all types are also organized into large nationwide associations such as the National Mining Association, the National Association of Realtors, and the National Federation of Independent Business.

The broadest business trade association is the Chamber of Commerce of the United States. Organized in 1912, the Chamber is a federation of thousands of local Chambers of Commerce representing tens of thousands of firms. Loosely allied with the Chamber on most issues is the National Association of Manufacturers, which, since its founding in the wake of the depression of 1893, has tended to speak for the more conservative elements of American business.

TABLE 6–1   PACs That Gave the Most to Federal Candidates, 2000–2004 (Millions of Dollars)

	2000	2002	2004
National Association of Realtors	3.42	3.65	3.77
Wal-Mart Stores	0.46	1.08	1.65
National Association of Home Builders	1.85	1.92	2.06
Association of Trial Lawyers of America	2.66	2.81	2.17
International Brotherhood of Electrical Workers	2.62	2.22	2.33
National Auto Dealers Association	2.50	2.58	2.58
Laborers Union	1.79	2.26	2.63
Carpenters and Joiners Union	1.72	2.09	1.88
United Parcel Service	1.76	1.62	2.14
SBC Communications	1.29	1.47	1.95

SOURCE: www.opensecrets.org/pacs/topacs.asp?strid=&cycle=2004&type=C&filter=P&txt=A&Format=Print.

History Makers

John Sherman and the Sherman Antitrust Act

One of the most important pieces of legislation relating to the economy is the Sherman Antitrust Act. This was the first legislation enacted by Congress prohibiting trusts or monopolies. In the 1880s some corporations formed "trusts" to gain greater control of the market. They assigned shares of stock to a single set of trustees, thus forming a monopoly that could control prices and deter competition. The Sherman Act permitted the government to take action against these trusts and break them up.*

The act is named for Senator John Sherman of Ohio, who served in the U.S. Senate for 16 years. He was a candidate for president in 1880 and also served as secretary of the treasury and secretary of state. Beginning in 1888, Sherman began to take an active interest in antitrust legislation. Because he was one of the most senior Republicans in the Senate and was a ranking member of the Senate Finance Committee, Sherman was uniquely positioned to take on the problem of corporate monopolies. He was the primary author of the Sherman Act, which is his most lasting legacy.[†]

Only five years after the Sherman Act was enacted, the Supreme Court did not permit its application in a case involving the American Sugar Refining Company, which controlled 98 percent of all sugar refining in the United States. But with the election of Theodore Roosevelt as president in 1904 and his "trust busting" agenda, the government began to use the Sherman Act with considerable success. The act remains relevant today. In the late 1990s the federal government used the Sherman Act against Microsoft.[‡] John Sherman's leadership in fostering economic competition lives on through the legislation that bears his name. ∎

> *... Sherman was uniquely positioned to take on the problem of corporate monopolies.*

*George Bittlingmayer, "Antitrust and Business Activity: The First Quarter Century," *The Business History Review* 70 (Autumn 1996), p. 377.
[†]William Letwin, *Law and Economic Policy in America* (Random House, 1965), pp. 87–88.
[‡]*Commonwealth of Massachusetts* v. *Microsoft Corporation*, at www.usdoj.gov/atr/cases/f204400/204468.htm, accessed July 7, 2006.

LABOR Workers' associations have a range of interests, from professional standards to wages and working conditions. Labor unions are one of the most important groups representing workers. The American workforce is the least unionized of almost any industrial democracy (see Figure 6–1) and disagreements among unions about tactics and leadership have grown more public and more intense in recent years.

Probably the oldest unions in the United States were farm organizations. The largest farm group now is the American Farm Bureau Federation, which is especially strong in the Corn Belt. Originally organized around government agents who helped farmers in rural counties, the federation today is almost a semigovernmental agency, but it retains full freedom to fight for such goals as price supports and expanded credit. As farms grow bigger and farm workers are less and less likely to be members of the farmer's family, there have been efforts to organize farm workers into unions. Noteworthy here have been the efforts of the late César Chávez and others to organize migrant farm workers.

Throughout the nineteenth century, workers organized political parties and local unions. Their most ambitious effort at national organization, the Knights of Labor, claimed 700,000 members in the 1890s. But by the beginning of the twentieth century, the American Federation of Labor (AFL), a confederation of strong and independent-minded national unions mainly representing craft workers, was the dominant organization. During the ferment of the 1930s, unions more responsive to industrial workers broke away from the AFL and formed a rival national organization organized by industry, the Congress of Industrial Organizations (CIO). In 1955, the AFL and CIO reunited. In the last few years, more than a third of AFL-CIO members (4.5 of 13 million

FIGURE 6-1 **Union Membership in the United States Compared to Other Countries (Estimated Percentage of the Workforce).**

SOURCE: European Industrial Observatory On-line, "Industrial Relations in the EU, Japan, and the US, 2001," at www.eiro.eurofound. eu.int/2002/12/feature/tn0212101f.html.

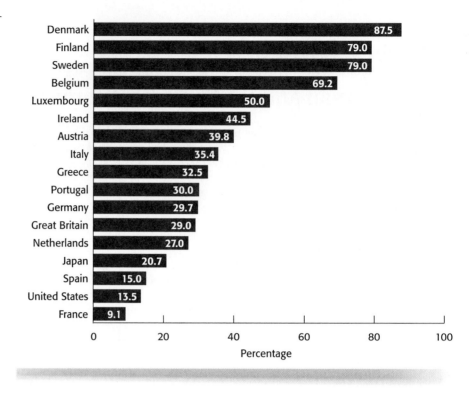

members) affiliated with the Service Employees International Union (SEIU), the International Brotherhood of Teamsters, and two other unions split off from the AFL-CIO, forming a new group named the Change to Win Federation.[13] As a result, unions are less unified and dues payments to the AFL-CIO have fallen by approximately $25 million a year.[14]

Union membership is optional in states whose laws permit the **open shop**, in which workers cannot be required to join a union as a condition of employment. In states with the **closed shop**, workers may be required to join a union to be hired at a particular company if most employees at that company vote to unionize. In both cases, the unions negotiate with management, and all workers share the benefits the unions gain. In open-shop states, many workers may choose not to affiliate with a union because they can secure the same benefits that unionized workers enjoy without incurring the costs of joining the union. When a person benefits from the work or service of an organization like a union (or even a public TV or radio station) without joining or contributing to it, this condition is referred to as the **free rider** problem. We discuss how groups and government deal with the free rider challenge later in the chapter.

The AFL-CIO speaks for about 57 percent of unionized labor,[15] but unions represent just under 14 percent of the nation's workforce (see Figure 6–2).[16] The proportion of the workforce belonging to all unions has fallen in part because of the shift from an industrial to a service and information economy. Dwindling membership limits organized labor's influence. Recently, however, public sector unions have begun to expand, and even some doctors have unionized.

For some years, the Committee on Political Education (COPE) of the AFL-CIO was one of the most respected—and feared—political organizations in the country. In the Kennedy and Johnson years (1961–1969), it won a reputation for political effectiveness. It encouraged and supervised grassroots political activity, and at the national level, it prepared and adopted a detailed platform that spelled out labor's position on issues. Labor contributed money to candidates, ran voter registration and get-out-the-vote

open shop
A company with a labor agreement under which union membership cannot be required as a condition of employment.

closed shop
A company with a labor agreement under which union membership can be a condition of employment.

free rider
An individual who does not join a group representing his or her interests yet receives the benefit of the group's influence.

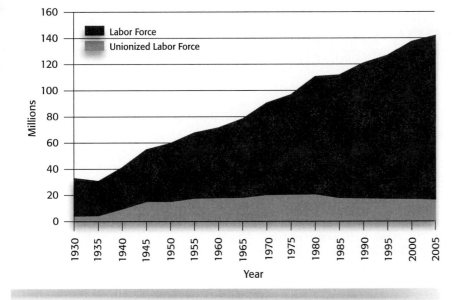

FIGURE 6-2 Labor Force and Union Membership, 1930–2005.

SOURCE: *The World Almanac and Book of Facts, 2000.* Copyright © 1999 Primedia Reference, Inc. Reprinted with permission; all rights reserved. U.S. Bureau of Labor Statistics, at www.stats.bls.gov/news .release/union2.toc. htm and www.bls.gov/cps/ cpsaat40.pdf. 2005 data taken from Department of Labor, Bureau of Labor Statistics. "Union Members in 2005," January 20, 2006, at www.bls.gov/news. release/pdf/union2.pdf, accessed September 25, 2006.

campaigns, and otherwise supported its favorite candidates. In recent elections, COPE has had a fairly successful record of wins for its endorsed House and Senate candidates.[17] In 1993, labor unions invested heavily in the fight against the North American Free Trade Agreement (NAFTA), claiming it would cost jobs. Labor's defeat in this battle was compounded by the 1994 election, which put Republicans in charge of Congress for the first time in 40 years.

Unions have become more effective in communicating with their members and organizing them for political purposes. From 1998 through 2006, unions sent mailings to their members, organized get-out-the-vote drives, and paid for television advertising. In the 2004 presidential primaries, unions were divided; most supported former Missouri Congressman Dick Gephardt, but some—like the Service Employees International Union (SEIU) and the American Federation of State, County, and Municipal Employees—supported former Vermont governor Howard Dean, while the firefighters supported John Kerry. Unlike 2000, when unions were seen as important to securing Al Gore's nomination, in 2004 they did not play that role in the Iowa caucus or other primaries.[18]

Traditionally identified with the Democratic Party, unions have not enjoyed a close relationship with Republican administrations. Given labor's limited resources, one option for unions is to form temporary coalitions with consumer, public interest, liberal, and sometimes even with industry groups, especially on issues related to foreign imports. Few of labor's recent legislative initiatives have been successful, and turning to the courts has yielded mixed results.[19]

PROFESSIONAL ASSOCIATIONS   Professional people have organized some of the strongest unions in the nation. Some are well known, such as the American Medical Association (AMA) and the American Bar Association (ABA). Others are divided into many subgroups. Teachers, for example, are organized into large groups such as the National Education Association, the American Federation of Teachers, and the American Association of University Professors and also into subgroups based on specialties, such as the Modern Language Association and the American Political Science Association.

Government, especially at the state level, regulates many professions. Lawyers, for example, are licensed by states, which, often as a result of pressure from lawyers themselves, have set up standards of admission to the state bar. Professional associations also use the courts to pursue their agendas. In the area of medical malpractice, for

How Other Nations Govern

Unions in Sweden

Interest groups are stronger in some countries and weaker in others. Organized labor, or unions, is a common feature of advanced democracies and industrial and postindustrial economies, but unions do not exercise the same influence over policy or politics in all countries.

In Sweden, unions are large and cohesive.* Nearly 79 percent of the Swedish workforce is unionized, compared with 14 percent in the United States.† In Sweden, moreover, unions form a single large labor federation, the Swedish Trade Union Confederation, which provides a powerful and cohesive voice in public policy. By contrast, American unions are fragmented into several federations, and even within federations there are tensions between particular unions.

The Swedish Trade Union Confederation has a close relationship with the dominant political party in Sweden, the Social Democratic Party (SDP). Union leaders form part of the party's leadership, and the Confederation supports the SDP with "money, manpower, and influence with the rank and file."* In the United States, most, but not all, unions support the Democratic Party, but they are less important for the Democratic coalition than unions are to Sweden's SDP.

Swedish unions are also more powerful in collective bargaining. In 2004, four industrial sectors in Sweden agreed to a new three-year deal that would provide generally for a 6.8 percent pay raise, plus cuts in working time that were worth a further 0.5 percent. Swedish unions are also working to further reduce the statutory 40-hour work week.† Because of the close relationship the unions have with the governing party, they can significantly influence legislation. In the United States, labor unions opposed the reelection in 2004 of George W. Bush, whose administration they considered hostile.‡ But with Republicans in control of both houses of Congress and the White House in recent years, labor unions in the United States were much less involved in policy making than were Swedish unions. ∎

Nearly 79 percent of the Swedish workforce is unionized, compared with 14 percent in the United States.

---

*Michael Roskin, *Countries and Concepts: Politics, Geography, Culture*, 8th ed. (Prentice Hall, 2004), p. 205.
†See "Overall Union Membership Declines," "2001-Annual Review for the USA," "First Agreements in 2004 Bargaining Round Concluded in Industry," and "Working Time Developments-2003," at European Industrial Relations Observatory On-line, www.eiro.eurofound.eu.int.
‡Steven Greenhouse, "A.F.L.-C.I.O. Plans to Spend $44 Million to Unseat Bush," *The New York Times*, March 11, 2004, p. A26.

---

example, doctors lobby hard for limited liability laws, while trial lawyers resist such efforts. Teachers, hairstylists, and marriage therapists work for legislation or regulations that concern them. It is not surprising, then, that groups representing professional associations such as the AMA and the National Association of Home Builders, are among the largest donors to political campaigns through political action committees (PACs).

Ideological or Single-Issue Interest Groups

Ideological groups focus on issues and often on a single issue. Members of the group generally share a common view of the issue and a desire for government to pursue policies consistent with their views. Some of these groups are *single-issue groups*, often highly motivated, that see politics primarily as a means to pursue one issue. Such groups are often unwilling to compromise. Right-to-life and pro-choice groups on abortion fit this description, as do the National Rifle Association (NRA) and anti-immigration groups.

Countless groups have organized around other specific issues, such as civil liberties, environmental protection, nuclear energy, and nuclear disarmament.[20] Such associations are not new. The Anti-Saloon League of the 1890s was single-mindedly devoted to barring the sale and manufacture of alcoholic beverages, and it did not care whether legislators were drunk or sober as long as they voted dry. One of the best-known ideological groups today is the American Civil Liberties Union (ACLU), with roughly 250,000 members committed to protecting civil liberties.[21] Other ideological groups include the Club for Growth, a generally libertarian and antitax group. In part as a reaction to the tendency of single-issue and ideological groups to be strongly liberal or strongly conservative, some centrist or moderate groups have been formed. Examples include the Concord Coalition, an organization concerned about government deficits and what it calls "responsible fiscal policy."[22]

Public Interest Groups

Out of the political ferment of the 1960s came groups that make a specific claim to promote "the public interest." For example, Common Cause, founded in 1970 by independent Republican John W. Gardner and later led by noted Watergate prosecutor Archibald Cox, campaigns for electoral reform and for making the political process more open. Its Washington staff raises money through direct-mail campaigns, oversees state chapters, publishes research reports and press releases on current issues, and lobbies Congress and government departments.

Ralph Nader started a conglomerate of consumer organizations that investigates and reports on governmental and corporate action—or inaction—relating to consumer interests. Public Interest Research Groups (PIRGs) founded by Nader are among the largest interest groups in the country. PIRGs have become important players on Capitol Hill and in several state legislatures, promoting environmental issues, safe energy, consumer protection, and good government. Nader ran for president in 2000 as the nominee of the Green party and in 2004 as an independent. Despite his reputation as an advocate for consumers, he received only 3 percent of the popular vote in 2000 and .03 percent in 2004.

A specific type of public interest group is the tax-exempt public charity. Examples include the American Heart Association, the Girl Scouts of the U.S.A., and the American Cancer Society. These organizations must meet certain conditions, such as educational or philanthropic objectives, to qualify for this preferred status. Not only

The Women's Christian Temperance Union, a movement dedicated to the prohibition of drinking liquor, succeeded in passing the Eighteenth Amendment, which outlawed the manufacture and sale of alcoholic beverages. It was later repealed by the Twenty-first Amendment.

Interest groups such as Greenpeace stage demonstrations to call attention to environmental issues.

are public charities tax-exempt, but donations to them are tax-deductible, and the organizations are not required to disclose information about their donors. These organizations "may not attempt to influence legislation as a substantial part of its activities and it may not participate at all in campaign activity for or against political candidates,"[23] nor can they benefit an individual or small group. Despite these limitations, tax-exempt charitable organizations have been active in voter registration efforts and in advertising campaigns to influence public opinion.

Foreign Policy Interest Groups

Interest groups also organize to promote or oppose foreign policies. Among the most prestigious foreign affairs groups is the Council on Foreign Relations in New York City. Other groups, devoted to narrower areas of American foreign policy, exert pressure on Congress and the president to enact specific policies. For example, interest group pressure influenced U.S. policy toward South Africa and played a role in South Africa's decision to abandon its system of racial segregation called apartheid in the early 1990s. Groups ranging from student organizations to national lobbies like the American Committee on Africa urged divestment, sanctions, or other policy measures that ultimately promoted change in South Africa. Other groups support or oppose free trade. Foreign policy groups should not be confused with foreign groups, which are banned from making campaign contributions but which often seek to influence policy through lobbying firms.

The American-Israel Political Action Committee (AIPAC) has more than 50,000 members. Because AIPAC's primary focus is lobbying and not distributing campaign funds, it is not required to disclose where its money comes from or goes. Included in the long list of AIPAC lobbying successes are enactment of aid packages to Israel, passage of the 1985 United States–Israel Free Trade Agreement, and emergency assistance to Israel in the wake of the 1992 Gulf War. Its counterpart, the National Association of Arab Americans, lobbies to support Arab causes. Efforts to secure a negotiated settlement between the Palestinians and Israel have meant that American interest groups on both sides of the dispute remain visible and important.

Another type of interest group with frequent international implications is called a **nongovernmental organization (NGO)**. These groups are nonprofit groups or associations that operate outside of the institutions of government but often pursue public policy objectives, lobby governments, and so on. The most frequent types of NGOs are social, cultural, or environmental groups. Examples of prominent NGOs are Greenpeace, Amnesty International, and the Humane Society of the United States.

Public Sector Interest Groups

Governments are themselves important interest groups. Many cities and most states retain Washington lobbyists, and cities also hire lobbyists to represent them at the state legislature. Governors are organized through the National Governors Association, cities through the National League of Cities, and counties through the National Association of Counties. Other officials—lieutenant governors, secretaries of state, mayors—have their own national associations.

Government employees form a large and well-organized group. The National Education Association (NEA), for example, claims 2.7 million members.[24] The NEA fits the definition of a professional association, labor union, and a public sector interest group. Bush administration Secretary of Education Rod Paige had to apologize after he labeled the NEA a terrorist organization in 2004.[25] At the time, Paige was at odds with teachers' unions because they disagreed with his agenda. His remarks may have helped motivate teachers to participate even more in the election of 2004 than they had in the past. Public employees are increasingly important to organized labor, because they are the fastest-growing unions.

nongovernmental organization (NGO)
A nonprofit association or group operating outside of government that advocates and pursues policy objectives.

Agents of Change

Katrina Brown, Vanessa Kirsch, and Public Allies

Public Allies was created in 1991 to prove that young adults were deeply committed to active citizenship and community change. Confronting the stereotype that young Americans were "slackers," the program created an apprenticeship program in Washington, D.C., to place young people ages 18 to 30 in positions of power in the city's charitable organizations. Two years later, the program created local chapters in Milwaukee, Wisc.; Raleigh-Durham, N.C.; and Wilmington, Del.; and has been expanding ever since. Apprentices work for ten months and receive anywhere from $1,300 to $1,500 a month in pay.

Vanessa Kirsch got the idea for Public Allies while she was still in college at Tufts University. Having battled dyslexia in col-

lege, Kirsch was convinced that young adults were anything but slackers. She learned more about young adult attitudes as a staffer at a nationally known public opinion firm. Eventually she concluded that she had to do something to increase the supply of future leaders. Starting a new organization was not easy. "We knew that what we were doing was extremely important work, but we felt like we were banging our heads against a wall," Kirsch remembers. "It's so hard to grow something."

Kirsch later left Public Allies to start a new organization called New Profit, Incorporated, which provides money to help other young Americans launch new organizations. Her new goal is to create hundreds of local charities that provide funding to new organizations en-

gaged in breaking the stereotype that young adults are only interested in themselves. ■

Read more about Public Allies at www.publicallies.org.

Vanessa Kirsch

QUESTIONS

Why do young adults have such a bad reputation for engaging in civic life?

Is Public Allies an interest group, and who does it represent?

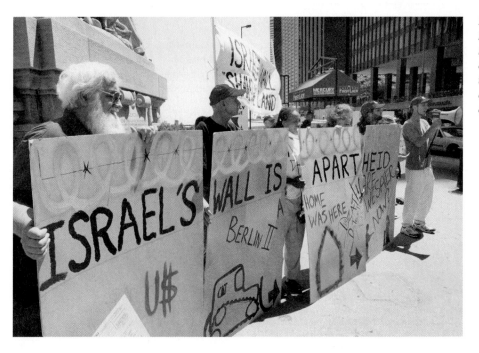

Some interest groups focus on foreign policy issues, such as U.S. aid to Israel in light of Israel's construction of a separation wall along the West Bank. Opponents argue that the wall is tantamount to apartheid and the Israeli government argues that it is a necessary security measure.

Jack Abramoff leaves federal court after pleading guilty to three counts of fraud, tax evasion, and conspiracy to bribe political officals. The plea bargain required the once-powerful lobbyist to provide evidence about members of Congress.

Other Interest Groups

Americans are often emotionally and financially involved in a variety of groups: veterans' groups such as American Legion or Veterans of Foreign Wars; nationality groups such as the multitude of German, Irish, Hispanic, Palestinian, and Korean organizations; or religious organizations such as the Knights of Columbus or B'nai B'rith. More than 150 nationwide organizations are based on national origin alone. In recent years, the number and variety of interests and associations have exploded. This is especially true for environmental groups (see Table 6–2).

Characteristics and Power of Interest Groups

Political scientists, sociologists, and economists have described how groups form and organize to pursue their goals or objectives as the pursuit of **collective action**, or what is also called **public choice**.[26] Groups vary in their goals, methods, and power. Among the most important group characteristics are size, incentives to participate, resources, cohesiveness, leadership, and techniques. As we will demonstrate, these different resources and objectives help us understand the characteristics and power of interest groups.

Size and Resources

Obviously, size is important to political power; an organization representing 5 million voters has more influence than one speaking for 5,000. Perhaps even more important than size is the extent to which members of a group are actively involved and willing to fight for policy objectives. Often people join an organization for reasons that have little

collective action
How groups form and organize to pursue their goals or objectives, including how to get individuals and groups to participate and cooperate. The term has many applications in the various social sciences such as political science, sociology, and economics.

public choice
Synonymous with "collective action," it specifically studies how government officials, politicians, and voters respond to positive and negative incentives.

TABLE 6–2 Some Environmental Groups and How They Do Business

Group	Membership	Issues	Activities
Greenpeace USA	250,000	Forests, global warming, genetically engineered foods, oceans, persistent organic pollutants, nuclear weapons	Media events; mass mailings; grassroots activity; does not lobby government
Natural Resources Defense Council	1,200,000	Resources, energy, global warming, pollution, nuclear weapons	Lobbying; litigation; watchdog; its scientists compete with experts from agencies and industry
Sierra Club	750,000	Wilderness, pollution, global warming, human rights, population, suburban sprawl	Grassroots action; litigation; news releases
Wilderness Society	250,000	Wilderness areas, public lands, energy development	Scientific studies; analysis; advocacy group

SOURCE: Greenpeace USA at www.greenpeaceusa.org; Natural Resources Defense Council at www.nrdc.org; Sierra Club at www.sierraclub.org; Wilderness Society at www.wilderness.org.

to do with its political objectives. They may want to secure group insurance, take advantage of travel benefits, participate in professional meetings, or get a job.

How do associations motivate potential members to join them? Organizations must provide incentives, material or otherwise, that are compelling enough to attract the potential free rider.[27] As discussed, groups provide benefits—like exclusive magazines, special discounts on insurance, and other services—to members beyond whatever advantages are exploited by free riders. Groups also attempt to sanction or punish free riders, which is why unions prefer to have a requirement that only union workers may be employed. When this is not possible, group leaders try to reduce the free rider problem through persuasion or group pressure.

Many government programs involve services that benefit everyone; examples include clean air, national defense, and public fireworks on July 4th. One solution to this free rider problem for government is to pay for these widely shared benefits through taxes. In the economy more generally, a service provider can require a number of people to pay for the service before it is provided. It is then in everyone's interest to pay for the service or face the prospect that no one will have it. It is unlikely that groups ever fully overcome the problem of free riders, but unless there is some compensation for these easily shared goods and services they are not likely to be universally produced.

Many groups face the free rider challenge but it is especially acute for labor unions. Unions are organized not just for lobbying but also to perform other important services for their members. They derive much of their strength from their ability to negotiate with corporations, which they use to try to improve wages or working conditions. Similarly, the AARP, in addition to lobbying on issues of concern to older citizens, offers incentives such as a free subscription to one of its magazines and member discounts at businesses and cultural institutions. The size and member commitment of the AARP make it an important supporter and feared opponent. For example, the AARP was part of the coalition pushing the partial prescription drug benefit that President Bush signed into law in 2003. Some AARP members, as well as former allies in Congress, expressed irritation at the AARP's support for this partial benefit, which they thought was inadequate.[28] Only two years later the AARP asked Congress to change the prescription drug program to provide extra help to low-income seniors. It has also asked the government to take a more active role in setting drug prices.[29]

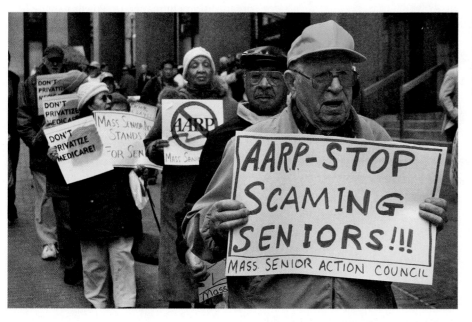

In 2003, the AARP successfully lobbied for passage of a prescription drug plan that many seniors argued would ultimately increase the cost of their prescription medications. To protest the AARP's position, some people burned their AARP cards.

While the size of an interest group is often important, so, too, is its *spread*—the extent to which membership is concentrated or dispersed. Because automobile manufacturing is concentrated in Michigan and a few other states, the auto industry's influence does not have the same spread as that of the AMA, which has an active chapter in virtually every congressional district. Concentration of membership, especially when in a key battleground state as is the case with the Cuban-Americans in Florida or ethanol producers in Iowa, enhances that group's influence. These interests, however, lack the influence of large groups dispersed broadly.

Interest groups also differ in the extent to which they preempt a policy area or share it with other groups. Doctors and the AMA have effectively preempted the health care policy area because they play such an important role in health care. But in setting transportation policy, for example, railroads must compete with interstate trucking and even air freight companies.

Groups also differ in their *resources*, which include money, volunteers, expertise, and reputation. Some groups can influence many centers of power—both houses of Congress, the White House, federal agencies, the courts, and state and local governments—while others cannot.

Cohesiveness

Usually, a mass membership organization is made up of three types of members: (1) a relatively small number of formal leaders who may hold full-time, paid positions or devote much time, effort, and money to the group's activities; (2) a few hundred people intensely involved in the group who identify with its aims, attend meetings, pay dues, and do a lot of the legwork; and (3) thousands of people who are members in name only and cannot be depended on to vote in elections or act as the leadership wants.[30]

Another factor in group cohesiveness is its *organizational structure*. Some associations have a strong formal organization; others are local organizations that have joined together in a loose state or national federation in which they retain a measure of separate power and independence. Separation of powers may also exist in groups. The national assembly of an organization establishes, or at least ratifies, policy; an executive committee meets more frequently; a president or director is elected to head and speak for the group; and permanent paid officials form the organization's bureaucracy. Power may be further divided between the organization's main headquarters and its Washington office. An organization of this sort tends to be far less cohesive than a centralized, disciplined group such as some trade unions and associations for trial lawyers and realtors.

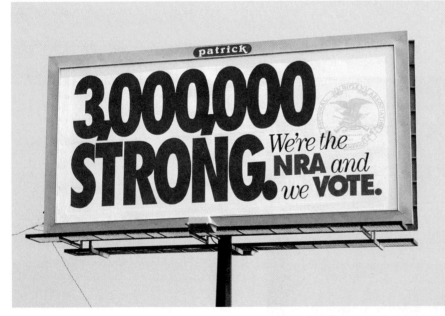

The NRA is a large, powerful interest group with considerable political clout, dedicated to fighting all gun control legislation and to electing candidates who oppose any form of gun control.

Leadership

Closely related to cohesion is the nature of the leadership. In a group that embraces many attitudes and interests, leaders may either weld the various elements together or sharpen their disunity. The leader of a national business association, for example, must tread cautiously between big business and small business, between exporters and importers, between chain stores and corner grocery stores, and between the producers and the sellers of competing products. The group leader is in the same position as a president or a member of Congress; he or she must know when to lead and when to follow.

Techniques

Interest groups seeking to wield influence choose from a variety of political weapons and targets. They present their case to Congress, the White House staff, state and local governments, and federal agencies and departments. This activity is called lobbying. They also become involved in litigation. Other techniques include protests, election activities, and even establishing their own political parties.

PUBLICITY AND MASS MEDIA APPEALS   One way to attempt to influence policy makers is through the public. Interest groups use the media—television, radio, newspapers, leaflets, signs, direct mail, and word of mouth—to influence voters during elections and to motivate constituents to contact their representatives between elections. Business enjoys a special advantage in this arena, and businesspeople have the money and staff to use propaganda machinery. As large-scale advertisers, they know how to deliver their message effectively or can find an advertising agency to do it for them. But organized labor is also effective in communicating with its membership through shop stewards, mail, and phone calls.

As people communicate more and more via e-mail, this technology has become an important means of political mobilization. Business organizations like the Business and Industrial Political Action Committee (BIPAC) have used the Internet to communicate with members and employees of affiliated businesses. Their Web site provides downloadable forms to request absentee ballots and the roll call votes of legislators on issues of interest to their businesses.[31] E-mail will likely become even more important to political communication at the workplace as management tells its workers about candidates and ballot issues.

MASS MAILING   One means of communication that has increased the reach and effectiveness of interest groups is computerized and targeted mass mailing.[32] Before computers, interest groups had to cull lists of people to contact from telephone directories and other sources. Managing these lists was so time-consuming that some groups sent out mailings indiscriminately. Today the computer permits easy data storage and efficient management of mailing lists, so all kinds of interest groups now use mass mailing. Today's technology can target personalized letters to specific groups. Such targeted direct mail can also appeal to people who share a common concern. Environmental groups make extensive use of targeted mail and e-mail.[33]

INFLUENCE ON RULE MAKING   Organized groups have ready access to the executive and regulatory agencies that write the rules implementing laws passed by Congress. Government agencies publish proposed regulations in the ***Federal Register*** and invite responses from all interested persons before the rules are finalized—what is called the "notice and comments period." (The *Federal Register* is published every weekday. You can find it at the library or on the Internet at www.gpoaccess.gov.) Well-staffed associations and corporations use the *Register* to obtain specific language of pending regulations, as well as deadlines that will affect their interests. Lobbyists prepare written responses to the proposed rules, draft alternative rules, and make their case at the hearings. These lobbyists seek to be on good terms with the staff of the agencies, so that they can learn what rules are being considered long before they are released publicly and thus have early input. Administrative rules are defined over time through legal cases and agency modifications, so even if an interest group fails to get what it wants, it can fight the rules in court or press for a reinterpretation when the agency changes leadership.

Finally, an interest group can seek to modify rules it does not like by pressuring Congress to change the legal mandate for the agency or reduce the agency's budget, making it difficult to enforce existing rules. In short, interest groups and lobbyists never really quit fighting for their point of view.

LITIGATION   When groups find the political channels closed to them, they may turn to the courts.[34] The Legal Defense and Education Fund of the National Association for

Federal Register
An official document, published every weekday, which lists the new and proposed regulations of executive departments and regulatory agencies.

The use of both conventional and electronic mail is an effective way of reaching a large number of people during political campaigns. The Montana Democratic Party sent this ad to potential voters informing them of Republican candidate Mike Taylor's misuse of student loan money several years prior when he operated a beauty school in another state. The ad prompted Taylor to withdraw from the race.

Taylor clipped the taxpayers by abusing student loans.

Mike Taylor made a fortune in the hair care industry. He also made up his own rules for awarding student loans.

Michael Taylor, Beauty Corner, Denver, Colorado.

Abusing Student Loans

In a hair-raising scheme to ensure the success of his "Institute of Hair Design," Mike Taylor improperly gave out thousands of dollars in federal student loan funds. Mike Taylor's "Institute of Hair Design" profited from the misuse of money that was meant for educational purposes.[1]

Ability to Directly Issue Student Loans Revoked

In 1998, based on "repeat findings" of violations, the U.S. Department of Education revoked Mike Taylor's authority to directly disperse federal student loan monies.[2] In 1999, the U.S. Department of Education followed up on this action by assessing the Institute of Hair Design about $159,000 for the numerous violations uncovered by department investigators.[3]

With Mike Taylor, There's no telling who will get clipped.

the Advancement of Colored People (NAACP), for example, initiated and won numerous court cases in its efforts to end racial segregation and to protect the right to vote for African Americans. Urban interests and environmental groups, feeling underrepresented in state and national legislatures, turned to the courts to influence the political agenda.[35] Women's groups, such as the National Organization for Women and the ACLU's Women's Rights Project, also used the courts to pursue their objectives.[36] Conservative religious groups like the Washington Legal Foundation and groups identified with the Religious Right have also used litigation to pursue their objectives.[37]

In addition to initiating lawsuits, associations can gain a forum for their views in the courts by filing ***amicus curiae*** briefs (literally, "friend of the court" briefs) in cases in which they are not direct parties. Despite the general impression that associations achieve great success in the courts, groups are no more likely than individuals to win their cases at the district court level.[38]

PROTEST Movements arise around particular issues but often lack widespread support. To generate interest and support for their cause, movements often use protest demonstrations. For example, after the House of Representatives passed new laws on illegal immigration, pro-immigrant groups mounted protests in cities like Phoenix and Washington, D.C. with more than 1 million participants.[39] Two months later, in a protest called "A Day Without Immigrants," more than 600,000 protestors gathered in Los Angeles to focus greater media attention on the important role immigrants play in the economy; similar rallies in Chicago drew more than 400,000 people.[40] Other move-

amicus curiae brief
Literally, a "friend of the court" brief, filed by an individual or organization to present arguments in addition to those presented by the immediate parties to a case.

ments or groups that have used protest include the civil rights movement and antiwar, environmental, and antiglobalization groups.[41]

ELECTION ACTIVITIES Although nearly all large organizations say they are nonpolitical, almost all are politically involved in some way. By nonpolitical they usually mean that they are *nonpartisan*. Most organized interest groups try to work through *both* parties and want to be friendly with the winners, which often means that they contribute to incumbents. But as competition for control of both chambers of Congress has intensified and with presidential contests also up for grabs, interest groups have generally invested more in one party or the other.

Many interest groups endorse candidates for office, either directly by issuing a statement or hosting an event where the endorsement is announced or more indirectly by publishing scorecards of how candidates performed on roll-call votes or in response to questionnaires administered by the group. Some groups give candidates letter grades from "A" to "F." The League of Conservation Voters calls attention to candidates they oppose by naming them to their "environmental dirty dozen," while praising other candidates as "environmental champions."[42] Endorsements are communicated to group members at the workplace, through the mail, electronically, and often to the broader public through mailings and on television and radio.

Labor usually favors Democrats. The AFL-CIO has supported every Democratic candidate for president since the New Deal in the 1930s. Although the Teamsters Union has often endorsed Republicans, in 2004, it joined most other unions in backing John Kerry. Business groups generally favor Republicans. The differing views of their members prevent some organizations from taking a firm position. A local retailers' group, for example, might be composed equally of Republicans and Democrats, and many of its members might refuse to openly support a candidate for fear of losing business.

Ideological groups target certain candidates, seeking to change a candidate's positions or, failing that, to influence voters to vote against that candidate. Americans for Democratic Action and the American Conservative Union publish ratings of members of Congress' voting records on liberal and conservative issues; so do the U.S. Chamber of Commerce, the AFL-CIO, and other groups on issues important to them.

FORMING A POLITICAL PARTY Another interest group strategy is to form a political party. These parties are organized less to win elections than to publicize a cause. The Free Soil Party was formed in the mid-1840s to work against the spread of slavery into the territories, and the Prohibition Party was organized two decades later to ban the sale of liquor. Farmers have formed a variety of such parties. More often, however, interest groups prefer to work through existing parties.

Today, environmental groups and voters for whom the environment is a central issue must choose between supporting the Green Party, which has yet to elect a person to federal office, an independent candidate like Ralph Nader in 2004, or one of the two major parties. Sometimes minor-party candidates can spoil the chances of a major-party candidate. In a New Mexico congressional special election in 1997, the Green Party candidate won 17 percent of the vote, taking some votes from the Democrat and thereby helping elect a Republican to what had been a Democratic seat. In the 1998 election, environmental groups campaigned aggressively for the Democrat in the same district, who obtained 53 percent of the vote, while all minor parties combined got only 4 percent.[43] In South Dakota's 2002 Senate race between Tim Johnson (D) and John Thune (R), the Libertarian candidate got more than 3,000 votes. Johnson defeated Thune by just over 500 votes. In the 2000 presidential election, most environmental groups supported Al Gore over Green Party nominee Ralph Nader. Many Democrats, however, blame Nader for diverting votes from Gore in such battlegrounds as Florida and New Hampshire, thereby costing him the election. Democrats again worried that Nader would cost them the White House in 2004, but explicit appeals from the party and from interest groups may have helped reduce Nader's impact. Early in the cam-

Personal contact with and access to decision makers continue to be key elements of lobbying today, as they were at the time of President Grant's administration.

paign, Nader described Democrat John Kerry as very presidential, but he later said that a vote for Kerry is "a vote for war—an endless, Vietnam-type quagmire."[44]

COOPERATIVE LOBBYING   Like-minded groups often form cooperative groups. In 1987, the Leadership Conference on Civil Rights and People for the American Way brought together many groups to defeat the nomination of outspoken federal judge Robert Bork to the U.S. Supreme Court.[45] Different types of environmentalists work together, as do consumer and ideological groups on the right and on the left. For example, while a large variety of groups that reflect diverse interests represent women, the larger the coalition, the greater the chance that members may divide over such issues as abortion. Another example of a cooperative group is the Business Roundtable, an association of chief executive officers of the 200 largest U.S. corporations, which promotes policies that help large businesses, such as free trade and less government regulation.

The Influence of Lobbyists

I ndividuals who represent interests are called **lobbyists**. Lobbyists are the employees of associations who try to influence policy decisions and positions in the executive and especially in the legislative branches of our government. Some lobbyists, like Jack Abramoff described earlier, work as hired representatives of individuals or groups who pay for their services.

The terms "lobbying" and "lobbyist" were not generally used until around the mid-nineteenth century in the United States. These words refer to the lobby or hallway outside the House and Senate chambers in the U.S. Capitol and to those who hung around the lobby of the old Willard Hotel in Washington, D.C., when presidents dined there. The noun "lobby" has been turned into a verb in this political context. Thus "to lobby" is to seek to influence legislators and government officials, and we call this **lobbying** even if no lobby is in sight.

Despite their negative public image, lobbyists perform useful functions for government. They provide information for the decision makers of all three branches of government, they help educate and mobilize public opinion, they help prepare legislation and testify before legislative hearings, and they contribute a large share of the costs of campaigns. Yet many people are concerned that lobbyists have too much influence on government and add to legislative gridlock by being able to stop action on pressing problems.

Who Are the Lobbyists?

The typical image is of powerful, hard-nosed lobbyists who use a combination of knowledge, persuasiveness, personal influence, charm, and money to influence legislators and bureaucrats. Lobbyists are experienced in government, often having been public servants before going to work for an organized interest group, association, or corporation. They might start as staff in Congress, perhaps on a congressional committee. Later, when their party wins the White House, they gain an administration post, often in the same policy area as their congressional committee work. After a few years in the administration, they are ready to make the move to lobbying, either by going to work for one of the interests they dealt with while in the government or for a lobbying firm.

Moving from a government job to one with an interest group—or vice versa—is so common it is called the **revolving door**. Although it is illegal for former national government employees to directly lobby the agency from which they came, their contacts made during government service are helpful to interest groups. Many former members of Congress make use of their congressional experience as full-time lobbyists.

The revolving door between government and interest groups produces networks of people who care about certain issues. These **issue networks** consist of relationships among interest groups, congressional committees and subcommittees, and the gov-

lobbyist
A person who is employed by and acts for an organized interest group or corporation to try to influence policy decisions and positions in the executive and legislative branches.

lobbying
Engaging in activities aimed at influencing public officials, especially legislators, and the policies they enact.

revolving door
Employment cycle in which individuals who work for governmental agencies that regulate interests eventually end up working for interest groups or businesses with the same policy concern.

issue network
Relationships among interest groups, congressional committees and subcommittees, and the government agencies that share a common policy concern.

The Changing Face of American Politics

Breaking into a Male-Dominated Profession

Relatively few women and minorities are lobbyists. The first woman to own a lobbying firm was Anne Wexler, who started her own firm after leaving the Carter administration in 1981. Wexler observes that when she started, "there were very few women in lobby-

ing. It was completely male dominated."* That remains the case today. In a 2001 study, nearly four-fifths of lobbyists were male and nearly all (99 percent) were white.†

Women have begun to make inroads into the lobbying profession, especially in areas

like health care, reproductive rights, and education. Because the number of women serving in senior congressional and White House staffs has grown, the pool of women that may become senior lobbyists has similarly grown. ■

In a 2001 study, nearly four-fifths of lobbyists were male and nearly all (99 percent) were white.

*Jeffrey H. Birnbaum, "Women, Minorities Make up New Generation of Lobbyists," *The Washington Post*, May 1, 2006, p. D1.
†Paul C. Light and Virginia Thomas, "Posts of Honor: How America's Corporate and Civic Leaders View Presidential Appointments," *Presidential Appointee Initiative Paper* (Brookings Institution, 2001).

ernment agencies that share a common policy concern. Sometimes these networks become so strong and mutually beneficial that they become a sort of subgovernment. A former senior staff person from a House or Senate agriculture committee now working for an agricultural corporation as a lobbyist who has ongoing friendships with his former staff colleagues, including some who now work at the Department of Agriculture, is an example of how personal relationships work within an issue network.

Legal and political skills, along with specialized knowledge, have become so crucial in executive and legislative policy making that they have become a form of power in themselves. Elected representatives increasingly depend on their staffs for guidance, and these issue specialists know more about "Section 504" or "Title IX" or "the 2002 amendments"—and who wrote them and why—than most political and administrative leaders, who are usually generalists.[46] Since a lot of the implementation and rule making associated with public policy occurs at the agency level of government, issue networks assume even more significance.

What Do Lobbyists Do?

Thousands of lobbyists are active in Washington, but few are as glamorous or as unscrupulous as the media suggest, nor are they necessarily influential. One limit on their power is the competition among interest groups. Rarely does any one group have a policy area all to itself. For example, transportation policy involves airplanes, trucks, cars, railroads, consumers, suppliers, state and local governments—the list goes on and on.

To members of Congress, the single most important thing lobbyists provide is money for their next reelection campaign. "Reelection underlies everything else," writes political scientist David Mayhew.[47] Money from interest groups has become instrumental in this driving need among incumbents. Interest groups also provide volunteers for campaign activity. In addition, their failure to support the opposition can enhance an incumbent's chances of being reelected.

Some people defend lobbyists as a kind of "third house" of Congress. Whereas the Senate and House are set up on a geographical basis, lobbyists represent people on the basis of interests and money. Small but important groups can sometimes get representation in the "third house" when they cannot get it in the other two. In a nation of vast and important interests, this kind of functional representation, if it is not abused, can supplement geographical representation.

Beyond their central role in campaigns and elections, interest groups provide another essential commodity to legislators: information of two important types, political and substantive. The *political information* lobbyists provide includes such matters as who supports or opposes legislation and how strongly they feel about it.[48] For example, knowing the views of other legislators, the executive branch, and key interest groups is important to passing or killing legislation. *Substantive information*, such as the impact of proposed laws, might not be available from any other source. Lobbyists often provide technical assistance for drafting bills and amendments, identifying persons to testify at legislative hearings, and formulating questions to ask administration officials at oversight hearings.

The battle over providing a prescription drug benefit for senior citizens illustrates how lobbyists influence the electoral and legislative process. The pharmaceutical industry invested more than $10 million in both the 2000 and 2002 elections in limited and disclosed contributions to candidates and parties,[49] and another $15 to $20 million in unlimited soft money contributions to the parties in both of these elections.[50] (See Chapters 7 and 9 for a discussion of soft money.) In addition, "Citizens for Better Medicare" spent an estimated $65 million in 2000 on issue ads targeted to battleground states. In 2002, "The United Seniors Association" spent an estimated $9 to $13 million on issue ads in competitive contests.[51] Issue ad spending is only an estimate because until 2004 groups could avoid disclosure and spending limits by claiming an ad was about issues and not candidates, when, in fact, the ads often were targeted to particular races. Lobbying was also part of the pharmaceutical industry strategy. In 2002, they spent an unprecedented $94 million on lobbying activities, hiring almost 700 lobbyists from 138 different firms.[52] Congress enacted a prescription drug benefit for seniors that had the support of the pharmaceutical industry and the largest seniors' organization, the AARP. Some people criticized the new benefit as being too costly and confusing,[53] others for not being comprehensive enough.[54] The intense electioneering and lobbying helped define the issue and set the stage for the legislation that was enacted.

Money and Politics

Interest groups also seek to influence politics and public policy by spending money on elections. They can do this in several ways. One way is by contributing money to candidates for their election campaigns; another is by contributing to political parties that assist candidates seeking office, especially in contested races. They can also contribute money to other interest groups; communicate to the members of their group, including employees; and spend money independently of the parties and candidates. Groups are a central part of the way candidates and parties fund campaigns and are major players acting independently in competitive federal elections.

Helping elect candidates creates a relationship between the interest group and the elected official that a group may exploit in the policy process. At a minimum, substantial involvement in the election process helps provide access to policy makers.[55] We discuss in greater detail the dynamics of campaign finance and efforts to reform or regulate it in Chapter 9. Here we discuss the most important ways interest groups organize and participate in funding campaigns and elections.

political action committee (PAC)
The political arm of an interest group that is legally entitled to raise funds on a voluntary basis from members, stockholders, or employees to contribute funds to candidates or political parties.

Political Action Committees (PACs)

A **political action committee (PAC)** is the political arm of an interest group that is legally entitled to raise limited and disclosed funds on a voluntary basis from members, stockholders, or employees in order to contribute funds to favored candidates or political parties. PACs link two vital techniques of influence—giving money and other

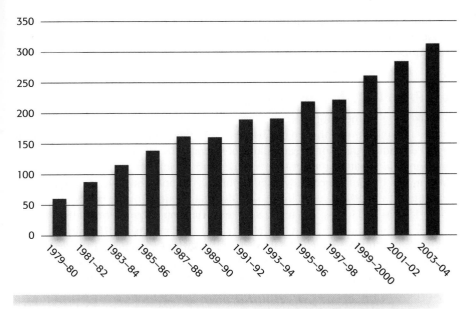

FIGURE **6–3 Total PAC Contributions to Federal Candidates, 1979–2004 (in millions).**

SOURCE: Federal Election Commission, "PAC Activity Increases for 2004 Elections," press release, April 13, 2005, at www.fec.gov/press/press2005/20050412pac/PACFinal2004.html, accessed April 19, 2005.

political aid to politicians and persuading officeholders to act or vote "the right way" on issues. Thus PACs are one important means by which interest groups seek to influence which legislators are elected and what they do once they take office.[56] PACs can be categorized according to the type of interest they represent: corporations, trade and health organizations, labor unions, ideological organizations, and so on.

PACs grew in number and importance in the 1970s, in part due to campaign finance reform legislation enacted in that decade. The number of PACs registered rose from 608 in 1974 to 4,210 today.[57] Corporations and trade associations contributed most to this growth; today their PACs constitute the majority of all PACs. Labor PACs, by contrast, represent less than 7 percent of all PACs.[58] But the increase in the number of PACs is less important than the intensity of PAC participation in elections and lobbying (see Figure 6–3).

Surprisingly, considering the growth in numbers of PACs that has occurred mainly in the business world, organized labor invented this device. In the 1930s, John L. Lewis, president of the United Mine Workers, set up the Non-Partisan Political League as the political arm of the newly formed Congress of Industrial Organizations (CIO). When the CIO merged with the American Federation of Labor (AFL), the new labor group established the Committee on Political Education (COPE), whose activities we have already described. This unit came to be the model for most political action committees: "From the outset, national, state, and local units of COPE have not only raised and distributed funds, but have also served as the mechanism for organized and widespread union activity in the electoral process, for example, in voter registration, political education, and get-out-the-vote drives."[59] Some years later, manufacturers formed the Business and Industry Political Action Committee, but the most active business PAC today is the one affiliated with the National Federation of Independent Business.[60]

A more recent phenomenon is the formation by officeholders of political action committees of their own that collect contributions from individuals and PACs and then make contributions to other candidates and political parties.[61] These committees, called **leadership PACs**, were initially used by aspiring congressional leaders to curry favor with candidates in their political party. For example, House Speaker Nancy Pelosi has a leadership PAC that raised and spent more than $1 million dollars in the 2000, 2002, and 2004 election cycles. During this same period House Republican leader Tom DeLay's leadership PAC raised and spent more than $3 million in each election.[62] Creation of a leadership PAC has the additional benefit of allowing members to

leadership PAC
A PAC formed by an office holder that collects contributions from individuals and other PACs and then makes contributions to other candidates and political parties.

raise more money from individuals and groups. They could ask for the maximum allowable contribution to their own reelection account but then ask for an additional contribution to their leadership PAC.

How PACs Invest Their Money

PACs take part in the entire election process, but their main influence lies in their capacity to contribute money to candidates. Candidates today need a lot of money to wage their campaigns. House candidates often spend more than $1 million on their campaign, and Senate campaigns can cost several million dollars.[63] And as PACs contribute more, their influence grows. What counts is not only how much they give, but to whom they give it. PACs give to the most influential incumbents, to committee chairs, to party leaders and whips, and to the Speaker of the House. More pragmatic PACs give not only to the majority party, but also to key incumbents in the minority party because today's minority could be tomorrow's majority. One scholar of congressional elections states that although PACs' "avowed intention is 'to keep our friends in office and elect those who are our friends,' it is perhaps more accurate to say that they aim to ensure that those in office remain their friends."[64]

PACs are important not only because they contribute such a large share of the money congressional candidates raise for their campaigns, but also because they contribute so disproportionately to incumbents. In the most recent election cycle, House incumbents seeking reelection raised 40 percent of the funds for their campaigns from PACs compared to only 14 percent for the challengers opposing them. In total, House incumbents raised more than ten PAC dollars for every one PAC dollar going to a challenger. Senate incumbents raise proportionately more from individuals, but also enjoy a fundraising advantage among PACs compared to Senate challengers (see Figures 6–4 and 6–5). One reason members of Congress become entrenched in their seats is that PACs fund them. Many members of Congress thrive on the present arrangements, and the leaders and members of both parties actually compete for PAC dollars (see Table 6–4).

The law limits the amount of money that PACs, like individuals, can contribute to any single candidate in an election cycle. But for a candidate, raising money from PACs is more efficient than from individuals. Since the 1970s, PAC contributions to any federal candidate have been limited to $10,000 per election cycle (primary and general elections) while individuals are limited to $4,000 per candidate per election cycle. The Bipartisan Campaign Reform Act (BCRA) doubled individual contribution limits while

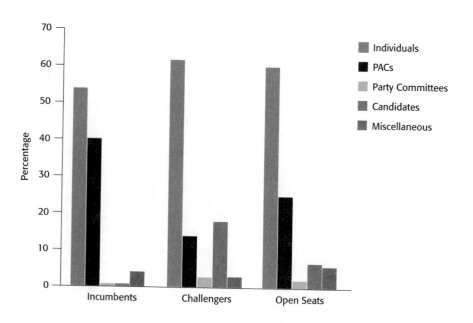

FIGURE 6–4 Sources of House Candidates' Receipts, 2003–2004.

SOURCE: Paul S. Herrnson, *Financing the 2004 Election* (Brookings Institution Press, 2006), p. 168.

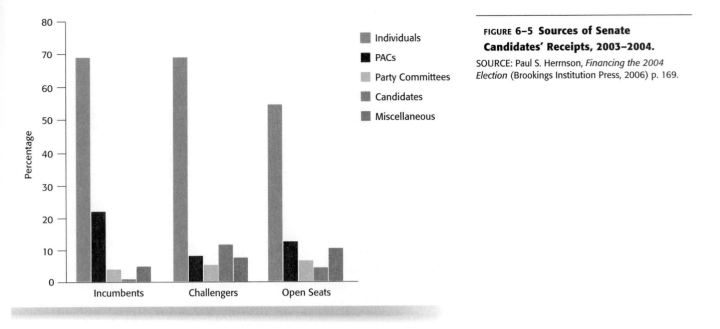

FIGURE 6–5 **Sources of Senate Candidates' Receipts, 2003–2004.**

SOURCE: Paul S. Herrnson, *Financing the 2004 Election* (Brookings Institution Press, 2006) p. 169.

leaving PAC contribution limits unchanged. This probably reflected the view of the legislators and the court that upheld this law that actual corruption or the appearance of corruption is more likely to come from organized interests like unions, trade associations, and businesses. PACs have found creative ways around this limit. They can host fund-raisers attended by other PACs to boost their reputation with the candidate, or they can collect money from several individual contributors and give it to the candidate as a bundle, a process called **bundling**. Through bundling, PACs and interested individuals can increase their clout with elected officials. Two of the most important groups doing bundling in 2003–2004 were EMILY's List and the Club for Growth. EMILY's List, which stands for "Early Money Is Like Yeast," raises money from individuals committed to electing Democratic women who are pro-choice on abortion. It identifies candidates who fit its criteria and then solicits checks for them at an early stage in a campaign. The Club for Growth, a conservative group, sees itself as applying the same bundling techniques as EMILY's List but for pro-growth and antitax candidates who are mainly Republicans.

As noted, PAC contributions are especially made to committee chairs and party leaders. To reinforce this relationship, the Republicans developed a strategy, the "K Street Project," to do even better in getting PAC contributions. (K Street in Washington, D.C., houses many of the lobbying and law firms that represent trade associations and corporations that make contributions.) Former House Republican leader Tom DeLay, a prime mover in the K Street Project, once said, "If you want to play in our revolution you have to live by our rules."[65] DeLay, under indictment in Texas for money laundering, resigned his seat in 2006. As recent examples have demonstrated, the process of seeking to influence public policy can go too far.

Mobilizing Employees and Members

Another way interest groups can influence the outcome of elections is by persuading their employees, members, or stockholders to vote in a way consistent with the interests of the group. Interest groups accomplish this mobilization through targeted communications at the workplace, through the mail, or on the Internet. As we discuss elsewhere in this chapter, labor unions have been especially effective in member communications. Corporations and business associations have been following labor's lead. Membership organizations like the National Rifle Association (NRA) have also been able to mobilize their members and allied individuals and groups.[66]

"If you want to play in our revolution you have to live by our rules."

FORMER HOUSE REPUBLICAN LEADER TOM DELAY

bundling
A tactic in which PACs collect contributions from like-minded individuals (each limited to $2,000) and present them to a candidate or political party as a "bundle," thus increasing the PAC's influence.

Other Modes of Electioneering

Until the 2004 election cycle, interest groups and individuals could avoid the contribution limitation to political parties by contributing so-called **soft money**. Originally justified as an exception to contribution limits to help the political parties by funding get-out-the-vote drives or party appeals that are not specific, soft money came to be used for candidate-specific electioneering.[67] Corporations and unions, long banned from giving directly to candidates and parties from their general funds for election-specific purposes, were permitted to give soft money, and they did so in large amounts. Soft money also diminished disclosure of a possible **quid pro quo** between an interest group and a politician. For example, a large donor could give millions to a party with the expectation that it was going to a particular U.S. Senate campaign, but such a connection is not traceable because the soft money passes through the party before it reaches candidates. By the 2000 and 2002 election cycles, soft money had climbed to around $500 million. BCRA banned soft money in 2002. We discuss party soft money in greater detail in Chapter 7 and BCRA in Chapter 9.

Some corporations had complained before BCRA was passed that elected officials were "shaking them down" for large soft money contributions. The BCRA ban on soft money gave corporations an excuse to spend less overall on politics in 2004. As noted, BCRA left other avenues open to corporations and unions, including organizing PACs, sending internal communications to members, and encouraging employees and other members to contribute to campaigns. It is important to remember that BCRA has only been in effect for two elections, 2004 and 2006, and history teaches us that groups adapt to new rules over multiple elections.

Between 1996 and 2002, interest groups could also help fund so-called "issue ads" supporting or opposing candidates as long as the ads did not use certain words. BCRA defines election broadcast ads more realistically (see Chapter 9). It also restores the long-standing ban on corporations and unions using their general funds for this purpose. Interest groups can continue to skirt disclosure if they communicate with voters through the mail, in newspaper ads, on billboards, on the phone, and by e-mail—even in the period leading up to the election.

Interest groups typically made the presidential campaign their highest priority in 2004. Some groups, like the League of Conservation Voters (LCV), in the past had invested some of their resources in presidential races but made House and Senate races higher priorities. LCV did just the opposite in 2004. With the presidential race so competitive and with so much passion behind supporting or opposing the incumbent president, interest groups' decision to emphasize the presidential contest is not surprising.

One example of an interest group that diversified its approach in 2004 is the United States Chamber of Commerce. The Chamber did not endorse a candidate for president but strongly supported the reelection of President Bush—a position that was only strengthened when John Kerry chose as his running mate a former trial lawyer, John Edwards. But the Chamber also invested heavily in races for state attorneys general, state supreme court justices, and state legislators in an effort to influence state policies and court decisions involving business.

Independent Expenditures

The Supreme Court in 1976 declared that limits on independent expenditures were unconstitutional when they were truly independent of a party or candidate. Hence, groups, like individuals, can campaign for or against a candidate independently of a party or candidate committee. They can do this in addition to making contributions from their PAC to candidates and party committees. These **independent expenditures** are unlimited but must be disclosed to the Federal Election Commission (FEC). In total interest group spending on elections, independent expenditures fall well below PAC contributions to candidates and parties. Groups that have made heavy use of independent expenditures include MoveOn PAC, NRA, several unions, National Right to

soft money
Unlimited amounts of money that political parties previously could raise for party-building purposes. Now largely illegal except for limited contributions to state and local parties for voter registration and get-out-the-vote efforts.

quid pro quo
Something given with the expectation of receiving something in return.

independent expenditures
The Supreme Court has ruled that individuals, groups, and parties can spend unlimited amounts in campaigns for or against candidates as long as they operate independently from the candidates. When an individual, group, or party does so, they are making an independent expenditure.

TABLE 6–3 Independent Expenditures
By Top Interest Groups, 2004

Interest Group	Expenditure
MoveOn PAC	$12,379,808
NRA Political Victory Fund	7,013,703
AFSCME–P E O P L E, Qualified	6,891,586
United Auto Workers–VCAP	5,156,529
Service Employees International Union	4,216,147
National Right to Life PAC	3,661,986
Planned Parenthood	2,684,061
National Association of Realtors PAC	2,603,143
NARAL Pro-Choice America	2,128,638
American Medical Association PAC	1,792,655
NEA Fund for Children and Public Education	1,508,808
Club for Growth PAC	1,499,446
AFSCME, AFL-CIO (D.C.)	1,254,232

SOURCE: Federal Election Commission, at ftp://ftp.fec.gov.FEC, accessed June 10, 2005.
NOTE: Expenditures for all national affiliates of an organization are combined, but expenditures for state affiliates are excluded.

Life PAC, Planned Parenthood, and the National Association of Realtors. (See Table 6–3.) Independent expenditures enable groups to direct more money to a particular race than they can through PAC contributions, while still getting credit with their members for their activity because the source of independent expenditures is clearly communicated.

Campaigning through Other Groups

In 1996, interest groups found a way to circumvent disclosure and contribution limits through **issue advocacy**. Reformers for more than a century sought disclosure of money in politics. This is consistent with efforts to have more complete disclosure of conflicts of interest in potential executive branch appointees and among legislators and judges. In campaigns and elections, disclosure was often incomplete, and groups quickly found ways to avoid it . The disclosure provisions of the Federal Election Campaign Act of 1971, later amended in 1974, defined electioneering ads as communications that used words like "vote for" or "vote against."

Until the mid-1990s, citizens, journalists, and scholars had a complete picture of who was giving what to whom, and who was spending money and in what ways, to influence elections. That changed with the discovery of issue advocacy as an electioneering tool in the 1996 election cycle. Electioneering ads were subject to disclosure and spending limits. To get around this law, groups simply made election ads without those words and then spent millions attacking or promoting particular candidates. Labor unions were the first to exploit this tactic in a major way, spending an estimated $35 million in 1996, mostly against Republican candidates.[68] Corporations and ideological groups quickly followed labor's lead. Groups could and did spend millions of their general funds on issue ads in 1996–2002. Not only did groups avoid contributions limits, but they could mask their identity by creating a new name behind which to campaign. Citizens for Better Medicare was largely funded by the pharmaceutical industry, and the Coalition to Make Our Voices Heard was funded in part by labor unions.[69] Perhaps the best-known example was Republicans for Clean Air, which attacked John McCain's

issue advocacy
Unlimited and undisclosed spending by an individual or group on communications that do not use words like "vote for" or "vote against," although much of this activity is actually about electing or defeating candidates.

environmental record in the 2000 presidential primaries. This group was really two Texans, businessmen Sam and Charles Wyly.[70]

BCRA limits issue advocacy by providing a new and more realistic definition of electioneering communications, requires greater disclosure by those funding broadcast electioneering ads, and restores the ban on corporations and unions using general funds in this way in the month before a primary and two months before a general election. BCRA does not regulate what any of these groups may do on the phone, through the mail, or in person. Consistent with prior Supreme Court decisions, BCRA excludes from regulation some interest groups that were not established by a business or labor union, or that are funded by individuals whose purpose is to "promote political ideas and cannot engage in business activities."[71] In 2004, four groups had this special status and therefore could spend unlimited amounts of money raised from individuals on competitive races. These groups were NARAL Pro-Choice America, Planned Parenthood, League of Conservation Voters, and Defenders of Wildlife. These groups are known as MCFL groups, an acronym that originated from one of the named parties in *FEC* v. *Massachusetts Citizens for Life*, a Supreme Court case that established that these qualifying groups can accept unlimited amounts of money.

In the post-BCRA elections of 2004 and 2006, interest groups continued to mount their own campaigns against or for candidates in ways similar to the old issue advocacy. The most visible example of this in the 2004 election was a group of Vietnam War veterans who formed a group they named Swift Boat Veterans for Truth whose ads attacked Senator John Kerry's Vietnam War record.[72] Groups like Swift Boat Veterans for Truth are called **527 organizations** because they are tax-exempt groups organized under section 527 of the Internal Revenue Service Code. These organizations can run ads against or for candidates under somewhat more restrictive conditions than existed before 2004 (see Table 6–4).

527 organization
A political group organized under section 527 of the IRS Code that may accept and spend unlimited amounts of money on election activities so long as they are not spent on broadcast ads run in the last 30 days before a primary or 60 days before a general election in which a clearly identified candidate is referred to and a relevant electorate is targeted.

TABLE 6–4 Top Twenty 527 Committees By Expenditures, 2003–2004

Rank	Committee	Total Expenditures
1	America Coming Together	$78,040,480
2	Joint Victory Campaign 2004	72,588,053
3	Media Fund	54,494,698
4	Service Employees International Union	39,579,709
5	Progress for America	35,631,378
6	Swift Boat Veterans and POWs for Truth	22,565,360
7	AFSCME	22,332,587
8	MoveOn.org	21,346,380
9	College Republican National Committee	17,260,655
10	New Democrat Network	12,524,063
11	Citizens for a Strong Senate	10,228,515
12	Club for Growth	9,034,364
13	Service Employees International Union	8,115,937
14	EMILY's List	8,100,752
15	Int'l Brotherhood of Electrical Workers	7,368,841
16	Voices for Working Families	7,202,695
17	AFL-CIO	6,473,110
18	Sierra Club	6,261,811
19	League of Conservation Voters	5,074,790
20	Club for Growth.net	4,039,892

SOURCE: The Center for Responsive Politics, "527 Committee Activity," at www.opensecrets.org/527s/527cmtes.asp, accessed July 21, 2005.

TABLE **6–5**   Top Ten Contributors to 527 Committees, 2003–2004

Rank	Contributor	Total Contributed
1	Joint Victory Campaign 2004*	$56,654,391
2	Service Employees International Union	53,187,817
3	AFSCME	30,327,630
4	Soros Fund Management/George Soros	23,881,000
5	Peter B Lewis/Progressive Corporation	22,395,000
6	Shangri-La Entertainment/Steve Bing	13,802,381
7	Victory Campaign 2004	13,365,000
8	Golden West Financial	13,012,959
9	AFL-CIO	11,424,853
10	Perry Homes	8,085,199

*Joint Victory Campaign 2004 is a joint fund-raising committee run by America Coming Together and the Media Fund. Money raised by JVC is divided between these two beneficiaries. Combining receipts for these three groups would result in double counting.

SOURCE: The Center for Responsive Politics, "Top-Twenty Contributors to 527 Committees," at www.opensecrets.org/527s/527contribs.asp?cycle=2004, accessed July 21, 2005.

Another notable example of one of these "527" groups is America Coming Together (ACT), which launched reportedly the largest voter mobilization project in American history,[73] utilizing voter lists and door-to-door canvassing to target voters for mobilization on election day. ACT's stated purpose was to "defeat George W. Bush and elect Democrats in federal, state, and local elections in 2004."[74] One of the most visible donors to this group was financier George Soros (see Table 6–5).

During the 2004 election cycle, 527 groups were much more active on the liberal or Democratic side than on the conservative or Republican side. There are several reasons for this. Democratic activists and allied interest groups understood that the BCRA ban on soft money would leave the party and its presidential candidate at a disadvantage against the fund-raising prowess of President Bush and the Republicans. As we discuss in Chapter 7, the Democrats were more dependent on soft money before BCRA. They thus started early and invested heavily in their 527 groups. Republicans and conservatives were less inclined to put money behind their Section 527 groups, in part because Republicans controlled the government and had been able to raise so much hard money in the past. The Republicans also doubted whether BCRA or the new 527 groups would survive the court challenge in *McConnell* v. *FEC* and the Federal Election Commission review process. When both BCRA and the 527 groups survived these challenges, the Republicans had lost valuable time in organizing and funding their 527 organizations. Interest groups allied to Democrats, including 527 groups, were again more active in 2006 than Republican-allied groups. Labor unions, teachers unions, trial lawyers, and 527 organizations like America Votes all were active in competitive federal races. The Chamber of Commerce and the NRA are examples of groups that tend to support Republicans.

Interest groups also utilized other sections of the tax code to involve themselves in the election. Section 501 of the tax code permits groups to organize, and, under Section 501(c)3, donations to the group are tax deductible. Because of their tax-deductible status, 501(c)3 groups avoid endorsing candidates but can get involved in voter registration and other nonpartisan activity. Other 501(c) organizations can be more political. More expressly political organizations like the AARP, the NRA, and MoveOn are 501(c)4 organizations. Contributions to these groups are not tax deductible. Labor unions are 501(c)5 organizations, while business groups like the Chamber of Commerce are 501(c)6 groups.[75] In 2004, several such groups were involved in the election. 501(c) groups supported both parties, but unlike the 527 groups, Republicans found more allies in the 501(c) organizations.[76] In 2006 the 501(c) organizations were involved in activities that helped register and inform voters, often with an indirect benefit to one party.

The heavy reliance of both sides in recent elections on 527 organizations and wealthy individual 527 donors raised questions about undue influence over elections from these individuals and what they expected in return if their side won the election. Regulation of 527 organizations is a topic President Bush, Senators John McCain and Russ Feingold, and others have pledged to pursue.

How Much Do Interest Groups Influence Elections and Legislation?

"Who, after all, can seriously contend that a $100,000 donation does not alter the way one thinks about—and quite possibly votes on— an issue?"

FORMER SENATOR ALAN SIMPSON

As discussed earlier, the pattern of PACs in giving more money to incumbents has meant that challengers face difficulties funding their campaigns. They have to rely more on individual contributors. Even with the larger individual contribution limits allowed in 2004, most challengers still had less money than their incumbent opponents.

How much does interest group money influence election outcomes, legislation, and representation? Former U.S. Senator Alan Simpson (R-Wyo.) testified in *McConnell* v. *FEC*, the court case to decide the constitutionality of BCRA, that "too often, members' first thought is not what is right or what they believe, but how it will affect fundraising. Who, after all, can seriously contend that a $100,000 donation does not alter the way one thinks about—and quite possibly votes on—an issue?"[77] Another former Senator, Warren Rudman (R-N.H.), said in the same court case that "you can't swim in the ocean without getting wet; you can't be part of this system without getting dirty."[78] In this area, as in others, money obviously talks. But it is easy to exaggerate its influence. Although a candidate may receive a great amount of interest group money, only a fraction of that total comes from any single group. It is also debatable how much campaign contributions affect elections, and there is no guarantee that winning candidates will be willing or able to "remember" their financial angels or that in the end the money produces a payoff in legislation.

Much depends, however, on the context in which money is given and received. Many campaigns—especially state and local campaigns—are small-scale undertakings in which a big contribution makes a difference. Amid all the murk of campaigning, a candidate may feel grateful for so tangible and useful a contribution as money. Studies demonstrate a significant relationship between the frequency of lobbying contacts and favorable treatment in the House Ways and Means and Agriculture committees. Campaign contributions are correlated with lobbying patterns, meaning that contributions to Representatives and Senators are more likely to result in committee action, "formulating amendments, negotiating specific provisions or report language behind the scenes, developing legislative strategy, and in other activities that require substantial time, information, and energy on the part of member and staff."[79]

Communicating with Voters and Members

One result of the recent campaign finance reforms was a surge in 2004 of interest groups communicating with voters via the mail and on the telephone. By closing down party soft money and limiting issue advocacy in television and radio ads in the weeks leading up to an election, the most recent reform makes issue advocacy via mail and telephone more attractive to individuals and groups. Examples of groups with

Campaign fundraisers such as this one often charge donors $1,000 a plate or more for the privilege of meeting the candidates and mingling with influential policymakers.

substantially enlarged issue advocacy efforts in 2004 included the U.S. Chamber of Commerce, NARAL Pro-Choice America, the NRA, and the Sierra Club.

How effective is electioneering by interest groups? In general, mass membership organizations fail to mobilize their full membership in elections, although these groups can effectively mobilize their membership when their interests are directly attacked, as was the case with the antiunion "paycheck protection" ballot initiatives in 1998 and 2000.[80] More typically, too many cross-pressures operate in the pluralistic politics of the United States for any one group to assume a commanding role. Some groups reach their maximum influence only by allying themselves closely with one of the two major parties. They may place their members on local, state, and national party committees and help send them to party conventions as delegates, but such alliances mean losing some independence.

Numerous groups sought to mobilize their membership in the 2004 presidential election. Groups created Web sites for members to obtain information on their organization's view of candidates and provided voter registration materials and absentee ballot request forms. They also solicited contributions to help fund these efforts. Organized labor, long perceived to be the leader in voter mobilization, was also especially active in 2004, as was the NRA. The Republican Party and allied groups, having learned from the techniques used by labor unions, mounted a successful party-based voter mobilization effort in 2006. Business groups like the Chamber of Commerce have come to use the Internet as a way to help members and supporters register to vote, request absentee ballots, and remind them to vote on election day. But most voter mobilization on the Republican side is done by the party. Democrats rely much more on allied groups like unions, environmental and pro-choice groups, and 527 organizations like America Votes. Their activity plus an energized base of supporters resulted in higher voter turnout in 2006.

Curing the Mischiefs of Faction— Two Centuries Later

I f **James Madison** were to return today, neither the existence of interest groups nor their variety would surprise him. However, the varied weapons of group influence, the deep involvement of interest groups in the electoral process, and the vast number of lobbyists in Washington and the state capitals might come as a surprise. And

Government's Greatest Endeavors

The Medicare Program

President Lyndon Johnson signs the Medicare bill.

QUESTIONS

How has Medicare helped your parents or grandparents?

Should younger, low-income Americans have access to Medicare?

Like Social Security, the Medicare program is one of the federal government's most popular initiatives. It provides medical coverage for more than 40 million Americans, covers most hospital bills, and allows beneficiaries to purchase additional federal insurance for outpatient care, physician visits, and laboratory fees. Under legislation passed in 2003, it now also provides coverage for prescription drugs. As national health care costs have risen over the decades, Medicare has emerged as one of the federal government's most expensive programs.

Medicare would not be a federal program at all, however, if not for heavy lobbying by interest groups for the elderly. President Harry S Truman originally raised the idea of some kind of national health care system in the late 1940s, but it was immediately opposed by the American Medical Association, which represents physicians. However, it was soon embraced by labor unions, who worried about helping their retired members cover health care costs, and by new interest groups such as the Council of Senior Citizens, which produced 17 million letters calling for action.

Despite growing demands for action, the bill remained stalled in Congress until the 1964 election, when President Lyndon Johnson won by a landslide and brought 65 new Democrats into Congress. With the increased support, Medicare quickly reached the top of the legislative agenda. Knowing that the bill was destined to become law, half the congressional Republicans broke with the American Medical Association and voted for passage. Johnson signed the bill in Independence, Missouri, Truman's hometown, and immediately enrolled the former president and his wife, Bess, as the nation's first two Medicare recipients. ■

doubtless Madison would still be concerned about the power of faction, especially its tendency to foster instability and injustice.

One of the main arguments against interest groups is that they do not represent people equally. For example, fewer interest groups represent young or low-income people than represent senior citizens or corporations. Further, some groups are better organized and better financed, allowing them a decided advantage over more general groups. And the existence of a multiplicity of interests often leads to incoherent policies, inefficiency, and delay as lawmakers try to appease conflicting interests. In addition, the propensity of interest groups to support incumbents in elections increases the advantages of incumbency, which is often seen as undesirable.

Concern about the evils of interest groups has been a recurrent theme throughout U.S. history. President Ronald Reagan in his Farewell Address warned of the power of "special interests,"[81] and President Dwight Eisenhower used his Farewell Address to warn against the "military-industrial complex," the alliance of defense industries and the U.S. military formed to pursue mutually beneficial policies.

Single-issue interest groups organized for or against particular policies—abortion, handgun control, tobacco subsidies, animal rights—have aroused concern in recent years. "It is said that citizen groups organizing in ever greater numbers to push single issues ruin the careers of otherwise fine politicians who disagree with them on one emotional issue, paralyze the traditional process of governmental compromise, and ignore the common good in their selfish insistence on getting their own way."[82] But which single issues reflect narrow interests? Women's rights—even a specific issue such as sexual harassment—are hardly "narrow," women's rights leaders contend, because women represent over half the population. Peace groups, too, claim that they represent the whole population, as do those who support prayer in schools. These issues may seem different from those related to subsidies for dairy farmers, for example.

What—if anything—should be done about factions? For decades, Americans have tried to find ways to keep interest groups in check. They have agreed with James Madison that the "remedy" of outlawing factions would be worse than the disease. It would be absurd to abolish liberty simply because it nourished faction. And the Constitution solidly protects the existence and activity of interest groups and lobbies. Moreover, interest groups provide important services. They supply needed and accurate information to government officials. But by safeguarding the value of liberty, have Americans allowed interest groups to threaten equality, the second great value in our national heritage? The question remains: How can we regulate interest groups in a way that does not threaten our constitutional liberties?

Federal and State Regulation

Americans have generally responded to this question by seeking to regulate lobbying in general and political money in particular. Concern over the use of money—especially corporate funds—to influence politicians goes back well over a century, to the Crédit Mobilier scandal during the administration of Ulysses S. Grant in the 1870s, when members of Congress promoted the Crédit Mobilier construction company in exchange for the right to make huge profits by buying its stock below market value. In the "progressive" era during the first two decades of the twentieth century, Congress legislated against corporate contributions in federal elections and required disclosure of the use of the money.

In 1921, President Warren G. Harding's administration allowed private companies to secretly lease public land that contained oil deposits that had been reserved for the navy. In response to this "Teapot Dome scandal," Congress passed the Federal Corrupt Practices Act of 1925. It required disclosure reports, both before and after elections, of receipts and expenditures by Senate and House candidates and by political committees that sought to influence federal elections in more than one state. Note that these were *federal* laws applying to *federal* elections; the states were left to regulate their own lobbying and elections.

But federal legislation was not very effective and was loosely enforced. Many candidates filed incomplete reports or none at all. The reform mood of the 1960s and the Watergate scandal of 1972 brought basic changes. The outcome was the Federal Election Campaign Act of 1971 (FECA), which was amended in 1974. We discuss FECA and the more recent BCRA in greater detail in Chapter 9.

During President Bill Clinton's first term, and after the Republicans won control of Congress in 1994, Congress passed the first major overhaul of lobbying laws since 1946. Under the Lobbying Disclosure Act of 1995, the definition of a lobbyist was expanded to include part-time lobbyists, those who deal with congressional staff or executive branch agencies, and those who represent foreign-owned companies and foreign entities. This act was expected to increase the number of registered lobbyists to as much as ten times its then current level.[83] In fact, the number of registered "clients" nearly doubled eight years after enactment of the act.[84] The act also included specific disclosure and information requirements.

As we have seen, groups are an important part of how democracy functions. They grow out of our associations, interests, and attitudes. Groups provide important political information and assistance to their members. They also are important participants in elections, policy making, the judicial process, and much of what our government does.

But groups can pose challenges and dangers to democracy, something Madison called the "mischiefs of faction." The excesses of lobbyist Jack Abramoff described at the beginning of this chapter illustrate some of these problems. But the excessive power of groups extends to many spheres. President Eisenhower, as noted, warned of a military-industrial complex, or the combination of large and powerful groups in and out of government.

How government seeks to limit the negative impact of corruption, the appearance of corruption, and undue influence by some groups to the detriment of other groups or the country as a whole is a formidable challenge. While fostering competition among groups is one important response, the need for government regulation including full disclosure of group activity has also proven necessary. At the same time government must be careful in its regulation of group activity to not stifle or limit the positive role groups play in the functioning of a constitutional democracy.

Summary

1. Interest groups exist to make demands on government. The dominant interest groups in the United States are economic or occupational, but the memberships of other groups—ideological, public interest, foreign policy, government itself, as well as ethnic, religious, and racial—cut across the big economic groupings. This both reduces and stabilizes their influence.

2. Many Americans have always been frustrated with government policies. Black people, women, and the economic underdogs have at various times organized themselves into movements.

3. Size, resources, cohesiveness, leadership, and techniques, especially the ability to contribute to candidates and political parties and to fund lobbyists, affect interest group power. But the actual power of an interest group stems from how these elements relate to the political and governmental environment in which the interest group operates.

4. Interest groups have long engaged in lobbying, but these efforts have become more significant as groups have become more involved in the electoral process, especially through the expanded use of political action committees (PACs). Interest groups also take their messages directly to the public through mass mailings and advertising. Other interest-group techniques include influencing rule making, litigation, election activities, and cooperative lobbying.

5. How PACs raise money and spend it on elections, especially for incumbents, has led to proposals to ban PACs or more strictly limit their activities. Yet the First Amendment protects their existence and rights.

6. Reforms of interest group excesses often include regulations about fairness, disclosure, and balance. All reform efforts must not infringe on the basic constitutional rights of individuals. The key issues today in "controlling factions" is whether to allow groups to proliferate and hope

a competition among groups will serve to check abuse or concentration of power or to seek reforms outside the groups by regulating them in their financing and limiting what they can give to policy makers.

7. Congress has enacted laws to regulate and reform excesses of interest groups in electoral democracy. The Federal Election Campaign Act (FECA) was passed in the 1970s in response to the Watergate scandal and the Bipartisan Campaign Reform Act (BCRA) was passed in 2002 in response to the soft money abuses by political parties and interest groups. The impact of these laws is debated and is often criticized for infringing on such rights as freedom of speech and freedom of association. Defenders of the reforms point to their success in removing large contributors from federal elections, at least for a couple of decades until groups found ways to circumvent the laws.

Further Reading

SCOTT H. AINSWORTH, *Analyzing Interest Groups: Group Influence on People and Policies* (Norton, 2002).

JEFFREY M. BERRY, *New Liberalism: The Rising Power of Citizen Groups* (Brookings Institution Press, 1999).

ROBERT BIERSACK ET AL., EDS., *After the Revolution: PACs, Lobbies, and the Republican Congress* (Addison-Wesley, 1999).

JEFFREY H. BIRNBAUM, *The Money Men: The Real Story of Fund-Raising's Influence on Political Power in America* (Crown, 2000).

WILLIAM P. BROWNE, *Groups, Interests, and Public Policy* (Georgetown University Press, 1998).

ALLAN J. CIGLER AND **BURDETT A. LOOMIS,** EDS., *Interest Group Politics*, 6th ed. (CQ Press, 2002).

MARTHA A. DERTHICK, *Up in Smoke* (CQ Press, 2002).

KENNETH M. GOLDSTEIN, *Interest Groups, Lobbying, and Participation in America* (Cambridge University Press, 1999).

GENE GROSSMAN AND **ELHANAN HELPMAN,** *Special Interest Politics* (MIT Press, 2001).

PAUL S. HERRNSON, RONALD G. SHAIKO, AND **CLYDE WILCOX,** *The Interest Group Connection: Electioneering, Lobbying, and Policymaking in Washington* (Chatham House, 1998).

ALLEN D. HERTZKE, *Representing God in Washington: The Role of Religious Lobbies in the American Polity* (University of Tennessee Press, 1988).

KEVIN W. HULA, *Lobbying Together: Interest Group Coalitions in Legislative Politics* (Georgetown University Press, 1999).

DAVID LOWERY AND **HOLLY BRASHER,** *Organized Interests and American Government* (McGraw-Hill, 2004).

DAVID B. MAGLEBY, ANTHONY D. CORRADO, AND **KELLY D. PATTERSON,** EDS., *Financing the 2004 Election* (Brookings Institution Press, 2006).

DAVID B. MAGLEBY, J. QUIN MONSON, AND **KELLY D. PATTERSON,** EDS., *Electing Congress: New Rules for an Old Game* (Prentice Hall, 2006).

MICHAEL J. MALBIN, ED., *The Election After Reform: Money, Politics, and the Bipartisan Campaign Reform Act* (Rowman & Littlefield, 2006).

ANTHONY J. NOWNES, *Pressure and Power: Organized Interests in American Politics* (Houghton Mifflin, 2001).

MANCUR OLSON, *The Logic of Collective Action* (Harvard University Press, 1965).

DAVID VOGEL, *Kindred Strangers: The Uneasy Relationship Between Politics and Business in America* (Princeton University Press, 1996).

JACK L. WALKER JR., *Mobilizing Interest Groups in America: Patrons, Professions, and Social Movements* (University of Michigan Press, 1991).

KeyTerms

faction, p. 144

pluralism, p. 144

interest group, p. 144

movement, p. 145

open shop, p. 148

closed shop, p. 148

free rider, p. 148

nongovernmental organization (NGO), p. 152

collective action, p. 154

public choice, p. 154

Federal Register, p. 157

amicus curiae brief, p. 158

lobbyist, p. 160

lobbying, p. 160

revolving door, p. 160

issue network, p. 160

political action committee (PAC), p. 162

leadership PAC, p. 163

bundling, p. 165

soft money, p. 166

quid pro quo, p. 166

independent expenditures, p. 166

issue advocacy, p. 167

527 organization, p. 168

Make It Real

INTEREST GROUPS

This unit lets students represent an interest group and try to get their legislation passed.

often problematic. In such democracies, holding power may be more important than the principle of democratic competition. Well-established parties help stabilize democracy.

This chapter begins by examining why parties are so vital to the functioning of democracy. We then examine the evolution of American political parties. Although American political parties have changed over time, they remain important in three different settings: as institutions, in government, and in the electorate. It is important to understand how parties facilitate democracy in all three settings. Finally, we discuss the strength of parties today and the prospects for party reform and renewal.

What Parties Do for Democracy

Party Functions

Political parties are organizations that seek political power by electing people to office, so that their positions and philosophy become public policy. American political parties serve a variety of political and social functions, some obvious and some not so obvious. They perform some functions well and others not so well, and how they perform them differs from place to place and time to time.

ORGANIZE THE COMPETITION One of the most important functions of parties is to organize the competition by designating candidates to run under their label. Parties exist primarily as an organizing mechanism to win elections and thus win control of government. For some races, parties recruit and nominate candidates for office; they register and activate voters; and they help candidates by training them, raising money for them, providing them with research and voter lists, and enlisting volunteers to work for them.[4] For more visible contests, especially ones in which there is a real chance of winning, multiple candidates often compete with each other for the nomination, often without party efforts to recruit them. Recently, campaign consultants rather than party officials have taken over some of these responsibilities; we explore this topic at some length in Chapter 10.[5]

The ability of parties to influence the selection of candidates varies by the type of nominating system used in the state. As discussed in Chapter 8, a few states use a *caucus* or *convention system*, which permits party leaders to play a role in the selection of nominees by placing their selection in the hands of people willing to attend party meetings called caucuses or conventions. Most people are not willing to invest this much time in a nomination process. Other states hold *primary elections* where voters cast ballots to select the party nominees. As more and more states turn to primary elections, the ability of party leaders to influence who runs under their party label is reduced. Candidates with little party experience but with well-known names or ample personal funds can often win in a primary over a person with a known track record of prior party service or success in a less visible office. Jon Corzine had never run for office and was not well known in New Jersey before spending $60 million in his successful 2000 campaign for the U.S. Senate. He left the Senate in 2005 to run successfully for governor of New Jersey; in this campaign he spent another $43 million of his own money.[6] Not all little-known, self-financed candidates win; in fact, they are often defeated. For example, Steve Forbes spent a combined $129 million in unsuccessful bids for the Republican presidential nomination in 1996 and 2000. Examples of former athletes who made successful candidates include Jim Bunning, a former baseball player and now senator from Kentucky; Bill Bradley, an All-American basketball player at Princeton who played for ten years with the New York Knicks and later served as a senator from New Jersey for three terms before unsuccessfully seeking the 2000 Democratic presidential nomination; University of Nebraska football coach Tom Osborne, who served three terms in the House of Representatives; and former NFL football player Jack Kemp, who served in the House of Representatives and was the Republican nominee for vice president in 1996.

Local and judicial elections in most states are **nonpartisan elections**, which

political party
An organization that seeks political power by electing people to office so that its positions and philosophy become public policy.

nonpartisan election
A local or judicial election in which candidates are not selected or endorsed by political parties and party affiliation is not listed on ballots.

"The political parties created democracy, and modern democracy is unthinkable save in terms of the parties."

POLITICAL SCIENTIST E. E. SCHATTSCHNEIDER

often problematic. In such democracies, holding power may be more important than the principle of democratic competition. Well-established parties help stabilize democracy.

This chapter begins by examining why parties are so vital to the functioning of democracy. We then examine the evolution of American political parties. Although American political parties have changed over time, they remain important in three different settings: as institutions, in government, and in the electorate. It is important to understand how parties facilitate democracy in all three settings. Finally, we discuss the strength of parties today and the prospects for party reform and renewal.

What Parties Do for Democracy

Party Functions

Political parties are organizations that seek political power by electing people to office, so that their positions and philosophy become public policy. American political parties serve a variety of political and social functions, some obvious and some not so obvious. They perform some functions well and others not so well, and how they perform them differs from place to place and time to time.

ORGANIZE THE COMPETITION   One of the most important functions of parties is to organize the competition by designating candidates to run under their label. Parties exist primarily as an organizing mechanism to win elections and thus win control of government. For some races, parties recruit and nominate candidates for office; they register and activate voters; and they help candidates by training them, raising money for them, providing them with research and voter lists, and enlisting volunteers to work for them.[4] For more visible contests, especially ones in which there is a real chance of winning, multiple candidates often compete with each other for the nomination, often without party efforts to recruit them. Recently, campaign consultants rather than party officials have taken over some of these responsibilities; we explore this topic at some length in Chapter 10.[5]

The ability of parties to influence the selection of candidates varies by the type of nominating system used in the state. As discussed in Chapter 8, a few states use a *caucus* or *convention system*, which permits party leaders to play a role in the selection of nominees by placing their selection in the hands of people willing to attend party meetings called caucuses or conventions. Most people are not willing to invest this much time in a nomination process. Other states hold *primary elections* where voters cast ballots to select the party nominees. As more and more states turn to primary elections, the ability of party leaders to influence who runs under their party label is reduced. Candidates with little party experience but with well-known names or ample personal funds can often win in a primary over a person with a known track record of prior party service or success in a less visible office. Jon Corzine had never run for office and was not well known in New Jersey before spending $60 million in his successful 2000 campaign for the U.S. Senate. He left the Senate in 2005 to run successfully for governor of New Jersey; in this campaign he spent another $43 million of his own money.[6] Not all little-known, self-financed candidates win; in fact, they are often defeated. For example, Steve Forbes spent a combined $129 million in unsuccessful bids for the Republican presidential nomination in 1996 and 2000. Examples of former athletes who made successful candidates include Jim Bunning, a former baseball player and now senator from Kentucky; Bill Bradley, an All-American basketball player at Princeton who played for ten years with the New York Knicks and later served as a senator from New Jersey for three terms before unsuccessfully seeking the 2000 Democratic presidential nomination; University of Nebraska football coach Tom Osborne, who served three terms in the House of Representatives; and former NFL football player Jack Kemp, who served in the House of Representatives and was the Republican nominee for vice president in 1996.

Local and judicial elections in most states are **nonpartisan elections**, which

political party
An organization that seeks political power by electing people to office so that its positions and philosophy become public policy.

nonpartisan election
A local or judicial election in which candidates are not selected or endorsed by political parties and party affiliation is not listed on ballots.

PAUL S. HERRNSON, RONALD G. SHAIKO, AND **CLYDE WILCOX,** *The Interest Group Connection: Electioneering, Lobbying, and Policymaking in Washington* (Chatham House, 1998).

ALLEN D. HERTZKE, *Representing God in Washington: The Role of Religious Lobbies in the American Polity* (University of Tennessee Press, 1988).

KEVIN W. HULA, *Lobbying Together: Interest Group Coalitions in Legislative Politics* (Georgetown University Press, 1999).

DAVID LOWERY AND **HOLLY BRASHER,** *Organized Interests and American Government* (McGraw-Hill, 2004).

DAVID B. MAGLEBY, ANTHONY D. CORRADO, AND **KELLY D. PATTERSON,** EDS., *Financing the 2004 Election* (Brookings Institution Press, 2006).

DAVID B. MAGLEBY, J. QUIN MONSON, AND **KELLY D. PATTERSON,** EDS., *Electing Congress: New Rules for an Old Game* (Prentice Hall, 2006).

MICHAEL J. MALBIN, ED., *The Election After Reform: Money, Politics, and the Bipartisan Campaign Reform Act* (Rowman & Littlefield, 2006).

ANTHONY J. NOWNES, *Pressure and Power: Organized Interests in American Politics* (Houghton Mifflin, 2001).

MANCUR OLSON, *The Logic of Collective Action* (Harvard University Press, 1965).

DAVID VOGEL, *Kindred Strangers: The Uneasy Relationship Between Politics and Business in America* (Princeton University Press, 1996).

JACK L. WALKER JR., *Mobilizing Interest Groups in America: Patrons, Professions, and Social Movements* (University of Michigan Press, 1991).

KeyTerms

faction, p. 144

pluralism, p. 144

interest group, p. 144

movement, p. 145

open shop, p. 148

closed shop, p. 148

free rider, p. 148

nongovernmental organization (NGO), p. 152

collective action, p. 154

public choice, p. 154

Federal Register, p. 157

amicus curiae brief, p. 158

lobbyist, p. 160

lobbying, p. 160

revolving door, p. 160

issue network, p. 160

political action committee (PAC), p. 162

leadership PAC, p. 163

bundling, p. 165

soft money, p. 166

quid pro quo, p. 166

independent expenditures, p. 166

issue advocacy, p. 167

527 organization, p. 168

Make It Real

INTEREST GROUPS

This unit lets students represent an interest group and try to get their legislation passed.

Chapter 7

Political Parties

ESSENTIAL TO DEMOCRACY

★

SOME YEARS AGO, A COMMUNITY COLLEGE DISTRICT IN LOS ANGELES HELD A NONPARTISAN ELECTION FOR ITS TRUSTEES IN WHICH ANY REGISTERED VOTER COULD RUN IF HE OR SHE PAID THE $50 FILING FEE AND GATHERED 500 VALID SIGNATURES ON A PETITION. A TOTAL OF 133 CANDIDATES RAN, AND EACH VOTER COULD CAST UP TO SEVEN VOTES IN THE ELECTION. POLITICAL PARTIES WERE NOT ALLOWED TO NOMINATE CANDIDATES, AND PARTY LABELS DID NOT APPEAR ON THE BALLOT TO HELP ORIENT VOTERS TO THE CANDIDATES.

How did people vote in an election without parties? Candidates were listed alphabetically, and those whose names began with the letters A to F did better than those later in the alphabet. Being well known was an advantage. Endorsements by the *Los Angeles Times* also influenced the outcome, as did campaigning by a conservative group. A Mexican American surname also helped. In this election, an important voting cue was absent: incumbency. Because the board of trustees was newly created, none of the candidates were incumbents. Can-

didates who are incumbents have an advantage because they are generally better known and have been active, and have provided services for their constituents.[1]

Rarely do American voters face such unorganized and plentiful choices, because parties give structure to national and state elections. E. E. Schattschneider, a noted political scientist, once said, "The political parties created democracy, and modern democracy is unthinkable save in terms of the parties."[2] This provocative statement is true, but such a favorable evaluation of political parties runs counter to a long-standing and deep-seated American fear and distrust of them. Experience has taught us that free people create political parties to promote their own goals. Even though our founders hoped to discourage them, political parties quickly became an integral part of our political system.

Parties serve many functions, including the important one of narrowing the choices for voters.[3] They also help organize the government, a topic we also explore in this chapter. They are both a consequence of democracy and an instrument of it. As institutions, parties need not be strong and cohesive like those in Britain and most European democracies, but few, if any, democratic systems do not have political parties. Elections serve the vital task of deciding who can legitimately exercise political power, and parties are an integral part of making national and state elections work. We Americans take for granted the peaceful transfer of power from one elected official to another and from one party to another, yet in new democracies, the transfer of power after an election is

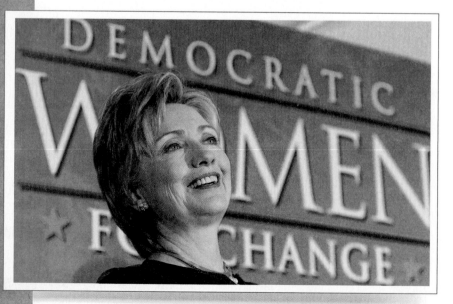

means that no party affiliation is indicated. Such systems make it more difficult for political parties to operate—precisely why many jurisdictions have adopted this reform. Proponents of nonpartisan local and judicial elections contend that party affiliation is not important to being a good judge or school board member. As with our example of the community college board at the beginning of this chapter, many voters in these nonpartisan elections rely more on how recognizable the name of a candidate is, or whether he or she now holds office (incumbency). In addition, fewer voters tend to turn out for nonpartisan elections than for standard partisan elections.[7]

UNIFY THE ELECTORATE   Parties are often accused of creating conflict, but they actually help unify the electorate and moderate conflict, at least within the party. Both parties have a strong incentive to fight out their differences inside the party but then come together to take on the opposition. Moreover, to win elections, parties need to reach out to voters outside their party and gain their support. This action also helps unify the electorate, at least into the two large national political parties in our system.

Parties have great difficulty building coalitions on controversial issues like abortion or gun control. Not surprisingly, candidates and parties generally try to avoid defining themselves or the election in single-issue terms. Rather, they hope that if voters disagree with the party's stand on one issue, they will still support the party because they agree with it on other issues. Deemphasizing single issues in this way helps defuse conflict and unify the electorate.

HELP ORGANIZE GOVERNMENT   Although political parties in the United States are not as cohesive as in some other democracies, parties are important when it comes to organizing our state and national governments. Congress is organized along party lines. The political party with the most votes in each chamber elects the officers of that chamber, selects the chair of each committee, and has a majority on all the committees. State legislatures, with the notable exception of Nebraska, are also organized along party lines. The 2004 election enlarged the Republican majorities in the U.S. Senate and U.S. House of Representatives. In the Senate, the GOP rose from 51 to 55 members, but this number remained below the number needed to override a filibuster. Republicans continued to control all committee chairs, but due to party rules, there was some rotation among Republicans. The Senate Judiciary Committee chairmanship, for example, switched in 2005 from Orrin Hatch (R-Utah) to Arlen Specter (R-Penn.). In 2007, when the Democrats regained control of the Senate, Senator Patrick Leahy (D-Vt.) became committee chair. In 2006 the Republican party nominated former Pittsburgh Steelers wide receiver and Hall of Fame member Lynn Swann for governor of Pennsylvania. Democratic incumbent Ed Rendell defeated Swann, getting 60 percent of the vote.

The party that controls the White House, the governor's mansion, or city hall gets **patronage**, which means it can select party members as public officials or judges. Such appointments are limited only by civil service regulations that restrict patronage typically to the top posts, but these posts, which number about 3,000 in the federal government without including ambassadors, U.S. Marshals, and U.S. Attorneys, are also numerous at the state and local levels. Patronage provides an incentive for people to become involved in politics and gives the party leaders and elected politicians loyal partisans in key positions to help them achieve their policy objectives. Patronage, sometimes called the spoils system, has declined dramatically from what it once was.

TRANSLATE PREFERENCES INTO POLICY   One of the great strengths of our democracy is that even the party that wins an election usually has to moderate what it does to win reelection. For that reason, public policy seldom changes dramatically with each election. Nonetheless, the party that wins the election has a chance to enact its policies and implement its campaign promises.

American parties have had only limited success in setting the course of national policy, especially when compared to countries with strong parties. The European model of party government, which has been called a *responsible party system*, assumes that parties discipline their members through their control over nominations and campaigns. Officeholders in such party-centered systems are expected to act according to party wishes and vote along party lines—or they will not be allowed to run again under

patronage
The dispensing of government jobs to persons who belong to the winning political party.

the party label, generally eliminating officeholders' prospects of winning reelection. Moreover, candidates run on fairly specific party platforms and are expected to implement those policies if they win control in the election.

Although we lack a European-type party system, most but not all Democrats in Congress vote together, as do most but not all Republicans. There are times, however, when a president of one party receives more congressional votes from the opposing party than from his own, as President Bill Clinton did in 2000 on legislation granting China permanent normal trade relations status with the United States.[8] And when the House passed the Enhanced Border Security and Visa Entry Reform Act of 2002, which President Bush wanted, nearly twice as many Democrats voted yes—182, compared to 92 yes votes from the Republicans.[9]

Because American parties do not control nominations, they are less able to discipline members who express views contrary to those of the party.[10] The American system is largely *candidate-centered;* politicians are nominated largely on the basis of their qualifications and personal appeal, not party loyalty. In fact, it is more correct to say that in most contests, we have *candidate* politics rather than *party* politics. As a consequence, party leaders cannot guarantee passage of their program, even if they are in the majority.

Even though parties cannot exert tight control over candidates, their ability to raise and spend money has had a significant influence. Through the 2002 election, parties played an important role in competitive federal elections through their **soft money** expenditures in particular contests.[11] In the 2002 South Dakota Senate race, for example, the party committees and allied interest groups spent a combined $12 million, equaling what the two major party candidates spent in that race.[12]

The Bipartisan Campaign Reform Act (BCRA), which took effect in the 2003–2004 election cycle, abolished soft money donations to political parties at the federal level. Soft money consisted of contributions given to the political parties by individuals, corporations, labor unions, and political action committees (PACs) for "party-building" purposes that came to be used for candidate promotion. Corporations and unions could also give the parties soft money from their general funds, something they could not do in support of candidates or other party activities. Because such contributions were unlimited, parties put a premium on raising them. The ads soft money paid for were often candidate-centered and focused on themes important to that race.[13]

Political parties responded to the soft money ban by raising more of the limited **hard money** from individuals and PACs. BCRA made this easier by raising the contribution limits for individuals from $1,000 to $2,000.[14] In an election cycle, an individual who wanted to give the maximum possible amount to candidates and parties could give $95,000, up from $50,000.[15] Both parties raised record-setting amounts of hard money in 2003–2004, surpassing what they had raised in hard and soft money combined in 1999–2000 or 2001–2002. Party hard money in 2004 was spent on a range of activities including get-out-the-vote efforts, contributions to candidates, and advertising. Parties may contribute $5,000 of hard money to House candidates and $35,000 to Senate candidates per election cycle, and additional money in hard money coordinated expenditures. The law permits political parties to spend limited amounts of hard money on campaign activities that are coordinated with the candidate and in which the candidate pays part of the cost. Between 1996 and 2004, parties had scaled back their coordinated spending and contributions to candidates, focusing instead on soft money.

More recently, political parties may spend unlimited amounts of hard money on **independent expenditures** for or against candidates. The Supreme Court gave parties and groups the same right to independent expenditures in a 1996 decision, *Colorado Republican Federal Campaign Committee* v. *FEC.*[16] In 2003–2004, with soft money not an option and with more success in raising hard money, both parties made substantial independent expenditures. For example, in the 2004 special election in South Dakota, the two parties combined spent nearly $3 million, mostly in independent expenditures.[17]

soft money
Money raised in unlimited amounts by political parties for party-building purposes. Now largely illegal except for limited contributions to state or local parties for voter registration and get-out-the-vote efforts.

hard money
Political contributions given to a party, candidate, or interest group that are limited in amount and fully disclosed. Raising such limited funds is harder than raising unlimited funds, hence the term "hard money."

independent expenditure
The Supreme Court has ruled that individuals, groups, and parties can spend unlimited amounts in campaigns for or against candidates as long as they operate independently from the candidates. When an individual, group, or party does so, they are making an independent expenditure.

PROVIDE LOYAL OPPOSITION Accountability in a democracy comes from the party out of power closely monitoring and commenting on the actions of the party in power. When national security issues are involved or the country is under attack, parties restrain their criticism, as the Democrats in Congress did for some time after September 11, 2001. There is usually a polite interval following an election—known as the **honeymoon**—after which the opposition party begins to criticize the party that controls the White House, especially when the opposition party controls one or both houses of Congress.[18] The length of the honeymoon depends in part on how close the vote was in the election, on how contentious the agenda of the new administration is, and on the leadership skills of the new president. Early success in enacting policy can prolong the honeymoon; mistakes or controversies can shorten it.

The Nomination of Candidates

From the beginning, parties have been the mechanism by which candidates for public office are chosen. The **caucus** played an important part in pre-Revolutionary politics and continued to be important in our early history as elected officials organized themselves into groups or parties and together selected candidates to run for higher office, including the presidency. This method of nomination operated for several decades after the United States was established.

As early as the 1820s, however, charges of "secret deals" were made against this method. Moreover, it was not representative of people from areas where a party was in a minority or nonexistent, since only officeholders took part in the caucus. Efforts were made to make the caucus more representative of rank-and-file party members. The *mixed caucus* brought in delegates from districts in which the party had no elected legislators.

Then, during the 1830s and 1840s, a system of **party conventions** was instituted. Delegates, usually chosen directly by party members in towns and cities, selected the party candidates, debated and adopted a platform, and built party spirit by celebrating noisily. But the convention method soon came under criticism that it was subject to control by the party bosses and their machines.

To involve more voters and reduce the power of the bosses to pick party nominees, states adopted the **direct primary**, in which people could vote for the party's nominees for office. Primaries spread rapidly after Wisconsin adopted them in 1905—in the North as a Progressive Era reform and in the South as a way to bring democracy to a region that had seen no meaningful general elections since the end of Reconstruction in the 1870s, due to one-party rule by the Democrats. By 1920, direct primaries were the norm for some offices in almost all states.

Today the direct primary is the typical method of picking party candidates. Primaries vary significantly from state to state. They differ in terms of (1) who may run in a primary and how one qualifies for the ballot; (2) whether the party organization can or does endorse candidates before the primary; (3) who may vote in a party's primary—that is, whether a voter must register with a party to vote; and (4) how many votes are needed for nomination—a plurality, a majority, or some other number determined by party rule or state law. The differences among primaries are not trivial; they have an important impact on the role played by party organization and on the strategy used by candidates.

In states with **open primaries**, any voter, regardless of party, can participate in the

A precinct captain takes a head count during the caucus in Burlington, Iowa, on January 19, 2004. John Kerry easily won the precinct.

honeymoon
Period at the beginning of a new president's term during which the president enjoys generally positive relations with the press and Congress, usually lasting about six months.

caucus
A meeting of local party members to choose party officials or candidates for public office and to decide the platform.

party convention
A meeting of party delegates to vote on matters of policy and in some cases to select party candidates for public office.

direct primary
Election in which voters choose party nominees.

open primary
Primary election in which any voter, regardless of party, may vote.

primary of whichever party he or she chooses. This kind of primary permits **crossover voting**—Republicans and Independents helping determine who the Democratic nominee will be, and vice versa. Other states use **closed primaries**, in which only persons already registered in that party may participate. Some states, like Washington and California, experimented with *blanket primaries*, in which all voters could vote for any candidate, regardless of party. Blanket primaries permitted voters to vote for a candidate of one party for one office and for a candidate from another party for another office, something that is not permitted under either closed or open primaries. In 2000, the Supreme Court held that California's blanket primary violated the free association rights of political parties, in part because blanket primaries permit people who have "expressly affiliated with a rival" party to have a vote in the selection of a nominee from a different party.[19] In a detailed study of California's blanket primary, political scientists found that less than 5 percent of voters associated with one party actually voted for nominees from another party. More broadly, they concluded that the rules of a primary are important in determining the winner.[20]

Along with modern communications and fund-raising techniques, direct primaries have diminished the influence of leaders of political parties. Many critics believe that this change has had more undesirable than desirable consequences. Party leaders now have less influence over who gets to be the party's candidate, and candidates are less accountable to the party both during and after the election.

Direct primaries are used to nominate most party candidates for most offices. Yet in some states, local caucuses choose delegates to attend regional meetings, which in turn select delegates to state and national conventions, where they nominate party candidates for offices. The Iowa presidential caucuses, in which 122,000 Iowans participated in 2004,[21] are highly publicized as the first important test of potential presidential nominees.[22]

In a few states, conventions still play a role in the nominating process for state and federal candidates. In Connecticut, for example, convention choices become the party nominees unless they are challenged. Candidates who attain at least 15 percent of the vote in the convention have an automatic right to challenge the winner at the convention, but they do not always exercise this right.[23] In Utah, if a candidate gets 60 percent of the delegate vote at the convention, there is no primary election for that office. If no candidate gets 60 percent, only the top two candidates are listed on the primary ballot. In other states, convention nominees are designated as such on the primary ballot; they may or may not receive help from the party organization. Conventions are also used to invigorate the party faithful by enabling them to meet with their leaders.

In most states, candidates can get their names on the ballot as an Independent or minor party candidate by securing the required number of signatures on a nomination petition. This is hard to do, but it can be done, as Ross Perot demonstrated in his campaign for president in 1992. He spent his own money to build an organization of volunteers who put his name on the ballot in all 50 states. Minor party gubernatorial candidates like the Minnesota Reform party's Jesse Ventura in 1998 or the Green party's presidential candidate Ralph Nader in 2000 secured their nominations as candidates of existing minor parties. Nader was on the ballot in 34 states and the District of Columbia as an independent candidate in 2004. Democrats successfully challenged his efforts to qualify for the ballot in Ohio, Arizona, and Pennsylvania. Some Republicans supported Nader's efforts to be on the ballot in more states, a move Democrats suspected was intended to draw support from John Kerry. Ballot access remains a major hurdle for minor party candidates.

Party Systems

Ours is a two-party system; most other democracies have a multiparty system. Although we have many minor parties, only the two major parties have much of a chance to win elections. Multiparty systems are almost always found in countries that have a parliamentary government, in contrast to our presidential system.

Parliamentary systems usually have a *head of state*, often called the president, but

crossover voting
Voting by a member of one party for a candidate of another party.

closed primary
Primary election in which only persons registered in the party holding the primary may vote.

How Other Nations **Govern**

Israel's Coalition Government

Israel has a multiparty system. Though Israelis vote for prime minister and parliament separately, the prime minister must still have the support of the majority of the members of parliament. If he doesn't, he is in danger of facing a parliamentary vote of no confidence. A vote of no confidence can lead to new elections for prime minister and parliament. Because there are many parties, it is difficult—if not impossible—for any one party to gain a majority of the seats in the Knesset, the Israeli parliament. Usually one party can get only a plurality of the seats. A party with only a plurality of seats must form a coalition with other parties to maintain power. Concessions like key cabinet positions may need to be made to those parties to convince them to join. If the ruling party loses the support of its coalition partners, the prime minister and his party must form a new coalition or else their government will be toppled by a parliamentary vote of no confidence.

The conflicts with the Palestinians and disagreement over how best to coexist with them have sometimes destabilized Israeli coalition governments. In July 2000, Prime Minister Ehud Barak, after upsetting rightist parties within his coalition by having peace talks with the Palestinians, called an early election for prime minister to avoid a vote of "no confidence." Ariel Sharon, an outspoken critic of Barak, soundly defeated him in the election. As the conflict with the Palestinians escalated, Sharon in early 2004 surprised many, including the rightist members of his governing coalition, by announcing that Israel would withdraw all its settlements from the Gaza strip and some settlements from the West Bank. Facing opposition from some in his cabinet and coalition,* Sharon invited the more leftist Labor party to join his coalition.† This in turn prompted Sharon's own Likud party to vote against Labor joining their coalition. By late 2005 Sharon left the Likud Party and formed the Kadima party, which won the most seats in the Knesset in the March 2006 election.

In early 2006, however, Sharon, who had created the new party and whose reputation helped it win power, suffered two incapacitating strokes leaving him unable to govern. In his place Ehud Olmert became leader of Kadima and prime minister in a coalition with Labor and several other parties.‡ Such a change in leadership can occur without another election. Olmert faced not only the challenges of carrying on Sharon's policies but a Palestinian government headed by Hamas, an Islamist group that denounces Israel's right to exist and is classified by the United States and other countries as a terrorist organization.

The shifting coalitions and changes in leadership in Israel illustrate the scrambling and compromising that often occur within countries that have multiparty systems. But this example also illustrates that strong leaders like Sharon can make bold policy changes, and even leave their party to form a new party and win the most seats in the next parliamentary election. ■

Because there are many parties, it is difficult—if not impossible—for any one party to gain a majority of the seats in the Knesset, the Israeli parliament.

---

*Gil Hoffman, "Sharon: Settlements in Gaza Cannot Remain," *The Jerusalem Post,* February 3, 2004, p. 1.
†Greg Myre, "Sharon Invites His Favorite Dove to Help Build a Coalition," *The New York Times*, July 13, 2004, p. 4.
‡"Ehud Olmert" at www.mfa.gov.il/MFA/MFAArchive/2000_2009/2003/3/Ehud+Olmert.htm Accessed 21 September, 2006.

---

they also have a *head of the government*, often called the prime minister or chancellor, who is the leader of one of the large parties in the legislature. In Germany, the chancellor, currently Angela Merkel, is elected by parliament and holds the greatest share of executive power. Typically, the chancellor comes from the largest party of a coalition of two or more parties and maintains power throughout a four-year term. In Germany, the president's responsibilities are mostly ceremonial, and he is expected to function in a politically neutral way. In democracies with multiparty systems, such as Israel and Italy, because no one party has a majority of the votes, *coalition* governments are necessary. Minor parties can gain concessions—positions in a cabinet or support of policies they want implemented—in return for joining a coalition. Major parties need the minor parties and are therefore willing to bargain. Thus the multiparty system favors the existence of minor parties by giving them incentives to persevere and disproportionate power if they will help form a government.

In some multiparty parliamentary systems, parties run slates of candidates for legislative positions, and winners are determined by **proportional representation**, in which the parties receive a proportion of the legislators corresponding to their proportion of the vote. In our **winner-take-all system**, only the candidate with the most votes in a district or state takes office.[24] Because a party does not gain anything by finishing second, minor parties in a two-party system can rarely overcome the assumption that a vote for them is a wasted vote.[25] Even if a third-party candidate can keep either major party candidate from receiving more than 50 percent (a *majority*) of the vote, the candidate with the most votes (a *plurality*) wins.

In multiparty systems, parties at the extremes are apt to have more influence than in our two-party system, and in nations with a multiparty system, their legislatures more accurately reflect the full range of the views of the electorate. Political parties in multiparty systems can be more doctrinaire than ours because they do not have to appeal to masses of people. Even though parties that do not become part of the governing coalition may have little to say in setting government policy, they survive because they appeal to some voters. Under such a system, third, fourth, or additional parties have an incentive to run because they may win some seats. In contrast, our two-party system tends to create *centrist* parties that appeal to moderate elements and suppress the views of extremists in the electorate. Moreover, once elected, our parties do not form as cohesive a voting bloc as ideological parties do in multiparty systems.

Multiparty parliamentary systems often make governments unstable as coalitions form and collapse. In addition, swings in policy when party control changes can be dramatic. In contrast, two-party systems produce governments that tend to be stable and centrist, and as a result, policy changes occur incrementally.

Minor Parties: Persistence and Frustration

Although we have a primarily two-party system in the United States, we also have **minor parties**, sometimes called *third parties*. Candidate-based parties that arise around a candidate usually disappear when the charismatic personality does. Examples of such parties are Theodore Roosevelt's Bull Moose party and George Wallace's American Independent party. Wallace's party polled more than 13 million votes and won 46 electoral votes in 1968. Ross Perot won 19 million votes, 19 percent of the total vote in 1992.[26] He did only about half as well in 1996, despite having organized a political party. Without Perot to lead it, the Reform party was badly divided in 2000. Its presidential candidate, Pat Buchanan, failed to reach 1 percent of the national popular vote and thus lost the Reform party much of the ground it had gained under Perot in terms of ballot access and federal campaign funding.

Minor parties that are organized around an *ideology* usually persist over a longer time than those built around a particular leader. Communist, Prohibition, Libertarian, Right to Life, and Green parties are of the ideological type. Minor parties of both types come and go, and several minor parties usually run in any given election.[27] Some parties arise around a single issue, like the Right to Life party active in states like New York. The Green Party is an example of an ideological third party, although it had a more recognized presidential nominee in Ralph Nader in 2000. Although not on the ballot in seven states, it mounted a major effort to reach 5 percent of the popular presidential vote for Nader and thereby qualify the party for federal funding in the 2004 elections. The effort failed. The Green Party mustered only 3 percent of the popular vote. In 2004, Nader, running as an independent, but endorsed by the Reform party, received just one-third of 1 percent of the vote.

Major parties have criticized minor parties as "spoilers," diverting votes away from the major party candidate and costing that candidate the election. Nader was accused of doing this to Al Gore in 2000, just as Perot was accused of costing George Bush reelection in 1992. In 2000, interest groups identified with environmental issues ran ads urging voters not to waste their vote on Nader, who could not win the election. The closeness of the 2000 election and the perception that Nader may have cost Gore the White House meant that Democrats aggressively tried to block access to the ballot for Nader in 2004 and stressed his potential to again be a spoiler. Early in

proportional representation
An election system in which each party running receives the proportion of legislative seats corresponding to its proportion of the vote.

winner-take-all system
An election system in which the candidate with the most votes wins.

minor party
A small political party that rises and falls with a charismatic candidate or, if composed of ideologies on the right or left, usually persists over time; also called a *third party*.

the campaign, Kerry and Nader met and the candidates were on good terms. This later dissipated as Nader criticized the Democratic party and the lack of differences between Kerry and George W. Bush.

Minor parties have had an indirect influence in our country by drawing attention to controversial issues and by organizing such groups as the antislavery and the civil rights movements.[28] Ross Perot, for example, elevated the importance of balanced budgets in 1992 and made it more difficult for George Bush to attack Bill Clinton on character issues.[29] However, they have never won the presidency or more than a handful of congressional seats (see Table 7–1).[30] They have done somewhat better in gubernatorial elections.[31] They have never shaped national policy from *inside* the government, and their influence on national policy and on the platforms of the two major parties has been limited.[32]

Examples of minor parties operating in recent elections include the Libertarian, Green, and Reform parties. The **Libertarian party** (www.lp.org) emphasizes individual liberties, personal responsibility, and freedom from government. Its agenda calls for an end to the federal government's role in education and crime control. Libertarians believe that "if government's role were limited to protecting our lives, rights and property, America would prosper and thrive as never before." Libertarians also believe that "every service supplied by the government can be provided better *and* cheaper by private business." Libertarians favor, in their terms, "re-legalizing" drugs and prostitution and also support open immigration. In 2006, 603 Libertarians ran for federal, state, and local office.[33]

The **Green party** (www.gp.org) takes its name from other pro-environment parties in many countries. In the United States, the Greens not only embrace pro-environment positions but are also committed to social justice, decentralization, respect for diversity, community-based economics, nonviolence, feminism, ecological wisdom, grassroots democracy, and personal and global responsibility. The party's 2004 presidential candidate, David Cobb, called for public campaign financing, greater environmental protection, and affordable housing. The party seeks to achieve social justice, eliminate discrimination, and promote self-reliance.

The **Reform party** (www.reformparty.org) was organized in 1995 by Ross Perot. It focuses on national government reform, fiscal responsibility, and political accountability. Internal division and a poor showing by the candidate it endorsed in 2004—Ralph Nader—means the future of the Reform party is uncertain.

In 2004, independent presidential candidate Ralph Nader received one-third of 1 percent of the popular vote.

"If I could not go to heaven but with a party, I would not go there at all."

THOMAS JEFFERSON

A Brief History of American Political Parties

Our First Parties

To the founders of the young Republic, parties meant bigger, better-organized, and fiercer factions, which they did not want. Benjamin Franklin worried about the "infinite mutual abuse of parties, tearing to pieces the best of characters." In his Farewell Address, George Washington warned against the "baneful effects of the Spirit of Party." And Thomas Jefferson said, "If I could not go to heaven but with a party, I would not go there at all."[34]

How, then, did parties start? They came largely out of practical necessity. The same early leaders who so frequently stated their opposition to political parties also recognized the need to organize officeholders who shared their views so that government could act. In 1787, parties began to form as citizens debated over ratifying the U.S. Constitution. To get Congress to pass its measures, the Washington administration had to fashion a coalition among factions. This job fell to Treasury Secretary Alexander Hamilton, who built an informal Federalist party, while Washington stayed "above politics."

Secretary of State Jefferson and other officials, many of whom despised Hamilton and his aristocratic ways as much as they opposed the policies he favored, were uncertain about how to deal with these political differences. Their overriding concern was the success of the new government; personal loyalty to Washington was a close second. Thus

Libertarian party
A minor party that believes in extremely limited government. Libertarians call for a free market system, expanded individual liberties such as drug legalization, and a foreign policy of nonintervention, free trade, and open immigration.

Green party
A minor party dedicated to the environment, social justice, nonviolence, and a foreign policy of nonintervention. Ralph Nader ran as the Green party's nominee in 2000.

Reform party
A minor party founded by Ross Perot in 1995. It focuses on national government reform, fiscal responsibility, and political accountability. It has recently struggled with internal strife and criticism that it lacks an identity.

TABLE 7–1   Minor Parties in the United States

Year	Party	Presidential Candidate	Percentage of Popular Vote Received	Electoral Votes
1832	Anti-Masonic	William Wirt	8%	7
1856	American (Know-Nothing)	Millard Fillmore	22	8
1860	Democratic (Secessionist)	John C. Breckinridge	18	72
1860	Constitutional Union	John Bell	13	39
1892	People's (Populist)	James B. Weaver	9	22
1912	Bull Moose	Theodore Roosevelt	27	88
1912	Socialist	Eugene V. Debs	6	0
1924	Progressive	Robert M. La Follette	17	13
1948	States' Rights (Dixiecrat)	Strom Thurmond	2	39
1948	Progressive	Henry A. Wallace	2	0
1968	American Independent	George C. Wallace	14	46
1980	National Unity	John Anderson	7	0
1992	Independent	Ross Perot	19	0
1996	Reform	Ross Perot	8	0
2000	Reform	Pat Buchanan	0	0
2000	Green	Ralph Nader	3	0
2004	Reform	Ralph Nader	0	0

Jefferson stayed in the cabinet, despite his opposition to administration policies, during most of Washington's first term. When he left the cabinet at the end of 1793, many who joined him in opposition to the administration's economic policies remained in Congress, forming a group of legislators opposed to Federalist fiscal policies and eventually to Federalist foreign policy, which appeared "soft on Britain." This party was later known as Republicans, then as Democratic-Republicans, and finally as Democrats.[35]

Realigning Elections

American political parties have evolved and changed over time, but some underlying characteristics have been constant. Historically, we have had a two-party system with minor parties. This differentiates us from most nations which have one-party or multiparty systems. Our parties are moderate and accommodative, meaning that they are open to people with diverse outlooks. Political scientist V. O. Key and others have argued that our party system has been shaped in large part by **realigning elections**. Also called critical elections, they are turning points that define the agenda of politics and the alignment of voters within parties during periods of historic change in the economy and society. Realigning elections are characterized by intense voter involvement, disruptions of traditional voting patterns, changes in the relations of power within the community, and the formation of new and durable electoral groupings. They have occurred cyclically, not randomly. These elections tend to coincide with expansions of the suffrage or changes in the rate of voting.[36] We focus here on four realigning elections: 1824, 1860, 1896, and 1932.

1824: ANDREW JACKSON AND THE DEMOCRATS   Party politics was invigorated following the election of 1824, in which the leader in the popular vote—the hero of the battle of New Orleans, Democrat Andrew Jackson—failed to achieve the necessary majority of the electoral college and was defeated by John Quincy Adams in the runoff election

realigning election
An election during periods of expanded suffrage and change in the economy and society that proves to be a turning point, redefining the agenda of politics and the alignment of voters within parties.

in the House of Representatives. Jackson, brilliantly aided by Martin Van Buren, a veteran party builder in New York State, later knitted together a winning combination of regions, interest groups, and political doctrines to win the presidency in 1828. The Whigs succeeded the Federalists as the opposition party. By the time Van Buren, another Democrat, followed Jackson in the White House in 1837, the Democrats had become a large, nationwide movement with national and state leadership, a clear party doctrine, and a grassroots organization. The Whigs were almost as strong; in 1840, they put their own man, General William Henry Harrison ("Old Tippecanoe"), into the White House. A two-party system had been born, and we have had that competitive two-party system ever since—one of few such systems worldwide.

1860: THE CIVIL WAR AND THE RISE OF THE REPUBLICANS   Out of the crisis over slavery evolved the second Republican party—the first being the National Republican Party that existed for barely a decade in the 1820s. The second Republican party ultimately adopted the nickname, "Grand Old Party" (GOP).[37] Abraham Lincoln was elected in 1860 with the support not only of financiers, industrialists, and merchants but also of many workers and farmers. For 50 years after 1860, the Republican coalition won every presidential race except for Grover Cleveland's victories in 1884 and 1892. The Democratic party survived with its durable white male base in the South.

1896: A PARTY IN TRANSITION   Economic changes, including industrialization and hard times for farmers, led to changes in the Republican party in the late 1800s.[38] Some Republicans insisted on maintaining their party's Reconstruction policies into the 1890s until it became obvious that such policies would jeopardize their electoral base.[39] A combination of western and southern farmers and mining interests sought an alliance with workers in the East and Midwest to "recapture America from the foreign moneyed interests responsible for industrialization. The crisis of industrialization squarely placed an agrarian-fundamentalist view of life against an industrial-progress view."[40] The two parties also differed over whether U.S. currency should be tied to a silver or gold standard, with Republicans favoring gold and Democrats silver. William Jennings Bryan, the Democratic candidate for president in 1896, was a talented orator but lost the race to William McKinley.[41] The 1896 realignment differs from the others, however, in that the party in power did not change hands. In that sense it was a *converting realignment* because it reinforced the Republican majority status that had been in place since 1860.[42]

The Progressive Era, the first two decades of the twentieth century, was a period of political reform led by the Progressive wing of the Republican party. Much of the agenda of the Progressives focused on the corrupt political parties. Civil service reforms shifted some of the patronage out of the hands of party officials. The direct primary election took control of nominations from party leaders and gave it to the rank-and-file. And a number of cities instituted nonpartisan governments totally eliminating the role of a party. With the ratification of the Seventeenth Amendment to the Constitution in 1913, U.S. senators came to be popularly elected. Women obtained the right to vote when the Nineteenth Amendment was ratified in 1920. Thus within a short time, the electorate changed, the rules changed, and even the stakes of the game changed. Democrats were unable to build a durable winning coalition during this time and remained the minority party until the early 1930s, when the Great Depression overwhelmed the Hoover administration.

1932: FRANKLIN ROOSEVELT AND THE NEW DEAL ALIGNMENT   The 1932 election was a turning point in American politics. In the 1930s, the United States faced a devastating economic collapse. Between 1929 and 1932, the gross national product fell more than 10 percent per year, and unemployment rose from 1.5 million to more than 15 million, with millions more working only part-time. Herbert Hoover and the Republican majority in Congress had responded to the Depression by arguing that the problems with the economy were largely self-correcting and that their long-standing policy of following **laissez-faire economics**, a hands-off approach in which the government did not attempt to interfere in the economy, was appropriate.

laissez-faire economics
Theory that opposes governmental interference in economic affairs beyond what is necessary to protect life and property.

Government's Greatest Endeavors

Promoting Technology

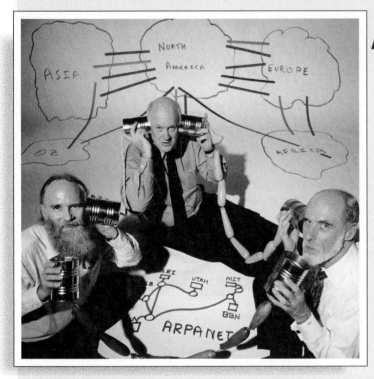

Founders of the Internet with their tin can and zucchini telephones.

QUESTIONS:

Why does the federal government promote science and technology?

What kind of government research has helped you today?

America's political parties are becoming increasingly effective at exploiting new technologies such as the Internet. They raise money on the Internet, promote candidates through sophisticated Web sites, and target specific groups of voters through e-mail, blogs, and podcasts.

Americans generally believe that the Internet and other new technologies come entirely from private investment. But many of the nation's greatest scientific and technological breakthroughs have started with federal support.

The Internet is a good example. Although major corporations such as Amazon, e-Bay, Google, and Microsoft have all exploited the Internet for profit, the Internet was actually conceived in the 1950s under a secret Defense Department program that sought to protect communications between nuclear missile bases. Convinced that a nuclear attack would destroy normal telephone and telegraph communications, the Defense Department provided the money to develop a computer-based system for splitting information into digital packets that could be sent through many channels to a single destination. By the early 1960s, this Advanced Research Projects Agency net (ARPANET) was up and running, but it did not become the Internet until computer technology began to catch up in the 1990s.

The federal government has funded other technological breakthroughs through the National Science Foundation, which was created in 1950. This government agency made just 28 grants to colleges and universities for advanced research in 1952, but has since expanded its funding to more than 10,000 grants and $5 billion today. Congress also funds basic research at the National Aeronautics and Space Administration (NASA), the National Institutes of Health, and the departments of Defense, Health and Human Services, Homeland Security, and Transportation. Much of this research is eventually used by private businesses to create new products and services. ∎

Voters wanted more. Franklin D. Roosevelt and the Democrats were swept into office in 1932 by a tide of anti-Hoover and anti-Republican sentiment. Roosevelt rode this wave and promised that his response to the Depression would be a "New Deal for America." He rejected laissez-faire economics and instead relied on **Keynesian economics**, which asserted that government could influence the direction of the economy through fiscal and monetary policy. After a century of sporadic government action, the New Dealers fundamentally altered the relationship between government and society by providing government jobs for the unemployed and by using government expenditures to stimulate economic growth.

The central issue on which the Republicans and Democrats disagreed in the New Deal period was the role government should play in the economy. Roosevelt Democrats argued that the government had to act to pull the country out of the Depression, but Republicans objected to enlarging the scope of government and intruding it into the economy. This basic disagreement about whether the national government should

Keynesian economics
Theory based on the principles of John Maynard Keynes, stating that government spending should increase during business slumps and be curbed during booms.

play an active role in regulating and promoting our economy remains one of the most important divisions between the Democratic and Republican parties today, although, with time, the country and both parties accepted many of the New Deal programs.

For the two decades following the 1932 election, the Republican party was relegated to watching the majority Democrats—a new coalition of union households, immigrant workers, white southerners, and people hurt by the Great Depression—implement their domestic policies. During World War II, both parties embraced a bipartisan foreign policy.

We have gone a long time since the last critical or realigning election. You will note that each realignment lasted roughly 36 years, or a couple of generations. Close and competitive elections like the 2000 and 2004 elections do not appear to be critical or realigning elections. There have not been disruptions of traditional voting patterns, major economic or social changes, or formations of new and durable electoral groupings. Some political scientists anticipated that we were ripe for realignment in 1968 or 1972, but it did not happen. A shift in party allegiances among many southern white people, from the Democratic to the Republican party, coincided with the enfranchisement of southern black people, who largely identify with the Democratic party. But this was more important regionally and did not constitute a national realignment. Now, as memories of the New Deal fade and the agenda of American politics shifts, the alignments of the 1930s and 1940s hold less and less relevance. Yet, to a surprising degree, the parties are stable and closely competitive, as recent elections demonstrated. Whether one party can seize the agenda of politics and fashion itself as the new majority party is one of the interesting political questions for the future.

Divided Government

Major shifts in the demographics of the parties have occurred in recent decades. The once "Solid South" that the Democrats could count on to bolster their legislative majorities and help win the White House has now become the "Solid Republican South" in presidential elections and increasingly in congressional elections as well. Republican congressional leaders have often been from Southern states that once rarely elected Republicans. Further evidence of partisan change in the South is the sweep of U.S. Senate victories Republicans had in 2004 in Florida, North Carolina, South Carolina, and Georgia, picking up seats Democrats had held going into the 2004 elections. This shift in the South is explained by the movement of large numbers of white people out of the Democratic party, in part as a result of the party's position on civil rights but also because of national Democrats' stand on abortion and other lifestyle issues. The rise of the Republican South reinforced the shift to conservatism in the GOP. This shift, combined with the diminished ranks of conservative southern Democrats, made the Democratic party, especially the congressional Democrats, more unified and more liberal than in the days when more of its congressional members had "safe" southern seats.[43]

Since 1953, **divided government**, with one party controlling Congress and the other the White House, has been in effect twice as long as united government where one party controls both legislative and executive branches, and at other times Congress has had divided control with one party having a majority in the House and the other in the Senate. Until the 1992 and 1994 elections, the Republicans' strength had been in presidential elections, where they often won with landslide margins. Part of the explanation was their ability to attract popular candidates like Dwight Eisenhower and Ronald Reagan, but Republicans also reaped the rewards of Democratic party divisiveness and generally weaker Democratic presidential candidates. Evidence that voters are inclined to favor divided government came in the 1990s, when voters elected a Republican congressional majority in 1994 and then retained it in 1996 and 1998. Building on the Republicans' securing unified party control of government in 2002, the GOP in 2004 expanded its congressional majorities. This was especially the case in 2005 when the Republican majority in the U.S. Senate climbed to 55 Republicans versus 44 Democrats, and 1 Independent. Since 2000 the Republicans have skillfully

divided government
Governance divided between the parties, as when one holds the presidency and the other controls one or both houses of Congress.

History Makers

Franklin Delano Roosevelt and the Democratic Party

From the critical election of 1860 until the election of 1932 in the midst of the Great Depression, the Republicans were the majority party. The economic and social challenges the country faced going into the 1932 presidential election gave the Democratic party the opportunity to emerge as the majority party. They did this under the leadership of Franklin D. Roosevelt. Roosevelt, who is sometimes known by his initials, FDR, and the Democrats gained widespread acceptance of their response to unemployment and the other challenges facing the nation, which they called the New Deal.

The new Democratic coalition expanded on the party's long-standing base of Southern voters to include strong support from labor union members, farmers, urban ethnic voters, the academic community, and African Americans who, since emancipation, had been more predictably Republican. The Democrats' inroads among black Americans were noteworthy because of the Democrats' strong support among Southern white people. FDR and his party not only included black people in the design and benefits of New Deal programs but had formed a new party organization, the National Colored Committee of the Good Neighbor League. This group turned out 16,000 black voters for a Roosevelt rally at New York's Madison Square Garden.* As one author put it, "the struggle to survive took precedence over the struggle for equality."†

Roosevelt's leadership and style held the party coalition together and even expanded party membership. Part of the strength of the attachment to Roosevelt was personal. For Democrats and "New Dealers," it was a positive attachment; for Republicans, and those who felt he had "sold the country down the river," it was negative. Later—as the country faced the challenge of World War II, followed closely thereafter by the cold war—Roosevelt and his successor Harry S. Truman demonstrated leadership in defense and foreign policy as well. ∎

> *The economic and social challenges the country faced going into the 1932 presidential election gave the Democratic party the opportunity to emerge as the majority party.*

*Jules Witcover, *Party of the People: A History of the Democrats* (Random House, 2003) pp. 372–376.
†John F. Bibby, *Politics, Parties, and Elections in America* (Nelson-Hall Publishers, 1992), pp. 32–33.

exploited incumbency, recruited strong candidates, and carefully managed the agenda of elections to retain unified government. However, in 2006 the Republicans lost control of both houses of Congress. The Democrats gained six Senate seats in the 2006 election, and in the 110th Congress held a majority in the Senate with 51 seats to the Republicans' 49 seats. The Democratic majority includes two Independents, Bernie Sanders (Vermont) and Joe Lieberman (Connecticut), who caucus with the Democrats.

Republican victories in presidential elections between 1952 and 1992 were achieved with the support of some elements of Roosevelt's New Deal coalition. New Deal programs that benefited these voters had expanded the middle class and made possible the conservative "hold onto what we've got" thinking of voters in the 1980s, 1990s, and 2000 elections.

The terrorist attacks on September 11, 2001, provided President Bush and the Republican party with an opportunity to assert strong leadership against terrorism. The "war on terror," as President Bush has labeled it, has been an important issue in the 2002, 2004, and 2006 elections. The Democrats have not had a unified response to the terrorism challenge as is typical for the party out of power. By 2006 the mood of the country had changed to concern with the war in Iraq and it was not necesary to present a distinct solution for the security issue. Instead, the Democrats focused on the need for change.

American Parties Today

Americans typically take political parties for granted.[44] If anything, most people are critical or even fearful of the major parties. Parties are, in a word, distrusted. Some see parties as corrupt institutions, interested only in the spoils of politics.

Critics charge that the parties evade the issues, fail to deliver on their promises, have no new ideas, follow public opinion rather than lead it, or are just one more special interest.

Still, most Americans understand that parties are necessary. They want party labels kept on the ballot, at least for congressional, presidential and statewide elections. Most voters think of themselves as Democrats or Republicans and typically vote for candidates from their party. They collectively contribute millions of dollars to the two major parties with more individual contributions generally going to the Republicans than to the Democrats.[45] Thus Americans appreciate, at least vaguely, that you cannot run a big democracy without parties.

Both the Democratic and Republican national parties and most state parties are moderate in their policies and leadership.[46] Successful party leaders must be diplomatic; to win presidential elections and congressional majorities, they must find a middle ground among competing and sometimes hostile groups. Members of the House of Representatives, to be elected and reelected, have to appeal to a majority of the voters from their own district. As more districts have become "safe" for incumbents, the House has become less moderate and has seen more partisan ideological clashes than the Senate.

Although each party usually takes its extremist supporters more or less for granted and seeks out the voters in the middle, both parties retain some ideological diversity. The Democratic coalition includes the conservative Coalition for a Democratic Majority, the moderate Democratic Leadership Council, a new group in 2004 called "Democrats for the West" composed of moderate western Democrats, and the liberal Americans for Democratic Action. The Democratic coalition embraces activists in the civil rights and other liberal-left movements. Republicans, while more homogeneous, have their contentious factions as well. On the more conservative side are the Religious Right, staunch supporters of the right to bear arms, and antitax activists, but also young professionals who are conservative economically but moderate or liberal on social issues like abortion and gay marriage.

As noted in Chapter 5, a gender gap exists in voting in presidential and congressional elections, with women voting Democratic more than men. As political scientist Virginia Sapiro has written, "Women and men may still be socialized to think about politics somewhat differently, or at least some groups of women and men are. The two sexes play different kinds of roles in society and family life and thus have different kinds of experiences."[47] Some interest groups also seek to reinforce the gender gap, emphasizing issues like reproductive rights, gun control, or the environment as they relate to women and urge them to vote Democratic. Some individual Republican candidates have succeeded in narrowing the gender gap.

Among Republican elected officials, the split has been between more liberal northeastern Republicans like Senator Lincoln Chafee of Rhode Island and Governor George Pataki of New York and the dominant conservative wing. Democratic officeholders also have substantial policy differences. Examples include a group of U.S. House members who are called "Blue Dog Democrats." The moniker is derived from the old reference to "yellow dog Democrats," a description of party loyalty, where a person would supposedly vote for a yellow dog before voting for a Republican. The "blue dogs" were representatives whose "moderate-to-conservative-views had been 'choked blue' by their party in the years leading up to the 1994 election."[48] Former Georgia Governor and U.S. Senator Zell Miller, a conservative Democrat, endorsed President George W. Bush and gave an impassioned speech at the 2004 Republican National Convention. He described the Democrats running for president in a *Wall Street Journal* article as indistinguishable. He said, "Look closely, there's not much difference among them. I can't say there's 'not a dime's worth of difference' because there's actually billions of dollars' worth of difference among them. Some want to raise our taxes a trillion, while the others want to raise our taxes by several hundred billion. But, make no mistake, they all want to raise our taxes."[49]

"Women and men may still be socialized to think about politics somewhat differently, or at least some groups of women and men are. The two sexes play different kinds of roles in society and family life and thus have different kinds of experiences."

POLITICAL SCIENTIST VIRGINIA SAPIRO

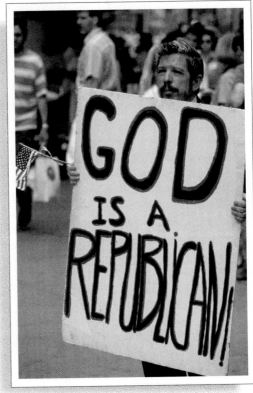

Religion is sometimes linked to partisanship. In reality, devoutly religious people are found in both major parties.

Howard Dean took over as chairman of the Democratic National Committee after his unsuccessful bid for the party's presidential nomination in 2004.

Republicans also have their differences, although in recent years, with their party in control of the White House, they have been less visible. A major divide in the GOP is over the primacy of social policy in areas like gay marriage, stem cell research, and abortion as compared to those who want lower taxes and less government, especially government spending. The 2008 presidential election will likely make the divisions in both parties more visible.

Parties as Institutions

Like other institutions of American government—Congress, the presidency, and the courts—political parties have rules, procedures, and organizational structure. What are the institutional characteristics of political parties?

NATIONAL PARTY LEADERSHIP   The supreme authority in both major parties is the **national party convention**, which meets every four years for four days to nominate candidates for president and vice president, to ratify the party platform, and to adopt rules.

In charge of the national party when it is not assembled in convention is the *national committee*. In recent years, both parties have strengthened the role of the national committee and enhanced the influence of individual committee members. The committees are now more representative of the party rank-and-file. But in neither party is the national committee the center of party leadership.

Each major party has a *national chair* as its top official. The national committee formally elects the chair, but in reality it is the choice of the presidential nominee. For the party that controls the White House, the chair actually serves at the pleasure of the president and does the president's bidding. Party chairs often change after elections. During the 2006 election cycle, the Republican National Committee (RNC) Chair was Ken Mehlman who previously served as campaign manager for the Bush-Cheney campaign in 2004. He served as White House Political Director from 2001 to 2003 and was the National Field Director for Bush-Cheney 2000.[50]

Howard Dean, the Democratic National Committee (DNC) Chair, was elected after the Democratic presidential election defeat in 2004. Dean served in the Vermont legislature before running successfully for lieutenant governor and governor in Vermont eight times. His 2004 presidential campaign made widespread use of the Internet, a tool he has taken with him into his role as DNC chair. Dean has made party organizing a priority, even in strongly Republican states.

The chair of the party without an incumbent president has considerable independence yet works closely with the party's congressional leadership. The national committee often elects a new head after an electoral defeat. Although chairs are the heads of their national party apparatus, they remain largely unknown to the voters. The chair may play a major role in running the national campaign; after the election, the power of the national chair of the victorious party tends to dwindle.

National party organizations are often agents of an incumbent president in securing his renomination. When there is no incumbent president seeking reelection, the national party committee is generally neutral until the nominee is selected. Although heated primary contests often preclude having a united party in the general election, national and state parties can attempt to dissuade candidates but in the end cannot prevent them from running.[51]

In addition to the national party committees, there are also congressional and senatorial *campaign committees*. In recent years, congressional and senatorial campaign committees have become much more active—recruiting candidates, training them, and assisting with campaign finance.[52] Senatorial campaign committees are composed of senators chosen for two-year terms by their fellow party members in the Senate; congressional campaign committees are chosen in the same manner by the House. Chairs of campaign committees are nominated by their party leadership and typically ratified by their party caucus. For information on the party committees

national party convention
A national meeting of delegates elected in primaries, caucuses, or state conventions who assemble once every four years to nominate candidates for president and vice president, ratify the party platform, elect officers, and adopt rules.

and their leadership, go to www.nrcc.org, www.nrsc.org, www.dccc.org, and www.dscc.org. These committees have a lot of say about which candidates get party campaign funds. With the abolition of soft money, the power of the party committees was presumed to lessen. In fact, the party committees continued to be active in competitive races and battleground states through independent expenditures. While this spending did not rival the old soft money, it was substantial in 2004.

PARTY PLATFORMS   While national party committees exist primarily to win elections and gain control of government, policy goals are also important. Every four years each party adopts a platform at the national nominating convention. The typical party platform—the official statement of party policy—is often a vague and ponderous document that hardly anyone reads. The platforms are the result of many meetings and compromise between groups and individuals. Platforms are ambiguous by design, giving voters few obvious reasons to vote against the party. This generalization about party platforms does not mean that political parties do not stand for anything. Most business and professional people believe the Republican party best serves their interests, while working people tend to look to the Democrats to speak for them. The proportion of voters discerning important differences between the parties has increased sharply as the parties have become more polarized (see Figure 7–1).[53]

Senator Mel Martinez (R-Fla.), took over as chairman of the Republican National Committee after Ken Mehlman resigned following the party's defeat in the midterm elections of November, 2006.

Many politicians contend that platforms rarely help elect anyone, but platform positions can hurt a presidential candidate. Because the nominee does not always control the platform-writing process, presidential candidates can disagree with their own party platform. But the platform-drafting process gives partisans, and generally the nominee through people he appoints, an opportunity to express their views, and it spells out the most important values and principles on which the parties are based. Once elected, politicians are rarely reminded of what their platform position was on a given issue. One major exception to this was former President George H.W. Bush's memorable promise not to raise taxes if elected in 1988, "Read my lips—no new taxes." He was forced to eat those words when taxes were raised in 1990.[54] In reality, the winning party actually seeks to enact much of its party platform.[55]

In 2004, the Bush and Kerry campaigns carefully controlled the party platforms. The Republican platform played to the conservative base of the party on such issues as abortion, gay marriage, and taxes. The Democratic platform, like the Democratic convention, sought to reassure the country that the party was strong on national security while also retaining its long-standing commitment to seniors, education, and social justice.

PARTIES AT THE STATE AND LOCAL LEVELS   The two major parties are decentralized, organized around elections in states, cities, or congressional districts. They have organizations for each level of government: national, state, and local. Party organization at the state and local levels is structured much like the national level. Each state has a *state committee* headed by a *state chair*. State law determines the composition of the state committees and regulates them. Members of state committees are usually elected from local areas. Party auxiliaries such as the Young Democrats or the Federation of Republican Women are sometimes represented as well. In many states, governors, senators, or coalitions of locally elected business and ethnic leaders dominate these committees. State committees normally elect state chairs, although in approximately one-quarter of the states they are chosen at state conventions. When the party controls the governorship, chairs are often agents of the governor.[56]

FIGURE 7–1 Important Difference in What Democratic and Republican Parties Stand for, 1984–2004.

SOURCE: *2004 National Election Study*, "Important Difference in What Democratic and Republican Parties Stand for, 1952–2004" (Center for Political Studies, University of Michigan, 2004).

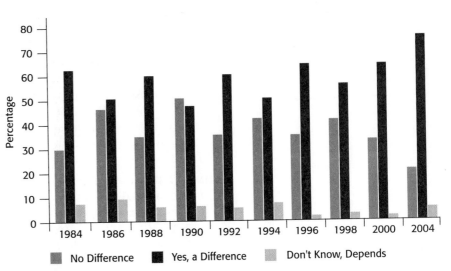

Powerful state parties have developed in recent years. Despite much state-to-state variation, the trend is toward stronger state organizations, with Republicans typically being much better funded.[57] Some states have significant third and fourth parties. New York, for instance, has a Conservative party in addition to the Democratic and Republican parties. The role minor parties play in statewide elections can be important, even though they rarely win office themselves.

Below the state committees are *county committees*, which vary widely in function and power. These committees recruit candidates for such offices as county commissioner, sheriff, and treasurer. This often involves finding a candidate for the office, not deciding among competing contenders. For a party that rarely wins an election, the county committee has to struggle to find someone willing to run. When the chance of winning is greater, primaries, not the party leaders, usually decide the winner.[58] Many county organizations are active, distributing campaign literature, organizing telephone campaigns, putting up posters and lawn signs, and canvassing door-to-door. Other county committees do not function at all, and many party leaders are just figureheads.

Parties in Government

Political parties are central to the operation of our government. They help bridge the separation of powers and facilitate coordination between levels of government in a federal system.

IN THE LEGISLATIVE BRANCH   Members of Congress take their partisanship seriously, at least while they are in Washington. Their power and influence are determined by whether their party is in control of the House or Senate; they also have a stake in which party controls the White House. The chairs of all standing committees in Congress come from the majority party, as do the presiding officials of both chambers. Members of both houses sit together with fellow partisans on the floor and in committee. We discuss the role of parties in Congress in greater detail in Chapter 11. Political parties help bridge the separation of powers between the legislative and executive branches by creating partisan incentives to cooperate. Partisanship can also help unify the two houses of Congress.

Members of congressional staffs are also partisan. From the volunteer intern to the senior staffer, members of Congress expect their staff to be loyal, first to them and then to their party. Should you decide to go to work for a representative or senator, you would be expected to identify yourself with that person's party, and you would have difficulty working for the other party later. Employees of the House and Senate—from elevator operators to the Capitol Hill police and even the chaplain—hold patronage jobs. With few exceptions, such jobs go to persons from the party that has a majority in the House or the Senate.

IN THE EXECUTIVE BRANCH   Presidents select almost all senior White House staff and cabinet members from their own party. Presidents, however, typically surround themselves with advisers who have campaigned with them and have proved their party loyalty.

Partisanship is also important in presidential appointments to the highest levels of the federal workforce. The party that wins the White House has around 3,000 non-career positions to fill,[59] not including ambassadors, U.S. Marshals, and U.S. Attorneys. Party commitment, including making campaign contributions, is expected of those who seek these positions.

IN THE JUDICIAL BRANCH   The judicial branch of the national government, with its lifetime tenure and political independence, is designed to operate in an expressly non-partisan manner. Judges, unlike Congress, do not sit together by political party. But the appointment process for judges has been partisan from the beginning. The landmark case establishing the principle of judicial review, *Marbury* v. *Madison* (1803), concerned the efforts of one party to stack the judiciary with fellow partisans before leaving office.[60] Today, party identification remains an important consideration when nominating federal judges. Although no form requires a judicial nominee to list his or her party affiliation, the people responsible for screening and evaluating candidates do take party and ideology into account.[61] Appointees must be acceptable to certain power centers in the party. For example, Republicans in the Ronald Reagan and George Bush administrations insisted on conservative judges; Bill Clinton, although nominating Democrats, placed more importance on gender and race than on ideology in selecting judges.[62] The confirmation process has also become increasingly partisan. Republicans claimed that Democrats were delaying hearings for George W. Bush's judicial nominees, and Democrats countered that they were responding in kind to what Republicans did to Clinton nominees when the GOP controlled the Senate.

AT THE STATE AND LOCAL LEVELS   The importance of party in the operation of local government varies among states and localities. In some states, such as New York and Illinois, local parties play an even stronger role than they do at the national level. In others, such as Nebraska, parties play almost no role. In Nebraska, the state legislature is expressly nonpartisan, though factions perform like parties and still play a role. Parties are likewise unimportant in the government of most city councils. But in most states and many cities, parties are important to the operation of the legislature, governorship, or mayoralty. Judicial selection in most states is also a partisan matter. Much was made by the 2000 Bush campaign of the fact that six of the seven Florida Supreme Court justices deciding the 2000 ballot-counting case in favor of Gore were Democrats. Democrats noted that the five U.S. Supreme Court justices who decided the election in favor of Bush were Republicans.

Parties in the Electorate

Political parties would be of little significance if they did not have meaning to the electorate. Adherents of the two parties are drawn to them by a combination of factors, including their stand on the issues; personal or party history; religious, racial, or social peer grouping; and the appeal of their candidates. The emphases among these factors change over time, but they are remarkably consistent with those political scientists identified more than 40 years ago.[63]

PARTY REGISTRATION   For citizens in most states, "party" has a particular legal meaning—**party registration**. When voters register to vote in these states, they are asked to state their party preference. They then become registered members of one of the two major parties or a third party. Voters can subsequently change their party registration. The purpose of party registration is to limit the participants in primary elections to members of that party and to make it easier for parties to contact people who might vote for their party.

PARTY ACTIVISTS   Activists tend to fall into three broad categories: party regulars, candidate activists, and issue activists. *Party regulars* place the party first. They value winning elections and understand that compromise and moderation may be necessary to reach that objective. They also realize that it is important to keep the party together, because a fractured party only helps the opposition.

Candidate activists are followers of a particular candidate who see the party as the means to elect their candidate. Candidate activists are often not concerned with the other operations of the party—with nominees for other offices or with raising money for the party. For example, people who supported Pat Buchanan in his unsuccessful run for the presidency as a Reform party candidate in 2000 would be classified as candidate activists. Buchanan, a conservative television commentator and unsuccessful candidate for the Republican nomination in 1996, built a personal following. Reform party members who traced their roots in the party to Ross Perot found Buchanan so repellent that they split from him and nominated their own candidate for president. Buchanan got less than 1 percent of the vote in the 2000 election. As a

party registration
The act of declaring party affiliation; required by some states when one registers to vote.

The Changing Face of American Politics

Portrait of the Electorate

Over a 40-year period the demographic composition of the two major political parties has undergone some changes while at the same time retaining some important similarities. Consistent with the Republican party's having become stronger, we find near parity in partisanship among men in 2004. In 1964, men were twice as likely to be Democrats as Republicans. Women continued to be disproportionately Democratic in 2004 as they were in 1964. Lower-income voters have consistently been more Democratic and higher-income voters more Republican. Younger voters in both 1964 and 2004 were more likely to be Democrats; in 2004, Republicans were at near parity with Democrats for those ages 35–64, something that was not the case in 1964. In 1964, Democrats enjoyed strong support from Protestants, Catholics, and Jews. By 2004, Protestants were evenly divided and the Democratic margin among Catholics had dropped significantly. Jewish voters remained heavily Democratic. In 1964, 59 percent of whites were Democrats; by 2004, the white population was more Republican than Democratic. Blacks were heavily Democratic in both 1964 and 2004. The changing face of party composition has implications for electoral competition and campaign strategy. ■

[I]n 2004, Republicans were at near parity with Democrats for those ages 35–64, something that was not the case in 1964.

	1964				2004			
	Republican	Democrat	Independent	Other	Republican	Democrat	Independent	Other
Sex								
Male	30%	61%	8%	1%	44%	45%	10%	1%
Female	30	61	7	1	37	53	9	2
Race								
White	33	59	8	1	49	41	9	2
Black	8	82	6	4	8	81	12	0
Hispanic	–	–	–	–	23	60	14	2
Age								
18–34	26	64	9	1	34	56	8	2
35–45	32	59	8	1	43	44	11	2
46–55	26	65	8	1	44	45	9	1
56–64	28	66	6	0	46	45	8	1
65+	43	49	6	2	37	50	11	2
Income*								
Less than $14,999	24	65	9	3	27	56	16	1
$15,000–$34,999	24	66	9	0	34	55	11	0
$35,000–$64,999	25	66	8	1	43	50	7	1
$50,000–$124,999	38	55	6	0	47	47	6	0
$125,000+	48	44	8	1	51	45	4	0
Religion								
Protestant	34%	58%	7%	1%	44%	46%	9%	1%
Catholic	22	70	9	0	37	48	13	1
Jewish	11	76	13	0	29	71	0	0
Other	28	55	16	1	33	55	9	2
Ideology†								
Liberal	–	–	–	–	12	85	3	0
Moderate	–	–	–	–	31	57	11	1
Conservative	–	–	–	–	76	19	4	1
Don't know/Haven't thought about it	–	–	–	–	26	51	19	4

*Income is given in 2000 dollars.
†Respondents were not asked about their ideology in the 1964 survey.

Portrait of the Electorate *continued*

	1964				2004			
	Republican	Democrat	Independent	Other	Republican	Democrat	Independent	Other
Region								
Northeast	36	54	10	0	37	51	12	0
North-Central	36	55	8	0	42	43	13	3
South	20	71	7	2	41	50	7	2
West	30	63	7	0	40	51	8	1
Total	30	61	8	1	40	49	10	2

SOURCE: *1964 National Election Study* (Center for Political Studies, University of Michigan, 1964), *2004 National Election Study* (Center for Political Studies, University of Michigan, 2004).
NOTE: Numbers may not add to 100 due to rounding. Independents who lean toward a party are classified with the party toward which they lean. Race is defined by the first race with which a respondent identifies. Income is classified as the respondent's household income.

result, the Reform party was ineligible for millions of dollars in federal subsidies for the 2004 elections.

Issue activists wish to push the parties in a particular direction on a single issue or a narrow range of issues: the war in Iraq, abortion, taxes, school prayer, the environment, or civil rights among others. To issue activists, the party platform is an important battleground because they want the party to endorse their position. Issue activists are also often candidate activists if they can find a candidate willing to embrace their position.

Both issue activists and candidate activists insist on making their "statement" regardless of the electoral consequences. They would rather lose the election than compromise. Party activists thus include a diverse group of people who come to the political party with different objectives. It is not surprising, then, that some of the most interesting politics are over candidate selection and issue positions within the political parties. Fights over strategy and party position are conducted in open meetings and under democratic procedures. Political parties foster democracy not only by competition *between* the parties but *within* the parties as well.

Party Identification

Party registration and party activists are important, but many voters are not registered with a political party. Most Americans are mere spectators of party activity. They lack the partisan commitment and interest needed for active involvement. This is not to say that parties are irrelevant or unimportant to them. For them, partisanship is what political scientists call **party identification**—an informal and psychological attachment to a political party that most people acquire in childhood; it is a standing preference for one party over another.[64] This type of voter may sometimes vote for a candidate from the other party, but without a compelling reason to do otherwise, most will vote according to their party identification. Peers and early political experiences reinforce party identification, which is generally acquired from parents. It is part of the political socialization process described in Chapter 4.

Political scientists and pollsters use the answers to the following questions to measure party identification: Generally speaking, in politics do you usually think of yourself as a Republican, a Democrat, an Independent, or what?

Persons who answer Republican or Democrat to this question are then asked: Would you call yourself a strong or a not very strong Republican/Democrat?

party identification
An informal and subjective affiliation with a political party that most people acquire in childhood.

"Very Republican. I love it."

Persons who answer Independent to the first question are asked: Do you think of yourself as closer to the Republican or the Democratic party?

Persons who do not indicate Democrat, Republican, or Independent to the first question rarely exceed 2 percent of the electorate and include those who are apolitical or who identify with one of the minor political parties.

Party identification is the single best predictor of how people will vote.[65] Unlike candidates and issues, which come and go, party identification is a long-term element in voting choice. The strength of party identification is also important in predicting participation and political interest. Strong Republicans and strong Democrats participate more actively in politics than any other groups and are generally better informed about political issues. Pure Independents are just the opposite; they vote at the lowest rates and have the lowest levels of interest and awareness of any of the categories of party identification. This evidence runs counter to the notion that persons who are strong partisans are unthinking party adherents.[66]

Partisan Realignment and Dealignment

As discussed earlier in this chapter, with the exception of the shift of southern white people to the Republican party[67] and the enfranchisement of black voters who remain Democrats, the current system of party identification is built on a foundation of the New Deal and the critical election of 1932, events that took place nearly three-quarters of a century ago. How can events so removed from the present still shape our party system? When will there be another realignment—an election that dramatically changes the voters' partisan identification? Or has such a realignment already occurred? The question is frequently debated. Most scholars believe that we have not experienced a major realignment since 1932.[68] Partisan identification has been stable for more than four decades, and even though new voters have been added to the electorate—minorities and 18- to 21-year-olds—the basic nature of the party system has trended slightly Republican but not changed dramatically. Table 7–2 presents the party identification breakdown from the 1950s to 2004.

Evidence of a possible voting realignment came in the early 1980s, when Republicans won several close Senate elections and gained a majority in that body.[69] Democrats, however, won back the Senate in 1986, and until 1994 they appeared to have a permanent majority in the House. All that changed with the 1994 election, as Republicans were swept into office on a tidal wave of victories. Republicans made major inroads in the South and strengthened their share of the vote among white males.

TABLE 7–2 Party Identification, 1950s–2000s

Decade	Strong Democrat	Weak Democrat	Independent-Leaning Democrat	Independent	Independent-Leaning Republican	Weak Republican	Strong Republican	Other
1950s*	23%	23%	8%	7%	7%	15%	13%	4%
1960s	22	25	8	10	7	15	12	2
1970s	17	24	12	14	10	14	9	2
1980s	18	26	11	12	11	14	11	2
1990s	18	19	13	10	12	15	13	1
2000s	17	17	16	11	11	12	13	1

*1950s percentages based on years 1952, 1956, and 1958.

SOURCE: *2000, 2002, and 2004 National Election Study* (Center for Political Studies, University of Michigan, 2004).
NOTE: Data may not sum to 100 percent due to averaging.

In presidential voting, Republicans have done well, winning seven of the last ten presidential elections. Their success ratio masks a much more evenly divided electorate. Democrats would also be quick to point out that their party won the popular vote in 2000, only reinforcing the point that the country is evenly divided. Why have the Republicans done better than Democrats in winning presidential elections? The answer is that they have been more effective in activating their core supporters and those few undecided voters in recent elections. Republicans also have a larger set of states they can predictably count on, forcing Democrats to win most of the populous states, which are often more competitive. Yet the fact that Republicans have won more than they have lost in the last 40 years does not indicate a realignment toward the GOP. (See Figure 7–2.)

We may therefore conclude from recent national elections that American voters overall have no consistent preference for one party over the other. In a time of such electoral volatility, the basics of politics determine the winners and losers: who attracts positive voter attention, who strikes themes that motivate voters to participate, who communicates better with voters. Party identification remains important for those voters who come out to vote, and strength of partisanship remains positively correlated with turnout.

Signs of voter disengagement are stronger than signs of voter realignment. Some observers feel that we are experiencing a rejection of partisanship in favor of becoming independent, and the number of persons who characterize themselves as Independents has increased. Journalist Hedrick Smith has expressed a widespread view: "The most important phenomenon of American politics in the past quarter century has been the rise of independent voters, who have at times outnumbered Republicans."[70]

The **dealignment** argument—that people have abandoned both parties to become Independents—would be more persuasive were it not that two-thirds of all self-identified Independents are really partisans in their voting behavior and attitudes. One-third of those who claim to be Independents lean toward the Democratic party and vote Democratic in election after election. Another third of Independents lean toward Republicans and just as predictably vote Republican. The remaining third, who appear to be genuine Independents and who do not vote predictably for one party, turn out to be people with little interest in politics. Despite the reported growth in Independents, there are proportionately about the same number of Pure Independents now as there were in 1956.[71] There are, in short, at least three types of Independents, and most of them are predictably partisan. Table 7–3 summarizes voting behavior in recent contests for president and the House of Representatives.

Why has realignment moved so slowly? Why are not all conservatives now happily ensconced in the Republican party and all liberals gladly lodged in the Democratic

"The most important phenomenon of American politics in the past quarter century has been the rise of independent voters, who have at times outnumbered Republicans."

JOURNALIST HEDRICK SMITH

dealignment
Weakening of partisan preferences that points to a rejection of both major parties and a rise in the number of Independents.

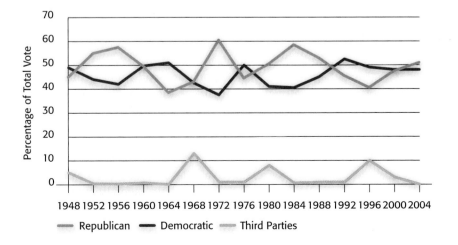

FIGURE 7–2 Presidential Vote by Party.

SOURCE: Data obtained from CQ Voting and Elections Collections, at library.cqpress.com/elections/.

TABLE 7–3 Voting Behavior of Partisans and Independents, 1992–2004

	Percent Voting for Democratic Presidential Candidate			
	1992	**1996**	**2000**	**2004**
Strong Democrats	93%	96%	97%	96%
Weak Democrats	68	82	89	84
Independent-leaning Democrats	70	76	72	83
Pure Independents	41	35	44	51
Independent-leaning Republicans	11	20	13	14
Weak Republicans	14	20	14	10
Strong Republicans	3	5	2	3

	Percent Voting for Democratic House Candidate					
	1994	**1996**	**1998**	**2000**	**2002**	**2004**
Strong Democrats	88%	87%	77%	90%	89%	90%
Weak Democrats	73	70	57	73	71	85
Independent-leaning Democrats	68	69	63	73	67	80
Pure Independents	55	41	41	50	35	54
Independent-learning Republicans	25	21	24	26	27	33
Weak Republicans	21	21	25	18	25	17
Strong Republicans	7	3	7	12	8	10

SOURCE: *2004 National Election Study* (Center for Political Studies, University of Michigan, 2004).

party? Americans do not casually cross party lines. If you grew up in a conservative New Hampshire family whose forebears voted Republican for a century, you are pretty much conditioned to stay with the GOP. Even if that party took a direction you disliked, you might continue to register as a Republican but quietly vote Democratic to avoid friction in the family. Or if you come from a "yellow dog" Democratic family in Texas, you might continue to vote for Democrats locally even though you disliked various Democratic candidates for president or senator. This pattern was once common throughout the South.[72]

The party identification questions produce seven categories of persons: strong Democrats, weak Democrats, Independent-leaning Democrats, pure Independents, Independent-leaning Republicans, weak Republicans, and strong Republicans. Over the nearly 50-year period during which political scientists have been conducting such surveys, the partisan preferences of the American public have remained remarkably stable.

Another reason for slow realignment is the local nature of the parties. For decades, conservative Democrats in the South have been voting for Republican candidates for president—not just George W. Bush and Ronald Reagan but also Richard Nixon and even Dwight Eisenhower—without changing their identification from the Democratic Party to the Republican.[73] Why? Partly because they still see themselves as Democrats, but also because the Democratic party remains stronger at the state and local levels in many southern states. So, if candidates and voters want to have an impact on local politics, in which the only meaningful elections may be in the Democratic primaries, they retain their Democratic affiliation.

Financing the Parties

Political parties, like candidates, rely on contributions from individuals and interest groups to fund their activities. Because of their close connection to officeholders, the courts have long permitted regulation of the source and amount of money people can contribute to parties. Under the post-Watergate reforms (Federal Election Campaign Act or FECA, as amended in 1974), contributions to the parties from individuals were limited to $20,000, while the limit for PACs was $15,000.[74] After the 1976 election, both parties pressed for further amendments to FECA, claiming that campaign finance reforms resulted in insufficient money for generic party activities like billboard advertising and get-out-the-vote drives. The 1979 amendments to FECA and the interpretations of this legislation by the Federal Election Commission (FEC) permitted unlimited soft money contributions to the parties by individuals and PACs for these party-building purposes. Soft money was thus easier to raise and could come from corporate and union general treasuries, which were monies that could not otherwise be given to candidates or political parties. Then in the 1996 election cycle, both parties found ways to spend this soft money to promote the election or defeat of specific candidates effectively circumventing party spending limits.[75]

The Rise in Soft Money

In the 1998, 2000, and 2002 elections, congressional campaign committees, following the lead of the national party committees in the 1996 presidential election, raised unprecedented amounts of soft money. In 2000, all party committees combined raised $500 million in soft money, a figure equaled in 2002, even though there was no presidential election that year. Soft money was spent in large amounts in the most competitive races where it could help determine which party controlled Congress or in the most competitive states in the 1996 and 2000 contests for the White House. The focus of these expenditures was candidate promotion. In many instances, broadcast ads paid for with soft money did not even mention the party.[76] This is why banning soft money became such a dedicated cause for Arizona Senator John McCain, a cosponsor of the McCain-Feingold campaign finance reform legislation. McCain, who beat George W. Bush in the New Hampshire presidential primary, in part on the basis of his challenging the party establishment on soft money, eventually lost to Bush in the 2000 nomination fight. Despite repeated defeats in one or both houses of Congress over 15 years, Congress passed the Bipartisan Campaign Reform Act (BCRA) in 2002.

What were the implications of this surge in soft money in presidential and congressional elections? First, because soft money contributions were unlimited, the priority given to raising soft money elevated the importance of large contributors. Parties came to rely heavily on these large donors. Among the largest soft money donors to the Democrats were the Affiliated Federal State County and Municipal Employees (AFSCME), the Service Employees International Union, and the Communications Workers of America. The largest Republican soft money donors were Phillip Morris and AT&T.

One uncertainty following BCRA was whether soft money donors would attempt to find another way to spend money on electing or defeating candidates. Some donors abandoned large donations altogether, instead making the limited and disclosed PAC or individual contributions. As we noted in Chapter 6, 2004 saw growth in PAC contributions. Other donors and some new contributors, however, pursued an alternative way to spend unlimited sums of the 2004 elections. As we have seen, they typically did this through groups formed under Section 527 of the tax code or other groups, which allowed them to spend unlimited amounts on voter registration, mobilization, mail and phone communications (see Chapters 6 and 8).

Effects of BCRA

A major element of BCRA was a near-complete ban on soft money in federal elections. The only remaining soft money provisions were limited contributions to state and local party committees for voter registration and mobilization and unlimited contributions to the party committees to help fund their conventions.

Central to the arguments for banning party soft money was the contention that the ability of individuals and groups to donate unlimited amounts of money to the parties gives these donors extraordinary access to and influence over elected officials. Since party leaders were often the ones asking for the unlimited soft money contributions, a majority of the Supreme Court cited the potential for corruption as justification for upholding BCRA. They noted, "There is substantial evidence in these cases to support Congress' determination that such contributions of soft money give rise to corruption and the appearance of corruption. For instance, the record is replete with examples of national party committees' peddling access to federal candidates and officeholders in exchange for large soft-money donations."[77]

Both parties, but especially the Democrats, had developed a dependence on soft money. In 1992, the Democrats raised more than four hard dollars for every soft dollar, and total Democratic party hard-money fund-raising, including by state and local parties, was $209 million, compared to $46 million in soft money. By 2002, for the first time, all Democratic committees collectively raised more in soft money ($246 million) than they did in hard money ($217 million). The gap between hard and soft money narrowed for Republicans between 1992 and 2002 but not to the same degree as for Democrats.[78] How would the parties cope without soft money in 2004? Many speculated that taking away soft money would significantly weaken the parties. Scholar Sidney Milkis speculated in his expert testimony on the case to determine the constitutionality of BCRA that "the reform act will diminish the national character of party organizations and, like FECA, will strengthen the influence of interest groups in American politics."[79] But in 2004, individual giving to both parties set new records, and the DNC and RNC raised as much in hard money from individuals and PACs as they had raised in hard and soft money combined in 2000 or 2002 (see Figure 7–3).

The parties' congressional campaign committees were not able to raise as much in hard money in 2004 as they had raised in hard and soft money combined in 2000 or 2002, but individual contributions did grow significantly. For all party committees this increase in individual contributions was driven in part by the unusual dynamics of 2004, with a highly contested contest for the White House and several competitive congressional races. Part of the surge in individual giving is attributable to BCRA, which increased the maximum amount any individual could give in combined contributions in a two-year cycle from $50,000 to $97,500, and for people who wanted to give the maximum possible to candidates and party committees, BCRA required that at least $20,000 go to the party committees.[80] For more affluent donors, this created an incentive to give more to the political parties. The surge in contributions in larger amounts is less surprising than the surge in small individual contributions for the Democrats. Since the 1970s, the Republicans have done better than Democrats among this donor group. That began to change in 2004, due in part to individuals giving via the Internet.[81]

It is debatable whether soft money had a positive effect on the parties. In competitive contests, parties became major players, mounting their own campaigns, often against the other party and its candidate. Most party spending was on ads placed on television and radio, sent through the mail, or delivered over the telephone. To a lesser extent, parties worked to register voters and mobilize them on election day. This latter type of activity is more likely to have an enduring effect on state and local parties.

FIGURE 7–3 **Hard Money, Soft Money, and Combined Receipts, 1992–2004.**

SOURCE: Federal Election Commission, "Party Financial Activity Summarized for the 2004 Election Cycle," press release, March 2, 2005, www.fec.gov/press/press2005/20050302party/Party2004final.html, accessed March 21, 2005.

NOTE: The totals for each party do not equal the sum of the party committee receipts because the numbers provided by the FEC have been adjusted to account for transfers between party committees so as not to double count money in the total receipts. The total also includes state and local hard money receipts, which are not shown.

BCRA provides for limited contributions to state and local party committees; individuals and groups may donate up to $10,000 per party committee for voter registration and mobilization efforts. This provision could encourage parties to continue to invest in mobilizing voters.

Independent Expenditures

As discussed in Chapters 6 and 8, individuals and groups have long been allowed to spend unlimited amounts for and against candidates as long as the expenditures were independent of the candidate or a party committee. As noted, spending money in this way is fully disclosed and is called an independent expenditure. In a case brought by the Republican Party, the U.S. Supreme Court said that party committees could also make independent expenditures.[82] Unlike soft money, party independent expenditures had to use money raised with the normal hard money contribution limits. As long as the party committees could use soft money, independent expenditures were of lesser importance, but with the BCRA ban on soft money, there was a surge in party independent expenditure activity in 2004 and again in 2006.

Independent expenditures by the party committees became an important way for the party to try to influence battleground states in the 2004 presidential election and competitive contests for Congress in 2004 and 2006. As Table 7–4 shows, the DNC was the most active party committee in independent expenditures in 2004, spending more than $120 million, which is noteworthy because before 2004 it had not engaged in independent expenditures at all. The RNC spent more than $18 million independently in 2004, about one-fifth what the DNC spent. Rather than match the DNC in independent expenditures, the RNC experimented, in coordination with the Bush-Cheney campaign, with another way to spend hard money. Few expected the RNC, and especially the DNC, to have these kinds of hard money resources in 2004.

TABLE 7-4 Independent Expenditures by Party Committee, 1994–2004

	1994	1996	1998	2000	2002	2004
DNC	$0	$0	$0	$0	$0	$120,333,466
DSCC	0	1,386,022	1,359,000	133,000	0	18,725,520
DCCC	0	0	0	1,916,489	1,106,113	36,923,726
RNC	0	0	0	0	500,000	18,268,870
NRSC	0	9,875,130	194,573	267,600	0	19,383,692
NRCC	0	0	0	548,800	1,203,854	47,254,064

SOURCE: Federal Election Commission, "Party Financial Activity Summarized for the 2004 Election Cycle," press release, March 2, 2005, www.fec.gov/press/press2005/20050302party/Party2004final.html, accessed March 21, 2005.

The congressional campaign committees were more evenly matched in independent expenditures than were the DNC and RNC. Both the Democratic and Republican Senatorial Campaign Committees spent about $19 million in 2004. The House Republicans (NRCC) spent about $10 million more than the House Democrats (DCCC). The congressional party committees targeted highly competitive contests with independent expenditures. Money was spent on television advertising, mail, phone-campaigning, and voter mobilization.[83]

During the debate over BCRA, and in the court case on its constitutionality, there was a great deal of speculation about whether political parties could survive a ban on soft money and the other BCRA provisions relating to parties. The surge in individual contributions has demonstrated that the DNC and RNC could and did find an alternative to soft money. It remains unclear whether the four congressional party committees can make up for the loss of soft money. The independent expenditure option allowed parties to continue to direct money well in excess of the normal limits to races they thought were more competitive.

Are the Political Parties Dying?

Critics of the American party system make three allegations against it: (1) parties do not take meaningful and contrasting positions on most issues, (2) party membership is essentially meaningless, and (3) parties are so concerned with accommodating the middle of the ideological spectrum that they are incapable of serving as an avenue for social progress. Are these statements accurate? And if they are accurate, are they important?

Some analysts fear that parties are in a severe decline or even mortally ill. They point first to the long-run adverse impact on political parties of the Progressive movement reforms early in this century, reforms that robbed party organizations of their control of the nomination process by allowing masses of independent and "uninformed" voters to enter the primaries and nominate candidates who might not be acceptable to party leaders. They also point to the spread of nonpartisan elections in cities and towns and to the staggering of national, state, and local elections that made it harder for parties to influence the election process.

Legislation limiting the viability and functions of parties was bad enough, say the party pessimists, but parties suffer from additional ills. The rise of television and elec-

Agents of Change

Michael Brown, Alan Khazei, and City Year

City Year is a nationally known organization founded in 1988 by Michael Brown and Alan Khazei. Built around the recruitment of 1,000 young adults each year, City Year seeks to increase civic engagement by putting its "youth service corps" to work in 16 cities teaming up with a range of local organizations to address social problems such as homelessness, poverty, education, domestic violence, and community renewal.

Wearing their signature City Year jackets and joining for morning calisthenics in a city square, City Year recruits learn how they can work together to become active citizens in a democracy. Over the past 15 years, they have also contributed 11 million hours of volunteer time to their cities.

City Year's founders, Brown and Khazei, started talking about how to heal the nation's divisions when they were seniors at Cornell University, and soon decided that City Year was the answer. "My father came from a country with a dictatorship, so he appreciated the value of democracy . . . But he also raised me to have a critical eye. We Americans have these ideals that we don't always live up to," Khazei said.

As Khazei remembers the start of City Year, "We'd have late-night discussions about how to change the world, and about how the United States is the richest country in the world but it still has homeless people and illiteracy and gang violence. Why do we have disparity? If you are exposed to an injustice or a need, you want to do something about it." By bringing together diverse groups of young people in public every day, City Year shows that it is possible to find common ground in helping others. ∎

Learn more about City Year at www.cityyear.org.

Michael Brown and Alan Khazei, founders of City Year

QUESTIONS

How does City Year help the nation address political polarization?

Should young Americans be required to engage in some form of national service—such as City Year—after graduation?

tronic technology and the parallel increase in the number of campaign, media, and direct-mail consultants have made parties less relevant in educating, mobilizing, and organizing the electorate. Television, radio, the Internet, and telephones have strengthened the role of candidates and lessened the importance of parties. (See Chapter 10 for more on the media in this role.)

Advocates of strong parties concede that parts of this diagnosis may be correct, including the demise of political machines at the local level, the decline in strong partisan affiliations, and the weakness of grassroots party membership, but they also see signs of party revival, or at least the persistence of party. The national party organizations—the national committees and the congressional and senatorial campaign committees—are significantly better funded than they were in earlier days; they even own permanent, modern headquarters buildings in Washington, D.C., located a few blocks from the U.S. Capitol. Moreover, the parties remain capable of providing assistance to candidates in competitive races and to state and local party organizations because of their financial base. Until 2004, they did this with soft money, and in 2004 and 2006 they did it with independent expenditures.[84]

Since the first years of the Reagan administration, both the Republican and Democratic parties have demonstrated a remarkable cohesiveness in Congress. This trend can be measured by the *party unity score*, defined as the percentage of members of a party who vote together on roll call votes in Congress on which a majority of the members of one party vote against a majority of the members of the other party. During the first session of the 109th Congress (2005), House and Senate Republicans voted together 90 percent of the time. Democrats were only slightly less united at 88 percent, setting a new unity record.[85] These numbers demonstrate the growing partisanship within the two chambers. Thus, while rank-and-file voters do not display strong partisan ties, party organizations and the party in government do show significant signs of strength.[86]

Reform Among the Democrats

In Chicago in 1968, the Democratic National Convention saw disputes inside the hall and riots outside, largely because of protests against the country's policy in Vietnam. Responding to the disarray and to disputes about the fairness of delegate selection procedures, members of the party agreed to a number of reforms. They established a process that led to greater use of direct primaries for the selection of delegates to the national convention and greater representation of younger voters, women, and minorities as elected delegates. Another reform was the abolition of the rule that a winner of a state's convention or primaries got all the state's delegates (the *unit rule*). This rule was replaced by a system of *proportionality* in which candidates won delegates in rough proportion to the votes they received in the primary election or convention in each state.

Mayor Richard J. Daley of Chicago, father of the city's current mayor, and many other party stalwarts argued that these reforms would make the party reflect the views of minorities within the party, such as college professors and intellectuals who would have time and resources to invest in the political process, and not working-class people, unionists, the elderly, and elected officials who depend more on group leaders to make their case. The new process also meant that elected officials who wanted a voice in determining presidential candidates had to run for delegate to the national convention. Responding to this criticism, the party created "superdelegate" positions for elected officials and party leaders who were not required to run for election as delegates.

Reform Among the Republicans

Republicans have not been immune to criticism that their conventions and procedures were keeping out the rank-and-file. They did not make changes as drastic as those made by the Democrats, but they did give the national committee more control over presidential campaigns, and state parties were urged to encourage broader participation by all groups, including women, minorities, youth, and the poor.

The Republican party has long been better organized than the Democrats. In the 1970s, the GOP emphasized grassroots organization and membership recruitment. Seminars taught Republican candidates how to make speeches and hold press conferences, and weekend conferences were organized for training young party professionals. The Democrats have become better organized and more professional. Both parties now conduct training sessions for candidates on campaign planning, advertising, fund raising, using phone banks, recruiting volunteers, and campaign scheduling.[87] But Republicans have cultivated a larger donor base and have been less reliant on the large-donor soft money contributions that became so controversial in recent elections.

As we have demonstrated in this chapter, political parties are vital to the functioning of democracy. They organize electoral competition, unify large portions of the electorate, simplify democracy for voters, help transform individual preferences into policy, and provide a mechanism for opposition. The United States has long had a two-party system in which minor parties can be spoilers but not winners. Such parties can, however, influence the agenda of politics. At present we have near parity in party preferences. Our political history has been marked by periods during which one party or the other was dominant.

Parties are just as important in organizing the government. They help straddle the separation of powers as fellow partisans cooperate between the executive and legislative branches, or between the House and Senate. Senior government appointees get their jobs in part because of their party loyalty.

The parties are well organized with national leadership, platforms, and state and local offices. While some opponents of campaign finance reform worried that recent reforms would weaken parties, in fact they have seen substantial growth in the numbers of individuals willing to contribute to them. Parties are also remarkably permeable organizations that provide citizens who want to influence the course of their government an accessible and often consequential way to get involved. Finally, parties continue to reinforce federalism through the distinctive nature of many state parties.

Summary

1. Political parties are essential to democracy—they simplify voting choices, organize the competition, unify the electorate, help organize government by bridging the separation of powers and fostering cooperation among branches of government, translate public preferences into policy, and provide loyal opposition.

2. Political parties help structure voting choice by nominating candidates to run for office. Before the advent of direct primaries, in which voters determine the party nominees, the parties had more control over who ran under their label. States determine the nomination rules. While most states employ the direct primary, some use a caucus or mixed caucus system in which more committed partisans have a larger role in the decision of who gets nominated. Recently, some states adopted a blanket primary in which voters could vote for a candidate from any party. These primaries were declared unconstitutional.

3. American parties are moderate. Bringing factions and interests together, they are broad enough to win the presidency and other elections. Third parties have been notably less successful. One reason for this is our single-member-district, winner-take-

all election rules. In systems with proportional representation or multi-member districts, there is a greater tendency for more parties to form and consequently a need to assemble governing coalitions of several parties.

4. American parties have experienced critical elections and realignments. Most political scientists agree that the last realignment occurred in 1932. In recent years, there has been divided government and an increase in the number of persons who call themselves Independents. This trend is sometimes called dealignment, but most Independents are closet partisans who vote fairly consistently for the party toward which they lean.

5. For half a century, it has been routine to have divided government, with one party in control of the presidency and the other in control of one or both houses of Congress. Successful presidents have found ways to cope with divided government and enact important parts of their agenda. The 2002 election gave Republicans unified government with control of both houses of Congress and the White House. Republican control of national government was strengthened by the 2004 elections.

6. Parties are governed by their national and state committees, and the focal points of party organization are the

national and state party chairs. When the party controls the executive branch of government, the executive (governor or president) usually has a determining say in selecting the party chair. With the rise of soft money in recent elections, parties had more resources to spend on politics. In 2002, Congress banned soft money except for some narrowly defined and limited activities.

7. Party platforms are vague and general by design, giving the other party and voters little to oppose.

8. Parties are vital in the operation of government. They are organized around elected offices at the state and local levels. Congress is also organized around parties, and judicial and many executive branch appointments are based in large part on partisanship.

9. Parties are also active in the electorate, seeking to organize elections, simplify voting choices, and strengthen party identification.

10. Frequent efforts have been made to reform our parties. The Progressive movement saw parties, as then organized, as an impediment to democracy and pushed direct primaries as a means to reform them. Following the 1968 election, the Democratic party took the lead in pushing primaries and stressing greater diversity among the individuals elected as delegates.

Republicans have also encouraged broader participation, and they have improved their party structure and finances.

11. The Bipartisan Campaign Reform Act (BCRA) significantly changed the role of party committees by banning soft money and raising hard money contribution limits to the parties.

One consequence of BCRA was a renewed emphasis on building a large individual donor base. Donors wanting to spend more than the BCRA limits did so in 2004 through a range of interest groups, many of which were allied 527 groups that ran parallel campaigns with the candidates and parties in 2004.

12. Compared to some European parties, ours remain organizationally weak. There has been some party renewal in recent years as party competition has grown in the South and the parties themselves have initiated reforms.

Further **Reading**

JOHN H. ALDRICH, *Why Parties? The Origin and Transformation of Party Politics in America* (University of Chicago Press, 1995).

JOHN F. BIBBY, *Politics, Parties, and Elections in America,* 5th ed. (Wadsworth, 2002).

DAVID BOAZ, *Libertarianism: A Primer* (Free Press, 1998).

MARY C. BRENNAN, *Turning Right in the Sixties: The Conservative Capture of the GOP* (University of North Carolina Press, 1995).

BRUCE E. CAIN AND **ELISABETH R. GERBER,** EDS., *Voting at the Political Fault Line: California's Experiment with the Blanket Primary* (University of California Press, 2002).

LEON EPSTEIN, *Political Parties in the American Mold* (University of Wisconsin Press, 1986).

DONALD GREEN, BRADLEY PALMQUIST, AND **ERIC SCHICKLER,** *Partisan Hearts and Minds* (Yale University Press, 2002).

JOHN C. GREEN AND **DANIEL J. COFFEY,** EDS., *The State of the Parties: The Changing Role of Contemporary American Parties,* 5th ed. (Rowman & Littlefield, 2006).

JOHN C. GREEN AND **PAUL S. HERRNSON,** EDS., *Responsible Partisanship? The Evolution of American Political Parties Since 1950* (University Press of Kansas, 2002).

PAUL S. HERRNSON AND **JOHN C. GREEN,** EDS., *Multiparty Politics in America: Prospects and Performance,* 2d ed. (Rowman & Littlefield, 2002).

MARJORIE RANDON HERSHEY, *Party Politics in America,* 12th ed. (Longman, 2006).

WILLIAM J. KEEFE AND **MARC J. HETHERINGTON,** *Parties, Politics, and Public Policy in America,* 9th ed. (Congressional Quarterly Press, 2003).

BRUCE E. KEITH, DAVID B. MAGLEBY, CANDICE J. NELSON, ELIZABETH ORR, MARK C. WESTLYE, AND **RAYMOND E. WOLFINGER,** *The Myth of the Independent Voter* (University of California Press, 1992).

DAVID B. MAGLEBY, ANTHONY D. CORRADO, AND **KELLY D. PATTERSON,** EDS., *Financing the 2004 Election* (Brookings Institution Press, 2006).

DAVID B. MAGLEBY, J. QUIN MONSON, AND **KELLY D. PATTERSON,** EDS., *Electing Congress: New Rules for an Old Game* (Prentice Hall, 2006).

L. SANDY MAISEL AND **KARA Z. BUCKLEY,** *The Electoral Process,* 4th ed. (Rowman & Littlefield, 2005).

KELLY D. PATTERSON, *Political Parties and the Maintenance of Liberal Democracy* (Columbia University Press, 1996).

STEVEN J. ROSENSTONE, ROY L. BEHR, AND **EDWARD H. LAZARUS,** *Third Parties in America: Citizen Response to Major Party Failure,* 2d ed. (Princeton University Press, 1996).

JEFFREY M. STONECASH, MARK D. BREWER, AND **MACK D. MARIANI,** *Diverging Parties: Social Change, Realignment, and Party Polarization* (Westview Press, 2003).

JAMES SUNDQUIST, *Dynamics of the Party System: Alignment and Realignment of Political Parties in the United States,* rev. ed. (Brookings Institution Press, 1983).

Make It Real

POLITICAL PARTIES

In this module, students have the opportunity to write their own party platforms.

Chapter 8

Public Opinion, Participation, and Voting

★

N BOTH 2000 AND 2004, CONCERNS ABOUT THE VOTING PROCESS LINGERED LONG AFTER THE ELECTION. THE CENTER OF ATTENTION IN 2000 WAS FLORIDA, WHERE CONTESTED BALLOTS AND OUTDATED VOTING MACHINES ADDED TO THE DRAMA OF A CLOSE ELECTION AND DETERMINED THE OUTCOME OF THE PRESIDENTIAL ELECTION. SOME OF THE PROBLEMS THAT BECAME FRONT-PAGE STORIES INCLUDED THE HANDLING OF ABSENTEE BALLOTS AND, IN SOME FLORIDA COUNTIES, PUNCH-CARD BALLOTS WITH PUNCHES THAT DID NOT perforate the card, leaving what are called "dangling chads." (A chad is the part of a punch-card ballot that the machine should remove as part of the voting process.) Other counties in Florida had ballots called "butterfly ballots," on which the candidates' names are staggered on opposite sides of the ballot with the punch holes in a straight line in the middle. As the candidates were not listed in a straight line, many people claimed

that they were confused about which hole corresponded with which candidate.

Lingering perceptions of partisanship in the Florida outcome include the way the Republican Florida Secretary of State, Katherine Harris, handled the recounts and other aspects of the election under her control. To many foreign observers, the fact that partisan officials, including secretaries of state and county clerks, administer U.S. elections raises concerns about objectivity and fairness. Such observers often ask whether neutral, nonpartisan—or at least bipartisan—commissions should administer elections.

The 2000 election in Florida demonstrated the acute need to modernize the way we vote in the United States. Many states and the federal government responded by authorizing money to provide new voting equipment. Some of that new equipment was used for the first time in the 2004 election. But in Ohio, the new machines and how they were administrated nearly generated the same kind of controversy Florida and the rest of the country experienced in 2000. Indeed, if the Ohio outcome had been as close as Florida was in 2000, the country would have faced another set of legal challenges to the presidential election. In 2004, the Ohio Secretary of State, Republican Kenneth Blackwell, was criticized like Harris had been in Florida four years before for his decisions about voter eligibility. In Florida, the state had purged from the voter list felons who were arguably, under Florida law, eligible to vote. In Ohio, Blackwell required voter

"Nonvoting is not a social disease."

POLITICAL SCIENTIST AUSTIN RANNEY

OUTLINE

★

Public Opinion

★

Participation: Translating
Opinions into Action

★

Voting Choices

★

Counting Votes

registration to be on cardstock of a certain weight, even though his office had distributed voter registration materials on paper that did not meet this standard. Blackwell also restricted the use of provisional ballots in ways Democrats claimed reduced the pool of votes cast.

In some Ohio counties, voters in precincts that were predominantly minority and Democratic had to wait in line for hours to vote because not enough new voting machines had been allocated to these precincts, while voters in more Republican areas had shorter lines. As is often the case, both sides were quick to accuse the other of improprieties. Democrats accused the Republicans of voter intimidation and pointed to mail sent to 35,000 voters telling them their voter registration was being challenged in court. These court hearings were later cancelled, but no subsequent mailing was sent to these voters informing them of the cancellation. Republicans accused Democrats and their allies of registering fictitious people like Dick Tracy and Mary Poppins, and of employing felons to register voters.[1]

The Florida and Ohio cases in 2000 and 2004 demonstrate that our country has a lot of work to do to make how we vote fair and transparent to all voters. In this chapter, we study issues like those that affected voting in Florida and Ohio. We also look at the nature and level of political participation in the United States, and why people vote the way they do. We begin by exploring public opinion, how to measure it, and what factors affect the formation of opinions.

Public Opinion

All governments in all nations must be concerned with public opinion. Even in nondemocratic nations, unrest and protest can topple those in power. And in a constitutional democracy, citizens can express opinions in a variety of ways, including through demonstrations, in conversations, by writing to their elected representatives and to newspapers, and by voting in free and regularly scheduled elections. In short, democracy and public opinion go hand in hand.

What Is Public Opinion?

Politicians frequently talk about what "the people" think or want. But social scientists use the term "public opinion" more precisely: **public opinion** is the distribution of individual preferences for or evaluations of, a given issue, candidate, or institution within a specific population. *Distribution* means the proportion of the population that holds a particular opinion, compared to people who have opposing opinions or no

public opinion
The distribution of individual preferences for or evaluations of a given issue, candidate, or institution within a specific population.

In addition to polls conducted by Gallup, Pew, and other such organizations, newspapers and TV networks conduct polls on election preferences and numerous other subjects.

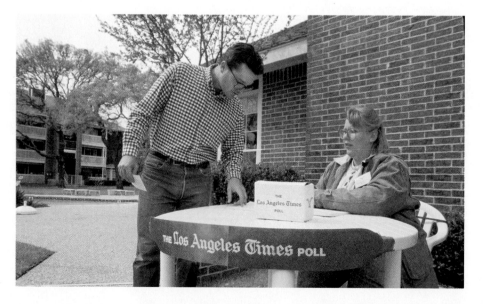

opinion at all. The most accurate way to study public opinion is through systematic measurement in polls or surveys. For instance, final preelection polls in 2004 by the Gallup Organization found that among potential voters, 49 percent reported they would vote for George W. Bush, 49 percent for John Kerry, and 1 percent for Ralph Nader. The actual vote was Bush 51 percent, Kerry 48 percent, and Nader 0.35 percent.

TAKING THE PULSE OF THE PEOPLE In a public opinion poll, a relatively small number of people can accurately represent the opinions of a larger population through the use of random *sampling* of people to survey. In a **random sample**, every individual has a known chance of being selected. The sample of randomly selected respondents should be appropriate for the questions being asked. For instance, a survey of 18- to 24-year-olds should not be done solely among college students, since roughly three-quarters of this age group do not attend college. Even with proper sampling, surveys have a *margin of error*, meaning that the sample accurately reflects the population within a certain range—usually plus or minus 3 percent for a sample of at least 1,500 individuals. If, for example, a preelection poll had one candidate at 50 percent and another at 48 percent, and the margin of error was plus or minus 3 percent, the first candidate could be as high as 53 percent or as low as 47 percent and the second candidate could be as high as 51 percent or as low as 45 percent. Such a race would be within the margin of error and too close to call or to even really say who was ahead. If the sample is sufficiently large and randomly selected, these margins of error would apply in about 95 out of 100 cases. The final preelection survey results in 2004 were within this margin of error for the actual vote.

How samples are selected is critical to the accuracy of polls. Accuracy requires random selection. One classic example of an erroneous poll was the 1936 *Literary Digest* poll, which predicted that Republican Alf Landon would defeat Democrat Franklin D. Roosevelt. However, the sample was drawn from people who owned cars and had telephones and was conducted by the *Literary Digest,* a magazine. In fact, Roosevelt decisively defeated Landon in the actual election, carrying every state except Vermont and Maine. Problems with the *Literary Digest* poll were not limited to its flawed sample but included bias in the response rate.[2] A much more reliable way to draw a sample is with random-digit dialing in which a computer generates phone numbers at random, allowing the researcher to reach unlisted numbers, and cell phones as well as home phones. Exit polls, when properly administered, interview voters at random as they leave the polls at a randomly selected set of precincts.

The *art of asking questions* is also important to scientific polling. How questions are worded and the order in which they are asked can influence the respondents' answers. Questions must be clear and as specific as possible. Good questions have to be pretested to be sure that the way they are worded does not bias how they are answered. Professional interviewers, who can read the questions exactly as written and without any bias in their voices, should ask survey questions. Questions can be worded in different ways to measure factual knowledge, opinions, the intensity of opinion, or views on hypothetical situations. *Open-ended questions* permit respondents to answer in their own words rather than in set categories. These questions are harder to record and compare, but they allow respondents to express their views more clearly and may provide deeper insight into their thinking. (See Table 8–1.)

In addition to random sampling, clearly worded questions, and the absence of bias in how questions are asked, scientific polls also require thorough *analysis and reporting of the results*. Scientific polls must specify the sample size, the margin of error, and when and where the poll was conducted. Moreover, because public opinion can change from day to day and even from hour to hour, polls are really snapshots of opinion at a particular point in time. One way to track opinion change is to interview the same sample at more than one point in time. Such surveys are called *panel surveys*. While panel surveys can be informative, those in the sample may know they will be interviewed again, which may influence their responses. Contacting respondents for a second or third set of interviews is more difficult and expensive than drawing a new random sample, but is effective for measuring opinion change over time.

random sample
In this type of sample, every individual has a known and random chance of being selected.

TABLE 8–1 How You Ask the Question Matters

How you ask a polling question makes a lot of difference in how people answer it, as four different polls that asked about a proposed constitutional amendment defining marriage demonstrated. The first two questions were part of national surveys that CBS conducted. The third question was part of an ABC/*Washington Post* poll. The Pew Research Center for the People and the Press asked the fourth question.

1. Would you favor or oppose an amendment to the U.S. Constitution that would allow marriage ONLY between a man and a woman?

Favor	60%
Oppose	37%
Don't Know	3%

2. Would you favor or oppose an amendment to the U.S. Constitution that would allow marriage only between a man and a woman, and outlaw marriages between people of the same sex?

Favor	51%
Oppose	42%
Don't Know	7%

3. Would you support amending the U.S. Constitution to make it illegal for homosexual couples to get married anywhere in the United States, or should each state make its own laws on homosexual marriage?

Amend Constitution	44%
State Laws	53%
Don't Know	3%

4. Do you strongly favor, favor, oppose, or strongly oppose allowing gays and lesbians to marry legally? IF OPPOSE GAY MARRIAGE ASK: There has been a proposal to change the U.S. Constitution to ban gay marriage. Do you think amending the Constitution to ban gay marriage is a good idea or a bad idea?

Total Favor	32%
Total Oppose	59%
(for those opposed) Good idea/ favor Const. amendment	36%
Bad idea/oppose Const. amendment	21%
Don't Know/Refused	2%
Don't Know/Refused	9%

SOURCE: The Pew Research Center for the People and the Press, "Reading the Polls on Gay Marriage and the Constitution," July 13, 2004, at www.people-press.org/commentary/display.php3?AnalysisID=92.

Defining public opinion as the distribution of *individual preference* emphasizes that the unit of measurement is *individuals*—not groups. The correct *universe* or *population* is the group of people to whom the question is asked. As noted, the universe of subscribers to the *Literary Digest* was not representative of the universe of all voters in 1936, a major reason why the poll incorrectly predicted the election.[3] When a substantial percentage of a sample agrees on an issue—for example, that we should honor the American flag—there is a *consensus*. But on most issues, opinions are divided. When two opposing sides feel intensely about an issue, the public is said to be *polarized*. On such issues it can be difficult to compromise or find a middle ground. The Vietnam War in the 1960s and 1970s was a polarizing issue. A more recent example is gay marriage. Neither those who favor legalizing gay marriage nor those who unequivocally oppose it see much room for compromise. Somewhere in the middle are those who oppose gay marriage but favor giving gay couples legal rights through "civil unions." (See Table 8–2.)

INTENSITY *Intensity*—how strongly people feel about their opinions—produces the brightest and deepest hues in the fabric of public opinion. The fervor of people's

TABLE 8-2 Differing Opinions on Gay Marriage

	Gay marriage should not be allowed	Gay marriage should not be allowed, but civil unions should be allowed	Gay marriage should be allowed
Total	63%	3%	34%
Gender			
Men	64	3	32
Women	61	3	36
Region			
Northeast	55	3	42
Midwest	71	3	25
South	70	2	28
West	47	5	48
Age			
18–29	49	2	49
30–44	59	4	37
45–64	64	4	32
65+	85	2	13
Church Attendance			
Every week	84	2	14
Almost every week	78	5	17
Once or twice a month	66	5	29
A few times a year	51	4	45
Never	44	0	56
Race			
White	63	3	34
African American	69	3	29
Hispanic	53	5	42
Other	56	8	36
Party			
Republican	80	4	17
Democrat	54	3	43
Independent	57	3	41
Other	60	5	35
Political Philosophy			
Conservative	82	4	14
Moderate	57	4	39
Liberal	32	2	66
Don't know/Haven't thought about it	66	2	32
Marital Status			
Married	68	3	29
Widowed	81	2	17
Divorced	57	8	35
Separated	74	0	26
Single, never married	49	1	50
Partnered, not married	37	5	59
Education			
High school or less	72	2	25
Some college	60	5	35
College degree or more	49	3	48

SOURCE: 2004 National Election Study (Center for Political Studies, University of Michigan, 2004).
NOTE: Numbers may not add to 100 due to rounding. Independents who lean toward a party are classified with the party toward which they lean. Race is defined by the first race with which a respondent identifies.

beliefs varies greatly. For example, some individuals mildly favor gun control legislation, and others mildly oppose it; some people are emphatically for or against it; and some have no interest in gun control at all. Others may not have even heard of it. People who lost their jobs or retirement savings because of corporate scandals are likely to feel more intensely about enhanced regulation of corporations and accounting firms than those not directly affected by corporate scandals. Intensity is typically measured by asking people how strongly they feel about an issue or about a politician. Such a question is sometimes called a *scale*.

LATENCY   *Latency* refers to political opinions that people may hold but have not fully expressed. These opinions may not have crystallized, yet they are still important, because they can be aroused by leaders or events and thereby motivate people to support them. Latent opinions set rough boundaries for leaders who know that if they take certain actions, they will trigger either opposition or support from millions of people. If leaders understand people's unexpressed wants, needs, and hopes, they will know how to mobilize people and draw them to the polls on election day. Many people who lived in communist Poland, East Germany, Czechoslovakia, or Hungary must have had latent opinions favorable to democracy—opinions supporting majority rule, freedom, and meaningful elections. As a result, these countries quickly embraced democratic reforms when new leaders openly encouraged such ideas. A more recent example of a latent opinion is the concern for security from foreign enemies, which had not been an issue in the United States before the terrorist attacks of September 11, 2001. The need for homeland security has now become a **manifest opinion**.

SALIENCE   *Salience* measures the extent to which people believe issues are relevant to them. Most people are more concerned about personal issues like paying their bills and keeping their jobs than about national issues, but if national issues somehow threaten their security or safety, the salience of national issues rises sharply. Salience and intensity, while different, are often correlated on the same issue.

The salience of issues may change over time. During the Great Depression of the 1930s, Americans were concerned mainly about jobs, wages, and economic security. By the 1940s, with the onset of World War II, foreign affairs came to the forefront. In the 1960s, problems of race and poverty were important to many Americans. In the 1970s, Vietnam and then the Watergate scandals became the focus of people's attention. By the early 2000s, concerns about Social Security, health care, education, terrorism, and national security had become salient issues. Events like terrorist attacks or the ongoing strife in Iraq tend to reinforce or elevate the salience of an issue.

How Do We Get Our Political Opinions and Values?

No one is born with political views. We develop our political attitudes from many mentors and teachers through a process called **political socialization**. As we discussed in Chapter 4, this process starts in childhood, and families and schools are usually the two most important political teachers. Children learn about our culture in childhood and adolescence but reshape it as they mature.[4] Socialization—how we come to see ourselves and society, how we learn to interact with other individuals and groups—lays the foundation for political beliefs, values, ideology, and partisanship.

A common element of political socialization in most cultures is *nationalism*, a consciousness of the nation-state and of belonging to it. Robert Coles describes nationalism this way:

> As soon as we are born, in most places on this earth, we acquire a nationality, a membership in a community. . . . A royal doll, a flag to wave in a parade, coins with their engraved messages—these are sources of instruction and connect a young person to a country. The attachment can be strong, indeed, even among children yet to attend school, wherever the flag is saluted, the national anthem sung. The attachment is as parental as the words imply—homeland, motherland, fatherland. . . . Nationalism works its way into just about every corner of the mind's life.[5]

manifest opinion
A widely shared and consciously held view, like support for homeland security.

political socialization
The process—most notably in families and schools—by which we develop our political attitudes, values, and beliefs.

Government's Greatest Endeavors

Helping Veterans Readjust to Civilian Life

Americans are currently divided on many issues, including immigration reform, the Iraq war, and energy policies. However, they also agree on many issues, including the need to help veterans adjust to civilian life after war. They may oppose the Iraq war, for example, but want the federal government to do everything possible to help veterans who have served in the war when they come home.

The most significant expansion of veterans' benefits occurred just before the end of World War II, when Congress passed the GI Bill. Enacted with overwhelming pubic support, the GI Bill helped veterans get a college education, buy homes, and prepare for new jobs, all of which helped the economy grow as they entered the job market. Of the 15 million veterans eligible for the GI Bill's education benefits, nearly eight million went to college or received employment training, at a cost of $15 billion.

Helping veterans readjust to civilian life is a more complicated task today, in part because of the changing nature of war. Many veterans are returning with new kinds of injuries caused by the kinds of bombs used in the Afghanistan and Iraq wars. Because of advanced battlefield medical care, more soldiers are surviving their wounds. This means that more are returning to the United States with serious injuries that take months, or even years, to heal. They are also returning with more serious mental illnesses caused by the intensity of combat.

Much of their care is provided by the Department of Veterans Affairs, which runs a network of veterans' hospitals and clinics staffed by more than 200,000 medical professionals. These hospitals are only open to veterans, but they are often linked to teaching hospitals that help the rest of the nation as well. ∎

Rehabilitation and physical therapy for a soldier who lost part of his leg in Iraq.

QUESTIONS

Should the veterans' hospitals be opened to Americans in general?

Why has the nation provided care for veterans since the Revolutionary War?

The pluralistic political culture of the United States means that the sources of our views are immensely varied. Political attitudes may stem from religious, racial, gender, or ethnic backgrounds, or economic beliefs and values. But we can safely make at least one generalization: We form our attitudes through participation in *groups*. This includes families, schools, social organizations, and more political groups like the National Rifle Association (NRA) or Planned Parenthood. Close-knit groups like the family are especially influential. When we identify closely with the attitudes and interests of a particular group, these attitudes color how we see things.[6] Group affiliation does not necessarily mean that individual members do not think for themselves. Each member brings his or her own emotions, memories, and resistance to groups.

Children in the United States tend at an early age to adopt common values that provide continuity with the past and that legitimate the American political system. Young children know what country they live in, and their loyalty to the nation develops early. Although the details of our political system may elude them, most young Americans acquire a respect for the Constitution and for the concept of participatory democracy, as well as an initially positive view of the most visible figure in our democracy, the president.[7]

"It should be 'yes' or 'no' or 'undecided'—we don't accept a 'don't give a damn' answer!"

Cartoon Features Syndicate.

Most American children have ample opportunities to learn the importance of participatory democracy.

FAMILY Most social psychologists agree that family is the most powerful socializing agent.[8] American children typically show political interest by the age of ten, and by the early teens their interest may be fairly high. Consider your own political learning process. You probably formed your picture of the world by listening to a parent at dinner or by absorbing the stories your older brothers and sisters brought home from school. Perhaps you also heard about politics from grandparents, aunts, and uncles. You, in turn, influenced your family, if only by bringing some of your own hopes and concerns home from school. What we first learn in the family is not so much specific political opinions as basic *attitudes,* which are more broad or general, that shape our opinions—attitudes toward our neighbors, political parties, other classes or types of people, particular leaders (especially presidents), and society in general.

Studies of high school students indicate a high correlation between their partisan identification and their parents' political party. This relatively high degree of correspondence continues throughout life. People, in other words, tend to belong to the same political party that their parents did. Such a finding raises questions: does the direct influence of parents create the correspondence? Or does living in the same social environment—neighborhood, church, socioeconomic group—influence parents and children? The answer is *both*. One influence often strengthens the other. For example, a daughter of Republican parents growing up in a small southern town with strong Republican leanings will be affected by friends, by other adults, and perhaps by youngsters in a church group, all of whom may reinforce the attitudes of her parents.[9] What happens when a young person's parents and friends disagree? Young people tend to go along with parents rather than friends on underlying political attitudes such as party affiliation, with friends rather than parents on some specific issues like the death penalty or gun control, and somewhere in between in their actual political behavior, such as how they vote in presidential elections.[10] Fathers' party preference has a greater impact on sons and mothers' on daughters. The same is true when parents have different party identifications.[11]

SCHOOLS Schools also mold young citizens' political attitudes. American schools see part of their purpose as preparing students to be citizens and active participants in governing their communities and the nation. Especially important are extracurricular activities like student government and debate in fostering later political involvement.[12] At an early age, schoolchildren begin to pick up specific political values and basic attitudes toward our system of government. Education, like the family, prepares Americans to live in society.

From kindergarten through college, students generally develop political values consistent with the democratic process and supportive of the American political system. In their study of American history, they are introduced to our nation's heroes and

"[M]ost young people do not seek out political information and . . . they are not very likely to do so in the future."

NATIONAL ASSOCIATION OF SECRETARIES OF STATE study

heroines, the important events in our history, and the ideals of our society. Other aspects of their experience, such as the daily Pledge of Allegiance and school programs or assemblies, seek to reinforce respect for country. Children also gain practical experience in how democracy works through elections for student government. In many states, high school and even college students are required by law to take courses in U.S. history or American government to graduate.

Do school courses and activities give young people the skills needed to participate in elections and democratic institutions? A study of 18- to 24-year-olds commissioned by the National Association of Secretaries of State found that young people "lack any real understanding of citizenship . . . information and understanding about the democratic process . . . and information about candidates and political parties."[13] Furthermore, the Secretaries of State report noted that "most young people do not seek out political information and that they are not very likely to do so in the future."[14] You and your classmates are not a representative sample in part because you are taking this course and therefore have more interest and knowledge than most people.

The debate about whether there is peer pressure on college campuses to conform to certain acceptable ideas or to use particular language highlights how higher education can shape attitudes and values. How does college influence political opinion? One study suggests that college students are more likely than people of the same age who are not attending college to be knowledgeable about politics, more in favor of free speech, and more likely to talk and read about politics.[15] Is this the influence of the professors, the curriculum, the other students, or the background of people attending college? The answer is difficult to generalize. While parents sometimes fear that professors have too much influence on their college-age children, most professors doubt that they can significantly influence their students' political views.

MASS MEDIA Like everyone else, young people are exposed to a wide range of media—school newspapers, national and local newspapers, the Internet, movies, radio, television—all of which influence what they think. They, like adults, often pick and choose the media with which they agree, so their exposure is *selective*. The mass media also serve as agents of socialization by providing a link between individuals and the values and behavior of others. Media influence is greater on attitudes about issues and individual politicians.[16] The popular media help shape the attitudes and opinions of the people who watch, listen to, or read them. News broadcasts present information about our society. Events that get intensive media coverage often focus our attention on certain issues. For example, TV coverage of the war in Iraq directed widespread attention to that country's ethnic groups and to the difficulty of establishing a lasting peace there. Similarly, many Americans began to pay attention to Islamic fundamentalism after the terrorist attacks of September 11, 2001.

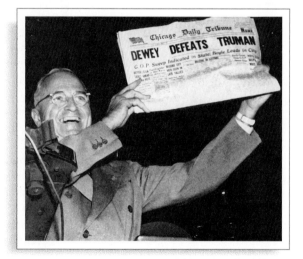

The Chicago Herald Tribune *was so sure of its polling data in the 1948 election, they predicted a win for Republican Thomas Dewey before the results were final. A victorious Harry Truman displays the mistaken headline.*

OTHER INFLUENCES Religious, ethnic, and racial backgrounds as well as the workplace can also shape opinions, both within and outside the family. Some scholars have found, for example, that the religious composition of a community has a direct impact on knowledge, discussion, and self-confidence in dealing with politics.[17] Generalizations about how people vote are useful, but we have to be careful about stereotyping people. For example, not all African Americans vote Democratic, and many Catholics disagree with their church's opposition to abortion. It is a mistake to assume that because we know a person's religious affiliation or racial background, we know his or her political opinions.

Stability and Change in Public Opinion

Adults are not simply the sum of their early experiences, but adults' opinions tend to remain stable. Even if the world around us changes rapidly, we are slow to shift our loyalties or to change our minds about things that matter to us. In general, people who remain in the same place, in the same occupation, and in the same income group

TABLE 8–3 Changes in Public Perception After Terrorist Attacks of September 11, 2001

	Increased	Decreased	Net Change
Trust national government	51%	7%	44%
Trust local government	32	13	19
Hours watching TV	40	24	16
Interest in politics	29	15	14
Trust local police	26	12	14
Interracial trust	31	20	11
Trust shop clerks	28	17	11
Support for unpopular book in library	28	18	10
Trust neighbors	23	13	10
Contributions to religious charity	29	20	9
Expect crisis support from friends	22	14	8
Trust "people running my community"	32	24	8
Worked with neighbors	15	8	7
Trust local news media	30	23	7
Gave blood	11	4	7
Volunteered	36	29	7
Expect local cooperation in crisis	23	17	6
Worked on community project	17	11	6
Attend political meeting	11	6	5
Newspaper readership	27	24	3
Visit with relatives	43	40	3
Attended club meeting	29	26	3
Attended public meeting	27	26	3
Contributions to secular charity	28	27	1
Attend church	20	19	1
Organizational memberships (number)	39	39	0
Had friends visit your home	39	45	−6
Support for immigrants rights	21	32	−11

SOURCE: The Saguaro Seminar: Civic Engagement in America, January 15, 2002, www.ksg.harvard.edu/saguaro/press.html.

> *"Following the attacks, Americans expressed confidence that people in their community would cooperate, for example, with voluntary conservation measures in an energy or water shortage."*
>
> POLITICAL SCIENTIST ROBERT D. PUTNAM

throughout their lives tend to have stable opinions. People often carry their attitudes with them, and families who move from cities to suburbs often retain their big-city attitudes after they have moved, at least for a time. Political analysts are becoming more interested in how adults modify their views. A harsh experience—a war, an economic depression, or the loss of a job—may be a catalyst that changes attitudes and opinions.

The September 11, 2001, terrorist attacks had at least a short-term impact on public trust and confidence in government. Political scientist Robert D. Putnam has studied how the public views political institutions and community interaction. Putnam conducted a national survey in the summer of 2000. Following the terrorist attacks, he interviewed the same respondents again to see how their views had changed. Table 8–3 shows some of the changes. Putnam found that more than half of his sample expressed greater confidence in government after the attacks. Interest in public affairs grew by 27 percent among people age 35 and under and by 8 percent among older respondents. Putnam concludes, "Americans don't only trust political institutions more: We also trust one another more, from neighbors and co-workers to shop clerks and perfect strangers. Following the attacks, Americans expressed confidence that people in their community would cooperate, for example, with voluntary conservation measures in an energy or water shortage." The events of September 11 also appear to have led people to be "somewhat more generous."[18] How enduring these changes are is not yet clear and may be more consequential in people's private lives than in their public activities like voting, volunteering, or becoming more involved in politics. Putnam's subsequent research found that trust in community leaders, neighbors, other races, and so on, declined by

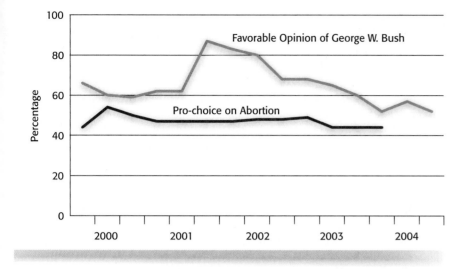

FIGURE 8–1 Comparison of Opinion of President George W. Bush and Attitude on Abortion Over Time.

SOURCE: Abortion/Pro-choice: Polling Report, at www.pollingreport.com/abortion.htm; Opinion of George W. Bush: Polling Report, at www.pollingreport.com/BushFav.htm9; *USA Today*/CNN/Gallup Poll reports, at www.usatoday.com/news/politicselections/nation/polls/usatodaypolls.htm.

the spring of 2002, but it remained higher than before 9/11. Confidence in community cooperation also "tended to fade over time." On the other hand, civic engagement has continued at its post-9/11 level and may even have become stronger.[19]

Some of our political opinions do not change much because they are part of our core values. For example, views on abortion, the death penalty, and doctor-assisted suicide tend to remain relatively stable over time. On issues that are less central to our values, such as our view of how a president is performing his job, opinions can change substantially. For example, Figure 8–1 contrasts the public's opinion toward President George W. Bush with its views on abortion over time. Although the electorate's opinion of President Bush changed a lot over time, opinions on abortion remained remarkably stable. On many issues, opinion can change once the public learns more about the issue or perceives that there is another side to the question. These are the issues that politicians can help shape attitudes about by calling attention to them and by leading the debate on them. The decisions by Presidents Dwight Eisenhower, John Kennedy, and Lyndon Johnson to enforce school desegregation are examples of leadership of public opinion, as were the positions of Presidents Jimmy Carter on the Panama Canal Treaty and George H. W. Bush and Bill Clinton on the North American Free Trade Agreement (NAFTA).[20]

Public Opinion and Public Policy

For much of human history, public opinion has been difficult to measure. "What I want," Abraham Lincoln once said, "is to get done what the people desire to be done, and the question for me is how to find that out exactly."[21] Politicians in our day do not face such uncertainty about public opinion—far from it.[22] Polling informs them about public opinion on all major policy issues. Politicians can commission polls themselves, or they can turn to public or media polls. More than 80 percent of newspapers and half of all television stations conduct or commission their own polls.[23]

There are many examples from history that show how public opinion can shape policy and, in turn, of how policies shape opinion. During the Vietnam War, antiwar demonstrations on college campuses spread to cities across the country. Benjamin Page and Paul Robert Shapiro found that "public opinion had a substantial impact on the rate of troop withdrawals."[24] In the Persian Gulf War of 1990–1991, opposition to the use of U.S. forces fell substantially after a few days of success in the air and ground war. When American forces were dispatched to Somalia in East Africa in Operation Restore Hope in January 1993, 79 percent of the public approved of using troops to ensure the delivery of humanitarian aid. But when U.S. soldiers were killed and dragged through the streets of Mogadishu, the capital of Somalia, support for the mission fell to only 17 percent in October of the same year.[25] On May 3, 2003, the day after President Bush announced "Mission Accomplished" in the Iraq War on an aircraft carrier, 72 percent of Americans approved of the way he had handled the situation with

"What I want is to get done what the people desire to be done, and the question for me is how to find that out exactly."

ABRAHAM LINCOLN

Iraq. About a year later, after the Abu Ghraib prison torture and repeated attacks on American forces in Iraq, the Bush approval rating had fallen to 34 percent.[26]

Typically, elected officials focus on issues of importance to the public.[27] In a sense they follow public opinion by using polls to learn how to talk about issues in ways that resonate with the public. Members of Congress want to win reelection by showing greater attention to public opinion as election day looms.[28] Candidates use polls to determine where to campaign, how to campaign, and even whether to campaign. The decision in 2004 about which states John Kerry and George W. Bush most aggressively campaigned in was driven by the polls and a preoccupation with securing 270 electoral votes. Both campaigns lavished time and attention on Ohio, Florida, Wisconsin, Iowa, and Pennsylvania. Even smaller states like New Hampshire and New Mexico received substantial attention. Larger states like New York, California, Illinois, and Texas were taken for granted because one side or the other was so far ahead in them, and gaining a plurality in the national popular vote was a secondary objective.

When properly conducted, polls provide valuable data on public opinion and voting behavior. When they have flawed samples or poorly worded questions, they are inaccurate and give scientific polling a bad name. Before taking the results of a poll seriously, it is important to know the nature of the sample, the timing of the survey—events might have occurred since the survey that make the results questionable—and the wording and order of the questions. The order of questions is important because a leading question preceding one that is reported in the media can alter the responses to the later questions.

Polls are no substitute for elections. With a ballot before them, voters must translate their opinions into concrete decisions. They must decide what is important and what is not. Democracy is more than the expression of views, more than a simple mirror of opinion. It also involves choosing leaders, taking sides on issues, and deciding how governments should act. Democracy is the thoughtful participation of people in the political process. Elections are the critical link between the many opinions "We the People" hold and how we select our leaders.

Awareness and Interest

For most people, politics is of secondary importance to earning a living, raising a family, and having a good time. Some Americans are more concerned about which team wins the World Series or the Super Bowl than they are about who wins the school board elections, who gets to be mayor, or even who gets to be president of the United States.

These college students feel responsible to vote and line up on campus to fill out absentee ballots.

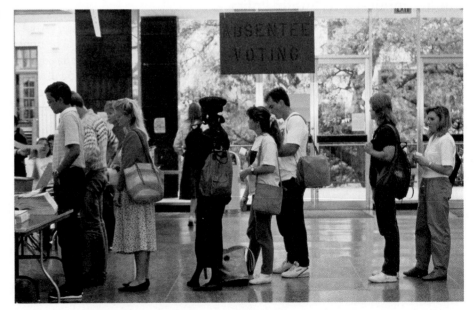

Most people find politics complicated and difficult to understand. And they should, because democracy *is* complicated and difficult to understand. The mechanics and structures of our government, such as how the government operates, how the electoral college works, how Congress is set up, and the length of terms for the president and for members of the Senate and House of Representatives are examples of such complexity that are important to our constitutional democracy.

Younger adults, who remember learning the details in school, typically know most about how the government works. In general, however, most adults fare poorly when quizzed about their elected officials.[29] Just over 15 percent of Americans know the names of the congressional candidates from their district.[30] With so few voters knowing the candidates for their congressional district, it is not surprising that "on even hotly debated congressional issues, few people know where their Congress member stands."[31]

The public knows even less about important public policy issues. In 1982, after approximately 59 years of debate over ratification of the Equal Rights Amendment, nearly one-third of the adults in the United States indicated they had never heard of it. The same is true for many other issues.[32] In 2004, only 28 percent could identify William Rehnquist as the then Chief Justice of the U.S. Supreme Court. Fortunately, not all Americans are uninformed or uninterested. About 25 percent of the public is interested in politics most of the time. This is the **attentive public**, people who know and understand how the government works. They vote in most elections, read a daily newspaper, and "talk politics" with their families and friends. They tend to be better educated and more committed to democratic values than other Americans.

At the opposite end of the spectrum are *nonvoters,* people who are rarely interested in politics or public affairs and seldom vote. About 67 percent of Americans have indicated that they are interested in politics "some of the time," "only now and then," or "hardly at all."[33] A subset of this group might be called *political know-nothings.* These individuals not only avoid political activity but also have little interest in government and limited knowledge about it.

Between the attentive public and the political know-nothings are the *part-time citizens,* roughly 40 percent of the American public. These individuals participate selectively in elections, voting in presidential elections but usually not in others. Politics and government do not greatly interest them; they pay only minimal attention to the news; and they rarely discuss candidates or elections with others.

Democracy can survive even when many citizens are passive and uninformed, as long as many other people serve as opinion leaders and are interested and informed about public affairs. Obviously, these activists will have much greater influence than their less active fellow citizens.

Participation: Translating Opinions into Action

Americans influence their government's actions in several ways, many of which the Constitution protects. In addition to voting in elections, they participate in Internet political chat rooms, join interest groups, go to political party meetings, ring doorbells, urge friends to vote for issues or candidates, sign petitions, write letters to newspapers, and call radio talk shows. This kind of "citizen-to-citizen" participation can be important and may become more important as more people use the Internet.

Protest is also a form of political participation. Our political system is remarkably tolerant of protest that is not destructive or violent. Boycotts, picketing, sit-ins, and marches are all legally protected. Rosa Parks and Martin Luther King Jr. used nonviolent protest to call attention to unfair laws (see Chapter 17). Few Americans participate in protests, but the actions of those who do can substantially shape public opinion.

A distinguishing characteristic of democracy is that citizens can influence government decisions by participating in politics. In 2004, millions of citizens in Kiev and other parts of the Ukraine protested what they saw as a fraudulent presidential election.

attentive public
Those citizens who follow public affairs carefully.

Agents of Change

Liz Erickson, Diane Ty, and YouthNoise

YouthNoise Web site

YouthNoise was created in 1999 as a global organization designed to inspire young people everywhere to engage in political action. By creating "NOISE-makers" around the world, the organization hopes to "inspire and empower young people everywhere to catapult their passion and idealism into movements to sustain the planet." Although YouthNoise looks like many organizations that seek to activate young people, its work focuses on social problems such as hunger, violence, HIV/AIDS, and hate crimes that it hopes young people will address in their lives. As such, it is an incubator of future leaders.

Liz Erickson and Diane Ty founded YouthNoise with the same question that motivates so many agents of change: "What next?" As graduates of Williams College and Duke University, they both felt that they had been ignored in their own efforts to improve the reputation of young adults. "We saw that, for teens, getting involved suffered from what I'd call an 'image problem.' Kids say, 'It's not for me. That's for goody two-shoes.' We also saw that the Internet is the preferred medium for this generation. We knew we really needed to have an online resource offering information and the connection to other young people."

With help from *Seventeen* magazine and powered by Google, the YouthNoise Web site gives young people access to a wide range of opportunities to make a difference in their communities and the world. The award-winning Web site has options for quick engagement such as signing electronic petitions, and access to blogs and chatrooms for discussing tough issues such as global hunger. It also has an electronic playground, conference center, and is one of the first youth organizations to win a People's Choice Award as the best Web site for political activism. ∎

Learn more about YouthNoise at www.youthnoise.com.

QUESTIONS

How does YouthNoise change public opinion?

Does its state-of-the-art Web site make a difference in public opinion?

The "Orange Revolution," so named because orange was the campaign color of Viktor Yushchenko, the primary opposition candidate, called attention to the public outcry and helped lead to the ordering of a second, run-off election, which Yushchenko won with 52 percent of the vote.[34]

But protests and demonstrations are not always peaceful or successful. In totalitarian societies, participation is limited, forcing people who want to change government policies to resort to violence or revolution. The 1989 protest of Chinese students in Tiananmen Square in Beijing failed to stop the onslaught of tanks and the repression that followed. Americans sometimes forget that our democracy was born of revolution and that maintaining a constitutional democracy after a revolution is difficult and demands public participation.

Even in an established democracy, people may feel so strongly about an issue that they would rather fight than accept the verdict of an election. The classic example is the American Civil War. Following the election of 1860, in which Abraham Lincoln, an antislavery candidate who did not receive a single electoral vote from a slave state, won the presidency, most of the South tried to secede from the Union. The ensuing war marked the failure of democracy to resolve sectional conflict. Examples in our own time include antiabortion or animal rights groups that use violence to press their political agenda and militia groups that arm themselves for battle against government regulations.

When the student pro-democracy protest was stopped by Chinese government tanks in Tiananmen Square on June 5, 1989, one man stood up in defiance until he was pulled to safety by bystanders.

Participation can also include less intense activity and even engaging in patriotic rituals. For example, many Americans routinely sing the national anthem or recite the Pledge of Allegiance. They communicate their views about government and politics to their representatives in Washington and the state capitals. They write letters to the editor or call into a radio talk show. They serve as jurors in courtrooms and enlist in the military. They express concern about the involvement of American military forces overseas. They complain about taxes and government regulations. And many families make a point to take their children to Washington, D.C., and other historic sites.

For most people, politics is a private activity. Some still consider it impolite to discuss politics at dinner parties. To say that politics is private does not mean that people do not have opinions or will not discuss them when asked by others, including pollsters. But many people avoid discussing politics with neighbors, coworkers, or even friends and family because it is too divisive or upsetting. Typically, fewer than one person in four attempts to influence how another person votes in an election. But in 2004 the proportion reporting that they tried to influence another person's vote rose to nearly 50 percent (see Table 8–4). Even fewer actually work for a candidate or party. Only about 13 percent contribute financially to a candidate,[35] and only 11 percent of taxpayers designate $3 of their taxes to the fund that pays for presidential general elections.[36] Few individuals attempt to influence others by writing letters to elected officials or to newspapers for publication. Fewer still participate in protest groups or activities. Despite the small number of persons who engage in these activities, small numbers of people can make a difference in politics and government. An individual or small group can generate media interest in an issue and thereby expand the issue's impact. Peaceful protests for civil rights, about environmental issues, and both for and against abortion have generated public attention and even changed opinions.[37]

TABLE 8–4 Political Participation and Awareness in the United States

Watch campaign on TV	86%
Vote in presidential elections	58
Vote in congressional elections	42
Try to persuade vote of others	48
Display campaign button, sticker, or sign	21
Give money to help a campaign	13
Attend dinner, meeting, or rally for candidate	7

SOURCE: U.S. Bureau of the Census, *Statistical Abstract of the United States: 2006* (U.S. Government Printing Office, 2006), p. 263; The 2004 National Election Study, Center for Political Studies, University of Michigan; The NES Guide to Public Opinion and Electoral Behavior, at www.umich.edu/~nes/nesguide/gd-index.htm#6; See also www.census.gov.

Voting

Voting is Americans' most typical political activity. The United States is a constitutional democracy with more than 200 years of free and frequent elections and a tradition of the peaceful transfer of power between competing groups and parties.

Originally, the Constitution left it to the individual states to determine who could vote, and the qualifications for voting differed considerably from state to state. All

History Makers

Lyndon Johnson and the Voting Rights Act of 1965

Even though the Fifteenth Amendment granted African Americans the right to vote in 1870, it took another 95 years for Congress to enact laws that made this right an actuality. Through a variety of means, including literacy tests, poll taxes, and physical violence, black persons were effectively denied the right to vote.

An important leader in extending the right to vote to all Americans was a son of the segregated South, Lyndon Johnson. As president, Johnson pushed for passage of the Twenty-Fourth Amendment ban-ning poll taxes and, in 1965, for passage of the National Voting Rights Act. This act outlawed the use of literacy tests as a requirement for voting, pro-vided for federal registrars for voter registration, and required the Department of Justice to approve in advance any change in voting laws in districts where black people made up at least 5 percent of the population.*

Johnson made passage of the Voting Rights Act a major pri-ority and used his considerable talents of persuasion to defeat a Senate filibuster against this leg-islation. In a nationwide broad-cast, Johnson signed the act in a ceremony at the U.S. Capitol Rotunda. On that occasion he said the act would "strike away the last major shackle of the Negro's 'ancient bonds.'"[†] The impact of the act was immedi-ate and continues today. For example, Mississippi saw voting registration for black people climb from under 7 percent in 1965 to over 74 percent in 1988.[‡] The act was extended in 1970, 1975, 1982 (with amendments), and most re-cently in 2006 by President George W. Bush. ∎

> *Johnson made a passage of the Voting Rights Act a major priority and used his considerable talents of persuasion . . .*

*National Voting Rights Act of 1965, 89th Cong., 1st sess., H.R. 1564.
[†]*Congress and the Nation, 1965–68: A Review of Government and Politics During the Johnson Years*, Volume 11, (Congressional Quarterly, 1969) p. 362.
[‡]United States Department of Justice: Civil Rights Division Voting Section, "Introduction to General Voting Rights Law." Accessed October 23, 2006, at http://www .usdoj.gov/crt/voting/intro/intro_c.htm.

states except New Jersey barred women from voting, most did not permit African Americans or Native Americans to vote, and until the 1830s, property ownership was often a requirement. By the time of the Civil War (1861–1865), however, every state had extended the franchise to all white male citizens. Since that time, eligibility standards for voting have been expanded seven times by congressional legislation and constitu-tional amendments (see Table 8–5).

The civil rights movement in the 1960s made voting rights a central issue and led to the adoption of the Twenty-Fourth Amendment and passage of the 1965 Voting Rights Act. The Twenty-Fourth Amendment prohibits Congress or any state from imposing a poll tax, or any other tax, on the right to vote. The Voting Rights Act banned literacy tests, eased registration requirements, allowed for official U.S. government poll watchers, and authorized federal registrars to replace local election officials in areas where the right to vote had been flagrantly denied. Anticipating that some state or local governments would change election rules to foster discrimination, the act also required that any changes to voting practices, requirements, or procedures must be cleared in advance with the U.S. District Court for the District of Columbia. The ban on the poll tax and the provisions of the Voting Rights Act resulted in a dramatic expan-sion of registration and voting by black Americans. Once African Americans were per-mitted to register to vote, "the focus of voting discrimination shifted . . . to preventing them from winning elections."[38] In southern legislative districts where black people are in the majority, however, there has been a "dramatic increase in the proportion of African American legislators elected" (see Figure 8–2).[39] The Voting Rights Act was again extended for another 25 years in 2006.[40]

voter registration
System designed to reduce voter fraud by limiting voting to those who have established eligibility to vote by submitting the proper documents.

REGISTRATION One legal requirement that is particularly American—**voter registra-tion**—arose in response to concerns about voting abuses, but it also discourages

TABLE 8–5 Changes in Voting Eligibility Standards Since 1870

Timeline	Change
1870	Fifteenth Amendment forbade states from denying the right to vote because of "race, color, or previous condition of servitude."
1920	Nineteenth Amendment gave women the right to vote.
1924	Congress granted Native Americans citizenship and voting rights.
1961	Twenty-Third Amendment permitted District of Columbia residents to vote in federal elections.
1964	Twenty-Fourth Amendment prohibited the use of poll taxes in federal elections.
1965	Voting Rights Act removed restrictions that kept African Americans from voting.
1971	Twenty-Sixth Amendment extended the vote to citizens age 18 and older.

voting. Most other democracies have automatic voter registration. Average turnout in the United States is more than 30 percentage points lower than in countries like Austria, Denmark, Germany, and Israel.[41] This was not always the case. In fact, in the 1800s, turnout in the United States was much like that of these countries today. Turnout began to drop significantly around 1900, in part as a result of election reforms (see Figure 8–3). Voter registration requirements substantially affect rates of voting.[42]

American elections in the 1800s were different from those of today. The parties printed the ballots, often using different colored papers for each party, and ballots were cast in public, so that party officials could monitor how people had voted. In some areas, charges of multiple voting generated a reform movement that replaced the party-printed ballots with the **Australian ballot**, a ballot that the government prints and is cast in secret (see Chapter 9). The same reformers also pressed for voter registration to prevent multiple voting and limit voting to those who had previously established their eligibility.

Registration laws vary by state, but every state except North Dakota requires registration in order to vote. Idaho, Maine, Minnesota, New Hampshire, Wisconsin, and Wyoming permit election day registration. The most important provision regarding voter registration may be the closing date. Until the early 1970s, closing dates in many states were six months before the election. Now, federal law prevents a state from closing registration more than 30 days before a federal election.[43] Voter registration requires voters to take an extra step—usually filling out a form at the county courthouse, when renewing a driver's license, or with a roving registrar—days or weeks before the election and every time they move to a new address. Other important provisions include places and hours of registration.[44]

Australian ballot
A secret ballot printed by the state.

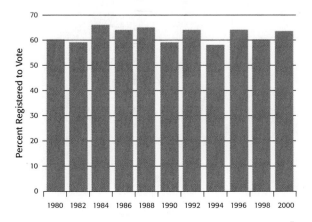

FIGURE 8–2 Percentage of African Americans Registered to Vote, 1980–2004.

SOURCE: U.S. Bureau of the Census, *Statistical Abstract of the United States,* 2001 (U.S. Government Printing Office, 2001), p. 251.

FIGURE 8–3 Voter Turnout in Presidential Elections, 1800–2004.

SOURCE: Howard W. Stanley and Richard G. Niemi, *Vital Statistics on American Politics, 1999–2000* (CQ Press, 2000). See also "National Voter Turnout in Federal Elections, 1996–2000," at www.infoplease.com/ipa/A0781453.html. 2004 update by authors.

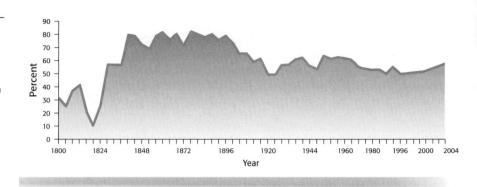

MOTOR VOTER   The burdens of voter registration were eased a bit when, on May 20, 1993, President Bill Clinton signed the National Voter Registration Act—called the "Motor Voter" bill because it allows people to register to vote while applying for or renewing a driver's license. Offices that provide welfare and disability assistance can also facilitate voter registration. States may also include public schools, libraries, and city and county clerks' offices as registration sites. The law requires states to allow registration by mail using a standardized form. To purge the voting rolls of voters who may have died or changed residence, states must mail a questionnaire to voters every four years. But Motor Voter forbids states from purging the rolls for any other reasons, such as because a person has not voted in multiple previous elections.

As a result of the law, more new voters have registered.[45] Data on the impact of Motor Voter suggest that neither Democrats nor Republicans are the primary beneficiaries because most new voters who have registered claim to be Independent.[46] Yet, Motor Voter does not appear to have increased turnout.

Reforming How We Vote

Following the controversy of the 2000 election, Florida enacted legislation modernizing its election process and establishing minimum standards for polling places and voting machines. These standards include certification of electronic voting machines and requirements for the use and storage of these machines. Despite this legislation and the purchase of more than $30 million worth of new electronic machines, their first use in the 2002 primary reminded many Florida voters of the problems with

In an effort to make registration easier, states have made registration forms available at motor vehicle stations, schools, public buildings, and even highway tollbooths.

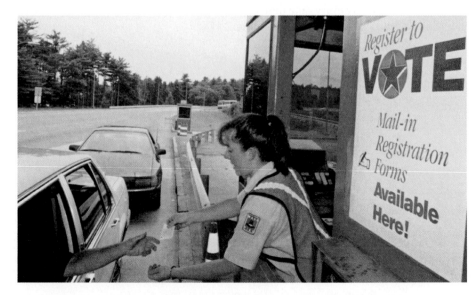

How Other Nations Govern

The Contested 2006 Election in Mexico

Exit polls in the 2006 Mexican presidential election did the unusual—they said the race was too close to call, and they were right. When the result was announced, the winner, Felipe Calderon of the conservative National Action Party (PAN), was ahead by 0.6 percent over Andrés Manuel López Obrador of the leftist Party of the Democratic Revolution.*

With the vote so close, Obrador refused to accept defeat and insisted that the vote count was invalid. Citing evidence of irregularities, including arithmetic errors and poll worker fraud (canceling Obrador's votes and padding Calderon's), Obrador initiated an official challenge with Mexico's Federal Election Tribunal. Meanwhile, hoping to broaden their margin of victory, the PAN also challenged the results. The Tribunal had until August 31 to rule on these challenges as a decision had to be made by the 6th of September due to election law. The Federal Electoral Tribunal certified Calderon's victory, finding Obrador's objections to be unfounded. The court showed Calderon beating Obrador by 233,831 votes out of 41 million cast, or by .56 of a percentage point.†

In addition to contesting the election results, Obrador also called on his supporters to protest and rally for a recount. Hundreds of thousands attended pro-Obrador rallies to protest the alleged fraud. Obrador supporters focused their protests at Mexican businesses, an important base of support for Calderon, and thronged the capital of Mexico City.‡ Protesting an election outcome on the streets is not customary in most democracies, but Obrador stated that if he was not granted a recount he would not give up, but would act in accordance with the will of the people. "If the people say that we have to carry out actions of civil disobedience, rough and forceful, we will carry them out. If the people say that we should act with less belligerence, that's how it will go."§ Obrador rejected the decision of the Federal election tribunal and planned to form a parallel government, stating he held a mandate to create "a new republic."‖ He intends to tour the country as an alternative president.¶ ∎

"If the people say that we have to carry out actions of civil disobedience . . . we will carry them out."

ANDRÉS MANUEL LÓPEZ OBRADOR

*The Associated Press, "Ruling Party Candidate Wins Mexico Vote," July 6, 2006.
†Hector Tobar, "Judges Name Calderon Winner of Vote," *Los Angeles Times*, September 6, 2006, p. 1.
‡Stevenson, Mark, "Mexican leftists push for vote recount," *The Washington Post*, July 24, 2006.
§Obrador, Andrés Manuel López, qtd. in James C. McKinley, Jr., "Mexico's losing leftist defiantly awaits election ruling," *The New York Times*, July 23, 2006.
‖Adam Thomson, "Mexico's leftwing candidate proclaims himself president-elect of 'new republic,'" *Financial Times*, September 18, 2006, p. 8.
¶James C. McKinley, Jr., "Mexican Leftist Suffers Setback in Local Race," *New York Times*, October 16, 2006, A4.

punch-card ballots in 2000. Some new machines failed to record votes, others recorded too many votes, and precinct workers were not adequately prepared to help voters with the new technology.

At the national level, Congress passed the Help America Vote Act (HAVA) providing $3.9 billion in federal funds to modernize American voting procedures and mandating that states maintain accurate statewide voter registration lists.[47] The legislation also permits voters to cast provisional ballots if there is uncertainty about their registration. Advocates of the new voting technology hope that it will improve accuracy and make voting more accessible for persons who have disabilities or who do not speak English.[48] Opponents of the changes see the funding as inadequate to meet the need and worry about the accuracy and security of the new systems.[49] In the days just before the 2004 election, both parties were preparing for legal challenges to the voting process. Issues included whether felons could vote and whether the parties could challenge the registration of new voters at the polls. The implementation of HAVA provisional ballots was also a possible source of litigation. States like Florida and Ohio were the likely battlegrounds for this legal battle, which did not materialize because of Bush's victory margin.

HAVA is just the start of a broader effort to modernize democracy. It is likely that state legislatures and Congress will eventually debate permitting people to vote via the Internet. If people can make purchases over the Internet, why not let them vote electronically as well? Some states experimented with "e-voting" on a small scale in presidential primaries in 2000, and some counties in California have also experimented with it since then. A shift to e-voting is in some respects an extension of the Oregon vote-by-mail experience since 1996. Oregon now largely conducts elections using mail ballots, a process that reduces costs and has increased participation. Yet critics worry that important elements of community and democracy are lost when people do not vote collectively at the local schoolhouse or fire station. Another concern is that e-voting may encourage more elections and referendums. If we can vote from home, why not vote on more things and more often?

Turnout

Americans hold more elections for more offices than the citizens of any other democracy. In part because there are so many elections, American voters tend to be selective about which elections they vote in. Americans elect officeholders in **general elections**, determine party nominees in **primary elections**, and replace members of the House of Representatives who have died or left office in *special elections*.

Elections held in years when the president is on the ballot are called **presidential elections**; elections held midway between presidential elections are called **midterm elections**, and elections held in odd-numbered calendar years are called *off-year elections*. Midterm elections (like the ones in 2002 and 2006) elect about one-third of the U.S. Senate; all members of the House of Representatives; and many governors, other statewide officeholders, and state legislators. Many local elections for city councils and mayors are held in the spring of odd-numbered years.

Turnout—the proportion of the voting-age public that votes—is highest in presidential general elections (see Figure 8-4). Because states have different voter registration requirements, the Census Bureau's estimate of the population over the age of 19 is the better baseline from which to compare state differences in turnout. Turnout is higher in general elections than in primary elections and higher in primary elections than in special elections. Turnout is higher in presidential general elections than in midterm general elections, and higher in presidential primary elections than in midterm primary elections.[50] This is due to greater interest in and awareness of presidential elections. Turnout is also higher in elections in which candidates for federal office are on the ballot (U.S. senator, member of the House of Representatives, president) than in state elections in years when there are no federal contests. Some states—for example, New Jersey, Virginia, and Kentucky—elect their governor and other state officials in odd-numbered years to separate state from national politics. The result is generally lower turnout. Finally, local or municipal elections have lower turnout than state elections, and municipal primaries generally have the lowest rates of participation.

---

general election
Elections in which voters elect officeholders.

primary election
Elections in which voters determine party nominees.

presidential election
Elections held in years when the president is on the ballot.

midterm election
Elections held midway between presidential elections.

turnout
The proportion of the voting-age public that votes, sometimes defined as the number of registered voters that vote.

FIGURE 8-4 **Voter Turnout in Presidential and Midterm Elections, 1990-2006.**

SOURCE: U.S. Bureau of the Census, *Statistical Abstract of the United States, 1998* (U.S. Government Printing Office, 1998), p. 97; Louis V. Gerstner, "Next Time, Let Us Boldly Vote as No Democracy Has Before," *USA Today*, November 16, 1998, p. A15; www.infoplease.com/ipa/A0781453.html; National Voter Turnout in Federal Elections: 1960-2000. 2004 update by authors.

How Other Nations Govern

Registration and Voting in the World's Parliamentary Elections

	Average Voter Turnout*	Compulsory Voting†	Automatic Registration‡
Australia	81.7%	Yes	No
Austria	72.6	No	Yes
Belgium	83.2	Yes	Yes
Canada	54.6	No	Yes
Denmark	83.1	No	Yes
Finland	65.2	No	Yes
France	59.9	No	No
Germany	75.3	No	Yes
Greece	89.0	Yes	No
Ireland	66.7	No	Yes
Israel	84.4	No	Yes
Italy	84.9	Yes	Yes
Japan	59.0	No	Yes
Netherlands	70.1	No	Yes
New Zealand	72.5	No	No
Norway	73.1	No	Yes
Spain	73.8	No	Yes
Sweden	77.7	No	Yes
Switzerland	34.9	No	Yes
United Kingdom	57.6	No	Yes
United States	46.6	No	No

*Percentage of turnout for total voting age population (VAP).
†In a *compulsory voting* system, registered voters have to vote or suffer some penalty, such as a small fine.
‡Automatic registration uses another form of citizen identification, such as a national identity card or a driver's license.

SOURCE: Richard S. Katz, *Democracy and Elections* (Oxford University Press, 1997), pp. 234–235; International Institute for Democracy and Electoral Assistance, "Voter Turnout from 1945 to Date: A Global Report on Political Participation," at www.idea.int/voter_turnout/voter_turnout.html.

Turnout reached more than 65 percent of persons eligible to vote in the presidential election of 1960, but it has since declined to just over 60 percent in 2004.[51] In midterm elections, turnout was 40 percent nationally in 2006, up about 1 percent from 2002 and up more than 2 percent since 1998. Competition tends to encourage turnout, as was the case in Ohio and Florida in 2004 and in states like Ohio and Pennsylvania in 2006. More competitive elections generate more interest among the public and more spending by the candidates, which in turn stimulate participation. The number of potential voters has increased since the 1960s because the Voting Rights Act of 1965 added many African Americans to the pool of registered voters. In 1971, the Twenty-Sixth Amendment, which gave voters aged 18–20 the right to vote, further increased the number of eligible voters. However, more than 80 million eligible Americans failed to vote in the 2004 presidential election, and even more did not vote in midterm, state, and local elections.[52]

Who Votes?

The extent of voting varies widely among different groups. Level of education especially helps predict whether people will vote; as education increases, so does the propensity to vote. "Education increases one's capacity for understanding complex and intangible subjects such as politics," according to one study, "as well as encouraging the ethic of civic responsibility. Moreover, schools provide experience dealing with a variety of bureaucratic problems, such as coping with requirements, filling out forms, and meeting deadlines."[53]

Race and ethnic background are linked with different levels of voting, largely because they correlate with education. In other words, racial and ethnic minorities with college degrees vote at about the same rate as white people with college degrees. As a group, black people vote at lower rates than white people, although this is beginning to change.[54] African American participation in the 2004 election increased over the 2000 election, but this still only counted for 11 percent of the electorate. Turnout among black voters had already surged in many states in 2000. Nationwide, African Americans accounted for 10 percent of the total vote that year, the same percentage as in 1996, yet some states experienced exceptional increases. For example, in Florida, African American turnout increased by 68 percent, from 530,000 in 1996 to 893,000 in 2000. One of the major reasons was that the National Association for the Advancement of Colored People (NAACP) mounted an unprecedented voter mobilization effort. The NAACP's National Voter Fund spent $10 million on a get-out-the-vote campaign. Such mobilization efforts can affect election outcomes in races as close as those of 2000 and 2004. In 2004, groups like America Coming Together, the NAACP, and others were especially active.

In 2004, both parties mounted major efforts to register and mobilize Hispanic voters as Hispanics have become the largest minority group in the United States. Despite these efforts, the proportion of Hispanics voting in 2004 was no higher than in 1992 and the same as in 2000. As the illegal immigrant issue took center stage in 2006, Democrats, Republicans, and allied groups again sought to expand the number of Hispanic voters.

Women, another historically underrepresented group, have voted in greater numbers than men since 1984.[55] Women's higher turnout is generally attributed to increasing levels of education and employment. Interest groups including prominent pro-choice groups have sought to mobilize women supporters of their agenda in recent elections.

Age is also highly correlated with the propensity to vote. As age increases, so does the proportion of persons voting. Older people, unless they are very old and infirm, are more likely to vote than younger people. The greater propensity of older persons to vote will amplify the importance of this group as baby boomers age and retire.

A major initiative to register and encourage young persons to vote was undertaken in 2004 by parties and groups. For example, the cable station MTV had a "Rock the Vote" effort. The mobilization effort appeared to work: 4.6 million more young voters between ages 18 and 29 voted in 2004 than in 2000. In absolute numbers this was an impressive gain, but because more people voted in 2004, young voters as a percentage of all voters did not increase. Young voters saw the 2004 election as more consequential than the 2000 election. Studies found that 57 percent of young adults said that the election would have a "great deal" or "quite a bit" of impact on the country's future. Only 33 percent of young adults had responded this way during the 2000 election.[56]

Income also influences voting. Those with higher family incomes are more likely to vote than those with lower incomes. Income, of course, largely corresponds to occupation, and those with higher-status jobs are more likely to vote than those with lower-status jobs. Poor people are less likely to feel politically involved and confident, and their social norms tend to deemphasize politics.[57]

Mobilization

In a nation as evenly divided politically as the United States is now, candidates must also mobilize their most loyal supporters, or what is often called their "base." To do this, they reaffirm their support for issues or groups that matter to the base. In 2004

The Changing Face of American Politics

Voter Turnout by Demographic Factors

Over the course of U.S. history, the right to vote has been extended and protected for women and racial minorities. Over time, groups that had not had the franchise, or had been effectively barred or discouraged from using it have become as active in their rates of voting as white men.

In the data presented below, note that women have voted at a higher percentage than men in each election since 1992. It took decades for women to reach this milestone and dismiss the old adage that "politics was men's business." The rate of voting among black persons was about ten percent-

age points below white persons in 1992 and 1994 but more recently has lagged by only about four percentage points. Hispanics are not yet participating at rates similar to women and black persons. History teaches that over time this will change. ■

. . . women have voted at a higher percentage than men in each election since 1992.

	1992	1994	1996	1998	2000	2002	2004
Sex							
Men	60%	44%	53%	41%	53%	41%	56%
Women	62	45	56	42	56	43	60
Race							
White	64	47	56	43	56	44	60
Black	54	37	51	40	54	40	56
Hispanic	29	19	27	20	28	19	28

SOURCE: U.S. Census Bureau, *Statistical Abstract of the United States, 2006* (U.S. Government Printing Office, 2006), p. 263.

and 2006, President Bush sought to mobilize his base by supporting a constitutional amendment that defined marriage as a union between a man and a woman. Democrats also appeal to their base, by communicating with black people, Hispanics, union members, and people who are pro-choice on abortion, among others.

In the 2004 battleground states, postcards reminding residents to vote and phone calls reminding them that it was election day bombarded those voters who were already likely to vote and who had already decided which candidate to support. For example, the candidates and parties mobilized their supporters to vote early in states where that was possible. This effort, sometimes called "banking the vote," reduced the list of people the campaigns needed to mobilize on election day when poll watchers would track those who had not yet voted and urge those who had pledged support to vote.

Campaigners learn which issues matter to potential voters and which candidates these voters prefer by conducting interviews on the telephone or in person, a process called a *canvass*. Individuals who are undecided and probable voters in competitive races are likely to receive communications designed to persuade them to vote for a particular candidate. Interest groups and political parties may also conduct a canvass, followed by mail and phone calls that often reinforce the same themes the candidates themselves express.

In 2004, the Republican Party took the lead in mobilizing voters for the Bush/Cheney campaign. On the Democratic side, a consortium of interest groups working together under the name "America Votes" shared data from the canvass and coordinated follow-up contacts. Among these groups were America Coming Together

(ACT), the AFL-CIO, the Sierra Club, the League of Conservation Voters, Planned Parenthood, NARAL Pro-Choice America, and more than 25 other groups. Both the Republican Party and America Votes focused on the presidential election in "battleground" states where the vote seemed highly competitive. Although some Congressional races were also hotly contested, such as the Senate races in South Dakota and Alaska, relatively few Senate or House contests were competitive in 2004, and most of these were not in presidential battlegrounds. Overall, less than 10 percent of House races and less than 20 percent of Senate races were competitive in 2004. The number of competitive House races in 2006 grew as the election approached and peaked on election day as states like Wyoming, Idaho, and New Hampshire saw races become competitive.

Undecided or "swing voters" are a major focus of mobilization efforts, and they received a lot of attention in competitive states in recent elections. Both sides intensely courted these voters through numerous person-to-person contacts, mailings, telephone calls, and efforts to register new voters. Candidates, groups, and parties are all part of this "ground war."

The volume of communication in competitive contests and battleground states in 2004 and 2006 was extraordinary. In 2004, voters in competitive presidential states received on average more than ten different pieces of mail in the last three weeks of the election about the presidential race compared to only two pieces of mail in noncompetitive states. One voter in Florida received 44 pieces of mail about the presidential race in the last three weeks. In the same year, voters in competitive U.S. Senate races received more than three pieces of mail in the last three weeks compared to an average of less than one piece of mail in noncompetitive states. One voter in South Dakota, a very competitive Senate race in 2004, received 55 pieces of mail about the race in the last three weeks.[58]

How Serious Is Nonvoting?

Although Americans can hardly avoid reading or hearing about political campaigns, especially during an election as intensely fought as that of 2004, about 40 percent of all Americans fail to vote. Who are they? Why don't they vote? Is the fact that so many Americans choose not to vote a cause for alarm? If so, what can we do about it?

There is considerable disagreement about how to interpret low voter turnout. The simplest explanation for low turnout is that people are lazy, but there is more to it than that. Of course, some people are apathetic, but most Americans are not. Paradoxically, we compare favorably with other nations in political interest and awareness, but for a variety of institutional and political reasons, we fail to convert this interest in politics into voting (see Table 8–6).

In the United States, voting is more difficult and takes more time and effort than in other democracies. In our system, as we have seen, people must first register to vote and then must decide how to vote not only for many different offices but also often for referendums on public policy or constitutional amendments. The United States also holds elections on weekdays rather than on holidays or weekends as other countries often do. Another factor in the decline of voter turnout since the 1960s is, paradoxically, the Twenty-Sixth Amendment, which, by lowering the voting age to 18 increased the number of eligible voters. But young people are the least likely to vote. After the amendment was ratified in 1971, turnout in the presidential election fell from 62 percent in 1968 to 57 percent in 1972.[59]

Some political scientists argue that nonvoting is not a critical problem. "Nonvoting is not a social disease," contends Austin Ranney, a noted political scientist. He points out that legal and extralegal denial of the vote to African Americans, women, Hispanics, persons over 18, and other groups has now been outlawed, so nonvoting is voluntary. He quotes the late Senator Sam Ervin of North Carolina: "I don't believe in making it easy for apathetic, lazy people to vote."[60] Some might even contend that nonvoting is a sign of voter satisfaction.

Those who argue that nonvoting is a serious problem cite the "class bias" of those who do vote. The social makeup and attitudes of nonvoters differ significantly from

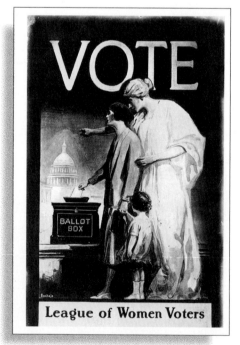

This poster, published by the League of Women Voters, urged women to use the vote the Nineteenth Amendment had given them.

TABLE 8-6   Why People Don't Vote

Too busy, conflicting schedule	19.9%
Illness or disability	15.4
Other reason	10.9
Not interested	10.7
Did not like candidates or campaign issues	9.9
Out of town	9.0
Don't know or refused	8.5
Registration problems	6.8
Forgot to vote	3.4
Inconvenient polling place	3.0
Transportation problems	2.1
Bad weather conditions	0.5

SOURCE: U.S. Bureau of the Census, "Reasons for Not Voting, by Sex, Age, Race and Hispanic Origin, and Educational Attainment: November 2004," at http://www.census.gov/population/www/socdemo/voting/cps2004.html.

those of voters and hence distort the representative system. "The very poor . . . have about two-thirds the representation among voters than their numbers would suggest." Thus the people who need the most help from the government lack their fair share of electoral power to obtain it. And, it is argued, this situation is growing worse.[61] Some might contend that younger voters, the poor, and minority citizens do not vote because politicians pay less attention to them. But politicians understandably cater to people who vote more than they do to people who do not vote.

Declining participation through voting and other political acts has puzzled some political scientists because voting rates have continued to drop even as the overall level of education, a strong predictor of voting, has increased. Part of the answer to the puzzle may be that political parties and other groups have done less voter mobilization over time. In other words, some people don't vote because no one asks them to. Furthermore, advances in technology allow parties and campaigns to target their appeals narrowly to people who are already likely to turn out.[62]

Low voting, according to those who see a class bias in voting, reflects "the underdevelopment of political attitudes resulting from the historic exclusion of low-income groups from active electoral participation."[63] In short, part of the problem of nonvoting among low-income, less-educated people is their failure to be aware of their own interests. Dynamic leadership or strong party organization, or both, would not only attract the poor to the polls but also make clear their "class grievances and aspirations."[64] Others reject this class bias argument. They admit that nonvoters are demographically different but cite polls showing that nonvoters' attitudes are not much different from those of voters. One study, comparing the party identification of voters with that of all Americans, found that the proportion of Democrats was nearly identical (51.4 percent of all citizens and 51.3 percent of voters), while Republicans as voters were slightly overrepresented (36 percent of citizens and 39.7 percent of voters). All other political differences were much smaller than this 3.7 percent gap in terms of party identification. Further, voters are not "disproportionately hostile" to social welfare policies compared to citizens generally.[65]

How might increased voter turnout affect national elections? It might make a difference, since there are partisan differences between different demographic groups and poorer persons are more likely to be Democrats. Candidates would have to adjust to the demands of this expanded electorate. A noted political scientist, while acknowledging that no political system could achieve 100 percent participation, pointed out that if the large nonvoter population decided to vote it could overturn the balance of power in the political system.[66] However, others persuasively contend that the difference might not be that pronounced because on many issues, nonvoters have much the same attitudes as voters. For example, nonvoters do not favor government ownership or regulation of industry more than voters do. Nor are nonvoters more egalitarian. They are, however, more inclined to favor additional spending on welfare programs.[67]

Finally, for better or worse, low voter turnout could indicate approval of the status quo, whereas high voter turnout might signify disapproval and widespread desire for change.

Voting Choices

Why do people vote the way they do? Political scientists have identified three main elements of the voting choice: party identification, candidate appeal, and issues. These elements often overlap.

Voting on the Basis of Party

Party identification is the subjective or self-defined sense of identification or affiliation that a person has with a political party (see Chapter 7). Party identification often predicts a person's stand on issues. It is part of our national mythology that Americans vote for the person and not the party, but as you will see, in fact we vote most often for a person from the party we prefer.

As we discussed, partisanship is typically acquired in childhood or adolescence as a result of the socialization process in the family and then reinforced by peer groups in adolescence. In the absence of reasons to vote otherwise, people depend on party identification to simplify their voting choices. Party identification is not the same as party registration or party membership in the sense of being a dues-paying, card-carrying member, as in some European parties. Rather, it is a psychological attachment to one party or another.

The number of self-declared Independents since the mid-1970s has increased dramatically. Nominally, Independents in the electorate today outnumber Republicans. But two-thirds of all Independents are, in fact, partisans in their voting behavior. There are three distinct types of Independents: Independent-leaning Democrats, Independent-leaning Republicans, and Pure Independents. Independent-leaning Democrats are predictably Democratic in their voting behavior, and Independent-leaning Republicans vote heavily Republican. Independent "leaners" are thus different from each other and from Pure Independents. Pure Independents have the lowest rate of turnout, but most of them generally side with the winner in presidential elections. Independent leaners vote at about the same rate as partisans and more than Pure Independents. Independent leaners vote for the party toward which they lean at about the same rate, or even more so, than weak partisans do. This data on Independents only reinforces the importance of partisanship in explaining voting choice. When we consider Independent-leaning Democrats and Independent-leaning Republicans as Democrats and Republicans respectively, only 10 percent of the population were Pure Independents in 2004.[68] This proportion is consistent with earlier election years. In short, there are few genuinely independent voters.

Although party identification has fluctuated in the past 40 years, it remains more stable than attitudes about issues or political ideology. Fluctuations in party identification appear to come in response to economic conditions and political performance, especially of the president. The more information voters have about their choices, the more likely they are to defect from their party and vote for a candidate from the other party.

party identification
An informal and subjective affiliation with a political party that most people acquire in childhood.

Voting on the Basis of Candidates

While long-term party identification is important, it is clearly not the only factor in voting choices. Otherwise, the Democrats would have won every presidential election since the last major realignment in partisanship, which occurred during the Great Depression in the election of Franklin Roosevelt in 1932. In fact, since 1952, Republicans have won nine presidential elections to the Democrats' five. The answer to this puzzle is largely found in a second major explanation of voting choice—**candidate appeal**.

Candidate-centered politics means that rather than rely on parties or groups to build a coalition of supporters for a candidate, the candidates make their case directly to the voters. In many races, the parties and groups also make the candidate the major focus of attention, minimizing partisanship or group identification.[69] The fact that we vote for officials separately—president, senator, governor, state attorney general, and so on—means voters are asked repeatedly to choose from among competing candidates. While the party of the candidates is an important clue to voters, in most contested races voters also look to candidate-specific information.

Candidate appeal often involves an assessment of a candidate's character. Is the candidate honest? Is the candidate consistent? Is the candidate dedicated to "family values"? Does the candidate have religious or spiritual commitments? In recent elections the press has sometimes played the role of "character cop," asking questions about candidates' private lives and lifestyles. The press asks these questions because voters are interested in a political leader's background—perhaps even more interested in personal character than in a candidate's political position on hard-to-understand health care or regulatory policy issues.

In 1980, Ronald Reagan generated positive candidate appeal. His opponent, President Jimmy Carter, had hoped that Reagan would behave more like Barry Goldwater, who in his speech accepting the nomination for president in 1964 had said, "Extremism in the defense of liberty is no vice. . . . Moderation in the pursuit of justice is no virtue."[70] President Lyndon Johnson, Goldwater's opponent, benefited from public perception that Goldwater and those who nominated him were out of the mainstream of American politics, an impression Goldwater's acceptance speech reinforced. Instead of repeating Goldwater's mistake, Reagan projected characteristics voters thought that Carter lacked—leadership and strength.

Like Barry Goldwater in 1964, George McGovern, who ran as the Democratic candidate for president in 1972, had negative appeal. Many perceived him as too liberal, a view bolstered by images of his supporters, who by their dress and manner appeared out of the mainstream of American politics. McGovern also raised doubts about his judgment and leadership by how he handled his choice of a running mate. McGovern first named Missouri Senator Tom Eagleton for vice president only to discover that Eagleton had once been hospitalized for emotional exhaustion and depression and had received electric shock therapy. McGovern initially stood behind Eagleton, but as press coverage and criticism of McGovern's lack of investigation into Eagleton's past grew, McGovern dropped Eagleton and named a new running mate. In the end, "only about one-third of the public thought McGovern could be trusted as president."[71]

Candidate appeal or the lack of it—in terms of leadership, experience, good judgment, integrity, competence, strength, and energy—is sometimes more important than party or issues. Many voters saw Bill Clinton in 1992 and 1996 as a regular working-class person who had risen against the odds. Dwight Eisenhower, who was elected president in 1952 and reelected in 1956, had great candidate appeal. He was a five-star general, a legendary hero of the Allied effort in World War II. His unmilitary manner, his moderation, his personal charm, and his appearance of seeming to rise above partisanship appealed across the ideological spectrum. In the 2004 presidential primaries, Howard Dean was initially perceived in positive terms, but that changed with his speech following the Iowa caucus. "The Scream," as the media labeled it, called into question his self-control.[72]

Increasingly, campaigns today focus on the negative elements of candidates' history and personality. Opponents and the media are quick to point out a candidate's limitations or problems. George W. Bush was attacked in 2004 for his policies in Iraq, his failure to build broader coalitions with other countries, his tax cuts that lowered taxes for rich people as well as for others, and for rising deficits. Bush's record in the National Guard during the Vietnam War became the subject of a CBS "60 Minutes" segment, only to have CBS admit that it could not authenticate the documents it used in

candidate appeal
How voters feel about a candidate's background, personality, leadership ability, and other personal qualities.

FIGURE 8–5 Which Quality Mattered Most in the 2004 Vote for President?

SOURCE: 2004 Exit Polls from Edison Media Research and Mitofsky International at www.cnn.com/ELECTION/2004/pages/results/states/US/P/00/epolls.0.html.

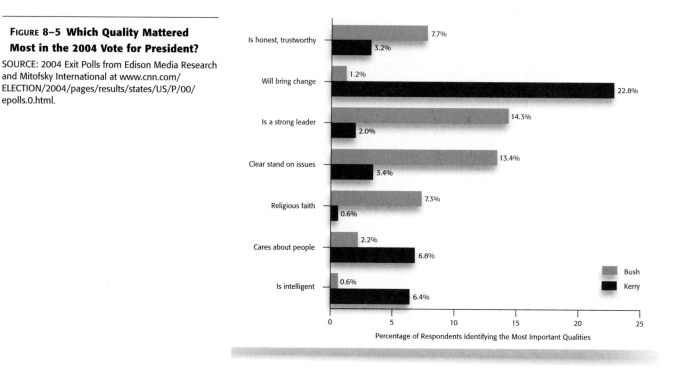

this critical story. John Kerry was attacked for flip-flopping over issues and for his liberal voting record in the Senate. A group called Swift Boat Veterans for Truth also attacked Kerry for his war record in Vietnam. (See Chapter 6.) This attack put the Kerry campaign on the defensive for days. (See Figure 8–5 for a list of which qualities mattered most to voters in 2004.)[73]

Voting on the Basis of Issues

Most political scientists agree that issues, while important, have less influence on how people vote than party identification and candidate appeal do.[74] This is partly because candidates often intentionally obscure their positions on issues—an understandable strategy.[75] When he was running for president in 1968, Richard Nixon said he had a plan to end the Vietnam War, which was clearly the most important issue that year, but he would not reveal the specifics. By not detailing his plan, he stood to gain votes both from those who wanted a more aggressive war effort and from those who wanted a cease-fire.

For issue voting to become important, a substantial number of voters must find the issue itself important, opposing candidates must take opposite stands on the issues, and voters must know these positions and vote accordingly. Rarely do candidates focus on only one issue. Voters often will agree with one candidate on one issue and with the opposing candidate on another. In such cases, issues will probably not determine how people vote. But lack of interest in issues by voters does not mean that candidates can take any position on issues that they please.[76]

Political parties and candidates often look for issues that motivate particular segments of the electorate to vote and on which the opposing candidate or party has a less popular position. These issues are sometimes called wedge issues. In recent elections examples of wedge issues have been gay marriage, raising the minimum wage, and abortion. One way to attempt to exploit a wedge issue is to place on the ballot an initiative for voters to decide a proposed law or amendment on the issue. Both parties and allied groups are expanding their use of ballot initiatives in this way.

More likely than **prospective issue voting** (voting based on what a candidate pledges to do in the future about an issue if elected) is **retrospective issue voting** (holding incumbents, usually the president's party, responsible for past performance on issues, such as the economy or foreign policy).[77] In times of peace and prosperity, voters will reward the incumbent. If the nation falls short on either, voters are more likely to elect the opposition.

prospective issue voting
Voting based on what a candidate pledges to do in the future about an issue if elected.

retrospective issue voting
Holding incumbents, usually the president's party, responsible for their records on issues, such as the economy or foreign policy.

But good economic times do not always guarantee that an incumbent party will be reelected, as Vice President Al Gore learned in 2000 when he was the Democratic candidate for president. Part of Gore's problem in that election was that only half the public saw their family's financial situation as having improved during the Clinton administration. Sixty-one percent of these voters voted for Gore.[78] But his inability to effectively claim credit for the good economic times hurt him, especially when Republicans contended that the American people, not the government under President Bill Clinton, had produced the strong economy. A similar debate arose in 2004 over the state of the economy and the extent to which President George W. Bush's policies or the terrorist attacks of September 11, 2001, had resulted in lost jobs and other economic problems. Democrats argued that the tax cuts Bush had sponsored had been irresponsible, especially when the country was at war. The Republicans countered that the tax cuts had helped stimulate the economy.

The state of the economy is often the central issue in both midterm elections and presidential ones. Studies have found that the better the economy seems to be doing, the more congressional seats the "in" party retains or gains. The reverse is also true. The worse the economy seems to be doing, the more seats the "out" party gains.[79] Political scientists have been able to locate the sources of this effect in how individual voters decide to vote. Voters tend to vote against the party in power if they perceive that their personal financial situations have declined or stagnated.[80]

Voters hold the president and Congress more responsible than governors or local officials for the state of the economy.[81] In 2004, the electorate was divided over the economy, jobs, and Bush's tax cuts. More voters felt that the economy was "not good or poor" than felt it was "excellent or good." The candidate voters preferred appeared to influence how they felt about the economy. Bush supporters were more positive, Kerry supporters more negative.[82] In fact, Kerry often tried to make the election about the economy and jobs, but more voters saw national security and terrorism as the more vital issues, which worked to Bush's advantage.

The Impact of Campaigns

Candidates and campaigns are important to the voting choice. Given the frequency of elections in the United States and the number of offices people vote for, it is not surprising that voters look for simplifying devices like partisanship to help them decide how to vote. In more visible and contested elections, voters rely on the campaigns to help them sort out for whom to vote. Effective campaigns give the voters reasons to vote for their candidate and reasons to vote against the other candidate.

Campaigns are a team sport, with the political parties and interest groups also important to the process of persuading and motivating voters. Groups and parties are heavily involved in all aspects of campaigns, and their efforts are often indistinguishable from the candidate's campaigns.

Effective campaigners find ways to communicate with voters that are memorable and persuasive. Ineffective candidates flounder in their efforts at persuasion and motivation. While adequate money is needed to run a competitive campaign, spending more money does not guarantee that a candidate will win.

Campaigns are not for the faint of heart. Electoral politics is intensely competitive, and campaigns are often negative and personal. Campaigns give voters a sense of how politicians react to adversity, because most competitive races involve adversity. Skills learned in the campaign environment in some respects at least carry over into the skill set needed to govern.

Counting Votes

Until the 2000 election, most Americans took the counting of ballots for granted. But with the closeness of that election and the controversy surrounding how the election was administered in Florida, the public became aware that counting votes is not a simple matter.

Votes are counted in the United States according to state law as administered by local officials. The technology used in voting varies greatly from state to state and in different parts of the same state. In Florida in 2000, some counties used paper ballots, others voting machines, and others punch-card ballots, and at least one county used ballots that a computer could scan. More recently, Florida and other states have moved to computerized voting systems with touch screens.

Another lesson the recent ballot-counting controversies have reinforced is that in every election, in every jurisdiction, and with every technology, voting is imperfect. Touch-screen software can be manipulated; people can miscount paper ballots; punch cards may not always be completely perforated, and so on. The goal in election administration is to minimize errors and eliminate as much bias and outright fraud as possible.

But counting votes is more complicated than the means by which we vote. Election officials have to make judgment calls about incomplete or flawed ballots. Decisions about which ballots to count and which ones not to count mattered in an election decided by only 537 votes as Florida's was in 2000. With the growth in absentee voting and with military personnel and civilians living abroad allowed to vote by mail, a close election may not be decided until days after the polls officially close.

Who is and who is not allowed to vote on election day is also a source of controversy. As discussed, in most states persons must be registered voters in order to vote. Voters are expected to vote in designated voting places. In 2004, as a result of the 2002 redistricting, some voting places and precincts in parts of the country had changed, which confused some voters who only voted in presidential elections and had not voted since 2000. The law permits voters who think they should be allowed to vote but who are not on the rolls to cast what are called provisional ballots. These ballots are only counted if the voter is, in fact, registered to vote.

In the wake of the 2000 election, federal and state governments have invested billions of dollars in new voting technology, established new rules on provisional ballots, and modernized voting methods. Interest groups, political parties, and candidates made the integrity of the 2004 voting process a high priority. Thousands of people worked as poll watchers. Groups established toll-free hot lines for voters to call if they felt they were not being treated fairly, and in key jurisdictions, lawyers were on call to file immediate challenges when a person's right to vote was contested. Nonetheless, while there were some delays on election day, they were more the result of insufficient voting booths and machines than of large-scale challenges to the voting lists.

Summary

1. Public opinion is the distribution across the population of a complex combination of views and attitudes that individuals acquire through various influences from their childhood on. Public opinion takes on qualities of intensity, latency, consensus, and polarization—each of which is affected by people's feelings about the salience of issues.

2. The American public has a generally low level of interest in politics, and most people do not follow politics and government closely. The public's knowledge of political issues is poor.

3. Americans who are interested in public affairs can participate by voting; joining interest groups and political parties; working on campaigns; writing letters to newspaper editors or elected officials; attempting to influence how another person will vote; donating money to a candidate, party, or group; or even protesting.

4. The better-educated, more affluent, and older people, and those who are involved with parties and interest groups, tend to vote more. The young tend to vote the least. Voter turnout tends to be higher in national than in state and local elections, higher in presidential than in midterm elections, and higher in general than in primary elections.

5. Counting ballots has generated controversy in recent elections. After the controversy over how Florida had voted in 2000, Congress passed HAVA. In 2004, voter turnout increased, in part because of a close election and in part because of voter mobilization efforts.

6. Party identification remains the most important element in determining how most Americans vote. It represents a long-term attachment and is a "lens" through which voters view candidates and issues as they make their voting choices. Candidate appeal, including character and record, is another key factor in voter choice. Voters decide their vote less frequently on the basis of issues.

Further **Reading**

R. MICHAEL ALVAREZ AND **JOHN BREHM,** *Hard Choices, Easy Answers: Values, Information, and American Public Opinion* (Princeton University Press, 2002).

HERBERT ASHER, *Polling and the Public: What Every Citizen Should Know,* 6th ed. (CQ Press, 2004).

BARBARA A. BARDES AND **ROBERT W. OLDENDICK,** *Public Opinion: Measuring the American Mind* (Wadsworth, 2006).

M. MARGARET CONWAY, *Political Participation in the United States,* 4th ed. (CQ Press, 2000).

ROBERT M. EISINGER, *The Evolution of Presidential Polling* (Cambridge University Press, 2002).

ROBERT S. ERIKSON AND **KENT L. TEDIN,** *American Public Opinion: Its Origins, Content and Impact,* updated 6th ed. (Longman, 2002).

WILLIAM H. FLANIGAN AND **NANCY H. ZINGALE,** *Political Behavior of the American Electorate,* 11th ed. (CQ Press, 2005).

DONALD P. GREEN AND **ALAN S. GERBER,** *Get Out the Vote!: How to Increase Voter Turnout* (Brookings Institution Press, 2004).

ROBERT HUCKFELDT AND **JOHN SPRAGUE,** *Citizens, Politics, and Social Communica-tion: Information and Influence in an Election Campaign* (Cambridge University Press, 1995).

LAWRENCE R. JACOBS AND **ROBERT Y. SHAPIRO,** *Politicians Don't Pander: Political Manipulation and the Loss of Democratic Responsiveness* (University of Chicago Press, 2000).

KATHLEEN HALL JAMIESON, *Everything You Think You Know About Politics and Why You're Wrong* (Basic Books, 2000).

BRUCE E. KEITH, DAVID B. MAGLEBY, CANDICE J. NELSON, ELIZABETH ORR, MARK C. WESTLYE, AND **RAYMOND E. WOLFINGER,** *The Myth of the Independent Voter* (University of California Press, 1992).

V. O. KEY JR., *Public Opinion and American Democracy* (Knopf, 1961).

JAN E. LEIGHLEY, *Strength in Numbers? The Political Mobilization of Racial and Ethnic Minorities* (Princeton University Press, 2001).

MICHAEL B. MACKUEN AND **GEORGE RABINOWITZ,** EDS., *Electoral Democracy* (University of Michigan Press, 2004).

MICHAEL MARGOLIS AND **DAVID RESNICK,** *Politics as Usual: The Cyberspace 'Revolution,"* 6th ed. (Sage Publications, 2000).

RICHARD G. NIEMI AND **HERBERT F. WEISBERG,** *Classics in Voting Behavior* (CQ Press, 1993).

RICHARD G. NIEMI AND **HERBERT F. WEISBERG,** *Controversies in Voting Behavior,* 4th ed. (CQ Press, 2001).

FRANK R. PARKER, *Black Votes Count: Political Empowerment in Mississippi After 1965* (University of North Carolina Press, 1990).

THOMAS E. PATTERSON, *The Vanishing Voter: Public Involvement in the Age of Uncertainty* (Vintage, 2003).

JAMES A. THURBER AND **CANDICE J. NELSON,** EDS., *Campaigns and Elections American Style,* 2d ed. (Westview Press, 2004).

MICHAEL W. TRAUGOTT AND **PAUL J. LAVRAKAS,** *The Voter's Guide to Election Polls,* 3d ed. (Rowman & Littlefield, 2004).

MARTIN P. WATTENBERG, *Where Have All the Voters Gone?* (Harvard University Press, 2002).

JOHN ZALLER, *The Nature and Origins of Mass Opinion* (Cambridge University Press, 1992).

See also *Public Opinion Quarterly, The American Journal of Political Science,* and *American Political Science Review.*

KeyTerms

Make It Real

PUBLIC OPINION, PARTICIPATION, AND VOTING

Students look at the 2000 presidential election and how the outcome was affected by using Congressional Districts to allocate Presidential Electors.

Chapter 9

Campaigns and Elections
DEMOCRACY IN ACTION

★

SOME CYNICS CONTEND THAT ELECTIONS DO NOT MATTER AND THERE IS LITTLE POINT IN VOTING. STRONG EVIDENCE TO THE CONTRARY COMES FROM THE 2000 ELECTIONS, IN WHICH AL GORE WON THE NATIONAL POPULAR VOTE BY 539,947 VOTES, OR ONLY SLIGHTLY MORE THAN 180 VOTES PER COUNTY! THE CONTEST WAS ESPECIALLY CLOSE IN FLORIDA, WHICH BUSH CARRIED BY 537 VOTES, AND NEW MEXICO, WHICH GORE WON BY 366 VOTES. THE CONTEST FOR THE PRESIDENCY WAS NOT THE ONLY ONE THAT REQUIRED recounts. In Michigan, Mike Rogers won election to the House by 88 votes. In the 2000 election, you could truthfully say that every vote counted. In 2002, the Colorado Seventh district Congressional race was decided by 121 votes and the South Dakota Senate race was won by only 524 votes. In 2006, there were again some close elections. The Montana Senate race was decided by 2,847 votes and the Connecticut 2nd Congressional race was decided by 91 votes. Several other House races were unusually close in 2006. At the state and local levels, races are often decided by only a few votes.

Another reason voting is important is that elections matter. Our recent history demonstrates that election outcomes are meaningful. The outcome of the 2000 presidential election has had important policy consequences. Presidents elected by the slimmest of margins still get to appoint Supreme Court Justices and other federal judges, select their entire cabinet and other executive branch officials, and exercise all of the other powers of the office. Had Al Gore won in the electoral college in 2000, he would not have selected John Roberts or Samuel Alito for the Supreme Court. The president's role in nominating justices can influence public policy for generations. Bush clearly understood that by selecting relatively young nominees. A Gore presidency would have differed from the Bush presidency in other respects, including environmental policy and the U.S. commitment to international environmental treaties.

In the United States, citizens vote more often and for more offices than citizens of any other democracy. We hold thousands of elections for everything from community college directors to county sheriffs. About half a million persons hold elected state and local offices.[1] In 2006, we elected 33 U.S. senators,[2] all 435 members of the U.S. House of Representatives, 36 state governors, about a dozen state treasurers, nine secretaries of state, and, in many states, judges.

In addition to electing people, state laws allow voters in 27 states to vote on laws or constitutional amendments proposed by initiative petitions or on popular referendums put on the ballot by

"I am John Kerry, and I'm reporting for duty."

JOHN KERRY, 2004 DEMOCRATIC PARTY CONVENTION

OUTLINE

★

petition. In every state except Delaware, voters must approve all changes in the state constitution.

In this chapter, we explore our election rules. We note four important problems: the lack of competition for some offices, the complexities of nominating presidential candidates, the distortions of the electoral college, and the influence of money. We also discuss proposed reforms in each of these areas.

Elections: The Rules of the Game

The rules of the game—the electoral game—make a difference. Although the Constitution sets certain conditions and requirements, state law determines most electoral rules. Our focus in this chapter is on presidential and congressional elections, although much of the discussion is also relevant to state and local elections.

Regularly Scheduled Elections

In our system, elections are held at fixed intervals that the party in power cannot change. It does not make any difference if the nation is at war, as we were during the Civil War, or in the midst of a crisis, as in the Great Depression; when the calendar calls for an election, the election is held. Elections for members of Congress occur on the first Tuesday after the first Monday in November of even-numbered years. Although there are exceptions (for special elections or peculiar state provisions), participants know *in advance* just when the next election will be. In most parliamentary democracies, such as Great Britain and Canada, the party in power can call elections at a time of its choosing. The predetermined timing of elections is one of the defining characteristics of democracy in the United States.

Fixed, Staggered, and Sometimes Limited Terms

Our electoral system is based on *fixed terms*, meaning that the length of a term in office is specified, not indefinite. The Constitution has set the term of office for the U.S. House of Representatives at two years, the Senate at six years, and the presidency at four years.

Our system also has *staggered terms* for some offices; not all offices are up for election at the same time. All House members are up for election every two years, but only one-third of the senators are up for election at the same time. Since presidential elections occur two or four years into a senator's six-year term, senators can often run for the presidency without fear of losing their seat, as John Kerry did in 2004. But if their Senate term expires the same year as the presidential election, the laws of many states require them to give up their Senate seat to run for president, vice president, or any other position. An example of a state that permits a candidate to run for election to two offices is Connecticut, where Joseph Lieberman was reelected to the U.S. Senate in 2000 while being narrowly defeated in his race for vice president. Had he been victorious in both campaigns, he would have resigned his Senate seat.

Term Limits

The Twenty-Second Amendment to the Constitution, adopted in 1951, limits presidents to two terms. Knowing that a president cannot run again changes the way members of Congress, the voters, and the press regard the president. A politician who cannot, or has announced he or she will not, run again is called a *lame duck*. Lame ducks are often seen as less influential because other politicians know that these officials' ability to bestow or withhold favors is coming to an end. Efforts to limit the terms of other offices have become a major issue in several states. The most frequent targets have been state legislators. One consequence of term limits is more lame ducks.

Term limits are popular. Voters in 15 states have enacted them for their state legislature, and in two states, the legislature imposed term limits on themselves. Four states have rescinded term limits. In 2006 an Oregon measure to restore voter-approved term limits that had been struck down by the courts was defeated, another sign that public support for term limits may be waning. Even more states limit the terms of governors.[3] Three-fourths of all voters favor term limits, including nine out of ten strong Republicans and seven out of ten strong Democrats.[4] Still, despite their popularity, proposals for term limits on federal legislators have repeatedly been defeated when they have come to a vote in Congress. The Supreme Court, by a vote of 5 to 4, declared that a state does not have the constitutional power to impose limits on the number of terms for which its members of the U.S. Congress are eligible, either by amending its own constitution or by state law.[5] Congress has refused to propose a constitutional amendment to impose a limit on congressional terms.

Winner Take All

An important feature of our electoral system is the **winner-take-all system**, or what is sometimes referred to as "first past the post" in other countries.[6] In most American electoral settings, the candidate with the most votes wins. The winner does not need to have a *majority* (more than half the votes cast); in a multicandidate race, the winner may have only a *plurality* (the largest number of votes). In the 1992 presidential election, Bill Clinton (D) got 43 percent of the vote, George H. W. Bush (R) got 37 percent, and Ross Perot, an independent candidate, got 19 percent. Clinton's margin in the electoral college was greater—370 electoral votes compared to 168 for Bush and none for Perot.[7] Senators and House members are often elected by pluralities. Winner-take-all electoral systems tend to reinforce moderate and centrist candidates because they are more likely to secure a plurality or a majority. Candidates in a winner-take-all system often stress that a vote for a minor party candidate is a "wasted vote" and that it might actually help elect the voter's least desired candidate.

Most American electoral districts are **single-member districts**, meaning that in any district for any given election—senator, governor, U.S. House, state legislative seat—the voters choose *one* representative or official.[8] When the single-member-district and winner-take-all systems are combined, minor parties find it hard to win. For example, even if a third party gets 25 percent of the vote in several districts, it still gets no seats.

The combination of single-member districts and winner-take-all is different from a **proportional representation** system, in which political parties secure legislative seats and power in proportion to the number of votes they receive in the election. Let us assume that a state has three representatives up for election. In each of the three contests, the Republican defeats the Democrat, but in one district by only a narrow margin. If you add up the statewide vote, the Republicans get 67 percent and the Democrats 33 percent. Under our single-member-district and winner-take-all system, the Republicans get all three seats. But under a system of proportional representation, in which the three seats represent the whole state, the Democrats would receive one seat because they got roughly one-third of the vote in the entire state. Proportional representation thus rewards minority parties and permits them to participate in government. Countries that practice some form of proportional representation include Germany, Israel, Italy, and Japan.

Proportional representation more accurately reveals the division of voter preferences and gives those who do not vote with the plurality some influence as a result of their vote. For this reason, proportional representation may encourage greater turnout for people who identify with parties that rarely win elections, like Democrats in Utah or Republicans in Massachusetts. Proportional representation may also encourage issue-oriented campaigns and enhance the representation of women and minorities.

But proportional representation can cause problems. It may make it harder to have a clear winner, especially if minor parties are likely to win seats. As a result, it may

winner-take-all system
An election system in which the candidate with the most votes wins.

single-member district
An electoral district in which voters choose one representative or official.

proportional representation
An election system in which each party running receives the proportion of legislative seats corresponding to its proportion of the vote.

encourage the proliferation of minor parties. Opponents of proportional representation worry that it can contribute to political instability and ideological extremism. For another example of this, see the "How Other Nations Govern" box on Israel in Chapter 7.

The Electoral College

We elect our president and vice president not by a national vote but by an indirect device known as the **electoral college**. The framers of the U.S. Constitution devised this system because they did not trust the choice of president to a direct vote of the people. Under this system, each state has as many electors as it has representatives and senators. California therefore has 55 electoral votes (53 House seats and two Senate seats) while seven states and the District of Columbia have three electoral votes each.

Each state legislature is free to determine how its electors are selected. Each party nominates a slate of electors, usually longtime party workers. Electors are expected to cast their electoral votes for the party's candidates for president and vice president if their party's candidates get a plurality of the vote in their state. In our entire history, no "faithless elector"—an elector who does not vote for his or her state's popular vote winner—has ever cast the deciding vote. There was one faithless elector in 2000 from the District of Columbia who abstained rather than cast her vote for Al Gore in order to protest the lack of congressional representation for Washington, D.C.[9] The electoral college vote in 2004 had one faithless elector: an elector from Minnesota who voted for John Edwards instead of John Kerry. This happened even though both parties named party faithful as electors on the assumption that the election would be close.

The Twelfth Amendment requires electors to vote separately for president and vice president. To demonstrate how this works, if you voted for the Republican candidate in 2004, you actually voted for the Republican slate of electors in your state who pledged to vote for George W. Bush for president and Dick Cheney for vice president in the electoral college.

Candidates who win a plurality of the popular vote in a state secure all that state's electoral votes, except in Nebraska and Maine, which allocate electoral votes to the winner in each congressional district plus two electoral votes for the winner of the state as a whole. Winning electors go to their state capital on the first Monday after the second Wednesday in December to cast their ballots. These ballots are then sent to Congress, and early in January, Congress formally counts the ballots and declares who won the election for president and vice president.

It takes a majority of the electoral votes to win. If no candidate gets a majority of the electoral votes for president, the House chooses among the top three candidates, with each state delegation having one vote. If no candidate gets a majority of the electoral votes for vice president, the Senate chooses among the top two candidates, with each senator casting one vote.

When there are only two major candidates for the presidency, the chances of an election being thrown into the House are remote. But twice in our history, the House has had to act: In 1800, before the Twelfth Amendment was written, the House had to choose in a tie vote between Thomas Jefferson and Aaron Burr; and in 1824, the House picked John Quincy Adams over Andrew Jackson, who had won the popular vote, and William Crawford. Henry Clay, who was forced out of the race when he came in fourth in the electoral college, threw his support behind Adams, who subsequently picked Clay as his secretary of state. His defeat in the House infuriated Jackson, who won the electoral college vote by a wide margin four years later.

electoral college

The electoral system used in electing the president and vice president, in which voters vote for electors pledged to cast their ballots for a particular party's candidates.

The Electoral Commission of 1877 met in secret session to decide the controversial presidential election between Rutherford B. Hayes and Samuel Tilden. After many contested votes the presidency was eventually awarded to Hayes.

Government's Greatest Endeavors

Expanding Voting Rights

Expanding voting rights is one of the government's greatest achievements of the past half-century, but it is also one of its most difficult achievements to maintain. African Americans won the right to vote under the Fifteenth Amendment, which was ratified in 1870, but Southern states soon invented a number of devices to keep African Americans from actually voting. These included poll taxes, or payments required to vote, and "literacy tests," often given only to blacks and including complicated and difficult questions.

Voting participation increased dramatically in the mid-1960s with passage of the Voting Rights Act, which was a top priority of President Lyndon Johnson. It applied only to Southern states. Voting rights also expanded with ratification of the Twenty-Fourth Amend-ment, which abolished the use of the poll tax.

African Americans have not been the only ones to benefit from the effort to expand voting rights, however. Young Americans won the right to vote under the Twenty-Sixth Amendment, which was ratified in 1971 and allowed anyone over the age of 18 to vote. The 1993 National Voter Registration Act, or "Motor Voter Act," created new incentives for states and localities to register voters whenever and wherever they receive public services, such as is the case with obtaining driver's licenses.

As the 2000 election shows, however, being allowed to cast a ballot is not necessarily enough to assure that a vote counts. The ballots must also be counted on reliable machines. Flawed voting machines in Florida eventually led to the 2000 presidential election impasse, which led to the Supreme Court's decision that gave the election to President Bush. The controversy also eventually led Congress to pass the Help America Vote Act (HAVA), which provides federal funding to help states and localities upgrade their voting systems. ∎

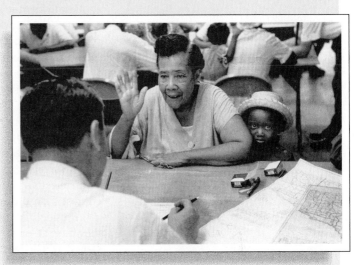

The Voting Rights Act removed voting roadblocks for many African Americans.

QUESTIONS

Do you exercise the right to vote?

How easy is it to vote, and why would some Americans conclude that it is not worth the effort?

As we were reminded in 2000, our electoral college system makes it possible for a presidential candidate to receive the most popular votes, as Al Gore did, and yet not get enough electoral votes to be elected president. Gore lost the electoral college 271 to 266.[10] This also happened in 1824, when Andrew Jackson won 12 percent more of the vote than John Quincy Adams; in 1876, when Samuel Tilden received more popular votes than Rutherford B. Hayes; and in 1888, when Benjamin Harrison won in the electoral college despite receiving fewer popular votes than Grover Cleveland. It almost happened in 1916, 1960, and 1976, when the shift of a few votes in a few key states could have resulted in the election of a president without a popular majority. As illustrated by the 1992 presidential election, in a year with a serious minor-party candidate, election of a president without a plurality of the vote is more likely, especially if the third-party candidate draws support from what otherwise would be the prevailing party in a few states with close votes. Some believe this was also the case with the Nader vote in 2000. (See Chapter 7.)

In two of the four elections in which winners of the popular vote did not become president, the electoral college did not decide the winner. The 1824 election was decided by the U.S. House of Representatives. In 1876, the electoral vote in three southern states and Oregon was disputed, resulting in the appointment of an electoral commission to decide how those votes should be counted. In 1888 and 2000, the electoral college awarded the presidency to the candidate with fewer popular votes.

Concern about the electoral college is renewed every time a serious third-party candidate runs for president. People began to ask, if no candidate receives a majority in the electoral college and the decision is left to Congress, which Congress casts the vote, the one serving during the election or the newly elected one? The answer is the new one, the one elected in November and taking office the first week in January. Since each state has one vote in the House, what happens if a state's delegation is tied, 2 to 2 or 3 to 3? The answer is its vote does not count. Would it be possible to have a president of one party and a vice president of another? Yes, if the election were thrown into the House and Senate, and a different party controlled each chamber.

The electoral college sharply influences presidential politics. To win a presidential election, a candidate must appeal successfully to voters in populous states like California, Texas, Ohio, Illinois, Florida, and New York. California's electoral vote of 55 in 2004 exceeded the combined electoral votes of the 14 least populous states plus the District of Columbia. Sparsely populated states like Wyoming and Vermont also have disproportionate representation in the Electoral College because each state has one representative, regardless of population. When the contest is close, as it was in 2000, every state's electoral votes count, and so greater emphasis is given to states in which the contest is close, even less populated states.[11]

Presidential candidates do not ordinarily waste time campaigning in a state unless they have at least a fighting chance of carrying that state; nor do they waste time in a state in which their party is a sure winner. Richard Nixon in 1960 was the last candidate to campaign in all 50 states, but he lost valuable time traveling to and from Alaska, while John Kennedy focused on the more populous states in which he had a chance to win. The contest usually narrows down to the medium-sized and big states, where the balance between the parties tends to be fairly even. In 2000 and 2004, voters in competitive states received extraordinary attention from the candidates, parties, and allied groups (see Table 9–1).

Running for Congress

How candidates run for Congress differs, depending on the nature of their district or state, on whether candidates are incumbents or challengers, on the strength of their personal organization, on how well known they are, and on how much money they have to spend on their campaign. There are both similarities and differences between House and Senate elections.

TABLE 9–1 2004 Battleground States

State	Electoral Votes	% Difference in 2004 Popular Vote
Wisconsin	10	.39% Kerry
New Mexico	5	.80% Bush
Iowa	7	.91% Bush
New Hampshire	4	1.36% Kerry
Pennsylvania	21	2.27% Kerry
Ohio	20	2.49% Bush
Nevada	5	2.62% Bush
Michigan	17	3.40% Kerry
Oregon	7	3.90% Kerry
Florida	27	5.02% Bush
Missouri	11	7.31% Bush

SOURCE: www.cbsnews.com/htdocs/politics/campaign2004/03%20battleground.pdf, and "2004 Battleground," at usinfo.state.gov/dhr/democracy/elections/battleground_states.html.

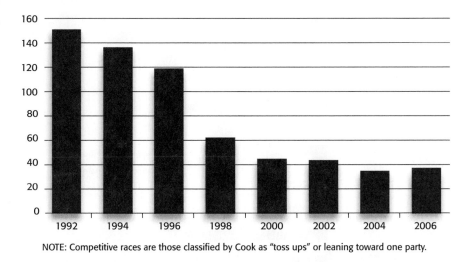

FIGURE 9–1 **Competitive House Seats, 1992–2006.**

SOURCE: Charlie Cook, "National Overview," The Cook Political Report, October 4, 2002, p. 6; "2004 Races at a Glance," The Cook Political Report, July 22, 2004; "Charlie Cook's National Overview," The Cook Political Report, November 6, 2006. http://www.cookpolitical.com/races/house/chart.php.

NOTE: Competitive races are those classified by Cook as "toss ups" or leaning toward one party.

First, most congressional elections are not close. In districts where most people belong to one party or where incumbents are popular and enjoy fund-raising and other campaign advantages, there is often little competition.[12] Congressional districts have become less competitive on the whole in the 2000s, in large part because of the way state legislatures have drawn district boundaries (see Figure 9–1). Districts in the 2002 redistricting were often drawn in ways that enhanced the reelection prospects of incumbents or one party, a process called *partisan gerrymandering*. We explore this process in greater detail in Chapter 11, which deals with Congress. Those who believe that competition is essential to constitutional democracy are concerned that so many officeholders have **safe seats**. When officeholders do not have to fight to retain their seat, elections are not performing their proper role.[13]

Competition is more likely when both candidates have adequate funding, which is not often the case in U.S. House elections. Elections for governor and for the U.S. Senate are more seriously contested and more adequately financed than those for the U.S. House.

Presidential popularity affects both House and Senate races during both presidential election years and in midterm elections. The boost candidates from the president's party get from running along with a popular presidential candidate is known as the **coattail effect**. But winning presidential candidates do not always provide such a boost. The Republicans suffered a net loss of six House seats in 1988, even though George H. W. Bush won the presidency, and the Democrats suffered a net loss of ten House seats in 1992 when Bill Clinton won the presidential election. Democrats fared better in 1996, registering a net gain of nine House seats. There were no discernible coattails in the 2000 elections. In 2004, Republicans picked up U.S. Senate seats in states carried by Bush, such as South Dakota, North Carolina, and South Carolina, and held contested seats in Oklahoma and Alaska. Overall, "measurable coattail effects continue to appear," according to congressional elections scholar Gary Jacobson, but their impact is "erratic and usually modest."[14]

In midterm elections, presidential popularity and economic conditions have long been associated with the number of House seats a president's party loses.[15] These same factors are associated with how well the president's party does in Senate races, but the association is less strong.[16] Figure 9–2 shows the number of seats in the House of Representatives and U.S. Senate gained or lost by the party controlling the White House in midterm elections since 1942. Republicans did better in 1994 than in any midterm election since 1946, picking up 53 seats. The Republican tide was not limited to the House but included a net gain of nine Senate seats.[17] In all of the midterm elections between

safe seat
An elected office that is predictably won by one party or the other, so the success of that party's candidate is almost taken for granted.

coattail effect
The boost that candidates may get in an election because of the popularity of candidates above them on the ballot, especially the president.

FIGURE 9–2 Seats Lost by the President's Party in Midterm Elections for the House of Representatives and the Senate, 1942–2006.

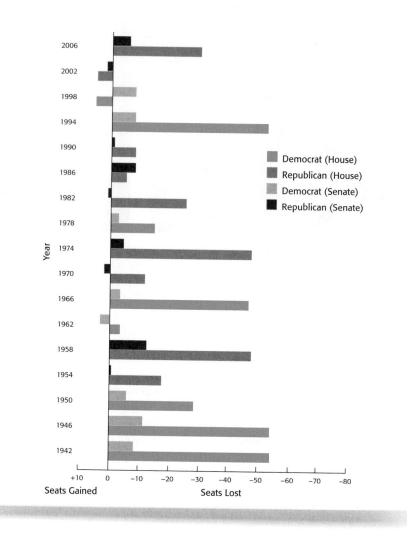

1934 and 1998, the party controlling the White House lost seats in the House. The range of losses, however, is wide, from a low of four seats for the Democrats in 1962 to a high of 71 seats for the Democrats in 1938. But in 2002, as in 1998, the long-standing pattern of the president's party losing seats did not hold. Republicans picked up a net gain of two seats in the Senate and six seats in the House. As noted, there were comparatively few competitive races in 2002, the most recent midterm election, especially for a year following redistricting. In 2006, however, the longstanding pattern of the president's party losing seats reemerged with the Republicans losing 30 House seats and 6 Senate seats.

Until the last few months of the 2006 election cycle most observers gave the Democrats only a slim chance of picking up the House or Senate. Republicans enjoyed advantages of incumbency and, as a result of gerrymandering in 2002, what Karl Rove labeled "structural advantages" in the House, and a net gain of six seats in the Senate seemed out of reach for the Democrats. What changed? Exit polls and other surveys show that the Bush administration's handling of the war in Iraq troubled many voters. Lingering worries about the general competence of the administration's handling of relief efforts after Hurricane Katrina in 2005 also created a climate where voters wanted change. Also fostering a mood for change was the perception of scandal in Congress, especially among Republicans. Troubles multiplied for Republicans in the months running up to the election as it became known that Representatives Tom DeLay (then house majority leader), Bob Ney, and Mark Foley were either under indictment or had behaved inappropriately in office. As a result, far more Republicans had competitive elections that would normally be the case and enough Republicans lost their elections for the Democrats to claim majorities in both houses of Congress.

Lois Murphy, Democratic candidate for Pennsylvania's 6th Congressional District, kicks off her campaign in the 2006 midterm election. Murphy, who was narrowly defeated in 2004 by Rep. Jim Gerlach (R-Pa.), lost another close race in 2006.

The House of Representatives

Every two years, as many as 1,000 candidates—including approximately 400 incumbents—campaign for Congress. Incumbents are rarely challenged for renomination from within their own party, and when they are, the challenges are seldom serious. In the 1990s, for example, on average only two House incumbents were denied renomination in each election, In 2006, 81% of all U.S. Representatives[18] and 54% of all U.S. Senators had no opponent in the primaries.[19] Challengers from other parties running against incumbents rarely encounter opposition in their own party.[20] In 2004 and 2006 two Republican incumbent Senators, Specter (Pa.) and Chafee (R.I.), and one incumbent Democratic Senator, Lieberman (Conn.), were seriously challenged for renomination. Specter and Chafee survived the primary challenge, while Lieberman lost to Ned Lamont. Fortunes reversed in the general election, with Lieberman easily gaining reelection as an Independent and Chafee losing his seat to Democratic challenger Sheldon Whitehouse.

MOUNTING A PRIMARY CAMPAIGN The first step for would-be challengers is to raise hundreds of thousands of dollars (or even more) to mount a serious campaign. This requires asking friends and acquaintances as well as interest groups for money. Candidates need money to hire campaign managers and technicians, buy television and other advertising, conduct polls, and pay for a variety of activities. Parties can sometimes help, but they shy away from giving money in primary contests. The party organization usually stays neutral until the nomination is decided.

Another early step is to build a *personal organization.* A congressional candidate can build an organization while holding another office, such as a seat in the state legislature, by serving in civic causes, helping other candidates, and being conspicuous without being controversial.

A candidate's main hurdle is gaining visibility. Candidates work hard to be mentioned by the media. In large cities with many simultaneous campaigns, congressional candidates are frequently overlooked, and in all areas, television is devoting less time to political news.[21] Candidates rely on personal contacts, on hand shaking and door-to-door campaigning, and on identifying likely supporters and courting their favor—the same techniques used in campaigns for lesser offices. Despite these efforts, the turnout in primaries tends to be low, except in campaigns in which large sums of money are spent on advertising.

CAMPAIGNING FOR THE GENERAL ELECTION The electorate in a general election is different from a primary election. Many more voters turn out in general elections, especially the less-committed partisans and independents. Partisanship is more important in a general election, as many voters use it as a simplifying device to select from among candidates in the many races they decide. Not surprisingly, candidates in districts where their party is strong make their partisanship clear. In districts where candidates come from a minority party, they deemphasize it. General elections also focus on the strengths and weaknesses of the candidates, their background, experience and visibility. Political scientists describe this dimension as **candidate appeal**. Issues can also be important in general elections, but they are often more local than national issues. Occasionally a major national issue arises that can help or hurt one party. The impact of a **national tide** can be reduced by the nature of the candidates on the ballot who might have differentiated themselves from their party or its leader if the tide is negative. Some elections for Congress or the state legislature are in part referendums on the president or governor, but this is rarely the only factor. How competitive the district is in underlying partisanship is also related to the impact of a national tide. In 2006, 88% of House incumbents won reelection.

As we have mentioned, most incumbent members of Congress win reelection.[22] Since 1970, just over 95 percent of incumbent House members seeking reelection have won, and since 2000, over 98 percent of incumbent House members running for reelection have been successful (see Figure 9–3).[23] Of the seven incumbents who were defeated in 2002, two ran against other incumbents when their districts were changed because of redistricting.

Why is reelection to a House seat so much easier than defeating an incumbent or winning an open seat? Incumbents have a host of advantages that help them win reelection. These "perks" come with the job of communicating with constituents and include: free mailings (the *franking privilege*) and telephone calls to constituents; the free use of broadcast studios to record radio and television tapes to be sent to local media outlets; and perhaps most important, a large staff to perform countless favors for constituents and send a stream of press reports and mail back to the district.[24] Representatives also try to win committee posts, even on minor committees, that relate to the needs of their districts and build connections with constituents.[25] Incumbents are generally better known than challengers, something called **name recognition**, and benefit from years of media coverage of their generally positive efforts on behalf of the district.

Incumbents also win so often because they are able to outspend challengers in campaigns by roughly 3 to 1 in the House and about 1.75 to 1 in the Senate.[26] Most challengers spend much less than incumbents do on campaigns, run campaigns that are much less visible than incumbents, contact few voters, and lose badly. Serious

candidate appeal

The tendency in elections to focus on the personal attributes of a candidate, such as his/her strengths, weaknesses, background, experience, and visibility.

national tide

The inclination to focus on national issues, rather than local issues, in an election campaign. The impact of a national tide can be reduced by the nature of the candidates on the ballot who might have differentiated themselves from their party or its leader if the tide is negative, as well as competition in the election.

name recognition

Incumbents have an advantage over challengers in election campaigns because voters are more familiar with them, and incumbents are more recognizable.

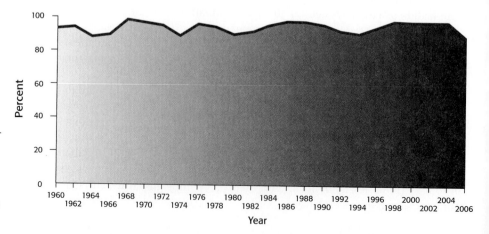

FIGURE 9–3 U.S. House Incumbents Reelected, 1960–2006.

SOURCE: Harold W. Stanley and Richard G. Niemi, eds., *Vital Statistics on American Politics 2001–2002* (CQ Press, 2001), pp. 53–55. 2004 and 2006 updates by authors.

challengers in House races are hard to find. Many potential challengers are scared away by the prospect of having to raise more than $1 million in campaign funds, and some do not want to face the media scrutiny that comes with a serious race for Congress. Nonetheless, in each election, a few challengers mount serious campaigns because of the incumbent's perceived vulnerability, the challengers' own wealth, party or political action committee efforts, or other factors.

In addition, many incumbents win so frequently because their districts are predominantly made up of voters who favor their party. The 2002 redistricting process largely protected incumbents in both parties by making districts less competitive. Retirements and redistricting create *open seats,* which can result in more competitive elections. But open seats have been rare. Potential candidates, as well as political action committees and political party committees, all watch open-seat races closely. If, however, the district is heavily partisan, the predominant party is likely to retain the seat, and once elected the incumbent then reaps the other incumbency advantages as well. In these cases the contest for the nomination in the predominant party effectively determines who will be the new representative. But as noted, most races have incumbents and most incumbents win, lending credibility to the charge that we have a "permanent Congress." Occasionally, one party has a big victory, as the Republicans did in 1994 with a 57-seat gain in the House, securing the majority for the first time in 40 years.

The Senate

Running for the Senate is generally more high-profile than running for the House. The six-year term, the fact that there are only two senators per state, and the national exposure many Senators enjoy make a Senate seat a glittering prize, leading to more intense competition. Senate campaigns cost more than House races and are more likely to be seriously contested than House races (see Figure 9–4).[27] The essential tactics are to raise large amounts of money, hire a professional and experienced campaign staff, make as many personal contacts as possible (especially in the states with smaller populations), avoid giving the opposition any positive publicity, and have a clear and consistent campaign theme. Incumbency is an advantage for senators, although not as much as it is for representatives.[28] Incumbent senators are widely known, but often so are their opponents, who generally raise and spend significant amounts of money.[29]

When one party controls the Senate by only a few seats, as has been the case in recent years, both parties and the White House become more involved in recruiting competitive candidates. Sometimes the party leadership attempts to "clear the field"

"My former opponent is supporting me in the general election. Please disregard all the things I said about him in the primary."

Dunagin's People. Tribune Media Services.

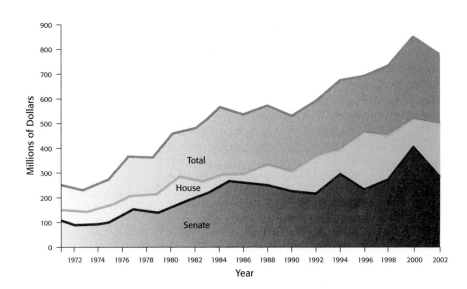

FIGURE 9–4 **Rising Campaign Costs in General Elections.**

SOURCE: Federal Election Commission, "Congressional Campaign Expenditures Total $772 Million," January 2, 2003, at www.fec.gov.

for a preferred candidate by discouraging other candidates from running while endorsing a candidate it considers to be more competitive. The Bush White House was especially active in clearing the field and candidate recruitment in 2002 and to a lesser extent in 2004 and 2006.[30]

Some candidates who initially appear promising can encounter difficulty as media attention and opposition candidates surface. Illinois Republicans were excited about their 2004 candidate for U.S. Senate, Jack Ryan, only to see him drop out of the race after allegations of sexual improprieties surfaced.[31] Other times, despite lots of effort, a party is not able to persuade a strong candidate to enter a race.

The cost of Senate campaigns can vary greatly. California has nearly 70 times the number of potential voters as Wyoming; not surprisingly, running for a seat from Wyoming is much cheaper than running for a seat from California. As a result, interest groups and parties direct more money to competitive races in small states where their campaign dollars reach more voters.[32]

Running for President

Presidential elections are major media events, with candidates seeking as much positive television coverage as possible and trying to avoid negative coverage. The formal campaign has three stages: winning the nomination, campaigning at the convention, and mobilizing support in the general election.

Stage 1: The Nomination

Presidential hopefuls must make a series of critical tactical decisions. The first is when to start campaigning. For the presidential election of 2004, some candidates, like John Kerry, John Edwards, and Howard Dean, began soon after the 2000 presidential election.[33] Early decisions are increasingly necessary for candidates to raise the money and assemble an organization. Campaigning begins well before any actual declaration of candidacy as candidates try to line up supporters to win caucuses or primaries in key states and to raise money for their nomination effort. This period in the campaign has been called the "invisible primary."[34]

One of the hardest jobs for candidates and their strategists is calculating how to deal with the complex maze of presidential primaries and caucuses that constitutes the delegate selection system. The system for electing delegates to the national party convention varies from state to state and often from one party to the other in the same state. In some parties in some states, for example, candidates must provide lists of delegates who support them months before the primary. The presidential campaign finance system provides funds to match small individual contributions during the nomination phase of the campaign for candidates who agree to remain within spending limitations. George W. Bush declined the federal funds in the 2000 and 2004 nomination phase, as did Democrats John Kerry and Howard Dean in 2004. Forgoing the public matching funds allows greater flexibility in when and where campaign money is spent and removes the overall limit for this phase of the process.

PRESIDENTIAL PRIMARIES   State presidential primaries, unknown before 1900, have become the main method of choosing delegates to the national convention. A delegate is a person chosen by local partisans to represent them in selecting nominees, party leaders, and party positions. Today, more than three-fourths of the states use presidential primaries. In 2000, 84 percent of the Democratic delegates and 89 percent of the Republican delegates were chosen in the primaries.[35] The rest of the delegates were chosen by state party caucuses or conventions, or were party leaders who serve as "super delegates." In 2004, 85 percent of Democratic delegates and 69 percent of GOP delegates were chosen in the primaries. Several states (Arizona, Colorado, Delaware, Maine, Michigan, South Carolina, Utah, Virginia, and Washington) that held GOP primaries in 2000 switched to state caucuses or other methods in 2004.[36]

The Iowa caucuses are an important first step in terms of media exposure for candidates running for president. Here, Democrat John Kerry speaks at a caucus site in Muscatine, Iowa, on January 12, 2004.

Presidential primaries often have two features: a *beauty contest,* or popularity vote, in which voters indicate which candidate they prefer but do not actually elect delegates to the convention, and *actual voting* for delegates pledged to a candidate. Since 1996, the Democrats require primary votes to be linked to delegate selection. The Republicans allow states to separate a popularity vote from delegate selection. States that use this system include Montana, Nebraska, Illinois, New Jersey, Pennsylvania, and West Virginia.[37]

Candidates may win the beauty contest but gain fewer delegates than their opponents because they failed to put a full slate of delegates on the ballot or because local notables were listed on the ballot as delegates pledged to another candidate. Different combinations of the popularity vote and the actual vote for delegates have produced the following systems:[38]

■ *Proportional representation:* Delegates to the national convention are allocated on the basis of the percentage of votes candidates win in the beauty contest. This system has been used in most of the states, including several of the largest ones. The Democrats mandate proportional representation for all their primaries.[39] In some states, Republicans use this same system, but Republicans are much more varied in how they select their delegates.[40]

■ *Winner take all:* Whoever gets the most votes wins all that state's delegates or the share of delegates from each congressional district. Republicans still use the winner-take-all system at the state level, and in 2004, most states used this rule at either the state or congressional district levels.[41] To win all the delegates of a big state like California is an enormous bonus to a candidate.

■ *Delegate selection without a commitment to a candidate:* New York Republicans allow the state committee to select 12 at-large delegates who are officially unpledged, as are the party chair and national committee representatives.[42]

■ *Delegate selection and separate presidential poll:* In several states, voters decide twice: once to indicate their choice for president and again to choose delegates pledged, or at least favorable, to a presidential candidate.

Voters in states like Iowa and New Hampshire, which are the first states to pick delegates, bask in media attention for weeks and even months before they cast the first ballots in the presidential sweepstakes. Because these early contests have had the effect of limiting the choices of voters in states that come later in the process, states have tended to move their primaries up. This process is called "front loading." California, which traditionally held its primary in June, moved it to March in 2000, so that its voters would play a more important role in selecting the nominee. Other states did the same thing. Front loading was even more prominent in 2004.[43] Democratic National Committee Chair Terry McAuliffe's hoped that his party's nominee would be chosen by March 2004 to cement party unity and give the party more time to raise money.[44]

In both 2000 and 2004, both the Democratic and Republican nominations were decided by March. This had the effect of compressing the nomination battle into several weeks of intense activity in the spring followed by months of much less activity before the fall general election campaign. For 2004, as in the past, states that felt overlooked in 2000 pushed to revise the schedule, including possibly having four regional groupings (East, South, Midwest, and West).[45] States that gain visibility and importance through early primaries continue to want to maintain that advantage.

CAUCUSES AND CONVENTIONS A meeting of party members and supporters of various candidates that may elect delegates to state or national conventions who in turn vote for the presidential nominee is called a **caucus**. In about a dozen states, one or both parties use a caucus or convention system (or both) to choose delegates.[46] Each state's parties and legislature regulate the methods used. The caucus or convention is the oldest method of choosing delegates and, unlike the primary system, it centers on staffing local party positions like voting district chair and often includes party discussions of issues and candidates in addition to a vote on candidates or policies.

In caucus or convention states, delegates who will attend the national party conventions are chosen by delegates to state or district conventions, who themselves are chosen earlier in county, precinct, or town caucuses. The process starts at local meetings open to all party members, who discuss and take positions on candidates and issues and elect delegates to represent their views at the next level. This process is repeated until conventions of delegates from a district or state choose delegates to the national nominating convention.

The best-known example of a caucus is in Iowa, because Iowa has held the earliest caucuses in the most recent presidential nominating contests. Every January or February in a presidential election year, Iowans have the opportunity to attend Republican and Democratic precinct meetings. Many voters attend these neighborhood or town meetings where they exchange views on issues and candidates, elect delegates to county and state conventions and express their preferences for presidential candidates.[47]

STRATEGIES Presidential hopefuls face a dilemma: To get the Republican nomination, a candidate has to appeal to the more intensely conservative Republican partisans, those who vote in caucuses and primaries and actively support campaigns. Democratic hopefuls have to appeal to the liberal wing of their party as well as to minorities, union members, and environmental activists. But to win the general election, candidates have to win support from moderates and pragmatic voters, many of whom do not vote in the primaries. If candidates position themselves too far from the moderates in their nomination campaign, they risk being labeled extreme in the general election and losing these votes to their opponent.

Strategies for securing the nomination have changed over the years. Some candidates think it wise to skip some of the earlier contests and enter first in states where their strength lies. John McCain pursued such a strategy in 2000, ignoring Iowa and concentrating on New Hampshire. In 2004 retired General Wesley Clark also bypassed Iowa, but unlike McCain he did not win in New Hampshire and dropped out of the race a few weeks later. Most candidates choose to run hard in Iowa and New Hampshire, hoping that early showings in these states, which receive a great deal of media attention, will move them into the spotlight for later efforts.

During this early phase, the ability of candidates to generate momentum by managing the media's expectations of their performance is especially important. Winning

caucus
A meeting of local party members to choose party officials or candidates for public office and to decide the platform.

The Changing Face of American Politics

More Diversity Among National Party Nomination Convention Delegates

One of the criticisms of the Democratic and Republican parties in the contentious 1968 election was that the delegates to the national party nominating conventions were not representative. A commission was formed in the Democratic Party to reform the process of delegate selection. One result of that reform was a growth in the number of presidential primaries. Another consequence was a much more diverse group of delegates in nominating conventions.

In 1968 delegates were mostly older white males. By 1972, in response to the recommendations of the Democratic Party reform commission, the proportion of males had dropped from nearly 90 percent to 60 percent. In that same four-year period the proportion of black delegates tripled and the proportion of younger delegates rose from 4 percent to 21 percent. In all cases except young delegates, the 2004 Democratic delegates approximated the composition of the 1972 Democratic delegates.

Republicans have also become more diverse in their delegate composition. In 2004 half of GOP delegates were women, compared to 43 percent for Democrats. There were fewer minority and young delegates at the 2004 Republican convention than at the 2004 Democratic convention. Both parties are sensitive to the symbolism of diversity and showcase delegates and others who can help the party connect to different demographic groups. ■

Demographic Makeup of Democratic National Delegates

	1968	1972	2004
Sex			
Male	87%	60%	57%
Female	13	40	43
Race			
Black	5	15	18
White	95	85	68
Other	0	0	14
Age*			
Young	4	21	7
Old	96	79	93

*Note that the 2004 source lists "young" as 18–29 years old, whereas the 1968 and 1972 source lists "young" as 30 years old and under.

SOURCE: 1968 and 1972 data from Austin Ranney, *Curing the Mischiefs of Faction: Party Reform in America* (University of California Press, 1975), p. 155. 2004 data from the *New York Times*/CBS News Poll "2004 Republican National Delegate Survey" August 29, 2004, and "2004 Democratic National Delegate Survey" July 23, 2004, at www.nytimes.com/packages/html/politics/20040829_gop_poll/2004_gop_results.pdf, accessed September 25, 2006/.

in the primaries thus centers on a game of expectations, and candidates may intentionally seek to lower expectations so that "doing better than expected" will generate momentum for their campaign. The media generally set these expectations in its coverage of candidates and pollsters. Lyndon Johnson actually won the New Hampshire primary in 1968, yet because his challenger, Eugene McCarthy, did better than the press had predicted, McCarthy was interpreted as the "winner." Both John Kerry and John Edwards did better than expected in Iowa in 2004, giving them momentum for New Hampshire and beyond.

It is also important to maintain a presidential bearing even in the primaries. In 2004, the frontrunner going into Iowa was Vermont Governor Howard Dean. In a speech to supporters after losing the Iowa caucuses, placing third after Kerry and Edwards, an animated Dean, attempting to rally his followers, uttered what came to be called the "Dean scream," or "I have a scream" speech.[48] As Dean learned, such a mistake, when replayed countless times on cable and broadcast news and when made the brunt of jokes elsewhere on television, becomes a defining moment and makes it difficult for a candidate to reestablish a positive campaign agenda. While Dean's ascendancy and sudden demise were both notable features of the 2004 election, a more enduring aspect of his candidacy was his extensive use of the Internet, especially for fundraising, and his demonstrating to the other Democrats the depth of anti-Bush passion among Democratic voters.[49]

"Extremism in the defense of liberty is no vice."

BARRY GOLDWATER,
1964 REPUBLICAN PARTY CONVENTION

national party convention
A national meeting of delegates elected in primaries, caucuses, or state conventions who assemble once every four years to nominate candidates for president and vice president, ratify the party platform, elect officers, and adopt rules.

Stage 2: The National Party Convention

The delegates elected in primaries, caucuses, or state conventions assemble at their **national party convention** in the summer before the election to pick the party's presidential and vice presidential candidates. Conventions follow standard rules, routines, and rituals. Usually, the first day is devoted to a keynote address and other speeches touting the party and denouncing the opposition; the second day, to committee reports, including party and convention rules and the party platform; the third day, to presidential and vice presidential balloting; and the fourth day, to the presidential candidate's acceptance speech. In 2004, with both parties' nominees having only limited broadcast television time, the focus was on major speeches each night.

For a half century, conventions have ratified a candidate who has already been selected in the primaries and caucuses. National party conventions used to be events of high excitement because there was no clear nominee before the convention. In the past, delegates also arrived at national nominating conventions with differing degrees of commitment to presidential candidates; some delegates were pledged to no candidate at all, others to a specific candidate for one or two ballots, and others firmly to one candidate only. Because of reforms encouraging delegates to stick with the person to whom they are pledged, there has been less room to maneuver at conventions.

Despite the lack of suspense about who the nominee will be, conventions continue to be major media events. As recently as 1988, the major networks gave the Democratic and Republican national conventions gavel-to-gavel coverage, meaning that television covered the conventions from the beginning of the first night to the end of the fourth night. Now the major networks leave comprehensive coverage to C-SPAN. The long-term decline in viewership and the reduced hours of coverage have altered the parties' strategies.[50] The parties feature their most important speakers and highlight their most important messages in the limited time the networks give them. In 2004, viewership of the conventions increased slightly.

Acceptance speeches provide the nominees with an opportunity to define themselves and their candidacy. An example of an acceptance speech that worked more to the benefit of the opposition was Barry Goldwater's speech to the Republican convention in 1964 when he said "extremism in the defense of liberty is no vice."[51] This only helped to define Goldwater as "dangerous" and "extreme," themes his opponent, Lyndon Johnson, exploited. Democrats hoped Ronald Reagan would also self-destruct in 1980. Instead, Reagan came off as warm and confident. At two places in his acceptance speech, he quoted Franklin D. Roosevelt, once by name. Candidates of one party rarely quote a president of the other party in favorable terms as Reagan did.[52] This was clearly an effort to reach out to Democrats. In 2004, John Kerry attempted to emphasize his military background and heroism in Vietnam by saluting the delegates and saying "I'm John Kerry, and I'm reporting for duty."[53] Soon after, his war record became an issue as outside groups ran ads claiming he exaggerated his heroism and helped the enemy by criticizing the Vietnam War.

THE PARTY PLATFORM   Delegates to the national party conventions decide on the *platform,* a statement of party perspectives on public policy. Why does anyone care what is in the party platform? Critics have long pointed out that the party platform is binding on no one and is more likely to hurt than to help a candidate by advocating positions unpopular to moderate or independent voters, whose support the candidate may need to win in the general election. But presidential candidates as well as delegates take the platform seriously because it defines the direction a party wants to take. Also, despite the charge that the platform is ignored, most presidents try to implement much of it.[54] For example, when President George W. Bush signed an education bill into law, he pointed to his party's commitment to "leave no child behind."[55] Neither party had a platform fight in 2004.

THE VICE PRESIDENTIAL NOMINEE   The choice of the vice presidential nominee garners widespread attention. Rarely does a person actually "run" for the vice presidential nomination, because only the presidential nominee's vote counts. But there is a good deal of maneuvering to capture that one vote. Sometimes the choice of a running mate is made at the convention—not a time conducive to careful and deliberate thought. But usually the choice is made before the convention, and the announcement is timed to enhance media coverage and momentum going into the convention. The last time a presidential candidate left the choice of vice president to the delegates happened at the Democratic convention in 1956.

Traditionally, the presidential nominee chooses a running mate who will "balance the ticket." Democratic presidential nominee Walter Mondale raised this tradition to a dramatic new height in 1984 by selecting a woman, New York Representative Geraldine A. Ferraro, to run with him. Mondale's bold decision was an effort to strengthen his appeal to women voters. But presidential candidates can also ignore the idea of a balanced ticket, as George W. Bush did when he chose Richard Cheney, another Texan from the oil industry, to be his running mate. Cheney moved his official residence to Wyoming and registered to vote there so that if the Bush-Cheney ticket won the popular vote in Texas, Republican Texas electors could vote for him, since the Constitution (Article II, Section 1) prohibits electors from voting for more than one person for president and vice president from their own state.

John Kerry's selection of John Edwards for his running mate in 2004 helped energize the Democratic campaign. Edwards was seen as appealing to young, rural, Southern, and moderate voters.[56] On most issues his positions were identical to Kerry's, but the two had fought aggressively against each other in the primaries despite these similarities. During the primaries, Kerry had criticized Edwards for his inexperience, especially in defense and foreign policy. Edwards helped motivate trial lawyers to contribute even more substantially to the Democratic ticket, but some parts of the business community were activated even more against Kerry because of its desire to enact limits on damages in law suits.

THE VALUE OF CONVENTIONS   Why do the parties continue to have conventions if the nominee is known in advance and the vice presidential nominee is the choice of one person? What role do conventions play in our system? For the parties, they are a time of "coming together" to endorse a party program and to build unity and enthusiasm for the fall campaign. For candidates as well as other party leaders, conventions are a chance to capture the national spotlight and further their political ambitions. For nominees, they are an opportunity to define themselves in positive ways. The potential exists to heal wounds festering from the primary campaign and move into the general election united, but the potential is not always achieved. Conventions can be potentially divisive, as the Republicans learned in 1964 when conservative Goldwater delegates loudly booed New York Governor Nelson Rockefeller and as the Democrats learned in 1968 in Chicago when the convention spotlighted divisions within the party over Vietnam, as well as ugly battles between police and protesters near the convention hotels.

NOMINATION BY PETITION   There is a way to run for president of the United States that avoids the grueling process of primary elections and conventions—if you are rich enough or well-known enough. John Anderson in 1980, as a third-party candidate, and H. Ross Perot in 1992, as an independent, met the various state requirements and made it onto the general election ballot in all 50 states. In 1996, Perot also qualified for the general election ballot in all 50 states as a third-party candidate for the Reform party. In 2000, Patrick Buchanan, candidate of the Reform party, was able to get his name on the ballot in all but one state and the District of Columbia, and Ralph Nader, candidate of the Green party, in all but seven states.[57] In 2004, the petition process was as simple as submitting the signatures of 1,000 registered voters in Washington State,[58] or by paying $500 in Colorado or Louisiana,[59] or as difficult as getting the signatures of currently registered voters equal to 2 percent of total votes cast in the last election in North Carolina (100,532 signatures).[60] In 2004, independent candidate Ralph Nader made the ballot in 34 states and the District of Columbia. He was excluded from 16 states, including Ohio and Pennsylvania.[61]

Stage 3: The General Election

The national party convention adjourns immediately after the presidential and vice presidential candidates deliver their acceptance speeches to the delegates and the national television audience. Traditionally, the weeks between the conventions and Labor Day were a time for resting, for binding up wounds from the fight for the nomination, for gearing up for action, and for planning campaign strategy. In recent elections, however, the candidates have not paused after the convention but launched directly into all-out campaigning. In 2004, both major-party candidates campaigned aggressively from March through the general election. The intensity of the early campaign was noteworthy, with Bush spending more than $80 million on advertising between March and June and Kerry more than $60 million.[62] Anti-Bush interest groups spent an estimated $32 million during this critical early period,[63] meaning that the anti-Bush/pro-Kerry spending exceeded the pro-Bush/anti-Kerry spending during this time. The early going in battleground states was unusually intense.

PRESIDENTIAL DEBATES   Televised presidential debates are a major feature of presidential elections. Presidential debates have come to be more of a joint appearance with opening and closing statements than a debate where the candidates interact much with each other.

Since 1988, the nonpartisan Commission on Presidential Debates has sponsored and produced the presidential and vice presidential debates. The commission includes representatives from such neutral groups as the League of Women Voters. Before the commission became involved, there was often a protracted discussion about the format, timing, and even whether to have debates. No detail seemed too small to the candidates' managers—whether the candidates would sit or stand, whether they would be able to ask each other questions, whether they would be allowed to bring notes, and whether a single journalist, a panel of reporters, or a group of citizens would ask the questions. By negotiating in advance many of the contentious details and arranging for debate locations, the commission now facilitates the presi-

dential and vice presidential debates. In 2000, George W. Bush proposed alternative formats and locations and dates, only to back down as it appeared he was avoiding debates.[64] The 2004 debates were again run by the Commission on Presidential Debates. The candidates again negotiated such things as whether they would be standing or sitting. An important departure from the presumed format was the use of split screens by the networks that showed one candidate reacting while the other was speaking. President Bush, especially during the first debate, reacted with what was widely described as a "scowl" to some of the criticisms leveled by Senator Kerry. In a later debate, Bush even made mention of his scowl. However, the president seemed more comfortable in the format where questions came from the audience.

Presidential debates give candidates an opportunity to show how quickly and accurately they can respond to questions and outline their goals. In the debates of the 2004 elections, the consensus was that John Kerry outperformed George W. Bush in all three presidential debates; however, his performance did not propel Kerry to victory in the election.

The 1960 debates between John Kennedy and Richard Nixon boosted Kennedy's campaign and elevated the role of television in national politics.[65] In 1976, President Gerald Ford debated Jimmy Carter and said that each country in eastern Europe "is independent, autonomous, it has its own territorial integrity, and the United States does not conceive that those countries are under the domination of the Soviet Union."[66] Ford's words inaccurately described Soviet-dominated countries like Poland and led to criticism in the media. A few days later Ford issued a statement clarifying his position. Ronald Reagan's performance in the 1980 and 1984 debates confirmed the public view of him as decent, warm, and dignified. Bill Clinton's skirmishes with George Bush in 1992 and with Bob Dole in 1996 showed him to be a skilled performer.

The 2004 presidential debates were widely watched and largely reinforced the candidate preferences of the viewers. Neither candidate made a major mistake, and both candidates were able to state their positions and draw contrasts with their opponent. Challengers generally benefit more from debates because it increases their visibility and permits ready comparison to the incumbent. In 2004, Kerry was seen as the "winner" in public opinion surveys following all three debates. The vice presidential debate followed the same pattern as the presidential debates, with no major mistake and few surprises.

Minor-party candidates often charge that those organizing debates are biased in favor of the two major parties. To be included in presidential debates, such candidates must have an average of 15 percent or higher in the five major polls the commission uses for this purpose. Candidates must also be legally eligible and on the ballot in enough states to be able to win at least 270 electoral votes.[67] In 2004 Ralph Nader failed to meet these criteria for inclusion, as did both he and Patrick Buchanan in 2000. In 1992, Ross Perot and his running mate, James Stockdale, had been included in the presidential and vice presidential debates, which generated large audiences, averaging more than 80 million viewers for each debate. Including or excluding minor-party candidates remains a contentious issue. Including them takes time away from the major-party candidates, especially if two or more minor-party candidates are invited. Including them may also reduce the likelihood of both major parties' candidates' participating. But excluding them raises issues of fairness and free speech.

Although some critics are quick to express their dissatisfaction with presidential candidates for being so concerned with makeup and rehearsed answers, and although the debates have not significantly affected the outcomes of elections, they have provided important opportunities for candidates to distinguish themselves and for the public to weigh their qualifications. Candidates who do well in these debates are at a great advantage. They have to be quick on their feet, seem knowledgeable but not overly rehearsed, and project a positive image. Most presidential candidates are adept at these skills.

The vice presidential debate tends to be a more contentious exchange than presidential debates, providing each running mate with an opportunity to assail the opposition on various issues without the constraints that govern the presidential debates. The Iraq war, terrorism, and the economy all figured prominently in the 2004 vice presidential debate between John Edwards and Dick Cheney.

TELEVISION AND RADIO ADVERTISING Presidential candidates communicate with voters in a general election and in many primary elections through the media: broadcast television, radio and cable television, and satellite radio. Approximately 630,000 commercials were run across the country during the 2004 presidential election.[68] Radio and television ads are expensive: An estimated $623 million was spent on ads in 2000.[69] In 2004, that spending increased to $1.6 billion.[70]

As with campaign activity generally—candidate visits, mail or phone calls about the candidates—the competitive or battleground states see much more activity. The 2004 presidential election is a good example of this trend. In March, early in the primary season, most of the television campaign ads were run in battleground states such as Florida, Ohio, Missouri, Wisconsin, Oregon, and Michigan. By October, when it had become clear that George W. Bush would win in Missouri, advertisers had mostly dropped out of the state. In a two-week period in September and October 2004, an estimated 27 percent of the electorate was targeted with 87 percent of the advertising in the presidential campaign.[71] Candidates and their consultants believe that advertising on television and radio helps motivate people to vote and persuade voters to vote for them—or against their opponent. With the growth in cable television, candidates can target ads to particular audiences—people who watch the Golf Channel or FOX News. Political party committees and interest groups also run television and radio ads for and against candidates.

THE OUTCOME Though each election is unique, politicians, pollsters, and political scientists have collected enough information to agree broadly on a number of basic factors that they believe affect election outcomes. Whether the nation is prospering probably has the most to do with who wins a presidential election, but as we have noted, most voters vote on the basis of party and candidate appeal.[72] Who wins depends on voter turnout, and here the strength of party organization and allied groups is important. The Democrats' long-standing advantage in the number of people who identify themselves as Democrats has declined in recent years and is mitigated by higher voter turnout among Republicans. Republicans also usually have better access to money, which means they can run more television ads in more places and more often.

History Makers

Henry George and the Secret Ballot

One of the elements of democracy we take for granted is the secrecy of the ballot, but for much of the nineteenth century, voters in the United States cast ballots printed and distributed by the political parties. They were on different colored paper, and poll monitors could easily determine which party a voter supported by the color of the ballot he cast. Party machines often rewarded loyal supporters with jobs and other compensation. Parties could also stuff ballot boxes since the government did not know how many ballots had been printed.* Party-printed ballots also made it hard for people to vote for candidates from more than one party for different offices, what we call split-ticket voting.[†]

The person most responsible for the introduction of a "public" ballot (sometimes called the Australian ballot), which is printed by the government and provided to voters at the polls, was an economist and author named Henry George. The secret ballot made the following changes:

■ Ballots were printed and distributed at government expense

■ Ballots contained the names of all legally nominated candidates

■ Ballots were only distributed by election officials at the polling place

■ Provisions were made for privacy and secrecy in casting ballots

Kentucky was first to adopt the secret ballot in 1888. Massachusetts followed one year later. By 1910, nearly all states had adopted the secret ballot. Although it had many positive benefits, the secret ballot led to a decline in turnout. Political scientists attribute this decline to the diminished role of party bosses and the reduction in voting fraud.[‡]

George's efforts to secure the secret ballot started with a December 1871 article in *Overland Monthly.* In another article in the *North American Review*, George contended that the secret ballot would "be the greatest single reform possible."[§] The author of the law establishing the secret ballot in Kentucky credited George's article in *North American Review* with influencing him and his state. George and his supporters formed the United Labor Party, which encouraged adoption of the secret ballot, as did other groups. As Americans shift to new voting technologies in the 2006 and 2008 elections, it is important to remember that an even more fundamental change was the introduction of secret ballots more than a century ago.[‖] ■

> *[F]or much of the nineteenth century, voters in the United States cast ballots that were printed and distributed by the political parties.*

*John C. Fortier and Norman J. Ornstein, "The Absentee Ballot and the Secret Ballot: Challenges for Election Reform," *University of Michigan Journal of Law Reform* 36 (Spring 2003), pp. 483–517.

[†]Jerrold G. Rusk, "The Effect of the Australian Ballot Reform on Split Ticket Voting: 1876–1908," *The American Political Science Review* 64 (December 1970), pp. 1220–1238.

[‡]John C. Fortier and Norman J. Ornstein, "The Absentee Ballot and the Secret Ballot: Challenges for Election Reform," *University of Michigan Journal of Law Reform* 36 (Spring 2003), pp. 483–517.

[§]Fortier and Ornstein.

[‖]L. E. Fredman, "The Introduction of the Australian Ballot in the United States," *Australian Journal of Politics and History* 13 (June 1967), pp. 204–220.

Incumbency, as we have shown, is typically an advantage, especially in U.S. House races. The underlying partisanship of a district or state is also important, including how the state counts its electoral votes for president. Democrats rarely carry Utah, and Republicans seldom win Massachusetts. Finally, candidates matter and so do their campaigns. The candidate's personal appeal, character, knowledge of issues, speaking ability, and experience all factor into the voting choice. Advertising, person-to-person politics, and voter registration drives can all make a difference. A candidate's personal wealth or ability to raise money for the campaign is another important factor.

After the votes are cast, as we saw in the last chapter, they must be counted. And the way they are counted can be critical in close races. Even before the votes were counted in 2004, both parties had deployed thousands of lawyers to observe the voting and ballot counting and to launch legal challenges if necessary. The Bush victory was large enough that these challenges did not materialize. As we have been reminded, the popular vote is not necessarily the deciding vote in presidential elections. The electoral college has an important role to play and courts may have to determine whether state and federal laws have been fairly applied. The peaceful transfer of power from one individual or party to another, especially after such contested elections, is the culminating event in electoral democracy.

Money in U.S. Elections

Election campaigns cost money, and the methods of obtaining the money have long been controversial. Campaign money can come from a candidate's own wealth, political parties, interested individuals, or interest groups. Money is contributed to candidates for a variety of reasons, ranging from altruism to self-interest. Individuals or groups, in hopes of influencing the outcome of an election and subsequently influencing policy, give what can be best described as **interested money**. Concern about campaign finance stems from the possibility that candidates or parties, in their pursuit of campaign funds, will decide that it is more important to represent their contributors than their conscience or the voters. The potential corruption that can result from politicians' dependence on interested money concerns many observers of American politics.

Scandals involving the influence of money on policy are not new. In 1925, responding to the Teapot Dome scandal, in which a cabinet member was convicted of accepting bribes in 1922 for arranging for the lease of federal land in Wyoming and California for private oil developments,[73] Congress passed the Corrupt Practices Act, which required disclosure of campaign funds but was "written in such a way as to exempt virtually all [members of Congress] from its provisions."[74]

The 1972 Watergate scandal—in which persons associated with the Nixon campaign broke into the Democratic Party headquarters to steal campaign documents and plant listening devices[75]—led to media scrutiny and congressional investigations that discovered that large amounts of money from corporations and individuals had been deposited in secret bank accounts outside the country for political and campaign purposes. Nixon's 1972 campaign spent more than $60 million, more than twice what it had expended in 1968.[76] Investigators discovered that wealthy individuals and corporations made large contributions to influence the outcome of the election or to secure ambassadorships and administrative appointments.[77]

Efforts at Reform

Reformers have tried three basic strategies to prevent abuse in political contributions: (1) imposing limits on giving, receiving, and spending political money; (2) requiring public disclosure of the sources and uses of political money; and (3) giving governmental subsidies to presidential candidates, campaigns, and parties to reduce their reliance on campaign contributors. Recent campaign finance laws have tended to use all three strategies.

THE FEDERAL ELECTION CAMPAIGN ACT In 1971, Congress passed the Federal Election Campaign Act (FECA), which limited amounts that candidates for federal office could spend on advertising, required disclosure of the sources of campaign funds and how they are spent, and required political action committees to register with the government and report all major contributions and expenditures.

In 1974, Watergate helped push Congress to amend the FECA in what was the most sweeping campaign reform measure in U.S. history. These amendments established more realistic limits on contributions to candidates and parties and spending by candidates, strengthened disclosure laws, created the **Federal Election Commission (FEC)** to administer the new laws and provided for partial public funding for presidential primaries and a grant to major party presidential candidates in the general election. The money to fund the presidential candidates comes from a checkoff that

interested money
Financial contributions by individuals or groups in the hope of influencing the outcome of an election and subsequently influencing policy.

Federal Election Commission (FEC)
A commission created by the 1974 amendments to the Federal Election Campaign Act to administer election reform laws. It consists of six commissioners appointed by the president and confirmed by the Senate. Its duties include overseeing disclosure of campaign finance information and public funding of presidential elections, and enforcing contribution limits.

allowed taxpayers to allocate $1 of their income taxes by checking a box on their tax form. This checkoff option is now $3.

The 1974 law was extensively amended after the Supreme Court's 1976 *Buckley* v. *Valeo* decision, which overturned several of its provisions on grounds that they violated the First Amendment.[78] The *Buckley* decision allowed limitations on contributions and full and open disclosure of all fund-raising activities by candidates for federal office, as well as the system of public financing for presidential elections.[79] The Supreme Court made a distinction between campaign spending and campaign contributions, holding that the First Amendment protects spending; therefore, legislatures may not limit how much of their own money people spend on their own campaigns independent of a candidate or political party, but Congress may limit how much people contribute to somebody else's campaign. The 1976 and 1978 elections, the first after FECA, saw less generic party activity and prompted parties to seek legislation to allow for individuals or groups to avoid the contribution limits if the money they were giving was going to the political parties for "party-building purposes."[80] This money came to be defined as **soft money**,[81] in contrast to the limited and more-difficult-to-raise **hard money** contributions to candidates and party committees that are committed to candidate-specific electoral activity. Over time, soft money became more important. The 1996 election saw aggressive soft money fundraising by the Clinton-Gore campaign, including opportunities for donors to have meetings with the president, to fly with him on Air Force One, and to spend the night in the Lincoln Bedroom at the White House. A congressional investigation into these and related concerns about campaign finance in the 1996 cycle reinforced the case for reform.[82] Both parties made raising and spending soft money a major priority after 1996, spending the money in targeted contests or battleground states. From the perspective of the voter, the advertising purchased by soft money was indistinguishable from other campaign expenditures.[83] Banning soft money became the primary objective of reformers in recent years and led to the passage of the **Bipartisan Campaign Reform Act (BCRA)** in 2002.

One of the success stories of FECA was that presidential candidates of both parties for 20 years chose to accept the limitations on fundraising and campaign spending that were part of the public financing provisions. Candidates could have had no spending limits by bypassing the public subsidizing and matching funds. During the nomination phase candidates receive federal matching funds for campaign contributions up to $250. Accepting the federal matching funds means candidates accept state-by-state spending limits for the caucuses and the primaries. Major-party candidates receive a grant for the general election but also stop their own fundraising. Until 2000, presidential candidates (except wealthy, self-financed candidates) accepted the voluntary limitations that come with partial public financing of presidential nomination campaigns. That changed, however, when George W. Bush, who raised more than $125 million for his campaign, declined federal matching funds in the 2000 primaries but accepted the public funding grant of $67.5 million for the general election. In 2004, having raised more than $366 million, he again turned down the matching funds in the primaries, as did two of the Democrats, Howard Dean and John Kerry (Kerry raised more than $322 million and Dean raised $60 million).[84] Figure 9–5 plots the money Bush and Kerry raised, by month, for the 2004 election. Note the steep rise in Kerry's fundraising as he became the likely nominee. In 2004, both Bush and Kerry accepted the federal general election grant of roughly $75 million, along with the general election spending limit. Whether future candidates will also decline federal funds for their campaigns depends on how well funded their opponents are, and on their own ability to raise money.

THE BIPARTISAN CAMPAIGN REFORM ACT (BCRA) After years of legislative debate, Senate filibusters and even a presidential veto, Congress passed and President Bush signed into law in 2002 the Bipartisan Campaign Reform Act (BCRA). This legislation, often known as the McCain–Feingold bill after its two chief sponsors in the Senate, was written with the understanding that it would immediately be challenged in court—and it was. The Supreme Court upheld most of the provisions of BCRA in *McConnell* v.

soft money
Contributions to a state or local party for party-building purposes.

hard money
Donations made to political candidates, party committees, or groups which, by law, are limited and must be declared.

Bipartisan Campaign Reform Act (BCRA)
Largely banned party soft money, restored long-standing prohibition on corporations and labor unions for using general treasury funds for electoral purposes, and narrowed the definition of issue advocacy.

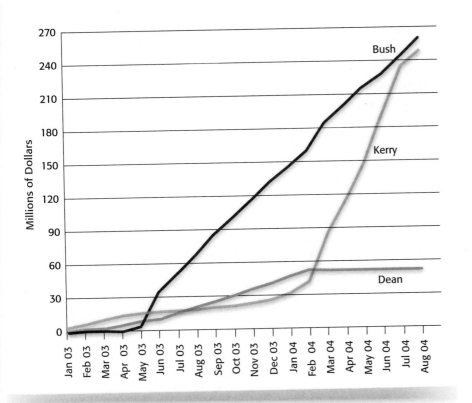

FIGURE 9–5 Presidential Primary Cumulative Receipts, 2003–2004 (millions of dollars).

SOURCE: Data prepared by author based on Federal Election Commission data.

FEC.[85] BCRA is best understood as incremental change. It kept the FEC with its six commissioners appointed by the president with the consent of the Senate, and continued the public financing of presidential campaigns with funds from the income tax checkoff. It left unchanged the limits on spending by candidates for presidential nominations (on a state-by-state basis and in total) and in the presidential general elections for those candidates who accept public funding. It also continued public subsidies for the two national parties' convention expenses and allowed subsidies for minor parties that had polled 5 percent of the total vote in the previous election. While recognizing that individuals are free to spend unlimited amounts on their own campaigns, BCRA provided increased contribution limits for candidates running against an opponent who was spending substantial amounts of his own money. Finally, it left unchanged the limits on the amounts the national parties can spend on presidential campaigns and on individual congressional and senatorial campaigns.

The hard money limits in BCRA for 2005–2006 for individuals giving to candidates are $2,100 for each primary, general, or runoff election. Runoffs are rare in the United States, so for most individuals the contribution limit to a candidate is $4,200. Individuals can give $10,000 per cycle to a PAC or federal or state party committee. Contribution limits under BCRA are indexed to inflation. Individuals had a typical two-year cycle limit in giving to a candidate of $4,000 in 2003–2004. Individuals also have an aggregate two-year election cycle limit. They can give up to $40,000 to federal candidates, and up to $61,400 to national party committees, federal PACs, and state party federal accounts. Of the $61,400, only $37,500 can be given to federal PACs and state party federal accounts. Individuals who want to give the maximum total of $101,400 allowable in hard money can thus allocate money to candidates, party committees, and PACs under the constraints noted.[86]

Soft Money The most frequently given justification for BCRA was the need to ban soft money. Soft money, as noted, had been allowed initially to help parties with such party-building activities as voter registration drives, mailings, and generic party advertising. The parties came to use it to influence the election of federal candidates by

TABLE 9–2 Effects of the 2002 Campaign Finance Reforms

	Before 2002 Reform	2006 Elections
Party contributions to candidates	$5,000 per election or $10,000 per election cycle	National Party Committees are limited to $5,000 per election, although there are special limits for Senate candidates. National committees and Senate campaign committees share a contribution limit of $37,300 per campaign.
Party-coordinated expenditures with candidates	*Senate:* State voting-age population times 2 cents, multiplied by the cost-of-living adjustment (COLA), or $20,000 multiplied by the COLA, whichever is greater *House:* $10,000 multiplied by the COLA; if only one representative in the state, same as the Senate limit	*Senate:* State voting-age population times 2 cents, multiplied by the cost-of-living adjustment (COLA), or $20,000 multiplied by the COLA, whichever is greater *House:* $10,000 multiplied by the COLA; if only one representative in the state, $20,000 multiplied by COLA
Party soft money contributions to the national party committee	Unlimited	Banned
Soft money to national or state and local parties for voter registration and get-out-the-vote drives	Unlimited	Limit of $10,000 per group to each state or local party committee (Levin Amendment)
Contributions to parties for buildings	Unlimited	Banned
Party-independent expenditures	Unlimited	Unlimited, except if ad falls under "electioneering communications definition." Then source of funding is subject to FECA regulations and limits, and the ad may not be broadcast within 30 days of a primary or 60 days of a general election. Parties may choose either independent expenditures or coordinated but not both.
Individual contributions to candidates per two-year election cycle	$2,000	$4,200
Individual contribution to Political Action Committee per year	$5,000	$5,000
Individual contribution to national party committee	$26,700	$26,700
Aggregate individual contribution limit to candidate or parties per two-year election cycle	$50,000	$101,400
PAC contribution to candidates per election	$5,000	$5,000
Political Action Committee to National Party Committee	$15,000	$15,000

SOURCE: Federal Election Commission, "Contribution Limits and Prohibitions," www.fec.gov/pages/bcra/rulemakings/part_110_rules.shtml; and "Quick Answers to Party Questions," at www.fec.gov/ans/answers_party.shtml.

transferring funds to state parties, which then ran ads for and against local federal candidates. Both parties made raising soft money a high priority, and soft money spending rose dramatically. All national party committees combined raised more than $509 million of soft money in the 1999–2000 election cycle, up from $110 million adjusted for inflation in 1991–1992[87] (see Figure 9–6). In 2001–2002, the party committees raised more than $495 million combined in soft money.[88]

Until 1998, soft money had been more important in presidential contests than in congressional contests. The most dramatic growth in 2000 and 2002 came among Senate Democrats. Figure 9–6 plots the surge in soft money funds for the four congressional campaign committees. The 2002 election cycle also saw extraordinary soft money activity by all party committees. Overall, the parties raised nearly as much soft money in 2001–2002 as they raised in 1999–2000, which was a presidential

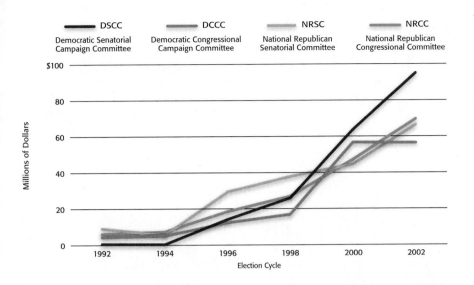

FIGURE 9–6 **Congressional Campaign Committee Soft Money Spending, 1994–2002.**

SOURCE: Federal Election Commission, "Party Committees Raise more than $1 Billion in 2002–2003," press release, March 20, 2002, at, www.fec.gov, April 29, 2003. Adjusted by CPI, at ftp://ftp.bls.gov/pub/special.requests/cpi/cpiai.txt, January 15, 2003.

NOTE: The totals for each party do not equal the sum of the party committee receipts because the numbers provided by the FEC have been adjusted to account for transfers between party committees so as not to double count money in the total receipts.

election cycle. When we compare 2002 with the previous midterm year, 1998, we see soft money more than doubling. With President Bush leading the way, the Republican National Committee raised nearly $114 million, up from $74 million in 1998. Again in 2002, the Democratic Senatorial Campaign Committee outpaced all other committees, raising more than $95 million.[89]

Soft money enabled large donors to be major players in campaign finance. It also strengthened the power of the national party committees, which allocate the money to state parties and indirectly to candidates. To the Supreme Court, which upheld the BCRA soft money ban, one of the major problems with soft money was that it purchased access to elected officials, and with that access came influence and the possibility or appearance of corruption.[90]

BCRA banned most forms of soft money. All soft money contributions to national party committees were banned, as was soft money spending by state parties for or against federal candidates. However, BCRA permits state and local party committees to raise and spend limited amounts of soft money for voter registration and get-out-the-vote efforts. Such activities may be funded with soft money contributions of no more than $10,000 per individual or group to a state or local party committee. The funds raised under this provision of BCRA are called "Levin Funds," after Michigan Senator Carl Levin, who sponsored this as an amendment.

ISSUE ADVOCACY ADVERTISING   Another way the post-Watergate election reforms were undermined was with the upsurge of interest groups running election ads. These ads typically attack a candidate, but the sponsor can avoid disclosure and contribution limitations because the ads do not use electioneering language, such as "vote for" or "vote against" a specific candidate. The Supreme Court in its 1976 *Buckley* v. *Valeo* decision on FECA defined election communication as "communications containing express words of advocacy of election or defeat, such as 'vote for,' 'elect,' 'support,' 'cast your ballot for,' 'Smith for Congress,' 'vote against,' 'defeat,' 'reject.' "[91] Communications that did not use these "magic words" were defined as issue ads, not subject to disclosure required by FECA restrictions. Not surprisingly, interest groups and media consultants found a way to communicate an electioneering message without using the magic words.

The 1996 election saw a surge in **issue advocacy**. Money spent on issue advocacy ads is unlimited and undisclosed because it presumably deals with issues, not

issue advocacy
Promoting a particular position or an issue paid for by interest groups or individuals but not candidates. Much issue advocacy is often electioneering for or against a candidate, and until 2004 had not been subject to any regulation.

A billboard seen along eastbound Interstate 70 near Boonville, Missouri, promotes an ethanol standard for Missouri fuel. Issue advocacy ads are often tied to campaigns for or against particular candidates.

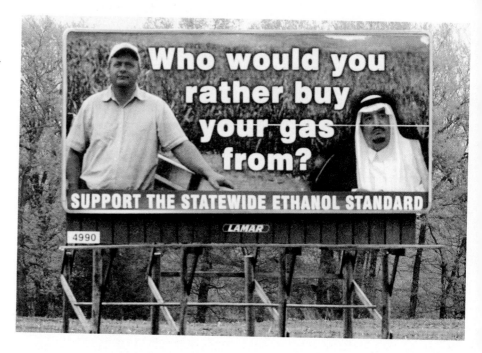

candidates. Issue ad spending in some U.S. House races exceeded $1 million in recent elections, and in 2000, one group, the Alliance for Quality Nursing Home Care, spent more than $1 million on issue ads in the Delaware U.S. Senate race.[92] A prominent example of issue advocacy against a candidate was two Texans who formed a group named Republicans for Clean Air and ran ads in some 2000 presidential primaries attacking John McCain.[93] In the 1998, 2000, and 2002 elections, businesses, labor unions, health maintenance organizations, environmental groups, the Business Roundtable, pro- and anti-gun groups, pro- and anti-abortion groups, and the pharmaceutical industry ran issue ads (see Table 9–3).

Campaign issue ads sponsored by interest groups have been nearly indistinguishable from candidate-run ads.[94] The same was also true for party ads paid for with soft money. In some competitive contests, interest groups and parties spent more money than the candidates did themselves. Typically these ads are even more negative than the ads run by candidates. Often the group identified as paying for the ad gave itself a nondescript name like "Citizens for . . ." or "Coalition against . . ." Many candidates have disavowed ads intended to help them and hurt their opponent. One of the problems with noncandidate ads in an election context is who is accountable for the content of the ads.

BCRA only partially addressed the issue ads loophole of 1996–2002. It redefines "electioneering communications" to include much of what claimed to be issue ads. Under BCRA an electioneering communication is "any broadcast, cable, or satellite communication which refers to a clearly identified candidate for Federal office [and in the case of House and Senate candidates is targeted to their state or district], is made within 60 days before a general, special, or runoff election for the office sought by the candidate; or 30 days before a primary or preference election."[95] BCRA prohibits unions and corporations from using treasury funds to pay for broadcast ads that fit this definition. BCRA does not extend to other forms of interest-group campaigning like mail, phone calls, e-mail, and get-out-the-vote efforts. Groups can spend substantial amounts on these activities.[96]

Section 527 and 501(c) Organizations

One predictable consequence of BCRA's ban on soft money, while leaving open the possibility of some electioneering communications, was increased interest-group electioneering through what are called 527 or 501(c) groups. These groups get their names from the section of the Internal Revenue Service code under which they are organized. Section **527 organizations** existed long before BCRA, but after BCRA these groups had an incentive to expand their efforts.

527 organizations
Interest groups organized under Section 527 of the Internal Revenue Code may advertise for or against candidates. If their source of funding is corporations or unions, they have some restrictions on broadcast advertising. 527 organizations were important in recent elections.

TABLE 9-3 Some Frequent Issue Advertisers in 2000

Advertiser	Amount Spent (in millions of dollars)*
Citizens for Better Medicare	$64
AFL-CIO	45
Coalition to Protect America's Health Care	30
National Rifle Association	25
U.S. Chamber of Commerce	15
Planned Parenthood Action Fund	14
Business Roundtable	13
Federation for American Immigration Reform	12
NAACP National Voter Fund	11
Americans for Job Security	10

*The numbers estimate total spending on issue advocacy and express advocacy; however, a large proportion went to issue advocacy.

SOURCE: Data from David B. Magleby, ed., *Election Advocacy: Soft Money and Issue Advocacy in the 2000 Congressional Elections* (Center for the Study of Elections and Democracy, Brigham Young University, 2001); Erika Falk, "Issue Advocacy Advertising Through the Presidential Primary, 1999–2000 Election Cycle," Annenberg Public Policy Center, press release, September 20, 2000.

Section 527 groups are formed to influence elections. Section 501(c) groups include nonprofit groups whose purpose is not political. Money given to these groups is tax deductible (Section 501(c)3 groups), and they can engage in nonpartisan voter registration and turnout efforts but cannot endorse candidates. Other 501(c) groups can and are expressly political and money contributed to them is not tax deductible. Disclosure of contributions to these groups and spending by them are less frequent than for Section 527 groups, political parties, or PACs.[97]

BCRA restricted the way 527 groups communicate with voters. Any 527 organization wishing to broadcast an electioneering communication within one month of a primary or two months of a general election must not use corporate or union treasury funds, it must report the expenditures associated with the broadcast, and it must disclose all the sources of all funds it has received since January 1 of the preceding calendar year. While contribution sources are restricted in this case, contribution amounts are not. Individuals spending their own money individually, and not as part of a group, are also not limited. This Supreme Court permitted this exemption on free speech grounds.

In 2004, the first post-BCRA election, the most visible 527 organization was America Coming Together (ACT), which raised and spent an estimated $76 million in presidential battleground states in 2004. Much of the early money for ACT came from wealthy investor George Soros. ACT helped organize many other interest groups to register and mobilize voters. A related group, The Media Fund, spent $54 million in ads against President Bush up until 60 days before the election.[98] The advent of groups like ACT and The Media Fund, while benefiting John Kerry and the Democrats, constitutes a shift in power toward groups and away from candidates and parties. Republicans, in part because they were in power and had the fundraising abilities of President Bush, did not see as many allied 527 groups as did the Democrats. Some examples of Republican 527 groups in 2004 included Progress for America, Leadership Forum, and the Republican Governors Association. The 527 group that may have had the greatest impact on the campaign was the Swift Boat Veterans for Truth, which attacked Senator Kerry's war record. The modest initial budget for this group's ads generated widespread news coverage, especially on cable news stations. The message of the ads cut to the core of the persona that Kerry had presented at the Democratic National Convention. President Bush was not drawn into the controversy, but former Senator Bob Dole's assertion that there might be something to the Swift Boat Veteran charges added to the attention the group received.

How Other Nations Govern

Campaign Financing in Britain and Canada

United States election campaigns go on for months or even years and are expensive. In contrast, Canadian general election campaigns are limited by law to about five weeks. Public opinion polls cannot be published during the last three days of a campaign, and the media are prohibited from reporting results from earlier time zones on the evening of the election in any district where voting is still taking place.

Expenditures are strictly limited for Canadian political parties and individual candidates. During the 1997 general election campaign to fill the 301 seats in the House of Commons, political parties that fielded candidates in all districts were limited by law to spending no more than approximately $8 million each for the entire election, and individual candidates could spend about $35,000 to $45,000, depending on the number of voters per district. In return, media outlets were required to sell a certain amount of airtime to the parties, and national and regional television and radio networks had to donate free airtime to these parties. If individual candidates received more than 15 percent of the vote in their districts, the government reimbursed 50 percent of their election-related expenses. Political parties receiving at least 2 percent of the national vote or at least 5 percent of the votes cast in electoral districts where they ran candidates were reimbursed 22.5 percent of their expenses.

In the 2004 Canadian elections, 1,685 candidates ran for office, and 12 political parties received registered status. Total spending by the parliamentary candidates and political parties was approximately $212 million in Canadian dollars—less than a fifth of the $1.16 billion spent by congressional candidates alone in the United States during the 2004 election campaign ($660 million on seats in the House of Representatives and $496 million on seats in the Senate).

British general elections also offer an interesting contrast to elections in the United States. The election campaign lasts only three weeks. Candidates for the British House of Commons, the most critical election in Britain, are allowed to raise and spend only $15,000. If they spend more, they are disqualified. Each candidate gets the same amount of free airtime and is allowed to mail one free election leaflet to each voter in the constituency. About 75 percent of voters turn out, and about 95 percent of eligible voters are registered to vote. At the voting booth, the voter is handed a slip of paper with the names of three or four candidates for the House of Commons. No other offices or ballot questions are voted on at that time. ■

> *Expenditures are strictly limited for Canadian political parties and individual candidates. . . . Candidates for the British House of Commons are allowed to raise and spend only $15,000.*

SOURCE: Adapted from Dudley Fishburn, "British Campaigning—How Civilized!" *New York Times*, April 14, 1992, p. 25. See also, Alexander MacLeod, "Britain Leads in Campaign Finance Reform," *Christian Science Monitor*, July 30, 1999, World section, p. 6. See also, FEC, "Candidates Spend $1.16 Billion During 2003–2004," press release, June 9, 2005, at www.fec.gov; Office of the Auditor General of Canada, "2005 Report of the Auditor General of Canada: Elections Canada—Administering the Federal Election Process," at www.oag-bvg.gc.ca/domino/reports.nsf/html/20051106ce.html.

The attack by the Swift Boat Veterans was effective in part due to the lack of a strong response and rebuttal from Kerry, his campaign, or his party. Nearly two years later, Kerry himself acknowledged his mistake by saying he should have responded and "we should have put more money behind it. . . . I take responsibility for it; it was my mistake. They spent something like $30 million, and we didn't. That's just a terrible imbalance when somebody's lying about you."[99] Given the effectiveness of this attack on Kerry, similar attacks can be expected in the future and candidates will likely respond much more aggressively to these attacks than Kerry did.

Without a presidential election in 2006, some 527 organizations shifted their focus and funds from federal races to state and local issues, where many groups felt they could be more effective. At the federal level groups selected key battleground areas and often communicated with voters in targeted ways. Unions, the Chamber of Commerce, environmental groups, and pro-choice groups were all very active in this election. Some groups like America Votes focused on turning out voters. The Campaign Money Watch, a 527 group, spent hundreds of thousands of dollars in select contests attacking Republicans on the scandal issues. A new progressive group named Catalyst invested heavily in building a voter file that was used in some key states and will be enhanced for use in the 2008 presidential election. Some of the donors who funded Democratic-leaning 527s in 2004 did not invest nearly as much in 2006, but these outside groups remain an important element of competitive elections at the federal and state levels.

INDEPENDENT EXPENDITURES   The Supreme Court made clear in its ruling on FECA in 1976 that individuals and groups have the right to spend as much money as they wish for or against candidates as long as they are truly independent of the candidate and as long as the money is not corporate or union treasury money. Individuals have made large independent expenditures, like Michael Goland, a California entrepreneur who spent $1.1 million against Senator Charles Percy (R-Ill.) in the 1984 election. At the time, it was the largest ever independent expenditure by an individual. Goland considered Percy unfriendly to Israel. In the 2000 presidential election, Stephen Adams, owner of an outdoor advertising firm, spent $2 million to support George W. Bush.[100] In 2004, billionaire George Soros, who gave millions to 527 organizations opposing the reelection of Bush, also spent $2.3 million in independent expenditures against the president. He used the money to run full-page newspaper ads against Bush and to fund a speaking tour during which he expressed his opposition to Bush's reelection. Soros also maintained a Web site and sent mailings to voters in key states.

Some groups have long tried to influence elections independently rather than through a party committee or a candidate's campaign. Membership organizations like the American Medical Association, National Education Association, or National Rifle Association often do this. Some ideological groups like Club For Growth, a libertarian antitax group, also have made substantial independent expenditures. As discussed in Chapter 7, the Supreme Court extended to political parties the same rights to make independent expenditures afforded to groups and individuals.[101]

BCRA does not constrain **independent expenditures** by groups, political parties, or individuals, as long as the expenditures by those individuals, parties, or groups are independent of the candidate and fully disclosed to the FEC.

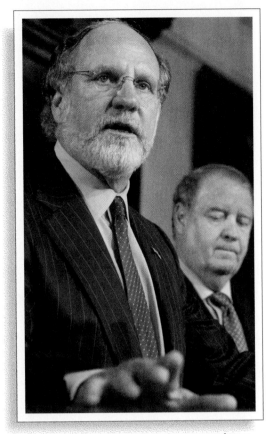

Jon S. Corzine was elected governor of New Jersey in 2005. A quote by his ex-wife claiming that Corzine "let his family down, and he'll probably let New Jersey down, too" was used by his opponent in a campaign attack ad. Corzine won the election by 54% of the vote.

Continuing Problems with Campaign Finance

The continuing problems with federal election fund raising are easy to identify: dramatically escalating costs, a growing dependence on PAC money, decreasing visibility and competitiveness of challengers (especially for the House), and the ability of wealthy individuals to fund their own campaigns. BCRA reduced the danger of large contributions influencing lawmakers directly or indirectly through political parties. But large contributions can still influence the outcome of elections, as 527 and other groups demonstrated in 2004 and 2006.

RISING COSTS OF CAMPAIGNS   The American ideal that anyone—even a person of modest or little wealth—can run for public office and hope to win has become more of a myth than a reality.[102] And rising costs also mean that incumbents spend more time raising funds and therefore less time legislating and representing their districts. Since the FECA became law in 1972, total expenditures by candidates for the House of Representatives have more than doubled after controlling for inflation, and they have risen even more in Senate elections (see Table 9–4). One reason for escalating costs is television. Organizing and running a campaign is expensive, limiting the field of challengers to those who have their own resources or are willing to spend more than a year raising money from interest groups and individuals.

DECLINING COMPETITION   Unless something is done to help finance challengers, incumbents will continue to have the advantage in seeking reelection. Nothing in BCRA addresses this problem. Challengers in both parties are typically underfunded. House Democratic challengers averaged $147,300 in spending in 2004,[103] while incumbents in both parties spent an average of about $1 million each in 2004.[104] In today's expensive campaigns, candidates are generally invisible if they only have $100,000 to $200,000 to spend.

independent expenditures
Money spent by individuals or groups not associated with candidates to elect or defeat candidates for office.

TABLE 9–4 Average Campaign Expenditures of Candidates for the House of Representatives, 1988–2004 General Election (In Thousands of 2004 Dollars)

	Incumbent	Challenger	Open Seat
Republican			
1988	$646.5	$101.7	$272.3
1990	573.5	100.7	266.5
1992	725.9	123.2	212.5
1994	568.4	172.1	280.5
1996	874.0	129.8	250.4
1998	785.5	157.5	314.9
2000	945.7	156.8	489.9
2002	931.7	117.2	446.5
2004	1,086.1	142.4	534.5
Democrat			
1988	$566.1	$124.0	$335.3
1990	582.1	91.1	325.1
1992	808.5	87.8	229.1
1994	744.6	96.0	251.4
1996	672.7	198.5	267.2
1998	634.4	150.8	473.5
2000	792.8	217.6	437.0
2002	842.7	203.6	436.5
2004	919.8	147.3	445.2

SOURCE: Federal Election Commission, "FEC Reports on Congressional Financial Activity for 2000," press release, May 15, 2001; Federal Election Commission, "Congressional Candidates Spend $1.16 Billion During 2003–2004," press release, June 9, 2005.

The high cost of campaigns dampens competition by discouraging individuals from running for office. Potential challengers look at the fund-raising advantages incumbents enjoy—at incumbents' campaign war chests carried over from previous campaigns that can reach $1 million or more and at the time it will take them to raise enough money to launch a minimal campaign—and they decide not to run. Moreover, unlike incumbents, whose salaries are being paid while campaigning and raising money, most challengers have to support themselves and their families throughout the campaign, which for a seat in Congress lasts roughly two years.

The high costs of television advertising diminish the ability of challengers to mount visible campaigns, resulting in declining competition. Only months after passage of the 2002 reforms, John McCain announced his support and sponsorship of legislation creating a "broadcast bank" where political parties would be given vouchers for free advertising time, with one-third of the time to go to challengers. Television stations, under McCain's proposal, would be required to devote at least two hours per week to political coverage in which the candidates were on camera during the last month of the general election campaign.[105] For more information on broadcast time proposals, see The Alliance for Better Campaigns at www.reclaimthemedia.org.

INCREASING DEPENDENCE ON PACS AND WEALTHY DONORS Where does the money come from to finance these expensive election campaigns? For most House incumbents, it comes from political action committees (PACs), which we discussed in Chapter 6. In recent years nearly two-out-of-five incumbents seeking reelection raised more money from PACs than from individuals (see Figure 9–7).[106] Senators get a smaller percentage of their campaign funds from PACs, but because they spend so

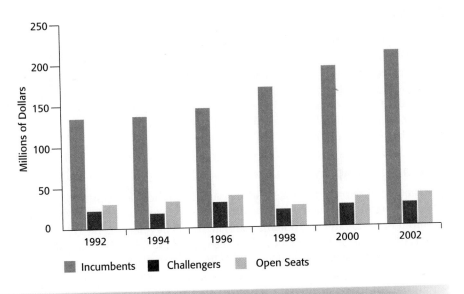

FIGURE 9–7 PAC Contributions to Congressional Candidates.
SOURCE: FEC, "PAC Activity Increases for 2002 Elections," March 27, 2003, at www.fec.gov.

much more, they need to raise even more money from PACs than House incumbents do. PACs are pragmatic, giving largely to incumbents. Challengers receive little from PACs because PACs do not want to offend politicians in power. BCRA raised the individual contribution limit to a candidate in the two-year campaign cycle to $4,000, but did not raise PAC contribution limits above the pre-BCRA levels of $10,000 for the primary and general election combined. Incumbents will continue to rely on PACs because relatively few individuals have the means to give $4,000 to a campaign. It also often takes less time to raise money from PACs than from individuals.

To be sure, PACs and individuals spend money on campaigns for many reasons. Most of them want certain laws to be passed or repealed, certain funds to be appropriated, or certain administrative decisions to be rendered. At a minimum, they want access to officeholders and a chance to talk with members before key votes.

Defenders of PACs point out that there is no demonstrable relationship between contributions and legislators' votes. But influence in the legislative process depends on access to staff and members of Congress, and most analysts agree that campaign contributions give donors extraordinary access. PACs influence the legislative process in other ways as well. Their access helps them structure the legislative agenda with friendly legislators and influence the drafting of legislation or amendments to existing bills. These are all advantages that others do not have.

Candidates' Personal Wealth   Campaign finance legislation cannot constitutionally restrict rich candidates—the Rockefellers, the Kennedys, the Perots—from spending heavily on their own campaigns. Big money can make a big difference, and wealthy candidates can afford to spend big money. In presidential politics, this advantage can be most meaningful before the primaries begin. The personal wealth advantage also applies to Congressional races. The 2000 New Jersey U.S. Senate race, for example, set new records for a candidate's personal spending in an election. Wall Street investment banker Jon Corzine, a newcomer to elections, spent a total of $60 million, $35 million of it on the primary alone.[107] Corzine was elected to the U.S. Senate and later spent another $45 million of his own money on his successful 2005 gubernatorial election in New Jersey.[108] BCRA includes a millionaire's provision that the Supreme Court upheld in *McConnell* v. *FEC*. The provision allows candidates running against self-financed opponents to have higher contribution limits from individuals or parties contributing to their campaigns.

Improving Elections

A combination of party rules and state laws determines how we choose nominees for president. Reformers agree that the current process is flawed but disagree over which aspects should be changed. Concern over how we choose presidents now centers on three issues:[109] how we fund presidential elections; the number, timing, and representativeness of presidential primaries; and the role of the electoral college, including the possibility that a presidential election might be thrown into the House of Representatives.

Reforming Campaign Finance

The incremental reforms of BCRA and the Supreme Court decision in *McConnell* v. *FEC* upholding them have not resolved the issues of campaign finance. Among the unresolved issues are how presidential campaigns will be financed, the role of Section 527 and 501(c) groups, the adequacy of disclosure, and the strength and viability of the political parties. More broadly, the FEC's inability to reach decisions because of its partisan deadlock, as demonstrated by its inaction on Section 527 groups, has helped generate growing pressure to reform the agency.

The 2004 election cycle, with its substantial interest group activity through Section 527 and 501(c) organizations, was seen by those who favor deregulation of campaign finance as another example of the impossibility of limiting money in elections. This school of thought will continue to push for disclosure as the regulatory aim of government in this area.

Another group of reformers will press for more aggressive reforms than those found in BCRA. Included in this agenda will be reining in the 527 and 501(c) groups, restructuring the public financing of presidential elections to sustain this element of FECA, and possibly extending public financing of congressional elections. Both sides are likely to agree that the FEC needs change but will not agree on how to change it.

Central to the functioning of a constitutional democracy like that in the United States is a system of fair elections that is well administered, so that the outcome of these elections has legitimacy. Voter trust and confidence in elections centers on the kinds of issues we have examined in this chapter. Over time we have learned ways to make elections better, including the secret ballot, disclosure and limitation of campaign contributions, and expanding the role of citizens through primaries and referendums. As important as these structural and institutional changes are, without the participation of people in politics the system will not function well.

Reforming the Nominating Process

As noted, in 2004 once again the choice of presidential nominees was most influenced by the voters in early primary or caucus states like Iowa and New Hampshire. The fact is that most citizens do not have a say in who the nominees are. Moreover, these early states are not broadly representative of the country or of their respective parties. Participation in primaries has been low in recent years (see Figure 9–8). In the 2004 primaries, turnout was generally under 17 percent of the voting-age population, and it declined as the primary season progressed and the field of candidates narrowed.[110] Voters in primaries also tend to be more ideological than voters generally, a further bias in the current nominating process.

None of these concerns are new. What would the critics substitute for state presidential primaries? Some argue in favor of a *national presidential primary* that would take the form of a single nationwide election, probably held in May or September, or separate state primaries held in all the states on the same day.[111] Supporters contend that a one-shot national presidential primary (though a runoff might be necessary) would be simple, direct, and representative. It would cut down the wear-and-tear on candidates, and the media coverage would attract a large turnout. Opponents argue that such a reform would make the present system even worse. It would enhance the role of showmanship and gamesmanship, and because it would be enormously expensive, it would hurt the chances of candidates who lack strong financial backing.

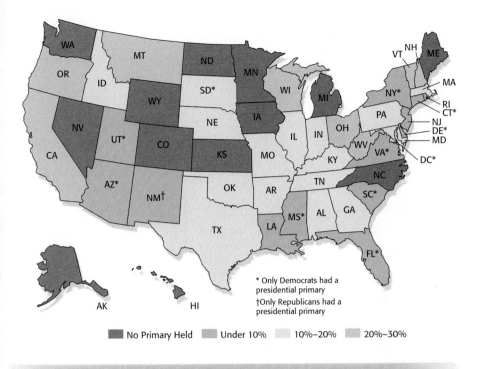

FIGURE 9–8 Voter Turnout in the 2004 Presidential Primaries.

SOURCE: Curtis B. Gans, Director, Committee for the study of the American Electorate, facsimile to author, September 22, 2004.

* Only Democrats had a presidential primary

†Only Republicans had a presidential primary

No Primary Held   Under 10%   10%–20%   20%–30%

A more modest proposal is to hold *regional primaries,* possibly at two- or three-week intervals across the country. Regional primaries might bring more coherence to the process and encourage more emphasis on issues of regional concern. But such primaries would retain most of the disadvantages of the present system—especially the emphasis on money and media. Clearly, they would give an advantage to candidates from whatever region held the first primary, and this advantage would encourage regional candidates and might increase polarization among sections of the country. In recent years, many states have sought to move their primaries to the week(s) soon after the New Hampshire primary, although few states have actually done it.

A different proposal is to drastically reduce the number of presidential primaries and make more use of the caucus system. The turnout of voters in the Iowa caucuses in recent elections shows that participation can be high, and the time participants spent discussing candidates and issues shows that such participation can be thoughtful and informed. However, if more states adopted caucuses, their turnout would not likely be as high as in Iowa because they would lack the media and candidate attention that Iowa gets by being first. In caucus states, candidates are more dependent on convincing political activists, who will show up for a political meeting. By relying on party meetings to select delegates, the caucus system would also, some say, enhance the role of the party.[112]

Still another idea—used by Colorado for nominations to state offices and by Utah for nominations to federal and state offices—would turn the process around. Beginning in May, local caucuses and then state conventions would be held in every state. They would then send delegates—a certain percentage of whom would be unpledged to any presidential candidate—to the national party conventions, which would be held in the summer. The national conventions would select two or three candidates to compete in a national primary to be held in September. In this plan, voters registered by party would be allowed to vote for their party nominee in the September primaries.[113] Such a plan would likely add voter engagement in the party process but would also be more expensive since candidates would have to fund three campaigns, one in the caucuses, one in September, and another in November.

Given the problems with the current nomination process, why has it not been reformed? Part of the answer is strong resistance from the states that benefit from the

Agents of Change

Bev Harris and Black Box Voting

Bev Harris

QUESTIONS

How much confidence do you have in electronic voting?

What are the risks of using the new technology?

What are the costs of using paper-ballot machines?

Black Box Voting was founded in 2002 to oppose the use of electronic voting machines that record each vote with the touch of a screen. Created after the 2000 election impasse in Florida, Black Box Voting took the controversial position that states and localities should return to old-fashioned paper ballots that can be recounted after an election is over.

Bev Harris created Black Box Voting after writing a book by the same title. A 52-year-old resident of a Seattle suburb, she seemed an unlikely person to take on a cause such as voting reform. Indeed, she says that she once thought voting was boring.

However, Harris became one of the nation's leading experts on voting technology. Although she understands that paper ballots are not perfect, she argues that electronic voting has its own flaws, including breakdowns that can erase every vote on a single machine, and potential security breaches that can allow invisible election fraud. Once an electronic vote disappears from a computer's memory in the "black box" that only experts can penetrate, it is gone for good and cannot be counted. Since starting her organization to oppose the increasing use of touch-screen voting machines, she has started to ask questions about other new voting technologies, including Internet voting.

Facing strong opposition from the electronic voting industry, Harris is not sure she can win her battle to return to simpler technologies. "Actually, it is going to be a long shot that we will win this battle on voting machines," she says. "We have proven our case, but they are still just barreling ahead." ∎

Learn more about Black Box Voting at www.blackboxvoting.org.

---

current system. In our federal system, imposing a national or regional primary means those states would lose power.

While many voters are effectively denied a vote in determining their party's nominee, news coverage of the primaries allows them to evaluate the candidates' political qualities and their abilities to organize campaigns; communicate through the media; stand up under pressure; avoid making mistakes (or recover if they do make them); adjust their appeals to shifting events and to different regions of the country; control their staffs as well as make good use of them; and be decisive, articulate, resilient, humorous, informed, and ultimately successful in winning votes. In short, supporters of the current system claim, primaries test candidates on the very qualities they must exhibit in the presidency.[114]

Reforming the Electoral College

The Florida ballot counting and recounting after the 2000 election and the fact that the winner of the popular vote did not become president prompted a national debate on the electoral college. The most frequently proposed reform is *direct popular election* of the president. Presidents would be elected directly by the voters, just as governors are, and the electoral college and individual electors would be abolished. Such proposals usually provide that if no candidate receives at least 40 percent of the total popular vote, a *runoff election* would be held between the two contenders with the most votes.

Supporters argue that direct election would give every voter the same weight in the presidential balloting in accordance with the one-person, one-vote doctrine. Plus, each voter would feel that their vote counts, even Republican voters in Massachusetts and Democratic voters in Utah. Winners would take on more legitimacy because their victories would reflect the will of the voters.

Opponents contend that the plan would further undermine federalism, encourage unrestrained majority rule and hence political extremism, and hurt the most populous and competitive states, which would lose some of their present influence. Others fear that the plan would make presidential campaigns more remote from the voters; candidates might stress television and give up their forays into shopping centers and city malls.[115]

From time to time, Congress considers proposals for a constitutional amendment to elect presidents directly.[116] Such proposals, however, seldom get far because of the strong opposition of various interests that believe they may be disadvantaged by such a change, especially small states and minority groups whose role is enlarged by the electoral college. Groups such as African Americans and farmers, for example, fear they might lose their swing vote power—their ability to make a difference in key states that may tip the electoral college balance.

Another alternative to the electoral college is sometimes called the National Bonus Plan. This plan adds to the current 538 electoral college members another 102 electoral votes, to be awarded on a winner-take-all basis to the candidate with the most votes, so long as that candidate received more than 40 percent of the popular vote. This system would avoid elections' being thrown into the House of Representatives and would help ensure that the candidate who won the popular vote became president. The most serious liabilities of the plan are that it is complicated and that it requires a runoff election if there is no winner.

Finally, two states, Maine and Nebraska, have already adopted a district system in which the candidate who carries each congressional district gets that electoral vote and the candidate who carries the state gets the state's two additional electoral votes. This quasi-proportional representation system has the advantage of not shutting out a candidate who is strong in some areas of a state but not others, but otherwise it does not address the larger concerns with the electoral college.

The failure of attempts to change the system of elections points to an important conclusion about procedural reform: Americans normally do not focus on procedures. Even after the intense controversy on the outcome of the 2000 election, including the role of the electoral college, reform was not seriously considered.

As we have demonstrated in this chapter, elections matter in a constitutional democracy. They determine who holds office and what policies the government adopts. Elections are complex, and the rules of the game affect how it is played. Our winner-take-all system is an example of a rule that has influenced the nature of our party system, the strategy of candidates, and the stability of our institutions. Over time the rules of the electoral game have been changed. Today party nominees are largely selected by voters in primaries, whereas early in our nation's history candidates were selected by party caucuses. Over time our system has expanded the role of citizens and voters as illustrated by the predominance of primaries.

There are important differences between congressional and presidential elections, but there are also similarities. The intensity of the campaign, the attention of voters, and the money spent are all greater in presidential elections. But congressional elections also find voters reacting to the party of the nominees, the appeal of the candidates, and the issues. One other constant is that candidates need money to mount viable campaigns. How candidates raise these campaign funds has been a recurrent concern to reformers. Recent reforms have sought to limit the ability of large contributors to have undue influence over elections and office holders.

In campaign finance, as in reform of the nomination process and the electoral college, there are ongoing efforts to make our system more accountable and democratic. But reforms often have unintended consequences, and sometimes these consequences prompt calls for further reform. Elections and democracy are best seen as works in progress.

The touch-screen voting machine is an example of a new way for voters to register their choice. This computerized machine prevents voters from choosing more than one candidate, as many did erroneously during the 2000 election in Florida; however, there is considerable controversy over the fact that these machines are not required to produce a paper receipt for each vote cast, making recounts impossible should they become necessary.

Summary

1. American elections, even presidential elections, are largely governed by state law and administered by local election officials. Following the 2000 elections, governments at all levels began to look for ways to improve the system.

2. Our electoral system is based on winner-take-all rules, typically with single-member districts or single officeholders. These rules encourage a moderate, two-party system. Fixed and staggered terms of office add predictability to our electoral system.

3. The electoral college is the means by which presidents are actually elected. To win a state's electoral votes, a candidate must have a plurality of votes in that state. Except in two states, the winner takes all. Thus candidates cannot afford to lose the popular vote in the most populous states. The electoral college also gives disproportionate power to the largest and smallest states, especially if they are competitive. It has the potential to defeat the popular vote winner.

4. Many congressional, state, and local races are not seriously contested. The extent to which a campaign is likely to be hotly contested varies with the importance of the office and the chance a challenger has of winning. Senate races are more likely to be contested, though most incumbents win.

5. The race for the presidency actually takes place in three stages: winning enough delegate support in presidential primaries and caucuses to secure the nomination, campaigning at the national party convention, and mobilizing voters in enough states to win the most votes in the electoral college.

6. Even though presidential nominations today are usually decided weeks or months before the national party conventions, these conventions still have an important role in setting the parties' direction, unifying their ranks, and generating enthusiasm.

7. Because large campaign contributors are suspected of improperly influencing public officials, Congress has long sought to regulate political contributions. The main approaches to reform have been (1) imposing limitations on giving, receiving, and spending political money; (2) requiring public disclosure of the sources and uses of political money; and (3) giving governmental subsidies to presidential candidates, campaigns, and parties, including incentive arrangements. Present regulation includes all three approaches.

8. Loopholes in federal law—including soft money and issue advocacy—led to the passage of BCRA. These loopholes became bigger and more important in the 1996 election cycle and led to substantial soft money and issue advocacy in the 1998, 2000, and 2002 elections.

9. The rising costs of campaigns have led to declining competition for congressional seats and increasing dependence on PACs and wealthy donors.

10. The present presidential selection system is under criticism because of its length and expense, because of uncertainties and biases in the electoral college, and because it seems to test candidates for media skills less needed in the White House than the ability to govern, including the capacity to form coalitions and make hard decisions.

11. Reform efforts center on presidential primaries, the electoral college, and campaign finance.

Further Reading

R. MICHAEL ALVAREZ, *Information and Elections* (University of Michigan Press, 1998).

LARRY M. BARTELS, *Presidential Primaries and the Dynamics of Public Choice* (Princeton University Press, 1988).

EARL BLACK AND MERLE BLACK, *The Vital South: How Presidents Are Elected* (Harvard University Press, 1992).

DAVID W. BRADY, JOHN F. COGAN, AND MORRIS P. FIORINA, EDS., *Continuity and Change in House Elections* (Stanford University Press, 2000).

BRUCE BUCHANAN, *Presidential Campaign Quality: Incentives and Reform* (Pearson Education, 2004).

ANN N. CRIGLER, MARION R. JUST, AND EDWARD J. MCCAFFERY, EDS., *Rethinking the Vote: The Politics and Prospects of American Election Reform* (Oxford University Press, 2004).

RONALD KEITH GADDIE, *Born to Run: Origins of the Political Career* (Rowman & Littlefield, 2004).

RONALD KEITH GADDIE AND CHARLES S. BULLOCK III, EDS., *Elections to Open Seats in the U.S. House: Where the Action Is* (Rowman & Littlefield, 2000).

PAUL GRONKE, *The Electorate, the Campaign, and the Office: A Unified Approach to Senate and House Elections* (University of Michigan Press, 2000).

RODERICK P. HART, *Campaign Talk* (Princeton University Press, 2000).

PAUL S. HERRNSON, *Congressional Elections: Campaigning at Home and in Washington*, 4th ed. (CQ Press, 2004).

PAUL S. HERRNSON, *Playing Hardball: Campaigning for the U.S. Congress* (Prentice Hall, 2000).

GARY C. JACOBSON, *The Politics of Congressional Elections,* 6th ed. (Longman, 2003).

KATHLEEN HALL JAMIESON, *Everything You Think You Know About Politics . . . and Why You're Wrong* (Basic Books, 2000).

KIM F. KAHN AND **PATRICK J. KENNEDY,** *The Spectacle of U.S. Senate Campaigns* (Princeton University Press, 1999).

DAVID B. MAGLEBY, ED., *Financing the 2000 Election* (Brookings Institution Press, 2002).

DAVID B. MAGLEBY AND **J. QUIN MONSON,** EDS., *The Last Hurrah?: Soft Money and Issue Advocacy in the 2002 Congressional Elections* (Brookings Institution Press, 2004).

L. SANDY MAISEL AND **KARA Z. BUCKLEY,** *Parties and Elections in America: The Electoral Process,* 4th ed. (Rowman & Littlefield, 2004).

MICHAEL J. MALBIN, ED., *The Election After Reform: Money, Politics, and the Bipartisan Campaign Reform Act* (Rowman & Littlefield, 2006).

MICHAEL J. MALBIN, ED., *Life After Reform: When the Bipartisan Campaign Reform Act . . . Meets Politics* (Rowman & Littlefield, 2003).

JEREMY D. MAYER, *Running on Race: Racial Politics in Presidential Campaigns, 1960–2000* (Random House, 2002).

WILLIAM G. MAYER AND **ANDREW E. BUSCH,** *The Front-Loading Problem in Presidential Nominations* (Brookings Institution Press, 2004).

STEPHEN K. MEDVIC, *Political Consultants in U.S. Congressional Elections* (Ohio State University Press, 2001).

NELSON W. POLSBY AND **AARON B. WILDAVSKY,** *Presidential Elections: Strategies and Structures of American Politics,* 11th ed. (Rowman & Littlefield, 2004).

SAMUEL L. POPKIN, *The Reasoning Voter: Communication and Persuasion in Presidential Campaigns,* 2d ed. (University of Chicago Press, 1994).

PAUL D. SCHUMAKER AND **BURDETT A. LOOMIS,** EDS., *Choosing a President: The Electoral College and Beyond* (Seven Bridges Press, 2002).

JAMES A. THURBER, ED., *The Battle for Congress: Consultants, Candidates, and Voters* (Brookings Institution Press, 2001).

JAMES A. THURBER AND **CANDICE J. NELSON,** EDS., *Campaign Warriors: Political Consultants in Elections* (Brookings Institution Press, 2000).

STEPHEN J. WAYNE, *The Road to the White House 2004* (Wadsworth, 2004).

See also *Public Opinion Quarterly, the American Journal of Politics,* and *American Political Science Review.*

KeyTerms

winner-take-all system, p. 245	national tide, p. 252	soft money, p. 264
single-member district, p. 245	name recognition, p. 252	hard money, p. 264
proportional representation, p. 245	caucus, p. 256	Bipartisan Campaign Reform Act (BCRA), p. 264
electoral college, p. 246	national party convention, p. 258	issue advocacy, p. 267
safe seat, p. 249	interested money, p. 263	527 organizations, p. 268
coattail effect, p. 249	Federal Election Commission (FEC), p. 263	independent expenditures, p. 271
candidate appeal, p. 252		

Make It Real

ELECTIONS

Learn how to run for office and get elected
as well as about the extension of voting rights
and alternate means of tabulating electoral votes.

Chapter 10

The Media and American Politics

★

POLITICIANS AND PUBLIC OFFICIALS OFTEN ENGAGE IN THE SELECTIVE "LEAKING" OF INFORMATION TO THE NEWS MEDIA. LEAKS ARE OFTEN INTENDED TO INFLUENCE THE PUBLIC BY REVEALING INFORMATION THAT OTHERWISE WOULD NOT BE KNOWN, OR TO PUSH A STORY ONTO THE PUBLIC AGENDA. OCCASIONALLY THE LEAK IS OF CLASSIFIED OR SECRET INFORMATION, AS WAS THE CASE WITH THE LEAKED DOCUMENTS THAT CAME TO BE KNOWN AS THE PENTAGON PAPERS DURING THE VIETNAM WAR.[1] REPORTERS TO WHOM INFORMATION IS leaked often promise not to reveal the identity of the person doing the leaking.

Reporters also gather information from many sources so that they can piece together with other information to generate news stories. In 2003, syndicated columnist Robert Novak, building on information provided by Deputy Secretary of State Richard Armitage, disclosed the identity of a CIA operative, Valerie Plame, a few months after the war with Iraq began.[2] Former U.S. Ambassador Joseph Wilson, Plame's husband, had written that the Bush Administration "twisted" intelligence to "exaggerate" the Iraqi threat.[3] The CIA had sent Wilson to the African nation of Niger in 2002 to investigate claims that Iraq had tried to purchase uranium there. Novak's story questioned the credibility of Wilson, stating that Plame had "suggested sending Wilson to Niger."[4] Novak's disclosure potentially endangered Plame's past contacts from when she was a spy.

The possible criminal action by persons in the administration in disclosing the identity of a CIA agent prompted an investigation and the appointment of a special prosecutor. Novak and Washington Post editor Bob Woodward refused to identify the source of their information. Other reporters who had been leaked the information about Wilson and Plame included Matthew Cooper of Time magazine and Judith Miller of the New York Times.[5] Both Cooper and Miller also initially declined to reveal their sources to the special prosecutor. Miller was jailed for contempt of court for refusing to testify. Cooper obtained a waiver from his source and testified. Cooper's source was revealed to be Karl Rove, President Bush's senior political advisor.[6] After Miller spent 12 weeks in jail, her source, I. Lewis "Scooter" Libby, Vice President Dick Cheney's chief of staff, freed her from her pledge of confidentiality and allowed her to cooperate with the special prosecutor. A grand jury indicted Libby for obstruction of justice, perjury, and making false statements. News reports also indicated that Libby first heard

"Americans have never been truly fond of their press. Through the last decade, however, their disdain for the media establishment has reached new levels."

JOURNALIST JAMES FALLOWS

Valerie Plame's name from Vice President Cheney a month before the Novak column made her CIA affiliation public knowledge. Rove testified before the grand jury five times before being cleared of charges in the case.

The public is seldom able to trace the sources of information given to reporters in cases like this. In this instance the leak may have been illegal because it involved staff closely connected to the president and vice president and the secretary of state. The dispute about the administration's justification for going to war with Iraq has added to the controversy about the efforts to discredit Wilson. The role of reporters in the case was also dramatic, with Miller going to jail rather than reveal her sources. Whether the information provided by Mr. Armitage to Robert Novak was in fact a "leak" later became the subject of a column by Mr. Novak, which he titled "Armitage's Leak," while Mr. Armitage claimed the information was given inadvertently.[7] Presidents and their advisors typically criticize leaks, but in cases like these, the administration may try to use the news media for its own purposes. In this chapter we examine the role the media plays in our system of government.

The Influence of the Media on Politics

The media, in particular the print media, have been called the "fourth estate," and the "fourth branch of government."[8] Evidence that the media influence our culture and politics is plentiful. In one form or another, the **mass media**—newspapers and magazines, radio, television (broadcast, cable, and satellite), the Internet, films, recordings, books, and electronic communication—reach almost everyone in the United States.[9] The **news media** are the parts of the mass media that tell the public what is going on in the country and the world, although the distinctions between entertainment and news have become increasingly blurred. News programs often have entertainment value, and entertainment programs often convey news. Programs in this latter category include TV newsmagazines such as *60 Minutes* and *Dateline*; talk shows with hosts like Larry King, Oprah Winfrey, Sean Hannity, and Alan Colmes; and Jon Stewart's parody of the news, *The Daily Show*.

By definition, the mass media disseminate messages to a large and often heterogeneous audience. The mass media make money by appealing to this large audience. Because they must have broad appeal, their messages are often simplified, stereotyped, and predictable. But how much political clout do the media have? Two factors are important in answering this question: the media's pervasiveness and their role as a link between politicians and government officials and the public.

Where do Americans get their news? Until 1960, most people got their news from newspapers. Today, they rely primarily on television. Whenever there is a crisis—from the assassination of President John F. Kennedy in 1963 to the *Challenger* explosion in 1986 to the terrorist attacks on September 11, 2001—people are glued to their TV sets.

The Internet has become an increasingly important source of news for Americans, taking its place alongside print, radio, and television. The number of Americans going online for news has grown dramatically and promises to become even more politically important organizations like MoveOn increasingly use the Internet to reach the public.[10] The Internet enables people to obtain information on any subject and to get that information from multiple sources—some of which may be unreliable—at any time of the day or night.

The Pervasiveness of Television

Television has changed American politics more than any other invention. Television, with its concreteness and drama, has an emotional impact that print media can rarely match.[11] Television cuts across age groups, educational levels, social classes, and races. In contrast, newspapers provide more detail about the news and often contain contrasting points of view, at least on the editorial pages, that help inform the public.

mass media
Means of communication that reach the public, including newspapers and magazines, radio, television (broadcast, cable, and satellite), films, recordings, books, and electronic communication.

news media
Media that emphasize the news.

For more than 40 years, Americans have been getting their news primarily from television. Whenever there is a crisis, most people turn first to television for information. No event in recent history has done more to underscore the importance of television as the primary source of news in contemporary U.S. society than the terrorist attacks that took place on September 11, 2001.

Most Americans watch some kind of television news every day. The average American watches over four and one-half hours of television a day, and most homes have more than two television sets.[12] Television provides instant access to news from around the country and the globe, permitting citizens and leaders alike to observe firsthand events such as the capture of Saddam Hussein, a kidnapping in southern California, or an earthquake in Indonesia. This instant coverage increases the pressure on world leaders to respond quickly to crises, enables terrorists to gain widespread coverage of their actions, and elevates the president's role in both domestic and international politics.

The growth of around-the-clock cable news and information shows is one of the most important developments in recent years. Until the late 1980s, the network news programs on CBS, NBC, and ABC captured more than 90 percent of the audience for television news at set times in the morning and early evening. With the rise of cable television and the advent of the Internet, the broadcast networks now attract only about 44 percent of the viewing public.[13] CNN and FOX News attract 46 percent.[14]

Satellites, cable television, Internet search engines like Google or Yahoo, and DVDs make vast amounts of political information available 24 hours a day. These technologies eliminate the obstacles of time and distance and increase the volume of information that can be stored, retrieved, and viewed. They have also reduced the impact of single sources of broadcast or cable news. Competition from cable stations for viewing has put pressure on broadcast networks to remain profitable, which has meant reduced budgets for news coverage and a tendency to look for ways to boost the entertainment value of broadcast news.

One of the biggest changes in American electoral politics of the last half-century is that most voters now rely more on television commercials for information about candidates and issues and less on news coverage. Although debates and speeches by candidates generate coverage, the more pervasive battleground for votes is radio and TV ads. As a result, electoral campaigns now focus on image and slogans rather than on substance. Successful candidates must be able to communicate with voters through this medium. To get their message across to TV audiences, politicians increasingly rely on media advisers to define their opponent as well as themselves. These consultants also seek positive news coverage for their candidates, but news coverage of most congressional campaigns tends to be limited and shallow.

History Makers

Walter Cronkite

Walter Cronkite

For nearly 20 years (from 1962 to 1981), Walter Cronkite anchored the *CBS Evening News*. Throughout his long tenure, the public saw him as authoritative and fair—the "most trusted figure" in American life.* His reporting of such events as the assassination of President Kennedy and the NASA space flights, especially the Apollo XI flight to the moon, made him not only an observer of history but a part of it.

Cronkite began his career by working for small public relations firms, newspapers, and radio stations in the Midwest. In 1939, he went to work for United Press (UP), a "wire service" that provided news stories to many newspapers. While at the United Press, Cronkite reported extensively on World War II and the Nuremberg trials and helped open the UP'S Moscow bureau.† Cronkite joined CBS television in 1950, doing both news and entertainment programming. He hosted a documentary series named *Twentieth Century* (1957–1967) and later *21st Century* (1967–1970).

It was Cronkite's hosting of the *CBS Evening News*, however, that linked him to the growing importance of television news and to the visual imagery that reinforced its impact. His voice and manner made him seem mainstream and believable. He rarely showed emotion, which made the tears he shed during his reporting of the Kennedy assassination all the more exceptional.‡ He ended each nightly news program with the words, "And that's the way it is." Chet Huntley and David Brinkley of NBC led in the ratings until 1967, but from then on until his retirement, Cronkite was the ratings leader. Early news anchors like Cronkite, Huntley and Brinkley, and Edward R. Murrow not only reported the news but helped make television the most influential source of news for most Americans. ∎

*"Cronkite: Trust is 'Individual Thing,'" *USA Today*, July 16, 2002, p. 1A.
†Smithsonian Associates, *Walter Cronkite: A Lifetime Reporting the News*, at http://smithsonian associates.org/programs/cronkite/cronkite.asp, May 9, 2006.
‡Charles Wheeler, "Kennedy: The Enduring Allure," *British Broadcasting Company* (November 19, 2003) at http://news.bbc.co.uk/1/hi/world/americas/3265185.stm, September 1, 2006.

It was Cronkite's hosting of the CBS Evening News, however, that linked him to the growing importance of television news and to the visual imagery that reinforced its impact.

Candidates are not the only ones who have used television and radio to reach voters. Ads paid for by party soft money (unlimited until banned after the 2002 election), party independent expenditures, and electioneering by interest groups has equaled or exceeded what the candidates spent in a competitive race.[15] To voters, the messages from the parties and interest groups were indistinguishable from the messages from the candidates,[16] except that the tone was generally more negative.[17] Interest groups have also run ads for and against President Bush's Supreme Court nominees in hopes of mobilizing opinion.[18]

The amount of television news devoted to politics has been declining and now constitutes less than one minute per half-hour broadcast.[19] A major effort to get local television stations to devote a few minutes to candidate debate in their nightly local news ended up with stations averaging 45 seconds a night, or as one observer put it, just enough time to "let candidates clear their throats."[20] In 2002, a majority (56 percent) of local news broadcasts did not mention the campaigns in the seven weeks leading up to the election.[21] In 2004, local news focused more on the election, with 64 percent of local news broadcasts having at least one election story.[22]

In large urban areas, viewers rarely see stories about their member of Congress, in part because those media markets usually contain several congressional districts. Newspapers do a better job of covering politics and devote more attention to it than television stations do. The decline in news coverage of elections and voting, especially on television, has only increased the importance of political advertising on television, through the mail, and over the telephone.

In most contested referendums, advertising is the most important source of information for voters.[23] The campaign finance reforms enacted in 2002 will only increase the amount of **issue advocacy**, especially through the mail and over the telephone. As we discussed in Chapters 6 and 9, the Bipartisan Campaign Reform Act (BCRA) bans issue advocacy on television or radio that mentions a candidate by name in the two months before a general election or one month before a primary election. But it does not limit what groups can do through the mail, over the phone, or in person, and in 2004, a wide range of groups communicated directly with voters in these ways. This "ground war" had been growing in importance before passage of BCRA, but the reforms intensified the groups' use of these techniques. In battleground states or districts, voters were often canvassed by groups and then received mail and phone calls to reinforce the message. Even more effective are face-to-face conversations, especially with people the voter knows.

The Persistence of Radio

Television and the newer media have not displaced radio. On the contrary, radio continues to reach more American households than television does. Only one household in 100 does not have a radio, compared with two in 100 without a TV.[24] More than nine out of ten people listen to the radio every week, and eight out of ten do so every day.[25] Many Americans consider the radio an essential companion when driving. Americans get more than "the facts" from radio: They also get analysis and opinion from commentators and talk show hosts.

Political campaigns continue to use radio to communicate with particular types of voters. Because radio audiences are distinctive, campaigns can target younger or older voters, women, Hispanics, and so on. The Bush reelection campaign in 2004 made greater use of radio ads in these ways.[26] One particularly important source of news on the radio is National Public Radio (NPR). An estimated audience of 26 million listens to programs like *Morning Edition*.[27] NPR even rivals conservative radio commentator Rush Limbaugh for size of audience.[28]

The Continuing Importance of Newspapers

Despite vigorous competition from radio and television, Americans still read newspapers. Daily newspaper circulation has been declining for the past 30 years to less than 55 million nationwide—or less than one copy for every five people.[29] The circulation figures for newspapers reflect a troubling decline in readership among younger persons: The number of young people who read newspapers on a regular basis declined by almost a third between 1967 and 2005.[30]

In addition to metropolitan and local newspapers, we now have national newspapers. Created in 1982 by the Gannett Corporation, *USA Today*, with a circulation of more than 2.1 million, recently replaced the *Wall Street Journal* as America's top-circulating newspaper.[31] the *Wall Street Journal*, with a circulation of over 2 million, has long acted as a national newspaper specializing in business and finance. the *New York Times* has a national edition that is read by more than 1.6 million people.[32] Some major newspapers like the *Washington Post* have experienced sharp declines in readership.[33]

issue advocacy
Promoting a particular position or an issue by interest groups or individuals but not candidates. Much issue advocacy is often electioneering for or against a candidate and, until 2004, had not been subject to regulation.

The Changing Face of American Politics

Toward a More Representative Newsroom

The newspaper industry has worked hard to achieve greater diversity in the newsroom. The American Society of Newspaper Editors has stated that diverse newsrooms cover America's communities more effectively. Because many stories involve contacts with a diverse public, the industry adopted a goal to make all newsrooms representative of the nation as a whole by 2025. Although America's largest newspapers, such as the *New York Times* and *Washington Post*, have made progress toward a more representative newsroom, smaller papers have had much more difficulty attracting and retaining minority reporters. Thus, 100 percent of newspapers with circulations over 500,000 readers employ at least some minority reporters, compared to less than 30 percent of newspapers with circulations under 10,000 readers. Moreover, the percentage of minority journalists varies greatly from one region of the country to another. Newspapers in the Midwest and New England have the smallest percentage of minority reporters, while newspapers in the Western states have the highest percentage. ■

Diversity at U.S. Newspapers

	Women		Minority*	
	1999	**2006**	**1999**	**2006**
Position				
Supervisors	34%	36%	9%	11%
Copy-Layout Editors	40	42	11	12
Reporters	40	40	13	15
Photographers	26	27	15	18

*African American, Asian American, Native American, Hispanic.

SOURCE: American Society of Newspaper Editors, "Diversity in Newspaper Newsrooms," at www.asne.org/index.cfm?id=1, June 9, 2006.

The Internet

From its humble beginnings as a Pentagon research project in the 1960s,[34] the World Wide Web (WWW) has blossomed into a global phenomenon. There are now more than 8 billion documents on the Web,[35] and more than 85 million unique domains have been registered worldwide.[36] Many people mistakenly think the Internet and the WWW are the same thing. The truth is that the Internet was the original "giant international plumbing system" for accessing information. It permits information to travel between computers. The WWW is now the most popular way of using the Internet because it transmits pictures, data, and text. However, the WWW incorporates all of the Internet services and much more.

The Internet opens up resources in dramatic ways. One study found that nearly half of Americans go online to search for news on a particular topic; somewhat smaller proportions go online for updates on stock quotes and sports scores. For about 23 percent of people, the Internet is a primary source of news.[37] Internet users can also interact with other people or politicians about politics through electronic mail, chat rooms, and blogs. Younger people, including teenagers, use the Internet extensively for schoolwork, and nearly three in four of them prefer it to the library.[38] A remarkable 76 percent of teens get news online, and 51 percent of teens use the Internet every day.[39]

Candidates are now using the Web for fundraising. Once a candidate gains recognition, as Howard Dean did in his campaign to win the Democratic nomination for president in 2004, he or she can raise money quickly and inexpensively via the Web. Half of the estimated $40 million Dean raised in 2003 came through the Internet.[40] Ironically, Dean himself didn't use a computer until 1998 and had initially refused to have a government e-mail address when he was governor of Vermont.[41] John Kerry also found the Internet to be a boon to his fundraising in the

Extensive use of computers by young children has left them vulnerable to sexual predators and commercial fraud, opening the issue of whether government regulation is needed. Parental supervision remains the best protection.

general election campaign in 2004. The success of the parties and candidates in Internet fundraising may significantly change the way politics is financed. As people gain confidence in making credit card transactions via the Internet, they will probably contribute more to parties and candidates in this way.

The Web provides an inexpensive way to communicate with volunteers, contributors, and voters and promises to become an even larger component of future campaigns. Candidates now regularly maintain home pages where voters can learn about them and their stand on issues. While much is still unknown about the impact of the Internet, it has the potential to fragment the influence of other media.[42]

The Changing Role of the American News Media

The public has an appetite for instant news and analysis, at least when it comes to a crisis or major controversy. Americans spend on average an hour per day consuming news, and the older they are, the more time they devote to it.[43] Yet people are quick to criticize the media. As journalist James Fallows put it, "Americans have never been truly fond of their press. Through the last decade, however, their disdain for the media establishment has reached new levels. Americans believe that the news media have become too arrogant, cynical, scandal-minded, and destructive."[44]

How often have you or your friends blamed the media for being biased, criticized the frenzy that surrounds a particular story, or denounced the "if it bleeds, it leads" mentality of nightly television news? Yet the content and style of news coverage are driven by market research in which viewers and readers are asked what they want to see reported and how they want it presented. Advertising revenue is directly linked to the number of readers or viewers a media outlet has.

Media bashing has become a national pastime. Americans blame the media for everything from increased tension between the races, biased attacks on public officials, sleaze and sensationalism, increased violence in our society, and for being more interested in making money than in conveying information. Many in the media agree with these charges and think that the media are headed in the wrong direction.[45] But complaints about the media may simply be a case of criticizing the messenger to avoid dealing with the message. Assertions like "It's the media's fault that we have lost our social values" or "The media's preoccupation with the private lives of politicians turns Americans off to politics" are too broad. Americans tend to blame far more problems on the media than are warranted.

There are also occasional examples of fabrication or plagiarism, as in the case of Jayson Blair of the *New York Times*, who made up stories and plagiarized others, including one from a Texas newspaper about the family of Iraqi prisoner of war Jessica Lynch;[46] and Jack Kelley, a top reporter for *USA Today* who fabricated parts of many stories, including one article that made him a Pulitzer Prize finalist.[47] Cases like these have prompted these newspapers and the media in general to evaluate editorial review and standards of integrity, but they also provoked criticism of the media.

The news media have changed dramatically over the course of U.S. history. When the Constitution was being ratified, newspapers consisted of a single sheet, often published irregularly by merchants to hawk their services or goods. Delinquent subscribers and high costs meant that newspapers rarely stayed in business more than a year.[48] But the framers understood the importance of the press as a watchdog of politicians and government, and the Bill of Rights guaranteed freedom of the press.

Political Mouthpiece

The new nation's political leaders, including Alexander Hamilton and Thomas Jefferson, recognized the need to keep voters informed. Political parties as we know them did not exist, but the support the press had given to the Revolution had fostered a growing awareness of the political potential of newspapers. Hamilton recruited staunch Federalist John Fenno to edit and publish a newspaper in the new national capital of Philadelphia. Jefferson responded by attracting Philip Freneau, a

Agents of Change

Takema Robinson, Risë Wilson, and the Laundromat Project

Takema Robinson and Risë Wilson

QUESTIONS

How are the arts a form of political media?

Can the arts influence politics?

The media, including the arts, are rarely accessible to low-income Americans, which is why the Laundromat Project was launched in 2002 in a single laundromat in the Bedford-Stuyvesant neighborhood in Brooklyn, New York. The Laundromat Project seeks to provide information through the spoken word rather than through newspapers and television.

Two Columbia University graduates—Takema Robinson and Risë Wilson—began the Laundromat Project in 1992 because they wanted to create a way for low-income citizens to experience the arts and solve community problems at the same time. "The idea is to create a space that invites anyone to experience art in a meaningful way, without entering a museum and without having to have a background in art," says Wilson. "I've always been interested in art, but never gave myself permission to pursue it as a career."

Robinson and Wilson view art as an important, but often neglected form of media. By featuring HIV/AIDS, homelessness, and other local problems in the art they produce and show, Robinson and Wilson hope to engage visitors in conversations about how to solve the problems and make them more visible to the print and electronic media. Wilson is convinced that art has the power to "transform passive viewers into critical thinkers and actively engaged citizens." Moreover, coverage of the Laundromat Project has also generated concern about the problems it features through its art.

The Laundromat Project does not have a Web site, in part because its constituents rarely have Internet access. However, it has already generated significant coverage from the traditional news media. More important, it has created a new forum for Bedford-Stuyvesant residents to get information and a way to talk about tough problems through the art they experience. ∎

"Independent journalism! That is the watchword of the future in the profession. . . . an end of assaults that are not believed fully just but must be made because the exigency of party warfare demands them."

NEW YORK TRIBUNE EDITOR WHITELAW REID

talented writer and editor and a loyal Republican, to do the same for the Republicans. (Jefferson's Republicans later became the Democratic party.) The two papers became the nucleus of a network of competing partisan newspapers throughout the nation.

Although the two newspapers competed in Philadelphia for only a few years, they became a model for future partisan newspapers. The early American press served as a mouthpiece for political leaders. Its close connection with politicians and political parties offered the opportunity for financial stability—but at the cost of journalistic independence.

Financial Independence

During the Jacksonian era of the late 1820s and 1830s, the right to vote was extended to all free white adult males through the elimination of property qualifications. The press began to shift its appeal away from elite readers and toward the mass of less educated and less politically interested readers. The rising literacy rate reinforced this trend. These two forces—increased political participation by the common people and the rise of literacy among Americans—began to alter the relationship between politicians and the press.

Some newspaper publishers began to experiment with a new way to finance their newspapers. They charged a penny a paper, paid on delivery, instead of the traditional annual subscription fee of $8 to $10, which most readers could not afford. The "penny press," as it was called, expanded circulation and increased advertising, enabling newspapers to become financially independent of the political parties.

The changing finances of newspapers also affected the definition of news. Before the penny press, all news was political—speeches, documents, editorials—directed at politically interested readers.[49] The penny press reshaped the definition of news as it sought to appeal to less politically aware readers with human interest stories and reports on sports, crime, trials, fashion, and social activities.

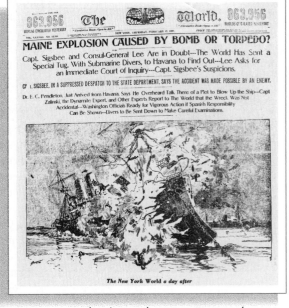

"Objective Journalism"

By the early twentieth century, many journalists began to argue that the press should be independent of the political parties. *New York Tribune* editor Whitelaw Reid eloquently expressed this sentiment: "Independent journalism! That is the watchword of the future in the profession. An end of concealments because it would hurt the party; an end of one-sided expositions . . . ; an end of assaults that are not believed fully just but must be made because the exigency of party warfare demands them."[50] Objective journalism was also a reaction to exaggeration and sensationalism in the news media, something called yellow journalism at the time.

As the nineteenth century progressed, literacy grew among the U.S. masses and more people began to get their news from newspapers. The popularization of the print media forced politicians and public officials to devote growing attention to their relationship with the press.

Journalists began to view their work as a profession and established professional associations with journals and codes of ethics. This professionalization of journalism reinforced the notion that journalists should be independent of partisan politics. Further strengthening the trend toward objectivity was the rise of the wire services, such as the Associated Press and Reuters, which remained politically neutral to attract more customers.

The Impact of Broadcasting

Radio and television nationalized and personalized the news. People could now follow events as they were happening and not have to wait for the publication of a newspaper. From the 1920s, when radio networks were formed, radio carried political speeches, campaign advertising, and coverage of political events such as national party conventions.[51] Politicians could now speak directly to listeners, bypassing the screening of editors and reporters. Radio also increased interest in national and international news because it enabled its audience to follow faraway events as if the listeners were actually there.

Beginning in 1933, President Franklin Roosevelt used radio with remarkable effectiveness. Before then, most radio speeches were formal orations, but Roosevelt spoke to his audience on a personal level, seemingly in one-on-one conversations. These "fireside chats," as he called them, established a standard that politicians still follow today. When Roosevelt began speaking over the microphone, he would visualize a tiny group of average citizens in front of him. He "would smile and light up" observers said, "as though he were actually sitting on the front porch or in the parlor with them."[52]

Television added a dramatic visual dimension, which increased audience interest in national events and allowed viewers to witness lunar landings and the aftermath of political assassinations, as well as more mundane events. By 1963, the two largest networks at the time, CBS and NBC, had expanded their evening news programs from 15 to 30 minutes. Today news broadcasting has expanded to the point that many local stations provide 90 minutes of local news every evening as well as a half-hour in the morning and at noon. Programs such as *20/20* and other newsmagazine shows are among the most popular in the prime-time evening hours.

Franklin D. Roosevelt was the first president to recognize the effectiveness of radio to reach the public. His fireside chats were the model for later presidents.

Cable television brought round-the-clock news coverage. During the Clinton impeachment hearings in 1998 and the 2000 Florida ballot-counting controversy, audiences around the world watched American cable news for its instantaneous coverage. C-SPAN now provides uninterrupted coverage of congressional deliberations, trials, and state and local governments.

Investigatory Journalism

News reporters today do more than convey the news; they investigate it, and their investigations often have political consequences. Notable examples of influential investigatory reporters include Seymour Hersh of the *New York Times*, who exposed what became known as the *Pentagon Papers*, revealing how the United States became involved in the Vietnam War; Nina Totenberg of National Public Radio, whose reporting on sexual harassment charges against Clarence Thomas helped force the Senate Judiciary Committee to extend the hearings on his confirmation to the U.S. Supreme Court; and Michael Isikoff of *Newsweek*, who broke the story of Bill Clinton's alleged perjury involving sexual misconduct with Monica Lewinsky.

In many ways the best example of the power of investigatory journalism is in the role the media played in the Watergate scandal.[53] Without persistent reporting by columnist Jack Anderson and two young *Washington Post* reporters, Robert Woodward and Carl Bernstein, the story would probably have been limited to a failed burglary of the headquarters of the Democratic National Committee at the Watergate building.[54] The news reporting, coupled with Congressional investigations, put a spotlight on the inner workings of the Nixon White House and the Nixon reelection committee, which had funded the attempted burglary and other political dirty tricks. Critical to the reporting on the broadening scandal, which ultimately brought down the president, was a confidential source, nicknamed Deep Throat, by Woodward and Bernstein.[55] In 2005, more than 30 years after these events, the former deputy director of the FBI, W. Mark Felt, identified himself as Deep Throat.

Media Consolidation

Australian-born Rupert Murdoch owns the FOX network, dozens of U.S. television stations, magazines, publishing organizations, and movie studios.

Local firms used to own the regional newspapers, radio, and television stations. As in other sectors of the economy, media companies have merged and created large conglomerates of many newspapers and broadcasting stations. Some of these conglomerates are multinational. Rupert Murdoch, founder of the FOX network, owns 35 television stations in the United States, 20th Century-Fox, HarperCollins publishers, and *TV Guide*, which has the largest magazine circulation in America. Murdoch's News Corporation recently purchased DirecTV and has moved its corporate headquarters to the United States.[56] Murdoch also owns seven newspapers abroad and two TV networks—one in Asia and one in the United Kingdom.[57]

When television was in its infancy, radio networks and newspapers were among the first to purchase television stations. These mergers established cross-ownership patterns that persist today. The Gannett Corporation, for example, owns 107 daily newspapers in the United States and United Kingdom and 21 television stations and cable television systems—assets that provide news coverage to nearly 20 million households in the United States.[58] The *Chicago Tribune* purchase of the Times-Mirror, publisher of the *Los Angeles Times*, resulted in combined assets of 16 newspapers, 26 TV stations, one radio station, and a growing online business.[59] More recently, newspapers like the *San Jose Mercury News* and the *Philadelphia Inquirer*, which were owned by the Knight Ridder Company, were purchased by the McClatchy Company, publisher of newspapers like the *Star Tribune* in Minneapolis-St. Paul and the *Sacramento Bee*. In such acquisitions some newspapers are subsequently sold to other conglomerates.

Making media companies more profitable is frequently cited as a reason for consolidation of media firms. Some conglomerates combine different kinds of media companies like movie studios, broadcast stations, cable stations, and newspapers.

Expanding to include global markets is another reason media companies have grown larger.[60] Some newspapers have purchased other newspapers in the same region, allowing consolidation of advertising and printing operations, and "in some cases even news divisions."[61]

The courts and the Federal Communications Commission (FCC)—an independent regulatory commission charged with licensing stations—are reinforcing the trend toward media conglomeration by relaxing and striking down regulations that limit cable and television network ownership by the same company.[62] In response to Congressional opposition, the FCC had lowered the maximum population a conglomerate could reach.[63] An appeals court called the FCC limits on media ownership "arbitrary and capricious" and overturned them,[64] a decision the Supreme Court let stand.[65] This is a matter the FCC is likely to consider again.

Will greater concentration of ownership of newspapers, television and radio stations, and broadcast, satellite, and cable networks limit or restrict the free flow of information to the public? Some see this as reducing the number of independent news providers, which are sometimes called news "gatekeepers." Such a concern is most evident in cities that had had two or more competing daily newspapers and now have only one newspaper that is owned by a large conglomerate. When reporting national news, local outlets depend heavily on news that national organizations like the Associated Press gather, edit, and distribute. As a result, some people contend that information is more diluted, homogenized, and moderated than it would be if the newspapers and broadcast stations were locally owned and the news was gathered and edited locally.[66] While the number of local broadcast stations has not declined to the same extent, conglomerates without ties to the community now own more of these stations.

At the national level, the cable networks—CNN, Fox, and others like Court TV and C-SPAN—have expanded the number of news sources available to the 86 percent of households with TV cable or satellite service.[67]

Regulation of the Media

The government has regulated the broadcast media in some form since their inception. Because of the limited number of television and radio frequencies, the national government through the FCC oversees their licensing, financing, and even content. The FCC continues to regulate licensing issues and occasionally fines or penalizes broadcasters who violate decency standards. For example, the FCC fined CBS for broadcasting as part of its Superbowl halftime show an incident in which Justin Timberlake removed part of Janet Jackson's costume, exposing her left breast.[68]

Mediated Politics

When dramatic events like the terrorist attacks on September 11, 2001, occur, we realize television's power to bring world events into our lives. Osama bin Laden, the purported mastermind behind those attacks, also understands the power of the media both inside and outside the United States, as evidenced by his continued release of videotapes of himself since the attacks.

The pervasiveness of newspapers, magazines, radio, and television confers enormous influence on the individuals who determine what we read, hear, and see because they can reach so much of the American public so quickly. With a large population scattered over a continent, both the reach and the speed of the modern media elevate the importance of the people in charge of them. The main source of campaign news in 2004 for more than two-thirds of Americans was television (68 percent), a proportion that has held relatively constant since 1992. Fifteen percent mentioned newspapers as the most important source. All other media trailed these two.[69]

Political parties and interest groups have long been political mediators that help organize the world of politics for the average citizen. Their role is less important today because the media now serve that function and political parties have largely lost

How Other Nations Govern

A Less-than-Free Press in Russia

Russia is a country struggling to establish a free press. After the fall of communism and its state-controlled media in the early 1990s, multiple, independent print and broadcast media emerged in Russia. Over time, both the number of these outlets and their ability to reach an audience has declined. NTV, an independent television channel, had been critical of Presidents Vladimir Putin and Boris Yeltsin, and of the Russian war against Islamic separatists in Chechnya. Russian government officials, claiming the station was corrupt,* took it over in 2001.

The government appointed Boris Jordan to head NTV after the takeover, only to fire him two years later over the way the channel covered a bloody takeover of a Moscow theater by Chechen terrorists, in which the Russian government's aggressive response resulted in many deaths among both the terrorists and their hostages. The moves against NTV have had a chilling impact on stations that are critical of the Putin government.† Today Russia has no independent national TV networks. Harassment of the media has not been limited to television. Journalists have been killed in suspicious circumstances, and the offices of independent newspapers have been ransacked.‡

Muzzling and intimidating the media or putting them out of business helped Putin's United Russia Party monopolize the news in the 2003 and 2004 elections, giving the party even more seats in Parliament and helping reelect Putin to the presidency. Putin justifies his media policies as preventing media moguls from becoming "king makers."§ A *Washington Post* article reported that the Kremlin's Web site, in publishing a news conference at which Presi-dent Bush criticized the lack of a free press in Russia, deleted all of Bush's critical statements and answers.‖ The waning of a free press casts a deepening shadow over Russian democracy itself. ∎

---

*"Media Muzzle," *The Economist*, April 21, 2001.
†"Unplugged," *The Economist*, U.S. Edition, June 28, 2003.
‡Christian Caryl and Eve Conant, "The Dead and the Silent," *Newsweek*, November 11, 2002, p. 39.
§Russia—Looking East," *Campaign*, September 27, 2002, p. 16.
‖Peter Baker, "In Russian Media, Free Speech for a Select Few," *Washington Post*, February 25, 2005, p. A18.

---

control over the nominating process (see Chapters 7 and 9). As a result, the candidates' perceived character and competence matter more than their party affiliations or platforms. The press, not the parties, evaluates these qualities.

The news media have also assumed the role of "speaking for the people." Journalists report what "the people" want and think, and then they tell the people what politicians and policy makers are doing about it. Politicians know they depend on the media to reach voters, and they are well aware that a hostile press can hurt or even destroy them. That explains why today's politicians spend so much time developing good relations with the press.

The Media and Public Opinion

Television's ability to present images and communicate events has influenced American public opinion. Television footage of the violence done to black and white protesters during the civil rights revolution of the 1950s and 1960s made the issue more real and immediate. News coverage of the war in Vietnam galvanized the antiwar movement in the United States because of the horrible images news shows brought into people's homes. The testimony of White House staff before the Senate Watergate and later House Judiciary committees further weakened confidence in the Nixon administration. Television coverage of the terrorist attacks on the World Trade Center and the Pentagon and the devastation left by Hurricane Katrina left indelible impressions on all who watched.

For a long time, analysts argued that political leaders wielded more influence in American politics than the media did. FDR's fireside chats symbolized the power of the politician over that of the news editor. Roosevelt spoke directly to his listeners over the radio in a way and at a time of his own choosing, and no network official could block or influence that direct connection. President John Kennedy's use of the televised press conference established similar direct contact with the public. President Ronald Reagan was nicknamed the "Great Communicator" because of his ability to talk persuasively and often passionately about public policy issues with the people through television. Both in office and in his reelection campaign, the terrorist attacks of September 11, 2001, were central to the image of President Bush as a strong leader. Controversy over the justification for going to war with Iraq, as discussed earlier in the chapter, became a major focus of the media in his second term and helped explain his substantial decline in the proportion of the public viewing his performance favorably. While his approval ratings had been as high as 80% in early 2002, President Bush spent most of 2006 dealing with approval ratings that hovered around 40% and even lower. Another measure of declining popularity was the smaller number of visits the President made to key battleground races in the midterm elections, and some campaigns signaled they did not welcome a presidential visit.

However, broadcasters and journalists are now so important to the political process that elected officials and politicians spend considerable time trying to learn how to use them to their advantage. Presidential events and "photo opportunities" are planned with the evening news and its format in mind.[70] Members of Congress use Capitol Hill recording studios to tape messages for local television and radio stations. The evening news frequently includes clips from White House press briefings.

Factors That Limit Media Influence on Public Opinion

The media can influence public opinion. Nevertheless, people are not just empty vessels into which politicians and journalists pour information and ideas. How people interpret political messages depends on a variety of factors: political socialization, selectivity, needs, and a person's ability to recall and comprehend the message.

POLITICAL SOCIALIZATION   We develop our political attitudes, values, and beliefs through an education process that social scientists call **political socialization**.[71] (See Chapters 4 and 8 for more detail on this process.) While not as important as family in influencing our values and attitudes,[72] the media are a socializing force and help shape public perceptions and knowledge. Face-to-face contacts with friends and business associates (*peer pressure*) often have far more impact than the information or views we get from an impersonal television program or newspaper article. Strong identification with a party also acts as a powerful filter.[73] A conservative Republican from Arizona might watch the "liberal Eastern networks" and complain about their biased news coverage while sticking to her own opinions. A liberal from New York will often complain about right-wing talk radio, even if he listens to it some nights on the way home from work (see Figures 10–1 and 10–2).

SELECTIVITY   People practice **selective exposure**—screening out messages that do not conform to their own biases. They subscribe to newspapers or magazines or turn to television and cable news outlets that support their views.[74] People also practice

political socialization
The process by which we develop our political attitudes, values, and beliefs.

selective exposure
The process by which individuals screen out messages that do not conform to their own biases.

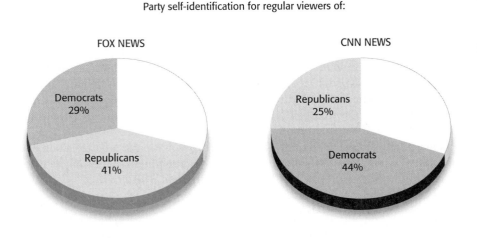

Party self-identification for regular viewers of:

FOX NEWS

CNN NEWS

FIGURE **10–1 Partisanship and Preferred News Source.**
SOURCE: *New York Times*, July 18, 2004.

FIGURE 10–2 Partisanship and News Source Credibility.

SOURCE: *New York Times*, July 18, 2004.

Do you believe all or most of what comes from:

	REPUBLICANS	DEMOCRATS
CBS News		
ABC News		
NBC News		
CNN		
FOX News		
MSNBC		
NPR		
C-SPAN		
Wall St. Journal		
New York Times*		

■ 2000   ■ 2004   * No data for 2000

---

selective perception

The process by which individuals perceive what they want to in media messages.

"Hey, do you want to be on the news tonight or not? This is a sound bite, not the Gettysburg Address. Just say what you have to say, Senator, and get the hell off."

selective perception—perceiving what they want to in media messages.[75] One dramatic example was the differing reactions of Democrats and Republicans to reports of President Clinton's sexual misconduct with Monica Lewinsky, a former White House intern, and the possibility that he encouraged her to lie under oath. In the first weeks after the story broke, Republicans were four times more likely than Democrats to believe that Clinton had been sexually involved with Lewinsky.[76] More than two-thirds of Republicans and Democrats agreed that Clinton committed perjury before the grand jury, but they had dramatically different opinions on whether Clinton should remain in office. Nearly two-thirds of Republicans wanted Clinton removed from office, while 63 percent of Independents and 87 percent of Democrats felt that Clinton should remain president.[77]

NEEDS People read newspapers, listen to the radio, or watch television for different reasons, often out of habit or because they want information.[78] Media affect people differently depending on whether they are seeking information about politics or want to be entertained. For those seeking entertainment, gossip about politicians' sex lives is more important than what those politicians' think about issues or how they vote. Members of the broader audience are also more likely to pay attention to news that directly affects their lives, such as interest rate changes or the price of gasoline.[79]

AUDIENCE FRAGMENTATION The growth of cable television and new media like the Web have reduced the dominance of broadcast media and newspapers in transmitting information. Because people are scattered across more press outlets and these outlets cover politics in varied ways, the impact of the press has become more diffuse. People can now tailor their news to their preferred point of view. A study of the 2004 election noted that "today's fractionalized media environment has taken the heaviest toll on local news, network news, and newspapers."[80] Fragmentation of the media audience has tended to counteract the impact of media conglomeration. But as media giants acquire both cable and broadcast stations and outlets (NBC, CNBC, MSNBC, for example), the trends may converge.

Are the Media Biased?

Americans tend to blame the media for lots of things. Conservatives complain, "The media are too liberal." Radio talk show host Rush Limbaugh even once said, "They all just happen to believe the same way. . . . They are part of the same culture as Bill Clinton."[81] Some liberals contend that the ruling class controls the mainstream press and that government propaganda distorts the facts. Conservatives say the press is too liberal in how it selects and interprets the news it covers. Liberals point to newspaper endorsements of Republican presidential candidates to support their claim that newspapers are biased in favor of conservative policies and candidates and cite FOX News as an example of conservative cable TV.

Newspapers, magazines, and television stations are business corporations concerned about profits. They work to boost circulation and ratings and must please their advertisers, sponsors, and stockholders. This leads some liberal critics to contend that the media reflect a conservative bias not only in what they report but also in what they choose to ignore. Political scientist Michael Parenti states that journalists "rarely doubt their own objectivity even as they faithfully echo the established political vocabularies and the prevailing politico-economic orthodoxy."[82]

Newspapers and television management go to some lengths to insulate reporters from their advertising and business operations, in part to reduce criticism about favorable treatment of large advertisers or the corporate owners. When the management of the *Los Angeles Times* attempted to foster closer relations between the business and news divisions, it was criticized.[83] News coverage also involves many reporters and a host of editors, all of whom have input into what is covered and how it is presented. This can provide another internal check on media bias.

Some commentators have suggested that a possible bias flows from the fact that reporters and editors become too friendly with the people and organizations they write about. According to David Broder of the *Washington Post*, many members of the print and television media have crossed the line that should divide objective journalism from partisan politics. Broder opposes the idea of journalists becoming government officials and vice versa.[84] Others argue that journalists with previous government service have close working relationships with politicians and can give us a valuable perspective on government without losing their professional neutrality.

Most reporters and editors pride themselves on impartial reporting of the facts.[85] But most reporters are liberal. Conservatives claim that even though many reporters and editors try to be impartial their personal political preferences influence the topics they cover and how they cover them.[86] Critics of this view counter that the idea that the media have a liberal bias is a myth. Rather, they point to conservative forces in the media like corporate ownership, which leads to a bias against unions, and to the disproportionate time and influence given to conservative radio, TV, and print pundits like Bill O'Reilly and Rush Limbaugh.[87]

A frequent criticism is the media's alleged political bias, whether liberal or conservative (see Table 10–1). But to whom are these critics referring? To reporters, writers, editors, producers, or owners of TV stations and newspapers? Do they assume that a journalist's personal politics will be translated into biased reporting? And does the public think so? Journalists are usually more liberal than the population as a whole; editors tend to be a bit more conservative than their reporters are; and media owners are more conservative still. Elite journalists—those who work for national news media organizations—tend to share a similar culture: cosmopolitan, urban, and upper-class. Their common worldview, which they may derive from their professional training, tends to govern their approach to the issues they cover and to what stories are covered.[88] The result, some critics contend, is that elite journalists give greater weight to points of view that correspond to their own version of reality.[89] The question of whether there is an ideological bias in the media has not been authoritatively answered; this has not stopped both liberals and conservatives from asserting a biased media.

One bias of the media that does not have a particular partisan or ideological slant is the bias toward sensationalism. Scandals of all types happen to liberals and conser-

"[Journalists] rarely doubt their own objectivity even as they faithfully echo the established political vocabularies and the prevailing politico-economic orthodoxy."

POLITICAL SCIENTIST MICHAEL PARENTI

TABLE 10–1 Partisanship and Ideology of Journalists, Policy Makers, and the Public

	Journalists	Policy Makers	Public
Party Identification			
Democrat	27%	43%	34%
Republican	4	24	28
Independent	55	26	21
Other	5	5	12
Don't Know/Refused	9	2	2
Self-Described Ideology			
Liberal	25%	25%	21%
Moderate	59	52	37
Conservative	6	18	35
Don't Know/Refused	11	5	7

SOURCE: The Kaiser Foundation, *The Role of Polls in Policy Making*, Combined Topline Results, June 2001, p. 27. www.kff.org/kaiserpolls/loader.cfm?url=/commonspot/security/getfile.cfm&PageID=13842.

vatives, Republicans and Democrats. Once the province of tabloids like the *National Enquirer,* stories about scandal have recently become commonplace in the mainstream media. For years, the media have seemed to gravitate to stories involving celebrities, sex, or both. From the O. J. Simpson murder trial in 1995 to the coverage of a missing intern who had been involved in an affair with a congressman, we have seen what some observers have called a media "feeding frenzy."[90] The intense and unrelenting focus on the scandal involving former President Bill Clinton and White House intern Monica Lewinsky is a clear example of the media's fondness for sensational coverage.

Newspapers and television news often set a tone of dissatisfaction with the performance of the national government and cynicism about politics and politicians. A critical tone may be an inevitable element of the mind-set of the press, but to whose benefit does that critical tone work? The media are accused of having an antireligion bias, a bias in favor of young viewers, and a bias toward fostering continuing crises.[91] The question is not whether the press is biased but whether a press bias—whatever the direction it may take—seeps into the content of the news. The answer to that question remains unclear.

Public Opinion

Two important influences of print and broadcast media on public opinion are *agenda setting* and *issue framing.*

AGENDA SETTING[92]   By calling public attention to certain issues, the media help determine what topics will become subjects of public debate and legislation.[93] However, the media do not have absolute power to set the public agenda. The audience and the nature of any particular issue limit it.[94] According to former Vice President Walter Mondale, "If I had to give up . . . the opportunity to get on the evening news or the veto power, . . . I'd throw the veto power away. [Television news] is the President's most indispensable power."[95] Ronald Reagan, more than any president before him, effectively used the media to set the nation's agenda. Reagan and his advisers carefully crafted the images and scenes of his presidency to fit television. Thus television became an "electronic throne."

Communicating through the media works, especially when it is—or at least appears to be—natural and unscripted. When President Bush first visited the scene of the destruction of the World Trade Center in New York City in September 2001, he took a bullhorn and said, "I can hear you. The rest of the world hears you, and the people who knocked these buildings down will hear all of us soon."[96] This action projected presidential leadership and empathy to a nation that was still shocked by the attacks.

ISSUE FRAMING Politicians, like everyone else, try to frame issues to win support, and they try to influence the "spin" the media will give to their actions or issues. The media provide the means for those seeking to communicate to define an issue or policy choice. Examples abound. Opponents of U.S. intervention in Bosnia in the 1990s tried to portray such action as another Vietnam. Objectors to normal trade relations with Communist China framed that relationship as a human rights travesty. When President Bill Clinton wanted to forestall a tax cut by the Republicans in Congress, he decried the resulting need to dip into the budget surplus to "rescue Social Security." People who favor the right to have an abortion define the issue as one of freedom of choice; those who oppose it define it as murder. In referendum campaigns, the side that wins the battle of defining what the referendum is about wins.[97]

In the 2004 election, voters indicated that the Iraq war and terrorism, the economy and jobs, and moral values were the most important issues. All of these issues had received a lot of attention in the media except "moral values," which prompted intense discussion after the election about what people meant by this response. The fact that gay marriage was on the ballot in 11 states and frequently mentioned in the campaign may help explain why one in five voters mentioned moral values.[98]

The Media and Elections

News coverage of campaigns and elections is greatest in presidential contests, less in statewide races for governor and U.S. senator, and least for other state and local races. Generally, the more news attention given the campaign, the less likely voters are to be swayed by any one source. Hence news coverage is likely to be more influential in a city council contest than in an election for president or the Senate. For most city elections, there are only one or two sources of information about what candidates say and stand for; for statewide and national contests, there are multiple sources.

Diversification of the news media lessens the ability of any one medium to influence the outcome of elections. Newspaper publishers who were once seen as key figures in state and local politics are now less important because politicians and their media advisers are no longer so dependent on newspapers and other news media to communicate their messages. Candidates can use ads on radio and television, direct mail, phone, the Web, and cable television to reach voters. In local contests, or even in larger settings like the Iowa caucuses or the New Hampshire primary, personal contact can also be important.[99]

Choice of Candidates

The extensive use of television has made looking and sounding good on television much more important. It has also led to the growth of the political consulting industry and made visibility the watchword in politics. Television strongly influences the public's idea of what traits are important in a candidate. A century ago, successful candidates needed a strong pair of lungs; today they need a telegenic appearance, a pleasing voice, and no obvious physical impairments. Back in the 1930s, the press chose not to show Franklin Roosevelt in his wheelchair or using crutches, whereas today the country wants to know every intimate detail of the president's health. The importance of the public's perception of these traits is evident in the ridicule often directed at candidates. In 2004, Kerry was described as "French-looking"[100] and flip-flopping on issues, and Bush as stubborn and smirking when Kerry spoke in the televised debates.

"I'm still undecided—I like Leno's foreign policy, but Letterman makes a lot of sense on domestic issues."

Consistent with the media's focus on personality is its highlighting of mistakes and gaffes by candidates and office holders. Long before Jon Stewart and *The Daily Show*, print and broadcast media devoted considerable attention to such things as Gerald Ford mistakenly classifying Poland as a free country in the 1976 presidential debates.[101] More recently, John Kerry made the mistake of ordering provolone on his Philly Steak sandwich (the only cheese option on an authentic Philly Steak sandwich is Cheez Whiz).[102] Some mistakes can be more than silly; George Romney's statement in 1968 that he had been brainwashed while on a tour of Vietnam by U.S. government officials helped end his campaign when it was mostly mistaken phrasing.[103]

Although the media insist that they pay attention to all candidates who have a chance to win, they also influence who gets such a chance. Consequently, candidates have to come up with creative ways to attract media attention. The late Paul Wellstone, in his 1996 campaign for the Senate in Minnesota, said in his advertisements that he did not have much money to pay for ads, so he would have to talk fast to cram what he had to say into fewer commercials. His witty commercial became a news event itself—it got Wellstone additional coverage. Sometimes a limited ad buy can generate funding for a much larger one. This was the case with the group that attacked the credibility and heroism of John Kerry in the 2004 presidential election; the Swift Boat Veterans for Truth turned a $550,000 ad buy[104] into millions of dollars in contributions to the group funding the airing of additional ads. Critical to this was the widespread news coverage generated by the controversy the first ad set off.[105] Without a presidential race in 2006 most ads focused on local races. One national group, VoteVets.org, ran ads on national cable television in the last days of the campaign criticizing President Bush's record in Iraq, Afghanistan, and the war on terror.

Campaign Events

Candidates schedule events—press conferences, interviews, and "photo ops"—in settings that reinforce their verbal messages and public image. A much-publicized example of such a staged event was President George W. Bush landing on the aircraft carrier USS *Lincoln* to announce the end of "major combat operations" in Iraq. While the event provided a dramatic backdrop for the president in his flight jacket, a debate ensued about the cost of the carrier remaining at sea an extra day,[106] and, more fundamentally, as the resistance to American forces in Iraq continued and intensified, Bush's declaration on the *Lincoln* seemed increasingly inappropriate. Many campaigns events fail to receive attention from reporters because they are edged out by other news stories and a sense that the events were staged to generate news coverage.

The parties' national conventions used to capture national attention. However, since party primaries now select candidates, the conventions no longer provide much suspense or make news except perhaps over who will be the vice presidential nominee. This is one reason why the networks have cut back their coverage of presidential nominating conventions. In 1952, the average television set was tuned to the political conventions for 26 hours, or an average of more than three hours a night for the eight nights of convention coverage.[107] During the 2000 presidential conventions, by contrast, the major networks provided only one or two hours of prime-time coverage each evening. Political parties have sought, in vain, to regain audience interest by relying on "movie stars, entertainment routines, and professionally produced documentaries to spice up their conventions."[108]

Technology

Although the expense associated with television advertising has contributed to the skyrocketing costs of campaigning, it has also made politics more accessible to more people. Thanks to satellites, candidates can conduct local television interviews without having to travel to local studios. Specific voter groups can be targeted through cable television or low-power television stations that reach homogeneous neighborhoods and small towns. Videocassettes with messages from the candidates further extend the campaign's reach.[109] All serious candidates for Congress and governor in

2000 and 2002 made themselves and their positions available through a home page on the World Wide Web.

Campaigns have primarily used the Internet and e-mail to reinforce voter preferences or help answer questions more than to reach and persuade more passive citizens. But with the Web, citizens can now interact with each other on a wide range of political topics. In this sense, the Web is something like a town meeting, but one that people can attend without leaving their homes or offices. In chat rooms on the Internet, people express ideas and respond to each other's opinions. Examples of chat rooms include Abortion Chat, Democrat Chat, Environment Chat, Republican Chat, and Congress Chat. Most chat rooms offer group discussions in which anyone can read and send messages, but in some chat rooms participants can also send private messages. As discussed earlier, the Internet has also become an important way for candidates and groups to raise funds.

Younger voters are much more likely to use the Internet to get campaign news than middle-aged and older voters. In a study of the 2004 election, nearly three times as many 18- to 29-year-olds said they used the Internet for news (20 percent), compared with only 7 percent of those over age 50 and 16 percent of persons aged between 30 and 49. Younger voters also relied much more on comedy TV shows like *The Daily Show* for campaign news.[110]

Image Making and Media Consultants

Candidates recognize that their messages about issues are often ignored. The press tends to emphasize goofs and gossip or tension among party leaders. Candidates in turn try to spin the news. Attempts to shape the news and portray candidates in the best possible light are not new. Presidential campaign sloganeering such as "Tippecanoe and Tyler Too" in 1840, "Honest Abe the Rail Splitter" in 1860, and "I Like Ike" in 1952 tried to convey the candidate's image. Radio, television, and the Web have expanded the ability to project images, and that expansion has in turn affected candidates' vote-getting strategies and their manner of communicating messages. Television is especially important because of the power of the visual image.

Television has contributed to the rise of new players in campaign politics: *media consultants,* campaign professionals who provide candidates with advice and services on media relations, advertising strategy, and opinion polling.[111] For example, candidates regularly receive consultants' advice on what colors work best for them, especially on television. Male U.S. senators often appear in light blue shirts with red ties, sometimes called "power ties." A primary responsibility of a campaign media consultant is to present a positive image of the candidate and to reinforce negative images of the opponent.

Some media consultants have been credited with propelling candidates to success. Dick Morris was seen as important to Clinton's resurgence after the Democrats lost control of Congress in 1994, until Morris had to resign from the White House staff because of a personal scandal. Republican consultant Mark McKinnon produced ads for President George W. Bush's 2000 and 2004 campaigns. Both parties have scores of media consultants who have handled congressional, gubernatorial, and referendum campaigns. These consultants have also been blamed for the negative tone and tactics of recent campaigns.

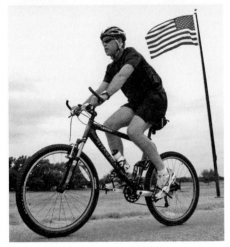

Media consultants have taken over the role party politicians formerly played. Before World War II, party professionals groomed candidates for office at all levels. Such leaders selected candidates whom they thought could win. They watched how potential candidates behaved under fire and judged their decisiveness, conviction, political skill, and other leadership qualities. Party professionals advised candidates which party and interest group leaders to placate, which issues to stress, and which topics to avoid.

Today, consultants coach candidates about how to act and behave on TV and what to discuss on the air. Consultants report the results of *focus groups* (small sample groups of people who are asked questions about candidates and issues in a discussion

A candidate's image often takes precedence over that candidate's message in the mass media. This was as true in the mid-nineteenth century as it is today. This is why image makers and media consultants have been in such high demand for so long. On the top, we see a portrait of Abraham Lincoln as "Abe the Rail Splitter." On the bottom, we see George W. Bush riding a mountain bike.

Government's Greatest Endeavors

Promoting Space Exploration

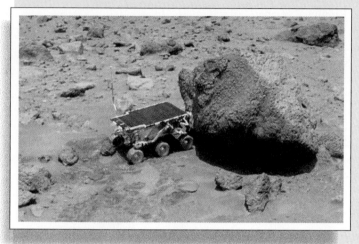

The robotic Sojourner rover vehicle on the surface of Mars

QUESTIONS

Should the United States go back to the moon and on to Mars?

What are the benefits of space exploration for the nation?

The media focuses on many stories about the latest crisis or scandal in the federal government. However, there is also sometimes good news, especially when the federal government gives the public a cause for national pride.

Space exploration has often supplied the government's best news of all. The race to the moon was one of the great stories of the 1960s, and generated intense national interest. Having challenged the nation in 1961 to send a man to the moon and bring him back safely by the end of the decade, President John F. Kennedy set a goal that seemed nearly impossible. The United States had not yet sent its first human into orbit when he announced the goal, let alone begun developing the technology to orbit and land on the moon.

Nevertheless, the United States met Kennedy's goal with five months to spare when members of the crew of *Apollo 11* planted the American flag on the moon in the summer of 1969. The astronauts also left a plaque that read in part, "We came in peace for all mankind."

The space program has produced many successes, including spectacular pictures from unmanned space probes to Mars and the outer planets, and important knowledge about the history of the universe from the Hubble Space Telescope. But it has also produced great failures, including the *Challenger* shuttle disaster in 1985, which generated the greatest public interest of any story during the past 25 years.

The United States has now announced that its next great goal is to return to the moon, and then on to Mars within the next two decades. ∎

---

setting) and *public opinion polls,* which in turn determine what the candidate says and does. Some critics allege that political consultants have become a new "political elite" who can virtually choose candidates by determining in advance which men and women have the right images or at least images that the consultants can restyle for the widest popularity.[112] But political consultants who specialize in media advertising and image making know their own limitations in packaging candidates. As one media consultant put it, "It is a very hard job to turn a turkey into a movie star; you try instead to make people like the turkey."[113]

The Media and Voter Choice

As television has become increasingly important to politics, and as such reforms as primary elections have weakened the political parties, and made news coverage of candidates more important, the question arises, what difference does the media make?

SUBSTANCE OVER PERSONALITY   Some critics think reporters pay too much attention to candidates' personality and background, and not enough attention to issues and policy. Others say character and personality are among the most important characteristics for readers and viewers to know about. The public appetite for stories on candidates' personal strengths and weaknesses is not new and is likely to continue. Making our campaigns more substantive and fostering election news coverage that reflects this is challenging in part because of the many contests in each media market. Some groups have called for television stations to include brief three-to-five-minute live candidate debates in their evening news programs.[114] To date, only a few stations have implemented the idea.

The influence of the media on the public varies by level of sophistication of the voters. Better informed and more educated voters are more sophisticated and therefore less swayed by new information from the media.[115] But for the public generally, other scholars contend that "television news is news that matters."[116]

THE HORSE RACE   A common tendency in the media is to comment less on a candidate's position on issues than on a candidate's position in the polls compared with other candidates—what is sometimes called the **horse race**.[117] "Many stories focus on who is ahead, who is behind, who is going to win, and who is going to lose, rather than examining how and why the race is as it is."[118] Reporters focus on the tactics and strategy of campaigns because they think such coverage interests the public.[119] The media's propensity to focus on the "game" of campaigns displaces coverage of issues.

NEGATIVE ADVERTISING   Paid political advertising, much of it negative in tone, is another source of information for voters. Political advertising has always attacked opponents, but recent campaigns have taken on an increasingly negative tone. A rule of thumb in the old politics was to ignore the opposition's charges and thus avoid giving one's rival importance or standing. Today candidates trade charges and counter-charges.

Voters say the attack style of politics turns them off, but most campaign consultants believe that negative campaigning works. This seeming inconsistency may be explained by evidence suggesting that campaigns that foster negative impressions of the candidates contribute to lower turnout.[120] Negative advertising may thus discourage some voters who would be inclined to support a candidate (a phenomenon known as *vote suppression*) while making supporters more likely to vote.

INFORMATION ABOUT ISSUES   In recent elections, the media have experimented with a more issues-centered focus, what has been called *civic journalism*. With funding from charitable foundations, some newspapers have been identifying the concerns of community leaders and talking to ordinary voters and then writing campaign stories from their point of view.[121] Some newspaper editors and reporters disagree with this approach; they believe the media should stick to responding to newsworthy events. Advocates of civic journalism counter that news events like murders and violence often overshadow coverage of issues that concern the community.

MAKING A DECISION   Newspapers and television seem to have more influence in determining the outcome of primaries than of general elections,[122] probably because voters in a primary are less likely to know about the candidates and have fewer clues about how they stand. By the time of the November general election, however, party affiliation, incumbency, and other factors diminish the impact of media messages. The mass media are more likely to influence undecided voters who, in a close election, can determine who wins and who loses.

ELECTION NIGHT REPORTING   Does TV coverage on election night affect the outcome of elections? Election returns from the East come in three hours before the polls close on the West Coast. Because major networks often project the presidential winner well before polls close in western states, some western voters have been discouraged from voting. This has dampened voter turnout in congressional and local elections. In a close presidential election, however, such early reporting may stimulate turnout because voters know their vote could determine the outcome. In short, television reporting may make voters believe their vote is meaningless when one candidate appears to be winning by a large margin.[123]

At 7:50 P.M. (EST) on election night, November 7, 2000, television networks projected that Al Gore had won Florida, but they soon had second thoughts and revoked

horse race
A close contest; by extension, any contest in which the focus is on who is ahead and by how much rather than on substantive differences between the candidates.

their announcement. Hours later FOX News projected Bush winning Florida. The truth was that the vote in Florida was by every measure too close to call and no network should have called the race. In the days and weeks after the election, the Voter News Service (VNS) admitted that its Florida sample was flawed, that it underestimated the Florida absentee vote, and that it relied on incomplete actual vote totals. The mistaken projections by the networks were embarrassing. Tom Brokaw of NBC said, "That's not 'an egg' on our faces; that's 'an omelet.'"[124]

In 2002 and 2004, the media exit polls were again controversial. On election day in 2002, the networks that sponsor the VNS, which conducts the media exit polling, announced that they would not be releasing exit poll numbers nor would they be projecting winners. VNS gathered data on election day but did not have confidence in its ability to accurately predict contests. Viewers on election night 2002 thus got what many had wanted, a night with only local exit polling. Exit polls caused additional controversy in the aftermath of the 2004 presidential election. The controversy arose because leaks of early exit polls in the media showed John Kerry winning Ohio.[125]

The Media and Governance

The press rarely follows the policy process to its conclusion. Rather, it leaves issues at the doorstep of public officials. By the time a policy about a political issue has been formulated and implemented, the press has moved on to another issue. When policies are being formulated and implemented, decision makers are at their most impressionable, yet the press has little impact at this stage.[126]

Lack of press attention to how policies are implemented explains in part why we know less about how government officials go about their business than we do about heated legislative debates or presidential scandals. Only in the case of a policy scandal, such as the lax security surrounding nuclear secrets at Los Alamos, does the press take notice.

Some critics contend that the media's pressuring policy makers to provide immediate answers forces them to make untimely decisions. Such quick responses may be a particular danger in foreign policy:

> If an ominous foreign event is featured on TV news, the president and his advisers feel bound to make a response in time for the next evening news broadcast. . . . If he does not have a response ready by the late afternoon deadline, the evening news may report that the president's advisers are divided, that the president cannot make up his mind, or that while the president hesitates, his political opponents know exactly what to do.[127]

Political Institutions and the News Media

Presidents have become the stars of the media, particularly television, and have made the media their forum for setting the public agenda and achieving their legislative aims. Presidential news conferences command attention (see Table 10–2). Every public activity a president engages in, both professional and personal, is potentially newsworthy; a presidential illness can become front-page news, as can the president's vacations and pets.

A president attempts to manipulate news coverage to his benefit. Examples of this include the Bush administration's decision to embed reporters with the American forces during the early stages of the Iraq war. Presidents or their staff also selectively leak news to reporters. Presidents use speeches to set the national agenda or spur congressional action. Presidential travel to foreign countries usually boosts popular support at home, thanks to largely favorable news coverage. Better yet for the president, most coverage of the president—either at home or abroad—is favorable to neutral.[128] President Clinton's trip to Israel during the height of the furor surrounding his impeachment may have helped distract attention from his domestic problems in both senses of that word.

TABLE 10–2 Presidential Press Conferences: Joint and Solo Sessions, 1913–April 20, 2006

President	Total	Solo	Joint	Joint as Percentage of Total	Months in Office	Solo Sessions per Month	Solo Sessions per Year
Wilson	159	159	0	0	96	1.7	19.9
Harding	No Transcripts Available				29		
Coolidge	521	521	0	0	67	7.8	93.4
Hoover	268	267	1	0.4	48	5.6	66.8
Roosevelt	1020	984	33	3.2	145.5	6.8	81.1
Truman	324	311	13	4.0	94.5	3.3	39.5
Eisenhower	193	192	1	0.5	96	2.0	24.0
Kennedy	65	65	0	0	34	1.9	23.0
Johnson	135	118	16	11.9	62	1.9	22.8
Nixon	39	39	0	0	66	0.6	7.1
Ford	40	39	1	2.5	30	1.3	15.6
Carter	59	59	0	0	48	1.2	14.8
Reagan	46	46	0	0	96	0.5	5.8
G. H. W. Bush	143	84	59	41.3	48	1.8	21.0
Clinton	193	62	131	67.9	96	0.7	7.8
G. W. Bush	125	27	98	78.4	63	0.4	5.1

SOURCE: Chart from Martha Joynt Kumar, "Presidential Press Conferences: The Evolution of an Enduring Forum," *Presidential Studies Quarterly*, vol. 35, no. 1, March 2005, and Kumar 2006 updates.
NOTE: A joint press conference is one where the president answers questions along with someone else, most often a foreign leader. In a solo session, only the president answers questions. There are three missing transcripts for Roosevelt and one for Johnson, which makes it impossible to determine whether those sessions were solo or joint ones.

Members of Congress have long sought to cultivate positive relations with news reporters in their states and districts. Members of Congress typically have a press relations staffer who informs local media of newsworthy events, produces press releases, and generally tries to promote the senator or representative.[129] Congress also provides recording studios for taping of news segments, and both parties have recording studios near the Capitol explicitly for electoral ads. Finally, politicians often appear on talk radio, which they can readily do from their offices in Washington. But the focus of this media cultivation is on the individual member and not the institution as a whole.

Congress is a fragmented body that is usually unable to act quickly, made up as it is of 435 representatives, 100 senators, scores of committees and subcommittees, and complex rules. It is also more likely to get negative coverage than either the White House or the Supreme Court. Unlike the executive branch, it lacks an ultimate spokesperson, a single person who can speak for the whole institution.[130] Congress does not make it easy for the press to cover it. Whereas the White House attentively cares for and feeds the press corps, Congress does not arrange its schedule to accommodate the media; floor debates, for example, often compete with committee hearings and press conferences.[131] Singularly dramatic actions rarely occur in Congress; the press therefore turns to the president to describe the activity of the federal government on a day-to-day basis and treats Congress largely as a foil to the president. Most coverage of Congress is about how it reacts to the president's initiatives.[132]

The federal judiciary is least dependent on the press. The Supreme Court does not rely on public communication for political support. Rather, it depends indirectly on public opinion for continued deference to or compliance with its decisions.[133] The Court does not allow television cameras to cover oral arguments, rarely allows audio taping, and bars reporters when it votes. The Court has strong incentives to avoid being seen as manipulating the press, so it retains an image of aloofness from politics and public opinion. The justices' manipulation of press coverage is far more subtle and complex than that of the other two institutions.[134] For example, the complexity of the Supreme Court's decision in 2000's Florida vote recount case, with multiple dissents and concurrences and no press release or executive summary, made broadcast reporting on the decision difficult.

The news media may be most influential at the local level.[135] Most of us have multiple sources for finding out what is happening in Washington that act as a check on the biases and limitations of reporters who cover national government and policy. But when it comes to finding out about the city council, the school board, or the local water district, most of us depend on the work of a single reporter. Consequently, the media's influence is much greater because there are fewer news sources.

Not all who think the media are powerful agree that their power is harmful. After all, they argue, the media perform a vital educational function. Almost 70 percent of the public thinks the press is a watchdog that keeps government leaders from doing bad things.[136] At the least, the media have the power to mold the public agenda; at most, in the words of the late Theodore White, they have the power to "determine what people will talk and think about—an authority that in other nations is reserved for tyrants, priests, parties, and mandarins."[137]

Summary

1. The news media include newspapers, magazines, radio, television, films, recordings, books, and electronic communications, in all their forms. These means of communication have been called the "fourth branch of government."

2. The news media are a pervasive feature of American politics and generally help define our culture. New communications technologies have made the media more influential. The news media are a link between politicians and government officials and the public.

3. Our modern news media emerged from a more partisan and less professional past. Today the media is independent from political parties, and journalists strive for objectivity and see themselves as important parts of the political process. They also engage in investigative journalism.

4. Broadcasting on radio and television has changed the news media, and most Americans use television and radio as primary news sources. The role of corporate ownership of media outlets, especially media conglomerates, raises questions about media competition and orientation.

5. The mass media's influence over public opinion is significant but not overwhelming. People may not pay much attention to the media or may not believe everything they read or see or hear. They may be critical or suspicious of the media and hence resistant to it. People tend to filter the news through their political socialization, selectivity, needs, and ability to recall or comprehend the news.

6. Both conservatives (who charge that the media are too liberal) and liberals (who claim that the media are captives of corporate interests and major advertisers) criticize the media as biased. Little evidence exists of actual, deliberate bias in news reporting.

7. Mass media news helps set the public agenda—determining what problems will become the issues that people think about and discuss. The media are also influential in defining issues for the general public.

8. Media coverage both before and after the national convention dominate presidential campaigns. Because of the way the media cover elections, most people seem more interested in the contest as a game or "horse race" than in seriously discussing issues and candidates. Another effect has been the rise of image making and the media consultant.

9. The press serves as both observer and participant in politics, as a watchdog, agenda setter, and check on the abuse of power, but it rarely follows the policy process to its conclusion.

Further Reading

ERIC ALTMAN, *What Liberal Media? The Truth About Bias and the News* (Basic Books, 2003).

STEPHEN ANSOLABEHERE AND **SHANTO IYENGAR,** *Going Negative: How Attack Ads Shrink and Polarize the Electorate* (Free Press, 1996).

BEN H. BAGDIKIAN, *The New Media Monopoly* (Beacon Press, 2004).

BRUCE BIMBER AND **RICHARD DAVIS,** *Campaigning Online: The Internet in U.S. Elections* (Oxford University Press, 2003).

TIMOTHY E. COOK, *Governing with the News: The News Media as a Political Institution* (University of Chicago Press, 1998).

TIMOTHY E. COOK, *Making Laws and Making News: Press Strategies in the U.S. House of Representatives* (Brookings Institution Press, 1990).

RICHARD DAVIS, *The Press and American Politics: The New Mediator,* 3d ed. (Prentice Hall, 2000).

ROBERT M. ENTMAN AND **W. LANCE BENNETT,** EDS., *Mediated Politics: Communication in the Future of Democracy* (Cambridge University Press, 2000).

JAMES FALLOWS, *Breaking the News: How the Media Undermine American Democracy* (Pantheon Books, 1996).

STEPHEN J. FARNSWORTH AND **S. ROBERT LICHTER,** *Mediated Presidency: Television News & Presidential Governance* (Rowman & Littlefield, 2005).

JAMES G. GIMPEL, J. CELESTE LAY, AND **JASON E. SCHUKNECHT,** *Cultivating Democracy: Civic Environments and Political Socialization in America* (Brookings Institution Press, 2003).

BERNARD GOLDBERG, *Bias: A CBS Insider Exposes How the Media Distort the News* (Harper Paperbacks, 2003).

DORIS A. GRABER, *Mass Media and American Politics,* 7th ed. (CQ Press, 2005).

KENNETH M. GOLDSTEIN AND **PATRICIA STRACH,** *The Medium and the Message: Television Advertising and American Elections* (Prentice Hall, 2004).

RODERICK P. HART, *Campaign Talk: Why Elections Are Good for Us* (Princeton University Press, 2000).

SHANTO IYENGAR AND **DONALD R. KINDER,** *News That Matters: Television and American Opinion* (University Of Chicago Press, 1989).

KATHLEEN H. JAMISON, *The Press Effect: Politicians, Journalists, and the Stories That Shape the Political World* (Oxford University Press, 2003).

PHYLISS KANISS, *Making Local News* (University of Chicago Press, 1991).

HOWARD KURTZ, *Spin Cycle: Inside the Clinton Propaganda Machine* (Free Press, 1998).

S. ROBERT LICHTER, STANLEY ROTHMAN, AND **LINDA S. LICHTER,** *The Media Elite* (Adler & Adler, 1986).

PIPPA NORRIS, *A Virtuous Circle: Political Communications in Post-Industrial Societies* (Cambridge University Press, 2000).

DONALD A. RITCHIE, *Reporting from Washington: The History of the Washington Press Corps* (Oxford University Press, 2006).

CASS SUNSTEIN, *Republic.com* (Princeton University Press, 2001).

DARRELL M. WEST, *Air Wars: Television Advertising in Election Campaigns, 1952–1992,* 4th ed. (CQ Press, 2005).

KeyTerms

mass media, p. 282

news media, p. 282

issue advocacy, p. 285

political socialization, p. 293

selective exposure, p. 293

selective perception, p. 294

horse race, p. 301

IT WAS MEANT TO BE A VICTORY THAT COULD BE SAVORED ALL THE

Price of Victory

ORIGINALLY AIRED: 3/25/04

PROGRAM: **Nightline**

RUNNING TIME: 14:34

way through the 2004 election. When the president signed the Medicare bill into law last December, it was a landmark event. This bill had managed to achieve what seniors had been demanding for years — prescription drug coverage. That's definitely something to celebrate. Well, a funny thing happened on the way to the bill becoming law: accusations of bribery, lying, intimidation, political shenanigans — it has become quite a Washington drama. A bureaucrat who you probably wouldn't normally hear about testified on Capitol Hill. Richard Foster is the chief actuary of the Medicare program and he says that his boss threatened to fire him if he publicized his estimates of how much the Medicare bill would actually cost. His boss happens to be a political appointee. The bill that passed had a cost estimate of around $400 billion. Foster's estimate — $534 billion — became public a month after the signing of the bill. Needless to say, people are furious, including Republicans who now say if they knew then what they know now, they would not have voted for the bill.

Then there is that story of the endless vote in the House — a fifteen-minute roll call that stayed open for three hours. A lot of arm-twisting occurred that night, including allegations that retiring Congressman Nick Smith (R-Michigan) was told that if he voted for the bill his son would get $100,000.00 worth of help for his upcoming congressional race. Smith voted against the bill but there is another investigation of this allegation.

There are some people who roll their eyes at the very thought of the congressional process, but this is a dramatic one. People are really emotional about it, as you will see in this program.

Critical Thinking Questions

After viewing "PRICE OF VICTORY" *on your* ABCNEWS DVD *answer the following questions.*

1. IN "PRICE OF VICTORY," of what does Medicare actuary Richard Foster accuse the administration?

2. IN THE PROCESS OF PASSING the 2003 Medicare bill, what was unusual in regard to the timing of the vote?

3. IN "PRICE OF VICTORY," of what does Representative Nick Smith accuse the House leadership?

4. YOUR TEXT DESCRIBES THE PROCESS by which bills become laws. How does the process in the text differ from the process in the video?

PRESCRIPTION
DRUGS
NOW

307

Chapter 11

Congress

THE PEOPLE'S BRANCH

★

T IS DIFFICULT TO REMEMBER A MEMBER OF CONGRESS WHO FELL SO FAR AND SO FAST AS TEXAS REPUBLICAN TOM DELAY. ONCE KNOWN AS "THE HAMMER" FOR HIS ABILITY TO EN-FORCE PARTY DISCIPLINE AFTER REPUBLICANS CAPTURED THE HOUSE MAJORITY IN 1994, DELAY MOVED QUICKLY UPWARD TO BECOME WHIP IN 1994 AND MAJORITY LEADER IN 2002. HIS FUTURE SEEMED LIMITLESS.

ONLY TWO YEARS LATER, HOWEVER, DELAY WAS FIGHTING FOR HIS POLITICAL LIFE. THE FIRST BLOW CAME IN SEPTEMBER 2004, when the House Committee on Standards of Official Conduct formally punished him for improper conduct during the 2003 Medicare prescription drug debate. The second blow came a month later when the committee warned DeLay for creating the appearance that donors could buy his special attention on energy legislation with campaign contributions. The third blow came in late 2005 when DeLay was charged with violating Texas election laws in the effort to redraw the state's 32 congressional districts to favor Republican candidates. Although he temporarily stepped down as majority leader to fight the charges, he remained immensely popular among House conservatives, and seemed likely to return to the House.

DeLay had yet to face his greatest challenge, however. Only two months after his arrest, DeLay was linked to an emerging scandal involving a Washington, D.C., "super-lobbyist" named Jack Abramoff. Abramoff had made more than $80 million in lobbying fees by protecting certain Native American tribes from federal gambling regulation, as well as by preventing other Native American tribes from opening new casinos. But most of the money never went to lobbying at all. On January 6, 2006, Abramoff pled guilty to federal charges that he had taken much of the money for himself, none of which he reported as taxable income to the Internal Revenue Service. He also admitted that he had used some of the money to give DeLay and other members of Congress free golfing trips, meals, and concert tickets in direct violation of congressional ethics rules.

Abramoff's guilty plea led to even further allegations of congressional corruption, including a *Time* magazine cover story that labeled Abramoff "The Man Who Bought Washington." As the investigation moved ever closer to DeLay's own conduct, House Republicans privately demanded his resignation as majority leader. Only four years after he took the post, DeLay became just another member of Congress. And only a few months later, he resigned from Congress to return to private life and a fight to stay out of prison.

DeLay's resignations show just how important the ethics issue is to most Americans. They may not know the fine points of campaign finance law, but they believe that campaign contributions matter to legislative action. They also may not know how lobbyists work the legislative process, but they believe that free trips, meals, and concert tickets are wrong. And they may not know how a bill becomes a law, but they believe that members of Congress often make special

"Democrats and Republicans may disagree on 75% of the issues. But if we agree and implement the remaining 25%, the country is 100% better off than before."

REPRESENTATIVE STEVE ISRAEL (D-N.Y.)

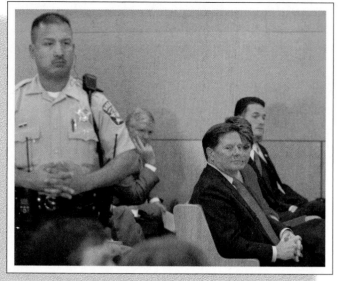

Representative Tom DeLay awaits court action on charges that he violated Texas state election laws by accepting corporate money that was then directed toward the election of state legislators. Using corporate money in state legislative campaigns is illegal in Texas.

"In the short run, everybody plays and nearly everybody wins. Yet the institution bleeds from 435 separate cuts."

POLITICAL SCIENTIST RICHARD F. FENNO JR.

deals to pass legislation. Not surprisingly, most Americans believe that members of Congress will say almost anything to get elected, then forget the public once they enter office.

Americans expect Congress to act on important issues such as immigration reform, gasoline prices, and taxes, all of which were on the legislative agenda as the lobbying scandal intensified. And most members of Congress do just that. Although some members are corrupt, the vast majority of members turn to conscience and the national interest when they have to make hard decisions on budgets, taxes, and war. Although they define the national interest differently, most members take their jobs very seriously, which is why DeLay's fall is so troubling. His behavior confirms the public's distrust of Congress during a time when Congress has never needed trust more.

In this chapter, we examine how the framers designed the legislative branch, and how it actually works today. We will also explore the role of interest groups, colleagues, congressional staff, the two parties, and the president in shaping decisions; explore the ethics issue in more detail; and discuss how a bill becomes a law.

Before turning to these questions, however, it is first important to ask how members of Congress reach office in the first place. The way we elect members of the House and Senate has a great deal to do with how they behave once in office, and it influences everything from committee assignments to legislative interests. We will also ask why individual members of Congress win reelection so easily.

Congressional Elections

There is only one Congress in the Constitution, but the 435 House members and 100 senators serve under very different election calendars. Because all House members serve two-year terms, while senators serve six-year terms, House members start worrying about the next election earlier in their terms of office. And because all House seats are up for election every two years, while only a third of Senate seats are up for election every two years, the House as a whole is more sensitive about issues that might affect elections than is the Senate as a whole. The framers believed that these rules would make the House and its members much more sensitive than senators to the opinions of their **constituents**, meaning residents of their districts or states.

House members and senators also run for their first elections under slightly different entry rules. House members must be 25 years old at the time they take office and must have been citizens for seven years, while senators must be 30 years old and have been citizens for nine years. House and Senate candidates must be residents of the states from which they are elected. By setting the Senate's requirements higher and giving its members a six-year term, the framers hoped the Senate would act as a check against what they saw as the less predictable House. Concerned about the "fickleness and passion" of the House of Representatives, James Madison in particular saw the Senate as "a necessary fence against this danger."[1]

Because all House members must defend their record every two years, the public has more influence over the House than the Senate. The willingness of "House members to stand and defend their own votes or voting record contrasts sharply with their disposition to run and hide when a defense of Congress might be called for," writes political scientist Richard F. Fenno Jr. "Members of Congress run *for* Congress by running *against* Congress. The strategy is ubiquitous, addictive, cost-free, and foolproof. . . . In the short run, everybody plays and nearly everybody wins. Yet the institution bleeds from 435 separate cuts."[2]

However, this does not mean that senators are free to ignore their constituents. Because the framers did not limit the number of terms House members or senators can serve, they must defend their records at some point if they want to stay in office.

constituents
The residents of a congressional district or state.

Drawing District Lines

The framers of the Constitution set the Senate apart from the House in respect to what population each serves. Every state has two U.S. senators, each of whom represents the entire state. Seats in the House of Representatives serve districts within their states, while senators serve the entire state. A state's population determines the number of districts in the state—hence, states with more citizens have more districts. The only restriction is that every state must have at least one member of the House. In states with fewer citizens, such as South Dakota and Wyoming, there are two senators and one representative, which means that all three represent the state as a whole, although on different electoral calendars. Because states with more citizens have more House members, they have a stronger voice in the House; because all states have two senators, and two senators only, states with fewer citizens have a stronger voice in the Senate.

The exact number of districts in each state is determined by a national census of the population taken every ten years, which is also specified in the Constitution. When population changes, so does the potential number of districts in each state. This process of changing the number of seats is called **reapportionment**. There are 435 seats in the House of Representatives, each one representing roughly 650,000 citizens. House members from small states often represent even fewer—Wyoming has just 580,000 citizens, for example, but is guaranteed one House member. Congress ordered states to stop creating new districts after the 1910 census.

Although states have the power to determine what areas each district covers, they cannot change the number of districts they have. When the number of districts changes, states control the **redistricting** process needed to make the new number fit. These decisions are subject to federal review, but only to the extent that they violate laws against racial discrimination. Otherwise, states decide where the district lines are drawn.[3] Under the Constitution, states, not the federal government, are responsible for determining the time, place, and manner of elections, which includes district lines.

There are several ways that district lines can be drawn to favor one party—a district can be packed with a large number of party voters, thereby diluting that party's strength in the districts next door, or it can be cracked into several districts, thereby weakening that party's strength in several districts. In extreme cases, this process is known as **gerrymandering**, which is a term dating back to the early 1800s when Massachusetts Governor Elbridge Gerry won passage of a redistricting plan that created a salamander-shaped district drawn to help his party win another seat.

Ordinarily, redistricting occurs just once every ten years. However, Texas changed the tradition in 2003 by redistricting the state a second time. The difference between 2001 and 2003 was a change in the party controlling the governor's office. With unified control of government, Republicans decided to redraw district lines a second time. Whereas Democrats had a 17 to 15 edge under the 2001 redistricting plan, Republicans ended up with a 21 to 11 edge after the 2003 process.

Advantages of Incumbency

It only takes one defeat to end a House or Senate career, which is why so many House members and senators work so hard to create safe seats. As we saw in Chapter 9, a **safe seat** is almost certain to be won by the current office holder, or **incumbent**. Although there are still competitive seats in the House, the vast majority is considered invulnerable to challenge. Of the 435 seats up for reelection in 2006, only a handful, perhaps no more than fifty, were considered winnable by a nonincumbent.

In contrast, Senate seats are considered much more vulnerable. Opponents are often well financed, in part because Senate elections are so visible nationally. With just a third of the Senate up for reelection at any one time, the public can pay closer attention to campaign issues and advertisements, and the two parties can invest more money in their candidates.[4] Although contests in large states tend to attract the most money, even small states such as South Dakota can host very expensive campaigns. This is exactly what happened in 2004 when South Dakota Senator Tom Daschle was

The word "gerrymander" comes from the name of the governor of Massachusetts, Elbridge Gerry, and the salamander-shaped district that was created to favor his party in 1811.

reapportionment
The assigning by Congress of congressional seats after each census. State legislatures reapportion state legislative districts.

redistricting
The redrawing of congressional and other legislative district lines following the census, to accommodate population shifts and keep districts as equal as possible in population.

gerrymandering
The drawing of legislative district boundaries to benefit a party, group, or incumbent.

safe seat
An elected office that is predictably won by one party or the other, so the success of that party's candidate is almost taken for granted.

incumbent
The current holder of elected office.

defeated. Daschle was a particularly tempting target for a well-financed Republican opponent. As Senate Majority Leader, he was one of the most visible Democrats in the nation. By defeating Daschle, Republicans were able to claim a mandate for their party.

In contrast, House elections tend to be local affairs. Although current members of Congress are sometimes judged by what they do in Washington, particularly on nationally visible issues such as prescription drug coverage, the war in Iraq, or education, most citizens have a favorable view of their own member of Congress. They might not recognize their member on the street, but they will recognize their member's name on the ballot. Incumbents benefit from several advantages. For example, incumbents:

- Do not have to pay postage on any mail to their district, except during the last 90 days before an election.

- Are allowed to send bulk e-mails any time.[5]

- Have greater access to the media, especially on local or state issues.

- Can raise campaign money more easily than challengers—donors like to put their support behind winners.

- Usually have more campaign experience than their challengers, and they are usually better campaigners.

- Often help constituents solve problems with government, and they often take credit for federal spending in their districts or state.

Democratic incumbents did not lose a single seat in 2006, while Republicans lost at least 15 seats. Still, the 2006 election was very good to incumbents, with more than 80 percent returned to office.

The 2006 Congressional Elections

Like the handful of past midterm congressional elections that occurred during periods of war, the 2006 congressional elections brought dramatic changes to Congress. With the elections framed as a national referendum on the Bush Administration's handling of the war in Iraq, the economy, and terrorism, the Republican Party lost control of both the House and the Senate to the Democrats. Although the vast majority of Democratic and Republican incumbents were reelected, Republicans lost at least 30 seats in the House, including 17 incumbents, while losing six seats in the Senate, including five incumbents. (See Table 11–1 for the overall changes as of November 17, 2006.)

Democrats needed at least 51 seats to control the Senate, and received the extra support required to meet the mark from independent senators Bernard Sanders (I-VT) and Joseph Lieberman (I-CT), both of whom promised to vote with Democrats in organizing the Senate. Democrats in the House had more than enough seats to pass the 218 needed for a majority. The gains may have been similar to past wartime presidents, but were enough to lead President Bush to declare that Republicans had taken a "thumping" on election night, while his press secretary described the election as a "whupping."

The gains in the House produced a dramatic change in power. The top leadership of the chamber changed overnight, with Nancy Pelosi (D-CA) becoming the first woman ever to occupy the top job. Every committee also gained a new chair in both chambers, even as Democrats moved into the bigger and better offices occupied by Republicans only days before. Democrats also won the power to set the congressional policy agenda, including everything from the Senate's power to approve the president's nominations for key executive jobs to the House's power to set taxes.

The battle for Congress was not the only story from the 2006 elections, however. Democrats won six governorships on election day, giving them a 28-to-22 edge over the Republicans. They also won control of four more state legislatures, giving them a 23-to-16 edge over the Republicans, with 10 states divided between the two parties, and Nebraska retaining its standing as the only state legislature to have one chamber in the legislature and no party affiliation among its members.

TABLE 11–1 Congressional Election Results, 2006

Senate

	2004	2006
Republican	55	49
Democrat	44	49
Independent	1	2

House

	2004	2006
Republican	232	201
Democrat	202	233
Independent	1	0

House figures do not include one undecided race as of December 15, 2006.

Voters also resolved a number of ballot initiatives. South Dakota rejected a sweeping ban on abortions, for example, while California and Oregon rejected requirements that doctors and clinics notify parents before performing an abortion on a woman under the age of eighteen. At the same time, seven states adopted ballot initiatives defining marriage as a union between a man and a woman, while one state, Arizona, rejected the ban on gay marriage. Another six states adopted higher minimum wages, while Missouri adopted an initiative to protect the rights of scientists to conduct stem cell research, and Michigan rejected the use of any form of affirmative action to help minorities win preferential treatment in winning admission to state colleges and universities and state jobs.

EXPLAINING THE RESULTS   There are several explanations for the midterm election results, including the war in Iraq, worries about the economy, and corruption in Washington. House Republicans lost at least five seats because of scandals, including the lobbying investigation that cost the party Delay's seat in Texas, marital infidelity by a member of Congress in Pennsylvania, or the discovery of lewd e-mails between a Florida member of Congress and the young congressional pages who run errands for the House. Although corruption appeared to affect only a handful of races, many voters mentioned it as a very important reason for their vote for Democrat candidates.

California Democratic Minority Leader Nancy Pelosi became the House's senior leader after her party won enough seats to become the majority.

Many voters were also deeply concerned about the growing violence in Iraq and the Bush administration's handing of the war. According to exit polls of more than 12,000 voters who were interviewed after they cast their ballots, 68 percent of Americans said that the war in Iraq was extremely or very important to their vote, while large percentages said that the war was no longer worth fighting.

Much of the campaign advertising against Republicans mentioned the war and the administration's commitment to "stay the course" in Iraq. Contrary to conventional wisdom, which says that House races involve local issues such as jobs and gasoline prices, two-thirds of voters said they cast their ballots on the basis of national issues such as corruption and Iraq. Almost 60 percent said they strongly or somewhat disapproved of the war, while 37 percent of voters said they had cast their vote to express opposition for Bush.

These results suggest that Democrats were highly successful in "nationalizing" the election by tying Republicans to the president and his agenda. The president's own approval was at or near all-time lows for his presidency at the time of the election, and many Republican candidates refused to have Bush campaign on their behalf.

Late in the campaign, for example, Bush went to the Florida panhandle to campaign on behalf of the Republican candidate for governor, Charlie Crist. The only problem was that Crist, who was running well ahead of his Democratic opponent at the time, did not want to be tied to the president and decided not to attend the rally. Crist decided to campaign in South Florida that day with Senator John McCain (R-AZ), a front-runner for the 2008 presidential nomination.

Similarly, many Republican candidates did not want to campaign with Vice President Dick Cheney, who was widely associated with the stay-the-course strategy in the Iraq war. Although Cheney remained very popular with religious conservatives, he was an unwelcome ally in many Republican districts, where incumbents and challengers alike worked hard to break any ties with the administration. Some never mentioned that they were Republicans, and very few talked about their potential influence in helping their districts through their connections to the administration.

Republicans did benefit from a gaffe late in the campaign involving 2004 Democratic presidential candidate John Kerry, but many candidates found it impossible to escape their own support for the president's programs, let alone photographs showing them side by side with the president earlier in the administration. As a result, the election increasingly became a way to express anger toward the president, not how well their own representatives had done serving their districts.

The results also reflected careful recruitment of more conservative Democratic candidates by the national Democratic committee. Instead of supporting traditional liberals, the party consciously sought candidates who would appeal to moderate

Republican voters through their support for gun control, restrictions on abortion, and budget control. Several Democratic candidates were also veterans of the war in Iraq, including Tammy Duckworth, who lost both her legs in the conflict, and Pennsylvania Democrats lined up solidly behind their Senate candidate, Bob Casey, even though he was anti-abortion.

Democrats also worked hard to provide enough money to make campaigns competitive. Although Republicans have traditionally enjoyed a commanding edge in campaign financing, Democrats were able to narrow the gap—the Republican Party spent more than $400 million on the campaigns, while the Democratic Party spent more than $300 million. Candidates spent at least another $1.2 billion, with incumbents in both parties almost always outspending challengers.

IMPACTS   The impact of the election was felt immediately in both the presidency and Congress. The day after the election, Bush announced that his secretary of defense and key Iraq advocate, Donald Rumsfeld, would resign from office. Although the resignation was not explicitly tied to the election, many observers interpreted the decision as an acknowledgment of the public's desire for change in the war strategy. The Republican Party also accepted the resignation of its chairman only days later.

Democrats also began crafting a legislative agenda for the new Congress, including issues such as raising the minimum wage to keep up with the many states that had already moved to increase the rate, reforms in the government's prescription drug coverage, tax reforms to lighten the burden on middle-income Americans, new ethics rules on members of Congress, and efforts to control the federal budget. At the same time, Democrats recognized they would need the president's help to pass any new legislation, and vice versa. Both immediately changed their political tone from election attack to promising a new period of bipartisanship on national policy.

The newfound commitment to working together was tested soon after the elections, however. Democrats began talking about setting a deadline for ending the war in Iraq. Having promised to address the mistakes that had led to the increasing chaos in Iraq, Democrats seemed poised to abandon their commitment to cooperation in an effort to bring more than 140,000 U.S. troops home as soon as possible.

The Structure and Powers of Congress

The framers expected that Congress, not the president or the courts, would be the most important branch of government. Hence, they worried most about how to keep Congress from dominating the other branches. In an effort to control Congress, they divided the legislative branch into two separate chambers, the House of Representatives and the Senate, which would "be as little connected with each other as the nature of their common functions and their common dependence on the society will admit."[6] Not only would House members and senators have different terms of office and represent different groups of voters (districts versus states), the framers originally wanted them to be selected through very different means. Until 1913, when the Seventeenth Amendment was ratified, senators were chosen by their state legislatures, not directly by voters.

The framers allowed each chamber to set its own rules for making the laws. Because it is so much larger than the Senate, the House has more rules governing debate, and limited time for debate. House members also have smaller staffs, receive less media coverage, and are not permitted to offer certain kinds of amendments to pending legislation. In contrast, the Senate has looser rules governing debate, rarely considers legislation unless all 100 senators agree on a schedule, and generally allows its members to offer an unlimited number of amendments to pending legislation, again as long as all senators agree to allow an open-ended process.

A Divided Branch

Bicameralism, or a two-house legislature, remains the most important organizational feature of the U.S. Congress. Each chamber meets in its own wing of the Capitol Build-

bicameralism
The principle of a two-house legislature.

Members of Congress are expected to fight for federal funding of projects in their district. Here Nancy Pelosi (D-CA) takes part in an official groundbreaking for the new Federal Building in San Francisco.

ing (see Figure 11–1); each has offices for its members on separate ends of Capitol Street; each has its own committee structure, its own rules for considering legislation, and its own record of proceedings (even though the records are published together as the *Congressional Record*); and each sets the rules governing its own members (each establishes its own legislative committees, for example).[7]

Bicameral legislatures were common in most of the colonies, and the framers believed that the arrangement was essential for preventing strong-willed majorities from oppressing individuals and minorities.[8] As James Madison explained in *The Federalist*, No. 51, "In order to control the legislative authority, you must divide it." (*The Federalist*, No. 51, is reprinted in the Appendix.)

Defenders of bicameralism point to its moderating influence on partisanship or possible errors in either chamber. This constitutionally mandated structure also guarantees that many votes will be taken before a policy is finally approved. The arrangement also provides more opportunities for bargaining and allows legislators with different policy goals a role in the shaping of national laws.

The Powers of Congress

The framers gave the most important powers to Congress. This list of **enumerated powers** was spelled out in a long list that even included the power to make war.

enumerated powers
The powers explicitly given to Congress in the Constitution.

FIGURE 11–1 **The Capitol Building.**

Because the Revolutionary War had been sparked by unfair taxation, the framers listed the power "to lay and collect Taxes" as the very first duty of Congress. They then gave Congress the power to borrow and coin money, regulate citizenship, build post offices and postal roads, and establish the lower courts of the federal judiciary, meaning every court below the Supreme Court. The framers also gave Congress the power to protect the nation against foreign threats by declaring war, raising armies, and building navies; and the power to protect the nation from domestic threats by regulating commerce and immigration.

The framers also gave Congress the power to "make all Laws which shall be necessary and proper for carrying into Execution the foregoing Powers, and all other Powers vested by this Constitution in the Government of the United States, or in any Department or Officer thereof." This clause is sometimes called the *elastic clause* because it stretches to cover much of what Congress might do. The Constitution also gave Congress complete authority to set its own rules for its proceedings.

Finally, the Constitution gave Congress important checks on government, including the power to remove the president and judges from office through the impeachment process. Under the process, the House has the authority to charge, or impeach, a president or judge for committing "high crimes and misdemeanors," while the Senate has the responsibility to conduct the trial to determine guilt or innocence. Impeachment requires a majority vote in the House, while conviction requires a two-thirds vote of the Senate. In 1999, for example, the House impeached President Bill Clinton for lying to a federal court about his affair with a White House intern, but the Senate acquitted him.

As the impeachment power shows, the Constitution gives different duties to each chamber. The Senate has the power to confirm (or not confirm) many presidential nominations, including nominations to the Supreme Court. In 2005, the Senate confirmed John Roberts as the new chief justice of the Supreme Court (replacing William Rehnquist, who died in 2005), and in 2006 it confirmed Samuel Alito Jr. (replacing Sandra Day O'Connor, who retired). The Senate must also play a crucial "advise and consent" role in making treaties—formal agreements between the United States and other countries. All treaties must be approved by a two-thirds vote in the Senate before they can be ratified by the president.

The House has its own responsibilities, too, most notably the power to impose taxes. But these powers are generally not as important as those given to the Senate, in part because the framers worried that House members would be too close to the people, and therefore, more likely to act in haste. Although all revenue bills must originate in the House, for example, the Senate can freely amend spending bills even to the point of changing everything except the title.

Despite its position as the first branch of government and its substantial powers, Congress has difficulty keeping pace with its great rival, the presidency. The president's national security responsibilities, preparation of the budget, media visibility, and agenda-setting influence have all enhanced the position of the presidency relative to Congress. Moreover, presidents often argue that the Constitution gives them the power to act without congressional consent during war. President George W. Bush made just such a claim in justifying his decision to allow government to eavesdrop on its own citizens without a court order. Although federal law specifically prohibited such action, Bush argued that this authority rests on his broader constitutional duty to protect the nation.

TABLE 11–2   Differences Between the House of Representatives and the Senate

House	Senate
Two-year term	Six-year term
435 members	100 members
Elected by districts	Elected by states
Fewer personal staff	More personal staff
Tighter rules	Looser rules
Decision to act made by majority	Decision to act made by unanimous consent of all members
Tax bills must come from the House	Foreign treaties must be ratified by the Senate
Less media coverage	More media coverage
Less prestige	More prestige
More powerful committee leaders	More equal distribution of power
Nongermane amendments (riders) not allowed	Nongermane amendments (riders) not allowed
Rules Committee sets terms of debate	Senate as a whole sets terms of debate
Limited debate	Extended debate
Some bills permit no floor amendments (closed rule)	Amendments generally allowed
No filibuster allowed	Filibuster allowed

How Other Nations Govern

The Palestinian Parliament

The Palestinian Authority's legislature is one of the most controversial in the world. Led by a majority composed of members of Hamas, a radical Middle East organization, the legislature represents two divided strips of land that lie to the east and west of Israel.

Promising that its members had no plans to pursue peace talks with Israel or disarm its soldiers, Hamas won a stunning victory in parliamentary elections in early 2006. Having won 74 of the legislature's 132 parliamentary seats, Hamas gained the authority to pick a speaker, two deputies, and a secretary. However, with eight of its new members held in Israeli prisons for terrorist acts, Hamas was able to occupy only 65 seats.

The Palestinian legislature represents an international authority created by Israel in the wake of 1994 negotiations with the Palestinian Liberation Organization, which had fought a decades-long war for independence. Although it is not yet a separate nation acknowledged by Israel or the international community, the Palestinian government has the authority to speak for the Palestinian people. The government blends elements of several models. It has a strong president modeled on the U.S. separated-powers system, and a unicameral parliament modeled on the British parliamentary system.

The Palestinian legislature may be one of the most controversial in the world, but is also one of the weakest. The president, not the legislature or prime minister, is the most powerful official in government. He is commander in chief, has the power to veto laws, can issue decrees with the force of law when the parliament is not in session, and is even responsible for picking the prime minister from the majority in parliament. Moreover, in spite of its surprising election victory, Hamas is far short of the two-thirds majority needed to override the president's veto.

Nevertheless, the Hamas election victory provoked international concern, especially in Israel and the United States. Both nations promised to withhold desperately needed aid to the Palestinians if Hamas did not renounce its long-standing opposition to Israel's right to exist. As of this writing, Hamas remains unwilling to reverse its stand.

Instead, Hamas has continued its fight with Israel. In June, 2006, for example, Israel and the Palestinian Authority began waging war over the Hamas kidnapping of an Israeli solder. The battles continued through October, when Israel and Hamas announced a general ceasefire of hostilites. But violence has continued to today. In December 2006, Palestinian Authority president Mahmoud Abbas called for a new presidential and parliamentary election in an effort to build a government that could regain international support and avoid civil war between Hamas and other less radical groups in the Palestinian territories. ∎

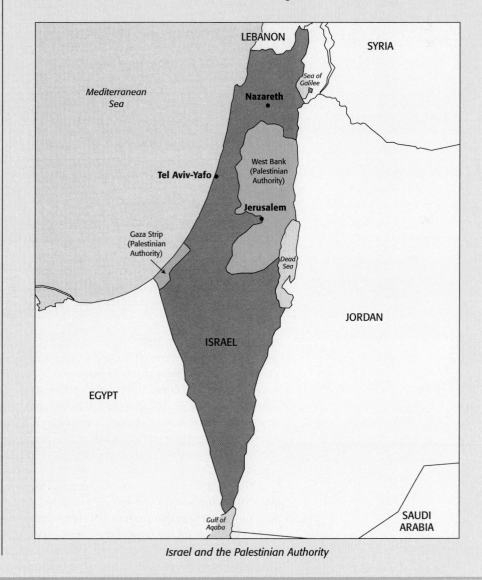

Israel and the Palestinian Authority

The two-year period between congressional elections is called a single Congress, and is divided into two one-year sessions. Each Congress is numbered dating back to the very first Congress in 1789–1791. Hence, the Congress that convened in January 2007 is the 111th, and comes 220 years after the first.

Congressional Leadership and Rules

Many Americans believe Congress is too slow to act on important national issues such as health care, raising the minimum wage, immigration reform, or finding new sources of energy, but the framers clearly preferred the delays as a way to protect the people from themselves. They worried that decisions made in haste might turn out to be bad for the nation.

Two hundred years later, the framers would still worry about decisions made in haste, particularly given the lingering war in Iraq, the confusion over prescription drug coverage, and the new budget deficits. Although they might agree with Congress on each one of these decisions, they would almost certainly wonder whether Congress did its homework in making the choices. They might also ask why so many spending and tax bills are passed into law with so little debate. They might also complain that too many members vote on legislation that they have never read. It is not that the framers expected Congress to be a perfect haven of judgment and deliberation, but they expected it to take its legislative powers seriously enough to think about issues before voting for passage.

Leading the House of Representatives

The organization and procedures in the House are different from those in the Senate, largely because the House is more than four times larger than the Senate. A larger membership requires more rules, which means that *how* things are done affects *what* is done. The House assigns different types of bills to different calendars. For instance, financial measures—tax or appropriations bills—are put on a special calendar for quicker action.

The House has other ways to speed up lawmaking, including electronic voting. Ordinary rules may be suspended by a two-thirds vote, or immediate action may be taken by *unanimous consent* of the members on the floor. By acting as a *committee of the whole*, the House is able to operate more informally and more quickly than under its regular rules. A *quorum* in the committee of the whole requires only 100 members, rather than a majority of the whole chamber, and voting is quicker and simpler. Members are limited in how long they can speak, and debate may be cut off simply by majority vote.

THE SPEAKER OF THE HOUSE   Again because of its size, the House gives its leaders more power than the Senate, where individual senators can and do derail legislation by merely refusing to approve the legislative schedule. The most powerful leader on Capitol Hill is the **Speaker** of the House.[9] Although the Speaker is formally elected by the entire House, the post is always filled by the majority party, which gives the party even more power to enforce its power. The Speaker is second in line to be president of the United States (after the vice president) in case of the death, resignation, or impeachment of the president, and must keep the White House informed about his or her whereabouts.

The Speaker has the power to recognize members who rise to speak, rule on questions of parliamentary procedure, and appoint members to temporary committees (but not the major committees that help make the laws). In a nutshell, the Speaker directs business on the floor of the House. More significant, of course, is the Speaker's political and behind-the-scenes influence. The Speaker has the power to reorganize House committees, name committee chairs, appoint his allies to leadership posts, and reduce the size of committee staffs, all of which give the Speaker enormous power to reward and punish individual members.[10]

Speaker
The presiding officer in the House of Representatives, formally elected by the House but actually selected by the majority party.

History Makers

Speaker Uncle Joe Cannon

Joseph Gurney Cannon, or "Uncle Joe" Cannon, was the first modern Speaker of the House. Born in North Carolina and raised in Indiana, he was first elected to the House from Illinois in 1873 and served until 1891, when he was defeated. He was reelected in 1893 and immediately became chairman of the powerful House Appropriations Committee. He ran for Speaker four times before finally capturing the post in 1903.

Whereas past Speakers had used the post to build compromises across the two parties, Cannon turned it into an engine of party discipline. He controlled virtually every committee appointment in the House, decided which committees would get the most important bills, and dictated the terms of legislative debate through tight control of the House Rules Committee. He also used his powers to punish Republicans who failed to support his positions. Called

"Czar Cannon" and the "Brakeman of the House," Cannon was widely regarded as a tyrant who would not tolerate dissent. Although there is some evidence that he was not as powerful as folklore suggests, Cannon did use the job to create much greater party discipline.*

Cannon was not just a Republican, however. He was a conservative Republican who opposed his own party's president, Theodore Roosevelt, and the "progressive," or moderate Republicans who supported legislation to regulate the meatpacking industry, abolish child labor, and break the industrial monopolies that exercised so much control over the national economy. Republican progressives eventually joined ranks with moderate and liberal Democrats to remove him from the job in 1911.

Cannon's vision of the Speaker's job lives on to this day. Today's Speakers do not

always use Cannon's harsh tactics to control the House, but do have the power to control committee assignments and set the agenda for legislative action. ■

---

*See Keith Krebbiel and Alan E. Wiseman, "Joe Cannon and the Minority Party: Tyranny or Bipartisanship," research paper no. 1858, Stanford University Graduate School of Business, July 2004.

The Cannon House Office Building, Washington, DC

The Speaker is usually selected on a vote by the majority **party caucus**, which is called *the party conference* by Republicans. The caucus elects party officers and committee chairs, approves committee assignments, and often helps the Speaker decide which issues will come first on the legislative calendar. However, because the Speaker is always selected first, he has the most important voice in determining all of these choices. The House selected its first woman as Speaker in 2007, Nancy Pelosi (D-Calif.), following the Democrats gaining a majority in the 2006 elections.

The powers of Speakers are not enough to protect them from their own members, however. They are subject to the same ethics rules that affect all members. This is how Republican Speaker Newt Gingrich (R-Ga.) was removed from office in 1998 after a long investigation into his use of special funds to help his allies win reelection. Although he insisted that there was little overlap between his political spending and his responsibilities as Speaker, the House fined him $300,000 for misusing funds and misleading the House Ethics Committee about his activities. Gingrich retired both as Speaker and as a member of Congress after the 1998 election.

After Gingrich's retirement, Republicans selected Illinois Representative J. Dennis Hastert as Speaker. Hastert, a former high school teacher and wrestling coach, had served for six years in the Illinois state legislature and 12 years in the U.S. House of

party caucus
A meeting of the members of a party in a legislative chamber to select party leaders and to develop party policy. Called a *conference* by the Republicans.

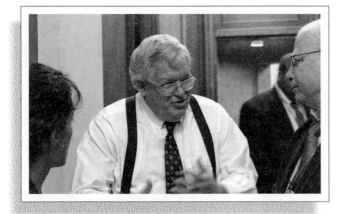

Former Speaker of the House Dennis Hastert (R-Ill.). Hastert lost his post following the 2006 midterm election when the Democrats became the majority party in the House.

Representatives before becoming Speaker of the House. "It's an orange and an apple," Hastert said about being Speaker. "However, it is a duty that I cannot ignore."[11] Hastert continues to earn praise from Republicans and Democrats alike because of his quiet style, but he also continues to use his powers to enforce party discipline.[12] Hastert lost his job to California Democrat Nancy Pelosi after Democrats retook the House majority in 2006. She was elected Speaker by a unanimous vote of her caucus.

OTHER HOUSE OFFICERS The Speaker is assisted by the **majority leader**, who helps plan party strategy, confers with other party leaders, and tries to keep members of the party in line. The minority party elects the **minority leader**, who usually becomes Speaker when his or her party gains a majority in the House. (These positions are also sometimes called majority and minority *floor leaders.*) Assisting each floor leader are the party **whips**. (The term comes from *whipper-in,* the huntsman who keeps the hounds bunched in a pack during a foxhunt.) The whips serve as liaisons between the House leadership of each party and the rank-and-file. They inform members when important bills will come up for a vote, prepare summaries of the bills, do vote counts for the leadership, exert pressure (sometimes mild and sometimes heavy) on members to support the leadership, and try to ensure maximum attendance on the floor for critical votes.

THE HOUSE RULES COMMITTEE The House Rules Committee is almost certainly the most powerful committee in either chamber. Under the much tighter rules that govern the larger House, the Rules Committee decides the rules governing the length of the floor debate on any legislative issue and sets limits on the number and kinds of floor amendments that will be allowed. By refusing to grant a *rule,* which is a ticket to the floor, the Rules Committee can delay consideration of a bill. A **closed rule** prohibits amendments altogether or provides that only members of the committee reporting the bill may offer amendments; closed rules are usually reserved for tax and spending bills. An **open rule** permits debate within the overall time allocated to the bill.

From the New Deal era in the mid-1930s until the mid-1960s, a coalition of Republicans and conservative Democrats used the Rules Committee to block significant legislation on civil rights, health care, and poverty. Liberals denounced it as unrepresentative, unfair, and dictatorial. More recently, the Rules Committee membership has come to reflect the views of the general makeup of the majority party. It has become much less an independent obstacle to legislation and more a place to design rules that help advance the general goals of the majority party. Once again, the Speaker has considerable power in appointing the majority party's members to the committee.

Leading the Senate

The Senate has the same basic committee structure, elected party leadership, and decentralized power as the House, but because the Senate is a smaller body, its procedures are more informal, and it permits more time for debate. It is a more open, fluid, and decentralized body now than it was a generation or two ago. Indeed, it is often said that the Senate has 100 separate power centers and is so splintered that the party leaders have difficulty arranging the day-to-day schedule.[13]

The Senate is led by the Senate majority leader, who is elected by the majority party in the Senate. When the majority leader is from the president's party, the president becomes the party's most visible leader on Capitol Hill and in the nation as a whole. However, when the majority leader and the president are from different parties, the Senate majority leader is considered his or her party's national spokesperson.

As the Senate's power broker, the majority leader has the right to be the first senator heard on the floor. In consultation with the Senate minority leader, the majority leader controls the Senate's agenda and recommends committee assignments for members of the majority party. But because the position is less powerful than being Speaker of the House, its influence depends on the leader's political and parliamentary

majority leader
The legislative leader selected by the majority party who helps plan party strategy, confers with other party leaders, and tries to keep members of the party in line.

minority leader
The legislative leader selected by the minority party as spokesperson for the opposition.

whip
Party leader who is the liaison between the leadership and the rank-and-file in the legislature.

closed rule
A procedural rule in the House of Representatives that prohibits any amendments to bills or provides that only members of the committee reporting the bill may offer amendments.

open rule
A procedural rule in the House of Representatives that permits floor amendments within the overall time allocated to the bill.

The Changing Face of American Politics

Diversity in Congress

Although the Constitution does not mention race, gender, or wealth among the qualifications for office, the framers expected members of Congress to be white male property owners. After all, women, slaves, and freed slaves could not vote, let alone hold office.

The framers would therefore be surprised at the face of Congress today. Recent Congresses have had record numbers of women and minorities. The framers would therefore be surprised at the face of Congress today. Recent Congresses have had record numbers of

women and minorities. In 2006, women added six seats to their total in Congress, including two new U.S. Senators, one from Minnesota and one from Missouri. More important perhaps, the second largest number of women ever ran for Congress, which gives even women who were defeated important experience for future campaigns. Despite these gains for women, there was little change in the racial diversity of Congress following 2006.

These numbers would not have increased without the rise of a new generation of women

U.S. Senator Barbara Mikulski (D-Md.), shown at the podium, with the other female Democratic senators onstage at the 2004 Democratic National Convention in Boston.

and minority candidates, however. Although voting participation by women and minority groups has increased dramatically over the past half-century, it took time for women and minority candidates to gain the experience needed for a successful congressional campaign. As the number of talented women and minority candidates increased, so did their odds of winning office.

Although Congress is becoming more diverse by race and gender, it still remains very different from the rest of America in income and oc-

cupation. Almost one-third of the senators who served in the 108th Congress were millionaires, and more than half were lawyers. Moreover, old customs die hard. Even with the Democratic senator from Washington, Patty Murray, sitting on his Appropriations Committee, Chairman Robert Byrd still addressed committee members as "Gentlemen." At the current rate of change in the number of women, for example, it will take another 400 years before women constitute a majority in the House.* ∎

---

*See the United States Capitol Historical Society, "Outstanding African-American Members of Congress" and "Women Members of Congress" at www.uschs.org/04_history/subs_articles/04e.html.

Number of Women in U.S. House and Senate

SOURCE: Rutgers University, Eagleton Institute of Politics, Center for American Women and Politics, November, 2006.

---

skills and on the national political situation.[14] Lyndon Johnson (D-Tex.) served in this post during the 1950s, and is still considered one of the most effective persuaders in Senate history.

The majority leader does have substantial influence over the Senate's legislative calendar. Senator Harry Reid was elected as the current Senate majority leader after Democrats won enough Senate seats to assure a slim majority in 2007. He replaced Senator Bill Frist (R-TN), who retired.

Party machinery in the Senate is similar to that in the House. There are party caucuses (conferences), majority and minority floor leaders, and party whips. Each party has a *policy committee,* composed of party leaders, which is theoretically responsible for the party's overall legislative program. In the Senate, the party policy committees help the leadership monitor legislation and provide policy expertise. Unlike the House

"We are prepared to govern in . . . partnership, not partisanship."

SPEAKER OF THE HOUSE NANCY PELOSI

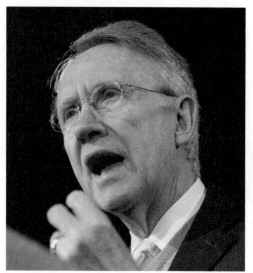

Harry Reid (D-NV) was named Senate Majority Leader after Democrats took control of the Senate by a slim majority in the 2006 elections. The one-vote Democratic majority depended on two independents who promised to organize with the Democrats, but was placed in jeopardy when Senator Tim Johnson (D-SD) had a stroke in mid-December 2006.

president pro tempore
Officer of the Senate selected by the majority party to act as chair in the absence of the vice president.

hold
A procedural practice in the Senate whereby a senator temporarily blocks the consideration of a bill or nomination.

filibuster
A procedural practice in the Senate whereby a senator refuses to relinquish the floor and thereby delays proceedings and prevents a vote on a controversial issue.

cloture
A procedure for terminating debate, especially filibusters, in the Senate.

party committees, the Senate's party policy committees are formally provided for by law, and each has a regular staff and a budget. Although the Senate party policy committees have some influence on legislation, they have not asserted strong legislative leadership or managed to coordinate policy.

The president of the Senate (the vice president of the United States) also has little influence over Senate proceedings. A vice president can vote only in the case of a tie. The Senate elects a **president pro tempore**, usually the most senior member from the majority party, who acts as chair in the absence of the vice president. Presiding over the Senate on most occasions is a thankless chore, so the president pro tempore regularly delegates this responsibility to junior members of the chamber's majority party. The vice president is officially president of the Senate, and occasionally casts the deciding vote when the Senate is evenly split, 50 to 50. Otherwise, the vice president works at 1600 Pennsylvania Avenue with the president. In 2003, Vice President Dick Cheney threatened to cast the deciding vote on what was called the "nuclear option" to change Senate rules to prevent filibusters against the president's judicial nominations, which must be confirmed by the Senate. (See the discussion of filibusters in the following section.) However, an agreement between the parties prevented this.

Despite these various leaders and offices, the Senate is far less structured than the House. It has always operated under rules that give individual senators great power. Extended debate allows senators to hold the floor as long as they wish unless a supermajority of 60 colleagues votes to end debate. Moreover, the Senate's rules allow individual senators to offer amendments on virtually any topic to a pending bill, allowing them to amend a bill to death.[15]

One relatively recent expression of this individualism is a practice called the **hold**, which is a delaying tactic designed to stop legislation. Holds were originally designed to give individual senators a short period to prepare for a debate or delay a vote for personal reasons. Over time, however, they have become a powerful device for blocking action on legislation and nominations, and are often viewed as a way to threaten a filibuster on a particular issue or nomination.

Although successful Senate leadership still depends on personal relationships, individual members have become more loyal to their parties in recent decades. "Senators known for compromise, moderation and institutional loyalty," observe political scientists Nicol Rae and Colton Campbell, "have been replaced with more ideological and partisan members who see the chamber as a place to enhance their party fortunes."[16] Partisanship in the Senate was vehement during the Bill Clinton impeachment proceedings and to a lesser extent in the confirmation battle of George W. Bush's nominee, John Ashcroft, as his first attorney general.

THE FILIBUSTER Because of the smaller size and looser rules of the Senate, debate is more open there than in the House. A senator who gains the floor may go on talking until he or she relinquishes the right to talk voluntarily or through exhaustion. This right to unlimited debate, known as the **filibuster**, may be used by a small group of senators to delay Senate proceedings by talking continuously so as to postpone or prevent a vote. Filibusters often begin with a legislative hold that puts a stop to all action, issued by individual senators. At one time, the filibuster was a favorite weapon of southern senators for blocking civil rights legislation.

A filibuster, or the threat of a filibuster through the use of a hold, is typically most potent at the end of a congressional session, when a date has been fixed for adjournment, because it could mean that many bills that have otherwise made it through the legislative process will die for lack of a floor vote. The knowledge that a bill might be subject to a filibuster is often enough to force a compromise satisfactory to its opponents. Sometimes the leaders, knowing that a filibuster will tie up the Senate and keep it from enacting other needed legislation, do not bring a controversial bill to the floor.

A filibuster can be defeated. Until 1917, the Senate could terminate a filibuster only if every member agreed. That year, however, the Senate adopted its first debate-ending rule, or **cloture**. The rule specifies that the question of curtailing debate must be put to a vote two days after 16 senators sign a petition asking for cloture. If three-fifths of the total number of the Senate (60 of the 100 members) vote in favor of cloture, no senator may speak on the measure under consideration for more than one hour. Once invoked, cloture requires that the final vote on the measure be taken after no more than 30 hours of debate. Under Vice President Cheney's threatened "nuclear option," the number of votes needed to break, or stop, a filibuster, would have been reduced to 50 plus 1, or a simple majority. To date, the Senate has avoided the kind of controversial issues or judicial nominations that might trigger such a fight.

There has been an increase in the use and threat of filibusters in recent years, and these tactics have often been used for partisan purposes. Indeed, as noted, senators usually anticipate a filibuster on controversial measures, and the threat is often sufficient to force the majority to compromise and modify its position.[17] Both parties have learned to use the filibuster when they are in the minority. The Senate has averaged almost two dozen filibusters each year since 2001. Most cloture votes fail.[18]

THE POWER TO CONFIRM The Constitution leaves the precise practices of the confirmation process somewhat ambiguous: "The President . . . shall nominate, and by and with the Advice and Consent of the Senate, shall appoint Ambassadors, other public Ministers and Consuls, Judges of the Supreme Court, all other officers of the United States." The framers of the Constitution regarded the Senate's "advise and consent" power as an important check against the executive.

As with other legislative business, the confirmation process starts with a review by the committee that oversees the particular position. For example, the Judiciary Committee considers federal judges and Supreme Court nominees; the Foreign Relations Committee considers ambassadorial appointments. Nominees appear before the committee to answer questions, and they typically meet individually with key senators before the hearing. Once the hearing is over, the committee approves or disapproves the nomination. Although the Senate Majority Leader can ask that the nomination be considered even on a vote of disapproval, the committee vote is usually honored.

Presidents have never enjoyed exclusive control over hiring and firing in the executive branch. The Senate jealously guards its right to confirm or reject or even delay major appointments; during the period of strong Congresses after the Civil War, presidents had to struggle to keep their power to appoint their top officers. For most of the past century, the Senate has generally confirmed the vast majority of the president's nominees, and has only rejected nine cabinet secretaries since 1789.

Nevertheless, the use of holds against lower-level presidential appointees has often forced the president to either withdraw those nominees or appoint them under the recess power, which allows presidents to put particularly controversial nominees into office while the Senate has taken a formal recess during holidays or at the end of each year. In 2004, for example, President George W. Bush used the recess power to appoint John R. Bolton as the U.S. ambassador to the United Nations, even though Bolton had once said that the United Nations should be abolished. Under a recess appointment, an officer can only serve until the end of the next session of Congress.

The Senate's role in the confirmation process was never intended to prevent a president from taking political considerations into account when appointments are made. Rather, the Senate was given the power to protect the executive and judicial branches against weak or controversial nominees. During the Bush administration, conservatives complained that Senate Democrats were interfering with the executive power of the president by rejecting nominees because of their political beliefs. Only a few years before, during the Clinton administration, however, liberals complained that Senate Republicans were doing the same thing.

Because federal judges serve for life, judicial appointments are particularly controversial. For the most part, the Senate gives the president the benefit of the doubt in selecting executive appointees, but it plays a greater role in judicial appointments. Federal judges constitute an independent check on both Congress and the executive branch, in part because of their lifetime terms.[19] In 2005, for example, Senate Democrats threatened to filibuster the proposed appointment of Harriet Miers, the president's counsel, to replace Sandra Day O'Connor on the Supreme Court. Miers was seen as

As part of her confirmation process, Labor Secretary Elaine Chao answered questions for congressional committee members on Capitol Hill.

only minimally qualified for her post, and asked to be withdrawn from consideration before her nomination even reached the hearing stage.[20]

Even with judicial appointments, however, the Senate and the president often work closely to reach agreement, especially on district court judges. Under the tradition of **senatorial courtesy**, presidents confer with the senators from the state in which a judge will serve, giving special consideration to the senator or senators from the president's own party. However, the president cannot discount a politically powerful senator from the opposition party. A nomination is less likely to secure Senate approval against the objection of these senators, especially if they are members of the president's party.

Congressional Committees

Committees are the workhorses of Congress. They draft legislation, review nominees, conduct investigations of executive branch departments and agencies, and are usually responsible for ironing out differences between House and Senate versions of the same legislation. They determine who gets what, when, where, and how from government—in short, they shape the politics of legislation.

It is sometimes said that Congress is a collection of committees that come together in a chamber every once in a while to approve one another's actions. Congress has long relied on committees to get its work done. Woodrow Wilson, a political science professor before he became president, expressed a similar thought: "Congress in session is Congress on display. Congress in committee is Congress at work."[21] Committees rarely make the first decisions on legislation, however. This duty belongs to the many subcommittees that start the process moving with hearings and first drafts of legislation.[22]

TYPES OF COMMITTEES   In theory, all congressional committees are created anew in each new Congress. In reality, however, most continue with little change from Congress to Congress. **Standing committees** are the most durable and are the sources of most bills, while **special or select committees** come together to address temporary priorities of Congress such as aging or taxes, and rarely author legislation. **Joint committees** have members from both the House and the Senate and exist either to study an issue of interest to the entire Congress or to oversee congressional support agencies such as the Library of Congress or the U.S. Government Printing Office. Almost all standing committees have subcommittees that help handle the legislative workload.

Of the various types of committees, standing committees are the most important for making laws and representing constituents, and they fall into four types: authorizing, appropriations, rules, and revenue. There are more than three dozen standing committees in the House and Senate.

Authorizing committees   Authorizing committees pass the laws that tell government what to do. The House and Senate education and labor committees, for example, are responsible for setting the rules governing the Pell Grant student loan program, including who can apply, how much they can get, where the loans come from, and how defaults are handled. Simply stated, authorizing committees make the most basic decisions about who gets what, when, and how from government. In 1999–2000, there were 15 authorizing committees in the House and 17 in the Senate. The number of committees remained unchanged in 2005–2007.

Authorizing committees are also responsible for oversight of the federal bureaucracy. Some of this oversight is designed to ask whether programs are working well, and some is designed to reduce fraud, waste, or abuse in an agency of government. The amount of congressional oversight is increasing. Political scientist Joel Aberbach found, for example, that just 8 percent of all legislative hearings focused on oversight in 1961, compared with over 25 percent just two decades later.[23]

Appropriations committees   Appropriations committees make decisions about how much money government will spend on its programs and operations. Although there is just one appropriations committee in each chamber, each appropriations commit-

Bono has been extremely active in lobbying Congress on issues of world hunger and poverty. Here he is testifying before the U.S. Senate Appropriations Committee in 2004 on AIDS funding.

senatorial courtesy
Presidential custom of submitting the names of prospective appointees for approval to senators from the states in which the appointees are to work.

standing committee
A permanent committee established in a legislature, usually focusing on a policy area.

special or select committee
A congressional committee created for a specific purpose, sometimes to conduct an investigation.

joint committee
A committee composed of members of both the House of Representatives and the Senate; such committees oversee the Library of Congress and conduct investigations.

TABLE 11–3 Congressional Standing Committees

House	Senate
Agriculture	Agriculture, Nutrition, and Forestry
Appropriations	Appropriations
Armed Services	Armed Services
Budget	Banking, Housing, and Urban Affairs
Education and the Workforce	Budget
Energy and Commerce	Commerce, Science, and Transportation
Financial Services	Energy and Natural Resources
Government Reform	Environment and Public Works
Homeland Security	Finance
House Administration	Health, Education, Labor, and Pensions
International Relations	Homeland Security and Governmental Affairs
Judiciary	Judiciary
Resources	Rules and Administrations
Rules	Small Business and Entrepreneurship
Science	Veterans' Affairs
Small Business	
Standards of Official Conduct	
Transportation and Infrastructure	
Veterans' Affairs	
Ways and Means	

tee has one subcommittee for each of the 13 appropriations bills that must be enacted each year to keep government running. Because they decide who gets how much from government, these subcommittees have great power to undo or limit decisions by the authorizing committees. The 13 appropriations bills often contain special projects, or **earmarks**, for individual members. Members of Congress use earmarks for everything from new highways to university buildings, and these expenditures increase the incumbency advantage. According to one recent analysis, the number of such earmarks increased from 1,400 in 1995 to nearly 16,000 ten years later.[24]

Rules and Administration Committees Rules committees in both chambers determine the basic operations of their chamber—for example, how many staffers individual members get, and what the ratio of majority to minority members will be. Again because of the number of members it must control, the House Rules Committee is more powerful than its twin in the Senate. As noted earlier, the House Rules Committee has special responsibility for giving each bill a rule, or ticket, to the floor of the House and determines what, if any, amendments to a bill will be permitted.

Revenue and Budget Committees Revenue and budget committees deal with raising the money that appropriating committees spend while setting the broad targets that shape the federal budget. As such, they determine how much money will actually go toward programs such as the Pell Grants. Authorizing committees may set the maximum amount that can be spent, but appropriations committees commit the actual dollars, and often provide less than the authorizing committees want.

Because it exists to raise revenues through taxes, the House Ways and Means Committee is arguably the single most powerful committee in Congress, for it both raises and authorizes spending. As the only committee in either chamber that can originate tax and revenue legislation, it is also responsible for making basic decisions on the huge Social Security and Medicare programs.

CHOOSING COMMITTEE MEMBERS Each political party controls the selection of standing committee members. The chair and a majority of each committee come from the

earmarks
Special spending projects that are set aside on behalf of individual members of Congress for their constituents.

majority party. The minority party is represented on each committee roughly in proportion to its membership in the entire chamber, except on some powerful committees on which the majority may want to enhance its position. Because some committees are more prestigious than others, the debate over committee assignments can be intense. These committees control more important programs or more money, and give their members important advantages in helping their home districts.

There are only four prestigious committees in the House: Appropriations; Rules; Ways and Means; and Commerce. House members can serve on only one of these "exclusive" committees. The chairs of these four committees cannot chair any other committees. House members can also serve on any two of 11 nonexclusive committees: Agriculture; Armed Services; Banking and Financial Services; Education and the Workforce; International Relations; Judiciary; Natural Resources; Science; Small Business; Transportation; and Veterans Affairs.

There are only four prestigious committees in the Senate, as well: Appropriations, Armed Services, Finance, and Foreign Relations. Senators can only serve on two of these "Super A" committees, and cannot be chairs of more than one. Senators can serve on two "A" committees, which cover everything from Agriculture, Nutrition, and Forestry to Commerce, Science, and Transportation; Homeland Security; and Judiciary. Senators can also serve on any number of "B" and "C" committees.

Getting on a politically advantageous committee is important to members of Congress. A representative from Kansas, for example, would rather serve on the Agriculture Committee than on the Banking and Financial Services Committee. Members usually stay on the same committees from one Congress to the next, although junior members who have had less desirable assignments often seek better committees when places become available.

The House and Senate choose committee members in different ways. House Republicans choose their committee members through their Committee on Committees, which is composed of one member from each state that has Republican representation in the House. Because each member has as many votes in the committee as there are Republicans in the delegation, senior members from the large state delegations dominate the group. Democrats in the House choose committee members through the Steering and Policy Committee of the Democratic caucus in negotiation with senior Democrats from the state delegations.

Veteran party members also dominate the Senate assignment process, where both parties have small Steering Committees that make committee assignments. In making assignments, leaders are guided by various considerations: how talented and cooperative a member is, whether his or her region is already well represented on a committee, and whether the assignment will aid in reelecting the member. Sometimes fierce battles erupt within these committees, reflecting ideological, geographical, and other differences.

Organizing its committees by subject matter is one way Congress copes with its legislative workload. This specialization allows members to develop technical expertise in specific areas and to recruit skilled staffs. Thus Congress is often able to challenge experts from the bureaucracy. Interest groups and lobbyists realize the great power a specific committee has in certain areas and focus their attention on its members. Similarly, members of executive departments are careful to cultivate the committee and subcommittee chairs and members of "their" committees.

THE ROLE OF SENIORITY   Most committee chairs are selected on the basis of the **seniority rule**; the member of the majority party with the longest continuous service on the committee becomes chair upon the retirement of the current chair or a change in the party in control of Congress. The seniority rule gives power to representatives who come from safe districts where one party is dominant and a member can build up years of continuous service. Conversely, the seniority rule lessens the influence of states or districts where the two parties are more evenly matched and where there is more turnover.

seniority rule
A legislative practice that assigns the chair of a committee or subcommittee to the member of the majority party with the longest continuous service on the committee.

Although it is not uncommon for the party leadership to reward a junior member with a prestigious committee assignment, seniority has long been respected in Congress for several reasons: it encourages members to stay on a committee, it encourages specialization and expertise, and it reduces the interpersonal politics that would arise if several members of a committee sought to become chair. Under new rules adopted in the mid-1990s, however, both House and Senate Republicans agreed to limit committee chairs to serving no more than three consecutive two-year terms.[25]

Senator Patrick Leahy became chairman of the Senate Judiciary Committee in 2007.

INVESTIGATIONS AND OVERSIGHT
Committees do more than produce legislation. They also have two additional roles in making government work.

The first is the power to *investigate*. Congress conducts investigations to determine if legislation is needed, to gather facts relevant to legislation, to assess the efficiency of executive agencies, to build public support, to expose corruption, and to enhance the image or reputation of its members.[26] Hearings by standing committees, their subcommittees, or special select committees are an important source of information and opinion. They provide an arena in which experts can submit their views. Congress launched immediate hearings on the Shuttle *Columbia* disaster in 2003, for example, and held hearings on Hurricane Katrina in 2006.

The second power committees have is *oversight* power—the responsibility to question executive branch officials to see whether their agencies are complying with the wishes of the Congress and are conducting their programs efficiently. Authorization committees regularly hold oversight hearings, and appropriations committees—exercising "the congressional power of the purse"—often use appropriations hearings to communicate committee members' views about how agency officials should conduct their business. Congress has held dozens of oversight hearings over the past five years on the operations of the Department of Homeland Security, which is responsible for protecting the nation against terrorism, and it summoned Federal Emergency Management Agency director Mike Brown to Capitol Hill in 2005 to defend his agency's slow response to Hurricane Katrina.

THE SPECIAL ROLE OF CONFERENCE COMMITTEES
Given the differences between the House and the Senate, it is not surprising that the version of a bill passed by one chamber may differ substantially from the version passed by the other. Only if both houses pass an absolutely identical measure can it become law. Most of the time, one house accepts the language of the other, but about 10 to 12 percent of all bills passed, usually major ones, must be referred to a **conference committee**—a special committee of members from each chamber that settles the differences between versions.[27] Both parties are represented, but the majority party has more members.

The proceedings of a conference committee are usually an elaborate bargaining process. When the revised bill is brought back to the two chambers, the conference

conference committee
Committee appointed by the presiding officers of each chamber to adjust differences on a particular bill passed by each in different form.

report can be accepted or rejected (often with further negotiations ordered), but it cannot be amended. Conference members of each chamber must convince their colleagues that any concessions made to the other chamber were on unimportant points and that nothing basic to the original version of the bill was surrendered.

Conference committees have considerable leeway in reaching agreement, prompting President Ronald Reagan to note, "You know, if an orange and an apple went into conference consultations, it might come out a pear."[28] Ordinarily, members are expected to end up somewhere between the different versions. On matters for which there is no clear middle ground, members are sometimes accused of exceeding their instructions and producing an entirely new bill. For this reason, the conference committee has been called a "third house" of Congress and one of the most significant congressional institutions.[29]

It is not clear whether the House or the Senate wins more often in conference committees. On the surface, it appears that the Senate's version wins more often, but this is partly because the Senate often acts on its legislation after the House. But by approving the initial bill first and thereby setting the agenda on an issue, the House often has more of an impact on the final outcome than the Senate.

CAUCUSES In contrast to conference committees, which are appointed by the House and Senate leadership to perform a specific legislative role, caucuses are best defined as informal committees that allow individual members to promote shared legislative interests. There are caucuses for House members only, for senators only, and for members of both chambers together. By the 1990s, according to one count, House members actually served on more informal caucuses than on committees and subcommittees.[30]

The growing diversity of the caucuses parallels the rest of society. They include the Black Caucus, Hispanic Caucus, Women's Issues Caucus, Rural Health Caucus, Children's Caucus, Cuba Freedom Caucus, Pro-Life Caucus, Homelessness Task Force, Urban Caucus, and Ethiopian Jewry Caucus. The diversity also parallels the fragmentation of interest groups, with caucuses on nearly every business and public interest issue—including steel, beef, wheel bearings, the Internet, mushrooms, mining, gas, sweeteners, wine, footwear, soybeans, animal rights, Chesapeake Bay, clean water, drug enforcement, adoption, the arts, energy, military reform, AIDS, and antiterrorism. There are also caucuses composed of friends of the Caribbean Basin, animals, human rights monitors, and Ireland.

> *"You know, if an orange and an apple went into conference consultations, it might come out a pear."*
>
> **PRESIDENT RONALD REAGAN**

The Job of the Legislator

Membership in Congress was once a part-time job. Members came to Washington for a few terms, averaged less than five years of continuous service, and returned to private life. Congressional pay was low, and Washington was no farther than a carriage ride from home.[31]

Congress started to meet more frequently in the late 1800s, pay increased, and being a member of Congress became increasingly attractive.[32] In the 1850s, roughly one-half of all House members retired or were defeated at each election; by 1900, the number who left at the end of each term had fallen to roughly one-quarter; by the 1970s, the number had fallen to barely a tenth. Even in the 1994 congressional elections, when Republicans won the House majority for the first time in 40 years, 90 percent of House incumbents who ran for reelection won.[33]

By the 1950s, being a member of Congress had become a full-time job and a long-term career. Members came to Washington to stay and began to exploit the natural advantages that come with running for reelection as an incumbent: name recognition, service to citizens back home, campaign funding, nearly unlimited access to the media, and free postage under the *franking privilege* for mailings back home. In 1954, for example, members of Congress sent 44 million pieces of mail back home. Fifty years later, the number had grown by more than 1,000 percent. Include the amount of e-mail, and the average member of Congress is in touch with his or her district almost daily.[34]

The workday also got longer. Most members work more than 70 hours a week, dividing their time among committee and subcommittee hearings, floor debates, meetings with citizens and interest groups, and raising money for the next election. Despite the workload, the vast majority of members report that they are very, or mostly, satisfied with their jobs, and only a fraction say the job has become less satisfying since they first entered Congress. Although they believe their jobs have become more complex and are frustrated by the lack of time with their families and friends, the vast majority does not want to leave.[35]

As members of Congress became attached to their careers, they began to abandon many of the norms that once guided their behavior in office.[36] The old norms were simple. Members were supposed to specialize in a small number of issues (the norm of specialization), defer to members with longer tenure in office (the norm of seniority), never criticize anyone personally (the norm of courtesy), and wait their turn to speak and introduce legislation (the norm of apprenticeship). As longtime House Speaker Sam Rayburn once said, new members were to go along in order to get along, and to be seen and not heard.

The new norms are equally simple. New members are no longer willing to wait their turn to speak or introduce legislation and now have enough staff to make their opinions known on just about any issue at just about any point in the legislative process. Although the norm of courtesy still lives on as members refer to each other with great respect, the new congressional career allows little time for the old norms of specialization, seniority, and apprenticeship. Members must take care of their electoral concerns first.

Legislators as Representatives

Congress has a split personality. On the one hand, it is a *lawmaking institution* that writes laws and makes policy for the entire nation. In this capacity, all the members are expected to set aside their personal ambitions and perhaps even the concerns of their own constituencies. Yet Congress is also a *representative assembly*, made up of 535 elected officials who serve as links between their constituents and the national government (see Table 11–4). The dual roles of making laws and responding to constituents' demands force members to balance national concerns against the specific interests of their states or districts.

Individual members of Congress perceive their roles differently. Some believe they should serve as **delegates** from their districts. These legislators believe it is their duty to find out what "the folks back home" want and act accordingly. Other members see their role as that of **trustee**. Their constituents, they contend, did not send them to Congress to serve as mere robots or "errand runners." They act and vote according to their own view of what is best for their district, state, and the nation. As Senate Judiciary Chairman Arlen Specter (R-Pa.) said at the beginning of hearings on the Bush administration's domestic eavesdropping policy in 2006, this was not a Democratic or Republican issue, but a national issue about privacy and liberty.

Most legislators shift back and forth between the delegate and trustee roles, depending on their perception of the public interest, their standing in the last and next elections, and the pressures of the moment. Most also view themselves more as free agents than as instructed delegates for their districts. And recent research suggests that they often *are* free, since about 50 percent of citizens are unaware of how their representatives voted on major legislation and often believe their representative voted in accordance with constituent policy views. Still, nearly everyone in Congress spends a lot of time building constituency connections, mending political fences, reaching out to swing voters, and worrying about how a vote on a controversial issue will "play" back home.[37]

delegate
An official who is expected to represent the views of his or her constituents even when personally holding different views; one interpretation of the role of the legislator.

trustee
An official who is expected to vote independently based on his or her judgment of the circumstances; one interpretation of the role of the legislator.

TABLE 11–4   Profile of the 109th Congress, 2005–2007

	Senate	House
Party Affiliation		
Republican	55	229
Democratic	45	202
Independent	0	1
Sex		
Male	86	368
Female	14	67
Religion		
Catholic	24	129
Jewish	11	26
Protestant	51	213
Other	14	67
Average Age	60	55
Racial/Ethnic Minorities	5	67
Major Occupations*		
Law	64	178
Education	13	91
Business, banking	40	205
Real estate	3	39
Agriculture	5	29
Medicine	4	16
Journalism	7	11

*Numbers exceed 100 and 435 because Senators and Representatives often had more than one occupation upon entering office.

SOURCE: *Congressional Quarterly Weekly*, January 31, 2005, pp. 240–243.

NOTE: Figures for the 111th Congress, 2007–2009, were not available for every category when this table was revised in late December 2006.

Making Legislative Choices

About 8,000 bills are introduced in the House and Senate during a two-year Congress, but only a handful of bills receive hearings, even fewer reach the floor, and one in eight become law. Although House members and senators cast 1,000 votes each year, the vast majority involve voice votes on noncontroversial legislation and procedures.[38] When they do take a vote on a controversial issue such as authorizing the use of force in Iraq, prescription drug coverage for the elderly, tax cuts, or more school testing, members of Congress are influenced by a number of actors, from the views of trusted colleagues to the wishes of the president.

COLLEAGUES   Legislators are often influenced by the advice of their close friends in Congress. Their busy schedules and the great number of votes force them to depend on the advice of like-minded colleagues. In particular, they look to respected members of the committee who worked on a bill.[39] Legislators find out how their friends stand on an issue, listen to the party leadership's advice, and take the various committee reports into account. Sometimes members are influenced to vote one way merely because they know a colleague is on the other side of the issue. For some legislators, the state delegation (senators and representatives from their home state) reinforces a common identity.

A member may also vote with a colleague in the expectation that the colleague will later vote for a measure about which the member is concerned—called **logrolling**. Some vote trading takes place to build coalitions so that members can "bring home the bacon" to their constituents. Other vote trading reflects reciprocity in congressional relations or deference to colleagues' superior information or expertise.

CONGRESSIONAL STAFF   Representatives and senators used to be at a distinct disadvantage in dealing with the executive branch because they were overly dependent on information supplied by the White House or lobbyists. The complexity of the issues and increasingly demanding schedules created pressures for additional staff. Congress

logrolling
Mutual aid and vote trading among legislators.

responded and gradually expanded its staffs, and this expansion has strengthened the role of Congress in the public policy process.

Because both chambers have roughly equal amounts of money for staff, Senate members and committees have much larger staffs than their House counterparts. Most congressional staff do not work in Washington, but in district and state offices back home. These offices are run very much like a continuous political campaign. Members of Congress return home every weekend to make speeches, appear on television, raise money, and greet voters, all of which are arranged in advance by their district or state staffs.

CONSTITUENTS Members of Congress rarely vote against the strong wishes of their constituents, but often think their constituents are more interested in a particular issue than they really are.[40] Members mostly hear from the **attentive public**—citizens who follow public affairs closely—rather than the general public. Nearly 70 percent of constituents say they have not visited, faxed, phoned, e-mailed, or written their member of Congress in the past four years.[41] Still, members of Congress are generally concerned about how they will explain their votes, especially as election day approaches. Even if only a few voters are aware of their stand on a given issue, this group might make the difference between victory and defeat.

Representative Carolyn McCarthy shows an assault rifle once covered under a federal ban. McCarthy's husband was killed in a handgun shooting, which led her enter to politics.

CONVICTIONS Members of Congress are influenced by their own experiences and attitudes about the role of government.[42] A liberal on social issues is also likely to be a liberal on tax and national security issues. Ideology is closely related to party as a predictor of congressional voting. In 2005, for example, the most liberal members of the House and Senate were all Democrats and mostly came from the Northeast or West, while the most conservative members of the House and Senate were all Republicans and mostly came from the South or Midwest. According to the 2006 rankings by the *National Journal*, Mac Collin (R-Ga.), Jack Kingston (R-Ga.), and Ed Schrock (R-Va.) were tied as the most conservative House members, while Pete Stark (D-Calif.) was the most liberal. In turn, Don Nickles (R-Okla.) and Craig Thomas (R-Wyo.) were tied as the most conservative senators, while Daniel Akaka (D-Hawaii) was the most liberal.[43]

This is not to argue that party is a perfect predictor of ideology. In 2004, for example, a group of moderate Democrats and Republicans created the "Center Aisle Caucus" to show their joint agreement on issues. As Rep. Steve Israel (D-N.Y.) said of his new coalition, "Democrats and Republicans may disagree on 75% of the issues. But if we agree and implement the remaining 25%, the country is 100% better off than before."[44] Moreover, as the *National Journal* rankings show, there are ideological mavericks in both parties. In 2006, there were several Northeastern Republicans in both chambers that were more liberal than many Southern Democrats.

INTEREST GROUPS Interest groups influence the legislative process in many ways. They make contributions to congressional campaigns, testify before committees, provide information to legislative staff, and build public pressure for or against their cause. Congressional lobbying has existed since the early 1800s and is a perfectly legal exercise of the First Amendment right to petition government.

However, it is sometimes difficult to tell where lobbyists end and Congress begins, especially in the heat of the legislative debate over major legislation such as the 2003 prescription drug bill. Republicans worked closely with the insurance industry to put

attentive public
Those citizens who follow public affairs closely.

Government's Greatest Endeavors

Creating a Strong National Defense

QUESTIONS

Why does Congress buy more military weapons than the military wants?

How does coordination between the armed services make the military stronger?

America has the strongest national defense in the world. It spends more money on defense than any other nation, and it has invested heavily in sophisticated technologies that make the United States almost impossible to defeat in war.

Although presidents support a strong national defense,

Congress often buys more and different kinds of weapons than either presidents want or the military needs. Defense spending is spread across most of the states and many congressional districts, and congressional incumbents eagerly seek spending in their districts.

It is one thing to have the equipment to fight a war, however, and quite another to use it effectively. That is why Congress passed a 1986 reform designed to improve coordination between the armed services. The 1986 law gave the Secretary of Defense much more authority to force the Army, Navy, and Air Force to work together in battle.

The reforms helped the military win the early battles

in Afghanistan (2001) and Iraq (2003). Army troops and Marines often called on the Air Force to help them destroy enemy defenses, while the Navy often worked with the Air Force to protect U.S. troops against enemy attacks.

The reforms also forced the military to work together in designing a single fighter airplane to use far into the future. The new Joint Strike Fighter is the most sophisticated fighter plane in the world, but it is much easier to fly and repair. It is also the most expensive fighter plane in the world, which may yet require Congress to make tough decisions about which weapons the nation can afford. ■

The Joint Strike Fighter is the most sophisticated war plane in the world.

the prescription program in their hands, Democrats worked with senior citizen groups to create the largest drug benefit possible, while both parties worked with the drugmakers to cover as many drugs as possible. Although the final bill tilted toward the insurance industry, the lobbying paid off for most of the interest groups involved in the debate.

Interest groups often cancel each other out by taking opposing positions on issues, thereby killing a bill. Some of this maneuvering occurs at the subcommittee level and is almost invisible to the public. But it is always visible to the interest groups and Congress. "The result," says Senator Joe Lieberman of Connecticut, "is that everyone on Capitol Hill is keeping a close eye on everyone else, creating a self-adjusting system of checks and balances."[45] Lieberman's comment may have been more hopeful than realistic, however.

Interest groups are almost always most effective when they mobilize public pressure on members of Congress. For example, higher education lobbying groups have effectively mobilized students and educators to write and call members of Congress on behalf of student aid and related provisions in various measures before Congress.[46] And tobacco companies spent large sums to fight taxes on cigarettes. Although most members of Congress reject the popular perception that interest groups "buy" their

U.S. Senator James Jeffords of Vermont, on the steps of the Capitol with prominent Democrats the day before he left the Republican party to become an Independent. Jeffords's decision gave the Democrats control of the Senate until 2003. He left the Republican party because he believed it had grown too conservative and was putting undue pressure on him to vote the party line.

votes, political contributions certainly do influence the parties and help provide access to members of Congress.

However, the vast majority of campaign contributions go to incumbents, which creates the image that lobbyists are buying future votes. Moreover, many members of Congress go to work as lobbyists once they retire, which also creates the image that members are cashing in past votes for future employment.

PARTY Members generally vote with their party. Whether as a result of party pressure or natural affinity, on major bills there is a tendency for most Democrats to be arrayed against most Republicans. Partisan voting has increased in the House since the early 1970s and has intensified even more since the 1994 elections. Indeed, party-line voting has been greater in recent years than at any time in recent decades. Party discipline is strongest on domestic issues such as health care, social welfare, economic policy, and judicial appointments. For example, all but four Democratic senators voted against Samuel Alito's confirmation to the Supreme Court in 2006, while all but one Republican voted in favor.

Members of both parties have become more loyal over the past thirty years, in part because each party has become more liberal or conservative. Since 2000, almost 90 percent of congressional Democrats and Republicans have voted with their party on key votes, compared with less than 70 percent on average during the 1970s, and less than 80 percent in the 1980s.[47] Party discipline also explains the increase—leaders of both parties have become more effective in holding their members together on key votes, in part because their members have drifted toward more liberal or conservative convictions. Liberal Democrats and conservative Republicans stick together on most votes.

"[E]veryone on Capitol Hill is keeping a close eye on everyone else, creating a self-adjusting system of checks and balances."

SENATOR JOE LIEBERMAN (I-CT)

President George W. Bush sits on a motorcycle in the "roll test" booth at the Harley-Davidson assembly plant in August 2006. Bush enjoyed nearly unprecedented congressional support his first year in office. His influence on congress remained high in the five years after that, though taking fewer and fewer positions on congressional votes contributed to his support scoring.

PRESIDENTS Presidents have a variety of tools for influencing Congress, not the least of which is the ability to distribute government resources to their friends. Presidents also help set the legislative agenda through their annual State of the Union Address, the budget, and assorted legislative messages, and lobby Congress on particularly important issues.

When asked why they vote one way or the other, members of Congress tend to deny the president's influence. Far better to say they are voting on behalf of their constituents or convictions than because of presidential pressure. But presidents work hard to influence public opinion, and they have a long list of incentives to encourage congressional support, not the least of which are invitations to special White House dinners and federal grants to support key projects back home. Congress is also likely to rally 'round the president during times of national crisis, which is what helped George W. Bush win 87 percent of the 120 congressional votes on which he took a clear position in 2001, easily besting every president since Lyndon Johnson, who won 93 percent of these key votes in 1965.[48]

Bush's support scores remained high through his first five years: He won 88 percent of his votes in 2002, 78 percent in 2003, 75 percent in 2004, and 78 percent again in 2005. Although the percentages would seem to make Bush the most influential president in modern history, Bush earned the scores by taking fewer and fewer positions. Whereas Bill Clinton took a position on an average of 86 House votes a year during his eight years in office, Bush took a position on only 46 of 669 key House votes in 2005 and just 45 of 366 key Senate votes. Moreover, when Bush did take a position, it was mostly in favor of bills that Congress was about to pass. He was influential, but only on a handful of votes. (We will return to presidential influence in Congress in Chapter 12.)

Legislative Ethics

Members of Congress have never been under greater scrutiny regarding their conduct, in part because they have never had so many rules governing their conduct. Despite the recent scandals, members of Congress have worked hard to improve individual conduct through rules that place limits on the value of gifts and meals they receive, but not yet on who pays for travel. Republicans even argued that Tom DeLay's resignation from the Minority Leader's position was proof that the ethics process works—after all, the House Committee on Standards of Official Conduct reprimanded him several times before the Abramoff lobbying scandal emerged. However, the measure of an effective ethics system is not in its ability to catch members after they have violated the rules, but in preventing the violations before they take place. By that measure, the ethics process has improved over the past 30 years, but is still not strong enough.

Under the Constitution, Congress is responsible for punishing its own members. Although individual members are subject to federal prosecution for bribery and other criminal acts, the House and Senate set the more general rules for ethical conduct, and investigate all complaints of misbehavior. Under the rules, members of Congress cannot solicit or receive gifts valued at more than $50, though they may accept larger gifts from family members and friends. Similarly, they cannot solicit or receive a meal val-

Agents of Change

J. B. Schramm and College Summit

College Summit was created in 1993 to help low-income high school students enter college. Knowing that thousands of high school seniors have the ability to succeed in college but simply do not know how to apply, College Summit provides knowledge and training to make sure they send in the strongest applications possible. This help involves basic guidance counseling, easy-to-use information on how to apply, and a four-day summer workshop on lifelong leadership skills. Students who attend the workshop are also trained to help other students apply to college, which multiplies the effect of the program once a senior is accepted.

The program was created by J. B. Schramm, who had the idea while directing a teen drop-in center in the basement of a low-income housing project in Washington, D.C. Having worked as an academic advisor to college freshmen at Harvard University, Schramm knew that many students were well coached in applying to college. Knowing that the average high school counselor handles 350 students a year, Schramm decided to make College Summit a new form of high school counseling. "If all the kids who could go to college went, there would be a benefit to the government of more than $60 billion a year in federal taxes," Schramm says, not to mention the simple value of helping kids succeed.

College Summit also teaches low-income seniors to believe in themselves, and encourages them to pursue any career they desire, including politics and government. Almost 80 percent of College Summit students attend college, which is more than twice the national average of 34 percent for low-income students. And almost 80 percent of College Summit students graduate. ■

Read more about College Summit at www.collegesummit.org.

J. B. Schramm

QUESTION
How might College Summit help Congress make decisions about student loan programs and other educational assistance?

ued at more than $50, but can accept meals of any value at large meetings, conventions, discussions, and events where admission is free to other members. Finally, they cannot accept any payment for making a speech, attending an event, or writing an article. Although they may accept free travel and expenses for making speeches and attending events, such travel must be related to their official duties as a member of Congress.

The House and Senate enforce the rules through separate ethics committees (the House Committee on Standards of Official Conduct and the Senate Ethics Committee). Because the seats on both committees are divided equally between Democrats and Republicans (four on each side in the House, and three on each side in the Senate), and are filled through the normal committee selection process, members are under tremendous pressure not to hurt their own party.

There are two types of congressional ethics, however. The first involves *individual conduct*, which refers to each member's willingness to obey the current rules on accepting gifts and taking trips. The second involves *institutional conduct*, which refers to Congress as a whole. Individual members can be perfectly ethical, for example, even though Congress allows unlimited campaign fundraising when members are in session, gives interest groups unlimited access to committee members and their staff, and permits former members to return as lobbyists the day they retire. It is difficult for individual members to remain ethical when the institution as a whole creates the conditions that foster potential corruption.[49]

This is not to argue that Congress ignores potential violations, as DeLay's resignations prove. Even after DeLay left office, however, Congress remained unwilling or unable to create tougher rules against the conduct that led to the lobbying scandal. Although the House and Senate tightened their ethics rules after DeLay resigned, the changes were relatively minor and merely required more reporting of potential conflicts, not actual bans on accepting free trips, travel on corporate jets, or gifts.

The Legislative Obstacle Course

Congress operates under a system of multiple vetoes. The framers intentionally dispersed powers so that no would-be tyrant or majority could accumulate enough authority to oppress the nation. Follow a bill through the legislative process, and there are at least 23 ways it can die—some visible, others completely hidden from public view.

1. The Speaker of the House can refuse to give the bill to a committee

2. The chair of the House authorizing subcommittee can refuse to forward a bill to a subcommittee

3. The House authorizing subcommittee as a whole can reject the bill

4. The chair of the House authorizing committee can refuse to schedule a hearing

5. The House authorizing committee as a whole can reject the bill

6. The House Rules Committee can refuse to send the bill to the floor

7. A majority of the House can reject the bill

8. The House appropriations subcommittee can refuse to provide money for the bill

9. The Senate majority leader can refuse to give the bill to a committee

10. The chair of the Senate authorizing subcommittee can reject the bill

11. The Senate authorizing subcommittee as a whole can reject the bill

12. The chair of the Senate authorizing committee can refuse to schedule a hearing

13. The Senate authorizing committee as a whole can reject the bill

14. The Senate appropriations committee can refuse to provide money for the bill

15. A senator or senators can place a hold on the bill or mount a filibuster

16. The majority of the Senate can reject the bill, or fail to gain enough votes to remove a hold or stop a filibuster

17. The floor leaders in either chamber can refuse to schedule the bill for debate

18. A majority in the Senate can reject the bill

19. A House–Senate conference committee can fail to resolve the differences between two versions of the same bill

20. A majority of the House can reject the conference committee agreement

21. A majority of the Senate can reject the conference committee agreement

22. The president can refuse to sign the bill

23. The Senate or House can fail to override the president's decision

Given these options, it is hardly surprising that so many bills never reach a final vote. It is much easier to kill a bill than to pass one. Nevertheless, hope springs eternal, and many bills are introduced to make a statement about a member's personal interests and desire for change.

How Ideas Become Bills

Name a domestic or international problem, and Congress has almost certainly considered legislation to solve it, largely because the vast majority of members come to Washington to make a difference for their country. Some bills are designed to advance government's past success, such as reducing disease, increasing access to college, strengthening the highway system, or reducing poverty among the elderly. Others are designed to address the lack of progress on long-standing problems such as workplace discrimination, human rights abuses, air and water pollution, or poverty among children.

Members also care about making a difference on issues that have affected them personally. "Politicians are human beings," said Massachusetts representative Joe Kennedy II, whose father was assassinated with a handgun during his 1968 presidential campaign and whose cousin suffered from bone cancer. "When there is a degree of very personal pain that one feels toward an issue—it might be gun control or my uncle's interest in fighting cancer—commitment level is higher and your willingness to compromise is lower."[50] Kennedy has been a strong supporter of both handgun control and increased health care research.

"Politicians are human beings."

REPRESENTATIVE JOE KENNEDY II (D-MA)

How Bills Become Laws

A bill must win many small contests on the way to final passage (see Figure 11–2). There are four broad steps from beginning to end: (1) introduction, which involves putting a formal proposal before the House or the Senate; (2) committee review, which involves holding a hearing and "marking up" the bill; (3) floor debate and passage, which means getting on the legislative calendar, passing once in each chamber, surviving a conference to iron out any differences between the House and Senate versions, and passing once again in each chamber; and (4) presidential approval.

INTRODUCING A BILL   House members introduce a bill by placing it into a mahogany box (called the hopper) on a desk at the front of the House chamber; senators introduce a bill by either handing it to the clerk of the Senate or by presenting it to their colleagues in a floor speech. In the more informal Senate, members sometimes short-circuit the formalities by offering a bill as an amendment to pending legislation. A bill that comes from the House is always designated H.R. (House of Representatives) followed by its number, and a bill from the Senate is always designated S. (Senate) followed by its number. Although presidents often recommend legislation to Congress, a member of the House or Senate must introduce all bills.

COMMITTEE REVIEW   Once a bill is introduced in either chamber, it is "read" into the record as a formal proposal and referred to the appropriate committee—tax bills to Ways and Means or Finance; farm bills to Agriculture; technology bills to Science, Space, and Technology; small business to Small Business; and so forth. The parliamentarian in each chamber decides where to send each bill.

The Referral Decision   Although most bills are referred to a single committee, particularly complex bills may be referred simultaneously or sequentially to multiple committees. President Bush's proposed Department of Homeland Security bill was so complicated and touched so many agencies that it was managed by a temporary

FIGURE 11–2 **How a Bill Becomes a Law.**

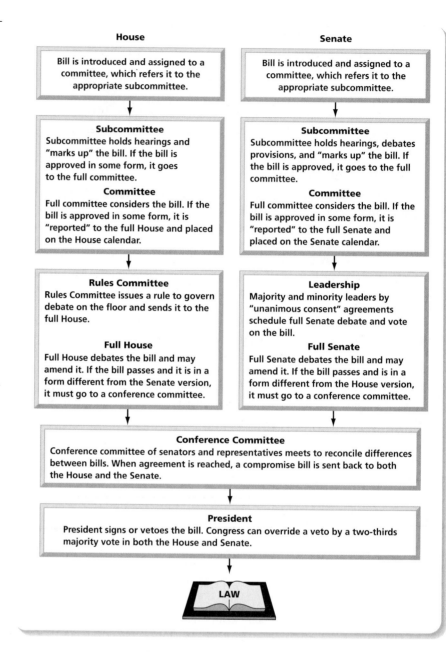

special committee in the House. The bill was referred to at least ten committees, including Judiciary, Ways and Means, and Government Reform, all of which held hearings on specific provisions of the largest government reorganization since the Department of Defense was created in 1947. The bill went into the House as a 35-page proposal and came out almost 500 pages long. Committees and their subcommittees are responsible for building a legislative record in support of a given bill. This *legislative record* also helps the president and federal courts interpret what Congress intended.

Markup Once a committee or subcommittee decides to pass the bill, it "marks it up" to clean up the wording or amend its version of the bill. The term *markup* refers to the pencil marks that members make on the final version of the bill.

Markups can produce significant changes in a bill, however. Amendments are often adopted, major provisions deleted, and new text written. Although the public is usually invited to attend, most markups involve members of Congress, their staffs, and lobbyists. The conversations are fast, agreements quick, and most of the agreements prearranged through one-on-one meetings between key members. The goal of a markup is to move forward, not spend endless hours debating specific language.

Once markup is over, the bill must be passed by the committee or subcommittee and forwarded to the next step in the process. If it is passed by a subcommittee, for example, it is forwarded to the full committee; if it is passed by a full committee in the House, it is then forwarded to the House Rules Committee for a rule that will govern debate on the floor; if it is passed by a full committee in the Senate, it is forwarded to the full chamber.

Discharge   Most bills die in committee without a hearing or further review, largely because the majority party simply does not favor action. However, a bill can be forced to the floor of the House through a **discharge petition** signed by a majority of the membership. In 2002, for example, House members were able to collect enough signatures to discharge the Rules Committee on a campaign finance reform bill that had been stalled for six months. Because most members share a strong sense of reciprocity, or mutual respect, toward the work of other committees, few discharge petitions are successful. The Senate does not use discharge petitions.

FLOOR DEBATE AND PASSAGE   Once reported to the full chamber directly from committee in the Senate or through the Rules Committee in the House, a bill will usually be scheduled for floor action or dropped entirely. Having come this far, most bills are passed into law.

Final passage sometimes comes at a very high price, however, especially when spending bills are involved. Although House members must accept the terms of debate set by the House Rules Committee, senators often attach **riders**, or unrelated amendments, to a bill either to win concessions from the sponsors or to reduce the odds of passage. Riders can also be used by sponsors to sweeten a bill and improve the odds of passage.[51]

Except for tax bills, which must originate in the House, the two chambers generally move forward on legislation independently. Bills that do not pass both chambers by the end of a two-year Congress must be reintroduced at the start of the next Congress and go through the entire process again.

Once a bill has passed both houses in identical form, it is inscribed on parchment paper and hand-delivered to the president, who may *sign* it into law or *veto* it. If Congress is in session and the president waits ten days (not counting Sundays), the bill becomes law *without* his signature. If Congress has adjourned and the president waits ten days without signing the bill, it is defeated by what is known as a **pocket veto**. After a pocket veto, the bill is dead. Otherwise, when a bill is vetoed, it is returned to the chamber of its origin by the president with a message explaining the reasons for the veto. Congress can vote to **override** the veto by a two-thirds vote in each chamber, but assembling such an extraordinary majority is often difficult. Just the threat of a veto may be enough to derail a bill, but the threat must be real. During his first five years in office, for example, George W. Bush did not veto a single bill, thereby weakening the believability of his veto threats.

An Assessment of Congress

More than two centuries after its creation, Congress is a larger, more vital, and very different kind of institution from the one the framers envisioned. It has become much more complex, more divided, and much more active. Yet most of its major functions remain the same, and their effective exercise is crucial to the health of our constitutional democracy. Even in the twenty-first century, Americans still look to Congress to solve problems, check the president, and oversee the executive branch.

discharge petition
Petition that, if signed by a majority of the House of Representatives' members, will pry a bill from committee and bring it to the floor for consideration.

rider
A provision attached to a bill—to which it may or may not be related—in order to secure its passage or defeat.

pocket veto
A veto exercised by the president after Congress has adjourned; if the president takes no action for ten days, the bill does not become law and is not returned to Congress for a possible override.

override
An action taken by Congress to reverse a presidential veto, requiring a two-thirds majority in each chamber.

On Tuesday, September 11, 2001, the leadership of the House of Representatives and the Senate gathered on the steps of the Capitol with other congressional members in a gesture of unity after the terrorist attacks.

Although most incumbents are easily reelected, most campaign constantly to stay in office, creating what some observers have called the "permanent campaign." Members appear driven by their desire to win reelection, so that much of what takes place in Congress seems mainly designed to promote reelection. These efforts usually pay off for members of Congress: Members who seek reelection almost always win.

The permanent campaign also affects legislative progress. In an institution where most members act as individual entrepreneurs and consider themselves leaders, the task of providing institutional leadership is increasingly difficult. With limited resources, and only sometimes aided by the president, congressional leaders are asked to bring together a diverse, fragmented, and independent institution. The congressional system acts only when majorities can be achieved. That the framers accomplished their original objective—creating a body that would not move with imprudent haste—has been generally well realized.

Newly elected presidents and members of Congress always arrive in Washington enthusiastically ready to enact the people's wishes. But they find that governing is invariably tougher and slower than they expected because government deals with complex issues about which there is often little consensus. Building policy majorities is hard because complex problems generate complex solutions, and the structure of Congress requires supermajorities to agree to serious changes. Thus the president's veto, the filibuster, and the use of holds and legislative riders all make consensus more difficult to find.

Criticism of Congress—its alleged incompetence, its responsiveness to organized interests, its inefficiencies, its party divisions—is difficult to separate from the context of policy preferences and democratic procedures. Sometimes criticism tells us more about the critic than it does about the effectiveness of Congress. Constitutional democracy is not the most efficient form of government. Congress was never intended to act swiftly; it was not created to be a rubber stamp or even a cooperative partner for presidents. Its greatest strengths—its diversity and deliberative character—also weaken its position in dealing with the more centralized executive branch.

The framers would not be troubled by the lack of action, however. By dividing power, they hoped to control it. The odds against action are high precisely because the framers did not want any one branch of the government to become a threat to individual liberty.

Summary

1. Congress plays a crucial role in our system of shared powers, controlling key decisions and constraining presidents. Yet over time, Congress has lost some influence as the presidency has gained influence. In recent decades, however, Congress has become more capable as a policy-making competitor for presidents. Redistricting and reapportionment have shaped a Congress that somewhat more accurately reflects the population.

2. The most distinctive feature of Congress is its bicameralism, which the framers intended as a moderating influence on partisanship and possible error. Each chamber has a few distinctive functions. The organization and procedures of the two houses also differ slightly, as do their political environments.

3. Congress performs these functions: representation, lawmaking, consensus building, overseeing the bureaucracy, policy clarification, and investigating. The Senate also confirms or denies presidential appointments and participates in the ratification of treaties.

4. Congress manages its workload through a leadership system that is different in both chambers. The House is led by the Speaker, a majority and a minority leader, and whips in each party, while the Senate is led by a majority and a minority leader. The Senate is more difficult to lead because of its greater individualism, which is sometimes expressed through the use of holds and filibusters to control the legislative process.

5. Most of the work in Congress is done in committees and subcommittees. Congress has attempted in recent years to streamline its committee system and modify its methods of selecting committee chairs. Seniority practices are still generally followed. Subcommittees are important, as they can prevent or delay legislation from being enacted. But there are numerous other stages when bills can be killed, making it easier to stop legislation than to enact it.

6. As a collective body, Congress must attempt to accomplish its tasks even as most of its members serve as delegates or trustees for their constituents. When they vote, members are influenced by their philosophy and values, their perceptions of constituents' interests, and the views of trusted colleagues and staff, partisan ties and party leaders, lobbyists, and the president.

7. The members of Congress do an excellent job of representing the values and views of most of their constituents. But they are cautious about enacting measures proposed by their own colleagues or the legislative agenda put forward by presidents. Most proposed legislation dies for lack of majority support.

8. Members of Congress are motivated by the desire to win reelection, and much of what Congress does is in response to this motive. Members work hard to get favors for their districts, to serve the needs of constituents, and to maintain high visibility in their districts or states. Incumbents have advantages that help explain their success at reelection: They have greater name recognition, they have large staffs, they are much better able to raise campaign money, and they have greater access to the media.

9. A bill becomes a law through a process that involves many opportunities for defeat. Although all formal bills are referred to committees for consideration, very few receive a hearing, even fewer are marked up and sent to the floor, and fewer still are enacted by both chambers and signed into law by the president. In addition, the legislative obstacle course sometimes involves filibusters, riders, holds, and the occasional override of a presidential veto.

10. Individual members of Congress are more popular than the institution. Congress is criticized for being inefficient, unrepresentative, unethical, and lacking in collective responsibility. Yet criticisms of Congress are difficult to separate from the context of policy preference and democratic procedures. Congress's greatest strengths—its diversity and its deliberative character—also contribute to its weaknesses.

Further Reading

JOEL D. ABERBACH, *Keeping a Watchful Eye: The Politics of Congressional Oversight* (Brookings Institution Press, 1990).

E. SCOTT ADLER, *Why Congressional Reforms Fail: Reelection and the House Committee System* (University of Chicago Press, 2002).

SARAH A. BINDER, *Stalemate: Causes and Consequences of Legislative Gridlock* (Brookings Institution Press, 2003).

SARAH A. BINDER AND **STEVEN S. SMITH,** *Politics or Principles? Filibustering in the United States Senate* (Brookings Institution Press, 1997).

BILL BRADLEY, *Time Present, Time Past: A Memoir* (Knopf, 1996).

DAVID W. BRADY AND **CRAIG VOLDEN,** *Revolving Gridlock: Politics and Policy from Carter to Clinton* (Westview Press, 1998).

ADAM CLYMER, *Edward M. Kennedy: A Biography* (Morrow, 1999).

ROGER H. DAVIDSON AND **WALTER J. OLESZEK,** *Congress and Its Members,* 10th ed. (CQ Press, 2005).

CHRISTOPHER J. DEERING AND **STEVEN S. SMITH,** *Committees in Congress,* 3d ed. (CQ Press, 1997).

LAWRENCE C. DODD AND **BRUCE J. OPPENHEIMER,** EDS., *Congress Reconsidered,* 8th ed. (CQ Press, 2005).

RICHARD F. FENNO JR., *Home Style: House Members in Their Districts* (Little, Brown, 1978).

RICHARD F. FENNO JR., *Learning to Govern: An Institutional View of the 104th Congress* (Brookings Institution Press, 1997).

RICHARD F. FENNO JR., *Senators on the Campaign Trail: The Politics of Representation* (University of Oklahoma Press, 1996).

MORRIS P. FIORINA, *Congress: Keystone of the Washington Establishment,* 2d ed. (Yale University Press, 1989)

LEE H. HAMILTON, *How Congress Works and Why You Should Care* (Indiana University Press, 2004).

PAUL HERRNSON, *Congressional Elections,* 4th ed. (CQ Press, 2003).

JOHN R. HIBBING AND **ELIZABETH THEISS-MORSE,** *Congress as Public Enemy: Public Attitudes Toward American Political Institutions* (Cambridge University Press, 1995).

GODFREY HODGSON, *The Gentleman from New York: Daniel Patrick Moynihan* (Houghton Mifflin, 2000).

GARY JACOBSON, *Politics of Congressional Elections,* 6th ed. (CQ Press, 2003)

LINDA KILLIAN, *The Freshmen: What Happened to the Republican Revolution?* (Westview Press, 1998).

FRANCES E. LEE AND **BRUCE I. OPPENHEIMER,** *Sizing Up the Senate: The Unequal Consequences of Equal Representation* (University of Chicago Press, 1999).

JOSEPH I. LIEBERMAN, *In Praise of Public Life* (Simon & Schuster, 2000).

TOM LOFTUS, *The Art of Legislative Politics* (CQ Press, 1994).

JANET M. MARTIN, *Lessons from the Hill: The Legislative Journey of an Education Program* (St. Martin's Press, 1993).

DAVID R. MAYHEW, *America's Congress: Actions in the Public Sphere, James Madison Through Newt Gingrich* (Yale University Press, 2002).

BARBARA MIKULSKI ET AL., *Nine and Counting: The Women of the Senate* (Morrow, 2000).

WALTER J. OLESZEK, *Congressional Procedures and the Policy Process,* 6th ed. (CQ Press, 2004).

NORMAN J. ORNSTEIN, THOMAS MANN, AND **MICHAEL MALBIN,** *Vital Statistics on Congress, 2002–2004* (AEI Press, 2004).

RONALD M. PETERS JR., ED., *The Speaker: Leadership in the U.S. House of Representatives* (CQ Press, 1995).

DAVID E. PRICE, *The Congressional Experience: A View from the Hill* (Westview Press, 1993).

NICOL RAE AND **COLTON CAMPBELL,** EDS., *New Majority or Old Majority: The Impact of Republicans on Congress* (Rowman & Littlefield, 1999).

WARREN B. RUDMAN, *Combat: Twelve Years in the U.S. Senate* (Random House, 1996).

BARBARA SINCLAIR, *Unorthodox Lawmaking: New Legislative Processes in the U.S. Congress,* 2d ed. (CQ Press, 2000).

DARVELL M. WEST, *Patrick Kennedy: The Rise to Power* (Prentice Hall, 2001).

KeyTerms

constituents, p. 310

reapportionment, p. 311

redistricting, p. 311

gerrymandering, p. 311

safe seat, p. 311

incumbent, p. 311

bicameralism, p. 314

enumerated powers, p. 315

Speaker, p. 318

party caucus, p. 319

majority leader, p. 320

minority leader, p. 320

whip, p. 320

closed rule, p. 320

open rule, p. 320

president pro tempore, p. 322

hold, p. 322

filibuster, p. 322

cloture, p. 322

senatorial courtesy, p. 324

standing committee, p. 324

special or select committee, p. 324

joint committee, p. 324

earmarks, p. 325

seniority rule, p. 326

conference committee, p. 328

delegate, p. 329

trustee, p. 329

logrolling, p. 330

attentive public, p. 331

discharge petition, p. 339

rider, p. 339

pocket veto, p. 339

override, p. 339

★ ★ ★
Make It Real
CONGRESS
★ ★
The simulation makes the student
a member of Congress.

Chapter 12

The Presidency

THE LEADERSHIP BRANCH

✦

GEORGE W. BUSH MADE A SECRET DECISION IN EARLY 2002. CONVINCED THAT FOREIGN TERRORISTS WERE CALLING THEIR CONTACTS INSIDE THE UNITED STATES, BUSH AUTHORIZED THE NATIONAL SECURITY AGENCY (NSA) TO START EAVESDROPPING ON TELEPHONE CONVERSATIONS. THE NATIONAL SECURITY AGENCY IS SO SECRET THAT ONLY A HANDFUL OF SENIOR OFFICIALS AND MEMBERS OF CONGRESS KNOW ITS BUDGET, NUMBER OF EMPLOYEES, AND PROGRAMS. UNDER THE PRESIDENT'S ORDER, THE NSA LISTENED TO thousands of telephone conversations and read thousands of e-mails from inside the United States to potential terrorists abroad. The program allowed the NSA to spy on U.S. citizens without any congressional or judicial review.

President Bush later argued that the secret program was fully consistent with his authority, as commander in chief, to defend the nation from foreign attack. Although federal law explicitly requires a court order for the government to listen to private conservations, Bush said, "The American people expect me to do everything in my power under our laws and Constitution to protect them and their civil liberties. And that is exactly what I will continue to do, so long as I am President of the United States."[1]

The program became national news after the *New York Times* reported that Bush had not only authorized the program only months after the September 11, 2001, terrorist attacks on New York City and Washington, D.C., but had reauthorized the program dozens of times afterward. The newspaper reminded readers that the president already had the authority to eavesdrop under the 1978 Foreign Intelligence Surveillance Act (FISA), which created accelerated procedures for requesting judicial authorization of just such secret surveillance. Under that act, presidents were allowed to listen to conversations for 72 hours; after that, they had to request a judicial order before a secret court. Although FISA seemed to provide ample authority for the spying program, President Bush and his advisors wanted the NSA to engage in such sweeping eavesdropping that the individual approvals would overwhelm the court.

Some members of Congress were angered by the program. As Republican Senator Lindsey Graham said in late February 2006, "If you're going to follow an American citizen around for an extended period of time believing they're collaborating with the enemy, at some point in time, you need to get some judicial review, because mistakes can be made."[2] As pressure mounted, the Bush administration reluctantly agreed to seek congressional approval for the program. Despite the president's concern that terrorists might change their communication channels after learning about the secret program, Congress decided to assert its role in questioning the president's broad powers to suspend civil liberties during times of war. Presidents

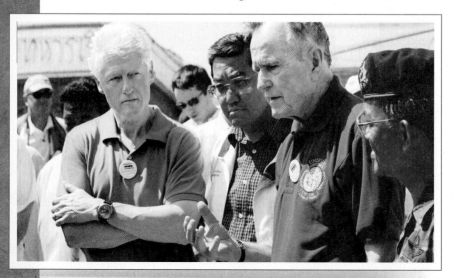

> "The American people expect me to do everything in my power under our laws and Constitution to protect them and their civil liberties."
>
> PRESIDENT GEORGE W. BUSH

OUTLINE

★

The Structure and Powers of the Presidency

★

Controversies in Presidential Power

★

Evolution of the Presidency

★

Managing the Presidency

★

The President's Job

★

Congress and the Presidency

★

Judging Presidents

345

may have the power to wage war, but not to violate laws created to protect U.S. citizens from their government. Although some argued that there was a precedent for such action, such as when Abraham Lincoln had used similar powers to suspend civil liberties during the Civil War, Congress began working on legislation to authorize the program and set limits on its reach. As of September 2006, Congress was still working to pass the legislation.

The framers of the Constitution both admired and feared centralized leadership. Although they knew that a strong president was needed to protect the nation against foreign and domestic threats, they also worried about the potential abuse of power. This chapter will examine the framers' intent in designing the presidency, review the president's powers, and then turn to the continuing controversies surrounding the exercise of these powers. We will also explore the many jobs of the president and ask how Congress and the president work together and against each other in making the laws. We conclude with a discussion of how history judges presidents.

The Structure and Powers of the Presidency

The framers wanted the president to act with "dispatch" against threats, but they also worried that presidents could become too powerful. Although they gave the president the power to run the executive branch, which includes the White House and all departments and agencies, they limited the president's other powers to a relatively short list, including the power to wage wars declared by Congress, report to the nation from time to time on the state of the union, nominate judges and executive appointees for Senate confirmation, and negotiate treaties.

The framers believed that the "jarrings of parties" in Congress were perfectly appropriate in making the laws, but not in fighting wars and running the executive branch. They did not believe the president should have unlimited freedom to act, however. Having given a much longer list of powers to Congress, they saw the president as a powerful check on legislative action, and as essential to the administration of government. As Alexander Hamilton argued in *The Federalist*, No. 70, which explains the presidency in detail, "A feeble executive implies a feeble execution of the government. A feeble execution is but another phrase for a bad execution: And a government ill executed, whatever it may be in theory, must be in practice a bad government."[3]

Having given this executive responsibility to a single person who would be eligible for reelection, the framers insulated the presidency from public opinion. To this day, for example, presidents are not elected directly by the public, but by electors who are selected in winner-take-all systems in all but two states, Maine and Nebraska. As a result, presidents often claim to speak for the entire nation, not a single district or state.

At the same time, the framers created a presidency of limited powers. They wanted a presidential office that would steer clear of parties and factions, enforce the laws passed by Congress, handle communications with foreign governments, and help states put down disorders. They wanted a presidency strong enough to match Congress yet not so strong that it would overpower Congress.

Separate Powers

The framers created a system of separate powers that prevents any one branch from controlling all of government. However, merely having three branches of national government—legislative, executive, and judicial—does not by itself create a pure system of separated powers; the United Kingdom also has legislative and executive branches, but both are automatically headed by the same political party, since the prime minister is chosen by members of the majority party in Parliament.

In the United States, the legislative, executive, and judicial branches are independent of one another. Although there are times when the legislative and executive

How Other Nations Govern

The Mexican President

The Mexican president is one of the most powerful elected chief executives in the democratic world, but was once also known as one of its most corrupt. Under the constitution of 1917, which was adopted after a decade of civil war, the president was given sweeping powers to run the country, including the authority to hire and fire most government employees. Many Mexican presidents used these powers to favor friends and party loyalists, sometimes for their own financial gain. Some also used the office to suppress opposition. Because Mexican presidents can only serve for one six-year term, they have sometimes been called the most powerful "six-year monarchs" in the world.

For most of its recent history the Mexican presidency was controlled by a single political party that the Mexican government itself created, the Institutional Revolutionary Party, or PRI. With party control ensured from term to term, presidents controlled the right to select their own successors. Although PRI candidates often faced opposition in the general election, the party earned a well-deserved reputation as the world's most efficient election machine.

Mexico took a dramatic step toward a more democratic system in 2000 when the nation elected Vicente Fox as president. A former Coca-Cola executive, Fox drew upon his populist roots as a rancher from the rural state of Guanajuato, saying he was the only candidate who had ever milked a cow. As a member of the National Action Party, which had opposed many of PRI's policies, Fox also drew upon Mexico's desire for a change from one-party rule. "From today forward, we need to unite," he said at a victory rally in 2000. "Let's celebrate today, because beginning tomorrow there's a lot of work to do." Fox was given all the powers of the presidency to do so, but left office after the July

2006 presidential elections with much of his agenda unfulfilled.

Fox did set one important precedent for his country. As the latest elections proved, Mexico is no longer governed by a single party.

Fox was replaced on December 1, 2006, by another member of his party, Felipe Calderón, who is expected to follow Fox's policies. However, the election was so close that Calderón's opponent demanded an immediate recount, and eventually appealed the results to Mexico's Federal Electoral Institute, which reviewed the election results in detail. After several months of review, the Institute declared Calderón the victor by just 0.56 percent of the vote, the closest margin of victory in Mexican history, and a source of continued conflict early in his administration. The ruling could not be appealed, however, and marked another step forward in Mexico's transition to a much more open democratic system. ■

Mexican President Vicente Fox

branch are headed by the same political party, there is nothing automatic about unified government—it can exist only if voters in enough states and districts vote for the same party over enough elections to control the House, Senate, presidency, and judiciary (whose members are nominated by the president and confirmed by the Senate).

The United States is one of the few world powers that is neither a parliamentary democracy nor a wholly executive-dominated government. Our Constitution plainly invites both Congress and the president to set policy and govern the nation. Leadership and policy change are likely only when Congress and the president, and sometimes the courts along with them, agree that new directions are desirable.

Defining the Presidency

The framers' most important decision about the presidency was also their first. Meeting on June 1, 1787, the Constitutional Convention decided that there would be a single executive. Despite worries that a single president might lay the groundwork for a future monarchy, the framers also believed that the new government needed energy in the executive. They were willing to increase the risk of tyranny in return for some efficiency.

Presidents can joke about themselves, as President Bush shows in a joint appearance with a Bush impersonator from Saturday Night Live. *The appearance was at the 2006 White House Correspondents Association dinner, which often pokes fun at the president.*

Once past this first decision, the framers had to decide just how independent that executive would be from the rest of the national government, which meant finding an appropriate method of selection or election. Had they wanted Congress to select the president from among its members, the framers would have created a **parliamentary system** that would look more like many European governments.

The convention was initially divided on how the president would be selected. A small number of delegates favored direct election by the people, which Pennsylvania's James Wilson thought would ensure that the president was completely independent of Congress. Convinced that the nation was too diverse to handle direct election and afraid that states might join together to support regional candidates who would favor their part of the country, the delegates never seriously considered direct election. A larger number of delegates favored selection by Congress, tying the president more closely to the legislative branch.

Eventually, the framers compromised by creating an electoral college: Voters would cast their ballots for competing slates of electors, who would in turn cast their electoral votes for president. It might be called a form of indirect direct election. The framers also gave the executive a four-year term of office, further balancing the House (two-year term) and Senate (six-year term). Although they were silent on the number of terms a president could serve, the nation's first president, George Washington, quickly established a two-term precedent, which held until Franklin Roosevelt's historic four-term presidency from 1932 to 1945. The Twenty-Second Amendment to the Constitution, ratified in 1951, restored Washington's precedent by limiting presidents to two terms.

The framers also created the position of vice president just in case the president left office before the end of the term. With little debate, the founders decided to give the vice president the power to break tie votes in the Senate. Otherwise, the vice president has no constitutional duties but to wait for the president to be incapacitated or otherwise unable to discharge the powers and duties of the presidency. In recent years, however, presidents have given their vice presidents greater responsibilities. Vice President Richard Cheney was involved in virtually every major decision made during the first six years of the Bush administration, including the war with Iraq and energy policy.

The framers also established three simple qualifications for both offices. Under the Constitution, the president and vice president must be (1) at least 35 years old; (2) natural-born citizens of the United States, as opposed to immigrants who become citizens by applying to the U.S. government for naturalization; and (3) residents of the

parliamentary system
A system of government in which the legislature selects the prime minister or president.

United States for the previous 14 years. The citizenship and residency requirements were designed to prevent a popular foreign-born citizen from capturing the office.

The Presidential Ticket

With this basic structure in place, the framers had to decide how the vice president would be selected. Once again, they created a remarkable electoral arrangement: The candidate who received the most Electoral College votes would become president, and the candidate who came in second would become vice president. Any tie votes in the Electoral College were to be broken by a majority vote in the House of Representatives.

It did not take long for the framers to discover the problem with this runner-up rule. The 1796 election produced Federalist President John Adams and Republican Vice President Thomas Jefferson. Because the two disagreed so sharply about the future of the country, Jefferson was rendered virtually irrelevant to government.

This rule created a constitutional crisis in 1800. The election could not have been more important, for it occurred during a time of rising public anger about the nation's direction. It also included multiple candidates from the same party. Jefferson and Aaron Burr both promised a smaller, simpler government, while Adams promised continued government expansion. Jefferson and Burr emerged from the balloting with 73 electoral votes each, leaving Adams behind with just 63. After 36 ballots, the House of Representatives finally selected Jefferson as president, and his defeated opponent became vice president.

Under the Twelfth Amendment, which was ratified in 1804, electors were allowed to cast separate votes for the president and vice president. This new practice encouraged candidates to run together as a **presidential ticket** that would rise or fall together.

Presidential Powers

Article II of the Constitution begins: "The executive Power shall be vested in a President of the United States of America." Some experts argue that the executive power covers almost everything not granted to the legislature or judiciary, while others believe that the president's relatively short list of enumerated powers suggests that the framers wanted a more limited executive.[4] Although short, Article II does address foreign threats and the day-to-day operations of government, establishing the president's authority to play three central roles in the new government: (1) commander in chief, (2) diplomat in chief, and (3) administrator in chief.

COMMANDER IN CHIEF The Constitution explicitly states that the president is to be commander in chief of the army and navy. It is a fundamental expression of the president's role in protecting the nation as a whole. The framers saw the president as the commander in chief but were divided over which branch would both declare and make war.[5]

The framers initially agreed that Congress would make war, raise armies, build and equip fleets, enforce treaties, and suppress and repel invasions, but eventually changed the phrase "make war" to "declare war." But they limited the presidential war power by giving Congress the power to appropriate money for the purchase of arms and military pay, and giving the Senate the power to approve military promotions. Although they also gave Congress sole authority to declare war, recent presidents have used their power as commander in chief to order U.S. troops into battle without formal declarations dozens of times over the past century, including the recent wars in Afghanistan and Iraq. Presidents have often interpreted the war power more broadly, as the Bush administration did in authorizing the domestic eavesdropping program.

DIPLOMAT IN CHIEF Article II also makes the president negotiator in chief of treaties with foreign nations, which must be approved by the Senate by a two-thirds vote. A **treaty** is a binding and public agreement between the United States and one or more nations that requires mutual action toward a common goal. Although presidents cannot make treaties without Senate approval, past presidents have argued that they

presidential ticket
The joint listing of the presidential and vice presidential candidates on the same ballot as required by the Twelfth Amendment.

treaty
A formal, public agreement between the United States and one or more nations that must be approved by two-thirds of the Senate.

President Bush meets with his national security advisors in the Situation Room of the White House soon after September 11, 2001.

have the power to terminate treaties without Senate consent. The U.S. has negotiated a number of treaties to reduce the number of nuclear, biological, and chemical weapons across the world.

Presidents can also make **executive agreements** with the leaders of foreign nations. Unlike treaties, executive agreements are negotiated without Senate participation. In 2003, for example, the Bush administration negotiated a 22-item executive agreement with Mexico to create a "smart border" that would limit the movement of illegal aliens into the United States, while improving the flow of goods between the two nations. Although some executive orders are secret, most are made public.

Finally, presidents can make **congressional–executive agreements**, which are also negotiated between the president and leaders of other nations. Like treaties, congressional–executive agreements require mutual action toward a common goal. Unlike treaties, they require approval by both houses of Congress. The 1994 North American Free Trade Agreement (NAFTA) is a congressional–executive agreement that provoked intense anger among some critics, who argued that the United States would lose jobs as a result.

ADMINISTRATOR IN CHIEF By giving the president the power to require the opinion of the principal officer in each of the executive departments "upon any subject relating to the duties of their respective offices," the Constitution puts the president in charge of the day-to-day operation of the federal departments and agencies. As we shall see, the president also has the responsibility to appoint ambassadors, judges, and all other officers of the United States, including the heads of executive departments, with the advice and consent of a majority of the Senate. Together, these powers give presidents the instruments needed to supervise and control the day-to-day operations of the federal departments and agencies.

ADDITIONAL EXECUTIVE POWERS Along with the specific powers associated with being commander, diplomat, and administrator in chief, the Constitution also gives the president five additional powers to lead government: (1) the power to appoint judges and officers of government; (2) the power to veto legislation, which serves as a check on Congress; (3) the power to grant pardons to individuals convicted of federal,

executive agreement
A formal agreement between the U.S. president and the leaders of other nations that does not require Senate approval.

congressional–executive agreement
A formal agreement between the U.S. president and the leaders of other nations that requires approval by both houses of Congress.

Government's Greatest Endeavors

Reducing Nuclear Weapons

Presidents have invested enormous amounts of time and energy over the past 30 years in trying to control and reduce the number of nuclear weapons around the world. Much of that work has involved efforts to stop the "arms race" between the United States and the Soviet Union, which together built enough nuclear weapons to destroy the world many times over.

Presidents negotiated a number of nuclear arms agreements during the long cold war, all of which had to be approved by the U.S. Senate under its treaty-making power. In 1972, for example, the Senate approved a freeze on the development of new weapons by the United States and Soviet Union that lasted through the 1970s. This Strategic Arms Limitation Treaty, negotiated by President Richard Nixon, froze the number of U.S. and Soviet missiles for five years.

In 1988, the Senate also approved a treaty banning the further development of shorter-range nuclear missiles that could be used in Europe and other "hot spots." This treaty, negotiated by President Ronald Reagan, marked the first time that the two nations also agreed to dismantle some of their existing weapons. Although both nations still have large numbers of nuclear weapons and missiles, further negotiations by presidents Bill Clinton and George W. Bush have reduced the numbers of weapons and created a much safer world.

Unfortunately, these negotiations and treaties have not stopped the development of nuclear weapons by other nations, such as North Korea. In addition, Iran is moving forward with what it describes as a peaceful nuclear power program that foreign observers argue will produce the material for a nuclear weapon. ■

U.S. nuclear missile in its silo

QUESTIONS

Why did the United States and Soviet Union develop so many nuclear weapons?

What can the United States do to reduce the spread of nuclear weapons to other nations?

but not state, crimes, thereby providing a check against the judiciary; (4) the power to take care that the laws are faithfully executed; and (5) the power to inform and convene Congress.

1. *The Appointment Power.* The Constitution gives the president authority to appoint judges, ambassadors, and other officers of the executive branch subject to the advice and consent of the Senate. This power gives presidents the ability to control what happens inside departments and agencies during their terms and to shape the federal judiciary far into the future. Presidents choose appointees on the basis of party loyalty, interest group pressure, and management ability. Although the appointments process has become more controversial in recent years, the vast majority of judicial and executive appointees are easily confirmed—the Senate has rejected only eight cabinet secretaries since the first Congress, and just 29 out of 145 nominations to the Supreme Court.

Moreover, many executive branch appointees serve entirely at the pleasure of the president, including the chiefs of staff to cabinet secretaries, who keep track of each department's political agenda. Because these jobs are not subject to Senate confirmation, they are often filled by campaign supporters, who act as the president's closest allies in the bureaucracy. Sometimes this can cause problems for the president, however. Although Federal Emergency Management Agency director Michael Brown had served on President Bush's 2000 campaign staff, he did not have any disaster management experience, and he failed to provide timely leadership in the hours and days after Hurricane Katrina came barreling ashore in 2005. All executive branch appointments, such as the head of FEMA, are considered "plums" for presidential friends, and are listed in a publication informally known as the "Plum Book."

Because judges can serve for life, presidents view judicial appointments as a way to exert influence far beyond the end of their term. Chief Justice William Rehnquist was just such an influential figure. Nominated by President Richard Nixon, Rehnquist served for more than 30 years and presided over vast changes in civil rights and civil liberties. The Bush administration had similar hopes for long service by its two Supreme Court appointments, John Roberts and Samuel Alito Jr. In addition, Presidents Clinton and Bush both nominated hundreds of federal judges who may have a similar impact at lower levels of the federal judiciary, perhaps even as future Supreme Court justices.

2. *The Veto Power.* The Constitution provides that bills passed by the U.S. House of Representatives and Senate "shall be presented to the President of the United States," and the president can then approve the measure or issue a **veto**. If a bill is vetoed by a president, it can be enacted only if the veto is overridden, which requires a two-thirds vote in each chamber of Congress.

A variation of the veto is the **pocket veto**. In the ordinary course of events, if a president does not sign or veto a bill within ten days after receiving it (not counting Sundays), the bill becomes law without the president's signature. But if Congress adjourns within the ten days, the president, by taking no action, can kill the bill.

The power of a veto lies in the difficulty of overriding a president's decision. Recall that two-thirds of both houses must vote to overturn a veto. Historically, Congress has overridden fewer than 10 percent of presidents' regular vetoes. This requirement gives presidents a vital bargaining chip in the legislative process, where the mere threat of a veto, announced publicly or through legislative aides, can strengthen a president's hand in persuading Congress to accommodate his wishes.

This veto threat is only credible, however, if the president is actually willing to use it. Whereas Ronald Reagan vetoed 78 bills in his two terms, and Bill Clinton vetoed 37 bills in his two terms, George W. Bush did not veto a single bill in his first six years. Although he had Republican majorities in both houses of Congress, he did not have enough votes to defeat potential overrides, especially given the intense party discipline in both chambers.

3. *The Pardon Power.* The pardon power can be traced directly to the royal authority of the king of England, and is probably the most delicate power presidents exercise. The pardon power can be used to shorten prison sentences, correct judicial errors, and protect citizens from future prosecution. It can also be used to address national controversies. On his last day in office in 2001, President Bill Clinton pardoned several of his associates who had been jailed in a long investigation of a real estate scandal dating back to his time as governor of Arkansas.

4. *The Take Care Power.* Presidents are also responsible to take care that the laws are faithfully executed under the **take care clause**. Located near the end of Article II is the simple statement that the president "shall take Care that the Laws be faithfully executed." This clause makes the president responsible for implementing the laws that Congress enacts, even ones that are enacted through the override of a presidential veto.

veto
A formal decision to reject a bill passed by Congress.

pocket veto
A formal decision to reject a bill passed by Congress after it adjourns—if Congress adjourns during the ten days that the president is allowed in order to sign or veto a law, the president can reject the law by taking no action at all.

take care clause
The constitutional requirement (in Article II, Section 3) that presidents take care that the laws are faithfully executed, even if they disagree with the purpose of those laws.

Presidents sometimes use the take care clause to claim **inherent powers**, meaning powers they believe are essential to protecting the nation. Jefferson drew on this broad notion in making the Louisiana Purchase in 1804, for example. Abraham Lincoln extended the concept early in the Civil War to suspend the rights of prisoners to seek judicial review of their cases, to impose a blockade of Confederate shipping, and to expand the size of the army beyond authorized ceilings, all without prior congressional approval as required under the Constitution's lawmaking power. Bush used a similar justification in authorizing the domestic eavesdropping program.

5. *The Power to Inform and Convene Congress.* Under Article II, presidents are required "from time to time to give to the Congress Information of the State of the Union, and recommend to their Consideration such Measures as he shall judge necessary." Over the years, the phrase "from time to time" has evolved to mean a constant stream of presidential messages, as well as the annual **State of the Union Address** in late January or early February. This power gives presidents a significant platform for presenting their legislative agenda to both Congress and the American people.

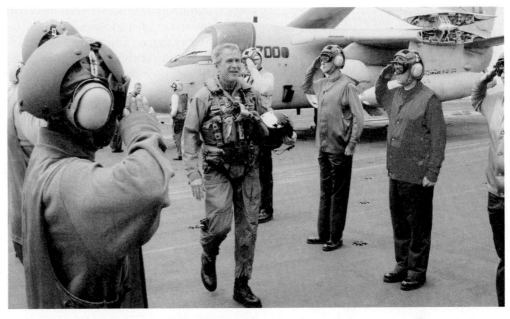

George W. Bush greets navy personnel after landing on the deck of the USS Abraham Lincoln in May 2003. Bush claimed inherent powers to justify the detention of Americans suspected of involvement with terrorism, arguing that they should be treated as a security threat to the nation.

The president also has the power to convene Congress in extraordinary circumstances and recommend "such Measures as he shall judge necessary and expedient." Those suggestions can range from simple ideas presented in a letter or news conference to specific proposals presented live before a joint session of the House and Senate. On September 20, 2001, for example, President George W. Bush appeared before Congress to ask for new legislation to strengthen antiterrorism programs, help airlines recover from the dramatic decline in air travel, and rebuild New York City.

Presidential Succession

Having decided how a president would enter office, the framers also decided how a president would leave. In addition to impeachment, defeat for reelection, retirement, resignation, or death, the Constitution was amended to provide two other ways to remove a president from office. Under the Twenty-Second Amendment, presidents must leave office after completion of two elected terms in office.

Under the Twenty-Fifth Amendment, presidents can also be removed from office temporarily if the vice president and a majority of either Congress or the president's own cabinet secretaries declares that the president is unable to discharge the powers and duties of the office—for example, because of illness or disability. In such a case, the vice president becomes the acting president until the duly elected president returns to office. The amendment also allows a president to appoint a new vice president in the event of the vice president's own resignation, death, impeachment, or rise to the presidency. Richard Nixon appointed Gerald Ford as his vice president after Spiro Agnew resigned in disgrace; in turn, Ford appointed Nelson Rockefeller as his vice president after becoming president when Nixon also resigned in disgrace.

inherent powers
Powers that grow out of the very existence of government.

State of the Union Address
The president's annual statement to Congress and the nation.

"Kings had always been involving and impoverishing their people in wars, pretending generally, if not always, that the good of the people was the object."

ABRAHAM LINCOLN

Under the Constitution, the vice president is the next in line if the president leaves office prematurely. Once past the vice president, Congress is responsible for determining the line of succession. Under current law, the Speaker of the House of Representatives is next in line, followed by the Senate president pro tempore, the secretary of state, secretary of the treasury, secretary of defense, and on down through the list of 15 cabinet secretaries by the date each department was established.

The framers gave Congress exclusive power to remove the president through the **impeachment** process. Under this process, the House drafts articles of impeachment that charge the president with treason, bribery, or other high crimes and misdemeanors. If the articles are approved by a majority vote, the Chief Justice of the Supreme Court oversees a trial before the entire Senate. If convicted by a two-thirds vote of the Senate, the president is removed immediately from office.

The impeachment process has been used only twice in history, in 1868 against Andrew Johnson and in 1998 against Bill Clinton. Both Senate trials resulted in acquittals. Richard Nixon resigned from office in 1974 before the House could finish drafting the articles of impeachment regarding his role in the Watergate cover-up. Nixon almost certainly would have been both impeached and convicted had he stayed in office.

Controversies in Presidential Power

The president, today more visible than ever as a national and international leader, is still constrained by constitutional checks and balances. These do not stop presidents from asserting powers that the framers intended for Congress or the judiciary, however.

The War Power

The Constitution divides the war power between the president and Congress. Article I states that Congress has the power to declare war, but Article II gives the president the power to wage war as commander in chief. The framers recognized that declaring war was both one of the most important powers of government and one of the most easily abused. Writing as a young member of Congress, Abraham Lincoln expressed the founders' intent as follows:

> The provision of the Constitution giving the war-making power to Congress was dictated, as I understand it, by the following reasons. Kings had always been involving and impoverishing their people in wars, pretending generally, if not always, that the good of the people was the object. This our convention understood to be the most oppressive of all kingly oppressions, and they resolved to so frame the Constitution that no one man should hold the power of bringing this oppression upon us.[6]

Over the past half-century, U.S. presidents have ordered troops into battle in Korea, Vietnam, Grenada, Panama, Iraq (twice), Kosovo, and Afghanistan, all without asking Congress for a formal declaration of war. If they have asked for congressional approval at all, they have usually sought broad resolutions of support. In 2002, for example, Bush merely asked Congress to give him the authority to deploy U.S. forces as "he determines to be necessary and appropriate" to defend national security against the threat posed by Iraq. Although the request was eventually approved by wide margins in the House and Senate, White House lawyers also argued that the president already had the authority to act with or without congressional approval.[7]

Presidents defend such actions by arguing that they have better information, much of it secret, than Congress. They also argue that presidents need the flexibility and secrecy to respond quickly to military threats to the nation's security interests. One State Department official described the president's war power authority as follows: "The Constitution leaves to the President the judgment to determine whether the circumstances of a particular armed attack are so urgent and the potential consequences

impeachment
Formal accusation against the president or other public official, the first step in removal from office.

so threatening to the security of the U.S. that he should act without formally consulting the Congress."[8]

Presidents and some scholars blame Congress for abdicating its constitutional authority to the presidency. Constitutional scholar Louis Fisher holds that Congress has repeatedly given up its fundamental war powers to the president. The framers knew what monarchy looked like and rejected it, writes Fisher. "Yet, especially in matters of the war power, the United States is recreating a system of monarchy while it professes to champion democracy and the rule of law abroad."[9]

Congress tried to reassert its role and authority in the use of military force at the end of the Vietnam War. In 1973, Congress enacted the War Powers Resolution over Richard Nixon's veto. The law, which is still in place, declares that a president can commit the armed forces of the United States only (1) after a declaration of war by Congress, (2) by specific statutory authorization, or (3) in a national emergency created by an attack on the United States or its armed forces. After committing the armed forces under the third circumstance, the president is required to report to Congress within 48 hours. Unless Congress declares war, the troop commitment must be ended within 60 days.

This resolution signaled a new determination by Congress to take its prerogatives seriously, yet presidents have generally ignored it. And many leading scholars now believe that this earnest and well-intentioned effort by Congress to reclaim its proper role actually gave away more authority than previous practices had already done. Because presidents can declare a national emergency under almost any circumstances and often act under broad legislation that authorizes the use of force in ambiguous situations, the War Powers Resolution is almost always ignored.

President Bush surprised U.S. military troops stationed in Iraq with a secret Thanksgiving Day visit in 2003. The president was in Baghdad for two hours and 32 minutes.

Executive Privilege

The Constitution does not give presidents the explicit power to withhold information from Congress or the public. However, courts have recognized that presidents have the power, or **executive privilege**, to keep secrets, especially if doing so is essential to protect national security.

Some experts argue that executive privilege has no constitutional basis.[10] Yet presidents have withheld documents from Congress at least as far back as 1792, when President George Washington temporarily refused to share sensitive documents with a House committee studying an Indian massacre of federal troops. Although he later shared the information with Congress, Washington set the precedent for the use of executive privilege. Thomas Jefferson and the primary author of the Constitution, James Madison, also withheld information during their presidencies.

Most scholars, the courts, and even members of Congress agree that a president does have the implicit, if not constitutionally explicit, right to withhold information that could harm national security. Presidents must keep secrets, and they often fight hard to do so. However, executive privilege cannot be asserted in either congressional or judicial proceedings when the issue is basically one of refusing to cooperate in investigations of personal wrongdoing.

executive privilege
The right to keep executive communications confidential, especially if they relate to national security.

Although the formal term "executive privilege" was first used in the 1950s during the Eisenhower administration, Richard Nixon created the controversy over the term.[11] In an effort to hide his own role in the Watergate scandal, President Nixon refused to release secret tapes of the Oval Office meetings that followed the failed burglary of Democratic Party headquarters in the Watergate building. He and his lawyers went so far as to claim that the decision to invoke executive privilege was not subject to review by Congress or the courts.

In its complicated decision, the Supreme Court acknowledged for the first time that presidents do indeed have the power to claim executive privilege if the release of certain information would be damaging to the nation's security interests. At the same time, the Court held that such claims are not exempt from review by the courts, and that national security was not threatened in the Watergate case. The Court ordered Nixon to yield his tapes, effectively dooming his presidency.[12]

Twenty-five years later, Congress asked the Bush administration to disclose the names of energy industry executives who had met with Vice President Dick Cheney's 2001 energy task force, which helped shape the administration's future energy plan. The White House refused, arguing that Congress has no constitutional right to investigate the process by which the president or his advisers make decisions about public issues. Although the White House never formally invoked executive privilege in the case, the refusal was clearly modeled on the notion that presidents have the right to keep secrets. Congress eventually sued Cheney for the information, but dropped the case in 2003 after losing the first round in a federal district court. The president's right to keep secrets will be revisited in each administration and tested by presidents and by the legislative branch. On occasion, courts will try to settle the dispute about the limits and conditions under which a president can invoke this well-established, if sometimes abused, presidential practice.

Executive Orders

Presidents execute the laws and direct the federal departments and agencies in part through **executive orders**, which are formal directives that are just as strong as laws and can be challenged in the courts. Although executive orders are not mentioned in the Constitution, they are considered essential to the faithful execution of the laws. According to past Supreme Court decisions, executive orders are generally accepted as the supreme law of the land unless they are in conflict with the Constitution or a federal law.

Beginning with George Washington, presidents have issued more than 13,000 executive orders. These orders have been used to declare American neutrality in the war between France and England (1793), to intern Japanese Americans during World War II, and to protect large tracts of federal land as "national monuments" in Arizona, Colorado, Oregon, Utah, and Washington in the Clinton administration. President George W. Bush has been just as active as recent presidents in using executive orders to manage government. He issued an order in October 2001 to create a White House Office of Homeland Security to coordinate the federal government's efforts to protect its borders, another in January 2003 to create a White House Council on Service and Civic Participation to encourage more Americans to volunteer, and still another in February 2004 to create a commission to investigate why the United States had been so wrong regarding Iraq's weapons of mass destruction. In his first four years Bush issued roughly 40 orders per year.[13]

The Budget and Spending Power

Battles over budgets and spending have been at the heart of national politics since the beginning of the Republic. The Constitution explicitly gives Congress the power to appropriate money, but presidents are responsible for actually spending the money.

Congress dominated the budget-making process until 1921, when it approved the Budget and Accounting Act. That law required the president to submit annual budgets to Congress, and it established the Bureau of the Budget, which in 1970 became the

executive orders
Formal orders issued by the president to direct action by the federal bureaucracy.

Office of Management and Budget. Although the 1921 act also created the General Accounting Office as an auditing and oversight arm of Congress, presidents have played an increasingly powerful role in shaping the federal budget.

President Nixon, however, overplayed his hand when his White House developed legal theories that justified a bold change in the traditional definition of **impoundment**, or refusal to spend appropriated money. Under the traditional definition, presidents were allowed to change the purpose of a spending bill to accommodate emergencies such as war or international crisis. Under the Nixon definition, impoundment was broadened to allow changes in a spending bill based on the president's ideology. Thus, if the president did not want appropriated funds to be spent for purposes he did not like, he could impound, or withhold, the money. In 1974, Congress approved the Congressional Budget and Impoundment Control Act, which sharply curtailed the president's use of impoundment. Enacted over Nixon's veto, the law gave Congress new powers to control its own budget process, created the Congressional Budget Office (CBO) to give the institution its own sources of economic and spending forecasts, and required the president to submit detailed requests to Congress for any proposed *rescission* (cancellation) of congressional appropriations.

Every budget cycle witnesses a new round of clashes between the branches. In recent years, Congress has almost always failed to pass all of the appropriations bills by the beginning of the fiscal year. Instead, the two branches have relied on *continuing resolutions,* proclamations extending the authority for federal spending a few days, weeks, or months.

In an effort to control its own tendency to overspend, Congress in 1996 voted to give the president greater budget power through the **line item veto**. Presidents were allowed to strike out specific sections of an appropriations bill while signing the rest into law. Although many governors have the line item veto, the Supreme Court decided that the law had disturbed the "finely wrought" procedure for making the laws, and declared it unconstitutional in a 6 to 3 vote in 1998. If Congress wanted a new procedure for making the laws, Justice John Paul Stevens wrote for the majority, it would have to pursue a constitutional amendment.[14]

The Use of Unilateral Powers

Presidents also have a set of unilateral powers to shape the implementation of the laws, even to the point of ignoring them. Presidents control much of the information that flows from federal departments and agencies, shape the national debate through messages to Congress and the public, direct the budget process that sets the initial debate about spending and taxation, control the behavior of their political appointees through tight White House oversight, and issue executive orders and presidential directives that can either slow or accelerate the implementation of the laws.[15] They can also express their unwillingness to implement parts of a congressional bill in the signing statement that accompanies their signature.[16] Although Congress or the judiciary can challenge all of these tools, such resistance is rare given the press of other business on the calendar.

Evolution of the Presidency

The history of presidential power is one of steady, if uneven, growth. Of the individuals who have filled the office, about one-third have enlarged its powers. Andrew Jackson, Abraham Lincoln, Theodore Roosevelt, Franklin Delano Roosevelt, and Harry Truman all redefined both the institution and many of its powers by the way they set priorities and responded to crises. Much of this expansion occurred during wartime or national crises such as the great economic depression of the 1930s.

Nevertheless, today's presidency reflects precedents established by the nation's first chief executive, George Washington. The framers could not have anticipated the kinds of foreign and domestic threats that now preoccupy the office, but they would recognize the importance of the presidency in protecting the nation in times of trouble.

impoundment
A decision by the president not to spend money appropriated by Congress, now prohibited under federal law.

line item veto
Presidential power to strike, or remove, specific items from a spending bill without vetoing the entire package; declared unconstitutional by the Supreme Court.

The First Presidency

The framers designed the presidency hoping that George Washington would be the first to occupy the post. Washington commanded the public's trust and respect and was unanimously elected as the first president of the new Republic in 1789. He understood that the people needed to have confidence in their fledgling government, a sense of continuity with the past, and a time of calm and stability free of emergencies and crises. He also knew that the new nation faced both domestic and foreign threats to its future.

Washington's presidency set important precedents for the future, not the least of which was how the president would be addressed in public. Vice President John Adams argued that the president should be called "His Highness the President of the United States and protector of Their Liberties," a title the popularly elected House immediately rejected. The president of the United States would be called "the President of the United States."[17]

Washington's presidency also produced a model against which to measure future presidents. Not only did he establish the legitimacy and basic authority of the office, Washington negotiated the new government's first treaty, appointed its first judges and department heads, received its first foreign ambassadors, vetoed its first legislation, and signed its first laws, thereby demonstrating just how future presidents should execute and influence the laws.

Washington also established a host of lesser precedents for running the presidency that still hold today. He started by assembling the first White House staff. It was hardly large, composed of just two clerks, but it was an office nonetheless. Indeed, it was so small that Washington paid for staff and office expenses from his own pocket. Washington also selected the first department secretaries, appointing Thomas Jefferson as secretary of state and Alexander Hamilton as secretary of the treasury.

Washington may have set his most important precedent in establishing the president's sole authority for supervising the executive branch. He was absolutely clear about the division of executive and legislative powers. Congress could appropriate money, confirm appointees, conduct oversight hearings, and always change the laws, but it could not run the departments. That was to be the president's job.

Washington's final contribution to the presidency involved his retirement after serving two terms. Although he would have been easily reelected to a third term, Washington believed that two terms were enough and returned to his Mount Vernon estate in 1796. It was a precedent that held until Franklin Roosevelt's four terms, and was finally enshrined in constitutional language under the Twenty-Second Amendment.

The First Modern Presidency

Designed in part to check what the founders thought would be a more powerful Congress, the presidency has evolved over the past two hundred years into a much more powerful institution than the framers ever imagined. However, the expansion of the presidency has involved more than inherent powers. It has also reflected a growing government role in regulating the U.S. economy and protecting national interests abroad, which has increased the size and mission of government, which in turn has increased the demand for presidential leadership. As the president has grown into a world power, so has the demand for presidential leadership.

Although the modern presidency was not formed by any single president, most historians and political scientists agree that Franklin Roosevelt was the first president to exploit the institution's inherent and enumerated powers to their fullest impact. Although conservatives do not always endorse the use of these powers to expand the federal departments and agencies, they agree with liberals that Roosevelt left an indelible mark on the institution of the presidency itself.

Over his 12 years in office, Roosevelt created an extraordinary record of achievement. He expanded the role of the president as commander, diplomat, and administrator in chief, while dominating Congress in both shaping and making the laws. Inaugurated for the first of his four terms in office in the midst of the Great Depression,

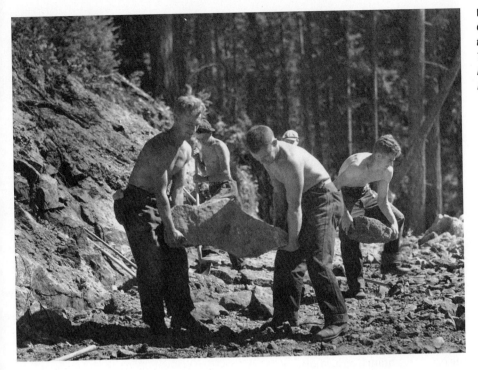

Workers from Camp F-24 of the Civilian Conservation Corps clear rocks from a truck trail in Snoqualmie National Forest in 1933. The CCC was created as part of Roosevelt's New Deal plan to ease the effects of the Great Depression.

Roosevelt took command, and his first 100 days in office in 1933 still stand as the most significant moment of presidential leadership in modern history. Most of his New Deal agenda for helping working and poor Americans is still law today, including Social Security for the aged, unemployment insurance, a guaranteed minimum wage for workers, banking and stock market regulation for investors, price supports for farmers, and a host of federal agencies that continue to build everything from nuclear weapons to highways.

Roosevelt clearly moved the presidency to the center of the legislative process. He created a new clearance process for sending legislative proposals to Congress, and used the State of the Union Address to focus the nation's attention on a specific list of presidential priorities. Although previous presidents had expressed their opinions about pending legislation, Roosevelt created new lobbying techniques that are still used to this day, the most notable of which involved the use of media to build public support for his program.

Roosevelt's impact extended well beyond the legislative agenda, however. He also exploited the powers of the presidency to build a highly personal relationship with the American public, using his "fireside chats" on radio to calm the public during the darkest days of the economic depression, while calling the nation to action during the early days of World War II. In doing so, he became the nation's communicator in chief, starting each broadcast with the simple phrase "My friends."

Roosevelt also changed the president's relationship with the federal departments and agencies, which grew from 600,000 employees before the New Deal to well over 1 million just before World War II. Not only did the New Deal produce a host of new federal agencies, it also demanded a larger White House staff to oversee the implementation of the laws. By 1937, Roosevelt's small White House staff was so overwhelmed that a national study group opened a report on the need for a stronger White House staff with the words: "The President needs help."

The Presidency Today

The formal powers the U.S. Constitution vests in a president have not been changed for more than 200 years, but the influence of modern presidents is considerably greater today than it has ever been, particularly at this moment in world history. Some observers have argued that the Bush administration has taken advantage of the war on terrorism to create an "imperial presidency" of unlimited powers.[18]

Nevertheless, some experts believe that presidential influence has declined in recent years, in part because of political scandals such as the burglary of the Democratic National Campaign offices at the Watergate Hotel in 1972 (Nixon), the illegal sale of weapons to Iran in return for aid to Nicaraguan rebels (Reagan), and the sexual affair between the president and an intern (Clinton). Nixon's resignation clearly diminished public respect for the presidency, Bill Clinton's impeachment clearly distracted the nation from more pressing problems such as the rising tide of anti-American sentiment in the Middle East, the controversy over the 2000 election raised questions about the legitimacy of the electoral process, and the war in Iraq led many Americans to doubt President Bush's leadership in the war on terrorism.

Managing the Presidency

Without help, presidents could not manage crises, build morale, set priorities and agendas, build legislative and political coalitions, mold public opinion, lead their parties, and otherwise take care that the laws are faithfully executed. Although some of that help comes from their *inner circle*, which is composed of their closest advisers including the first lady, presidents could not do their job without a vast array of support that extends well beyond 1600 Pennsylvania Avenue to include the executive branch as a whole.

The White House Staff

Presidents have come to rely heavily on their personal staffs. Nowhere else—not in Congress, not in the cabinet, not in the party—can presidents find the loyalty and single-mindedness that often develops among their closest White House aides.[19] Cabinet heads are often perceived as staunch advocates of their departments and the constituencies their departments serve and so cannot be assumed to give objective advice. By contrast, presidents presume that their aides will provide them with sound and unbiased policy guidance. But there are sometimes substantial costs to listening only to a small circle of advisers. The White House staff shaped much of the intelligence that led the United States into the Iraq War in 2003, for example, and made overly optimistic assumptions about the eventual course of the war. They also drew upon faulty intelligence about how the Iraqi people would react to the war, which helped convince Congress to give the president authority to commit U.S. troops to battle.

THE WHITE HOUSE ORGANIZATION The White House staff grew steadily from the early 1900s through the early 1990s, then stabilized at roughly 400 today. The **chief of staff**, who is considered the president's most loyal assistant, heads the staff. The White House staff also includes the president's chief lawyer, speechwriters, legislative liaison staff, and press secretary. The chief of staff supervises all other White House staff and is considered a member of the president's inner circle.

There are at least two kinds of White House offices. *Political* offices are designed to help the president run for reelection, control the national party, and shape the president's image through press conferences, television and radio addresses, polling, and travel. These offices provide the "spin" on the news that shows the president in the most favorable light, and allow the president to go over the heads of members of Congress to lobby the public directly. The list of political offices includes the Office of Communications, which contains the president's top political advisers, the Office of the Press Secretary, which coordinates most contacts with the media, and the Office of Speechwriting.

Policy offices are designed to shape the president's foreign and domestic program. Like congressional committees, these offices collect information and often write legislation. Unlike committees, they do not hold hearings, conduct investigations, or pass bills. They must rely on the president to make the case for legislative action, issue executive orders, negotiate treaties or executive agreements, and persuade the public of the need for action. The list of policy offices includes the National Economic Council,

chief of staff
The head of the White House staff.

which coordinates the president's economic agenda, the National Security Council, which helps set foreign policy, and the Office of Faith-Based Initiatives, which encourages the use of religious institutions to help address community problems.[20]

RUNNING THE WHITE HOUSE Over the past three decades, presidents have used three very different models for running the White House staff: competitive, collegial, and hierarchical. Among modern presidents, Franklin Roosevelt and Lyndon Johnson both used the competitive approach, a "survival of the fittest" situation in which the president allows aides to fight each other for access to the Oval Office. Johnson sometimes gave different staffers the same assignment, hoping that the competition would produce a better final decision.

In contrast, John Kennedy, Jimmy Carter, and Bill Clinton all used the collegial approach, in which presidents encourage aides to work together toward a common position. It is a much friendlier way to work than the competitive approach but may have the serious drawback of producing what some social psychologists call *groupthink*. Groupthink is the tendency of small groups to stifle dissent in the search for common ground.[21] Groupthink may have affected the White House as it moved toward the Iraq War, for example. The president, vice president, secretary of defense, and national security adviser shared a common vision of the war, and did not invite opponents into their internal debates about when and how to proceed.

Finally, Dwight Eisenhower, Richard Nixon, Ronald Reagan, and George W. Bush all used the hierarchical model, in which the president establishes tight control over who does what in making decisions. Presidents who use this approach usually rely on a "gatekeeper," or trusted adviser such as the chief of staff, to monitor the flow of information to and from the White House.

The Executive Office of the President

The **Executive Office of the President** was created in 1939 to give the president more help running the federal departments and agencies. The EOP consists of the Office of Management and Budget, the Council of Economic Advisers, and several other staff units (see Figure 12–1). It also contains the White House staff.

The **Office of Management and Budget (OMB)** is the central presidential staff agency. Its director advises the president in detail about the hundreds of government agencies—how much money they should be allotted in the budget and what kind of job they are doing. OMB seeks to improve the planning, management, and statistical work of the agencies. It makes a special effort to see that each agency conforms to presidential policies in its dealings with Congress; each agency has to clear its policy recommendations to Congress through OMB first.[22]

Through the long budget-preparation process, presidents use OMB as a way of conserving and centralizing their own influence. A budget is more than just a financial

Executive Office of the President
The cluster of presidential staff agencies that help the president carry out his responsibilities. Currently the office includes the Office of Management and Budget, the Council of Economic Advisers, and several other units.

Office of Management and Budget (OMB)
Presidential staff agency that serves as a clearinghouse for budgetary requests and management improvements for government agencies.

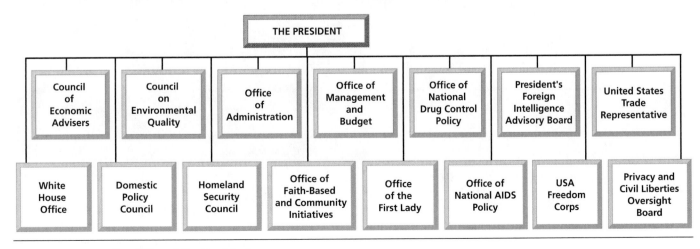

FIGURE **12–1 Executive Office of the President.**
SOURCE: *United States Government Manual, 2005–2006* (Government Printing Office, 2006).

plan. It reflects power struggles between the president and federal departments and agencies, and is used to signal the president's priorities to Congress. Although Congress is responsible for actually authorizing and appropriating money, the president's budget usually provides an initial outline of how much each department and agency will get.

The Cabinet

It is hard to find a more unusual institution than the president's **cabinet**. The cabinet is not specifically mentioned in the Constitution, yet since George Washington's administration, every president has had one. Washington's consisted of his secretaries of state, treasury, and war, plus his attorney general.

DEFINING THE CABINET   Defining the cabinet is the first major job for the president-elect. The cabinet consists of the president, the vice president, the heads of the 15 executive departments, and several others a president considers essential officials. The cabinet has always been a loosely designated body, and it is not always clear who belongs in it. In recent years, certain executive branch administrators and White House counselors have been accorded cabinet rank. Nineteen officials have had cabinet status in the George W. Bush administration, including the 15 cabinet secretaries, the vice president, the chief of staff, and the director of national intelligence.

CABINET GOVERNMENT   Cabinet government is generally defined as a system of advice in which the voice of individual cabinet members is of major importance. As such, cabinet government does not exist in the United States.[23] In fact, an American president is not required by the Constitution to form a cabinet or to hold regular meetings.

cabinet

Advisory council for the president, consisting of the heads of the executive departments, the vice president, and a few other officials selected by the president.

President Bush holds a press conference surrounded by his cabinet. The cabinet is made up of heads of executive departments and other key officials. While some department heads are expected to be included in every administration, the president has great leeway in deciding who is to be part of this powerful council.

The Changing Face of American Politics

Presidential Appointees

Presidents Bill Clinton and George W. Bush both promised to appoint administrations that were as diverse as the country. Although both presidents came surprisingly close on race, neither approached the 50 percent mark on gender.

Although the percentages of women and minority appointees are disappointing given the changing face of federal departments and agencies (discussed in the next chapter), both administrations did much better than their predecessors—less than 15 percent of the Carter administration's appointees were women, compared with just 8 percent of the Reagan administration's first-term appointees. And the fact that both Clinton and Bush were able to recruit many women and minority appointees at lower levels suggests that future administrations will be even more successful. Past research shows that the higher-level jobs almost always go to appointees with prior service at lower levels of government. By increasing the numbers of women and minorities in the pipeline, the Clinton and Bush administrations increased the odds that there will be more women and minority candidates for the top jobs for future Democratic and Republican administrations alike.

The commitment to diversity is particularly apparent at the very top of government. Clinton appointed five women, seven African Americans, three Hispanics, and one Asian American as secretaries of departments during his eight years in office, while Bush named five women, four African Americans, three Hispanics and two Asian Americans in his first four years in office.

Bush's second term brought more diversity. He appointed his White House lawyer, Alberto Gonzales, to be the first Hispanic attorney general, Condoleezza Rice to be the first female African American secretary of state, and Carlos Gutierrez to be the first Cuban American secretary of commerce. He also appointed dozens of women and minorities to lower-level posts, thereby giving them the experience for future promotions to higher-level jobs. ∎

	Clinton First-Term Appointees	Bush First-Term Appointees
Women	30%	23%
Men	70	77
African American	14%	9%
Hispanic	6	8
Asian American	3	

SOURCE: Data collected by the Presidential Appointee Initiative, analysis by authors.

Presidents John Kennedy, Lyndon Johnson, and Richard Nixon all preferred small conferences with individuals specifically involved in a problem and rarely held cabinet meetings. Kennedy saw no reason, for example, to discuss Defense Department matters with his secretaries of agriculture and labor, and he thought cabinet meetings wasted valuable time. Both Jimmy Carter and Ronald Reagan tried to revive the cabinet, and both met often with their cabinets during their first two years. But the longer they remained in office, the less frequently they met with their cabinets as a whole.

Despite their occasional praise of cabinet government, presidents tend to rely on their own advisers for most input on key issues. Proximity is power in Washington, and the White House staff is always close by (see Figure 12–2). Further, presidents are aware

West Wing

Cabinet Room

Vice President's Office

East Wing

Presidential Briefing Room

Oval Office

FIGURE 12–2 **The White House.**

History Makers

Condoleezza Rice

Condoleezza Rice

Although Condoleezza Rice was neither the first woman nor the first African American to be appointed as secretary of state, she entered the job as the first African American woman to have served as the president's national security adviser, and as the first African American woman to become secretary of state. In taking the job, she became instantly visible as a possible presidential candidate.

As the president's national security adviser during the first term, Rice had been a natural for one of the toughest foreign policy jobs in government. She sat only a few doors away from the president, advised the president on all foreign issues, and traveled with him on all missions abroad. She also helped him resolve disputes among his foreign policy team. Her appointment as secretary of state at the start of the second term gave her even greater influence over foreign policy.

Rice also had a nearly perfect résumé for both her jobs. She earned her bachelor's degree in political science from the University of Denver at 19 and received her Ph.D. from the Graduate School of International Studies at Denver seven years later. Already a full professor at Stanford University, she joined the first Bush administration in 1989 as the director of the Soviet and East European desk at the National Security Council, then returned to Stanford as provost, the second most important administrative post at the university.

That résumé would have been more than enough to qualify her for almost any foreign policy job in the Bush administration. But she also earned her status as a key adviser during the 2000 presidential campaign. By paying her dues on the campaign trail, she earned the president's trust. During the hours and days after the terrorist attacks, President Bush often asked her to give him her advice on the right course of action.

Her service in the Bush administration has not been without controversy, however. She was widely criticized for her role in shaping the case for war with Iraq, arguing for the existence of weapons of mass destruction that threatened the United States even though that claim had been discredited by the Central Intelligence Agency well before the president used it as part of his case for war. As such, she will likely be remembered more for what she did during the early days of the war on terrorism than for her current role as secretary of state.

Although she has said she had to be "twice as good" to get ahead, Rice made it to the top by believing her parents when they told her that "you may not be able to have a hamburger at Woolworth's but you can be president of the United States." ∎

---

that some cabinet members adopt narrow "advocate" views: the Agriculture Department secretary is a strong advocate for farmers; the Housing and Urban Development Department secretary is an ambassador for the housing industry and, to some extent, also for big-city mayors; and so on through much of the cabinet, especially in departments concerned primarily with domestic policy matters.

MANAGING THE GOVERNMENT Presidents are responsible for faithfully executing the laws, which means that they are in charge of the day-to-day operations of the federal departments, agencies, military personnel, and employees. All departments are not created equal, however. Some are much larger than others—the Department of Defense has nearly a million employees, while the Department of Education has barely 5,000; the Department of Health and Human Services has a budget of approximately $600 billion, while the Department of State has a budget of just $10 billion.

Some departments are also more important—presidents tend to pay the greatest attention to the departments of Defense, Justice, State, and Treasury. These four departments are often called the *inner cabinet* because they are so important to the president's foreign and domestic success. The economy (Treasury), crime (Justice), and international affairs (State and Defense) are rarely far from the top of the president's list of policy concerns. Presidents almost always appoint very close allies to the inner cabinet posts, even if those allies do not always have the best credentials for the jobs.

The other departments are generally called the *outer cabinet,* largely because they are more distant from the day-to-day worries that occupy the president and White House staff. The Department of Veterans Affairs, for example, is rarely in the headlines, even though its 250,000 full- and part-time employees make it the second-largest department in the federal bureaucracy.

The Vice Presidency

Despite Vice President Dick Cheney's visible role today, the vice presidency has not always been an important job. For most of American history, the vice president was seen as an insignificant officer at best and at worst a political rival who sometimes connived against the president. The office was often dismissed as a joke. One reason for the vice president's posture as an outsider was that presidential nominees usually chose running mates who were geographically, ideologically, demographically, and in other ways likely to "balance the ticket."

No matter how influential they become, vice presidents have only one major responsibility: to be ready to take the oath of office in case the president cannot discharge his duties. Vice presidents are not mere replacement parts, however. President Jimmy Carter included Walter Mondale in the daily processes of decision making in the White House, and President Clinton used Al Gore as an important adviser and confidant on domestic as well as foreign policy matters and key appointments. Even when recent presidents have mostly ignored their vice presidents, as the first President Bush did with his vice president, Dan Quayle, vice presidents enter office with substantial access, including an office just down the hall from the president in the West Wing of the White House, a substantial staff of their own, and access to all of the information flowing into the Oval Office.

Vice President Dick Cheney has more than just access to President Bush, however. He also has considerable influence. As a former member of Congress and secretary of defense during the first Bush administration, Cheney brought significant credibility to the 2000 campaign and reassured voters that the younger Bush was ready for the presidency. He was also a trusted advisor to the Bush family, and actually chaired the vice-presidential search process that produced his candidacy. Although he started his vice presidency as one of the most popular political leaders in the country, his approval fell dramatically as the war in Iraq continued. By February 2004, Americans were evenly divided on whether Cheney should even remain on the presidential ticket—even 28 percent of Republicans said the president should make a change.[24]

While the vice president's primary responsibility is to take the oath of office should the president become unable to carry out his or her term, some vice presidents have wielded more power and influence than others.

The President's Job

Presidents are always expected to perform roles not explicitly defined in the Constitution. Americans want the chief executive to be an international peacemaker as well as a national morale builder, a politician in chief as well as a commander in chief. They want the president to provide leadership on foreign, economic, and domestic policy. Americans also want presidents to be crisis managers and role models of a kind. They want them to be able to connect with ordinary Americans and be honest, yet be smarter, tougher, and more honest than the rest of us. (See Table 12–1 for what Americans say they care about most in picking a president.)

Presidents as Crisis Managers

The framers designed the president's job as commander in chief as a limited role. Congress, not the president,

TABLE 12–1	What Americans Want to Know about their Candidates	
Percentage of Americans who said it is very important to know the following about a presidential candidate:	**2000 Campaign**	**2004 Campaign**
How well a candidate connects with average people	67%	71%
A candidate's voting record or policy positions he or she previously held	60	64
A candidate's reputation for honesty	84	88
A candidate's major campaign contributors	42	39
A candidate's military background	19	21
Whether a candidate is an active churchgoer	25	27

SOURCE: Pew Research Center for the People and the Press, "Democratic Primary Campaign Impresses Voters," February 19, 2004, p. 1.

The first lady can be an important influence on a president. In recent decades, the first lady has evolved into a prominent policy advisor to the president as well as a champion of many important causes of her own choosing. Although Laura Bush has not been as influential on major policy issues as Hillary Clinton was, she is still a formidable adviser to the president, if only because she has instant access whenever she wishes.

declares war, makes the rules for the army and navy, and controls the funding of wars. Yet the president is still in charge of the military as commander in chief.

When presidents react quickly to crises, their approval ratings usually rise. These **rally points** are particularly strong when a military action, such as an invasion or a bombing, is both short and successful. Rally points do not necessarily last long, however. George W. Bush's ratings jumped dramatically following the September 11, 2001, attacks when he called on the nation to support the war on terrorism, but eventually fell back with the continued violence after the first moments of the war in Iraq. (See Table 12–2 for examples of recent rally points.)

Not all rally points involve foreign crises, however. Clinton's approval rose after the Oklahoma City bombing in 1995 in large part because Americans turned to him for leadership in the crisis. Presidential approval ratings can also rise during periods of great national pride. Reagan's public approval (and reelection chances) jumped during the 1984 Olympic Games as the United States won one gold medal after another, in part because the Soviet Union and its eastern European allies boycotted the event. In contrast, Bush's ratings fell when his administration was slow to help New Orleans after Hurricane Katrina hit.

Presidents as Morale Builders

As chief of state, the president must project a sense of national unity and authority as the country's chief ceremonial leader. The framers of the Constitution did not fully anticipate the symbolic and morale-building functions a president must perform. But over time, presidents have become the nation's number one celebrities, and command media attention merely by jogging, fishing, golfing, or going to church. By their actions, presidents can arouse a sense of hope or despair, honor or dishonor.

The morale-building job of the president involves much more than just ceremonial cheerleading or quasi-chaplain duties. Presidential leadership, at its finest, radiates national self-confidence and helps unlock the possibility for good that exists in the nation. Our best leaders have been able to provide this special and often intangible element. That is certainly what George W. Bush intended in the days and weeks that followed September 11, 2001. By his words and deeds, he sought to simultaneously calm the nation and warn the rest of the world that the United States would not tolerate further terrorist attacks.

Presidents as Agenda Setters

By custom and circumstance, presidents are now responsible for proposing initiatives in foreign policy and economic growth and stability. This was not always the case. But beginning with Woodrow Wilson, and especially since the New Deal, a president has been expected to propose reforms to ensure domestic progress. Presidential candidates searching for campaign issues seize on new ideas, and the ideas are later refined and implemented by the executive office staff, by special presidential task forces, and by Congress.[25]

rally point
A rise in public approval of the president that follows a crisis as Americans "rally 'round the flag" and the chief executive.

TABLE 12–2 Recent Rally Points

President and Event	Approval Before	Approval After	Change in Approval
George W. Bush			
September 11 terrorist attacks (2001)	51%	80%	+29%
Beginning of the Iraq War (2003)	55	67	+12
Bill Clinton			
Oklahoma City bombing (1995)	46	51	+ 5
George H. W. Bush			
Beginning of Gulf War (1991)	59	79	+20

President Bush, flanked by firefighters and rescue workers, addresses a crowd at the scene of the September 11 World Trade Center disaster in New York. In times of crisis, the nation often rallies around the president despite political differences.

NATIONAL SECURITY POLICY   The framers foresaw a special need for speed and unity in dealing with other nations. As a result, presidents generally have more leeway in foreign policy and military affairs than they have in domestic matters. The Constitution gives the president command of the two major instruments of foreign policy—the diplomatic corps and the armed services. It also gives the president responsibility for negotiating treaties and commitments with other nations, although the Senate must consent to treaty ratifications, and almost all international agreements require congressional action for their implementation.

Congress has granted presidents discretion in initiating foreign policy, for diplomacy frequently requires quick action. The Supreme Court has upheld strong presidential authority in this area. In *United States* v. *Curtiss-Wright* (1936), the Court referred to the "exclusive power of the president as the sole organ of the federal government in the field of international relations—a power which does not require as a basis for its exercise an act of Congress, but which, of course, like every other governmental power, must be exercised in subordination to the applicable provisions of the Constitution."[26] These are sweeping and much-debated words.[27] Still, a determined Congress that knows what it wants does not lack power in foreign relations. Congress must authorize and appropriate the funds that support the president's policies abroad, but it often gives the president wide latitude in protecting the nation.

ECONOMIC POLICY   Ever since the New Deal, presidents have been expected to promote policies to keep unemployment low, fight inflation, keep taxes down, and promote economic growth and prosperity. The Constitution does not specify these duties for the executive, yet presidents know that when the nation is not prosperous and jobs are scarce, they may suffer the fate of Herbert Hoover, who was denounced for his inaction at the beginning of the Great Depression. The growth and complexity of economic problems since the depression of the 1930s have placed more economic responsibility in the president's hands.

Although presidents receive economic advice from inside and outside government, the three most important advisers are the secretary of the treasury, the head of the White House economic office, and the director of the Office of Management and Budget. The chair of the Federal Reserve Board of Governors is also an influential, if independent, adviser on the economy.

DOMESTIC POLICY   Leadership is often defined as the art of knowing what followers want. John Kennedy and Lyndon Johnson did not launch the civil rights movement, for example. Nor did Bill Clinton or George W. Bush create public pressure for national health insurance or prescription drug coverage. But they all responded to the public demand by supporting legislation on each issue.

At the same time, presidents sometimes take highly unpopular positions for what they see as the good of the country. The vast majority of Americans opposed Harry Truman's decision to integrate the armed services, and many southerners left the Democratic Party when Lyndon Johnson demanded action on civil rights. Similarly, many Americans opposed the Bush administration's decision not to fund stem-cell research, which is seen as a potential tool in curing spinal-cord injuries and certain brain diseases.

Presidents as Persuaders

Presidents must build political coalitions if they are to have any chance of winning passage of their legislative priorities. As candidates, they make promises to the people and assemble an electoral coalition of supporters. To get things done and to get reelected, however, they must work with interest groups and people who have differing loyalties and responsibilities. Inevitably, presidents become embroiled in legislative, bureaucratic, and lobbying politics, and their approval ratings often suffer as a consequence.

Despite their formal powers, presidents spend most of their time *persuading* people. As Richard Neustadt argues, the power to persuade is the president's chief resource.[28] This power to persuade is based on the president's ability to communicate directly with members of Congress and the public, which rests on the skillful use of press conferences, speeches, and public events to maintain contact with the country. Although much of this communication is designed to support other presidential roles, today's presidents are making more prime-time television appearances, giving more speeches, and spending more time outside of Washington in efforts to influence the country. According to political scientist Samuel Kernell, the number of major and minor presidential addresses has grown from just a dozen or so in the first three years of the Hoover administration (1929–1931) to well over 100 in the first three years of the Bush presidency almost 60 years later. The greatest growth came in the number of minor addresses before specialized audiences—trade associations, college graduations, and advocacy groups.[29]

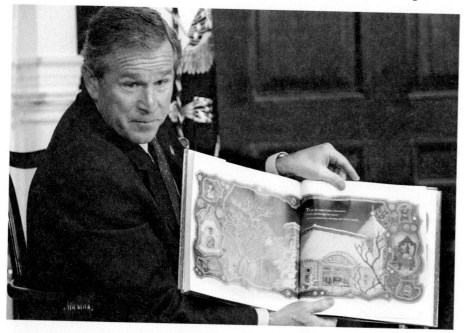

President Bush reads "The Night Before Christmas" to Washington area schoolchildren at the White House in 2002. Bush lobbied Congress to pass the No Child Left Behind act, which he described as "the cornerstone of my administration."

At the same time, presidents have been spending less time holding press conferences. Whereas Franklin Roosevelt averaged almost seven press conferences a month during his dozen years in office, the past four presidents averaged barely one. Presidents would much rather be interviewed by local reporters outside Washington than by members of the experienced White House press corps, much rather give exclusive interviews to a sympathetic interviewer than face a roomful of unpredictable reporters, and much rather use live satellite feeds to remote stations to get their message across than deal with the *Washington Post, New York Times,* or *Wall Street Journal.* (Presidential press conferences are covered in more detail in Chapter 10.) This strategy is often labeled as "going public," and it often involves carefully staged events before friendly audiences that show strong support for the president.

Agents of Change

Marie Wilson and the White House Project

QUESTIONS

Why does increasing the number of women at senior levels of lower-level organizations affect the potential for electing a woman as president?

What kind of training do women need to be effective candidates?

The nonpartisan White House Project was launched in 1998 to increase the political participation of women at all levels of government. As its name suggests, the organization's ultimate goal is to advance a woman all the way to the White House. But the organization believes that this goal is only possible if more women advance in all institutions, including government, businesses, universities, and charities.

The White House Project was launched by Marie Wilson, who had served as the president of the Ms. Foundation for Women since the mid-1980s. Having been the first woman elected to the Des Moines, Iowa, city council in 1983, Wilson had long understood the barriers that women face in any organization, political or otherwise. After cocreating Take Our Daughters to Work Day, Wilson turned her attention to women's political participation. "Our democracy suffers when women—who are over 51% of the population—are seriously underrepresented in both the voting booth and in public office," she says.

Under the White House Project, Wilson has created a long list of new projects designed to advance a range of issues, including increasing the number of women voters and elected officials across the country. She also led the Vote, Run, Lead program in 2004, which encouraged women to become more active in public life at all levels of government. She launched the Go Run project as a weekend intensive training program to encourage women to become candidates for election. The White House Project also works with local organizations to encourage young women to consider politics. As the group's motto asks, "If all you're told is to be a good girl, how do you grow up to be a great woman?" ∎

Read more about the White House Project at www.thewhitehouseproject.org.

Marie Wilson

Going public clearly fits with changes in the electoral process. Presidents now have the staff, the technology, and the public opinion research to tell them how to target their message, and the nearly instant media access to speak to the public easily. And, as elections have become more image-oriented and candidate-centered, presidents have the incentive to use these tools to operate a permanent White House campaign. Presidents are still welcome to bargain and persuade, to focus congressional attention and twist arms, but members of Congress may pay attention only when pressure is coming from the voters back home.

Presidential Personality

Presidential personality plays a central role in the president's ability to play these roles as crisis manager, agenda-setter, and morale builder. According to James David Barber, presidents who bring energy to these roles and enjoy the job are more successful in leading the public than those who have little energy and gain little emotional reward from their work.[30] Barber describes the first kind of president as an active-positive, and the second as a passive-negative. He also describes presidents who bring energy to the job but little joy as active-negative, and those who give little energy and are mostly unhappy as passive-negatives.

Barber puts Franklin Roosevelt, Harry Truman, John F. Kennedy, and Bill Clinton in the active-positive category—all worked hard and had fun in the job. He puts Lyndon

"Our democracy suffers when women are seriously underrepresented in both the voting booth and in public office."

MARIE WILSON

TABLE 12–3 Presidential Personality Types		
	Active: *Plays all the roles of being president aggressively*	**Passive:** *Rarely plays the roles of being president aggressively except during crisis*
Positive: *Enjoys the job of being president, flexible*	Roosevelt, Truman, Kennedy, Clinton, George W. Bush	Reagan, George H. W. Bush
Negative: *Unhappy in the job, anxious*	Johnson, Nixon	Eisenhower

Johnson and Richard Nixon in the active-negative—both also worked hard but received little joy from their engagement. He puts Ronald Reagan and George H. W. Bush in the passive-positive category, and Jimmy Carter in the passive-negative category. (See Table 12–3 for the comparisons.)

Although Barber did not rate George W. Bush, most observers put him in the active-positive category. Some observers argue that the second president Bush started out as a passive-positive president who became an active-positive president in response to the September 11, 2001, attacks. Bush appears to enjoy the job of being president, and he has clearly been extremely active in pursuing homeland security, fighting the war on terrorism, and pursuing domestic reforms in Social Security, tax cuts, and prescription drug coverage for older Americans. Bush's change suggests that presidential personality depends in part on the situations presidents confront. Although their basic attitude to the job may not change, their level of activity can rise and fall depending on the situations they face.

Congress and the Presidency

Congress and the presidency have a contentious relationship. On the one hand, they often work closely together to address critically important problems such as homeland security, prescription drugs, welfare reform, and civil rights.

On the other hand, Congress and the president are often unable to reach agreement on equally difficult issues such as global warming, energy independence, education reform, and increases in the minimum wage. They are most likely to agree in the first year of a president's first term, and when one party controls both the White House and Congress, and more likely to fight late in the president's first term and off and on throughout the entire second term.

Given the separation of powers, it is a wonder that Congress and the president ever agree at all, which is exactly what the framers intended. The framers did not want the legislative process to work like an assembly line. Rather, they wanted ambition to counteract ambition as a way to prevent tyranny. To the extent that they designed the legislative process to work inefficiently, they succeeded beyond their initial hopes. Hard as presidents work to win passage of their top priorities, they often complain that Congress is not listening. However, Congress listens more closely to its constituents, especially when the president's public approval is low. That is why so many of the Bush administration's second-term priorities never reached the floor of the House or Senate.

President John F. Kennedy understood the importance of direct communication with the American people and often addressed the public with television broadcasts.

Why Presidents and Congress Disagree

Congress and the president disagree for many reasons, not the least of which is the natural tendency of members of Congress to think about elections far into the future. Not only does the Constitution give each institution separate powers and checks and balances, it also provides competing constituencies, calendars, and campaigns, all of which put Congress and the presidency on a frequent course to stalemate.

COMPETING CONSTITUENCIES The framers guaranteed that members of Congress and the president would represent different constituencies, which often leads to conflict over major legislation. Members of Congress represent either states or local districts, while the president represents the nation as a whole. Although these constituencies often overlap, particularly in states that strongly support the president's election, members of Congress often worry most about how the laws and presidential actions will affect their home districts. Even members of the president's own party often put their own constituency first, as conservative Republicans did in demanding more administration support for reducing the deficit in 2005 and 2006.

COMPETING CALENDARS The Constitution also ensures that Congress and the president will not share the same terms of office. Presidents can serve a maximum of eight years before leaving office, while senators and members of the House can serve for decades. Presidents enter office wanting everything passed at once, while members of Congress have plenty of time to wait. Convinced that they must either move quickly or lose all hopes of any success at all, presidents tend to overload Congress with priorities in their first year, thereby actually reducing their chances of passage. Asked to do everything at once, many members of Congress decide to do nothing particularly fast.

COMPETING CAMPAIGNS Finally, the Constitution ensures that Congress and the president will run different kinds of election campaigns. Most members of Congress finance their election campaigns with only minimal assistance from their national political party. They usually run independently of the president or national party platform. Once again, even members of the president's own party have been known to ask the president not to visit their districts in particularly tight elections or when the president's public approval is falling. Whenever possible, members try to make elections about local, not national issues, which means that the president is often completely ignored during the campaign.

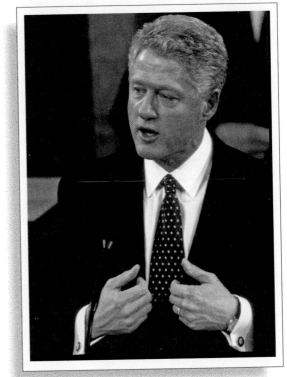

President Bill Clinton addresses Congress and the nation during a State of the Union Address. While Clinton often enjoyed popular support, he frequently faced opposition in the Republican-controlled Congress.

Influencing Congress

Presidents are clearly much more than faithful executors of the laws passed by Congress. They have long had a substantial, if not always dominant, role in shaping what Congress does. Their primary vehicle for doing so is the president's agenda, which is an informal list of top legislative priorities. Whether through the State of the Union address or through other messages and signals, presidents make clear what they think Congress should do.[31]

It is one thing to proclaim a presidential priority, however, and quite another to actually influence congressional action. As Richard Neustadt argued in *Presidential Power*, a president's constitutional powers add up to little more than a job as America's most distinguished office clerk. It is a president's ability to persuade others that spells the difference between being a clerk and being a national leader.[32] This power to persuade rests in the resources a president brings to office and the skills that he or she uses in making the most of those resources. (Figure 12–3, on page 372, compares recent presidents on their ability to influence Congress on key votes. Bush's support scores remained remarkably high through his fifth year in office, but this was in part because he took fewer positions on controversial congressional issues.)

Presidential Resources

There are two kinds of resources that shape both the size of a president's agenda and its ultimate impact on Congress. The first involves the political resources needed to convince Congress to support the president, while the second involves the decision-making resources that help presidents decide what they want.

POLITICAL RESOURCES Presidential influence comes from three external resources: (1) the mandate provided through the most recent presidential election, (2) the level of public approval, and (3) the number of party seats in Congress.

"It's a hard job being president. . . . Anybody who walks in there thinking he can punch a time clock at 9 in the morning and leave at 5 has got another think coming."

PRESIDENT GERALD FORD

Presidents who enter office with a large electoral margin, high public approval, and a party majority in Congress often claim a **mandate** to govern. The winner-take-all nature of the electoral-college system tends to make the president's popular vote look larger than it truly is. Ronald Reagan set the modern record in 1984 by winning every state but Massachusetts and the District of Columbia, rolling up 98 percent of the electoral votes with a popular total of 59 percent.

Mandates also reside in public approval for either the president or some policy issue. In 1993, for example, Clinton claimed a mandate for national health insurance, arguing that the issue was at the core of much of his public support. The claim would have been more believable if Clinton had won with a popular vote larger than 43 percent. George W. Bush made a similar claim for a broad agenda early in 2001, arguing that the American public wanted action in Washington. Again, the claim would have been more plausible had he won the popular vote.

The mandate to govern depends in part on public approval, which often falls over time. (See Figure 12–4 for presidential approval trends over the past half-century.) Bush became the first incumbent president in modern history to win reelection despite starting his campaign with an approval rating below 50 percent. Although he regained ground after his second inauguration, his ratings continued to fall as his second term continued, which helps explain the declining number of congressional votes on which he took a position. He simply did not have enough *political capital* to take more positions.

PERSONAL RESOURCES Presidential influence comes from three personal resources: (1) time and energy, (2) experience, and (3) the ability to focus congressional attention on the president's priorities.

The first resource always declines as presidents serve out their term and age in the job. One need only compare pictures of presidents at the start and end of their terms to see the impact of the long hours and constant stress. As Gerald Ford once remarked, "It's a hard job being president. . . . Anybody who walks in there thinking he can punch a time clock at 9 in the morning and leave at 5 has got another think coming. We do not elect presidents who want that kind of a life."

In contrast, experience increases over time as presidents learn their jobs. In a sense, the presidency is the nation's most intense American government course. Senators who become president tend to know more about policy issues than managing government, while governors who become president tend to know more about managing

mandate
A president's claim of broad public support.

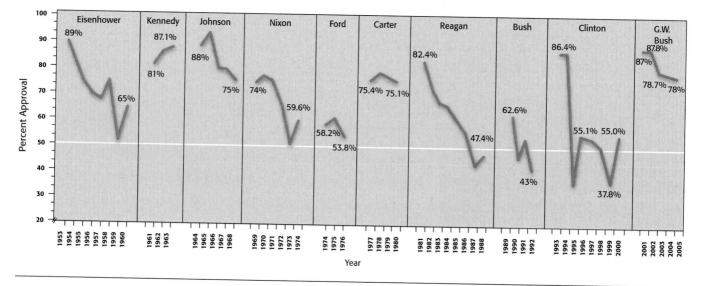

FIGURE **12–3 Legislative Support from Congress, 1953–2005.**
SOURCE: Gallup Organization, at www.gallup.com. Updated by the authors.

government than policy issues. Washington insiders tend to know more about how Congress and the presidency negotiate, while Washington outsiders may have a better sense of public opinion. But wherever they start, presidents learn over time.

Finally, the president's focusing skill depends on the personal ability to make the case for action. Ronald Reagan and Bill Clinton often used their personal charisma to persuade reluctant members, Lyndon Johnson often threatened to withhold campaign funding, and George W. Bush has often promised to provide federal funding for pet projects. Presidents can also increase support by providing small gifts such as tickets to special White House events. But whatever the technique, members of Congress rarely support the president unless they see some benefit back home.[33]

CYCLES OF PRESIDENTIAL INFLUENCE AND EFFECTIVENESS   These two sets of resources interact to create two cycles that shape the president's relationship with Congress. The first cycle is called the **cycle of decreasing influence**. As presidential approval falls over time, presidents become less influential on Capitol Hill. Although Republicans actually gained more seats in Congress during Bush's first six years, the steady declines in public approval made the seats less dependable for the president's cause.

The second cycle is called the **cycle of increasing effectiveness**. The longer presidents stay in office, the better they get at being president. They learn how Washington works, what powers they can use to influence congressional action, and who they need to convince to win passage of their top priorities. They also learn how to use unilateral powers to accomplish some of their goals.

The two cycles suggest that presidents have the greatest influence at the very point when they know the least about being president, and know the most about being president when they have the least influence. Nevertheless, presidents generally believe they must "move it or lose it," meaning that they have to use their political influence when they have it. Doing so creates great opportunities for mistakes, however. Clinton and Bush both flooded Congress with long lists of first-year priorities, which created confusion and delays on Capitol Hill as individual members and committees tried to decide which priorities came first.

cycle of decreasing influence
The tendency of presidents to lose support over time.

cycle of increasing effectiveness
The tendency of presidents to learn more about doing their jobs over time.

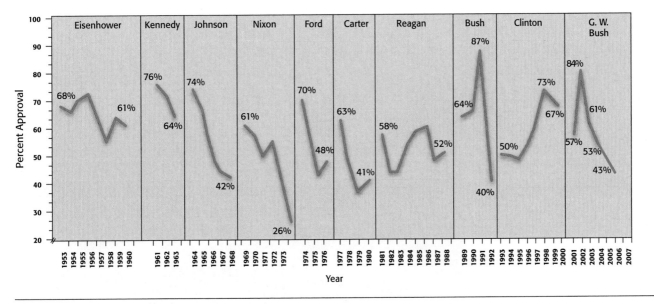

FIGURE **12–4 Presidential Approval Ratings, 1953–2006.**
SOURCE: *Congressional Quarterly Weekly*, January 12, 2002, p. 110. Updated by the authors.
NOTE: Percentages represent average scores for both chambers of Congress.

Judging Presidents

Presidents rise and fall in the historical rankings based on a number of factors. Some rise because they led the nation through periods of intense domestic or international crisis; others rise because they had a distinctive vision of where the nation should go on issues such as civil rights, social policy, or the economy. Rankings also involve at least some assessment of how presidents did as political and moral leaders of the nation. Some fall because of political or personal scandal, others because a president failed to grapple with a big issue such as national health insurance or economic crisis. In the end, rankings involve the overall measure of a president's impact in meeting the public's expectations.

History tends to judge wars as the most significant test of a president's leadership. Wars that end in stalemate tend to diminish a president's greatness, while wars that end in victory raise a president's ranking, especially when the nation's survival is threatened. Abraham Lincoln (the Civil War), Woodrow Wilson (World War I), and Franklin Delano Roosevelt (World War II) rank among the great presidents because of their leadership during just such wars, while Lyndon Johnson ranks much lower because of his role in the Vietnam stalemate.

War is not the only path to greatness, however. George Washington and Thomas Jefferson rank as great presidents because of their role in protecting the nation during its early years. Theodore Roosevelt ranks as a great president because of his role in making the United States an international power at the turn of the twentieth century. And Harry Truman and Dwight Eisenhower rank among the near-great presidents because they led the nation through the first decade of the cold war against communism. Ronald Reagan also ranks among the near-great presidents because he played an important role in ending the cold war 30 years later. These presidents also made difficult decisions about domestic issues such as civil rights, economic policy, and the need for a strong national government.

Corruption and inability to deal with economic problems are sure paths to presidential failure. Warren Harding and Richard Nixon both rank as failures because of scandals that tarnished their presidencies, while Herbert Hoover is ranked as a failure because of his lack of leadership at the start of the Great Depression. Although Lyndon

Residents of New Orleans' Lower Ninth Ward stranded on the roofs wait for rescue after Hurricane Katrina slammed into Louisiana in 2005. President Bush and his administration came under fire for a slow response to the disaster.

Johnson launched a number of great domestic programs such as Medicare for older Americans and helped secure civil rights for African Americans, his role in the Vietnam War continues to cast a shadow on his presidential greatness.

It is too early to guess where George W. Bush will be ranked by history. His response to September 11, 2001, was steady and reassuring, and Americans rallied to his side in the first few weeks of the war in Iraq. At the same time, soaring budget deficits and questions about the ever lengthening war in Iraq undermined both his credibility and his public support. So did rising gasoline prices and the government's sluggish response to Hurricane Katrina in 2005.

Ultimately, a president's place in history is determined years, even decades, after the president has left office. By remembering that there is a future accounting, presidents can find some inspiration for making the hard and sometimes unpopular choices that have led to greatness among their predecessors. Thus the judgment of history may be one of the most important sources of accountability that the nation has on its presidents. With less than two years to go in his term, Bush may well be remembered most for his two Supreme Court appointments and his early victories on tax cuts and education reform than anything yet to be accomplished. Moreover, unless the United States finds a way to end the war in Iraq, he may yet be viewed as one of history's least successful presidents.

Summary

1. The framers created a presidency with limited powers. To enact government business, the president must cooperate with Congress, but power is divided among the branches, and the politics of shared power has often been stormy. In general, however, both the role and the influence of presidents have increased over the course of the nation's history.

2. The framers gave the president three central roles in the new government: commander in chief, diplomat in chief, and administrator in chief. Presidents have expanded their powers in several ways over the decades. Crises, both foreign and economic, have enlarged these powers. When there is a need for decisive action, presidents are asked to supply it. Congress, of course, is traditionally expected to share in the formulation of national policy. Every president must learn anew the need to work closely with the members of Congress.

3. The Constitution is not always clear on which branch has what powers, which creates controversies over the president's war power, authority to assert executive privilege, issue executive orders, and control the budget and spending process. Congress has made several attempts in recent decades to clarify the president's war and spending power.

4. Presidents manage the executive branch with the assistance of a White House staff composed of roughly 400 individuals and a cabinet of department secretaries that oversees the civil servants. The vice president is also involved in helping the president manage government.

5. The presidency has evolved over the past two centuries to become one of the world's most powerful institutions. This evolution began with George Washington, who set many of the precedents for presidential leadership that exist to this day. It continued with the first modern president, Franklin Roosevelt, who built the presidency into an instrument for sweeping national policy.

6. Americans expect a great deal from their presidents. They want them to be crisis managers, morale builders, and agenda setters, yet also want them to be able to connect with average Americans.

7. The president and Congress often have a tense relationship because of different constitutional expectations and party divisions. Presidents have a variety of tools for influencing Congress, however, and use their political and personal resources to gain support for their policy proposals.

8. Presidential greatness is hard to define. Historians, political scientists, and the American public consider Washington, Jefferson, Lincoln, and Franklin Roosevelt as their greatest presidents. Greatness depends in part on how presidents deal with crisis and war.

Further Reading

DAVID GRAY ADLER AND **LARRY N. GEORGE**, EDS., *The Constitution and the Conduct of American Foreign Policy: Essays on Law and History* (University Press of Kansas, 1996).

PAUL BRACE AND **BARBARA HINCKLEY**, *Follow the Leader: Opinion Polls and the Modern Presidents* (Basic Books, 1992).

JOHN P. BURKE, *The Institutional Presidency: Organizing and Managing the White House from FDR to Clinton*, 2d ed. (Johns Hopkins University Press, 2000).

JEFFREY COHEN, *The Presidency* (McGraw-Hill, 2002).

THOMAS E. CRONIN, ED., *Inventing the American Presidency* (University Press of Kansas, 1989).

THOMAS E. CRONIN AND **MICHAEL A. GENOVESE**, *The Paradoxes of the American Presidency*, 2d ed. (Oxford University Press, 2004).

TERRY EASTLAND, *Energy in the Executive* (Free Press, 1992).

MICHAEL A. GENOVESE, *The Power of the American Presidency, 1989–2000* (Oxford University Press, 2000).

DAVID GERGEN, *Eyewitness to Power: The Essence of Leadership, Nixon to Clinton* (Simon & Schuster, 2000).

FRED GREENSTEIN, *The Presidential Difference* (Free Press, 2000).

ERWIN C. HARGROVE, *The President as Leader: Appealing to the Better Angels of Our Nature* (University Press of Kansas, 1998).

STEPHEN HESS, *Organizing the Presidency*, 2d ed. (Brookings Institution Press, 2003).

CHARLES O. JONES, *Passages to the Presidency: From Campaigning to Governing* (Brookings Institution Press, 1998).

SAMUEL KERNELL, *Going Public: New Strategies of Presidential Leadership* (CQ Press, 1997).

GARY KING AND **LYN RAGSDALE**, *The Elusive Executive: Discovering Statistical Patterns in the Presidency*, 2d ed. (CQ Press, 2002).

MARK LANDY AND **SIDNEY M. MILKIS**, *Presidential Greatness* (University Press of Kansas, 2000).

LEONARD W. LEVY AND **LOUIS FISHER**, EDS., *Encyclopedia of the American Presidency* (Simon & Schuster, 1994).

JOHN A. MALTESE, *Spin Control: The White House Office of Communications and the Management of the Presidential News* (University of North Carolina Press, 1992).

SIDNEY M. MILKIS, *The President and the Parties: The Transformation of the American Party System Since the New Deal* (Oxford University Press, 1993).

SIDNEY M. MILKIS AND **MICHAEL NELSON**, *The American Presidency: Origins and Development, 1976–2000*, 4th ed. (CQ Press, 2003).

MICHAEL NELSON, ED., *The Presidency and the Political System*, 8th ed. (CQ Press, 2005).

RICHARD E. NEUSTADT, *Presidential Power and the Modern Presidents* (Free Press, 1991).

HUBERT S. PARMET, *George Bush: The Life of a Lone Star Yankee* (Scribner, 1998).

BRADLEY H. PATTERSON JR., *The White House Staff: Inside the West Wing and Beyond* (Brookings Institution Press, 2000).

JAMES PFIFFER, *Understanding the Presidency*, 3d ed. (Longman, 2002).

JAMES P. PFIFFNER, *The Strategic Presidency: Hitting the Ground Running*, 2d ed. (University Press of Kansas, 1996).

GLENN A. PHELPS, *George Washington and American Constitutionalism* (University Press of Kansas, 1993).

STEPHEN PONDER, *Managing the Press: Origins of the Media Presidency* (Palgrave, 2000).

LYN RAGSDALE, *Vital Statistics on the Presidency*, rev. ed. (CQ Press, 1998).

ANDREW RUDALEVIGE, *The New Imperial Presidency: Renewing Presidential Power after Watergate* (University of Michigan Press, 2005).

STEPHEN SKOWRONEK, *The Politics Presidents Make* (Belknap, 1997).

SHELLEY LYNNE TOMKINS, *Inside OMB: Politics and Process in the President's Budget Office* (Sharpe, 1998).

KENNETH T. WALSH, *Feeding the Beast: The White House Versus the Press* (Random House, 1996).

SHIRLEY ANNE WARSHAW, *Powersharing: White House–Cabinet Relations in the Modern Presidency* (State University of New York Press, 1996).

KeyTerms

Make It Real

THE PRESIDENT

This module allows students to
pick the next Supreme Court Justice.

Chapter 13

The Federal Administrative System

EXECUTING THE LAWS

★

Hurricane Katrina crashed ashore near New Orleans, Louisiana, at dawn on August 29, 2005. Although Katrina had weakened somewhat before it reached land, it remained one of the strongest hurricanes in modern history. Despite Katrina's winds and the rising tides that came with her, most observers felt that the worst was over when Katrina headed inland. Unfortunately, the fragile system of levees that protected New Orleans from Lake Pontchartrain to its north soon began to collapse. By the next day, much of the city was under water.

Katrina did more than flood the city and devastate most of the Louisiana and Mississippi Gulf Coast. It also killed more than 1,300 people and left thousands stranded on rooftops or in desperate conditions at the Louisiana Superdome and the Convention Center in the heart of New Orleans. With the city government in disarray, and the Louisiana state government desperate for help, the federal government seemed to be the region's only hope, and the Federal Emergency Man-

agement Agency (FEMA) and its Senate-confirmed director, Michael Brown, its first responder. After all, the federal government had created FEMA in the late 1970s precisely to coordinate the response to emergencies such as Katrina.

Unfortunately, FEMA did not start moving until well after the levees collapsed. Some later argued that FEMA had been weakened when it was merged, along with 21 other agencies, into the new Department of Homeland Security. With the department focused on the war on terrorism, FEMA's budget and staffing dropped precipitously, while employee morale fell. Moreover, Michael Brown had no emergency management experience before being appointed to his job. His main claim to the post was service in the Bush 2000 presidential campaign. Given a lower-level political job at FEMA early in the administration, Brown had worked his way upward to the director's office based on his intense loyalty to the president, not his knowledge of emergency management.

As the nation would later discover, Brown did not inform his superiors of the growing crisis, nor were his superiors paying enough attention. Although Brown told senior White House officials that something bad was coming the night before the hurricane blew ashore, they waited for Brown to make the call on what the federal government should do. As the nation would soon learn, Brown seemed to be more concerned about how he looked on television than on organizing the federal response.

"With Katrina, there was no shortage of plans. There were plans, but there was not enough planning."

CONGRESSIONAL INVESTIGATORY COMMITTEE

379

Although Katrina was much worse than anyone had predicted, FEMA knew about the potential for catastrophe months before, and was simply unprepared to move food and water into the disaster zone quickly. Brown was soon removed from his job, but supplies did not reach the city until late in the first week, and only then in small amounts. Although Brown argued that he had had no choice but to wait until the federal government declared an "incident of national consequence," Americans could see the need for action on their own television screens, and many donated money to the Red Cross and other charities. With city and state governments in tatters from the storm, the region waited desperately for the federal government to act.

All federal agencies did not fail during the critical hours that followed Katrina, however. The U.S. Coast Guard rescued thousands of citizens from their rooftops, even as the Transportation Security Administration turned the New Orleans airport into an emergency hospital and evacuation center. Nevertheless, Katrina showed how vulnerable the nation can be when the federal government fails, and how important the federal government can be when it organizes quickly to act. "With Katrina, there was no shortage of plans," a congressional investigatory committee reported. "There were plans, but there was not enough planning. Government failed because it did not learn from past experiences, or because lessons thought to be learned were somehow not implemented." As the congressional investigation concluded, Katrina had not been a failure to imagine the possible consequences of a major hurricane on a fragile city. Rather, Katrina involved a failure to act.[1]

Most Americans saw Katrina as another example of how the federal administrative system fails. But the reality is that Americans have positive experiences with the federal government every day, even if they do not know it. Their air and water are guarded by the Department of the Interior and the Environmental Protection Agency (EPA), their food is protected by the Department of Agriculture and the Food and Drug Administration (FDA), threats to their health are being studied by the National Institutes of Health and Centers for Disease Control and Prevention, their college loans are either funded or insured by the Department of Education, at least part of their retirement income is being sheltered by the Social Security Administration (SSA), their workplaces are inspected by the Occupational Health and Safety Administration (OSHA), and their roads are smoothed in part by the Department of Transportation.

In this chapter, we examine the origins, functions, and realities of federal administration, which involves governmental bodies such as departments and agencies and the federal employees who administer the laws. We also explore how governmental departments, agencies, and employees are held accountable to the president, Congress, and the American public.

Understanding the Federal Administrative System

The **framers clearly understood** that the new national government would need an administrative system to protect the young Republic from foreign and domestic threats. They also understood that the new departments of government would need talented employees if they were to succeed. Although the framers hoped that government employees would be motivated by the desire to serve their country, they also knew that government would have to pay those employees for their work. They also understood that presidents would have to rely on talented executives to oversee the daily work of government, whether in repaying the costs of the Revolutionary War, building postal roads to carry the mail, training a national army and navy, caring for soldiers disabled in battle, administering treaties with other nations, or regulating commerce between the states.

"[A] government ill executed, whatever it may be in theory, must be, in practice, a bad government."

ALEXANDER HAMILTON, *THE FEDERALIST,* No. 70

The Undefined Branch

Federal administration is responsible for one task, and one task only: to faithfully execute all the laws. Although disagreements and factions were a normal and predictable part of making the laws, they were unacceptable when it came time for the laws to be executed. As Alexander Hamilton explained in *The Federalist,* No. 70, "a government ill executed, whatever it may be in theory, must be, in practice, a bad government."[2] The framers spent little time worrying about the administration of government, however. Instead, they left most of the details to future presidents. They believed that federal departments and agencies would be relatively small, and they expected Congress to establish the same departments that had existed under the Articles of Confederation.[3] They also expected George Washington to be the government's first chief executive and believed that he would lead the new government with the same skill that he had led the Continental Army. Nevertheless, the framers made three key decisions about executing the laws that continue to shape federal administration to this day.

This drawing depicts the assassination of President James Garfield on July 2, 1881. He was shot by an attorney who had been repeatedly rejected for a consular post in Garfield's administration.

First, they prohibited members of the House and Senate from holding executive branch positions. They drew a sharp line on the issue in Article I, Section 6, of the Constitution: "No Senator or Representative shall, during the Time for which he was elected, be appointed to any civil Office under the Authority of the United States, which shall have been created, or the Emoluments whereof shall have been increased during such time, and no Person holding any Office under the United States, shall be a Member of either House during his Continuance in Office." Under this provision, Congress could not create executive jobs for its members, which was a common form of corruption in England before the Revolutionary War.[4]

Second, the framers decided to give the president complete authority to nominate the senior officers of government. Although the framers also gave the Senate authority to confirm the president's appointees, it was not given any responsibility for selecting the names. The framers also decided that the president, not Congress, is responsible for filling any vacancies in those jobs without Senate review when the Senate is in recess. Although Article I does give Congress the power to create the departments of government and the Senate the power to confirm presidential appointees by a two-thirds vote, the president emerged from the final days of the Constitutional Convention as the nation's administrator in chief. This effort to create direct presidential control of government was seen as essential for faithfully executing the laws.

Third, the framers decided that the president, not Congress, is responsible for requiring the opinions of the "principal officer" of each executive department, which means that the president is in charge of what presidential appointees do. The president is not only responsible for hiring and supervising presidential appointees, however. The president also has the power to fire appointees for any reason. Although presidential appointees may resign at any time, which is how FEMA director Michael Brown left his job shortly after Hurricane Katrina, presidents usually fire appointees by asking for their resignations. Presidents routinely ask all of their appointees to resign at the end of their term in office to allow the next president complete freedom to select a new team.

These decisions about presidential power did not give the president unlimited authority to execute the laws, however. The framers gave Congress, not the president, the power to create the departments and agencies of government in the first place, and the responsibility for appropriating the money to administer programs and hire government employees. They also gave the Senate the power to confirm certain presidential appointees, and they clearly expected both houses of Congress to monitor the workings of the executive branch.

Federal Administration Today

More than two hundred years after the Constitution was written, federal administration is carried out by one of the largest organizations in the world. The federal administrative system now includes 15 departments, 50 agencies, the U.S. Postal Service, and the armed services. All told, almost 2.7 million Americans work for the federal administrative system, including 800,000 in the postal service and more than 1.8 million in federal departments and agencies. And another 1.4 million Americans serve in the armed forces.

Federal departments and agencies are traditionally referred to as the "bureaucracy," a term that dates from the early nineteenth century. Originally, the word "bureau" referred to a cloth covering the desks of French government officials in the eighteenth century, and eventually it came to be applied to the desk itself. The term was soon linked with the suffix "-ocracy" (as in "democracy" or "aristocracy") to describe government (essentially, "rule by people at desks").

At one time in history, **bureaucracy** actually meant fast, effective, and rational administration. In its ideal form, a bureaucracy made sure that every job was carefully designed to ensure faithful performance by well-trained, highly motivated **bureaucrats**, or employees. Over time, however, the term has taken on a negative meaning. "Bureaucracy" is now used to describe an inefficient organization clogged with red tape and staffed with security-conscious employees who care little about helping people.

Many American government textbooks use the words "bureaucracy" and "bureaucrats" to describe the federal administrative system, which creates an automatic negative reaction toward federal administration. Although many experts still use these words to describe government, especially when they talk about red tape and inefficiency, this book uses the terms "federal administration," "federal administrative system," "federal employees," and "federal workforce" to refer to the organizations and employees of government. These terms create a more neutral focus on the organizations and employees of government. Although some federal employees are "bureaucrats" in the negative sense, most are motivated by the chance to accomplish something worthwhile, are proud to work for government, believe they make a difference, and are ready to help their agencies succeed. And although some federal agencies behave like "bureaucracies," many are very effective in achieving their missions.

Nevertheless, federal departments and agencies can be difficult to manage. First, duplication and overlap across departments and agencies can create confusion about which agencies are responsible for a problem. For example, mad cow disease, which can be transmitted to human beings by eating meat from diseased cows, is the concern of several agencies. The Department of Agriculture's Animal and Plant Health Inspection Service keeps diseased cattle out of the United States, which is the best way to prevent the disease; the Department of Health and Human Services' Food and Drug Administration is supposed to monitor cattle feed, which is another way to prevent the disease, and the Department of Agriculture's Food Safety and Inspection Service inspects cattle as they go to slaughter, which is the last defense against letting diseased meat enter the food supply. All three may have failed in 2003 when the meat from a diseased cow entered the U.S. food supply. Similarly, many federal agencies are responsible for trying to prevent an outbreak of avian influenza, or "bird flu." The National Institutes of Health is responsible for developing a vaccine against the disease, the Centers for Disease Control is responsible for making the vaccine available to the public, the Department of Agriculture regulates how chickens are raised, and the Department of Labor is responsible for protecting poultry workers against contact with diseased birds.

Second, even within a single agency, federal administration often creates dense layers of management that keep information from moving up and down the organization quickly. Most federal organizations impose dozens of layers of management between the president and the federal employees who actually do the work. For example, the Department of Homeland Security has a secretary who heads the department, a chief of staff to the secretary, deputy chief of staff to the secretary, deputy secretary, five undersecretaries, and eight assistant secretaries, all of whom help direct the department's activities. Although each job is important, they often block the president's view of what is actually happening at the bottom of the department, where baggage and passenger screeners inspect bags at the airports, immigration officers check

bureaucracy
A form of organization that operates through impersonal, uniform rules and procedures.

bureaucrat
A career government employee.

passports at international terminals, and border police watch for illegal immigrants along the borders with Canada and Mexico.

How the Federal Administrative System Is Organized

Federal employees work for departments and agencies, which are classified into four broad categories: (1) *departments,* (2) *independent agencies,* (3) *independent regulatory commissions,* and (4) *government corporations.*

Departments tend to be the largest federal organizations and have the broadest missions. **Independent agencies** tend to be smaller and have more focused responsibilities. **Independent regulatory commissions** are similar to agencies but are designed to be free from direct presidential control. Finally, **government corporations** are designed to operate much like private businesses.

DEPARTMENTS   Departments are the most visible organizations in the federal administrative system. Today's 15 departments of government employ more than 70 percent of all federal civil servants and spend 93 percent of all federal dollars—the rest is spent by the other kinds of agencies to be described. Fourteen of the departments are headed by secretaries; the fifteenth, the Justice Department, is headed by the attorney general.

Measured by the total number of employees, the Defense Department is by far the largest department, followed by the Department of Veterans Affairs, which helps veterans return to civilian life after military service; the Department of Homeland Security, which was created to protect the nation from terrorism; the Department of the Treasury, which manages the economy and raises revenues through the Internal Revenue Service; and the Department of Justice, which enforces the laws through the federal courts and investigates crime through the Federal Bureau of Investigation.

Measured by prestige, the Defense, Justice, State, and Treasury departments are considered part of the inner circle closest to the president, while the rest of the departments are considered part of the outer circle of departments that rarely receive the president's attention (see Figure 13–1 for the inner and outer circles).

Measured by budget, the Department of Health and Human Services is the largest department of government. This department provides health insurance to the elderly through the huge Medicare program, helps states cover health care for the poor through the Medicaid programs, covers the cost of health insurance for children through the Children's Health Insurance Program (CHIP), and administers a variety of programs to help poor Americans. It also contains the Food and Drug Administration, the National

department
Usually the largest organization in government with the largest mission; also the highest rank in federal hierarchy.

independent agency
A government entity that is independent of the legislative, executive, and judicial branches.

independent regulatory commission
A government agency or commission with regulatory power whose independence is protected by Congress.

government corporation
A government agency that operates like a business corporation, created to secure greater freedom of action and flexibility for a particular program.

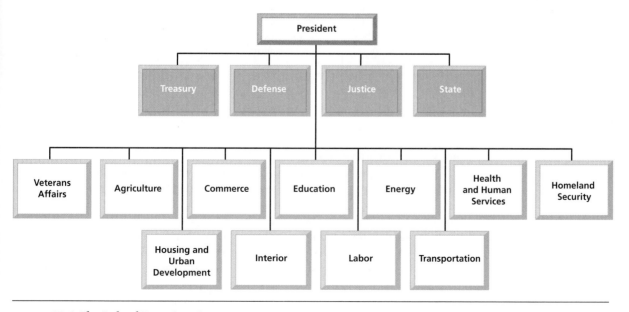

FIGURE 13–1 **The Federal Departments.**

The Changing Face of American Politics

A Representative Government

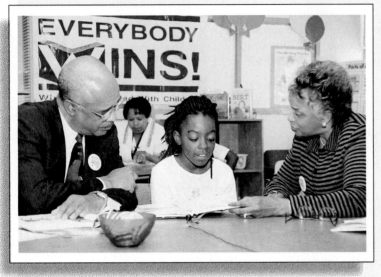

Education Department employee Claudia Gaines and then Education Secretary Rod Paige work with a fourth-grade student during National Volunteer Week.

female nursing corps), all of which have more than 50 percent female employees. Military and technical departments such as Defense, Energy, NASA, and Transportation have far fewer women. Health and Human Services has 65 percent women, while Transportation has just 25 percent; 50 percent of the Department of Education's employees are minorities, compared with just 16 percent of Agriculture's.

Second, women and minorities are not represented at all levels of the federal administrative system. Women held

70 percent of lower-paying technical and clerical positions in 2004, while minorities were also heavily represented at the bottom of government. Together, women and minorities held barely 15 percent of the top jobs. Nevertheless, women and minorities are moving into the top jobs at a fast rate. Between 1994 and 2004, the number of women and minorities jumped by 44 and 58 percent respectively. Although there is still a long way to go, women and minorities are closing the gap quickly. ■

The federal administrative system is clearly more representative of the public now than it was in the 1950s, when most of its employees were white and most women were clerk-typists. Women held 45 percent of all federal jobs in 2004, while minorities occupied nearly 30 percent.

Even though the number of women and minorities in the federal workforce is at an all-

time high, however, both groups still face barriers in rising to the top. First, women and minorities are not equally represented in all departments and agencies. They tend to be concentrated in departments with strong social service missions such as Education, Health and Human Services, Housing and Urban Development, and Veterans Affairs (which runs the VA hospital system, with its mostly

The Face of the Federal Workforce, 2004

Gender	
Men	56%
Women	44

Race	
White	69
African American	17
Hispanic	7
Asian and Pacific Islander	5
American Indian	2

Education*	
High school or some college	60
College graduate	40

*2003 figure.

SOURCE: Office of Personnel Management, *The Fact Book, 2004 Edition* (U.S. Government Printing Office, 2004).

Institutes of Health, and the Centers for Disease Control and Prevention, all of which protect Americans from disease.

The 15 federal departments are the result of two very different historical processes. One approach has been to create an umbrella department by combining a number of related programs. The Department of Homeland Security, for example, was created by combining elements of 22 separate agencies, including the Coast Guard, Immigration and Naturalization Service, Customs Service, Federal Emergency Management Agency, Secret Service, and portions of the Animal and Plant Health Inspection Service. The Departments of Health and Human Services, Commerce, and Defense also reflect large mergers of existing agencies.

The other approach has been the creation of a single-purpose department that owes much of its existence to the strength of an interest group. Congress created the

Department of Veterans Affairs in 1989 under pressure from veterans' groups such as the American Legion and Veterans of Foreign Wars, who wanted their own advocate in the president's cabinet. It was hardly the first time that Congress yielded to such pressure. Congress created the Department of Education in 1980 largely to satisfy the nation's largest teachers' union. One can easily argue that the Departments of Agriculture, Commerce, and Labor were also created in response to interest group pressure.

Creating a department does not necessarily guarantee that it will carry out its mission well. Three years after its creation, the Department of Homeland Security is still working to make the merger work. It took two years for the department to decide on a common uniform for customs agents, immigration inspectors, and passenger screeners, for example, and it is still looking for a permanent space for its Washington headquarters.

INDEPENDENT REGULATORY COMMISSIONS Independent regulatory commissions are insulated from presidential and congressional control. Over the decades, Congress has created dozens of independent regulatory commissions with the power to protect consumers (the Consumer Product Safety Commission), regulate stock markets (the Securities and Exchange Commission), oversee federal election laws (the Federal Election Commission), monitor television and radio (the Federal Communications Commission), regulate business (the Federal Trade Commission), control the supply of money (the Federal Reserve Board), and watch over nuclear power plants (Nuclear Regulatory Commission). These commissions are often small, but their influence over American life is large. Many experts contend that the Federal Reserve Board chair is the second most influential person in making economic policy, and others would argue that the current chair, Ben S. Bernanke, is the most important leader in influencing public confidence about the economy.[5] Bernanke was appointed to a 14-year term in 2006, replacing Alan Greenspan, who had served for almost 20 years.

Although independent regulatory commissions are part of the federal administrative system, they have a measure of independence from both Congress and the president through their leadership structure. By definition, these commissions are headed not by a single executive but by a small number of commissioners who are appointed

President Bush and Ben S. Bernanke (center), reach out to shake hands with Alan Greenspan. In 2005 Bernanke became Bush's choice to succeed the long-serving Greenspan as chairman of the Federal Reserve.

by the president, with Senate confirmation, for fixed terms of office. Unlike other presidential appointees, commissioners cannot be removed from office without cause, which is defined by law to mean "inefficiency, neglect of duty, or malfeasance in office." As a result, independent regulatory commissions are less responsive to political pressure from either end of Pennsylvania Avenue.

Independent regulatory commissions are not completely independent, however. Their commissioners are appointed by the president and subject to Senate confirmation, their annual budgets must be approved by Congress, and their decisions are subject to judicial review. Moreover, presidents make most appointments on the basis of party, which means that commissions are often highly political.

Moreover, the commissioners who lead these agencies often disagree on key issues, even to the point of being unable to reach majority decisions, especially during periods when the governing board has vacancies because of retirements or the end of terms. The Federal Communications Commission has often split votes in its effort to regulate television content, while the Federal Election Commission often splits on three-to-three votes between its Democratic and Republican commissioners.

Independent regulatory commissions tend to be much less visible than departments, at least until an issue such as corporate fraud becomes hot. The Securities and Exchange Commission was on the front pages for three years, for example, as one corporation after another disclosed accounting fraud in their annual reports to investors. The SEC was created in the 1930s to restore investor confidence in the stock market after the Great Depression, but it was accused of being negligent in monitoring accounting practices at big companies such as Enron and WorldCom in the early 2000s. It is currently rebuilding its staff and taking a much more aggressive stand on accounting standards. Independent regulatory commissions are also effectively insulated from public view, which may undermine their authority in enforcing their decisions. Moreover, many Americans do not know why independent regulatory commissions exist or how they operate.

INDEPENDENT AGENCIES   The word "independent" means at least two things in the federal administrative system. Applied to a regulatory commission, it means that the agency is outside the president's control. Applied to an agency or administration, it merely means "separate" or "standing alone." Whereas independent regulatory commissions do not report to the president, independent agencies do.

As a general rule, independent agencies are small federal organizations that serve specific groups of Americans or work on specific problems. Becoming an agency is often the first step toward becoming a department. The Veterans Administration was created in 1930, for example, but it only became a department in 1988.

Independent agencies are usually headed by an administrator, which is the second most senior title in the federal administrative system behind secretary or attorney general. There are roughly 60 such agencies today, including the Environmental Protection Agency (EPA), the Central Intelligence Agency (CIA), the National Aeronautics and Space Administration (NASA), the National Security Agency (NSA), and the Small Business Administration (SBA).

Although independence increases each agency's ability to focus on its mission, independence also weakens its willingness to cooperate. The spread of independent agencies can also increase confusion about who is responsible for what in the federal government. In late 2004, for example, Congress created a new national intelligence director to oversee the federal government's 15 different intelligence agencies, which include the Central Intelligence Agency, Defense Intelligence Agency, Federal Bureau of Investigation, and National Security Agency. These 15 agencies had a history of keeping secrets not just from the American people, but from each other, which contributed to the intelligence failures leading up to the war in Iraq.

Independent agencies come in many sizes, from small to very large. The National Aeronautics and Space Administration, for example, has an annual budget of over $11 billion and a workforce of more than 23,000, as well as several hundred thousand private business employees who help manage the space shuttle. NASA's budget ranks it ahead of four cabinet departments (Justice, Interior, State, and Commerce).

At times, independent agencies can be more important politically to the president than some cabinet departments. The director of the CIA or the administrator of the EPA may get a higher place on the president's agenda than the secretary of HUD or agriculture, particularly when an issue such as international spying or global warming is in the headlines.

The term "agency" does not just apply to independent agencies. Many highly visible agencies actually exist within departments, including the Forest Service (located in the Agriculture Department), the National Park Service (located in the Department of the Interior), the Occupational Safety and Health Administration (located in the Labor Department), and the Census Bureau (located in the Commerce Department). Unlike independent agencies, which report directly to the president, these agencies report to a department secretary, who, in turn, reports to the president.

GOVERNMENT CORPORATIONS   Government corporations are perhaps the least understood organizations in the federal administrative system. Because they are intended to act more like businesses than like traditional government departments and agencies, they generally have more freedom from the rules that control traditional government agencies. They often have greater authority to hire and fire employees quickly, and are allowed to make money through the sale of services such as train tickets, stamps, or home loans.[6]

Ultimately, no two government corporations are alike. The term is so loosely used that no one knows exactly how many corporations the federal administrative system has. What experts do know is that the number is between 31 and 47, including the Corporation for Public Broadcasting (which runs PBS television), the U.S. Postal Service, the National Railroad Passenger Association (better known as Amtrak), and Americorps (which runs a national service program created by the Clinton administration), along with a host of financial enterprises that make loans of one kind or another.

Franklin D. Raines testifies before Congress about accounting irregularities and Fannie Mae, a federal corporation that helps Americans buy homes. He soon resigned.

Once again, the fact that these organizations are not departments does not mean they are small or insignificant. The U.S. Postal Service employs almost 800,000 people, making it the second-largest organization in the federal administrative system. It also lost almost $1 billion in 2006, bringing the amount of money it owed to American taxpayers to more than $10 billion. The Postal Service may have no choice but to lose money, however. Unlike private firms such as FedEx and United Parcel Service, which can focus on the most profitable routes, the Postal Service delivers mail anywhere in the country. In 2005 alone, the Postal Service delivered more than 211 billion pieces of mail.

Federal Administrative Leaders

Every federal department and agency is headed by a presidential appointee, who is either subject to confirmation by the Senate or appointed on the sole authority of the president. As political officers, presidential appointees serve at the pleasure of the president and generally leave their posts at the end of that president's term in office. There are roughly 3,000 presidential appointees who run the federal government, including 600 administrative officers who are subject to Senate confirmation, and another 2,400 who serve entirely "at the pleasure of the president." The president also appoints roughly 1,000 U.S. marshals, U.S. attorneys, and ambassadors to foreign nations.

BECOMING A PRESIDENTIAL APPOINTEE   Presidential appointees have some of the toughest jobs in the world. They work long hours, resolve complex disputes, and make important decisions about how the laws will be executed. Although many presidential appointees are selected on the basis of political connections, the top positions in the most important departments are generally reserved for individuals with significant leadership skills and experience.

Federal Emergency Management Agency Director Michael Brown leaves the emergency operations center in Baton Rouge, Louisiana. Brown was removed as FEMA director after widespread criticism of his handling of the Hurricane Katrina rescue efforts.

Senior presidential appointees are selected through a four-step process. The first step is to be selected as a candidate. Except for individuals who are extraordinarily close to the president, candidates are selected by the White House Office of Presidential Personnel, which often turns to senators and representatives for names. Although the Bush administration received more than 100,000 résumés by mail and through the Internet in 2001, almost all successful candidates had political connections of some kind. Not surprisingly, most presidential appointees are members of the president's party, and many contributed either time or money to the president's campaign.

The second step in becoming an appointee is to survive the White House clearance process, which is designed to ensure that candidates are legally qualified for office and pose no potential embarrassment to the president. All candidates receive a packet of forms that require detailed disclosure on every aspect of their personal and professional life, including job history, drug use, personal counseling, financial investments, and even traffic fines of more than $150. They must list every job they have held over the past 15 years, including the name of a supervisor, as well as every place of residence they have lived, including the names of neighbors who might remember them, and every school they have attended, including the name of a high-school classmate who can vouch for them. Some candidates withdraw from consideration at this stage, either because they see potential problems in their past or simply do not have the time to fill out the forms. Every answer on the forms is subject to further review by the White House, the FBI, the IRS, the Office of Government Ethics, and the Senate committee that is responsible for confirming the candidate.

The third step in the process is the simplest: The president submits the name of the nominee on parchment paper to the clerk of the Senate. The document is placed in a special envelope, sealed with wax, and hand-delivered to the Senate when it is actually in session.

The fourth step involves Senate confirmation. The Senate refers each nomination to the appropriate committee, which conducts its own review of each candidate. Depending on the position and the nominee, the Senate may ask to review the entire file developed by the White House, including the FBI's investigation. Once the review is complete, the committee holds a hearing on the nomination and usually sends the nomination to the floor of the Senate with a favorable recommendation. In turn, most nominations are approved by the Senate on voice votes.

There are times, however, when the Senate uses nominations to send signals to the White House about political concerns. In 2005, for example, Senator Hillary Clinton (D-N.Y.) blocked the nomination of a new EPA administrator as a way to express her concern about air quality in New York City. Although she later withdrew her objections, she was able to delay the nomination long enough to force the Bush administration to make a promise to study air quality more closely in the future.

Senior Executive Service
Established by Congress in 1978 as a flexible, mobile corps of senior career executives who work closely with presidential appointees to manage government.

THE SENIOR LEADERSHIP CORPS Presidential appointees work closely with the 7,000 members of the **Senior Executive Service**, which includes roughly 6,400 career executives who are appointed through a rigorous review process, and another 600 political executives who are appointed by the president without Senate confirmation. Career

How Other Nations Govern

The Japanese Experience

Japan has one of the strongest federal government administrations in the world. This powerful system was created immediately after the Japanese surrendered at the end of World War II, and was given sweeping powers to run the country in an effort to prevent any return of imperial power. The Japanese parliament has little power over the administration of government, as does the Japanese judicial system. Although not completely independent, the administrative system drafts most legislation and makes key decisions on the Japanese economy.

Japan had strong administrative systems long before the end of World War II, however. Its samurai warriors eventually evolved from great fighters to great administrators, and helped establish one of the world's first administrative systems in which government employees would be selected on the basis of merit.

With few checks and balances to prevent mistakes, however, the Japanese administrative system made a series of disastrous economic decisions over the decades, which created an Asian financial crisis in the late 1990s. The bureaucracy also turned out to be riddled with corruption. Under Japanese custom, senior administrative officers often negotiated high-paying jobs with large private corporations before they retired.

On January 1, 2001, the legislature finally acted to reform the bureaucracy. It cut government employment by 25 percent and reduced the number of departments and agencies almost in half, from 24 to 13. At the same time, it gave the prime minister new powers to control the administrative system. However, the system has mostly resisted reform, in part because it is still considered to be more competent than its political leaders. Japanese administrators are also deeply respected in Japanese society. Only a handful of new administrators are hired each year. With few political appointments at the top of government, these administrators have instant influence over the nation's direction. Working in the Japanese government is considered one of the most prestigious careers for a top college graduate. ■

> *. . . samurai warriors eventually evolved from great fighters to great administrators, and helped establish one of the world's first administrative systems in which government employees would be selected on the basis of merit.*

senior executives continue in their posts regardless of who happens to be president and are selected on the basis of merit

Together with the president's political appointees, there are 10,000 senior executives who help run federal departments and agencies. The number has grown dramatically over the past three decades as the federal government has "thickened," with more layers of leadership and more leaders at each layer.[7] Some political scientists argue that Congress caused the pressure for thickening by creating highly complex programs that demand close supervision, while others believe that thickening is driven in part by a competition for power among competing organizations. According to this *theory of public bureaucracy*, bureaucratic organizations constantly seek to enhance their power, whether by creating new titles, adding more staff, or increasing their budgets.[8]

How the Federal Workforce Evolved

As already noted, the federal workforce started out small. As public administration scholar Leonard White once wrote, the entire federal administrative system of 1790 consisted of nothing more than a "foreign office with John Jay and a couple of clerks to deal with correspondence from John Adams in London and Thomas Jefferson in Paris; . . . a Treasury Board with an empty treasury; . . . a 'Secretary at War' with an

In November 1995, the vast bureaucracy of the federal government shut down for lack of funds.

TABLE 13–1 Measuring the Size of Government, 1940–2007

Year	Employment (in thousands)	Budget (in billions of current dollars)	Budget as a Percentage of Gross Domestic Product
1940	699	$ 9.5	9.9%
1945	3,370	92.7	43.7
1950	1,439	42.6	16.0
1955	1,860	68.4	17.8
1960	1,808	92.2	18.3
1965	1,901	118.2	17.6
1970	2,203	195.6	19.9
1975	2,149	332.3	22.0
1980	2,161	590.9	22.3
1985	2,252	946.4	23.9
1990	2,250	1,253.2	21.9
1995	2,018	1,788.8	21.9
2000	1,784	1,788.8	18.2
2005	1,875	2,396.7	16.9
2007	1,868	2,770.0	19.1

SOURCE: Office of Management and Budget, *Budget of the U.S. Government, Fiscal Year 2006, Historical Tables* (U.S. Government Printing Office, February 2006).

authorized army of 840 men; . . . [and] a dozen clerks whose pay was in arrears."[9] (See Table 13–1 for measures of the federal government's size since 1940.)

Creating the first departments was not easy, however. Congress fought to restrict the president's authority to fire appointees, and briefly considered creating a board to run the new Department of the Treasury. President Washington won the arguments, however, and settled any remaining worries about his judgment by appointing Thomas Jefferson as secretary of state, Alexander Hamilton as secretary of the treasury, and Henry Knox as secretary of war. All three were easily confirmed and quickly went about the business of running their departments. At roughly the same time, Congress also created the Post Office Department and allowed for the appointment of a U.S. attorney general.

Even though this early federal work force was but the tiniest fraction of its current size, it was not long before presidential candidates began promising smaller government. Indeed, Jefferson made waste in government a centerpiece of his first Inaugural Address in 1801, promising "a wise and frugal government, which shall restrain men from injuring one another, shall leave them otherwise free to regulate their own pursuits of industry and improvement, and shall not take from the mouth of labor what it has earned." Jefferson wanted a government that taxed lightly, paid its debts on time and in full, and sought "economy in the public expense." Jefferson set aside his promise long enough to make the Louisiana Purchase, which doubled the size of the nation and laid the groundwork for a vast expansion of America's economy.

Unfortunately, Jefferson's purchase also set off a wave of corruption at the federal government's General Land Office, where corrupt federal clerks reserved the best pieces of land to sell for themselves. The corruption eventually ignited the western anger that swept Andrew Jackson—and a new era in two-party competition—into office in 1828. Jackson soon introduced a **spoils system** into government—as in "to the victor belong the spoils."

Under Jackson's system, federal jobs were filled on the basis of political connections. Actual ability to do the work had almost nothing to do with obtaining an appointment. As such, the spoils system gave the president's party complete control

spoils system
A system of public employment based on rewarding party loyalists and friends.

The Louisiana Purchase doubled the land area of the United States, but also set off a wave of corruption in the General Land Office. Anger over the corruption contributed to the election of Andrew Jackson in 1828.

over almost every government job, from cabinet secretaries all the way down to post office clerks. This political job system became known as *patronage*—individuals would patronize, or support, the president's party with money before an election in return for a federal job.

The civil service was created in 1883 to end corruption in the spoils system. Indeed, it was a job seeker who started the federal bureaucracy down the road toward today's civil service system. Unfortunately for President James Garfield, that job seeker happened to be both disappointed and a good shot. Garfield's assassination prompted Congress to pass the Pendleton Act of 1883, which created an independent Civil Service Commission to assure that most federal jobs were awarded under a **merit system**, meaning on the basis of an individual's ability to do the work, not political connections. Federal service was placed under the control of a three-person bipartisan board called the Civil Service Commission, which functioned from 1883 to 1978.[10]

Ninety percent of federal employees are now selected on the basis of merit. Almost all the rest are selected through hiring systems that emphasize a special skill such as medicine, while only 3,000 out of 1.8 million are selected for their political qualifications. Nevertheless, these 3,000 presidential appointees occupy the very top jobs in government, and wield great influence over their agencies. They also occupy many of the management layers that presidents use to control department and agency decisions (see Figure 13–2 for types of federal employees).

Today, the **Office of Personnel Management (OPM)** administers civil service laws, rules, and regulations. The independent Merit Systems Protection Board is charged with protecting the integrity of the federal merit system and the rights of federal employees. It conducts studies of the merit system, hears and decides charges of wrongdoing, considers employee appeals against adverse agency actions, and orders corrective and disciplinary actions against an agency executive or employee when appropriate. (A sampling of current federal job offerings can be found at www.usajobs .opm.gov.)

merit system
A system of public employment in which selection and promotion depend on demonstrated performance rather than political patronage.

Office of Personnel Management (OPM)
Agency that administers civil service laws, rules, and regulations.

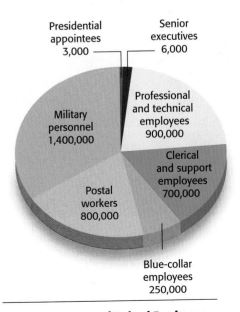

FIGURE 13–2 **Types of Federal Employees.**

Public Opinion toward Federal Employees

Americans have a love-hate relationship with the federal government. They want more of virtually everything government delivers, from health care to national parks, and from faster drug approval to home loans, yet they often complain that government is too big and wasteful. A majority of Americans believe that the federal government creates more problems than it solves, and that it controls too much of daily life.[11] In October 2003, for example, 93 percent of Americans said that the federal government wastes a great deal or fair amount of money.[12]

When problems arise, however, Americans often ask the federal government to respond. Like the "rally 'round" effect on presidential approval ratings, confidence in the federal administrative system rose dramatically in the days following the terrorist attacks on New York City and Washington in September 2001. The number of Americans who said they trusted the federal government to do the right thing almost always or most of the time jumped from 29 percent in July 2001 to 57 percent in October.

Yet, even as confidence went up, Americans remained skeptical about big government. Interviewed three weeks after the 2001 terrorist attacks, 70 percent of Americans assumed that most federal employees chose to work for the government because of the job security, and 68 percent cited the salary and benefits. Even at a time when Americans accepted the need for a strong federal government, they doubted the basic motivations of the people who work for it.[13]

Moreover, as September 11 faded from memory, so did trust in government. By May 2002, the number of Americans who said they trusted the government in Washington to do the right thing just about always or most of the time had fallen to 40 percent, which is where it stood two years later in July 2004. Although trust was still above its pre-September 2001 levels, Americans still viewed the federal government as wasteful and its employees as more motivated by the pay, benefits, and job security than the chance to make a difference and serve the country. Americans also believe that the president's own appointees are driven more by an interest in making connections and making money than serving the people.[14]

This general lack of trust has affected interest in federal careers among talented young Americans. Asked in 2003 what attracted them most to a job, the vast majority of these students said they wanted meaningful work, training, challenging work, the opportunity to gain new skills, and rewards for high performance. The opportunity to repay college loans and salary came in dead last. These students were not saying "show us the money," but "show us the work."[15] These students saw charities, not government, as the best place for making a difference, accomplishing something worthwhile, and gaining the respect of family and friends. They also said that charities, not government, had the best organizations for spending money wisely, helping people, and being fair in their decisions. Asked first what the words "public service" meant to them, these students talked about giving something back to their communities, volunteering, helping others, and selfless service. Asked next about

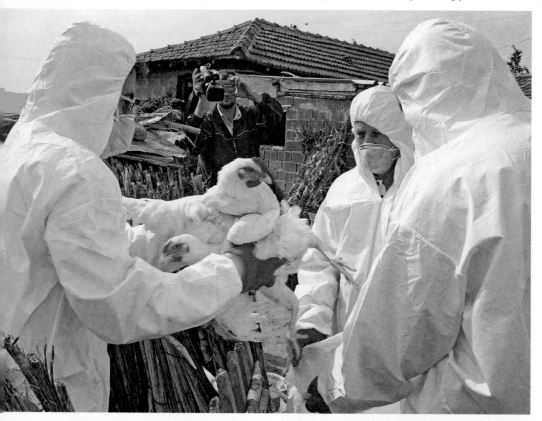

Officials in Turkey examine a flock of chickens for signs of avian flu. In the United States, citizens depend on the Department of Agriculture to protect them from animal-borne illnesses.

options for public service, nearly 60 percent said that working for a charity was completely about public service, compared with barely a quarter who said the same about government.

This declining interest in government as the sole destination for helping people reflects the rise of a new public service. Many of the best jobs in public service now exist in state and local governments, charities, faith-based organizations such as churches that help the needy, and private businesses that deliver goods and services under contract to the federal government. Not only can young job seekers find meaningful public service outside the federal government, they can and do switch jobs and sectors at will.[16]

Working for Government

Much of the public's distrust toward the federal administrative system is based on myths about federal employees. Polls show that many Americans think that most federal employees work in Washington, D.C., and that the federal government spends much more on welfare and assistance for the poor than it does on Social Security or defense.

The realities are much different:

- Only about 15 percent of the government's career civilian employees work in the Washington area. More federal employees work in California, Georgia, and Texas, for example, than in Washington.

- More than 25 percent of the civilian employees work for the Army, the Navy, the Air Force, or some other defense agency; another 30 percent work for the U.S. Postal Service.

- Social programs consume a sizable portion of the U.S. budget, yet the workforce that administers programs such as welfare and medical care for the poor is relatively small. Fewer than 10 percent of federal employees work for welfare agencies such as the Social Security Administration or the Department of Veterans Affairs.

- Almost half of federal employees work for the departments of Defense, Homeland Security, Justice, and State, which are all involved in the war on terror.

- Federal civil servants are much more likely to look like the rest of the nation in terms of race, sex, religion, education, and disability than are the political appointees or members of Congress who make the laws they execute.

- Although the civil service includes more than 450 different kinds of jobs, the vast majority of workers are white-collar employees, such as lawyers, contract managers, budget analysts, engineers, inspectors, and auditors.

Donald Rumsfeld served as Secretary of Defense under two presidents. Criticism of his handling of the war in Iraq contributed to his resignation only two days after Republicans lost control of both the House and the Senate in the 2006 midterm elections.

Nevertheless, there are reasons to worry about the health of the federal civil service. Substantial minorities of federal employees say their organizations do not provide the information, technological equipment, and training to do their jobs well, and a majority believe their organizations do not have enough employees to succeed. In addition, many federal employees believe that their organizations do not do well at disciplining poor performers. They also describe the federal hiring process as slow and confusing, and often complain that their senior leaders are not qualified for their jobs.[17]

The Hiring Process

Unlike appointees who are selected by the president, the vast majority of federal employees are recruited through the civil service. The civil service system was designed to reduce political corruption by promoting merit in the hiring process. But hiring on the basis of merit is not the only way government seeks to reduce corruption. As we shall see, it also regulates the political activities of civil servants.

As already noted, the Office of Personnel Management sets the federal government's rules for recruiting, hiring, promoting, and disciplining civil servants. However, individual agencies are responsible for hiring new personnel, subject to agency standards. Individual agencies may promote people from within or transfer a civil servant from another agency in the government. If, however, they wish to consider an "outsider," they request that OPM certify possible candidates from its roster of applicants. OPM typically certifies the top three applicants for the opening, and the agency normally selects one of these. However, the agency can decide not to make an appointment from the list or to request a longer list of applicants.

These procedures are intended to protect the merit principle and to meet agencies' needs for qualified personnel. In practice, the two objectives sometimes conflict. The trade-off is between central control by OPM and delegation of discretionary authority to the agencies. And sometimes the pursuit of both objectives is undermined by other goals, such as giving military veterans extra credit in the hiring process.

Regulating the Civil Service

In 1939, Congress passed the Act to Prevent Pernicious Political Activities, usually called the **Hatch Act** after its chief sponsor, Senator Carl Hatch of New Mexico. The act was designed to ensure that the federal civil service did not have disproportionate influence in the election of presidents and members of Congress. In essence, the Hatch Act permitted federal employees to vote in government elections but not to take an active part in partisan politics. The Hatch Act also made it illegal to dismiss civilian employees for political reasons.[18]

In 1993, Congress, with the encouragement of the Clinton administration, overhauled the Hatch Act and made many forms of participation in partisan politics permissible. The revised Hatch Act still bars federal officials from running as candidates in partisan elections, but it does permit most federal civil servants to hold party positions and involve themselves in party fund-raising and campaigning. This new law was welcomed by those who believed the old Hatch Act discouraged political participation by 3 million people who might otherwise be vigorous political activists.[19]

The new Hatch Act spells out many restrictions on federal bureaucrats: they cannot raise campaign funds in their agencies, and those who work in such highly sensitive federal agencies as the CIA, FBI, Secret Service, and certain divisions of the IRS are specifically barred from nearly all partisan activity. Those who work in the U.S. military have stricter rules regulating their political involvement. On the one hand, federal employees *may* register and vote as they choose; assist in voter registration; express opinions about candidates and issues; contribute money to political organizations; attend political fund-raising functions; wear or display political badges, buttons, or stickers; attend political rallies and meetings; and join political parties. On the other hand, they *may not* be candidates for public office in partisan elections, use their jobs or authority to interfere with or affect the results of an election, collect contributions or sell tickets to political fund-raising functions from subordinate employees, or solicit funds or discourage the political activity of any person who has business before the employee's office.

The Role of Government Employee Unions

Since 1962, federal civilian employees have had the right to form unions or associations that represent them in seeking to improve government personnel policies, and about one-third of them have joined such unions. Some of the most important unions representing federal employees today are the American Federation of Government Employees, the National Treasury Employees Union, the National Association of Government Employees, and the National Federation of Federal Employees.

Hatch Act
Federal statute barring federal employees from active participation in certain kinds of politics and protecting them from being fired on partisan grounds.

Unlike unions in the private sector, federal employee unions lack the right to strike and are not able to bargain over pay and benefits. But they can attempt to negotiate better personnel policies and practices for federal workers, they can represent federal employees at grievance and disciplinary proceedings, and they can lobby Congress on measures affecting personnel changes. They can also vote in elections. This is why members of Congress from districts that have large numbers of federal workers often sit on the House and Senate civil service subcommittees.

The Job of the Federal Administrative System

Whatever their size or specialty, all federal organizations share one job: to faithfully execute, or implement, the laws. **Implementation** covers a broad range of bureaucratic activities, from writing checks at the Social Security Administration to inspecting job sites at the Occupational Health and Safety Administration, swearing in new citizens at the Immigration and Naturalization Service, or monitoring airline traffic at the Federal Aviation Administration. Some agencies implement the laws by spending money, others by raising revenues or by issuing rules that govern what private citizens and businesses do, and still others by collecting information or conducting research. Whatever tool government uses, implementation is the act of converting a law into action.

Because Congress and the president could never pass laws that are detailed enough to deal with every aspect of their administration, they give federal departments and agencies **administrative discretion** to implement the laws in the most efficient and effective manner possible. This freedom varies from agency to agency, depending on both past performance and congressional politics. Political scientist Theodore Lowi believes that Congress often gives the federal administrative system vague directions because it is unable or unwilling to make the tough choices needed to resolve the conflicts that arise in the legislative process. Congress gets the credit for passing a law, while the federal workforce gets the challenge of implementing an unclear law.[20]

Whether a law is clear or ambiguous, most agencies implement the law through two means: administrative *regulations*, which are formal instructions for either running an agency or for controlling the behavior of private citizens and organizations, or *spending*, which involves the transfer of money to and from government.

Making Regulations

Regulations, or rules, are designed to convert laws into action. They tell people what they can and cannot do, as well as what they must or must not do. It is an Agriculture Department rule that tells meat and poultry processors how to handle food, an Environmental Protection Agency rule that tells automobile makers how much gasoline mileage their cars must get, a Social Security Administration rule that tells Americans how long they must work before they are eligible for a federal retirement check, an Immigration and Naturalization Service rule that tells citizens of other nations how long they can stay on a student visa, and a Justice Department rule that tells states what they must do to ensure that every eligible citizen can vote. Although all these rules can be traced back to legislation, they provide the details that most laws leave out.

Rules are drafted and reviewed through a quasi-legislative **rule-making process** that is governed by the Administrative Procedure Act. Enacted in 1946 to make sure that all rules are made visible to the public, the act requires that all proposed rules be published in the *Federal Register*. Publication in the federal government's newspaper marks the beginning of what is known as the "notice and comment" period during which all parties affected by the proposed regulation are encouraged to make their opinions known to the agency. Because rules have the force of law and can become the basis for legal challenges, the process can take years from start to finish and can

implementation
The process of putting a law into practice through bureaucratic rules or spending.

administrative discretion
Authority given by Congress to the federal bureaucracy to use reasonable judgment in implementing the laws.

regulations
The formal instructions that government issues for implementing laws.

rule-making process
The formal process for making regulations.

involve thousands of pages of records. Some agencies even hold hearings and take testimony from witnesses in the effort to build a strong case for a particularly controversial rule.

The rule-making process does not end with final publication and enforcement. All rules are subject to the same judicial review that governs formal laws, thereby creating a check against potential abuse of power when agencies exceed their authority to faithfully execute the laws. Rules, like laws, can also be changed by future action. In late 2003, for example, the Bush administration announced plans to change the rules governing coal-burning electric power plants. Under a Clinton administration rule, mercury had been declared extremely dangerous to public health. As a result of the ruling, power plants were about to be forced to install expensive new technology to reduce the amount of mercury released to the minimum amount possible. Under the new rules, power plants would have more freedom to release larger amounts of mercury, and save billions. Environmentalists charged that the new EPA administrator, former Utah governor Mike Leavitt, had been forced by the White House to accept the change in policy. Although Leavitt admitted that the proposal had been discussed within the administration, he argued that "the rules are ultimately made and signed here."[21] It was a nearly perfect statement of just how important making the rules can be to society.

uncontrollable spending
The portion of the federal budget that is spent on programs, such as Social Security, that the president and Congress are unwilling to cut.

entitlement program
Programs such as unemployment insurance, disaster relief, or disability payments that provide benefits to all eligible citizens.

Spending Money

The federal bureaucracy also implements laws through spending, whether by writing checks to more than 35 million Social Security recipients a year, buying billions of dollars worth of military equipment, or making grants to state governments and research universities. Viewed in relative terms as a percentage of gross domestic product (GDP), federal spending more than doubled over the past half-century but began to shrink with the end of the cold war in 1989. It began to rise after passage of the 2001 tax cuts, which cut federal revenues substantially. Moreover, viewed in constant dollars adjusted for inflation, federal spending continues to rise each year, driven in part by the cost of caring for a rapidly aging population.

Most of this spending goes to what political scientists and budget experts call **uncontrollable spending**, defined as spending. This kind of spending is for (1) **entitlement programs** that provide financial benefits for any American who is eligible, such as Social Security for older Americans, loans for college students, or help for the victims of natural disasters such as floods and hurricanes (in these programs, everyone who is eligible and applies automatically gets the help), and for (2) programs that require more federal spending each year automatically through cost-of-living increases or interest on the national debt.

Uncontrollable spending sharply limits the amount of the federal budget that is actually subject to debate in any given year. Even funding for programs such as defense, which is technically subject to yearly control, is almost impossible to cut without controversy, especially during a time of high public concern about terrorism.

Senior citizens line up to enroll in the Social Security program. Social Security is a popular entitlement program. The program is often discussed in Washington but presidents and Congress are wary of making cuts in Social Security benefits.

The largest share of uncontrollable spending comes from Social Security and Medicare, which are guaranteed to any American who has paid taxes into the program for enough years. As more Americans grow older, uncontrollable spending will almost certainly rise over the next few decades as Social Security and Medicare grow. The two programs are already the two largest programs in the federal budget, and will eventually account for more than half of all federal spending. In total, uncontrollable spending accounted for nearly $2 trillion in 2007, accounting for two-thirds of the federal government's $2.8 trillion budget.

A much smaller share of the uncontrollable budget involves welfare for the poor, which is linked to the performance of the economy. More unemployment, for example, means more federal unemployment insurance; more poverty means more food stamps, job training, temporary financial assistance, and other income support programs.

The uncontrollable budget is not growing just because more people are eligible for entitlements, however. Many of these entitlements are subject to **indexing**—that is, they grow automatically with inflation, regardless of how the economy is doing. Indexing affects a growing list of federal programs, again leaving Congress and the president little control over year-to-year increases. The number of programs indexed to automatic cost-of-living adjustments (COLAs) grew from 17 in 1966 to 100 by 2006.[22]

Holding the Federal Administrative System Accountable

Every president enters office promising to make federal agencies work better. Indeed, Jimmy Carter, Ronald Reagan, Bill Clinton, and George W. Bush all made bureaucratic reform a central part of their presidential campaigns. Carter promised to create a government as good as the American people, Reagan promised to reduce waste in government, Clinton and Vice President Al Gore promised to reinvent government, and Bush promised to make government more friendly to citizens.

Yet presidents leave office frustrated by their lack of success. As political scientist James Q. Wilson noted, "Presidents see much of the bureaucracy as their natural enemy and always are searching for ways to bring it to heel."[23] And presidents are not the only ones who want to control the federal administrative system. Congress, too, clearly worries about making the federal system work better. Together, both complain that federal departments and agencies can be more accountable to interest groups and themselves than to either branch of government.

A jury found David Safavian, a former Bush administration official, guilty of covering up his dealings with the lobbyist Jack Abramoff. Safavian was convicted on four of five felony counts of lying and obstruction of justice. In 2005, he resigned from his post as the federal government's chief procurement officer.

Accountability to the President

Modern presidents invariably contend that the president should be firmly in charge of the federal employees, for the chief executive is responsive to the broadest constituency. A president, it is argued, must see that popular needs and expectations are converted into administrative action. When the nation elects a conservative president who favors cutbacks in federal programs and less governmental intervention in the economy, for example, his policies must be carried out by the federal administrative system. The voters' wishes can be translated into action only if federal employees support presidential policies.

Yet under the American system of checks and balances, the party that wins the presidency does not acquire total control of the national government. Under our Constitution, the president is not even the undisputed master of the executive structure. Presidents come into an ongoing system over which they have little control and within which they have little leeway to make the bureaucracy responsive.

Still, the president has some control over federal departments and agencies through the powers of appointment, reorganization, and budgeting. A president can

indexing
Providing automatic increases to compensate for inflation.

History Makers

Louis Brownlow

Louis Brownlow is one of the least known but most important creators of the modern administrative system. Born in 1879, he worked as a journalist for most of his career, and spent time as a foreign correspondent in Europe, the Middle East, and Asia in the early 1900s. He also worked as city manager of Knoxville, Tennessee, where he had been a reporter. Having finished his careers in journalism and city government, he founded a public administration program at the University of Chicago in 1930 and eventually retired in 1945.

Despite his distinguished career, Brownlow was a surprise choice to head Franklin Delano Roosevelt's Committee on Administrative Management in 1936. He had few political connections to the president's party and no relationship with Roosevelt. Roosevelt picked Brownlow precisely because he was an independent expert whose advice would be based on careful analysis, not party politics. Facing growing political pressure to make sense of the rapidly expanding administrative system, Roosevelt understood that he needed help managing the dozens of new agencies he had created in his first term.

Brownlow's three-person committee agreed. Indeed, the very first sentence of the committee's famous 1937 report read "The President needs help." The committee argued that the president should reorganize dozens of agencies into larger departments, move the budget process into a new Executive Office of the President, and create a new White House staff composed of individuals with "a passion for anonymity."

The committee also recommended a series of budget cuts that would reduce federal spending. "Economy is not the only objective," the committee wrote, "though reorganization is the first step to savings; the elimination of duplication and contradictory policies is not the only objective, though this will follow; a simple and symmetrical organization is not the only objective, though the new organization will be simple and symmetrical." The sole objective of the effort was faithful execution of the laws.

Roosevelt created the Executive Office of the President in 1939, thereby assuring that future presidents would have greater control of the administrative system, especially through the budget process. Although Roosevelt also began work on creating several new departments, World War II distracted him from further action. By the 1950s, however, Congress had created the first of several new departments that the Brownlow Committee had recommended, and would eventually merge dozens of Roosevelt's agencies into what would become the departments of Health and Human Services, Transportation, and Housing and Urban Development.

Although Brownlow maintained his own passion for anonymity through the end of his life, the federal administrative system continues to operate under his design. The Executive Office of the President maintains tight control of federal departments and agencies, the federal budget reflects the president's priorities, and the president has greater control over federal employees. However, as the number of departments and agencies has continued to grow, the simple administrative system that Brownlow advocated has remained elusive, and White House staffers have become far less anonymous.* ∎

*Louis Brownlow, *A Passion for Anonymity: The Autobiography of Louis Brownlow* (University of Chicago Press, 1955).

Despite his distinguished career, Brownlow was a surprise choice to head Franklin Delano Roosevelt's Committee on Administrative Management in 1936. . . . Roosevelt picked Brownlow precisely because he was an independent expert whose advice would be based on careful analysis, not party politics.

Government's Greatest Endeavors

Improving Government Performance

Congress has passed dozens of laws to improve the federal government's performance, while presidents have launched a long list of reforms designed to reduce federal waste, improve efficiency, and "reinvent government" to make it more like a business.

Although many of these reform efforts have failed, Congress and the president continue to search for ways to reduce waste in government. In 1993, for example, the Clinton administration launched an eight-year effort to cut federal red tape in half, improve customer service at agencies such as the Social Security Administration and Internal Revenue Service, reduce the number of federal managers, and eliminate wasteful programs.

Led by Vice President Al Gore, this reinventing government campaign was supposed to cut the number of federal employees by 10 percent, while saving more than $100 billion by cutting waste. Gore campaigned hard for the program, even appearing on the *David Letterman Show* to ridicule the federal government's detailed rule for making ashtrays, which had to shatter into no fewer than 14 pieces if they were accidentally broken.

In 2001, President George W. Bush launched a similar reform plan. Under Bush's approach, the federal government was ordered to reduce the number of wasteful programs, while improving its management of the budget.

Congress and the president often disagree on how to improve government, however. Presidents want more freedom to direct the federal administrative system, while Congress prefers tighter rules that restrict presidential authority. The result is a confusing slate of reform plans, which are often reversed by the next administration to enter office. ∎

Vice President Al Gore took the Clinton administration's campaign to cut government waste to the people when he appeared on The David Letterman Show. *Gore and Letterman both wore goggles as Gore showed how to smash an ashtray under federal rules.*

QUESTIONS

Why do Americans believe that the federal government wastes so much money?

Can government be run more like a business?

---

attempt to control the federal system by appointing or promoting sympathetic personnel, mobilizing public opinion and congressional pressure, changing the administrative apparatus, influencing budget decisions, using extensive personal persuasion, and if all else fails, shifting an agency's assignment to another department or agency (although such a shift requires tacit if not explicit congressional approval).[24]

Accountability to Congress

Congress has a number of ways to control federal administration, whether by establishing agencies, formulating budgets, appropriating funds, confirming personnel, authorizing new programs or new shifts in direction, conducting investigations and hearings, or even terminating agencies.

Much of this authority is used to help constituents as they battle federal red tape. Members of Congress earn political credit by interceding in federal agencies on behalf of their constituents. Still, Congress deserves at least some of the blame for having created the red tape in the first place, whether by enacting pet programs, refusing to give federal agencies greater flexibility, delaying presidential appointments, or placing limits on bureaucratic discretion to protect some constituents but not others. Moreover, by demanding special attention for their constituents, members of Congress may undermine the fairness of the entire process. Like those who cut in line at a movie theater, they slow the progress for everyone but the special few who get their attention.

The brutal fact is that only a small minority of our 535 members of Congress would trade the present bureaucratic structure for one that was an efficient, effective agent of the general interest—the political payoffs of the latter are lower than those of the former. Congressional talk of inefficient, irresponsible, out-of-control bureaucracy is typically just that—talk—and when it is not, it usually refers to agencies under the jurisdiction of other legislators' committees. Congress can abolish or reorganize an agency. Congress can limit or expand an agency's jurisdiction or allow its authority to lapse entirely. Congress can slash an agency's appropriations. Congress can investigate. Congress can do all these things, but individual members of Congress generally find reasons not to do so.[25]

It is not Congress as a whole that shares direction over the bureaucracy with the president. More accurately, individual members and committees specialize in the appropriations and oversight processes. They oversee policies of a particular cluster of agencies—often the agencies serving constituents in their own districts. Some legislators stake out a claim over specific areas. Members of Congress, who see presidents come and go, come to think they know more about particular agencies than the president does (and often they do). Some congressional leaders prefer to seal off "their" agencies from presidential direction and maintain their influence over public policy. Sometimes their power is institutionalized; the Army Corps of Engineers, for example, is given authority by law to plan public works and report to Congress without going through the president.

The Role of Oversight

Congress and the president spend a great deal of energy monitoring the federal administrative system. The hope is that **oversight**, the process of monitoring day-to-day activities, will somehow encourage agencies to perform better or at least deter them from worse performance.

Presidents have a number of tools for keeping a watchful eye. They can put loyal appointees such as Attorney General Alberto Gonzales or Secretary of State Condoleezza Rice into the top jobs at key agencies; they can direct White House aides, such as national security adviser Stephen Hadley, to oversee the work of certain agencies; and they can always call cabinet meetings to learn more about what is happening in the various departments.

However, presidents tend to use the Office of Management and Budget for most routine oversight. Departments and agencies must get the president's approval before testifying before Congress on pending legislation, making legislative proposals, or answering congressional inquiries about their activities. Under this **central clearance** system, OMB forwards communications to Congress in three categories: "in accordance" with the president's program (reserved for the president's top priorities), "consistent with" the president's program (indicating the president's second-tier priorities), or "no objection." If the president objects to any communication, OMB simply does not forward the legislation to Congress. OMB also conducts oversight on all federal departments and agencies as it assembles the president's budget plan.

Congress also has a number of tools for overseeing the federal administrative system, not the least of which consists of the individual members of Congress themselves, who are free to ask agencies for detailed information on just about any issue. However, most members and committees tend to use the General Accounting Office or the Congressional Budget Office to conduct a study or investigation of a particular program.

Congress uses these and other sources of information as a basis for committee and subcommittee hearings on specific agencies or programs. Although the level of congressional oversight increased steadily during the 1970s and 1980s, it began declin-

oversight
Legislative or executive review of a particular government program or organization. Can be in response to a crisis of some kind or part of routine review.

central clearance
Review of all executive branch testimony, reports, and draft legislation by the Office of Management and Budget to ensure that each communication to Congress is in accordance with the president's program.

Agents of Change

Katya Fels and On the Rise

On the Rise is a tiny organization founded in 1995 to help homeless women receive help from city, state, and federal government. These often-forgotten women are rarely acknowledged in political campaigns, almost never vote, and struggle to get basic services such as food and nutrition and housing. Although homeless women qualify for government aid, they often need help to identify the programs and apply for help.

On the Rise was founded by Katya Fels after she graduated from Harvard in 1993. She had served as a volunteer counselor on the local response hotline for survivors of sexual assault and saw many similarities with the homeless women she later met as a codirector of the Harvard Square Homeless Shelter. "I was really profoundly struck by how similar their stories were," she remembers. As she describes her small center for homeless women, "It's different from a drop-in center because the outreach workers aren't just here to get a woman a toothbrush or clean clothes. It says to a woman, 'We're respecting the choices that you're making.' There's no one right way for a woman to better her own situa-tion. We're the mortar between the cracks."

Since its founding, On the Rise has helped more than 1,000 women find the help they need, especially after a crisis. Most women who use the program have a history of extreme abuse, but they often do not meet the traditional criteria of city social service programs. By creating the needed connections with city services, while giving Harvard an opportunity to improve its own community, On the Rise fills in when the administrative state fails those who need help. ■

Katya Fels

Read more about On the Rise at www.ontherise.org.

Questions

Why are programs such as On the Rise important in helping the federal administrative system do its job?

Why would a university participate in such programs?

---

ing in the 1990s and continues to decline. Members of Congress may be spending so much time on reelection that they have little energy left for the routine, but important, task of oversight. They may also be delegating at least some oversight responsibility to blue-ribbon commissions and other independent investigatory bodies that review major government failures such as the Shuttle *Columbia* disaster and the Hurricane Katrina response.[26]

Together, Congress and the president conduct two basic types of oversight. One is what can be called "police patrol" oversight, in which the two branches watch the bureaucracy through a routine pattern. They read key reports, watch the budget, and generally pay attention to how the departments and agencies are running. If they happen to see a "crime" in progress, all the better. But the general goal of the patrol is to deter problems before they arise. The other can be called "fire alarm" oversight, in which the two branches wait for citizens, interest groups, or the press to find a major problem and pull the alarm. The media play a particularly important role in such oversight, often uncovering a scandal before a routine "police patrol" can spot it.[27]

Sometimes, federal employees help oversee the government by leaking important information to the media and Congress. Such *whistleblowers* released the information on the Bush administration's domestic eavesdropping program in late 2005, for example. Although whistleblowers are protected by federal law, many are forced to leave government because of informal pressure.

The Problem of Self-Regulation

Career administrators are in a good position to know when a program is not operating properly and what action is needed. But many Americans believe that federal employees, whether selected on merit or not, fail to make things better. The problem is that many career employees act as if the expansion of their organization is vital to the public interest. They sometimes become more skillful at building political alliances to protect their own organization than at building political alliances to ensure their programs' effectiveness.

Career administrators usually try hard to be objective, but they are inevitably involved in politics. Some have more bargaining and alliance-building skills than the elected and appointed officials to whom they report. In one sense, agency leaders are at the center of action in Washington. Over time, administrative agencies may become much closer to the interests they regulate than to the public they protect.

Special-interest groups that perceive real or potential harm to their interests cultivate the bureau chiefs and agency staffs who have jurisdiction over their programs. They also work closely with the committees and subcommittees of Congress that authorize, appropriate, and oversee programs run by these key bureaucracies. Recognizing the power of interest groups, bureau chiefs frequently recruit them as allies in pursuing common goals. These officials, interest groups, and congressional allies share a common view that more money should be spent on their federal programs. These alliances among bureaucrats, interest groups, and subcommittee members and their staffs on Capitol Hill are sometimes described as *iron triangles*.

Government's Greatest Achievements

Despite their complaints about the federal bureaucracy, Americans are reluctant to support cutbacks in what government does. On the contrary. The vast majority say the federal government's big problem is not the wrong priorities, but inefficiency, and few support a drastic reduction in federal responsibilities. Americans may complain about the red tape and waste in Washington, but the federal administrative system continues to make progress in solving some of the most difficult problems of modern society.

The federal government helped rebuild Europe after the devastation of World War II, won the cold war against communism, strengthened voting rights for all Americans, reduced workplace discrimination, ended racial segregation in public schools, and won the race to the moon. Name an international or domestic problem facing the nation today, and the federal administrative system has almost certainly tried to solve it. The list of resulting achievements is impressive:

- Poverty among older Americans has fallen to modern lows.

- Air and water quality have improved.

- More women are graduating from college and professional school, and more are competing in college sports.

- Food and drugs have become safer and the drug approval process has become faster.

- More poor children are getting a head start in preschool.

- More pregnant women are receiving proper medical care.

- Home ownership rates have risen to their highest levels ever.

- Americans are living longer with greater financial security.

- Polio and tuberculosis have been virtually eliminated.

- The Internet (originally developed by the Defense Department) has revolutionized communications.

- Federal crime rates are much lower today than they were two decades ago.

Many of these achievements depend on making sure the federal government can recruit the next generation of civil servants. None of the laws on which these achievements are based can be faithfully executed without the help of talented public employees.

Of course, not every federal endeavor has produced success. Too many American children still go to bed hungry, too many people are still homeless, too many workers are unable to make ends meet with minimum-wage jobs, and too many citizens have too little access to health care. Americans are right to ask whether the federal administrative system is doing enough to address problems such as global warming, terrorism, the spread of new diseases such as the bird flu, and energy independence. But if the mark of a great society is what it asks its government to achieve, Americans can be proud of the federal workforce today.

Summary

1. The chief characteristics of the federal administrative system are continuity, predictability, impartiality, standard operating procedures, and "red tape." Federal administrative agencies are responsible for implementing the laws that Congress makes. Although the framers expected federal departments and agencies to remain small, the federal administrative state has grown to 15 departments, dozens of agencies, and 4 million employees.

2. The framers made two key decisions about the structure of government. First, they prohibited members of Congress from serving in the executive branch, thereby guaranteeing some independence in the execution of the laws. Second, they gave the president the power to appoint the officers of government, albeit with the advice and consent of the Senate. These two decisions ensured that the president would be the nation's administrator in chief.

3. Most of the federal government's civilian employees serve under a merit system that protects their independence of politics. They work in one of the 15 cabinet departments or elsewhere in a long list of government corporations, independent agencies, and independent regulatory boards or commissions. The administrative system is led by presidential appointees and senior career executives. Senior presidential appointees must be nominated by the president and confirmed by the Senate, and must answer dozens of questions about their personal life on the way into office.

4. The federal government's Office of Personnel Management sets policy for recruiting and evaluating federal workers. Various restrictions on federal workers prevent them from running for political office or engaging in political fund-raising activities. The federal workforce generally prizes continuity, stability, and following the rules more than risk taking or innovation.

5. The federal administrative system generally uses regulations or spending to implement the laws. The rule-making process is governed by the Administrative Procedure Act, while the spending process is governed by the federal budget. Most of the federal budget is uncontrollable, whether because of indexing to inflation or because Congress and the president are unwilling to cut highly popular programs such as Social Security.

6. The federal workforce is led by a small number of senior political and civilian executives, and includes 900,000 higher-level professional and technical employees, 625,000 lower-level clerical and support employees, 250,000 blue-collar employees, 800,000 postal employees, and 1,400,000 military personnel.

7. The federal administrative system has at least two immediate supervisors: Congress and the president. It must pay considerable attention as well to the courts and their rulings and to well-organized interest groups and public opinion. Despite their efforts to assure accountability, Congress and the president often give vague instructions to the administrative system, which gives the system significant discretion in implementing the laws.

Further **Reading**

JOEL D. ABERBACH, *Keeping a Watchful Eye: The Politics of Congressional Oversight* (Brookings Institution Press, 1990).

ROBERT D. BEHN, *Rethinking Democratic Accountability* (Brookings Institution Press, 2001).

BARRY BOZEMAN, *Bureaucracy and Red Tape* (Prentice Hall, 2000).

COUNCIL FOR EXCELLENCE IN GOVERNMENT AND **THE PRESIDENTIAL APPOINTEE INITIATIVE,** *The Survivor's Guide for Presidential Nominees* (Brookings Institution Press, 2001).

SHELLEY L. DAVIS, *Unbridled Power: Inside the Secret Culture of the IRS* (HarperBusiness, 1997).

JOHN J. DILULIO JR., ED., *Deregulating the Public Service: Can Government Be Improved?* (Brookings Institution Press, 1994).

JAMES W. FESLER AND **DONALD F. KETTL,** *The Politics of the Administrative Process* (Chatham House, 1991).

JANE E. FOUNTAIN, *Building the Virtual State: Information Technology and Institutional Change* (Brookings Institution Press, 2001).

STEPHEN GOLDSMITH AND **WILLIAM EGGERS,** *Government by Network: The New Shape of the Public Sector* (Brookings Institution Press, 2005).

CHARLES T. GOODSELL, *The Case for Bureaucracy*, 3d ed. (Chatham House, 1994).

AL GORE, *Creating a Government That Works Better and Costs Less: The Report of the National Performance Review* (Plume-Penguin, 1993).

PHILIP K. HOWARD, *The Death of Common Sense: How Law Is Suffocating America* (Random House, 1994).

RONALD N. JOHNSON AND **GARY D. LIBECAP,** *The Federal Civil Service System and the Problem of Bureaucracy* (University of Chicago Press, 1994).

HERBERT KAUFMAN, *The Administrative Behavior of Federal Bureau Chiefs* (Brookings Institution Press, 1981).

DONALD KETTL, *The Global Management Revolution*, 2d ed. (Brookings Institution Press, 2005).

ANDREW KOHUT, ED., *Deconstructing Distrust: How Americans View Government* (Pew Research Center for the People and the Press, 1998).

PAUL C. LIGHT, *The New Public Service* (Brookings Institution Press, 1999).

PAUL C. LIGHT, *Thickening Government: Federal Hierarchy and the Diffusion of Accountability* (Brookings Institution Press, 1995).

PAUL C. LIGHT, *The Tides of Reform: Making Government Work, 1945–1995* (Yale University Press, 1997).

AREND LIJPHART, *Patterns of Democracy: Government Forms and Performance in Thirty-Six Countries* (Yale University Press, 1999).

G. CALVIN MAKENZIE AND **MICHAEL HAFKIN,** *Scandal Proof: Do Ethics Laws Make Government Ethical?* (Brookings Institution Press, 2002).

DAVID OSBORNE, *The Tools of Government: A Guide to the New Governance* (Oxford University Press, 2002).

DAVID OSBORNE AND **TED GAEBLER,** *Reinventing Government: How the Entrepreneurial Spirit Is Transforming the Public Sector* (Addison-Wesley, 1992).

JAMES Q. WILSON, *Bureaucracy: What Government Agencies Do and Why They Do It* (Basic Books, 1989).

Four useful journals are the *Journal of Policy Analysis and Management, National Journal, Public Administration Review,* and *Government Executive.*

bureaucracy, p. 382

bureaucrat, p. 382

department, p. 383

independent agency, p. 383

independent regulatory
commission, p. 383

government corporation, p. 383

Senior Executive Service, p. 388

spoils system, p. 390

merit system, p. 391

Office of Personnel Management
(OPM), p. 391

Hatch Act, p. 394

implementation, p. 395

administrative discretion, p. 395

regulations, p. 395

rule-making process, p. 395

uncontrollable spending, p. 396

entitlement program, p. 396

indexing, p. 397

oversight, p. 400

central clearance, p. 400

KeyTerms

Chapter 14

The Judiciary

THE BALANCING BRANCH

★

THE SUPREME COURT MADE A GENERATIONAL CHANGE IN THE FALL OF 2005. EIGHTY-TWO-YEAR-OLD CHIEF JUSTICE WILLIAM H. REHNQUIST DIED IN OFFICE AND 75-YEAR-OLD JUSTICE SANDRA DAY O'CONNOR RETIRED. THEY WERE REPLACED BY YOUNGER JUDGES WHO ARE LIKELY TO SERVE FOR 20 TO 30 YEARS: CHIEF JUSTICE JOHN ROBERTS AND JUSTICE SAMUEL A. ALITO JR. WITH REHNQUIST AND O'CONNOR GONE, THE OLDEST JUSTICE IS JOHN PAUL STEVENS, WHO REMAINS HEALTHY AND ENGAGED AT 86 YEARS OF AGE.

Roberts and Alito were confirmed after a relatively calm review process in the Senate. Although Democrats worried that the two new justices were too conservative, both rode out the potential storm through their well-rehearsed testimony before the Senate Judiciary Committee. As other nominees have done before, Roberts and Alito declined to answer some senators' questions on controversial issues that may come before the court. Neither gave any hint of their position on issues of race, privacy, pornography, or abortion; and neither questioned past Supreme Court decisions. In short, they dodged every effort that senators made to get them to declare their positions on any case that might reach the Court.

The nomination process was not without controversy, however. President George W. Bush had originally nominated Roberts to replace O'Connor, but renominated him for Chief Justice after Rehnquist died. Bush then announced his intention to nominate his White House Counsel, Harriet Miers, to replace O'Connor. The nomination seemed doomed from the start. Although Miers had been the president's lawyer, she had little experience with the courts and had never argued a case before the Supreme Court.

Moreover, in the view of many, Miers seemed to lack the experience and background to be a Supreme Court Justice. On the one hand, Republicans complained that she was not conservative enough to fill O'Connor's post. O'Connor had been a deciding vote in favor of abortion rights, and Republicans wanted her replaced with a swing vote against. Although Bush tried to defend Miers by noting that she had been a member of an evangelical Christian church that opposed abortion, Republicans were not convinced.

On the other hand, Democrats questioned her credentials for appointment. Running for a Dallas city council seat in 1989, she had supported a constitutional amendment against abortion, thereby giving Democrats the ammunition to attack her claims that she had no position on abortion. That one position, old as it was, fueled Democratic plans to stop her nomination.

Miers also become the butt of late-night television jokes about her intense loyalty to the president. As White House Counsel, she had often been a cheerleader

Judge John Roberts

"Legislatures make law wholesale, judges retail."

FORMER SUPREME COURT JUSTICE
FELIX FRANKFURTER

for his policies, and she was portrayed as a naïve, unquestioning advocate of whatever the president wanted. Democrats took the jokes seriously, arguing that she would be little more than a conduit for the president's positions on key cases before the Court.

With so much pressure against her from both sides, Miers withdrew herself from consideration less than a month after the president had nominated her. In doing so, she became just the ninth nominee out of 120 in history to be withdrawn or rejected. Bush soon nominated Alito to fill the post, no doubt because Alito was very skilled, but also because he had never taken a visible position on abortion and other controversial issues.

With the new justices in office, the Supreme Court began work on a variety of new issues, including freedom of religion, the war on terrorism, gay rights, limits on the federal government's power to regulate the states, and the treatment of immigrants. Many of these issues have only recently reached the judicial branch, confirming the conventional wisdom that cases can take years, if not decades, to rise all the way to the top of the federal judiciary as lower courts and state courts make the preliminary decisions.[1]

The Roberts, Miers, and Alito nominations raise important questions about how the federal judiciary works, who gets nominated for the Supreme Court, and why potential judges are so cautious not to reveal their preferences before they reach the "bench," or a given court. Before turning to these issues later in the chapter, it is first important to understand more about how the framers designed the federal judiciary and what its key characteristics are today. It is also important to understand the three levels of the federal judiciary, how judges are selected for their posts, and limits on judicial action. Once past these basic discussions, we will turn to the Supreme Court in detail, asking how justices are nominated and how they make decisions.

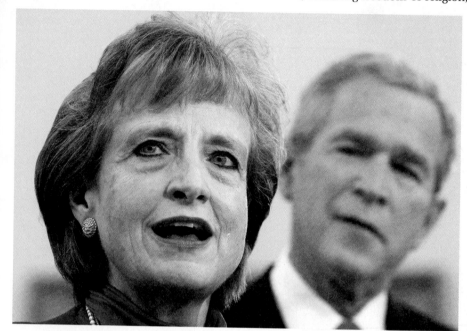

President Bush nominated Harriet Miers to replace Sandra Day O'Connor on the Supreme Court. Questions about her qualifications from Democrats and Republicans led her to withdraw from consideration.

Understanding the Federal Judiciary

The framers viewed the federal judiciary as an important check against both Congress and the president. Hence, they insulated the judiciary against both public opinion and the rest of government. In an effort to protect the judiciary from shifts in public opinion, the framers rejected the direct election of judges, which had been used to select many judges in the colonies, and is still used today to select some state and local judges. They also excluded the House, the more representative of the two bodies of Congress, from any role in either selecting or confirming federal judges.

In an effort to protect the judiciary from Congress as a whole, the framers rejected limits on judicial terms. Federal judges serve during good behavior, which ordinarily means for life. The framers also prohibited Congress from ever reducing a judge's salary after the judge is confirmed, thereby removing financial pressure as a possible way to interfere with judicial actions.

These early decisions were essential to protect the judiciary's independence in resolving public disputes. As Alexander Hamilton wrote, "The Executive not only dispenses the honors, but holds the sword of the community. The legislature not only commands the purse, but prescribes the rules by which the duties and rights of every citizen are to be regulated. The Judiciary, on the contrary, has no influence over either the sword or the purse."[2]

The federal judiciary has no army or police force to enforce its will or make the people obey its decisions. Although it can order Congress and the president to act, it must often rely on the public's respect to implement its decisions. The challenge is to maintain this respect in resolving controversial issues such as abortion rights; the death penalty; the rights of prisoners of war; protection from pornography; and basic freedoms of the press, religion, and speech. There are times when the federal judiciary opposes the public in rejecting popular laws, such as a ban on burning the American flag. Although the federal judiciary does consider public opinion as it tackles controversial issues, it is crucial that it maintain its independence.

Characteristics of the Federal Judiciary

Federal judges play a central role in American life. Not only do they resolve the kinds of controversial cases described above, they decide whether the laws are constitutional. Many of these decisions are based on Chief Justice John Marshall's successful claim of **judicial review**; that is, the power to authoritatively interpret the Constitution (see Chapter 2). Only a constitutional amendment or a later Supreme Court can modify the Court's decisions. Justice Felix Frankfurter suggested tersely: "The Supreme Court is the Constitution."

Federal judges are also asked to resolve disputes involving billions of dollars, decide conflicts among competing interest groups, supervise the criminal justice system, and make rules affecting the lives of millions of people. They not only settle legal conflicts but in some cases have overseen the operation of schools, prisons, mental hospitals, and complex businesses. Sometimes they decide the details of how these institutions should be run. Still, the scope and nature of judicial power limit the role of judges.

The federal judiciary has five basic characteristics that help distinguish it from Congress, the presidency, and the administrative system.

1. The federal judiciary is an **adversary system**. A court of law is a neutral arena in which two parties argue their differences and present their points of view before an impartial judge. The adversary system is based on the fight theory, which holds that arguing over law and evidence, which may or may not arrive at the truth, guarantees fairness in the judicial system.[3] The adversary system thus imposes restraints on the exercise and scope of judicial power. The courts handle many kinds of legal disputes, but the most common are **criminal law**, which defines crimes against the public order and provides for punishment, and **civil law**, which governs the relations between individuals and defines their legal rights. The federal government brings all federal criminal cases, and it can also be a party to a civil action.

2. The federal judiciary is both *passive* and *reactive*. Judges cannot instigate cases. Moreover, not all disputes are within the scope of judicial power. Judges decide only **justiciable disputes**—lawsuits that grow out of actual controversies and are capable of judicial resolution. Judges do not use their power unless a real case or controversy comes to their court. It is not enough for a judge merely to have a general interest in a subject or to believe that a law is unconstitutional.

3. The federal judiciary requires that anyone who appears before a court have *standing to sue*. Those who start a lawsuit (*plaintiffs*) must have sustained or be in immediate danger of sustaining a direct and personal injury. Plaintiffs may not raise hypothetical issues; they must have a real dispute and opposing interests with another party. They must also claim a personal injury—the violation of a constitutional or other legal right—and show a "personal stake in the outcome." But plaintiffs may also bring suits over environmental damages, defective consumer products, and other matters that affect interest groups and large numbers of people.[4] Plaintiffs occasionally band together to file *class-action lawsuits* that affect large numbers of Americans.

4. The federal judiciary decides cases, not whether to prosecute persons for allegedly committing crimes. This decision is left to government *prosecutors*, who act on behalf of the public in choosing whether and how to pursue cases against

"The Judiciary . . . has no influence over either the sword or the purse."

ALEXANDER HAMILTON

judicial review
The power of a court to refuse to enforce a law or government regulation that in the opinion of the judges conflicts with the U.S. Constitution or, in a state court, the state constitution.

adversary system
A judicial system in which the court of law is a neutral arena where two parties argue their differences.

criminal law
A law that defines crimes against the public order.

civil law
A law that governs relationships between individuals and defines their legal rights.

justiciable dispute
A dispute growing out of an actual case or controversy and that is capable of settlement by legal methods.

defendants who may have violated the law. They also decide whether to offer or accept a **plea bargain**, whereby defendants agree to plead guilty to a lesser offense to avoid having to stand trial and face a sentence for a more serious offense. Prosecutors also make recommendations to judges about what sentences to impose.

5. The federal judiciary does not settle all disputes, especially ones that involve issues that the Constitution explicitly assigns to Congress or the president. The federal judiciary has been particularly reluctant to intervene in foreign policy questions involving the power to declare war, economic questions such as the fairness of the federal tax system, or social questions such as the amount of money the federal government should spend on specific programs such as education, health care, or the environment. Although the federal judiciary does resolve questions about whether the federal government has followed the laws, it generally allows Congress and the president to resolve their differences through the normal legislative process.

Prosecuting Cases

The U.S. Department of Justice is responsible for prosecuting federal criminal and civil cases. The department is led by the attorney general, who is assisted by the solicitor general, 94 U.S. attorneys, and about 1,200 assistant attorneys.

The solicitor general represents the federal government whenever a case appears before the Supreme Court, while U.S. attorneys represent the government whenever a case appears before a lower federal court. U.S. attorneys are appointed by the president with the advice and consent of the Senate.

The appointment of U.S. attorneys is of great interest to senators. Not only are U.S. attorneys highly visible because of the cases they prosecute, they often run for higher office. Because there is at least one federal district court in every state, senators exercise significant influence over the selection process. And because U.S. attorneys are almost always members of the president's political party, it is customary for them to resign if the opposition party wins the White House.

The attorney general appoints each of the assistant U.S. attorneys after consulting with the U.S. attorneys in each district. Some districts have only one assistant U.S. attorney, while the largest has dozens.

The federal judiciary also provides help to defendants who cannot afford their own attorneys in criminal trials. Traditionally, private attorneys have been appointed to provide assistance, but many state and federal courts employ a **public defender system**. This system provides lawyers to any defendant who needs one, and is supervised by the federal judiciary to assure that the public defenders are qualified for their jobs.

The Three Types of Federal Courts

rticle III of the Constitution is the shortest of the three articles establishing the institutions of government. Yet, brief as it is, it provides a short list of the duties reserved for the judiciary, including controversies:

- To which the U.S. shall be a party—for example, the enforcement of the laws.

- Between two or more states—for example, oversight of harbors and state borders.

- Between a state and citizens of another state—for example, taxes on Internet purchases.

- Between citizens of two or more states—for example, disagreement over purchases of goods and services.

- Between citizens of the same state involving national issues—for example, disputes over a constitutional right.

defendant
In a criminal action, the person or party accused of an offense.

plea bargain
Agreement between a prosecutor and a defendant that the defendant will plead guilty to a lesser offense to avoid having to stand trial for a more serious offense.

public defender system
Arrangement whereby public officials are hired to provide legal assistance to people accused of crimes who are unable to hire their own attorneys.

Article III is not the only part of the Constitution dealing with the federal judiciary, however. The framers also gave Congress the power to establish "all tribunals inferior to the Supreme Court," which meant that Congress could establish the lower courts discussed below.

The first Congress used this power to create a hierarchy of federal courts. Under the Judiciary Act of 1789, which was the very first law that Congress passed, the federal judiciary was divided into a three-tiered system that exists to this day. The first tier consists of *district courts,* the middle tier consists of *circuit courts of appeal,* and the highest tier is composed of just one court, the *Supreme Court.* The Supreme Court has **original jurisdiction** in cases that affect ambassadors, other public ministers, and other diplomats, and cases that involve a state or states as a party, which is the authority of a court to hear a case "in the first instance." The Supreme Court has **appellate jurisdiction** in all other cases, which is the power to review decisions of other federal courts and agencies, as determined by Congress, and appeals from state supreme court decisions that raise questions of federal law. In general, federal courts may decide only cases or controversies arising under the Constitution, a federal law, a treaty, or admiralty and maritime law; cases brought by a foreign nation against a state or the federal government; and diversity suits—lawsuits between citizens of different states—if the amount of the controversy exceeds $50,000.

Level One: District Courts

Although the Supreme Court and its justices receive most of the attention, the work-horses of the federal judiciary are the district courts in the states, the District of Columbia, and U.S. territories. In 2005, they heard more than 250,000 civil cases and almost 70,000 criminal cases.[5] There are 665 judgeships in the 94 district courts that exist across the country, at least one in every state.

District courts are the trial courts where almost all federal cases begin. District judges are appointed by the president, subject to confirmation by the Senate, and hold office for life. District judges appoint and are assisted by clerks, bailiffs, stenographers, law clerks, court reporters, and probation officers. District judges normally hold trials and decide cases individually. However, because reapportionment of congressional districts and voting rights are so important to the nation, they hear cases concerned with these issues in three-judge panels.

As the federal judiciary's primary trial courts, district courts make the primary decisions on the death penalty, drug crimes, and major violations of the laws. Thus, they are on the front lines of questions about the unfair prosecution and heavy sentences that are often imposed on minority groups. They are also on the front lines of highly visible decisions involving stock market trading, environmental pollution, and fraud against the government. They also make rulings about federal crimes; for example, a district court put Martha Stewart in jail in 2004 for lying to investigators about the sale of stock in a drug manufacturing company called ImClone.

Level Two: Circuit Courts of Appeals

All district court decisions can be *appealed,* or taken to a higher court for further review. Almost all of these cases are reviewed by federal **courts of appeals.** Judges in these courts are bound by the **precedents,** or previous decisions made by courts of appeals and the Supreme Court, but they have considerable discretion in applying these earlier decisions to specific cases. Although the vast majority of their cases come upward from federal district courts, federal regulatory commissions bring their cases to the courts of appeal directly.

Courts of appeals are located geographically in 11 *judicial circuits* that include all the states and U.S. territories (see Figure 14–1 for a map of the states included in each of the 11 geographic circuits). A twelfth is located in the District of Columbia and hears the largest number of cases challenging federal statutes, regulations, and administrative decisions. The thirteenth appellate court is the Court of Appeals for the Federal Circuit, which is located in the District of Columbia and reviews cases from any state or

original jurisdiction
The authority of a court to hear a case "in the first instance."

appellate jurisdiction
The authority of a court to review decisions made by lower courts.

court of appeals
A court with appellate jurisdiction that hears appeals from the decisions of lower courts.

precedent
A decision made by a higher court such as a circuit court of appeals or the Supreme Court that is binding on all other federal courts.

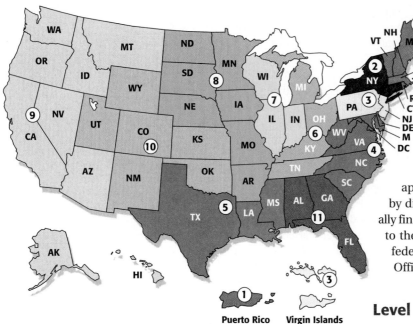

FIGURE 14-1 **States Covered by the Eleven U.S. Circuit Courts of Appeal.**

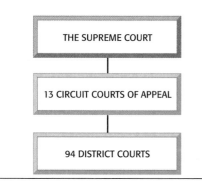

FIGURE 14-2 **The Structure of the U.S. Judiciary.**

region that deal primarily with appeals in patent, copyright, and international trade cases. The largest circuit is the ninth, with 28 circuit judges and 99 district judges. It is geographically the size of western Europe and contains 20 percent of the U.S. population.

Each circuit court consists of six to 28 permanent judgeships (179 in all). These courts normally hear cases in panels of three judges, and heard almost 70,000 cases per year in 2005.

Except in unusual circumstances, courts of appeals can only resolve cases that have been decided by district courts. Nevertheless, their decisions are usually final. Less than 1 percent of their decisions are appealed to the Supreme Court. (For more information about the federal judiciary, go to the Web site of the Administrative Office of the U.S. Courts at www.uscourts.gov.)

Level Three: The Supreme Court

The Constitution established only one court of appeal for the entire nation: the Supreme Court. As the only court named in the Constitution, the Supreme Court is considered the "court of last resort." Once the Supreme Court decides, the dispute or case is over. (See Figure 14–2 for the three-tiered structure of the federal judiciary.)

Compared with Congress and the presidency, the Supreme Court has changed the least since its creation. There are nine Supreme Court justices today, compared with six in 1789, and the Court only moved into its own building, which some call the "Marble Temple," in 1932. Before its move, the Court shared space with the House and Senate in the U.S. Capitol Building. Unlike the current practice in both houses of Congress, oral arguments before the Court about individual cases are not televised, and its justices still appear in robes.

Moreover, the justices still prefer to keep some distance from the public. They never endorse political candidates, rarely give speeches or interviews, and never talk to reporters or the public about specific cases. Although justices are sometimes recognized in public, it is one thing to become well known, and quite another to seek celebrity through press releases and photo opportunities. If justices appeared on the Sunday morning political talk shows such as *Meet the Press* or in televised interviews, they would lose some of their legitimacy.

Because it is so important in making decisions that affect the entire country, the Supreme Court will be discussed in a separate section later in this chapter.

Judicial Federalism: State and Federal Courts

Unlike most countries, which have a single national judicial system that makes all decisions on criminal and civil laws, the United States has both federal and state courts. Each state maintains a judiciary of its own, and many large cities and counties have judicial systems as complex as those of the states. Within both federal and state systems, judicial power is further divided between trial courts (and other lesser courts such as traffic courts) and one or more levels of appellate courts, which hear appeals from the lower courts.

State courts primarily interpret and apply their state constitutions and law. When their decisions are based solely on state law, their rulings may not be appealed to or reviewed by federal courts. Only when decisions raise a federal question, involving the application of the Bill of Rights or other federal law, are federal courts able to review them. Federal courts have **writ of *habeas corpus*** jurisdiction (the power to

writ of *habeas corpus*
A court order requiring explanation to a judge why a prisoner is being held in custody.

release persons from custody if a judge determines that they are not being detained constitutionally) and may review criminal convictions in state courts if they believe that an accused person's federal constitutional and legal rights have been violated. Except for *habeas corpus* jurisdiction, the Supreme Court is the only federal court that may review state court decisions, and only in cases involving a conflict with federal law. Other than the original jurisdiction the Constitution grants to the Supreme Court, no federal court has any jurisdiction except that granted to it by an act of Congress.

Most legal cases are heard in state courts, which annually face about 90 million civil and criminal cases. The type of litigation in state courts also tends to differ from that in federal courts. Apart from criminal cases, the largest portion of state court cases involves economic issues—state regulation of public utilities, zoning and small business, labor relations, natural resources, energy, and the environment. But state courts also handle controversial issues. For example, the constitution of the State of Minnesota contains an explicit right to privacy, which has been the subject of several cases questioning the use of "spyware" for tracking Internet browsing by citizens.

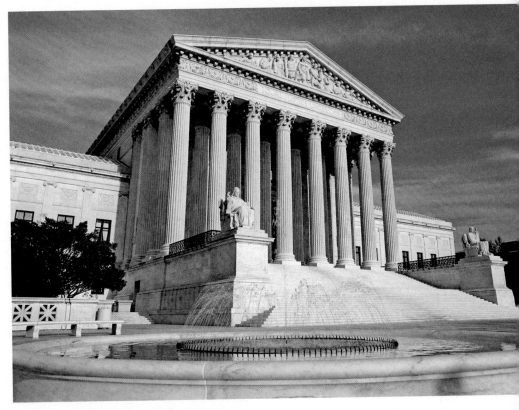

The U.S. Supreme Court Building, Washington, DC.

The U.S. Supreme Court, 2006: (First Row L to R), Justice Anthony M. Kennedy, Justice John Paul Stevens, Chief Justice John G. Roberts, Justice Antonin Scalia, Justice David H. Souter. (Second Row L to R), Justice Stephen G. Breyer, Justice Clarence Thomas, Justice Ruth Bader Ginsburg, and Justice Samuel Alito.

The Politics of Appointing Federal Judges

The Constitution sets absolutely no requirements for serving on the Supreme Court, nor did the first Congress create any requirements for the lower courts. Since judges were to be appointed by the president with the advice and consent of the Senate, the framers assumed that judges would be experienced in the law. As Hamilton explained, "there can be a few men in the society who will have sufficient skill in the laws to qualify them for the stations of judges. And making the proper deductions for the ordinary depravity of human nature, the number must be still smaller of those who unite the requisite integrity with the requisite knowledge."[6]

Much as the framers believed that the judiciary should be independent, the appointments process gives presidents and the Senate ample opportunity for influencing the direction of the courts. Indeed, George Washington established two precedents about judicial appointments that continue to this day. First, Washington's appointees were political and ideological allies of the president—indeed, all of Washington's appointees belonged to his Federalist Party. Second, every state was represented on some court somewhere, thereby assuring at least some representation across the nation.

Presidents continue to follow these precedents today. They nominate judges who are likely to agree with them on the key issues before the courts, and tend to nominate judges from their own party. And they routinely rely on the senators in a given state to make recommendations for lower-court appointments. Because judges serve for life, presidents see judicial appointments as an opportunity to shape the courts for decades to come. Moreover, because federal judges often move up from the lower courts to the Supreme Court, presidents pay great attention to the possibility that even the most obscure judge might eventually reach the highest court in the nation. As Table 14–1 shows, federal lower-court judges are the most likely to rise to the Supreme Court—in fact, ten of the last 15 Supreme Court justices were federal lower-court judges at the time of their nomination.

TABLE 14–1 Moving Up to the Supreme Court

Job	Number	Most Recent Example
Federal Judges	32	Samuel Alito Jr., 2005
Practicing Lawyers	22	Lewis F. Powell, 1971
State Court Judges	18	Sandra Day O'Connor, 1981
Cabinet Members	8	Labor Secretary Arthur Goldberg, 1962
Senators	7	Harold H. Burton (R-Ohio), 1945
Attorneys General	6	Tom C. Clark, 1949
Governors	3	Earl Warren (D-Calif.), 1953
Other	14	Solicitor General Thurgood Marshall, 1967

SOURCE: *Congressional Quarterly Weekly*, October 10, 2005, p. 2701.

Making the Initial Choices

Article II of the Constitution gives the president the power to appoint federal judges with the advice and consent of the Senate. Judges are selected through a complex bargaining process that involves the candidates for appointment, the president, and the White House staff. The process also involves consultation with the Department of Justice, the American Bar Association (ABA), senators, party leaders, and interest groups.

As a nonpartisan association of lawyers and some judges, the ABA rates all judicial candidates as well qualified, qualified, or not qualified. In 2006, it rated both Roberts and Alito as well qualified, which gave both greater legitimacy as their nominations proceeded in the Senate. Any "unqualified" votes from the ABA committee that reviews candidates can create controversy. In 1991, Clarence Thomas received 12 votes for

Chief Justice John Roberts, right, congratulates Justice Samuel A. Alito Jr. at Alito's swearing-in ceremony as a new member of the Supreme Court.

qualified, and two votes for unqualified, an unfavorable beginning of what would be a very controversial Senate review.

Despite its continuing influence, the ABA is no longer quite as powerful as it once was. Conservative groups have mounted a continuing attack on the ABA's role, contending that it reflects a liberal bias and has given low ratings to some conservative nominees. In response to this criticism, President George W. Bush announced in March 2001, shortly after he took office, that he would no longer ask the ABA to evaluate judicial candidates before nomination. Senators on the Judiciary Committee, however, continue to receive the ABA's evaluations of judicial nominees. Whereas it was once impossible for a judge to win confirmation with a hint of a poor ABA rating, it is now possible if a potential judge has the strong support of the president and liberal or conservative interest groups.

Because judicial appointments have become more controversial in recent years as presidents seek to control the judiciary by appointing more liberal or conservative judges, presidents have taken a much more active role in the selection process. Whereas most district and circuit court judges were once waved ahead on the basis of American Bar Association endorsement and the support of their local senator, they now go through an intense interview process that touches on all aspects of their personal life and judicial philosophy.

The Department of Justice also plays a significant role in selecting judges. Beginning with the Reagan administration, the assistant attorney general in charge of the Office of Legal Policy has overseen the screening of potential judicial nominees. After candidates' backgrounds and judicial philosophies have been checked, they are discussed by a White House working group that includes the legal counselor to the president and the attorney general. This group recommends nominees to the president. (For more information about the Office of Legal Policy and current judicial nominations, go to its Web site at www.usdoj.gov/olp.)

Before the White House submits nominees' names to the Senate for confirmation, it observes the practice of **senatorial courtesy**—the custom of submitting the names of prospective judges for approval to the senators from the states in which the appointees are to work. If the senators approve of the nomination, all is well. But if negotiations are deadlocked between the senators, or between the senators and the Department of Justice, a seat may stay vacant for years.[7] The custom of senatorial courtesy is not observed with Supreme Court appointments, since they have national jurisdiction; nevertheless, President Clinton consulted with Republican Senator Orrin Hatch, who at the time chaired the Senate Judiciary Committee because the Senate was controlled by Republicans, so as to avoid a confirmation battle over his nominees to the Supreme Court, Justices Ruth Bader Ginsburg in 1993 and Stephen Breyer in 1994.

senatorial courtesy
Presidential custom of submitting the names of prospective appointees for approval to senators from the states in which the appointees are to work.

In addition to this process within the government, liberal and conservative interest groups often provide their own views of nominees' qualifications for appointment. People for the American Way and the Alliance for Justice often support liberal nominees and oppose conservatives, while the Heritage Foundation and a coalition of 260 conservative organizations called the Judicial Selection Monitoring Project often support conservative judges and oppose liberals. These organizations once waited until after the president sent the name of a nominee to the Senate to express their opinions, but now they are active before the choice is known, informing the media of their support or opposition to potential nominees.

Senate Advice and Consent

The normal presumption is that the president should be allowed considerable discretion in the selection of federal judges. Despite this presumption, the Senate takes seriously its responsibility in confirming judicial nominations, especially when the party controlling the Senate is different from that of the president. However, because individual senators can always threaten or actually mount a filibuster, even party control of the Senate is no guarantee that a nomination will succeed.

All judicial nominations are referred to the Senate Judiciary Committee for a hearing and a committee vote before consideration by the entire Senate. Like legislation, judges are confirmed with a majority vote. Even before they receive a hearing, however, all district court nominees must survive a preliminary process that involves the nominee's two home-state senators. Each senator receives a letter from the committee asking for approval. This request is printed on blue paper, and is called a "blue slip." If either senator declines to return the slip, the nomination is dead, and no hearing will be held. During the last two years of Clinton's presidency, Republican senators delayed and defeated confirmation of many of his judicial nominees by simply refusing to respond. The blue-slip process is used for district court nominees only, not for circuit court or Supreme Court nominees.

There are other ways to delay or defeat a judicial nominee, including the threat of a filibuster. Just as the Republican Senate majority had stalled Clinton nominations in the late 1990s, the new Democratic majority stalled many of the Bush administration's nominees after it took control of the Senate in mid-2001. Democrats also stalled many of the Bush nominees even after Republicans regained control of the Senate following the 2002 midterm elections, using both the threat and actual use of filibusters.[8]

Even if the Senate delays or rejects a nomination, however, presidents always have the option of making *recess appointments* after the Senate adjourns at the end of a session. Bush did just that in early 2004 by using a recess appointment to place Charles W. Pickering on the court of appeals. Pickering's appointment had been stalled for almost four years by Senate Democrats, who believed that the Mississippi native had been too conservative on issues of race. Bush may have won the battle, but he did not win the war. Under a recess appointment, Pickering could only serve until the next Congress convened. Knowing that Senate Democrats would continue to oppose his nomination, Pickering decided to withdraw his name from consideration for another nomination, and he left the court in early 2005 just before the new Congress convened.

Before the mid-1950s, the Senate confirmation process was relatively simple and nonpartisan. Until then, the Senate Judiciary Committee did not even hold hearings to ask potential judges questions about their personal history and philosophy. However, as judges became more important in deciding civil rights cases, the committee began interviewing candidates on various questions, sometimes imposing a *litmus test* by asking nominees about their positions on specific issues such as abortion. Nominees almost always refuse to answer such questions to protect themselves from attack and reserve their judgment for actual cases.

As noted in the introduction to this chapter, most judicial nominees have refused to answer questions about their future decisions on controversial issues such as abortion rights. But in 1987, Supreme Court nominee Robert Bork adopted a different and ultimately unsuccessful strategy. Because he had written so many law articles, made so any speeches, and decided so many cases as a circuit court judge, he sought to clarify his constitutional views in defending himself before the Judiciary Committee. His candor may well have contributed to the Senate's rejection of him, and that has made subsequent nominees even more reluctant to respond to similar questions. Bork was also vigorously opposed by liberal interest groups, which led to the use of the term "Borking" to describe particularly angry opposition to a nominee for any judicial post.

Until recently, most judicial appointments, especially those for the district and circuit courts, were processed without much controversy. However, "now that lower court judges are more commonly viewed as political actors, there is increasing Senate scrutiny of these nominees."[9] The battle over judicial confirmations ordinarily takes place in hearings before the Senate Judiciary Committee, although debates can also occur on the Senate floor after the committee has acted.[10] Nominees for the Supreme Court are the most likely to face defeat. Indeed, the Senate has refused to confirm 29 of the 138 presidential nominations for Supreme Court justices since the first justice was nominated in 1789.

The Role of Party, Race, and Gender

Presidents so seldom nominate judges from the opposing party (around 90 percent of judicial appointments since the time of Franklin Roosevelt have gone to candidates from the president's party) that partisan considerations are taken for granted. Today more attention is paid to other characteristics, such as ideology, race, and gender.[11]

Although President Jimmy Carter had no opportunity to make an appointment to the Supreme Court, he brought increased diversity to the lower courts: 16 percent of Carter's appointees were women, 14 percent were African Americans, and 6 percent were Hispanics. President Ronald Reagan was the first to appoint a woman to the Supreme Court, but appointed fewer minority members or women to the lower courts than Carter did.[12] Of George H. W. Bush's appointees to the lower courts, 20 percent were women, 7 percent were African Americans, and 4 percent were Hispanics.[13]

Bill Clinton promised to appoint federal judges who would be more representative of the ethnic makeup of the United States. "We don't have litmus tests or judicial-philosophy tests," insisted Assistant Attorney General Eleanor Dean Acheson, who oversaw judicial selection during the Clinton administration, "but I do think we've put people on the bench who are interested in people and their problems."[14] Clinton lived up to his pledge by naming more women and minorities to the bench than his predecessors had; 182 of his 367 appointees were women and minorities, or 49 percent of his appointees.

George W. Bush appointed a number of women and minorities in his first year in office but fewer thereafter. As of late 2006, 32 percent of Bush's judicial nominees have been women and minorities, including 21 percent women, 7 percent African Americans, and 10 percent Hispanics.

"We don't have litmus tests or judicial-philosophy tests, but I do think we've put people on the bench who are interested in people and their problems."

FORMER ASSISTANT ATTORNEY GENERAL
ELEANOR DEAN ACHESON

The Role of Ideology

Finding a party member is not enough; presidents want to pick the "right" kind of Republican or "our" kind of Democrat to serve as a judge. They have usually been able to achieve this goal. Judges picked by Republican presidents tend to be judicial conservatives. Judges picked by Democratic presidents are more likely to be liberals. Both of these orientations are tempered by the need for judges to go through a senatorial confirmation process that during recent administrations has been rigorous and driven by opposition to the White House.[15]

President Ronald Reagan's two terms made it possible for him to join Presidents Franklin D. Roosevelt and Dwight D. Eisenhower as the only presidents in the last century to appoint a majority of the federal bench. All told, Reagan appointed 368 lifetime judges. His administration acted carefully to nominate only those whose views about the role of the courts and constitutional issues were consistent with Reagan's own.[16]

The Changing Face of American Politics

Diversity in the Federal Courts

Supreme Court Justices Clarence Thomas, left, and Anthony Kennedy testify before a House Appropriations Subcommittee hearing on funding for the judiciary.

T he federal judiciary has long been dominated by white males. But diversity on the federal bench has been increasing during the last several decades, largely due to the judicial appointments of Presidents Jimmy Carter, Bill Clinton, and George W. Bush.

Although the number of women and minorities appointed to the federal courts has only recently increased significantly, the first woman, Judge Florence Allen, was appointed in 1934 by President Franklin D. Roosevelt. President Harry Truman named the first African American, Judge William Henry Hastie, in 1950. President John F. Kennedy appointed the first Hispanic, Judge Reynaldo G. Garza, in 1961, and President Richard M. Nixon in 1971 appointed the first Asian American, Judge Herbert Choy. The first Native American, Judge Billy Michael Burrage, was appointed in 1994 by President Clinton. ∎

Justice Ruth Bader Ginsburg

**Former Justice
Sandra Day O'Connor**

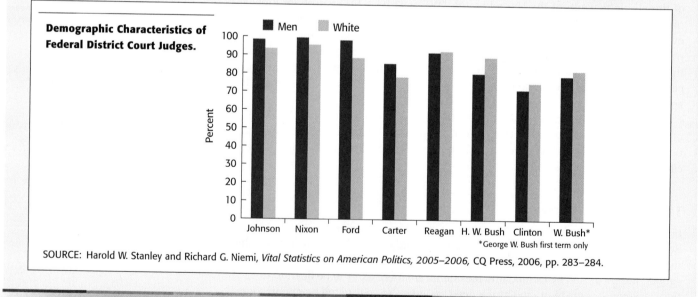

Demographic Characteristics of Federal District Court Judges.

Legend: ■ Men   ▦ White

(Bar chart, Percent on y-axis from 0 to 100, by president)

President	Men	White
Johnson	98	93
Nixon	99	95
Ford	97	88
Carter	84	77
Reagan	90	91
H. W. Bush	79	87
Clinton	69	73
W. Bush*	77	79

*George W. Bush first term only

SOURCE: Harold W. Stanley and Richard G. Niemi, *Vital Statistics on American Politics, 2005–2006*, CQ Press, 2006, pp. 283–284.

Not only were a large number of judicial conservatives appointed, but many of them—because they were comparatively young—will continue to have an effect on judicial policy well into the twenty-first century.

Because President George H. W. Bush was less committed to conservatism than Reagan, conservative organizations—the Heritage Foundation, the Pacific Legal Foundation, and the Federalist Society—focused more attention on his judicial nominees.

The first president Bush appointed 148 district judges, 37 appellate judges, and two Supreme Court justices—David Souter and Clarence Thomas. It turned out that his appointees, with the exception of Justice Souter, were among the most conservative in recent history.[17] His appointment of Justice Thomas helped consolidate the Court's "turn to the right."[18]

President Clinton gave Democratic senators clear guidelines about the kind of judges he wanted—competent professionals who would bring diversity to the bench.[19] But after the Republicans took control of the Senate in 1994, Clinton abandoned or declined to nominate several judicial candidates opposed by conservative interest groups and had to reach compromises with Republican senators. With increasing opposition from the Republican-controlled Senate, confirmation rates declined so much that Chief Justice Rehnquist scolded the Senate for jeopardizing the ability of the federal courts to do their work. Despite the slowdown in Senate confirmations, Clinton had named 367 of the 849 federal judges by the end of his second term, averaging more than 40 appointments per year; despite a similar slowdown, Bush appointed more than 200 federal judges by 2006, averaging 35 per year.

As older, conservative judges appointed during the Reagan administration continue to retire, the second Bush administration has been working hard to find younger conservative judges to fill the vacancies. Thus, Roberts and Alito were in their fifties when nominated for the Supreme Court, and are likely to serve for decades. Many of the second Bush administration's lower-court appointees are also relatively young, which assures their lasting impact.

Like Clinton, George W. Bush has had difficulty winning the support of opposition party senators for his judicial nominees. Democrats delayed Bush's most conservative nominees and held filibusters in order to prevent confirmation votes on ten circuit court nominees. In retaliation, Bush bypassed the Senate by naming two candidates—Charles W. Pickering and William H. Pryor—to recess appointments, which they held until the next session of Congress in 2005. Whereas Pickering removed himself from further consideration in early 2005, Pryor was nominated again for his post and was confirmed in July, 2005, under an agreement to allow votes on seven judges that Democrats had opposed.

Alabama's attorney general, William H. Pryor, testifies before the Senate Judiciary Committee considering his nomination as judge of the 11th U.S. Circuit Court of Appeals.

The Role of Judicial Philosophy

A candidate's judicial philosophy also influences the selection process. Does a candidate believe that judges should interpret the Constitution to reflect what the framers intended and what its words literally say; that is, does the candidate believe in **judicial restraint**, meaning that the courts should only act when the Constitution is clear? Or does the candidate believe that the Constitution should be adapted to reflect current conditions and philosophies; that is, does the candidate believe in **judicial activism**?

Throughout most of our history, federal courts have been more conservative than Congress, the White House, or state legislatures. Before 1937, judicial restraint was the battle cry of liberals who objected to judges' interpreting the due process clauses of the Fifth and Fourteenth Amendments to strike down many laws passed to protect labor and women and to keep the national and state governments from regulating the economy. These judges broadly construed the words of the Constitution to prevent what they thought to be unreasonable regulations of property.

With Presidents Richard Nixon, Ronald Reagan, George H. W. Bush, and George W. Bush, however, these positions changed dramatically, and it was conservatives who were advocates of judicial restraint. What is needed, they argued, are judges who will step back and let Congress, the president, and the state legislatures regulate or forbid abortions, permit prayer in public schools, impose capital punishment, and not hinder law enforcement.

Still, it would be wrong to assume that judicial philosophy is nothing more than another way to argue about political ideology. Some conservatives, for example, favor judicial activism because they want current judges to reverse the last half-century of precedents on civil rights and to protect property rights from government regulation. The conservative majority on the Rehnquist Court invited criticisms from liberals for

judicial restraint
Philosophy proposing that judges should interpret the Constitution to reflect what the framers intended and what its words literally say.

judicial activism
Philosophy proposing that judges should interpret the Constitution to reflect current conditions and values.

After a contentious confirmation process in 1987, the Senate rejected Judge Robert Bork by a vote of 58 to 42.

Despite extensive controversy surrounding his nomination, the Senate narrowly confirmed Justice Clarence Thomas in 1991.

its judicial activism in overturning precedents and striking down state and federal laws promoting affirmative action, for example, and invalidating congressional enactments for infringing on states' rights. In these areas, liberals favor judicial restraint because they believe that judges should defer to the democratic process and that democratic self-governance will flourish if judges stay out of such policy debates.

Hence the debate over the role of the Supreme Court and the federal judiciary today is less about activism and restraint than about competing conceptions of the proper balance between government authority and individual rights, between the power of democratically accountable legislatures and that of courts and unelected judges.

Reforming the Selection Process

The televised confirmation hearings of Supreme Court nominees Robert Bork in 1987 and Clarence Thomas in 1991 provoked widespread complaints about the judicial selection process. Not only were the hearings lengthy and bitter, they focused on personal issues that some critics believed were irrelevant to each nominee's qualification to serve. The hearings also included detailed questions about the nominees' positions on controversial issues, which neither was willing to answer.

The hearings produced a series of task forces and studies that recommended ways to reduce the intense politics that surround the judicial confirmation process. Some recommended that Supreme Court nominees should not be required to appear before the Senate, others argued for a shorter confirmation process, and still others suggested that the Senate should return to the practice of judging nominees on their written record and on the testimony of legal experts.[20]

Although all of the recommendations might improve the process, they ignored the new political realities of judicial confirmation. Confirmation is slower, for example, because more controversy surrounds each nomination, and senators question nominees extensively. Although this opposition clearly rises when the Senate leadership and the president are of different parties, it exists even when the president's party has a majority in the Senate. Unless the president's party has the 60 votes needed to stop a filibuster, a single senator can stop the confirmation process, as the Pickering and Pryor cases suggest. Although both delays began under a Democratic Senate, they continued after Republicans won control in 2002.[21]

The politics of judicial selection may shock those who like to think judges are picked strictly on the basis of legal merit and without regard for ideology, party, gender, or race. But as a former Justice Department official observed, "When courts cease being an instrument for political change, then maybe the judges will stop being politically selected."[22] Moreover, as another scholar put it, "Supreme Court Justices have always been appointed for political reasons by politicians, and their confirmation process has always been dictated by politicians for political purposes. . . . In fact," he concluded, "not despite the politicization of the appointment and confirmation process, but because of it, the Supreme Court has endured as a flexible, viable force in the American democracy for over 200 years."[23]

Limits on Judicial Action

Although the framers worked hard to create an independent federal judiciary, there have long been limits on the ability of any one judge to make decisions that conflict with the courts as a whole. Judges cannot make decisions that ignore earlier decisions unless they have a clear reason to break with the past.

Adherence to Precedent

stare decisis

The rule of precedent, whereby a rule or law contained in a judicial decision is commonly viewed as binding on judges whenever the same question is presented.

Just because judges make independent decisions does not mean they are free to do whatever they wish. They are subject to a variety of limits on what they decide—some imposed by the political system of which they are a part and some imposed by higher courts and the legal profession. Among these constraints is the policy of **stare decisis**, the rule of precedent.

Stare decisis pervades our judicial system and promotes certainty, uniformity, and stability in the law. Drawn from the Latin phrase "to stand by that which is decided," the term means that judges are expected to abide by previous decisions of their own courts and by rulings of superior courts. Although adherence to precedent is the norm, the doctrine of *stare decisis* is not very restrictive.[24] Indeed, lower-court judges sometimes apply precedents selectively to raise additional questions about an earlier higher-court decision or to give the higher courts a chance to change a precedent entirely.

The doctrine of *stare decisis* is even less controlling in the field of constitutional law. Because the Constitution itself, rather than any one interpretation of it, is binding, the Court can *reverse* a previous decision it no longer wishes to follow, as it has done hundreds of times. Supreme Court justices are therefore not seriously restricted by *stare decisis*. Liberal Justice William O. Douglas, for one, maintained that *stare decisis* "was really no sure guideline because what did the judges who sat there in 1875 know about, say, electronic surveillance? They didn't know anything about it."[25] Rehnquist was no less candid in holding that precedents dealing with civil rights that were handed down on a 5-to-4 vote should always be open for reconsideration, since they were decided by only a bare majority of the Court. Since 1789, the Supreme Court has reversed more than 200 of its own decisions and overturned almost 200 acts of Congress; nearly 1,000 pieces of state legislation and state constitutional provisions, including many ballot propositions; and more than 100 city ordinances.[26]

Precedents do not govern judicial decisions forever, however. Otherwise, the nation would still be racially segregated. Having ruled that separate-but-equal accommodations on railway cars were perfectly legal in 1896, the Court allowed states to set up a host of segregated systems that included separate public schools, public drinking fountains, and sections for whites and minorities on buses. It took almost 50 years for the Court to reverse itself and rule that separate-but-equal schools violated the Constitution.

Many Court observers expect the new, more conservative justices to slowly move the law away from the right to abortion established in *Roe* v. *Wade* in 1973. Although they do not expect the Court to overturn the decision in a single, sweeping case, they do expect the Court to chip away at the precedent as more limited opportunities come before it.[27] However, South Dakota's 2006 decision to ban all abortions, except those that might save the life of the mother, sets up the possibility that the Court will soon be presented with a sweeping opportunity to overturn the right to abortion.

Congressional and Presidential Action

Individual judges are protected from Congress and the president by their life tenure, but the judiciary as a whole can be affected by legislative decisions that alter both the number and composition of the courts. Because the district and circuit courts are both created through legislation, they can be expanded or altered through legislation.

CHANGING THE NUMBERS One of the first actions a political party takes after gaining control of the White House and Congress is often to increase the number of federal judgeships. With divided government, however, when one party controls Congress and the other holds the White House, a stalemate is likely to occur, and relatively few new judicial positions will be created. During Andrew Johnson's administration, Congress went so far as to reduce the size of the Supreme Court to prevent the president from filling two vacancies. After Johnson left the White House, Congress returned the Court to its former size to permit Ulysses S. Grant to fill the vacancies.

In 1937, President Franklin Roosevelt proposed an increase in the size of the Supreme Court by one additional justice for every member of the Court over the age of 70, up to a total of 15 members. Ostensibly, the proposal was aimed at making the Court more efficient. In fact, Roosevelt and his advisers were frustrated because the Court had declared much of the early New Deal legislation unconstitutional. Despite Roosevelt's popularity, his "court-packing scheme" aroused intense opposition and his proposal failed. Although he lost the battle, the Court began to sustain some important New Deal legislation, and subsequent retirements from the bench enabled him to make eight appointments to the Court.

CHANGING THE JURISDICTION   Congressional control over the structure and jurisdiction of federal courts has been used to influence the course of judicial policy making. Although unable to get rid of Federalist judges by impeachment, Jefferson's Republican party abolished the circuit courts created by the Federalist Congress just before they lost control of Congress. In 1869, radical Republicans in Congress altered the Supreme Court's appellate jurisdiction in order to remove a case it was about to review involving the constitutionality of some Reconstruction legislation.[28]

Each year, a number of bills are introduced in Congress to eliminate the jurisdiction of federal courts over cases relating to abortion, school prayer, and school busing, or to eliminate the appellate jurisdiction of the Supreme Court over such matters. These attacks on federal court jurisdiction spark debate about whether the Constitution gives Congress authority to take such actions. Congress has not yet decided to do so, because it would amount to a fundamental shift in the relationship between Congress and the Supreme Court. As one scholar concluded, "History suggests the public has seen such attempts for precisely what they are, as attacks on judicial independence, and such attacks have been resisted."[29]

Questioning Decisions

Federal judges are often accused of "making law" through their decisions, which affect both the selection process and public approval. Although judges rarely consider public opinion in their decisions, except in very significant cases where public opposition may weaken the legitimacy of the result, they do worry about the public's support. Recall that they must rely on the public's support to enforce their decisions.

Judges are particularly sensitive to charges that they somehow make laws through their decisions, and are reluctant to admit that they make, or shape, laws. Nevertheless, judges readily admit that they do make sense of the laws by interpreting what Congress and the president intended when a bill became law. Because Congress and the president often use vague language to get laws passed, the courts must often step in to interpret the actual meaning of words. As former Chief Justice Earl Warren once explained of those who file lawsuits (*litigants*), the courts do not make law consciously, and it does not make law to undermine Congress, but making law comes with the job of being a judge. "When two litigants come into court, one says the act of Congress means this, the other says the act of Congress means the opposite of that, and we say the act of Congress means something—either one of the two or something in between. We are making law, aren't we?"[30]

Nevertheless, some Americans might argue that the Court makes a new law when it picks a side or something in between, in part because they believe judges should only act like referees in a prizefight. They expect referees to be impartial and disinterested, treating both parties as equals, and to apply rules, not make them. However, much as lawsuits may seem like a prizefight, they often seek clarification of a law's actual intent. In that sense, judges must make laws, in part by defining the intent of a law.

In 2006, for example, the Supreme Court ruled on a law that was designed to protect the U.S. Postal Service from lawsuits involving the "negligent transmission" of the mail, which was generally understood to mean letters and packages that are delivered to the wrong address. Although the law was essential for preventing frivolous lawsuits, the Court ruled that it was not intended to protect the Postal Service against leaving mail in places where it could cause an accident.

Legislatures make law by enacting statutes, or laws, but judges must apply the statutes to real-life situations. Statutes are drawn in broad terms: Drivers shall act with "reasonable care"; no one may make "excessive noise" in the vicinity of a hospital; employers must maintain "safe working conditions"; postal workers must not "negligently transmit" the mail. Such broad terms must be used because legislators cannot know exactly what will happen in every circumstance. Courts must judge their application in specific cases. In the words of Justice Felix Frankfurter, "Legislatures make law wholesale, judges retail."[31]

The problems of interpreting and applying law are intensified when judges are required—as American judges are—to interpret a constitution that has existed for more than 220 years. The Constitution is full of generalizations: "due process of law," "equal protection of the laws," "unreasonable searches and seizures," "Commerce . . . among several States." Recourse to the intent of the framers or to the words of the Constitution may not help judges facing cases involving thermal imaging and other new forms of governmental surveillance, the Internet, reproductive rights, or same-sex marriages. This is why the philosophy of judicial restraint is so difficult to use in practice—it is hard to interpret the words of the Constitution on issues that no one could envision in 1787.

The Supreme Court and How It Operates

The Supreme Court's term runs from the first Monday in October through the end of June. The justices listen to oral arguments for two weeks each month from October to April and then adjourn for two weeks to consider the cases and to write opinions. By agreement, at least six justices must participate in each decision. Cases are decided by a majority vote. In the event of a tie, the decision of the lower court is sustained, although on rare occasions the case may be reargued.

At 10:00 A.M. on the days when the Supreme Court sits, the eight associate justices and the chief justice, dressed in their robes, file into the courtroom. As they take their seats—arranged according to seniority, with the chief justice in the center—the clerk of the Court introduces them as the "Honorable Chief Justice and Associate Justices of the Supreme Court of the United States." Those present in the courtroom, asked to stand when the justices enter, are seated, and counsel take their places along tables in front of the bench. The attorneys for the Department of Justice are at the right. The attorneys are dressed conservatively; sport coats are not considered proper. Dress and ceremony are all part of the high ritual of the Court.

1. Courtyards
2. Solicitor General's Office
3. Lawyers' Lounge
4. Marshall's Office
5. Main Hall
6. Court Room
7. Conference and Reception Rooms
8. Justices' Conference Room
9. Chief Justice's Chambers
10. Justices' Chambers

FIGURE 14–3 **The Supreme Court Building.**

"The Chief Justiceship does not guarantee leadership. It only offers its incumbent an opportunity to lead."

POLITICAL SCIENTIST DAVID DANELSKI

The Powers of the Chief Justice

The chief justice of the United States is appointed by the president and confirmed by the Senate, like other federal judges. Yet the chief justice heads the entire federal judiciary; as a result, he (in our history, all have been men) has greater visibility than if selected by rotation of fellow justices, as is the practice in the state supreme courts, or by seniority, as is the practice in the federal courts of appeals. The chief justice has special administrative responsibilities in overseeing the operation of the judiciary, such as assigning judges to committees, responding to proposed legislation that affects the judiciary, and delivering the Annual Report on the State of the Judiciary.

But within the Supreme Court, the chief justice is only "first among equals," even though periods in Court history are often named after the chief justice. As Rehnquist said when he was still an associate justice, the chief deals not with "eight subordinates whom he may direct or instruct, but eight associates who, like him, have tenure during good behavior, and who are as independent as hogs on ice."[32] As political scientist David Danelski observed, "The Chief Justiceship does not guarantee leadership. It only offers its incumbent an opportunity to lead." Yet the chief justice "sets the tone, controls the conference, assigns the most opinions, and usually, takes the most important, nation-changing decisions for himself."[33]

The ability of the chief justice to influence the Court has varied considerably. Chief Justice Charles Evans Hughes kept tight control over the Court's deliberations by keeping the justices on the point, moving the discussion along, and doing his best to work out compromises in order to achieve unanimous decisions, which carry greater weight with the public. By contrast, Chief Justice Harlan F. Stone encouraged justices to state their own points of view and let the discussions wander. Chief Justice Warren Burger was not very successful in leading conferences. He devoted much of his time to judicial reform, speaking to bar associations and trying to build political support for modernizing the judicial process. Unlike his predecessors, Rehnquist moved conferences along quickly with a dry sense of humor and concise statements of the cases. However, his main focus was to win a quick decision on each case. It is yet to be seen just how Chief Justice Roberts will lead the court, although he did present himself as a consensus builder in his confirmation hearings.

Which Cases Reach the Supreme Court?

When citizens vow to take their cases to the highest court of the land even if it costs their last penny, they underestimate the difficulty of securing Supreme Court review and misunderstand the Court's role. The rules for appealing a case are established by the Supreme Court and Congress. Until 1988, when Congress enacted the Act to Improve the Administration of Justice, the Supreme Court was obliged by law to review a large number of appeals. Today, however, almost all appeals come to the Court by means of a ***writ of certiorari***, which is a formal petition used to appeal a case to the Court (see Figure 14–4 for a simplified description of the two paths to the Supreme Court).

The writ, which can be denied, produces the Supreme Court's agenda, or **docket**, of potential cases. The docket has grown significantly since the 1970s as more Americans have brought more lawsuits, states have imposed more death sentences, federal regulation has increased, and federal punishment for crimes has become more severe. Once the docket is set, the Supreme Court has maximum discretion to decide the actual cases it will review. Of the 8,588 cases that were filed for review in 2004, for example, the Supreme Court made decisions on just 87. That is half the number of cases decided annually two decades ago (see Figure 14–5).[34]

The crucial factor in determining whether the Supreme Court reviews a case is its importance to the operation of the governmental system as a whole. The Supreme Court will review a case only if the claim involves a substantial question of federal law that has broad public significance—what kinds of affirmative action programs are permissible, whether individuals have a right to doctor-assisted suicide, or under what

writ of certiorari
A formal writ used to bring a case before the Supreme Court.

docket
The list of potential cases that reach the Supreme Court.

conditions women may have abortions. The Court also tends to review cases in which the courts of appeals disagree. Or a case may raise a constitutional issue on which a state supreme court has presented an interpretation with which the Court disagrees.

Supreme Court justices also consider the national interest in deciding whether to recommend a case for further consideration. Justices ask whether they care about the outcome of a case, whether the case can be won on the merits, and whether the case is worth deciding. They also ask:

- Is it constitutionally irresponsible not to take the case?

- Is the case an opportunity to answer a question that must be answered?

- Is there a better case for addressing the question?

- Is the case important?

- Is there a strong reason to resolve the case immediately?

- Is the case a good opportunity to resolve the disagreement?

As the list strongly suggests, the importance of the case is always first and foremost in recommending action.[35]

The Court decides whether to move forward based on the *rule of four*. If four justices are sufficiently interested in a petition for a *writ of certiorari*, it will be granted and the case brought up for review. The justices' law clerks read the petitions and write a memorandum on each, recommending whether a review should be granted. These memos circulate to all the justices except Justice John Paul Stevens, whose law clerks review the petitions for him, and he reads a few of them himself.[36]

Denial of a *writ of certiorari* does not mean that the justices agree with the decision of the lower court, nor does it establish precedent. Refusal to grant a review may indicate all kinds of possibilities. The justices may wish to avoid a political "hot potato," or the Court may be so divided on an issue that it is not yet prepared to take a stand, or it may want to let an issue "percolate" in the federal courts so that the Court

U.S. SUPREME COURT

↑

WRIT OF CERTIORARI

Decisions may be appealed if they raise a constitutional question

STATE SUPREME COURTS

↑

Cases may be appealed to next level

STATE COURTS OF APPEAL

↑

Cases may be appealed to next level

STATE TRIAL COURTS

Cases may be appealed to next level

U.S. CIRCUIT COURTS OF APPEAL

↑

Cases may be appealed to next level

U.S. DISTRICT COURTS

FIGURE **14–4 How Most Cases Rise to the Supreme Court.**

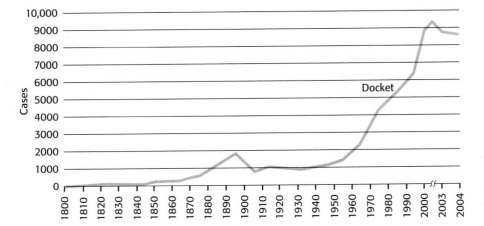

FIGURE **14–5 The Supreme Court Docket.**

SOURCE: David M. O'Brien, *Storm Center: The Supreme Court in American Politics*, 7th ed. (Norton, 2005), figures updated by authors.

How Other Nations Govern

The South African High Court

Lawyers argue a case before South Africa's highest court, the Constitutional Court.

From 1948 to the early 1990s, South Africa engaged in *apartheid,* which separated its citizens by race. Believing that the lack of a constitutional court had created the conditions for apartheid, South Africa created the South African Constitutional Court in 1994. The 11 members of the court sit atop a judicial system that consists of a Supreme Court of Appeal, the High Courts, the Magistrates' Courts, and other courts established by the South African parliament.

Although the Supreme Court of Appeal is ordinarily the last court to hear criminal and civil cases, it is not allowed to make decisions on cases involving the interpretation, protection, or enforcement of the South African constitution. That responsibility belongs solely to the South African Constitutional Court. Like the U.S. Supreme Court and many European constitutional courts, South Africa's constitutional court is the final destination for cases involving civil rights and liberties, as well as the interpretation of parliamentary laws. Also similar to the U.S. Supreme Court and many European constitutional courts, the South African Constitutional Court does not hear evidence questions or decide whether defendants are guilty of crimes.

However, unlike the U.S. Supreme Court, but like many European constitutional courts, South Africa's constitutional court cannot make decisions on the more ordinary criminal or civil cases that move upward from the nation's Magistrates' Courts. These Magistrate Courts resemble U.S. District Courts, but oversee South Africa's municipal (city/county) and provincial courts. As such, the South African judiciary divides into two types of courts—the first is regular, meaning that it handles all ordinary cases all the way up to the Supreme Court of Appeal, while the second is constitutional, which means it only reviews constitutional questions.

The South African Constitutional Court faces many of the same controversial cases that rise to the U.S. Supreme Court. In December 2005, for example, the Court recognized the marriage of two South African women and ordered the parliament a year to extend the same marital rights to all same-sex couples. As a result, South Africa became the first African nation to approve gay and lesbian marriages, and only the fifth nation in the world to make such marriages legal. It is not yet clear whether the parliament will agree, however. Unlike the U.S. Supreme Court, South Africa's Constitutional Court does not yet have the full respect of the legislature, which has ignored several of its most controversial decisions in the past. ∎

may benefit from their rulings before it decides. The Court tends to take cases on which two or more appellate courts have rendered conflicting rulings on an issue, in order to resolve their conflict and to provide uniformity to the law.[37]

After a case is granted review, each side prepares written *briefs* presenting legal arguments, relevant precedents, and historical background for the justices and their law clerks to study and on the basis of which to render their decisions.

The Role of the Law Clerks

Beginning in the 1920s and 1930s, federal judges began hiring the best recent graduates of law schools to serve as clerks for a year or two. As the judicial workload increased, more law clerks have been appointed. Today each Supreme Court justice is entitled to four clerks. These are young people who have graduated from a leading law school and have previously clerked for a federal or state court.

Each justice picks his or her own clerks and works closely with them throughout the term. Clerks screen writs of certiorari and prepare draft opinions for the justices. Some observers and former law clerks claim that the justices now depend too much on their clerks and that the Court is "clerk-driven."[38] As the number of law clerks and computers has increased, so has the number of concurring and dissenting opinions. Today's opinions are longer and have more footnotes and elaborate citations of cases and law review articles. This is the result of the greater number of law clerks and the operation of justices' chambers like "nine little law firms," often practicing law against each other.[39]

The Role of the Solicitor General

Attorneys in the Department of Justice and from other federal agencies participate in more than half of the cases that the Supreme Court agrees to decide and therefore play a crucial role in setting its agenda. As noted earlier in this chapter, the solicitor general is responsible for representing the federal government before the Supreme Court and is sometimes called the "tenth justice." Because the U.S. may not appeal any case upward without the solicitor general's approval, the solicitor general has significant influence in limiting the kinds of cases that the Supreme Court eventually sees.[40]

The solicitor general also files ***amicus curiae*** (Latin for "friend of the court") **briefs** in cases in which the federal government is not a party. The practice of filing *amicus curiae* briefs guarantees that the Department of Justice is represented if a suit questions the constitutionality of an act of Congress or the executive branch. The solicitor general may also use these briefs to bring to the Court's attention the views of the current administration.[41] On occasion, though, solicitors general appear to compromise their independence, as during the administrations of Ronald Reagan and George H. W. Bush, in too aggressively asking the Court to overturn precedents.[42] Still, when the solicitor general appears before the Supreme Court, only respectful formal attire is worn—dark vest, tails, and striped pants. Attire is all part of maintaining respect for the Court, as is the decision not to televise the actual arguments before the Court. The Court has long believed that television would demean the court, and seeks anonymity, not press attention, as part of maintaining a sense of respect surrounding its decisions. (Briefs filed by the solicitor general may be found on the Web at www.usdoj.gov/osg.)

The Role of *Amicus Curiae* Briefs

Individuals, interest groups, and organizations may also file *amicus curiae* briefs if they claim to have an interest in the case and to have information of value to the Court.[43] An *amicus* brief may help the justices by presenting arguments or facts that the parties to the case have not raised. In recent decades, interest groups have increasingly filed such briefs in an effort to influence the Court and to counter the positions of the solicitor general and the government.

In *Webster* v. *Reproductive Health Services,* dealing with a Missouri law regulating abortions and asking the Court to reverse *Roe* v. *Wade,* 78 *amicus* briefs were filed.[44] In *United States* v. *Lopez,* which challenged congressional authority to ban guns in and around schools, more than 40 parties filed a dozen *amicus* briefs. Ohio, New York, and the District of Columbia argued in favor of federal power, as did associations of police and school officials. On the other side were some conservative public interest firms, the National Governors Association, and the National League of Cities.[45]

Interest groups once filed *amicus curiae* briefs before the Supreme Court granted a *writ of certiorari,* in order to encourage the Supreme Court to review the case. Their doing so enhanced the probability that the Court would take the case for review but had almost no influence on how the case was decided.[46] More typically, these briefs are filed after the Court has granted a case review to urge the Court to reach a particular decision.

***amicus curiae* brief**
Literally, a "friend of the court" brief, filed by an individual or organization to present arguments in addition to those presented by the immediate parties to a case.

The Role of Oral Arguments

Once the justices receive printed briefs from each side, a case is set for oral arguments—usually in three to four months. Lengthy oratory before the Supreme Court, once lasting for several days, is a thing of the past. As a rule, counsel for each side is now allowed only 30 minutes. Lawyers use a lectern with two lights: A white light flashes five minutes before time is up. When the red light goes on, the lawyer must stop, even in the middle of a sentence.

The entire procedure is informally formal. Sometimes, to the annoyance of attorneys, justices talk among themselves or consult briefs or books during oral arguments. Other times, if justices find a presentation particularly bad, they will tell the attorneys so. Justices freely interrupt the lawyers to ask questions and request additional information. In recent years, "the justices seem barely able to contain themselves, often interrupting the answer to one question with another query."[47] Hence the 30-minute limit is problematic, especially when the solicitor general participates, since his ten minutes come out of the time of the two parties before the Court.

If a lawyer is having a difficult time, the justices may try to help out with a question. Occasionally, justices bounce arguments off a hapless attorney and at one another. Justice Antonin Scalia is a harsh questioner. "When Scalia prepares to ask a question, he doesn't just adjust himself in his chair to get closer to the microphone like the others; he looks like a vulture, zooming in for the kill. He strains way forward, pinches his eyebrows, and poses the question, like '. . . do you want us to believe?' "[48] Justice Ruth Bader Ginsburg is a particularly persistent questioner, frequently rivaling Scalia, while Justice Clarence Thomas almost never asks a question at all. (Oral arguments in landmark cases may be listened to on the Web by going to www.oyez.org.)

Behind the Curtains: The Conference

On Wednesday afternoons and Fridays, the justices meet in private conference. They have heard the oral arguments and studied the briefs. Each brings to the meeting a book in which the cases and the votes of the justices are recorded. These conferences are held in secret. They are usually a collegial but vigorous give-and-take.

The chief justice presides, usually opening the discussion by stating the facts, summarizing the questions of law, and suggesting how to dispose of each case. Each justice, in order of seniority, then gives his or her views and conclusions. Recently, the justices have not bothered with casting formal votes because their votes are clear from their discussion of the case.[49]

"[Dissenting opinions are] an appeal to the brooding spirit of the law, to the intelligence of a later day."

FORMER CHIEF JUSTICE CHARLES EVANS HUGHES

Opinions

The Supreme Court announces and explains its decisions in **opinions of the Court**. Opinions generally state the facts, present the issues, and explain the reasoning of the Court. These opinions are the Court's principal method of expressing its views to the world. Their primary function is to instruct judges of state and federal courts how to decide similar cases in the future.

One justice delivers the opinions of the Court, but the opinions do not reflect his or her thinking alone. They must explain the reasoning of the majority of the justices. Consequently, opinions of the Court are negotiated documents that require the author to compromise and at times bargain with other justices to attain agreement on an opinion.[50]

Judicial opinions may also be directed at Congress or at the president. If the Court regrets that "in the absence of action by Congress, we have no choice but to . . ." or insists that "relief of the sort that petitioner demands can come only from the political branches of government," it is asking Congress to act.[51] Justices also use opinions to communicate with the public. A well-crafted opinion may increase support for a policy the Court favors.

opinion of the Court
An explanation of a decision of the Supreme Court or any other appellate court.

History Makers

Justice Sandra Day O'Connor

Sandra Day O'Connor was nominated to the Supreme Court by Republican President Ronald Reagan in 1981, confirmed by the Senate on a 99 to 0 vote, and became the first woman to serve on the high bench. She was born in El Paso, Texas, grew up on a cattle ranch in Arizona, and graduated at the top of her class at Stanford Law School in the early 1950s.

Despite her academic achievements, she could not find a job with any law firm in California, and eventually took a post as deputy county attorney in San Mateo County, California. In time, she moved back to Arizona, was elected to the Arizona state legislature, and was appointed to the Arizona Court of Appeals, where she served until her Supreme Court appointment. Almost a quarter of a century later, *Forbes* magazine listed her as the fourth most powerful woman in the world.

As a Supreme Court Justice, O'Connor was conservative but less hard-line than the other Reagan appointees. She cast the deciding vote on controversial issues such as abortion, affirmative action, minority-majority voting districts, and some disputes involving the separation of church and state. She was also a central voice in cases involving federal–state relations.

However, O'Connor was also a moderating force on controversial issues. During her 24 terms on the Court, O'Connor was often the swing, or deciding, vote on many cases, often creating a 5-to-4 majority in favor of one decision or against another. In 2002, she cast the deciding vote both in favor of the University of Michigan's program for giving disadvantaged minority students special preference in the admissions process, and in favor of abortion rights. Just

before she left the court, she cast the deciding vote upholding the constitutionality of campaign finance reform.

O'Connor was also known as one of the most interesting of the Supreme Court justices. She never gave up her love of horses, battled breast cancer early in her Supreme Court career, and became a role model for many women. She was personable, had a good sense of humor, and managed to find consensus on most issues. She approached each case carefully, avoiding decisions that might "paint her into a corner" on future decisions, but was often criticized by conservatives for not taking a stronger position against abortion. ∎

Justice Sandra Day O'Connor

ASSIGNING OPINIONS   When voting with the majority, the chief justice decides who will draft the opinion of the Court. When the chief justice is in the minority, the senior justice among the majority makes the assignment. The justice assigned to write the opinion must give persuasive reasons for the outcome, for no vote in conference is final until the opinion of the Court has been agreed to. Justices are free to change their minds if not persuaded by draft opinions.

A justice is free to write a **dissenting opinion** if desired. Dissenting opinions are, in Chief Justice Charles Evans Hughes's words, "an appeal to the brooding spirit of the law, to the intelligence of a later day."[52] Dissenting opinions are quite common, as justices hope that someday these dissenting opinions will command a majority of the Court. If a justice agrees with the majority on how the case should be decided but differs on the reasoning, that justice may write a **concurring opinion**.

CIRCULATING DRAFTS   Writing the opinion of the Court is an exacting task. The document must win the support of at least four—and more, if possible—intelligent, strong-willed persons. Assisted by the law clerks, the assigned justice writes a draft and sends

dissenting opinion
An opinion disagreeing with the majority in a Supreme Court ruling.

concurring opinion
An opinion that agrees with the majority in a Supreme Court ruling but differs on the reasoning.

it to colleagues for comments. If the justice is lucky, the majority will accept the draft, perhaps with only minor changes. If the draft is not satisfactory to the other justices, it must be rewritten and recirculated until a majority reaches agreement.

The two weapons justices can use against their colleagues are their votes and the threat of writing dissenting opinions attacking the majority's opinion. Especially if the Court is closely divided, one justice may be in a position to demand that a certain point or argument be included in, or removed from, the opinion of the Court as the price of his or her vote. Sometimes such bargaining occurs even though the Court is not closely divided. An opinion writer who anticipates that a decision will invite critical public reaction may want a unanimous Court and will therefore compromise to achieve unanimity. For this reason, the Court delayed declaring school segregation unconstitutional, in *Brown* v. *Board of Education,* until unanimity was secured.[53] The justices understood that any sign of dissension on the bench on this major social issue would be an invitation to evade the Court's ruling.

RELEASING OPINIONS TO THE PUBLIC   In the past, justices read their entire opinions from the bench on "opinion days." Now they give only brief summaries of the decision and their opinions. Copies are immediately made available to reporters and the public and published in the official *United States Supreme Court Reports.* Since April 2000, the Court has made its opinions immediately available on its Web site (www.supreme-courtus.gov).

After the Court Decides

Victory in the Supreme Court does not necessarily mean that winning parties get what they want. Although the Court resolves many issues, it also sometimes *remands* the case, sending it back to the lower court with instructions to act in accordance with its opinion. The lower court often has considerable leeway in interpreting the Court's mandate as it disposes of the case.

The impact of a particular Supreme Court ruling on the behavior of individuals who are not immediate parties to a lawsuit is more uncertain. The most important rulings require a change in the behavior of thousands of administrative and elected officials. Sometimes Supreme Court pronouncements are simply ignored. For example, despite the Court's holding that it is unconstitutional for school boards to require students to pray within a school, some schools continue this practice.[54] And for years after the Supreme Court held public school segregation unconstitutional, many school districts remained segregated.[55]

The most difficult Supreme Court decisions to implement are those that require the cooperation of large numbers of officials. For example, a Supreme Court decision announcing a new standard for property searches is not likely to have an impact on the way police make arrests for some time, since not many police officers subscribe to *United States Supreme Court Reports.* The process is more complex. Local prosecutors, state attorneys general, chiefs of police, and state and federal trial court judges must all participate to give meaning to Supreme Court decisions. The Constitution may be what the Supreme Court says it is, but a Supreme Court opinion, for the moment at least, is what a trial judge or police officer or prosecutor or school board or city council says it is.

Judicial Power in a Constitutional Democracy

An independent judiciary is one of the hallmarks of a constitutional democracy and a free society. As impartial dispensers of equal justice under the law, judges should not be dependent on the executive, the legislature, parties to a case, or the electorate. But judicial independence is often criticized when judges make unpopular decisions. Perhaps in no other society do the people resort to litigation as a means

Government's Greatest Endeavors

Reducing Crime

QUESTIONS

Should the federal government be involved at all in state and local crime control?

What happens to state and local crime control efforts, such as hiring 100,000 police officers, when the federal money runs out?

The Reverend Jesse Jackson is a strong supporter of gun control.

State and local governments are responsible for enforcing most laws against criminal activities such as murder, rape, and theft. However, the federal government provides money to help them do so, and it also enforces federal drug laws and gun controls. It has also helped fund larger police forces and imposed tougher sentences against federal crimes such as kidnapping and terrorism.

The federal government's biggest investment has been in providing money to help states control both street crimes and organized crime by the Mafia and other criminal organizations. In 1968, for example, Congress passed the Crime Control and Safe Streets Act, which gave millions of dollars to the states to increase their police forces and patrol the streets. The law also raised the minimum age for purchasing a handgun to 21 years of age.

The 1968 law set an important precedent for federal involvement in state and local crime control, which led to further controls on handguns and a new Crime Control and Safe Streets Act in 1994. Under the new law, the federal government gave states even more money to hire 100,000 new police officers and banned 19 types of assault weapons, such as the M-16 and AK-47, which are rapid-firing rifles often used by the military. The law also banned hate crimes such as painting Nazi slogans and swastikas on Jewish synagogues.

In part because of increased state and local action, national crime rates have fallen dramatically over the past quarter-century, particularly in large urban settings such as New York City. Although violent crimes fell through the 1990s and early 2000s, recent statistics show a troubling increase in the number of murders, rapes, armed roberies, and assaults between 2005 and 2006. The increase will require more federal, state, and local government action to make sure the rates go down again. ∎

---

of making public policy as much as they do in the United States. For example, the National Association for the Advancement of Colored People (NAACP) turned to litigation to get relief from segregation practices in the 1930s, 1940s, and 1950s. More recently, an increasing number of women's organizations, environmental groups, and religious and conservative organizations have also turned to the courts.[56]

The involvement of courts in politics exposes the judiciary to political criticism. Throughout our history, the Supreme Court has been attacked for engaging in "judicial legislation." This is nothing new. Yet the active role of the federal courts on behalf of both liberal and conservative causes since 1937 and Republican efforts to enforce strict constructionism have returned these issues to the forefront of public debate. So did the Supreme Court's decision that resolved the 2000 election impasse, which gave the presidency to George W. Bush.

Whereas in earlier times judges occasionally told public officials what they could *not* do, today they often tell them what they *must* do. For example, federal judges, responding to class action complaints, have told Congress, state legislatures, and local officials that they must provide attorneys for the poor, ensure adequate care for mental patients, modernize prisons, and even break up the telephone system. Often judges retain jurisdiction for years as they preside over the implementation of the decrees they have issued.[57] Judges have always been policy makers; that role is not a matter of choice but flows from the roles they play in deciding cases.

The Great Debate over the Proper Role of the Courts

Whether judges are liberal or conservative, defer to legislatures or not, try to apply the Constitution as they think the framers intended or interpret it to conform to current values, there are linkages between what judges do and what the people want done. The linkages are not direct, and the people never speak with one mind, but these linkages are the heart of the matter.[60] In the first place, the president and the Senate are likely to appoint justices whose decisions reflect their values. Therefore, elections matter, because the views of the people who nominate and confirm the judges are reflected in the composition of the courts. For instance, in 1992, the Supreme Court, by a 5-to-4 vote in *Planned Parenthood* v. *Casey,* refused to overturn *Roe* v. *Wade* and upheld its core holding—that the Constitution protects the right of a woman to an abortion—although upholding state regulations that do not "unduly burden" that right.[61] This close vote on abortion made it clear that presidential elections could determine whether that right would continue to be protected.

The 2004 election results had an almost immediate impact when Chief Justice Rehnquist died and Justice O'Connor retired, and George W. Bush replaced both by conservatives. Although Rehnquist had already ruled against abortion, O'Connor had been a swing vote in favor. With her replacement, Samuel Alito, almost certain to vote against abortion, the court may yet overturn *Roe* v. *Wade*.

Scholars debate how public opinion influences what judges decide, whether it is direct or indirect through presidential selection and Senate confirmation of judges, but there is little question that there is a correlation between public opinion and judicial decisions.[62] Judicial opinions that reflect what the people want tend to survive. When a new political coalition takes over the White House or Congress, the old regime may stay on in the federal courts. New electoral coalitions eventually take over the federal courts, and before long, new interpretations of the Constitution reflect the dominant political ideology.[63]

Judges have neither armies nor police to execute their rulings. Although Congress cannot reverse Supreme Court decisions through legislation, and only six Supreme Court decisions have been reversed by formal constitutional amendment, the political system alters judicial policy in more subtle ways. Decisions are binding on the parties to a particular case, but the policies that result from judicial decisions are effective and durable only if the electorate supports them. To win a favorable Supreme Court decision is to win something of considerable political value.

"American courts are not all-powerful institutions."[64] If the Court's policies are too far out of step with the values of the country, the Court is likely to be criticized. In former Chief Justice William H. Rehnquist's words, "No judge worthy of his salt would ever cast his vote in a particular case simply because he thought the majority of the public wanted him to vote that way, but that is quite a different thing from saying that no judge is ever influenced by the great tides of public opinion that run a country such as ours."[65]

"The people" speak in many ways and with many voices. The Supreme Court also hands down rulings on controversies—abortion rights, affirmative action, and the rights of homosexuals—on which the public is deeply divided. And the justices are often likewise split in deciding those cases. The Supreme Court—and the other courts—thus generally represent and reflect the competing values of the people. Whether they agree or disagree with particular rulings, the public generally holds the Supreme Court in high regard. Notably, the Court's public approval rating remained high and virtually unchanged after its controversial decision in *Bush* v. *Gore* (2000), contrary to predictions by the four dissenting justices and critics that the Court's reputation would be badly damaged by the bare majority's ruling assuring George W. Bush's election.[66]

"No judge worthy of his salt would ever cast his vote in a particular case simply because he thought the majority of the public wanted him to vote that way. . . ."

FORMER CHIEF JUSTICE WILLIAM H. REHNQUIST

Agents of Change

Karen Tse and International Bridges to Justice

International Bridges to Justice (IBJ) was created in 2000 to help improve access to justice for citizens of Asian countries. Working with the governments of Cambodia, China, and Vietnam, IBJ is establishing legal aid networks that give individual citizens the advice and counsel they need to enter the judicial system. IBJ believes that independent judiciaries are a cornerstone of safe and stable societies, but also believes that such systems are of little value unless all citizens have access. According to IBJ, its mission is to guarantee all citizens the right to competent legal representation, the right to be protected from cruel and unusual punishment, and the right to a fair trial.

IBJ was founded by Karen Tse, whose parents immigrated to the United States from Hong Kong in search of more opportunity. Tse was born in 1964, lived in public housing in Cleveland for much of her childhood, and transformed the Asian Students Association at Scripps College from a social club into a strong advocacy organization on Asian issues. She attended law school at UCLA and worked for the San Francisco public defenders office. As she remembers, her decision to create IBJ reflected an initial contact with a 12-year-old boy held in a Cambodian prison with no lawyer to defend him and no trial date to determine his guilt or innocence for a crime that had yet to be determined. "Perhaps ten years ago, there might have been precious little that we could have done for this boy," she wrote in 2000. "Citizens like him were unimportant to the government and the denial of their basic rights had now less to do with present government policy and more to do with vestiges of a legal system that formerly tolerated and even condoned this denial of rights."

IBJ works with existing legal aid societies in Asia to expand access to help, provide training for new public defenders, and create strong advocacy groups that will push for greater access to justice. Tse's ultimate goal is an international coalition of groups that will advance reform across Asia. ■

Learn more about IBJ at www.ibj.org.

Karen Tse

Questions

How does International Bridges to Justice help create a legal system similar to that in the United States?

Why are public defenders so important to a fair judiciary?

Although the Court is not the defenseless institution portrayed by some commentators, and its decisions are as much shapers of public opinion as reflections of it, ultimately the power of the Supreme Court in a constitutional democracy rests on retaining the support of most of the people most of the time. The Court's power rests, as former Chief Justice Edward White observed, "solely upon the approval of a free people."[67] No better standard for determining the legitimacy of a governmental institution has been discovered.

Summary

1. The federal judiciary was designed as a powerful check on Congress and the presidency. Although Article III is the shortest article in the Constitution, it established the Supreme Court and provided a short list of cases that the Court could address. The federal judicial system was expanded under Congress's Article I power to create lower courts.

2. The American judicial process has five major characteristics: (1) it is an adversary system, in which disputes must have two sides, (2) the system is both passive and reactive, (3) individuals who bring a lawsuit must have standing to sue, (4) judges decide cases and cannot invent opportunities to decide, (5) the courts cannot make certain deci-sions—although they do interpret the laws, they do not settle issues that are expressly reserved for Congress and/or the president.

3. There are three levels of federal courts: (1) district courts, which hear original trials, (2) circuit courts of appeal, which can only review the process by which district courts made their decisions, and (3) the

Supreme Court, which makes the final decision. The caseload for this three-tiered judicial system has been rising over the past 30 years.

4. The Supreme Court has almost complete control over the cases it chooses to review as they come up from the state courts, the courts of appeals, and district courts. Law clerks and the solicitor general play important roles in determining the kinds of cases the Supreme Court agrees to decide. Its nine justices dispose of thousands of cases, but most of their time is concentrated on the fewer than 100 cases per year that they accept for review. The Court's decisions and opinions establish guidelines for lower courts and the country.

5. Partisanship and ideology are important factors in the selection of all federal judges, and these factors ensure a linkage between the courts and the rest of the political system, so that the views of the people are reflected, even if indirectly, in the work of courts. In recent decades, candidates for the presidency and the Senate have made judicial appointments an issue in their election campaigns. The president's judicial nominees must be confirmed by the Senate, where nominations are often delayed by philosophical and political disagreements.

6. The judiciary is limited in its ability to make decisions by precedents set by past courts, congressional and presidential restrictions on both the number and geographical location of the courts, and by continuing philosophical controversies about whether judges should make law.

7. The debate about how judges should interpret the Constitution is almost as old as the Republic. Almost 220 years after the Constitution was adopted, the argument between those who contend that judges should interpret the document literally and those who believe they cannot and should not remains in the headlines. Both liberals and conservatives have attacked judicial activism and urged judicial restraint.

Further **Reading**

HENRY J. ABRAHAM, *Justices, Presidents, and Senators: A History of U.S. Supreme Court Appointments from Washington to Clinton* (Rowman & Littlefield, 1999).

ROBERT A. CARP AND **RONALD STIDHAM,** *The Federal Courts* (CQ Press, 2001).

CORNELL CLAYTON AND **HOWARD GILMAN,** EDS., *Supreme Court Decision Making: New Institutionalist Approaches* (University of Chicago Press, 1999).

CLARE CUSHMAN, *The Supreme Court Justices: Illustrated Biographies, 1789–1995,* 2d ed. (CQ Press, 1996).

DEL DICKSON, *The Supreme Court in Conference, 1940–1995* (Oxford University Press, 2001).

LEE A. EPSTEIN AND **JEFFREY A. SEGAL,** *Advice and Consent: The Politics of Judicial Appointments* (Oxford, 2005).

LEE A. EPSTEIN, JEFFREY A. SEGAL, HAROLD SPAETH, AND **THOMAS WALKER,** EDS., *The Supreme Court Compendium,* 2d ed. (CQ Press, 2001).

HOWARD GILLMAN, *The Votes That Counted: How the Court Decided the 2000 Presidential Election* (University of Chicago Press, 2001).

SHELDON GOLDMAN, *Picking Federal Judges: Lower Court Selection from Roosevelt Through Reagan* (Yale University Press, 1997).

KERMIT L. HALL, ED., *The Oxford Companion to the Supreme Court of the United States* (Oxford University Press, 1992).

PETER IRONS, *A People's History of the Supreme Court* (Viking, 1999).

RANDOLPH JONAKAIT, *The American Jury System* (Yale University Press, 2003).

DAVID KLEIN, *Making Law in the U.S. Courts of Appeals* (Cambridge University Press, 2002).

LISA KLOPPENBERG, *Playing It Safe: How the Supreme Court Sidesteps Hard Cases and Stunts the Development of the Law* (New York University Press, 2001).

FOREST MALTZMAN, JAMES F. SPRIGGS II, AND **PAUL J. WAHLBECK,** *Crafting Law on the Supreme Court: The Collegial Game* (Cambridge, 2000).

ROBERT G. MCCLOSKEY, *The American Supreme Court,* 3d ed. (University of Chicago Press, 2001).

DAVID M. O'BRIEN, ED., *Judges on Judging: Views from the Bench,* 2d ed. (CQ Press, 2004).

DAVID M. O'BRIEN, *Storm Center: The Supreme Court in American Politics,* 7th ed. (Norton, 2005).

J. W. PELTASON, *Federal Courts in the Political Process* (Doubleday, 1955).

TERRI JENNINGS PERETTI, *In Defense of a Political Court* (Princeton University Press, 1999).

GERALD N. ROSENBERG, *The Hollow Hope: Can Courts Bring About Social Change?* University of Chicago Press, 1991).

C. K. ROWLAND AND **ROBERT A. CARP,** *Politics and Judgment in Federal District Courts* (University Press of Kansas, 1996).

PETER RUSSELL AND **DAVID M. O'BRIEN,** EDS., *Judicial Independence in the Age of Democracy: Critical Perspectives from Around the World* (University Press of Virginia, 2001).

ELLIOT E. SLOTNICK, *Judicial Politics: Readings from Judicature,* 3d ed. (American Judicature Society, 2005).

DONALD R. SONGER AND **SUSAN B. HAIRE,** *Continuity and Change on the United States Courts of Appeals* (University of Michigan Press, 2000).

Key Terms

judicial review, p. 409

adversary system, p. 409

criminal law, p. 409

civil law, p. 409

justiciable dispute, p. 409

defendant, p. 410

plea bargain, p. 410

public defender system, p. 410

original jurisdiction, p. 411

appellate jurisdiction, p. 411

court of appeals, p. 411

precedent, p. 411

writ of *habeas corpus*, p. 412

senatorial courtesy, p. 415

judicial restraint, p. 419

judicial activism, p. 419

stare decisis, p. 420

writ of *certiorari*, p. 424

docket, p. 424

amicus curiae brief, p. 427

opinion of the Court, p. 428

dissenting opinion, p. 429

concurring opinion, p. 429

Make It Real

THE JUDICIARY

This module allows students to become Supreme Court Justices.

Illegal Immigrant Workers

ORIGINALLY AIRED: 12/14/04

PROGRAM: **Nightline**

RUNNING TIME: 15:22

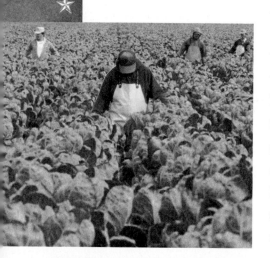

WHEN BERNARD KERIK, PRESIDENT BUSH'S FIRST CHOICE TO RUN the Department of

Homeland Security, withdrew his nomination because of a nanny who was an undocumented worker that he hired and failed to pay taxes on, it was a story that probably sounded familiar. Cabinet nominees have been tripped up on this issue before in both the Clinton and Bush administrations. So the question is, why does this keep happening?

One of the reasons it keeps happening is that it is pretty easy to get by hiring undocumented workers. It seems that the only way to get tripped up is if you undergo a background check for an important government post. You would be hard pressed to find any aspect of the nation's economy where undocumented workers are not making a contribution. It could be in the service industry or the construction business. You will eat something today that has been brought to you as a result of the labor of illegal immigrants working here. A conservative estimate is that at least 50 percent of agricultural laborers are undocumented workers. So is this a result of American employers being cheap or is it a result of the efficiency of market forces? Many employers say it is not easy to find Americans willing to do a lot of the low-paying, menial, and tedious tasks that immigrants are willing to do. Labor advocates say that illegal immigrants depress the wage market so Americans are shut out of these jobs. Everyone can find statistics to back their argument.

So what is the solution? When the president announced a proposal earlier this year to grant legal status to millions of undocumented workers in the United States, it wasn't greeted with unanimous enthusiasm. "Out of common sense and fairness, our laws should allow willing workers to enter our country and fill jobs that Americans are not filling" the president said. He wasn't calling for amnesty but a temporary guest worker program. But will that satisfy both sides? Michel Martin examines the arguments advanced on something that has always been a hot-button issue. We also speak with Senator John McCain of Arizona. His state has addressed the illegal immigration issue by voting for a sweeping proposition that bans all government services to illegal immigrants. He says that this is an issue that the nation has to wake up to and start dealing with as a high priority.

Critical Thinking Questions

After viewing "ILLEGAL IMMIGRANT WORKERS" *on your* ABCNEWS DVD *answer the following questions.*

1. **WHY AREN'T IMMIGRATION LAWS** more strictly enforced?

2. **EXPLAIN THE "GEOGRAPHIC"** component to immigration law enforcement.

3. **THE INABILITY TO BAR ILLEGAL ALIENS** from entering the country is not a question of power. Rather, the problems are political and practical. Briefly explain what this means.

437

Chapter 15

First Amendment Freedoms

★

IN ONE SENTENCE, OUR CONSTITUTION LAYS DOWN THE FUNDAMENTAL PRINCIPLES OF A FREE SOCIETY: FREEDOM OF CONSCIENCE AND FREEDOM OF EXPRESSION. THE FIRST AMENDMENT DECLARES, "CONGRESS SHALL MAKE NO LAW RESPECTING AN ESTABLISHMENT OF RELIGION, OR PROHIBITING THE FREE EXERCISE THEREOF, OR ABRIDGING THE FREEDOM OF SPEECH, OR OF THE PRESS, OR THE RIGHT OF THE PEOPLE PEACEABLY TO ASSEMBLE, AND TO PETITION THE GOVERNMENT FOR A REDRESS OF GRIEVANCES." THESE freedoms are essential to our individual self-determination and to our collective self-governance—to government by the people. Yet they have also been vulnerable during times of war and, many would argue, are now because of recent security measures put into place to combat international terrorism.[1]

These freedoms were not constitutionally guaranteed, though, until the addition in 1791 of the first ten amendments to the Constitution, the Bill of Rights. For that reason, we begin this chapter by discussing the rights in the original Constitution and in the Bill of Rights as applied to both the national and state governments before turning to the "first freedoms" of religion, speech, press, and assembly. Before doing so, though, it may be helpful to clarify certain terms—*liberties, freedoms, rights,* and *privileges*—that are often used interchangeably when discussing rights and freedoms. We offer these definitions. *Civil liberties* are the constitutionally protected freedoms of all persons against governmental restraint: the freedoms of conscience, religion, and expression, for example, which are secured by the First Amendment. The due process and equal protection clauses of the Fifth and Fourteenth Amendments also protect these civil liberties. *Civil rights* are the constitutional rights of all persons, not just citizens, to due process and the equal protection of the laws: the constitutional right not to be discriminated against by governments because of race, ethnic background, religion, or gender. These civil rights are protected by the due process and equal protection clauses of the Fifth and Fourteenth Amendments and by the civil rights laws of national and state governments. They are discussed further in Chapters 16 and 17. *Legal privileges* are granted by governments and these privileges may be subject to conditions or restrictions; for example, the right to welfare benefits or to a driver's license.

Rights in the Original Constitution

Even though most of the framers did not think a bill of rights was necessary, they considered certain rights important enough to spell them out in the Constitution (see Table 15–1). These rights included the writ of *habeas corpus* and protection against *ex post facto* laws and bills of attainder. These guarantees were secured because of the framers' experiences with the abuses of the English Crown.

Foremost among constitutional rights is the **writ of *habeas corpus*.** Literally meaning "produce the body" in Latin, this writ is a court order directing any

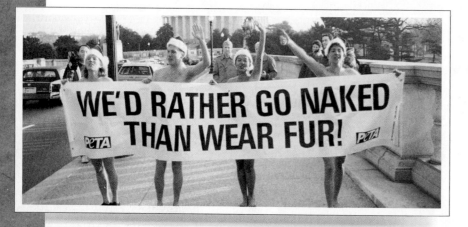

"One man's vulgarity is another man's lyric."

JUSTICE JOHN MARSHALL HARLAN

TABLE 15–1 Rights in the Original Constitution

1. *Habeas corpus*
2. No bills of attainder
3. No *ex post facto* laws
4. No titles of nobility
5. Trial by jury in national courts
6. Protection for citizens as they move from one state to another, including the right to travel
7. Protection against using the crime of treason to restrict other activities; limitation on punishment for treason
8. Guarantee that each state has a republican form of government
9. No religious test oaths as a condition for holding a federal office
10. Protection against the impairment of contracts

official holding a person in custody to produce the prisoner in court and explain why the prisoner is being held. As originally used in England, the writ was merely a judicial inquiry to determine whether a court had the proper jurisdiction to hold a person in custody. But over the years, it developed into a remedy for any illegal confinement. People who are incarcerated may appeal to a judge, usually through an attorney, stating why they believe they are being held unlawfully and should be released. The judge then orders the jailer or a lower court to show cause of why the writ should not be issued. If a judge finds a petitioner is detained unlawfully, the judge may order the prisoner's immediate release. Although state judges lack jurisdiction to issue writs of *habeas corpus* to find out why federal authorities are holding persons, federal district judges may issue writs to find out if state and local officials are holding people in violation of the Constitution or national laws.

In recent years, the use of the writ of *habeas corpus* by federal courts to review convictions by state courts has been widely criticized. Some people believe that state prisoners have abused the writ to get an endless and expensive round of reviews, which sometimes lead a federal judge to set aside their convictions even after two or more state courts have upheld them. Partly because of concerns about maintaining the principles of federalism and partly because of the growing caseloads of federal courts, the Supreme Court and Congress have restricted federal judges' *habeas corpus* jurisdiction. The Antiterrorism and Effective Death Penalty Act of 1996, for example, restricts the number of times a person may be granted a *habeas corpus* review, stops appeals for most habeas petitions at the level of the U.S. Court of Appeals, and requires federal judges to defer to the decisions of state judges unless those decisions are clearly "unreasonable."[2]

The Supreme Court nonetheless underscored the fundamental nature of the right to a writ of *habeas corpus* in two decisions rejecting the position of President George W. Bush's administration that it could hold indefinitely foreign nationals and U.S. citizens deemed "enemy combatants" in its war against terrorism. The Court held that detainees have a right to have an independent tribunal review why they are being held.[3] Subsequently, in *Hamdan* v. *Rumsfeld* (2006),[4] the Court rebuffed the Bush administration's position that it could try enemy combatants by military commissions, rather than in civilian courts or in courts martial, and that it could ignore the Geneva Conventions that specify that the accused has a right to see and hear the evidence for alleged crimes.

An *ex post facto* **law** is a retroactive criminal law making a particular act a crime that was not a crime when an individual committed it, increasing punishment for a crime after the crime was committed, lessening the proof necessary to convict for a crime after it was committed, or permitting prosecutions for crimes that statutes of limitations had barred from prosecution.[5] This prohibition does not prevent the retroactive application of laws that work to the benefit of an accused person—a law

writ of *habeas corpus*
Court order requiring explanation to a judge why a prisoner is being held in custody.

***ex post facto* law**
Retroactive criminal law that works to the disadvantage of a person.

decreasing punishment, for example—or the retroactive application of civil law, such as an increase in income tax rates applied to income already earned.

Bills of attainder are legislative acts inflicting punishment, including deprivation of property, on named individuals or members of a specified group without a trial. For example, when Congress adopted a rider to an appropriations bill in 1946 denying payment of the salaries of three federal employees for "disloyalty," the Supreme Court struck down the rider for being a bill of attainder.[6]

The Bill of Rights and the States

Although the framers wrote the Constitution, in a sense the American people drafted our basic charter of rights. The Constitution drawn up in Philadelphia included guarantees of a few basic rights but lacked a specific bill of rights similar to those in most state constitutions. The Federalists argued that the Constitution established a limited government that would not threaten individual freedoms, and therefore a bill of rights was unnecessary. The Antifederalists were not persuaded, and the omission of a bill of rights aroused widespread suspicion. (See Chapter 1.) To persuade delegates to the state ratification conventions to vote for the Constitution, the Federalists promised to correct this deficiency. In its first session, the new Congress made good on that promise by proposing 12 amendments, ten of which were promptly ratified by the states and became part of the Constitution.[7]

The guarantees of the Bill of Rights originally applied *only to the national government,* not to state governments.[8] Why not to the states? The framers were confident that citizens could control their own state officials, and most state constitutions already had bills of rights. It was the new and distant central government the people feared. As it turned out, those fears were largely misdirected. The national government has generally shown less tendency to curtail civil liberties than state and local governments have.

When the Fourteenth Amendment, which explicitly applies to the states, was adopted in 1868, supporters contended that its **due process clause**—which declares that no person shall be deprived by a state of life, liberty, or property without due

bill of attainder
Legislative act inflicting punishment, including deprivation of property, without a trial, on named individuals or members of a specific group.

due process clause
Clause in the Fifth Amendment limiting the power of the national government; similar clause in the Fourteenth Amendment prohibiting state governments from depriving any person of life, liberty, or property without due process of law.

The freedoms protected by the First Amendment, such as the freedom of religion and the separation of religion and government, sometimes clash in the opinion of citizens. Here supporters of allowing public displays of the Ten Commandments on government property protest in front of the Supreme Court.

process of law—limits states in precisely the same way the Bill of Rights limits the national government. But for decades, the Supreme Court refused to interpret the Fourteenth Amendment in this way. Then in *Gitlow* v. *New York* (1925), the Court announced that it assumed "that freedom of speech and of the press—which are protected by the First Amendment from abridgment by Congress—are among the fundamental personal rights and 'liberties' protected by the due process clause of the Fourteenth Amendment from impairment by the States."[9]

Gitlow v. *New York* was a revolutionary decision. For the first time, the U.S. Constitution protected freedom of speech from abridgment by state and local governments. In the 1930s and continuing at an accelerated pace during the 1960s, through the **selective incorporation** of provision after provision of the Bill of Rights into the due process clause, the Supreme Court applied the most important of these rights to the states.[10] Today the Fourteenth Amendment imposes on the states all the provisions of the Bill of Rights except those of the Second and Third Amendments, the Fifth Amendment provision for indictment by a grand jury, the Seventh Amendment right to a jury trial in civil cases, and the Ninth and Tenth Amendments (see Table 15–2).

Selective incorporation of most provisions of the Bill of Rights into the Fourteenth Amendment is probably the most significant constitutional development that has occurred since the Constitution was written. It has profoundly altered the relationship between the national government and the states. It has made the federal courts, under the guidance of the Supreme Court, the most important protectors of our liberties.

Recently, however, there has been renewed interest in state constitutions as independent sources of additional protections for civil liberties and civil rights.[11] Advocates of what has come to be called the *new judicial federalism* contend that the U.S. Constitution should set minimum but not maximum standards for protecting our rights. State bills of rights sometimes provide more protection of rights—the rights to equal education and personal privacy, for instance—than the national Bill of Rights or the

selective incorporation

The process by which provisions of the Bill of Rights are brought within the scope of the Fourteenth Amendment and so applied to state and local governments.

TABLE 15–2 Selective Incorporation and the Application of the Bill of Rights to the States

Right	Amendment	Year
Public use and just compensation for the taking of private property by the government	5	1897
Freedom of speech	1	1925
Freedom of the press	1	1931
Fair trial	6	1932
Freedom of religion	1	1934
Freedom of assembly	1	1937
Free exercise of religion	1	1940
Separation of religion and government	1	1947
Right to a public trial	6	1948
Right against unreasonable searches and seizures	4	1949
Freedom of association	1	1958
Exclusionary rule	4	1961
Ban against cruel and unusual punishment	8	1962
Right to counsel in felony cases	6	1963
Right against self-incrimination	5	1964
Right to confront witness	6	1965
Right of privacy	1, 3, 4, 5, 9	1965
Right to an impartial jury	6	1966
Right to a speedy trial and compulsory process for obtaining witnesses	6	1967
Right to a jury trial in nonpetty cases	6	1968
Protection against double jeopardy	5	1969

Supreme Court's rulings on its guarantees. Despite the revival of interest in state bills of rights, the U.S. Supreme Court and the national Bill of Rights remain the dominant protectors of civil liberties and civil rights.

Freedom of Religion

The first words of the First Amendment are emphatic and brief: "Congress shall make no law respecting an establishment of religion, or prohibiting the free exercise thereof." Note that there are *two* religion clauses: the *establishment* clause and the *exercise* clause. The Supreme Court has struggled to reconcile these two clauses, both of which are cast in absolute terms, and either of which, if expanded to a logical extreme, would clash with the other. Does a state scholarship for blind students given to a college student who decides to attend a college to become a clergyman violate the establishment clause by indirectly aiding religion? Or would denying the scholarship violate the student's free exercise of religion? The Supreme Court has held that giving such benefits does not violate the establishment clause, but also that the free exercise clause does not entitle individuals to receive such benefits or compel states to make them available.[12]

The Establishment Clause

In writing what has come to be called the **establishment clause**, the framers were reacting to the English system, wherein the crown was (and still is) the head not only of the government but also of the established church—the Church of England—and public officials were required to take an oath to support the established church as a condition of holding office. The establishment clause goes beyond merely separating government from religion by forbidding the establishment of a state religion. It is designed to prevent three evils: government sponsorship of religion, government financial support of religion, and government involvement in religious matters. However, the clause does not prevent governments from "accommodating" religious needs. To what extent and under which conditions governments may accommodate these needs are at the heart of much of the debate in the Supreme Court and the country over interpreting the clause.

Controversies over the establishment clause stir deep feelings and frequently divide the justices of the Supreme Court. The prevailing interpretation stems from the decision in *Everson* v. *Board of Education of Ewing Township* (1947) that the establishment clause creates a "wall of separation" between church and state and prohibits any law or governmental action designed to specifically benefit any religion, even if all religions are treated the same.[13] That decision, though, was decided by a bare majority and upheld state support for transportation of children to private religious schools as a "child benefit."

The separation of church and state was further elaborated in *Lemon* v. *Kurtzman* (1971), which laid down a three-part test: (1) A law must have a secular legislative purpose, (2) it must neither advance nor inhibit religion, and (3) it must avoid "excessive government entanglement with religion."[14] This so-called *Lemon test* is often, but not always, used because the justices remain divided over how much separation between government and religion the First Amendment requires.

Another test, championed by Justice Sandra Day O'Connor, is the *endorsement test*. Justice O'Connor believed that the establishment clause forbids governmental practices that a reasonable observer would view as endorsing religion, even if there is no coercion.[15] A series of decisions has honed the endorsement test as the Court has struggled with the question of whether governments may allow religious symbols to be displayed on, in, or near public properties and in public places. For example, the Court concluded that when a nativity scene was displayed in a shopping district together with Santa's house and other secular and religious symbols of the Christmas season,

establishment clause
Clause in the First Amendment that states that Congress shall make no law respecting an establishment of religion. The Supreme Court has interpreted this to forbid governmental support to any or all religions.

there was little danger that a reasonable person would conclude that the city was endorsing religion.[16] But the Constitution does not permit a city government to display the nativity scene on the steps of the city hall, because in this context, the city gives the impression that it is endorsing the display's religious message.[17]

The Court's three most conservative justices at the time—Chief Justice William Rehnquist and Justices Antonin Scalia and Clarence Thomas—supported a *non-preferentialist test*.[18] They believed the Constitution prohibits favoritism toward any particular religion but does not prohibit government aid to *all* religions. In their view, government may accommodate religious activities and even give nonpreferential support to religious organizations so long as government does not coerce individuals to participate in religious activities or give certain religious activities favorable treatment.[19]

By contrast, the more liberal justices—Justices David H. Souter, John Paul Stevens, Ruth Bader Ginsburg, and Stephen Breyer—usually maintained that there should be *strict separation* between religion and the state.[20] They generally have held that even indirect aid for religion, such as scholarships or teaching materials and aids for students attending private religious schools, crosses the line separating the government from religion.

Applying these generalizations, we find that the establishment clause forbids states—including state universities, colleges, and school districts—from introducing devotional exercises into the public school curriculum, including school graduations and events before football games.[21] However, the Supreme Court has not, as some people assume, entirely prohibited prayer in public schools. It is not unconstitutional for students to pray in a school building. What is unconstitutional is sponsorship or encouragement of prayer *by public school authorities*.[22] Devotional reading of the Bible, recitation of the Lord's Prayer, and posting the Ten Commandments on the walls of classrooms in public schools have also been ruled to be unconstitutional. A state may not forbid the teaching of evolution or require the teaching of "creation science"— the belief that life did not evolve but rather was created by a single act of God.[23]

Tax exemptions for church properties, similar to those granted to other nonprofit institutions, are constitutional. State legislatures and Congress may also hire chaplains to open each day's legislative session—a practice that has continued without interruption since the first session of Congress in 1789. But if done in a public school, this practice would be unconstitutional. Apparently, the difference is that legislators, as adults, are not "susceptible to religious indoctrination or peer pressure."[24] Also, as the joke goes, legislators need the prayer more.

A long-running controversy involves the public display of the Ten Commandments and other religious symbols. In *Stone* v. *Graham* (1980),[25] the Court held unconstitutional a Kentucky statute requiring the posting of the Ten Commandments in public school rooms. The Court then revisited the issue in two sharply divided 2005 rulings. In *Van Orden* v. *Perry*,[26] Chief Justice Rehnquist held that erecting a six-foot monument on which the Ten Commandments were chiseled did not violate the First Amendment. However, in *McCreary* v. *American Civil Liberties Union of Kentucky*,[27] the Court ruled that two Kentucky counties violated the First Amendment by prominently displaying the Ten Commandments in their courthouses. In both cases, Justice Steven Breyer cast the pivotal vote in bare majorities. He did so on the grounds that the Texas monument had stood unchallenged for 40 years, whereas the Kentucky displays had immediately sparked controversy and appeared to clearly aim at endorsing religion.

Another continuing controversy centers on whether requiring school children to recite the words "under God" in the Pledge of Allegiance violates the First Amendment. The Court avoided ruling on the issue in *Elk Grove Unified School District* v. *Newdow* (2004) by denying standing to Michael A. Newdow, an atheist, to sue on behalf of his daughter because he was not her legal guardian.[28] However, Chief Justice Rehnquist and Justices O'Connor and Thomas would have granted review and held that the Pledge does not violate the freedom of religion; Justice Scalia agreed with them but had to recuse himself because in an earlier speech he had criticized the lower court's ruling that the First Amendment was violated. Americans United for the Separation of Church and State and other supporters of Newdow plan other lawsuits; they also oppose the efforts of the American Family Association, an evangelical Christian group, to get states to require the display of the national motto, "In God We Trust," in public schools. The controversy over the Pledge and national motto is certain to return to the Supreme Court in another case.

Vouchers and State Aid for Religious Schools

Another troublesome area involving the separation of religion and government has revolved around states' providing financial assistance to parochial and other religious schools. The Supreme Court has tried to draw a line between permissible tax-provided aid to schoolchildren and impermissible aid to religion.

At the college level, the problems are relatively simple. Tax funds may be used to construct buildings and operate educational programs at church-related schools as long as the money is not spent directly on buildings used for religious purposes, such as chapels, or on teaching religious subjects. Even if students choose to attend religious schools and become clergymen, government aid to these students is permissible, because such aid has a secular purpose. Its effect on religion is the result of individual choice "and it does not confer any message of state endorsement of religion."[29]

At the level of elementary and secondary schools, however, the constitutional problems are more complicated because the secular and religious parts of institutions and instruction are much more closely interwoven. Also, students are younger and more susceptible to indoctrination, so the chances are greater that funding church-operated schools aids religion in violation of the establishment clause.

Despite the constitutional obstacles, some states have provided tax credits or deductions for parents who send their children to private, largely religious-run schools. Such deductions or credits available *only* to parents of children attending nonpublic schools are unconstitutional, but allowing taxpaying parents to deduct or take a credit from their state income taxes for what they paid for tuition and other costs to send their children to school—public or private—is constitutional, even if most of the benefit goes to those who send their children to private religious schools.[30]

The Supreme Court has also approved using tax funds to provide students who attend primary and secondary church-operated schools (except those that deny admission because of race or religion) with textbooks, standardized tests, lunches, transportation to and from school, diagnostic services, sign language interpreters, and teachers for remedial and enrichment classes, as well as computers and software.[31]

One hot controversy that the Supreme Court avoided for years involved whether states may also use tax money to give parents **vouchers** for the tuition of children to attend schools of their choice, including religious schools. Maine and Vermont have long had voucher programs for students living in rural areas. The cities of Cleveland, Milwaukee, and Washington, D.C., as well as the state of Florida experimented with voucher programs that permit the payment of tuition at religious schools. Opponents argue that such programs violate the establishment clause, while supporters argue that the denial of vouchers for attending religious schools violates the free exercise clause and denies parents the freedom to choose not to send their children to dysfunctional public schools.

The Supreme Court finally addressed the constitutionality of voucher programs in *Zelman* v. *Simmons-Harris* (2002),[32] and by a 5-to-4 vote found Ohio's program to be neutral and permissible. Ohio's law provides low-income families in Cleveland with vouchers of up to $2,250 per child to put toward the cost of their children's attending public or private schools outside of the failing inner-city school district, and 96 percent of the vouchers went to religious schools. As a result of this ruling, Congress authorized a $14 million voucher program for students of low-income families in the District of Columbia. In its first year of operation, however, not enough public school students there applied to fill all of the slots available. Officials with the Washington Scholarship Fund, a nonprofit organization that runs the District program, awarded grants of $7,500 per student.[33] There may be increased pressure on state legislatures and school boards to adopt voucher programs, though the programs have been challenged, and in 2006, the Florida supreme court declared its state's voucher program unconstitutional because it reduced funds for public schools.

vouchers
Money government provides to parents to pay their children's tuition in a public or private school of their choice.

The Free Exercise Clause

The right to hold any or no religious belief is one of our few absolute rights. The **free exercise clause** affirms that no government can compel us to accept any creed or to deny us any right because of what we do or do not believe. Requiring religious oaths as a condition of public employment or as a prerequisite for running for public office is unconstitutional. In fact, the original Constitution states, "No religious Test shall ever be required as a Qualification to any Office or public Trust under the United States" (Article VI).

Reverend Anthony Cummins, pastor of St. Peter the Apostle Church, in front of his church in Boerne, Texas, after a battle with city officials who denied the church permission to build an addition to the historic structure.

Although carefully protected, the right to practice a religion has had less protection than the right to hold particular beliefs. Before 1990, the Supreme Court carefully scrutinized laws allegedly infringing on religious practices and insisted that the government provide some compelling interest to justify actions that might infringe on someone's religion. In other words, the First Amendment was thought to throw a "mantle of protection" around religious practices, and the burden was on the government to justify interfering with them in the least restrictive way.

Then, in *Employment Division* v. *Smith* (1990), the Court significantly altered the interpretation of the free exercise clause by discarding the compelling governmental interest test for overriding the interests of religious minorities.[34] As long as a law is generally applicable and does not single out and ban religious practices, the law may be applied to conduct even if it burdens a particular religious practice.[35]

In reaction to *Employment Division* v. *Smith*, Congress enacted the Religious Freedom Restoration Act of 1993 (RFRA). RFRA aimed to override the *Smith* decision and to restore the earlier test prohibiting the government—federal, state, or local—from limiting a person's exercise of religion unless the government demonstrates a compelling interest that is advanced by the least restrictive means. Congress asserted its power to pass RFRA because the Fourteenth Amendment gives it the authority to enforce rights secured by that amendment, including the right to free exercise of religion.

However, when the Catholic archbishop of San Antonio, Texas, was denied a building permit in 1997 to enlarge a church, because the remodeling did not comply with the city of Boerne's historical preservation plan, he claimed that the denial of a building permit interfered with religious freedom as protected by RFRA. The Supreme Court then ruled RFRA unconstitutional because Congress was attempting to define, rather than enforce or remedy, constitutional rights and was thereby assuming the role of the courts, which contradicted "vital principles necessary to maintain separation of powers and the federal balance."[36]

In response to the invalidation of RFRA, Congress enacted the Religious Land Use and Institutionalized Persons Act (RLUIPA) of 2000, which specified that state and local governments that receive federal funding for services may not impose a substantial burden on the free exercise of religion of an individual in a prison or jail, unless the burden is necessary to achieving a compelling governmental purpose. When that law was challenged in *Cutter* v. *Wilkinson* (2005),[37] the Court unanimously upheld it as a permissible governmental accommodation of religious practices.

> *"The best test of truth is the power of the thought to get itself accepted in the competition of the market. . . . That any rate is the theory of our Constitution."*
>
> JUSTICE OLIVER WENDELL HOLMES

Tensions between the establishment and free exercise clauses have recently become more prominent. On the one hand, the University of Virginia denied a Christian student group funds to pay for printing its newspaper, *Wide Awake*, because it interpreted the establishment clause to forbid allocating student fee money to a newspaper that "primarily promotes a belief in or about a deity." The students argued that the university deprived them of their freedom of speech, including religious speech, and the Supreme Court agreed with them.[38] On the other hand, Christian students at the University of Wisconsin objected to the use of mandatory student activity fees for funding groups they deemed offensive and contrary to their religious beliefs. But the Court rejected their claim that they should be exempt from paying that portion of their fees.[39]

The Court, however, appeared to draw the line in addressing the tensions between the (dis)establishment and free exercise clauses in *Locke* v. *Davey*.[40] There, the Court held that a student awarded a scholarship who wanted to earn a degree in theology

free exercise clause
Clause in the First Amendment that states that Congress shall make no law prohibiting the free exercise of religion.

The Changing Face of American Politics

Growing Religious Intensity and Polarization

The United States is an intensely religious country, and the trend during the last two decades has been toward stronger religious belief. According to a study by The Pew Research Center for the People and the Press, eight of ten (81 percent) say that prayer is an important part of their daily lives, and even more (87 percent) agree with the statement "I never doubt the existence of God."*

The growing religious intensity is evident in how citizens characterize their religious faith. In the late 1980s, 41 percent of

Protestants and 24 percent of the population identified themselves as "born-again or evangelical" Christians, whereas today 54 percent of Protestants and 30 percent of the population describe themselves in that way. The trend is especially marked among African Americans: 50 percent now describe themselves that way, compared with 36 percent earlier. Fewer than one in ten (9 percent) report that they have no religion.

Moreover, recent generations are becoming more religious as they age. Almost two decades ago, 61 percent of

people in their late teens and twenties expressed deep religious faith, but 71 percent of the same people, who are now in their thirties and forties, do.

During the last two decades religion and religious faith have also grown more aligned with partisan and ideological identification. Republicans and Democrats remain equally likely to express strong religious attitudes, but Republicans have become increasingly united in that belief, with a widening gap between the parties (78 percent versus 71 percent of Democrats). While religiosity and

conservatism have always been correlated, that relationship has increased substantially among self-identified conservatives (81 percent today compared to 73 percent in the late 1980s), while liberals have become somewhat less religiously oriented (54 percent express strong religious belief today, compared to 59 percent in the late 1980s). ■

*The Pew Research Center for the People and the Press, *The 2004 Political Landscape: Evenly Divided and Increasingly Polarized* (November 3, 2003), at people-press.org/reports/display.php3?reported=196.

could be barred from using it for that purpose, under Washington state's constitutional bar against public expenditures for religion, over his objection that it violated the First Amendment guarantee of the free exercise of religion. Writing for the Court, Chief Justice Rehnquist cited other rulings permitting indirect aid for religious schools, such as vouchers and scholarships, on the ground that those programs directly benefit students and turned on student choices. In short, the Court ruled that the free exercise clause does not compel what the (dis)establishment clause permits.

Free Speech and Free People

Government by the people is based on every person's right to speak freely, to organize in groups, to question the decisions of the government, and to campaign openly against them. Only through free and uncensored expression of opinion can government be kept responsive to the electorate and political power transferred peacefully. Elections, separation of powers, and constitutional guarantees are meaningless unless all persons have the right to speak frankly and to hear and judge for themselves the worth of what others have to say. As Justice Oliver Wendell Holmes observed in 1919, "The best test of truth is the power of the thought to get itself accepted in the competition of the market. . . . That at any rate is the theory of our Constitution. It is an experiment, as all life is an experiment."[41]

Free speech is not simply the personal right of individuals to have their say; it is also the right of the rest of us to hear them. The British philosopher John Stuart Mill, whose *Essay on Liberty* (1859) is the classic defense of free speech, put it this way: "The peculiar evil of silencing the expression of opinion, is that it is robbing the human race. . . . If the opinion is right, they are deprived of the opportunity of exchanging error for truth; if wrong, they lose what is almost as great a benefit, the clearer perception and livelier impression of truth, produced by its collision with error."[42]

Americans overwhelmingly support the principle of freedom of expression in general. Yet some who say they believe in free speech draw the line at ideas they consider

"The peculiar evil of silencing the expression of opinion, is that it is robbing the human race."

JOHN STUART MILL

History Makers

Ernesto Pichardo

Ernesto Pichardo

A Cuban-born immigrant, Ernesto Pichardo, cofounded with other members of his family the first church of the Santeria religion, the Church of the Lukumi Babalu Aye, in Hialeah, Florida. Slaves brought to Cuba in the eighteenth and nineteenth centuries worshipped African gods alongside Catholic saints, and their religion became known as Santeria—"the way of the saints." Many followers of Santeria came to the United States from Cuba after Fidel Castro took power there in 1959 and again in 1980 with the Mariel "boatlift" that followed Castro's deportation of some 125,000 Cubans he considered undesirable.

The founding of the Hialeah church created a major controversy. In Cuba, the practice of Santeria was illegal and done in secret. Pichardo wanted to give the religion legitimacy, to institutionalize it, and to publicly perform rituals, including animal sacrifice. Both leaders of various other religions in Hialeah and animal rights organizations opposed the church.

Within weeks, the Hialeah city council passed ordinances making ritual animal sacrifice, except in slaughterhouses, a crime. The ordinances were defended as health and safety measures and as preventing cruelty to animals. But Pichardo challenged them for violating the First Amendment free exercise clause. The ordinances specifically targeted a religious practice, and Hialeah did not criminalize hunting, fishing, and other ways of killing animals.

In *Church of the Lukumi Babalu Aye, Inc. and Ernesto Pichardo* v. *City of Hialeah,** the Supreme Court struck down Hialeah's ordinances banning ritual animal sacrifice. The Court unanimously held that the city had targeted and discriminated against a particular religion, thereby violating the First Amendment. Pichardo thus won an important victory when the Court reaffirmed that government may not overtly discriminate against religious minorities. ∎

Church of the Lukumi Babalu Aye, Inc. and Ernesto Pichardo v. *City of Hialeah,* 508 U.S. 530 (1993); see also David M. O'Brien, *Animal Sacrifice and Religious Freedom* (University Press of Kansas, 2004).

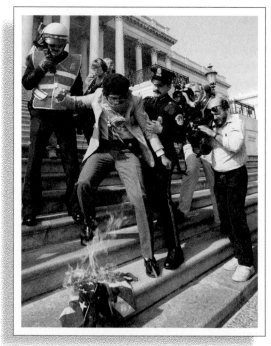

Police arrest Scott Tyler of Chicago after he set fire to an American flag on the steps of the Capitol building in Washington. The Supreme Court ruled that freedom of speech covers even "symbolic speech" like burning the U.S. flag.

dangerous or when speech attacks them or is critical of their race, religion, or ethnic origin. But what is a dangerous idea? Who decides? Who can find an objective, eternally valid standard to judge which political ideas are right? The search for truth involves the possibility—even the inevitability—of error. The search cannot go on unless everyone is free to think and talk about it. This means, in the words of Justice Robert Jackson, that "freedom to differ is not limited to things that do not matter much. That would be a mere shadow of freedom. The test of its substance is the right to differ as to things that touch the heart of the existing order."[43]

Even though the First Amendment explicitly denies Congress the power to pass any law abridging freedom of speech, the courts have never interpreted the amendment in absolute terms. Like almost all rights, the freedoms of speech and of the press are limited. In discussing the constitutional power of government to regulate speech, it is useful to distinguish among *belief, speech,* and *action.*

At one extreme is the right to *believe* as we wish. Despite occasional deviations in practice, the traditional American view is that government should not punish a person for beliefs or interfere in any way with freedom of conscience. At the other extreme is *action,* which the government may restrain. As has been said, "The right to swing your fist ends where my nose begins."

Speech stands somewhere between belief and action. It is not an absolute right, like belief, but neither is it as exposed to governmental restraint as is action. Some kinds of speech—libel, obscenity, fighting words, and commercial speech—are not entitled to constitutional protection. But many problems arise in distinguishing between what does and does not fit into the categories of nonprotected speech. People disagree, and it usually falls to the courts to decide what free speech means and to defend the right of individual and minority dissenters to exercise it.

Judging: Drawing the Line

Plainly, questions of free speech require that judges weigh a variety of factors: What was said? In what context and how was it said? Which level of government is attempting to regulate the speech—a city council speaking for a few people, or Congress, speaking for many? (The Supreme Court is much more deferential to acts of Congress than to those of a city council or state legislature.) How is the government attempting to regulate the speech—by prior restraint (censorship) or by punishment after the speech? Why is the government doing so—to preserve the public peace or to prevent criticism of the people in power? The never-ending process of determining what the First Amendment permits and what it forbids involve these and scores of other considerations.

Historical Constitutional Tests

It is useful to start with the three constitutional tests the judiciary used in the first part of the twentieth century: the bad tendency test, the clear and present danger test, and the preferred position doctrine. Although they are no longer applied, they provide a background for the current judicial approach to governmental regulation of speech and to the courts' expanding protection for free speech.

THE BAD TENDENCY TEST   This test was rooted in English common law. According to the **bad tendency test**, judges presumed it was reasonable to forbid speech that tends to corrupt society or causes people to engage in crime. The test was abandoned because it swept too broadly and ran "contrary to the fundamental premises underlying the First Amendment as the guardian of our democracy."[44] Some legislators still appear to hold this position today, however, and it also seems to be the view of college students, who want to see their institution punish students or faculty who express "hateful" or "offensive" ideas.

THE CLEAR AND PRESENT DANGER TEST   This is perhaps the most famous test. Justice Oliver Wendell Holmes Jr. in *Schenck* v. *United States* (1919) formulated the **clear and present danger test** as an alternative to the bad tendency test. In the words of Justice Holmes, "The question in every case is whether the words are used in circumstances and are of such a nature as to create a clear and present danger that they will bring about substantive evils that Congress has a right to prevent."[45] A government should not be allowed to interfere with speech unless it can prove, ultimately to a skeptical judiciary, that the particular speech in question presents an immediate danger—for example, speech leading to a riot, the destruction of property, or the corruption of an election.

Supporters of the clear and present danger test concede that speech is not an absolute right. Yet they believe free speech to be so fundamental that no government should be allowed to restrict it unless the government can demonstrate a close connection between the speech and an imminent lawless act. To shout "Fire!" falsely in a crowded theater is the most famous example of unprotected speech.

THE PREFERRED POSITION DOCTRINE   This was advanced in the 1940s when the Court applied all of the guarantees of the First Amendment to the states. The **preferred position doctrine** came close to the position that freedom of expression—the use of words and pictures—should rarely, if ever, be curtailed. This interpretation of the First Amendment gives these freedoms, especially freedom of speech and of conscience, a preferred position in our constitutional hierarchy. Judges have a special duty to protect these freedoms and should be most skeptical about laws trespassing on them. Once that judicial responsibility was established, judges had to draw lines between nonprotected and protected speech, as well as between speech and other forms of communication.

bad tendency test
Interpretation of the First Amendment that would permit legislatures to forbid speech encouraging people to engage in illegal action.

clear and present danger test
Interpretation of the First Amendment that holds that the government cannot interfere with speech unless the speech presents a clear and present danger that it will lead to evil or illegal acts.

preferred position doctrine
Interpretation of the First Amendment that holds that freedom of expression is so essential to democracy that governments should not punish persons for what they say, only for what they do.

Nonprotected and Protected Speech

Today the Supreme Court holds that all speech is protected unless it falls into one of four narrow categories—*libel, obscenity, fighting words,* and *commercial speech.* Such **nonprotected speech** lacks redeeming social value and is not essential to democratic deliberations and self-governance.

Still, the fact that nonprotected speech does not receive First Amendment protection does not mean that the constitutional issues relating to these kinds of speech are simple. How we prove libel, how we define obscenity, how we determine which words are fighting words, and how much commercial speech may be regulated remain hotly contested issues.

Libel

At one time, newspaper publishers and editors had to take considerable care about what they wrote to avoid prosecution for **libel**—published defamation or false statements—by the government or lawsuits by individuals. Today, as a result of gradually rising constitutional standards, it has become more difficult to win a libel suit against a newspaper or magazine.

Seditious libel—defaming, criticizing, and advocating the overthrow of government—was once subject to criminal penalties but no longer is. Seditious libel was rooted in the common law of England, which has no First Amendment protections. In 1798, only seven years after the First Amendment had been ratified, Congress enacted the first national law against **sedition**, the Sedition Act of 1798. Those were perilous times for the young Republic, for war with France seemed imminent. The Federalists, in control of both Congress and the presidency, persuaded themselves that national safety required some suppression of speech. But popular reaction to the Sedition Act helped defeat the Federalists in the elections of 1800, and the act expired in 1801. The Federalists had failed to grasp the democratic idea that a person may criticize the government, oppose its policies, and work to remove those in power yet still be loyal to the nation. They also failed to grasp the distinction between *seditious speech* and *seditious action*—conspiring to commit and engaging in violence against the government, which can be prosecuted and punished.

Another attempt to limit political criticism of the government was the Smith Act of 1940. That law forbade advocating the overthrow of the government, distributing material advocating the overthrow of government by violence, and organizing any group having such purposes. In 1951, during the cold war, the Supreme Court agreed that the Smith Act could be applied to the leaders of the Communist party who had been charged with conspiring to advocate the violent overthrow of the government.[46] More recently, the Bush administration has threatened prosecutions for violating espionage laws against the *New York Times* for disclosing plans and operations in the war in Iraq.

Since the 1950s, however, the Court has substantially modified constitutional doctrine, giving all political speech First Amendment protection. In *New York Times* v. *Sullivan* (1964), seditious libel was declared unconstitutional.[47] Now neither Congress nor any government may outlaw mere advocacy of the abstract doctrine of violent overthrow of government: "The essential distinction is that those to whom the advocacy is addressed must be urged to do something now or in the future, rather than merely to believe in something."[48] Moreover, advocacy of the use of force may not be forbidden "except where such advocacy is directed to inciting or producing imminent lawless action and is likely to incite or produce such action."[49]

In *New York Times* v. *Sullivan* and subsequent cases, the Court established guidelines for libel cases and severely limited state power to award monetary damages in libel suits brought by public officials against critics of official conduct. Neither public officials nor public figures can collect damages for comments made about them unless they can prove with "convincing clarity" that the comments were made with "actual

nonprotected speech
Libel, obscenity, fighting words, and commercial speech, which are not entitled to constitutional protection in all circumstances.

libel
Written defamation of another person. For public officials and public figures, the constitutional tests designed to restrict libel actions are especially rigid.

sedition
Attempting to overthrow the government by force or use violence to interrupt its activities.

malice." *Actual malice* means not merely that the defendant made false statements but that the "statements were made with a knowing or reckless disregard for the truth."[50]

Public figures cannot collect damages even when subject to outrageous, clearly inaccurate parodies and cartoons. Such was the case when *Hustler* magazine printed a parody of the Reverend Jerry Falwell; the Court held that parodies and cartoons cannot reasonably be understood as describing actual facts or events.[51] Nor does the mere fact that a public figure is quoted as saying something that he or she did not say amount to a libel unless the alteration in what the person said was made deliberately, with knowledge of its falsity, and "results in material change" in the meaning of the quotation.[52]

Constitutional standards for libel charges brought by private persons are not as rigid as those for public officials and figures. State laws may permit private persons to collect damages without having to prove actual malice if they can prove the statements made about them are false and were negligently published.[53]

Obscenity and Pornography

Obscene publications are not entitled to constitutional protection, but members of the Supreme Court, like everyone else, have difficulty defining obscenity. As Justice Potter Stewart put it, "I know it when I see it."[54] Or, as the second Justice John Marshall Harlan explained, "One man's vulgarity is another man's lyric."[55]

In *Miller* v. *California* (1973), the Court finally agreed on a constitutional definition of **obscenity**. A work may be considered legally obscene if (1) the average person, applying contemporary standards of the particular community, would find that the work, taken as a whole, appeals to a prurient interest in sex; (2) the work depicts or describes in a patently offensive way sexual conduct specifically defined by the applicable law or authoritatively construed (meaning that the legislature must define in law each obscene act); and (3) the work, taken as a whole, lacks serious literary, artistic, political, or scientific value.[56]

Before *Miller,* the distinction between *pornography* and *obscenity* was not clear. The *Miller* standard clarified that only hard-core pornography is constitutionally unprotected. X-rated movies and adult theaters that fall short of the constitutional definition of obscenity are entitled to some constitutional protection, but less protection than political speech, and they are subject to greater government regulation. Cities may, as New York City has done, also use zoning laws to regulate where adult theaters and bookstores may be located,[57] and they may ban totally nude dancing in adult nightclubs.[58] Under narrowly drawn statutes, state and local governments can also ban the sale of "adult" magazines to minors, even if such materials would not be considered legally obscene if sold to adults.

The Court has also held that the First Amendment does not protect *child pornography*—sexually explicit materials either featuring minors or aimed at them.[59] Just as the government may protect minors, so apparently may it protect members of the armed forces. The Supreme Court left standing a ruling of a lower court upholding an act of Congress forbidding the sale or rental on military property of magazines or videos whose "dominant theme" is to portray nudity "in a lascivious way."[60]

Pressure to regulate pornography came primarily from political conservatives and religious fundamentalists concerned that it undermines moral standards. Some feminists have joined them, arguing that pornography is degrading and perpetuates sexual discrimination and violence against women. They argue that just as sexually explicit materials featuring minors are not entitled to First Amendment protection, so should there be no protection for pornographic materials. They contend that pornography promotes the sexual abuse of women and maintains the social subordination of women as a class. Some feminists define pornographic materials more broadly than the Court has and would include sexually explicit pictures or words that depict women as sexual objects who enjoy pain and humiliation or that present abuse of women as a sexual stimulus for men.[61]

obscenity
Quality or state of a work that taken as a whole appeals to a prurient interest in sex by depicting sexual conduct in a patently offensive way and that lacks serious literary, artistic, political, or scientific value.

Not all feminists favor antipornography ordinances, yet those who do have joined social conservatives in a battle to regulate pornography. For this antipornography coalition to be successful, constitutional doctrine will have to be substantially altered. Unlike the Canadian Supreme Court, which redefined obscenity to include materials that degrade women,[62] the U.S. Supreme Court does not appear willing to substantially change current doctrine.

Fighting Words

Fighting words were held to be constitutionally unprotected because "their very utterance may inflict injury or tend to incite an immediate breach of peace."[63] That the words are abusive, offensive, and insulting or that they create anger, alarm, or resentment is not sufficient. Thus a four-letter word worn on a sweatshirt was not judged to be a fighting word in the constitutional sense, even though it was offensive and angered some people.[64] In recent years, the Court has overturned convictions for uttering fighting words and struck down laws that criminalized "hate speech"—insulting racial, ethnic, and gender slurs.[65] The Court, though, has indicated that cross-burning by the Ku Klux Klan may be punished because it has historically been associated with intimidation.[66]

Commercial Speech

Commercial speech—such as advertisements and commercials—used to be unprotected because it was deemed to have lesser value than political speech. But the Court has reconsidered and extended more protection to commercial speech, as it has to fighting words. In *44 Liquormart, Inc.* v. *Rhode Island* (1996), for instance, the Court struck down a law forbidding advertising the price of alcoholic drinks.[67] It now appears that states may forbid and punish only false and misleading advertising, along with advertising the sale of anything illegal—for example, narcotics. Although the Supreme Court has not specifically removed commercial speech from the nonprotected category, it has interpreted the First, Fifth, and Fourteenth Amendments to provide considerable constitutional protection for it.

Protected Speech

Apart from these four categories of nonprotected speech, all other expression is constitutionally protected, and courts strictly scrutinize government regulation of such speech. The Supreme Court uses the following doctrines to measure the limits of governmental power to regulate speech.

PRIOR RESTRAINT Of all the forms of governmental interference with expression, judges are most suspicious of those that impose **prior restraint**—censorship before publication. Prior restraints include governmental review and approval before a speech can be made, before a motion picture can be shown, or before a newspaper can be published. Most prior restraints are unconstitutional, as the Court has said: "Any system of prior restraints of expression comes to this Court bearing a heavy presumption against its constitutional validity."[68] About the only prior restraints the Court has approved relate to military and national security matters—such as the disclosure of troop movements[69]—and to high school authorities' control over student newspapers.[70] Student newspapers at colleges and universities receive the same protections as other newspapers because they are independent and financially separate from the college or university.

VOID FOR VAGUENESS Laws must not be so vague that people do not know whether their speech would violate the law and hence are afraid to exercise protected freedoms. Laws must not allow the authorities who administer them so much discretion that they may discriminate against people whose views they dislike. For these reasons, the Court strikes down laws using the void for vagueness doctrine.

fighting words
Words that by their very nature inflict injury on those to whom they are addressed or incite them to acts of violence.

commercial speech
Advertisements and commercials for products and services; they receive less First Amendment protection, primarily to discourage false and misleading ads.

prior restraint
Censorship imposed before a speech is made or a newspaper is published; usually presumed to be unconstitutional.

How Other Nations Govern

Hate Speech in Canada

Although the Supreme Court of Canada, in interpreting the nation's Charter of Rights, generally follows the rulings on freedom of speech of the U.S. Supreme Court, it refused to do so with respect to hate speech. Whereas the U.S. Supreme Court held that the First Amendment bars making hate speech a crime,* the Canadian Court upheld a law making it a crime to express "hatred against any identifiable group ... distinguished by colour, race, religion, or ethnic origin."

James Keegstra, a high school teacher, was convicted of teaching anti-Semitism to his students. However, an appeals court overturned his conviction on the ground that the law punishing hate speech violated the Charter's guarantee of freedom of expression. In reversing the lower court and upholding Keeg-

stra's conviction and Canada's hate speech law, the Supreme Court observed:

The international commitment to eradicate hate propaganda and, most importantly, the special role given equality and multiculturalism in the Canadian Constitution necessitate a departure from the view, reasonably prevalent in America at present, that the suppression of hate propaganda is incompatible with the guarantee of free expression.

At the core of freedom of expression lies the need to ensure that truth and the common good are attained, whether in scientific and artistic endeavors or in the process of determining the best course to take in our political affairs. ... Nevertheless, the argument from truth does not provide convincing support for

James Keegstra

the protection of hate propaganda. Taken to its extreme, this argument would require us to permit the communication of all expression, it being impossible to know with *absolute* certainty which factual statements are true, or which ideas obtain the greatest good. ... There is very little chance that statements intended to promote hatred against an identifiable group are true, or that their vision of society will lead to a better world. To portray such statements as crucial to truth and the betterment of the political and social milieu is therefore misguided.[†]

The Canadian court's ruling was not unique in departing from U.S. standards. Hate speech and blasphemy laws are common in Europe, the Middle East, and Africa. Austria, Finland, Ger-

many, Ireland, Italy, the Netherlands, Spain, Switzerland, and the United Kingdom, for example, have laws against blasphemy and other hate speech. ∎

R.A.V. v. St. Paul, 505 U.S. 377 (1992).
[†]*Regina v. Keegstra,* 3 S.C.R. 697 (1990).

LEAST DRASTIC MEANS   Even for an important purpose, a legislature may not pass a law that impinges on First Amendment freedoms if other, less drastic means are available. For example, a state may protect the public from unscrupulous lawyers but not by forbidding attorneys from advertising their fees for simple services. The state could adopt other ways to protect the public from such lawyers that do not impinge on their freedom of speech; it could, for example, disbar lawyers who mislead their clients.

CONTENT AND VIEWPOINT NEUTRALITY   Laws concerning the time, place, or manner of speech, that regulate some kinds of speech but not others, or that regulate speech expressing some views but not others are much more likely to be struck down than those that are content-neutral or viewpoint-neutral, that is, laws that apply to *all* kinds of speech and to *all* views. For example, the Constitution does not prohibit laws forbidding the posting of handbills on telephone poles. Yet laws prohibiting only religious handbills or only handbills advocating racism or sexism would probably be declared unconstitutional because they would relate to the kinds of handbills or what is being said rather than to all handbills regardless of what they say.

The lack of viewpoint neutrality was the grounds for the Court's striking down a St. Paul, Minnesota, ordinance that prohibited the display of a symbol that would arouse anger on the basis of race, color, creed, religion, or gender. The ordinance was not considered viewpoint-neutral because it did not forbid displays that might arouse anger for other reasons, for example, because of political affiliation.[71]

Freedom of the Press

Courts have carefully protected the right to publish information, no matter how journalists get it. But some reporters, editors, and others argue that this is not enough. They insist that the First Amendment gives them the right to ignore legal requests and to withhold information and a *right of access,* a right to go wherever they need to go to get information.

Does the Press Have the Right to Withhold Information?

Although most reporters have challenged the right of public officials to withhold information, they claim the right to do so themselves, including the right to keep information from grand juries and legislative investigating committees. Without this right to withhold information, reporters insist, they cannot assure their sources of confidentiality, and they will not be able to get the information they need to keep the public informed.

The Supreme Court, however, has refused to acknowledge that reporters, and presumably scholars, have a constitutional right to ignore legal requests such as subpoenas and to withhold information from governmental bodies.[72] In 2005, *New York Times* reporter Judith Miller was jailed for two months for refusing to disclose her sources to a grand jury. Many states have passed *press shield laws* providing some protection for reporters from state court subpoenas, and pressure is growing for Congress to pass a similar federal law.

Does the Press Have the Right to Know?

The press has argued that if reporters are excluded from places where public business is conducted or are denied access to information in government files, they cannot perform their traditional function of keeping the public informed. In similar fashion, some reporters argue that they should be able to enter facilities such as food markets, child care centers, and homes for the mentally ill, even using false identities, to expose discrimination, abuse, and fraud. The Supreme Court, however, has refused to acknowledge that the press has a constitutional right to know, although it did concede that the press, along with the public, has a First Amendment right to be present at criminal trials.[73]

Although they have no constitutional obligation to do so, many states have adopted *sunshine laws* requiring government agencies to open their meetings to the public and the press. Congress requires most federal executive agencies to open hearings and meetings of advisory groups to the public, and most congressional committee meetings are also open to the public. Federal and state courtroom trials are open, but judicial conferences, in which the judges discuss how to decide the cases, are not.

Congress has authorized the president to establish a classification system to keep some public documents and governmental files secret, and it is a crime for any person to divulge such classified information. So far, however, although they have been threatened, no newspapers have been prosecuted for doing so.

The Freedom of Information Act (FOIA) of 1966, since amended, liberalized access to nonclassified federal government records. This law makes the records of federal executive agencies available to the public, with certain exceptions, such as private financial transactions, personnel records, criminal investigation files, interoffice memorandums, and letters used in internal decision making. If federal agencies fail to act promptly on requests for information, applicants are entitled to speedy judicial hearings. The burden is on an agency to explain its refusal to supply material, and if the judge decides the government has improperly withheld information, the government has to pay the legal fees. Since the inception of FOIA, more than 250,000 people have requested information, and more than 90 percent of these requests have been granted.

President Bill Clinton issued an executive order requiring the automatic declassification of almost all government documents after 25 years. Any person who wants

Government's Greatest Endeavors

Making Government More Open to the Public

The public cannot learn about what the federal government does unless it has access to information. And the press cannot write stories about government unless it can learn the details. Until the end of World War II, however, most federal activities were invisible to the public. Decisions were made behind closed doors and were often kept secret.

Even though the federal government still keeps many secrets, sunshine in government has increased steadily over the past half-century. In 1958, Congress passed the first version of the Freedom of Information Act, which gives the press and public much greater access to public records.

Under the 1958 act, which has been strengthened at least three times since, government was required to keep careful records of its decisions and make them available to any person requesting access. The federal government still has the authority to deny public requests for information, but it must now publish indexes of internal records for review and release documents if there is no compelling reason to keep them secret. It must also search for documents when the press or public files a Freedom of Information Act request.

Under other laws, the federal government is no longer allowed to keep most of its internal meetings secret. Although the government can still hold secret meetings when sensitive issues are being discussed, the press and public are allowed into any meeting that involves a federal advisory commission, such as the ones that First Lady Hillary Clinton chaired in developing the proposed 1993 health care reforms. ∎

Hillary Clinton

QUESTIONS

Why does the federal government still keep secrets?

Should the press and public have access to all information or just the information government wants to provide?

access to documents that are not declassified can appeal to an Interagency Security Classification Appeals panel, which has a record of ruling in favor of releasing documents. The Electronic Freedom of Information Act of 1996 requires most federal agencies to put their files online and to establish an index of their records.

Free Press Versus Fair Trials

When newspapers and television journalists report in vivid detail the facts of a crime, interview prosecutors and police, question witnesses, and hold press conferences for defendants and their attorneys—as in the O. J. Simpson murder trial and the Oklahoma City bombing cases in 1995—they may so inflame the public that it becomes difficult to find a panel of impartial jurors and conduct a fair trial. In Britain, strict rules determine what the media may report, and judges do not hesitate to punish newspapers that comment on pending criminal proceedings. By contrast, in the United States free comment is protected. Yet the Supreme Court has not been indifferent to protecting persons on trial from inflammatory publicity. Judges may impose "gag orders" on lawyers and jurors, but not reporters, restraining them from talking about an ongoing trial, and new trials may be ordered as a remedy for prejudicial publicity. Trials may even, on rare occasions, be closed to the press and the public. Although federal rules of criminal procedure forbid radio or photographic coverage of criminal cases in federal courts, most states permit televising courtroom proceedings, and court TV programs have become popular.

Other Media and Communications

When the First Amendment was written, freedom of "the press" referred to leaflets, newspapers, and books. Today the amendment protects other media as well—the mails, motion pictures, billboards, radio, television, cable, telephones, fax machines, and the Internet. Because each form of communication entails special problems, each needs a different degree of protection.

The Mail

In 1921, Justice Oliver Wendell Holmes Jr. wrote in dissent, "The United States may give up the Post Office when it sees fit, but while it carries it on, the use of the mails is almost as much a part of free speech as is the right to use our tongues."[74] In 1965, the Court adopted that view by striking down an act that had directed the postmaster general to detain foreign mailings of "communist political propaganda" and to deliver these materials only upon the addressee's request.[75] The Court has also set aside federal laws authorizing postal authorities to exclude from the mails materials they consider obscene.

Although government censorship of mail is unconstitutional, household censorship is not. The Court has sustained laws giving householders the right to ask the postmaster to order mailers to delete their names from certain mailing lists and to refrain from sending any advertisements that they believe to be "erotically arousing or sexually provocative."[76] Moreover, Congress may forbid—and has forbidden—the use of mailboxes for any materials except those sent through the United States mails.

Handbills, Sound Trucks, and Billboards

Religious and political pamphlets, leaflets, and handbills have been historic weapons in the defense of liberty, and their distribution is constitutionally protected. So, too, is the use of their contemporary counterparts, sound trucks and billboards. A state cannot restrain the distribution of leaflets merely to keep its streets clean,[77] but it may impose reasonable restrictions on their distribution so long as they are neutrally enforced, without regard to the content.

Motion Pictures and Plays

Prior censorship of films to prevent the showing of obscenity is not necessarily unconstitutional; however, laws that require films to be submitted to a government review board are constitutional only if there is a prompt judicial hearing. The burden is on the government to prove to the court that the particular film in question is obscene. Prior censorship of films by review boards was once common, but no longer is. Live performances, such as plays, concerts, and revues, are also entitled to constitutional protection.[78]

Broadcast and Cable Communications

Despite the rise of the Internet, television remains an important means of distributing news and appealing for votes. Yet of all the mass media, broadcasting receives the least First Amendment protection. Congress has established a system of commercial broadcasting, supplemented by the Corporation for Public Broadcasting, which provides funds for public radio and television. The Federal Communications Commission (FCC) regulates the entire system by granting licenses, regulating their use, and imposing fines for indecent broadcasts.

The First Amendment would prevent censorship if the FCC tried to impose it. The First Amendment does not, however, prevent the FCC from imposing sanctions on sta-

> *"[The] use of the mails is almost as much a part of free speech as is the right to use our tongues."*
>
> **JUSTICE OLIVER WENDELL HOLMES JR.**

tions that broadcast indecent or filthy words, even if those words are not legally obscene.[79] Nor does the First Amendment prevent the FCC from refusing to renew a license if, in its opinion, a broadcaster does not serve the public interest. In 2006, President Bush signed a law authorizing the FCC to fine broadcasters up to $325,000 for each instance of indecent broadcasting.

The Supreme Court allows more governmental regulation of broadcasters than of newspaper and magazine publishers because space on the airwaves was historically limited. However, technological advances such as cable television, videotapes, and satellite broadcasting have opened up new means of communication and brought more competition to the electronic media. Recognizing these changes, Congress passed the Telecommunications Act of 1996, allowing telephone companies, broadcasters, and cable TV stations to compete with one another. In adopting the act, Congress did not abandon all government regulation of the airwaves. On the contrary, the act calls for many new regulations—for example, requiring that all new television sets sold in the United States be equipped with V-chips that allow viewers to block programs containing violent or sexual material.

The Court has upheld a congressional requirement that cable television stations must carry the signals of local broadcast television stations.[80] The Court has also held that Congress may authorize cable operators to refuse access to leased channels for "patently offensive" programs. The Court, however, struck down congressional requirements that if a cable operator allows such offensive programming, it must be blocked and unscrambled through special devices. In *United States* v. *Playboy Entertainment Group* (2000), the Court underscored the greater protection for cable than for broadcast television. Whereas broadcast television may be required to provide programming for children and not air violence at certain times, the Court held that such rules do not apply to cable television because homeowners can block unwanted programming.[81]

At a press conference, Howard Stern defends his use of raunchy language and subject matter that led to the FCC fining the Infinity Broadcasting network. Stern subsequently decided to leave the network to work on a satellite radio station.

Telecommunications and the Internet

Millions of Americans log on to the Internet to buy books, clothing, jewelry, airplane tickets, stocks, and bonds. Because the Internet has become a commercial marketplace and a major channel for communication, Congress has struggled with issues raised by cyberspace communication. Although Congress has imposed a moratorium on state taxation of commercial transactions on the Internet, debate continues over whether the national government should preempt state taxation. How do existing laws against copyright piracy apply to the World Wide Web? Should there be national regulation of junk e-mail, or can state laws take care of the problem? How may Congress regulate indecent and obscene communications on the Web? Should Congress try to protect the privacy of those who use the Web? (For more information about privacy and developments on the Web, go to the Electronic Privacy Information Center at www.epic.org.)

As Congress and the state legislatures deal with these and other new problems, legislators and judges will have to apply traditional constitutional principles to new technologies and means of communication. The Court distinguishes between a limited ban on indecent messages on radio and broadcast television and those on telephones, cable television, and the Internet. Radio and broadcast messages are readily available to children and can intrude into the privacy of the home without prior warning. By contrast, telephone messages may be blocked, and access by minors is more readily restricted.[82]

In its major ruling on First Amendment protection for the Internet, *Reno* v. *American Civil Liberties Union* (1997), the Court struck down provisions of the Communications Decency Act of 1996 that had made it a crime to send obscene or indecent messages to anyone under 18 years of age. In doing so, the Court emphasized the unique character of the Internet, holding that it is less intrusive than radio and broadcast television.[83] In response to *Reno* v. *ACLU,* Congress passed the Child Online Protection Act of 1998 (COPA), which made it a crime for a commercial Web site to knowingly make available to anyone under the age of 17 sexually explicit material considered "harmful to minors" based on "community standards." But the Supreme Court held that the law was unenforceable because imposing criminal penalties was not the least drastic means of achieving Congress's goals; Internet filters and adult checks could block minors' access to sites with sexually explicit material.[84] The Court also struck down the Child Pornography Prevention Act of 1996, which made it a federal crime to create or distribute "virtual child pornography" generated by computer images of young adults rather than actual children. The law went beyond punishing child pornography, which is a crime because it involves real children, the Court ruled, and had the potential to chill clear artistic and literary expression.[85]

Freedom of Assembly

Khallid Abdul Muhammad, a known racist and anti-Semite, organized what he called a "Million Youth March" in New York City in 1998. Then, Mayor Rudolph Giuliani denied a permit for the march on the grounds that it would be a "hate march." A federal appeals court upheld a lower court ruling that denial of the permit was unconstitutional. However, a three-judge panel placed restrictions on the event, limiting its duration to four hours, and scaling it back to a six-block area. The march proceeded, surrounded by police in riot gear who broke up the demonstration after Muhammad delivered a vitriolic speech against the police, Jews, and city officials.

It took judicial authorities to defend the rights of these unpopular speakers and marchers, but it is not always the "bad guys" whose rights the courts have to protect. It also took judicial intervention in the 1960s to preserve for Martin Luther King Jr. and those who marched with him the right to demonstrate in the streets of southern cities on behalf of civil rights for African Americans.

Such incidents present a classic free speech problem. It is almost always easier, and certainly politically more prudent, to maintain order by curbing public demonstrations by unpopular groups. However, if the police did not have the right to order groups to disperse, public order would be at the mercy of those who resort to street demonstrations to create tensions and provoke street battles.

A recent controversy surrounds the decision by then-Attorney General John Ashcroft to allow law enforcement agents to go undercover to monitor activities and assemblies in any public place—including mosques, churches, and chat rooms on the Internet—to combat international terrorism.[86] He thereby abandoned the Department of Justice's guidelines adopted in 1976 after Congress discovered that FBI agents were conducting surveillance and had infiltrated the civil rights movement and other groups engaged in lawful activities, as well as closely monitored Martin Luther King and other leaders. In response to criticisms that the new guidelines infringed on the

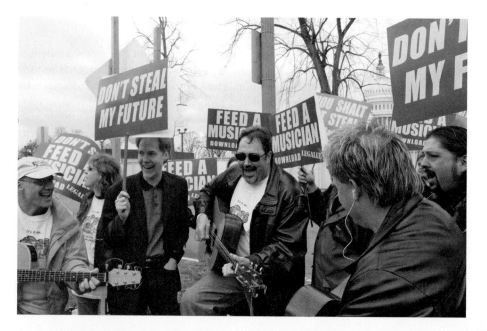

Demonstrators parade with posters in front of the U.S. Supreme Court in Washington, DC, as the nine justices heard oral arguments on the legality of music file-sharing networks. The right to assemble peaceably and protest is guaranteed by the Bill of Rights.

Agents of Change

Aaron Liberman and Jumpstart

Jumpstart was founded in 1993 to help children get access to quality preschool programs through federal/state programs such as Head Start. Jumpstart has two goals: (1) to increase access to preschool programs, and (2) to encourage college students to engage in community service by volunteering in programs like Head Start. In 2005, Jumpstart served 10,000 preschool children through a network of 6,000 volunteers at 200 Head Start programs around the nation.

Jumpstart was started by Aaron Liberman in his senior year at Yale University. After graduating from Yale, Liberman worked as a preschool teacher at South End Head Start in Boston, where he continued to learn about how to help all young children start school with

an equal chance at success. Liberman eventually left Jumpstart to create his own private business, Acelero Learning, to develop management systems to track and educate the same students Jumpstart serves. The only difference is that he is now selling the systems for a minimal profit. "We need everybody, in all sectors of our economy, to attempt to meet the challenge of helping every child successfully enter school," he says. "I believe we've just begun to show the impact of our approach—and I believe our network can grow to help support the use of $100 million in federal funds and directly impact 15,000 children every year."

Liberman is still active with Jumpstart, and he sees Acelero and Jumpstart as partners in his initial dream of a much more

effective Head Start program, and as key contributors to ensuring access to the basic education the framers wanted every citizen to have. ■

Learn more about Jumpstart at www.jstart.org.

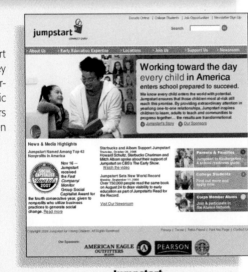

Jumpstart

QUESTIONS

How do organizations such as Jumpstart promote civil liberties?

What is the role of education in ensuring civil liberties?

freedoms of assembly and association, Ashcroft stressed that FBI agents were limited to investigating terrorist activities. Subsequently, though, in 2005 and 2006, it was revealed that the National Security Agency has monitored e-mails and cell phone calls to suspected international terrorists, as well as international financial transactions.[87]

Public Forums and Time, Place, and Manner Regulations

The Constitution protects the right to speak, but it does not give people the right to communicate their views to everyone, in every place, at every time they wish. No one has the right to block traffic or to hold parades or make speeches in public streets or on public sidewalks whenever he or she wishes. Governments may not censor what can be said, but they can make "reasonable" *time, place,* and *manner* regulations for protests or parades. The Supreme Court has divided public property into three categories: public forums, limited public forums, and nonpublic forums. The extent to which governments may limit access depends on the kind of forum involved.

Public forums are public places historically associated with the free exercise of expressive activities, such as streets, sidewalks, and parks. Courts look closely at time, place, and manner regulations that apply to these traditional public forums to ensure that they are being applied evenhandedly and that the government is not acting because of what is being said rather than how and where or by whom it is being said.

Other kinds of public property, such as rooms in a city hall or in a school after hours, may be designated as *limited public forums,* available for assembly and speech for limited purposes, for a limited amount of time, and even for a limited class of speakers (such as only students, only teachers, or only employees), provided the distinctions between the people allowed access and those excluded are not biased.

Nonpublic forums include public facilities such as libraries, courthouses, prisons, schools, swimming pools, and government offices that are open to the public but are not public forums. As long as people use such facilities within the normal bounds of conduct, they may not be constitutionally restrained from doing so. However, people may be excluded from such places as a government office or a school if they engage in activities for which the facilities were not created. They have no right to interfere with programs or to try to take over a building—especially facilities such as a university president's office—to stage a political protest.

Does the right of peaceful assembly include the right to violate a law nonviolently but deliberately? We have no precise answer, but in general, **civil disobedience**, even if peaceful, is not a protected right. When Martin Luther King Jr. and his followers refused to comply with a state court's injunction forbidding them to parade in Birmingham, Alabama, without first securing a permit, the Supreme Court sustained their conviction, even though there was serious doubt about the constitutionality of the injunction and the ordinance on which it was based.[88]

More recently, the First Amendment right of antiabortion protesters to picket in front of abortion clinics has come into conflict with a woman's right to go to an abortion clinic. Protesters have often massed in front of clinics, shouting at employees and clients and blocking entrances to the clinic. The Supreme Court has struck down provisions that prohibit protesters from expressing their views. But it has upheld injunctions that keep antiabortion protesters outside of a buffer zone around abortion clinics and also upheld injunctions that were issued because of the protesters, previous unlawful conduct. The proper constitutional test for such injunctions is "whether the challenged provisions . . . burden no more speech than necessary to serve a significant government interest," such as public safety or the right of women to go into such a clinic.[89]

The combination of First Amendment guarantees for rights and freedoms and their judicial enforcement is one of the fundamental features of our government and political system. As Supreme Court Justice Robert H. Jackson wrote:

> The very purpose of [the] Bill of Rights was to withdraw certain subjects from the vicissitudes of political controversy, to place them beyond the reach of majorities and officials and to establish them as legal principles to be applied by the courts. One's right to life, liberty, and property, to free speech, a free press, freedom of worship and assembly, and other fundamental rights may not be submitted to vote: they depend on the outcome of no elections.[90]

The connection between constitutional limitations and judicial enforcement is an example of the "auxiliary precautions" James Madison believed were necessary to prevent arbitrary governmental action. Citizens in other free nations rely on elections and political checks to protect their rights; in the United States, we also appeal to judges when we fear our freedoms are in danger.

civil disobedience
Deliberate refusal to obey a law or comply with the orders of public officials as a means of expressing opposition.

Summary

1. The Constitution protects our right to seek a writ of *habeas corpus* and forbids *ex post facto* laws and bills of attainder.
2. First Amendment freedoms—freedom of religion, of speech, of the press, and of assembly and association—are at the heart of a healthy constitutional democracy.
3. The Supreme Court has become the primary branch of government for giving meaning to these constitutional restraints. And since 1925,

these constitutional limits have been applied not only to Congress but to all governmental agencies—national, state, and local.
4. The First Amendment forbids the establishment of religion and also guarantees its free exercise. These two freedoms, however, are often in conflict with each other and represent conflicting notions of what is in the public interest.
5. The Supreme Court holds that there are only four categories of non-

protected speech—libel, obscenity, fighting words, and commercial speech. All other speech is protected under the First Amendment, and government may regulate that speech only when it has a compelling reason and does so in a content-neutral way.
6. Over the years, the Supreme Court has taken a pragmatic approach to First Amendment freedoms. It has refused to make them absolute rights above any kind of governmental regulation, direct or indirect, or to

say that they must be preserved at whatever price. But the justices have recognized that a constitutional democracy tampers with these freedoms at great peril. They have insisted on compelling justification before permitting these rights to be limited. How compelling the justification is, in a free society, will always remain an open question, but is especially difficult during war.

Further Reading

STUART BIEGEL, *Beyond Our Control? Confronting the Limits of Our Legal System in the Age of Cyberspace* (MIT Press, 2001).

STEVEN P. BROWN, *Trumping Religion: The Christian Right, The Free Speech Clause, and the Courts* (University of Alabama Press, 2002).

JAMES MACGREGOR BURNS AND **STEWART BURNS,** *A People's Charter: The Pursuit of Rights in America* (Knopf, 1991).

LOUIS FISHER, *Religious Liberty in America: Political Safeguards* (University Press of Kansas, 2002).

MIKE GODWIN, *Cyber Rights: Defending Free Speech in the Digital Age* (MIT Press, 2003).

ROBERT JUSTIN GOLDSTEIN, *Flag Burning and Free Speech: The Case of* Texas *v.* Johnson (University Press of Kansas, 2002).

ISAAC KRAMNICK AND **LAURENCE MOORE,** *The Godless Constitution: A Moral Defense of the Secular State* (Norton, 2005).

LAWRENCE LESSIG, *Code and Other Laws of Cyberspace* (Basic Books, 2000).

LEONARD W. LEVY, *Emergence of a Free Press* (Oxford University Press, 1985).

ANTHONY LEWIS, *Make No Law: The Sullivan Case and the First Amendment* (Random House, 1991).

CATHARINE A. MACKINNON, *Only Words* (Harvard University Press, 1993).

ALEXANDER MEIKLEJOHN, *Political Freedom: The Constitutional Powers of the People* (Harper & Row, 1965).

JOHN T. NOONAN JR., *The Lustre of Our Country: The American Experience of Religious Freedom* (University of California Press, 1998).

DAVID M. O'BRIEN, *Animal Sacrifice and Religious Freedom:* Church of the Lukumi Babalu Aye *v.* City of Hialeah (University Press of Kansas, 2004).

DAVID M. O'BRIEN, *Constitutional Law and Politics: Civil Rights and Civil Liberties,* 7th ed. (Norton, 2008).

J. W. PELTASON AND **SUE DAVIS,** *Understanding the Constitution,* 16th ed. (Harcourt, 2004).

SHAWN FRANCIS PETERS, *Judging Jehovah's Witnesses: Religious Persecution and the Dawn of the Right Revolution* (University Press of Kansas, 2002).

NADINE STROSSEN, *Defending Pornography: Free Speech, Sex, and the Fight for Women's Rights* (Scribner, 1995).

MELVIN UROFSKY, ED., *100 Americans Making Constitutional History* (CQ Press, 2005).

KeyTerms

Make It Real

CIVIL LIBERTIES

The simulation puts the student in the role of NSA policymaker.

Chapter 16

Rights to Life, Liberty, and Property

✦

RECENT MEASURES TO STRENGTHEN HOMELAND SECURITY—WHETHER IN SCHOOLS; AT CONCERTS; TRAVELING IN AIRPORTS, ON TRAINS, OR ON PUBLIC STREETS; OR IN OUR HOMES—ARE FORCING US TO RETHINK THE BALANCE BETWEEN LIBERTY AND SECURITY. WE ARE NOT LIKELY TO TAKE EITHER FOR GRANTED AGAIN. CONSIDER THE FEDERAL BUREAU OF INVESTIGATION'S (FBI) GROWING DNA DATABASE OF OVER THREE MILLION AMERICANS, WHICH EVEN INCLUDES PEOPLE WHO HAVE BEEN ARRESTED FOR MINOR crimes but not convicted[1]; the National Security Agency's (NSA) warrantless monitoring of e-mails and satellite communications for links to suspected terrorists[2]; and the use of drone airplanes to monitor the border with Mexico for illegal immigrants. Still, we are among the freest people in the world. And we need to remember how fortunate we are to live in a society that values *due process*—established rules and regulations that restrain officials who exercise power. Such procedures are not available to most people in the world; not, for example, in China or in much of Africa and South America.

Public officials in the United States have great power. Under certain conditions, they can seize our property, jail us, and—in extreme circumstances—even take our lives. The framers of our Constitution recognized that it is necessary—but dangerous—to give power to those who govern. It is so dangerous that we do not depend on the ballot box alone to keep our officials from becoming tyrants. Because political power may threaten our liberty, we parcel it out in small chunks and surround it with restraints. No single official can decide to take our lives, liberty, or property. Officials must act according to the rule of law. If they exceed their authority or act contrary to law, they can be restrained, dismissed, or punished. These rights to due process are the precious rights of all who live under the American flag—rich or poor, young or old, man or woman, and regardless of race, religion, or color.

In this chapter, we look at the rights of all persons to due process, but before we do, let us look at the precious freedoms and rights that American citizenship confers.

Citizenship Rights

Every nation has rules that determine nationality and define who is a member of, owes allegiance to, and is a subject of the nation. But in a constitutional democracy, citizenship is an *office,* and like other offices, it carries with it certain powers and responsibilities. How citizenship is acquired and retained is therefore important.

"All persons born or naturalized in the United States, and subject to the jurisdiction thereof, are citizens of the United States and of the State wherein they reside."

FOURTEENTH AMENDMENT TO THE U.S. CONSTITUTION

How Citizenship Is Acquired and Lost

The basic right of citizenship was not given constitutional protection until 1868, when the Fourteenth Amendment was adopted; before that, each state determined citizenship. The Fourteenth Amendment states, "All persons born or naturalized in the United States, and subject to the jurisdiction thereof, are citizens of the United States and of the State wherein they reside." This means that all persons born in the United States, except children born to foreign ambassadors and ministers, are citizens of this country regardless of the citizenship of their parents. (Congress has defined the United States for this purpose to include Puerto Rico, Guam, the Northern Marianas, and the Virgin Islands.) A child born to an American citizen living abroad or who has an American citizen as a grandparent is an American citizen if either the parent or grandparent has lived in the United States for at least five years, two years of which were after age 14. Although the Fourteenth Amendment does not make Native Americans citizens of the United States and of the states in which they live, Congress did so in 1924.

NATURALIZATION   Citizenship may also be acquired by **naturalization**, a legal act conferring citizenship on an alien. Congress determines naturalization requirements (see Table 16–1 for the list of requirements). Today, with minor exceptions, non-enemy aliens over age 18 who have been lawfully admitted for permanent residence and who have resided in the United States for at least five years and in the state for at least six months are eligible for naturalization. Any state or federal court in the United States or the Immigration and Naturalization Service (INS) can grant citizenship. The INS, with the help of the FBI, makes the necessary investigations.

Any person denied citizenship after a hearing before an immigration officer may appeal to a federal district judge. Citizenship is granted if the judge is satisfied that the applicant has met all the requirements after reviewing the FBI check that no disqualifying felony conviction has been found. The applicant renounces allegiance to his or her former country, swears to support and defend the Constitution and laws of the United States against all enemies, and promises to bear arms on behalf of the United States when required to do so by law. Those whose religious beliefs prevent them from bearing arms are allowed to take an oath swearing that if called to duty, they will serve in the armed forces as noncombatants or will perform work of national importance under civilian direction. The court or INS then grants a certificate of naturalization.

Proud naturalized citizens are sworn in at an emotional ceremony.

Naturalized citizenship may be revoked by court order if the government can prove that a person secured citizenship by deception. But citizenship cannot be taken from people because of what they have done—for example, for committing certain crimes, voting in foreign elections, or serving in foreign armies. In addition, any American may renounce citizenship. Even so, the government must prove that the citizen "not only voluntarily committed the expatriating act prescribed in the statute, but also intended to relinquish his citizenship."[3]

DUAL CITIZENSHIP   Because each nation has complete authority to define nationality for itself, two or more nations may consider a person a citizen. **Dual citizenship** is not unusual, especially for people from nations that do not recognize the right of individuals to renounce their citizenship, called the **right of expatriation**. Children born abroad to American citizens may also be citizens of the nation in which they were born. Children born in the United States of parents from a foreign nation may also be citizens of their parents' country.

Among the nations that allow dual citizenship are Canada, Mexico, France, and the United Kingdom. One expert estimates that based on the number of American children born to foreign-born parents, the number of Americans eligible to hold citizenship in another country grows by about 500,000 a year.[4] Moreover, with more than 7 million Mexican-born immigrants in the United States and their American-born

naturalization
A legal action conferring citizenship on an alien.

dual citizenship
Citizenship in more than one nation.

right of expatriation
The right to renounce one's citizenship.

TABLE 16–1 Requirements for Naturalization

An applicant for naturalization must:
1. Be over age 18.
2. Be lawfully admitted to the United States for permanent residence and have resided in the United States for at least five years and in the state for at least six months.
3. File a petition of naturalization with a clerk of a court of record (federal or state) verified by two witnesses.
4. Be able to read, write, and speak English.
5. Possess a good moral character.
6. Understand and demonstrate an attachment to the history, principles, and form of government of the United States.
7. Demonstrate that he or she is well disposed toward the good order and happiness of the country.
8. Demonstrate that he or she does not now believe in, nor within the last ten years has ever believed in, advocated, or belonged to an organization that supports opposition to organized government, overthrow of government by violence, or the doctrines of world communism or any other form of totalitarianism.

For more information about immigration and naturalization, go to the Web site of the Federation for American Immigration Reform, at www.fairus.org.

children now becoming eligible to apply for Mexican citizenship, the number of dual citizens in the United States is rising. Dual citizenship carries negative as well as positive consequences; for example, a person with dual citizenship may be subject to national service obligations and taxes in both countries.

Rights of American Citizens

An American becomes a citizen of one of our states merely by residing in that state. *Residence* as understood in the Fourteenth Amendment means the place one calls home. The legal status of residence should not be confused with the fact of physical presence. A person may be living in Washington, D.C., but be a citizen of California—that is, consider California home and vote in that state.

Most of our most important rights flow from *state* citizenship. In the *Slaughter-House Cases* (1873), the Supreme Court carefully distinguished between the privileges of U.S. citizens and those of state citizens.[5] It held that the only privileges of national citizenship are those that "owe their existence to the Federal Government, its National Character, its Constitution, or its laws." These privileges have never been completely specified, but they include the right to use the navigable waters of the United States and to protection on the high seas, to assemble peacefully and petition for redress of grievances, to vote if qualified to do so under state laws and have one's vote counted properly, and to travel throughout the United States.

In times of war, the rights and liberties of citizenship are tested and have been curbed. Although the Supreme Court overruled President Abraham Lincoln's use of military courts to try civilians during the Civil War,[6] it upheld the World War II internment of Japanese Americans in "relocation camps" and never questioned their loyalty or the government's argument that they posed a threat to national security. The Court drew a distinction between the rights of citizenship during peacetime and wartime, observing that, "hardships are part of war, and war is an aggregation of hardships. All citizens alike, both in and out of uniform, feel the impact of war in greater or lesser measure. Citizenship has its responsibilities as well as its privileges, and in time of war the burden is always heavier."[7] The Court also approved the use of military tribunals to try captured foreign saboteurs[8] who were held abroad, but ruled that citizens may not

Government's Greatest Endeavors

Reducing Disease

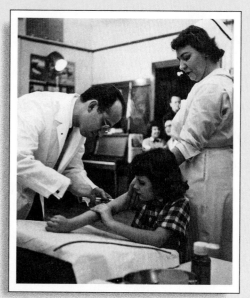

Jonas Salk administers his polio vaccine to children in 1954.

QUESTIONS

How has the effort to protect the nation from disease affected you or your family?

How much should the federal government do to promote healthy lifestyles through campaigns against smoking, speeding, and other life-threatening habits?

The framers guaranteed that the Constitution would protect life, liberty, and the pursuit of happiness, but these rights are impossible to exercise if Americans are haunted by life-threatening diseases. Indeed, the framers believed that science and reason were essential for self-government, and expected the new government to play a central role in supporting a healthy public.

The modern effort to reduce disease is one of the federal government's great achievements. Federal funding for research and vaccinations against diseases such as polio has rendered the disease virtually nonexistent, while ongoing research on heart disease, cancer, and HIV/AIDS has lengthened the lifespan of many Americans affected by these illnesses.

The modern campaign against disease began after World War II with the federal government's first programs for vaccinating children against deadly diseases. These national vaccination programs continue to this day with efforts to control the spread of the flu.

The federal vaccination program is administered by the Centers for Disease Control, which is also responsible for monitoring the spread of deadly diseases. Since the 1950s, when the federal government began its vaccination program, the incidence of most childhood diseases has fallen by 95 percent or more. The number of crippling polio cases fell from 15,000 annually in the early 1950s to zero today, while German measles is no longer a feared disease.

The federal government's research on other diseases, such as cancer, is led by the National Institutes of Health, which was created in 1887 when the federal government opened its first research institute on New York's Staten Island. Today's National Institutes of Health occupy a sprawling campus in Bethesda, Maryland, and conduct research on everything from aging to allergies and infectious diseases. ■

be subject to courts-martial or denied the guarantees of the Bill of Rights.[9] For that reason, John Walker Lindh, the young American captured fighting with the Taliban in Afghanistan in 2001, was accorded the assistance of counsel and tried in court.

In the war against international terrorism, President George W. Bush issued orders declaring U.S. citizens "enemy combatants" for plotting with the Al-Qaeda network, and authorized their and other captured foreign nationals' detention in military compounds, without counsel or access to a court of law. His orders were controversial and the Supreme Court ruled, in *Hamdi* v. *Rumsfeld* (2004) and *Rasul* v. *Bush* (2004), that U.S. citizens and foreign nationals may not be detained indefinitely without the opportunity to consult an attorney and to contest the basis for their detention before an independent tribunal.[10] In response to those rulings, President Bush ordered the trial of enemy combatants by military commissions. But when the commissions were challenged in *Hamdan* v. *Rumsfeld* (2006),[11] the Court held that the commissions' procedures violated basic tenets of military and international law, including the right to a speedy trial and the opportunity to respond to the charges and basis for detention. Writing for the Court, Justice Stevens held that the prisoners must be tried in civilian courts or in courts-martial according to the Uniform Code of Military Justice and the Geneva Conventions.

THE RIGHT TO LIVE AND TRAVEL IN THE UNITED STATES This right, which is not subject to any congressional limitation, is perhaps the most precious aspect of American citizenship. Aliens have no such right. They may be stopped on the high seas or at the borders and turned away if they fail to meet the terms and conditions stipulated by Congress for admission. Today millions of people around the world yearn to come and live in the United States, but only American citizens have a constitutionally guaranteed right to do so.

THE RIGHT TO TRAVEL ABROAD The right to international travel can be regulated within the bounds of due process. Under current law, it is unlawful for citizens to leave or enter the United States without a valid passport (except as otherwise provided by the president, as has been done for travel to Mexico, Canada, and parts of the Caribbean, although antiterrorism laws will soon eliminate these exceptions). Travel to Cuba is forbidden without special permission, as has increasingly been granted for journalists, artists, scholars, and politicians; however, the Bush administration tightened restrictions on Americans who want to visit their families in Cuba.

Rights of Aliens

During periods of suspicion and hostility toward aliens, the protections of citizenship are even more precious. Congress enacted the Enemy Alien Act of 1798, which remains in effect, authorizing the president during wartime to detain and expel citizens of a country with which we are at war. Citizens may not be expelled from the country, but aliens may be expelled for even minor infractions.[12] The Supreme Court also upheld the 1996 amendments to the Immigration and Naturalization Act that require mandatory detention during deportation hearings of aliens accused of certain crimes,[13] though they may not be held longer than six months.[14]

Still, the Constitution protects many rights of *all persons,* not just of American citizens. Only citizens may run for elective office and their right to vote may not be denied, but all other rights are not so literally restricted. Neither Congress nor the states can deny to aliens the rights of freedom of religion or freedom of speech. Nor can any government deprive any person of the due process of the law or equal protection under the laws.[15]

However, Congress and the states may deny or limit welfare and many other kinds of benefits to aliens. Congress has denied most federally assisted benefits to illegal immigrants and has permitted states to deny them many other benefits, making an exception only for emergency medical care, disaster relief, and some nutrition programs. The Court has also upheld laws barring the employment of aliens as police officers, schoolteachers, and probation officers.[16] While states have considerable discretion over what benefits they give to aliens, the Supreme Court has held that states cannot constitutionally exclude children of undocumented aliens from the public schools or charge their parents tuition.[17]

Admission to the United States

Although we are a nation populated largely by immigrants, throughout our history debates have flared among those wishing to open our borders and those wishing to close them. Americans have recently become increasingly concerned about illegal immigration and that admitting too many people from abroad will dilute our traditions and values. Recent polls found that nine out of ten Americans claim that immigration is a serious problem. According to the Census Bureau, there are more than 35 million immigrants in the United States, and racial and ethnic minorities now account for more than half of the population in California and Texas. Most immigrants are here legally, but an estimated 12 million are undocumented aliens—mostly from Mexico and Central and South America. They cross our borders not because they fear political persecution, but to secure greater economic opportunities.[18]

The inability to keep illegal aliens out of the country is not a question of constitutional power, for Congress has complete power over the admission of aliens. But the

Immigrants arriving at Ellis Island in 1900 came with high hopes but few material possessions.

problem of illegal immigration, and what to do about it, remains very divisive. Although Congress has authorized an increase in the number of border patrol guards and funded additional fencing of the U.S.-Mexico border, our borders extend for thousands of miles. Moreover, it is difficult to track down undocumented aliens once they are inside the United States and then expel them in a fashion consistent with the practices and policies of a free society. President Bush and the Senate favor a "guest worker" program, but the House favors achieving border security first. Conflicting pressures make compromises difficult. Latino groups are concerned that enforcing laws against hiring undocumented workers will make employers hesitate to hire any Latinos. Businesses contend that illegal immigrants are needed in service and construction jobs that would otherwise be difficult to fill. Some American workers argue that undocumented workers depress wages. State and local governments are under pressure to provide social services for undocumented aliens.

Congress has wide discretion in setting the numbers, terms, and conditions under which aliens can enter and stay in the United States. The Immigration Act of 1965, as amended in 1990 and 1996, sets an annual ceiling of 675,000 nonrefugee aliens allowed to come here as permanent residents, but when refugees and other exempt categories are added, about 800,000 people enter the United States legally each year. The law also sets an annual limit on immigrants from any single country. Preference is given for family reunification and to people who have special skills or who are needed to fill jobs for which U.S. workers are not available. Another provision allows for the admission of "millionaire immigrants" who are willing and able to invest a substantial sum to create or support a business in the United States that will provide jobs for Americans. Few have been admitted under this provision. There is also a "diversity" category to provide visas for 55,000 immigrants from 34 countries whether or not they have relatives living in the United States. These visas are drawn annually by lottery from a pool of qualified applicants.

In addition to regularly admitted aliens, the U.S. also admits political refugees. In recent years, more than 100,000 such refugees were admitted annually, but the Bush administration decreased the number to 70,000.[19] *Political refugees* are people who have well-founded fears of persecution in their own countries based on their race, religion, nationality, social class, or political opinions. People admitted as political refugees can apply to become permanent residents after one year. The attorney general, acting through the INS, may also grant *asylum* to applicants who have well-founded fears of persecution in the country to which they would be returned, based on the same criteria. Applicants, however, must not just face the same terrible conditions that all other citizens of their country face or wish to escape poverty. They must show specific danger of persecution.

The INS may turn back at the border persons seeking asylum if it considers their requests insubstantial; it may even hold them in detention camps. The president may order the Coast Guard—as Presidents George H. W. Bush and Bill Clinton did with respect to Haitian and Cuban refugees—to stop people on the high seas before they enter the territorial waters of the United States and return them to the country from which they have fled without determining whether they qualify as refugees.[20] Once in the United States, aliens are subject to the full range of obligations, including paying taxes. Aliens are counted in the census for the purpose of apportioning seats in the U.S. House of Representatives. Legally admitted aliens may be detained and deported for a variety of reasons—for example, conviction of crimes involving immoral acts, turpitude, incitement of terrorist activity, illegal voting in elections, and conviction of domestic violence. In the months following the September 2001 terrorist attacks, over 1,100 people were detained for questioning and their identities were not disclosed. Approximately 5,000 more people of Middle Eastern descent were questioned voluntarily.[21]

Property Rights

Constitutional Protection of Property

Property does not have rights. People do. People have the right to own, use, rent, invest in, buy, and sell property. Historically, American political thinking and political institutions have emphasized the close connection between liberty and owning property and between property and power. A major purpose of the framers of the Constitution was to establish a government strong enough to protect people's rights to use and enjoy their property. The framers also wanted to limit government so it could not endanger that right. As a result, the Constitution has a variety of clauses protecting **property rights**.

Of special concern to the framers were the efforts of some state legislatures to protect debtors at the expense of their creditors by issuing paper currency and setting aside private contracts. To prevent these practices, the legal tender and contract clauses in the Constitution forbid states from making anything except gold or silver legal tender to pay debts and from passing any "Law impairing the Obligation of Contracts."

The **contract clause** (Article I, Section 10) was designed to prevent states from extending the period during which debtors could meet their payments or otherwise evade contractual obligations. The framers had in mind an ordinary contract between private persons. However, beginning with Chief Justice John Marshall (1801–1835), the Supreme Court expanded the coverage of the clause to prevent states from taking away privileges previously conferred on corporations. In effect, the contract clause was used to protect property and to maintain the status quo at the expense of a state's power.

In the late nineteenth century, however, the Supreme Court gradually began to restrict the coverage of the contract clause and to subject contracts to what in constitutional law are known as **police powers**—the powers of states to protect the public health, safety, and welfare of their residents. By 1934, the Court actually held that state law could even modify contracts between individuals—the very ones the contract clause was intended to protect—to avert social and economic catastrophe.[22] Although the contract clause is still invoked occasionally to challenge state regulation of property, it no longer significantly limits governmental power.

What Happens When the Government Takes Our Property?

Both the national and state governments have the power of **eminent domain**—the power to take private property for public use—but the owner must be fairly compensated. This limitation, contained in the Fifth Amendment, was the first provision of the Bill of Rights to be enforced as a limitation on state governments as well as on the national government.[23]

What constitutes "taking" for purposes of eminent domain? Ordinarily, but not always, the taking must be direct, and a person must lose title and control over the property. Sometimes, especially in recent years, the courts have found that a governmental taking has gone "too far," and the government must compensate its owners, even when title is left in the owner's name.[24] These are called **regulatory takings**. Thus if a government creates landing and takeoff paths for airplanes over property adjacent to an airport, making the land unsuitable for its original use (say, raising chickens), compensation is warranted.[25] The government may, however, impose land use and environmental regulations, temporarily prohibiting the development of a property, without compensating the owners.[26]

In a major and controversial ruling with wide-ranging ramifications for urban planners and homeowners, a bare majority of the Court upheld the use of the government's

property rights
The rights of an individual to own, use, rent, invest in, buy, and sell property.

contract clause
Clause of the Constitution (Article I, Section 10) originally intended to prohibit state governments from modifying contracts made between individuals; for a while interpreted as prohibiting state governments from taking actions that adversely affect property rights; no longer interpreted so broadly and no longer constrains state governments from exercising their police powers.

police powers
Inherent powers of state governments to pass laws to protect the public health, safety, and welfare; the national government has no directly granted police powers but accomplishes the same goals through other delegated powers.

eminent domain
Power of a government to take private property for public use; the U.S. Constitution gives national and state governments this power and requires them to provide just compensation for property so taken.

regulatory taking
Government regulation of property so extensive that government is deemed to have taken the property by the power of eminent domain, for which it must compensate the property owners.

power of eminent domain to condemn and take, with just compensation, private property for the purpose of advancing the economic development of a community. *Kelo* v. *City of New London* (2005) held that "public use" was not limited to the use of eminent domain to build a road or a bridge, but includes "promoting economic development," even if the property was taken and sold for development to private developers.[27]

"Just compensation" is not always easy to define. When there is a dispute over compensation, the courts make the final resolution based on the rule that "the owner is entitled to receive what a willing buyer would pay in cash to a willing seller at the time of the taking."[28] An owner is not entitled to compensation for the personal value of an old, broken-down, dearly loved house—just the value of the old, broken-down house.

Due Process Rights

Perhaps the most difficult parts of the Constitution to understand are the clauses in the Fifth and Fourteenth Amendments forbidding the national and state governments to deny any person life, liberty, or property without "due process of law." Cases involving these guarantees have resulted in hundreds of Supreme Court decisions. Even so, it is impossible to explain *due process* precisely. In fact, the Supreme Court has refused to give due process a precise definition and has emphasized that "due process, unlike some legal rules, is not a technical conception with a fixed content unrelated to time, place and circumstances."[29] We define **due process** as rules and regulations that restrain those in government who exercise power. There are, however, basically two kinds of due process: procedural and substantive.

Procedural Due Process

Traditionally, **procedural due process** refers not to the law itself but to *how a law is applied.* To paraphrase Daniel Webster's famous definition, the due process of law requires a procedure that hears before it condemns, proceeds upon inquiry, and renders judgment only after a trial or some kind of hearing. Originally, procedural due process was limited to criminal prosecutions, but it now applies to most kinds of governmental proceedings. It is required, for instance, in juvenile hearings, disbarment proceedings, proceedings to determine eligibility for welfare payments, revocation of drivers' licenses, and disciplinary proceedings in state universities and public schools.

A law may also violate the procedural due process requirement if it is too vague or if it creates an improper presumption of guilt. A vague statute fails to provide adequate warning and does not contain sufficient guidelines for law enforcement officials, juries, and courts.

The liberties that due process protects include "the right of the individual to contract, to engage in any of the common occupations of life, to acquire useful knowledge, to marry, to establish a home and bring up children, to worship God according to the dictates of his own conscience, and generally to enjoy those common law privileges long recognized as essential to the orderly pursuit of happiness by free men."[30] The property due process protects includes a variety of rights that may be conferred by state law, such as certain kinds of licenses, protection from being fired from some jobs except for just cause (for example, incompetence) and according to certain procedures, and protection from deprivation of certain pension rights.

Substantive Due Process

Procedural due process limits *how* governmental power may be exercised; **substantive due process** limits *what* a government may do. Procedural due process mainly limits the executive and judicial branches because they apply the law and review its application; substantive due process mainly limits the legislative branch because it enacts laws. Substantive due process means that an "unreasonable" law, even if properly passed and properly applied, is unconstitutional. It means that governments *should not be allowed to do certain things.*

due process
Established rules and regulations that restrain government officials.

procedural due process
Constitutional requirement that governments proceed by proper methods; limits how government may exercise power.

substantive due process
Constitutional requirement that governments act reasonably and that the substance of the laws themselves be fair and reasonable; limits what a government may do.

Before 1937, substantive due process was used primarily to protect the right of employers to make contracts with employees freely, without government interference.[31] During this period, conservative jurists who considered almost all social welfare legislation unreasonable dominated the Supreme Court. They used the due process clause to strike down laws setting maximum hours of labor, establishing minimum wages, regulating prices, and forbidding employers to fire workers because they joined a union.

Since 1937, the Supreme Court has largely refused to apply the doctrine of substantive due process in reviewing laws regulating business enterprises and economic interests. The Court now believes that deciding what constitutes reasonable regulation of business and commercial life is a legislative, not a judicial, responsibility. As long as the justices find a conceivable connection between a law regulating business and the promotion of the public welfare, the Supreme Court will not interfere with laws passed by Congress or state legislatures.

This does not mean, however, that the Court has abandoned substantive due process. On the contrary, it has taken on new life as a protector of civil liberties, especially the right of privacy. Substantive due process has deep roots in concepts of natural law and a long history in the American constitutional tradition. For most Americans most of the time, it is not enough merely to say that a law reflects the wishes of the popular or legislative majority. We also want our laws to be just, and we rely heavily on judges to decide what is just.

Privacy Rights

The most important extension of substantive due process in recent decades has been its expansion to protect the right of privacy, especially marital privacy. Although the Constitution does not mention the right to privacy, in *Griswold* v. *Connecticut* (1965), the Supreme Court pulled together elements of the First, Third, Fourth, Fifth, Ninth, and Fourteenth Amendments to recognize that personal privacy is one of the rights the Constitution protects.[32]

This right has three aspects: (1) the right to be free from governmental surveillance and intrusion, especially with respect to intimate decisions on sexuality; (2) the right not to have the government make private affairs public; and (3) the right to be free in thought and belief from governmental regulations.[33]

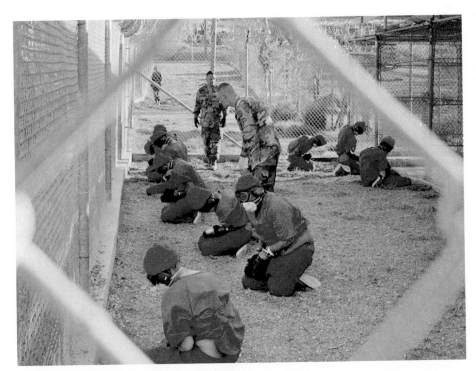

The USA PATRIOT Act, passed in the wake of the September 11, 2001, attacks, and renewed in 2006, removes those designated by the president as "enemy combatants" from many of the procedural due process protections that are the cornerstone of the U.S. legal system. Both U.S. citizens and noncitizens alike can be designated as "enemy combatants" at the president's discretion.

History Makers

Estelle Griswold

Estelle Griswold

Estelle Trébert Griswold was born in 1900 and became the executive director of the Planned Parenthood League of Connecticut (PPLC) in 1953. In that position, she led a fight to legalize birth control in Connecticut that resulted in a landmark Supreme Court ruling on the right of privacy and the Constitution's protection for intimate decisions on human sexuality.

Connecticut had prohibited the use of contraceptives in an 1879 law and had also made it a crime to "assist, abet, or counsel" someone on birth control. By the 1950s, contraceptives were nonetheless widely sold in drug stores in the state, and the law was generally ignored. But Griswold and some doctors and advocates of women's rights contended that the law had a chilling effect. Griswold and the PPLC lobbied the state legislature to repeal the law, but the Catholic-dominated Connecticut state senate blocked the repeal. Courts refused to strike down the law.

Griswold and Dr. Lee Buxton decided to open a birth control clinic in Connecticut and create a test case challenging the law. After opening the clinic, they held a press conference. A few days later, police arrived and, after receiving PPLC literature, arrested Griswold and Buxton, who were tried in state court, convicted, and fined $100 each for violating the law.

On appeal in *Griswold* v. *Connecticut* (1965),* the Supreme Court struck down Connecticut's law for violating a constitutionally protected right of privacy. The decision remains controversial because the Bill of Rights does not specifically enumerate a right to privacy. But the ruling laid the basis for other landmark decisions on a woman's right to choose, in *Roe* v. *Wade* (1973),[†] and on constitutional protection for private consensual sexual activities in *Lawrence* v. *Texas* (2003),[‡] which struck down Texas's law making homosexual sodomy a crime. ∎

---

*Griswold v. Connecticut, 381 U.S. 479 (1965).
[†]Roe v. Wade, 410 U.S. 113 (1973).
[‡]Lawrence v. Texas, 539 U.S. 558 (2003).

Abortion Rights

The most controversial aspect of constitutional protection of privacy relates to the extent of state power to regulate abortions. In *Roe* v. *Wade* (1973), the Supreme Court ruled that (1) during the first trimester of a woman's pregnancy, it is an unreasonable and therefore unconstitutional interference with her liberty and privacy rights for a state to set any limits on her choice to have an abortion or on her doctor's medical judgments about how to carry it out; (2) during the second trimester, the state's interest in protecting the health of women becomes compelling, and a state may make a reasonable regulation about how, where, and when abortions may be performed; and (3) during the third trimester, when the fetus becomes capable of surviving outside the womb, the state's interest in protecting the unborn child is so important that the state can prohibit abortions altogether, except when necessary to preserve the life or health of the mother.[34]

The *Roe* decision led to decades of heated public debate and attempts by Presidents Ronald Reagan and the first George Bush to select Supreme Court justices who might reverse it. Nonetheless, *Roe* v. *Wade* was reaffirmed in *Planned Parenthood* v. *Casey* (1992). A bitterly divided Court, by a five-person majority (O'Connor, Kennedy, Souter, Blackmun, and Stevens), upheld the view that the due process clause of the Constitution protects a woman's liberty to choose an abortion prior to viability. The Court, however, held that the right to have an abortion prior to viability may be subject to state regulation that does not "unduly burden" it. In other words, states may make "reasonable regulations" on how a woman exercises her right to an abortion so long as they do not prohibit any woman from making the ultimate decision on whether to terminate a pregnancy before viability.[35]

Applying the undue burden test, the Court has held, on the one hand, that states can prohibit the use of state funds and facilities for performing abortions; states may make a minor's right to an abortion conditional on her first notifying at least one parent or a judge; and states may require women to sign an informed consent form and wait 24 hours before having an abortion. On the other hand, a state may not condition a woman's right to an abortion on her first notifying her husband. The Court also struck down Nebraska's ban on "partial birth" abortions in *Stenberg* v. *Carhart* (2000) because it completely forbade one kind of medical procedure and provided no exception for when a woman's life is at stake and thus imposed an "undue burden" on women.[36] Nonetheless, Congress passed and President George W. Bush signed into federal law a similar ban on "partial birth" abortions that was immediately challenged in the courts, and which has been appealed to the Supreme Court. A number of states have also recently enacted laws that limit access to abortions in anticipation that the Supreme Court may uphold them or even overrule *Roe* v. *Wade*. South Dakota, for instance, passed a law banning all abortions if *Roe* is overturned.

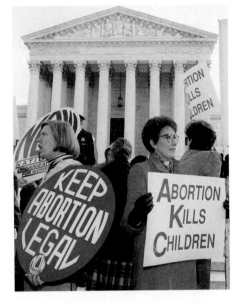

The battle over abortion has been fought in the courts and on the streets, and has been a key issue in recent presidential elections.

Sexual Orientation Rights

Although there is general agreement on how much constitutional protection is provided for marital privacy, in *Bowers* v. *Hardwick* (1986), the Supreme Court refused to extend such protection to private relations between homosexuals[37]; a bare majority of the Court also held that the Boy Scouts of America may exclude homosexuals.[38] By a 5-to-4 vote in *Bowers,* the Court refused to declare unconstitutional a Georgia law that made consensual sodomy a crime. But state supreme courts, including Georgia's, later found greater privacy protection in their state constitutions than the U.S. Supreme Court found in the U.S. Constitution. Finally, in *Lawrence* v. *Texas* (2003),[39] the Court struck down Texas's law making homosexual sodomy a crime. Writing for the Court and noting the trend in state court decisions that did not follow *Bowers,* Justice Kennedy held the law to violate personal autonomy and the right of privacy. Dissenting, Justice Scalia, along with Chief Justice Rehnquist and Justice Thomas, warned that the decision might lead to overturning laws barring same-sex marriages, as some state courts and Canadian courts had already done.

The U.S. Supreme Court, in *Romer* v. *Evans* (1996),[40] also struck down an initiative amending the Colorado constitution that prohibited state and local governments from protecting homosexuals from discrimination. Although the Court did not rule on the basis of substantive due process, it held that this provision violated the equal protection clause because it lacked a rational basis and simply represented prejudice toward a particular group.

The rulings in *Romer* v. *Evans* and *Lawrence* v. *Texas* ignited a continuing controversy over same-sex marriages, particularly after the Massachusetts supreme court ruled in 2003 that its state constitution forbids denying marriage licenses to same-sex couples. A number of states have recently adopted state constitutional amendments forbidding same-sex marriages, and in 2006 President Bush urged Congress to enact a federal constitutional amendment banning same-sex marriages. The state laws, though, have been challenged in the courts. Nebraska's law was struck down by a federal court, but high courts in New York and Georgia upheld their state laws defining marriage as between a man and a woman. While Massachusetts remains the only state to grant same-sex couples marriage licenses, Connecticut and Vermont recognize same-sex civil unions. The District of Columbia, California, Hawaii, Maine, and New Jersey also recognize some spousal benefits, like health care and inheritance rights, for same-sex couples.

The right of privacy as an element of substantive due process is one of the developing edges of constitutional law, one about which people both on and off the Court have strong disagreements. How the Supreme Court handles privacy issues has become front-page news.

Rights of Persons Accused of Crimes

Despite what you see in police dramas on television and in the movies, law enforcement officers have no general right to break down doors and invade homes. They are not supposed to search people except under certain conditions, and they have no right to arrest them except under certain circumstances. They also may not compel confessions, and they must respect other procedural guarantees aimed at ensuring fairness and the rights of the accused. Persons accused of crimes are guaranteed these and other rights under the Fourth, Fifth, Sixth, Eighth, and Fourteenth Amendments.

Freedom from Unreasonable Searches and Seizures

According to the Fourth Amendment, "The right of the people to be secure in their persons, houses, papers, and effects, against unreasonable searches and seizures, shall not be violated, and no Warrants shall issue, but upon probable cause, supported by Oath or affirmation, and particularly describing the place to be searched, and the persons or things to be seized."

Protection from unreasonable searches and seizures requires police, if they have time, to obtain a valid **search warrant**, issued by a magistrate after the police indicate under oath that they have *probable cause* to justify it. Magistrates must perform this function in a neutral and detached manner and not serve merely as rubber stamps for the police. The warrant must specify the place to be searched and the things to be seized. *General search warrants*—warrants that authorize police to search a particular place or person without limitation—are unconstitutional. A search warrant is usually needed to search a person in any place he or she has an "expectation of privacy that society is prepared to recognize as reasonable," for example, in a hotel room, a rented home, or a friend's apartment.[41] In short, the Fourth Amendment protects people, not places, from unreasonable governmental intrusions.[42]

Police may make reasonable *warrantless searches* in *public places* if the officers have probable cause, or at least a reasonable suspicion, that the persons in question have committed or are about to commit crimes. No later than two days after making such an arrest, the police must take the arrested person to a magistrate, so that the magistrate—not just the police—can decide whether probable cause existed to justify

search warrant

A writ issued by a magistrate that authorizes the police to search a particular place or person, specifying the place to be searched and the objects to be seized.

Police exercise a reasonable search of this man's car after having probable cause that a crime had been committed. The man was arrested after police found stolen goods in his car.

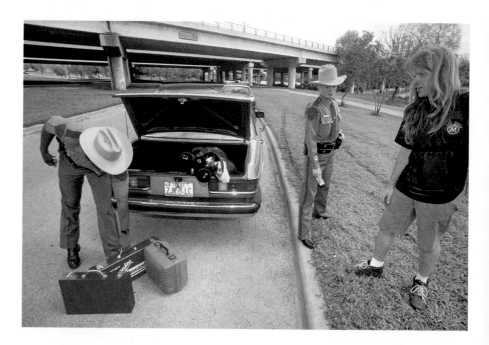

the warrantless arrest.[43] Probable cause, however, does not, except in extreme emergencies, justify a warrantless arrest of people in their own homes.

Under the common law, police officers apprehending a fleeing suspected felon can use weapons that might result in the felon's serious injury or even death. But the Fourth Amendment places substantial limits on the use of what is called *deadly force*. It is unconstitutional to shoot at an apparently unarmed, fleeing suspected felon unless the officer has probable cause to believe that the suspect poses a significant threat of death or serious injury to the officer or others. Also, when feasible, the officer must first warn the suspect, "Halt or I'll shoot."

Not every time the police stop a person to ask questions or seek that person's consent to a search is there a seizure or detention requiring probable cause or a warrant. If the police just ask questions or even seek consent to search an individual's person or possessions in a noncoercive atmosphere, there is no detention. "So long as a reasonable person would feel free 'to disregard the police and go about his business,' the encounter is consensual and no reasonable suspicion is required." But if the person refuses to answer questions or consent to a search, and the police, by either physical force or a show of authority, restrain the movement of the person, even though there is no arrest, the Fourth Amendment comes into play.[44] For example, if police approach people in airports and request identification, this act by itself does not constitute a detention. The same is true if police ask bus passengers for consent to search their luggage for drugs. But if the police do more, especially after consent is refused, then they must have some objective justification for the search beyond mere suspicion.[45]

The Supreme Court also upheld, in *Terry* v. *Ohio* (1968), a *stop and frisk* exception to searches of individuals when officers have reason to believe they are armed and dangerous or have committed or are about to commit a criminal offense. The *Terry* search is limited to a quick pat-down to check for weapons that might be used to assault the arresting officer, to check for contraband, to determine identity, or to maintain the status quo while obtaining more information.[46] If individuals who are stopped for questioning refuse to identify themselves, they may be arrested, though police must have a reasonable suspicion they are involved in criminal activities.[47] If an officer stops and frisks a suspect to look for weapons and finds criminal evidence that might justify an arrest, the officer can make a full search.[48] Police and border guards may also conduct *border* searches—searches of persons and the goods they bring with them at border crossings.[49] The border search exception also permits officials to open mail entering the country if they have "reasonable cause" to suspect it contains merchandise imported in violation of the law.[50]

There are several other exceptions to the general rule against warrantless searches and seizures of what is found by police and customs officials. The most important are the following:

1. *The Plain-View Exception.* The plain-view exception permits officers to seize evidence without a warrant if they are lawfully in a position from which the evidence can be viewed, it is immediately apparent to them that the items they observe are evidence of a crime or are contraband, and they have probable cause to believe—a reasonable suspicion will not do—that the evidence uncovered is contraband or evidence of a crime.[51] Police may also enter a dwelling if they have probable cause to believe someone inside is threatened with serious injury.[52]

2. *Exigent Circumstances.* Searches are permissible when officers do not have time to secure a warrant before evidence is destroyed, when a criminal escapes capture, or when there is a need "to protect or preserve life or avoid serious injury." For example, firefighters and police may enter a burning building without a warrant and may remain there for a reasonable time to investigate the cause of the blaze after the fire has been extinguished. However, after the fire has been put out, the police cannot use the emergency as an excuse to make an exhaustive, warrantless search for evidence.

3. *The Automobile Exception.* If officers have probable cause to believe that an automobile is being used to commit a crime, even a traffic offense, or that it contains persons who have committed crimes, or that it contains evidence of crimes, they may stop the automobile, detain the persons found in it, and search them and any containers or packages they find inside the car.[53] Once an automobile has been lawfully detained, the police officers may order the driver and passengers to get out of the car without violating the Fourth Amendment[54]; they may also use drug-sniffing dogs around cars stopped for routine traffic violations.[55] If police arrest the driver, they may search the contents of the car.[56]

4. *Foreign Intelligence and National Security.* Although the Supreme Court has never directly sustained it, Congress has endorsed the presidential claim that a president can authorize warrantless wiretaps and physical searches of agents of foreign countries. Congress created the Foreign Intelligence Surveillance Court to approve such requests; this court, consisting of federal district judges, meets in secret. The USA PATRIOT Act of 2001, which was renewed in 2006, expanded the size of this court, lowered the basis for its approval of warrants in cases involving terrorism, and permits searches for foreign intelligence and evidence of terrorist activities.

A recent controversy erupted over the revelation that President Bush issued a secret executive order authorizing the National Security Agency (NSA) to conduct warrantless electronic surveillance of "communications where one . . . party to the communication is outside the United States" and there is "a reasonable basis to conclude that one party" supports terrorists. The surveillance involves monitoring e-mails through Google-like searches, and tracking cell-phone calls. The administration defended the surveillance on three grounds. First, the president has the inherent power as commander in chief to do so during times of war. Second, the joint resolution for the Authorization for the Use of Military Force (AUMF) of 2001 provides for the use of "all necessary and appropriate" force to combat terrorists, and thus justifies the president's action. Third, the AUMF justifies not complying with the provisions of the Foreign Intelligence Surveillance Act (FISA), since it superseded FISA. But, some members of Congress and civil liberties groups counter that the president has no such inherent power and that neither the AUMF nor FISA permit such a program. After months of negotiations, in 2006 Congress enacted legislation reasserting the authority of the Foreign Intelligence Surveillance Court, while permitting wiretapping without a warrant for up to 45 days but requiring the attorney general to certify and explain why such wireless surveillance is necessary to a subcommittee of the Senate Intelligence Committee.[57]

In addition, various administrative searches by nonpolice government agents, such as teachers and health officials, do not require search warrants. Rules governing the conduct of such administrative searches are more lenient than those for searches by police investigating crimes. In certain limited circumstances, the courts have upheld administrative searches conducted without grounds for suspicion of particular individuals.[58]

One recent troublesome area relates to **racial profiling**—the police target members of certain racial groups for street questioning or traffic stops on the assumption that members of these groups are likely to be engaged in illegal activities. African Americans and civil rights organizations have complained for years about the practice because police do not need probable cause to stop someone and because it encourages racial discrimination.[59] In response, President George W. Bush issued guidelines governing 70 federal law enforcement agencies that bar the use of race and ethnicity in routine investigations; however, federal agencies may still use these racial and ethnic profiles to "identify terrorist threats and stop potential catastrophic attacks."[60]

The recent expansion of compulsory, random drug testing is also controversial. The Supreme Court has upheld the constitutionality of blood and urine tests of rail employees involved in train accidents, of federal employees, and of high school students engaged in interscholastic athletic competitions. But it struck down a Georgia

racial profiling
Police targeting of racial minorities as potential suspects of criminal activities.

Following Semptember 11, 2001, airport security was tightened throughout the country. Such extensive searches are lawful because they are technically voluntary.

law requiring candidates for designated state offices to certify that they had taken and passed a drug test because Georgia failed to show why this invasion of personal privacy was necessary.[61] In 2002, however, the Court on a 5-to-4 vote held that schools may require students who participate in extracurricular activities of any kind to submit to random drug tests.[62]

THE EXCLUSIONARY RULE In *Mapp* v. *Ohio* (1961), the Supreme Court adopted a rule excluding evidence from a criminal trial that the police obtained unconstitutionally or illegally.[63] This **exclusionary rule** was adopted to prevent police misconduct. Critics question why criminals should go free just because of police misconduct or ineptness,[64] but the Supreme Court has refused to abandon the rule. It has made some exceptions to it, however, such as cases in which police relied in "good faith" on a search warrant that subsequently turned out to be defective or granted improperly.[65]

THE RIGHT TO REMAIN SILENT During the seventeenth century, special courts in England forced confessions by torture and intimidation from religious dissenters. The British privilege against self-incrimination developed in response to these practices. Because they were familiar with this history, the framers of our Bill of Rights included in the Fifth Amendment the provision that persons shall not be compelled to testify against themselves in criminal prosecutions. This protection against self-incrimination is designed to strengthen the fundamental principle that no person has an obligation to prove innocence. Rather, the burden is on the government to prove guilt.

The privilege against self-incrimination applies literally only in criminal prosecutions. But it has always been interpreted to protect any person subject to questioning by any agency of government, such as a congressional committee. It is not enough, however, to contend that answering questions might be embarrassing or might lead to loss of a job or even to civil suits; persons must have a reasonable fear that their answers might support a criminal prosecution against them.

Sometimes authorities would rather have information from witnesses than prosecute them. Congress has established procedures so that prosecutors and congressional committees may secure a grant of **immunity** for such a witness. When immunity has been granted, a witness no longer has a constitutional right to refuse to testify, and the government cannot use the information derived directly from the compelled testimony in any subsequent prosecution, though it may use other evidence to prosecute the witness for crimes.

exclusionary rule
Requirement that evidence unconstitutionally or illegally obtained be excluded from a criminal trial.

immunity
Exemption from prosecution for a particular crime in return for testimony pertaining to the case.

THE *MIRANDA* WARNING   Police questioning of suspects is a key procedure in solving crimes. Roughly 90 percent of all criminal convictions result from guilty pleas and never reach a full trial. Police questioning, however, can easily be abused. Police officers sometimes forget or ignore the constitutional rights of suspects, especially those who are frightened and ignorant. Unauthorized detention and lengthy interrogation to wring confessions from suspects, common practice in police states, were not unknown in the United States.

Federal and state laws require police officers to take people they have arrested before a magistrate promptly, so that the magistrate may inform them of their constitutional rights and allow them to get in touch with friends and seek legal advice. Despite these requirements, police were often tempted to quiz suspects first, trying to get them to confess before a magistrate informed them of their constitutional right to remain silent.

To put an end to such practices, the Supreme Court, in *Miranda* v. *Arizona* (1966), announced that no conviction could stand if evidence introduced at the trial had been obtained by the police during "custodial interrogation" unless suspects were notified that they have a right to remain silent and that anything they say can and will be used against them; to terminate questioning at any point; to have an attorney present during questioning by police; and to have a lawyer appointed to represent them if they cannot afford to hire their own attorney.[66] If suspects answer questions in the absence of an attorney, the burden is on prosecutors to demonstrate that suspects knowingly and intelligently gave up their right to remain silent. Failure to comply with these requirements leads to reversal of a conviction, even if other evidence is sufficient to establish guilt.

Critics of the *Miranda* decision believe that the Supreme Court severely limited the ability of the police to bring criminals to justice. Over the years, the Court has modified the original ruling by allowing evidence obtained contrary to the *Miranda* guidelines to be used to attack the credibility of defendants who offer testimony at their trial that conflicts with their statements to the police. Congress tried to get around *Miranda* in the Crime Control and Safe Streets Act of 1968 by allowing confessions made in violation of *Miranda* to be used as evidence in federal courts. But in *Dickerson* v. *United States* (2000), the Court reaffirmed the constitutionality of the *Miranda* doctrine. In an opinion by Chief Justice William H. Rehnquist, the Court held that the *Miranda* warning is not merely a rule of evidence to enforce the constitutional guarantee but is itself constitutionally required and applies in both state and federal courts.[67]

The case of Ernesto Miranda (right) led to the Supreme Court decision in 1966 requiring suspects in police custody to be advised of their constitutional rights to remain silent and to have an attorney present during questioning.

Fair Trial Procedures

Many people consider the rights of persons accused of a crime to be less important than other rights. But as Justice Felix Frankfurter observed, "The history of liberty has largely been the history of observance of procedural safeguards." Further, these safeguards have frequently "been forged in controversies involving not very nice people."[68] Nonetheless, they guarantee that all persons accused of crimes will have the right to representation by counsel and to a fair trial by an impartial jury.

THE RIGHT TO COUNSEL   If after questioning by police the suspect is arrested and charged with a crime, the Supreme Court has ruled that the accused has a constitutional right to counsel at every stage of the criminal proceedings—preliminary hearings, bail hearings, trial, sentencing, and first appeal. Communications between the accused and counsel are privileged and may not be revealed to a judge or jury. However, in cases of terrorism, under new guidelines issued by Attorney General John Ashcroft, police may listen in, undercover, on consultations between lawyers and detainees if there is a reasonable suspicion that a detainee and attorney are facilitating.

INDICTMENT Except for members of the armed forces and foreign terrorists, the national government cannot require anyone to stand trial for a serious crime except on the basis of a grand jury indictment or its equivalent; states are not required to use grand juries, and those that do not use them vest prosecutors instead with the power to seek indictments. A **grand jury** is concerned not with a person's guilt or innocence but merely with whether there is enough evidence to warrant a trial. The grand jury has wide-ranging investigatory powers and "is to inquire into all information that might bear on its investigations until it is satisfied that it has identified an offense or satisfied itself that none has occurred."[69] The strict rules that govern jury proceedings do not apply. The grand jury may admit hearsay evidence, and the exclusionary rule to enforce the Fourth Amendment does not apply. If a majority of the grand jurors agree that a trial is justified, they return what is known as a *true bill*, or **indictment**.

The Constitution guarantees the accused the right to be informed of the nature and cause of the accusation, so that he or she can prepare a defense. After indictment for an offense, prosecutors and the attorney for the accused usually discuss the possibility of a **plea bargain** whereby the defendant pleads guilty to a lesser offense that carries a lesser penalty. Prosecutors, facing more cases than they can handle, like plea bargains because they save the expense and time of going to trial. Likewise, defendants are often willing to "cop a plea" for a lesser offense to avoid the risk of more serious punishment.

Once defendants plead guilty, they usually can no longer raise objections to their conviction. That is why, before accepting guilty pleas, the judge questions defendants to be sure their attorneys have explained the alternatives and they know what they are doing.

TRIAL After indictment and preliminary hearings that determine bail and what evidence will be used against the accused, the Constitution guarantees a *speedy and public trial*. Do not, however, take the word "speedy" too literally. Defendants are given time to prepare their defense and in fact often ask for delays because delays can work to their advantage. In contrast, if the government denies the accused a speedy trial, not only is the conviction reversed but the case must also be dismissed outright.

Under the Sixth Amendment, the accused has a right to trial before a **petit jury** selected from the state and district in which the alleged crime was committed. Although federal law requires juries of 12 members, the Supreme Court has held that states may try defendants before juries consisting of as few as six persons. Conviction in federal courts must be by unanimous vote, but the Court has ruled that state courts may render guilty verdicts by nonunanimous juries, provided that such juries consist of six or more persons.[70]

An *impartial jury,* one that meets the requirements of due process and equal protection, consists of persons who represent a fair cross section of the community. Although defendants are not entitled to juries on which there must be individuals of their own race, sex, religion, or national origin, government prosecutors cannot strike people from juries because of race or gender, and neither can defense attorneys use what are called *peremptory challenges* to keep people off juries because of race, ethnic origin, or sex.[71]

During the trial, the defendant has a right to obtain witnesses in his or her favor and to have the judge subpoena witnesses to appear at the trial and testify. Both the accused and witnesses may refuse to testify on the grounds that their testimony would tend to incriminate themselves. If witnesses testify, both the prosecution and the defense have the right to confront and cross-examine them.

Sentencing and Punishment

At the conclusion of the trial, the jury recommends a verdict of guilty or not guilty. If the accused is found guilty, the judge hands down the sentence. The Eighth Amendment forbids the levying of excessive fines and the inflicting of cruel and unusual punishment.

In federal courts, judges follow the sentencing guidelines set down by the United States Sentencing Commission. Such sentences are not considered cruel and unusual. Many states have also established guidelines for sentencing by state courts.

"The court finds itself on the horns of a dilemma. On the one hand, wiretap evidence is inadmissible, and on the other hand, I'm dying to hear it."

grand jury
A jury of 12 to 23 persons who, in private, hear evidence presented by the government to determine whether persons shall be required to stand trial. If the jury believes there is sufficient evidence that a crime was committed, it issues an indictment.

indictment
A formal written statement from a grand jury charging an individual with an offense; also called a *true bill.*

plea bargain
Agreement between a prosecutor and a defendant that the defendant will plead guilty to a lesser offense to avoid having to stand trial for a more serious offense.

petit jury
A jury of six to 12 persons that determines guilt or innocence in a civil or criminal action.

Agents of Change

Mark Hanis and the Genocide Intervention Network

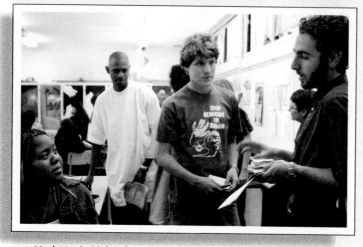

Mark Hanis (right), founder of the Genocide Intervention Network

QUESTIONS

Why don't students do more to combat human rights abuses or take on other political issues?

How can your college help?

The Genocide Intervention Network was created in 2003 at Swarthmore College to encourage students to protest international human rights abuses in Sudan and other nations. Still located on the Swarthmore campus, the Net-work attempts to engage other colleges and students in protesting such abuses on campuses and through traditional political engagement such as letters to Congress and protest marches. Its first target was the genocide in Darfur, which has claimed the lives of thousands of innocent civilians in a civil war between the Sudanese government and ethnic groups.

The Network was created by Mark Hanis, who asked why his fellow students were so passive in the face of such great abuse. "Hopefully, it's not due to our busy schedules," he wrote in the student newspaper. "Perhaps we haven't found any means of action here, even though professors and students in various disciplines across the country are writing letters and raising the political cost of failure to stop the genocide. With protests going on all over the country, it wouldn't be hard to organize one at Swarthmore and get the local media involved."

Thus far, the Network has expanded to include coalitions with other campus organizations and to provide training to students across the nation. The Network also provides links to news coverage of genocide and advice on how to get students involved through "virtual house-parties" and other Internet-based organizing. As Hanis wrote, "There's no excuse for inaction on Sudan. We should refuse to stand by as most of the world did during the Armenian genocide, the Holocaust, the Cambodian genocide and the Rwandan genocide...." ∎

Learn more about the Network at www.genocideintervention.net.

THREE STRIKES AND YOU'RE OUT   Although the crime rate has actually been going down in the past few years, public concern about crime remains high. At the national and state level, presidents, governors, and legislators vie with one another to show their toughness on crime. California, Virginia, Washington, and other states have "three strikes and you're out" laws, requiring a lifetime sentence without the possibility of parole for anyone convicted of a third felony, even if it is a minor offense. In some states, the felonies must be for violent crimes; in others, any three felonies will do. Scholars are skeptical that "three strikes and you're out" laws reduce crime, and constructing and staffing more jails to take care of aging felons is expensive. Nonetheless, the Supreme Court in *Ewing* v. *California* (2003) upheld California's tough law for committing three felonies, and the Court held that a 25-years-to-life sentence for stealing three golf clubs, each valued at $399, did not violate the prohibition against cruel and unusual punishment.[72]

APPEALS AND DOUBLE JEOPARDY   After trial, conviction, and sentencing, defendants may appeal their convictions if they claim they have been denied some constitutional right or the due process and equal protection of the law. The Fifth Amendment also provides that no person shall be "subject for the same offense to be twice put in jeopardy of life or limb." **Double jeopardy** does not prevent punishment by the national and the state governments for the same offense or for successive prosecutions for the same crime by two states. Nor does the double jeopardy clause forbid civil prosecutions, even after a person has been acquitted in a criminal trial for the same charge.[73]

double jeopardy
Trial or punishment for the same crime by the same government; forbidden by the Constitution.

★ ★ ★
How Other Nations Govern
★ ★

The Death Penalty Around the World

The United States and Japan are the only two industrialized countries that retain the death penalty. Most of the 77 countries that still impose capital punishment are in Africa, the Middle East, the Caribbean, and Central America.

According to Amnesty International, 118 countries have abolished capital punishment for all or most crimes. In the last 30 years, 66 countries joined this group, most recently the Philippines (2006), Bhutan and Samoa (2004), Armenia (2003), and Cyprus and Yugoslavia (2002).

Among the countries that abolished capital punishment for all crimes are the countries in the European Union, other Western and Eastern European countries,

Cambodia, and South Africa. Fourteen other countries have abolished capital punishment for ordinary criminal offenses: Albania, Argentina, Armenia, Bolivia, Brazil, Chile, the Cook Islands, El Salvador, Fiji, Israel, Latvia, Mexico, Peru, and Turkey.

Another 23 countries retain the death penalty but have abolished it in practice by not carrying out executions in a decade or more. Among these countries are Algeria, Brunei, Congo, Kenya, the Russian Federation, Sri Lanka, and Tunisia. ■

SOURCE: Amnesty International, at http://web.amnesty.org/pages/deathpenalty-index-eng.

Persons Executed, 1930–2003

Number of Death Row Inmates, 1953–2003

THE DEATH PENALTY Capital punishment remains controversial. Japan and the United States are the only two industrialized countries to retain the death penalty. The European Union has outlawed capital punishment as a requirement for membership, and courts in South Africa and several central and eastern European countries have declared it unconstitutional and a denial of human dignity.

After a ten-year moratorium on executions in the late 1960s and early 1970s, the U.S. Supreme Court ruled that the death penalty is not necessarily cruel and unusual punishment if it is imposed for crimes that resulted in a victim's death, if the courts "ensure that death sentences are not meted out wantonly or freakishly," and if these processes "confer on the sentencer sufficient discretion to take account of the character and record of the individual offender and the circumstances of the particular offense to ensure that death is the appropriate punishment in a specific case."[74]

The Rehnquist Court made it easier to impose death sentences, cut back on appeals, and carry out executions. More states have added the death penalty (38 states now have it), and the federal government has increased the number of crimes for which the death penalty may be imposed. As a result, the number of persons on death row has increased dramatically. Since capital punishment was reinstated in 1976, more than 600 people have been executed nationwide, and more than 3,500 are on death row. However, concerns have also grown about the fairness of how capital punishment is imposed. DNA tests that have established the innocence of a sizable number of those convicted of murder have increased these concerns.[75]

The prohibition against cruel and unusual punishment also forbids punishments grossly disproportionate to the severity of the crime. In 2002, the Supreme Court overruled a prior ruling and held that it is excessive and disproportionate to execute mentally retarded convicted murderers because they cannot understand the seriousness of their offense.[76] The Court noted that in recent years there has been a movement to bar executions of mentally retarded death-row inmates. And because 18 of the 38 states that impose capital punishment exempt the mentally retarded, the Court concluded that there was an emerging "national consensus" against executing mentally retarded inmates.[77]

How Just Is Our System of Justice?

Because the American system of criminal justice contains many guarantees for protecting the rights of the accused, critics often argue that these protections prevent justice from being done. Among the other criticisms are that the system is inefficient, biased, and unfair.

Too Many Loopholes?

Some observers argue that by overprotecting criminals and placing too much of a burden on the criminal justice system not to make mistakes, we delay justice, encourage disrespect for the law, and allow the guilty to go unpunished. Justice should be swift and certain without being arbitrary. But under our procedures, criminals may go unpunished because the police decide not to arrest them; the prosecutor decides not to prosecute them; the grand jury decides not to indict them; the judge decides not to hold them for trial; the jury decides not to convict them; the appeals court decides to reverse the conviction; the judge decides to release them on a writ of habeas corpus; or the president or governor decides to pardon, reprieve, or parole them if convicted. As a result, the public never knows whom to hold responsible when laws are not enforced. The police blame prosecutors, prosecutors blame the police, and both blame the juries and judges.

Others take a different view and point out that justice involves more than simply securing convictions. All the steps in the administration of criminal laws have been developed over centuries of trial and error, and each step has been constructed to protect ordinary persons from particular abuses by those in power. History warns against entrusting the instruments of criminal law enforcement to a single officer. For this reason, responsibility is vested in many officials.

Too Unreliable?

Critics who say that our system of justice is unreliable often point to trial by jury as the chief source of trouble. No other country relies as heavily on trial by jury as the United States. Jury trials are also time-consuming and costly. Trial by jury, critics argue, leads to a theatrical combat between lawyers who base their appeals on the prejudices and sentiments of the jurors. "Mr. Prejudice and Miss Sympathy are the names of witnesses whose testimony is never recorded, but must nevertheless be reckoned with in trials by jury."[78]

The jury system allows for what is called *jury nullification* when jurors ignore their instructions to consider only the evidence presented in court and vote for acquittal to express their displeasure with the law or the actions of prosecutors or police. Jury nullification has a long history. In colonial times, juries refused to convict colonists of political crimes against the royal government as a way to protest laws of which they disapproved. Before the Civil War, northern juries refused to convict people for helping runaway slaves. Before the 1970s, white southern juries sometimes refused to convict police for brutality against black people.

Responding to growing public disenchantment with juries after a raft of unpopular verdicts, states have been rewriting the rules for the jury system. These changes include making it more difficult for people to be excused from jury service, allowing for nonunanimous decisions, limiting how long jurors can be sequestered, and giving judges more control over lawyers' attempts to appeal to jurors' emotions.

"Mr. Prejudice and Miss Sympathy are the names of witnesses whose testimony is never recorded, but must nevertheless be reckoned with in trials by jury."

— JEROME FRANK, *COURTS ON TRIAL*

The Changing Face of American Politics

A Renewed Debate over the Death Penalty

Although 38 states retain capital punishment, the number of people executed in recent years has declined from a high of 98 in 1999 to 60 in 2005. In 2005, the New York state assembly voted not to reinstate the death penalty, after the state's high court struck down the state's law. The Kansas supreme court also declared its death penalty statute unconstitutional, and the New Jersey supreme court imposed a moratorium on executions. Capital punishment is not used in the District of Columbia and 12 other states, including Alaska, Hawaii, Iowa, Maine, Massachusetts, Michigan, Minnesota, North Dakota, Rhode Island, Vermont, West Virginia, and Wisconsin. In addi-

tion, the governor of Illinois declared a moratorium on executions in 2003, and a number of other governors have ordered DNA testing for death row inmates and, based on the test results, have pardoned them.

While some groups, like the U.S. Conference of Catholic Bishops, oppose the death penalty on moral grounds, the renewed debate now focuses on the fairness of the entire process of administering capital punishment. The American Bar Association (ABA) has called for a halt to executions because the death penalty is administered in arbitrary and capricious ways that deny fundamental due process and the equal protection of the law. Prominent Republicans and Democrats

also are questioning the system of imposing the death penalty.

The debate about the fairness of capital punishment was sparked by the increasing number of inmates who have been released because new DNA evidence proved their innocence—often after they had spent a decade or more on death row. Critics also point out the seeming randomness in imposing capital punishment. Public prosecutors seek the death penalty in less than 5 percent of all murder cases. Defendants often agree to plea bargains in return for life sentences. When murder trials are held, some juries refuse to impose the death sentence. And of the criminals sentenced to death, some receive clemency or are paroled. A study

of more than 4,500 capital cases found that more than two-thirds of all death sentences are overturned. Why? The primary reasons are that defense lawyers were incompetent, important evidence was overlooked, witnesses lied, or prosecutors withheld evidence from the defense. Racial discrimination in the imposition of capital punishment is also a major concern. Black people who murder white people are much more likely to receive death sentences than white people who murder black people or black people who kill other black people. ■

SOURCE: Death Penalty Information Center. See also Hudo Bedau and Paul Cassell, eds., *Debating the Death Penalty* (Oxford University Press, 2004).

Defenders of the jury system reply that trial by jury provides a check by nonprofessionals on the actions of judges and prosecutors. There is no evidence that juries are unreliable; on the contrary, decisions of juries do not significantly differ from those of judges.[79] Moreover, the jury system helps educate citizens and enables them to participate in the application of their country's laws.

Too Discriminatory?

During the past several decades, the Supreme Court has worked hard to enforce the ideal of equal justice under the law. Persons accused of crimes who cannot afford attorneys must be furnished them at government expense. If appeals require transcripts of court cases, such transcripts must be made available to those who cannot afford to purchase them. If appeals are permitted, the government must provide attorneys for at least one appeal of the decision of the trial court. Poor people cannot be imprisoned because they cannot pay a fine. Nor, once sentenced, can poor people be kept in jail beyond the term of the sentence because they cannot afford to pay a fine. Even for civil proceedings, courts cannot impose fees that deny poor people their fundamental rights, such as the right to obtain a divorce.

Unfair to Minorities?

One of the acute problems of our society is the tension between the police and the African American, Hispanic, and Middle Eastern communities congregated in inner cities. Many members of minorities believe they do not have equal protection under

"Whether the stated belief is well founded or not, is at least partly beside the point. The existence of the belief is damaging enough."

GEORGE EDWARDS,
THE POLICE ON THE URBAN FRONTIER

the law and that law enforcement officers target them. "Whether the stated belief is well founded or not," one political scientist observed, "is at least partly beside the point. The existence of the belief is damaging enough."[80]

Some black people consider the police to be enforcers of white law. Studies proving prejudice by some white police officers and examples of rough, even brutal, police treatment of black suspects support this viewpoint. One study in California found that "the rate of unfounded arrest was four times higher for African Americans than Anglos. Latino rates were double those of Anglos."[81] Police use of racial profiling, already a concern of black people and Hispanics, has also became a concern of Muslims and white people.[82]

In recent decades, police departments have recruited more African Americans, Hispanics, and women as officers and appointed them to command posts. Larger cities now have oversight boards with civilian members to which citizens can bring complaints about police misconduct. In some cities, **community policing** has also replaced traditional police procedures. Police departments work with churches and other local community groups and take officers out of patrol cars to walk the beat and work in neighborhoods. Community policing, when combined with police cooperation with community organizations to sponsor crime prevention programs, appears not only to reduce crime but also to improve minorities' confidence in the police.[83]

The Supreme Court and Civil Liberties

Judges play a major role in enforcing constitutional guarantees of our civil liberties. This focuses public attention on the Supreme Court. Yet few controversies are actually carried to the Supreme Court, and a Supreme Court decision is not the end of the judicial process. Lower court judges as well as police, superintendents of schools, local prosecutors, school boards, state legislatures, and thousands of others clarify the Court's doctrines.

Moreover, the Supreme Court can do little unless its decisions over time reflect a national consensus. As Justice Robert H. Jackson observed, "The attitude of a society and of its organized political forces, rather than its legal machinery, is the controlling force in the character of free institutions. Any court that undertakes by its legal processes to enforce civil liberties needs the support of an enlightened and vigorous public opinion."[84] Thus the Bill of Rights—and the other procedural and substantive liberties of our Constitution—cannot rest on a foundation merely of tradition. The preservation of these rights depends on wide, continuing, and knowledgeable public support.

community policing
Assigning police to neighborhoods where they walk the beat and work with churches and other community groups to reduce crime and improve relations with minorities.

Summary

1. One of the basic distinctions between a free society and a police state is that a free society restrains the way public officials, especially law enforcement officials, perform their duties. In the United States, the courts enforce these constitutional restraints.

2. The Constitution protects the acquisition and retention of citizenship. It protects the basic liberties of citizens as well as aliens, although in times of war, foreign saboteurs and terrorists may be detained and tried without the rights accorded citizens and other aliens.

3. The Constitution protects our property from arbitrary governmental interference, although debates about which interferences are reasonable and which are arbitrary are not easily settled. If the government takes private property or renders it worthless, it must pay just compensation to the owner.

4. The Constitution imposes limits not only on the procedures government must follow but also on the ends it may pursue. Some actions are out of bounds no matter what procedures are followed. Legislatures have the

primary role in determining what is reasonable and what is unreasonable. However, the Supreme Court exercises its own independent and final review of legislative determinations of reasonableness, especially on matters affecting civil liberties and civil rights.

5. The Supreme Court has pulled together elements from the First, Fourth, Fifth, Ninth, and Fourteenth Amendments to recognize a constitutionally protected right to personal privacy, especially with regard to marital privacy, including the right of a woman to choose an abortion.

6. The framers knew from their own experiences that in their zeal to maintain power and to enforce the laws, especially in wartime, public officials are often tempted to infringe on the rights of persons accused of crimes. To prevent such abuse, the Bill of Rights requires federal officials to follow detailed procedures in making searches and arrests and in bringing people to trial.

7. The Supreme Court continues to play a prominent role in developing public policy to protect the rights of the accused, to ensure that the innocent are not punished, and to guarantee that the public is protected against those who break the laws.

The Court's decisions influence what the public believes and how police officers and others involved in the administration of justice behave. But the Court alone cannot guarantee fairness in the administration of justice.

Further Reading

JEFFREY ABRAMSON, *We, the Jury: The Jury System and the Ideal of Democracy* (Harvard University Press, 2000).

LIVA BAKER, *Miranda: Crime, Law and Politics* (Atheneum, 1983).

STUART BANNER, *The Death Penalty: An American History* (Harvard University Press, 2002).

ROBERT P. BURNS, *A Theory of the Trial* (Princeton University Press, 1999).

DAVID COLE, *Enemy Aliens: Double Standards and Constitutional Freedoms in the War on Terrorism* (New Press, 2003).

DAVID COLE AND **JAMES X. DEMPSEY,** *Terrorism and the Constitution*, 3d ed. (New Press, 2006).

JOHN DENVIR, *Democracy's Constitution: Claiming the Privileges of American Citizenship* (University of Illinois Press, 2001).

LOUIS FISHER, *Nazi Saboteurs on Trial: A Military Tribunal and American Law* (University Press of Kansas, 2003).

GEORGE P. FLETCHER, *Basic Concepts of Criminal Law* (Oxford University Press, 1998).

DAVID J. GARROW, *Liberty and Sexuality: The Right to Privacy and the Making of* Roe *v.* Wade (Macmillan, 1994).

ROGER HOOD, *The Death Penalty: A Worldwide Perspective*, 3d ed. (Oxford University Press, 2002).

SADAKAT KADRI, *The Trial: A History from Socrates to O. J. Simpson* (Random House, 2005).

RANDALL KENNEDY, *Race, Crime, and the Law* (Pantheon, 1997).

ANTHONY LEWIS, *Gideon's Trumpet* (Random House, 1964).

JOHN R. LOTT JR., *More Guns, Less Crime: Understanding Crime and Gun Control Laws* (University of Chicago Press, 2000).

DAVID M. O'BRIEN, *Constitutional Law and Politics: Vol. 2, Civil Rights and Civil Liberties*, 7th ed. (Norton, 2008).

WILLIAM H. REHNQUIST, *All the Laws but One: Civil Liberties in Wartime* (Knopf, 1998).

BARRY SCHECK, PETER NEUFELD, AND **JIM DWYER,** *Actual Innocence: Five Days to Execution, and Other Dispatches from the Wrongly Convicted* (Doubleday, 2000).

MELVIN UROFSKY, ED. *The Public Debate Over Controversial Supreme Court Decisions* (CQ Press, 2006).

MARY E. VOGEL, *Coercion to Compromise: Plea Bargaining, the Courts, and the Making of Political Authority* (Oxford University Press, 2001).

WELSH S. WHITE, *Miranda's Waning Protections: Police Interrogation Practices After Dickerson* (University of Michigan Press, 2001).

PRISCILLA MACHADO ZOTTI, *Injustice for All:* Mapp *v.* Ohio *and the Fourth Amendment* (Peter Lang, 2005).

KeyTerms

naturalization, p. 464

dual citizenship, p. 464

right of expatriation, p. 464

property rights, p. 469

contract clause, p. 469

police powers, p. 469

eminent domain, p. 469

regulatory taking, p. 469

due process, p. 470

procedural due process, p. 470

substantive due process, p. 470

search warrant, p. 474

racial profiling, p. 476

exclusionary rule, p. 477

immunity, p. 477

grand jury, p. 479

indictment, p. 479

plea bargain, p. 479

petit jury, p. 479

double jeopardy, p. 480

community policing, p. 484

Chapter 17

Equal Rights Under the Law

✦

THE PRECIOUS RIGHTS OF *EQUALITY* AND *LIBERTY* ARE PROCLAIMED IN THE DECLARATION OF INDEPENDENCE: "WE HOLD THESE TRUTHS TO BE SELF-EVIDENT, THAT ALL MEN ARE CREATED EQUAL, THAT THEY ARE ENDOWED BY THEIR CREATOR WITH CERTAIN UNALIENABLE RIGHTS, THAT AMONG THESE ARE LIFE, LIBERTY, AND THE PURSUIT OF HAPPINESS." ALTHOUGH THE DECLARATION DOES NOT SPECIFY EQUALITY OF WHITE, CHRISTIAN, OR ANGLO-SAXON MEN (AT THAT TIME "ALL MEN" MEANT WHITE, PROPERTY-OWNING, ANGLO-SAXON MEN), IT TOOK ALMOST 200 YEARS TO EXPAND

that definition to include all races, all religions, and all women as well as men. This creed of individual dignity and equality is nonetheless older than our Declaration of Independence; its roots go back into the teachings of Judaism and Christianity.

The Constitution, however, does not make any reference to "equality" (the word never appears in the Constitution or in the original Bill of Rights). But we know the framers believed that all men—at least all white adult men—were equally entitled to life, liberty, and the pursuit of happiness. But like the Declaration, the Constitution refers only to "person," "people," "citizens," and "he," but not to women, and none of its lofty sentiments applied to slaves or Native Americans, who enjoyed neither liberty nor equality. The framers resolved their ambiguity about what kind of equality and for whom by creating a system of government designed to protect what they called *natural rights*. (Today we speak of *human rights,* but the idea is basically the same.) By **natural rights** the framers meant that every person by virtue of being a human being has an equal right to protection against arbitrary treatment and an equal right to the liberties that the Bill of Rights guarantees. These rights do not depend on citizenship; governments do not grant them. They are the rights of *all people*.

We often use the terms *civil liberties* and *civil rights* interchangeably to refer to rights that constitutional democracies protect. *Civil liberties* is sometimes used more narrowly to refer to freedoms of conscience, religion, and expression. *Civil rights* is used to refer to the right not to be discriminated against because of race, religion, gender, or ethnic origin. The Constitution protects civil rights in two ways. First, it ensures that government officials do not discriminate against us; second, it grants national and state governments the power to protect these civil rights against interference by private individuals.

"Our Constitution is color-blind and neither knows nor tolerates class among citizens."

JUSTICE JOHN MARSHALL HARLAN

487

This chapter is concerned with both the protection of our rights from abuse *by government* and the protection *through government* of our right to be free from abuse by our *fellow citizens*. Here, we focus on the struggles of African Americans, women, Hispanics, Asian Americans, and Native Americans to secure the basic civil rights to the vote, to an education, to a job, and to a place to live on equal terms with their fellow citizens.

Equality and Equal Rights

Americans are committed to equality. "Equality," however, is an elusive term. The concept of equality for which there is the greatest consensus and that is most clearly written into the Constitution is that everyone should have *equality of opportunity* regardless of race, ethnic origin, religion, and, in recent years, gender and sexual orientation. Advancing the equality of opportunity has led to the historic struggles for civil rights.

A variation of the concept of equal opportunity is *equality of starting conditions*. There is not much equal opportunity if one person is born into a well-to-do family, lives in a safe suburb, and receives a good education, while another is born into a poor, broken family, lives in a run-down inner-city neighborhood, and attends inferior schools. Thus, it is argued, if we are to have meaningful equality of opportunity, we must provide special opportunities for the disadvantaged through federal programs such as Head Start, which helps prepare preschool children from poor families for elementary school.

Traditionally, we have emphasized *individual* achievement, but in recent decades, some politicians and civil rights leaders have focused attention on the concept of *equality between groups*. When large disparities in wealth and advantage exist between groups—as between black and white people or between women and men—equality becomes a highly divisive political issue. Those who are disadvantaged emphasize economic and social factors that exclude them from the mainstream. They champion programs like **affirmative action** that are designed to provide special help to people who have been disadvantaged because they belong to a certain group. Those who are advantaged, however, often try to maintain the status quo and downplay socioeconomic disparities. As a result, whether such programs promote or deny equality remains one of the most controversial current debates.

Finally, equality can also mean *equality of results*. A perennial debate is whether social justice and genuine equality can exist in a nation in which people of one class have so much and others have so little and where the gap between them is growing wider.[1] There is considerable support for guaranteeing a minimum floor—a "safety net"—below which no one should be allowed to fall. Yet Americans generally do not support an equality of results—that everyone should have the same amount of material goods—but instead tend to believe that, regardless of current economic status, a person should be able to expect that things will get better and that hard work and an entrepreneurial spirit will be rewarded.

The Quest for Equal Justice

To gain some perspective on the court decisions, laws, and other government actions relating to civil rights for women and minorities, we review here the political history and social contexts in which these constitutional issues arise. These issues involve more than court decisions, laws, and constitutional amendments, however. They encompass the entire social, economic, and political system. And although the struggles of all groups are interwoven, they are not identical, so we deal briefly and separately with each.

natural rights
The rights of all people to dignity and worth; also called *human rights*.

affirmative action
Remedial action designed to overcome the effects of discrimination against minorities and women.

Racial Equality

Americans had a painful confrontation with the problem of race before, during, and after the Civil War (1861–1865). As a result of the northern victory in that war, the Thirteenth, Fourteenth, and Fifteenth Amendments became part of the Constitution.

During Reconstruction in the late 1860s and 1870s, Congress passed civil rights laws to implement these amendments and established programs to provide educational and social services for the freed slaves. But the Supreme Court struck down many of these laws, and it was not until the 1960s that progress was again made toward ensuring African Americans their civil rights.

SEGREGATION AND WHITE SUPREMACY   Before Reconstruction programs had any significant effect, the white southern political leadership regained power, and by 1877, Reconstruction was ended. Northern political leaders abandoned African Americans to their fate at the hands of their former white masters; presidents no longer concerned themselves with enforcing civil rights laws, and Congress enacted no new ones. The Supreme Court either declared old laws unconstitutional or interpreted them so narrowly that they were ineffective. The Court also gave such a limited construction to the Thirteenth, Fourteenth, and Fifteenth Amendments that these amendments failed to accomplish their intended purpose of protecting the rights of African Americans.[2]

For almost a century, white supremacy went unchallenged in the South, where most African Americans lived. They were kept from voting; they were forced to accept menial jobs; they were denied educational opportunities; they were segregated in public and private facilities.[3] African Americans were lynched on an average of one every four days, and few white people raised a voice in protest.

During World War I (1914–1918), African Americans began to migrate to northern cities to seek jobs in war factories. The Great Depression of the 1930s and World War II in the 1940s accelerated their relocation. Although discrimination continued, more jobs became available, and African Americans made social gains. As migration of African Americans out of the rural South shifted the racial composition of cities across much of America, the African American vote became important in national elections. These changes created an African American middle class opposed to segregation as a symbol of servitude and a cause of inequality. By the mid-twentieth century, urban African Americans were active and politically powerful. There was a growing demand to abolish color barriers.

SLOW GOVERNMENT RESPONSE   By the 1930s, African Americans were challenging the doctrine of segregation in the courts. And after World War II, this civil rights litigation began to have a major impact. The Supreme Court, beginning with the landmark 1954 ruling in *Brown* v. *Board of Education of Topeka,* prohibited racially segregated public schools[4] and subsequently struck down most of the devices that state and local authorities had used to keep African Americans from voting.[5]

In the late 1940s and 1950s, Presidents Harry S. Truman and Dwight D. Eisenhower used their executive authority to fight segregation in the armed services and the federal bureaucracy. They directed the Department of Justice to enforce whatever civil rights laws were on the books, but Congress still held back. In the late 1950s, an emerging national consensus in favor of governmental action to protect civil rights plus the political clout of African Americans in the northern states began to influence Congress. In 1957, Congress overrode a southern filibuster in the Senate and enacted the first federal civil rights laws since Reconstruction.

A TURNING POINT   Even after the Supreme Court declared racially segregated public schools unconstitutional, most African Americans still went to segregated schools, and there was widespread resistance to integration in the South. Many legal barriers to equal rights had fallen, yet most African Americans still could not buy houses where they wanted, secure the jobs they needed, send their children to well-equipped schools, or eat in restaurants or walk freely on the streets of "white neighborhoods."

But times were changing. What had once been deemed a "southern problem" was finally being recognized as a national challenge. A massive social, economic, and political movement began to supplement the struggles in the courts. It began in Montgomery, Alabama, on December 1, 1955, when Rosa Parks, an African American seamstress, refused to give up her seat to a white man on a bus as the law required her to do. She was removed from the bus, arrested, and fined. The black community responded by boycotting city buses.

"When my distinguished colleague refers to the will of the 'people,' does he mean his 'people' or my 'people'?"

Rosa Parks's decision not to give up her seat on the bus in Montgomery, Alabama, sparked a boycott by African Americans who, for more than a year, refused to ride the segregated city buses. Rosa Parks died in 2006.

"Our nation is moving toward two societies, one black, one white—separate and unequal."

THE KERNER COMMISSION, 1967

Firefighters in Birmingham, Alabama, turned their hoses full blast on civil rights demonstrators in the 1960s. At times the water came with such force, even on children, that it literally tore the bark off fully grown trees.

The boycott worked. It also produced a charismatic national civil rights leader, the Reverend Martin Luther King Jr. Through his doctrine of nonviolent resistance, King gave a new dimension to the struggle. By the early 1960s, new organizational resources arose in almost every city to support and sponsor "sit-ins," "freedom rides," "live-ins," and other nonviolent demonstrations. These measures were often met with violence, and some state and local governments failed to protect the victims or to prosecute those responsible for the violence.[6]

The simmering forces of social discontent boiled over in the summer of 1963. A peaceful demonstration in Birmingham, Alabama, was countered with fire hoses, police dogs, and mass arrests. More than a quarter of a million people converged on Washington, D.C., to hear King and other civil rights leaders speak while millions more watched them on television. By the time the summer was over, hardly a city, North or South, had not had demonstrations, protests, or sit-ins; some cities also erupted in violence.

This direct action had an effect. Many cities enacted civil rights ordinances, more schools were desegregated, and President John F. Kennedy urged Congress to enact a comprehensive civil rights bill. Late in 1963, the nation's grief over the assassination of President Kennedy, who had become identified with civil rights goals, added political fuel to the drive for decisive federal action to protect civil rights.[7] President Lyndon B. Johnson made civil rights legislation his highest priority, and on July 2, 1964, after months of debate, he signed into law the Civil Rights Act of 1964, which forbids discrimination on the basis of race, color, religion, sex, or nationality.[8]

RIOTS AND REACTION By the early 1970s, the legal phase of the civil rights movement had largely come to a close, but as things got better, discontent grew. Millions of impoverished African Americans demonstrated growing impatience with the discrimination that remained. This volatile situation gave way to racial violence and disorders. In 1965, a brutal riot took place in Watts, a section of Los Angeles. In 1966 and 1967, the disorders spread in scope and intensity. The Detroit riot in July 1967, the worst such disturbance up to that time in modern American history, made clear the deep divisions between the races and the urgency of taking corrective action.[9]

President Johnson appointed the special Advisory Commission on Civil Disorders in 1967 to investigate the origins of the riots and to recommend measures to prevent such disasters in the future. When the commission (called the Kerner Commission after its chair, Illinois Governor Otto Kerner) issued its report, it said in stark, clear language: "What white Americans have never fully understood—but what the Negro can

History Makers

Martin Luther King Jr.

Martin Luther King Jr. was born January 25, 1929, in Atlanta, Georgia. After graduating from high school, he entered Morehouse College in 1944 and majored in sociology, but in his junior year, he decided to enter the ministry. After Morehouse, King entered the Crozer Theological Seminary in Pennsylvania. There he became a follower of the Indian pacifist Mohandas Gandhi. Following graduation, King earned a doctorate from Boston University in 1955. He then became pastor of the Dexter Avenue Baptist Church in Montgomery, Alabama.

In 1957, King and another Baptist minister, Ralph Abernathy, founded the Southern Christian Leadership Conference to advance the cause of civil rights. In that year, King's home and church were bombed and violence against black protesters began to escalate. In March 1963, King was jailed in Birmingham, Alabama, for leading a protest parade without a permit. Subsequently, he led the March on Washington, on August 28, 1963, at which hundreds of thousands of civil rights activists focused national attention on the racial problems in the country. The march built support for the passage of the Civil Rights Act of 1964.

Speaking at the march from the steps of the Lincoln Memorial, King delivered his famous "I Have A Dream" speech, in which he said he dreamed of the day when "my four little children . . . will not be judged by the color of their skin but by the content of their character," and concluded with the memorable line, "Free at last! Thank God Almighty, we are free at last!"

In 1963, King became *Time* magazine's Man of the Year, and in 1964, he was awarded the Nobel Peace Prize for his leadership in the civil rights movement and advocacy of nonviolent protest. In 1968, King was assassinated, and riots erupted in more than 100 cities. ∎

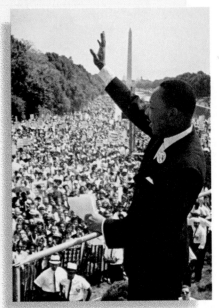

Martin Luther King Jr.

---

never forget—is that white society is deeply implicated in the ghetto. White institutions created it, white institutions maintain it, and white society condones it." The basic conclusion of the commission was that: "Our nation is moving toward two societies, one black, one white—separate and unequal. . . ." Only "a commitment to national action on an unprecedented scale" could change this trend.[10]

The commission made sweeping recommendations on jobs, education, housing, and the welfare system. But other events diverted attention from these recommendations: the Vietnam War; Watergate; the elections of Ronald Reagan and George H. W. Bush, who were reluctant to take government actions to enforce civil rights; and a growing skepticism in the country about the effectiveness of government in general.

The Clinton administration (1993–2001) was more sympathetic toward the use of government power to deal with inequality than its immediate predecessors had been, but because of budgetary constraints and Republican opposition to "big government" programs, it was largely unable to promote major initiatives directly aimed at the problems of the inner cities where many poor African Americans lived. The administration of George W. Bush has pursued more race-neutral policies like the No Child Left Behind program aimed at raising educational standards across the nation. Still, civil rights leaders like the Reverend Jesse Jackson continue efforts to eliminate the vestiges of racial discrimination through boycotts and lawsuits aimed at persuading businesses and corporations to reach out to, hire, and promote more African Americans.

Women's Rights

The struggle for equal rights for women was intertwined with the battle to secure equal rights for African Americans. The Seneca Falls Women's Rights Convention (1848), which launched the women's movement, involved men and women who actively campaigned to abolish slavery and to secure the rights of African Americans and women.

Susan B. Anthony and Elizabeth Cady Stanton were the two most influential leaders of the women's suffrage movement in the nineteenth century.

Agents of Change

Elizabeth Martin and WomensLaw

Elizabeth Martin

WomensLaw was founded in 2000 by a group of lawyers, teachers, activists, and Web designers to use the power of the Internet to help survivors of domestic violence. Convinced that women do not have enough information to protect their civil rights, WomensLaw provides basic information and resources to women living with or trying to escape domestic violence. The organization provides state-by-state information on laws against domestic violence for advocates of change, and it helps victims of abuse by guiding them to help in their own communities.

WomensLaw was created by Elizabeth Martin, who graduated from Duke University and received her law degree from the University of North Carolina. Before starting WomensLaw, she worked as a legal services attorney in Asheville, North Carolina, and as a volunteer attorney in domestic violence cases. She also serves on a number of boards of domestic violence organizations, and has worked to build coalitions within the domestic violence community. She has been instrumental in building the organization, and recently moved to New York City to work with the Blue Ridge Foundation, which provides basic support to young organizations.

WomensLaw has already helped thousands of women find help even though, as the WomensLaw Web site says, "We cannot give you legal advice." However, with more than 20,000 visits to its Web site each month, the information the site provides appears to be getting through. ∎

Learn more about WomensLaw at www.womenslaw.org.

QUESTIONS

Why is WomensLaw an important addition to the many organizations that work to reduce domestic violence?

Why do women need its help?

But as the Civil War approached, women were urged to abandon their cause and devote their energies to ending slavery.[11] The Civil War brought the women's movement to a halt, and the temperance movement to prohibit the sale of liquor, which gathered strength in the late nineteenth century, also diverted attention away from women's rights. The Fourteenth and Fifteenth Amendments did not advance voting rights for women, even as they guaranteed that right, in theory, to males regardless of race.

By the turn of the twentieth century, however, a vigorous campaign was under way for **women's suffrage**—the right to vote. The first victories came in western states, where Wyoming led the way. As a territory, Wyoming had given women the right to vote in 1869. When members of Congress in Washington grumbled about this "petticoat provision," the Wyoming legislators replied they would stay out of the Union 100 years rather than come in without women's suffrage. Congress gave in and admitted Wyoming to the Union in 1890. By the end of World War I, more than half the states had granted women the right to vote in some or all elections.

Many suffragists were dissatisfied with this state-by-state approach. They wanted a decisive victory—a constitutional amendment that would force all states to allow qualified women to vote. Finally, in 1919, Congress proposed the Nineteenth Amendment. Opposition to granting voting rights to women was intertwined with opposition to granting voting rights to African Americans. Many southerners opposed the amendment because it gave Congress enforcement power, which might bring federal officials to investigate elections to ensure that the amendment was being obeyed—an interference that could call attention to how black people were being kept from voting.

women's suffrage
The right of women to vote.

With the ratification of the Nineteenth Amendment in 1920, women won the right to vote, but they were still denied equal pay and equal rights, and national and state laws imposed many legal disabilities on them, such as the lack of comparable pay and health benefits. In the 1970s and 1980s, the unsuccessful struggle to secure the adoption of the Equal Rights Amendment occupied much of the attention of the women's movement. But there are now other goals, and women have mobilized their political clout behind issues that range from equal pay to world peace, sexual harassment, abortion rights, and electing more women to office.[12]

Since the late 1980s, the Supreme Court has been reluctant to expand the Fourteenth Amendment to extend protection against gender discrimination, though it did hold that Virginia could not create a separate military academy for women instead of admitting them into the all-male Virginia Military Institute, a 150-year-old state-run institution.[13]

The courts, however, have increasingly enforced the prohibition against sex discrimination in the 1964 Civil Rights Act and expanded it to forbid sexual harassment in the workplace. Ironically, members of the House of Representatives who opposed the act, which was designed primarily to end racial discrimination, added the section on gender in an effort to defeat its passage.[14] As a result, it was initially not taken seriously, and not until the 1980s did it apply to "quid pro quo" sexual harassment, in which an employer requires sexual favors from a person as a condition of employment (in hiring, promotions, and firing).[15] Sexual harassment was brought to national attention in 1991 by accusations made against Clarence Thomas by Anita Hill, a law professor and former colleague, at the time of his Senate confirmation hearings for the Supreme Court. Subsequently, the Supreme Court ruled that the law also applies to situations in which employees are forced to work in a "hostile environment." The Court defined a hostile environment as a workplace "permeated" with intimidation, ridicule, and insult that is severe and pervasive, and this includes same-sex harassment.[16]

Some women still complain that a "glass ceiling" in large corporations prevents their advancement. But there is no denying that major progress has been made, with more and more women going to college and professional schools and into the media and business. Indeed, during the past three decades, the number of women graduating from colleges and universities has outpaced that of men (see Figure 17–1).

Hispanics

The struggle for civil rights has not been limited to women and African Americans. Throughout American history, many native-born Americans have considered each new wave of immigrants suspect, especially if the newcomers were not white or English-speaking. Formal barriers of law and informal barriers of custom combined to deny equal rights to immigrants. But as groups established themselves—first economically and then politically—most of these barriers were swept away, and the newcomers or their children enjoyed the same constitutionally guaranteed rights as other Americans.

As discussed in Chapter 5, most Hispanics—many of whose ancestors have been Americans for generations—are bilingual, speaking Spanish as well as English. However, because English may not be their first language, it has been difficult for some Hispanics to do well in school or to become business executives and professionals. Although less visible than African Americans, Hispanics have suffered the same kinds of discrimination in employment, education, housing, and access to public accommodations.

In many parts of America, Hispanics have not been able to translate their numbers into comparable political clout because of political differences among the Hispanic population and because many Hispanics are not citizens or registered to vote. However, after California adopted Proposition 187 in 1994, which denied medical, educational, and social services to illegal immigrants, and Congress amended the federal welfare laws to curtail benefits to noncitizens, many immigrants rushed to become naturalized. Half of all Hispanic Americans live in two states: California and Texas. In 2001, California became the first big state in which white people are in the minority; Texas, the second most populous state, became the second majority-minority state in 2004.[17]

FIGURE 17–1 Percentage of Bachelor's Degrees Awarded to Men.

SOURCE: Michael A. Fletcher, "Degrees of Separation," *Washington Post*, June 25, 2002, p. A1.

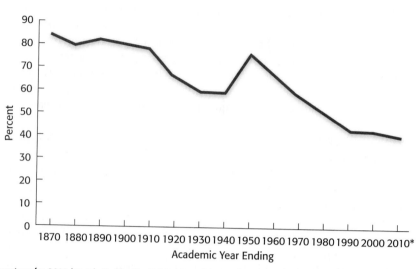

*Percentage for 2010 is projected by the Pell Institute for the Study of Opportunity in Higher Education, National Center for Education Statistics.

"Asian-Americans do face widespread prejudice, discrimination and barriers to equal opportunity."

U.S. CIVIL RIGHTS COMMISSION, 1992

Asian Americans

The term "Asian American" describes approximately 10 million people from many different countries and ethnic backgrounds. Most do not think of themselves as Asians but as Americans of Chinese, Japanese, Indian, Vietnamese, Cambodian, Korean, or other specific ancestry. They live chiefly in the western states, but their number has been increasing rapidly in New York and Texas.

Although Asian Americans are often considered a "model minority" because of their successes in education and business, the U.S. Civil Rights Commission found that "Asian-Americans do face widespread prejudice, discrimination and barriers to equal opportunity" and that racially motivated violence against them "occurs with disturbing frequency."[18]

CHINESE AMERICANS   The Chinese were the first Asians to come to the United States. Beginning in 1847, when young male Chinese peasants came to the American west to escape poverty and to work in mines, on railroads, and on farms, the Chinese encountered economic and cultural fears by the white majority, who did not understand their language or their culture. In response, the Chinese seldom tried to assimilate but instead gravitated to "Chinatowns," Chinese enclaves in cities like San Francisco and New York. Discriminatory restrictions on Chinese immigration and naturalization were first imposed in 1882 and were not removed until the end of World War II.

Since that time, the Chinese have moved into the mainstream of American society, and they are beginning to run for and win local political offices. Gary Locke, a Democrat and a graduate of Yale and Boston University Law School, became the first Chinese American to become governor of a continental state in 1996 when he was elected to the first of two terms as governor of Washington.

JAPANESE AMERICANS   The Japanese first migrated to Hawaii in the 1860s and then to California in the 1880s. Most Japanese immigrants remained in the West Coast states. By the beginning of the twentieth century, they faced overt hostility. In 1905, white labor leaders organized the Japanese and Korean Exclusion League, and in 1906, the San Francisco Board of Education excluded all Chinese, Japanese, and Korean children from neighborhood schools. Some western states passed laws denying the right to own land to aliens who were ineligible to become citizens—meaning aliens of Asian ancestry.

During World War II, anti-Japanese hysteria provoked the internment of West Coast Japanese—most of whom were loyal American citizens guilty of no crimes—in

In the hysteria following the outbreak of World War II, Japanese Americans were rounded up and transported to internment camps.

prison camps in California, Colorado, and other states. Their property was often sold at confiscatory rates, and many of them lost their businesses, jobs, and incomes. Following the war, the exclusionary acts were repealed. In 1988, President Ronald Reagan signed a law providing $20,000 restitution to each of the approximately 60,000 surviving World War II internees.

OTHER ASIAN AMERICANS Like other Asian Americans, Koreans faced overt discrimination in jobs and housing, but a Korean middle class has been growing, with many Korean Americans becoming teachers, doctors, and lawyers. Others operate small family businesses such as dry cleaners, florist shops, service stations, and grocery stores, often in inner cities.[19]

When Filipinos first came to the United States in the early twentieth century, they were considered American nationals because the Philippine Islands were an American possession. Nonetheless, they were denied rights to full citizenship and faced discrimination and even violence, including anti-Filipino riots in the state of Washington in 1928 and later in California, where nearly one-third of the more than 1.5 million Filipinos in the U.S. live.[20] Their economic status has improved, but their influence in politics remains as small as their numbers.

The newest Asian arrivals consist of more than a million refugees from Vietnam, Laos, and Cambodia, who first came to the United States in the 1970s and settled mostly in California and Louisiana. Although this group included middle-class people who left Vietnam after the communist victory there in 1975, it also consisted of many "boat people," so-called because they fled Vietnam in small boats and arrived in the U.S. without financial resources. In a relatively short time, most of these new Asian Americans established themselves economically. Although they are starting to have political influence, some remain socially and economically segregated.

Native Americans

Almost half of the more than 2 million Native Americans live on or near a *reservation*—a tract of land given to the tribal nations by treaties with the federal government—and are enrolled as members of one of the 550 federally recognized tribes, including 226 groups in Alaska.[21] Native Americans speak about 200 different languages, although most also speak English.

Native Americans speak of their tribes as "nations," yet they do not possess the full attributes of sovereignty. Rather, they are separate peoples with power to regulate their

The Changing Face of American Politics

Racial and Ethnic Identification

1860	1870	1880	1890	1900	1910	1920	1930	1940	1950
White	White	White	White	White	White	White	White	White	White
Black	Black	Black	Black	Black	Black	Black	Black	Black	**Negro**
Mulatto	Mulatto	Mulatto	Mulatto		Mulatto	Mulatto			
	Chinese	Chinese	Chinese	Chinese	Chinese	Chinese	Chinese	Chinese	Chinese
	Indian	Indian	Indian	Indian	Indian	Indian	Indian	Indian	American Indian
			Quadroon						
			Octoroon						
			Japanese	Japanese	Japanese	Japanese	Japanese	Japanese	Japanese
						Filipino	Filipino	Filipino	Filipino
						Hindu	Hindu	Hindu	
						Korean	Korean	Korean	
							Mexican		
					Other	Other	Other	Other	Other

Tiger Woods, the prize-winning golfer, is proud of his diverse heritage. He is both African American and Asian (Thai). He feels that ethnic background should not make a difference. It doesn't to him. As Woods says, "I am an American and proud of it."

Since 1860, the U.S. census has changed its classifications of race and ethnicity several times to reflect the nation's growing diversity and political developments. The classifications continue to provoke controversy. For example, in 1975, an ad hoc government committee picked the classification "Hispanic" over "Latino" to identify Spanish-speaking and Spanish-surnamed individuals. It chose the term because "Hispanic" connotes the cultural diaspora of centuries-old conquests by Spain in Mexico, Central America, and South America. In recent years "Latino" has become a more popular term because it refers to the Latin-based Romance languages of Spain, France, Italy, and Portugal, as well as to Portuguese-speaking Brazilians. But many still prefer "Hispanic" because it connotes a history of colonialism and does not include the French and Italians.*

Below are the categories used in the decennial counts from 1860 to 2000. Each new category is boldfaced at its first inclusion. ■

---

*Darrly Fears, "The Roots of 'Hispanic,'" *The Washington Post*, October 15, 2003, p. A21.

own internal affairs, subject to congressional supervision. States cannot regulate or tax the tribes or extend the jurisdiction of their courts over them unless Congress authorizes the states to do so.[22] In recent years, Congress has stepped in to mediate growing tensions between Indian tribes who have used their sovereignty over reservations to operate gambling casinos and the states in which these reservations are located.

By acts of Congress, Native Americans are citizens of the United States and of the states in which they live. They have the right to vote. Native Americans living off reservations and working in the general community pay taxes just like everyone else; off reservations they have the same rights as any other Americans. If they are enrolled members of a recognized tribe, they are entitled to certain benefits created by law and by treaty. The Bureau of Indian Affairs of the Department of the Interior administers these benefits.

During the period of assimilation that began in 1887 and lasted until 1934, tribal governments were weak, some reservations were dissolved, and the federal government severed its governing relationship with more than 100 tribes.[23] The civil rights movement of the 1960s created a more favorable climate for Native Americans. Their

1960	1970	1980	1990	2000
White	White	White	White	White
Negro	Negro/Black	Black/Negro	Black/Negro	Black/**African American**/Negro
Chinese	Chinese	Chinese	Chinese	Chinese
American Indian	American Indian	Indian	Indian	**American Indian or Alaska Native**
Japanese	Japanese	Japanese	Japanese	Japanese
Filipino	Filipino	Filipino	Filipino	Filipino
		Asian Indian	Asian Indian	Asian Indian
	Korean	Korean	Korean	Korean
Aleut		Aleut	Aleut	
Eskimo		Eskimo	Eskimo	
Hawaiian	Hawaiian	Hawaiian	Hawaiian	**Native Hawaiian**
Part Hawaiian				
		Vietnamese	Vietnamese	Vietnamese
		Guamanian	Guamanian	Guamanian or **Chamorro**
		Samoan	Samoan	Samoan
			Other Asian	Other Asian
			Pacific Islander	Pacific Islander
Other	Other	Other	**Other race**	**Some other race**
Ethnicity	Mexican	**Mexican American**	Mexican/Mexican American	Mexican/Mexican American
		Chicano	Chicano	Chicano
	Puerto Rican	Puerto Rican	Puerto Rican	Puerto Rican
	Central/South American			
	Cuban	Cuban	Cuban	Cuban
	Other Spanish	Other Spanish/Hispanic	Other Spanish/Hispanic	Other Spanish/Hispanic/**Latino**
	(None of these)	**Not Spanish**/Hispanic	Not Spanish/Hispanic	Not Spanish/Hispanic/Latino

goals were to reassert treaty rights and secure greater autonomy for the tribes. Under the leadership of the Native American Rights Fund (NARF), more Indian law cases were brought in the past several decades than at any time in our history.[24]

As a result of these efforts and of a greater national consciousness to minorities, most Americans are now aware that many Native Americans live in poverty. Native Americans "are in far worse health than the rest of the population, dying earlier and suffering disproportionately from alcoholism, accidents, diabetes, and pneumonia."[25] Although in recent years the rest of the United States has enjoyed about 4 percent unemployment, many reservations continue to experience 50 to 60 percent unemployment. Some reservations lack adequate health care facilities, schools, decent housing, and jobs. Congress has started to compensate Native Americans for past injustices and to provide more opportunities to develop tribal economic independence, and judges are showing greater vigilance in enforcing Indian treaty rights.

In 1986, Ben Nighthorse Campbell, a Colorado Democrat, became the first Native American to be elected to Congress. He later became a Republican after being elected to the Senate in 1992; he retired in 2005.

Equal Protection of the Laws: What Does It Mean?

The **equal protection clause** of the Fourteenth Amendment declares that no state (including any subdivision thereof) shall "deny to any person within its jurisdiction the equal protection of the laws." Although no parallel clause explicitly applies to the national government, courts have interpreted the Fifth Amendment's **due process clause**, which states that no person shall "be deprived of life, liberty, or property, without due process of law," to impose the same restraints on the national government as the equal protection clause imposes on the states.

The equal protection clause applies only to the actions of *governments,* not to those of private individuals. If a private person performs a discriminatory action, that action does not violate the Constitution, although it may violate federal and state laws. The equal protection clause does not, however, prevent governments from creating various classifications of people in its laws. What the Constitution forbids is *unreasonable* classifications. In general, a classification is unreasonable when there is no relation between the classes it creates and permissible governmental goals. A law prohibiting redheads from voting, for example, would be unreasonable. In contrast, laws denying persons under 18 the right to vote, to marry without the permission of their parents, or to apply for a driver's license appear to be reasonable (at least to most persons over 18).

Constitutional Classifications and Tests

One of the most troublesome constitutional questions is how to distinguish between constitutional and unconstitutional classifications. The Supreme Court uses three tests for this purpose: the *rational basis* test, the *strict scrutiny* test, and the *heightened scrutiny* test.

THE RATIONAL BASIS TEST   The traditional test to determine whether a law complies with the equal protection requirement places the burden of proof on the parties attacking the law. They must show that the law has no rational or legitimate governmental goals. Traditionally the rational basis test applied only to legislation affecting economic interests and, with two exceptions in the last 70 years,[26] the Court upheld the legislation and deferred to legislative judgments. But recently the Court has applied the test to challenges to legislation affecting noneconomic interests.[27] Notably, in *Romer* v. *Evans* (1996), the Court struck down an amendment to Colorado's constitution that barred local governments from adopting laws that forbid discrimination against homosexuals.[28] The Court held that the law lacked a rational basis and was based on animus and bias against gays and lesbians.

SUSPECT CLASSIFICATIONS AND STRICT SCRUTINY   When a law is subject to strict scrutiny, the courts must be persuaded that there is both a "compelling governmental interest" to justify such a classification and no less restrictive way to accomplish this compelling purpose. The Court applies the strict scrutiny test to suspect classifications. A *suspect classification* is a class of people deliberately subjected to such unequal treatment in the past or that society has made so politically powerless as to require extraordinary judicial protection.[29]

Classifications based on race or national origin are always suspect. It does not make any difference if the laws are designed for supposedly benign purposes—that is, to help persons of a particular race or national origin. For example, the Supreme Court has held that laws that give preference for public employment based on race are subject to strict scrutiny.

QUASI-SUSPECT CLASSIFICATIONS AND HEIGHTENED SCRUTINY   To sustain a law under this test, the government must show that its classification serves "important governmental objectives." Classifications based on gender are subject to heightened scrutiny. Not until 1971 was any classification based on gender declared unconstitutional. Before that time, many laws provided special protection for women—such as a Michigan law forbidding any woman other than the wife or daughter of a tavern owner to serve as a barmaid. As Justice William J. Brennan Jr. wrote for the Court, "There can be

equal protection clause

Clause in the Fourteenth Amendment that forbids any state to deny to any person within its jurisdiction the equal protection of the laws. By interpretation, the Fifth Amendment imposes the same limitation on the national government. This clause is the major constitutional restraint on the power of governments to discriminate against persons because of race, national origin, or sex.

due process clause

Clause in the Fifth Amendment limiting the power of the national government; similar clause in the Fourteenth Amendment prohibiting state governments from depriving any person of life, liberty, or property without due process of law.

TABLE 17–1 Major Civil Rights Laws

- **Civil Rights Act, 1957** Makes it a federal crime to prevent persons from voting in federal elections.
- **Civil Rights Act, 1964** Bars discrimination in employment or in public accommodations on the basis of race, color, religion, sex, or national origin; created the Equal Employment Opportunity Commission.
- **Voting Rights Act, 1965** Authorizes the appointment of federal examiners to register voters in areas with a history of discrimination.
- **Age Discrimination in Employment Act, 1967** Prohibits job discrimination against workers or job applicants aged 40 through 65 and prohibits mandatory retirement.
- **Fair Housing Act, 1968** Prohibits discrimination on the basis of race, color, religion, or national origin in the sale or rental of most housing.
- **Title IX, Education Amendment of 1972** Prohibits discrimination on the basis of sex in any education program receiving federal financial assistance.
- **Rehabilitation Act, 1973** Requires that recipients of federal grants greater than $2,500 hire and promote qualified handicapped individuals.
- **Fair Housing Act Amendments, 1988** Gave the Department of Housing and Urban Development authority to prohibit housing bias against the handicapped and families with children.
- **Americans with Disabilities Act, 1991** Prohibits discrimination based on disability and requires that facilities be made accessible to those with disabilities.
- **Civil Rights Act, 1991** Requires that employers justify practices that negatively affect the working conditions of women and minorities or show that no alternative practices would have a lesser impact. Also established a commission to examine the "glass ceiling" that keeps women from becoming executives and to recommend how to increase the number of women and minorities in management positions.

no doubt that our nation has had a long and unfortunate history of sex discrimination. Traditionally such discrimination was rationalized by an attitude of 'romantic paternalism' which in practical effect put women, not on a pedestal, but in a cage."[30]

Today the Court's view is that treating women differently from men (or vice versa) is forbidden when supported by no more substantial justification than "the role-typing society has long imposed upon women."[31] If the government's objective is "to protect members of one sex because they are presumed to suffer from an inherent handicap or to be innately inferior," that objective is illegitimate, and the government must have "an exceedingly persuasive justification" for discriminating between men and women.[32] In recent years, the Supreme Court has struck down most laws brought before it that were alleged to discriminate against women but has tended to do so on the basis of federal statutes like the 1964 Civil Rights Act (for other legislation see Table 17–1).

POVERTY AND AGE Just as racial minorities and women are entitled to special constitutional protection, it is argued, the poor and the elderly should be similarly protected. But the Supreme Court rejected the argument "that financial need alone identifies a suspect class for purposes of equal protection analysis."[33] However, state supreme courts in Texas, Ohio, Connecticut, and elsewhere have ruled that unequal funding for public schools as a result of "rich" districts spending more per pupil than "poor" districts violates their state constitutional provisions for free and equal education.[34]

Age is not a suspect class. Many laws commonly make distinctions based on age: to obtain a driver's license, to marry without parental consent, to attend schools, to buy alcohol or tobacco, and so on. Many governmental institutions have age-specific programs: for senior citizens, for adult students, for mid-career persons. The Supreme Court has repeatedly refused to make age a suspect classification requiring extra judicial protection. As Justice Sandra Day O'Connor observed, "States may discriminate on the basis of age without offending the Fourteenth Amendment if the age classification in question is rationally related to a legitimate state interest."[35]

"There can be no doubt that our nation has had a long and unfortunate history of sex discrimination. Traditionally such discrimination was rationalized by an attitude of 'romantic paternalism' which in practical effect put women, not on a pedestal, but in a cage."

JUSTICE WILLIAM J. BRENNAN JR.

How Other Nations Govern

Canadian Courts Forbid Discrimination Against Homosexuals

Within months of the Massachusetts state supreme court's ruling in 2003 that its state constitution forbids discrimination against same-sex marriages and the U.S. Supreme Court's decision striking down laws making homosexual sodomy a crime,* the High Court in the Canadian province of Ontario ruled that the government had to recognize same-sex marriages. In doing so the court extended a series of rulings barring discrimination against homosexuals in Canada.

The Supreme Court of Canada in 1995 held that sexual orientation was embraced by the equality guarantee of Section 15(1) of Canada's Charter of Rights and Freedom, which provides: "Every individual is equal before and under the law and has the right to the equal protection and equal benefit of the law without discrimination and, in particular, without discrimination based on race, national or ethnic origin, colour, religion, sex, age or mental or physical disability."†

Subsequent decisions further expanded protection for gays and lesbians in holding, for example, that they may not be discriminated against in employment.‡ On the basis of those rulings, courts in the provinces of Quebec and British Columbia invalidated prohibitions against same-sex marriages. And in *Halpern* v. *Attorney General of Canada* (2003), the Court of Appeal for Ontario held that Canada's Charter of Rights and Freedoms bars discrimination against same-sex marriages. The High Court rejected the government's arguments that it had compelling interests in barring same-sex marriages. Specifically, the court ruled that interests in uniting the opposite sexes, encouraging the birth and rearing of children by married couples, and promoting companionship, were not compelling justifications for discrimination against homosexuals and same-sex marriages.

In 2005, Canada's legislature enacted a law recognizing same-sex marriages, as did Spain. Gay marriages have also been recognized in the Netherlands (since 2001) and in Belgium (since 2003). A number of other countries have legalized same-sex civil unions, including Denmark (since 1989), Sweden (since 1995), France (since 1999), Germany (since 2001), Finland and Switzerland (since 2002), and Britain (since 2005).

The full text of the opinion in *Halpern* v. *Attorney General of Canada* is available on the Web site of the Court of Appeal of Ontario at www.ontariocourts.on.ca/decisions. ∎

Lawrence v. *Texas*, 539 U.S. 558 (2003).
†*Egan* v. *Canada*, 2 S.C.R. 513 (1995).
‡*Vriend* v. *Albert*, 1 S.C.R. 493 (1998); and *M.* v. *H.*, 2 S.C.R. 3 (1999).

Congress, however, responding to "gray power," frequently treats age as a protected category. Congress has made it illegal for most employers to discriminate on the basis of advancing age. Except for a few exempt occupations, employers may not impose mandatory retirement requirements. Congress also attempted to extend the protections against age discrimination to cover state employees, but the Supreme Court ruled that Congress lacks the constitutional authority to open the federal courts to suits by state employees for alleged age discrimination. State employees are limited to recovering monetary damages under state laws in state courts.[36]

FUNDAMENTAL RIGHTS AND STRICT SCRUTINY The Court also strictly scrutinizes laws impinging on *fundamental rights*. What makes a right fundamental in the constitutional sense? It is not the importance or the significance of the right that makes it fundamental but whether it is explicitly or implicitly *guaranteed by the Constitution*. Under this test, the rights to travel and to vote have been held to be fundamental, as well as First Amendment rights such as the right to associate to advance political beliefs. Rights to an education, to housing, or to welfare benefits have not been deemed fundamental. Important as these rights may be, no constitutional provisions specifically protect them from governmental regulation.

Proving Discrimination

Does the fact that a law or a regulation has a differential effect—what has come to be known as *disparate impact*—on persons of a different race or sex by itself establish that the law is unconstitutional? In one of its most important decisions, *Washington* v. *Davis* (1976), the Supreme Court said no.[37] "An unwavering line of cases" from the Supreme Court "hold that a violation of the Equal Protection Clause requires state action motivated by discriminatory intent; the disproportionate effects of state action are not sufficient to establish such a violation."[38] Or, as the Court said in another case, "the Fourteenth Amendment guarantees equal laws, not equal results."[39]

What do these rulings on disparate impact mean in practical terms? They mean, for example, that even when city ordinances permit only single-family residences and thus make low-cost housing projects impossible, they are not unconstitutional—even if their effect is to keep minorities from moving into the city—unless it can be shown that they were adopted with the *intent* to discriminate against minorities. For another example, preference for veterans in public employment does not violate the equal protection clause, even though its effect is to keep many women from getting jobs; the distinction between veterans and nonveterans was not adopted deliberately to create a sex barrier.

What is constitutional can nonetheless be illegal. For example, state laws creating legislative districts with no intent to discriminate against African Americans but that in effect do dilute their voting power are not unconstitutional. But in the Voting Rights Act of 1965, Congress made such laws illegal if the result is to dilute the voting power of African Americans, regardless of the laws' intent. The Voting Rights Act of 1965 tests the legality of state voting laws and practices by their *effects* rather than by the *intentions* of the legislatures that passed them.

Voting Rights

Under our Constitution, the states, not the federal government, regulate elections and voting qualifications. However, Article I, Section 4, gives Congress the power to supersede state regulations as to the "Times, Places and Manner" of elections for representatives and senators. Congress has used this authority, along with its authority under Article II, Section 2, to set the date for selecting electors, to set age qualifications and residency requirements to vote in national elections, to establish a uniform day for all states to hold elections for members of Congress and presidential electors, and to give American citizens who live outside the United States the right to vote for members of Congress and presidential electors in the states in which they are legal residents.

The Fourteenth Amendment (forbidding qualifications that have no reasonable relation to the ability to vote), the Fifteenth Amendment (forbidding qualifications based on race), the Nineteenth Amendment (forbidding qualifications based on sex), and the Twenty-Sixth Amendment (forbidding states to deny citizens 18 years of age or older the right to vote on account of age) limit the states' power to set voting qualifications. These amendments also empower Congress to enact the laws necessary to enforce their provisions.

Protecting Voting Rights

In the 1940s, the Supreme Court began to strike down one after another of the devices that states and localities had used to keep African Americans from voting. In the one-party South of the early twentieth century, the Democratic party would hold whites-only primaries, effectively disenfranchising black voters because in the absence of viable Republican candidates, the winner of the Democratic primary was guaranteed to win the general election. In *Smith* v. *Allwright* (1944), the Court declared the **white primary** unconstitutional.[40] In 1960, the Court held that **racial gerrymandering**—drawing election districts to ensure that African Americans would be a minority in all districts—was contrary to the Fifteenth Amendment.[41] In 1964, the Twenty-Fourth Amendment eliminated the **poll tax**—payment required as a condition for voting—in presidential and congressional elections. In 1966, the Court held that the Fourteenth Amendment forbade the poll tax as a condition in any election.[42]

Officials seeking to deny African Americans the right to vote were forced to rely on registration requirements. On the surface, such requirements appeared to be perfectly proper, but it was the way they were administered that kept black people from the polls. White election officers confronted African Americans trying to register while white police stood guard; white judges heard appeals of decisions that registration officials made. Officials often seized on the smallest error on an application form to disqualify a black voter. In one parish (county) in Louisiana, after four white voters

white primary
Democratic party primary in the old "one-party South" that was limited to white people and essentially constituted an election; ruled unconstitutional in *Smith* v. *Allwright* (1944).

racial gerrymandering
The drawing of election districts so as to ensure that members of a certain race are a minority in the district; ruled unconstitutional in *Gomillion* v. *Lightfoot* (1960).

poll tax
Tax required to vote; prohibited for national elections by the Twenty-Fourth Amendment (1964) and ruled unconstitutional for all elections in *Harper* v. *Virginia Board of Elections* (1966).

challenged the registration of black voters on the grounds that those voters had made an "error in spilling" [*sic*] in their applications, registration officials struck 1,300 out of approximately 1,500 black voters from the rolls.[43]

In many southern areas, **literacy tests** were used to discriminate against African Americans. Some states required applicants to demonstrate that they understood the national and state constitutions and that they were persons of good character. Although poor white people often avoided registering out of fear of embarrassment from failing a literacy test, the tests were more often used to discriminate against African Americans.[44] White people were often asked simple questions; black people were asked questions that would baffle a Supreme Court justice. "In the 1960s southern registrars were observed testing black applicants on such matters as the number of bubbles in a soap bar, the news contained in a copy of the *Peking Daily*, the meaning of obscure passages in state constitutions, and the definition of terms such as *habeas corpus*."[45] In Louisiana, 49,603 illiterate white voters were able to persuade election officials they could understand the Constitution, but only two illiterate black voters were able to do so.

The Voting Rights Act of 1965

For two decades after World War II, under the leadership of the Supreme Court, many limitations on voting were declared unconstitutional, but this approach still did not open the voting booth to African Americans. Finally Congress acted. The Civil Rights Act of 1964 had hardly become law when events in Selma, Alabama, dramatized the inadequacy of depending on the courts to prevent racial barriers in polling places. Led by Martin Luther King Jr., a voter registration drive in Selma sparked arrests, marches on the state capital, and the murder of two civil rights workers. Still there was no dent in the color bar at the polls. Responding to events in Selma, President Lyndon Johnson made a dramatic address to Congress and the nation calling for federal action to ensure that no person would be deprived of the right to vote in any election for any office because of color or race. Congress responded with the Voting Rights Act of 1965.

Section 2 of the Voting Rights Act prohibits voting qualifications or standards that result in a denial of the right of any citizen to vote on account of race and color. Section 5 requires that states with a history of denying African Americans or Hispanic citizens the right to vote must clear with the Department of Justice changes in voting practice or laws that might dilute the voting power of these groups.[46] What precisely constitutes "dilution" and how to measure it have been the subjects of much litigation. Examples include changes in the location of polling places, changes in candidacy requirements and qualifications, changes in filing deadlines, changes from ward to at-large elections, changes in boundary lines of voting districts, and changes that affect the creation or abolition of an elective office, and imposition by state political parties of fees for delegates to nominating conventions.[47]

Following the 1990 census, the Department of Justice pressured southern state legislatures to draw as many districts as possible in which minorities would constitute a majority of the electorate. Most of these districts tended to be Democratic, leaving the other congressional districts in these states heavily white and Republican. The lower federal courts sustained the Department of Justice's interpretation. As a result, the number of congressional districts represented by minorities and Republicans increased considerably.

The Supreme Court, however, in a series of cases beginning with *Shaw* v. *Reno* (1993), announced that although it was a legitimate goal for state legislatures to take race into account when they drew electoral districts to increase the voting strength of minorities, they could not make race the sole or predominant reason for drawing district lines. The Department of Justice, said the Supreme Court, was wrong to force states to create as many **majority-minority districts** as possible. A test case involved the North Carolina legislature's creation of a majority-minority district 160 miles long and in some places only an interstate highway wide. "If you drove down the interstate," said one legislator about this district, "with both car doors open, you'd kill most of the

literacy test
Literacy requirement some states imposed as a condition of voting, generally used to disqualify black voters in the South; now illegal.

majority-minority district
A congressional district created to include a majority of minority voters; ruled constitutional so long as race is not the main factor in redistricting.

people in the district." North Carolina's reapportionment scheme, the Court declared, was so "irrational on its face that it can be understood only as an effort to segregate voters into separate voting districts because of their race." To comply with the Voting Rights Act, the Court explained, states must provide for districts roughly proportional to the minority voters' respective shares in the voting-age population.[48]

Since then the Court has expanded *Shaw* by clarifying that it was not meant to suggest that a "district must be bizarre on its face before there is a constitutional violation." Legislatures may take racial considerations into account when they draw district lines, but when race becomes the overriding motive, the state violates the equal protection clause.[49] Even though many southern states had to redraw legislative districts, when African American incumbents ran in the newly drawn districts, with majority white electors, they were reelected.[50]

Problems with voting irregularities remain. After the 2000 presidential election, some black voters in several counties in Florida complained that they were discouraged from voting or that their votes were not counted. Also, Florida and other states denied felons who had served their sentences the right to vote. In the 2004 presidential election, both parties, as well as international observers, monitored and contested processes for violations of voting procedures.

The Voting Rights Act was renewed in 1982 and was due to expire in 2007. But in 2006, it was extended for another 25 years. Some southern Republicans in the House had opposed the extension of provisions for southern state and local governments to receive federal approval of changes in voting districts, to ensure that they do not have a discriminatory effect on minority voters. But House Democrats joined with moderate Republicans to defeat that and other changes and to extend the law. The Senate also endorsed extension of the act by a vote of 98 to 0.

Education Rights

Until the Supreme Court struck down such laws in the 1950s, southern states had made it illegal for white and black people to ride in the same train cars, attend the same theaters, go to the same schools, be born in the same hospitals, drink from the same water fountains, or be buried in the same cemeteries. **Jim Crow laws**, as they came to be called, blanketed southern life. How could these laws stand in the face of the equal protection clause? This was the question raised in *Plessy v. Ferguson* (1896).

In the *Plessy* decision, the Supreme Court endorsed the view that government-imposed racial segregation in public transportation, and presumably in public education, did not necessarily constitute discrimination if "equal" accommodations were provided for the members of both races.[51] But the "equal" part of the formula was meaningless. African Americans were segregated in unequal facilities and lacked the political power to protest effectively. The passage of time did not lessen the inequalities. However, in the late 1930s African Americans started to file lawsuits challenging the doctrine. They cited facts to show that in practice "separate but equal" was not equal and always resulted in discrimination against African Americans.

The End of "Separate but Equal":
Brown v. Board of Education

At first, the Supreme Court was not willing to upset the separate but equal doctrine, but in *Brown* v. *Board of Education of Topeka* (1954), the Court finally held that the *Plessy* doctrine did not apply to public schools by ruling that "separate but equal" is a contradiction in terms. *Segregation is itself discrimination.*[52] A year later, the Court ordered school boards to proceed with "all deliberate speed to desegregate public schools at the earliest practical date."[53]

But many school districts moved slowly or not at all, and in the 1960s, Congress and the president joined even more directly to fight school segregation. Title VI of the

Jim Crow laws
State laws formerly pervasive throughout the South requiring public facilities and accommodations to be segregated by race; ruled unconstitutional.

Thurgood Marshall (center), George C. E. Hayes (left), and James Nabrit Jr. (right) argued and won Brown v. Board of Education of Topeka *before the Supreme Court in 1954.*

Civil Rights Act of 1964, as subsequently amended, stipulated that federal dollars under any grant program or project must be withdrawn from an entire school or institution of higher education that discriminates "on the ground of race, color, or national origin," gender, age, or disability, in "any program or activity receiving federal financial assistance."

From Segregation to Desegregation—but Not Yet Integration

School districts that had operated separate schools for white children and black children now had to develop plans and programs to move from segregation to integration. For such school districts, desegregation would not be enough; they would have to bring about integration. If they failed to do so on their own initiative, federal judges would supervise the school districts to ensure that they were doing what was necessary and proper to overcome the evils of segregation.

But since most white people and most African Americans continued to live in separate neighborhoods, merely removing legal barriers to school integration did not by itself integrate the schools. To overcome this residential clustering by race, some federal courts mandated busing across neighborhoods, moving white students to once predominantly black schools and vice versa. Busing students was unpopular and triggered protests in many cities.

The Supreme Court sustained busing only if it was to remedy the consequences of *officially* sanctioned segregation, **de jure segregation**. The Court refused to permit federal judges to order busing to overcome the effects of **de facto segregation**, segregation that arises as a result of social and economic conditions such as housing patterns.

Following *Brown* v. *Board of Education*, federal courts oversaw lawsuits forcing integration in more than 500 desegregation cases. As a result, many southern cities now have more integrated schools than large northern cities do. However, in both North and South, many school districts in central cities today are predominantly African American or Hispanic. This segregated pattern of schools is partly the result of

de jure segregation
Segregation imposed by law.

de facto segregation
Segregation resulting from economic or social conditions or personal choice.

"white flight" to the suburbs in the 1970s and 1980s and the transfer of white students to private schools to escape court-ordered busing. In more recent years, it is also due to higher birthrates and immigration among African Americans and Hispanics.

After a period of vigorous federal court supervision of school desegregation programs, the Supreme Court in the 1990s restricted the role of federal judges.[54] It instructed some of them to restore control of a school system to the state and local authorities and to release districts from any busing obligations once a judge concludes that the authorities "have done everything practicable to overcome the past consequences of segregation."[55]

Political support for busing and for other efforts to integrate the schools also faded.[56] Many school districts eliminated mandatory busing, with the result that *Brown*'s era of court-ordered desegregation drew to a close. The percentage of southern black students attending white-majority schools fell from over 40 percent to 30 percent, or about the same level it had been in 1969.[57] Some African American leaders, while still supporting desegregation efforts, are now more concerned about improving the quality of inner-city schools than desegregating them. They are turning to state courts and state constitutions, which mandate equal public education, to force increases in public school financing and to make adequate educational resources available to all on equal terms.[58] But some also now demand greater community control over local schools that are racially segregated. In 2006, Omaha, Nebraska, for instance, split its school system into three districts based along racial lines. Omaha's schools are 41 percent white, 31 percent black, and 23 percent Hispanic or Asian, but are segregated by neighborhoods. The plan has been challenged in the courts and would not go into effect until 2008.

Rights of Association, Accommodations, Jobs, and Homes

Association

As we have noted, the Fifth and Fourteenth Amendments apply only to governmental action, not to private discriminatory conduct. As Justice William O. Douglas said, our Constitution creates "a zone of privacy which precludes government from interfering with private clubs or groups. The associational rights which our system honors permit all-white, all-black, all-brown, and all-yellow clubs to be established. They also permit all-Catholic, all-Jewish, or all-agnostic clubs. . . . Government may not tell a man or a woman who his or her associates must be. The individual may be as selective as he desires."[59]

Families, churches, or private groups organized for political, religious, cultural, or social purposes are constitutionally different from large associations organized along other lines. For example, the Supreme Court has upheld the application of laws forbidding sex or racial discrimination by organizations such as the Jaycees, the Rotary Club, and large (in this case, more than 400 members) private eating clubs. Such associations and clubs are not small, intimate groups. Nor were they able to demonstrate that allowing women or minorities to become members would change the content or impact of their purposes.[60] In *Boy Scouts of America* v. *Dale* (2000), however, the Court held that the Boy Scouts may exclude homosexuals because it is a private association and because of its overall mission.[61]

Accommodations

In 1883, the Supreme Court had declared unconstitutional an act of Congress that made it a federal offense for any operator of a public conveyance, hotel, or theater to deny accommodations to any person because of race or color on the grounds that the Fourteenth Amendment does not give Congress such authority.[62] Since the 1960s, however, the constitutional authority of Congress to legislate against discrimination by private individuals is no longer an issue because the Court has broadly construed the **commerce clause**—which gives Congress the power to regulate interstate and foreign commerce—to justify action against discriminatory conduct by individuals. Congress has also used its power to tax and spend to prevent not only racial discrimination but also discrimination based on ethnic origin, sex, disability, and age.

TITLE II: PLACES OF PUBLIC ACCOMMODATION   For the first time since Reconstruction, the Civil Rights Act of 1964 authorized the massive use of federal authority to combat privately imposed racial discrimination. Title II makes it a federal offense to discriminate against any customer or patron in a place of public accommodation because of race, color, religion, or national origin. It applies to any inn, hotel, motel, or lodging establishment (except those with fewer than five rooms and where the proprietor also lives—in other words, small boardinghouses); to any restaurant or gasoline station that serves interstate travelers or serves food or products that have moved in interstate commerce; and to any movie house, theater, concert hall, sports arena, or other place of entertainment that customarily hosts films, performances, athletic teams, or other sources of entertainment that are moved in interstate commerce. Within a few months after its adoption, the Supreme Court sustained the constitutionality of Title II.[63] As a result, public establishments, including those in the South, opened their doors to all customers.

TITLE VII: EMPLOYMENT   Title VII of the 1964 Civil Rights Act made it illegal for any employer or trade union in any industry affecting interstate commerce and employing 15 or more people (and, since 1972, any state or local agency such as a school or university) to discriminate in employment practices against any person because of race, color, national origin, religion, or sex. Employers must create workplaces that avoid abusive environments. Related legislation made it illegal to discriminate against persons with physical handicaps, veterans, or persons over age 40.

There are a few exceptions. Religious institutions such as parochial schools may use religious standards. Employers may take into account the age, sex, or handicap of prospective employees when occupational qualifications are absolutely necessary to the normal operation of a particular business or enterprise—for example, hiring only women to work in women's locker rooms.

The Equal Employment Opportunity Commission (EEOC) was created to enforce Title VII. The commission works together with state authorities to try to ensure compliance with the act and may seek judicial enforcement of complaints against private employers. The attorney general prosecutes Title VII violations by public agencies. Not only can aggrieved persons sue for damages for themselves, but they can also do so for other persons similarly situated in a **class action suit**. The vigor with which the EEOC and the attorney general have acted has varied over the years, depending on the commitment of the president and the willingness of Congress to provide an adequate budget for the EEOC.[64]

A 1965 presidential executive order requiring all contractors doing work for the federal government, including universities, to adopt and implement affirmative action programs to correct "underutilization" of women and minorities supplemented Title VII. Such programs may not establish racial or ethnic quotas for minorities or women, but they may require contractors to establish timetables and goals; to follow open recruitment procedures; to keep records of applicants by race, sex, and national origin; and to explain why their labor force does not reflect the same proportion of persons in the appropriate labor market pools. Failure of contractors to file and implement an approved affirmative action plan may lead to loss of federal contracts or grants.

THE FAIR HOUSING ACT AND AMENDMENTS   Housing is the last frontier of the civil rights crusade, the area in which progress is slowest and genuine change most remote. As political scientist Charles Lamb observes:

> Segregated housing contributes mightily to a vicious circle that also includes educational and employment discrimination. . . . Because of poor schools for many

commerce clause
The clause of the Constitution (Article I, Section 8, Clause 3) that gives Congress the power to regulate all business activities that cross state lines or affect more than one state or other nations.

class action suit
Lawsuit brought by an individual or a group of people on behalf of all those similarly situated.

Government's Greatest Endeavors

Reducing Workplace Discrimination

The United States has one of the most diverse workforces in the world. As diversity has grown, so have calls for protection against workplace discrimination. Most of these calls have been answered by the federal judiciary, where women, older Americans, and the disabled have won a series of victories assuring their basic rights.

Many of these victories involved the 1964 Civil Rights Act, the 1967 Age Discrimination Act, and the 1990 Americans with Disabilities Act. Together, these three acts have created protections that have made reducing workplace discrimination one of the federal government's greatest achievements.

The 1964 Civil Rights Act was particularly important for guaranteeing equal rights for women. Under the original bill, women were not included in the law. Ironically, it was a conserva-tive Democrat who added the word "sex" to the prohibition against discrimination on the basis of "race, color, religion, or national origin" in the act. He did so in the belief that Congress would not pass a bill guaranteeing equality of the sexes. However, the bill did pass, and women had the legislation that would provide the opportunity to take employers to court for sex discrimination.

Disabled Americans won similar protection under the 1990 Americans with Disabilities Act. The fight for passage was led by Senator Bob Dole (R-Kans.), who had lost the use of his right arm in World War II. In 1998, the Supreme Court ruled that people with HIV/AIDS were protected against discrimination under the law, demonstrating the important link between such laws and eventual judicial action in assuring basic rights. ∎

MARTA (Metropolitan Atlanta Rapid Transit Authority) allows disabled citizens access to Atlanta's mass transit system.

QUESTIONS

Have you ever experienced workplace discrimination, and, if so, how was it resolved?

What new forms of workplace discrimination need action?

minorities, they cannot find well-paying jobs. Without such jobs, they often cannot afford to live in nicer neighborhoods with decent housing. And because of their location in less desirable communities, good educational systems are less likely to be available.[65]

In 1948, the Supreme Court made racial or religious **restrictive covenants** (a provision in a deed to real property that restricts to whom it can be sold) legally unenforceable.[66] The 1968 Fair Housing Act forbids discrimination in housing, excluding from its protection what it called "Mrs. Murphy boardinghouses," housing owned by private individuals who own no more than three houses; dwellings that have no more than four separate living units in which the owner maintains a residence; and religious organizations and private clubs housing their own members on a noncommercial basis. The act forbids owners of all other housing to refuse to sell or rent to any person because of race, color, religion, national origin, sex, or physical handicap or because a person has children. Discrimination in housing also covers efforts to deny loans to minorities.

The Department of Justice has filed hundreds of cases, especially those involving large apartment complexes, yet African Americans and Hispanics still face discrimination in housing. Some real estate agents steer African Americans and Hispanics toward neighborhoods that are not predominantly white and require minority renters to pay larger deposits than white renters. Yet those affected complain about less than 1 percent of these actions because the discrimination is so subtle that victims are often

restrictive covenant
A provision in a deed to real property prohibiting its sale to a person of a particular race or religion. Judicial enforcement of such deeds is unconstitutional.

unaware that they are being discriminated against. However, more aggressive enforcement has increased the number of discrimination complaints that the Department of Housing and Urban Development and local and state agencies receive.

Voluntary segregation obviously exists. "It's a fact of life that blacks like to live in black neighborhoods and whites like to live in white neighborhoods," according to Daniel Mitchell, who added, "Real estate agents generally like to bring customers to places they will like and where the agent can make a sale."[67] Whatever the reasons, housing segregation persists.

The Affirmative Action Controversy

When white majorities were using governmental power to discriminate against African Americans, civil rights advocates cited with approval the famous words of Justice John Marshall Harlan when he dissented from the *Plessy* decision: "Our Constitution is color-blind and neither knows nor tolerates class among citizens."[68] But by the 1960s, there was a new set of constitutional and national policy debates. Many people began to assert that government neutrality is not enough. If governments, universities, and employers simply stopped discriminating but nothing else changed, individuals previously discriminated against would still be kept from equal participation in American life. Because discrimination had so disadvantaged some people from some groups, they suffered disabilities that white males did not share in competing for openings in medical schools, for skilled jobs, or for their share of government grants and contracts.

Supporters call remedies to overcome the consequences of discrimination against African Americans, Hispanics, Native Americans, and women *affirmative action*; opponents call these efforts *reverse discrimination*. The Supreme Court's first major statement on the constitutionality of affirmative action programs came in a celebrated case relating to university admissions. Allan Bakke—a white male, a top student at the University of Minnesota and at Stanford, and a Vietnam War veteran—applied in 1973 and again in 1974 to the medical school of the University of California at Davis. In each of those years, the school admitted 100 new students, 84 in a general admissions program and 16 in a special admissions program created for minorities who had previously been underrepresented. Both years, under the special admissions program, the school rejected Bakke's application and admitted students with lower grade-point averages, test scores, and interview ratings. After his second rejection, Bakke brought suit in federal court claiming he had been excluded because of his race, contrary to requirements of the Constitution and Title VI of the Civil Rights Act of 1964.

In *University of California Regents* v. *Bakke* (1978), the Supreme Court ruled the California plan unconstitutional[69] because the plan created a *quota*—a set number of admissions from which whites were excluded solely because of race. But the Court also declared that affirmative action programs are not necessarily unconstitutional. A state university may properly take race and ethnic background into account as "a plus," as one of several factors in choosing students to achieve a diverse student body.

After *Bakke*: Refinements and Uncertainty

Following *Bakke,* the Court dealt with a variety of affirmative action programs in public and private employment, sustaining most but not all of them. As the justices continued to disagree on the application of the equal protection clause, opposition to such programs became more heated.

In *Richmond* v. *Croson* (1989), the Court struck down a regulation by the city of Richmond requiring nonminority city contractors to subcontract at least 30 percent of the dollar amount of their contracts to one or more minority business enterprises. Writing for the Court, Justice Sandra Day O'Connor called into question the validity of most government affirmative action plans and stated, "Race-sensitive remedial measures are to be justified only after a strong basis in evidence has established that

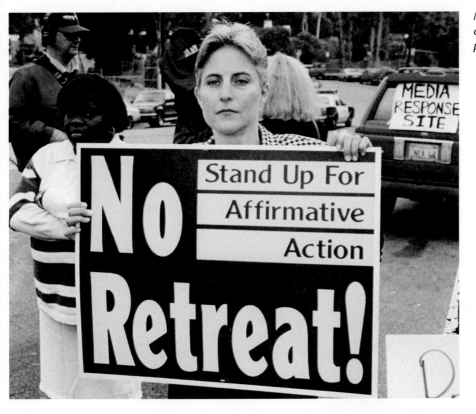

Many Americans believe that affirmative action is the best way to address the issue of past racial and ethnic quotas.

remedial action is necessary to overcome the consequences of past discriminatory action."[70]

Since *Croson,* a bare majority of the Court has rejected the view that racial classifications, whether benign or hostile, should ever be subject to less than strict scrutiny by either the national or state and local governments.[71] And as noted, the Court has also opposed using race as the sole criterion for drawing electoral districts.[72] The only permissible programs in government employment and contracting are those that are narrowly tailored remedies for past discrimination.

California's Proposition 209 and Other Plans

In 1995, the Regents of the University of California voted to eliminate race or gender as factors in employment, purchasing, contracting, or admissions. The following year, Californians voted overwhelmingly for Proposition 209 to amend the state constitution to forbid state agencies to discriminate against or grant preferential treatment to any individual or group on the basis of race, sex, color, ethnicity, or national origin in public employment, public education, or public contracting, except where necessary to comply with a federal requirement.

Although Proposition 209 clearly forbids universities and other state agencies to take race and gender into account, it did not make unconstitutional state-supported outreach programs designed to recruit more women and minorities to become scientists and engineers, nor does it prevent state universities from continuing outreach programs aimed at schools with large minority enrollments. Due to such outreach programs the percentage of students admitted to the University of California from "underrepresented groups"—African Americans, Native Americans, and Hispanics—gradually rebounded.[73] The University of California's board of regents also shifted policy to take into account the economic backgrounds and personal achievements, not just grades and SAT scores, of students applying for admission. As a result, the percentage of racial and ethnic minorities moved back to previous levels, though it is still low at Berkeley, where Asian Americans make up more than 40 percent of the student body.[74]

Opponents of affirmative action had hoped that the adoption of Proposition 209 in California would start a national movement to restrict or eliminate affirmative action programs, and some federal programs designed to give women- and minority-owned businesses greater access to federal contracts were cut back. Under pressure from the Office of Civil Rights, some universities stopped offering scholarships based solely on race or ethnicity. But Congress has not limited other federal affirmative action programs.

California and six other states (Texas, Louisiana, Mississippi, Georgia, Florida, and Washington) abandoned affirmative action programs—some like California and Washington because of voter opposition and others like Texas and Georgia because federal courts held that they were unconstitutional.[75] They adopted the strategy of automatic admissions for a certain percentage of all high school graduates to maintain diversity in colleges and expand educational opportunities for minorities. California offers admission to the top 4 percent of high school graduates, Texas to the top 10 percent, and Florida to the top 20 percent.

These programs, though, have been sharply criticized for accepting students from poor inner-city and rural schools who are not prepared to compete effectively in college with students from wealthier and more advantaged school districts. Critics also complain that under the program some students from the top high schools are denied admission to state flagship universities.

Reaffirming the Importance of Diversity

The controversy and the conflicting lower court decisions on the permissibility of affirmative action in higher education resulted in confusion and uncertainty about how colleges and universities may pursue diverse student bodies. The Supreme Court clarified the matter in 2003, reaffirming *Bakke* in two cases that challenged the admission policies for undergraduates and law students at the University of Michigan. Both policies sought to achieve diverse student bodies, but in different ways.

Jennifer Gratz, a white high school student with a 3.8 GPA, was denied admission to the undergraduate college at Michigan. She challenged its admissions policy based on a "selection index" that ranked on a 150-point scale applicants' test scores and grades for up to 100 points, and allocated 40 points for other factors, including 4 points for children of alumni, 16 points for residents of rural areas, and 20 points for students from underrepresented minor-

Jennifer Gratz (right) is the successful plaintiff in Gratz v. Bollinger, *a case that struck down the University of Michigan's undergraduate admissions policy that awarded points to applicants based on various factors including racial and ethnic background. Barbara Grutter (left) is the unsuccessful plaintiff in* Grutter v. Bollinger, *a case that challenged the admissions policy of the University of Michigan's law school. Unlike the undergraduate admissions policy, the law school took an applicant's racial and ethnic background into account when considering that applicant's qualifications but did not award points based on this information.*

ity groups or from socioeconomically disadvantaged families. Writing for the Court in *Gratz* v. *Bollinger* (2003), Chief Justice Rehnquist struck down the policy as too mechanical and not narrowly tailored to giving applicants "individualized consideration" as *Bakke* required.[76]

In *Grutter* v. *Bollinger* (2003), however, a bare majority of the Court upheld the law school's affirmative-action policy that made "special efforts" to achieve racial and ethnic diversity.[77] Unlike the undergraduate program, the law school did not use a point system based in part on race. Writing for the Court, Justice O'Connor held that law school admissions were based on a "highly individualized, holistic review of each applicant's file" and did not use race as a factor in a "mechanical way." For that reason, it was consistent with *Bakke*'s holding that race may be used as a "plus factor" to achieve a diverse student body.

Justice O'Connor reaffirmed the importance of diversity, observing: "In order to cultivate a set of leaders with legitimacy in the eyes of the citizenry, it is necessary that the path to leadership be visibly open to talented and qualified individuals of every race and ethnicity." But she also added that, "We expect 25 years from now, the use of racial preferences will no longer be necessary." Chief Justice Rehnquist and Justices Scalia, Kennedy, and Thomas dissented, maintaining that race may never be used as a consideration in college admissions.

The Court thus reaffirmed the importance of diversity in education and employment. Public support for affirmative action as measured in public opinion polls varies by race, social class, education, and life experience, but close inspection suggests that "whites and blacks are not separated by unbridgeable gaps on affirmative action issues, at least not insofar as college admissions decisions are concerned."[78] People's responses seem to depend to a significant degree on how the survey question is put. If the question asked is something like "Are you in favor of abolishing preferences in hiring or college admissions based on race or gender?" most people say yes. But if the question is something like "Do you favor affirmative action programs to increase the number of minorities in colleges or in jobs?" most people support such programs.

Equal Rights Today

Today, civil rights legislation, executive orders, and judicial decisions have lowered, if not removed, legal barriers. Important as these victories are, according to civil rights leader James Farmer, "They were victories largely for the middle class—those who could travel, entertain in restaurants, and stay in hotels. Those victories did not change life conditions for the mass of blacks who are still poor."[79]

As prosperous middle-class African Americans have moved out of inner cities, the remaining black *underclass,* as they have been called, has become even more isolated from the rest of the nation.[80] There are similar trends in Hispanic communities in Los Angeles, Dallas, and Houston.[81] Children are growing up on streets where drug abuse and crime are everyday events. They live in "separate and deteriorating societies, with separate economies, diverging family structures and basic institutions, and even growing linguistic separation within the core ghettos. The scale of their isolation by race, class, and economic situation is much greater than it was in the 1960s, with impoverishment, joblessness, educational inequality, and housing insufficiency even more severe."[82]

One of the difficulties is that as conditions have become better for many African Americans and Hispanics, the less fortunate see their lives as getting worse, while most Americans see conditions for minorities as improving. "Both perceptions will be correct. And the fact that both are correct in arriving at opposite perceptions of what is going on will itself lead to further misunderstanding."[83]

> Despite the lack of improvement in social conditions, the push for integration has lessened: In fact, power on both sides of the color line is based to some extent on acceptance of segregation. On the black side of the color line, it is advantageous to keep African Americans within black electoral areas and keep black-controlled resources within black institutions; integrationist policies are often viewed as posing larger threats than they actually do. On the white side of the line . . . some residents in outlying suburbs see critical advantages in their almost all-white and all middle-class status.[84]

Some contend that we should pay attention to the plight of the underclass and that instead of focusing on issues of race, we need to focus on class differences and policies that provide jobs and improve education.[85] Others say there has to be a revival of the civil rights crusade, a restoration of vigorous civil rights enforcement, more job training, and, above all, an attack on residential segregation.[86] In any event, questions about how best to provide equal opportunities for all citizens remain high on the national agenda.

"In order to cultivate a set of leaders with legitimacy in the eyes of the citizenry, it is necessary that the path to leadership be visibly open to talented and qualified individuals of every race and ethnicity."

— JUSTICE SANDRA DAY O'CONNOR

Summary

1. Americans are committed to "equality," an elusive term, with most support for equality of opportunity, some for equality of starting conditions, and some for equality of results.

2. Progress in securing civil rights for African Americans was a long time coming. After the Civil War, the national government briefly tried to protect the freed slaves and to enforce the Thirteenth, Fourteenth, and Fifteenth Amendments and the civil rights laws passed to implement them. But after the 1870s, the national government left black people to their own resources. Not for nearly a century did the national government act to prevent racial discrimination.

3. The crusade for women's rights was born partly out of the struggle to abolish slavery. Similarly, the modern women's movement learned and gained power from the civil rights movements of the 1950s and early 1960s. The fate of these two social movements has long been intertwined. Women secured the right to vote in the Nineteenth Amendment.

4. Concern for equal rights under the law continues today for African Americans and women. Hispanics, Asian Americans, and Native Americans have also experienced discrimination.

5. The Supreme Court uses a three-tiered approach to evaluate the constitutionality of laws that may violate the equal protection clause. The Court sustains laws touching economic concerns if they help accomplish a legitimate government goal. It sustains laws that classify people because of gender or sexual orientation only if they serve important governmental objectives. It subjects laws that touch fundamental rights or classify people because of race or ethnic origin to strict scrutiny and sustains them only if the government can show that they serve a compelling public purpose.

6. A series of constitutional amendments, Supreme Court decisions, and laws passed by Congress have now secured the right to vote to all Americans aged 18 and over. Following the Voting Rights Act of 1965, the Justice Department can oversee practices in locales with a history of discrimination. Recent Supreme Court decisions have refined the lengths to which legislatures can go, or are obliged to go, in creating minority-majority districts.

7. *Brown* v. *Board of Education of Topeka* (1954) struck down the "separate but equal" doctrine that had justified segregated schools, but school districts responded slowly. The Supreme Court demanded compliance, and some federal courts mandated busing children across neighborhoods to comply. Still, full integration has proved elusive, as "white flight" has left many inner cities, and their schools, predominantly black or Hispanic.

8. The Civil Rights Act of 1964 outlawed discrimination in public accommodations. This act also provided for equal employment opportunity. The Fair Housing Act of 1968 and its 1988 amendments prohibited discrimination in housing.

9. The desirability and constitutionality of affirmative action programs that provide special benefits to members of groups subjected to past discrimination divide the nation and the Supreme Court. Remedial programs tailored to overcome specific instances of past discrimination are likely to pass the Supreme Court's suspicion of classifications based on race, national origin, and gender. The Court has also reaffirmed the importance of diversity in education and employment.

Further Reading

RAYMOND ARSENAULT, *Freedom Riders: 1961 and the Struggle for Racial Justice* (Oxford University Press, 2006).

TALYOR BRANCH, *At Canaan's Edge: America in the King Years, 1965–1968* (Simon & Schuster, 2006).

TAYLOR BRANCH, *Parting the Waters: America in the King Years, 1954–1963* (Simon & Schuster, 1988).

TAYLOR BRANCH, *Pillar of Fire: America in the King Years, 1963–1965* (Simon & Schuster, 1998).

GORDON H. CHANG, ED., *Asian Americans and Politics* (Stanford University Press, 2001).

IRIS CHANG, *The Chinese in America: A Narrative History* (Viking, 2003).

CHARLES CLOTFELTER, *After Brown: The Rise and Retreat of School Desegregation* (Princeton University Press, 2004).

CLARE CUSHMAN, ED., *Supreme Court Decisions and Women's Rights* (CQ Press, 2000).

ARLENE M. DAVILA, *Latinos, Inc.: The Marketing and Making of a People* (University of California Press, 2001).

DAVID DENT, *In Search of Black America: Discovering the African American Dream* (Simon & Schuster, 2000).

JANET DEWART, ED., *The State of Black America* (National Urban League, published annually).

WILLIAM N. ESKRIDGE JR., *Gaylaw: Challenging the Apartheid of the Closet* (Harvard University Press, 2000).

JONATHAN GOLDBERG-HILLER, *The Limits to Union: Same-Sex Marriage and the Politics of Civil Rights* (University of Michigan Press, 2002).

RANDALL KENNEDY, *Race, Crime, and the Law* (Pantheon, 1997).

PHILIP A. KLINKER AND **ROGER M. SMITH,** *The Unsteady March: The Rise and Decline of Racial Equality in America* (University of Chicago Press, 2000).

RICHARD KLUGER, *Simple Justice: The History of* Brown v. Board of Education (Knopf, 1976).

PETER KWONG AND **DUSANKA MISCEVIC,** *Chinese America: The Untold Story of America's Oldest New Community* (New Press, 2006).

NANCY MCGLEN, KAREN O'CONNOR, LAURA VAN ASSELDFT, AND **WENDY GUNTHER-CANADA,** *Women, Politics and American Society,* 3d ed. (Pearson/Longman, 2005).

DAVID M. O'BRIEN, *Constitutional Law and Politics: Civil Rights and Civil Liberties,* 7th ed. (Norton, 2008).

GARY ORFIELD AND **CHUNGMEI LEE,** *Brown at 50: King's Dream or Plessy's Nightmare* (The Civil Rights Project, Harvard University, 2004).

J. W. PELTASON, *Fifty-Eight Lonely Men: Southern Federal Judges and School Desegregation* (University of Illinois Press, 1971).

RUTH ROSEN, *The World Split Open: How the Modern Women's Movement Changed America* (Viking, 2000).

JOHN DAVID SKRENTNY, ED., *Color Lines: Affirmative Action, Immigration, and Civil Rights Options for America* (University of Chicago Press, 2001).

GIRARDEAU A. SPANN, *The Law of Affirmative Action: Twenty-Five Years of Supreme Court Decisions on Race and Remedies* (New York University Press, 1999).

PHILIPPA STRUM, *Women in the Barracks: The VMI Case and Equal Rights* (University Press of Kansas, 2002).

SUSAN F. VAN BURKLEO, *"Belonging to the World": Women's Rights and Constitutional Culture* (Oxford University Press, 2001).

KeyTerms

natural rights, p. 488

affirmative action, p. 488

women's suffrage, p. 492

equal protection clause, p. 498

due process clause, p. 498

white primary, p. 501

racial gerrymandering, p. 501

poll tax, p. 501

literacy test, p. 502

majority-minority district, p. 502

Jim Crow laws, p. 503

de jure segregation, p. 504

de facto segregation, p. 504

commerce clause, p. 506

class action suit, p. 506

restrictive covenant, p. 507

Make It Real

CIVIL RIGHTS

This module contains an excellent interactive timeline on civil rights movements.

WHEN WE SAY "POOR" OR "POVERTY-STRICKEN AMERICANS," WHAT image comes

to mind? The homeless man sleeping on the grate? The unemployed person standing in line at the unemployment or welfare office? What about someone who has a full-time job making $9.00 an hour? That sounds like a decent wage, right? Well,

On the Edge

ORIGINALLY AIRED: **4/15/04**

PROGRAM: **Nightline**

RUNNING TIME: **16:16**

that actually comes out to just above $18,000.00 a year, and for a family with one adult and three children, that means poverty. We've decided to launch a new, occasional series that looks at the working poor: the millions of Americans who live on the edge of poverty.

The genesis of tonight's show was a new book by former *New York Times* reporter and Pulitzer Prize-winner David Shipler. "The Working Poor" takes a comprehensive look at the lives of people set to plunge into the abyss of financial ruin if just one payment isn't met, if their car breaks down, or if they call in sick at work. Such seemingly minor events can have catastrophic effects on this segment of the population, and Mr. Shipler has documented many of their lives, weaving economic analysis into the story of what these people face trying to survive from day to day. Ted Koppel sat down with Mr. Shipler for an extensive interview on his findings.

Critical Thinking Questions

*After viewing "*ON THE EDGE*" on your* ABCNEWS DVD *answer the following questions.*

1. HOW DOES AUTHOR David Shipler define "working poor"?

2. HOW DOES THE VIDEO'S TITLE, "On the Edge," apply to the working poor?

3. THE UNDERLYING PROBLEM of the working poor seems to be their vulnerability in every area of life. Explain how the working poor are vulnerable in ways not experienced by other economic groups.

4. AUTHOR DAVID SHIPLER disagrees with the concept of a "culture of poverty." Instead, he speaks of an "ecological system of interactions." What does he mean?

5. WHAT IS THE DIFFERENCE between an entitlement and a means-tested entitlement?

515

Chapter 18

Making Economic and Regulatory Policy

⭐

GEORGE W. BUSH ENTERED HIS SECOND TERM WITH A BOLD PROMISE TO REFORM THE FEDERAL TAX SYSTEM, WHICH IS AMONG THE MOST COMPLICATED IN THE WORLD. HAVING PILOTED A MASSIVE TAX CUT THROUGH CONGRESS IN 2001, HE CREATED A BLUE-RIBBON STUDY COMMISSION TO MAKE RECOMMENDATIONS FOR ACTION AND PLACED TAX REFORM HIGH ON HIS LEGISLATIVE AGENDA FOR 2005. WHEN APPOINTING THE COMMISSION, HE SAID THAT TAX REFORM IS ESSENTIAL FOR THE NATION AND VOWED that he was absolutely committed to getting something done.

Only a year later, tax reform was off the Bush agenda. He did not mention tax reform once in his 2006 State of the Union Address, and he refused to embrace the recommendations of his own blue-ribbon commission. Bush still believed that the federal tax system was riddled with loopholes and expensive tax breaks, and he also wanted Congress to extend his 2001 tax cuts, which contained dozens of provisions that were set to expire between 2005 and 2012. However, he found that legislators had little interest in either broad tax reform or extending his 2001 cuts. As Bush learned, everyone believes in tax reform until they actually have to give up a tax break.

Some breaks allow individuals and corporations to deduct the amount of income they have to count each year, others exempt cer-tain kinds of income from any taxes at all, and still others provide tax credits that encourage certain investments and decisions. In theory, all of these devices encourage taxpayers to be socially responsible, whether by encouraging home-ownership, investments in new energy sources, or having children. In 2006, for example, individual taxpayers took $76 billion in deductions for the amount of interest they paid on their home mortgages, or loans, another $35 billion for the amount they paid in state and local taxes, and $33 billion for the contributions they made to charities such as the Red Cross and the Salvation Army. They received another $33 billion in tax credits based on the number of their dependent children and saved $126 billion in taxes because the federal government does not tax the health insurance and medical care they get from their employers.

These deductions and exclusions make the federal tax system almost impossible to understand, which is why accountants are so busy in the weeks and months before Americans file their annual tax returns on April 15.

Deductions and exclusions also favor some taxpayers over others. Renters help pay the mortgage interest on their apartments, for example, but only the landlord, who pays the mortgage, receives the tax deduction.

Despite the unfairness (such as giving a benefit to property owners but not to renters), most deductions and exclusions have powerful supporters in Congress. The real estate industry has an obvious interest in protecting the mortgage-interest deduction, corporations have an interest in protecting tax breaks for investment and research, and

"*Protectionism will do little to create jobs, and if foreigners retaliate we will surely lose jobs.*"

FORMER FEDERAL RESERVE BOARD CHAIRMAN ALAN GREENSPAN

individual Americans resist any tax reform that might make the system even more confusing. Oil companies fight for the $2 billion in tax credits that encourages new investment in energy independence, while veterans campaign for the $4 billion in tax exemptions that protects their disability and death benefits.

Changing these and other tax breaks would not only be politically expensive, major reform would require the Internal Revenue Service to write thousands of pages of new rules to execute the changes. Reform would also take time. Individuals and corporations rely on tax rules to plan their futures years or even decades in advance, and they cannot react quickly to the elimination of a major deduction.

Like many presidents before him, Bush hoped that Americans would be drawn to a simpler system, such as a flat tax that everyone would pay regardless of income, or a national sales tax that would apply to every purchase. However, such a system could only work if the vast majority of current tax breaks were removed from law. In the end, even Bush could not accept his own study commission's recommendation to abolish the mortgage interest deduction, especially given the immediate uproar from real estate brokers and home builders, not to mention the millions of Americans who would lose the biggest deduction on their annual tax returns.[1]

Whereas the preceding chapters in this book described how the American political process works, this chapter and the two chapters that follow focus on what the federal government does to promote the general welfare, provide for the common defense, and secure the blessings of liberty for all its citizens. As we shall see, the federal government pursues these grand goals through economic, social, and foreign and defense policy. Before turning to economic policy in this chapter, it is first important to understand more about how public policy is made.

A Brief Introduction to Making Public Policy

When government decides to act, it does so through a **public policy**, which is a specific course of action that government takes to address a problem such as the federal budget deficit. A public policy can be conveyed to the public in the laws passed by Congress and signed by the president, opinions issued by the Supreme Court, and/or rules written within the administrative system. But whatever form it takes, a public policy tells the nation and the world who is about to get what, when, and how from the federal government.

The Policy-Making Process

Every policy reflects a series of separate decisions leading to final implementation and action. The process involves six steps: (1) making assumptions about the world, (2) identifying the problem to be solved, (3) deciding whether to act at all, (4) deciding how much to do, (5) choosing a tool for solving the problem, and (6) making rules for implementation.

The process does not always follow these six steps in order, however. Making public policy is an often unpredictable process in which problems and solutions are loosely connected. It can start anywhere in the circle and skip back and forth at will. The result is a policy-making process that is often unpredictable and almost always in flux.[2]

1. *Making Assumptions about the World.* Every government decision involves assumptions about the future. Is the economy going to get stronger? If so, perhaps employment will go up and the costs of supporting the unemployed will go down. Is teenage pregnancy going to increase? If so, perhaps childhood poverty, which increases as more single teenagers have children, will also increase. Is world terrorism going to increase? Answers to these and other questions about the future shape decisions about what the federal government might do.

    Because there is no sure way to choose among competing assumptions about such a distant future, policy makers often make choices that help sell their particular views of the world. They are often pessimistic about the future when they

public policy
A specific course of action taken by government to achieve a public goal.

New Orleans residents and their supporters pray against the rebuilt levee wall while honoring the victims of Hurricane Katrina during a Memorial Day service in 2006. The levee was rebuilt with federal funds.

define problems, but optimistic when they announce specific proposals to fix the problems. The result is that problems may look much worse than they truly are, while solutions may seem likely to work better than they possibly could.

2. *Picking the Problem.*   Choosing the problem to be solved is the essential decision in setting the **policy agenda**. The policy agenda, as John Kingdon defines it, "is the list of subjects or problems to which governmental officials, and people outside of government closely associated with those officials, are paying some serious attention at any given time."[3]

   Problems reach the list of possible agenda items from a variety of sources. Some arise from events such as the September 11 terrorist attacks, others because of newspaper or television stories about a controversial issue such as gay marriage, and still others because of interest group pressure. The government monitors a battery of assumptions on the state of the economy, for example, that can show the beginnings of an economic slowdown through the number of jobless claims, the rise of inflation through the consumer price index, or problems in credit through rising or falling interest rates. Readers need only visit www.fedstats.gov to see the range of information government provides to policy makers in search of problems.

3. *Deciding Whether to Act at All.*   The fact that a problem exists does not automatically mean that Congress and the president will try to solve it. Nothing forces presidents, members of Congress, or judges to act unless doing so will further some goal that they value such as reelection or a place in history. Some problems help policy makers achieve their personal or political goals, in which case they will decide to act, while others do not, in which case they pick other problems to solve.

   Policy makers clearly understand that public pressure for action ebbs and flows over time. In fact, writes political scientist Anthony Downs, "American public attention rarely remains sharply focused upon any one domestic issue for very long—even if it involves a continuing problem of crucial importance to society." According to Downs, attention to problems follows an issue-attention cycle in which each problem "suddenly leaps into prominence, remains there for a short time, and then—though still largely unresolved—gradually fades from the center of public attention."[4]

4. *Deciding How Much to Do.*   Once the federal government decides that it wants to do something about a problem, one of its most difficult decisions is how much to do. It can launch a comprehensive program such as Social Security or Medicare, or an incremental program that can be expanded bit by bit over time.

"American public attention rarely remains sharply focused upon any one domestic issue for very long—even if it involves a continuing problem of crucial importance to society."

POLITICAL SCIENTIST ANTHONY DOWNS

policy agenda
The informal list of issues that Congress and the president consider most important for action.

The first decision government makes on how much to do in response to a problem involves the size of the proposed solution. Will it be an incremental, or small-scale adjustment in an existing program, such as the Pell Grants program for college students, or a major new initiative, such as prescription drug coverage for older Americans? Although major policy reforms are generally much more difficult to pass, in part because they involve more federal spending and/or produce greater regulation, such initiatives allow Congress and the president to claim much greater credit for solving a problem.

The second decision involves the way in which government benefits are to be distributed across the various groups in society. Federal programs that offer new benefits to all groups in society and are funded by all citizens equally are usually described as **distributive policy**. National parks, air traffic control, the interstate highway system, education funding, national defense, and Social Security are all defined as distributive in nature.

In contrast, federal programs that take resources (usually through taxes) from one or more groups in society so that another group can benefit (usually in the form of an entitlement program) are described as **redistributive policy**. Such programs tend to provide benefits to the less fortunate in society, often provoking conflict between the haves and have-nots. Welfare, poverty programs, Head Start for poor preschool children, and special programs to help minority groups are often characterized as redistributive. Some political scientists call these programs zero-sum games, meaning that one group's gain (the program's benefits) is another's loss (the program's cost in taxes).

5. *Choosing a Tool.* Public policy scholars generally argue that the federal government has five basic tools available to solve most public problems: (1) spending money, (2) providing tax breaks to encourage certain activities, (3) providing goods or services directly, (4) providing protection against risk, and (5) enforcing restrictions and penalties.[5]

The federal government spends money on a variety of direct payments to individuals, hospitals, corporations, and other nations. Social Security is still the largest direct payment to individuals, while Medicare for older Americans is the largest direct payment to hospitals. The federal government also provides direct payments to corporations to purchase goods and services such as computers, build highways and bridges, or support the military, and helps other nations through foreign aid.

As we've already seen, the federal government provides tax breaks to encourage a variety of activities, such as charitable giving and home ownership.

The federal government provides goods and services to the public either completely free or for a fee. National parks such as Yosemite and the Grand Canyon generally charge an admission fee, the National Air and Space Museum on the Washington Mall is open to the public for free, and Americans do not pay anything directly for national defense. Ultimately, of course, nothing the government does is completely free—the National Air and Space Museum is supported by general taxes, as is defense.

Protections against risk involve a range of devices to encourage activities where the private sector might otherwise not go. The most familiar protections are federal loan guarantees, under which the government promises to cover the losses in the event that a student, farmer, small business, or other borrower fails to repay a debt. The federal government also provides protection against risk in the form of special exemptions from certain laws. Major league baseball, for example, is exempted from federal antitrust law. The exemption was designed to encourage the expansion of the national pastime, but was never given to professional football, hockey, or basketball.

Restrictions and penalties are designed to encourage or discourage certain behaviors. The list of laws and regulations that limit what individual citizens, associations, and businesses can do is seemingly endless, and includes everything from criminal laws to requirements that all cigarette packages carry the surgeon general's warning that smoking can be dangerous to your health. The violation of a law usually results in a government sanction of some kind, usually a fine or imprisonment.

distributive policy
A type of policy that provides benefits to all Americans.

redistributive policy
A type of policy that takes benefits (usually through taxes) from one group of Americans and gives them to another (usually through spending).

6. *Making Rules for Implementation.* As we shall see later in this chapter, almost everything the federal government does involves a rule. Technically, a government **rule** is a precise legal statement that implements a law. It is issued through a formal process that tells the public exactly who will get what, when, and how from government—whether, for example, by specifying the amount of sulfur dioxide that can be released from a smokestack, the required height of a wheelchair ramp in a private building, or the number of life jackets that must be on a ferryboat. As such, rules are essential for turning even the most detailed legislation into action, and rule making is the central device used to execute the laws.

Technically, rule making comes at the very end of the policy-making process and is almost invisible to most Americans. Nevertheless, it is the essential step in converting the abstract ideas and language of laws, presidential orders, and court rulings into precise rules governing what individual members of the public, companies, or agencies can or must do.

Policy-Making Alliances

Although formal decisions about public policy are made by Congress, the president, and/or the courts, most decisions involve collections of political leaders and interest groups that join together on behalf of a specific cause. Some of these collections exist for decades, while others come together for a specific cause, and then disband. The former are often called **iron triangles**, while the latter are labeled **issue networks**.

IRON TRIANGLES By definition, an iron triangle has three sides that hold together over long periods of time: (1) a federal department or agency, (2) a set of loyal interest groups, and (3) a House and/or Senate authorizing committee. Each side supports the other two. Congress gives money to the agency, for example, and gets campaign money and endorsements from the interest groups in return; the interest groups give money and endorsements to Congress and get special services from the agency in return; the agency gives special services to the interest groups and gets money from Congress in return. Policy making for veterans, for example, is made through an iron triangle composed of the Department of Veterans Affairs, the House and Senate Veterans Committees, and a long list of interest groups that represent veterans.

ISSUE NETWORKS As the number of interest groups has increased, iron triangles have been replaced by much looser collections of participants. As political scientist Hugh Heclo has argued, the notion that iron triangles make all policy was "not so much wrong as it was disastrously incomplete" in today's complicated policy environment.[6] Although iron triangles can exist for decades, even centuries, the increasing number of small, highly specialized interest groups makes an iron triangle almost impossible to create, if only because Congress and federal agencies can no longer identify a steady occupant for the third corner of the triangle. They have to find temporary allies, depending on the issue. There is nothing "iron" about such coalitions of smaller groups: They last only as long as a given issue is hot.

Issue networks tend to concentrate power in the relatively small number of individuals that organize and maintain the networks. These people make the key decisions about who participates and what they say. Because of this, some political scientists refer to the rise of well-financed issue networks such as the ones that promote prescription drug coverage for older Americans or tax cuts for business as a form of elitism, not pluralism, in which a very small number of actors accelerate or delay action. Medicare prescription drug coverage, for example, involved an issue network composed of drug companies, the American Association of Retired Persons, and hospitals.

Economic Policy

The federal government has been involved in economic policy since the end of the Revolutionary War. The framers wanted a government strong enough to promote free trade, protect patents and trademarks, and enforce contracts between

rule
A precise legal definition of how government will implement a policy.

iron triangle
A policy-making alliance that involves very strong ties among a congressional committee, an interest group, and a federal department or agency.

issue network
A policy-making alliance among loosely connected participants that comes together on a particular issue, then disbands.

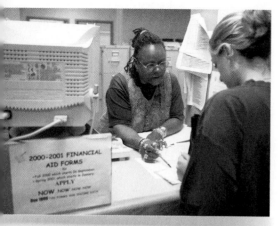

Many college students take advantage of financial aid. Changes in interest rates affect the affordability and availability of these programs.

fiscal policy

Government policy that attempts to manage the economy by controlling taxing and spending.

monetary policy

Government policy that attempts to manage the economy by controlling the money supply and thus interest rates.

inflation

A rise in the general price level (and decrease in dollar value) owing to an increase in the volume of money and credit in relation to available goods.

unemployment

The number of Americans who are out of work but actively looking for a job. The number does not usually include those who are not looking.

individuals and businesses. And they wanted a government with enough funding so that it could build the postal roads, bridges, railroads, and canals that would allow the young economy to grow.

As much as they worried about the state of the economy, the framers did not concentrate economic policy in any one branch. Instead, they divided economic policy-making control between the legislative and executive branches and between the House and the Senate. Article I, Section 8, of the Constitution gives Congress the power to borrow, coin, and print money, while Article II, Section 2, gives the president the power to appoint the officers of government, including the secretary of the treasury. In a similar vein, Article I gives Congress the power to regulate commerce with foreign nations, among the states, and with Native American tribes, while Article II gives the president authority to negotiate the treaties and enforce the laws. Finally, Article I gives Congress the power to establish post offices and build postal roads, which were as important to the free movement of commerce in the 1700s as the highways, rails, and Internet are today. Article II gives the president the power to appoint executive officials such as the postmaster general of the United States.

By creating a national government of limited powers and providing constitutional guarantees to protect property from excessive regulation, the framers succeeded in protecting capitalism. More than two centuries later, the U.S. economy is the strongest in the world, and the federal government continues to safeguard the basic conditions needed for capitalism to thrive. Part of the government's role is to stay out of the way as individuals and businesses create wealth through new ideas and hard work, but part is to promote the national welfare through **fiscal policy**, which uses federal spending and taxation to stimulate or slow the economy, and **monetary policy**, which manipulates the supply of money that individuals and businesses have in their hands to keep the economy from swinging wildly from boom to bust. In addition, the federal government promotes economic growth and trade and controls many economic decisions through regulations against certain kinds of business, labor, and environmental practices.

These tools are designed to smooth the ups and downs of the normal *business cycle.* Economists tend to focus on four discrete stages of the cycle: (1) expansion, in which the economy produces new jobs and growth; (2) contraction, as the economy starts to slow down; (3) recession, in which the economy reaches a trough of low growth; and (4) recovery, in which the economy rebounds. The goal of effective economic policy today is to make sure the peaks are not too high and the troughs are not too low. In general, **inflation**, or rising prices on goods and services such as gasoline, food, and housing, is considered the primary policy problem during expansion and recovery, while **unemployment**, or joblessness among employable Americans, is considered the greatest problem during contraction and recession.

Inflation is usually measured by the Consumer Price Index (CPI), which shows how much more or less consumers are paying for the same "basket of goods" over time. The major components of the CPI are food, shelter, fuel, clothing, transportation, and medical care. In turn, unemployment is measured simply by the percentage of able-bodied workers who are looking for jobs but cannot find them. The unemployment rate does not measure the number of able-bodied workers who have given up looking for work or who have taken jobs below their skill levels with lower pay.

The federal government exercises less control over the national economy than it does over social or foreign policy. Nevertheless, it keeps a firm hand on many of the gears and levers that guide not only the economy's general direction but the rate at which it moves. These controls are taxes, spending, and borrowing.

Fiscal Policy

Congress and the president** make fiscal policy by taxing, borrowing, and spending money. Nothing reflects the growth of federal programs and the rise of big government more clearly than the increased spending by the national government. In 1933, the federal government spent only $4 billion, about $30 per capita. In 2006, the figure was $2.7 trillion, or about $9,000 per person.

The Federal Budget

Today, federal, state, and local governments spend an amount equal to about one-third of the income of all Americans. The national government is the biggest spender of all—it spends more than all state and local governments combined. Annual spending by the federal government accounts for some 23 percent of the gross domestic product (GDP), or nearly one dollar out of every four spent in the U.S. economy.

WHERE THE MONEY COMES FROM Although Benjamin Franklin once said that nothing is more certain in life than death and taxes, he would be surprised at the range of revenue sources used to fund federal spending today (see Figure 18–1 for the percentages from each source):

1. *Individual income taxes.* Taxes on individual Americans accounted for nearly $1 trillion of the federal government's tax revenue in 2006. The income tax was prohibited under the Constitution until the Thirteenth Amendment was ratified in 1913.

2. *Corporate income taxes.* Taxes on corporations accounted for an estimated $277 billion of federal revenue in 2006. Tax cuts on corporations have steadily reduced the impact of this tax, which had reached 40 percent of revenue in 1943.

3. *Payroll receipts.* Payroll taxes are the second-largest and most rapidly rising source of federal revenue and accounted for an estimated $841 billion of federal revenue in 2006. Most Americans pay more in Social Security taxes than in federal income taxes.

4. *Excise taxes.* Federal **excise taxes** are placed on the sale of liquor, tobacco, gasoline, telephones, air travel, and other so-called luxury items, and accounted for an estimated $74 billion of federal revenue in 2006.

5. *Other Sources.* The federal government collects a number of smaller taxes and fees that add to its revenue, including admission to national parks and camping fees in national forests. The federal government also collects taxes on large estates left behind after death, and raises money through interest payments on its loans to college students. Separately, these sources often generate small amounts of revenue, but together they accounted for an estimated $96 billion in federal revenue in 2006.

6. *Borrowing.* The federal government borrows money when it does not raise enough revenue to cover all its services. The federal government borrows from investors such as individuals, banks, and foreign governments that buy Treasury notes, Treasury bills, and U.S. savings bonds. The federal government must borrow money when it runs a **deficit** between the amount it raises and spends. Borrowing accounted for an estimated $423 billion in federal revenues in 2006.

Putting power over taxation into the hands of the people was a major achievement in the development of self-government. "No taxation without representation" had been a battle cry in the Revolutionary War. The Constitution clearly provided that Congress "shall have Power to lay and collect Taxes, Duties, Imposts, and Excises." Under the Constitution, **tariffs** (taxes on imports from other countries) and excise taxes have to be levied, or collected, uniformly throughout the United States.

Taxes are not just a matter of raising money, however. As we've seen, taxes are also used to discourage certain activities such as smoking (with an excise tax) and encourage other activities such as home ownership (with a mortgage interest deduction). In a broad sense, all taxation involves decisions about who gets what, when, where, and how. For example, a **progressive tax** that places higher taxes on individuals and families with higher incomes tends to help individuals and families with lower incomes. In contrast, a **regressive tax**, such as a sales tax that is collected on all purchases of food and clothing, tends to hurt individuals and families with lower incomes.

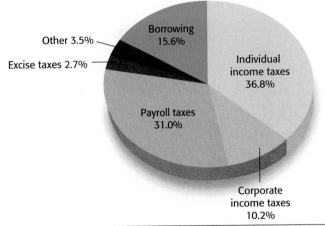

FIGURE 18–1 **Where the Money Comes From.**

excise tax
Consumer tax on a specific kind of merchandise, such as tobacco.

deficit
The difference between the revenues raised annually from sources of income other than borrowing and the expenditures of government, including paying the interest on past borrowing.

tariff
Tax levied on imports to help protect a nation's industries, labor, or farmers from foreign competition. It can also be used to raise additional revenue.

progressive tax
A tax graduated so that people with higher incomes pay a larger fraction of their income than people with lower incomes.

regressive tax
A tax whereby people with lower incomes pay a higher fraction of their income than people with higher incomes.

FIGURE 18–2 Where the Money Goes, 2006.

SOURCE: Summary Tables, *Budget of the United States, Fiscal Year 2007* (U.S. Government Printing Office, 2006).

Taxes also carry certain costs—it costs money to raise money. Like people who carry large balances on their credit cards, the U.S. must pay interest on its deficits.[7] Government borrowing adds to the total **national debt**, which is the cumulative total of all deficits over time. In spring 2006, Congress raised the amount of money the federal government could borrow to $9 trillion, which would generate nearly $200 billion in interest payments during the year. Even as members complained about the $9 trillion, they also voted to authorize another $100 billion to fund the Iraq war, thereby requiring more borrowing.

Americans might not be as troubled by the size of the debt if they understood two characteristics of federal borrowing. First, the government owes roughly 90 percent of the money to its own citizens rather than to foreign governments or investors, although the amount owed to foreigners is growing. Second, the economic strength and resources of the country are more significant than the size of the debt.

WHERE THE MONEY GOES Much of the money the federal government takes in is spent on benefit payments to individuals and on national defense. Measured in absolute dollars spent in 2006, almost half of federal spending went to required benefit payments for individuals such as Social Security, Medicare, Medicaid, and other major social programs. Of federal spending, the vast majority is mandatory, meaning the Congress and the president cannot use their discretion to change the spending rates. Mandatory programs include Social Security and Medicare for older Americans and other programs that pay any citizen who qualifies for support (see Figure 18–2). The rest of the spending is discretionary, meaning that Congress and the president can change the spending rates.

Of the spending, more than half goes to individuals outside of government, while the rest goes to the purchase of goods and services such as consulting, computers, and military equipment. Virtually all federal buildings are now guarded by private employees who work for contractors who receive their money from the federal government, while almost all defense spending goes to military and civilian employees, military equipment, and the cost of war.

Two hundred years ago, revenues and spending were so small that neither had a significant impact on the overall economy. In today's $2.7 trillion federal budget, even small changes in taxes and spending can alter the direction of the economy. However, because many federal programs are open to all eligible citizens, much of the federal budget is "uncontrollable" or nondiscretionary, meaning that the bills must be paid regardless of the cost.

THE FEDERAL BUDGET DEFICIT Congress and President Clinton received some stunning news in the summer of 1999: For the first time in two decades, the federal government's budget was balanced. Although Congress and the president had set the process in motion with budget agreements in 1990, 1993, and 1997, the news came nearly three years ahead of schedule and showed a much larger surplus in the future than anyone had predicted. Suddenly, the federal government was looking at almost $6 trillion in surpluses over the next ten years (see Figure 18–3 for figures on the appearance and disappearance of the surplus).

The balanced budget and projected surplus were the product of three events. Defense spending fell dramatically with the end of the cold war. Spending for domestic programs did not rise as fast, largely because the economy was growing, and tax revenues increased more than expected. Practically everything that could go right did go right, and the budget forecast became brighter with each passing month.

Just as surprisingly, perhaps, the budget surplus was gone within three years, in part because just about everything that could go wrong with the economy and the world did go wrong, and in part because Congress and the new Bush administration decided to give $1.3 trillion of the projected surplus back to the American public in the 2001 tax cuts, subtract another $300 billion for further tax cuts in 2003 and $400 billion for a new prescription drug plan for the elderly in 2004, and spend another $320 billion for the wars in Afghanistan and Iraq by 2006. Suddenly, the $6 trillion in projected surpluses became $3 trillion in projected deficits.

national debt
The total amount of money the federal government has borrowed to finance deficit spending over the years.

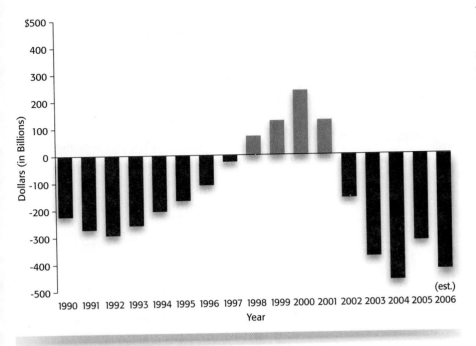

FIGURE 18-3 **The Disappearing Federal Budget Surplus.**

SOURCE: Summary Tables, *Budget of the United States, Fiscal Year 2007* (U.S. Government Printing Office, 2006).

The disappearing surplus shows just how sensitive federal budgets are to unexpected events such as wars and economic downturns, as well as political decisions such as cutting taxes. Having worked for 20 years to get the budget balanced, Congress and the president subtracted much of the money away over a three-month span, leading some critics to argue that Republicans were hoping to "strangle the beast" of big government by denying it the money to create new programs, such as national health insurance.

Although there may be some truth to the charge, Congress and the president did not stop spending. Moreover, as the budget deficit increases, so does the national debt and the interest payments the federal government must make to its lenders. In 2005, for example, the federal government paid almost $170 billion in interest, or almost five times as much as aid to college students and their schools.

The Budget Process

Before Congress enacted the Budget and Accounting Act of 1921, each executive agency dealt with Congress on its own, requesting that Congress appropriate funds for its activities with little or no presidential coordination. In 1921, the Bureau of the Budget (changed to the Office of Management and Budget in 1970) was created in the Treasury Department, and for the first time, the executive branch presented one budget to Congress.

THE EXECUTIVE BRANCH The federal government's fiscal year begins on October 1. The budget process begins nearly two years in advance, when the various departments and agencies estimate their needs and propose their budgets to the president.[8] While Congress is debating the budget for the coming fiscal year, the agencies are making estimates for the year after that (see Table 18–1). Agency officials take into account not only their needs as they see them, but also the overall presidential program and the probable reactions of Congress. Departmental budgets are detailed; they include estimates of expected needs for personnel, supplies, office space, and the like.

TABLE 18–1	Steps in the Budget Process, Fiscal Year 2007
February–December 2005	Executive branch agencies develop requests for funds, which are reviewed by the Office of Management and Budget and forwarded to the president for final decision.
December 2005	The formal budget documents are prepared.
January–February 2006	The budget is transmitted to Congress as a formal message from the president.
March–September 2006	Congress reviews the president's proposed budget, develops its own budget, and approves spending and revenue bills.
October 1, 2006	Fiscal year 2006 begins.
October 1, 2006–September 30, 2007	Executive branch agencies execute the budget provided in law.
October–November 2007	Figures on actual spending and receipts for the completed fiscal year become available.

How Other Nations Govern

Tax Policy in the United States and Denmark

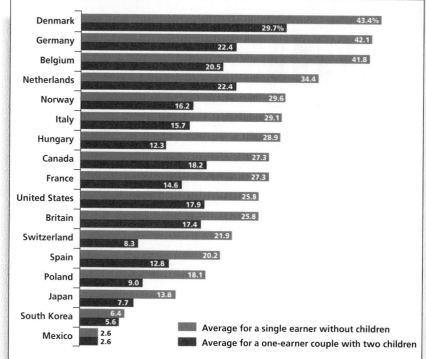

	Single earner	One-earner couple
Denmark	43.4%	29.7%
Germany	42.1	22.4
Belgium	41.8	20.5
Netherlands	34.4	22.4
Norway	29.6	16.2
Italy	29.1	15.7
Hungary	28.9	12.3
Canada	27.3	18.2
France	27.3	14.6
United States	25.8	17.9
Britain	25.8	17.4
Switzerland	21.9	8.3
Spain	20.2	12.8
Poland	18.1	9.0
Japan	13.8	7.7
South Korea	6.4	5.6
Mexico	2.6	2.6

■ Average for a single earner without children
■ Average for a one-earner couple with two children

Percentage of Wages Full-Time Workers Pay in Income Taxes in Selected Countries.

SOURCE: "Tax Burdens," *Washington Post*, September 30, 2000, p. A14.
NOTE: The rates include contributions to social insurance and retirement funds, less cash benefits paid, such as child allowances.

One way to compare nations is to ask how much citizens pay in income taxes. The higher the amount paid, the larger the national government is likely to be. Because income taxes are progressive in nature, they allow for the redistribution of income from wealthier house-holds to low-income households.

As much as Congress and the president complain that Americans are overtaxed, the United States actually ranks well down the list of Western democracies in its income tax rates. Although it makes up the difference through an across-the-board Social Security and Medicare tax on all workers, as well as state and local sales taxes, its overall tax rate is roughly half as high as that in Denmark and other Scandinavian countries.

The difference is in what Denmark provides in government services. Whereas the United States provides help for needy and older Americans on a more selective basis, Denmark has a universal system of support that covers every citizen regardless of income. The Danish government provides free health care, retirement pensions, and free college education, including some living expenses, for all of its citizens. It also provides child care, paid maternity leave, and unemployment support and welfare for those who qualify. Families also receive a government allowance for each child under the age of 18.

The Danish government also runs nursing homes, homeless shelters, children's homes, and alcohol and drug treatment centers, which are often provided in the United States through charitable institutions. These benefits are not only guaranteed for Danish citizens, they are often provided in government-run facilities such as hospitals and clinics.

Although the United States provides health coverage to older Americans and to poor families and children, its coverage is less generous and often requires copayments by participants. Moreover, the United States generally gives its citizens cash assistance to purchase health care and other services from private, not government, providers and sets time limits on how long needy Americans can receive services. In general, Denmark imposes few, if any, time limits.

As a result, Denmark's government spends more money on each citizen and must raise more money through taxes, hence the significant difference between what U.S. and Danish citizens pay each year to their governments. ■

Office of Management and Budget (OMB)
Presidential staff agency that serves as a clearinghouse for budgetary requests and management improvements for government agencies.

The **Office of Management and Budget (OMB)**, a staff agency of the president, handles the next phase. OMB budget examiners review each agency's budget and reconcile it with the president's overall plans. OMB then holds informal hearings with every department and agency to give each one a chance to clarify and defend its estimates.

Once this give-and-take is over, the OMB director gives the president a single, consolidated set of estimates of both revenue and expenditures—the product of perhaps a year's work. The president takes several days to review these figures and make adjustments. The budget director also helps the president prepare a budget message that will stress key aspects of the budget and tie it to broad national goals. The president must submit the budget recommendations and accompanying message to Congress between the first Monday in January and the first Monday in February. The president's budget recommendations cover thousands of pages.

THE LEGISLATIVE BRANCH The president's proposal is only the beginning of the budget process. Under the Constitution, Congress must appropriate the funds and raise the taxes. However, the White House also plays a role in all decisions, if only because all appropriations and tax proposals are subject to a presidential veto. Presidents often threaten to veto these bills as a way of winning passage of their priorities.

Congress acts on the budget in several steps. It starts its process by approving an initial budget resolution that sets the broad spending and revenue goals for the process. It then moves forward with hearings on the 13 giant appropriations bills that actually spend money, and it considers a final budget resolution that reconciles the actual spending with its initial guidelines. Because the budget resolution only sets broad guidelines, it does not go to the president for signature. But because the 13 appropriations bills spend real dollars, they all must be signed into law.

Congress adopted the Budget and Impoundment Control Act of 1974 to strengthen its role in the budget process. This act specifies that the president must include proposed changes in tax laws, estimates of amounts of revenue lost through existing preferential tax treatments, and five-year estimates of the costs of new and continuing federal programs. The act also calls on the president to seek authorizing legislation for a program a year before asking Congress to fund it.

The 1974 Budget Act also created the **Congressional Budget Office (CBO)**, an independent agency that prepares budget data on behalf of Congress, and Congress only. By February 15 of each year, CBO furnishes its analysis of the presidential recommendations to the House and Senate budget committees. CBO also provides Congress with biannual forecasts of the economy, analyzes alternative fiscal policies, prepares five-year cost estimates for bills proposed by congressional committees, and undertakes studies requested by committees. CBO also monitors the results of congressional action on individual appropriations and revenues against the targets or ceilings specified by legislation.

Such budget reform efforts did not by themselves balance the budget in 1999, but they did set in place a discipline and a mind-set that moved toward balancing the budget. Equally, if not more, important was the economic boom of the 1990s, which generated huge tax revenues that helped achieve the first budget surpluses in 30 years. However, as we have seen, the budget surplus was soon gone.

The Politics of Taxing and Spending

In addition to raising funds to run the government, taxes also promote economic growth and reward certain types of behavior, such as contributing to charities. Critics also suggest that tax legislation helps individual members of Congress raise campaign funds—several of the most popular corporate deductions must be renewed every year, for example, which gives members a chance to show their support for corporations regularly, and corporations a chance to show their support for Congress, too.[9]

Much as Americans complain about taxes, most want more of virtually everything the federal government provides. However, there is considerable disagreement about the best type of tax. Some experts argue that a progressive income tax (also called a *graduated income tax*) is best because it is relatively easy to collect, hits hardest those who are most able to pay, and hardly touches those with little income. Others argue that *excise taxes* are the fairest because they are paid by people who spend money for luxury goods and thus obviously have money to spare. In addition, by discouraging people from buying expensive goods, excise taxes occasionally have a deflationary (price-lowering) effect when prices are on the rise. However, excise taxes are more expensive to collect than income taxes. In some cases, such as the tax on tobacco, they

Congressional Budget Office (CBO)
An agency of Congress that analyzes presidential budget recommendations and estimates the costs of proposed legislation.

may hit the poor the hardest. Excise taxes also face strong resistance from affected industries—tobacco, liquor, and airlines, for example.

The most controversial tax is a general **sales tax**, which is levied by all but a few states on the sale of most goods, sometimes exempting food and drugs. Labor and liberal organizations see sales taxes as *regressive:* Because a sales tax is the same for all persons, these taxes are not related to a taxpayer's ability to pay, and poor persons pay a higher percentage of their income in sales taxes for the goods and services they buy than rich people do. Proponents of a national sales tax stress its potential anti-inflationary effect and point to its successful use in a number of states.

The sales tax is exclusively a state and local tax in the United States, but in Europe a similar tax, a **value-added tax (VAT)**, is used to raise revenues for central governments. The VAT differs from a sales tax in that it collects a tax on the increased value of a product *at each stage of production and distribution* rather than just at the point of sale, as with a sales tax. A loaf of bread would thus have value added several times: The farmer would pay a value-added tax on the grain before selling to the miller, who would be taxed before selling to the baker, and so forth. The value-added tax is seen by some as a way to infuse a large amount of new revenue into the federal government. Opponents of the tax see it as regressive and increasing the tax burden. States see a federal VAT as invading their turf. Since it taxes consumption and not savings, a VAT could encourage savings and investment, both of which are vital to economic growth.

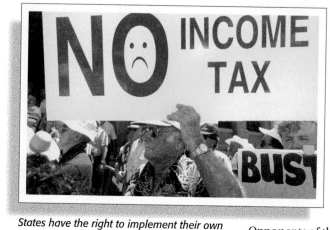

States have the right to implement their own income and sales taxes. Most states have one or the other. Only New Hampshire has thus far balked at instituting either.

Tax Expenditures

Tax expenditures are a final type of fiscal policy that uses the tax code to provide special tax incentives or benefits to individuals and businesses for economic goals such as home ownership, retirement savings, and college education. According to the Government Accountability Office, these benefits totaled more than $850 billion in 2004 and continue to rise.

Tax expenditures are one means by which the national government carries out public policy objectives. For example, the government encourages investment in research and development by allowing such costs to be deducted from a company's taxes. Federal grants could also achieve this objective.

Critics assert that the rich get their "welfare" through such loopholes, including protection against taxes on certain luxury items. In 2005, for example, the federal government provided tax incentives in support of Hummers and other large cars and trucks. This form of "welfare" does not require a visible appropriation of money plainly identified in the budget. However meritorious the objectives of tax expenditures are— encouraging home ownership, research and development, retirement savings—these tax benefits do not benefit all levels of society. In many instances, they lead investors to put their money into low-yield investments to obtain large tax benefits, which in turn pulls money out of more productive parts of the economy.

sales tax
General tax on sales transactions, sometimes exempting food and drugs.

value-added tax (VAT)
A tax on increased value of a product at each stage of production and distribution rather than just at the point of sale.

tax expenditure
Loss of tax revenue due to federal laws that provide special tax incentives or benefits to individuals or businesses.

monetarism
A theory that government should control the money supply to encourage economic growth and restrain inflation.

Monetary Policy

Monetary policy is the second way the federal government manages the economy. The core element of **monetarism** is the idea that prices, incomes, and economic stability reflect growth in the amount of money that circulates through the economy at any one time. Monetarists contend that the money supply is the key factor affecting the economy's performance and that restrained yet steady growth in the money supply will encourage solid economic growth but not inflation.

The Federal Reserve System

Monetary policy is not made by either Congress or the president but by the Board of Governors of the **Federal Reserve System** (often simply called "the Fed"), specifically its Federal Open Market Committee. The members of the committee, some of the most powerful people in the United States, have a lot to say about how much interest you pay on the car you are buying and whether you refinance your home because of lower interest rates. They can stimulate the economy so that it could be easier for you to find a job or slow it down so that it could be harder. Who are these people with so much power, and how do they influence economic policy?

The Fed's Board of Governors consists of a chair and six other members who are appointed by the president with the consent of the Senate to 14-year terms, with one member's term expiring every two years. These long, staggered terms are intended to insulate members from politics as much as possible. The governors supervise 12 regional Federal Reserve banks, each headed by a president and run by a nine-member board of directors chosen from the private banking business in that region.

The 12 members of the Fed's Open Market Committee are all professional economists or bankers. Though their names are unfamiliar to most people, this group, which meets every six to eight weeks, decides how much money will be allowed to enter the economy, manages foreign currency operations, and regulates banks. It does this by buying and selling government securities, which can encourage either lower or higher interest rates. Other lenders closely watch the decisions of the Fed and typically make their interest rates consistent with Fed decisions. Because lenders make it either more or less expensive to borrow money, they influence a wide range of economic activity.

The chair of the Board of Governors, by tradition an economist, is appointed by the president to a four-year term, and is now Ben S. Bernanke, who was appointed in 2006. The chair is automatically one of the most influential national public policy officials. The staff of the Fed reports directly to the chair, not to the board, and the chair is the one who appears before Congress and the country to explain the policies of the Federal Reserve System. The chair heads the Federal Open Market Committee and is credited or blamed for the decisions made by the Fed.

The Fed has three basic tools for influencing the economy. First, it can change the discount rate, which determines how much banks must pay for borrowing money.

Federal Reserve System
The system created by Congress in 1913 to establish banking practices and regulate currency in circulation and the amount of credit available. It consists of 12 regional banks supervised by the Board of Governors. Often called simply *the Fed.*

Alan Greenspan (right) served as chairman of the Federal Reserve under four presidents. He is seen here with his replacement, Ben Bernanke. Greenspan retired in 2006.

History Makers

Alan Greenspan

Alan Greenspan

Already regarded as one of the most important economic policy makers of the late twentieth century, former Federal Reserve Board chair Alan Greenspan may well be remembered more for stopping inflation than promoting growth. Appointed to his post in 1987 by Ronald Reagan, Greenspan served for almost 20 years and is best described as a monetarist who used the Fed to promote his view that the economy can only grow so fast before it ignites inflation.

Greenspan is best known for using interest rates to either stimulate or slow down the economy. As the economy worsened in late 2000 and early 2001, for example, the Fed began cutting interest rates to stimulate demand. In all, the Fed cut its federal funds rate 11 times in 2001, dropping the amount banks charge each other to borrow money from 6.5 percent in January to just 1.75 by December. When the economy did not respond, the Fed lowered the rate again to 1.25 percent in November 2002, and to just 1.0 percent in June 2003, where it remained through most of 2004. Worried about inflation, the Fed raised the rate to 1.25 percent in June 2004, and continued raising rates over the next two years. After 17 separate increases, the rate hit 5.25 percent in late June 2006 when the Fed stopped raising rates for a time.

Whether as an inflation fighter or a recession breaker, Greenspan became one of the world's most watched economic leaders. Although he once joked that he had learned "to mumble with great incoherence" early on at the Fed, he also knew the power of words to slow the economy. In December 1996, for example, he wondered out loud whether the stock market was suffering from what he called "irrational exuberance," which prompted an immediate 145-point drop in the Dow Jones Industrial Average, the most widely followed stock indicator.

Greenspan finished his doctorate in economics in 1977, after leaving the Ford administration. During his term at the Fed, he started each day with a 2½-hour hot bath to soothe his ailing back, using the time to read memos and analyze the latest economic data. "The unsung hero at the Fed is the assistant who has to read his waterlogged scribblings," said his wife, Andrea Mitchell. However he made his decisions, he was strongly supported by the business community for his continued efforts to restrain federal spending and encourage growth, even though he was often criticized for raising interest rates. ■

> "We saw a crowd of some fifty men fighting over a barrel of garbage which had been set outside the back door of a restaurant. American citizens fighting for scraps of food like animals!"
>
> **AN OBSERVER OF THE GREAT DEPRESSION**

Raising rates slows down the economy by increasing costs for money and credit; lowering rates stimulates the economy by making money more easily available for investment and growth.

Second, the Fed buys and sells federal debt. Selling federal debt to the public tends to slow down the economy by taking dollars out of circulation that could have been used for investment or growth, while buying federal debt back from the public tends to free up money that can be used for new activities, thereby stimulating the economy.

Third, the Fed determines how much money nationally chartered banks must keep in their reserves. Raising the requirement tends to slow down the economy by reducing the funds banks have available to lend to the public for investment and growth, while decreasing the requirement injects more money into the economy.

Government and Economic Policy

Depression is a hard teacher, and the 1930s had a tremendous impact on American thinking about the role of government in the economy. The Great Depression that began in 1929 brought mass misery. "One vivid, gruesome moment of those dark days we shall never forget," wrote one observer. "We saw a crowd of some fifty men fighting

Agents of Change

Darrell Hammond and KaBOOM!

KaBOOM! was created in 1995 to help build playgrounds and promote play as a step toward building strong communities. By creating "hangouts for success," KaBOOM! is dedicated to creating a safe place to play for every child in America, and, in doing so, engaging communities in building a safe place to live.

According to its mission, KaBOOM! is built on the belief that the process of organizing a community-built playground is as important as the product: the playground itself. It is the building that is most important to engaging citizens in the effort to create strong local economies. The organization also believes that happy children have a greater chance to succeed throughout life.

KaBOOM! was created by Darrell Hammond, who sees play as a fundamental right for children. Raised in an orphanage with his eight brothers and sisters, Hammond remembers the importance of play to his own survival. He built his first public playground as a junior at Ripon College in Wisconsin, and joined City Year after graduating. "KaBOOM! attempts to do what we know is so important," he says, "and that is to provide spaces and playgrounds in neighborhoods around the U.S., particularly in tough difficult neighborhoods where they haven't had a playground for many years because of violence and gangs...."

In 2003, KaBOOM! and Home Depot announced a unique national effort to build 1,000 playgrounds in 1,000 days across North America. Home Depot has invested $25 million of its profits and provided nearly 1 million volunteer hours to KaBOOM!, which will benefit 1.5 million parents and children. ■

Learn more about KaBOOM! at www.kaboom.org.

Darrell Hammond as a child

QUESTIONS

Why might a playground be an important part of a strong economy?

Why does building playgrounds improve local economies?

---

over a barrel of garbage which had been set outside the back door of a restaurant. American citizens fighting for scraps of food like animals!"[10]

The depression continued despite Franklin D. Roosevelt's New Deal economic agenda, which pumped new money into the economy, created hundreds of thousands of federally subsidized jobs, and established new regulations governing the financial markets. Faint signs of recovery could be seen in the mid-1930s, but a new recession in 1937 and 1938 indicated that the country was by no means out of the woods. Between 8 and 9 million people were jobless in 1939. Unemployment fell dramatically with World War II, which put millions of Americans back to work building military hardware and millions more into military uniforms.

There were several theories about what the federal government could do to stimulate the economy at the time. Some economists urged the government to reduce spending, lower taxes, curb the power of labor, and generally leave business and the economy alone. This first theory is called **laissez-faire economics**.

Another group, deeply influenced by the work of the English economist John Maynard Keynes,[11] recommended that when consumer spending and investment decline, government spending and investing should increase. Government must do the spending and investing during a recession because private enterprise will not or cannot.

This second theory is called **Keynesian economics**. When the economy is in a recession, Keynsians press for more government spending that will either purchase more goods and services for government or provide more money to help the needy. Keynesians believe that this spending will "prime the pump" for increased economic activity by putting more government money into the economy. More government

laissez-faire economics
Theory that opposes governmental interference in economic affairs beyond what is necessary to protect life and property.

Keynesian economics
Economic theory based on the principles of John Maynard Keynes stating that government spending should increase during business slumps and be curbed during booms.

spending, and the economic activity that goes with it, should also stimulate more jobs for unemployed Americans. When there is more money in the pockets of individuals, Keynesians believe that at least some of it will be spent, or in economic terms, consumer demand will increase. This theory is sometimes called demand-side economics.

Although Keynesian economics influences government economic policy to this day, Ronald Reagan and George W. Bush both argued that tax cuts were better for creating a strong economy. This new and untested theory was called *supply-side economics*, and is based on the notion that tax cuts increase the supply of money in the economy, which stimulates economic growth.

Promoting the Economy

ederal economic policy involves more than the effort to smooth the ups and downs of the business cycle. It also involves efforts to promote economic growth, often measured by the number of new jobs or businesses created. In doing so, it helps create jobs for individual Americans, which in turn produces higher revenues, which in turn produces either greater savings or more federal spending. U.S. economic policy has two goals: (1) to promote economic growth so the United States remains a world leader in terms of quality of life, and (2) to regulate business activity so no single industry or company has an unfair edge in competing for success.

Promoting Economic Growth

The framers believed that developing a strong economy was part of securing the "blessings of liberty," and they encouraged U.S. exports by creating a navy to protect cargo ships. Over history, the federal government created a number of departments and agencies to protect that hoped-for growth, including the departments of Agriculture and Commerce and the Small Business Administration.

The Department of Commerce is the most visible advocate of business within the federal administrative system, and is sometimes known as the nation's "service center for business." Its secretary is usually picked for his or her connections to business, and is an advocate for free enterprise and lower regulation.

The Department of Commerce also encourages innovation through the protection of intellectual property. Its Patent and Trademark Office administers the patent system that Congress established "to promote the Progress of Science and useful Arts" under Article I of the Constitution. Each year, the office issues more than 100,000 patents to cover new inventions. These patents generally give their users exclusive rights to use the patent for 17 years, after which anyone can use it. The number of patents issued annually almost doubled during the economic expansion of the 1990s, but fell back during the 2001–2002 economic recession. The rate reflects more than just poor economic performance, however. It also may reflect falling interest in math and science among U.S. students and the enormous cost of selling a new idea to consumers.

The Department of Agriculture is also an advocate of business, albeit focused entirely on farming. It also administers a long list of programs that support higher prices for basic products such as corn, barley, oats, wheat, soybeans, cotton, and rice. In 2006 alone, these agricultural *subsidies* cost more than $15 billion by either guaranteeing a minimum price for crops or paying fees for not planting fields. By altering the supply and price of crops, these subsidies increase the cost of everything from bread and eggs to soy milk. The department also provides a host of support services to improve agricultural production, many of which are administered by state agriculture extension offices, which operate out of large universities such as the California state university system, Cornell, Ohio State, and Texas A & M. Although these subsidies and support were originally designed to help small family farmers, most now go to large agricultural corporations such as Archer Daniels Midland, ConAgra, and Smithfield, all of which own millions of acres of farms.

Promoting International Trade

The United States experienced its first **trade deficit** in more than a century when the amount of imports exceeded the value of exports in 1971. In the 30 years since then, the nation has faced billions of dollars in ever growing trade deficits. Congress and the president are under continuing pressure from industry, unions, and regional political leaders to protect American jobs, companies, and communities from foreign competition. These pressures come not only from the textile and auto industries but also from glass, steel, shoes, lumber, electronics, book publishing, aluminum, farming, and domestic wine and spirit coalitions, to name just a few. These leaders claim that the trade deficit justifies the imposition of trade sanctions.

The problem, however, is not that the United States is importing too much but that it is exporting too little. German cars, Japanese technology, and Indonesian textiles are fine products; if other countries produce better cars or shoes at a lower price, free traders argue, the United States should buy from them and direct our labor and capital to areas in which it can do better.

The question is also whether U.S. products are given fair treatment by other nations. American agricultural products are denied entry into some countries and are subject to high tariffs in others. American automobile manufacturers complain of unfair restrictions imposed by the Japanese on our cars. Finally, some countries exploit the U.S. advantage in technology by slavishly copying our products and then selling them back to us or to other countries at a profit.

Another unfair trade practice is *dumping*—selling products below the cost of manufacturing or below their domestic price with the intention of driving other producers out of the market and then raising prices to profitable levels. Another practice is government *subsidizing* of certain industries. Some countries, for example, subsidize steel for export. Others require lengthy inspection procedures for imported goods. Japan has protected several of its industries—producers of automobiles, baseball bats, and even chopsticks, for example—by setting standards that are virtually impossible for U.S. manufacturers to meet. Japan also sets limits on rice imports.

In 1947, a group of countries formed a trade organization to negotiate free trade by lowering tariffs (taxes on imports that raise their price) and quotas (limits on the quantity of a particular product that may be imported) and other disadvantages countries face when trading. Today the **World Trade Organization (WTO)**, based on the **General Agreement on Tariffs and Trade (GATT)**, includes more than 130 countries, and its membership accounts for four-fifths of the world's trade. The WTO has negotiated agreements through eight rounds of trade negotiations (the most recent was called the Uruguay Round, named after the site of the conference).

The United States has tried to focus these negotiations on increased trade in agricultural items, foreign investment, and protection of technological innovations and intellectual property. Although U.S. imports and those of other countries still face many trade restrictions, the WTO and GATT have helped lower tariffs and quotas and increase fair trade throughout the world. Many analysts maintain that GATT is one of the most successful innovations in the history of international relations and one of the contributing factors to the United States' economic success since the end of the Cold War.[12]

Not everyone believes that free trade should be unlimited, however. Labor unions, environmentalists, and human rights advocates argue that U.S. trade policies spur the creation of low-wage jobs abroad and encourage child labor, pollution, and worker

Hong Kong is one of the world's financial centers.

trade deficit
An imbalance in international trade in which the value of imports exceeds the value of exports.

World Trade Organization (WTO)
International organization derived from the General Agreement on Tariffs and Trade (GATT) that promotes free trade around the world.

General Agreement on Tariffs and Trade (GATT)
An international trade organization with more than 130 members, including the United States and the People's Republic of China, that seeks to encourage free trade by lowering tariffs and other trade restrictions.

abuse in countries such as China and India that export large quantities of goods to the United States.

THE NORTH AMERICAN FREE TRADE AGREEMENT   In 1992, the United States, Canada, and Mexico signed the **North American Free Trade Agreement (NAFTA)**, which formed the largest geographical free trade zone in the world, even surpassing the European Community's 15-country conglomerate. Although President George H. W. Bush signed NAFTA near the end of his presidency, the agreement could not become law until ratified by Congress. President Bill Clinton promoted NAFTA, even though many members of his own party were its most vigorous opponents. Congress passed NAFTA by a thin margin in a bipartisan vote in which the Democrats were the minority.

Though trade among the United States, Canada, and Mexico is not absolutely "free" or unimpeded, the agreement has had a tremendous impact on the economies of all three countries. Today Mexico is the United States' third most important trading partner, and the United States is Mexico's most important trading partner. Critics of NAFTA remain concerned because Mexican antipollution laws are significantly less stringent than those in the United States, and Mexican workers work for considerably lower wages. Both of these factors make relocation to Mexico attractive to many U.S. companies seeking to lower labor and pollution control costs.

Recent reports suggest that many of those lower-paid jobs in Mexico have moved to China. Hourly wages in Tijuana, Mexico, range from $1.50 to $2.00, well below the U.S. minimum wage of $5.15 per hour but well above the 25 cents per hour paid in China. More than 500 low-wage assembly line factories in Mexico closed between 2000 and 2002, due largely to the migration of jobs in the global economy to Asia.[13] Nevertheless, the free trade movement has continued, with approval of the Central American Free Trade Agreement (CAFTA) in 2005.

REMOVING BARRIERS TO FREE TRADE   Worries about the loss of U.S. jobs to foreign countries often lead to calls for **protectionism**, which can take the form of special taxes, or tariffs, placed on imported goods. Most economists oppose protectionism because it prevents efficient use of resources and because consumers pay much more for protected products than they otherwise would in the world economy. Tariffs merely divert attention from real solutions like increased productivity and capital investments and inevitably invite retaliation from foreign countries.

In the 1930s, many nations faced high unemployment, low production, and general economic misery. The United States was no exception. In an effort to aid ailing American industries, Congress passed the Smoot-Hawley tariff, the highest general tariff the United States had ever had. Supporters hoped high tariffs on imported goods would increase the demand for goods produced in the United States and thus help get the country out of the Great Depression. The exact opposite occurred. Other nations retaliated with high tariffs on American goods. Demand fell, intensifying the depression.

Congress later gave the president the power to negotiate mutual tariff reductions with other nations, subject to certain restrictions, and by the early 1970s, tariffs on industrial products had been substantially reduced. Trade barriers are less severe today than they were in the 1930s. But restrictions still exist. Certain tariffs, quotas on imported goods, and import regulations limit American consumption of foreign products. Most exist to protect American farmers, businesses, or workers in certain industries. Thus we have restrictions on clothing and textile imports, and these restrictions cost U.S. consumers a lot more than they benefit workers' wages.

The United States has generally supported increased trade and fewer trade barriers, yet many Americans worry that globalization will hurt the country. Free trade and globalization policies do not confer equal benefits on everyone. Inevitably, some workers will be worse off as a result of a freer international flow of goods and capital. All told, trade barriers cost U.S. consumers approximately $80 billion a year—equal to more than $1,200 per family.[14]

North American Free Trade Agreement (NAFTA)
Agreement signed by the United States, Canada, and Mexico in 1992 to form the largest free trade zone in the world.

protectionism
Policy of erecting trade barriers to protect domestic industry.

THE "OFFSHORING" DEBATE Free trade has many benefits, including access to new markets in large nations such as Mexico. It also has a significant impact on U.S. jobs through **offshoring**, which involves the movement of jobs from higher-paying U.S. companies to lower-paying foreign companies, or to foreign branches of U.S. companies.

Although offshoring clearly hurts U.S. workers in the short term, most economists agree that efforts to stop the movement of jobs to other nations would hurt the U.S. economy in the longer term. "Protectionism will do little to create jobs," former Federal Reserve Board Chairman Alan Greenspan said in 2004, "and if foreigners retaliate, we will surely lose jobs. We need to discover the means to enhance the skills of our workforce and to further open markets here and abroad." Liberals tend to agree, but argue that the federal government should provide greater help for workers who lose their jobs to foreign nations. "The answer is not to try to stop outsourcing," says former Clinton administration Secretary of Labor Robert Reich in using another term for offshoring, "but we do have to get serious about job retraining, lifetime learning, extended unemployment insurance, and wage insurance."

Offshoring may make perfect economic sense in the long term, but it has very harsh consequences in the short term. Workers whose jobs move abroad often face years of unemployment, which is why the issue has been so controversial. Some estimates suggest that the United States has lost more than one million jobs, which were exported to Mexico and other Central American countries, and now to China.[15]

The United States' economic policy in the future will continue to combine free trade and selective protectionism. Though protectionism shields highly visible industries from competition at home or abroad, such measures often favor one industry over another, which reduces competition.

Even free trade advocates can occasionally find a political reason for protectionism. In March 2002, for example, President George W. Bush imposed 30 percent tariffs on a range of products made with imported steel in an effort to protect the ailing U.S. steel industry. In doing so, he honored a campaign promise he had made in Ohio, Pennsylvania, and West Virginia, steel-producing states that were also key battleground states in his 2000 campaign.

There is no question that steel imports hurt the U.S. steel industry. Nearly 50,000 jobs were lost between 1997 and 2002 because of bankruptcies and factory closings, and more than 300,000 jobs were at risk. As European steelmakers complained to the World Trade Organization, however, the international economy was merely working its will by rewarding more efficient foreign steelmakers with a bigger market. The WTO agreed that the U.S. tariffs violated free trade rules, forcing the United States to drop the tariffs or face international retaliation on a range of products from Florida oranges to North Carolina tobacco. In December 2003, the Bush administration dropped the tariffs.

> *"The answer is not to try to stop outsourcing, but we do have to get serious about job retraining, lifetime learning, extended unemployment insurance, and wage insurance."*
>
> **FORMER SECRETARY OF LABOR ROBERT REICH**

Leo Gerard, United Steelworkers of America president, addresses steelworkers who came to Washington, D.C. to protest the problems globalization and free trade have created in their industry.

Regulating the Economy

The second goal of U.S. economic policy is to regulate business activities that might create unfair advantages. Americans believe in competition among businesses, but they also want a level playing field, meaning that no industry or company cheats its way to the top or abuses its employees or the environment along the way.

The Constitution explicitly authorizes Congress to regulate commerce among the states and with foreign nations. In our earliest years, Congress used this regulatory

offshoring
The practice of exporting U.S. jobs to lower-paid employees in other nations.

Government's Greatest Endeavors

Clean Air and Water

Belching smokestacks were a primary target of the 1970 Clean Air Act.

QUESTIONS

How clean should the air and water be in order to be declared "clean"?

How can the federal government protect the environment without hurting industry and creating unemployment when dirty factories must close?

One of the most visible forms of economic regulation involves nearly 60 years of effort to protect the nation's air and water from pollution. Although early laws such as the 1948 Water Pollution Act and the 1963 Clean Air Act established a federal role in protecting the environment, the 1970 Clean Air and 1972 Clean Water acts provided much of the legal power to make progress in both areas.

Over the past 30 years, the levels of most air pollution covered by the Clean Air Act have fallen dramatically as the U.S. Environmental Protection Agency has established ever-tighter rules promoting more efficient automobiles and cleaner-burning fuels. Although it is hard to find a single American city where the air quality has not improved, air pollution continues to spread to rural areas such as national parks where automobile pollution is concentrated as tourists arrive in record numbers.

Similarly, it is hard to find a single body of water or river that is not significantly cleaner because of the Clean Water Act. However, as the nation has learned more about pollutants such as arsenic, the pressure to improve water quality has increased. In 2001, the Bush administration changed some of the rules governing arsenic and animal waste to give industry more time to change its practices. Citizen groups appealed both decisions and won victories in the courts reversing them.

Such victories come at a cost to industry, which is why the 1990 amendments to the Clean Air Act contained new incentives to reduce pollution in the hope that industry would find a good financial reason to act on the public's behalf. ∎

power to impose or suspend tariffs on imports from other nations. In the nineteenth century, the federal government created a number of agencies to regulate the conduct of citizens and commercial enterprises with an eye toward promoting economic development. Among these were the Army Corps of Engineers (1824), the Patent and Trademark Office (1836), the Steamboat Inspecting Service (1837), and the Copyright Office of the Library of Congress (1870). In 1887, Congress created the Interstate Commerce Commission to deal with widespread dissatisfaction over the practices of railroads.

Additional regulations were created to end monopolies, increase food safety, prevent environmental pollution, improve automobile safety, and prevent employment discrimination on the basis of race, color, national origin, religion, sex, and age. More recently, government has created regulations to protect citizens from raw sewage in rivers, lead in paint and gasoline, toxins in the air, radon gas in homes, and asbestos, cotton dust, and hazardous products in the environment. Federal regulations for environmental, health, and safety are estimated at about $200 billion in higher product cost, but equal or greater benefits in reduced disease and injury rates.[16]

Preventing Corporate Abuse

In a broad sense, *regulation* is any attempt by the government to control the behavior of corporations, other governments, or citizens. **Regulation** is commonly defined as any method the government uses to alter the natural workings of the open market to achieve some desired goal such as reducing child labor and the abuse that goes with it. Regulation by government interjects political goals and values into the economy in the form of rules that direct behavior in the marketplace. These rules have the force of law and are backed by the government's police powers. (See the discussion of rules earlier in this chapter.)

All economies are regulated by their governments, but the amount of government regulation varies. The United States has a competitive market economy, with relatively little government regulation. It allows wages, prices, and the allocation of goods and services to follow the laws of supply and demand, even when that produces unpopular results, such as the dramatic increase in gasoline prices in 2005–2006. The nation relies on private enterprise and market incentives to carry out most production and distribution.

Nevertheless, market economies have imperfections. Even opponents of regulation recognize that the market does not always solve every problem. Consider pollution. For a long time, no price was imposed on a business for using air and water to discharge toxic wastes. Therefore, market forces did not consider the social costs of its air and water pollution. When the market fails to set appropriate costs and benefits, pressures develop for the government to step in. The government can, for example, create regulations imposing penalties for air pollution. Market forces also do not encourage taking a bus instead of a car to work. If government enacted higher taxes on gasoline, our fuel costs would be brought more in line with Europe's. Such a policy would also reduce our dependence on Middle East oil and promote domestic energy production.

In 1935, there were 4,000 pages of regulations in the *Code of Federal Regulations,* which lists all federal rules; today, there are more than 70,000 pages of regulations.[17] Both political parties say regulatory overkill threatens to overwhelm entrepreneurs and divert them from building vital, innovative companies. Although some economists estimate that regulations can add as much as $3,000 to the cost of a new car, the regulations also purchase important benefits such as cleaner air and safer cars, which, in turn, reduce accidents and improve the overall quality of life.[18] The question is not

The risk of animal-borne diseases, such as mad cow disease, has led the federal government to institute regulation of the nation's agriculture industry.

regulation
Efforts by government to alter the free operation of the market to achieve social goals such as protecting workers and the environment.

whether there are both costs and benefits from regulation but whether the balance is right. Conservatives tend to overstate the costs of many regulations and understate the benefits, while liberals tend to overstate the benefits and understate the costs.

Types of Corporate Regulation

There are two general categories of regulation: economic and social regulation.

Economic regulation generally refers to government controls on the behavior of businesses in the marketplace: the entry of individual firms into particular lines of business, the prices that firms may charge, and the standards of service they must offer.

Although the national government has been regulating interstate commerce since 1789, it was generally reluctant to regulate private businesses until after the Civil War. As the U.S. economy grew, so did the need for rules governing business and labor. Congress created the Interstate Commerce Commission in 1887 as the first of what would become many independent regulatory commissions. The ICC was established to regulate the railroads and other transportation industries, but it was abolished in the late 1970s as part of the deregulation movement, which is discussed later in this chapter (see Table 18–2 for a list of key government regulatory agencies).

The second type of regulation, *social regulation,* refers to government attempts to correct a wide variety of side effects, usually unintended, brought about by economic activity. Concern for worker health and safety and for environmental hazards has led to much social regulation. Social regulation also includes efforts by government to ensure equal rights in employment, education, and housing. Whereas economic regulation is usually organized along industry lines, social regulation cuts across these lines.

The Environmental Protection Agency, the Consumer Product Safety Commission, and the Occupational Safety and Health Administration are regulatory agencies

TABLE 18–2 Selected Regulatory Agencies and Their Missions

Agency	Year Established	Primary Functions
Federal Trade Commission (FTC)	1914	Administers certain antitrust laws concerning advertising, labeling, and packaging to protect consumers from unfair business practices
Food and Drug Administration (FDA)	1931	Establishes regulations concerning purity, safety, and labeling accuracy of certain foods and drugs; issues licenses for manufacturing and distribution
Securities and Exchange Commission (SEC)	1934	Oversees the activities of the stock markets and assures that all publicly reported information is honest
Federal Communications Commission (FCC)	1934	Licenses civilian radio and television communication; licenses and sets rates for interstate and international communication
Environmental Protection Agency (EPA)	1970	Develops environmental quality standards; approves state environmental plans
Occupational Safety and Health Administration (OSHA)	1970	Develops and enforces worker safety and health regulations
Consumer Product Safety Commission (CPSC)	1972	Establishes mandatory product safety standards and bans sales of products that do not comply
Nuclear Regulatory Commission (NRC)	1974	Licenses the construction and operation of nuclear reactors and similar facilities and regulates nuclear materials; licenses the export of nuclear reactors and the export and import of uranium and plutonium
Transportation Security Administration (TSA)	2001	Controls passenger and baggage screening; regulates what passengers can carry; requires airlines to check bags through electronic screens; oversees all airport, land, and maritime security

The Changing Face of American Politics

Women and Minority Board Members

All corporations have boards of directors that wield great power—they oversee executive salaries and compensation, approve major decisions such as mergers and acquisitions of other companies, and are responsible for the honesty of corporate financial reports.

Although women and minorities now constitute a significant percentage of the U.S. workforce, they occupy relatively few of the seats on the boards of America's largest corporations. As of 2005, just 12 percent of board members at the nation's 1,500 largest companies were women, while 10 percent were minorities. These percentages have grown slightly over the past decade, but they still remain well below the per-

centage of women and minorities in the workforce. They are also well below the number of women and minorities who work as managers and executives in the largest U.S. corporations.

These percentages may increase in coming years as corporations seek to add more board members under new federal rules adopted in the wake of the accounting scandals at Enron, WorldCom, and other leading corporations. The problem is not a lack of names for nomination—in May 2002, for example, the New American Alliance, a nonprofit association of Latino business leaders, and the Hispanic Association for Corporate Responsibility joined together to create a database of

more than 1,000 Hispanic candidates for board openings. If the numbers do not grow, advocacy groups have promised to pressure the Securities and Exchange Commission for a rule requiring greater diversity. ■

Percentage of Women and Minorities in the Workforce and Board Room, 2005.

	Percent Women	Percent Racial Minorities
U.S. Workforce	47%	30%
Executives and Managers	35	16
Seats on the Boards of the 1,500 Largest Companies	12	10

SOURCE: Data from Susan Williams, "Board Diversity," Investment Responsibility Resource Center, 2006 Background Report A, March 1, 2006.

engaged in social regulation. In economic terms, producers affected by social regulation must now pay for external costs that once were free, such as using rivers, landfills, or the atmosphere for waste disposal. These costs, however, are then passed along to the consumer, so the true cost of the product is more accurately reflected in its price.

Congress has created two types of regulatory agencies: those within the executive branch and those with a degree of independence from Congress and the president. Members of executive branch agencies serve at the pleasure of the president. Executive branch regulatory agencies include the Food and Drug Administration, the Office of Surface Mining, and the National Highway Traffic Safety Administration. Commissioners of independent regulatory agencies are appointed by the president and confirmed by the Senate, and they cannot be removed by a president except for cause. Independent agencies, usually headed by a board composed of seven members, include the Federal Communications Commission, the Equal Employment Opportunity Commission, and the Nuclear Regulatory Commission.

Regulating Business

Business regulation increased in three major waves over the past century. The first came in the 1910s, the second in the 1930s, the third in the late 1960s through 1980. In each case, changing circumstances gave rise to the legislation.

Perhaps the most important responsibility of government regulation in a free market system is to maintain competition. When one company gains a **monopoly**, or

monopoly
Domination of an industry by a single company; also the company that dominates the industry.

several create an *oligopoly*, the market system operates ineffectively. The aim of **antitrust legislation** is to prevent monopolies, break up those that exist, and ensure competition. In the past, so-called natural monopolies, such as electric utilities and telephone companies, were protected by the government because it was assumed that in these fields competition would be grossly inefficient.

In the late nineteenth century, social critics and populist reformers believed that the oil, sugar, whiskey, and steel industries were deceiving consumers, in large part because of the rise of large monopolies, called **trusts**. Once they became aware of abuses in these industries, Americans began to call for more government regulation. In 1890, Congress responded by passing the Sherman Antitrust Act, which was designed "to protect trade and commerce against unlawful restraints and monopolies." Henceforth, persons making contracts, combinations, or conspiracies in restraint of trade in interstate and foreign commerce could be sued for damages, required to stop their illegal practices, and subjected to criminal penalties. However, the Sherman Antitrust Act had little immediate impact; presidents made few attempts to enforce it, and the Supreme Court's early interpretation of the act limited its scope.[19]

Congress added the Clayton Act to the antitrust arsenal in 1914. This act outlawed such specific abuses as charging different prices to different buyers in order to destroy a weaker competitor, granting rebates, making false statements about competitors and their products, buying up supplies to suppress competition, and bribing competitors' employees. In addition, *interlocking directorates* (having an officer or director in one corporation serve on the board of a competitor) were banned, and corporations were prohibited from acquiring stock in competing concerns if such acquisitions substantially lessened interstate competition. That same year, Congress established the Federal Trade Commission (FTC), run by a five-person board, to enforce the Clayton Act and prevent unfair competitive practices. The FTC was to be the "traffic cop" for competition.[20]

Regulating the Use of Labor

Government regulation of business is essentially restrictive. Most laws and rules curb business practices and steer private enterprise into socially useful channels. But regulation cuts two ways. In the case of American workers, most laws in recent decades have tended not to restrict labor but to confer rights and opportunities on it. Actually, many labor laws do not touch labor directly; instead they regulate relations with employers.

Federal regulations protect workers in the following important areas, among others:

1. *Public contracts.* The Walsh-Healy Act of 1936, as amended, requires that no worker employed under contracts with the federal government in excess of $10,000 be paid less than the prevailing wage and that he or she be paid overtime for all work in excess of eight hours per day or 40 hours per week.

2. *Wages and hours.* The Fair Labor Standards Act of 1938 set a maximum workweek of 40 hours for all employees engaged in interstate commerce or in the production of goods for interstate commerce (with certain exemptions). Work beyond that amount must be paid for at 1½ times the regular rate.

3. *Child labor.* The Fair Labor Standards Act of 1938 prohibits child labor (under 16 years of age, or under 18 in hazardous occupations) in industries that produce goods for interstate commerce.

4. *Industrial safety and occupational health.* The Occupational Safety and Health Act of 1970 created the first comprehensive federal industrial safety program. It gave the secretary of labor broad authority to set safety and health standards for companies engaged in interstate commerce.

antitrust legislation
Federal laws (starting with the Sherman Antitrust Act of 1890) that try to prevent a monopoly from dominating an industry and restraining trade.

trust
A monopoly that controls goods and services, often in combinations that reduce competition.

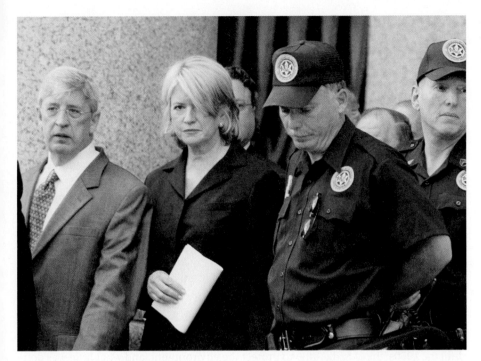

Martha Stewart was tried and convicted in 2004 for misleading federal investigators about why she sold her stock in a drug company called ImClone Systems.

Federal regulations also protect employee rights to organize unions. Under the 1935 National Labor Relations Act (usually called the Wagner Act), for example, the federal government gave workers significant new rights to organize unions, while prohibiting businesses from discriminating against union members or refusing to bargain in good faith with union representatives.

Congress passed a major modification of the labor laws in 1947, the Labor-Management Relations Act, commonly called the Taft-Hartley Act. The act outlawed the **closed shop** (a company in which only union members in good standing may be hired) and permitted the **union shop** (a company in which new employees are obligated to join the union within a stated period of time), prohibited employers from refusing to bargain with employees, allowed courts to issue **labor injunctions** forbidding specific individuals or groups from performing acts considered harmful to the rights or property of an employer or community, and structured the process of **collective bargaining** between unions and employers to set wages, benefits, and working conditions.

Regulating Corporate Markets

The stock market crash of 1929 did more than devastate the American economy and usher in the Great Depression. It also revealed deep problems in how stocks were sold to investors. Millions of new investors entered the stock market in the 1920s only to find out that the companies in which they had invested were virtually worthless.

Before 1934, when the Securities and Exchange Commission (SEC) was created, investors themselves had to determine whether a company was telling the truth about its stock. Since 1934, that responsibility has fallen to the SEC. Under the Securities Exchange Act of 1934 and a long list of later laws, companies that offer their stock for sale to the public must tell the truth about their businesses, which means full disclosure of all financial statements, as well as the stocks they are selling and the risks involved in investing.

At the same time, the act also required that anyone in the business of selling stocks, including brokers, dealers, and stock exchanges such as the New York Stock Exchange and NASDAQ, must treat investors fairly and honestly, putting investors'

closed shop
A company with a labor agreement under which union membership is a condition of employment.

union shop
A company in which new employees must join a union within a stated time period.

labor injunction
A court order forbidding specific individuals or groups from performing certain acts (such as striking) that the court considers harmful to the rights and property of an employer or a community.

collective bargaining
Method whereby representatives of the union and employer determine wages, hours, and other conditions of employment through direct negotiation.

interests first. That means, for example, that individuals who know about a new stock offering in advance or have other inside information on events that might increase or decrease the value of a given stock are prohibited from using that information to benefit themselves.

Congress added to the long inventory of other laws to protect investors when it passed a corporate reform bill in 2002. This law was designed to prevent the kind of deceptive accounting games that led to the collapse of the Enron Corporation in late 2001. As later trials showed, Enron misled investors about the health of the company, while contributing millions to the campaign funds of members of Congress and the president. Even as millions of investors put money into the company, its senior executives were taking money out in bonuses and illegal payments.

The new corporate reform law strengthened the SEC, created a new oversight board to monitor accounting practices, and set new disclosure requirements on how corporations report their profits. The Enron collapse was only one of many highly visible corporate scandals of the early 2000s that included communications companies such as WorldCom and Adelphia. In 2006, Enron executive Kenneth Lay went on trial for stealing money from his company, while WorldCom became part of Verizon Corporation, and Adelphia went out of business.

Regulating and Protecting the Environment

Until the 1960s, the U.S. did little to protect the environment, and what little was done was by state and local governments. In recent decades, however, the federal government has taken on new responsibilities, starting with passage of the Clean Air and Water Acts in the early 1970s. These two laws put new limits on the amount of pollution companies could release into the environment, and launched a long list of new laws designed to regulate everything from leaking underground storage tanks to garbage. New laws also encouraged energy conservation and recycling. Congress also created the Environmental Protection Agency to enforce the new laws.

Perhaps the most controversial environmental regulation involves **environmental impact statements**, which are used to assess the potential effects of new construction or development on the environment. Most projects using federal funds must file such statements, and since 1970, thousands have been filed. Supporters contend that such statements reveal major environmental risks in new construction projects and can lead to cost savings along with greater environmental awareness. Critics claim that environmental impact reviews simply represent more government interference, paperwork, and delays in the public and private sectors.

Environmental impact statements are only one form of environmental regulation, however. In 1990, Congress amended the Clean Air Act to tighten controls on automobiles and the fuel they use. Building on earlier mileage regulation, the 1990 amendments required automakers to install pollution controls to reduce emissions of hydrocarbons and nitrogen oxides, and set stiff standards for the kinds of gasoline that can be sold. The 1990 act also required power companies to cut pollution from coal-burning power plants, phased out the use of certain chemicals that harm the earth's protective ozone layer and may contribute to global warming, and set new limits on a long list of cancer-causing pollutants. In 2005, the Bush administration implemented a new set of regulations supporting its Clear Skies initiative. The new regulations placed limits on the release of certain pollutants, but were widely seen as a general weakening of environmental laws.

The 1990 amendments and Clear Skies initiatives used the profit motive to encourage self-regulation by private business. Under new rules and permits issued by the Environmental Protection Agency, businesses are allowed to generate a certain amount of pollution. If they produce less pollution than their allotment, they can sell the balance of their permits to other companies that are polluting more. By setting overall caps for certain regions of the country, this "cap-and-trade" system encourages individual companies to reduce the total amount of pollution they would have pro-

environmental impact statement
A statement required by federal law from all agencies for any project using federal funds to assess the potential effect of the new construction or development on the environment.

Global warming is being blamed for increased incidents of severe weather, such as Hurricane Katrina, which hit New Orleans and other areas of the Gulf region in 2005.

duced under traditional regulations. Initial efforts along these lines have been successful, while saving billions.

Protecting the Global Environment

As globalization has expanded, so have the environmental challenges and hazards associated with that growth. Global temperatures are rising, suggesting the possibility that economic development and the burning of carbon-based fuels that goes with it has created a blanket of carbon dioxide "greenhouse gases" that traps heat in the earth's atmosphere.

Concerns about the consequences of global warming led to negotiation of the Kyoto Protocol in 1997. Named for the Japanese city in which it was negotiated, this treaty required participating countries to make substantial cuts in greenhouse gas emissions year by year until 2012. Because not all nations participated in the negotiations and because the effort to control carbon-based fuels would slow the growth of less developed nations, the Kyoto Protocol immediately divided the world between North (developed countries) and South (less developed countries). Moreover, because the United States would be required to spend billions of dollars reducing the greenhouse gases from its cars and coal-fired electric plants, the Senate also signaled its reluctance to participate. As of 2006, the future of the Kyoto Protocol is uncertain.

Global warming is only one of several environmental problems the world faces, however. Greenhouse gases may be on the rise, but the world's ozone layer, which protects humans from cancer-causing ultraviolet radiation, is thinning. Unlike global warming, the world has made considerable progress in limiting the major chemicals that have contributed to the "ozone hole" in the atmosphere. The greatest progress came on two very different products, refrigerators that used Freon gas to keep food cold, and chemicals used in everything from deodorants to hairspray.

The Deregulation Movement

One solution to criticisms of government regulation has been **deregulation**, the reduction or complete abolition of federal regulation in a particular sector of the economy. Deregulation began in 1977 with the airline, trucking, and railroad industries, and has continued with banking and telecommunications.

deregulation
A policy promoting cutbacks in the amount of federal regulation in specific areas of economic activity.

At the same time the federal government has been working to deregulate certain industries, it has also created new procedures to limit the amount of regulation the federal government can impose. In 1993, for example, President Clinton issued an executive order prohibiting agencies from issuing regulations unless the benefits of the regulations (in lives saved, for example) outweighed the costs. In 2001, President Bush followed suit by imposing a 60-day hold on all regulations published by the Clinton administration until his administration could ensure that the regulations met the benefit/cost test.

Deregulating Transportation

No industry has undergone more extensive deregulation than the transportation industry. Over the past generation, airlines, trucking, and railroads have been granted considerable freedom in conducting their operations. No deregulation effort has been more visible to consumers than airline deregulation.

The federal government began regulating aviation when it established the Civil Aeronautics Board (CAB) in 1938 to protect airlines from unreasonable competition by controlling rates and fares. Critics charged that airlines competed only in the frequency of flights and in the services they offered, forcing consumers to pay higher fares than needed.

After years of debate, Congress abolished the CAB in 1978, allowing the market to set fares through competition. Although many fares fell, some medium-sized cities lost service because carriers found it more profitable to use their aircraft in busier markets. Airlines were raising fares on routes over which they had monopolies in order to subsidize lower fares on more competitive routes. Critics charged that safety precautions and maintenance suffered as a result of cutthroat competition and the ease with which new airlines could enter the market.

Although problems have been associated with airline deregulation, it has resulted in generally lower fares, greater choice of routes and fares in most markets, and more efficient use of assets by the industry.[21] Some airlines have been driven into bankruptcy and others have merged, but deregulation of the airlines has been judged a success by the surviving airlines and most observers of the industry. If an airline is overcharging passengers, a competitor will eventually steal those travelers away. Southwest Airlines is an example of a discount airline that took advantage of deregulation to take on larger airlines.[22] Deregulation has strengthened the industry by forcing companies to streamline their operations in order to survive in a competitive market.

But recent mergers of major airlines have worsened the problems caused by deregulation and cancellation of service to small and medium-sized cities in parts of states in the West. The post–September 11 collapse in travel pushed several airlines toward bankruptcy, which in turn prompted Congress to provide loans to many airlines to help them through the crisis. Under economic pressure, many airlines have stopped providing basic services such as meals, while some have demanded deep cutbacks in wages and benefits from their employees. However, some new airlines such as Jet Blue and Southwest have been highly profitable by offering low-cost services across the nation. Indeed, Jet Blue was rated the number one airline in customer satisfaction in 2006.

Deregulating Telecommunications

Airline deregulation may have been the most visible to consumers, but the deregulation of telecommunications may eventually have a greater impact on how Americans live, whether in the form of lower phone bills, easier access to the Internet, or better cellular technology. Unlike the deregulation of transportation, which came in a number of steps over time, deregulation of telecommunications came in a single, massive bill called the Telecommunications Act of 1996.

This act broke long-standing monopolies by companies such as AT&T, while creating new opportunities for competition in the phone, Internet, and cable-television industries. Telephone companies that were once divided into seven local "baby Bells" were allowed to offer services outside their defined regions. Local telephone companies won the freedom to provide long-distance service, manufacture communications equipment, and offer video service in competition with cable television. At the same time, local telephone companies opened their networks to competition for local telephone service from cable television and long-distance companies. In short, restrictions were removed so that cable television and local and long-distance telephone companies could effectively compete with one another. However, recent mergers of companies have stifled competition in cellular communication and cable television, which has put pressure on Congress to reregulate the industry.

The Telecommunications Act also contained two highly controversial provisions: new regulation on Internet content and a requirement that all television makers install a "V-chip" to allow parents to block out television shows with objectionable content. However, the Supreme Court struck down provisions making it a crime for any person knowingly to make indecent material accessible to minors on the Internet. The Court found the provision too vague and held that the Internet receives full protection under the First Amendment.[23] Although the debate continues about who will decide what is deemed violent or offensive, most surveys suggest that parents are unwilling or unable to use the V-chip to control their family viewing habits.[24]

A Continued Federal Role

Despite campaign promises to reduce the federal government's economic role and give more money back to citizens and corporations, members of Congress and the president understand that the federal government must be involved in the economic life of the nation. It will continue to collect taxes, regulate the money supply, prevent monopolies that would hurt consumers, and promote free trade. It will do all this while trying to let the market, not government regulators, shape the demand for and the price of products and services. Most Americans want their government to play only a limited role in the economy, but competing values such as fairness, equality, protecting workers and the environment, and encouraging healthy competition inevitably encourage elected officials to take on certain balancing or referee responsibilities in order to promote the common good.

Summary

1. The policy-making process involves a variety of choices made by Congress, the president, and the courts, including: (1) making assumptions about the world, (2) identifying the problem to be solved, (3) deciding whether to act at all, (4) deciding how much to do, (5) choosing a tool for solving the problem, and (6) making rules for implementation.

2. The federal government influences how wealth is produced and distributed primarily via fiscal policy (taxing and spending), monetary policy (control of the money supply), and regulatory policy.

3. Fiscal policy is implemented by the federal budget, which is annually negotiated between the president and Congress. Monetary policy is primarily under the control of the Federal Reserve System, which has considerable independence from both Congress and the president as it works to supply sufficient amounts of money and credit so that the economy will grow but not so much that it will lead to inflation.

4. Government's role in promoting growth and jobs is not new. It is as old as the Republic itself. The federal government has long been involved in promoting agriculture and concerned about helping farmers, even though large corporations own the vast majority of farmland. Working

through the Department of Commerce, it also promotes business. The federal government is also involved in promoting trade and commerce with other nations, which has involved efforts to reduce barriers to imports and exports. Globalization has led to sharp debates about offshoring.

5. Regulation, now a major activity of government, involves altering the natural workings of the open market to achieve some desired goal. Economic regulation aims to control the behavior of business in the marketplace. Social regulation aims to correct the unintended side effects of economic activity such as environmental pollution, and to ensure equal rights in employment, education, and housing. Government regulates labor to give workers the right to organize into unions. It regulates markets to protect investors. It regulates the environment to protect the public. And it is increasingly involved in regulating the global environment.

6. A deregulation movement designed to get the government out of the regulation of certain businesses has taken form over the past 30 years. Liberals sometimes favor deregulation if they believe it will foster more competition. Conservatives generally favor deregulation that will relieve business from complying with detailed safety, health, environmental, and consumer protection standards.

Further Reading

JEFFREY H. BIRNBAUM AND **ALAN S. MURRAY,** *Showdown at Gucci Gulch: Lawmakers, Lobbyists, and the Unlikely Triumph of Tax Reform* (Vintage, 1988).

STEPHEN G. BREYER, *Breaking the Vicious Circle: Toward Effective Risk Regulation* (Harvard University Press, 1993).

GARY BRYNER, *Blue Skies, Green Politics: The Clean Air Act of 1990 and Its Interpretation,* 2d ed. (CQ Press, 1995).

GARY BURTLESS, ROBERT J. LAWRENCE, ROBERT E. LITAN, AND **ROBERT J. SHAPIRO,** *Globaphobia: Confronting Fears About Open Trade* (Brookings Institution Press, 1998).

THOMAS W. CHURCH AND **ROBERT T. NAKAMURA,** *Cleaning Up the Mess: Implementation Strategies in Superfund* (Brookings Institution Press, 1993).

ROBERT W. CRANDALL AND **HAROLD FURCHTGOTT-ROTH,** *Cable TV: Regulation or Competition?* (Brookings Institution Press, 1996).

ROBERT W. CRANDALL AND **LEONARD WAVERMAN,** *Who Pays for Universal Service? When Telephone Subsidies Become Transparent* (Brookings Institution Press, 2000).

ROBERT W. CRANDALL ET AL., *An Agenda for Federal Regulatory Reform* (American Enterprise Institute/Brookings Institution, 1997).

ROBERT M. ENTMAN, *Competition, Innovation, and Investment in Telecommunications* (Aspen Institute, 1998).

THOMAS L. FRIEDMAN, *The Lexus and the Olive Tree: Understanding Globalization* (Anchor Books, 2000).

THOMAS L. FRIEDMAN, *The World Is Flat: A Brief History of the Twenty-First Century* (Farrar, Straus, and Giroux, 2005).

WILLIAM GREIDER, *Secrets of the Temple: How the Federal Reserve Runs the Country* (Simon & Schuster, 1987).

PHILIP K. HOWARD, *The Death of Common Sense: How Law Is Suffocating America* (Random House, 1994).

CORNELIUS M. KERWIN, *Rulemaking: How Government Agencies Write Law and Make Policy,* 2d ed. (CQ, 1998).

ROBERT KUTTNER, *Everything for Sale: The Virtues and Limits of Markets* (Knopf, 1997).

LAWRENCE LESSIG, *Code and Other Laws of Cyberspace* (Basic Books, 2000).

STEPHEN D. LEVITT AND **STEPHEN J. DUBNER,** *Freakonomics: A Rogue Economist Explores the Hidden Side of Everything* (Morrow, 2005)

CALVIN MACKENZIE AND **SARANNA THORTON,** *Bucking the Deficit: Economic Policy-Making in America* (Westview Press, 1996).

STEVEN A. MORRISON AND **CLIFFORD WINSTON,** *The Evolution of the Airline Industry* (Brookings Institution Press, 1995).

PETER G. PETERSON, *Facing Up: Paying Our Nation's Debt and Saving Our Children's Future* (Simon & Schuster, 1994).

ALLEN SCHICK, *The Federal Budget: Politics, Policy, Process,* rev. ed. (Brookings Institution Press, 2000).

JOSEPH E. STIGLITZ, *Globalization and Its Discontents* (Norton, 2002).

JOHN WARGO, *Our Children's Toxic Legacy: How Science and Law Fail to Protect Us from Pesticides* (Yale University Press, 1997).

BOB WOODWARD, *Maestro: Greenspan's Fed and the American Boom* (Simon & Schuster, 2000).

JEFFREY WORSHAW, *Other People's Money: Policy Changes, Congress, and Bank Regulation* (Westview Press, 1997).

DANIEL YERGIN AND **JOSEPH STANISLAW,** *The Commanding Heights: The Battle Between Government and the Marketplace That Is Remaking the Modern World* (Simon & Schuster, 1998).

KeyTerms

Make It Real

ECONOMIC POLICY

The simulation allows students to try to balance the federal budget.

Chapter 19

Making Social Policy

⭐

I N 2006, PRESCRIPTION DRUGS COST AMERICAN CONSUMERS MORE THAN $100 BILLION A YEAR, OR ROUGHLY $900 FOR EACH AMERICAN OVER 65. BEFORE 2006, OLDER AMERICANS HAD TO COVER THE COST OF THEIR PRESCRIPTION DRUGS MOSTLY ON THEIR OWN. ALTHOUGH MANY HAD PRIVATE INSURANCE AND SOME RECEIVED HELP FROM THE JOINT FEDERAL-STATE MEDICAID PROGRAM FOR THE POOR, MANY OLDER AMERICANS WERE FORCED TO CHOOSE BETWEEN FOOD AND DRUGS, OFTEN CUTTING THEIR DAILY MEDICATIONS TO MAKE ENDS MEET.

That all changed on an early Saturday morning in late 2003 when the House of Representatives held its final vote on a law designed to help older Americans pay for their prescription drugs. Although most members of Congress supported the new program, Democrats wanted the federal government to both spend more and administer the program, while Republicans wanted to spend less and allow private insurance companies to run the program.

Republicans eventually won the battle on party line votes in the House and Senate, and passed a huge new spending program. However, they lost the battle on the ultimate cost of the program. Although

they initially estimated that the program would cost $400 billion over its first ten years, current estimates put the ultimate cost at $1 trillion, largely because Republicans did not calculate either rising drug costs or the growing number of older Americans.[1]

Nevertheless, the bill moved quickly through the legislative process and to the president's desk on December 8 for a signature. In return for a $35 monthly premium, the federal government promised to cover 75 percent of all yearly drug costs between $250 and $2,250, thereby helping all participants regardless of need. In addition, the federal government promised to cover 95 percent of all drug costs above $3,600, thereby protecting participants who face extremely high, or catastrophic, drug costs.

Critics argued that the effort was flawed for several reasons. First, the program did not help the approximately 60 million Americans who have no health insurance at all, let alone those who have no prescription drug coverage.

Second, the new program created a "notch," or lack of coverage for older Americans caught between $2,251 and $3,600 in prescription costs.

Third, Congress and the president did nothing to address the long-term financial problems of paying for health care for older Americans under the Medicare program, which was created in 1965. According to the latest projections, the Medicare program will start to run a deficit in 2019, which means that the federal government will have to either raise taxes or cut benefits to cover the total cost. Unless something is done soon to control costs, Congress may yet have to cut the prescription drug program the government just implemented.

"It's unacceptable that some of the poorest and sickest people are having the most trouble, and it's not what Congreess intended."

A SENIOR REPUBLICAN CONGRESSMAN

549

Finally, and perhaps most important, the new law created enormous confusion among older Americans about how to actually get the coverage. By March 2006, only 15 million of the more than 40 million eligible Americans had signed up for the new benefit. Part of the problem was the sheer number of private insurers that offered the benefit—many older Americans were simply overwhelmed with information on competing plans, including one offered by the American Association of Retired Persons, which has more than 36 million members.

Part of the problem also involved a benefit for the seven million older Americans who had been enrolled in Medicaid, which had provided drug coverage for the poor. Under the new program, these older Americans either had to choose a private plan or lose their existing drug coverage. Although more than five million chose a plan by the December 31, 2005, deadline, another two million did not. The 50 state governments that administer Medicaid on behalf of the federal government faced a dilemma: Either the states had to continue covering the needy on their own or hope that the federal government would extend Medicaid coverage long enough to allow these older Americans to sign up with a new program.

These issues reached Congress almost immediately after the new prescription drug coverage went into effect. The media carried heartbreaking stories of older Americans who had been turned away from pharmacies or forced to pay regular prices for their drugs. Although some states stepped in to continue providing coverage at their own cost, most could not, or would not. Having opposed the original legislation, Democrats revived their opposition to letting private companies run the program, while Republicans worried that the issue might affect the 2006 elections. "It's unacceptable that some of the poorest and sickest people are having the most trouble," one senior Republican said, "and it's not what Congress intended."[2]

As of this writing, Congress has yet to reopen the original legislation to fix the problem. Republicans argue that it is just a matter of time before all eligible older Americans find a plan, while Democrats believe that the program must be changed to assure that everyone is covered whether they enroll or not.

These problems illustrate the difficulties in both designing and implementing a major new federal program. No matter how well intended new legislation may be, new programs require time to take hold. Unfortunately for low-income older Americans, time is of the essence if the federal government is to guarantee the Constitution's promise to promote the general welfare of its citizens.

Volunteers work on a new cottage for the Azleway Boys' Ranch in Chapel Hill, Texas. Volunteerism plays an important role in providing many types of assistance to Americans in need.

This chapter will explore how the federal government promotes the general welfare through a range of social programs, how that promise has expanded over the past century, and what remains to be done to protect the needy. It will also examine three areas of social policy that are likely to be active over the next few years: health, education, and crime control.

The Role of Government in Social Policy

From the beginning of the Republic, the nation has debated the federal government's role in promoting the general welfare. Some Americans ask whether government should be involved at all in social policies such as child care, help for the needy, and job training, all of which were once thought of as purely private, religious, or charitable responsibilities. Others ask which level of government should be involved in issues such as education, welfare distribution, and crime control, all of which were once thought to be solely state and local responsibilities. Today, these responsibilities are a large part of the agenda of our national government.

Nevertheless, Americans remain sharply divided on how much government should do to care for the less fortunate. Although the Preamble to the Constitution promises that the federal government will promote the general welfare, liberals and conservatives often differ sharply on just what this promise means. Liberals tend to believe that the federal government should take the lead in helping needy Americans, while conservatives tend to believe that the free market and state and local governments should be the source of support for those in need.

The two political parties tend to divide sharply in this debate along liberal and conservative lines. Republicans believe that the federal government is not the solution to poverty and other social ills but part of the problem, because it gets in the way of the free market. They tend to favor programs that create incentives for people to pull themselves out of poverty through hard work. By contrast, Democrats are more likely to believe that only the federal government has the resources and jurisdiction to provide adequate Social Security, help local governments improve the quality of education, and ensure that all Americans, rich and poor, have access to proper medical attention. They tend to favor programs that make sure all Americans are protected from the occasional failures of the free market system. They believe that the federal government must provide a safety net for individuals and a minimum standard of living—a job, an education, health care, housing, and basic nutrition—for all citizens.

These differences are clear in recent public opinion surveys. Just 27 percent of conservative Republicans interviewed in October 2005 said that America was dividing into two groups, the "haves" who live in prosperity and the "have-nots" who live in poverty, compared with 37 percent of moderate and liberal Republicans, 62 percent of conservative and moderate Democrats, and 65 percent of liberal Democrats. Overall, 48 percent of Americans said society was dividing into haves and have-nots, while 38 percent said they were have-nots themselves.[3] The percentages were even higher among African Americans.

Americans also disagree about whether the federal government should care for the needy. Some Americans argue that state and local governments should solve social problems such as poverty, in part because states and localities know more about the specific needs in their communities. Others believe that only the national government can ensure that every American is protected against misfortune, in part because poor states and localities do not have the resources to provide as much help as their richer neighbors.

In recent years, Democrats and Republicans have resolved the debate in part by setting national standards that require all states and localities to provide minimum levels of help. In turn, state governors have been increasingly critical of **unfunded mandates** to the states that require states to implement certain policies without federal support. The tendency of Congress to impose unfunded mandates forces state

unfunded mandates
Programs that the federal government requires states to implement without federal funding.

Americans are sharply divided on how involved the government should be in helping the nation's needy. Funding for homeless shelters, such as this one in Atlanta, comes from both public and private sources.

governments to raise taxes or reduce funding for other state programs. Governors argue that if Congress inaugurates a new program requiring states to take action, Congress should provide the federal funds to help pay for that program.

The Early History of Social Policy in the United States

Most **Western governments** expanded their social programs long before the United States did. Americans generally believed that people who could not succeed in a nation as big, rich, and open as the United States simply were not working hard enough. This commitment to *rugged individualism* meant that government, be it local, state, or federal, played only a limited role in people's lives. Rather grudgingly, state governments in the early twentieth century extended relief to needy groups, especially the old, the blind, and the orphaned. But government aid was limited, and much reliance was placed on private charity.[4]

This is not to suggest that the federal government ignored domestic policy, however. From its founding, the government took care of its military veterans. Indeed, with the Revolutionary War barely over, the Continental Congress established the nation's first programs to help soldiers who had been disabled in battle and to provide retirement pensions for officers. Thus, contrary to those who argue that government did little to care for older Americans until it created the Social Security system in 1935, the Continental Congress actually provided care for older veterans well before the new government was even created. Established in the 1780s, the financial security system for veterans expanded slowly but steadily as the soldiers aged into disability and poverty. Americans could not stand to see their veterans in tattered clothing and felt obliged to provide support for the less fortunate. In 1818, for example, Congress expanded retirement benefits to cover all veterans of the Revolutionary War, whether officers or not, and created the first old soldiers' homes for poor veterans. In 1840, Congress expanded the veterans program again to provide financial relief to the widows of soldiers killed in battle.[5]

These early programs set two important precedents for contemporary domestic policy. First, they established the notion that some Americans would be automatically entitled to certain government benefits on the basis of an eligibility requirement such as service in the nation's armed forces. Thus veterans' relief was the nation's first **entitlement**, under which the government provides benefits to any citizen who is eligible. In the original program, only soldiers met the eligibility requirement. Second, these early programs also established government's right to restrict some benefits only to those citizens who could actually prove their need for help. Thus veterans' programs were early examples of what are now called **means-tested entitlements**, under which citizens must prove they are poor enough to deserve the government's help. In the original program, only poor veterans could go to old soldiers' homes.

Veterans' benefits are also important because they eventually came to cover huge numbers of Americans. As political scientist Theda Skocpol has noted, the Civil War triggered a massive expansion in veterans' benefits. The war involved 2.2 million Union soldiers who would later qualify for veterans' benefits. "By 1910, about 28 percent of all American men aged 65 or more, more than half a million of them, received federal benefits averaging $189 a year," writes Skocpol. "Over three hundred thousand widows, orphans, and other dependents were also receiving payments from the federal treasury."[6] Because so many men served in the Civil War and because veterans' benefits were even more generous toward Spanish-American War and World War I veterans, veterans' benefits accounted for one-quarter of all federal spending by 1932. The numbers would have been even higher if Confederate soldiers had been entitled to benefits. However, Congress decided to leave their care to the former Confederate states.

entitlements
Programs such as unemployment insurance, disaster relief, or disability payments that provide benefits to all eligible citizens.

means-tested entitlements
Programs such as Medicaid and welfare under which applicants must meet eligibility requirements based on need.

Types of Social Policy

Having entered the twentieth century with only a handful of federal domestic programs, most of which were built around helping veterans, the federal government left the century with a deep inventory of domestic programs. According to the *Catalog of Federal Domestic Assistance*, which lists every one of the federal government's 1,425 domestic funding programs in a searchable database (at www.cfda.gov), there are at least 38 separate programs for farmers, another 142 for colleges and their students, 148 for women, and 257 for children.

The Goals of Social Policy

Because most of these programs are restricted to one group of citizens only, they are often described as *categorical* aid. One only needs to type in a search term on the Internet such as "students," "elderly," "children," "disabled," "workers," "farmers," "women," or "veterans" to see just how much help the federal government provides in each category. But regardless of category, federal domestic policy focuses on two broad goals.

The first goal is to protect citizens against poverty and personal misfortune, whether by providing relief for unemployed workers, health care for the elderly, emergency shelter for the homeless, or school lunches for poor children, most of which are available to citizens only on the basis of a means test. Although almost all Americans are covered by federal unemployment insurance through a payroll tax, only workers who have been laid off from their jobs through no fault of their own can qualify for benefits, and only then for a relatively brief period of time. (For an inventory of federal programs for helping workers, visit the Department of Labor Web site at www.dol.gov.)

The second goal of federal domestic policy is to raise the quality of life for all Americans, whether by improving air and water quality, building roads and bridges,

Thousands fill the National Mall during the 2005 Millions More Movement event in Washington, DC, which commemorated the tenth anniversary of the Million Man March and focused on concerns of education, housing, economic development, finance, health, and violence.

regulating air traffic, fighting crime, or strengthening local schools through federal aid. Almost all federal aid to the states for these purposes is distributed on the basis of formulas that allocate money on the basis of population, not need.

Most scholars trace the federal government's effort to protect citizens against economic and personal hard times to the Great Depression and the Social Security Act of 1935. Although there is no question that Franklin Roosevelt's New Deal agenda stimulated a remarkable expansion in the federal government's domestic policy role, there is also no question that federal, state, and local governments were helping citizens long before the depression began.

Until about a century ago, the poor were divided into two groups: the worthy poor, meaning people who were in poverty through no fault of their own, and the unworthy poor, meaning people who were in poverty because of idleness or unwillingness to work, which was considered the source of most unemployment at the time. As historian Joel Handler writes, this categorization emerged in the early 1800s as states began to place the worthy poor into separate government institutions such as schools for the blind and disabled. This movement was driven by a clear recognition that "those who were dependent by misfortune did not deserve the stigma of the unworthy poor."[7]

Types of Protection

By the early 1900s, however, public attitudes toward the poor had begun to change. Although the nation continued to distinguish between the worthy and unworthy poor, Congress and the president soon invented two very different types of federal programs to protect Americans against hardship, both of which continue to exist today.

The first type of help for the less fortunate is called **public assistance**, a term that is often used interchangeably with the word "welfare" to label government aid for the poor. The first public assistance programs were actually created in the late 1800s when states established aid programs to help single, poor mothers and their children. Although these programs were often described as "mothers' pensions" to create the impression that the beneficiaries had earned the benefits through some contribution, they created a precedent for many of the federal government's later antipoverty programs.

Most of this assistance flows through noncontributory programs, meaning that recipients do not have to pay anything in advance to receive benefits. Most federal assistance programs also impose a means test on all applicants. As noted earlier, these tests require applicants to disclose all financial assets and income to prove that they fall below the poverty line, which is generally calculated as three times the amount of money an individual or family needs to purchase the food for a nutritious diet. Defined as such, the poverty level changes with the size of the family. In 2006, the poverty line for participation in federal assistance programs was drawn at just under $10,000 for individuals, and exactly $25,000 for a family of four.[8]

The U.S. Bureau of the Census uses a somewhat different measure of income to determine how many Americans are poor at any given time. According to its measure, which runs a year or two behind the Department of Health and Human Services, 13 percent of Americans, or 37 million, were poor in 2004. The poverty rate was 18 percent among children, 10 percent among Asian Americans, 22 percent among Hispanics, and 25 percent among African Americans.[9]

Public assistance in the United States today incorporates elements of job training, transportation subsidies, housing subsidies, free school lunches, food aid for poor families and pregnant mothers with young children, and tax credits for low-income people. The federal government also provides what some critics label as "corporate welfare" to favored industries such as agriculture and steel, as well as "middle-class welfare" to college students, home buyers, and the citizenry as a whole in the form of college loans, tax deductions for home mortgages, and access to national parks and

public assistance
Aid to the poor; "welfare."

forests (supported by taxpayers but rarely used by poor people). However, the term "welfare" is generally used for public assistance to the needy, including the following forms:

■ Direct payments to single parents with young children, the unemployed, and the disabled

■ Food stamps

■ Low-cost and/or public housing

■ Reduced cost or free access to public transportation, higher education, or job training

■ Free or low-cost medical care

In absolute numbers, most poor people are white. As a percentage within their own population, however, a larger proportion of African Americans and Hispanics are poor. Moreover, in both absolute and proportional terms, more women than men are poor. Indeed, some scholars refer to the relatively recent rise in poverty among women as the "feminization of poverty."[10] Although more women than men tend to take jobs in lower-paying occupations, they earn less than men even when they are in the same jobs. They also save less money over their lifetimes than men, in part because they often take time off from paying work to care for their children and aging parents. As noted above, the poverty rate among children is 17 percent, which is much higher than the rate among working-age individuals aged 18 to 64 (12 percent) and individuals over the age of 65 (10 percent). The poverty rate among older Americans has fallen with automatic annual increases in Social Security benefits, while the rate among 18- to 64-year-olds and children has increased.

Food stamps allow needy families to purchase the food necessary for a nutritious diet.

The second type of protection against hardship is called **social insurance**, a term that refers to government programs that provide benefits to anyone who is eligible either because of past service (veterans, miners, merchant marines) or payments of some kind (payroll taxes for Social Security and Medicare, insurance premiums). Some social insurance programs, such as unemployment and disability insurance, provide benefits only to those in need, thereby acting like private automobile and life insurance, which pay off only when an accident or death occurs. Other social insurance programs, such as Social Security and Medicare, pay benefits regardless of wealth, thereby acting more like a private savings program or annuity, which pays off at a set point in time.

Many federal assistance programs involve partnerships with state governments. There are two reasons for the connection. First, except for veterans' policy, states have been responsible for protecting their citizens against hardship since the United States was formed. Second, states and local governments have the administrative agencies to stay in touch with recipients of aid, whether to make sure they are actually eligible for support or to provide services such as job training or school lunches.

Because states vary greatly in their generosity, most federal assistance is designed to set a minimum floor of support that individual states can raise on their own. The most generous states in the country tend to be located in the Northeast and West, where living costs tend to be higher and legislatures more liberal, while the least generous tend to be found in the South. In this way, states act as a check on the federal government's ability to raise benefits too far, frustrating those who believe that the federal government should set a uniform level of benefits for all citizens while ensuring the consent of the governed for helping those in need. (Table 19–1 shows the amount of federal payments to individuals in 2006.)

social insurance
Programs in which eligibility is based on prior contributions to government, usually in the form of payroll taxes.

TABLE 19–1 Federal Payments to Individuals, 2006

MAJOR PUBLIC ASSISTANCE PROGRAMS

Medicaid	$192 billion
State Children's Health Insurance	6 billion
Supplemental Security Income	35 billion
Food stamps	35 billion
Child nutrition	13 billion
Family support payments to states	21 billion
Low Income Tax Credit	35 billion

SOCIAL INSURANCE FUNDING

Social Security	$460 billion
Medicare	390 billion
Disability insurance	91 billion
Unemployment insurance	37 billion

SOURCE: Summary Tables, *Budget of the United States, Fiscal Year 2007*, Washington, D.C., U.S. Government Printing Office, February 2006.

The Expansion of Social Policy in the Twentieth Century

The federal government's commitment to helping the poor and improving the quality of life expanded rapidly during the Great Depression that followed the stock market crash of 1929. The "social safety net" built by state and local governments and private charities simply could not meet the needs of the huge increase in the homeless, unemployed, and poor.

The New Deal

The most significant expansion of federal social policy occurred in the five years that followed Franklin Roosevelt's inauguration in 1933. That year, as part of Roosevelt's New Deal agenda, the federal government began making loans to states and localities to help the poor, and soon it launched a long list of programs to help older Americans (Social Security), the jobless (unemployment insurance), and the poor (Aid to Families with Dependent Children).

THE FIRST 100 DAYS   Before creating these signature New Deal programs, however, the Roosevelt administration moved quickly to help the needy. The first 100 days of the administration produced the most significant list of legislation ever passed in American history, including the Federal Emergency Relief Administration (FERA), established in May 1933 to give unemployed workers cash grants to get them through the summer, and the Civil Works Administration (CWA), created in November 1933 to provide millions of public jobs to help many of those same workers make it through the winter.

The list of "alphabet agencies" grew longer as the administration created a host of new programs to help the poor, including the Works Progress Administration (WPA), which was created in 1935 to provide work for millions of unemployed Americans, and the Civilian Conservation Corps (CCC), which put millions of young Americans to work clearing trails and building roads in the national forests and parks. Between 1933 and 1945, for example, the WPA put 8.5 million Americans to work at a cost of $10 billion. All told, the WPA built 650,000 miles of roads, 125,000 public buildings, 8,200 parks, and 850 airports. The wages were hardly generous, however. The average WPA worker received just $55 a month, far below the $100 the federal government deemed a subsistence wage. The WPA was abolished during World War II when the economy finally rebounded.

Together, these and other New Deal programs created a national safety net to catch those in need. It is little wonder, therefore, that scholars would describe the New Deal as the "big bang" of domestic policy.[11] Although the distinction between the worthy and unworthy poor still remained, joblessness was no longer defined as merely a problem of individual idleness or the unwillingness to work.

HELP FOR OLDER AMERICANS   Once past the immediate crisis, the Roosevelt administration began designing the flagship programs of the New Deal. First on the list was **Social Security**, which was enacted in 1935 and stands today as the federal government's most popular social program. Social Security was designed to meet two goals: (1) to provide a minimum income floor for poor beneficiaries, and (2) to ensure that benefits bear a relationship to the amount of payroll taxes a beneficiary actually paid. Supported by equal contributions from employers and employees, the program now covers more than 90 percent of the American workforce.[12] The universal nature of Social Security is one reason it is politically so popular: Everyone benefits, regardless of need. In 2006, 18 million Americans received a Social Security number, while 53 million beneficiaries received a monthly check.

Social Security was expanded in 1939 to include financial support for survivors of workers covered by Social Security when the retired worker died, and in 1954, the program was again expanded to include support for disabled workers and the children of deceased or disabled workers. Benefit levels were raised repeatedly during the first 40 years of the program, often just before an election. The increases became so frequent and so costly that in 1975 Congress finally indexed benefits to rise with inflation. Under legislation enacted in 1983, the Social Security retirement age started to rise in 2003 and will reach 67 years of age by the year 2027. In 2006, for example, workers who retire at age 65 years and 6 months are eligible for full benefits, while workers who retire early at age 62 are eligible for a reduced amount. The average benefit in 2006 was $917, while the maximum benefit for a worker retiring at full retirement age was $2,053.[13]

Until the 1970s, growth in Social Security benefits was relatively uncontroversial, largely because "the costs were initially deceptively low," while the benefits increased

Many senior citizens rely on Social Security benefits to see them through their retirement years. The program covers more than 90 precent of the American workforce.

Social Security
A combination of entitlement programs, paid for by employer and employee taxes, that includes retirement benefits, health insurance, and support for disabled workers and the children of deceased or disabled workers.

History Makers

Marion Wright Edelman

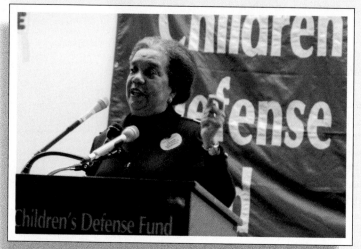

Marion Wright Edelman

Marion Wright Edelman is one of the nation's strongest advocates for children. Born in South Carolina in 1939, she experienced racial segregation firsthand. Denied the right to enter public parks in her birthplace of Bennettsville, she played in a park her father built behind his church.

Despite these early racial barriers, Edelman earned her undergraduate degree at Spellman College, a historically African American college, and a law degree from Yale University. She soon became the first African American woman to be admitted to practice law in Mississippi, and became an active advocate of children's issues. She was involved in making sure Mississippi implemented the new federal law to give poor children a head start before entering school, and soon moved to Washington, D.C., to help organize Martin Luther King's Poor People's Campaign, which sought to improve the lives of poor Americans, young and old.

As the Poor People's Campaign came to an end, Edelman decided to start an entirely new organization that eventually became the Children's Defense Fund (CDF), which focused on a host of childhood and adolescent issues such as preventing teenage pregnancy, increasing federal funding for the Head Start program, and providing better health benefits for children. With poverty rates growing fastest among children, Edelman focused her energies on making sure children had a voice on Capitol Hill and in the White House.

As one of the nation's most visible interest groups, the Children's Defense Fund has a long reputation for legislative success. It lists more than 20 major victories, on causes from improving foster care to increasing vaccination rates, providing greater access to child care, and increasing funding for food stamps. CDF is also deeply involved in reducing poverty among all Americans. ∎

Read more about
Marion Wright Edelman
and her organization at
www.childrensdefense.org.

steadily, making the system politically painless.[14] Since Social Security began, the program has experienced steady growth and is now the world's largest insurance program for retirees, survivors, and people with disabilities. In 2006, Social Security and Medicare expenditures totaled nearly $860 billion.

Social Security, unlike many welfare programs, is financed not from general taxes but from a trust fund into which taxes on employees and employers are paid under the Federal Insurance Contribution Act, commonly known as FICA. Over the years, Congress added benefits to the Social Security system without adding enough money to the trust fund to cover the added expense. In 1983, Congress tried to solve the problem by raising the retirement age at which one qualifies for Social Security benefits, increasing Social Security taxes, imposing the first-ever tax on the Social Security payments to upper-income individuals, and imposing a one-time cut in the annual cost-of-living increase in benefits.

Social Security taxes are now the largest tax paid by most Americans, and for three-quarters of Americans, their Social Security tax now exceeds their income tax. Employees paid a 6.2 percent FICA tax on all wages up to $94,200 in 2006, and an additional 1.45 percent on all wages up to any amount for Medicare. All employee taxes are matched dollar for dollar by employers, meaning that self-employed Americans must pay 15.3 percent total.

Although Social Security has been enormously successful in lowering the poverty rate among older Americans, it is under increasing pressure as Americans get older. In 1990, for example, the average American was 33 years old; by 2020, the average age will be 38 years. The average age is rising in part because Americans are having fewer children, and in part because medical advances have increased the lifespan. Medical advances have been particularly important in increasing the number of very old Americans—the number of Americans over the age of 85 is expected to grow from roughly 3 million in 2000 to 17 million in 2050, which means increased Social Security and Medicare costs.

These increases would not be a problem if the payroll taxes coming into Social Security and Medicare from today's workers were put away for their eventual retirement. But much of the revenue actually goes to payments for today's retirees. Social Security is thus a "pay-as-you-go" system, in which today's young workers finance the retirement of today's elderly. At some point in the not-too-distant future, there will not be enough workers paying into the two programs to cover all the benefits. Under current projections, Medicare is expected to start running deficits in 2019, and Social Security in 2029. Sooner or later, Congress will have to decide whether to raise taxes on workers, cut benefits for older Americans, increase the retirement age, or some combination of all three.

The Social Security system is still running a surplus, meaning that the amount of revenue collected through Social Security taxes is greater than the amount of money going out in benefits. The surpluses are invested in Treasury bonds, with the promise that they will be repaid with interest later. As the baby boomers retire and begin to collect Social Security, however, the bonds must be redeemed to pay benefits, and the program will start running annual deficits. Experts differ on when the next Social Security funding crisis will come, but there is little disagreement that something will have to be done to ensure the viability of Social Security for young people now paying into the system.[15]

Social Security is one of three programs that are designed to help older Americans. The second program is **Medicare**, which was created in 1965. Medicare provides hospital, medical, and prescription drug insurance to individuals who are also entitled to Social Security. The hospital insurance is funded by a portion of the Social Security taxes paid by people still working and pays for inpatient hospital care, skilled nursing care, and other services. The medical insurance is funded by monthly premiums paid by enrollees and from general revenues and pays for a portion of doctors' fees, outpatient hospital visits, and other medical services and supplies.

The third program for older Americans is Supplemental Security Income (SSI), which provides monthly payments to disabled persons or those over age 65 who meet an income test. Levels of SSI support vary by state to reflect cost-of-living differences. SSI recipients also qualify for Medicaid, food stamps, and other assistance. SSI benefits are financed by general tax revenues.

HELP FOR THE UNEMPLOYED Social Security was not the only strand of economic protection woven during the New Deal. The New Deal also produced the federal government's first unemployment insurance program, which was enacted as part of the 1935 Social Security Act. Under the program, which is administered by state governments but funded in part with federal unemployment taxes, eligible workers can receive benefits for up to 26 weeks in most states. In periods of high unemployment, the federal government also provides funds for extended benefits for a maximum of 39 weeks in most states.

HELP FOR THE POOR The federal government became involved in protecting women and children against poverty when Congress passed the Infancy and Maternity Protection Act of 1921. Supported by many of the same women's groups that had just won ratification of the Nineteenth Amendment, which gave women the right to vote, the act gave the newly created federal Children's Bureau funds to encourage states to create new maternal, infant, and early childhood health programs. Although the act was allowed to expire in 1929, it set a precedent for future federal involvement in protecting families against poverty.

Congress also established the school lunch program during the New Deal as both a way to help feed the hungry and to strengthen the ailing farm economy. The Federal Surplus Relief Corporation began purchasing surplus agriculture products for needy

Medicare
National health insurance program for the elderly and disabled.

Government's Greatest Endeavors

Helping Low-Income Workers

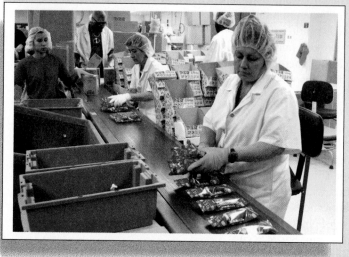

Many minimum-wage workers' incomes are below the poverty level.

QUESTIONS

Besides raising the minimum wage and increasing the EITC, what other ways might the federal government help low-income workers?

Have you ever held a minimum-wage job, and, if so, was it enough to live on by yourself?

The federal government has passed many laws to help low-income workers make ends meet, including increasing the minimum wage, providing help for day care centers, and creating job-training programs.

Between the end of World War II and today, the federal government has increased the minimum wage from 40 cents an hour in 1945 to $4.25 in 1989 and $5.15 in 1997. Although the federal minimum wage has not increased since, many states have raised the amount on their own, with Washington state currently at $7.63. At $5.15 an hour, even full-time workers cannot earn enough money to stay above the poverty level.

The federal government's greatest contribution to helping low-income workers came in 1975 with creation of the Earned Income Tax Credit (EITC), which reduces or completely eliminates all taxes for the working poor. Under the EITC, low-income workers also receive money back from the federal government to help raise their income. Because the money comes in the form of a tax refund, not a welfare check, many experts believe that low-income workers are less embarrassed to take the federal support.

The EITC has clearly reduced poverty rates among low-income workers. In 2004, for example, almost 21 million low-income workers received more than $36 billion through the program, which lifted almost five million out of poverty. The program has been particularly effective in helping unmarried working mothers, who often take minimum-wage jobs in the service industry (fast-food restaurants, dry cleaners, day care centers, grocery stores, and so forth). ∎

families in 1935 and launched the nation's first school lunch programs for poor children shortly thereafter. By 1941, more than 5 million children were receiving free school lunches, consuming more than 450 million pounds of surplus pork, dairy products, and bread. Although the program was disbanded during World War II because of food shortages, it was restored under the 1946 National School Lunch Act. As President Harry Truman said at the signing ceremony, "No nation is any healthier than its children." He could have added that many draftees had been rejected for service in World War II because of malnutrition.

Congress moved even further to help the needy when it passed the Aid to Families with Dependent Children (AFDC) program in 1935.[16] By its very name, AFDC tried to shift the focus away from what the mother had or had not done to deserve poverty and onto the children who suffered whatever the cause, thereby reducing public opposition to expanded benefits. Under the program, states were given federal money to establish cash grants for poor families under two conditions: (1) states had to match the federal funds with some contribution of their own, and (2) states had to establish a means test for all families receiving benefits. AFDC was abolished in 1996 when Congress and the president created an entirely new program that required states to set time limits on public assistance, thereby creating a greater incentive for welfare recipients to find work. We describe this program below, under "Reforming Welfare."

The Great Society

The second major expansion of social policy came in the 1960s with what became known as the Great Society. At a commencement speech at the University of Michigan in May 1964, President Lyndon Johnson described his vision of the Great Society:

> The Great Society rests on abundance and liberty for all. It demands an end to poverty and racial injustice. . . . But that is just the beginning. The Great Society is a place where every child can find knowledge to enrich his mind and to enlarge his talents. . . . It is a challenge constantly renewed, beckoning us toward a destiny where the meaning of our lives matches the marvelous products of our labors.[17]

Johnson's agenda was as broad as his rhetoric, and Congress enacted much of it in a fairly short period of time. Great Society programs dramatically increased the role of the federal government in health, education, and welfare through a number of programs that exist today:

- *Food stamps.* The food stamp program gives poor families coupons that can be used to purchase the basics of a healthy, nutritious diet. The average benefit is about $90 per person per month up to $200 per household.

- *Head Start.* Head Start is a preschool program designed to help poor children get ready for kindergarten. The program serves more than 900,000 children each year at a cost of roughly $7,000 per child. Almost 30 percent of Head Start teachers and staff are parents of Head Start children or were Head Start children themselves.

- *Medicare.* As noted above, Medicare was created in 1965 to provide health care to older Americans. It is now the largest medical program in the federal budget, and will soon cost more than Social Security.

- *Medicaid.* **Medicaid** was created in 1965 to provide basic health services for poor families. The program is administered and partially funded by state governments, and covers everything from hospital care to family planning.

- *Supplemental Security Income.* The SSI program was created in 1972, to provide an extra measure of support for the elderly poor and the blind or disabled. The program provides monthly benefit checks ranging from just $1 to roughly $800 and is administered by the Social Security Administration.

- *Housing assistance.* The Department of Housing and Urban Development, which was created in 1965, administers a number of programs designed to help low-income families find affordable, safe housing, in part by giving property owners subsidies to make up the difference between what tenants can pay and what the local housing market will bear.

The Great Society also produced a vast new social insurance program to cover all hospital and most other health care costs for older Americans. Under the Medicare program, the federal government pays all of the reasonable costs of all inpatient hospital care, including drugs, surgery, and postoperative care, regardless of the beneficiary's personal wealth. Like Social Security, this insurance is "purchased" through payroll taxes, which are set aside solely for Medicare expenditures. Medicare beneficiaries are also entitled to purchase additional federal health insurance to cover the costs of outpatient care, physician visits, and laboratory fees. Americans may also now enroll in the prescription drug program described at the beginning of this chapter.[18] Medicare beneficiaries must also pay a deductible on all hospital stays and a monthly premium for the additional insurance.

The Great Society also produced a long list of important changes in other social policies, including the following:

- *Civil Rights Act of 1964*—set forth the most comprehensive civil rights protections since Reconstruction

- *Elementary and Secondary Education Act of 1965*—established federal funding and programs in public education for disadvantaged children

"No nation is any healthier than its children."

PRESIDENT HARRY TRUMAN, SIGNING THE NATIONAL SCHOOL LUNCH ACT

Medicaid
Federal program that provides medical benefits for low-income persons.

- *Higher Education Act of 1965*—established federal funding for colleges and college students

- *Department of Housing and Urban Development Act of 1965*—created a new department with responsibility for low-rent housing and urban renewal programs

- *Child Nutrition Act of 1966*—expanded federal programs to reduce childhood hunger

- *Fair Packaging and Labeling Act of 1966*—expanded federal oversight of consumer labeling

- *Age Discrimination Act of 1967*—prohibited discrimination based on age

- *Housing and Urban Development Act of 1968*—expanded federal housing and urban development programs

- *Open Housing Act of 1968*—prohibited discrimination in housing

- *Omnibus Crime Control and Safe Streets Act of 1968*—provided federal aid for local law enforcement, crime prevention, and corrections programs

Although Great Society programs such as Medicare, Head Start, and food stamps remain essential threads in the social safety net today, they were enacted during a period of enormous domestic unrest over race relations and the Vietnam War. Unable to win public support for his "guns and butter" agenda, and unsure that he could even win his own party's presidential nomination, Johnson eventually decided not to seek reelection in 1968.

Reforming Welfare

Republicans have not been the only critics of the New Deal and Great Society welfare programs. President Bill Clinton made welfare reform a centerpiece of his reelection agenda in 1996, promising to "end welfare as we know it."[19]

Working with the new Republican congressional majority, Clinton won passage of the Personal Responsibility and Work Opportunity Reconciliation Act in 1996, which replaced AFDC with Temporary Assistance for Needy Families (TANF). Its name captures two themes of the new act—individuals should take more responsibility for themselves, and work, not welfare, is the goal of public assistance.

The burden of administering the new program was shifted entirely to the states. The federal government now gives *block grants* of money to the states and generally requires that the states match those funds. Under the new rules, federally funded public assistance is limited to five years over a person's lifetime, and all recipients must enter some kind of work training program within two months of receiving initial benefits. Although states can exempt up to 20 percent of cases from the work requirements and lifetime limits—an exemption intended for blind and disabled persons—the message to recipients is clear: Find work soon.

The law originally excluded legal immigrants from many welfare programs, but at the strong urging of the governors, most welfare benefits were later restored to legal immigrants. To discourage persons on welfare from moving to states with more generous assistance payments, the law gave states the option of limiting welfare to newcomers from other states. This provision was declared unconstitutional by a federal district court judge, however, who said it "denies 'equal protection of the laws' to indigent families moving from one state to another."[20]

There are several ways to measure the success of the 1996 welfare reform. One is simply to ask whether the number of welfare recipients has declined. By 2002, the number of welfare recipients was lower than it had been in more than three decades. As the authors of a 2002 study of welfare reform argue, "The welfare rolls have declined greatly, more mothers than ever are working, the average income of female-headed families is increasing, and poverty has dropped substantially."[21] The number continued to fall in 2003 despite the economic downturn. As of March 2004, which is the most recent information available, the total number of Americans who received federal welfare benefits had fallen to 4.8 million, 60 percent fewer than in August 1996 when the reforms were enacted.

Yet merely reducing the number of welfare recipients is no guarantee that they either have good-paying jobs or are moving out of poverty. It is one thing to remove a recipient from the welfare rolls and quite another to get the person into a good job with decent benefits. Research suggests that most mothers who leave welfare make $7 to 8 per hour, well above the minimum wage. However, most mothers who leave welfare have other expenses, such as transportation and child care, that may or may not be covered by state or local assistance, and many who go to work lose their food stamps and Medicaid, which means they are more dependent on food banks and have to go without preventive health care.

Although the 1996 welfare reform legislation focused on replacing welfare with work, it also ordered the federal government to promote marriage. Advocates argue that marriage improves the lives of both children and parents. Married adults, whether women or men, are happier, healthier, and wealthier than their unmarried peers and are more likely to give their children a healthier start in life. Some advocates even argue that more marriages would reduce health costs by reducing depression and crime.[22]

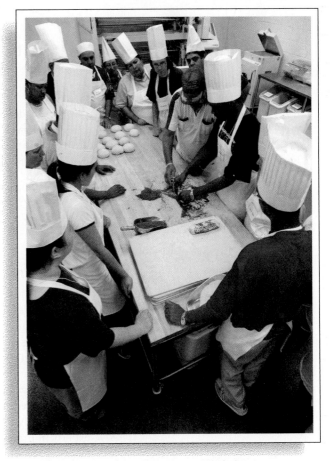

Job-training programs help low-income families improve their earning potential.

The federal government can promote marriage in two ways. First, it can reduce the penalties it imposes on welfare recipients who get married. Under current law, for example, a single mother working full time at a minimum-wage job who marries stands to lose as much as $8,000 a year in cash and noncash benefits. Second, it can promote marriage through advertising, counseling, or even providing cash grants for getting married. Although the federal government has long engaged in activities designed to promote good social behavior, such as vaccinating young children, and promoting smoking cessation, the use of seat belts, and driving under 55 miles an hour, not all Americans believe that promoting marriage is the answer to welfare. They note, for example, that domestic violence and child abuse occur almost as frequently in married as in unmarried households. They also worry that government grants for marriage would promote a rash of false marriages designed to get the cash. Most important, opponents believe that the best way to encourage marriage among welfare recipients is to find them good-paying jobs. They look to states such as Minnesota that have created strong welfare-to-work programs that do not punish married women for getting a job.

Social Policy Challenges for the Future: Health, Education, and Safety

Even if states take on a greater social policy role, the federal government is sure to remain the greatest source of funding for the safety net. As Table 19–2 shows, human resource spending for programs such as Social Security, Medicare, Medicaid, and child nutrition has more than doubled since 1950. Spending is almost certain to rise in coming years as the baby boom generation enters retirement and starts to draw down the Social Security surplus and use Medicare. Moreover, the federal social policy agenda will almost certainly expand as Congress and the president respond to public pressure for action on health care, education, and crime control.

TABLE 19–2 Changing Priorities in the Federal Budget

Function	1950	1960	1970	1980	1990	2000	2006
National defense	32%	52%	42%	23%	24%	15%	20%
Human resources	33	28	39	53	49	64	65
Physical resources	7	9	8	11	10	5	5
Interest on the debt	11	8	8	10	15	13	7

SOURCE: Historical Tables, *Budget of the United States, Fiscal Year 2007*, Washington, D.C., U.S. Government Printing Office, February 2006.

The Federal Role in Health Care

Medicare is just one of the federal government's many health programs. It has been involved in reducing disease since 1887, when the federal government opened a one-room laboratory on Staten Island, New York, to study infectious diseases carried to the United States on passenger ships. In time, that one-room laboratory expanded into the National Institutes of Health (NIH), a conglomeration of 37 separate institutes on a 300-acre campus in Bethesda, Maryland.

The surgeon general of the United States is arguably the most visible health care official in government. As head of the Public Health Service (PHS), the surgeon general works closely with the NIH. Researchers in these institutes, working closely with experts in private laboratories, study causes and seek cures for serious diseases. Fellowships for health research are granted to able scientists and physicians. The NIH administers billions of dollars in grants each year to support the research of university and other scientists and physicians. The PHS also administers grants to states and local communities to help improve public health. Another federal agency promoting health is the Food and Drug Administration (FDA), which oversees the development of new drugs and assures food safety through inspections of the nation's food supply.

There are dozens of other federal agencies that work to improve public health. The Centers for Disease Control and Prevention (CDC) in Atlanta is also intimately involved in preventing disease. The CDC and its 7,800 "disease detectives" have been at the forefront of identifying a host of mystery illnesses, including the respiratory disease that attacked attendees at an American Legion convention in 1976 (Legionnaire's disease), toxic shock syndrome in 1980, and hepatitis C in 1989, while tracking down the causes of major health disasters, including the outbreak of the SARS upper-respiratory virus in 2003 and 2004, and the bird flu starting in 2006.

Despite its success in improving the nation's health, the federal government faces two major health care challenges in the future: containing costs and expanding coverage.

THE RISING COST OF HEALTH CARE   Health care costs in the United States have nearly quadrupled, after controlling for inflation, since 1970.[23] Although they slowed with the rest of the economy in 2001, costs are expected to escalate rapidly as the nation ages over the next two decades.

All Americans pay for the increasing costs (see Figure 19–1). Although employers provide insurance to three out of five Americans, they have steadily increased the share of insurance that employees must pay, including increased premiums, deductibles, or partial payments for services. Taxpayers also pay for the increases through federal dollars that might otherwise go to other programs such as homeland security, college loans, or highway construction.

The good news is that costs have risen in part because people live longer. Average life expectancy increased by more than five years between 1970 and 1995. Most experts

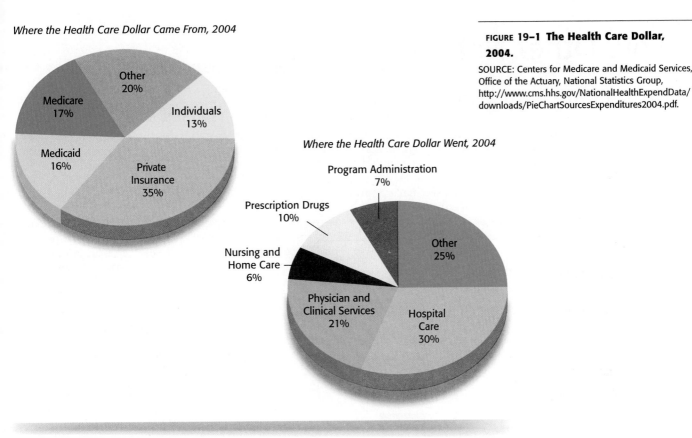

Where the Health Care Dollar Came From, 2004

Where the Health Care Dollar Went, 2004

FIGURE **19–1 The Health Care Dollar, 2004.**

SOURCE: Centers for Medicare and Medicaid Services, Office of the Actuary, National Statistics Group, http://www.cms.hhs.gov/NationalHealthExpendData/downloads/PieChartSourcesExpenditures2004.pdf.

believe it will rise another year by 2015, in part because of advanced treatments, including new drugs for battling HIV/AIDS.[24] In 1900, only one out of every 25 Americans was over the age of 65. By 1950, the number was one in 12 and by 1985, one in nine. According to experts, the number will rise to one in five by 2030. In 1900, the average American lived to age 47; by 2000, the average had increased to 79. Again according to experts, the number will rise into the mid-80s by 2030.

As people live longer, of course, they place greater demands on the health care system, as well as on the Social Security program. New and advanced medical technology—life-support systems, ultrasound, sophisticated x-ray equipment, and genetic counseling—have all increased the costs of health care. Longer life expectancies also place greater demands on other social policies.

The bad news is that some costs have nothing to do with saving lives or preventing disease. Some physicians claim that they have to perform procedures such as laboratory tests that may be medically unnecessary but are legally essential to reduce the risk of being sued by patients. These procedures are alleged to add up to billions in unnecessary costs, but they do not necessarily improve the quality of care provided to patients.[25] Physicians also complain about the high cost of malpractice insurance, nine times more costly in the United States than in Canada. Malpractice insurance costs for all physicians have more than doubled in a decade. A physician's insurance coverage routinely costs as much as $60,000 a year.[26] For specialists like obstetricians, premiums are 400 percent higher than for internists.[27]

At least part of the cost crisis is avoidable. Medicare alone spends billions of dollars each year treating smoking-related diseases, and over the next 20 years the costs to treat such diseases will continue to rise.[28] Other illnesses at least partly related to lifestyle include heart disease, liver disease, HIV/AIDS, and the epidemic of health disorders caused or made worse by obesity, such as diabetes.

COVERING THE UNINSURED Despite passage of the Medicare program, the nation has yet to develop a comprehensive insurance program for the approximately 60 million

How Other Nations Govern

Health Care in the United States and Canada

Advanced industrial democracies like Canada, Germany, Japan, the Netherlands, and the United Kingdom provide health care for their entire population either through national health insurance or a national health service. Although the United States outspends all these countries in terms of health expenditures as a percentage of gross domestic product (see chart), this high level of spending on health care does not mean that the United States has a healthier population. The nation's infant mortality rates, for instance, are among the worst of all industrialized countries, and the United States ranks below average for industrialized nations in male and female life expectancy at birth.

In Canada, about 9 percent of the nation's GDP is devoted to health care spending, and all Canadians are covered by provincial health insurance. Canada's administration of health care is based on a publicly funded system, whereas the program in the United States is divided among public and private insurers. Canada's administrative costs per patient are only one-fourth the size of those in the United States, and companies in the United States often pay three to five times more than Canadian companies to fund employee health and social benefits, including taxes collected by governments to pay for some of these benefits.

The Canadian health care system is not without its faults. Canadians are taxed at a much higher rate than Americans, in part to pay for the publicly funded system. In addition, patients may face delays in receiving services, especially for routine health problems and elective surgery. Doctors and nurses are also paid less in Canada, and thousands of them have moved to the United States, where salaries are much higher. Costs for health care are also increasing faster than the rate of inflation, and the Canadian federal and provincial governments have begun to cut back on funding certain services. Nevertheless, most Canadians express satisfaction with their health care system, and Canada manages to provide health insurance for all of its citizens while spending far less per capita than the United States. ■

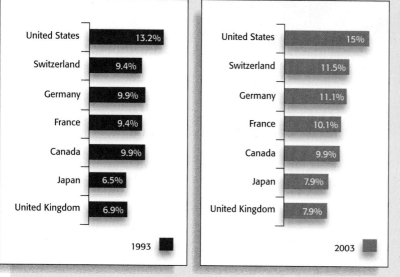

Total Health Care Expenditures as a Share of Gross Domestic Product, 2003.
SOURCE: Organization for Economic Cooperation and Development, Health Data, 2005.

Americans who are uninsured at some point in any given year.[29] Although some rely on public clinics, emergency room care, or charity, many people go without any health or dental care.[30] Many of the uninsured have jobs, but their employers do not provide health insurance, and because their incomes are above the poverty line, they do not qualify for Medicaid. Uninsured individuals usually seek care in hospital emergency rooms only when their illness has reached a critical stage. Postponing medical care drives up costs because critical care is much more expensive than preventive medicine or early treatment.

But it is not just the poor who are uninsured. People who change jobs may often go without coverage for several months before their new insurance takes effect. Those who lose jobs lose their insurance. And people with serious medical conditions may find a new insurance company unwilling to cover their expenses, claiming that the illness is a "preexisting condition." Some insurance companies set caps on their coverage, meaning that families coping with very expensive illnesses end up essentially uninsured.

Although there are many different proposals for health care reform, the essential approaches include a single-payer system, prepaid health plans, employer-mandated coverage, spending caps, individual responsibility, and medical savings accounts.

Single payer   Under a single-payer system, the national government, using broad-based taxes, covers the costs of health care and hospitalization and sets the rates. Like the system in Canada, such a plan would provide universal coverage and benefits to *all* Americans. No longer would people need to worry about the costs of catastrophic illnesses or a change in jobs that would exclude them from coverage. Proponents claim that a single-payer system would save billions of dollars in administrative expenses by reducing the number of insurers from about 1,200 to 1. Opponents of the single-payer system claim it would lead to a bureaucratic mess, with little incentive for innovation, cost control, or diversity of coverage. They further claim that the government would be put in the position of deciding which procedures to pay for and how to ration access to these procedures. As a result, they contend, Americans would lose not only quality in their health care but their freedom of choice as well.

Business leaders generally oppose single-payer coverage out of concern for costs and what the program would do to taxes and the federal budget. The American Medical Association, U.S. Chamber of Commerce, Health Insurance Association of America, and other interest groups representing health care providers oppose the single-payer system. Labor unions, some senior citizens' groups, and most consumer groups advocate this type of plan, in part because Medicare has been so successful in covering older Americans, albeit at a growing cost. If Medicare works for older Americans, or so the argument goes, perhaps it could work for younger Americans as well.

Prepaid health plans   Cost containment has been a frequent refrain of large corporations and consumer groups. In the 1970s and 1980s, business owners reduced benefits, increased payments by employees, and encouraged employees to join managed care plans called **health maintenance organizations (HMOs)**, in which individuals or their employees pay a set amount for each person covered each year in return for health care and hospital coverage. During the 1980s and 1990s, HMO enrollment increased fourfold, from fewer than 10 million in 1980 to more than 80 million Americans in 2006. Most HMOs guarantee access, but many do not guarantee that a patient can see the same physician.

Because there are no national standards of heath care quality, consumer groups are pressing HMOs to improve treatment of specific conditions and are urging Congress and the president to enter the battle.[31] HMOs counter that they provide adequate care at reasonable costs and that national standards would drive up costs. Consumers want the reduced costs associated with HMOs but do not like the limitations on choice of physicians and the right to sue health plans or the lack of coverage for some procedures.[32]

The quality of HMO care and limitations on patient choice remain controversial political issues. Both parties have endorsed competing variations of what they call a "patient's bill of rights." Such a bill of rights would permit a woman to see a gynecologist as her primary care physician, allow for review of the need for medical procedures, leave it to the doctor to determine the length of stay in the hospital, require coverage of emergency care a "prudent layperson" would deem necessary, and remove rules that deny doctors permission to talk to patients. George W. Bush called for granting HMO patients the right to appeal denials of care to an independent review panel, providing report cards on HMOs, giving women direct access to their obstetrician-gynecologist, and in some cases being able to sue HMOs. To date, HMOs have successfully resisted efforts to expand patient rights.

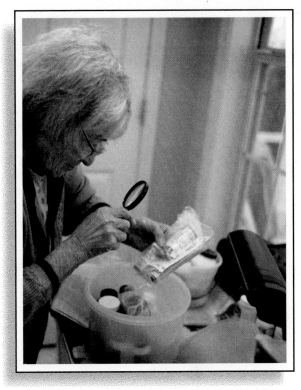

The cost of prescription drugs places a strain on senior citizens and underinsured wage earners.

health maintenance organization (HMO)
Alternative means of health care in which people or their employers are charged a set amount and the HMO provides health care and covers hospital costs.

Employer-mandated coverage   Currently more than 161 million Americans get some form of medical insurance from their employers.[33] But many small businesses contend that they cannot afford to provide this benefit and stay in business. Some have estimated that the costs of health care for small businesses may be 10 to 40 percent higher than for large businesses. In businesses with fewer than 25 employees, only about one-third of the workers receive coverage directly from their employer.[34] Mandating coverage does not solve this problem, nor does it take care of individuals who do not have jobs or who are self-employed.

Proponents counter that the negative consequences can be mitigated through tax credits and government subsidies. They also point out that if all small businesses provide health insurance, none of them will be put at a disadvantage compared with other small businesses. As noted, the federal government allows businesses to deduct what they pay in health benefits to employees as a business expense and gives tax credits to low-income families to purchase coverage for their children.

Spending caps   Because the cost of providing health care each year consumes a larger and larger share of our gross domestic product, some have proposed that the national government impose an overall expenditure cap on health care that applies not only to public expenditures but to private ones as well. Supporters of a cap include some prominent Democrats. The American Hospital Association, American Medical Association, and Pharmaceutical Manufacturers Association vigorously oppose the idea. They argue that spending caps would limit research and development in medicine and deter talented young people from pursuing medical careers. However, the costs associated with an aging population may yet lead to some form of spending caps and the health rationing that would clearly go with them.

Individual responsibility for coverage   Another reform proposal is to apply a free market approach to health care by abolishing *all* employer-provided benefits and encouraging individuals to buy health insurance on their own, in much the same way that individuals are responsible for purchasing their own automobile insurance. Those with low incomes, including people not now insured, would have tax credits or vouchers to assist in the purchase of insurance.

Advocates of such a market solution say that if individuals purchased their own insurance, they might pay more attention to costs and more closely monitor doctor and hospital fees. When higher wages are combined with tax credits, some individuals could end up with improved benefits tailored to their individual needs. Such a plan would also eliminate the need to impose price controls or pay for a large health care bureaucracy. It is unlikely, however, that employees would recover all they now spend on health care from their employers, so costs to individual consumers might increase. It is also unlikely that all uninsured persons who need government assistance could be taken care of without a tax increase to pay for it. Nevertheless, Massachusetts launched just such a plan in 2006. Although it is too early to tell whether the state can cover the full costs of the insurance, the program may set an important precedent that other states may follow.

Medical savings accounts   In 1996, Congress authorized an experiment with **medical savings accounts**. As of 2004, individuals may make tax-deductible contributions of roughly $2,600 a year ($5,150 for a family) to a special medical savings account that can be used to pay medical expenses not covered by insurance or government.[35] Withdrawals for other purposes are taxable and subject to an early withdrawal penalty.

Supporters of medical savings accounts say that they will eventually lower health care costs by giving people the incentive to spend their own money more carefully. They also allow people to go to a doctor of their own choosing without prior approval from their insurance company. Opponents of medical savings accounts say that they amount to nothing more than a tax break for the wealthy and the healthy. Because of high deductibles, people may decide not to seek needed services and preventive care. Opponents also argue that because healthier people are more likely to sign up for

medical savings account
Alternative means of health care in which individuals make tax-deductible contributions to a special account that can be used to pay medical expenses.

medical savings accounts, sicker people pay higher insurance premiums. Older and less wealthy people cannot afford to invest in medical savings accounts, critics charge, and will be forced to depend on more expensive insurance.

The Federal Role in Education

The federal government has been involved with education at least since the Northwest Ordinance of 1785, in which Congress set aside one section in each township for support of a public school. In 1862, the Morrill Land Grant Act provided grants of land to states for universities specializing in the mechanical or agricultural arts. The U.S. Office of Education was established in 1867 to oversee these programs, but the scope of federal involvement was modest by today's standards. Even the G.I. Bill, which helped provide a college education for approximately 20 million World War II veterans, was seen more as an employment program than an educational one.

During the cold war, however, education became one part of the national defense. When the Soviet Union launched *Sputnik*—the first man-made satellite to orbit the earth—in 1957, Congress responded in 1958 by passing the National Defense Education Act to upgrade science, language, and mathematics courses.

ELEMENTARY AND SECONDARY EDUCATION Kindergarten through high school education is generally seen as a state and local responsibility. Most children go to public schools run by local school boards and funded, at least partly, by property taxes. Because school districts vary greatly in the wealth of their residents, children from poor districts are much more likely to have lower-quality public schools than those from wealthier districts. As a result, public schools vary in the quality of teacher preparation, student performance, dropout rates, and educational opportunities provided to minority students.

Although the federal government has been reluctant to make direct investments in poor school districts, it has tried to help the children those districts serve. For example, in 1964, Congress created the Head Start program for preschool children. Under the program, needy children get help learning to read and understand numbers. Head Start centers also provide healthy meals and snacks and monitor child health care. Many also work with parents to encourage greater involvement and literacy.

Recent evaluations of the program suggest that Head Start increases learning, but they have also revealed a need for improvement. In 2006, Head Start provided funding to more than 20,000 child-care centers with almost 50,000 classrooms, some of which reported chronic shortages of well-trained teachers. In addition, the student–teacher ratio varied significantly across the centers. Moreover, the program is not an entitlement, meaning that funding only covers roughly a third of all eligible children. When the dollars run out, Head Start centers stop enrolling participants.

Head Start is not the federal government's only education program, however. In 1965, Congress passed the Elementary and Secondary Education Act (ESEA), which supplied educational materials for underprivileged public school students and provided funding for research on how to help children from disadvantaged backgrounds. Over the years, the act was amended to provide federal support for special education, as well as additional funding for textbooks, teacher training, and other support for poor schools. In 2006, the federal government contributed just 9 cents on the dollar of public school spending.

As concerns about the quality of public education increased during the 1990s, however, the federal government became more involved in local education, first by setting national goals for student achievement, then by passing the No Child Left Behind Act in 2001. In return for federal funding, states were required to annually test at least 95 percent of all third and eighth graders in reading and math. In addition, states were required to grade schools as passing or failing, set higher standards for teachers, and give students in failing schools the option to move to higher-performing schools. Schools must either improve test scores each year or risk being labeled "in

Agents of Change

Dave Levine, Mike Fenberg, and the Knowledge Is Power Program

QUESTIONS

How does KIPP increase the odds that other social programs will work?

How is knowledge a form of power?

The Knowledge Is Power Program (KIPP) was created in 1994 after Dave Levine and Mike Fenberg completed their two-year fellowships with Teach for America. Launched in a poor neighborhood of Houston, Texas, KIPP is designed to help schools improve student performance. KIPP currently runs its own schools in several cities and has launched a leadership academy that trains teachers to give young people a stronger leadership role in their schools. Funded in part by GAP, Inc., KIPP has expanded steadily over the past decade to train 400 teachers who serve over 9,000 students in 15 states.

Levine and Fenberg learned about the value of such training in Teach for America, but they have expanded their idea in collaboration with Stanford University, which is responsible for the teacher training. Levine learned firsthand about the need for better teaching in New York City, where he suffered from a learning disability. In turn, Fenberg describes himself as "the loudest introvert you'll ever meet," and draws inspiration from his mother, who is a psychotherapist working in alternative schools.

KIPP's leadership training focuses on how teachers can develop their students into future leaders. The effort involves four basic techniques: (1) students complete over two hours of homework each night, while teachers must be available on cell phone for assistance; (2) students, parents, and teachers make a commitment to excellence that confirms their commitment to the school and to each other toward achieving success; (3) rigorous college preparatory instruction is balanced with extracurricular activities like martial arts, music, chess, and sports; and (4) the school year culminates with academically oriented experiential field lessons to national parks, historically significant regions, and college campuses. ■

Read more about KIPP at www.kippschools.org.

KIPP helps students in poor communities improve their performance in school.

need of improvement." Under the act, all students are supposed to be proficient in reading and math by 2014.

Although the new law set higher standards, it increased federal spending for education by only a tiny percentage. By 2006, many states were complaining that they did not have enough funding to test every student every year, nor enough to meet the law's requirement for teacher training and certification. In addition, schools with many disabled or special-needs-type students were being unfairly categorized as "failing" because they could not meet the test-score requirement.

Americans ask more of their schools than just to educate their children. Schools have become one-stop social policy centers and are now a major means by which basic nutrition is provided to millions of poor children. Schools screen at-risk children and attempt to get them medical and psychological assistance; they seek to socialize students into acceptable behaviors, often in the face of increasing violence in the surrounding neighborhoods; and they often reach out to families to provide basic help in parenting.

HIGHER EDUCATION The federal government also provides help to colleges and universities. In 2006, the federal government provided roughly 70 percent, or more

The Changing Face of American Politics

Access to College

	1996-97	2002-03
Associate Degrees		
Men	51.8%	40.0%
Women	48.2	60.0
White	84.5	66.0
African-American	8.2	11.4
Hispanic	4.1	10.0
Asian/Pacific Islander	1.7	4.9
American Indian/Alaska Native	0.6	1.1
Nonresident alien	0.8	2.1
Bachelor's Degrees		
Men	53.8%	42.5%
Women	46.2	57.5
White	88.0	70.0
African-American	6.4	8.7
Hispanic	2.0	6.3
Asian/Pacific Islander	1.5	6.2
American Indian/Alaska Native	0.4	0.7
Nonresident alien	1.7	3.2

SOURCE: U.S. Department of Education, National Center for Education Statistics, *Postsecondary Institutions in the United States: Fall 2003 and Degrees and Other Awards Conferred: 2002–03* (Washington, D.C., 2006), accessed at nces.ed.gov/fastfacts.

Federal aid to education has increased access to college for all Americans, but it has had a particularly significant effect on women and students of color. The effect has been pronounced at both the community college and four-year college levels, where women now earn the majority of associate and bachelor degrees, and where students of color have more than doubled over the decades. Under the 1998 Higher Education Act, the number of students of color should increase even faster as the federal government puts more dollars into preparing students for college.

Although two-year and four-year colleges have both seen an increase in women and minority enrollment, the growth has been fastest at two-year colleges, which tend to have lower tuition. Two-year colleges are increasingly the destination of choice for many students who are unable to afford four-year colleges, or who start at two-year colleges to save money, then transfer to four-year colleges. Wherever they go, however, women and minorities have made significant advances in enrollment since the 1960s, with women now occupying more than half of the seats in college at both levels. ∎

than $25 billion, of the financial aid that college students receive. Pell grants for low-income students and low-interest guaranteed student loans continue to be the most available and most used subsidies for college expenses. In 1998, Congress added three new programs to improve the odds that needy children will make it to college: (1) GEAR-UP, which supports early interventions to help students complete high school; (2) the Learning Anytime Anywhere Partnerships (LAAP), which provide federal funding for distance learning through the Internet; and (3) a new initiative designed to improve teacher quality in primary and elementary schools. Although the three programs account for less than 1 percent of federal spending for education, they acknowledge the link between the quality of primary and elementary education and college success, as well as the need to act early to increase the odds of success for needy students.

The Federal Role in Crime Control

Controlling crime is also considered primarily a state and local matter. The federal government usually acts more as a banker than a police officer, providing grants to states and local governments to hire their own police officers, build more prisons, improve drug enforcement, and prosecute organized crime.

Crime is hardly unimportant to national politics, however. The federal government must enforce its own laws against everything from counterfeiting to pollution while protecting its borders and preventing drugs from flowing into the country.

Congress has intervened on such matters as gun control. Because guns are manufactured and transported across state lines, Congress has the power to regulate sales under the Constitution's commerce clause and has used it to ban the sale and ownership of semiautomatic weapons and assault rifles and set age minimums for the purchase of handguns (21 years of age) and long guns such as rifles and shotguns (18 years of age).

In 1993, for example, Congress passed landmark legislation imposing a waiting period on the purchase of handguns. Under the Brady Handgun Violence Prevention Act, federally licensed firearms dealers have five days to check with local law enforcement officials regarding the background of a potential purchaser. If local law enforcement officials fail to respond within five business days, the handgun can be sold. The National Rifle Association has been powerful enough to stop most other antigun legislation, even though such legislation has had the support of most police chiefs and most of the general public. The debate over gun control at the local, state, and national levels remains intense.

In 1994, Congress passed an omnibus anticrime bill that authorized more than $30 billion in spending on federal crime initiatives. The money funded the hiring of as many as 100,000 new police officers and the construction of new prisons and "boot camps" for juvenile offenders. The bill also added new assault rifle restrictions, made a long list of federal offenses punishable by death, imposed federal penalties and programs aimed at curbing domestic violence, and, with its "three strikes and you're out" provision, mandated life imprisonment upon conviction for a third violent felony. This "three strikes" provision exists at both the federal level and in many states.

The federal government enforces its laws primarily through the Department of Justice, which contains the Federal Bureau of Investigation (FBI). The FBI was created in 1908 and charged with gathering and reporting evidence in matters relating to federal criminal laws. In addition, the FBI provides investigative services on a cooperative basis to local law enforcement in fingerprint identification and laboratory services, and has new responsibilities in the war on terrorism. Other law enforcement agencies of the federal government include the Drug Enforcement Agency (DEA), which is responsible for preventing the flow of illegal narcotics and other illegal drugs into the United States, patrolling U.S. borders, and conducting joint operations with countries where drugs are produced, and the Bureau of Alcohol, Tobacco and Firearms, which monitors the sale of destructive weapons and guns inside the United States, regulates alcoholic beverage production, and oversees the collection of taxes on alcohol and tobacco.

Although the number of violent crimes decreased through the 1990s, it began rising in 2001, reinforcing the widespread perception that crime and violence are increasing and the federal government needs to step in. As a result, Congress has made more and more crimes federal ones and increased the severity of punishments for them. As more people are put in prisons, the cost of keeping them in prison has increased dramatically.

Terrorism is clearly the federal government's top crime priority today. Only weeks after the September 11, 2001, terrorist attacks on New York City and Washington, D.C., Congress passed a massive antiterrorism law, and it created the new Department of Homeland Security the following summer. For his part, the president created the Office of Homeland Security within the White House in October 2001 and ordered a complete reorganization of the Federal Bureau of Investigation in early 2002 to create a stronger focus on preventing terrorism.

Two years later, Congress created an entirely new department to police U.S. borders. The new Department of Homeland Security merged 22 agencies and 180,000 federal employees. Although the nation is no doubt safer as a result, if only because the 22 agencies did not cooperate well with each other before the merger, the department has been criticized as too large to move quickly against terrorist threats. It failed to react quickly to Hurricane Katrina in August and September 2005, for example, and has yet to implement new policies to police cargo containers that enter U.S. ports. These containers are seen as a major threat because they can be used to hide a potential biological, chemical, or nuclear weapon.

Under the USA PATRIOT Act of 2001 (the letters stand for Uniting and Strengthening America by Providing Appropriate Tools Required to Intercept and Obstruct Terrorism), the federal government was given sweeping authority to conduct secret investigations of suspected terrorists, use "roving wiretaps" to intercept conversations on any phones that a suspect might use, and detain any noncitizens believed to be a national security risk for up to seven days without being charged with a crime. Although the USA PATRIOT Act expired on December 31, 2005, the Bush administration made its renewal a centerpiece of the president's 2004 State of the Union Address. "Key provisions of the Patriot Act are set to expire next year," the president told Congress. "The terrorist threat will not expire on that schedule. Our law enforcement needs this vital legislation to protect our citizens." The administration also asked Congress to expand the government's authority to investigate what it called "lone-wolf" terrorists who are not affiliated with a foreign government or known terrorist organization such as Al-Qaeda, which planned the September 11 attacks. The act was finally reauthorized in February 2006.[36]

"Key provisions of the Patriot Act are set to expire next year. The terrorist threat will not expire on that schedule."

**PRESIDENT GEORGE W. BUSH,
2004 STATE OF THE UNION ADDRESS**

The Politics of Social Policy

Despite the nation's current focus on terrorism and homeland security, social policy still dominates the agenda of American politics. Welfare, health care, education, and crime—and their costs—are today's political battleground between the parties and between contending interest groups. Education reform was at the forefront of the 2000 presidential election, the war on terrorism was part of the 2004 campaign, and problems implementing the prescription drug bill became an issue in the 2006 midterm elections.

The nation long ago answered questions about whether the national government has a role in providing decent housing, adequate health care, and a solid education for all of its citizens. The question is not whether the nation will provide a safety net for its needy citizens, but how strong the net will be and who will be responsible for providing it. Although the vast majority of Americans support Social Security and Medicare, for example, they are sharply divided over how much the nation should do for its poorest citizens. They are also increasingly divided about reforms such as the No Child Left Behind Act and its mandatory testing, which have prompted some states to sue the federal government to recover some of the costs of implementing the unfunded mandate portions of the act.

Nevertheless, social policy will be part of the federal agenda far into the future. Although presidents and Congress cannot always know what Americans will support and how much they are willing to pay, they can be sure that most Americans want government to take care of citizens who are needy through no fault of their own.

Summary

1. Conservatives advocate private solutions for most social problems, while liberals argue that it is the responsibility of government to provide a minimum standard of living—including a job, an education, health care, housing, and nutrition—for all citizens. Since the New Deal, some national government involvement in social programs has been widely accepted, although the extent of involvement has waxed and waned. Conservatives generally prefer state and local government action over federal programs.

2. Social Security, inaugurated in 1935 as part of the New Deal, is perhaps the most significant social legislation in U.S. history. Through a system of employee and employer taxes, retired workers and disabled individuals receive monthly payments and health benefits. With the country's aging population, strains on the system are likely to increase.

3. Welfare takes many forms, including direct payments to the poor, the

unemployed, and the disabled; food stamps; job training; housing subsidies; free school lunches; tax credits; and subsidized medical care. Public assistance programs began with the New Deal and have grown ever since.

4. Welfare has long been criticized as discouraging work, and many proposals have been put forward to make programs more effective and efficient. The most recent welfare reform, which became law in August 1996, transferred the administrative burden to the states, giving them more discretion over recipients and benefits while helping to fund welfare programs through block grants of federal money.

5. The federal government supports medical research and has increased its role in health care cost control and access as the country's mostly private health care system is beset by rising costs, increasing numbers of uninsured Americans, unnecessary procedures, endless paperwork, high litigation costs, avoidable illnesses, and limited access. A variety of proposals for reform are under consideration, including a single-payer system, prepaid health plans, employer-mandated coverage, spending caps, individual responsibility for coverage, and medical savings accounts.

6. Education continues to be primarily a state and local government function in the United States. The federal government plays an important role in funding public schools and pushing national goals for better education, and is also heavily involved in helping finance college and university education.

7. Crime control has been part of the national agenda for decades, especially related to drugs, but has become much more visible as part of the war on terrorism.

Further Reading

ANNE MARIE CAMMISA, *From Rhetoric to Reform? Welfare Policy in American Politics* (Westview Press, 1998).

BARBARA EHRENREICH, *Nickle and Dimed: On (Not) Getting By in America* (Metropolitan Books, 2001).

FRANK FISCHER, *Evaluating Public Policy* (Nelson-Hall, 1995).

LAURENE A. GRAIG, *Health of Nations: An International Perspective on U.S. Health Care Reform* (CQ Press, 1993).

CHRISTOPHER JENCKS, *The Homeless* (Harvard University Press, 1994).

PAUL C. LIGHT, *Still Artful Work: The Continuing Politics of Social Security Reform* (McGraw-Hill, 1995).

THOMAS E. MANN AND **NORMAN J. ORNSTEIN,** EDS., *Intensive Care: How Congress Shapes Health Policy* (Brookings Institution Press, 1995).

DANIEL PATRICK MOYNIHAN, *Miles to Go: A Personal History of Social Policy* (Harvard University Press, 1996).

CHARLES MURRAY, *Losing Ground: American Social Policy, 1950–80* (Basic Books, 1984).

B. GUY PETERS, *American Public Policy: Promise and Performance*, 4th ed. (Chatham House, 1996).

PAUL E. PETERSON AND **MARTIN R. WEST,** EDS., *No Child Left Behind: The Politics and Practice of School Accountability* (Brookings Institution Press, 2004).

FRANCES FOX PIVEN AND **RICHARD A. CLOWARD,** *Regulating the Poor: The Functions of Public Welfare* (Vintage, 1993).

THEDA SKOCPOL, *Social Policy in the United States: Future Possibilities in Historical Perspective* (Princeton University Press, 1995).

R. KENT WEAVER, *Ending Welfare as We Know It* (Brookings Institution Press, 2001).

MARGARET WEIR, ED., *The Social Divide: Political Parties and the Future of Activist Government* (Brookings Institution Press, 1998).

BOB WOODWARD, *Agenda: Inside the Clinton White House* (Simon & Schuster, 1994).

Make It Real

SOCIAL POLICY

In this unit, students consider immigration policy options.

Chapter 20

Making Foreign and Defense Policy

⭐

THE UNITED STATES HAD THREE GOALS WHEN IT INVADED IRAQ IN 2003. FIRST, IT WANTED TO REMOVE IRAQ'S BRUTAL DICTATOR, SADDAM HUSSEIN, FROM OFFICE, AND REPLACE HIM WITH AN ELECTED PRESIDENT. SECOND, IT WANTED TO FIND AND DESTROY IRAQ'S CAPABILITY TO MANUFACTURE AND USE BIOLOGICAL, CHEMICAL, AND NUCLEAR WEAPONS, WHICH ARE OFTEN REFERRED TO AS WEAPONS OF MASS DESTRUCTION. AND THIRD, IT WANTED TO CONVERT IRAQ INTO ONE OF THE MIDDLE EAST'S FEW DEMOCRACIES IN THE hope that the idea would spread across a region that supplies most of the world's oil.

The U.S. clearly succeeded in its first goal. Hussein's army was crushed only days after the war began. Later Hussein himself was captured, and then stood trial for crimes against the Iraqi people. However, the United States never found the alleged weapons that created so much concern about Hussein, nor any labs for making them, and democracy in Iraq is still a hope, not a reality.

Indeed, more than three years after the war began, Iraq's young democracy is still threatened by intense divisions between a Shiite Arab majority of 60 percent, a Sunni Arab minority of between 15 and 20 percent, and the independence-minded Kurdish minority of roughly 20 percent. Although Iraqis had approved a new constitution and elected their first democratic parliament by December 2005, the election occurred in the midst of growing violence against U.S. troops and among ethnic groups.

The parliamentary election had followed overwhelming ratification of the Iraqi constitution in a first election only a year earlier. Although turnout in the two elections was high, both were marked by threats of violence. Throughout the first three years of the war, much of that violence had been directed against U.S. forces, which suffered high casualties from roadside bombs and suicide attacks.

By 2006, however, much of the violence had shifted to battles between the Sunnis and Shiites. On February 22, 2006, for example, a sacred Shiite shrine in the holy city of Samara was bombed by what were believed to be Sunni forces, leaving 200 dead and sparking counter-attacks against Sunnis in Iraq's capital

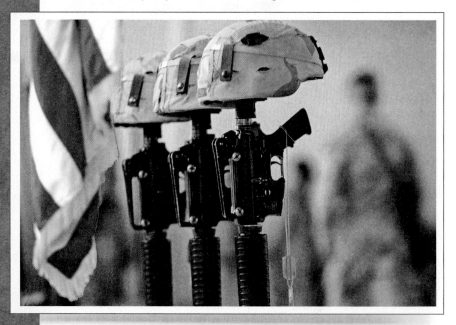

"*[Power is] the ability to influence others to get them to do what you want.*"

HARVARD PROFESSOR JOSEPH NYE

577

The U.S. war against Iraq began on March 20, 2003, with a bombing campaign designed to produce "shock and awe" within Iraq and thereby assure the collapse of military resistance.

city of Baghdad. In early March, three car bombings in a Shiite-controlled neighborhood in Baghdad set off another round of counterattacks against Sunni targets. Reprisal attacks continued into the spring and summer, weakening efforts to prevent a civil war.

The conflict between the Shiites and Sunnis dates back well before the U.S.-led invasion in 2003, and reflects the repeated abuse of both the Shiites and Kurds by Hussein. With the Kurds geographically isolated and well armed to defend their lands to the north, the future of Iraq depended on cooperation between the Shiites and Sunnis. But faced with a choice between civil war and democracy, Iraqis were torn between the need to work together to rebuild their war-torn nation, and the desire to avenge the past and protect their power.

The rising tide of violence shows just how difficult it is to build a democracy from scratch, especially one that starts with a war led from the outside. Although Hussein almost certainly would still be in power if the United States had not invaded Iraq, the lack of a democratic tradition, a fragile sense of common nationhood, and centuries-old violence between Iraqi's religious traditions may yet force the nation to divide into a bloody battle over the future of the nation.

Experts have argued that the United States simply does not have enough troops in Iraq to enforce the peace needed to support a young democracy. Unlike the United States, which moved toward its own democracy after it rose up against the British, the Iraqi people have long been divided between the oppressed and the oppressors.

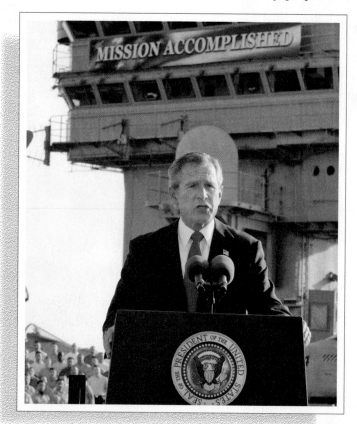

President Bush on the deck of the USS Abraham Lincoln on May 1, 2003, declares an end to major combat operations in Iraq. Since that time, thousands of injuries and deaths have occurred on both sides of the conflict.

Merely removing Hussein and his army from power may not be enough to create the conditions for a young democracy to flourish, especially when Shiite and Sunni militants alike have access to all the weapons they need to fight. Nevertheless, Iraq's president finally broke a stalemate between the Shiites and Sunnis in late April 2006, by appointing a Shiite to form a new government. Only time will tell whether the decision will heal the strife, but it was an important step toward democracy.

Democracy cannot flourish in the midst of civil violence, however, which appears to be increasing to dangerously high levels. September 2006 was the third bloodiest month on record for U.S. casualties in the war, and the Iraqi Army remains relatively small and under-trained. Despite promises to reduce the number of U.S. troops in Iraq by the end of 2006, military commanders decided that the level of violence was too high to do so. The troops are spread thinly across the country, trying to restore a level of calm, as battles between religious radicals have escalated and the cost of the war has soared. Back in the U.S., Iraq became a central issue in the 2006 election as Democrats took the position that the U.S. should withdraw.

This chapter will ask how choices are made in planning and executing foreign policy, such as the effort to create democracy in Iraq. We will first examine key debates in making foreign and defense policy, look at basic terms and concepts of foreign and defense policy, and examine some of today's greatest foreign policy challenges, such as the war in Iraq. Then we will turn to a discussion of the key actors in making U.S. foreign policy and appraise the range of tools the United States uses to accomplish its international goals. The chapter concludes with a more detailed assessment of defense policy.

Understanding Foreign and Defense Policy

In the broadest sense, the primary goal of U.S. foreign and defense policy is to protect the nation from harm. As George Washington argued in his 1797 farewell address to the nation, the U.S. should keep itself as separate from the rest of the world as possible:

The great rule of conduct for us in regard to foreign nations is, in extending our commercials relations, to have with them as little *political connection* as possible. . . . Trust to temporary alliances for extraordinary emergencies, steer clear of permanent alliances with any portion of the foreign world. . . . Such an attraction of a small or weak nation toward a great and powerful nation dooms the former to be the satellite of the latter.[1]

More than 200 years later, the United States does not have the luxury of avoiding the rest of the world. As one of the world's great superpowers, it has accepted a range of obligations, including promoting democracy abroad in nations such as Iraq, providing help to victims of disaster such as the 2005 Asian tsunami, promoting greater economic ties across all nations, and steering the world away from the use of weapons of mass destruction, which many nations now possess. It has also become one of the world's great advocates of freedom. (Figure 20–1 shows the map of freedom in 2005.)

Although the United States supports greater freedom in the world, it has long been divided about its own role in international affairs. Some Americans believe the United States should defend itself against its enemies, but remain isolated from the rest of the world; others believe it should always remain realistic about the basic motives of other nations, while others promote a more hopeful vision of a peaceful world; still others believe that the United States should use its substantial military strength to force other nations to support its positions, while others argue that it should use its own history of civil liberties and rights to lead the world through example.

In general, these debates start with basic questions about how the United States views the world, how it should respond to threats from other nations, and how it should use its substantial military and diplomatic power. Each of these issues will be discussed below.

How the United States Views the World

Historically, U.S. foreign and defense policy has been built on two very different views of the world. The first view involves **realism**, which reflects a belief that other nations are interested first and foremost in their own advancement, whether economic, political, or social. Realists believe that other nations are primarily concerned with strengthening their own power.

For the most part, realists were in charge of policy during the 40-year cold war between the United States and the Soviet Union, which involved great tension—but no actual war—between the two superpowers. Realists viewed the Soviet Union as a formidable enemy that was committed to the ultimate destruction of the United States

realism
A theory of international relations that focuses on the tendency of nations to operate from self-interest.

Map of Freedom 2005

Map Legend ■ Free ■ Partly Free ■ Not Free

FIGURE 20–1 **The Map of Freedom, 2005.**

and its freedom. They saw the world through the lens of *domino theory*: every nation that fell to the Soviet Union was part of a chain of countries that would eventually fall, too. Thus, the United States fought the Korean War and the Vietnam War to prevent the spread of Soviet power to other nations in Asia.

Critics of realism argue that the world is composed of nations that seek cooperation and stability, not power. This view involves **idealism**, a belief that nations can work together to solve common problems such as global hunger and poverty, with peace, not war, as the ultimate aim. Idealists view national power as a tool for good, not merely as a way to amass more military and economic resources. They also view national power as a force for promoting democracy in other nations.

Although these two terms are often used to represent two competing views of the world, they can be used as part of a broader, more integrated foreign and defense policy. Thus, the United States could be realistic about the need to remove Saddam Hussein from power, yet still believe that democracy could take hold in a nation with little history of free elections and civil rights and liberties. As President Bush often argued in the months leading to the war in Iraq, the United States had to be realistic about Iraq's interest in building biological, chemical, and nuclear weapons, even as he also argued that democracy would lead those nations toward international cooperation and peace.

At least in retrospect, Bush's view of the world turned out to be more idealistic than realistic. Much as he believed that Iraq constituted a clear threat to the United States, he moved ahead with the war believing that the Iraqi people would embrace a free Iraq without resorting to violence against each other. His idealism about the future of Iraq clearly affected his willingness to go to war.

Responding to the World

Whether based on realism or idealism, American foreign policy has reflected very different views of how it should respond to the rest of the world. Some Americans back an approach based on **isolationism**, which is a belief that the United States should stay out of international affairs unless other nations constitute a direct threat to its existence. The term was first used during the years leading to World War I, when many Americans believed that the United States should stay out of the global conflict.

But isolationism is still alive and well in the debate about whether the United States should remain in Iraq. Isolationists argue that the United States should follow George Washington's advice to avoid international "entanglements," lest those entanglements lead the United States into wars that either cannot be won or have a high cost in U.S. lives. They also argue that the United States should always focus first on its own interests by staying away from other nations.

Other Americans, including most foreign and defense policy experts, believe in **internationalism**, which reflects a belief that the United States must be involved in international affairs if it is to protect its own interests. Realists and idealists can disagree on the goals of U.S. foreign and defense policy, but they can still agree that the United States should engage the world on economic, political, and social issues such as human rights for oppressed people, global hunger, or the war on terrorism. Internationalists tend to view themselves as citizens of the world, not just as citizens of the United States. As citizens of the world, they feel that there are times when the United States should intervene, even when it is not directly threatened by another nation.

Internationalists have two very different views about how the United States should respond to international issues, however. Supporters of **unilateralism** believe that the United States has the right to act alone in response to threats, even if other nations are unwilling to help. Like many isolationists, they look back to George Washington's farewell address for inspiration. But unlike isolationists, they interpret Washington's words as a warning that the United States must protect itself regardless of what other nations think. They argue that the United States should never give other nations (or the

idealism
A theory of international relations that focuses on the hope that nations will act together to solve international problems and promote peace.

isolationism
The desire to avoid international engagement altogether.

internationalism
The belief that nations must engage in international problem solving.

unilateralism
A philosophy that encourages individual nations to act on their own when facing threats from other nations.

United Nations) a veto over its actions, even if that means it acts alone in using its great military power. President Bush sought help from other nations in the Iraq war. He eventually convinced Britain, Italy, and Spain to send troops, but not France, Germany, and Turkey. Despite this support, most of the troops that engaged in combat were American, which made the war unilateral in reality.

In fact, President Bush even announced a new unilateral policy immediately after the September 11, 2001, terrorist attacks on New York City and Washington. Under the **Bush Doctrine**, any nation that threatens the United States is automatically a potential target for unilateral action. The Bush Doctrine led immediately to the war in Afghanistan, the country that had harbored Osama bin Laden and his terrorist organization, Al-Qaeda, as they planned the September 11, 2001, attacks. As in Iraq, the United States has attempted to introduce democracy in a country long dominated by a radical religious group, in this case the Taliban. Also as in Iraq, Afghanistan held successful democratic elections after the Taliban was forced from power, but it remains deeply divided and may yet collapse into civil war. The United States also continues to maintain a military presence in the country, which may need to continue for years, if not decades.

The Bush Doctrine is built around four basic concepts that the president announced in the weeks and months following September 11, 2001. First, Bush declared that the United States would attack any nation that either harbored terrorists or constituted a serious threat to the United States. In the past, the United States had only gone to war after another nation had issued a direct challenge to the nation. But under the Bush doctrine, the United States can go to war when another nation constitutes a threat, even if that nation has yet to attack.

Second, Bush announced that the United States would act unilaterally against other nations even if it did not have the support of all or even some of its allies. In the past, the United States had usually sought help from other nations in fights against its enemies. Under the Bush Doctrine, the United States was prepared to act alone.

Third, Bush warned the world that the United States would use massive force against its enemies. Unlike the Korean and Vietnam wars, which were both fought to stalemates in part because the United States pledged not to use nuclear weapons or bomb certain cities, Bush promised that the United States would use every means at its disposal to win future wars. As he noted in April 2006 regarding Iran's development of nuclear weapons, no options are off the table when another nation becomes a threat.

Finally, Bush promised that the United States would actively promote democracy and freedom across the world. Although this commitment to freedom existed before September 11, 2001, Bush returned to the theme repeatedly as the war in Iraq lingered on.

Opponents of the Bush Doctrine support **multilateralism**, which is a belief that the United States should only act with the active support of other nations. According to its advocates, multilateralism not only increases the odds that the United States will share the burdens of war with its allies, it also increases the potential that other nations will support the U.S. position once a war is over. Three years after announcing the Bush Doctrine, the Bush administration itself began backing away from the policy. Faced with mounting costs of rebuilding Iraq and reducing international tension with other Middle Eastern nations, the Bush administration began working to bring other nations such as Russia, France, and Germany into the debate.

The Use of Power

Internationalists have different views of just how the United States should influence other nations. Some favor the use of **hard power**, which is a term used to describe military and economic strength, while others favor the use of **soft power**, which involves negotiation and diplomacy. Hard power depends almost entirely on a nation's ability to threaten or force another nation to act a certain way to avoid an attack. Thus, the Bush administration initially threatened Iraq with war if Hussein did not allow international

Bush Doctrine
A policy adopted by the Bush administration in 2001 that asserts America's right to attack any nation that has weapons of mass destruction that might be used against U.S. interests at home or abroad.

multilateralism
A philosophy that encourages individual nations to act together to solve international problems.

hard power
The reliance on economic and military strength to solve international problems.

soft power
The reliance on diplomacy and negotiation to solve international problems.

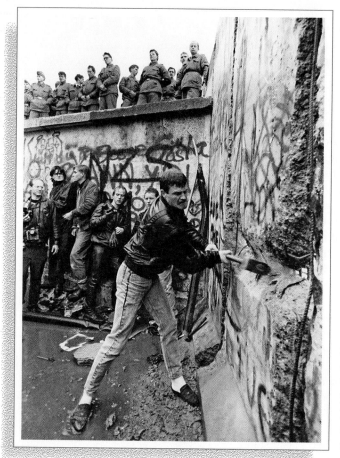

Built in 1961, the Berlin Wall separating East and West Berlin was a longtime symbol of the division between communism and democracy. Economic hard times in 1989 led to a wave of refugees fleeing East Germany, which eventually forced the government there to relax exit restrictions. The fall of the Berlin Wall became symbolic of the fall of the communist Soviet Union that followed.

weapons inspectors to prove that Iraq did not possess either weapons of mass destruction or the means to produce them. Although Hussein did allow international inspectors to look for such weapons and factories, the United States argued that he was still resisting full inspections and used hard power to remove him from office.

Hard power is often associated with the **theory of deterrence**, which was most visible during the cold war between the United States and Soviet Union. Under this theory, a nation creates enough military strength to assure a massive response to any attack. The term is often associated with nuclear weapons, which cause massive destruction. During the cold war, the United States maintained more than enough nuclear weapons to deter the Soviet Union from using its nuclear weapons first. The United States argued that enough of its weapons would survive any Soviet attack to assure the destruction of the Soviet Union. This notion of *mutual assured destruction*, sometimes called MAD, was enough to keep both nations from using their nuclear weapons, but it kept both nations on constant alert just in case the other dared to act first.

Soft power is based on a nation's international reputation and more traditional diplomacy, which is discussed later in this chapter as a tool of foreign policy. The term was first used by Harvard University professor Joseph Nye, who defined power as "the ability to influence others to get them to do what you want." According to Nye, there are three tools for exercising power. One is to threaten other countries with hard power, a second is to pay them with carrots such as foreign aid, and a third is to attract them to a position based on negotiation and diplomacy. Soft power is often more persuasive if it is supported by hard power, but it is much less costly, especially if a nation wants to maintain a reputation for international cooperation on other, nonmilitary issues.[2]

Foreign and Defense Policy Priorities

Balancing political, economic, and social values is critical in setting foreign and defense priorities. Although U.S. policy leaders do not always agree on how much the United States should do in each area, the current foreign and defense policy agenda generally focuses on seven major issues: (1) controlling the spread of weapons of mass destruction, (2) winning the war on terrorism, (3) securing lasting peace in the Middle East, (4) promoting free trade abroad, (5) addressing global climate change, (6) promoting democracy and international understanding, and (7) winning the war in Iraq.

Controlling Weapons of Mass Destruction

The international community has been working for decades to reduce the threat of biological, chemical, and nuclear weapons, which are often called **weapons of mass destruction**. Although the world is particularly concerned about the development of such weapons in North Korea and Iran, the effort to reduce the spread of nuclear weapons actually started with nuclear disarmament talks between the United States and the Soviet Union in the 1970s. With the cold war over in 1989, the United States and Russia began to look for new ways of reducing their nuclear arsenals and agreed in 2002 to reduce the number of nuclear warheads dramatically.

The world is still threatened by biological, chemical, and nuclear weapons, however. Although chemical weapons were outlawed by international agreement after

theory of deterrence
A theory that is based on creating enough military strength to convince other nations not to attack first.

weapons of mass destruction
Biological, chemical, or nuclear weapons that can cause a massive number of deaths in a single use.

World War I, at least nine countries have declared that they have developed chemical weapons, such as nerve gases, that kill on contact. Others continue to develop biological weapons that spread disease or poisons, and still others already have or intend to develop nuclear weapons.

The United States has been particularly concerned in recent years about Iran's effort to develop nuclear weapons, which the United States and many other nations believe might be used against Israel. In April 2006, for example, Iran declared its intent to continue building its nuclear power program, which has the potential to generate the uranium used in nuclear weapons.

At the same time, the United States made an agreement with India to support its peaceful nuclear power program, even though the program could also produce the uranium needed for a nuclear weapon. Nuclear power has been used by many nations across the world, but the nuclear materials can be converted into a weapons program with relative ease. Although India promised the United States that it would only use the program to generate electricity for its rapidly growing economy, the agreement may have undermined the U.S. case against Iran's nuclear program, which Iran said would only be used for peaceful means.

Winning the War on Terrorism

The war on terrorism is a broad term used to describe efforts to control terrorist acts sponsored by other nations, such as Afghanistan, or acts undertaken by independent groups that operate without any connection to a government.

Although the war is most often associated with Osama bin Laden and Al-Qaeda, there are dozens of other terrorist organizations. These other terrorist groups have executed bombings in London, Madrid, Moscow, the Middle East, and throughout Southeast Asia, including Thailand, Malaysia, the Philippines, and Indonesia, where terrorists have carried out several bombings at or near popular tourist hotels. For example, in October 2005, terrorists exploded several bombs near Bali's Four Seasons Hotel, killing more than 20 people, including six U.S. citizens.

Nevertheless, the United States has generally treated international terrorists as if they are part of Al-Qaeda. President Bush claimed that Iraq was harboring Al-Qaeda terrorists before the war began, for example, even though experts could find no evidence of connection. Bush has also linked many other groups to Al-Qaeda, again in spite of evidence that they operate on their own.

The war on terrorism is often associated with radical Islamic religious groups that are committed to a global Jihad, which is actually a term that covers everything from the personal struggle to attain perfect faith to a violent struggle to protect or expand Islam. Even though most followers of Islam are peace-loving, Islamic terrorist groups have used a range of violent means to advance their strategy, which has prompted a backlash against Islam across the world.[3]

Osama bin Laden became America's public enemy number one after his Al-Qaeda organization took credit for destroying the World Trade Center on 9/11.

Beyond direct efforts to bring terrorist leaders to justice, the U.S. war against terrorism has concentrated on three broad goals. First, the United States has destroyed many of the camps where terrorists train for attacks. Second, the United States has tried to prevent the funding of terrorist operations, in part by policing U.S. charities that might provide money for the purchase of weapons and other supplies. Finally, the United States often collects intelligence about terrorist movements that might

President Bush addresses the General Assembly at the United Nations on September 12, 2002, seeking approval for military action against Iraq. The U.N. Security Council ultimately did not grant its approval and in 2004, U.N. Secretary General Kofi Annan (left) charged that the U.S. war against Iraq was in violation of international law because it did not have the backing of the U.N. Security Council.

normal trade relations
Trade status granted as part of an international trade policy that gives a nation the same favorable trade concessions and tariffs that the best trading partners receive.

threaten its citizens both at home and abroad. In late 2005, the *New York Times* reported that part of this intelligence effort had involved a secret domestic eavesdropping program that focused on potential terrorists inside the United States.

Although these efforts have weakened terrorist organizations such as Al-Qaeda, terrorist groups have proved difficult to locate. Moreover, they tend to operate through highly secretive networks that are difficult to destroy. Immediately after September 11, 2001, Bush promised to capture bin Laden "dead or alive." Five years later, bin Laden was presumed to be alive and hiding in the remote mountains between Afghanistan and Pakistan, and Bush declared that he was no longer as concerned about capturing him.

Securing Lasting Peace in the Middle East

Long before the war on terrorism began, the United States was working to secure peace between Israel and its neighbors, in part because the Middle East is such an important source of the world's oil, and in part because the United States has long considered Israel an important ally. However, despite decades of U.S. effort to promote peace in the region, the Middle East remains locked in a violent struggle over Israel's right to exist. Although the region has made some progress toward peace, much of this progress has been threatened by ongoing conflict with Arab nations and terrorist groups that continue to deny Israel's right to exist.

In 2002, however, the United States, Israel, and most Arab nations embraced what is now known as "The Road Map to Peace." Under this agreement, which was formally signed in April 2003, Israel and its adversaries agreed to two broad steps toward eventual peace. For its part, the Palestinian Authority, which represents citizens in territories captured by Israel in past wars, agreed to arrest, disrupt, and restrain individuals and groups that plan and conduct violent attacks on Israel. Israel in turn agreed to start dismantling settlements of Israeli citizens in the occupied territories to its south and east. Israel honored its part of the agreement starting in 2005 by dismantling all settlements, thereby turning over complete control of the territories to the Palestinian Authority.

Although the Palestinian Authority initially agreed to try to stop violence against Israel, it has yet to acknowledge Israel's right to exist. Moreover, in 2006, the Palestinian people gave a majority of seats in their new parliament to members of Hamas, a political party that had long waged war against Israel. Although there has been strong international pressure on Hamas to renounce violence, its leaders continue to support violence against Israel even though other nations have threatened to cut international aid unless Hamas changes its view.

Promoting International Trade

As the world economy has grown, so has international competition with the United States. The United States has generally responded to this *globalization* with a basic policy of free trade, meaning a commitment to the free movement of goods across international borders. It does not allow the unrestricted export of technologies that can be used to build nuclear weapons, however, and has long protected certain defense industries that would be essential should it ever be forced into another world war. It has also used trade as a tool to promote human rights and democratic reform. Nevertheless, as noted above, the United States recently relaxed its policies on the export of nuclear materials to improve relations with India.

The United States has pursued a mix of goals in the battle over free trade with China. On the one hand, China has a long history of violating basic human and democratic rights. On the other hand, China has one of the fastest-growing economies in the world. U.S. exports to China have tripled over the past decade, and imports from China have grown rapidly. This balancing effort caused great controversy when the Clinton administration asked Congress to grant **normal trade relations** status to China. Under

Young boys wave the flag of Hamas outside a polling station in Gaza City while Palestinians held their first parliamentary election in a decade in 2006. Victory in the election for the radical Islamic faction led to western governments distancing themselves from the Palestinians. Later in the year, President Mahmoud Abbas called for a new election in an effort to regain international support.

normal trade relations, China would be given the same favorable trading terms, such as low tariffs, or taxes, on imports and exports, that other favored nations receive.

Under the normal process, Congress grants normal trade relations under a "fast-track," or accelerated basis by limiting its own debate to a simple yes-or-no, up-or-down vote with no amendments. Although Congress initially refused to use this process for China, it eventually approved the status and extended the president's authority to negotiate such trade agreements in the Trade Act of 2002.

The Bush administration has used this authority to pursue open trade with Chile, Singapore, South Africa, and several Arab nations in the Middle East. In 2005, for example, the Bush administration asked Congress to approve the Central American Free Trade Agreement (CAFTA) as part of its broader campaign to expand the North American Free Trade Agreement (NAFTA). Under both agreements, the United States and its neighbors agreed to remove most barriers to trade. Although NAFTA and CAFTA were opposed by U.S. labor unions, which worried about the export of high-paying U.S. jobs to lower-paying workers in Mexico and other Central American countries, and by environmental groups, which worried about pollution in less developed economies, both agreements were approved by Congress on sharply divided votes.

Addressing Global Climate Change and Potential Epidemics

The United States has a mixed record in efforts to control the global climate change often associated with greenhouse gases that trap heat in the environment and raise the world's temperature. Much of the recent increase in greenhouse gases is related to the release of carbon dioxide from the burning of fossil fuels such as gasoline and coal by automobiles and power plants.

There is increasing agreement that the world's average temperature has risen over the past few decades. Although experts disagree on the amount of the increase and its potential impact on oceans and climate, there appears to be growing agreement that temperature increases threaten the world's climate in two ways. First, as the average temperature rises, the polar ice caps and glaciers melt. As the water melts, the oceans rise, threatening low-lying areas across the world. By some estimates, New York City, Washington, Florida, Louisiana, and other coastal areas could be completely under water within several hundred years. Second, as average temperatures rise, the weather becomes more unpredictable and potentially severe. Some experts attribute the recent increase in violent hurricanes such as Hurricane Katrina to global warming, and predict more violent storms in the future.

The world acknowledged these problems when it adopted an international treaty called the Kyoto Protocol in 1997. Under the treaty, all participating nations agreed to reduce their emission of greenhouse gases by set amounts over the coming decades. Although 55 nations, including the United States, most European nations, and Russia signed the agreement, the United States has never ratified the treaty and has yet to embrace limits on the burning of fossil fuels, even though the United States produces a significant amount of the world's greenhouse gases. The United States has argued that the limits imposed by the Kyoto Protocol would weaken its economy.

The world also suffers from an increase in chemical pollution related to rapidly expanding manufacturing in nations such as China. According to international monitoring, China contains 16 of the world's 20 most polluted cities, and is a major contributor to water contamination through the release of chemicals into its rivers. In December 2005, for example, China accidentally poisoned a major river with the cancer-causing chemical benzene. As the spill drifted toward the river, it penetrated the drinking water of millions of Chinese citizens, and will eventually reach the world's oceans, where it may poison millions of citizens in other nations.

Global climate change and pollution are not the only international environmental issues that face the United States. The recent spread of bird flu is considered one of the greatest threats to global health, and has prompted worries about a massive epidemic that could kill millions of people across the world. Although the disease has yet to enter the United States, many experts believe that it is only a matter of time before it does. The United States has been storing medicines to treat the disease, but has admitted that it is not prepared for a major epidemic.

Promoting Democracy and International Understanding

The United States has long engaged in promoting democracy and its freedoms. It does so through a mix of incentives and punishments, providing economic aid to nations that it believes are moving toward democracy, such as Iraq and Afghanistan, while refusing to provide aid to nations that are led by dictators, such as communist Cuba.

However, some of these efforts involve conflicts with other U.S. goals such as promoting international trade and fighting the war on terrorism. Although China continues to deny its citizens basic rights such as a free press, for example, the United States continues to promote international trade with one of the world's fastest-growing economies. In addition, the United States continues to provide aid to many Middle Eastern nations that are ruled by dictatorships in order to gain their help in the war on terrorism.

The United States also provides humanitarian aid to nations affected by natural disasters such as the 2004 tsunami in southern Asia. Although dictators led many of the countries affected, the United States has long believed that citizens should not suffer during crises even though their governments are not free.

Finally, the United States uses programs such as the Peace Corps to promote international understanding. Peace Corps volunteers are expected to serve in another nation for two years and become part of the community they are serving. Volunteers work on a variety of projects, such as teaching math and science, doing community development work, and improving water and sanitation systems. Most volunteers either have a college degree, specific international experience, or a combination of both. About 10 percent of the 7,300 current volunteers are over 50 years old. The Peace Corps covers travel and a minimum salary and typically trains volunteers in language and job skills for about three months before their service abroad.[4]

Winning the Iraq War

The decision to launch the Iraq war reflected a blend of several foreign policy priorities, including the effort to control weapons of mass destruction, fight terrorism, and

History Makers

Woodrow Wilson

Woodrow Wilson, the twenty-eighth president of the United States, won election in 1912 after a brutal campaign against the Republican incumbent, William Howard Taft, and former president Theodore Roosevelt, who ran on a third-party ticket. Taft and Roosevelt split the Republican vote, thereby giving Wilson the victory. As a former professor of political science at Princeton University, and former governor of New Jersey, Wilson was the first Democrat to win the presidency in two decades, and easily won reelection to a second term in 1916.

Although Wilson made important contributions to the nation's domestic and economic policies, he is often celebrated most for leading the United States during World War I, which led to his vision of a League of Nations that would prevent future wars. Having helped the countries involved end what was called the "war to end all wars," he campaigned hard for the creation of the League. However, he was rebuffed by the U.S. Senate, which voted not to join the international organization in 1920.

Wilson's vision of the League of Nations involved a number of duties that are now part of the United Nations, which was created at the end of World War II. Like the United Nations, which is discussed later in this chapter, Wilson's League was designed to improve international understanding through a body of nations that would cast votes on major world issues. Located in Geneva, Switzerland, the League was originally designed to encourage all nations to disarm their militaries, to settle disputes between nations by providing an opportunity for negotiation in a neutral setting, and to prevent the use of the kind of chemical weapons used in World War I.

The League had the authority to deal with any issue that threatened world peace, but it lacked both the membership and military strength to enforce its decisions. Unlike the United Nations, the League did not have a peacekeeping force, and it was only effective in the first years following its creation. It failed to stop Germany's military buildup in the 1930s, and it did little to prevent World War II, which produced more casualties than any war in modern history.

Wilson remained deeply committed to international understanding until the end of his life in 1924. Although his presidency was effectively over after a stroke in 1919, his work to create a lasting world peace marked him as one of America's great presidents. In 1919, for example, he won the Nobel Peace prize for his effort to establish the League of Nations. Unfortunately, he was never able to convince the American public to support the idea. As one of the nation's international idealists, he also failed to prevent the new isolationism that emerged after World War I and lasted for 20 years, until the start of World War II. ∎

Woodrow Wilson

promote democracy. Some also argued that the war was also based in part on George W. Bush's effort to finish what his father had started in the 1991 Gulf War, which followed Iraq's invasion of its oil-rich neighbor to the south, Kuwait. Although the United States and its allies easily defeated the Iraqi army in that conflict, they had stopped well short of Baghdad, leaving Hussein in power.

Iraq moved rapidly up the list of foreign-policy priorities in the days and weeks following the September 11, 2001, terrorist attacks. Convinced that Iraq possessed weapons of mass destruction that it was ready and willing to use against the United States, Bush ordered the military to start planning for a possible invasion only six days after September 11.[5] He also began building the case for action with the American public, arguing in his 2002 State of the Union Address that Iraq was part of an "axis of evil" that threatened the peace of the world.

Believing that Iraq continued to be a great threat to U.S. security, the Bush administration decided to force Iraq to prove that it had destroyed its weapons of mass destruction, while making the argument for preemptive war if Iraq refused to allow international inspectors to enter the country. Despite Iraq's limited willingness to allow the inspections, the Bush administration was convinced that the weapons not only existed, but constituted a clear and present danger to the United States.

The administration was sharply divided on how to disarm Iraq, however. Defense Secretary Donald Rumsfeld, Vice President Dick Cheney, and then-national security advisor Condoleezza Rice argued that the United States had a moral obligation to remove Hussein from power, even if doing so meant war. "This is an evil man who, left to his own devices, will wreak havoc again on his own population, his neighbors, and, if he gets weapons of mass destruction and the means to deliver them, on all of us," Rice told the British Broadcasting Corporation in August 2002. "There is a very powerful moral case for regime change. We certainly do not have the luxury of doing nothing."[6]

In contrast, Secretary of State Colin Powell argued that the United States needed to consider the impact of such an attack on other foreign and defense policy goals, as well as on the war on terrorism itself. Although he also believed the world would be better off without Hussein in power, he worried about both the cost and the impact of war. Having overseen the first war with Iraq as the U.S. Army's most senior officer in 1991, Powell knew that U.S. military power would win any war against Iraq, but he also believed that a prolonged war in Iraq, especially one waged with minimal international support, might increase hostility toward the United States, while giving terrorist organizations more targets for violence.

Two years after the terrorist attacks, Bush made his case for war to the international community. According to Bush, Iraq was not only expanding and improving facilities that it had used for building chemical weapons, it also had made several attempts to buy the equipment needed to build a nuclear weapon. Bush also made the case for removing Hussein from power:

> The United States has no quarrel with the Iraqi people; they've suffered too long in silent captivity. Liberty for the Iraqi people is a great moral cause, and a great strategic goal. The people of Iraq deserve it; the security of all nations requires it. Free societies do not intimidate through cruelty and conquest, and open societies do not threaten the world with mass murder. The United States supports political and economic liberty in a unified Iraq.[7]

Nine months later, the United States launched a massive attack on Iraq. American troops quickly reached the outskirts of the nation's capital city, Baghdad. They secured the city over the next two days, and helped topple a statue of Hussein at the center of the city. On May 1, 2003, President Bush stood on the deck of the USS *Abraham Lincoln* underneath a banner that read "MISSION ACCOMPLISHED" and told the nation that "Major combat operations in Iraq have ended."

However, despite an intense search, Iraq's weapons of mass destruction were never found. According to a U.S. Intelligence Committee report released in July 2004, most of the key judgments in the intelligence community's assessment of Iraq's weapons programs were "either overstated, or were not supported by, the underlying intelligence reporting."[8] In addition, the intelligence community "did not accurately or adequately explain to policy makers the uncertainties behind the judgments" contained in a key October 2002 assessment that the Central Intelligence Director, George Tenet, had called a "slam dunk case" that Iraq had the weapons.[9] Tenet resigned three weeks before the report was released.

Moreover, the battle for Iraq was only beginning. By September 2006, more than 2,700 U.S. troops had been killed, and more than 10,000 wounded. As already noted, Iraq was also teetering on the brink of civil war as Shiite and Sunni Muslims began using suicide bombings and open military action to strengthen their positions in the future.

The continued uncertainty about the future of Iraq had several effects on the Bush administration's foreign and defense policy goals. First, it undermined the president's case for unilateral action—it was one thing to declare a unilateral position at the start of the Iraq war, and quite another to maintain it as U.S. casualties mounted. But having decided that he needed more international cooperation, Bush's use of hard power in Iraq undermined his call for help.

"[Saddam Hussein] is an evil man who, left to his own devices, will wreak havoc again on his own population, his neighbors, and, if he gets weapons of mass destruction and the means to deliver them, on all of us."

CONDOLEEZZA RICE,
THEN-NATIONAL SECURITY ADVISOR, 2002

Second, the uncertainty weakened public support for the war, and created increasing pressure to resolve the stalemate by bringing at least some U.S. forces home. In April 2006, for example, a long list of retired military officers called on the president to bring the war to a close, arguing that it had been a mistake to go to war in the first place, especially given the failure to find weapons of mass destruction.

Finally, and perhaps most important, the lingering conflict reduced the military's ability to recruit new troops. With violence on the rise, young Americans became less likely to join the all-volunteer force (discussed later in this chapter), thereby threatening U.S. troop strength abroad. The effects have been particularly visible in the National Guard, which is composed of part-time soldiers who are called to duty in the event of a national emergency. As much as half the troops in Iraq are members of the National Guard, many of whom have been kept in Iraq much longer than originally promised. The result has been a significant decline in the willingness to serve in the Guard.

The Foreign and Defense Policy Administrative System

Even in troubled times, the president does not have absolute authority to act. Congress has the power to declare war, to appropriate funds for the armed forces, and to make rules that govern them. But the president is commander in chief and is authorized to negotiate treaties and receive and send ambassadors—that is, to recognize or refuse to recognize other governments. The Senate confirms U.S. ambassadorial appointments and gives consent (by a two-thirds vote) to treaty ratification. The courts have the power to interpret treaties, but by and large they have ruled that relations with other nations are matters for the executive to decide. The primacy of the executive in foreign policy is a fact of political life of all nations, including constitutional democracies.

Officially, the president's principal foreign policy adviser is the secretary of state, although others, such as the national security adviser or the vice president, are sometimes equally influential. The secretary of state administers the State Department, receives visits from foreign diplomats, attends international conferences, and usually heads the U.S. delegation in the General Assembly of the United Nations. The secretary also serves as the administration's chief coordinator of all governmental actions that affect our relations with other nations. In practice, the secretary of state delegates the day-to-day responsibilities for running the State Department and spends most of the time negotiating with the leaders of other countries.

The interdependence of foreign, economic, and domestic policies requires more than just one or two advisers. The conduct of foreign affairs is now the business of several major departments and agencies, including State, Defense, Treasury, Agriculture, Commerce, Labor, Energy, the Central Intelligence Agency (CIA), and the Department of Homeland Security. The need for immediate reaction and full preparedness has transferred many responsibilities directly to the president and to a great extent to the senior White House aides who assist in coordinating information and advice. Yet no matter what the system for advice and coordination, there are always overlaps of responsibilities, redundancy, and competition among agencies.

The National Security Council

The key coordinating agency for the president is the National Security Council (NSC). Created by Congress in 1947, it is intended to help presidents integrate foreign, military, and economic policies that affect national security. The NSC serves directly under the president. By law, it consists of the president, vice president, secretary of state, and secretary of defense. Recent presidents have sometimes included the director of the

CIA, the White House chief of staff, and the national security adviser as assistants to the NSC.

The national security adviser, appointed by the president, has emerged as one of the most influential foreign policy makers, sometimes rivaling the secretary of state in influence. Presidents come to rely on these White House aides both because of their proximity (down the hall in the West Wing of the White House) and because they owe their primary loyalties to the president, not to any department or program. Each president has shaped the NSC structure and adapted its staff procedures to suit his personal preferences, but over the years, the NSC, as both a committee and a staff, has taken on a major role in making and implementing foreign policy.

The State Department

The State Department is responsible for the diplomatic realm of foreign and defense policy. The department is organized around a series of "desks" representing different parts of the world and foreign policy missions. The State Department is also responsible for negotiating treaties with other nations and international organizations, protecting U.S. citizens abroad, promoting U.S. commercial interests in other nations, and granting visas to foreign visitors. The State Department also runs all U.S. embassies and consulates abroad. Embassies provide full diplomatic services on behalf of the United States and its citizens, while consulates are smaller branch offices of embassies that help foreign citizens enter the United States through visas, or entry papers.

The State Department also plays a significant role in homeland security. Many of the September 11, 2001 attackers had entered the United States on student visas granted by the State Department's Bureau of Consular Affairs. Although their movements once in the United States were supposed to be monitored by the Justice Department's Immigration and Naturalization Service, the State Department was criticized for being too lax in granting visas to almost anyone with enough money to purchase an airline ticket.

The State Department's budget of about $6 billion (not counting foreign aid) is the lowest of all the cabinet departments—only a fraction of the Department of Defense's much larger budget.[10] Considering the State Department's role and prestige, its worldwide staff of 25,000 is small, especially compared with the more than two million civilian and military personnel in the Department of Defense.

Its role is particularly impressive given recent cutbacks. The United States has closed at least 30 consulates and embassies over the past two decades, and many operate with obsolete technology and in antiquated and unsafe buildings. These cutbacks help explain the breakdowns in the visa issuance process. The State Department simply did not have enough employees to interview every applicant for a visa.

STAFFING THE DIPLOMATIC SYSTEM   U.S. embassies are staffed largely by members of the U.S. Foreign Service. Although part of the State Department, the service represents the entire government and performs jobs for many other agencies. Its main duties are to carry out foreign policy as expressed in the directives of the secretary of state; gather political, economic, and intelligence data for American policy makers; protect Americans and American interests in foreign countries; and cultivate friendly relations with host governments and foreign peoples.

The Foreign Service is composed of highly trained civil servants who are comparable to army officers in the military. They are a select, specially trained group expected to take assignments anyplace in the world on short notice. There are approximately 4,000 such officers; in recent years, fewer than 225 junior officers have won appointment each year. Approximately two-thirds of our U.S. ambassadors to about 160 nations come from the ranks of the Foreign Service. The others are usually presidential appointees confirmed by the senate.

The Foreign Service is one of the most prestigious yet most criticized career services of the national government. Criticism sometimes comes as much from within as from outside. Critics claim that the organizational culture of the Foreign Service stifles

In 2005, President Bush named John Negroponte as the first Director of National Intelligence, a position created at the recommendation of the 9/11 Commission.

creativity; attracts officers who are, or at least become, more concerned about their status than their responsibilities; and requires new recruits to wait 15 years or more before being considered for positions of responsibility. Like other federal agencies, most notably the Central Intelligence Agency and the Federal Bureau of Investigation, the Foreign Service has had great difficulty recruiting officers with Arabic-language skills, which clearly weakens each agency's ability to interpret, let alone collect, intelligence on the terrorist networks that have emerged in the Middle East and Asia.

The Central Intelligence Agency and the Intelligence Community

Accurate, timely information on foreign nations is essential for making wise decisions, as the failure to find weapons of mass destruction after the initial stages of the Iraq war demonstrated. As the Senate Intelligence Committee and the national commission created to investigate the September 11, 2001 attacks both noted, the intelligence community failed to provide that information in time to prevent the attacks or change the course of the Iraq war.[11]

Much of the failure in both these cases occurred within the Central Intelligence Agency, which was created in 1947 to coordinate the gathering and analysis of information that flows into various parts of the U.S. government from all over the world. In recent years, the CIA has had about 20,000 employees, who both collect information and shape the intelligence estimates that policy makers use to set priorities.

Although most of the information the CIA gathers comes from open sources such as the Internet, the CIA does use spies and undercover agents to monitor foreign threats. This secret intelligence occasionally does supply crucial data. But it is not all glamour; much is routine. Intelligence work involves three basic operations: reporting, research, and dissemination. *Reporting* is based on the close and rigorous observation of developments around the world; *research* is the attempt to detect meaningful patterns in what was observed in the past and to understand what appears to be going on now; *dissemination* means getting the right information to the right people at the right time.

The CIA is only one of 15 intelligence agencies in the federal government, including the State Department's Bureau of Intelligence and Research; the Defense Department's Defense Intelligence Agency (which combines the intelligence operations of the Army, Navy, Air Force, and Marine Corps); the Federal Bureau of Investigation; the Treasury Department's Office of Terrorism and Finance Intelligence; the Energy Department's Office of Intelligence; the Homeland Security Department's Directorate of Information Analysis and Infrastructure Protection and Directorate of Coast Guard Intelligence; and the National Security Agency (which specializes in electronic reconnaissance and code breaking), National Reconnaissance Office (which runs the U.S. satellite surveillance programs), and National Geospatial-Intelligence Agency (which collects and analyzes photographic imagery). Together, the 15 agencies constitute the *intelligence community.*

Because each of these agencies was created to collect unique information (imagery, electronic intelligence, and so forth) for a unique client (the president, the secretary of defense, or others), they rarely share information with each other. The lack of cooperation clearly affected the government's ability to prevent the September 11, 2001 attacks. "Many dedicated officers worked day and night for years to piece together the growing body of evidence on Al-Qaeda and to understand the threats," the 9/11 Commission concluded. "Yet, while there were many reports on bin Laden and his growing Al-Qaeda organization, there was no comprehensive review of what the intelligence community knew and what it did not know, and what that meant."[12]

Congress responded by creating a **National Intelligence Director** in 2004 to oversee all of the intelligence offices. Under its legislation, the new director was responsible for providing the primary advice to the president on intelligence issues, and was given the authority to increase or decrease the budgets of all other intelligence agencies. Bush named the first director in 2005, John Negroponte. The director also oversees a

"[W]hile there were many reports on bin Laden and his growing Al-Qaeda organization, there was no comprehensive review of what the intelligence community knew and what it did not know, and what that meant."

9/11 COMMISSION

National Intelligence Director
The federal government's primary intelligence officer, responsible for overseeing all national intelligence agencies and providing advice to the president on terrorist threats.

new federal counterterrorism center, which is responsible for making sense of all national intelligence on potential terrorist threats to the United States. Despite the promise of more coordination, however, Negroponte came under fire in mid-2006 for merely adding a new layer of bureaucracy to the already confused intelligence system. According to congressional critics in both parties, there was less coordination and more confusion than ever.

The Department of Defense

The president, Congress, the National Security Council, the State Department, and the Defense Department all make overall defense policy and attempt to integrate U.S. national security programs, but the day-to-day work of organizing for defense is the job of the Defense Department. Its headquarters, the Pentagon, houses within its 17.5 miles of corridors 23,000 top military and civilian personnel. The offices of several hundred generals and admirals are there, as is the office of the secretary of defense, currently Robert M. Gates, who provides civilian control of the armed services.

Although the Department of Defense has existed for more than half a century, its leaders are still working to ensure both strategic vision and practical coordination among the military services. Until 1947, there were two separate military departments—War and Navy. The difficulty of coordinating them during World War II led to demands for their unification. In 1947, the Air Force, already an autonomous unit within the War Department, was made an independent department, and all three military departments—Army, Navy, and Air Force—were placed under the general supervision of the secretary of defense. The Unification Act of 1947 was a bundle of compromises between the Army, which favored a tightly integrated department, and the Navy, which wanted a loosely federated structure, but the act at least brought the military services onto a common organizational chart.

The committee known as the Joint Chiefs of Staff serves as the principal military adviser to the president, the National Security Council, and the secretary of defense. It includes the heads of the three armed services, plus the commandant of the Marine Corps, and the chair and vice chair of the Joint Chiefs. The president, with the consent of the Senate, appoints all the service chiefs to four-year nonrenewable terms. Note that the twice-renewable two-year term of the chair of the Joint Chiefs is part of the process of ensuring civilian control over the military.

Before 1986, the members of the Joint Chiefs of Staff were, collectively, very powerful. They advised the president and the secretary of defense. Because they functioned as a committee and could not act until unanimous agreement was reached, however, they often produced overly broad decisions. Critics therefore viewed much of the work of the Joint Chiefs as wasteful and even dangerous.

The Department of Defense Reorganization Act of 1986 shifted considerable power to the chair. Reporting through the secretary of defense, the chair now advises the president on military matters, exercises authority over the forces in the field, and is responsible for overall military planning. In theory, the chair of the Joint Chiefs can even make a military decision that the chiefs of the other services oppose. On paper at least, these other chiefs now serve the chair merely as advisers, and even the chair's deputy, the vice chair, outranks the other service chiefs. The chair has a mandate to encourage "jointness" in military education and in other spheres to integrate the services for maximum effectiveness. The chair of the Joint Chiefs today is the most powerful peacetime military officer in the Defense Department. These changes clearly contributed to military success in the Afghanistan and Iraq wars, where special operations forces and U.S. Marines worked closely with Navy and Air Force pilots to target precision-guided weapons on enemy positions.

It is crucial to recognize, however, that the chair of the Joint Chiefs is *not* the head of the military. The chair and the Joint Chiefs are advisers to the secretary of defense and the president, but the president can disregard their advice and on occasion

The Changing Face of American Politics

Diversity in the Military

The U.S. military has become much more diverse over the past three decades, in part due to much more aggressive recruiting of women and minorities. In 1990, for example, just 11 percent of all military personnel were women, while 28 percent were people of color. By 2003, which is the latest information available, 15 percent were women, and 39 percent were people of color.

The four armed services—Army, Navy, Marine Corps, and Air Force—vary greatly in terms of diversity, however. As of 2003, roughly 42 percent of the Army, 37 percent of the Navy, 32 percent of the Marine Corps, and 26 percent of the Air Force were African American, Hispanic, Asian American, or another minority group. At the same time, 19 percent of the Air Force, 16 percent of the Army, 14 percent of the Navy, and just 6 percent of the Marine Corps were women.

There are several reasons why the armed forces have done better recruiting people of color than recruiting women. First, the military has worked hard to improve its reputation as an equal opportunity employer. Colin Powell's rise to the highest post in the armed services has often been used to show recruits of color that anything is possible in the military. Powell

Year	Percentage of Minority Personnel	Percentage of Women Recruits
1990	28%	11%
1995	28	13
2000	38	15
2003	39	15

SOURCE: Department of Defense, *2003 Demographic Characteristics*, Defense Department, 2005.

entered the military as a second lieutenant in 1958, served two tours of duty in Vietnam, and eventually became the first African American officer to chair the Joint Chiefs of Staff.

Second, the military has long focused on recruiting high school graduates who are not college-bound, which is a group that contains more people of color. The military has also developed several new programs that set aside substantial amounts of funding for future college tuition, which has also been effective in recruiting people of color. ∎

---

has done so. A president must weigh military action or inaction against the larger foreign and security interests of the nation.

Understanding the Defense Administrative System

The defense administrative system is best understood as a *confederation* or a bargaining arena rather than a highly focused system. Although recent changes have improved cooperation between the military services, the system continues to face problems coordinating its actions.

Disputes among the military services involve more than professional jealousies. The technological revolution in warfare has made many military concepts obsolete, thereby threatening the traditional roles of some of the services. In the past, it made sense to divide command among land, sea, and air forces. Today, defense research and development are constantly altering formerly established roles and missions, yet the individual services are reluctant to give up their traditional functions or to serve each other's crucial needs. The Navy, for example, is interested in waging sea warfare, not in running a freight service for the Army. Rivalries between the services erupt when the Army and Air Force quarrel over who should provide air support for ground troops. Each branch also supports weapons that bring it prestige. The Air Force and Navy dispute, for example, the effectiveness of land-based versus sea-based missiles.[13]

Whether strategic policies are worked out by the Defense Department, the White House, or Congress, the decisions result from a political process in which some measure of consensus is essential. The Joint Chiefs engage in the same type of vote trading used in Congress. On budget issues, the chiefs often endorse all the programs desired by each service. When forced to choose on an issue of policy, the chiefs have traditionally compromised among the different service positions rather than attempt to develop a position based on a unified military point of view.

The Department of Homeland Security

The Department of Homeland Security plays a small but important role in foreign policy by policing U.S. borders. Created in late 2002, the department is composed of 22 agencies and a workforce of 170,000 full-time civil servants. It includes the Border Patrol, the Coast Guard, the Customs Service, the Secret Service, the Immigration Service, and the Transportation Security Administration.

The department has three basic goals: (1) to prevent the entry of terrorists into the country, (2) reduce the chances of a terrorist attack, and (3) help the nation recover from an attack if and when it occurs. Toward these goals, it is responsible for screening all passengers and baggage on U.S. domestic flights (Transportation Security Administration), checking all cargo (Customs Service, Coast Guard) and visitors (Immigration Service) entering the United States, patrolling the borders (Border Patrol, Coast Guard), and providing aid and assistance to communities affected by human and natural disasters (Federal Emergency Management Agency). Although the Bureau of Consular Affairs remains in the State Department, the secretary of homeland security now has primary responsibility for making sure that visas are not issued to potential terrorists.

Despite making significant progress toward tighter airport security over its first three years, the department still needs time to develop similar programs for the nation's ports, subways, and airports, nuclear power plants, chemical factories, sports facilities, and shopping malls. The September 11th investigation recommended that the department move as quickly as possible to create a biometric screening system that uses fingerprints and digital photographs to identify U.S. citizens and visitors alike. As of this writing, these new systems have yet to be widely used, however, and complaints continue about the failure to inspect cargo that arrives at U.S. ports of entry.

Participants in Foreign and Defense Policy

Foreign policy flows through the same institutional and constitutional structures as domestic policy. Public opinion, interest groups, foreign countries, political parties, and Congress all affect the making of foreign policy. Yet these structures operate somewhat differently from the way they do in domestic affairs.

The Public

In crisis situations, presidents and their military and intelligence advisers make the key decisions, often operating from a high-tech operations center in the basement of the White House. Yet even in these situations, presidents and their advisers know that their decisions will ultimately require support from the public and from Congress.

At first glance, many Americans appear indifferent or uninformed about foreign and defense policy. Foreign affairs issues are more remote than domestic issues. Most Americans have a poor sense of world geography and an even weaker grasp of world politics. However, Americans—whether ill informed or not—have strong opinions about the nation's vital interests. Interviewed only days after the September 11, 2001, attacks, 77 percent said the United States should go to war with Afghanistan even if it meant taking heavy casualties, and 44 percent said military action to attack terrorism abroad was a wiser investment than building up the nation's defenses at home. As Table 20–1 shows, Americans also became much more concerned about increasing defense spending.

Individual Americans have also been deeply involved in the war on terrorism, whether by attending rallies and protests for or against the Iraq war, donating blood and money to the victims of the September 11 attacks, or writing letters to their members of Congress or the president. Many Americans have also joined together to create new organizations both in support of and opposition to the Iraq war. In August 2005,

TABLE 20–1 Views of Foreign Policy Before and After September 11, 2001

	Before	After
THE UNITED STATES SHOULD FORMULATE FOREIGN POLICY BASED ON		
Mostly U.S. interests	38%	30%
Interests of allies	48	59
Neither or both	8	7
THE U.S. LEADERSHIP ROLE SHOULD BE		
Single leader or first among equals	38	45
Just one of leading nations	50	46
No leadership role	8	3
NATIONAL DEFENSE SPENDING SHOULD BE		
Increased	32	50
Kept the same	44	41
Cut back	20	7

SOURCE: Pew Research Center for the People and the Press, *Public Opinion in a Year for the Books* (Pew Research Center, 2002), p. 12.

for example, Cindy Sheehan, the mother of a U.S. soldier killed in Iraq, staged a vigil outside the president's ranch in Crawford, Texas. Although Cindy Sheehan was never able to meet with the president, she galvanized public opposition to the war and became a national celebrity for her nonviolent protest.

Interest Groups

It is difficult to generalize about the impact of interest groups on American foreign policy. At times of international crisis, the president is usually able to mobilize public support so that interest groups find it difficult to exert much influence. As a general rule, special-interest groups that do not have major economic interests rarely have a decisive role in the formulation of foreign policy.

Ethnic interest groups, however, sometimes play an important role in foreign and defense policy decisions. As a nation of immigrants and the children and grandchildren of immigrants, our citizens often retain a special bond with their country of origin. Thus Irish Americans, Jewish Americans, Cuban Americans, African Americans, Asian Americans, Polish Americans, Greek Americans, Arab Americans, and Mexican Americans take a keen interest in decisions affecting Ireland, Israel, Cuba, South Africa, China, Japan, Vietnam, the Philippines, South Korea and other Pacific Rim nations, Poland, Greece, the Middle East, and Mexico. Such groups sometimes exert great pressures on policy makers to support (or in the case of Cuba, contest) the country to which they are emotionally linked.

Business groups also play a role in foreign and defense policy decisions. Defense contractors are heavily involved in decisions about defense spending and contribute large amounts of campaign money to presidential and congressional candidates. They also lobby hard on behalf of their projects before Congress and the executive branch, which can and does raise questions of conflict of interest and special favors. In July 2004, for example, executives of Houston-based Halliburton, Inc., were called before Congress to address allegations of waste and abuse in administering more than $8 billion in defense contracts that had been awarded without competition from other

Agents of Change

Victoria Hale

Victoria Hale and the Institute for OneWorld Health

The Institute for OneWorld Health was created in 2000 to identify and develop new medicines that are particularly effective in reducing disease in poor countries. The Institute also helps build partnerships for the distribution of the medicines and works to ensure that the medicines are affordable. Driven to combat life-threatening diseases such as malaria, the Institute has a single goal: to save lives.

Convinced that new medicines hold great promise for helping poor countries build strong economies, protect their most vulnerable citizens, and prevent corruption in the sale of medicines, the Institute is working with other international groups such as the Bill and Melinda Gates Foundation and government agencies as the first nonprofit pharmaceutical company in the world.

The Institute was founded by Victoria Hale, who believes that the world has reached a "tipping point," meaning "that moment when the fulcrum shifts and incremental change becomes sweeping change." She earned her doctorate in pharmaceutical chemistry from the University of California, San Francisco, and worked at the U.S. Food and Drug Administration and several universities before she started the Institute. At the Institute, she writes, "we're tapping the extraordinary power of pharmaceutical research to identify and develop treatments and cures for diseases that have long been neglected—diseases that affect millions around the world....The challenge we've taken on—to erase the terrible inequities in global health—is huge." If OneWorld Health succeeds, it will save millions of lives and prevent needless suffering abroad. ∎

Learn more about the Institute for OneWorld Health at www.oneworldhealth.org

QUESTIONS

Why is global health often neglected in U.S. foreign policy?

Why is it an important issue for the future?

---

potential contractors. The charges were particularly visible because the company had been led by Vice President Dick Cheney during the 1990s, which created the appearance of favoritism in the contracting process. His former company continues to face investigations of waste in its Iraq reconstruction contracts, for example, and remains a target of continued criticism for overcharging on basic supplies such as gasoline. Moreover, contractors remain under fire for not supplying enough body armor to protect the troops in Iraq from roadside bombing.

Defense contractors are not the only business interests involved in foreign and defense policy. Agricultural interests have lobbied successfully for expanded grain and food exports, the steel industry has lobbied successfully for import quotas on foreign steel, the entertainment industry has campaigned against piracy of music and film abroad, and the high-tech industry has pressed Congress to allow the immigration of more computer programmers.

U.S. businesses also participate in foreign policy. In 2002, General Electric and several other companies urged India to seek a more peaceful relationship with its neighbor, Pakistan. Having become highly dependent on millions of English-speaking, low-wage workers in India for computer programming and service, these firms warned India that they would move their operations to other countries if the tensions with Pakistan continued to grow.[14] Bush pursued the same goal in 2006 when he offered U.S. support for India's nuclear power industry, even though the industry could be used to create nuclear weapons.

Even rock stars have their own agendas. Bono has become a strong advocate on behalf of ending global hunger and reducing the spread of HIV/AIDS, for example, and has lobbied Congress, the president, and international officials for greater spending to help African nations address these problems. Although he is not a U.S. citizen, he has become a highly visible advocate of change.

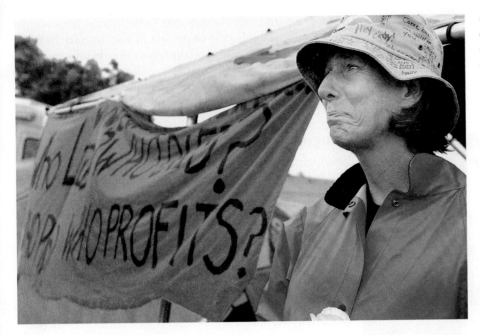

Cindy Sheehan, whose son was killed in Iraq, attracted national attention in 2005 for her extended protest of the war outside President Bush's ranch in Texas.

Foreign Nations

Most countries have embassies that lobby for their interests in Washington. In addition, some countries like Japan have built up a powerful network of lawyers, lobbyists, and Washington-based publicists who are retained by Japanese companies and trade associations, as well as by the Japanese government, to defend their extensive economic interests in the United States.[15] Lobbyists representing industrialized countries like South Korea, Taiwan, Singapore, Brazil, and Mexico have also expanded their Washington lobbying efforts to fight U.S. protectionism and import quotas on textiles, shoes, and other products. Such lobbying is legal, provided that the lobbyists register and report their activities to Congress.

Foreign nations have occasionally tried to influence U.S. policy through less visible means. In 1996, for example, the fact that China and Indonesia had made large contributions to the Clinton–Gore reelection campaign came to light. Although the president vigorously denied any connection between the contributions and administration policy, the Democratic National Committee returned the money. George W. Bush's inaugural committee returned a $100,000 gift in early 2001 to a donor who had questionable ties to foreign leaders.[16] Nevertheless, most foreign countries continue to retain lobbyists in Washington, and some even have lobbyists working with state governments to promote trade.

Political Parties

Political parties do not usually play a major role in shaping foreign and defense policy, for two reasons: (1) Many Americans still prefer to keep partisan politics out of foreign policy, and (2) parties usually take less clear and candid stands on foreign policy than they do on domestic policy. Party platforms often obscure the issues instead of highlighting them, and many members of Congress fail to follow any strict party line when it comes to foreign policy.

At the end of World War II, sentiment grew strong for a bipartisan approach to foreign policy. An ambiguous concept, **bipartisanship** in foreign affairs generally means (1) collaboration between the executive and the congressional leaders of both parties, (2) support of presidential foreign policies by both parties in Congress, and (3) downplaying major foreign policy differences in national elections and in presidential debates. Overall, bipartisanship is an attempt to remove the issues of foreign policy from partisan politics.

bipartisanship
A policy that emphasizes a united front and cooperation between the major political parties, especially on sensitive foreign policy issues.

Not everybody agrees that bipartisanship is desirable. There is virtue, critics say, in debating contending ideas—such as foreign aid or the war in Iraq. In early 2006, for example, Senator Russell Feingold (D-Wis.) called on the Senate to formally censure, or criticize, the president for misleading the nation on the intelligence that helped make the case for the Iraq war, even as several congressional committees opened investigations into the failure to train enough Iraqi soldiers to replace U.S. troops in the future.

The spirit of bipartisanship is reflected in the report of the 9/11 Commission, issued on July 22, 2004. The commission was made up of both Democrats and Republicans who managed to put their ideological differences aside and to ultimately issue a report that is critical of both the Clinton and Bush administrations in their handling of terrorism. Shown here are 9/11 Commission Chairman Thomas Kean and Vice Chairman Lee Hamilton.

Congress

Although Congress seldom initiates foreign policy on its own, it has taken the lead on some trade and economic assistance questions and, of course, it controls the power of the purse. In addition, Congress is authorized to define the limits of presidential war powers.[17]

Congress is a crucial link between policy makers and the public. Regardless of their party, members of Congress want a voice in foreign policy, or at least what some members call "meaningful consultation." After all, they represent the constituents who must fight the wars, pay the taxes, and bear the burdens of wartime. Congress also represents a check on presidential power through its spending and oversight power.

To date, however, Congress has not been a significant check in the Iraq war. With U.S. troops at risk, Congress has approved the president's requests for additional spending, including an additional $25 billion in 2004 on top of the $65 billion already approved and spent on the wars in Afghanistan and Iraq. By the start of 2007, the cost of the Iraq war had reached $320 billion.

Making Foreign Policy in a Democracy

A democratic foreign policy is presumably one in which policy makers are known and are held accountable to the people. This is a tough test for any policy, yet it is especially tough for foreign policy because of the frequent need to act with speed and sometimes with secrecy, the generally low level of information among the general public, the anonymity of most foreign policy leaders, and the complexity of most international issues and strategic policy options. Still, the American public wants to be consulted and informed, and it wants its leaders held accountable.[18]

A constitutional democracy may not be able to keep leaders from making mistakes. However, it can make sure that policy mistakes eventually become public, such as the early failure to anticipate the possibility that Iraq did not have any weapons of mass destruction. That is when the safeguarding agencies of democracy—the opposition party, the press, and public opinion—play a crucial role in demanding accountability. The public's opposition to the Vietnam War eventually forced the United States to withdraw, for example, and widespread worries about the cost of the Iraq war may eventually have the same effect.

The temptation during times of crisis is to rally around the president and the flag in support of the country. But as noted elsewhere in this book, dissent is an essential element of maintaining accountability during such moments.

Foreign and Defense Policy Options

The United States has a number of tools for achieving foreign policy success, not the least of which is military might. But military might, or hard power, is no longer enough to ensure success, or even deter foreign threats. Without conventional diplomacy, or soft power, to send its message clearly, foreign aid to help nations in need, economic sanctions to isolate its adversaries, and public diplomacy to help other nations understand its agenda, the nation will not succeed in reaching its foreign policy goals.

Conventional Diplomacy

Much of U.S. foreign policy is conducted by the Foreign Service and ambassadors in face-to-face discussions in Washington and other capitals, at the United Nations in New York and Geneva, at North Atlantic Treaty Organization or World Trade Organization meetings, and elsewhere around the world in regional or international organizations and world conferences. International summit meetings, with their high-profile pomp and drama, are another form of conventional diplomacy. Even though traditional diplomacy appears more subdued and somewhat less vital in this era of personal leader-to-leader communication by telephone, fax, and teleconferencing, it is still an important, if slow, process by which nations can gain information, talk about mutual interests, and try to resolve disputes.

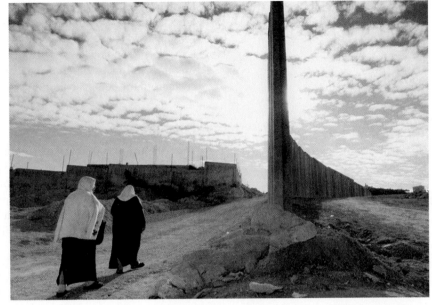

The inability of both the Israelis and the Palestinians to reach an agreement on Israeli settlements in the West Bank by means of conventional diplomacy has led to the use of violence on both sides of the issue and ultimately to Israel's construction of a "separation wall" that it believes will protect Israeli settlers from further violence.

Much of the conventional diplomacy carried out by the State Department may not produce important breakthroughs, yet it is difficult to measure the value of diplomatic representation. No price tag can be placed on close personal relations with foreign officials or on information gathered and arguments made to promote American interests around the world. The closing of one embassy or the withdrawal from an international organization is unlikely to cause major setbacks for the United States, yet a less active diplomatic corps could mean a less effective foreign policy.

When relations between nations become strained, diplomatic relations are sometimes broken as a means of political coercion. When the United States breaks diplomatic ties, the consequences are more than merely symbolic. Doing so greatly restricts tourist and business travel to a country and in effect curbs economic as well as political relations with the nation. Breaking diplomatic relations, however, is a next-to-last resort (force is the last resort), for such action undermines the ability to reason with a nation's leaders or to use other diplomatic strategies to resolve conflicts. The act also undermines our ability to get valuable information about what is going on in a nation and to have a presence there.

THE ROLE OF THE UNITED NATIONS The United Nations is one of the most important arenas for traditional diplomacy. Established in 1945 by the victors of World War II, the United Nations now has 189 nation members.

Despite its promise as a forum for world peace, the United Nations has been frustrated during its first 45 years. Critics contend that it either ducked crucial global issues or was politically unable to tackle them. During much of that time, the U.N. General Assembly, dominated by a combination of Third World and communist nations, was hostile to many U.S. interests. The General Assembly often became a talk shop, passing vague resolutions. More recently, the five permanent members of the U.N. Security Council—the United States, China, Russia (which replaced the Soviet Union), Britain, and France—have usually worked in harmony. Moreover, the United Nations' assumption of responsibilities in the Persian Gulf War and its extensive peacekeeping missions in Cyprus and Lebanon won it respect. U.N. efforts in Cambodia, Somalia, and Sudan are considered much less successful, in part because peacekeepers are rarely given enough authority or military equipment to stop a civil war.

In addition, several of the specialized agencies of the United Nations—including the World Health Organization, the United Nations High Commission for Refugees, and the World Food Program—are considered major successes. But the review is much more mixed with respect to the United Nations' peacekeeping efforts, of which it has conducted more than 50. These operations are plagued by inadequate and often underprepared personnel. "First-world countries with first-rate armies are usually

Kofi Annan, secretary general of the United Nations. Annan came under intense criticism in late 2004 for his role in managing the Iraqi oil accounts during the 1900s when Iraq was allowed to sell oil to purchase medical supplies and food. He was replaced in 2007 by South Korea's Ban K. Moon.

unwilling to put their troops at risk," writes former United States Ambassador Dennis Jett. "Thus these operations are often left to third-world countries, and the United Nations sends some of the worst soldiers in the world off to situations where it can only hope they are not called on to actually do anything."[19] As of 2006, the United Nations was involved in 16 different peacekeeping missions, including the effort to protect civilians in the Sudan civil war.

Foreign Aid

The United States offers aid to more than 100 countries directly and to other nations through contributions to various U.N. development funds. Since 1945, the United States has provided about $400 billion in economic assistance to foreign countries. In recent years, however, foreign aid spending has amounted to around $15 billion per year, or less than 50 percent of what it spent in inflation-adjusted dollars back in 1985.[20]

Most foreign aid goes to a few countries that the United States deems to be of strategic importance to our national security: Israel, Egypt, Ukraine, Jordan, India, Russia, South Africa, and Haiti. That list is sure to change in the future as the nation reallocates its budget to nations central to the war on terrorism. However, regardless of which nation receives the aid, most foreign aid is actually spent in the United States, where it pays for the purchase of American services and products being sent to those countries. It thus amounts to a hefty subsidy for American companies and their employees.

Many Americans and members of Congress oppose foreign aid. A recent poll of American citizens found that only 9 percent supported increasing foreign aid, while 47 percent favored reducing it. Another 40 percent would keep it pretty much at the same level.[21] Few powerful interest groups or constituencies back foreign aid initiatives. State Department officials are invariably the biggest advocates of foreign aid. Presidents also recognize the vital role foreign aid plays in advancing U.S. interests. Successive presidents have all wanted to maintain the leverage with key countries that economic and military assistance provides. One major debate today is how much debt relief to provide for the world's poorest nations, some of which spend up to 50 percent of their budgets to pay interest on old loans. The problem is particularly severe in Central and South America, where international debt has brought high inflation, unemployment, and civil unrest.

Despite these arguments, Congress invariably trims the foreign aid budget, responding in part to polls that show most Americans believe that the United States spends more on foreign aid than it does on Medicare and other domestic priorities. Members of Congress often criticize foreign aid as a "Ghana versus Grandma" case. How, they say, can you give away taxpayers' money to some foreign country when we have poor older people who can't afford their prescription drugs and decent medical help?[22]

Critics also note that U.S. foreign aid has subsidized the most autocratic and most corrupt of dictators. And there are plenty of instances in which foreign aid money has been stolen or misspent. Defenders counter that some corruption is inevitable. "You can't engage in bone-poor countries that lack laws and independent journalists and elections, and expect American standards of transparency," writes *Washington Post* editorial writer Sebastian Mallaby. "Yes, many aid programs fail and will continue to do so. But you don't give up trying to educate and house people just because it's hard. And you don't give up on international engagement just because it's as daunting as it is important."[23]

Economic Sanctions

The United States has frequently applied economic pressure in response to a nation's unwillingness to abide by what we perceive to be international law or proper relations. Indeed, the United States has employed economic sanctions more than any other nation—more than 100 times in the past 50 years. **Economic sanctions** entail a denial

"You can't engage in bone-poor countries that lack laws and independent journalists and elections, and expect American standards of transparency."

WASHINGTON POST EDITORIAL WRITER SEBASTIAN MALLABY

economic sanctions
Denial of export, import, or financial relations with a target country in an effort to change that nation's policies.

Government's Greatest Endeavors

Rebuilding Europe After World War II

Rebuilding democracies in Europe after World War II is considered by historians and political scientists to be the federal government's greatest achievement of the past 60 years.

It was also one of its most controversial following World War II. Many Americans opposed helping Germany recover from the war, but eventually most supported the effort as way to both protect these nations against the Soviet Union and provide humanitarian aid to the hungry and homeless in the defeated nations.

Rebuilding Germany involved providing military aid, which was also controversial. Germany's army and air force had been destroyed in the war, and Japan had been completely disarmed at its surrender. By providing limited aid for police and relatively small militaries, the United States helped protect both nations from possible invasion by the Soviet Union, which emerged from World War II as a superpower.

Named in honor of its director, General George C. Marshall, the federal government's Marshall Plan spent more than $12 billion rebuilding Germany, as well as other war-torn nations. The Marshall Plan also provided money for basic services such as medical care and food and clothing to millions who had lost their homes in the war. It also helped the U.S. economy by creating new markets for U.S. goods.

The Marshall Plan is still widely viewed as a form of humanitarian aid, but its greatest impact may have been in protecting Western Europe from internal unrest. "The seeds of communism are nurtured by misery and want," President Harry Truman said in lobbying Congress for funding. "They spread and grow in the evil soil of poverty and strife. ∎

Something as simple as a new pair of shoes could bring joy to the children of war-torn Germany.

QUESTIONS

Why was rebuilding Europe so important to U.S. foreign policy?

How do we know it was a success?

---

of export, import, or financial relations with a target country in an effort to change that country's policies. Economic sanctions imposed on South Africa doubtless helped end apartheid and encourage democracy in that nation, while sanctions on Libya helped end its nuclear weapons program. But sanctions imposed on Cuba have not had much effect in dislodging that nation's dictatorial regime. The United States imposed sanctions on India and Pakistan in 1998 when both nations began a round of nuclear testing, but because of economic distress both in Pakistan and among U.S. wheat growers, Congress and the president lifted most of the sanctions within months of imposing them.

The popularity of economic sanctions has risen and fallen over the years. They are especially unpopular among farmers and corporations that have to sacrifice part of their overseas markets to comply with government controls, and they rarely work as effectively as intended. They can also be costly to U.S. businesses and workers while intensifying anti-American sentiment.

Senator Richard Lugar (R-Ind.) believes that sanctions seldom work unless they are multilateral rather than imposed by the United States alone.[24] Scholars suggest that when dealing with authoritarian regimes, the United States should direct sanctions at rulers, not the populace at large. "Iraqis are not our enemies. Nor are the Cubans,"

TABLE 20–2 The Costs of War

Number Killed

Revolutionary War	4,435
War of 1812	2,260
Civil War	214,939
Spanish-American War	385
World War I	53,402
World War II	291,557
Korean War	35,516
Vietnam War	58,516
Persian Gulf War	382
Afghanistan War	220
Iraq War	2,700*

*Figures as of October 2006.

SOURCE: *Washington Post*, May 26, 2003; figures updated by authors.

writes Gary Hufbauer. "Where the president imposes comprehensive sanctions on an authoritarian regime, he should view those sanctions as a prelude to the exercise of military force, not as a substitute for force. Unless we are prepared to remove bad governments with military force, we have no business heaping prolonged punishment on innocent people."[25]

Military Intervention

War is not merely an extension of diplomacy but rather the complete and total breakdown of diplomatic efforts. The United States has used military force in other nations on the average of almost once a year since 1789, although usually in short-term initiatives such as NATO's military activities in Bosnia and Kosovo. Although presidential candidate John Kerry argued that the Iraq war was the first time in history that the United States had gone to war because it chose to, not because it had to, it has actually sent forces into combat many times without a clear threat. It did not have to go to war against Spain in 1898 or send troops to Cuba, Haiti, the Dominican Republic, Lebanon, Mexico, Nicaragua, Somalia, South Vietnam, or even Europe in World War I.[26] (See Table 20–2 for the number of Americans killed in the nation's major wars.)

Experts tend to agree that the use of force is most successful when it is used in small and even medium-sized countries for short engagements (Grenada, Panama, Kuwait, Kosovo, and Afghanistan). They also agree that it "often proves ineffective in the context of national civil wars (the United States in Vietnam; Israel in Lebanon)."[27]

Not all military action is visible to the public or even the intended target. Covert activities are planned and executed to conceal the identity of the sponsor. The United States repeatedly engaged in covert operations during the Cold War, including early intervention in Vietnam and Central America, as well as in Afghanistan, where it supported rebels fighting the Soviet invasion. But covert activities in Cuba, Chile, and elsewhere have backfired, and support for this strategy has cooled in the post–Cold War era.[28] Ironically, U.S. covert aid to the Afghan rebels eventually led to the Soviet withdrawal, which in turn led to the establishment of the Taliban, which allowed Osama bin Laden and his followers to establish training bases in its territory.

Members of the United Nations Peacekeeping Force, in their distinctive blue helmets, are called in around the world when the UN determines they are necessary to keep or restore order.

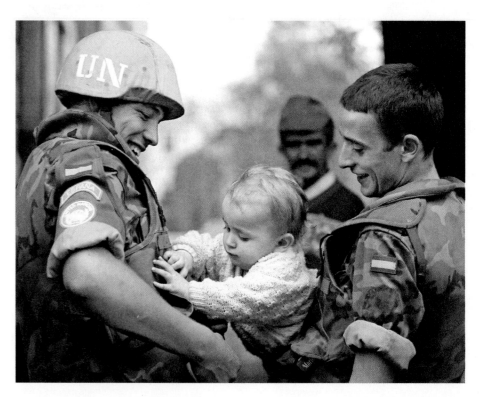

How Other Nations Govern

Norway's Foreign Aid

Wealthy nations can do many things to help other countries around the world, not the least of which is provide direct foreign aid. According to the Organization for Economic Cooperation and Development, which monitors international governance, the United States was the largest foreign aid contributor in the world in 2003, giving $15 billion to a variety of projects around the globe.

The United States is far from the most generous, however. Although Norway gives less foreign aid in total dollars, it contributes a much greater amount measured against its gross national income. By that measure, it is nearly five times more generous than the United States.

Norway is more generous for several reasons. First, some experts argue that Norway has a longer history of international trade with Africa, which is a major target of its aid. Having visited many nations over the centuries, its people may have a more natural desire to help others. Second, Norway is a very liberal nation—it has higher taxes than most nations, which allows it to spend more money on foreign aid. Third, although Norway does participate in international peacekeeping missions and has been an ally of the United States, it does not have a large military, which also gives it more money to contribute.

Norway is more generous than the United States and most other nations in other ways, too. According to the Center for Global Development, a nonpartisan Washington, D.C., think tank, Norway and other Scandinavian nations have a long tradition of free trade with other nations and have been very welcoming to foreign immigrants who want to help their nations. When all its contributions are added up into a single index of commitment to helping poorer nations, Norway emerges as the most generous nation in the world, followed by Denmark, Sweden, and the Netherlands. By these same measures, the United States is number 20 on the list of the world's 21 richest nations. ∎

Foreign Aid Spending, 2004

Nation	Total Spending (billions of U.S. dollars)	Percentage of Gross National Income
Norway	$2.20	0.87%
Denmark	2.04	0.85
Sweden	2.72	0.76
Netherlands	4.20	0.73
France	8.47	0.41
Switzerland	1.56	0.41
United Kingdom	7.88	0.36
Germany	7.53	0.28
Canada	2.60	0.27
Spain	2.44	0.24
Japan	8.91	0.19
Italy	2.46	0.19
United States	19.70	0.17

SOURCE: Organization for Economic Cooperation and Development, December 2005.

Public Diplomacy

In July 2002, President George W. Bush created the White House Office of Global Communications to address the question he asked before a joint session of Congress only a week after the terrorist attacks on New York City and Washington, D.C.: "Why do they hate us?" The office is designed to enhance America's image abroad, thereby countering the image of the United States as the "Great Satan," as some of its enemies describe it.[29] In 2005, Bush put his former political adviser and White House aide Karen Hughes in charge of the public diplomacy effort. Although the administration hoped that she would bring a more effective political perspective to the job, her initial efforts to rebuild the U.S. image in Arab nations were unsuccessful.

Bush was not the first president to worry about the U.S. image abroad. President Franklin Roosevelt created the Office of War Information early in World War II, which in turn established the Voice of America program to broadcast pro-American information into Nazi Germany. President Harry Truman followed suit early in the Cold War with the Soviet Union by launching the Campaign of Truth, which eventually led to the creation of the United States Information Agency under President Dwight Eisenhower. Both agencies exist today and are being strengthened as part of the "new public diplomacy." In this case, the word "public" refers to citizens of other nations, not the United States.

Public diplomacy is a blend of age-old propaganda techniques and modern information warfare. It has three basic goals: (1) to cast the enemy in a less favorable light among its supporters, (2) to mold the image of a conflict such as the war in Afghanistan, and (3) to clarify the ultimate goals of U.S. foreign policy. The United States has tried to convince the people of Afghanistan that Osama bin Laden is the true enemy of the people, the war is not between Muslims and Western democracies, and that the war is about preventing the deaths of innocent women and children in both Afghanistan and the United States.

Special Problems in Defense Policy

The United States has a long history of military involvement in world affairs. Since 1945, more than 100,000 U.S. military personnel have died in undeclared wars such as Vietnam and Iraq; more than 400,000 have suffered battle injuries.[30] But Congress has formally declared war on only a few occasions. The war in Afghanistan was never formally declared, nor was the current war in Iraq. Although Congress passed joint resolutions authorizing the use of force in both cases, the president moved military forces into position well before passage.

Americans believe that the United States should use its military power carefully. As noted earlier in this chapter, almost three out of five Americans said the United States should use military force to prevent future terrorism, compared with just one out of five who said it should use force to punish the terrorists. Even after the events of September 11, 2001, substantial numbers of Americans continued to believe that the United States should not send forces into regional conflicts when other means are available to achieve our objectives. Many also continued to believe that the United States should not intervene in conflicts without a broad public consensus at home and an alliance of nations abroad.

The All-Volunteer Force

The Constitution authorizes Congress to do what is "necessary and proper" in order to "raise and support Armies," "to provide and maintain a Navy," and "to provide for calling forth the Militia." The problem is that the role of the United States in the world has changed dramatically since 1789, as have the nation's military needs. Although our boundaries once defined our major national interest, U.S. interests now reach around the globe.

Military conscription (the draft) was first instituted in 1862, during the Civil War. It was used during World War I, when Congress passed the Selective Service Act. This act called for a draft of males between the ages of 21 and 30, with exemptions for certain public officials and for clergy. In both instances, conscription ended when the conflicts ended. The first peacetime draft began in 1940, with the Selective Service and Training Act. By the time of Pearl Harbor, in late 1941, men between the ages of 18 and 35 were eligible for the draft. When World War II ended, however, the draft continued, in various forms, for almost three decades.

Shortly before the Vietnam War ended, Congress replaced the draft with an *all-volunteer force*, which is composed entirely of citizens who choose to serve. The armed services offer a variety of benefits to make sure they meet their annual recruiting targets, including signing bonuses, special training, college tuition, and even help finding a job after service is completed. The all-volunteer concept has worked well during peacetime, particularly when the quality of recruits is measured by their educational achievement and performance on standardized intelligence tests. However, all services began having difficulty recruiting new troops as the Iraq war lingered on. With troops in constant danger, military service lost some of its luster as the place to be all you can be.

It is not yet clear that the all-volunteer force will be able to recruit enough Army troops to fight future wars. "I worry about this every single day—recruiting and retention," said the Army's top personnel officer in July 2004. "We are recruiting a volunteer force during a time of war. We've never done that before."[31] Although the Air Force and Navy continue to meet their annual recruiting targets, the Army failed to meet its targets in the spring of 2004, in part because of the increased death toll in Iraq, and in part because of the Abu Ghraib prison abuse scandal.

The Army is far from a crisis point, however, and expects to meet its targets by increasing recruitment and retention bonuses—soldiers now receive a one-time $10,000 bonus for reenlisting at the end of their two-year tour. But the United States may eventually have to return to a draft to fill hard-to-recruit positions in information technology, medicine, and intelligence, where the military faces intense competition from the private sector. Because all males must register with the Selective Service at age 18, the list of potential draftees is already on file.

In the first major offensive of the war on terrorism, American troops invaded Afghanistan. Women now make up approximately 15 percent of the total enlistment in the U.S. armed forces.

Women in Combat

As the number of women in the armed forces has increased, so has the number of women who serve in combat zones. Whereas women constituted 6 percent of U.S. forces in the first war in Iraq in 1991, they constituted 15 percent of forces in Iraq in 2000. Although most of their jobs were in noncombat positions, Iraq has been a very dangerous place to serve—by October 2006, more than 60 women had been killed and 300 wounded. The first female casualty in Iraq was Army private Lori Piestewa, a member of the Hopi Indian Tribe, who was killed when her supply convoy got lost in the desert only days after the war began.

Federal law already allows women to fly Air Force and Navy combat aircraft, and the Pentagon has now opened thousands of combat-related positions in the military services to women. The military is redesigning its assignments to ensure that equal opportunity exists within its ranks but has yet to assign women to specific combat roles.

Despite their accomplishments in battlefield support positions, women have faced significant barriers to advancement in the armed services, most notably sexual harassment.[32] In March 2003, for example, the Air Force removed the senior leadership at the Air Force Academy in Colorado Springs following repeated allegations of sexual abuse. Further congressional investigation found 142 specific complaints of verbal and physical abuse between 1993 and 2003, many of which had been received with indifference or retribution. Most of the Academy's senior leadership was removed in the wake of the scandal, including the superintendent, commandant and vice commandant of cadets, and dean of the faculty. Despite these efforts, women continue to report harassment in all branches of the armed services.

The Politics of Defense Spending

The U.S. defense budget reached $535 billion in 2006, a figure that covers everything from weapons and ammunition to salaries for soldiers, sailors, pilots, and civil servants, and pensions for more than 1.5 million retired Defense Department personnel (see Figure 20–2). The defense budget also includes more than $12 billion dedicated to nuclear weapons research and maintenance and environmental cleanup projects that are actually run by the Department of Energy.[33] However, the $535 billion does not include the cost of the wars in Iraq or Afghanistan.

Defense spending fell dramatically at the end of the Cold War as weapons systems were canceled or postponed, bases closed, ships retired, and large numbers of troops brought home from Germany, the Philippines, and elsewhere. The Army was cut by over 30 percent, and the National Guard and the military reserve were cut back about

FIGURE **20–2 Defense Expenditures, 2006.**

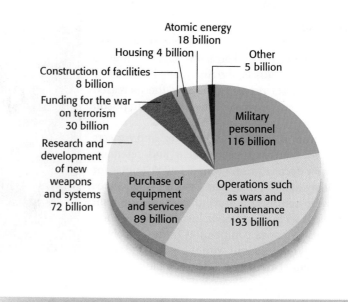

25 percent. As a result, defense spending also fell, dropping from 25 percent at the height of the Cold War in the mid-1980s to 15 percent in 2000. The defense budget surged with the war on terrorism and the Iraq war, however, rising to 19 percent of the budget in 2006.

Even as defense spending rises, some experts argue that the nation needs a much lighter, highly mobile force to combat terrorism and that further spending on "Cold War legacy" systems such as nuclear attack submarines and heavy tanks is wasteful.[34] Moreover, some experts argue that investment in such systems reduces funding for lighter equipment and body armor needed to protect soldiers in Iraq. They argue that the United States cannot have it all—meaning old Cold War systems, high-tech space defenses, decent military pay, and the kind of expensive precision weaponry used in Afghanistan and Iraq.

Despite the logic, Congress can rarely muster the will to kill a weapons system. Cutting defense spending means cutting jobs, and cutting jobs, especially those in the home districts of powerful members of Congress, is politically painful.[35]

Weapons are, in fact, a major American industry, one that members of Congress work hard to promote and protect. As former World War II hero Dwight Eisenhower warned in his presidential Farewell Address in 1960, the United States must be wary of the *military-industrial complex* that supports increased defense spending as a way to protect jobs. Eisenhower's words are well worth rereading today:

> This conjunction of an immense military establishment and a large arms industry is new in the American experience. The total influence—economic, political, even spiritual—is felt in every city, every State house, every office of the Federal government. We recognize the imperative need for this development. Yet we must not fail to comprehend its grave implications. Our toil, resources and livelihood are all involved; so is the very structure of our society.
>
> In the councils of government, we must guard against the acquisition of unwarranted influence, whether sought or unsought, by the military industrial complex. The potential for the disastrous rise of misplaced power exists and will persist.[36]

The military-industrial complex has become even more significant as the U.S. military has privatized many of the jobs that are essential for war. Private contractors were responsible for building the bases and feeding U.S. troops in Iraq, for example, as well as maintaining and repairing military equipment, providing security for foreign diplomats, and even interrogating prisoners.[37] As of April 2006, more than 150 contractors had been killed in the Iraq war. Contractors have provided much of the security for

U.S. diplomats and Iraqi officials, and have often been used to support U.S. combat operations.

The military is also dealing with a dramatic number of mergers and acquisitions in the defense industry. In the 1950s, for example, 11 different companies were building fighter aircraft; by 2006, just three companies remained: Boeing, Lockheed-Martin, and Northrop Grumman. As the consolidation has increased, the amount of competition between firms has declined, making the U.S. more dependent on a handful of firms to build the next generation of weapons.[38]

Prospects for the Future

The world has become a much more uncertain place since the end of the Cold War, if only because the U.S. now faces many potential "hot spots" where individual nations and groups can challenge its views. Moreover, the Internet has increased access to information across the world; the global economy has increased competition for jobs and markets; and the war on terrorism has increased anti-American sentiment in many nations.

The United States is clearly struggling to address this uncertainty without frustrating the public or compromising basic democratic principles. On the one hand, for example, Americans favor open borders, easy movement of imports and exports, short lines at airports, quick access to information, and protection of their privacy. On the other hand, they want government to monitor terrorists, detect dangerous cargo, ensure airport security, keep secrets from the enemy, and make sure that no one slips through the border to bring harm to the nation.

Although the goals are not necessarily contradictory, they do require a careful balance of individual liberty and national interest. They also involve an effort to prevent the spread of terrorism by promoting global peace and understanding. The war on terrorism will not be won in a single battle with a single adversary, nor will weapons of mass destruction disappear without a broad international commitment to action. As the United States has learned over the hard months of combat in Iraq, coalition building may be difficult, frustrating, and most certainly time-consuming, but, ultimately, it may be the only option available. Having fought the Iraq war largely on its own, the U.S. has come to realize that it needs help to accomplish its goals. Whether it will be able to find that help given its recent unilateralism is still in doubt.

Summary

1. U.S. foreign and defense policy reflects debates about three basic issues: how the United States views the world, how the United States engages the world, and how the United States uses power. Idealists believe in a world of cooperation, while realists believe that conflict is inevitable based on each nation's self-interests. Isolationists believe the United States should limit contact with the world, while internationalists think the United States must be involved in securing world peace and protecting the nation through deterrence. Finally, advocates of hard power believe the United States should make its case through economic and military strength, while advocates of soft power believe the United States should use diplomacy to solve most international problems.

2. The United States has a number of competing foreign and defense policy goals, but the top seven today are: (1) controlling the spread of weapons of mass destruction, (2) winning the war on terrorism, (3) securing lasting peace in the Middle East peace, (4) promoting free trade abroad, (5) addressing global climate change, (6) promoting democracy and international understanding, and (7) winning the war in Iraq.

3. The war in Iraq has dominated U.S. foreign and defense policy for the past three years. The war had three goals: to remove Saddam Hussein from power, to destroy Iraq's capacity

to make and use weapons of mass destruction, and to convert Iraq into a democracy. Although Hussein was deposed, no weapons of mass destruction were found. Democracy may take years to establish in view of continuing violence.

4. The president has the primary responsibility to shape foreign and defense policy. The principal foreign policy adviser is the secretary of state, although other cabinet secretaries, including the secretary of defense, are also influential. The National Security Council and the intelligence agencies also play key roles. Public opinion, interest groups, foreign countries, political parties, and Congress also affect the making of foreign policy.

5. Presidents, Congress, and the American people all become involved in defining our vital national security interests, but they often have contradictory views. Presidents must sometimes act swiftly and decisively. The role of the president in foreign affairs was strengthened during the cold war years as the United States developed an enormous standing military capability and an extensive intelligence network. Presidents are often in a good position to see the nation's long-term interests above the tugging of bureaucratic and special interests. But in our constitutional democracy, presidents and their advisers must consult with Congress and inform the American people. The media and special interests also play a role.

6. U.S. foreign policy interests are advanced by one or a combination of the following strategies: diplomacy, foreign aid, economic sanctions, political coercion (including the breaking off of diplomatic relations), covert action, and military intervention. Traditional diplomacy is often augmented by the U.S. role in the United Nations.

7. The U.S. military is an all-volunteer force. Although the military does provide enormous opportunities for women and minorities, women have yet to play a significant role in combat. The all-volunteer force has been weakened in recent years by the Iraq war, which has put more stress on soldiers and exposed many to the dangers of combat.

Further Reading

GEORGE H. W. BUSH AND **BRENT SCOWCROFT,** *A World Transformed* (Knopf, 1998).

WARREN CRISTOPHER, *In the Stream of History: Shaping Foreign Policy for a New Era* (Stanford University Press, 1998).

IVO H. DAALDER AND **MICHAEL E. O'HANLON,** *Winning Ugly: NATO's War to Save Kosovo* (Brookings Institution Press, 2000).

JOSEPH G. DAWSON III, ED., *Commanders-in-Chief: Presidential Leadership in Modern Wars* (University Press of Kansas, 1993).

LOUIS FISHER, *Presidential War Power,* 2nd ed. (University Press of Kansas, 2004).

JOHN LEWIS GADDIS, *The Cold War: A New History* (Penguin Press, 2005).

JOHN LEWIS GADDIS, *The United States and the End of the Cold War* (Oxford University Press, 1992).

RICHARD N. HAASS, *The Reluctant Sheriff: The United States After the Cold War* (Council on Foreign Relations, 1997).

RICHARD N. HAASS AND **MEGHAN L. O'SULLIVAN,** EDS., *Honey and Vinegar: Incentives, Sanctions, and Foreign Policy* (Brookings Institution Press, 2000).

OLE HOLSTI, *Public Opinion and American Foreign Policy* (University of Michigan Press, 1996).

SAMUEL HUNTINGTON, *The Clash of Civilization and the Remaking of World Order* (Simon & Schuster, 1996).

LOCH K. JOHNSON, *Secret Agencies: U.S. Intelligence in a Hostile World* (Yale University Press, 1996).

HAROLD HONGJU KOH, *The National Security Constitution: Sharing Power After the Iran-Contra Affair* (Yale University Press, 1990).

STEVEN KULL AND **I. M. DESTLER,** *Misreading the Public: The Myth of a New Isolationism* (Brookings Institution Press, 1999).

THOMAS W. LIPPMAN, *Madeleine Albright and the New American Diplomacy* (Westview Press, 2000).

ROBERT LITAN, *Globalphobia* (Brookings Institution Press, 2002).

ROBERT S. LITWAK, *Rogue States and U.S. Foreign Policy: Containment After the Cold War* (Johns Hopkins University Press, 2000).

NATIONAL COMMISSION ON TERRORIST ATTACKS ON THE UNITED STATES, *The 9/11 Commission Report* (W.W. Norton, 2004).

JOSEPH NYE, *Soft Power: The Means To Success In World Politics* (PUBLIC AFFAIRS, 2005).

MICHAEL E. O'HANLON, *How to Be a Cheap Defense Hawk* (Brookings Institution Press, 2002).

WILLIAM PERRY, *Preventive Defense: A New Security Strategy for America* (Brookings Institution Press, 1999).

JOHN PRADOS, *Keepers of the Keys: A History of the National Security Council from Truman to Bush* (Morrow, 1991).

ROSEMARY RIGHTER, *Utopia Lost: The United Nations and World Order* (Twentieth Century Fund, 1995).

JOSEPH ROMM, *Defining National Security: The Nonmilitary Aspect* (Council on Foreign Relations, 1993).

GEORGE SHULTZ, *Turmoil and Triumph: My Years as Secretary of State* (Scribner, 1993).

RONALD STEEL, *Temptations of a Superpower* (Harvard University Press, 1995).

STEPHEN R. WEISSMAN, *A Culture of Deference: Congress's Failure of Leadership in Foreign Affairs* (Basic Books, 1995).

GEORGE C. WILSON, *This War Really Matters: Inside the Fight for Defense Dollars* (CQ Press, 2000).

BOB WOODWARD, *Plan of Attack* (Simon & Schuster, 2004).

KeyTerms

realism, p. 579

idealism, p. 580

isolationism, p. 580

internationalism, p. 580

unilateralism, p. 580

Bush Doctrine, p. 581

multilateralism, p. 581

hard power, p. 581

soft power, p. 581

theory of deterrence, p. 582

weapons of mass
destruction, p. 582

normal trade relations, p. 584

National Intelligence
Director, p. 591

bipartisanship, p. 597

economic sanctions, p. 600

Make It Real

FOREIGN POLICY

In this simulation, students articulate
their foreign policy views.

PUBLIC EDUCATION IS ONE OF THE GREAT PROMISES OF THIS

country. But is America keeping that promise? This ABC News program offers a timely report card on the nation's public education system. Hard hit by state budget cuts in recent years, the system is also under immense pressure from the No Child Left Behind Act—legislation that demands much of schools but, say critics, provides little funding to help them meet the mandated goals. California has particular challenges because of a growing and diverse student population.

Report Card

ORIGINALLY AIRED: 10/8/03

PROGRAM: Nightline

RUNNING TIME: 17:24

Critical Thinking Questions

After viewing "REPORT CARD" *on your* ABC-NEWS DVD *answer the following questions.*

1. WHAT IS AN UNFUNDED MANDATE?
Give examples of unfunded mandates in the No Child Left Behind Act that are discussed in "Report Card."

2. IN "REPORT CARD," AUTHOR JONATHAN KOZOL
says the "way we finance education in the United States is archaic, chaotic, and utterly undemocratic." What about our education financing leads him to say this?

3. ARNOLD SCHWARZENEGGER RECENTLY VETOED
a bill that would have redefined proficiencies in core areas measured by the No Child Left

Behind Act. What are arguments against the Federal Government setting standards and defining things like proficiency?

611

Chapter 21

State and Local Politics

WHO GOVERNS?

★

MANY OF THE MOST CRITICAL DOMESTIC AND ECO-
NOMIC ISSUES FACING THE UNITED STATES ARE
DECIDED BY OUR STATE AND LOCAL OFFICIALS.
ELECTED AND APPOINTED OFFICIALS IN OUR STATES AND
LOCALITIES DECIDE HOW OUR SCHOOLS ARE RUN, HOW
WELFARE POLICY IS SHAPED, WHO GOES TO PRISON OR GETS
PROBATION, AND HOW MUCH PROPERTY AND SALES TAXES
WE PAY. SUCH CHALLENGING RESPONSIBILITIES AS OVERSEE-
ING THE TRANSITION FROM WELFARE TO WORK, MAINTAINING
prisons and jails (almost 92 percent of the people incarcerated in Amer-
ica are in state and local facilities, not federal prisons), and bringing the
residents of the inner cities into the economic mainstream require
leadership and thoughtful public policy at the state and local levels of
government, as well as in Washington, D.C.

State and local governments have recovered from the economic
downturn of the early 2000s, but now face longer-run fiscal challenges.
As the federal government confronts large budget deficits federal officials feel pressure to cut federal spending on domestic programs, and
state and local governments are increasingly forced to rely on their own
resources. Yet state and local governments also feel political pressure to
keep taxes low. Supporters of different
issue areas must therefore compete for
scarce dollars from state and local governments. Spending on health and elementary and secondary education
programs has grown in recent years
despite this competition, while state
budget cuts have more typically been
imposed on public libraries, colleges and
universities, prisons and other correctional facilities, transportation projects,
parks, and environmental and natural
resource programs. Many states have
also cut the size of their own bureaucracies. Thus, a major question facing many
states is how to sustain financial support
for their many functions outside of
health and education.[1]

State and local governments flourished long before there was a national
government. Indeed, the framers of our
Constitution shaped the national government largely according to their practical
experience with colonial and state governments. What happens today in state
and local governments continues to influence the policies of the national government. The reverse, of course, is also
true: The national government and its
policies have an important impact on
local and state government. The national
government's activities—such as the
war against international terrorism, key
Supreme Court decisions, and major
congressional investigations and legislation—receive such great publicity that we
often overlook the countless ways governments closer to home affect our lives.

Studying state and local governments to find out how they operate and
who governs them is also a challenge.
It is one thing to study our national
system, vast and complex as it is; it is
some thing else to study 50 separate

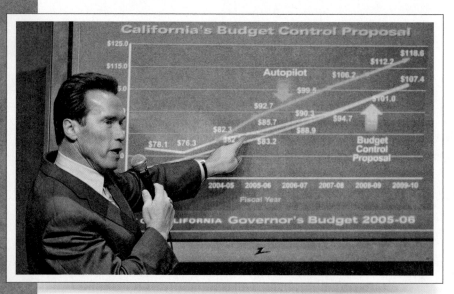

"It is difficult for the common good to prevail against the intense concentration of those who have a special interest, especially if the decisions are made behind locked doors."

OUTLINE

★

Who Has the Power?

★

The Stakes in the Political Struggle

★

Participation Patterns in Small and Medium-Sized Cities

★

Challenges for State and Local Governments

613

Actor Arnold Schwarzenegger was elected governor of California in a special election held because of the state's budget crisis and his promise not to raise taxes.

state governments, each with its own legislature, executive, and judiciary and each with its own intricate politics and political traditions. Moreover, state and local governments are only part of a much larger picture. To discuss the government of the state of Mississippi or the city of Detroit without mentioning race, the government of New York City or Los Angeles without noting the politics of ethnic groups, or the government of Texas without referring to the cattle and oil industries would be to ignore the real dynamics of the political process. State and local governments, like the national government, are more than organizational charts. They are systems of politics and people with their own unique histories that affect how and what public policies are enacted. The great variations among the states and localities—in population, economic resources, and environment—make comparisons and generalizations difficult.

Still, every government system is part of a larger social system. A government is a structure and a process that resolves, or at least attempts to manage, conflicts. It regulates, distributes, and sometimes redistributes property and wealth. It is also a means for achieving certain goals and for performing services desired both by those who govern and by the governed. It operates in the context of an economic system, class structure, and lifestyle that are often more important than the structure of the government itself, or even the nature of its political processes. The interrelations among the economic, social, and political systems are complex and difficult to unscramble.[2]

This picture is complicated further by the fact that almost 88,000 cities, counties, towns, villages, school districts, water control districts, and other governmental units are piled one on top of another within the states.[3] If all states or cities or towns were alike, the task might be manageable. But of course they are not. Each city, like each state, has distinct characteristics.

Who Has the Power?

How can we grasp the operations and problems of state and local government without becoming bogged down in endless detail? We can do so by focusing on the core components of democratic governance: citizen participation, liberty, constitutional checks and balances, representation, and responsible leadership. Further, we can address several questions that throw light on all these problems: Who governs? How much influence or control is in the hands of the business community? Does political power tend to gravitate toward a relatively small number of people? If so, who are these people? Do they work closely together, or do they oppose each other?

Do the same people or factions shape the agenda for public debate and dominate all decision making? Or do some sets of leaders decide certain questions and leave other questions to other leaders or simply to chance?

In 1924, two sociologists from Columbia University, Robert and Helen Lynd, decided to study a typical American city as though they were anthropologists investigating a tribe in Africa or Indonesia. For two years, they lived in Muncie, Indiana—at that time a city of 38,000 residents—asking questions and watching how people made their living, raised their children, used their leisure time, and joined in civic and social associations. The Lynds reported that despite the appearance of democratic rule, a social and economic elite actually ran things.[4] Their work stimulated studies in all kinds of communities to find out whether power is concentrated in the hands of the few, is dispersed among the many, or operates in some other way.

Relying on a mix of research methods, social scientists since the Lynds' time have studied patterns of power in communities and arrived at a variety of findings. Floyd Hunter, a sociologist who analyzed Atlanta in the 1950s, found a relatively small and stable group of top policy makers drawn largely from the business class. This elite operated through secondary leaders who sometimes modified policy, but the power of the elite was almost always important.[5] In contrast, Robert Dahl and his graduate students at Yale studied New Haven at the same time and concluded that although some people had a great deal of influence, there was no permanent elite. Instead, there were shifting coalitions of leaders who sometimes disagreed among themselves but who always had to keep in mind what the public would accept when making decisions.[6]

Rule by a Few or Rule by the Many?

One group of investigators, chiefly sociologists such as Hunter, have been concerned with **social stratification** in the political system—how politics is affected by divisions among socioeconomic groups or classes in a community. These social scientists assume that political influence is a function of social stratification. They try to find out who governs particular communities by asking various citizens to identify the people who are most influential. Then they study those influential people to determine their social characteristics, their roles in decision making, and the interrelations among them and between them and the rest of the citizens. Using this technique, they find that the upper socioeconomic groups make up the *power elite*. Elected political leaders are subordinate to that elite, and the major conflicts within the community are between the upper and the lower socioeconomic classes.

Other investigators question these findings and raise objections to the research techniques used. They contend that the evidence in social stratification studies does not support the conclusion that communities are run by a power elite. Rather, the notion of a power elite is merely a reflection of the techniques used and the assumptions made by stratification theorists. Instead of studying the activities of those who are thought to have "clout," these researchers insist, one should study how decisions are actually made.

Researchers conducting *community power* studies analyzing the making of decisions usually find a relatively open, pluralistic power structure. Some people do have more influence than others, but that influence is shared among many people and tends to be limited to particular issues and areas. For example, those who decide how the public schools are run may have little influence over other economic policies. For many communities and issues, there is no identifiable group of influential people. Policies emerge not from the actions of a small group but rather from the unplanned and unanticipated consequences of the behavior of a relatively large number of people, especially from the countless contending groups that form and win access to those who make the important decisions. According to community power theorists the social structure of the community is certainly important, but it is not the determining factor in how goods and services are distributed.

Comparing power elite and community power studies highlights the fact that how we ask questions often influences the answers we get. If we ask highly visible and

social stratification
Divisions in a community among socioeconomic groups or classes.

actively involved citizens for their opinions of who is powerful, we find that they name a relatively small number of people as the real brokers of power. But if we study dozens of local events and decisions, we find that a variety of people are actually involved—different people in different policy areas.

Other studies of local politics suggest that local values, traditions, and the structure of governmental organizations also determine which issues get on the local agenda.[7] Thus tobacco, mining, or steel interests may be so dominant in some areas that tax, regulation, or job safety policies are kept off the local policy agenda for fear of offending the "powers that be." Those "powers" may indeed go to great lengths to prevent what they deem to be adverse policies. This type of research alerts us to weigh carefully the possibility that defenders of the status quo can mobilize power resources in such a way that nondecisions may be more important than decisions. In effect, these researchers tell us not only to study who governs but also to study the procedures and rules of the game. They urge us to determine which groups or interests would gain and which would lose by political decisions.[8]

On many economic policy matters, local corporations and business elites are involved. Studies of cities in Michigan and Georgia, employing refined and contextual analysis of political decision making, concluded that business elites are indeed important but they are not necessarily the controlling factor in city governance:

> There is, then, no controlling hand in community politics. No conspiracy of business and government exists. Business interests do not invariably dominate government policy even where a single industry dominates the community. However, the giant industrial companies do provide the backdrop against which the public policy process operates in the industrial city. They are always there, seldom intervening in specific policy matters but never far from the calculations of policy makers.[9]

Studies of states and communities have now produced enough findings to infer how formal government institutions, social structure, economic factors, and other variables interact in a working political system.

The Stakes in the Political Struggle

The national government has become the driving force behind the nation's economic strength and security. It assumes major responsibility for protecting civil rights, fighting inflation and unemployment, regulating economic sectors, and subsidizing weaker sectors of the economy—not to mention its position in matters of war and peace. State and local governments cannot claim so central a role. Yet the role of states and localities is increasing over a range of domestic policies, even though they diverge in their priorities and policies as a result of the maze of interests in each state. In response to health concerns and budget deficits, for example, five states charge $2 or more per pack of cigarettes in taxes, while 14 charge less than 50 cents; some cities, like New York, impose additional taxes both to discourage smoking and to raise revenue.

Since World War II, state and local government activities have increased much faster than the nondefense activities of the federal government. In the past decade, the federal government has been downsizing while state and local governments have been growing. About six times as many people work for state and local governments—16 million—than work for the federal government, which has fewer than 3 million civilian employees.[10] Most state and local employees work in education (8.5 million), hospitals (919,000), law enforcement (902,000), and corrections (707,000).[11]

State and local governments deal more directly with the average person than the national government does, because neighborhood, school, and housing problems are closely regulated at the state and local levels. States have had to assume greater responsibilities for collecting taxes, setting economic and social priorities, and administering most welfare and job creation programs as a result of cutbacks in federal funds and devolution of responsibilities to the states.

The points at which people come into contact with government services and officials most often involve schools, streets and highways, parks and playgrounds, police and fire protection, zoning, and health care. But even in these areas, the mix of national, state, and local programs and responsibilities is such that it is often hard to isolate what each level of government is doing. In addition, there are some national-to-individual relationships that bypass state and local governments altogether, such as the Internal Revenue Service, the U.S. Postal Service, and Social Security.

The Maze of Interests

Special-interest groups can be found in varying forms in every state and locality. For example, industrial Rhode Island has farm organizations, and rural Wyoming has trade unions. Influential economic pressure groups and political action committees, organized to raise and disburse campaign funds to candidates for public office, operate in the states much as they do nationally. They try to build up the membership of their organizations, they lobby at the state capitals and city halls, they educate and organize the voters, and they support their political friends in office while opposing their enemies. They also face the same internal problems all groups face: maintaining unity, dealing with subgroups that break off in response to special needs, and balancing democracy with discipline.

Government reaches into many trivial aspects of our lives, such as restrictions on our pets.

One great difference, however, is that group interests can be concentrated and highly influential in states and localities, whereas their strength tends to be diluted in the national government. Big business does not really run things in Washington, D.C., any more than the Sierra Club, the Catholic Church, or the American Legion does. But in some states and localities, certain interests clearly dominate because they represent the social and economic majorities of the area. Few politicians in Wisconsin will attack dairy farmers, few candidates for office in Florida will oppose benefits for senior citizens, and few officeholders in Idaho will support gun control. In other areas, industries such as timber or energy are influential because of their role in the local economy.

It is the range and variety of these local groups that give American politics its special flavor, excitement, and challenge: auto unions and manufacturers in Michigan, corn and hog farmers in Iowa, gas and oil dealers in Texas, gun owners in New Hampshire and Idaho, tobacco farmers in North Carolina and Virginia, poultry growers in Arkansas, Boeing and Microsoft in the Seattle, Washington area, coal miners in West Virginia, and sheep ranchers in Utah.

However, the power of interest groups should not be exaggerated. Because of internal divisions, we have to be cautious about lumping all workers, all businesspeople, all teachers, all Hispanics, or all African Americans together. The union movement is sometimes sharply divided among the truckers, building trades, machinists, auto workers, and so on. The business community is often divided between big industrial, banking, and commercial firms on the one hand and small merchants on the other. In New England, Irish and Italian fraternal societies express the opinions of their respective groups on public issues; other organizations speak for people of French Canadian or Polish descent. New England politicians fear the power of ethnic groups to influence elections, especially primaries, yet there are plenty of examples of "Yankees" winning in heavily ethnic areas. Similarly, Asian American, Latino, and African American communities are playing an increasingly important role in elections in states such as California, Florida, and Texas.

Compared to the other considerations affecting voters' choices, the ethnic factor may be small. Still, even a small percentage of the populace voting according to their ethnic interests can have a decisive effect on an election. Much depends on the character of the candidates and their personal appeal. Any group, no matter how strong, must cope with a variety of cross pressures, including a general sense that the voter does not vote for "one of our own" on that basis alone.

Other interests that are more specialized may also have a close relationship with local government. Many businesspeople either sell products or perform services for the state: milk dealers, printers, contractors, parking meter manufacturers, computer and communications technology firms, makers of playground equipment, textbook publishers, and so on. They often organize, formally or informally, to improve their relations with purchasing officials. At the local level, developers and home builders and their lawyers press for zoning and planning commission action. Millions of dollars are often at stake, and the resulting action or inaction frequently shapes both the economic growth and the environmental quality of a community.

The September 11, 2001 attack on the World Trade Center was a blow not only to the United States, but also to New York City and New York state.

Business interests are inevitably involved in city and county politics and policy making. As one study of Atlanta found, the business elite is rarely a passive or reluctant partner in setting local priorities. "Atlanta's postwar political experience is a story of active business-elite efforts to make the most of their economic and organizational resources in setting the terms on which civic cooperation occurs."[12] Businesses everywhere depend on local governments for parking, good roads and transportation, safety, urban renovations, and much more. Business elites get involved in long-range community planning, are keenly interested in who gets elected, and are ever watchful of changes in taxation structures.

Another type of interest group intimately concerned with public policy is the professional association. States license barbers, beauticians, architects, lawyers, doctors, teachers, accountants, dentists, and many other occupational groups. At the statehouse you will find lobbying representatives from the Beauticians Aid Association, the Funeral Directors and Embalmers Association, the Institute of Dry Cleaning, and the Association of Private Driver-Training Schools. Associations representing such groups are concerned with the nature of the regulatory laws and the makeup of the boards that do the regulating. They are especially concerned about the rules for admission to their profession or trade and about the way in which professional misconduct is defined and punished. Stiffening licensing requirements for physicians will decrease the supply of new doctors, for example, and thereby raise the incomes of those in practice. Bar associations, for the same reason, closely monitor licensing standards for the legal profession and the appointment of state and local judges.

Today, other groups of citizens are also likely to organize to influence decisions in the state capital: those who are pro-life and those who are pro-choice, those who want stiffer sentences for drunken driving, and those who favor three-strikes-and-you're-out legislation to send repeat criminals to jail for life. Environmental, antitax, and antismoking groups, animal rights activists, and prison guards are also well organized. Increasingly significant are environmental groups such as the Sierra Club, both in forging public policies and as forces in election contests.

Lobbyists at the Statehouse

Many businesses, especially large corporations, employ lobbyists, public relations specialists, political consultants, or law firms to represent them.[13] Consulting is a growing business in state politics, usually performed by specialized lawyers or former state legislators. For a fee, lobbyists push desired bills through the legislature or block unwanted ones. This kind of activity again raises the question of who has clout or who governs. Clearly, those who can hire skilled lobbyists and other experts to shape the public agenda often wield more influence than unorganized citizens, who rarely even follow state and regional governmental decision making.

The Changing Face of American Politics

The Growing Diversity of State Populations

The 2000 Census showed significant changes in both the number and location of minority Americans. The percentage of whites declined from 76 percent of the population in 1990 to 69 percent in 2000, while the percentage of Hispanics increased from 9 percent to 12.5 percent, blacks from 11.7 percent to 12.1 percent, and Asian-Pacific Islanders from 2.8 percent to 3.7 percent.

America's growing minority population is not equally distributed across the states and cities, however. Roughly three-quarters of all Hispanics live in the West or South, accounting for a quarter of the population in the West and 12 percent of the population in the South. In turn, over half of all blacks live in the South, making up 20 percent of the total population; while half of the Asian-Pacific Islander population live in just three states, California, New York, and Hawaii; and two-

fifths of all Native Americans live in the West.

Although Hispanics are counted as a single minority group, almost 60 percent of Hispanics identified themselves in the 2000 Census as Mexican, 10 percent as Puerto Rican, and 4 percent as Cuban. Similarly, the Asian-Pacific Islander population includes Asian Indians, Chinese, Filipinos, Japanese, Koreans, Native Hawaiians, and Samoans; while Native Americans include members of six American Indian tribes—Cherokee, Navajo, Latin American Indian, Choctaw, Sioux, and Chippewa—as well as Eskimo.

By 2025, the U.S. Census Bureau predicts that the percentage of white Americans will decline to 62 percent. By then, four states and the District of Columbia will be "majority minority," and several others will be closing in on the 50 percent mark. ■

Top Ten States by Minority Population in 2000		Top Ten States by Minority Population Projected in 2025	
District of Columbia	72%	Hawaii	77%
Hawaii	71	District of Columbia	74
New Mexico	52	California	66
California	50	New Mexico	60
Texas	44	Texas	54
Mississippi	38	New York	47
Louisiana	36	Maryland	46
Maryland	35	New Jersey	45
New York	35	Alaska	43
Georgia	33	Louisiana	43

SOURCE: U.S. Census Bureau, "State Projections by Single Year of Age, Sex, Race, and Hispanic Origin, 1995–2025," accessed online at www.census.gov/population/www/projections/stproj.html on February 15, 2004.

By 2025, the U.S. Census Bureau predicts that the percentage of white Americans will decline to 62 percent.

Lobbyists are present in every state capital, and they are there to guide through the legislature a small handful of bills their organization wants passed or to stop those their organization wants defeated.[14] Legislators process hundreds or even thousands of bills each year, in addition to doing casework on behalf of constituents and worrying about reelections. Shrewd lobbyists usually get a chance—sometimes several chances—to influence the fate of their bills of interest.

There is a widespread impression that lobbyists have freer rein in state legislatures than they do in the U.S. Congress and, what is more, that bribes or informal payoffs by lobbyists are cruder and more obvious in state legislatures. Certainly lobbying restrictions in the majority of states are more relaxed than at the federal level, although in some of the larger states they may be more stringent. There is less media coverage of state politics in many states than is focused on national politics in Washington, D.C. Corruption of legislators and state officials is usually hard to prove. However, exposure of scandals in several states pushed many legislatures to curb election abuses and pass ethics codes with stringent conflict-of-interest provisions.[15] Several legislatures have enacted comprehensive financial disclosure laws, and today most state governments are more open, professional, and accountable than in the past.[16] Former President Jimmy Carter, who served in the Georgia Senate and then became governor, recalled that only a "tiny portion" of the 259 members of the Georgia legislature were dishonest. But Carter found that "it is difficult for the common good to prevail against the intense concentration of those who have a special interest, especially if the decisions are made behind locked doors."[17]

In a few states, one corporation or organization may exercise considerable influence; in others, a "big three" or "big four" dominate politics. But in most states, there is

YOU KNOW WHAT THIS COUNTRY NEEDS? THIS COUNTRY NEEDS MORE PRISONS!

SIMPLY PUT THE CRIMINALS IN THE JUG AND THROW AWAY THE KEY!

DID YOU KNOW THEY WERE BUILDING ONE JUST THREE BLOCKS OVER?

WHAT?! NOT IN MY NEIGHBORHOOD THEY AIN'T!!

Don Wright/Don Wright, Inc.

competition among many organizations; no single group or coalition of groups stands out. In no state does only one organization control legislative politics, although the powerful Anaconda Company once came close in Montana. For example, some 400 lobbyists are registered in Arkansas. Of these, 125 represent utilities; more than 200 represent individual businesses, industry, or professions; nine represent labor interests; eight work on behalf of senior citizens; and three lobby for environmental interests. The Arkansas Power and Light Company, the railroads, the poultry and trucking industries, the teachers, and the state Chamber of Commerce are the most effective lobbyists. "It is still true that ordinarily those with greater economic resources, greater numbers, and higher status have far more impact than those who lack these attributes," writes political scientist Diane Blair. "Nevertheless, an increasingly complex economy has produced many more actors in the political system, and especially when there is division among the economic elite, some of the lesser voices can be heard."[18]

In Michigan, about 1,250 lobbyists are registered with the state, including representatives of the "big three" automakers, the United Auto Workers, the AFL-CIO, the Michigan Education Association, the Michigan Manufacturers Association, the city of Detroit, the Michigan Chamber of Commerce, certain conservation and environmental groups, and various antitax groups.[19]

As a result of the influence and growing number of lobbyists, states have adopted ethics laws that regulate their activities. Five states completely ban lobbyists from contributing to campaign contributions at any time; for instance 22 states prohibit lobbyists from making contributions during a legislative session. Eighteen states restrict the monetary value of gifts that public employees may receive.[20]

Not to be overlooked are the growing number of groups and media outlets that view themselves as "watchdogs" of the public policy process. Groups such as the League of Women Voters, Common Cause, and various citizens' groups regularly monitor state politics for questionable fund-raising or lobbying practices. Their "watchdog" efforts are sometimes aided by reporters who cover state capitals.

Participation Patterns in Small and Medium-Sized Cities

Although it is widely believed that citizens feel "closer" to city and county governments than the more remote national government in Washington, D.C., citizens generally take less interest in, vote less often in, and are less informed about their local governments than they are about the national government. There are understandable reasons for the lower involvement in local government. Although issues about where to locate a garbage dump or a prison or how to deal with police brutality can arouse considerable attention, most of the time local governments are preoccupied with relatively noncontroversial routine matters, such as keeping the roads in shape, providing fire and police service, attracting businesses that can create more jobs, or applying for state and federal financial assistance.

Local communities want to keep their tax rates down and promote their cities as "nice places" in which to live, work, and raise families. Mayors and city officials generally try to avoid controversy and criticism that will divide a community. Although they do not always succeed, they go to considerable lengths to be reasonable and work for the good of the community. Few aggressively seek to alter the status quo. They do not, as a rule, try to promote equality by redistributing various resources to needier citizens. **Redistributive policies** are programs to shift wealth or benefits from one segment of the population to another, usually from the rich to the poor. Local officials tend to believe that this is the task of the national or state authorities—if they think it should be done at all. Typically, they say their communities do not have the funds for such programs. They might add, "Go see the governor" or "Go talk to your member of Congress." This may be good advice, because various programs (educational loans, unemployment compensation, disability assistance, and so on) explicitly designed to help the less fortunate are administered at the state or federal level.

redistributive policies
Governmental tax and social programs that shift wealth or benefits from one segment of the population to another, often from the rich to the poor.

Neighborhood groups sometimes become involved in protecting their neighborhoods and petitioning for improvements. One concern that often activates neighborhood groups is the possibility that "undesirable" facilities might be located in their neighborhood, such as drug rehabilitation clinics, prisons, dumps, or homeless shelters. Although attendance at local government meetings is usually low, the announcement of a landfill area or a prison construction project often stimulates the reaction that local officials call NIMBY, an acronym for "Not In My Back Yard!" This can have the perverse effect of forcing facilities like airports to remain in densely populated areas, since it is too difficult to find alternative sites for them.

The Role of Local Media

Most communities have only one newspaper, and in small communities it is often a weekly. Some newspapers and local radio and television stations do a good job of covering city and county politics, but this is the exception rather than the rule. Reporters assigned to cover local politics are often inexperienced beginners, yet they provide the only news that citizens get about their city council or zoning board. Even the best of them have difficulty conveying the full complexities of what is going on in a column or two of newsprint.

Some local newspapers enjoy a cozy relationship with elected local officials. Sometimes the owners or editors are social friends or golfing buddies of local officials. Friendships and mutual interests develop, and close scrutiny of what goes on in city hall takes a backseat to city boosterism. In effect, "newspapers boost their hometown, knowing that its prosperity and expansion aid their own. Harping on local faults, investigating dirty politics, revealing unsavory scandals, and stressing governmental inefficiencies only provide readily available documentary material to competing cities."[21]

Editors and station managers recognize that their readers, viewers, or listeners are more interested in state or national news, and especially in sports, than in what is going on at municipal planning meetings or county commission sessions. Much of what takes place in local government is rather dull. It may be important to some people, yet it strikes the average person as decidedly less exciting than what goes on at the White House, whether Congress has finally solved the Social Security problem, whether their stocks have gone up or down, or whether the New York Jets or the Los Angeles Lakers won last night. We have dozens of ways to find out about Congress and the White House, but we usually have only one source for stories about the mayor or sheriff or school board. Of course, we could attend board meetings or even talk with our mayor, but that is not what most people are likely to do.

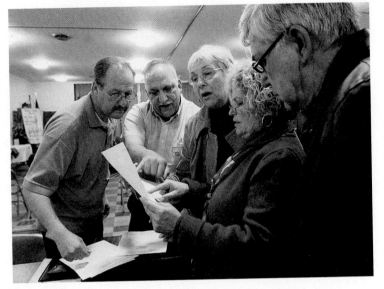

National issues often start at or filter down to the local level. Members of Dover C.A.R.E.S. (Citizens Actively Reviewing Educational Strategies) in Dover, Pennsylvania, examine a list of school board candidates in 2005. The group was formed to oppose the school board's vote to require biology teachers to read a statement in class saying that Charles Darwin's theory of evolution is not fact and alternative theories exist, including "intelligent design."

Apathy in Grassroots America

Voter apathy in local elections is summed up in the bumper sticker "DON'T VOTE. IT ONLY ENCOURAGES THEM." Many important political and economic transactions in communities are ignored by the press and citizens. Charter revision and taxation often galvanize only those directly affected by the new taxes or regulations. Even New England town meetings have difficulty getting people to participate—despite the fact that decisions made at these meetings have major consequences for local tax rates and the quality of the schools, the police force, and the parks and recreational areas. Thomas Jefferson once proclaimed the town meeting to be the noblest, wisest instrument yet devised for the conduct of public affairs, but today most towns find that only about 2 or 3 percent of the population cares enough to come.[22]

The major reason for grassroots apathy is that local politics simply does not interest the average person. Most people are content to leave politics and political responsibilities to a relatively small number of activists while they pursue their own private concerns—their bowling leagues, their children's Little League or soccer games, golf, or fishing. In a healthy democracy, we can expect that most people will be involved with their families and jobs; other than voting occasionally, they tend to leave civic responsibilities to a relatively small number of their fellow citizens. This is probably a reasonable choice. It may also be an indication of satisfaction with the state of the community.

Cynicism about the effectiveness and fairness of local political processes is sometimes reflected in the politics of protest—mass demonstrations, economic boycotts, even civil disorders—to make demands on government. When certain issues become intense, people become politically active. African Americans, Hispanics, homosexuals, and others form political organizations to present their grievances and marshal votes. Neighborhood organizations work for better housing and enforcement of inspection ordinances and to prevent crime and drug dealing.

Civic Initiatives in Local Governments

Just as there will always be indifference toward politics and apathy about government, there will also be creative, entrepreneurial people who are willing to step forward and find new ways of solving problems. States such as Oregon and Minnesota seem to encourage a climate of innovation and civic enterprise, and a wider look at the United States finds buoyant, optimistic, creative problem solvers in nearly every corner of the nation.

Enterprising local activists have advocated and implemented cost-saving energy programs, environmental cleanup campaigns, recycling and solar energy initiatives, job training centers, AIDS prevention efforts, housing for the elderly, tutoring for the illiterate, housing for the poor, and hundreds of other problem-solving and opportunity-enhancing community efforts.[23] In almost every case, they create partnerships with elected officials at city hall, sometimes with the Urban League or Chamber of Commerce, and often with local foundations and business corporations.

Sometimes it takes a tragedy to get community groups mobilized. Such an event happened in Boston when gang members burst into the funeral of a young man. "In the presence of the mourners, the gang killed one of those in attendance," writes the Reverend Eugene Rivers of the Azusa Christian Community:

> That brazen act told us we had to do more. Now. That young man's death galvanized us, and soon the Ten Point Coalition was reaching out to at-risk youth. Our mission was to pair the holy and the secular, to do whatever it took to save our kids. The black churches worked hand-in-hand with the schools, courts, police, and social service agencies. We called on anyone and everyone who had the means to help our children. We formed programs for teens, neighborhood watches, and patrols . . . We established ourselves in the neighborhood, standing on the same street corner where the drug dealers once stood. We tracked down the thieves, dealers, and gangs. We tried to give people a chance, but if they wouldn't take it, we staked our claim and ran them out of our neighborhood.[24]

There are persistent debates about how to solve social, economic, and racial problems in our large metropolitan areas. Some people contend that government cannot undertake this task and that private initiatives can be more effective. Others insist that state and local governments are best suited to deal with these challenges. Still others contend that imaginative public–private collaboration is needed to fashion the strategies and mobilize the resources to revive cities and bring about greater opportunity. Whatever the merits of such contending interpretations, it is clear that neighborhood organizations and spirited civic renewal are critical to the vitality of local government.[25]

Challenges for State and Local Governments

Most states and communities are confronting difficult times. People want better schools, a clean environment, and safe roads. About one-third of our inner-city governments and school systems are in financial distress. The cycle of poverty in the inner cities remains one of the greatest threats to the economic health

History Makers

De Witt Clinton

No one demonstrated more dramatically how the actions of a single state could shape American history than did De Witt Clinton, whose vigorous efforts in support of the digging of the Erie Canal made possible the "Wedding of the Waters" in 1825, the connecting of the Great Lakes to the Atlantic Ocean by means of a continuous navigable waterway. Clinton was not the first New York State politician to press for a canal between Lake Erie and the Hudson River but once a few state legislators convinced him to take up the cause in 1810, his commitment to the canal helped make a reality out of a project that most observers thought was an impossibility only a few years before its construction began.

Clinton was born in 1769 to a politically prominent New York family; he studied and briefly practiced law after graduating from Columbia College. He then served as secretary to George Clinton, the governor of New York and De Witt's uncle, from 1790 to 1795. He entered the New York State legislature in 1797 and was U.S. Senator from 1802 to 1803. He served ten one-year terms as mayor of New York (1803–1815), usually while he also held state offices, including state senator (1806–1811) and lieutenant governor (1811–1813). He later served as governor from 1817 to 1823, and from 1825 until his death.

Clinton advocated many causes during his political career, including public education, sanitation, antislavery, hospitals for the mentally ill, and assistance for the poor. But he applied his prodigious energy, intellect, and charisma most persistently to the building of the 350-mile canal between Buffalo and Albany—what eventually came to be called "Clinton's ditch." After the state legislature appointed him, in 1810, to the commission charged with developing a plan for linking Lake Erie with the Hudson, Clinton fought hard for the canal—overseeing technical analyses, writing reports arguing its feasibility, giving innumerable speeches, enlisting powerful allies (including state senator and future president, Martin Van Buren), lambasting the canal's many opponents in vivid language, and seeking ways to fund the unprecedented endeavor.

He and other canal supporters faced many obstacles. The terrain that had to be cleared and dug was full of trees, dense brush, and large rocks; the engineering profession in the United States at the time was nearly nonexistent; and federal financial support never materialized. But Clinton used his florid rhetoric, and exploited the failure to secure federal funding, to build public support for the canal within New York and put pressure on the state legislature to underwrite the project. Finally, in 1817

the legislature passed a bill that guaranteed funds for the completion of the project, largely by selling bonds to be paid off with tolls from the canal.

Eight years later, the canal was completed. It rendered the Great Lakes region an economic tributary to the port of New York—and contributed greatly to New York's rapid growth into the nation's largest city and its financial center. It spurred economic and urban development around the Great Lakes, as well as in upstate New York. It inspired canal construction elsewhere in the country, resulting in 3,000 miles of waterways by 1837. And it helped to unify the new nation by knitting the eastern and western states and territories together, culturally as well as economically. In all these ways, De Witt's Erie Canal project showed that American states could step in and take on enormous tasks with national, not just local, consequences.

For more on De Witt Clinton and the Erie Canal, see Peter L. Bernstein, *Wedding of the Waters: The Erie Canal and the Making of a Great Nation* (W. W. Norton, 2005). ∎

De Witt Clinton

[T]he 350-mile canal betweeen Buffalo and Albany . . . eventually came to be called "Clinton's Ditch."

---

of the country. Cities, though, usually cannot raise enough funds through local taxes to create jobs and to provide adequate educational opportunities and housing. Federal and state initiatives have attempted to create economic opportunities for inner-city residents. Community development banks, "empowerment zones," Head Start, charter schools, and national service (Americorp) programs have all been tried in an attempt to bring residents of depressed inner cities into the economic mainstream. However, these efforts have been inadequate and must compete with other demands on financially pressed states and localities. Meanwhile, federal officials are proposing cuts in many of

Not all citizens are apathetic. These young people are spending their free time rehabilitating a community center.

the domestic programs that aid state and local governments, while continuing to add mandates that force additional spending by those same governments.[26]

The following central issues in state and local communities command the attention of the country. They vary depending on location, of course, yet these urgent challenges are part of the unfinished business of a government by the people:

■ *People want more services* yet at the same time would like to see their taxes cut. City and state officials are constantly trying to do more with less and introduce efficiencies into city and state operations. Voters in many communities have enacted spending limits that constrain growth in public budgets.

■ *Racism still exists in many communities.* As our nation has become more diverse, most Americans have learned to appreciate the strength that comes from multiple cultures and races. Yet racist groups still thrive in some areas, and bigotry and discrimination persist.

■ *Drugs, gangs, and drug-related crime impose tough policy challenges.* The costs of corrections and prisons have skyrocketed in recent years, yet gangs, drugs, and crime are still a menace in some urban and even rural areas.

■ *The costs of homeland security are rising.* Due to the continuing threat of international terrorism, states and localities must assume a greater role in safeguarding airports and other public places, as well as assume the role of "first responders" in the event of an attack. Mayors of major cities and some governors, however, complain that the national government has failed to provide the funding necessary for these expanded responsibilities.

■ *Poverty in the inner cities persists.* We have extremes of rich and poor within metropolitan regions, and often the wealthier suburbs turn their backs on the problems and poverty of the older cities. Indifference to these inequalities and lack of opportunities may undermine a sense of community and fairness in America.

■ *We need to guarantee the best possible education for all our young people.* Parents are demanding better education and more parental involvement. Communities have been experimenting with educational choice and competition, school vouchers, and charter schools. Improving the public schools is necessary, but their resources and the salaries of teachers are often too low to attract and retain the best-qualified teachers. State and local governments have the responsibility to pay for public education, so educational reform and the search for excellent teachers and learning processes will remain a top state and local priority. Many states, though, object to the Bush administration's push for national standards, under its No Child Left Behind program, as an intrusion on the states and too costly in the current economic environment. Utah decided to forgo federal funds and declined to participate in the program, and some other states may do likewise.

Local residents often form groups to handle and discuss issues that are important to their neighborhood, as illustrated by this gathering of Neighborhood Watch volunteers.

■ *Environmental regulation, land use, and recycling are also major challenges at the local level.* Every city and state wants economic growth and economic opportunities for its workers and businesses, but many forms of economic development impose costs in terms of the quality of air, water, landscapes, and health. Local officials face tough decisions about the need to balance economic and environmental concerns.

■ *Health care costs and delivery are challenges to all levels of government.* Health care reform has been an important policy issue for many years. Massachusetts has enacted universal health insurance; others have worked to control costs. Still, many of the uninsured end up obtaining health care in emergency rooms in local public hospitals, which in turn seek funding from the local and state governments.

For more information on these and other issues confronting state and local governments, go to our home page at www.prenhall.com/burns, or to the Web site of the Council of State Governments at www.csg.org, or that of the National Conference of State Legislatures at www.ncsl.org.

Summary

1. Many of the most critical domestic and economic issues facing the United States today are decided at the state and local levels of government.

2. Studies of states and communities have investigated how formal government institutions, social structure, economic factors, and local traditions interact to create a working political system. Some studies find that a power elite dominates, whereas community power studies find pluralism and diverse interest groups competing for influence over a range of policy areas. Special-interest groups operate in every state and locality, but their influence varies.

3. Although it is widely believed that local governments are "closer to the people" than the national government, voting and other forms of participation at the local level are low.

4. Innovative programs at the local level address problems in education, the environment, crime and violence, and ways to improve community life. Local civil action is one of the most important forms of citizen participation in politics.

Further Reading

JOHN R. BAKER, ED., *The Lanahan Readings on State and Local Government* (Lanahan Press, 2001).

BUZZ BISSINGER, *A Prayer for the City* (Random House, 1997).

ALLAN CIGLER AND **BURDETT LOOMIS,** EDS., *Interest Group Politics,* 6th ed. (CQ Press, 2002).

FRANK J. COPPA, *County Government* (Praeger, 2000).

THOMAS E. CRONIN AND **ROBERT D. LOEVY,** *Colorado Politics and Government: Governing the Centennial State* (University of Nebraska Press, 1993).

E. J. DIONNE JR., ED. *Community Works: The Revival of Civil Society in America* (Brookings Institution Press, 1998).

THOMAS D. DYE AND **SUSAN A. MACMANUS,** *Politics in States and Communities,* 12th ed. (Prentice Hall, 2006).

ROBERT S. ERIKSON, GERALD C. WRIGHT, AND **JOHN P. MCIVER,** *Statehouse Democracy: Public Opinion and Policy in the American States* (Cambridge University Press, 1993).

STEPHEN GOLDSMITH, *The Twenty-First Century City* (Regnery, 1997).

VIRGINIA GRAY, RUSSELL HANSON, AND **HERBERT JACOB,** EDS., *Politics in the American States,* 8th ed. (CQ Press, 2003).

VALERIE C. JOHNSON, *Black Power in the Suburbs* (State University of New York Press, 2002).

DANIEL KEMMIS, *The Good City and the Good Life* (Houghton Mifflin, 1995).

MADELEINE KUNIN, *Living a Political Life* (Vintage, 1995).

JOHN O. NORQUIST, *The Wealth of Cities* (Addison-Wesley, 1998).

ROBERT F. PECORELLA AND **JEFFREY M. STONECASH,** *Governing New York State* (State University of New York Press, 2006).

DOUGLAS W. RAE, *City: Urbanism and Its End* (Yale University Press, 2003).

ALAN ROSENTHAL, *The Third House: Lobbyists and Lobbying in the States,* 2d ed. (CQ Press, 2001).

KEVIN B. SMITH, *State and Local Government 2005–2006* (CQ Press, 2005).

JON C. TEAFORD, *The Rise of the States* (Johns Hopkins University Press, 2002).

JOSEPH F. ZIMMERMAN, *The New England Town Meeting: Democracy in Action* (Praeger, 1999).

See also the *State Politics and Policy Quarterly* and the Web site of the Council of State Governments at www.csg.org.

KeyTerms

social stratification, p. 615

redistributive policies, p. 620

★ ★ ★
Make It Real

STATE GOVERNORS

The simulation allows students to sign or veto bills.

Chapter 22

State Constitutions
CHARTERS OR STRAITJACKETS?

O N NOVEMBER 18, 2003, THE MASSACHUSETTS SUPREME JUDICIAL COURT RULED THAT DISCRIMINATING AGAINST SAME-SEX MARRIAGES VIOLATED THE STATE CONSTITUTION. IN RESPONSE THE MASSACHUSETTS STATE LEGISLATURE CALLED A SPECIAL CONVENTION IN 2004 TO PROPOSE AN AMENDMENT BANNING SAME-SEX MARRIAGES. THE CONVENTION, WHICH MET IN FEBRUARY AND AGAIN IN MARCH, APPROVED AN AMENDMENT BARRING SAME-SEX MARRIAGES, BUT RECOGNIZING "CIVIL UNIONS" THAT CONFER THE same benefits, rights, and privileges on same-sex couples that legally married couples enjoy. But under Massachusetts's Constitution, the amendment must be resubmitted in the next legislative session for approval, and then submitted to the voters for ratification in a statewide vote. The amendment was submitted to the legislature and subsequently voted down in September of 2005.

Massachusetts is not alone in considering constitutional reforms growing out of the controversy over same-sex marriages. States often use constitutional changes to address a wide variety of issues, and their constitutions are typically easier to amend than is the federal Constitution. For example, to head off state court decisions like the one in Massachusetts, 20 states have adopted constitutional amendments prohibiting same-sex marriage, and at least six more states will vote on similar bans before the end of 2006. Seven states approved constitutional amendments to restrict marriage to a man and a woman in 2006: Colorado, Idaho, South Carolina, South Dakota, Tennessee, Virginia, and Wisconsin. The total of such states to approve an amendment is now 23. Arizona was the first state to reject a constitutional amendment.[1]

Massachusetts is, however, unusual in its attempt to use a constitutional convention to change its fundamental document. Even though constitutional conventions were both common and important in the nineteenth century, they have rarely been successful since then. New York, for example, has had only four constitutions since 1777. Yet, by constitutional mandate, every 20 years the people of New York are asked on a general election ballot if they want to convene a constitutional convention to propose a new constitution. In addition, the legislature—with the concurrence of the governor—put the question of a new constitutional convention before voters in 1965. The voters approved, and a convention was held in 1967, but then voters rejected its work. Voters were asked again in 1977 if they wanted to convene another convention, however, this time they said no.

"Whenever these great objects are not obtained, the people have a right to alter the government and to take measures necessary for their safety, happiness, and prosperity."

JOHN ADAMS, PREAMBLE TO THE MASSACHUSETTS CONSTITUTION

OUTLINE

★

The Roots of
State Constitutions

★

Amending State Constitutions

★

The Politics of
Constitutional Revision

★

The Future for
State Constitutions

The question of a new constitutional convention was placed before voters again in 1997. In preparation for the vote, the Temporary Commission on Constitutional Revision was set up to identify issues and to inform voters about the need for a new constitution. The commission called for a convention of ordinary citizens and suggested that New Yorkers take advantage of new technology such as cable television and electronic town meetings to observe convention proceedings. The commission targeted the budget process, state–local relations, education, and public safety as being of special importance.[2] A constitutional convention, commission members argued, could then write a new constitution in clear English, simplify voter registration, improve voting rules and ballot access, regulate campaign finance and lobbying, reform the legislative process, restore confidence in the courts, reform the tax structure, and improve protection for the environment.[3]

Opposed to calling a constitutional convention were the American Federation of Labor–Congress of Industrial Organizations (AFL-CIO), the Conservative party, the Sierra Club, the National Abortion Rights Action League (NARAL), select antitax groups, and some legislative leaders from both parties. They saw a convention as a threat to their right to organize; trial lawyers worried about limits on lawsuits; environmentalists feared that a convention might jeopardize provisions protecting open spaces; some women's groups were fearful that the convention might restrict abortion rights; and some conservatives feared that liberal interests would control the convention.

Two weeks before the election, however, polls indicated that voters, upset by the apparent inability of the state government to get anything done, were overwhelmingly in favor of calling for a constitutional convention to make government work better. But opponents of constitutional revision got busy. Unions and other anticonvention groups launched television advertisements, direct-mail operations, and phone banks, arguing that the convention was a waste of money and would open the door to dangerous changes. On November 5, 1997, 62 percent of New York voters rejected the call for the convention.[4] The voters will again get a chance to answer this question in 2017.

New York's experience in 1997 is not unusual. In recent years, voters in several states have rejected calls for a constitutional convention. For example, in 1994 Michigan voters rejected the call for a convention by almost 3 to 1 in all 183 counties; Arkansas voters in December 1995 rejected the call by 4 to 1 in all 75 counties.[5] No constitutional conventions have been held since Rhode Island had one in 1986, and it won approval of the voters for only eight of 14 proposed revisions.

Now, you might give some thought to your own state constitution. Like the U.S. Constitution, state constitutions are both instruments of government and limitations on government. Unlike the federal Constitution, however, state constitutions are not popular symbols. On a trip to your state capitol, you are unlikely to find the state constitution "displayed [like] the federal Constitution, in a setting similar to a Shinto shrine."[6]

In this chapter, we examine the roots of state constitutions and some of the ways we work around constitutional rigidity. Then we look at methods of amending state constitutions, ending with a few case studies of states that have tried, for the most part unsuccessfully, to adopt new constitutions.

The Roots of State Constitutions

The first state constitutions were outgrowths of colonial charters. Massachusetts and New Hampshire can boast of charters still in effect that are older than the federal Constitution. Virginia added a bill of rights to its constitution in 1776— 13 years before the national one was proposed by Congress. In 1787, the framers of the U.S. Constitution drew heavily on their experience with these state charters. "What is the Constitution of the United States but that of Massachusetts, New York, and Mary-

"What is the Constitution of the United States but that of Massachusetts, New York, and Maryland! There is not a feature in it which cannot be found in one or the other."

JOHN ADAMS

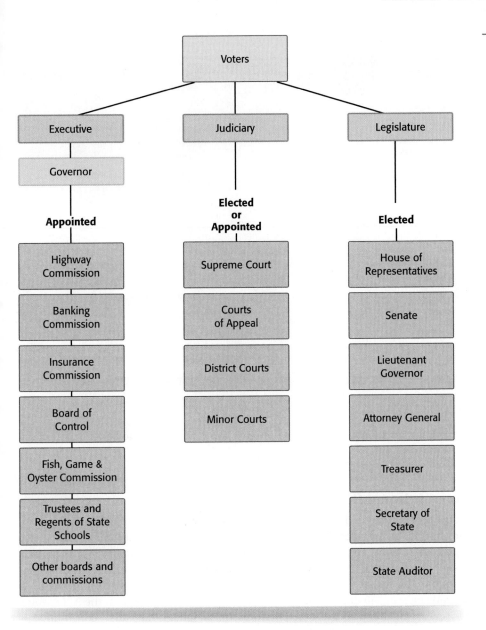

FIGURE 22–1 **Government Under a Typical State Constitution.**

land!" remarked John Adams, who drafted the Massachusetts constitution in 1779. "There is not a feature in it," he said, "which cannot be found in one or the other."[7]

Subject only to the broad limitations of the U.S. Constitution, the people of each state are free to create whatever kind of republican government they wish. All state constitutions are similar in general outline (see Figure 22–1). A state constitution typically consists of a preamble, a bill of rights, articles providing for the separation of powers, a two-house legislature, an executive branch, and an independent judiciary with the power of judicial review. It will also have a description of the form and powers of local units of government, an article on how to amend the constitution, and miscellaneous provisions dealing with election procedures, corporations, railroads, finances, education, and other specific topics.

The bills of rights in state constitutions are, in general, similar to the federal Bill of Rights, although they sometimes use different language and cover different rights. For example, "Twenty-seven states have speech and press guarantees quite different from the First Amendment's, thirty-eight have equality guarantees dissimilar to the equal protection clause, and thirty-nine have guarantees of a separation of church and state that differ from the federal establishment clause."[8] Fourteen states adopted

FIGURE **22–2 Amending State Constitutions.**

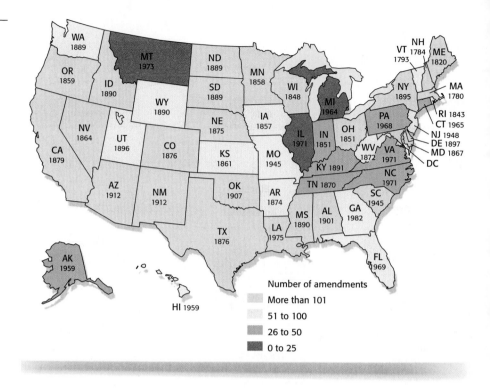

FIGURE **22–2 Amending State Constitutions.**

Number of amendments
More than 101
51 to 100
26 to 50
0 to 25

"Until changed by the Legislature, the flash test for all kerosene oil for illuminating purposes shall be 115 degrees Fahrenheit; and the specific gravity test for all such oil shall be 40 degrees."

THE OKLAHOMA CONSTITUTION

the Equal Rights Amendment even though it was never ratified to become part of the U.S. Constitution.

Constitutional Rigidity and Evasion

State constitutions contain more details than the U.S. Constitution does. They are longer and more specific, and they require more frequent amendment[9] (see Figure 22–2). Louisiana has had 11 constitutions; Georgia has had ten; South Carolina, seven; and Alabama, Florida, and Virginia, six.[10] Only 19 states have their original constitution. The average state constitution is more than 100 years old and has been amended about 140 times.[11] State constitutions vary in length—from the 9,200 words of New Hampshire's to the 340,136 words of Alabama's. Alabama's constitution is almost 40 times as long as the U.S. Constitution, which has only 7,400 words; the median state constitution has around 26,000.[12]

Although most state constitutional provisions deal with matters of significance, some also deal with seemingly trivial subjects. California's much-amended constitution (more than 500 amendments since it was adopted in 1879) goes into great detail about the taxation of fish and the internal organization of various departments.[13] The Oklahoma constitution proclaims, "Until changed by the Legislature, the flash test for all kerosene oil for illuminating purposes shall be 115 degrees Fahrenheit; and the specific gravity test for all such oil shall be 40 degrees."[14] The South Dakota constitution declares that providing hail insurance is a public purpose and authorizes the legislature to levy a tax to provide for it.[15] The Alabama constitution authorizes the legislature to indemnify peanut farmers for losses incurred as a result of *Aspergillus flavus* (a fungus) and freeze damage in peanuts.[16] In 2000, Florida voters approved an amendment declaring the development of high-speed ground transportation in the public interest of reducing traffic congestion. And in 2003, Wisconsin voters approved one guaranteeing the people's right to fish, hunt, trap, and take game.

In addition to the inclusion of these statute-like details, state constitutions and their more frequently adopted amendments tend to be longer than the U.S. Constitution because their bills of rights cover, in addition to the traditional rights, more recently emerging protections, such as the right to an equal public education and the rights of victims of crimes. Finally, state constitutions have to deal with a much wider range of functions, educational provisions, and criminal codes than the U.S. Constitution, which created a national government of intentionally limited powers to deal with a limited range of functions.[17] It has long been asserted that the length and detail of state constitutions account for the fact that many of them have not had the longevity of the national Constitution. However, a careful empirical study shows that "longer and more detailed design of state constitutions actually enhances rather than reduces their longevity."[18]

Constitutions as Roadblocks

The earliest state constitutions granted authority to the legislatures without much restriction on how their powers should be exercised. However, after many legislatures gave special privileges to railroads, canal builders, and other interests, constitutional amendments were adopted to prevent such abuses. Distrusting the legislatures, reform groups began to insist that certain controls be incorporated into state constitutions. In time, state constitutions became encrusted in layer upon layer of procedural detail.

What does this mean for democratic government? It means that state constitutions—intended as charters of self-government—are often like straitjackets imposed on the present by the past. Some outdated provisions do no harm, but more often they are roadblocks to effective government. For example, fixed salaries do not reflect changing economic conditions, and a rigidly organized administrative structure is incapable of adjusting to new needs. When a constitution allocates revenues, elected officials are deprived of discretion to deal with budget difficulties as they arise. Under such conditions, the legislature cannot act, and voters then turn to constitutional amendments.

Getting Around the Constitution

Can state constitutions forever prevent the wishes of the people from being carried out? Not necessarily. The constitutional system of the states, like that of the national government, includes more than the formal written document. Unwritten rules, practices, political parties, and interest groups also shape events. When people see a need for change, they usually find ways to overcome formal barriers.

One device for constitutional change is **judicial interpretation**, whereby judges modify a constitutional provision by a new interpretation of its meaning. The more complex and detailed the constitution, the easier it is for judges to redefine meanings. Actually, one reason for the growing length of some constitutions is that amendments are often required to reverse judicial interpretations. In addition, some sections of state constitutions have been invalidated by federal action, especially in the area of civil rights and suffrage.

The New Judicial Federalism

In what is called **new judicial federalism**, state constitutions have taken on greater importance. For decades, state judges tended to look only to the U.S. Constitution and Bill of Rights and how the U.S. Supreme Court interpreted these documents. But since the 1970s, as the Supreme Court has become more conservative, some state supreme courts have been relying on their own state constitutions and state bills of rights in overruling state laws and the actions of state and local officials. In recent years, state supreme courts have refused to follow the U.S. Supreme Court's rulings and on the basis of their state constitutions have held unconstitutional sobriety checkpoints for

judicial interpretation
A method by which judges modify the force of a constitutional provision by reinterpreting its meaning.

new judicial federalism
The practice of some state courts using the bill of rights in their state constitutions to provide more protection for some rights than is provided by the Supreme Court's interpretation of the Bill of Rights in the U.S. Constitution.

The Changing Face of American Politics

Affirmative Action in the 2006 Congressional Elections

Although the vast majority of Americans believe that everyone should be given an equal start in achieving a good education, job, housing, and so forth, they do not agree on just how to remedy past discrimination. Americans are especially divided on affirmative action, which is designed to address past discrimination against women, minorities, and other disadvantaged groups.

In 2006, Michigan voters spoke on the issue in the elections by enacting an amendment to their state constitution to "ban public institutions from using affirmative action programs that give preferential treatment to groups or individuals based on their race, gender, color, ethnicity or national origin for public employment, education or contracting purposes." The amendment also contained

a specific list of public institutions affected by the ban, including the University of Michigan. The University had waged a long fight to give minority applicants extra points toward admission, and had won a Supreme Court case upholding the approach.

Michigan voters rejected the approach in the November 2006 elections by a 58 percent to 42 percent margin. Although the ban on any kind of special help may not survive another Supreme Court challenge, it did reflect a statewide sentiment that all applicants should be treated the same, and specifically rejected any effort to use quotas or provide extra points in state job and university applications. Michigan voters were not saying that the demographics of state institutions should remain mostly white or male, but were

saying they did not want to give any group special status.

The vote itself reflected a division over just how to help these and other groups, with white males giving the largest share of support. According to exit polls of voters, the vote was clearly split (see table).

The constitutional ban echoes similar bans in California and Washington states, but was much more specific regarding opposition to affirmative action. It is no surprise that non-white women expressed the greatest opposition, since they are likely to be the most affected, but the University of Michigan was also intensely opposed. Like many colleges and universities, Michigan has

	Yes	No
Vote by Gender		
Men	64%	36%
Women	52%	48%
Vote by Race		
White	64%	14%
African-American	14%	89%
Vote by Race and Gender combined		
White Men	70%	30%
White Women	59%	41%
Non-White Men	30%	70%
Non-White Women	18%	82%

SOURCE: CNN.com, accessed on November 21, 2006.

used a variety of tools to increase the number of minority students, and made clear its intention to fight the ban through the federal court system. Michigan voters may want the face of American politics to continue changing, but not if it involves affirmative action. ■

drivers,[19] the random drug testing of public employees,[20] and restrictions on minors who seek abortions.[21]

This trend takes its inspiration from the U.S. Supreme Court, which sent clear messages to state supreme court judges that they are free to interpret their own state constitutions to impose greater restraints than the U.S. Constitution does. The U.S. Supreme Court and the U.S. Constitution set the floor, not the ceiling, for the protection of rights.[22] As a result, some state judges are now using their constitutions to require state legislatures to provide better schools for children living in poor neighborhoods, build low-income housing, provide public financing of abortions for poor women, and regulate business enterprises to protect the environment.[23]

When state judges rely on their own state constitutions to protect rights beyond those required by the U.S. Constitution, they do so at some political peril, since most judges are dependent on voter approval to keep their office. This risk has increased now that the Supreme Court requires state judges who wish to escape a review of their decisions by the Supreme Court to make it clear they have decided a case on adequate and independent state constitutional grounds.[24]

Amending State Constitutions

Amendments may be proposed by the state legislature, citizen-initiated ballot petitions, or constitutional conventions. After an amendment has been proposed, it must be ratified. In all states except Delaware, where the legislature can ratify as well as propose amendments, ratification is by the voters. In most states, an amendment becomes part of the constitution when approved by a majority of those voting on the amendment. In a 2003 special election in New Mexico, voters approved constitutional amendments that created a cabinet-level secretary of education and authorized more spending for public education by just 195 votes (92,198 to 92,003).[25] In some other states—such as Minnesota—approval by a majority of all those voting in the election is required. This provision makes ratification difficult, because some people who vote for candidates do not vote on amendments. In recent years, state voters have typically adopted about three-quarters of all constitutional amendments proposed by legislatures, but voter approval declined in 2004, when only half of the constitutional amendments on the ballots were adopted.[26]

Legislative Proposals

All states permit their legislature to propose amendments; in fact, this is the most commonly used method. Although provisions vary, the general practice is to require the approval by a super-majority, usually two-thirds or three-fifths, of each chamber of the legislature. Some states, however, permit proposal of an amendment by a simple majority in two successive legislatures.

A legislature may appoint a **revision commission** to make recommendations for constitutional change that, except in Florida, have no force until acted upon by the legislature and approved by the voters. The legislature creates a commission of a relatively small number of people—some selected by the governor and some by the legislature—and charges it with presenting proposals for constitutional revision. A commission is less expensive than a full-blown constitutional convention, does not require initial voter approval, and gives the legislature final control of what is presented to the electorate.

California, for instance, turned to a revision commission to overcome its budgetary gridlock after its senate rejected a 1992 proposal asking voters if they wanted a constitutional convention (the first in 113 years). California's constitution has been so frequently amended that about 85 percent of the state's annual revenues are allocated before the governor and legislature even start working on the budget! Eventually, if this trend were to continue, *all* state revenues could be allocated in this way, and there might be no state funds available for programs such as higher education and health care.[27] A 23-member revision commission was created in 1993 to examine the budget process and the configuration of state and local duties. Two years later, the commission made its recommendations. However, the legislature failed to act on any of them, in part because it was an election year. Also, because the state senate was Democratic and the state assembly Republican, it proved impossible to work out any compromise.

Constitutional commissions are in fact infrequently used. Utah is the only state that had such a commission in operation in 2004.[28] The recommendations of revision commissions are also seldom implemented quickly, perhaps because the commissioners have not been responsive to political currents or are not representative of broad enough interests. Still, a commission may provide less partisan consideration of amendments and be more resistant to single-interest groups than either the legislature or a convention. Mississippi has tried, so far unsuccessfully, to use a commission for changing its 1890 constitution, which was designed to keep African Americans out of the political process.[29]

Nonetheless, Florida, Virginia, and Louisiana have used the commission procedure to bring about significant constitutional change. Utah's Constitutional Revision Commission is a permanent body, required by law to submit recommendations for

revision commission
A state commission that recommends changes in the state constitution for action by the legislature and vote by the voters.

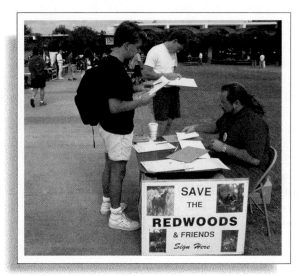

Initiative petitions deal with a great variety of reforms.

constitutional revision to the legislature 60 days before each regular session.[30] It has initiated revisions relating to the rights of crime victims as well as to changes in revenue and taxation. Florida has a Taxation and Budget Reform Commission that is called into session every ten years. Unlike other such commissions, in addition to making recommendations to the legislature, it may propose constitutional amendments directly to the voters. In 1998, the commission recommended nine amendments; Florida voters approved eight of them.

Initiative Petitions

At the end of the nineteenth century, revelations of corruption diminished the prestige of state governments, especially state legislatures. Out of this disillusionment came a variety of reforms as part of the Progressive Movement. Among the reforms was the **constitutional initiative petition**, a device that permits voters to place specific constitutional amendments on the ballot by petition. Eighteen states allow amendments to their constitutions to be proposed by initiative petitions.

The number of signatures required on petitions varies from four to 15 percent of either the total electorate or the number of voters who voted in the last election.[31] Although it takes more signatures to propose a constitutional amendment than to place other kinds of initiatives on the ballot, "the higher threshold is no longer a significant impediment to well-financed special-interest groups."[32]

Once the appropriate state official (attorney general or secretary of state) approves the precise wording of a petition, the amendment is placed on the ballot at the next general election. (California allows initiatives to appear even on primary election ballots.) The number of votes required to approve a constitutional amendment is typically a majority vote, although a few states have a more demanding requirement. Illinois requires a majority of those voting in the election or three-fifths of those voting on the amendment, and Nevada requires a majority vote on the same measure in two successive elections.

In some states, initiative proposals are limited to *amending* the state constitution, not to *revising* it. The distinction between revision and amendment is that revision refers to a comprehensive change to the basic governmental plan, a substantial alteration in the basic governmental framework, or a substantial alteration of the entire constitution, rather than to a less extensive change in one or more of its provisions.[33] Some states exclude certain subjects from amendment by initiative. Massachusetts, for example, does not allow amendments by popular initiative that concern religion, the judiciary, or judicial decisions; that are restricted to a particular town, city, or political division; that appropriate money from the state treasury; or that restrict rights such as freedom of speech.

In recent years, voters have approved about 50 percent of amendments proposed by initiative petitions. This figure compares with a slightly more than 75 percent approval rate for amendments proposed by state legislatures.[34] A variety of factors may account for the lower adoption rate of initiative measures. Initiatives tend to be used for controversial issues that have already been rejected by the legislature and engender an organized opposition. Initiatives are also often proposed by narrow-based groups or by reform-minded elites who lack broad support for their views. Sometimes initiatives are proposed in order to launch educational campaigns rather than to actually win adoption.

People anxious to limit the power of state and local governments are using the initiative process in more states. Since California in 1978 adopted Proposition 13, which limited the state government's right to raise property taxes, other states have followed suit. In addition, these "new reformers" have produced "a series of state constitutional amendments that, taken together, fundamentally altered the character and powers of state governments by limiting the tenure of governmental officials, reducing their powers, and transferring policy-making responsibilities to the people."[35] In addition,

constitutional initiative petition
A device that permits voters to place specific amendments to a state constitution on the ballot by petition.

History Makers

John Adams

One of John Adams's most enduring and important achievements was accomplished not as the second American president, a diplomat to the European powers, or a leader in the American Revolution—all roles he performed during his long and consequential life—but as an elected delegate from his hometown of Braintree, Massachusetts, to the state's constitutional convention of 1779. As a delegate, Adams eventually became the primary author of the Massachusetts constitution, which remains in effect today and is the world's oldest functioning written constitution—and is a document that greatly influenced the content of the national Constitution, which was written in 1787.

The Commonwealth of Massachusetts was making its second attempt to adopt a constitution in 1779. The first effort failed after voters in the state rejected a constitution drafted by the legislature. After this failure, the legislature called for a constitutional convention, a special body composed of persons elected by the people to write a constitution and submit it to voters for approval. This was the first use of a constitutional convention, which, by directly representing the people and not the legislature, established a sharp distinction between ordinary legislation and the state's constitutional framework—and which was used several years later to write and ratify the national Constitution.

Adams worked on the Massachusetts constitution during a very pleasant time in his life, a brief reunion with his family in Braintree between difficult diplomatic missions in France and Great Britain. Upon meeting in Cambridge, the convention of 312 persons created a committee of 30 to draft a constitution. The committee in turn appointed three persons to a subcommittee to perform that function; from that subcommittee, Adams was selected to write the first draft.

After reviewing his own past political writings, a few state constitutions already in place, and the works of a few political thinkers, Adams began writing at home and completed a draft within several weeks. He submitted a constitution of three main parts: a preamble, which laid out the aims of self-government; a bill of rights; and a section prescribing the structure of the government. Although the convention made some changes before the final draft was adopted, the changes were mostly minor and the constitution was subsequently ratified by the people in 1780.

The Massachusetts constitution contained many provisions that helped to shape the national Constitution. It provided protection against unreasonable searches and seizures. It divided governmental power into separate legislative, executive, and judicial departments—and created a bicameral legislature to ensure "that it might be a government of laws, and not of men." The state house of representatives was given the right to make impeachments and the senate to try them. The executive was given a veto over legislation. And the judiciary enjoyed considerable independence, as judges were appointed during good behavior, not elected, and thus not subject to political pressures, either from the elective branches of government or from the voters.

Some of the provisions that Adams wrote were interesting even though they were not repeated in the national document. His preamble included an explicit right to revolution: "Whenever these great objects are not obtained, the people have a right to alter the government and to take measures necessary for their safety, happiness, and prosperity." He considered religious worship to be more of a duty than a right. And he added that government had an obligation to encourage education and the arts and sciences, and to promote commerce.

After his long and distinguished public career, Adams retired to Braintree, which was renamed Quincy, and lived to the age of 90. He died on July 4, 1826, 50 years after the original Independence Day, and the same day as Thomas Jefferson, who was an author of the Virginia constitution, and the president who succeeded Adams.

For more on John Adams, see David McCullough, *John Adams* (Simon & Schuster, 2002); and Joseph J. Ellis, *Passionate Sage: The Character and Legacy of John Adams* (W. W. Norton, 1993). ■

John Adams

Adams eventually became the primary author of the Massachusetts constitution, which remains in effect today and is the world's oldest functioning written constitution.

"the focus of constitutional initiatives . . . has shifted from questions of governmental structure . . . to questions of substantive policy," such as initiatives on tort liability, the rights of gays, affirmative action, and the rights of immigrants.[36]

Constitutional Conventions

Americans once loved state constitutional conventions: 144 were held in the nineteenth century. But the twentieth century produced only 63 constitutional conventions, and only one has been convened in the twenty-first century.[37] One scholar noted that calling conventions of the people is a uniquely American idea, emphasizing that legislators cannot be trusted and that the supreme power belongs to the people.[38]

Forty-one state constitutions authorize their legislature to submit the calling of a convention to the voters; the other states assume that the legislature has the power to do so. Fourteen state constitutions require the legislature to question voters about a convention at fixed intervals, varying from every nine to every 20 years. For example, Missouri is required to submit the question to the voters every 20 years; Hawaii raises the issue every 9 years; Michigan, every 16 years.

If the voters approve, the next step is to elect delegates to a convention. Some state constitutions contain elaborate procedures governing the number of delegates, the method of election, and the time and place of the convention. Others leave the details to the legislature. The way convention delegates are selected seems to affect the kind of document the convention proposes. Selection by nonpartisan, multimember districts is more likely to result in a reform convention that makes major changes than one in which political parties play a major role.[39]

After delegates have been chosen, they usually assemble at the state capital. When the convention has prepared a draft of the new constitution, the document is submitted to the voters. First the convention delegates have to make a difficult choice: Should the voters be asked to accept or reject the new constitution as a whole? Or should they vote on each section separately?

The advantage of the first method is that each provision of a constitution ties in with another, and to secure all the advantages of revision, the entire constitution should be adopted. The disadvantage is that those who oppose a particular provision may vote against the entire constitution. When convention delegates know that a particular provision is controversial, they may decide to submit that provision separately. Whichever method they choose, the supporters of change must rally their forces to gain voter approval of their work.

The Politics of Constitutional Revision

Constitutions are not a neutral set of rules perched above the world of everyday politics. Rather, they significantly affect who gets what from government. Therefore, the way a constitution is changed can help or hinder various groups.

Although there have recently been campaigns for constitutional reform in Alabama, Oklahoma, and Texas, most people tend not to care about these reforms.[40] It is difficult to work up public enthusiasm for state constitutional revisions except among special interests, and these interests are more likely to oppose than to favor reform. Supporters of the status quo, consequently, thus have a systemic advantage, which, combined with the difficulty inherent in the amending process, helps explain the lack of revision. "Revision is time-consuming, requiring sophisticated legal and drafting skills of the highest order, and involves negotiation and compromise. To be successful, revision requires gubernatorial as well as legislative leadership. . . . An effective political campaign is essential. . . . Success at the polls is not assured. Constitutional revision can be a high-risk endeavor."[41] Following are some case studies that illustrate the risky nature of constitutional revision.

Rhode Island Amends Its Constitution

Rhode Island's biennium constitutional convention began in 1984 and produced 14 separate propositions for amending its 1843 constitution. On November 4, 1986, voters approved eight of the 14 provisions, rejecting attempts to increase compensation of state legislators, to provide for merit selection of judges, and to create a paramount right to life which would have banned abortions or public funding of them. The voters approved provisions strengthening free speech, due process, equal protection rights, and expanding fishing rights and access to the shore; they also approved a statement that the rights protected by the Rhode Island constitution are independent of the U.S. Constitution.[42]

The Rhode Island constitution calls for voters to be asked every ten years if they want to convene a constitutional convention. In November 1994, the voters rejected a convention by a vote of 173,693 to 118,545.[43] Despite this defeat in November 2001 the issue resurfaced in the form of a 2-to-1 vote in favor of a nonbinding ballot question for a constitutional convention focused on separation of powers issues. This was a response to a decision of the Rhode Island Supreme Court to the effect that the Rhode Island Constitution allows the state legislature to both make and execute state laws. After years of debate and continued pressure from Common Cause and 30 other organizations, in 2003 Rhode Island's legislature approved a constitutional amendment strengthening the separation of powers and placed it on the 2004 ballot for voters' approval. State voters passed the separation of powers amendment by a 78 percent majority, and in 2005, the state's legislature began developing legislation implementing the new constitutional provisions.[44]

Louisian7a Revises Its Constitution

The Louisiana Constitutional Revision Commission set out during 1973 and 1974 to write a streamlined "people's constitution"—one the average person could understand.[45] The AFL-CIO, National Association for the Advancement of Colored People, League of Women Voters, Committee for a Better Louisiana, National Municipal League, and many other lobbying groups became involved in shaping the new constitution. It took well over a year to write, and it cost the taxpayers approximately $4 million. In the end, a readable 26,000-word document replaced the existing 265,000-word document that contained some 536 amendments. In April 1974, Louisiana voters approved the new charter by a large margin.

The Louisiana constitution can no longer be cited as the prime example of an unworkable state constitution, although more than 100 amendments have been added since 1974 and the length has inched back up to about 54,112 words. "Indeed," according to one commentator, constitutional amendment in Louisiana is "sufficiently continuous to justify including it with Mardi Gras, football, and corruption as one of the premier components of state culture."[46]

Changing the Hawaii Constitution

More than 800 proposals for constitutional changes were submitted to the Hawaii state constitutional convention of 1978. The League of Women Voters and other groups conducted extensive information and discussion meetings, and the convention held many public hearings on key issues. The 102 delegates to the convention met for nearly three months. After extensive debate, the convention narrowed the proposals to 34 questions to be placed on the fall ballot. Convention delegates rejected proposals for the initiative, referendum, and recall; for a unicameral legislature; and for an elected (instead of an appointed) attorney general.

The delegates were not opposed to all government reforms, for they endorsed a two-term limit for governor and lieutenant governor, moved to make Hawaii's party primaries more open by allowing voters to cast ballots without declaring party preference, and authorized the state legislature to provide partial public funding for election campaigns and to establish spending limits. The convention reflected concern over government spending by setting tougher overall debt and spending limits for the state. It also strengthened environmental safeguards and gave further constitutional and financial protection to the special status of native Hawaiians. In November 1978, 74 percent of the voters went to the polls; all 34 amendments were adopted.

However, in 1986, Hawaiians rejected the periodic question of whether to call a convention by a vote of 173,977 to 139,236. Again in 1996, the question of calling a convention was put to the voters, and the vote was 163,869 in favor and 160,153 against, but 45,245 people left the question unanswered. Blank ballots were tallied as a no, in response to a decision of the state supreme court that the Hawaii constitution required approval by a majority of all ballots cast. The Ninth U.S. Circuit Court of Appeals, which refused to order a new election, sustained this decision.

Other proposals for a convention had been backed by several interests, including those who wanted to overturn a decision of the Hawaii Supreme Court favoring the legalization of same-sex marriages, by those who wanted to impose term limits, and by those who wanted to limit the power of state courts to restrict police searches.

Hawaii's experiences with the revision process are reminders that constitution making is not just an exercise in abstract argument or logical reasoning but flows directly from a state's political life.

Texas Keeps Its Old Constitution

Texas has a lengthy constitution. Adopted in 1876, it has been amended more than 370 times. The most recent effort to thoroughly revise it was in 1972, after political scandals brought in a new governor, Dolph Briscoe, and a reform-oriented state legislature. After pushing through a variety of reforms dealing with the ethics of officeholders, campaign practices, and registration of lobbyists, the legislature did an unconventional thing by calling into being a constitutional convention consisting of members of the legislature rather than a specially elected body.

After working for 17 months, the legislator-delegates came up with a much revised and shortened document intended to modernize many obsolete governmental practices. The convention deadlocked, however, over whether to give constitutional status

After three years of preparations and deliberation, the proposed Texas constitution of 1974 failed by three votes in the final hectic session of the constitutional convention.

to the state's right-to-work law, which prohibits labor contracts that require union membership as a condition of employment, so this issue was referred to the voters. In the end, neither the AFL-CIO nor Governor Briscoe supported all of the convention's recommendations. The governor was especially opposed to the proposal that legislative sessions be held annually, rather than every two years, which he argued would cause higher taxes. Advocates of the revised constitution tried to salvage their work by offering substantial parts of the new charter to the voters as amendments to the existing constitution.

Conservatives praised the old constitution, claiming it had served Texas well for 100 years. Progressives complained that the old constitution was elitist, permitted only the narrowest governmental objectives, and made real change nearly impossible. In November 1975, amid charges and countercharges, Texas voters rejected the amendments by a 2-to-1 margin.[47] Since then, Texans have approved 143 amendments and rejected 33 but have not held another convention.

The Arkansas Constitution

Arkansas's eighth constitutional convention was a protracted affair. The 100 delegates who were elected in 1978 held their organizational session in the winter of that year but did not get down to work until the spring of 1979. Having reconvened in June 1980 to revise the final draft, they submitted the proposed constitution to the voters in November 1980.

Opposition developed to a provision in the new constitution allowing the legislature, by a two-thirds vote, to set interest rates rather than limit them, as in the current constitution. Other groups opposed a provision enlarging the taxing powers of local governments. Even though then Governor Bill Clinton, the Democratic party, and the Arkansas Education Association endorsed the new constitution, the voters rejected it, 2 to 1.

The question of a constitutional convention was again put to Arkansas voters in December 1995. Those planning the 1995 convention structured the convention call in such a way that the convention would avoid addressing "issues which were not critical to state government but which would inflame folks" and would concentrate on "issues of pure governance."[48] Nonetheless, the call for the convention was decisively rejected.

Alabama Considers a New Constitution

Alabama has had six constitutions. The most recent, written in 1901 and adopted in 1902, was "a document of the Old South,"[49] unashamedly and openly designed to keep African Americans segregated in public schools and from voting or participating in governmental matters.[50] It has been amended more than 740 times and there have been many unsuccessful attempts to modernize and replace it.

The issue of constitutional reform remains on Alabama's agenda. A 21-member, independent commission called the Alabama Citizens for Constitutional Reform has been pushing the idea for years.[51] It proposed that the legislature put the issue of whether a constitutional convention should be held to a statewide vote and if voters approved, they would select in a special election delegates from each of the 105 House districts, who would convene to propose a new constitution, which then would be presented to the people for approval or rejection. One poll showed that 61 percent of the state's residents favored constitutional reform.[52]

The proposal for putting the issue of calling a constitutional convention before the voters in November 2002 was nonetheless defeated in the House of Representatives by a vote of 33 to 105.[53] However, both of the Democratic and Republican candidates for governor supported constitutional reforms and a statewide vote on the matter, though Republican candidate Bob Riley opposed holding a citizens' constitutional convention. Shortly after his inauguration as governor in 2003, Riley instead addressed the matter by establishing a 35-member Alabama Citizens' Constitutional Commission to propose constitutional reforms in five areas: strengthening the governor's line-item veto power, giving more home rule back to counties, requiring more than a simple majority of the legislature to raise taxes, changing provisions that earmark 90 percent of all tax revenues for specific purposes, and studying how the constitution might be shortened and reformed. The commission's recommendations went to the legislature for approval. The legislature proposed an amendment eliminating language in the constitution that requires segregated schools and poll taxes, which remain even though federal courts invalidated them more than 40 years ago.[54] In 2004, however, voters defeated that amendment by just 1,850 votes out of the more than 1.3 million cast. Nonetheless, the issue has not died: there are still many in Alabama who want to call a convention to reform the constitution and are pushing to get the question placed on the ballot.[55]

The Future for State Constitutions

Unlike the federal Constitution, which has only been amended 27 times in almost 220 years, the constitutions of most states are amended on a regular basis. While there has not been an entirely new state constitution adopted since the 1980s, the process of constitutional amendment allows state governments and voters to modify and modernize the existing constitutions to fit changing conditions. Almost 900 amendments were proposed in the period from 1998 to 2004, affecting almost every state constitution. Many of these amendments were limited in scope, concerning only local issues or the organization of specific state agencies. However, there were also amendments that affected states' bills of rights, broad finance and taxation issues, and electoral revision.[56]

It is certain that state constitutions will continue to be modified as new issues arise and conditions change in the states. The recent move to add bans on same-sex marriages to state constitutions is not exceptional. Indeed, it reflects the fact that it is the voters in the states who are the ultimate judges of the meaning and content of their state's constitution, and which rights the state will recognize and policies it will follow.

Summary

1. State constitutions spell out the fundamental laws of the states. Although they vary considerably in detail, each outlines the organizational framework of the state, vesting powers in the legislature and other departments. Each includes a bill of rights, sets procedures for holding elections, provides for local governments, and contains a variety of provisions dealing with finances, education, and other state issues.

2. Most state constitutions are cumbersome documents containing much more detail than the U.S. Constitution. Although reformers may have introduced such detail to prevent abuse, most constitutional scholars believe such matters are better left to statutory law.

3. In the past 20 years, there has been a flurry of renewed interest in state constitutions as they have been discovered to be additional instruments for protecting and expanding rights in what is known as the new judicial federalism.

4. State constitutions can be amended by ratification by the voters of proposals submitted by the legislature, by popular initiative petitions, or by constitutional conventions. Conventions tend to revise the entire constitution rather than just amend portions of it.

5. In recent decades, there has been an expanded use of the initiative process in several states to bring about constitutional reforms.

6. Despite the considerable constitutional change brought about during the last half-century through amendments, voters have usually resisted sweeping constitutional revision.

Further Reading

The Greenwood Publishing Group has commissioned reference guides for the constitution of each state, written by an expert on the state. As of 2006, guides for 42 states have been published, including Alabama, Alaska, Arizona, Arkansas, California, Colorado, Connecticut, Delaware, Florida, Hawaii, Idaho, Indiana, Iowa, Kansas, Kentucky, Louisiana, Maine, Maryland, Michigan, Minnesota, Mississippi, Montana, Nebraska, Nevada, New Hampshire, New Jersey, New Mexico, New York, North Carolina, North Dakota, Ohio, Oklahoma, South Carolina, Tennessee, Texas, Utah, Vermont, Virginia, Washington, Wisconsin, West Virginia, and Wyoming.

WILLI PAUL ADAMS, *The First American Constitutions: Republican Ideology and the Making of State Constitutions in the Revolutionary Era* (Rowman & Littlefield, 2001).

RICHARD J. ELLIS, *Democratic Delusions: The Initiative Process in America* (University Press of Kansas, 2003).

PAUL FINKELMAN AND **STEPHEN E. GOTTLIEB,** EDS., *Toward a Usable Past: Liberty Under State Constitutions* (University of Georgia Press, 1991).

JENNIFER FREISEN, *State Constitutional Law* (Michie, 1996).

SANFORD LEVINSON, ED., *Responding to Imperfection: The Theory and Practice of Constitutional Amendment* (Princeton University Press, 1995).

CHARLES LOPEMAN, *The Activist Advocate: Policy Making in State Supreme Courts* (Praeger, 1999).

ROBERT L. MADDEX, *State Constitutions of the United States,* 2d ed. (CQ Press, 2005).

JAMES T. McHUGH, *Ex Uno Plura: State Constitutions and Their Political Cultures* (State University of New York, 2003).

LAURA J. SCALIA, *America's Jeffersonian Experiment: Remaking State Constitutions, 1820–1850* (Northern Illinois University Press, 1999).

G. ALAN TARR, *Understanding State Constitutions* (Princeton University Press, 2000).

ROBERT F. WILLIAMS, *State Constitutional Law: Cases and Materials* (Michie, 1993).

See also the quarterly review *State Constitutional Commentaries and Notes,* published by the Edward McNail Burns Center for State Constitutional Studies at Rutgers University.

Key Terms

judicial interpretation, p. 631

new judicial federalism, p. 631

revision commission, p. 633

constitutional initiative petition, p. 634

Chapter 23

Parties and Elections in the States

★

THE CHAOS IN THE COUNTING OF BALLOTS IN FLORIDA IN THE 2000 ELECTION SURPRISED MANY AMERICANS, WHO ASSUMED THAT VOTE COUNTING IS SIMPLE AND PRECISE. THEY WERE WRONG. THE PROBLEMS WERE NOT ISOLATED TO FLORIDA'S CLOGGED VOTING MACHINES, DEFECTIVE PUNCH CARDS, AND INCONSISTENT STANDARDS FOR DEALING WITH PROBLEMS. BALLOTS WERE MISPLACED IN NEW MEXICO; VOTING MACHINES BROKE DOWN IN SEVERAL STATES; PEOPLE'S NAMES WERE INCORRECTLY PURGED FROM VOTING LISTS; AND long lines of people waiting to vote led to court challenges in many states. In the weeks and months following the election, at least half the states launched efforts to study the problems and propose solutions; in addition, national commissions, advisory groups, and experts undertook extensive analyses of our voting procedures.

Most people agree that many communities need new voting equipment and that the antiquated and flawed punch-card technology used by "roughly 30 percent of the nation's voters" need to be replaced.[1] As a result of the widespread problems in election administration in 2000, Congress passed the Help America Vote Act (HAVA) in 2002. HAVA provides federal funds to help states replace antiquated punch-card and

lever voting machines. By accepting the funding, states were to have these new machines in place by the November 2004 election or apply for a waiver to delay implementation until 2006. Although the process of replacing the old voting machines has not been as rapid as many HAVA supporters had hoped, big changes have already occurred in how Americans vote. About half of all registered voters in the United States used punch cards or levers in November 2000. By January 2006, only 16 percent of registered voters were estimated to be living in places where these outmoded technologies were still in use, and even fewer voters were expected to use these methods in the November 2006 elections.[2]

At the same time, the percentage of registered voters using electronic voting more than doubled, from 13 percent in 2000 to 38 percent in 2006. However, the spread of e-voting prompted new debates about the accuracy and accountability of computerized voting machines, especially if the machines were paperless and did not allow voters to be sure their votes had been tallied correctly. As a result, many states are now requiring electronic voting machines to print out paper ballots that can be checked in case of problems in the electronic tally.

Still other problems are being identified and addressed. The National Association of Secretaries of State—the state officials charged with election administration—issued recommendations that included better pay for poll workers; aggressive voter education on matters like how to ask for a second ballot if the first is spoiled; equal access to balloting

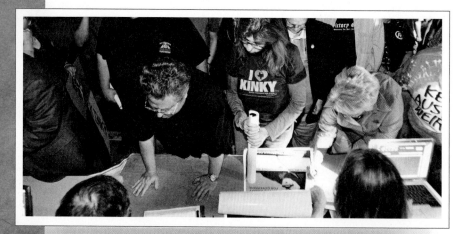

"The Times, Places and Manner of holding Elections for Senators and Representatives shall be prescribed in each State by the Legislature thereof; but the Congress may at any time by Law make or alter such Regulations, except as to the Places of choosing Senators."

U.S. CONSTITUTION, ARTICLE I, SECTION 4

643

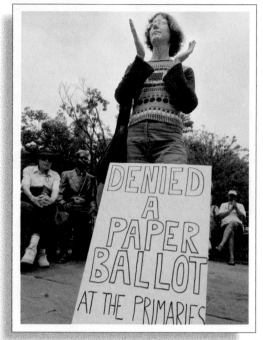

Antiquated punch-card and lever voting machines received considerable notoriety during the 2000 presidential election. These machines were blamed for many of the problems that plagued certain precincts in Florida, leading to the controversy over recounts and disqualified ballots. The new touch-screen voting machines, however, come with their own problems, among them no legal requirement that they provide a paper record of each vote cast in case verification should become necessary and a potential vulnerability to hackers who may wish to disrupt the election results.

for minorities, the poor, and elderly voters; maintaining up-to-date voter lists; ensuring the integrity of absentee ballots; and providing federal money to local communities to upgrade their voting systems.[3]

The 2002 elections saw no repeats of the troubled recounts in Florida in 2000. There was, however, some controversy in South Dakota about the registration drives among Native Americans. Charges of fraud in Native American voter registration surfaced before the election but were dismissed by the South Dakota attorney general. Despite widespread concerns before the election, there were no major problems with voting technology in the 2004 presidential election, though there were charges of irregularity in the voting in Ohio, including lack of sufficient voting machines in some heavily Democratic counties, and unlikely turnout reports in other areas. A partial recount did not change the outcome in Ohio, and a challenge to the election results in Congress was rejected.[4]

These controversies, and especially the 2000 election and its aftermath, taught us to not take election administration for granted. The states have the responsibility to manage elections and to ensure the right of participation to every citizen. The central role of states in our electoral democracy is the subject of this chapter.

Electoral Politics in the States and Localities

The U.S. Constitution provides only the most general guidelines to the states concerning the regulation of elections for members of the U.S. Congress. Article I, Section 4, says, "The Times, Places and Manner of holding Elections for Senators and Representatives shall be prescribed in each State by the Legislature thereof; but the Congress may at any time by Law make or alter such Regulations, except as to the Places of choosing Senators." The constitutional language regarding presidential elections also defers to state law: "Each State shall appoint, in such Manner as the Legislature thereof may direct, a Number of Electors."

Amendments to the U.S. Constitution relating to elections do not alter the central role of state constitutions and state law regarding voting rights. Rather, these amendments expressly forbid the states to restrict the right to vote in any election, for state and local as well as for national offices, to certain kinds of people. States cannot deny the franchise on the basis of "race, color, or previous condition of servitude" (Fifteenth Amendment), gender (Nineteenth Amendment), failure to pay a poll tax (Twenty-Fourth Amendment), or age for persons over age 18 (Twenty-Sixth Amendment).

Federalism and Elections

Political federalism in this country is noteworthy. Most elected officials, including even the president, are elected in a process that reinforces the importance of states. State identities are important to both politicians and voters. We think of ourselves as citizens of a particular state as well as of the United States. States have distinctive political traditions and political cultures. Because of these strong state identities and differences between the states in laws and practices, it should not be surprising that state parties are in many ways more important than national parties. Indeed, national parties, aside from their congressional campaign committees, are largely federations of state parties. Moreover, since our national parties as electoral organizations have never been strong, the activities they undertake usually end up being carried out by the state parties. The independence of state parties also helps explain why, for instance, Democratic voters in one state can be so different from those in another and why Republicans from different states can come down on opposite sides of some major issues.

The electoral process in the United States is *decentralized* in its rules and administration. Elections in the United States are administered by state and local governments, not by the national government. Even the president is chosen in state elections

The Changing Face of American Politics

A Demographic Profile of Local Government Officials

Number of Local Elected Officials	494,093
Gender	
Male	76.3%
Female	23.7

Race	
White	96.7
Black	2.8
American Indian or Alaskan Native	0.4
Asian or Pacific Islander	0.1
Hispanic	1.4

SOURCE: U.S. Bureau of the Census, "Popularly Elected Officials in 1992," *1992 Census of Governments* (U.S. Government Printing Office, 1992). Note: This is the most recent census of elected officials and these proportions may have changed somewhat since the data were collected.

conducted according to state rules. Because of the electoral college and the winner-take-all system, presidential politics focuses not on getting the most popular votes but instead on getting a plurality of votes in as many states as possible. State elections also determine who will serve as members of Congress, as governor, and as other statewide officials like attorney general, as well as the outcome of many ballot measures.

Most states prescribe the organization of the state parties, the means by which their officers are elected, and the nomination process for president and other offices.[5] In states that have some form of public financing of elections or parties, such as Maine and Arizona, the state also regulates the distribution of public funds to the parties and the reporting of how those funds are spent.

States differ in the hours the polls are open, how close to the voting place campaigning may be conducted, and whether they require voter registration. Largely because of overriding federal legislation, differences between the states in how long you must have lived in the state before voting and how you may register to vote have diminished in recent years.

As we learned in the 2000 presidential election in Florida, there is great variation in the way people vote, even from county to county. Some Florida counties used ballots read by optical scanners, and others used punch card ballots. Other states use these same types of ballots as well as paper ballots, voting machines, and even the Internet. Following the 2000 election, Florida mandated that voting in statewide elections be by computerized touch screens or ballots read by optical scanning machines.[6] Some of these devices malfunctioned in the 2002 Florida primary election. Despite these mishaps, a substantial amount of variation in voting systems continued through the 2004 election. In nearly half of the states (22), some voters continued to have punch-card ballots, for example.[7] Delays in funding the 2002 legislation delayed implementation of new voting technologies in 2004 in many states. For a state-by-state summary of election reforms, see www.electionline.org.

Along with the variation in ballots, we have many types of elections, including *general elections* to determine who holds office and *primary elections* to determine who will run in the general elections. Most statewide elections are partisan, whereas most local elections for school boards, water districts, and city governments are nonpartisan. State legislative elections are partisan except in Nebraska, where the legislature is nonpartisan. Voters in all states but Delaware must ratify changes to the state constitution in a referendum. Roughly half of the states allow votes on initiatives and referendums put on the ballot by petition. The initiative and referendum are also found in many local governments.

The Role of Political Parties

Although political parties are not mentioned in the U.S. Constitution, they are vital not only to our national government but also to the functioning of the electoral system within the states. Parties organize the competition by recruiting and nominating candidates, function as the loyal opposition when out of power, unify and organize the electorate, and provide a link between the people and their government. The existence of political parties is acknowledged in many state constitutions.

Election rules in general favor the two major parties over minor parties. The Republican and Democratic parties have a "preferred position"—that is, their candidates will definitely be placed on the ballot. Ballot access for minor party and independent candidates is less certain. State laws typically require minor parties to garner a minimum number of votes in the previous election or submit a prescribed number of signatures of registered voters in order to appear on the ballot. States vary in the difficulty of ballot access for minor parties, depending on three factors: the number of signatures required, the time allowed to collect them, and whether signatures must be distributed across several counties.

State election ballots are of two kinds. The **party column ballot** (also known as the *Indiana ballot*), which encourages party-line voting, is organized by parties, with the party name and symbol at the top of a column that lists all the party's candidates running for offices in that election (see Figure 23–1). Typically, there is an option at the top of the ballot column that allows voters to cast votes for all candidates of that party. When voters choose such an option, they cast a **straight ticket** vote. Voters may also have to work their way through state constitutional amendments, referendums, and initiatives on the ballot.

Partly to discourage straight ticket voting, some states use the **office block ballot** (also known as the *Massachusetts ballot*), which lists all the candidates running for an

party column ballot
Type of ballot that encourages party-line voting by listing all of a party's candidates in a column under the party name.

straight ticket
A vote for all of one party's candidates.

office block ballot
Ballot on which all candidates are listed under the office for which they are running.

FIGURE 23–1 A Sample Party Column Ballot.

office together in one block or on one screen, all those running for another office in another block/screen, and so on (see Figure 23–2). If voters want to cast a straight ticket vote, they have to hunt through each block/screen for their preferred candidate. Office block ballots encourage **split ticket** voting, or voting for candidates from more than one party. One consequence of computerized ballots will be a shift to office block formats.

Party Organization and Officers

AN EARLIER ERA: MACHINES AND BOSSES   In the nineteenth century, political *machines* became established in a number of American cities. Typically, these were organizations in which one political party dominated the political life of the city, often by recruiting new immigrants as supporters and voters by offering them patronage jobs and social welfare benefits. For many years, the epitome of a political machine in the United States was Tammany Hall, the building where the Tammany Society (named after a Delaware Indian chief) met and ran New York City politics. Tammany Hall was closely identified with Democrats and was ruled by William Tweed, the boss of New York City politics.

A *boss* is a party leader who uses patronage, government contracts, and access to power to dictate policy. Some bosses, like Tweed, were never elected to office but were powers behind the scenes who told the mayor and other city officials what to do. Party bosses were common after the Civil War and well into the twentieth century. Other cities with powerful political machines were Chicago, Los Angeles, Boston, Pittsburgh, Cincinnati, Philadelphia, Indianapolis, San Francisco, and Baltimore.

The principal objective of the urban reform movement in the early twentieth century was to overthrow the bosses and the political machines. Reformers advocated nonpartisan local elections, competitive bids for projects, and civil service in place of

split ticket
A vote for some of one party's candidates and some of another party's.

FIGURE 23–2 **A Sample Office Block Ballot.**

Touch-screen voting machines are designed to speed up the vote counting process and provide uniformity in the balloting system. However, some experts argue that the machines break down too frequently. Moreover, these machines do not produce a paper record that can be used to assure accuracy.

patronage. They achieved most of their goals, although it is not clear whether the power of political machines was reduced by these reforms or by other social and economic forces.

PARTY ORGANIZATIONS TODAY   Although state party organizations are not all alike, most organize themselves along the same lines as the national parties. In all states, there is a *party chair* who is elected by the party's central committee or delegates to a party convention. Other statewide party officers include the *vice chair*, who by state law or party bylaws often must be of the opposite gender from the party chair,[8] plus officers like treasurer and secretary. Party leaders generally answer to a *central committee*, which consists of 20 or more persons who are elected or otherwise chosen for specified terms.

The state party chair is the spokesperson for the party, especially when the party does not control the governorship. He or she raises money for the party and its candidates. When the party controls the governorship, the central committee defers to the governor in the selection of the chair. Because overt expressions of partisanship are thought to be unbecoming of elected officials, often the party chair defends the party and, when necessary, goes on the offensive against the opposition party.

The day-to-day operations of the party are usually carried out by the party's *executive director*, a full-time employee who oversees the staff, assists the chair, and coordinates the work of the central committee and other party officials. The executive director schedules functions and serves as a liaison with the national organizations.

At the local level, political parties generally have a structure patterned after the state party organization. In some counties, party organizations are fully staffed and functioning, but in most counties, they are run by volunteers and are mostly inactive until just before an election. Local parties provide opportunities for ordinary citizens to become involved in politics, a first step that can eventually lead to running for office. Some states, like Minnesota, have congressional district parties as well.[9]

Although party bosses and strong party machines are a thing of the past, local politics is still organized on a partisan basis in many of our largest cities. More typically, as noted, local politics is nonpartisan with three-quarters of U.S. cities having nonpartisan elections.[10]

Party Activities in Elections

American politics is candidate-centered. Candidates create their own campaign organizations. Yet parties serve important secondary roles in elections. They provide the structure for elections; in some places, they recruit candidates, register voters, mobilize voters on election day, and supply resources and campaign help to their candidates.

STRUCTURE FOR ELECTIONS   Our election system would function in a dramatically different way if we had no political parties to organize the competition. Parties narrow the field of candidates through a primary election or convention process, providing voters with relatively few choices in the general election. Candidates, to one degree or another, must secure the support of fellow partisans to win a place on the ballot as the party's nominees for the offices they are seeking.

CANDIDATE RECRUITMENT   Party officials often seek out candidates to run for office, help train them in how to run, and occasionally provide modest financial support. One sign of the weakness of our parties is that many offices go uncontested, including some members of Congress. The number of unopposed candidates increases as you go down the ballot. To be sure, some incumbents have done such a good job that to oppose them would be an exercise in futility. Yet lack of competition in elections violates American assumptions about democracy and is reminiscent of politics in the former communist states, where party officers ran unopposed. One important characteristic of American parties at all levels is that they are extremely open to would-be candidates. Virtually anybody can run for the state legislature. Generally speaking, the greater the likelihood that a party nomination will help with winning the general election, the more competition there is for that nomination.

VOTER REGISTRATION   All states except North Dakota require citizens to register before voting. In California, you can register online, at www.ss.ca.gov/elections/elections .htm, and some states, like Wisconsin, allow registration at the polls on election day. Voter registration became easier when Congress passed the National Voter Registration, or Motor Voter, Act in 1993. People are now able to register to vote when they apply for or renew their driver's license or visit certain public agencies. The half-dozen states that permit election day registration or do not require voter registration are exempt from the law. The idea behind Motor Voter is to ease the registration process, thereby increasing the number of registered voters and turnout.

What difference has Motor Voter made? During 2003 and 2004, almost 22 million people registered through motor vehicle or other agencies, about 43 percent of total registrations in that period.[11] Many of the new Motor Voter registrants are registering as Independents. In terms of party balance, Motor Voter does not appear to have made much difference, contrary to expectations that it would result in a bias in favor of Democrats.[12]

At the time of registration, some states ask voters to register with a political party; in other states, party registration is optional. Most states do not register voters by party. To see what your state requires, visit the voter registration section of the Federal Election Commission Web site at www.fec.gov. Even in states that require party registration, voters have the option to decline to state their party at the time of registration. For example, in California in 2006, 18.5 percent of the registered voters declined to state their party preference.[13] Opting out of party registration often means voters may not vote in a party primary, which in some states may be the election that effectively decides the officeholder. An excellent data bank on voter registration and turnout is maintained by the National Conference of State Legislatures at www.ncsl.org.

Helping register sympathetic voters is important to candidates, parties, and interest groups. These efforts are typically aimed at citizens they anticipate will vote for their party's candidate. Voter registration drives targeted at African Americans often help Democrats in key states and congressional districts. Both parties have worked to register Hispanic voters. Interest groups with active voter registration efforts include organized labor, business groups, and groups concerned about the environment and abortion.

Political parties favor laws requiring voters to disclose their party preference at the time they register. First, this requirement permits parties to limit participation in their primaries to registered party members in states that have a closed primary system. Second, party registration creates voter registration lists, which parties find extremely useful for campaigning and fund raising. In addition, *list vending*—selling voter lists with addresses, phone numbers, and party preferences—is a multimillion-dollar industry. Third, voter registration helps the parties in the redistricting process because state legislators, using party registration, voting, and other data, can draw new congressional and state legislative district boundaries in ways that give their party an advantage. Examples of states where partisanship was a major factor in redistricting after the 2000 census were Colorado, Georgia, Utah, and Texas. In Georgia the Democrats managed to put in place a plan favoring their candidates, while in Utah the plan favored the Republicans.[14]

VOTER MOBILIZATION   Just over three-quarters of eligible voters are registered, and of that number, only about two-thirds vote in presidential elections, meaning that *as little as half the voting-age population bothers to vote* in a presidential election and fewer still in a midterm election.[15] Turnout in the 2004 presidential election was heavier than any election since 1968 but was still less than 56 percent of the voting-age

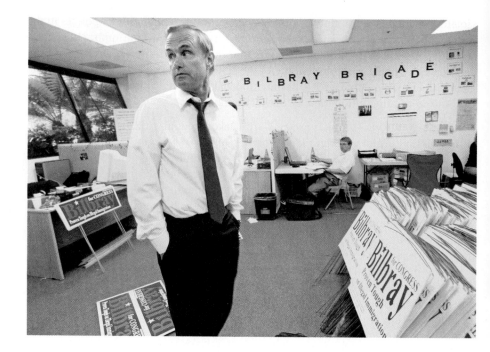

Brian Bilbray, Republican representative of California's 50th House District, in his campaign office in Carlsbad, California. Bilbray won reelection in 2006.

population. Only 35 percent of the voting-age population voted in the 2002 congressional midterm elections, and just 17 percent of voting-age population in the 1998 state and local primaries.[16] Get-out-the-vote drives are therefore a major activity of candidates and parties. Elections are often decided by which party does better at turning out its supporters. Party workers, through telephone or door-to-door canvassing, identify registered voters who are likely to support their party and then contact those voters personally on election day, perhaps more than once, to encourage them to go to the polls. Where resources permit, the parties may even provide transportation to the polls or baby-sitting services.[17]

In states that permit registration by mail or by roving registrars, volunteers register voters at the same time they find voters who will support their party's candidates in the election. When absentee or mail ballots are options, voter mobilization efforts help voters fill out the form requesting an absentee ballot and then mail the form for them. A few weeks later, a party volunteer checks to make sure a ballot has arrived and has been filled out and returned. Because most voters prefer one party over another, it makes sense for candidates from the same party to consolidate their efforts.

CAMPAIGN RESOURCES American political parties, with some notable exceptions, are organizationally weak. In better-organized states, parties often provide campaign funds and campaign help. They raise funds for their party organization and finance voter registration and mobilization efforts, often with the help of national parties. As at the national level, control of the executive branch helps in fund raising because interest groups are much more likely to contribute to the governor's party. Texas Governor George W. Bush not only tapped into his base of affluent Texans but also won the support of other governors to finance much of his 2000 presidential campaign. He built on this network to raise record-setting amounts as a candidate in his 2004 reelection campaign.

In states with well-organized parties, the parties train the candidates they have recruited. Wisconsin and New York have strong state legislative campaign committees that distribute resources to candidates, as the national party committee does to congressional candidates.[18] Sometimes the state parties provide polling data to state and local candidates, help establish campaign themes, or prepare generic advertising that can be used in several state legislative districts.

Until 2004, parties also channeled money from the national congressional and senatorial campaign committees to local candidates for U.S. Senate or U.S. House involved in competitive races. This **soft money**, which could come in disclosed but unlimited amounts, was banned at the national level by the Bipartisan Campaign Reform Act (BCRA) in 2002.[19] State parties operate under their own rules, and all but Connecticut permit soft money for state and local candidates. Moreover, the 2002 reforms permit limited amounts of soft money, $10,000, to go to state and local parties for voter registration and mobilization.[20] Between 1996 and 2002, Republican and Democratic national party committees, including the congressional and senatorial campaign committees, raised and distributed large amounts of soft money. Because state parties largeiy spend the soft money for the national parties, this expenditure has not generally made state parties stronger.

One reason parties raised soft money was to respond to **issue advocacy**, in which an interest group attacks some political candidates or supports others but carefully avoids specifically telling voters to vote for or against that individual. Though much of the soft money and issue advocacy advertising focuses on presidential and congressional elections, both parties have also devoted these resources to gubernatorial, judicial,[21] and state legislative races.[22]

Issue advocacy, which aims to defeat or elect a particular candidate, has been important since the 1996 elections.[23] The pharmaceutical industry ran significant issue advocacy campaigns in 2000 and 2002. Tort reform was an important topic for issue ads in 2004. Issue advocacy groups also tried to change the balance of state governments, such as Colorado where there were close races for governor and control of the state legislature in 2006.[24]

Voting Choices

Voters generally base their election decisions on three factors, listed in decreasing order of importance: political party identification, candidate appeal, and issues. But in many local elections, since party labels are absent from the ballot, voters rely more on candidate appeal, issues, and factors like incumbency, media endorsements, and name recognition.

PARTY IDENTIFICATION Party identification is the most important predictor of voting behavior. Parties provide a party label that guides voters in making their decisions. Party labels are especially important in elections in which voters have little information about candidates, as in contests for attorney general, state senator, state representative, or county commissioner. The simplifying device of party labels helps voters sort through the many candidate choices they encounter on election day.

People who identify themselves as strong Democrats and strong Republicans are remarkably loyal to their party when voting for governor and other state and local offices. Independent-leaners have clear partisan preferences in the direction of one party or the other. Pure Independents have no party preference and are most inclined to vote for one party and then another with changing circumstances, but there are few Pure Independents in the total electorate.[25]

CANDIDATE APPEAL Although party identification is important, it is not decisive. Candidate appeal can be crucial. For example, in the 2003 California recall election, voters not only viewed Governor Gray Davis negatively,[26] they were positive about Arnold Schwarzenegger's success in business, his independence from special interests because of his personal wealth, and his sponsorship of a ballot initiative that provided for after-school programs.[27] In some respects the 2003 California recall election resembled the 1998 Minnesota gubernatorial election, in which Reform party candidate Jesse Ventura was elected largely because his style and approach generated interest among voters, and a plurality preferred him over the established candidates in the major parties.

In fact, this sort of appeal explains why states in which one major party has large advantages in voter registration, and usually are carried easily by that party's presidential candidate, often elect governors from the other major party. For example, Massachusetts is one of the most Democratic states in presidential elections, and routinely

soft money
Unlimited contributions to political parties for party-building purposes.

issue advocacy
Promoting a particular position on an issue, often funded by interest groups and designed to influence voters' choices on election day.

elects large Democratic party majorities to both houses of its state legislature. However, Massachusetts has had Republican governors since 1991. Wyoming, a very Republican state in most respects, has elected Democratic governors in five of seven elections since 1974.

In state and local elections, name identification and the advantages of incumbency are important. Incumbents generally have an advantage in candidate appeal because of greater name recognition and access to campaign resources. Candidates sometimes use creative means to generate positive name recognition. For example, when Bob Graham was governor of Florida, he often worked one day a week in different jobs around the state to demonstrate his desire to relate to his constituents.

ISSUE VOTING Issues can be very important to the outcome of elections. Economic conditions are an important factor in state and local elections, as they are in national ones. William Weld, a Republican, was able to win his first Massachusetts gubernatorial election in 1990, despite the fact that Massachusetts is a very strong Democratic state, because the state's economy at the time was so bad. Former New Jersey Governor Christine Todd Whitman won election in part because her incumbent opponent had raised state taxes and she promised a 30 percent tax cut. Although issues are important in state and local elections, it is fair to say that they are probably less important than at the national level.[28]

JUDICIAL ELECTIONS Judicial elections in some states are partisan and resemble campaigns for other offices in intensity. In 2000, the Michigan Democratic party ran ads attacking incumbent candidates for the Michigan supreme court who had been appointed by a former Republican governor. One of the ads showed an insurance executive sitting at his desk searching through papers and asking the secretary, "Where are my judges?" She replies, "Just where they've always been, right in your pocket." The executive looks in his suit coat pocket to see three justices frolicking in handfuls of money. Three pictures appear on the screen and a voice says, "Justices Markman, Taylor, and Young have accepted hundreds of thousands from insurance and big business. Justice should not be for sale."[29]

Ads attacking judicial candidates like this were not unique to Michigan in 2000. Ohio, Illinois, Alabama, and Idaho had races in which political parties or interest groups used similar ads[30]; this occurred again in several states in 2002. A 2002 Supreme Court decision, *Republican Party of Minnesota* v. *White*, allows judicial candidates to state their views on disputed legal and political issues. More than $24 million was spent on television ads in state judicial campaigns in 2004, with candidates increasingly stating positions on issues like abortion, gun control, and school choice.[31] Substantial spending by political parties and interest groups in judicial elections has prompted criticism by good-government groups and led the American Bar Association to form a task force on this topic.

NONPARTISAN LOCAL ELECTIONS Nonpartisan elections were intended to weaken political parties in local elections, and they have been successful. Arguing that political parties had little to contribute to the administration of local government, reformers during the first half of the twentieth century introduced nonpartisan elections. The two parties were, in effect, blocked from exerting an open influence on local politics.

Some observers contend that nonpartisan local elections make it more difficult for poor persons, minorities, and the less educated to participate effectively. For such people, the party label serves to identify politicians who share their values and perspectives on government. Well-educated and wealthy voters know more about who is running and what they stand for, even without party labels. Nonpartisan elections sometimes help Republican candidates, especially in cities with populations of more than 50,000, because Republican voters tend to vote more in low-turnout elections and are more likely to know which candidates are Republicans.[32] Others have found that there is not generally an advantage to Republican candidates in nonpartisan elections.[33]

Parties in State Government

PARTIES IN THE EXECUTIVE BRANCH Just as winning the presidency is the big prize at the national level, so is winning the governorship at the state level. The party that controls the governorship has the power to appoint executive department officials and some state judges. Governors are usually perceived as the leaders of their party, and they establish the political agenda and help define the party for their state. They customarily win office with the help of fellow partisans, and they know from the day they take office that the other party is planning ways to defeat them and their party in the next election.

Governors often assist in recruiting candidates for the state legislature; they usually campaign on behalf of their party, even when they are not on the ballot for reelection. Presidential candidates often seek the help of governors. Governors raise money for campaigns as well as for the state party. They have wide latitude in appointing boards, commissions, judges, and state administrators, and they almost always take party affiliation and activity into account when making appointments.

PARTIES IN THE LEGISLATURE Like Congress, state legislatures (excluding Nebraska, which is nonpartisan) are organized largely along party lines. The *speaker of the house or assembly* and the *president of the senate* are elected by the majority party in most states. They preside over floor proceedings and make key assignments to standing committees and study committees. Most state legislatures have floor leaders, called *majority leaders* and *minority leaders* and majority and minority *whips.*

In most states, parties sit on different sides of the aisle in the legislative chambers and are separated in committee meetings as well. Committee chairs in most state legislatures go to members from the majority party in that chamber, with the leaders of the majority party wielding great power in the final decision. The **party caucus** is often important in state legislatures. The caucus is a meeting of party leaders and legislators to discuss party policy. Because some state legislatures meet for only a few months a year, the party caucus can help hammer out agreements rapidly.

One area in which legislatures are predictably partisan is **redistricting**. Each decade, following the national census, state legislatures are constitutionally required to realign congressional and state legislative district boundaries to make them equal in population and reflect population changes. The redistricting following the 2000 Census was especially important because the two parties were so evenly divided in numbers of legislative chambers controlled. Going into the 2006 elections, the Democrats controlled 47 chambers, the Republicans 49, and two were tied.[34]

How district lines are drawn can help or hurt a party. Where one party controls both houses and the governorship or has a veto-proof majority in the legislature, the majority party can do pretty much what it wants with district boundaries, so long as it keeps the districts equal in population and respects the rights of racial minorities. Where power is divided between the parties, the result is often a redistricting that protects incumbents.

Although traditionally it has been the practice to redistrict only once per decade, usually right after the decennial Census data become available, redistricting might become more frequent and perhaps even more sensitive to shifts in control of the state legislatures. In 2003, Texas replaced a congressional districting plan that a state court had drawn up the previous year with one that was much more favorable to Republicans. The new plan was challenged in court, eventually reaching the Supreme Court, which upheld the constitutionality of most of the second plan, overturning only one district's boundaries that were held to dilute Hispanic votes in violation of the Voting Rights Act.[35] However, a similar attempt to replace a court-drawn plan in Colorado was struck down by the state supreme court, since the state constitution only allowed redistricting once a decade.[36]

Typically, after redistricting occurs, several U.S. House incumbents retire rather than face the uncertainty of an election in a newly drawn district or the prospect of running against another incumbent. This was less the case in 2002 because to a very large extent, state legislatures drew district boundaries to protect incumbents.

party caucus
A meeting of the members of a party in a legislative chamber to select party leaders and develop party policy. Called a *conference* by the Republicans.

redistricting
The redrawing of congressional and other legislative district lines following the census, to accommodate population shifts and keep districts as equal as possible in population.

California, with its 53 congressional districts, emerged from redistricting with only one or two districts considered competitive in 2002 and 2004. Three notable exceptions to this are the partisan gerrymandering carried out in Utah and Texas by Republicans and in Georgia by Democrats. In these cases, the parties controlled the process and sought to create districts more favorable to their party, even if it gave incumbents from their party districts that were less safely partisan.

In five states, commissions rather than the legislature do the redistricting. Commissions tend to be more neutral and often create districts that are more competitive. This was the case in Arizona with the last redistricting. Arizona's new congressional district, the First District, had nearly equal numbers of registered Democrats and Republicans and was seen as a toss-up by political prognosticators.

Parties in Local Government

Political parties are still important in the politics of many cities, especially the larger ones, although they are in a much weaker position now than they were 25 or 50 years ago. Mayors often lead city party organizations and play a role in the campaigns of presidents, senators, and governors. The mayor's office is sometimes a stepping-stone to other offices. Former Governor Jesse Ventura began his political career as mayor of Brooklyn Park, Minnesota; U.S. Senator Richard Lugar was once mayor of Indianapolis; George Voinovich was mayor of Cleveland and became governor of Ohio before going on to the U.S. Senate; and U.S. Senator Dianne Feinstein was mayor of San Francisco. In 2002, former St. Paul mayor Norm Coleman was elected to the U.S. Senate from Minnesota.

Parties rarely get involved in initiative and referendum elections at the local or state level, but some nonpartisan local elections have partisan overtones as candidates may be identified with the parties, or the parties may want to advance the career of a local nonpartisan candidate.

Party Balance and Imbalance

State politics may be classified according to how the parties share public offices. In a **two-party state**, the Republican and Democratic parties can each regularly assemble winning majorities. Two-party states include Indiana, Illinois, and Missouri. In a **one-party state**, one party wins all or nearly all the offices, and the second party usually receives only one-third or less of the popular vote. One-party Republican states currently include Utah, Idaho, and Kansas. Massachusetts is an example of a Democratic one-party state. It is possible for Democrats to win in Utah, and the same is true for Republicans in Massachusetts, but the more predictable tendency is to support the predominant party.

Since the end of World War II, there has been an accelerating trend toward two-party politics. The Democratic party lost its previously solid support in the South as more and more white southerners moved over to the Republican party. At first, Republican resurgence in the South was mainly evident in presidential and congressional elections, but in recent years, Republicans have regularly been elected to southern state legislatures. Since the mid-1970s, the number of Republicans in southern state legislatures has increased from about 12 percent to near parity.[37]

Republican gains have also been evident in contests for governor. Since 1966, all southern states have at least once elected a Republican governor, and in 2006, Republican governors led seven southern states. In terms of the popular vote for president, the South has voted more Republican than the country as a whole in nine of the last 11 presidential elections.[38] In 2004, all 11 former confederate states went to George W. Bush. Even with southerner Al Gore on the ballot, the Democrats carried no southern state in 2000.

Outside the South, there has also been a gradual spread of two-party politics, with the rise of Democratic strength in the formerly solid Republican states of Iowa, Maine, and New Hampshire. Democrats have lost strength in parts of the Rocky Mountain

two-party state
A state in which the two major parties alternate in winning majorities.

one-party state
A state in which one party wins all or nearly all the offices and the other party receives only a small proportion of the popular vote.

area; however, the Democratic party has been gaining loyalists in the Northeast and Pacific Coast states.

What are the consequences of party balance? When parties and their candidates compete on an equal basis, they are more likely to be sensitive to public opinion, for the loss of even a fraction of the voters can tip the scales to the other side in the next election. Party competition tends to push leaders within each party to work together, at least as elections draw near. Any defection may throw a race to the opponents, so competition generally produces more teamwork and efficiency in government. It may also generate more service to constituents by legislators.

In a one-party state, party imbalance may have a serious effect on the accountability that is part of electoral competition. Competition that otherwise would occur *between* the major parties occurs *within* the majority party. The most important contests in some states like Massachusetts are generally not between Democrats and Republicans but among Democrats in the primary; the same is true for Republicans in Utah. In these intraparty fights, personalities dominate the campaign. Voters do not participate as much as they do in two-party contests.

If party imbalance disorganizes the dominant party, it pulverizes the minority party. With faint hope of winning, minority party leaders do not put up much of a fight. They find it difficult to raise money for campaigns and to persuade people to become candidates. They have no state or local patronage to give out. Volunteers are slow to come forward. Young people wishing to succeed in politics drift into the dominant party. The second party is likely to be concerned only with national politics, where it may win an election, and the patronage that could come its way if its candidate wins the White House.

Party imbalance can be found in more extreme forms in cities and towns than at the state level. Republicans hardly ever carry Chicago, Boston, Washington, Baltimore, Albany, Hartford, Pittsburgh, and many other cities throughout the industrial North. Nevertheless, party balance is not always a determining factor. In heavily Democratic New York City, for example, voters elected a Republican, Michael Bloomberg, as mayor in 2001, and Rudolph Giuliani in 1993 and 1997. Bloomberg had been a Democrat but ran for mayor as a Republican.

Elections at the State and Local Levels

Each year, there are thousands of state and local elections. Europeans, who are used to voting for one or two candidates at the national and local levels and voting only once every two or three years, are flabbergasted to learn that we engage in elections almost continuously. Selection of town and local officials in the late winter may be followed in the spring by primaries to choose delegates to conventions, then primaries to choose party candidates, then general elections in the fall in which the actual officeholders are chosen—all interspersed with special elections, elections for school boards or to adopt school budgets, special town or state referendums, and even, in some states, recall elections to throw officials out of office as in California in 2003 when voters removed Gray Davis from the governorship and replaced him with Arnold Schwarzenegger.

Even more bewildering to some is the number of offices we vote on, from president to probate judge, from senator to sheriff, from governor to library board member. This is the *long ballot*. Europeans are more accustomed to electing a handful of key officials, who in turn appoint career officials. Given this volume of election activity, it is fair to conclude that Americans like elections, even though most of them choose not to vote in most of those elections.

Differences in Who May Vote

Subject to constitutional constraint, states can regulate who may vote. Most, for example, do not permit prison inmates to vote. If a state wanted to permit 16-year-olds to vote, it could do so. Voter registration rules can discourage people from participating in elections. States differ in the length of their residency requirement, as well as in whether they permit roving registrars, postcard registration, online registration, or election day registration. Most states require a periodic purge of the voter registration list to remove people who have moved or died.

A common reason why people do not register is that they have moved and have not registered at their new address. Fifteen percent of Americans change their residence every year.[39] After moving, they may not realize that they need to register at their new address until only a few days before the election, and then it is too late. Maryland, North Carolina, and the District of Columbia allow college students who have moved within a city or county to vote without registering if they notify election officials of their move. All told, a state's registration rules can lower turnout by as much as 9 percent.[40]

Differences in How We Vote

Although millions of Americans carry cell phones, own computers, and shop on the Internet, only a few years ago we still voted in an antiquated way. One of the surprises of the 2000 presidential election was the extent to which we were still using outdated technology. Nearly one in five counties in the United States used punch-card ballots, which are subject to problems like dangling or dimpled chads that do not clearly indicate the voter's intent. Another two in five communities used optical scan ballots on which the voter uses a pencil to mark the ballot and a scanner records the vote.[41] Although much more reliable than punch cards, scanned ballots are also subject to problems if voters mark outside the box or do not use a pencil.

Voting machines with levers were used in 14 percent of counties, and paper ballots were used in 12 percent. Unlike punch cards, optical scanners, and paper ballots, voting machines do not permit an audit of the vote.[42]

However, state and local governments responded quickly to the well-publicized problems of ballot counting in Florida in 2000 as well as to the enactment of the Help America Vote Act of 2002, which granted funding to states to help them modernize their voting methods. By 2006, 34 percent of counties used electronic or computer voting systems, up from 10 percent in 2000. The expanded use of electronic voting systems came largely at the expense of punch cards, levers, and paper ballots, methods that were used by only 13 percent of the counties in 2006, down from 44 percent in 2000.[43]

Nonetheless, there are still concerns about relying on electronic voting systems. One concern is security: Can votes remain secret and tamper proof? Another problem is how to do a recount in case a dispute arises. Some see the use of an audit device, perhaps a paper printout of each person's vote, as a necessary precaution in the move to electronic voting. But even these systems—called a "voter verified paper trail"—can be vulnerable to efforts to tamper with votes.[44] Overcoming these problems is not impossible, but most observers agree that voting processes and machinery will continue to change in the near future.

The biggest voting problem in 2004 was long lines in several states. This was more the result of insufficient voting machines and booths than a breakdown in voting technology. The margin of victory for President Bush was large enough that the process was not as contested as in 2000.

Voting by Mail and by Absentee Ballot

Modern technology makes it possible to vote by other means than appearing in person at a voting place on election day. Cities like San Diego, Berkeley, and Vancouver first experimented with holding *elections by mail*. Voters are mailed a pamphlet that describes the questions to be decided in the election and gives instructions on how to complete the ballot and return it by mail. Voters sign the return envelope, and their signature is compared against their signature on the voter registration form. There have been no major problems in administering these local mail ballot elections, and the response has been considerably higher than the norm for in-person special elections.[45]

In January 1996, Oregon voters elected a U.S. senator in a special election through the mail rather than in person. Oregonians had 20 days from the date the ballots were mailed to return them to county clerks, and two-thirds of those who received ballots returned them. In 1998, Oregon voters approved an initiative to conduct all elections by mail. There appear to have been few instances of fraud, and vote-by-mail elections are popular with the voters in Oregon.[46] Opponents of the vote-by-mail system worry about fraud, and that voters might be pressured to vote a certain way. A husband might press his wife to vote for his preferred candidates, or parents might try to direct the vote of their young adult children still living at home. Another problem might be if supporters of a candidate visit voters at home soon after the ballots are delivered and pressure people to vote on the spot, perhaps offering to mail the ballot.

Supporters point to the higher turnout and lower costs in administering vote-by-mail elections. They also point to the absence of fraud or abuse in the vote-by-mail elections.

A less dramatic reform of election laws is the *absentee ballot*. In most of the country, voters may request a ballot by mail, often without having to state a reason for doing so.[47] Absentee balloting is especially useful for initiative measures. In states like California or Washington, where voters may face 20 or more complicated ballot questions, those who vote by absentee ballot can take their time researching and pondering how they are going to vote and do not have to decide within the few minutes they would have in a voting booth.

Increased ease in obtaining ballots has significantly expanded the rate of absentee voting in California. It has been used especially by Republicans to activate retirees and other voters who find it difficult to get from their homes to polling places. In Washington, absentee ballots made up nearly 85 percent of all ballots in 2006.[48] Other states have also liberalized their absentee voting provisions. Oklahoma and Texas, for instance, have *early voting*, whereby voters may vote for several days before an election at several locations in each county.

Absentee ballots also figured in the controversy in the Florida 2000 presidential voting. In two counties, absentee ballot request forms had incorrect voter identification numbers, but the county clerk permitted the Republican party to correct the mistake after the forms were returned to the county. In other Florida counties, some absentee ballots from military personnel did not have postmark dates or were otherwise technically not in compliance with the law. Initially, some counties did not count these ballots, but eventually, most military ballots were counted.

These absentee ballots will be sent to voters in Missouri as an alternative to the conventional practice of going to the polls to vote.

Differences in Nomination Processes

State law establishes the process by which party nominees are selected. Most states use a *primary election*, but some permit the parties to nominate their candidates through a *caucus* or *convention*. In the caucus system, party delegates who are elected in local voting district meetings decide on the party nominee. In some states, a convention narrows the field to two candidates if no candidate gets a set percentage of delegate votes at the party convention.

The dynamics of winning a nomination in states with a caucus system are different from those in states with a primary. In a caucus system, having a grassroots organization that can mobilize voters to attend a neighborhood meeting is essential for candidates. The state best known for the caucus system is Iowa, whose party caucuses yield the first decision in our presidential election system and are covered extensively by the media. Some form of the caucus or convention system is used in about a dozen states.

There are two kinds of party primaries, closed and open. In a **closed primary**, only voters registered in a party may vote in that party's primary. Such a primary discourages **crossover voting**—allowing voters from outside the party to help determine the party's nominee—which is why partisans prefer closed primaries. In an **open primary**, any voter can participate in any party's primary. Wisconsin has long had open primaries. California voters rejected an initiative to establish an open primary in 2004.

Some states, like Montana, Washington, and California, allowed voters to vote for more than one party in the same primary election; this is called a **blanket primary**. Thus, a voter could choose a Democratic nominee for governor and Republican nominees for U.S. senator and attorney general. The blanket primary, according to those who advocated it, encouraged voters to select the best nominees regardless of party and was thought to help moderate candidates. Opponents said it further weakened parties, made our system even more candidate-driven, and gave voters from one party the opportunity to choose the weakest candidate from the opposing party. However, research shows that less than 5 percent of voters actually vote for the weakest candidate from the opposing party.[49] In July 2000, the Supreme Court ruled that blanket primaries are unconstitutional because they violate the right to political association under the First Amendment.[50]

Louisiana has a unique system. All candidates, regardless of party, run in a single election. If no candidate gets a majority of the votes, there is a runoff election to determine the winner. It is not uncommon for both candidates in a runoff to be from the same party.

In a primary election, when all the candidates are from the same party, voters make their choices based on candidate appeal and issues. They may also vote for the candidate they perceive has the best chance of winning the general election.[51]

Differences in Timing and Frequency of Elections

Federal law sets the date of the presidential election as "the Tuesday next after the first Monday in November, in every fourth year," with similar language applying to elections for the House and Senate. States are free to determine the dates of all other elections, but for ease of administration, they usually consolidate gubernatorial and state general elections on the first Tuesday after the first Monday in November. Two states elect their governor every two years. Five states conduct their elections (primary and general) for governor, other state officials, and the state legislature in odd-numbered years, leaving the even-numbered years for federal elections. Two-thirds of the states (including the two-year states) elect governors in presidential midterm years, halfway between presidential elections.

Separating state elections from presidential or federal elections permits voters to focus more closely on state issues than if they had to vote for state and federal candidates at the same time. Separating elections also means that state and local officials are not as likely to be hurt by an unpopular presidential candidate at the top of the

closed primary
Primary election in which only persons registered in the party holding the primary may vote.

crossover voting
Voting in another party's primary.

open primary
Primary election in which any voter, regardless of party, may vote.

blanket primary
Primary election open to all voters, who may vote for a candidate from any party for each office.

ticket. The passage of campaign finance reform at the federal level may prompt some states to consider off-year state elections. Having state elections in a different year from federal elections may reduce federal oversight and encourage soft money donors to contribute more to state parties.

Some states hold their primaries in late spring, others in mid-September. Primary elections are under the control of state law. Some states have two primaries in presidential years, one for the presidency in the spring and one for other contests in the fall.

State law establishes the rules for local elections but often allows cities and towns some discretion in setting the dates of elections. Many municipal elections are held in the spring of odd-numbered years, again to avoid any positive or negative carryover from candidates running for federal or statewide office. Counties usually conduct their elections at the same time state officials are elected.

State governments can also hold *special elections* to vote on a ballot initiative, a statewide constitutional change, or even a completely new constitution or to replace a U.S. senator who has died or resigned. Participation in special elections varies greatly, depending on what is being decided, but turnout is generally lower than in midterm general elections. Before states hold special elections to fill a vacated U.S. Senate seat, they often have a special primary election to determine the party nominees for that election. In these primaries, turnout is even lower than in the special general election.

The frequency of our elections and the range of choices sometimes make it hard for voters to pay enough attention to cast informed votes. For this reason, some reformers have proposed consolidating elections to once or twice every couple of years.

Participation

What are the consequences of holding so many elections at so many different times? One is that Americans pick and choose which elections, if any, they participate in. States vary significantly in their rate of **turnout**, the proportion of the voting-age public that votes. Note that political scientists do not calculate turnout on the basis of voter registration because there is such variability in state registration rules that it is unfair to compare the turnout in a state with difficult registration laws with the turnout in a state whose laws make voting registration much more accessible. Rather, turnout is calculated on the Census Bureau's estimate of the voting-age population in each state.

Primaries usually draw fewer voters than general elections, and sometimes the turnout is quite low. Low turnout raises concerns about whether voters in primary elections reflect the general public. Primary voters are generally better educated, earn more money, and are more likely to be white than voters in general elections, who themselves are not representative of the voting-age population.[52] Primary election turnout is also related to strength of partisan identification, ease of voter registration, and the issues in the campaign.

Campaign Finance

In the early 1970s, many states enacted campaign finance disclosure laws, a few instituted partial public financing of elections, and others provided partial underwriting of the costs of parties. **Disclosure** is a common element of campaign finance legislation at the state and local levels. Candidates are typically asked to file disclosure statements specifying where the money came from to finance their campaign. Interest groups are often required to file reports on how they distribute their campaign contributions. Once elected, most state and local officials are required to file a different kind of disclosure form, one that indicates their personal wealth, investments, and other financial matters that may reveal conflicts of interest.

Roughly three-fourths of the states have enacted campaign finance reforms that limit individual contributions, and several states provide some form of public financing. State laws are often patterned after federal law, but some states have experimented with

turnout
The proportion of the voting-age public that votes.

disclosure
A requirement that candidates specify where the money came from to finance their campaign.

lower contribution limits than those allowed in federal elections.[53] Other states have experimented with tax credits to encourage small contributions. In 1996, Maine voters passed a ballot initiative that provided what supporters call a "clean money" option of public financing.[54] Under this system, candidates who agree to raise a small amount of private money and accept spending limits receive public funds for their campaigns.

However, fashioning and sustaining effective campaign finance laws are not easy tasks. Maine's reform laws are aimed at reducing state candidates' reliance on private contributors, especially those who make large contributions. The success of its laws depends on, among other things, the availability of public funding to encourage candidates to accept spending limits and forgo private contributions. Yet Maine, like many other states that have tried to implement public financing reforms, has found that it is hard to maintain adequate funding to support its program.[55] Maine's legislators, for example, borrowed considerable sums from the state's Clean Election Fund after the state's general revenues dropped.[56] Other states, such as Vermont, have tried to avoid this funding challenge by simply imposing spending limits and very low limits on contributions. But the U.S. Supreme Court struck down Vermont's restrictions in 2006 as unconstitutional infringements on free speech and reaffirmed its 1976 holding that spending limits are only constitutional when candidates voluntarily accept them in exchange for public funds.[57]

Voting on Ballot Questions

Voting on ballot questions is heavily influenced by campaign spending. Presumably, greater expenditures make the most difference when there is a low level of information, as is the case with many ballot propositions. And opinions on ballot propositions are more volatile because voters' views on such matters are not deeply rooted in party affiliation, feelings toward an incumbent, or party appeal.[58]

Because many initiatives are supported by well-funded interests, and because a vote in one state can start a national movement on an issue, initiative campaigns can attract large sums of money. Some examples of heavy spending include a 1988 election in Maryland in which the National Rifle Association and other groups spent a record $6.8 million in an unsuccessful attempt to defeat a handgun registration referendum. The tobacco industry spent more than $21 million in California in 1988 to defeat an initiative raising the cigarette tax. More than $101 million was spent in California in that year on five initiatives that dealt with automobile insurance reform. A decade later, in what remains one of the most expensive initiative battles in U.S. history, more than $92 million was spent for and against a successful initiative to permit casinos on Native American lands in California.[59]

Voting on ballot questions is different from voting for candidates because voters do not have such simplifying factors as party identification and candidate appeal to rely on. More people vote for candidates than vote on ballot questions. Confused voters tend to vote no. "Ballot fatigue," tiring from too many contests and questions on the ballot, also makes people more likely to vote no.[60]

Voting in Recall Elections

Recall elections permit citizens to attempt to remove elected public officials from office before the end of their term of office. As with initiatives and referendums, recalls require sufficient petition signatures from registered voters to meet a preestablished threshold. Recall elections have been relatively rare at the statewide level. For example, before the successful 2003 recall of Governor Gray Davis there had been 31 unsuccessful attempts to recall California governors, none of which made it to the ballot.[61] Only two governors in American history have ever been recalled, including Davis.[62] While there were significant political problems in California at the time, including large budget deficits, it has been argued that Davis was recalled largely

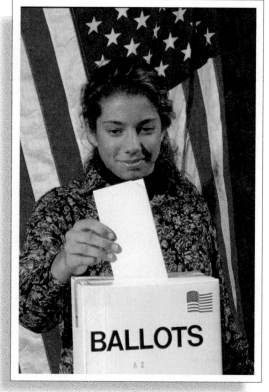

Urging young people to take an interest in government and to vote is a top priority for both major parties.

History Makers

Hiram Johnson and Direct Legislation

The California recall election in 2003 and frequent initiative and referendum elections in 24 states across the country highlight the important role that citizens play in deciding state laws and state elections. However, until the early 1900s most of these decisions were made by state legislatures and not directly by voters. This was an era marked by party machines that controlled politics in cities and states. They rewarded supporters with patronage, jobs, and access to politicians. In response to this, the Progressive Movement arose.

By working at the state and national level, the Progressives encouraged more widespread citizen participation through direct legislation, including popular control over nominees for elected offices, expanded suffrage rights, and initiatives and referendums. Progressives believed that "enlightened, dispassionate, independent" citizens should hold political power.*

The Progressive Party was founded in part by Hiram Johnson, who was selected as Theodore Roosevelt's running mate in the 1912 presidential election. Johnson was the governor of California from 1911 to 1917, and later served in the U.S. Senate for almost 30 years. While governor of California, he advocated reforms such as the direct election of U.S. senators; suffrage for women; initiative, referendum, and recall laws; and allowing candidates to register in multiple parties.[†] More than any other state today, California is identified with the use of the initiative and referendum or direct legislation.

In the 1912 presidential election, Roosevelt and Johnson received 27 percent of the popular vote and 88 electoral college votes. The Progressive Party had more success on the state level, electing 13 members of Congress and approximately 260 local officials.[‡] Although the Progressive Party's influence had leveled off by 1920, it was not before the Sixteenth Amendment allowing for the direct election of U.S. senators and the Nineteenth Amendment allowing women to vote were passed. Hiram Johnson and the Progressive Party left a legacy of trust in individual voters and direct participation of citizens in democracy. ∎

Hiram Johnson

---

*David B. Magleby, *Direct Legislation: Voting on Ballot Propositions in the United States* (Johns Hopkins University Press, 1984), p. 23.
†Benjamin Parke DeWitt, *The Progressive Movement* (The Macmillan Company, 1915), pp. 66–67. See also *Sacramento Bee*, "People of the Century: Hiram Johnson," at www.sacbee.com/static/archive/news/projects/people_of_century/century_special/johnson.html.
‡John Allen Gable, *The Bull Moose Years: Theodore Roosevelt and the Progressive Party* (Kennikat Press, 1978), p. 146.

---

because of negative views regarding his political character, which caused him to lose the goodwill and trust of voters.[63]

The 2003 California recall ballot consisted of two questions: the first asking whether or not to remove Governor Davis from office, and the second asking who should replace Davis if he were recalled.[64] If a majority had voted no on the first question, the results of the second question would not have mattered. Because a majority voted yes on the first question, the person who got the most votes on the second question became the new governor. Other states divide the questions, first having an election to decide whether to recall the official and if a majority votes yes, a second election to determine the replacement.

Recall elections have been more common at the local level, including in elections for school board.

The Future of Grassroots Democracy

Political parties are vital to the operation of our democracy. Many political scientists believe that our system would be strengthened if we had stronger political parties. The first step in the renewal of the parties would be to change their negative image and persuade citizens that political activity is essential to a healthy constitutional democracy. The next would be to give people who support parties a greater say in choosing the candidates who run under their party's label. Although our candidate-centered tradition will certainly remain, it is important to moderate it with strengthened parties that can discipline candidates, at least by withholding resources that candidates cannot easily acquire elsewhere. We would do well to make ballots and elections more voter-friendly. The proliferation of elections, including special elections, turns off even the most committed citizens. Why not, many reformers argue, consolidate elections so that voters might exercise their vote only once or twice, rather than three or four times, a year?

Getting qualified people to run for office is another challenge. The spiraling cost of campaigns and the advantages enjoyed by incumbents have deterred many good potential candidates. Others are repelled by the nasty and negative tone of recent elections. However, unless a democracy produces able citizens who are willing to run for office, it loses its ability to hold incumbents accountable.

One of the advantages of 50 states and thousands of communities is that they afford citizens a multitude of opportunities for participation, making involvement less intimidating. The fact that our states do not all have the same approach to elections, parties, or voting also provides valuable data for states considering changing their process. One disadvantage of so many governmental units and so many different elected officials is that they make politics seem more complicated. Citizens willing to become involved, however, often find they can have more influence than they expected.

Summary

1. In the United States, there are no national elections, only state elections. Even the presidential election is really a set of 51 different elections to choose electors who will in turn cast their ballots for president. Elections for U.S. senators and representatives are conducted largely under state law.

2. Political parties are essential to the functioning of democracy at all levels, but they are principally organized at the state, congressional district, or county levels. This arrangement makes state parties vitally important. Routinely, they are patterned after the national party organization and include a chair, a vice chair, and a central committee. State parties are often run by full-time party administrators called executive directors.

3. Political parties play important roles in candidate recruitment, voter registration, voter mobilization, and fund raising, and they provide a link between people and government. Parties are also important to the operation of most state legislatures. The governor is the head of his or her party. Governors consider party loyalty when appointing people to executive and judicial openings.

4. Voters usually vote along party lines in state and local elections, although candidate appeal and issues can also influence them.

5. Political parties were once strong and well organized at the local level; in some cities, these organizations were called machines and were led by party bosses. Reaction to the abuses of these machines led to reform efforts. One of these reforms was to make most local politics officially nonpartisan.

6. States vary in whether the two parties are competitive. In one-party states, elections are generally won by one party, while in two-party states, the parties alternate in holding power.

7. State election law is important in defining who may vote, when elections will be held, how party nominees are chosen, and which candidates will appear on the ballot. State election law also establishes a framework for ensuring fair elections.

8. State registration laws make voting more or less difficult, depending on their requirements. States may require persons to register by party to vote in primary elections; when voting is thus limited, the primaries are called closed primaries. Over the course of U.S. history, states have gradually eased registration requirements.

9. Turnout varies by type of election; it is higher in general than primary elections and higher in presidential than midterm elections. Turnout is higher in state than local elections, and regularly scheduled elections typically have higher turnout than special elections. Turnout in vote-by-mail elections is also higher than in in-person elections in most cases. More people vote for major candidate races than vote on ballot questions.

Further **Reading**

MARK BALDASSARE, *A California State of Mind: The Conflicted Voter in a Changing World* (University of California Press, 2002).

BRUCE E. CAIN AND **ELISABETH R. GERBER,** EDS., *Voting at the Political Fault Line: California's Experiment with the Blanket Primary* (University of California Press, 2002).

THOMAS M. CARSEY, *Campaign Dynamics: The Race for Governor* (University of Michigan Press, 2000).

THOMAS E. CRONIN, *Direct Democracy: The Politics of Initiative, Referendum, and Recall* (Replica Books, 2000).

PAUL S. HERRNSON, *Party Campaigning in the 1980s* (Harvard University Press, 1988).

MALCOLM E. JEWELL AND **SARAH M. MOREHOUSE,** *Political Parties and Elections in American States,* 4th ed. (CQ Press, 2001).

V. O. KEY JR., *American State Politics: An Introduction* (Knopf, 1956).

NORMAN R. LUTTBEG, *The Grassroots of Democracy* (Lexington Books, 1999).

DAVID B. MAGLEBY, *Direct Legislation: Voting on Ballot Propositions in the United States* (Johns Hopkins University Press, 1984).

L. SANDY MAISEL AND **KARA Z. BUCKLEY,** *Parties and Elections in America: The Electoral Process,* 4th ed. (Rowman & Littlefield, 2005).

MARK MONMONIER, *Bushmanders and Bullwinkles: How Politicians Manipulate Electronic Maps and Census Data to Win Elections* (University of Chicago Press, 2001).

A. JAMES REICHLEY, ED., *Elections American Style* (Brookings Institution Press, 1987).

ALAN ROSENTHAL, *Governors and Legislators: Contending Powers* (CQ Press, 1990).

BYRON E. SHAFER, *The Two Majorities and The Puzzle of Modern American Politics* (University Press of Kansas, 2003).

LINDA WITT, KAREN M. PAGET, AND **GLENNA MATTHEWS,** *Running as a Woman: Gender and Politics in American Politics* (Free Press, 1994).

JOSEPH FRANCIS ZIMMERMAN, *The Initiative: Citizen Lawmaking* (Greenwood Press, 1999).

KeyTerms

party column ballot, p. 646
straight ticket, p. 646
office block ballot, p. 646
split ticket, p. 647
soft money, p. 651
issue advocacy, p. 651

party caucus, p. 653
redistricting, p. 653
two-party state, p. 654
one-party state, p. 654
closed primary, p. 658
crossover voting, p. 658

open primary, p. 658
blanket primary, p. 658
turnout, p. 659
disclosure, p. 659

Chapter 24

State Legislatures

★

STATE LEGISLATURES EXISTED LONG BEFORE THE CONTINENTAL CONGRESS WAS FORMED IN 1776 AND EXERTED GREAT POWER UNDER THE ARTICLES OF CONFEDERATION. HAVING EXISTED AS THE PRIMARY FORM OF GOVERNMENT EVEN UNDER BRITISH COLONIAL RULE, STATE LEGISLATURES WERE RELUCTANT TO GIVE UP THEIR POWER TO EITHER THE NATIONAL GOVERNMENT OR THEIR OWN GOVERNORS. MOST STATES HAD RELATIVELY WEAK EXECUTIVES, AND SEVERAL HAD NO EXECUTIVE AT ALL. INDEED, THE CREATION OF THE

Constitution was in part a reaction against the excessive power of the state legislatures, which is why the framers of the Constitution imposed limits on the powers of the state legislatures (see especially Article I, Section 9).

The Tenth Amendment to the U.S. Constitution makes it clear that any power not given to the national government or denied to the states lies with the states or with the people. State constitutions, in turn, give some of this reserved power exclusively to nonlegislative agencies and specifically deny some to the legislature. What is left is inherited by the state legislatures.

Although state legislatures today do not dominate state policy making the way they did in 1787, they do play a vital role in state politics and policy. State legislators strive to solve problems and provide services—and do so, whenever possible, without raising taxes or creating larger bureaucracies. Legislators these days seek to make the legislature a counterbalance to powerful governors and powerful state bureaucracies.

In recent years, legislatures have been involved in a remarkable variety of activities:

- Legislatures in Massachusetts, Vermont, and Maine enacted health care programs designed to ensure that all residents were covered by health insurance.

- Utah's legislature passed a law allowing local schools to ignore federal mandates under the national education program, No Child Left Behind.

- Connecticut legislators appropriated funds for stem cell research.

- Illinois approved the nation's first universal preschool program for three-year-old children, and many other states have expanded their preschool programs.

- In the first four months of 2006, state legislators in 43 states introduced 461 bills related to immigration or immigrants.

- Legislatures in several states have taken action to limit the use of eminent domain for economic development.

"*Legislators represent people, not trees or acres. Legislators are elected by votes, not farms or cities or economic interests. The right to elect legislators in a free unimpaired fashion is a bedrock of our political system.*"

CHIEF JUSTICE EARL WARREN

665

■ Several state legislatures have scheduled citizen referendums that would ban same-sex marriages, while the Colorado legislature supported a ballot proposal to give same-sex couples most of the rights of marriage.

■ By 2006, 20 states had established minimum wages higher than the federal minimum wage.

■ Many states have adopted some form of election reform, including new ballots, a ban on punch cards, and new computer voting systems.

In short, legislatures everywhere make or modify policies on all kinds of issues by balancing conflicting political pressures, while facilitating compromises between political factions or different parts of the state. They also make laws and modify and approve budgets. Legislatures perform countless constituency services and, along with the governor and the courts, help keep state agencies accountable to both the laws and the citizens. Legislators must constantly reconcile pressures among competing interest groups. Representing local views at the state level, they dramatize issues and bring them into the open. A state legislature serves as a lightning rod to which most of the conflicting pressures of American society are drawn.

This chapter will examine state legislatures in greater detail by asking what they do, how they are organized, and how they have adapted to a much more complex world. As they have grown into more professional bodies, state legislatures are claiming a greater role in how government works and are important partners in both state policy and federal action.

The Legislative Branch

The 50 state legislatures share many characteristics—all states except Nebraska have a two-house **bicameral legislature**. Nebraska has a one-house **unicameral legislature**.[1] The larger chamber is generally called the house of representatives. (In a few states, it is called the assembly or house of delegates.) It contains from as few as 40 members in Alaska and 41 in Delaware to as many as 400 members in New Hampshire and 203 in Pennsylvania; the average number is around 100. In all but five states, representatives serve two-year terms; in Alabama, Louisiana, Maryland, Mississippi, and North Dakota, representatives serve for four years. The smaller chamber, known as the senate, is typically composed of about 40 members. State senators serve four-year terms in most states.

How Are Legislatures Organized?

State legislatures look very much like the United States Congress. A *speaker,* usually chosen by the majority party, presides over the lower house. In many states, speakers have more power to control proceedings than their national counterpart has. For example, most state speakers have the right to appoint committees and thus play a key role in determining policy. However, the power of speakers varies greatly: Speakers have great powers in West Virginia, New Hampshire, and Arizona but minimal powers in Alaska, Mississippi, Hawaii, and Wyoming.[2] In 25 states, lieutenant governors preside over the senate, though they are usually mere figureheads; in other states, the majority party in the senate chooses its presiding officer, the president of the senate.[3]

As in the U.S. Congress, the committee system prevails. In several states, such as Maine and Massachusetts, *joint committees* are used to speed up legislative action. However, state legislative committees usually do not have the same power over bills as their national counterparts: Some still lack adequate professional assistance, the seniority system is not as closely followed as in Congress, and membership turnover is usually higher, especially where term limits have taken effect.

bicameral legislature
A two-house legislature.

unicameral legislature
A one-house legislature.

Every legislature has committees on education, transportation, agriculture, and energy or natural resources. Most also have important committees on rules, appropriations, and taxes (sometimes called the Ways and Means Committee). Legislators generally specialize and become experts on one or two substantive matters, such as education, crime, taxation, or the budget process. As in any organization or large assembly, an individual earns respect and influence primarily by developing specialized knowledge about either policy or procedural matters.

There are striking differences among state legislatures. Some have excellent staff and splendid information technology and are well-run professional organizations. The New York legislature has nearly 3,100 permanent staffers, Pennsylvania has nearly 3,000, and California has 2,300. Other legislatures get by with much smaller staffs. Wyoming has just 29 permanent staff for the entire legislature, while North Dakota has 32, Vermont has 52, and South Dakota has 56.[4]

Legislatures also differ in how members interact and conduct legislative politics—differences that sometimes stem from historical or ethnic traditions. They can also arise from urban-rural or east-west factional splits and sometimes from regional differences, as is the case with the "Hill people" versus the "Delta people" in Mississippi. Here is how one expert on state politics viewed some of the more distinctive characteristics shaping state politics in the United States:

> In New York professional politics, political wheeling and dealing and frantic activity are characteristic. In Virginia, one gets a sense of tradition, conservatism, and gentility. . . . Louisiana's politics are wild and flamboyant. By contrast, moderation and caution are features of Iowa. A strong disposition of compromise pervades Oregon, with politicians disposed to act as brokers and deal pragmatically rather than dogmatically. In Kansas, hard work, respect for authority, fiscal prudence, and a general conservatism and resistance to rapid social change are pervasive features of the state environment. Indiana is intensely partisan. Wyoming is mainly individualistic, and Ohio is fundamentally conservative. In Hawaii, the relatively recent political dominance of Japanese and the secondary status of Chinese, native Hawaiians, and Haoles (whites) makes for tough ethnic politics. Yankee Republicans used to run Massachusetts, but now the Irish dominate. Their personalized style, which blends gregariousness and political loyalty, results in a politics of the clan. Mormonism of course dominates Utah.[5]

How Do Legislatures Compare?

State legislatures differ in important ways, not the least of which is their basic level of professionalism, generally defined as having full-time legislators, more staff, and higher pay, which in turn may draw more ambitious candidates for office and longer service.

Legislators in larger states tend to represent districts with larger populations, and therefore have to deal with more constituent concerns and interest group pressures. Larger states also generally dedicate more resources to the operation of their legislatures. Smaller states typically have smaller districts and less money. However, professionalism does not simply track state size: Alaska is a very small state in population but has a professionalized legislature. Georgia is a fairly large state with a much less professionalized legislature (see Table 24–1).

In the New Hampshire House of Representatives, legislators are essentially volunteers. These "citizen-legislators" represent districts of about 3,000 people. They earn just $200 for the two-year term and meet for no more than 45 days a year. In contrast, the California Assembly has 80 members, each representing a district of about 450,000 people. California legislators earn $111,000 a year in addition to expense allowances, meet nearly all year long, and consider their legislative work a full-time occupation.

Legislative salaries are most often set by the legislature. Most legislators are reluctant to increase their salaries, and as a result, lawmakers' salaries lag well behind the rate of inflation and increases in the cost of living. Most people run for the legislature for reasons other than compensation. "No one goes into politics to get rich," notes

TABLE 24–1 The Diversity of State Legislatures

State legislatures across the country vary greatly in many respects. The National Conference of State Legislatures grouped them into three types based on their length of session.

RED: Full- or Near-Full-Time, High-Pay, Large-Staff "Professional Legislatures"

Alaska	New York
California	New Jersey
Florida	Ohio
Illinois	Pennsylvania
Massachusetts	Wisconsin
Michigan	

WHITE: In-Between Hybrid

Alabama	Minnesota
Arkansas	Missouri
Arizona	Nebraska
Colorado	North Carolina
Connecticut	Oklahoma
Delaware	Oregon
Hawaii	South Carolina
Iowa	Tennessee
Kentucky	Texas
Louisiana	Virginia
Maryland	Washington

BLUE: Part-Time, Low-Pay, Small-Staff "Citizen Legislatures"

Georgia	New Mexico
Idaho	North Dakota
Indiana	Rhode Island
Kansas	South Dakota
Maine	Utah
Mississippi	Vermont
Montana	West Virginia
Nevada	Wyoming
New Hampshire	

SOURCE: National Conference of State Legislatures, "Full-Time and Part-Time Legislatures," www.ncsl.org/programs/press/2004/backgrounder_fullandpart.htm, updated October 2005.

"No one goes into politics to get rich, but you can't have a system where only the rich get into politics."

FORMER MASSACHUSETTS STATE SENATOR TOM BIRMINGHAM

former Massachusetts state senator Tom Birmingham. "But you can't have a system where only the rich get into politics."[6]

Legislatures also differ by the level of activity. Forty-three state legislatures meet every year from January through May or June. Legislatures in seven states, including Arkansas, Montana, Nevada, and Texas, meet only every other year. Some state constitutions limit their legislatures to regular sessions of a fixed number of days, usually 60 or 90. Such restrictions reflect both a distrust of government and the desire to allow legislators to serve and still maintain other careers. *Special sessions* have been developed to get around these limitations. The governor has the power to call the legislature into special session and in some states to determine the issues that may be discussed in the special session—a power governors frequently use. The trend in many states has been to somewhat longer annual legislative sessions and higher salaries.

Who Serves in the State Legislature?

Like members of the U.S. Congress, the vast majority of state legislators run for reelection and win. Indeed, about one-third of state legislative elections are uncontested; this is especially true in smaller, one-party states and in the South.[7]

An incumbent seeking reelection has many advantages over a challenger: name recognition, better access to campaign funds, experience in running campaigns, and a record of helping with constituent problems. Also like members of the U.S. Congress, few legislators feel politically secure, even when they have not been opposed in the last election.

In an incumbent's mind, there is seldom such a thing as a "safe district" and a sure reelection. "Whatever their margins of victory in prior elections, however 'safe' their district may appear to the analyst, incumbents know that lightning can strike. . . . They have seen colleagues relax their efforts and subsequently lose their seats. They live in perpetual danger of casting a roll-call vote that upsets their constituency or mobilizes a key interest group to seek their defeat."[8] Incumbents also worry about scandals in their party or having to run with an unpopular candidate at or near the top of their party ticket.

THE PERSONAL PROFILE The typical American state legislator is a 48-year-old white male, well educated and well-off, often a businessman or lawyer of Anglo-Saxon origin who has had some type of previous political experience—not always elective—at the city or county level. Some have worked as a staff member in the legislature or in state government.[9] Most state legislators have held some type of local party position and have been active in political campaigns. Surprisingly, about one-third were born in some other state, a reflection of our increasingly mobile population.

State legislators tend to have more education and higher incomes than other citizens do in their states. They are usually hardworking, public-spirited citizens who believe being in the legislature is a good opportunity for service. Yet state legislators enjoy less prestige than members of Congress, especially in states that have large legislatures. Discouraged by modest salaries and long hours, many serve a few terms and then either retire voluntarily or run for higher office. Some leave after just a couple of terms because they find they are spending much of their time on matters that do not interest them. As one one-termer explained, "A great deal in the political process does not—repeat, does not—involve the glamorous policy issues. Most of the work is sheer routine and hardly awe-inspiring."[10] And, of course, some are now leaving because of term limits in their states that prevent more than two or three terms.

PARTY AFFILIATION At the start of 2006, the state legislatures were almost evenly divided between the two parties. Democrats occupied 2,709 of the 5,411 House seats, while Republicans occupied 2,680; similarly, Democrats held 954 of the 1,971 Senate seats, while Republicans held 963. Only 72 of the nation's state legislators consider themselves Independents or nonpartisan, including all 49 members of Nebraska's unicameral legislature.[11] Given these margins, a change of just three seats would alter party control of 29 legislative chambers, House or Senate, in 24 states. Republicans controlled both houses of the state legislature in 20 states, the Democrats controlled 19 states and the District of Columbia, and 10 states had divided control.

OCCUPATION Lawyers continue to be the largest occupational group in most state legislatures, yet the percentage of attorneys has leveled off; today attorneys constitute only about 17 percent of state legislators nationwide. There has been an increase in those who consider themselves full-time legislators, and there has been a slight increase as well of teachers, homemakers, retirees, and students.[12] Real estate and insurance dealers and sales representatives are also commonly found in legislatures (see Figure 24–1).

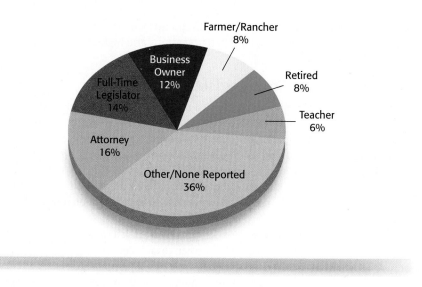

FIGURE 24–1 A Profile of State Legislators.

SOURCE: National Conference of State Legislatures.

The number of farmers continues to fall as redistricting continues to shift power away from rural areas and as the number of farms declines. Moreover, longer sessions of the legislatures make it less possible to be both a farmer and a legislator. When legislatures used to meet for just a few months in winter, farmers were able to fit their schedules to the legislative cycle.

Because legislators must have flexible schedules, the job often attracts retired people and those whose businesses or professional practices have been so successful that they can afford to take time off. Legislators used to identify themselves by their occupations outside the legislature, but this is less the case now; many refer to their occupation as legislator.

PROSPECTS Many state legislators go on to fill other elected offices. Fully 51 percent of the members of the United States Congress in 2005 were former state legislators, 235 of the 435 members of the House of Representatives and 39 of the 100 United States Senators.[13] Many statewide elected officials are also former state legislators.

What State Legislators Do

The nation's 7,382 state legislators engage in many of the same lawmaking and oversight activities as members of the U.S. Congress: They enact laws that create state parks; specify salaries for state officials; draw up rules governing state elections; fix state tax rates; set workers' compensation policies; determine the quantity and quality of state correctional, mental health, and educational institutions; and oversee welfare programs. State legislators approve all appropriations and thereby confirm or modify a governor's proposed budget. Legislators in most states are also responsible for overseeing the administration of public policy. Although they do not administer programs directly, legislators can and do determine whether programs are being carried out according to legislative intentions through hearings, investigations, audits, and the budgetary process. Bill passage rate varies greatly from state to state, depending on a variety of factors, including procedural necessities, constitutional requirements, and local culture. Figure 24–2 outlines the steps involved in passing state laws.

State legislatures perform various functions within the larger federal system, such as ratifying proposed amendments to the U.S. Constitution, exercising the right to petition Congress to call for a constitutional convention in order to propose an amendment to the U.S. Constitution, and approving interstate compacts on matters affecting state policies and their implementation. The national government has recently turned back some health and welfare responsibilities to the states.

Each state's constitution prescribes the procedures its legislatures must follow and sets limits on the rate of taxation, the kinds of taxes, the subjects that may be taxed,

The Changing Face of American Politics

Women in the Statehouse

In the late 1960s, state legislatures were dominated by men and often had the look of a "good old boys' club." This has changed in recent years as more women have been elected, bringing the national average up from just 4.5 percent in 1971 to 22.6 percent in 2006. Thirty-five percent of the Maryland legislative seats are occupied by women, followed by Delaware at 34 percent, and Arizona, Colorado, Kansas, Nevada, and Vermont at 33 percent. In South Carolina, by contrast, only 9 percent of the lawmakers are women.

As women have won more legislative seats, their influence has grown, particularly as more women win election to key legislative posts. In addition, women increasingly occupy key committee positions and often meet to plan strategies on women's issues.

It is not clear if the election of women to state legislatures has made a significant difference in how women are represented. Although some analysts believe female legislators are more likely to offer leadership on women, family, and children's policy issues,[*] other scholars have found little or no difference in how men and women deal with gender policy issues.[†]

Although more women, African Americans, and Hispanics are winning election to state legislatures, these groups are still notably in the minority. Of the 7,382 state legislators in 2005, 23 percent were women, 8 percent were African American, and just 3 percent were Hispanic. ∎

Female members of the Washington legislature constitute the highest percentage of women in any legislature in the nation's history.

[*]See Sue Thomas, *How Women Legislate* (Oxford University Press, 1996). See also Kathleen Bratton and Kerry L. Haynie, "Agenda Setting and Legislative Success in State Legislatures: The Effects of Gender and Race," *Journal of Politics* 61 (August 1999), pp. 658–679.
[†]Beth Reingold, *Representing Women: Sex, Gender, and Legislative Behavior in Arizona and California* (University of North Carolina Press, 2000).

SOURCE: National Conference of State Legislatures, "Legislator Demographics," www.ncsl.org/programs/legman/about/demographic_overview.htm, accessed January 13, 2006.

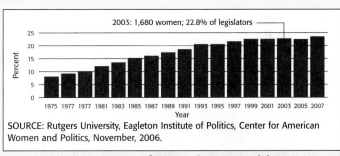

SOURCE: Rutgers University, Eagleton Institute of Politics, Center for American Women and Politics, November, 2006.

Current Percentage of Women in State Legislatures.

and the purposes of taxation. State legislatures participate in amending their states' constitutions by proposing amendments for voter ratification. Legislatures also have authority to impeach and try state officials, and they also are involved in the appointive process.

State legislators help translate public wants and aspirations into laws and regulations. In addition to their lawmaking functions, they also try to be ombudsmen—to listen, learn, and find solutions to problems. Invariably, state legislators wind up doing a lot of favors: getting a merchant a license to sell lottery tickets, persuading some state agency to look into safety standards at the local hospital, pushing for funds to repair county roads, arranging for a campaign supporter to be appointed to the state labor commission, and so on. State legislators are accessible. Citizens and students can nearly always contact their legislators directly and communicate with them in person, by telephone, or via e-mail.

FIGURE 24–2 How a Bill Becomes a State Law.

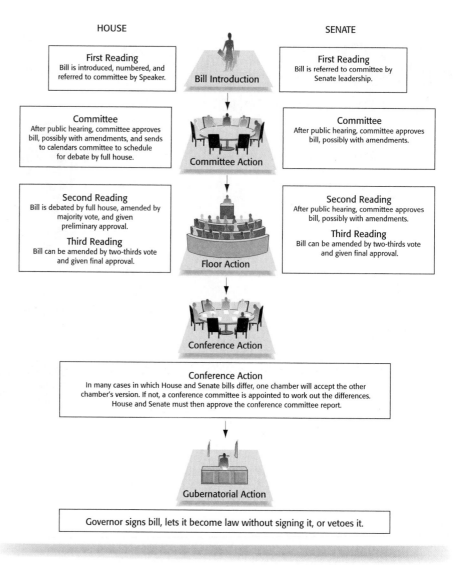

HOUSE | SENATE

First Reading
Bill is introduced, numbered, and referred to committee by Speaker.

Bill Introduction

First Reading
Bill is referred to committee by Senate leadership.

Committee
After public hearing, committee approves bill, possibly with amendments, and sends to calendars committee to schedule for debate by full house.

Committee Action

Committee
After public hearing, committee approves bill, possibly with amendments.

Second Reading
Bill is debated by full house, amended by majority vote, and given preliminary approval.

Third Reading
Bill can be amended by two-thirds vote and given final approval.

Floor Action

Second Reading
After public hearing, committee approves bill, possibly with amendments.

Third Reading
Bill can be amended by two-thirds vote and given final approval.

Conference Action

Conference Action
In many cases in which House and Senate bills differ, one chamber will accept the other chamber's version. If not, a conference committee is appointed to work out the differences. House and Senate must then approve the conference committee report.

Gubernatorial Action

Governor signs bill, lets it become law without signing it, or vetoes it.

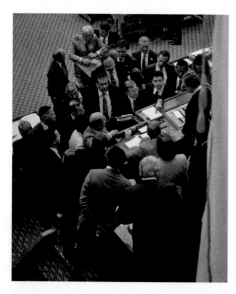

Members of the Texas House of Representatives gather around the speaker's podium to iron out a disputed point.

The agenda of issues that legislators confront varies over time and from state to state. Some issues, however, have severely challenged many states' legislatures in recent years. Legislatures have had to confront many kinds of pressures on the state budget. Rapid increases in health care costs, and the growing number of Americans without health insurance, have made it very difficult for state legislatures to slow government spending in this area. Public demands for state spending have also been strong in recent years for the building and repair of roads and highways; for environmental protection, particularly as the federal government has cut back its support for such functions; for correctional facilities, as more and more criminals have been given lengthy sentences; and for primary and secondary education, as society has come to expect greater performance from schools in a competitive world economy. Yet these demands for public spending are often hard to meet now as state politicians have either become increasingly reluctant to raise taxes or unable to do so because of new constitutional restrictions on their powers of taxation.

Legislators have also had to face some difficult and divisive issues involving fundamental rights in recent years—and the questions show little sign of going away. The nomination of new justices on the U.S. Supreme Court has led some state legislators to believe that states may now exercise greater control over access to abortions. The growing number of immigrants living in more and more states has put pressure on state legislatures to deal with questions about the enforcement of immigration laws and the rights of undocumented immigrants. Competing groups have also been fighting in state legislatures over whether couples of the same sex may marry or join

History Makers

Jesse Unruh

Jesse M. Unruh was Speaker of the California State Assembly from 1961 to 1968, holding the position longer than any previous speaker. Unruh led the transformation of the California legislature from a part-time body to a full-time professionalized organization that was able to hold its own with the governor. He was one of the most powerful and colorful individuals in California politics in a career spanning four decades.

Unruh was born in Kansas, a sharecropper's son. He served in the military in World War II and then went to the University of Southern California on the G.I. Bill, which paid the college expenses of veterans. Unruh started his political career with election to the California assembly in 1954. California was at that time undergoing rapid economic growth, and a power vacuum had developed in the state's political system. Unruh was one of the individuals that filled this leadership void. Unruh was politically liberal, authoring the Unruh Credit Regulation Act to protect consumers. His 1959 Unruh Civil Rights Act prohibited discrimination by businesses, such as restaurants and hotels, that offered services to the public; the act served as a model for later federal civil rights legislation. Unruh also authored the first detailed campaign finance disclosure act for public officials. However, Unruh was often in conflict with liberal political reformers who resented his political dominance and heavy-handed tactics, which included locking the doors of the assembly in order to force members to stay in the chamber and vote.

Unruh was one of the more quotable politicians of his day, and many of his best quotes reflected his practical view of politics, including, "Money is the mother's milk of politics," and "Sometimes we must rise above principles."

Unruh was also active in national politics. He headed John F. Kennedy's campaign in California in 1960 and helped Robert Kennedy win the 1968 California primary. Unruh was present when Robert Kennedy was assassinated after that primary, and assisted in capturing the shooter.

In 1970, Unruh ran for governor of California and lost to Ronald Reagan. He then ran unsuccessfully for mayor of Los Angeles in 1973. In 1974, he was elected treasurer of California and served in that position until his death in 1987. ■

Jesse Unruh

SOURCE: Jesse M. Unruh Institute of Politics, University of California, "About Jesse M. Unruh," www.rcf.usc.edu/~unruhins/about_jesse_m__unruh.htm; James Q. Wilson, *The Amateur Democrat: Club Politics in Three Cities* (University of Chicago Press, 1962).

---

in civil unions and enjoy some or all of the rights typically granted to heterosexual marriages.

With the growth of state functions, legislators are spending increasing amounts of time on casework or constituency services. Constituent relations are often the most time-consuming aspect of a legislator's job. Local city and school officials always need the help of legislators, and interest groups back home are always pressing their views. Legislators usually try hard to perform constituent casework because they recognize its political value. The more help they give to home-district citizens and businesses, they reason, the more they will earn respect, win reelection, or perhaps gather support for election to higher office.

What Legislative Committees Do

A legislative committee is where bills are drafted, hearings are held, and the general policy making and preliminary lawmaking take place. Committees vary in power and influence from state to state. In general, however, the influence of committees has increased in recent decades. They used to be pale shadows of their counterparts in the U.S. Congress, and they often still are in the less populous states because of short sessions, limited staffing, and turnover of both staff and legislators. Still, legislative committees process and shape hundreds or even thousands of bills and resolutions every year.[14] In many of the more professionalized legislatures, committees may also meet between sessions of the legislature, conducting hearings and preparing for the next session.

Committees do the legislature's work. They consider and amend legislation, oversee the implementation of the laws, interview judges, and serve as the major access point for citizens, interest groups, and lobbyists. The functions of a legislative committee are advisory; all of its proposals are subject to review, approval, or rejection by the legislative body of which it is a part. However, it is rare that the full body will adopt a bill that is not screened and favorably reported by a committee.

The committee system allows members to concentrate their energies on specific areas of governmental operations. Over time, legislative committees and their members develop extensive knowledge about particular activities and provide greatly valued information about the content and desirability of proposed bills to their colleagues. Since it is impossible for everybody to be an expert on all aspects of state government, properly staffed and run committees can evaluate the merits and faults of a proposed law more effectively than any individual legislator can.

How State Legislators Decide

State legislators are influenced by many of the same factors that affect members of the U.S. Congress, including legislators' personal ideology and policy positions and the views of their constituencies. For part-time, less professionalized legislatures, however, party membership and interest group pressure are much more important to legislative outcomes.

POLITICAL PARTIES   Except in Nebraska, candidates for state legislatures are nominated by political parties in primaries or by party conventions and caucuses, and they are elected *as party members.* Although the official party organization is sometimes not a dominant influence in recruiting state legislative candidates, a candidate nonetheless has to go through the party to gain the nomination. Figure 24–3 shows the current party control of the state legislatures.

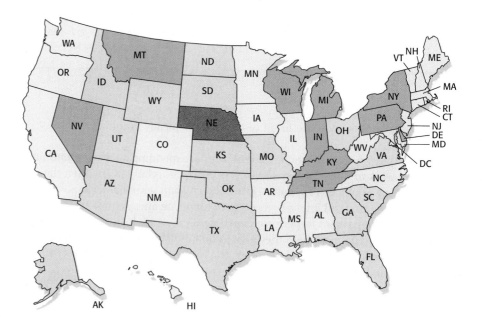

FIGURE 24–3 Party Control of State Legislatures, 2007.

Democratic Control (23)   Republican Control (16)   Split Control (10)   Nonpartisan (1)

The role of political parties in the governance of legislatures and in policy making varies widely from state to state. In nearly half the states—especially in the urban, industrialized states and in the Northeast—the political party is a key factor in decision making. In other states—in the Southwest, for example—parties appear less significant. Coalitions there tend to form along rural–urban, conservative–liberal, or regional lines.

Parties in most states are less influential than they used to be. Candidates welcome what help they can get from the parties, but that is often not much. However, in some states, party leaders in the legislature raise and allocate campaign contributions that prove helpful to those running for the first or second time, particularly in competitive races. Party organizations and political action committees are major sources of money for many legislative candidates. Still, legislative candidates almost always have to form their own personal organization, separate from the local party apparatus, to wage a winning campaign.

In nearly every state where there are two active parties, the political party selects legislative leaders and assigns members to committees. Party leaders in many state legislatures distribute sought-after perks, ranging from committee assignments to parking spaces. **Party caucuses**—meetings of all the members of one party in the chamber—also distribute campaign funds to their members and to specifically targeted districts.

Party unity on policy matters is typically found in states with a highly competitive two-party system. In those states, party caucuses develop party positions, and party members are expected to support them in the legislative chambers. In a few states, binding votes in party caucuses virtually (although not legally) force party members to vote as a unified bloc on the floor of their chamber. Binding caucus votes are taken on relatively few issues, however. Voting regularly with the party and being a member of the majority party can help legislators win discretionary grants or other favors for their districts.

The party caucus is a principal instrument for legislative decision making in about half the states, including Colorado, Delaware, Idaho, Montana, California, and Utah. In states where a party holds a slim majority of the seats in a legislative chamber, representatives are more likely to feel pressure to "toe the party line" than where a party commands a large majority.[15] Similarly, legislators are more likely to vote with their party in states where the political party plays an important role in recruiting and nominating candidates.

In legislatures in which a single party has had long-standing dominance or control, as used to be in some southern states, parties are less important in conducting and shaping legislative business. Because of the recent rise of the Republican party in the South and Southwest, however, parties and partisanship are gradually increasing in strength in such states as Florida, Texas, and North Carolina. A rebirth of partisanship and growing attention to elections of legislators are apparently making the parties more important than they have been in the past.

INTEREST GROUPS Interest groups are a significant and growing source of influence on state legislatures. Teacher organizations, trade associations, labor groups, trial attorneys, taxpayer associations, insurance, mining, real estate, road builders, and banking interests are often the most visible single-interest groups. In states with an obvious major economic interest, such as agriculture, mining, lumbering, or fishing, legislators pay close attention to the needs of that interest, regardless of whether the group employs lobbyists. The legislatures in these states seldom pass legislation hostile to their own state's principal economic interests.

Most state interest groups use lobbying as a major tool of influence. **Lobbying** is attempting to influence the decisions of public officials, especially legislators. The right to lobby is secured by the First and Fourteenth Amendments to the Constitution, which protect the right of the people to petition the government for redress of grievances. State constitutions provide similar protections.

party caucus
A meeting of the members of a party in a legislative chamber to select party leaders and develop party policy.

lobbying
Engaging in activities aimed at influencing public officials, especially legislators, and the policies they enact.

Representing the next generation of politics, Scott A. Merrick was reelected to the New Hampshire House of Representatives for a second term in 2006 at age 19.

"If you happen to know the four people on a certain senate committee, it's pretty damn easy to kill a bill."

A COLORADO LEGISLATOR

lobbyist
A person who is employed by and acts for an organized interest group or corporation to influence policy decisions and positions in the executive and legislative branches.

Anyone can try to influence how a state legislator votes. States usually define a professional **lobbyist** as someone who is paid to influence legislators on behalf of a client or clients. States now require lobbyists to register annually, either with the secretary of state's office or with an election or lobbyist commission. In most states, lobbyists must pay a fee for lobbying. In Texas, for example, professional lobbyists pay a $300 fee, although lobbyists for tax-exempt public interest groups pay only $100.

Hundreds of lobbyists operate in the committee rooms and corridors of the state capitols. The more populated states register thousands of lobbyists. In one recent year, Texas and New York each registered as many as 1,800 professional lobbyists. At least 1,200 lobbyists work the state capitol in California. Even less-populated Vermont had more than 600 lobbyists registered with the secretary of state.

Most lobbyists are regular employees of corporations, unions, or trade associations. Many are members of law firms; others are former state employees. Effective lobbyists are specialists in both subject matter and legislative procedure. Lobbyists for organized interests know the schedule of general hearings, committee meetings, floor debates, and social events. They also know as much as possible about the legislators, their electoral support, their values, their hobbies, and who has their "ear." They are present and prepared when their interests are affected. Veteran lobbyists know how to influence legislators. Lobbyists live by two important rules: First, it's a lot easier to kill a bill than to pass it. And second, work in such a way that you have no permanent allies and no permanent enemies. Today's opponent may be your supporter on the next issue for which you are lobbying.[16]

Some of the most effective lobbyists are retired state legislators. They not only have good contacts with their former colleagues, they know where the leverage points are in the legislative process. "If you happen to know the four people on a certain senate committee," said one Colorado legislator, "it's pretty damn easy to kill a bill."[17]

Lobbyists have two sources of influence: (1) information and (2) campaign support. Information is usually the key ingredient in gaining or losing a vote. Lobbyists are useful providers of such information to anyone who can influence state policy making. "Lobbyists are strategists, tacticians, builders of coalitions among groups, experts and communicators. They testify in committees, buttonhole lawmakers one-on-one, organize meetings between their members and legislators, stage rallies and demonstrations, and try to put a favorable 'spin' on media coverage of their issues."[18] Some of the information lobbyists provide may be quite technical, such as how a particular environmental regulation works; but effective lobbyists typically explain how these sometimes complicated laws or proposals affect or are likely to affect real businesses, institutions, and individuals, especially those in a legislator's own district.

In addition, interest groups are usually the major financial backers of incumbent legislators, and in return the lobbyists for those groups get unusual access. As the costs of state legislative races climb, so does the dependence of legislators, legislative leaders, and political parties on organized interests.[19]

Illegal use of lobbying techniques, primarily bribery, has been found in some states. Scandals have been exposed in Arkansas, Arizona, Kentucky, Massachusetts, New Mexico, and South Carolina, among others, in recent years.

Still, bribery is not a widespread problem in most states. Writing about his own experiences in the Vermont Senate, Frank Smallwood observed that as a rule, most of the lobbyists "were articulate, hard-working, and extremely well informed in their particular areas of expertise. This last attribute—information—represented their chief weapon and gave them real clout. As far as I could find out, the lobbyists didn't offer legislators any money or other direct inducements, at least, they never offered me anything, not even a sociable drink. Instead they relied on information."[20]

In recent years, states have sought to regulate lobbying activities, conflicts of interest, and the financing of political campaigns. Wisconsin and Minnesota ban such favors as buying meals for a legislator. In the wake of a 1992 Federal Bureau of Investigation sting, lawmakers in Kentucky are now barred from taking anything from a lobbyist except $100 per year in meals and drinks. State senators in New York voluntarily declined the meals and gifts worth more than $25 that interest groups had routinely lavished on them.[21]

Not all these reforms have been easy to implement, nor have they all worked according to the original intentions. Laws that control lobbying and regulate how much individuals may spend to influence either elections or the legislative process are difficult to enforce. It is sometimes unclear, too, whether they infringe on the constitutional right of persons to petition their government and to spend their own money for political purposes.[22]

OTHER INFLUENCES ON STATE LEGISLATORS   Usually the greatest influence on legislators comes from the people that elect them, their constituents.

Much as they promise to clean up state government and cut wasteful spending, many legislators fight hard to see that their own district gets a fair share of state government construction projects and subsidies. Voting for one's home district makes sense to many legislators. Former state legislator John E. Brandl writes that state legislators understand that on election day, their constituents who are grateful for favors received "are more apt to express positive sentiments on the ballot than those not receiving benefits from the capitol. . . . A former colleague of mine in the Minnesota House of Representatives seemed bewildered when he heard the suggestion that his first responsibility as a legislator might not be to look out for his district but rather to be concerned for the good of the whole state. 'Nobody who thinks like that could ever get elected from my district,' he maintained."[23]

But if state legislators are elected to represent the people and their views at the statehouse, few lawmakers think they should merely mirror or "re-present" the views of their district's constituents. Most legislators like to consider themselves **trustees** of their constituents, claiming to rely on their own conscience or on their considered judgments in making decisions. Legislators who view themselves as **delegates**, by contrast, adhere more closely to instructions from their constituents. Not surprisingly, the trustee role is not only more popular but also easier and more realistic to practice. Given the complexity of government and the difficulty of finding out where citizens stand on a wide variety of issues, the trustee role is a more workable one in the day-to-day decision making of a legislator during legislative sessions.

Views of constituents back home are influential on matters such as taxes and major construction on highway projects, yet on most issues, the people back home have little direct influence on lawmaking. On issues that are of keen local interest, legislators certainly do take their constituents into account when they vote. In other words, state lawmakers act as trustees on some issues and delegates on others. Yet conscience and personal philosophy are seldom the only, or even the most important, guide. Colleagues, committee recommendations, party leadership, staff counsel, and lobbying by the affected interests are also influential.

Another aspect of state politics that often fuels legislation is action taken by other states. Legislators frequently ask their staffs, "What is California, Minnesota, or Oregon doing on this problem?" Legislators are always on the lookout for innovative tax, educational, or welfare policies implemented elsewhere. Legislators are keenly interested in how their state compares to others in certain areas—on sales taxes, teen driving privileges, high school dropouts, clean air, the minimum wage, or federal moneys coming to the state. The press often uses such rankings in headlines and editorials.

The National Conference of State Legislatures, a nonpartisan professional organization funded by all 50 state legislatures, acts as an effective clearinghouse for new ideas (www.ncsl.org). With about 180 staff members located mainly in Denver, Colorado, it distributes studies to legislators across the country. A rival yet smaller and more conservative group, the American Legislative Exchange Council, has developed in recent years (www.alec.org). The Council of State Governments (www.csg.org) and the State Legislative Leaders Foundation (www.sllf.org) are two groups that also help serve state legislative leaders.

trustee
An official who is expected to vote independently, based on his or her judgment of the circumstances; one interpretation of the role of a legislator.

delegate
An official who is expected to represent the views of his or her constituents even when personally holding divergent views; one interpretation of the role of a legislator.

Actions taken by the federal government also influence state laws and regulations. Over the past 30 years, state legislatures have been burdened by **federal mandates**, which require states to allocate state funds to match federally stipulated programs such as Medicare. Funding for federal mandates was often the fastest-growing part of a state's budget, a sore point with state legislators. In the 1990s, Congress began to place some mild restraints on the growth of federal mandates.

Modernization and Reform

As states are asked to take on increasing responsibility, their legislatures face greater pressure to modernize: Lobbying is more intense than ever, campaign costs have increased, and fewer members follow the old folkways that used to make for an almost clubhouse collegiality in most legislatures. The greater participation of women, minorities, and more independent-minded legislators has meant a broader mix of agendas and ideas. The influence of legislative leaders has decreased, and that of the media and staff has grown.[24] According to state legislative scholar Alan Rosenthal, "Earlier, leaders were truly in command, and power was tightly held. Partly as a consequence of modernization and reform, legislatures have been democratized. Resources are more broadly distributed, and the gap between leaders and other legislators is narrower."[25]

State legislatures in the past were criticized as inefficient, ineffective, poorly staffed, scandal-ridden, secretive, sexist, unrepresentative, and often dominated by rural interests. Most legislatures had little or no staff and high rates of turnover among members. Legislators had to rely primarily on information that came to them from lobbyists or the governor's office. Legislatures were often run by factions that could not be held accountable, and parliamentary procedures and inadequate committee systems either prevented action or served narrow or specially favored interests.

> Given the goals of members, the demands of groups, and the heavy workload, deliberation gives way to expediency. Members frequently are unwilling to say no to their colleagues, lest their colleagues say no to them. They also are averse to saying no to constituents, lest their constituents withdraw support. The process has become porous; much seeps through that probably should not. Standing committees do not screen the wheat from the chaff as diligently as they might.[26]

Most state legislatures have adopted internal reforms to address these perceived shortcomings. Legislatures typically now have longer annual sessions, expanded and more competent staffs, more effective committee systems, streamlined procedures such as automated bill status and statute retrieval systems, higher salaries, and modern information systems.[27] In 1979, for example, state legislatures had 16,930 permanent staffers; by 2003, the number had climbed to 28,067.

Legislatures have also become more sensitive to new technologies. Every legislature now has a colorful Web site with detailed information about the workings of the lawmaking body. Hawaii has a fully equipped and staffed "public access room," making it easy for citizens to lobby their state legislators.[28] Virginia is considered a leader in e-government technology for its commitment to citizen–legislator communication through e-mail.[29] And most important, prodded by federal court rulings, legislative districts are now approximately equal in population and thus more representative of the people.

In short, amateur, part-time state legislatures are much less common now than a few decades ago. The new professionalism reflects a determination on the part of most legislators—especially the leaders—to take charge of their own branch as major players in shaping state public policy.

The movement to encourage full-time professional legislatures with substantial staffs, however, has not been universally praised. In fact, in recent years, some political scientists and some citizens have contended that we were better off when we had part-

federal mandate
A requirement imposed by the federal government as a condition for the receipt of federal funds.

time citizen-legislators. The groundswell in the early 1990s to enact term limits was in many ways a voters' protest against professionalized legislators who appeared to be making their job of representation into a career.

Legislative Term Limits: Problem or Solution?

Although the complexity of state problems may well require professional legislators who devote full-time attention to legislative issues, this professionalism "runs counter to the traditional theory of American politics in which citizens come together, conduct the public's business and return to their other occupations."[30] In the 35 states where there are no term limits, many legislators have served for a very long time—and hence are perceived by some persons as less connected to the people they represent.

Term limits were the most talked-about legislative "reform" in the 1990s. Reform began in 1990 when voters in California, Colorado, and Oklahoma approved the first term-limit restrictions through citizen-instigated ballot initiatives. Two years later, another 11 states enacted voter initiatives along the same lines. Several more approved term-limit provisions of some type for their constitutions, while voters in three states rejected them. In addition, state legislators in Utah and Louisiana voted to impose term limits on themselves. State supreme courts in five states—Massachusetts, Nebraska, Oregon, Washington, and Wyoming—have struck down term limits as unconstitutional. Note, however, that Nebraska voters in 2000, four years after their court nullified voter-approved limits, voted to reinstate them. In 2004, voters in Arkansas and Montana rejected ballot measures that would have relaxed term limits. In 2005, the Florida legislature also asked the voters to relax term limits, from eight years to 12 years.[31] Only two states had term limits initiatives on their ballots in 2006.

There is some evidence that the term-limit movement has run out of energy. In 2002, Idaho legislators voted to repeal term-limit provisions that had been approved on several occasions by Idaho voters. Term-limit supporters complained that this legislative repeal constituted "a slap in the face to all Idaho voters. The arrogance of the Legislature to repeal an issue that has been supported by four separate votes is unconscionable."[32] But Idaho legislative leader Bruce Newcomb responded that term limits won approval only because out-of-state money influenced the votes: "We were a cheap state to buy; it was not in the public interest. . . . There was never a real debate. . . . They had no opposition."[33] In 2003, the Utah legislature followed suit, repealing the limits it had imposed on itself only five years earlier.[34]

Nevertheless, term-limit provisions exist in 15 states (see Table 24–2). These provisions limit state legislators to legislative service of six to 12 years. In some states, lawmakers are barred from serving in the same office beyond a set number of years. In nine other states, they must skip one term (more in some states) before running again for office. In 2002, for example, 71 percent of Michigan's legislators were forced out of office under term limits.

Voters in California went even further and enacted a measure that slashed legislative staffs and curbed legislative pension benefits as well as limited the number of terms legislators could serve. This citizen-sponsored and citizen-enacted law also prohibited legislators from ever running again for the legislature.

Voters can, of course, dispatch legislators from office by voting for challengers. But voters seem to want the added constitutional device of doing for them what most voters do not do themselves—throw the rascals out! All the drama about term limits diverts attention from other serious problems, including weak parties, too many safe-seat districts where one party virtually always wins, and neglect of educational investment and economic development in the states.

Term limits have serious consequences for state legislative activity. In California, novice lawmakers now chair committees and hold leadership positions, and there are signs in California and elsewhere that term limits discourage legislative cooperation, decrease institutional expertise, and generally weaken legislatures relative to governors, bureaucrats, and lobbyists.

"We were a cheap state to buy; it was not in the public interest. There was never a real debate. They had no opposition."

IDAHO LEGISLATIVE LEADER BRUCE NEWCOMB

TABLE 24–2 Term Limits in the States

State	Year Enacted	House Limit (years)	House Year of Impact	Senate Limit (years)	Senate Year of Impact	Popular Vote in Favor
Maine	1993	8	1996	8	1996	67.6%
California	1990	6	1996	8	1998	52.2
Colorado	1990	8	1998	8	1998	71.0
Arkansas	1992	6	1998	8	2000	59.9
Michigan	1992	6	1998	8	2002	58.8
Florida	1992	8	2000	8	2000	76.8
Missouri*	1992	8	2002	8	2002	75.0
Ohio	1992	8	2000	8	2000	68.4
South Dakota	1992	8	2000	8	2000	63.5
Montana	1992	8	2000	8	2000	67.0
Arizona	1992	8	2000	8	2000	74.2
Oklahoma	1990	12	2004	12	2004	67.3
Nevada†	1996	12	2008	12	2008	70.4
Louisiana	1995	12	2007	12	2007	76.0
Nebraska‡	2000	8	2008	—	—	55.8

*Because of special elections, term limits became effective in 2000 for eight current members of the House and one senator in 1998.
†The Nevada Legislative Council and Attorney General have ruled that Nevada's term limits cannot be applied to those legislators elected in the same year term limits were passed (1996). They first apply to persons elected in 1998.
‡Nebraska has a unicameral legislature.

SOURCE: National Conference of State Legislatures, "The Term-Limited States," www.ncsl.org/programs/legman/about/states.htm, accessed October 13, 2006.

However, term limits thus far have changed the general profile of state legislators.[35] Indeed, opponents contend correctly, it takes several years for new legislators to become acquainted with rules, procedures, and regulations; therefore, to jettison politicians just as they begin to feel comfortable, confident, and knowledgeable is to lose a wealth of accumulated experience.

The Politics of Drawing Legislative District Lines

State legislatures are required by their state constitutions, by federal laws, and by court rulings to draw district boundaries for both their state legislature and U.S. House of Representative seats after each population census. The 2000 census once again triggered redistricting of congressional and state legislative lines.

Redistricting is the action of a state legislature or other body in redrawing legislative electoral district lines. About a dozen states delegate these responsibilities to independent redistricting or reapportionment commissions. In Alaska, the governor's office draws the legislative districts. Most legislatures, however, consider these once-a-

redistricting
The redrawing of congressional and other legislative district lines following the census, to accommodate population shifts and keep districts as equal as possible in population.

decade responsibilities so important that they are unwilling to turn control of this task over to anybody else.

The drawing of legislative district boundaries has always been controversial, in large part because redistricting decisions are made by partisan majorities in legislatures. The highly political nature of the undertaking is usually reflected in the results. "Redistricting is the political equivalent," says one observer, "of moving the left field fence for a right-handed pull hitter. By changing the boundaries, redistricting helps some, hurts others—and leaves just about everyone else scrambling."[36]

The politics and debate about redistricting are most intense in the years immediately after a census is taken. Drawing district boundaries to benefit a party, group, or incumbent is called **gerrymandering**. The term was first used in 1811 to describe a strange, salamander-shaped legislative district drawn in northeastern Massachusetts when Elbridge Gerry was governor. A district does not need to be odd in shape, however, to be gerrymandered.

As a result of huge differences in population among the districts, state legislative districts used to face problems of **malapportionment**. State legislatures for decades had given rural and small-town voters more votes in the legislature than they were entitled to on the basis of their declining share of the population. In Georgia, for instance, the 1960 reapportionment gave the largest county, with 556,326 inhabitants, no more representation than the three smallest counties, whose combined population was 6,980.[37] City officials complained bitterly that small-town and farmland-dominated legislators were unsympathetic to their problems and had different legislative priorities.

But no matter how much they protested, people who were underrepresented in the state legislatures made little progress. Legislators from small towns and farm areas naturally did not wish to reapportion themselves out of jobs, and their constituents did not wish to lose their influence. Even though the failure of state legislatures to reapportion often violated express provisions of state constitutions and raised serious questions under the U.S. Constitution, state and federal judges took the position that issues having to do with legislative districting were "political questions" and outside the scope of judicial authority.

Finally, the U.S. Supreme Court stepped in. In 1962, in *Baker* v. *Carr*, the Court held that voters do have standing to challenge legislative apportionment and that such questions should be considered by the federal courts. Arbitrary and capriciously drawn districts deprive people of their constitutional rights of representation, and federal judges may take jurisdiction over such cases.[38]

One Person, One Vote

In *Wesberry* v. *Sanders* (1964), the U.S. Supreme Court announced that as far as congressional representation is concerned, "as nearly as practicable one man's vote in a congressional election is to be worth as much as another's."[39] The Court extended this principle to representation in the state legislatures, although it subsequently modified this decision allowing for somewhat more population discrepancies among state legislative districts than for congressional districts.

In *Reynolds* v. *Sims* (1964), the Court held that "the fundamental principle of representative government in this country is one of equal representation for equal numbers of people, without regard to race, sex, economic status, or place of residence within a state." In the Court's view, this principle applied not only to the more numerous house of the state legislature, which was usually based on population, but also to the state senate, where representation was often based on area, such as the county or some other governmental unit. Defenders of this pattern had argued that as long as the more numerous chamber represented population, the senate could represent geographical units. Look at the federal system embodied in the U.S. Constitution, they said. Isn't representation in the U.S. Senate based on area? Although many thought this

> "[T]he fundamental principle of representative government in this country is one of equal representation for equal numbers of people, without regard to race, sex, economic status, or place of residence within a state."
>
> **U.S. SUPREME COURT, 1964**

gerrymandering
The drawing of legislative district boundaries to benefit a party, group, or incumbent.

malapportionment
Having legislative districts with unequal populations.

a compelling argument, a majority of the Court did not. Chief Justice Earl Warren explained: "Legislators represent people, not trees or acres. Legislators are elected by voters, not farms or cities or economic interests. . . . The right to elect legislators in a free unimpaired fashion is a bedrock of our political system."[40] The U.S. Senate analogy, in short, did not hold.

The Supreme Court has been especially strict about how states draw districts for the U.S. House of Representatives. A state legislature must justify any variance from mathematical equality by showing it made a good-faith effort to come as close as possible to the standard. The Supreme Court is, however, less insistent on absolute equality for state legislative districts. Thus, the Court in 1983 upheld a Wyoming plan that allocated at least one state legislative seat per county, saying that Wyoming's policy was rational and appropriate to the special needs of that sparsely populated state.[41] This ruling was a rare exception to the general principle of allowing at most a 10 percent deviation between state legislative districts. Nevertheless, the requirement that the districts be established in accordance with the one-person, one-vote principle still remains.

New Rules for Redrawing the Districts

Even though the one-person, one-vote principle is firmly established, many issues affecting the nature of legislative representation continue to be hotly debated. In northern metropolitan areas, for instance, the general pattern has been for the center city to be Democratic and the outlying suburbs Republican. If legislative district lines in these areas are drawn like spokes from the center city to the suburbs, fewer Republicans will probably be elected than if the district lines are drawn in concentric circles.

In recent decades, African Americans and Hispanics have begun to charge that state legislatures have an obligation under the Voting Rights Act of 1965 to redraw legislative districts to avoid dilution of the influence of minorities at the ballot box. They have gone to court to force legislators to create **majority-minority districts**. The U.S. Supreme Court, however, has put restraints on implementation of the act. The Court has held that although legislatures may take race into account in drawing state and federal legislative district lines and must act to avoid diluting the voting strength of minorities, a legislature violates the constitutional rights of white voters if race becomes the overriding motive.[42]

Controversy continues to surround reapportionment, no matter what processes are used. No one ever doubts the ability of incumbents in the majority to rig elections through reapportionment. In the words of the old-time politicians, "You tell me the results you want, and I'll draw the district map to do it." Today, computers are shaping the districts, and the people who control the computers, their programming, and their data can influence the outcome.

A case can be made that the vast majority of state legislative elections offer little meaningful competition. Whether designed by legislative party leaders or redistricting commissioners, those who carve up legislative districts every ten years do so primarily with the intent to protect incumbents or create districts that at least leave their party no worse off than it was before. The Supreme Court has ruled that partisan gerrymandering can be challenged in court as a violation of the Constitution. However, the Supreme Court did not find that a particularly controversial redistricting plan in Texas was an unconstitutional gerrymander, and has not yet stated a standard by which to judge exactly what would make a gerrymander unconstitutional.[43]

"Real competition, where a challenger to an incumbent might have some actual chance of winning, is evident in elections that are won by margins of less than 10 percent of the vote," writes Columbia University law professor Samuel Issacharoff.[44] But this is rarely the case in state after state. The wonder is "that anyone bothers to participate at all in such hollow elections."[45] And this was, in part, the reason that the term-limit crusade gained support in the first place.

majority-minority district
A legislative district created to include a majority of minority voters; ruled constitutional so long as race is not the main factor in redistricting.

Direct Legislation: Policy Making by the People?

Many states, mostly in the West, believe that citizens should have the power to create legislation through the initiative, referendum, and recall. This "direct democracy" movement began with populist reformers in Utah in 1900 and spread quickly to Oregon in 1902, Montana in 1904, Maine and Michigan in 1908, and Arizona and Colorado in 1910. Of the nearly 2,200 initiatives that the public has placed on the ballot in the 24 states that allow this form of direct democracy, nearly 1,100 have been in five states: Oregon, California, Colorado, North Dakota, and Arizona.

Reformers had good reason to bypass their legislatures in the early 1900s—legislatures in several states were either incompetent or under the domination of the political machines. For example, the Southern Pacific Railroad's political machine in California had dominated the selection of state legislators, governors, and U.S. senators for years.[46] The Progressives placed enormous trust in the wisdom of the people, assuming that voters would inform themselves about issues and make responsible decisions on a variety of policy questions put before them.

Initiative

The **initiative** permits a designated minimum number of voters to propose a law or constitutional amendment by petition. It becomes law if approved by a majority of the voters at a subsequent election. Twenty-four states, mostly in the West, authorize the making of laws by means of the initiative petition (see Figure 24–4). In California, Oregon, Washington, North Dakota, Arizona, Colorado, Michigan, and Massachusetts, the initiative has become an important feature of state political life.

In some states, the *direct initiative* applies to constitutional amendments and to legislation; in others, it can be used only for one or the other. Thus in Florida, the direct initiative can be used only to change the state constitution, while in Idaho, direct

initiative
Procedure whereby a certain number of voters may, by petition, propose a law or constitutional amendment and have it submitted to the voters.

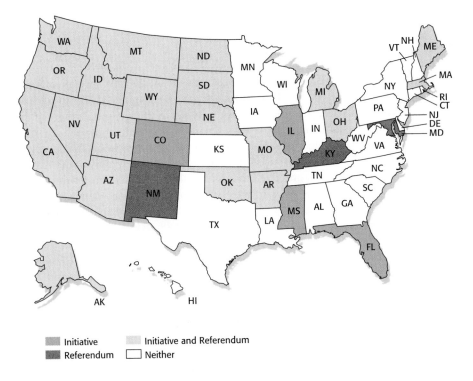

Initiative
Referendum
Initiative and Referendum
Neither

FIGURE 24–4 **Citizen-Initiated Initiative and Referendum at the State Level, 2007.**

initiative can be used only for statutory lawmaking. In a state that permits the direct initiative, any individual or interest group may draft a proposed law and file it with a designated state official, usually the secretary of state. Supporters have only to secure a certain number of signatures (between 2 and 15 percent of the vote in the last election) to place the measure on the next general election ballot. Only California permits initiatives on primary election ballots.

The *indirect initiative* is used in a few states, including Alaska, Maine, and Massachusetts. After a certain number of petition signatures have been collected, the state legislature is given an opportunity to act on the measure without alteration; if approved, the law simply goes into effect. If not approved, the proposed legislation is then placed on the ballot, although in some states, additional signatures are required before the proposal can be placed before the voters.

Referendum

A **referendum** permits voters to vote on, and possibly overturn, recently passed laws or legislatively proposed amendments to a state's constitution. A majority vote is required to overturn legislatively approved laws. The referendum, it should be noted, is required in every state except Delaware for the ratification of constitutional amendments.

Legislation may be subject to mandatory or optional referendums. The *mandatory referendum* calls for a waiting period, usually 60 to 90 days, before legislation goes into effect. If during this period a prescribed number of voters sign a referendum petition requesting that the act be referred to the voters, the law does not go into effect unless a majority of the voters give their approval at the next election. The *optional referendum* permits the legislature, at its discretion, to provide that a measure shall not become law until it has been approved by the voters at an election. This second kind is the more common.

Although statewide initiatives and referendums get the most attention, the same processes also flourish at the local level in many states. Nearly 90 percent of cities have some form of referendum process.[47] The annual volume of measures presented to voters in school districts, cities, and counties runs to several thousand, and covers a wide range of issues: bonds for school buildings, fluoridation of water, banning of glass bottles, restrictions on nuclear power facilities, and approval or rejection of convention facilities or sport stadiums.

Recall

Recall is the means by which voters may remove elected public officials before the end of their term. Eighteen states, mostly in the West, provide for the recall of state officers, but many others permit the recall of local officials (see Figure 24–5). Recall also requires a petition, but it needs more signatures (typically 25 percent of voters in the last election for the position in question) than the initiative or referendum.

The most famous recall in recent history involved the removal of California Governor Gray Davis and the election of former bodybuilder and movie star Arnold Schwarzenegger. In California and five other states, the recall election for the officeholder was held on the same ballot with the election of a successor—hence, the recall of Davis and election of Schwarzenegger occurred at the same time. In eight states, the recall election is held first and is followed by a special election for a successor at a later time. And in four states the recall election is held first and the successor is appointed by either a special board or the governor.

There are various kinds of recall elections. In some, the official must run and try to win reelection in a yes-or-no vote-of-confidence election; in others, candidates are permitted to file and run against the incumbent, making it, in effect, a new election. If in the former case an incumbent is voted out of office, a new election is required.

Recall is akin to impeachment by the public. But unlike impeachment, formal charges of wrongdoing against the incumbent are not required. Rather, recall permits throwing people out of office merely because of policy differences. For recall, voters

referendum
Procedure for submitting to popular vote measures passed by the legislature or proposed amendments to a state constitution.

recall
Procedure for submitting to popular vote the removal of public officials from office before the end of their term.

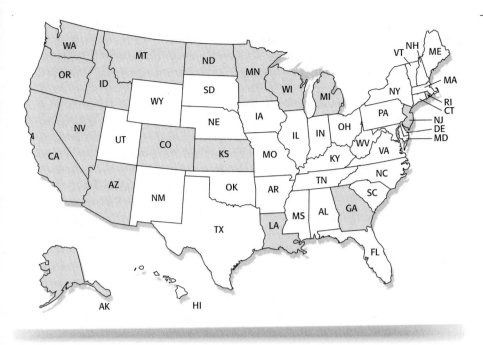

FIGURE 24–5 **States That Provide for Citizen-Initiated Recall of Elected State Officials.**

need only circulate petitions and obtain the required number of signatures. Recall is seldom used at the state level, although one governor and several state legislators have been recalled. Although the recall is rarely used successfully in the 18 states that now permit it, even the threat of a recall serves to remind legislators and other state officials of their obligations to the voters.

Recall is also used surprisingly often against local officials—although only 18 states allow recall of statewide officials, 36 allow recall of local officials such as mayors, county commissioners, and school board superintendents. From 1977 to 2001, nearly 10 percent of all U.S. cities held a recall election of a mayor or city council member.[48]

The Debate Over Direct Democracy

Hundreds of issues have been placed on state election ballots by citizen initiative in recent years. Citizens have turned to the initiative process to try to regulate handguns in California, to protect the moose in Maine, to encourage the death penalty in Massachusetts, to approve the sale of wine in grocery stores in Colorado, to abolish daylight savings time in North Dakota, and in several states to allow marijuana to be used for specific medicinal purposes.

In 2004, voters in 34 states cast ballots on 162 initiatives and referendums, including $3 billion for stem cell research in California (approved), education reform in five states (three approved, two rejected), legalized gambling in Washington State (rejected), relaxation of term limits on state legislators in Arkansas and Montana (rejected), legalization of marijuana for any usage in Alaska (rejected), and bans on same-sex marriage in 11 states (all approved).

Of the 162 ballot measures, 50 were initiatives and the rest were referendums of some kind. Nebraska voters actually faced four ballot choices on gambling, including one referendum from the legislature and three initiatives from the voters (all four failed).

Contrary to election-night hunches, the gay-marriage initiatives did not bring large numbers of voters to the polls in hotly contested battleground states such as Michigan and Ohio in 2004—voters in the battleground states were already engaged by the presidential campaigns. However, the bans appear to have boosted turnout in states that were not hotly contested by the campaigns.

Voters approved 67 percent of the initiatives and referendums in 2004. In 2005, a much less active year due to the absence of a national election and few statewide races, there were only 39 initiatives and referendums on the ballot in seven states. Just over half of these—and only two of the 18 initiatives—were approved. There was significant activity in California, however, where Governor Schwarzenegger attempted to implement much of his agenda through four initiatives. California voters rejected all four.

Political scientists, law professors, and lawmakers are often critical of direct legislation.[49] Early opponents had argued that such measures would undermine the legitimacy of representative government and open the way for radical or special-interest legislation. Critics of the initiative and the referendum believe that the Progressives who advocated direct legislation were naively idealistic and that these mechanisms are more likely to be used by special interests. Only well-organized interests can gather the appropriate number of signatures and mount the required media campaigns to gain victory. Critics of direct democracy say that this is indeed what has happened in California, Oregon, and elsewhere.[50]

In addition to giving advantages to well-organized interests, direct legislation often introduces confusion because some petitions are worded not so much for clarity but to win votes. Moreover, the 30-second ads that support or oppose many initiatives also tend to confuse rather than clarify.

The results of direct democracy have been both positive and negative. Historically, direct legislation by initiative has resulted in progressive victories on many consumer and economic issues and conservative victories on social issues. Direct democracy has not weakened our legislatures; seats in state legislatures are still valued, sought after, and competed for by able citizens. However, direct democracy has clearly had a considerable impact on state taxes and spending, especially in states that have enacted budget and tax limits. These measures have pleased many conservatives, upset liberals, and made life difficult for governors and state legislators.

Another serious problem has arisen in western states. Political consulting firms, for a price, will gather signatures and put nearly anything you want on the ballot. Deceptive pitches are sometimes made to get people to sign petitions. It takes a small fortune to do this, and only well-organized, well-financed, single-interest groups can afford it.[51]

Still another problem with the initiative process is that it can be used to target minorities, as California's limitations on illegal immigrants in 1994 and affirmative action in 1996 did. Similarly, Colorado's controversial Measure 2 in 1992 targeted gays and lesbians. How far can the majority go in using the initiative process against minorities? The courts have generally reversed part or all of discriminatory initiatives that were successful at the polls, yet such reversals put the courts in the awkward position of opposing a vote of the people.

The initiative process has become a powerful tool used by interest groups, politicians, and ideologues. "A vote on an issue in a single state can propel an issue onto the national agenda because of the widespread media attention given to some controversial initiatives."[52] Interest groups have set state policy by means of the initiative and have used it to reduce local government options in taxing, zoning and planning, and related matters. "One reason for this tendency to take on matters that were previously local and decide them at the statewide level is interest group efficiency. It is easier to restrict local taxing powers, strike local rent control laws, and eliminate ordinances protecting gays and lesbians by mobilizing a single statewide vote" rather than by campaigning to reverse or defeat local initiatives.[53]

Viewed from another perspective, most of the perceived flaws of the populist processes of direct democracy are also the flaws of democracy. When we vote in an election, we often wish we had more information about issues and candidates. Delegates at constitutional conventions or national party conventions frequently have similar misgivings when they are forced to render yes-or-no votes on complicated issues.

So, too, members of state legislatures—especially in those frantic days near the end of their sessions—yearn for more information, more clarity about consequences, and more discussion and compromise than time will permit.

Critics lament the rise in what they call "public policy making by bumper sticker." Opponents of direct legislation fear that the very fabric of legislative processes and representative government is at stake. To be sure, lack of faith in legislative bodies has sometimes prompted the use of direct legislation devices, but the best way to restore faith in the legislature is not to bypass it but to elect better people to it.

Supporters of populist democracy say they have not given up on the legislative process. Rather, they wish to use direct legislation primarily when legislatures prove unresponsive. If our legislature will not act, they say, give us the opportunity to debate our proposals in the open arena of election politics. Supporters further contend that the people are capable of making decisions on complex matters.

Voters throughout the country say that citizens ought to have the right, at least occasionally, to vote directly on policy issues. Surveys find that both voters and non-voters say they would be more likely to become interested in politics and vote if some issues appeared along with candidates on their ballots.[54] Moreover, Californians, who have had to deal with more ballot issues than voters in any other state, continue to say statewide ballot propositions elections are overall "a good thing for California" (74 percent), even as they acknowledge limits to their own grasp of the process.[55]

The legislative process is never perfect. Even with larger professional staffs, hearings, new technologies, bicameralism, and other distinctive features of constitutional democracy, mistakes are made and defective bills are enacted into law in our legislatures. The Supreme Court has overturned hundreds of laws passed by state legislatures as unconstitutional, and state legislatures often spend much of their time amending or otherwise improving measures they passed in previous years. As a practical matter, however, Americans should be at least as skeptical and questioning of the initiative and referendum process as they already are of their state legislators.

Summary

1. State legislatures were the most powerful institutions in the nation during the Revolutionary War, and remain powerful to this day. Although some state legislatures still rely on part-time legislators with little or no staff, many now elect full-time legislators who receive significant pay and staff support. In many ways, state legislatures are becoming more like the U.S. Congress every day.

2. The nation's 7,387 state legislators are called on to represent diverse views, help formulate state public policy, oversee the administration of state laws, and mediate political con-flicts that arise in the state. State legislatures have become more diverse in recent decades as population changes have improved the election prospects of women and minority candidates.

3. The main influences on a state legislator's voting decisions are political parties, lobbyists and interest groups, district considerations, constituent views, colleagues, committee recommendations, the party leaders, the media, and actions taken by other states and the federal government. State legislators use many of the same tools for making deci-sions as members of the U.S. Congress.

4. State legislators are constantly subjected to intense lobbying by organized interests. Although lobbyists and interest group representatives are important sources of information, legislatures have become increasingly concerned about potential conflicts of interest and ethical conduct. Many states have created special rules covering campaign contributions and lobbying activities in the wake of scandals in their own legislatures.

5. As a result of legislative reform efforts, most states now have longer

annual sessions, larger and more competent staffs, open-meeting laws, and a variety of electronic-age information systems. As they have become more professionalized, they have also become more capable of producing legislative impacts in a variety of policy areas such as the environment, education, and crime control.

6. Seventeen states have limited the number of terms legislators can serve. Most state legislators and political scientists oppose term limits for a variety of reasons, yet voters in many states have viewed them as a way of keeping their representatives accountable and encouraging the notion of citizen representation.

7. The politics of redistricting, or redrawing legislative boundaries, heats up every ten years after the census is taken. Redistricting is never easy; political careers can be ruined by redrawn boundaries. Major controversies have arisen over partisan and racially motivated drawing of legislative district lines, and the federal courts are increasingly asked to establish guidelines that will limit such outcomes.

8. Direct legislative procedures, especially the initiative petition, are a prominent part of the legislative process, particularly in the West. Other direct mechanisms, such as the referendum and the recall, are also available to voters in many states.

Further Reading

SHAWN BOWLER AND **TODD DONOVAN,** *Demanding Choices: Opinions, Voting, and Direct Democracy* (University of Michigan Press, 1998).

SHAWN BOWLER, TODD DONOVAN, AND **CAROLINE J. TOLBERT,** EDS., *Citizens as Legislators: Direct Democracy in the United States* (Ohio State University Press, 1998).

DAVID S. BRODER, *Democracy Derailed: Initiative Campaigns and the Power of Money* (Harcourt, 2000).

WILLIAM M. BULGER, *While the Music Lasts: My Life in Politics* (Houghton Mifflin, 1996).

BRUCE E. CAIN, *The Reapportionment Puzzle* (University of California Press, 1984).

JOHN M. CAREY, RICHARD G. NIEMI, AND **LYNDA W. POWELL,** *Term Limits in the State Legislatures* (University of Michigan Press, 2000).

THOMAS E. CRONIN, *Direct Democracy: The Politics of the Initiative, Referendum, and Recall* (Harvard University Press, 1989).

RICHARD J. ELLIS, *Democratic Delusions: The Initiative Process in America* (University Press of Kansas, 2002).

VIRGINIA GRAY AND **RUSSELL HANSON,** EDS., *Politics in the American States,* 8th ed. (CQ Press, 2003).

JOHN J. KENNEDY, *The Contemporary Pennsylvania Legislature* (University Press of America, 1999).

TOM LOFTUS, *The Art of Legislative Politics* (CQ Press, 1994).

BURDETT A. LOOMIS, *A Legislative Year: Time, Politics, and Policies* (University Press of Kansas, 1994).

DAVID B. MAGLEBY, *Direct Legislation: Voting on Ballot Propositions in the United States* (Johns Hopkins University Press, 1984).

JAY MICHAEL AND **DAN WALTERS,** *The Third House: Lobbyists, Money, and Power in Sacramento* (Berkeley Public Policy Press, 2002).

GARY MONCRIEF, PEVERILL SQUIRE, AND **MALCOLM E. JEWELL,** *Who Runs for the Legislature?* (Prentice Hall, 2001).

NATIONAL CONFERENCE OF STATE LEGIS-LATURES AND AMERICAN SOCIETY OF LEGISLATIVE CLERKS AND SECRETARIES, *Inside the Legislative Process* (National Council of State Legislatures, 1998).

ALBERT J. NELSON, *Emerging Influentials in State Legislatures: Women, Blacks, and Hispanics* (Praeger, 1991).

BETH REINGOLD, *Representing Women: Sex, Gender, and Legislative Behavior in Arizona and California* (University of California Press, 2000).

JAMES RICHARDSON, *Willie Brown: A Biography* (University of California Press, 1996).

ALAN ROSENTHAL, *The Decline of Representative Democracy* (CQ Press, 1998).

ALAN ROSENTHAL, *Drawing the Line: Legislative Ethics in the States* (University of Nebraska Press, 1996).

ALAN ROSENTHAL, *Heavy Lifting: The Job of the American Legislature* (CQ Press, 2004).

PETER SCHRAG, *Paradise Lost: California's Experience, America's Future* (New Press, 1998).

FRANK SMALLWOOD, *Free and Independent: The Initiation of a College Professor into State Politics* (Stephen Greene Press, 1976).

JOHN A. STRAAYER, *The Colorado General Assembly,* 2d ed. (University Press of Colorado, 2000).

SUE THOMAS, *How Women Legislate* (Oxford University Press, 1994).

SUE THOMAS AND **CLYDE WILCOX,** EDS., *Women and Elective Office* (Oxford University Press, 1998).

JOEL A. THOMPSON AND **GARY F. MONCRIEF,** EDS., *Campaign Finance and State Legislative Elections* (CQ Press, 1998).

See *State Legislatures,* published ten times a year by the National Conference of State Legislatures. *Legislative Studies Quarterly* often has articles on state legislatures; it is published by the Legislative Studies Section of the American Political Science Association. *Governing,* published monthly by Congressional Quarterly, Inc., regularly covers state politics and state legislative issues. *Spectrum: The Journal of State Government* is a useful quarterly published by the Council of State Governments.

KeyTerms

Chapter 25

State Governors

★

THE JOB OF GOVERNOR IS ONE OF THE MOST IMPORTANT AND EXACTING IN AMERICAN POLITICAL LIFE. OVER THE PAST TWO DECADES, CONGRESS AND THE WHITE HOUSE HAVE TRANSFERRED, OR DEVOLVED, MANY ACTIVITIES TO THE STATES THAT WERE FOR A TIME CONSIDERED NATIONAL RESPONSIBILITIES, SUCH AS WELFARE ASSISTANCE. THIS TRANSFER HAS MEANT THAT GOVERNORS NOW HAVE TO BE EVEN MORE EFFECTIVE MANAGERS. THEY HAVE TO ASK THE RIGHT QUESTIONS AND CONSIDER THE LONG-TERM IMPLICATIONS and side effects of their policies more carefully than ever.

During the boom economic times of the 1990s, governors, with the concurrence of the state legislatures, got to spend vast sums of new money on state priorities such as education, economic development, transportation, health, and environmental protection. Then came the recession of the early 2000s, which brought dramatic revenue shortfalls in more than 40 states. To balance state budgets, governors had to recommend cuts in services, project delays, state employee layoffs, payraise postponements, and in some cases, higher taxes. After the recession, governors still faced many demands for action, in some cases restoring the cuts made to get through the recession, and also addressing issues like homeland security and the rising cost of health care. In good economic times and bad, governors are invariably at the center of public policy developments.

Governors are also frequently involved in national politics and are often viewed as national leaders. Seventeen governors have gone on to serve as U.S. president, including four of the last five, and at least 17 members of the current U.S. Senate served earlier as governors in their states. Presidents frequently pick current or former governors for their cabinet; for instance, George W. Bush selected Christine Todd Whitman of New Jersey, Tom Ridge of Pennsylvania, Tommy Thompson of Wisconsin, Dirk Kempthorne of Idaho, Mike Johanns of Nebraska, and Mike Leavitt of Utah. Moreover, as California's 2003 recall election proved, gubernatorial campaigns can generate enormous national attention. Arnold Schwarzenegger's successful campaign to unseat Governor Gray Davis was a top national news story, and his subsequent troubles also received national attention.

In this chapter, we look at how governors come into and keep office, a typical governor's power and influence, efforts to bring modern management techniques to the governor's office, ways that governors interact with other elected state officials, and the rewards of being governor. But first we examine the rising expectations we have for governors.

Rising Expectations for Governors

Although the constitutional powers of governors vary from state to state, Americans evaluate and rate their governors using many of the

"*[A governor needs to see] the state's few most urgent needs, develop strategies to address them, and persuade at least half the people that he or she is right.*"

FORMER TENNESSEE GOVERNOR LAMAR ALEXANDER

same criteria for rating presidents.[1] Governors in the large and even medium-sized states are responsible for running complex enterprises that are at least as complicated as *Fortune* 500 corporations. Lamar Alexander, former governor of Tennessee, said that a governor needs to "see the state's few most urgent needs, develop strategies to address them, and persuade at least half the people that he or she is right."[2] An effective governor also has to perform countless symbolic and ceremonial functions and win the respect of the people and the legislature in order to exercise fully the executive functions of the office.

Today, a governor is expected to be, among other things, the state's chief policy maker, shaper of the state budget, a savvy political party leader, chief recruiter of the best available advisers and administrators, and an inspiring renewer of confidence in state programs. The governor must also champion the state's interests against the encroachments of federal or local governments and be the state's chief booster to attract business and tourism. In order to be effective, governors are expected to take trips abroad to encourage foreign investment in their states and promote their local products.[3] Thirty-eight states even operate some form of overseas office, including trade mission posts in Harare and Kuala Lumpur.[4] Governors also work with their legislatures to raise revenues for such programs as welfare, education, and economic development. Governors act as crucial links among the states and between the local and the national governments.

Becoming and Remaining Governor

Each state's constitution and laws spell out the rules of eligibility, tenure, and salary for its governor. Thirty-three states require their governors to be at least 30 years of age and a state resident for at least five years immediately preceding the election. Although California, Ohio, Rhode Island, Vermont, Washington, and Wisconsin set the minimum age at 18, the odds against election at age 18 are staggering.[5] In theory, any qualified voter of the state who meets a state's age qualification is eligible for the office of governor; in practice, there are well-traveled career paths to the governor's office.

Most governors are white males about 40 to 55 years old, and a substantial minority hold law degrees. As the number of women legislators has grown, so has the number of women governors. Most governors were state legislators or held statewide elective office, and some have had law enforcement experience. Of the governors in office in 2006, for example, nine were former members of Congress, 21 had served in their state legislatures, six had been state attorney general, and six had been mayors.

One of the most common paths upward is election to the state legislature, followed by election to a statewide office such as lieutenant governor, secretary of state, or attorney general, followed by a run for governor. Vermont Governor James Douglas was elected to the state legislature right out of college, and served as secretary of state and state treasurer before becoming governor. Mayors often run for governor; the mayors of Albuquerque, Phoenix, Indianapolis, Las Vegas, and Maui have all run for governor in their states in recent years.

Although serving in office is certainly helpful for building a political base, it is hardly essential. Eleven governors in 2006 had not held elected or appointed office at all, including Massachusetts Governor Mitt Romney, Mississippi Governor Haley Barbour, and Montana Governor Brian Schweitzer. Former Texas Governor George W. Bush was a businessman and baseball executive who enjoyed widespread

Bill Richardson, the Democratic governor of New Mexico.

The Changing Face of American Politics

Women Governors

Arizona Governor Janet Napolitano

Hawaii Governor Linda Lingle

Kansas Governor Kathleen Sebelius

There have been only 28 women governors in all of U.S. history. But of the 28, 20 were elected to office since 1974, and 14 since 1990. Eight women served as governors in 2006, seven of whom were elected and an eighth who entered the governor's office in Connecticut after the governor resigned. As women have occupied increasingly powerful positions in state legislatures and in lower-level statewide offices such as lieutenant governor, attorney general, and secretary of state, they have become much more visible as potential candidates for the governorship. African Americans and Hispanics have not made similar gains, however. As of 2007, there was only one Hispanic governor in office, Bill Richardson of New Mexico, and there was one African American, Deval Patrick of Massachusetts. ∎

Women Governors Elected Since 1975

Governor	State	Term of Office	Governor	State	Term of Office
Ella Grasso	Connecticut	1975–1980	Judy Martz	Montana	2001–2005
Dixie Lee Ray	Washington	1977–1981	Ruth Ann Minner	Delaware	2001–
Martha L. Collins	Kentucky	1983–1987	Jane Swift	Massachusetts	2001–2002
Madeleine Kunin	Vermont	1985–1991	Janet Napolitano	Arizona	2003–
Kay Orr	Nebraska	1987–1991	Linda Lingle	Hawaii	2003–
Rose Mofford	Arizona	1988–1991	Kathleen Sebelius	Kansas	2003–
Joan Finney	Kansas	1991–1995	Jennifer Granholm	Michigan	2002–
Ann Richards	Texas	1991–1995	Olene Walker	Utah	2003–
Barbara Roberts	Oregon	1991–1995	Kathleen Blanco	Louisiana	2004–
Christine Todd Whitman	New Jersey	1994–2001	M. Jodie Rell	Connecticut	2004–
Jeanne Shaheen	New Hampshire	1997–2002	Christine Gregoire	Washington	2005–
Jane Dee Hull	Arizona	1998–2002	Sarah Palin	Alaska	2007–

SOURCE: *The Book of the States, 2005* (Council of State Governments, 2005) p. 197.

name recognition as the son of a former president, as did his younger brother, Jeb Bush, who also went from a business career to the Florida governorship.

Two hundred years ago, most states had one- or two-year terms for their governors. Today, all states except New Hampshire and Vermont have four-year terms, and all states except Virginia allow governors to run for more than one consecutive term. Some governors, such as William Janklow of South Dakota, Roy Romer in Colorado, John Engler in Michigan, George Pataki in New York, Jim Hunt in North Carolina, and Tommy Thompson in Wisconsin, have recently been elected to three or four terms as governors, but 35 states now have a two-term limit on governors, and Utah has a three-term limit.

Governors under Pressure

Once elected, governors enjoy high visibility in their states. Governors earn more than $100,000 in most states; salaries range from $179,000 in New York to $70,000 in Maine. In addition, governors receive an expense allowance; all but five are provided an executive mansion; 43 of them have regular access to a state plane or helicopter or both.[6]

Even as governors have become increasingly important in recent decades, they have also had to deal with the twin problems of rising aspirations and scarcity of resources. People want better schools, highways that do not spoil the environment, adequate welfare programs, protections for civil rights, safe streets, and clean air and water. However, citizens usually want their taxes kept as low as possible.

Former New York Governor Mario Cuomo (who served from 1983 until 1995) used to say he was always running into people who wanted him to expand programs. He would look them in the eye and say, "Now what are you going to give me so that I can pay for it? Do you want to wait longer in line at the Motor Vehicle office to get your license renewed? Do we stop paving the road in front of your home? Do you mind if we plow the snow less often?" Typically, of course, he heard that the people requesting additional spending did not want to forgo any of those things, which prompted him to say, "Well, then, I don't understand. Where do I get what I need to do what you want?" His point is simple. Given limited resources, choices must be made. Elected officials cannot afford to do everything people would like. Politicians are elected to negotiate trade-offs. You must "give to get."[7]

Governors and state legislators face the challenge of administering federally mandated welfare programs with fewer federal dollars. They have campaigned for the federal government to give more dollars to the states—without strings. The Republican-controlled U.S. Congress in the late 1990s responded by terminating some underfunded federally mandated programs and shifting a few other federal programs to the states. Governors and state legislators now face the challenge of reworking old federal welfare programs as state welfare programs with cutbacks in federal grants. On the other hand, Congress has also passed new legislation such as the No Child Left Behind education bill that some governors have said is underfunded.[8]

Reelection

About 74 percent of incumbent governors who run for reelection are reelected.[9] In 34 states, elections for governor are scheduled for nonpresidential or midterm election years (for example, 2006); Kentucky, Louisiana, Mississippi, New Jersey, and Virginia elect governors in odd-numbered years. Reformers have, for the most part, successfully argued that presidential and gubernatorial elections should be separated so that governors are not subject to the tides of national politics. Governors in New Hampshire and Vermont are elected for two-year terms in even-numbered years, while nine states elect governors at the same time as presidential elections. In 2006, 36 governorships were up for election. (See Figure 25–1 for the party affiliations of the governors who held office in 2007.)

California Governor Gray Davis (top) enjoyed serving as governor during the boom times of the late 1990s but faced staggering state deficits after his reelection in 2002. Davis was recalled in 2003 and replaced by Arnold Schwarzenegger (bottom), who won reelection in November 2006.

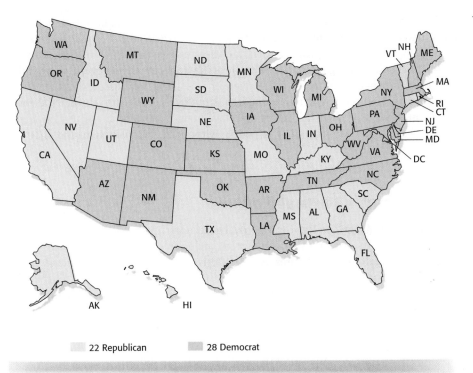

FIGURE 25-1 Party Control of the Governor's Office, 2007.

22 Republican   28 Democrat

Incumbency is not always an advantage for reelection. Governors have to make tough decisions, which can antagonize major interests and arouse public criticism. Governors in Arizona, Alabama, Arkansas, Connecticut, and New Jersey left office in recent years because of personal scandals. Governors in Ohio, Oregon, and Kansas left because they had such low approval ratings in the polls that they chose not to run again. Incumbents sometimes lose because of a depressed state economy or because they increased state taxes and became unpopular.

Public anger over taxes and budgets was clearly behind the 2003 California recall election. Gray Davis was widely criticized for having tripled the registration fee, or "car tax," that motorists paid on their vehicles. As future governor Arnold Schwarzenegger said repeatedly in his campaign, "I feel Californians have been punished enough. From the time they get up in the morning and flush the toilet they're taxed. When they go get a coffee they're taxed. When they get in their car they're taxed. When they go to the gas station they're taxed. When they go to lunch they're taxed. This goes on all day long. Tax. Tax. Tax. Tax. Tax."[10]

Similarly, in New Jersey in 1993, Governor James Florio was narrowly defeated by Christine Todd Whitman due in part to a recession but mostly because Florio had recommended, and the legislature had enacted, a major tax increase. That tax increase came back to haunt Florio when he ran for U.S. senator in the New Jersey Democratic primary in 2000. His opponent, Jon Corzine, ran ads stressing Florio's role as a big spender and won the primary.

Circumstances often dictate what a governor can or cannot do. Certainly, the health of the state's economy is a critical factor. The good economic times in the late 1990s plainly helped most governors who ran for reelection, while bad economic times hurt them in the early 2000s. In November 2004, only three incumbent governors won reelection, three were defeated in the primary or general election, and five retired.

Promises to cut taxes have been effective campaign strategies for several candidates. Many governors in the 1990s, including Christine Todd Whitman in New Jersey and George Pataki in New York, made tax cutting a central part of their campaigns for election and reelection. Republican James Gilmore in Virginia won a landslide victory in his 1997 race for governor by repeatedly saying "No Car Tax"—a reference to a highly unpopular personal property tax on cars, trucks, and motorcycles.[11] On the

"I feel Californians have been punished enough. From the time they get up in the morning and flush the toilet they're taxed."

CALIFORNIA GOVERNOR ARNOLD SCHWARZENEGGER, IN HIS 2003 CAMPAIGN

other hand, Gilmore's successor, Governor Mark Warner, suspended Gilmore's car tax cut and increased spending on education and infrastructure, and left office with much greater popularity. While proposing tax increases can be politically risky, it may not be political suicide for governors.[12] Many other factors can affect governors' agendas and their prospects for reelection. Governor Jim Doyle of Wisconsin made stem cell research a central issue of his campaign, and this issue has also entered the campaigns in other states.[13] Other issues that have been important in recent campaigns have been the increasing number of people without health insurance, and environmental protection.

A Governor's Formal Powers

Before the American Revolution, royal governors, appointed by and responsible to the British crown, had broad powers, including extensive veto power over the elected colonial legislatures. As anti-British sentiment increased, royal governors became more and more unpopular. The position of state governor in the new Republic was born in this atmosphere of distrust. In the 1770s and 1780s, state legislatures elected state governors, a method that ensured that governors would remain under the control of the people's representatives. The early state constitutions also limited governors to few powers and terms of just a year or two.

Gradually, however, the office of governor grew in importance. In New York, the position of chief executive was sufficiently developed and effective by 1787 that it became one of the main models for the proposed American presidency. If we compare the formal sources of authority in the U.S. Constitution and in a typical state constitution, we see significant differences. "The executive Power," says the Constitution, "shall be vested in a President of the United States of America." Compare this statement with its counterpart in a typical state constitution: "The executive department shall consist of a Governor, Lieutenant Governor, Secretary of State, Treasurer, Attorney General," and perhaps other officials. Unlike the president, the governor *shares* executive power with other elected officials. Most state constitutions go on to say, however, "the supreme executive power shall be vested in the Governor, who shall take care that the laws be faithfully executed." Thus, the public looks to the governor for law enforcement and the management of the state administrative system. In some states, the governor also has the authority to supervise the activities of local prosecutors.

Twenty-four states have strengthened the governorship by making the lieutenant governor run with the governor as a team so that the chief executive is less likely to be paired with a hostile lieutenant governor. In 42 states, the lieutenant governor, like the U.S. vice president, takes over executive responsibilities if for any reason the governor cannot fulfill the duties of the office. In 2005, New Jersey voters approved a constitutional amendment to establish a lieutenant governor, who will run on the ticket with the governor beginning in 2009. Most important, in almost all states, the governor presents the state budget to the legislature and controls spending after the budget has been approved. Thus, state officials must look to the governor as well as the legislature for funds.

The constitutional powers of governor vary from state to state (see Table 25–1). Yet regardless of a governor's formal constitutional authority, a governor's actual power and influence depend on his or her ability to persuade.[14] This power, in turn, usually depends on the governor's reputation, popularity, knowledge of what should be done, and, of course, ability to communicate. Governors usually also benefit from being the informal leader of their party in the state. Governors must have political skills as well as constitutional authority if they are to provide leadership.

To supplement their formal constitutional powers, governors may hold town meetings around the state, appear on radio and television talk shows, or invite legislators and other influential party and policy leaders to the executive mansion for lobbying and consultation sessions. Remember, however, that not all states vest great

TABLE 25–1 Rankings of States According to the Formal Powers of the Governor

Strong

Maryland	Ohio
New Jersey	Pennsylvania
New York	Utah

Moderately Strong

Alaska	Nebraska
Colorado	North Dakota
Connecticut	South Dakota
Iowa	Tennessee
Kansas	West Virginia
Michigan	Wisconsin
Minnesota	Wyoming
Montana	

Moderate

Arizona	Louisiana
California	Maine
Delaware	Massachusetts
Florida	Missouri
Hawaii	Nevada
Idaho	New Mexico
Illinois	Oregon
Indiana	Texas
Kentucky	Virginia

Weak

Alabama	Oklahoma
Arkansas	Rhode Island
Georgia	South Carolina
Mississippi	Vermont
North Carolina	Washington
New Hampshire	

SOURCE: Adapted from Thad L. Beyle, "The Governors," in *Politics in the American States: A Comparative Analysis*, 7th ed., Virginia Gray, Russell Hanson, and Herbert Jacob, eds. (CQ Press, 1999), pp. 210–211.
NOTE: Rankings are based on budget powers, appointive and organizational powers, tenure potential, veto powers, and party control.

constitutional power in the governor. Whether the state constitution defines a strong role is just one of the factors in determining the effectiveness of a governor.

Most governors have the following constitutional authority:

- To make appointments

- To prepare the state budget

- To veto legislation and to exercise an item veto over appropriations measures

- To issue executive orders

- To command the state National Guard

- To pardon or grant clemency

- To help establish the legislature's agenda

Appointive Power

Perhaps a governor's most important job is to recruit talented leaders and managers to head the state's departments, commissions, and agencies.[15] Through recruitment of effective people and prudent delegation of responsibilities to them, a governor can provide direction for the state government.

In most states, the governor is one executive among many, with only limited authority over elected officials, whom the governor can neither appoint nor dismiss. Moreover, if these officials are from a different political party than the governor, they are likely to oppose the governor's recommendations. Governors have greater, yet still limited, power over officials they appoint. Some governors appoint hundreds of key officials; others, such as those in Mississippi, South Carolina, and Texas, have severe restrictions on their appointive power. Moreover, in most states, governors must share their appointive power with the state senate and may remove people only when they have violated the law or failed in their legal duties. State administrators whose programs are supported by federal funds also have a measure of independence from the governor.

Along with the appointive power comes a host of challenges. First, salaries for cabinet and agency administrators are modest in many states, especially in the smaller ones, and it is often hard to get people to leave better-paying jobs in private industry. The situation is even worse when the state capital is in a remote or rural section of the state. Second, powerful politicians may demand that their friends be appointed to certain top posts, and they may threaten to be uncooperative if the governor does not go along with their "suggestions." Finally, relatively high turnover in many state positions often hampers a governor's efforts to carry out programs.

Fiscal and Budgetary Power

A governor's financial planning and budgetary powers are key weapons in getting programs passed. Purchasing, budgeting, and personnel matters are centralized under the governor. When implemented by a strong staff and backed by a strong political base, a governor's fiscal powers are extremely important.

In almost all states, the governor has responsibility for preparing the budget and presenting it to the state legislature. This takes place every year in 30 states and every second year in 20 states. The art of budget making involves assessing requests from various departments and agencies and balancing them against available resources. Governors and their staffs have to calculate the costs of existing and newly proposed programs and weigh those costs against estimated revenues for the state.

The budget process is similar in most states. In May and June, the governor's budget office, which is called different things in different states, including Office of Management and Budget or Department of Administration, sends request forms to the various executive agencies. From July to October, the agencies complete their detailed requests and send them back for consideration. Their requests are invariably 10 to 15 percent higher than what is available and also much higher than the governor's proposed guidelines. The governor's budget chief evaluates all requests, sometimes holds internal administrative hearings, and then makes recommendations to the governor. Finally, the governor presents the recommendations to the legislature at the beginning of the new year. Governors frequently use their annual State of the State address to present these recommendations, and continue to promote them during speeches given throughout the budget process.

Although the governor and chief budget officials may appear to control the budgetary process, considerable budgeting influence remains in the hands of the executive branch agencies. Further, a governor's budget reflects to a very high degree budgetary decisions made over the years (costs such as prisons or state universities that will not be shut down), so what governors end up doing in practice is tinkering or adjusting at the edges of the overall budget.

The final budget document is presented to the legislature for adoption as an *appropriations measure*. State moneys cannot be spent without legislative appropriations. Legislators can, and usually do, make a number of alterations in a governor's budget. In theory, a legislature controls all state activities through the budget process because it has the final say in approving the budget. In practice, however, most legislatures do not review every budgetary item; they merely trim or make additions at the margins. Hence, budgets reflect the policy views of those responsible for their preparation—namely, the governor and the governor's budget office. A governor who has control over the budget and uses this power effectively has an important asset.

States spent about a third of their budgets on education in 2004. The Medicaid program for poor people alone accounted for over 22 percent of state spending.[16] Other welfare assistance, highways, prisons and criminal justice programs, health and rehabilitation efforts, and state parks and recreation also make up large portions of the budget. About 50 percent of a state's revenue usually comes from taxes; a third comes from federal sources. When state revenues do not match expenses, governors have to cut or delay programs because state constitutions as a rule require a balanced budget, and states cannot print money as the federal government can. In addition, states spend roughly 9 percent of their funds implementing federal mandates, such as student testing under the No Child Left Behind Act.[17]

Veto Power

veto
Rejection by a president or governor of legislation passed by a legislature.

line item veto
Right of an executive to veto parts of a bill approved by a legislature without having to veto the entire bill.

reduction veto
The power of governors in a few states to reduce a particular appropriation.

amendatory veto
The power of governors in a few states to return a bill to the legislature with suggested language changes, conditions, or amendments. Legislators then decide either to accept the governor's recommendations or to pass the bill in its original form over the veto.

Among the most useful gubernatorial powers is the **veto**, the power to conditionally reject legislative bills, especially appropriations measures. Michigan Governor Jennifer Granholm vetoed more than 30 bills in her first 18 months in office, including one that would have banned late-term abortions, another that would have created a process for creating specialty license plates, and another that would have given suburbs more control over the Detroit Water and Sewer Board, even though the board sets their rates. Her veto activity led the *Detroit Free Press* to title a story on her tenure "Granholm stars in her own 'Kill Bill.'"[18]

In all but eight states, governors have the **line item veto**, which permits them to veto individual items in an appropriations bill while signing the remainder of the bill into law. Thus, they can influence the flow of funds to the executive departments and thereby attempt to control their activities. In May 2006, for example, Florida Governor Jeb Bush vetoed $448.7 million from the state's $74 billion budget.[19]

In several states, a governor can reduce particular appropriations; this power is called the **reduction veto**. In 19 states, governors can exercise what is called an **amendatory veto**, which allows the governor to return a bill to the state legislature with suggested language changes, conditions, or amendments. In this last case, legislators must decide to accept the governor's recommendations or approve the bill in its original form, which in some cases requires a majority vote and in other cases a three-fifths or supermajority vote. Since the president does not have line item, reduction, or amendatory vetoes, these tools give governors a much greater ability to shape legislation.

State legislatures can override a governor's veto; in most states, it takes a two-thirds majority of both legislative chambers. Some governors, like Wisconsin's Tommy Thompson, vetoed thousands of legislative measures. New York Governor George Pataki vetoed 1,379 provisions the legislature sent him in 1998.[20] Governors on average veto about 4 percent of the bills sent to them, but only about 2 percent of gubernatorial vetoes are overridden by legislatures.[21] Most governors believe the veto power should be used sparingly. Indeed, some observers think too frequent use of the veto is a sign of gubernatorial weakness because an effective governor usually wins battles through negotiations rather than by confronting state legislators.[22]

Legislators in several states have established a *veto session*—a short session following adjournment—so they can reconsider any measures vetoed by their governor. This is clearly an effort to reassert the legislature's check-and-balance authority in relation to the governor. Most states using veto sessions have legislatures that meet for a limited time; in full-time legislatures, a veto session would be unnecessary.

Executive Orders

One long-standing power of governors is their authority to issue **executive orders** that have the force of law. Even though executive orders differ from statutes or formal acts passed by the legislature, they have almost the same binding effect. Depending on the state, governors get their authority to issue executive orders from implied powers as chief executive, from specific constitutional grants, or from delegations of authority by their state legislatures. Executive orders supplementing a law are both more detailed and more important than the general guidelines contained in legislation. Governors have issued executive orders during such emergencies as natural disasters and energy crises, in compliance with federal rules and regulations, and to create advisory commissions. However, governors can also use executive orders to make policy. Governor Arnold Schwarzenegger of California, for example, used executive orders in 2006 to promote the use of biofuels, to set up a system to identify high-risk sex offenders, and to promote state contracts with small businesses. State legislators are sometimes angered by sweeping executive orders. They insist that they, not the governors or the courts, should be the primary lawmakers in a state.

Governors do not have to issue executive orders to have an impact on state and local government, however. Even though he opposed same-sex marriages, Governor Mitt Romney of Massachusetts reminded local officials in 2004 they had to follow the state's Supreme Judicial Court decision allowing same-sex marriage of state residents. At the same time, however, he also said he intended to use a 1913 law to prohibit the marriage of same-sex couples from other states. Such marriages would be null and void under his interpretation, he argued, thereby preventing Massachusetts from drawing same-sex couples from across the United States.[23]

Commander in Chief of the National Guard

Emergencies can enhance the authority of an executive because they call for decisive action. As commander in chief of the state's National Guard when it is not in federal service, a governor may use this force when local authorities are inadequate—in case of riots, floods, and other catastrophes. The National Guard has played a role in the aftermath of floods in midwestern states, riots and earthquakes in California, fires in Florida, and hurricanes throughout the southeastern states. In most states, the state police are also available for emergencies.

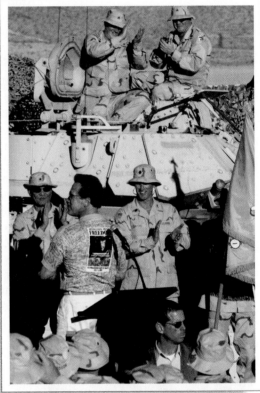

As commander in chief of the state's National Guard when it is not in federal service, a governor may use this force to handle state emergencies such as fires, floods, earthquakes, and other disasters. The war in Iraq necessitated the deployment of National Guard troops from all over the country to aid in the fighting. Here, Governor Arnold Schwarzenegger provides a morale boost for a California National Guard unit.

executive order
Directive issued by a president or governor that has the force of law.

Congress provides most of the money to operate the National Guard. This fact, along with the supremacy clause of the U.S. Constitution, gives Congress and the president the power to take charge of a state's National Guard even against the wishes of a governor. In 1990, the Supreme Court ruled unanimously that Congress can authorize the president to call National Guard units to active duty and send them outside the United States despite the objections of the governors, several of whom had tried to keep President Ronald Reagan from calling their respective National Guards to training exercises in Honduras.[24] States could if they wish provide and maintain from their own funds a defense force exempt from being drafted into the armed forces of the United States, but none has done so.

Although governors are technically in charge of their state's National Guard, the president can call their troops into service during national emergencies. In late 2005, 80,000 of the states' 333,000 National Guard troops were deployed in Iraq, with more in Afghanistan or preparing to be deployed, and then 21,000 were called out to help after Hurricane Katrina hit the Gulf Coast.[25] In 2006, President Bush called for 6,000 National Guard troops to help stop illegal immigration from Mexico.[26]

Pardon Power

In half the states, governors may pardon violators of state law; in the other states, they share this duty with a pardoning board. Except in cases of impeachment or certain specified crimes, the governor may pardon the offender, commute a sentence by reducing it, or grant a reprieve by delaying the punishment. The governor is normally assisted by pardon attorneys or pardon boards that hold hearings and determine whether there are sufficient reasons for a pardon.

A Tennessee governor, Ray Blanton (1975–1979), caused considerable controversy and sparked a federal investigation when he pardoned or paroled several dozen convicts just before leaving office in 1979. Critics charged that some of these convicts allegedly "purchased" their releases. Blanton's misuse of his pardon powers created such outrage that his elected successor, Lamar Alexander, was sworn in early and the locks to the governor's office were quickly changed so that Blanton was not able to enter the office, let alone grant any additional pardons. Governor Ernie Fletcher of Kentucky in 2005 pardoned officials who were charged with illegally forcing out civil service employees in order to replace them with supporters of the governor, leading to calls for Fletcher's resignation.[27] Seldom, however, is the pardon power the subject of such controversy, because it is generally administered with appropriate care.

Similar to a governor's pardon power is a governor's authority to grant a stay of execution in death penalty cases. This is one of the most controversial aspects of executive power in states that permit the death penalty.[28] Texas Governor George W. Bush came under attack during the 2000 presidential campaign for allowing more than 130 executions during his time in office, in part because another Republican governor, George Ryan of Illinois, had imposed a moratorium on executions earlier in the year. Before leaving office in early 2003, Ryan commuted all Illinois death sentences to prison terms of life or less.

Policy-Making Influence

A governor's policy influence in the legislature depends in part on his or her popularity and formal powers. Obviously, governors can send detailed policy and program messages to their legislature and argue for their programs. In some states, they can trade appointive jobs for legislative support, and they can also use their veto power to trade for votes. They can attract more public attention to their views than any single legislator can. Much depends on a governor's ability, political base, and personal popularity, as well as on the political situation in which he or she operates.

Some states have a long tradition of strong executive leadership, while others give their governors relatively weak powers. On paper at least, the governors of Pennsylvania and New York, for example, have strong constitutional powers, and usually have

A conventional politician in most ways, former Illinois Governor George Ryan was plagued by various scandal accusations. Yet he will be remembered mostly for his bold and controversial review of death penalty practices in Illinois and for his criticism of state-sponsored executions. He commuted the death sentences of 163 men and four women to prison sentences of life or less.

strong party organizations behind them, which enhance close ties with followers in their respective legislatures.[29]

On paper, again, the governors of Nevada and Texas have much less formal power and preside over relatively independent departments and agencies. Yet governors of rural and smaller states generally have few other competing institutions or interests when it comes time to exercise policy leadership, while governors in large states face a number of competitors. "Power governors in large urbanized states have many others with whom they must compete—heads of major industries, media personalities, mayors of large cities, and even presidents of prestigious universities," comments political scientist Thad Beyle. "There are lots of big fish in a larger pond, which can mean that a governor may not be as powerful as it might first appear."[30]

Consider these two contrasting evaluations of the governorships in New York and Mississippi:

> The office of governor of the Empire State is surely not small. On the contrary, because of substantial grants of formal power in the state constitution, the historical exercise of such power by formidable incumbents, and widespread expectations that the governor provide leadership, the New York governor is one of the strongest in the nation.[31]
>
> Mississippi's governor remained less powerful than the state legislature. The large number of independent boards and commissions and independently elected executive officials limits his ability to effectively manage the executive branch. It is easy for agency heads to "go native" and reflect the views of their co-workers and clients rather than those of the chief executive. . . . The office of governor in Mississippi has nevertheless become more influential in recent years.[32]

Balanced against a governor's formal powers are great obstacles, which may include a hostile legislature, cutbacks in federal funding, a depressed state economy, corrupt party or administrative officials, regional tensions in the state (downstate versus upstate, east versus west, urban versus rural), special interests and lobbyists, a cynical press, an indifferent or apathetic public, the sheer inertia of a vast bureaucracy, antiquated civil service systems, and the reluctance of most citizens to get involved.[33]

Some western governors complain that absentee landlords or the federal government causes many of their states' problems, which together control much land in the West. The federal government owns 83 percent of Nevada, 68 percent of Alaska, 65 percent of Utah, and 53 percent of Oregon. This land is managed, regulated, and overseen by a score of federal agencies, such as the National Park Service, the Forest Service, the Bureau of Land Management, the Fish and Wildlife Service, and the Department of Defense. Governors of western states find that they must constantly negotiate with these many federal agencies. In contrast, states east of the Rockies have only small amounts of land owned by the federal government. In Kansas and Maine, for example, the federal government owns less than 1 percent of the land.[34]

Governors also find that they must become preoccupied with daily housekeeping tasks, and this focus often collides with their efforts to define long-range priorities. Former Vermont governor Madeleine Kunin recalls that she had to fix problems as they happened and yet simultaneously had to define her policy vision for the future. "Finding the time, energy, and perspective to carry out a dual strategy was to be the physical and mental challenge of governing."[35] Even though management duties occupy a fair amount of time, many governors consider these the least glamorous of their responsibilities (see Table 25–2).

Although governors come to office hoping to introduce new programs and reforms, they often spend most of their time raising money just to keep things going; hence some governors are viewed as merely budget balancers rather than as leaders or shapers of a state's future. The governor's role as leader of his or her political party also has an important impact on policy. The coalitions that governors form within their political parties help them put into effect the policies they desire. A governor's power increases in a state that has a competitive two-party system. In such a state, legislators of the governor's party are likely to work more closely with the governor to produce a successful legislative record.

"There are lots of big fish in a larger pond, which can mean that a governor may not be as powerful as it might first appear."

POLITICAL SCIENTIST THAD BEYLE

TABLE 25–2 How Governors Say They Spend Their Time

Activity	Percentage of Time Spent*
Managing state government	29%
Working with the legislature	16
Meeting the general public	14
Performing ceremonial functions	14
Working with press and media	9
Working with federal government	7
Working with local governments	7
Carrying out political activities	6†
Recruiting and appointing	6
Doing miscellaneous activities (staff, interstate, reading, phoning)	16

*Totals do not add to 100 percent but are averages of the governors' estimates of the time they devoted to the particular activities. Percentages based on responses from those scheduling gubernatorial time in 40 states.
†Plainly, some governors understate time spent campaigning for reelection.

SOURCE: Thad L. Beyle, "The Governor as Chief Legislator," *State Government*, Winter 1978, p. 3.

> *"Finding the time, energy, and perspective to carry out a dual strategy was to be the physical and mental challenge of governing."*
>
> **FORMER VERMONT GOVERNOR MADELEINE KUNIN**

Recent years have witnessed the election of a new breed of well-educated and able governors who have been effective in enlarging their policy-making roles: Jennifer Granholm in Michigan, Bill Richardson in New Mexico, Frank Murkowski in Alaska, and Jeb Bush in Florida. Because many governors come to office with impressive legislative and administrative experience, they are more likely to be real executive heads of government, not mere figureheads. Some have initiated experimental welfare and job-training programs that have become models for others to emulate. Because states are now playing a larger role in planning and administering a wide range of social and economic programs, the managerial and planning ability of a governor is clearly important.

Governors and Media Relations

Governors often attempt to shape their influence through aggressive media outreach. Many worked effectively with the media during their gubernatorial campaign and therefore understand their potential. Once in office, however, governors are thrust into a defensive role rather than the offensive role they played during the election. Instead of running aggressive advertisements for their campaign, they are now under the media's magnifying glass, subject to scrutiny and investigation by reporters. They are quickly evaluated in light of their campaign promises and in comparison with previous governors.[36]

Past governors have been very aware of the media, with a handful having professional backgrounds in reporting or public relations. For example, former governors Tom McCall of Oregon and Thomas Kean of New Jersey both had prior experience in public relations positions—McCall as a journalist and radio announcer and Kean as a state campaign chair for President Ford and a television reporter during the Reagan campaign. Governor Kean notes the importance of communication with the media: "The most important power the governor has is the power of communicating. If that isn't done properly, you lose your power very fast."[37] Governor Arnold Schwarzenegger of California, like his predecessor Ronald Reagan, was a movie actor and was able to use his skill in front of a camera both to win election and to press for the issues he supported.

Not all governors are effective in dealing with the media, nor do they necessarily enjoy it. As Minnesota's former governor Jesse Ventura says of the media: "The American media are suffering from very serious problems, and now I've seen them first-hand. They

Governor Christine Gregoire talks about her views on running the State of Washington from the governor's office in Olympia.

have the most twisted set of biases I've ever seen. As their whipping-boy-of-choice, I've been in a unique position to see what the media have become. There are a few honorable exceptions, but for the most part, they're corrupt, shameless, and irresponsible as hell."[38]

Each governor tends to have a personal style in dealing with the media. Some are very vocal, preferring to host daily radio or television talk shows, while others prefer to avoid the spotlight unless necessary. To capitalize on the media's ability to disseminate information, governors have been known to request special time on television attempting to explain and make an argument for policy changes, especially tax increases. Others become visible by attending community functions such as building dedications or opening ceremonies or even crowning beauty queens. It is especially important for governors to be publicly active as a calming influence during an emergency situation. During a disaster, such as an earthquake, hurricane, or terrorist action, governors have the ability to call out the National Guard and organize official aid groups. To visit, show concern for, and help ameliorate the suffering of involved families can do wonders for a governor's public opinion ratings. Governors must face public scrutiny, yet they can use the media to set and gain support for the state's agenda.[39]

Managing the State

Governors and their senior staffs are also responsible for managing their state's executive branch, whether by providing strategic planning and vision, initiating policy, settling disputes among different agencies, promoting the state (attracting tourism, exports, and investment), recruiting top state administrative and judicial officials, developing the budget, or negotiating disputes with the federal government and with nearby states.

Much recent federal legislation turning programs over to the states specifically designates the governor as the chief planning and administrative officer. This role has given governors both more flexibility and more headaches. On one hand, governors can now dispense federal funds as a form of patronage, supporting services and programs for influential professional and local communities. On the other hand, this new intergovernmental relations role requires more time, more staff, and constant negotiations both with the "feds" and with local interest group leaders vying for the money or services involved.

Some reformers have suggested that all state agencies should be accountable to the governor all the time, but others believe that politics should be kept out of the day-to-day operations of a state agency. For example, how much influence should a governor have over the running of the department of corrections in a state? Should public agencies respond to fluctuations in public opinion or to a governor's political mood? Which policy decisions should be made by professionals and experts, and which should be controlled by elected officials or by partisan appointees?

Modernizing State Government

Governors in recent years have had more managerial control over their states as a result of the use of modern management techniques: strategic planning, systems analysis, and sophisticated information technology and budgeting systems. In fact, a modern system of professional management has gradually replaced the old "buddy system," in which governors relied on political pals to get things done.

In urban states with competitive party systems, such as New York, Illinois, New Jersey, Pennsylvania, Washington, and California, governors have considerable formal constitutional authority to organize their administrations as they see fit. Even in more rural states, such as South Dakota, scores of agencies have been consolidated into a few comprehensive units as the result of executive orders from the governors.

A few years ago, in the wake of highly publicized scandals, the South Carolina legislature agreed to abolish 75 state boards, folding them into 17 larger executive agencies. This restructuring also gave the governor the authority to hire and fire the directors of most of these agencies.[40] In 2003, Texas enacted a plan to replace 11 health and human services agencies with four departments in order to increase efficiency and improve services.[41]

During the past several decades, various reformers have urged that the governor be made the true manager of the executive branch, whether by consolidating agencies into a smaller number of more tightly controlled departments, giving the governor greater power to hire and fire senior executives, or modernizing state government through better information technology.

However, attempts to reorganize state governments have not received universal praise. In some states, reorganization commissions have submitted reports that were filed away and forgotten. Groups that profit from the existing structure can be counted on to resist change. So, too, can officials who fear loss of jobs or prestige. Also, legislators are sometimes reluctant to approve recommendations that might make a governor too powerful.

Many critics oppose not so much the idea of reorganization as the basic principle of strengthening executive power and responsibility, which has dominated the reorganization movement. Often, they say, there is little evidence to support the adoption of these reforms, and there is a real danger that reorganizers are overlooking basic values in their concern with saving money. Intent on efficiency and economy, reformers often fail to foresee the risks involved in creating a powerful chief executive where no effective party or legislative opposition exists to keep a strong governor in check.

Reformers agree that no one size of reform is right for every state. However, they maintain that the basic ideas—integrated authority, centralized direction, simplified structure, clear responsibility—are sound. In fact, it is more likely that narrow special interests not responsible to the voters will take over government when the administrative structure is cumbersome, confusing, and too spread out. The legislature can more effectively supervise an administration integrated under the governor's control than one in which responsibility is split.

Effects of Reorganization

Although large savings have been realized through centralized purchasing and the adoption of modern money management practices, it is difficult to measure the results of consolidating departments, strengthening the governor's control over the executive branch, or establishing an ombudsman office to handle citizen complaints. However, the best-governed states do seem to be those in which the administrative structure has been closely integrated under the governor.

Overall, formal reorganization is not the only way states modify and modernize their governmental structures. Often they change in stages, copying innovations from other states. Certain states, in fact, serve as exporters of innovations. So does the federal government. When the federal government creates, say, the Department of Housing and Urban Development, states often respond by creating similar departments; when the federal government establishes the Department of Transportation, so do several of the states; and when the federal government creates a special White House–level office for trade, many governors set up their own offices for trade and export responsibilities.

Although governors are more powerful today than they have ever been, vigorous gubernatorial direction of a state's bureaucracy is still more the exception than the rule. Some governors fail to exploit their powers of appointment or budget setting. "Governors also have other tasks than functioning as chief bureaucrat.... Bureaucratic complexity also discourages involvement. Given these realities, involvement with state bureaucracies is very much a matter of governors picking their spots."[42]

Several former governors, including Mario Cuomo of New York and Pete Wilson of California, experimented with private sector reforms such as total quality management (TQM) and performance-based pay initiatives, but these reforms were opposed by public employee labor unions. Such proposals have also been viewed as impractical: "From TQM to vision statements to performance measurements to virtual organizations, the management theories and trends come thick and fast—faster than a lot of government employees can keep up with them."[43] Moreover, management reform often gets cast aside when one governor takes over from another, as when Republican Governor George Pataki replaced Democratic Governor Mario Cuomo in New York.

"Although the analogy between a governor and a private sector chief executive is apt," writes political scientist Thad Beyle, "governors have a distance to go before possessing comparable power of appointment and removal."[44] Many governors don't have the flexibility in hiring and firing personnel that business executives have, and they must share control with various boards, commissions, and elected officials.

In sum, governors can be influential in leading certain reforms and introducing management improvements, but they are rarely as influential and as effective as most citizens assume is the case. All kinds of constitutional, legal, and political restraints put brakes on their attempts to bring about fundamental change. Still, in good economic times, governors are generally able to begin new programs and improve the performance of existing state operations.

Other Statewide Elected Officials

Other executive officials elected by the people in most states include the lieutenant governor, secretary of state, attorney general, treasurer, and auditor. These offices each have important duties and powers, but often also constitute rungs on the ladder of political ambition. (See Table 25–3 for an inventory of state elected officials.)

Lieutenant Governor

Forty-two states have a lieutenant governor, a post similar to vice president at the national level. In nearly half the states, the lieutenant governor is elected on the same ticket as the governor, and in those states, the job is indeed like that of the vice president—the job and its influence depend very much on the mood of the governor. In 26 states, the lieutenant governor presides over the state senate. In 42 states, the lieutenant governor becomes governor or acting governor in case of the death, disability, or absence of the governor from the state. Doubtless for this reason, more governors

TABLE 25–3 States with Elected Officials

Governor	50
Attorney general	43
Lieutenant governor	42*
State treasurer	37
Secretary of state	35
Superintendent of education	14
Agriculture commissioner	13
Auditor	18
Insurance commissioner	11

*In Alaska, Hawaii, and Utah, one elected official serves as both lieutenant governor and secretary of state. In Tennessee, there is no lieutenant governor, but the Speaker of the state senate has the additional statutory title of lieutenant governor.

SOURCE: *The Book of the States, 2005* (Council of State Governments, 2005).

have sprung from this office than from other statewide elective offices. For example, in 2000, two lieutenant governors were elected governor: Judy Martz of Montana and Ruth Ann Minner of Delaware, and a third, Rick Perry of Texas, became governor there when George W. Bush moved to the White House. Perry won his own election in 2002. In 2004, Connecticut's lieutenant governor, M. Jodi Rell, became governor when Governor John Rowland resigned in the wake of allegations that he accepted special gifts from state contractors. In 2005, Lieutenant Governor Tim Kaine of Virginia was elected governor.

In states where the governor and lieutenant governor are elected on the same ticket, the lieutenant governor is likely to be given some significant responsibilities. Still, many lieutenant governors have no statutory duties, and in some smaller states, being lieutenant governor is really a part-time job. In the states where the lieutenant governor is elected independently of the governor, the lieutenant governor can sometimes be a member of the opposition party, and he or she can become a thorn in the side of the chief executive. In states like Texas, where the lieutenant governor is elected separately, the lieutenant governor is sometimes as politically powerful as the governor.[45]

There is some reason to question whether lieutenant governors are really necessary. After all, eight states, including Arizona, Georgia, and Oregon, run perfectly well without one. If their only job is to stand in waiting in case the governor dies, resigns, or is impeached, a state's attorney general, secretary of state, or the ranking member of the governor's party in the legislature could perform the replacement function. However, in New Jersey the successor to the governor is the president of the senate, who retains that position while acting as governor, and this can lead to conflicts between that person's legislative and executive roles. New Jersey voters therefore decided to create a separate office of lieutenant governor, effective with the 2009 election.

Although the position of lieutenant governor has worked well in some states, the view persists that lieutenant governors are often in search of job assignments that make them look important. The staffs and cabinets that are currently growing up around governors make the governor's chief of staff more of a deputy governor than most lieutenant governors. Moreover, many candidates for lieutenant governor appear to seek the post primarily for the name recognition and statewide experience to advance their political careers. In sum, the value to the state of the often obscure office of lieutenant governor is debatable.[46]

Attorney General

The attorney general—the state's chief lawyer—gives advice to state officials, represents the state before the courts, and in some states supervises local prosecutors. Some state attorneys general have real authority over local prosecutors and may prosecute cases on their own initiative, although in most states, criminal prosecution remains under the control of the local county prosecutor. In many states, attorneys general have taken the lead as champions of the consumer and protectors of the environment. They often have their own legislative agendas, separate from the governors. They can issue advisory opinions to state and local officials, and in many cases review legislation. They have launched major investigations into the insurance industry and into business practices. They have also led the fight against the tobacco companies and have waged antitrust investigations against corporations such as Microsoft. New York State's attorney general, Eliot Spitzer, became a nationally recognized figure and *Time* magazine's 2002 Crusader of the Year through his investigations of Wall Street fraud, and he used that visibility to build a formidable campaign for governor in 2006. The office of attorney general has become a frequent launching pad for governors. In 2006, six governors were former attorneys general.

An additional power of the attorney general is to make sure the state's laws are implemented properly. Attorneys general work in narcotics enforcement, investigate illegal activities, and often concentrate on laws that affect public safety. In California, due to power companies' recent noncompliance with laws and allegations of overcharging customers, Attorney General Bill Lockyer has filed complaints against four major power companies.[47]

Disputes between attorneys general and governors can be partisan if they belong to different parties or have conflicting ambitions, but disputes can also be issue-oriented. Thus, governors in many states have their own staff lawyers to represent them in contests with attorneys general. The office is sometimes a stepping-stone to the governorship—indeed, the acronym AG is often said to stand for both Attorney General and Almost Governor.

Secretary of State

The secretary of state publishes the laws, supervises elections, and issues certificates of incorporation. In some states, the secretary issues automobile licenses and registers corporate securities. Voters in 36 states elect secretaries of state. In eight states, governors appoint people to this position. In three states, secretaries of state are elected by the legislature. And three states don't have this position at all.

Although all secretaries of state have some duty to oversee state elections, their responsibilities differ greatly from state to state. However, all share a general commitment to increasing voter education and turnout. In 1998, the National Association of Secretaries of State launched the "New Millennium Project" to encourage greater participation among young Americans. Several states now send birthday cards with voter registration forms to every 18-year-old, while others have created challenges that pit colleges against each other in registration contests.

Treasurer and Auditor

The treasurer is the guardian of the state's money. Although in some states the job is largely ministerial, state treasurers generally have the responsibility of ensuring that cash is available to meet the obligations of the state and that all available funds are invested to maximize interest return. Treasurers are elected in 37 states, and appointed in the rest.

The auditor in most states has two major jobs: to authorize payments from the state treasury and to make periodic audits of officials who handle state money. In Montana,

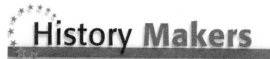

History Makers

George Wallace

George Wallace

Throughout his career as state legislator and governor, Wallace supported expanded state governmental responsibilities and expenditures for economic development, health care, elementary and secondary education, higher education, consumer protection, and workers' compensation.

One of the most controversial, complicated, and influential American political figures in the second half of the twentieth century was Governor George Wallace of Alabama. Wallace served his first term from 1963 to 1967, when the civil rights movement was at its height and southern resistance was intense. He then served two terms from 1971 to 1979, and a fourth term in 1983–1987.

Wallace's political career was full of contradiction and ironic twists. His defense of racial segregation was often virulent, including his 1963 inaugural speech, when he called for "segregation now, segregation forever," and, in the same year, his "stand at the schoolhouse door" when he briefly blocked the admission of two African American students who had legally enrolled at the University of Alabama. But in his first campaign for the governorship in 1958, he ran as a moderate on racial matters, spoke out against the Ku Klux Klan, and received the support of the National Association for the Advancement of Colored People. Moreover, during his last gubernatorial administration, in the 1980s, he appointed a record number of black Alabamians to government positions and constructed the "Wallace Coalition," composed of teachers, black political organizations, trial lawyers, and labor unions.

Although his disdain for the federal government contributed to the rise of the national conservative movement in the 1980s, Wallace was never a principled conservative. Throughout his career as state legislator and governor, Wallace supported expanded state governmental responsibilities and expenditures for economic development, health care, elementary and secondary education, higher education, consumer protection, and workers' compensation. President Lyndon Johnson played on Wallace's support for progressive programs when he chastised the governor in 1965: "Why are you off on this black thing?" the president asked. "You ought to be down there calling for help for Aunt Susie in the nursing home."

Finally, Wallace was an intense advocate of states' rights and state political autonomy. In 1966, he said, "I am an Alabama Democrat, not a national Democrat. I'm not kin to those folks." Yet more than any other governor of his day, he succeeded in using his state position to build a national constituency, as he spread his politics of resentment among white, working-class Protestants in northern states during his presidential primary campaigns of 1964, 1972, and 1976—and during his campaign in the 1968 presidential election as the candidate of the American Independent Party.

George Wallace was born to a farming family in Clio, Alabama, in 1919. He graduated from a law program at the University of Alabama in 1942, paying his tuition by waiting tables and fighting in boxing matches. He was elected to the state legislature in 1947 and first ran for governor, unsuccessfully, in 1958. However, after he was soundly defeated by his opponent on racial issues, he took a hard line on race relations, and in 1962 he got the largest vote of any gubernatorial candidate in the state's history. While campaigning in the presidential primaries in 1972, he was shot by a would-be assassin and lost the use of his legs. His last term as governor and his final years were marked by a more conciliatory tone, even a reaching out for support from black Alabamians. Wallace died in 1998.

For more on George Wallace, see Dan T. Carter, *The Politics of Rage: George Wallace, the Origins of the New Conservatism, and the Transformation of American Politics*, 2d ed. (Louisiana State Press, 2000). For the source of President Johnson's remark and the history of the civil rights movement during Wallace's first term, see Taylor Branch, *At Canaan's Edge: America in the King Years 1965–68* (Simon & Schuster, 2006). ∎

the state auditor serves as insurance commissioner. Before money can be spent, the auditor must sign a *warrant* certifying that the expenditure is authorized by law and that the money is available in the treasury. This job is more accurately called the *preaudit* and is increasingly being assigned to a comptroller appointed by and responsible to the governor. Auditing *after* money has been spent, however, is a job most observers believe should be given to an officer responsible to the legislature. Even advocates of much more centralized administration believe that the auditor should not be responsible to the governor, and most auditors are appointed, but in 18 states they are elected.

Other Officials

Such positions as superintendent of public education, agriculture commissioner, public utilities commissioner, comptroller, and insurance commissioner are less likely to be elected than treasurers or auditors. Putting positions like these on the ballot results in a longer ballot and voters will sometimes pay little attention to the minor offices; in one election, fully half the people who went to the polls failed to vote for superintendent of public instruction. The proliferation of elected officials also makes it more difficult for governors to manage and lead state government.

As part of the trend toward integrated administration, the duties of elected state officials have generally been limited to those specified in the state constitution. Some important functions have been given to officials appointed by the governor. In many states, the budget director appointed by the governor has a more important role than the elected treasurer or secretary of state. Yet elected officers can often control patronage, attract a following, and thus develop a political base from which to attack the governor's program and administration.

Sometimes progressive and controversial initiatives in state governments come from elected officials. An attorney general in Texas helped design and pass the Texas Open Records Act, one of the broadest and most strictly enforced freedom-of-information statutes in the country. A secretary of state in Massachusetts modernized election laws, helped enact campaign finance laws, and championed conflict-of-interest reforms. A state treasurer in Colorado battled to transfer some of his state's revenue deposits from a few large Denver banks to smaller banks around the state and devised incentives for these banks to lend money to students and small businesses and to support low-income housing and family farms.

The Rewards of Being a Governor

No one thinks governors have an easy job. However, most governors earn praise for their leadership, and most governors enjoy solid public approval ratings.[48] Some recent governors—Bob Riley of Alabama, Marc Racicot of Montana, Thomas J. Vilsack of Iowa, Gary Locke of Washington, Frank O'Bannon of Indiana, and Mark Warner of Virginia—became popular despite the political "heat" and the need to make tough decisions. "A governor achieves his personal best by being honest and by staying in touch with the people who elected him to serve them," says former governor Lamar Alexander of Tennessee.[49] Former governor Tom Kean of New Jersey echoed similar thoughts: "I have tried to show during my political career, and especially my years as governor, that responsible government can meet people's needs and bring them together, that government can make a difference in the way we live."[50]

Ultimately, the best governors are ones who have a keen sense of history and their own circumstance. A popular former governor of Utah, the late Scott Matheson, wrote that they have been the men and women who have the right combination of values "for quality service, the courage to stick to their convictions, even when in the minority, integrity by instinct, compassion by nature, leadership by perception, and the character to admit wrong, and when necessary, to accept defeat."[51]

Summary

1. The job of governor is one of the most important and exacting in American political life. Governors are usually white male lawyers in their forties or fifties. At least three out of four governors who run again win reelection.

2. Today, a governor is expected to be the state's chief policy maker, the architect of the state budget, the chief manager of the state administration, and the political and symbolic leader of the state. The governor also plays an increasingly complex role as the crucial link between the national and local governments.

3. Governors have many formal powers. The most important are their appointive and budgetary powers. Governors also have veto and pardon powers and the power to issue executive orders. They are commanders in chief of the National Guard. But a governor's formal powers mean little if he or she is not a persuasive communicator with good judgment and the capacity to focus simultaneously on daily tasks and long-range priorities. Governors who are effective with the media find this an additional source of informal power. Governors help set the policy agenda and frame the debate on important public issues. Yet governors, as a general rule, have more responsibility than power.

4. Over the past generation, reforms in management and organization have strengthened most governorships. Most governors have gained powers that enable them to achieve more of their goals. But constitutional, legal, and political restraints continue to limit their efforts. Thus, few governors have an easy tenure, and it is generally agreed that public demands and expectations on governors today are higher than ever.

5. In addition to a governor, the voters in most states also elect other statewide officials such as a lieutenant governor, secretary of state, attorney general, and state treasurer. In about half of the states, the governor and lieutenant governor run as a team ticket, but elsewhere this is not the case, and all other statewide elected officials run separately. Many of the officials play important political and policy roles in their states, and many current governors previously served in some other statewide elected capacity.

Further Reading

LAMAR ALEXANDER, *Steps Along the Way: A Governor's Scrapbook* (Nelson, 1986).

CECIL ANDRUS AND **JOEL CONNELLY,** *Cecil Andrus: Politics Western Style* (Sasquatch Books, 1998).

THAD L. BEYLE, ED., *Governors and Hard Times* (CQ Press, 1992).

THOMAS M. CARSEY, *Campaign Dynamics: The Race for Governor* (University of Michigan Press, 2000).

THOMAS E. CRONIN AND **ROBERT D. LOEVY,** *Colorado Politics and Government* (University of Nebraska Press, 1993).

ROBERT S. ERIKSON ET AL., *Statehouse Democracy: Public Opinion and Policy in the American States* (Cambridge University Press, 1993).

ALVIN S. FELZENBERG, *Governor Tom Kean: From the New Jersey Statehouse to the 9-11 Commission* (Rutgers University Press, 2006).

EARL H. FRY, *The Expanding Role of State and Local Governments in U.S. Foreign Affairs* (Council on Foreign Relations Press, 1998).

VIRGINIA GRAY AND **RUSSELL HANSON,** EDS., *Politics in the American States: A Comparative Analysis,* 8th ed. (CQ Press, 2003).

MADELEINE M. KUNIN, *Living a Political Life* (Vintage, 1995).

GERALD C. LUBENOW AND **BRUCE E. CAIN,** EDS., *Governing California* (Institute of Governmental Studies Press, 1997).

SARAH M. MOREHOUSE, *The Governor as Party Leader* (University of Michigan Press, 1998).

DAVID OSBORNE, *Laboratories of Democracy: A New Breed of Governor Creates Models for National Growth* (Harvard Business School Press, 1988).

GEORGE PATAKI WITH **DANIEL PAISNER,** *Pataki: An Autobiography* (Viking, 1998).

ALAN ROSENTHAL, *Governors and Legislatures: Contending Powers* (CQ Press, 1990).

SUE THOMAS AND **CLYDE WILCOX,** *Women and Elective Office* (Oxford University Press, 1998).

TOMMY G. THOMPSON, *Power to the People: An American State at Work* (HarperCollins, 1996).

JESSE VENTURA, *Do I Stand Alone?* (Pocket Books, 2000).

JESSE VENTURA, *I Ain't Got Time to Bleed* (Signet, 2000).

See also the quarterly *Spectrum: The Journal of State Government; Governing; State Policy Reports;* and *State Government News;* see also the valuable University of Nebraska Press series on state politics in the individual states, each of which has a chapter on governors.

The National Governors' Association publishes a variety of surveys, reports, and studies, including the weekly *Governors' Bulletin* and the *Proceedings of the National Governors' Association* annual meetings. These and related documents can be purchased by writing to the National Governors' Association, 444 N. Capitol Street NW, Washington, D.C., 20001.

veto, p. 690

line item veto, p. 690

reduction veto, p. 690

amendatory veto, p. 690

executive order, p. 691

Make It Real
STATE GOVERNORS

The simulation allows students
to sign or veto bills.

Chapter 26

Judges and Justice in the States

★

A LTHOUGH WE HEAR MORE ABOUT FEDERAL JUDGES THAN ABOUT THEIR STATE COUNTERPARTS, MOST OF THE NATION'S JUDICIAL BUSINESS IS CONDUCTED BY THE ALMOST 30,000 STATE AND MUNICIPAL JUDGES. PUT INTO PERSPECTIVE, FEDERAL COURTS HAVE ALMOST 2 MILLION ANNUAL CRIMINAL, CIVIL, AND BANKRUPTCY FILINGS, WHEREAS STATE COURTS CONFRONT OVER 100 MILLION CASES, MOST OF WHICH ARE TRAFFIC RELATED (ALMOST 55 MILLION).[1] STATE JUDGES PRESIDE OVER MOST CRIMINAL TRIALS, SETTLE MOST

lawsuits between individuals, and administer most estates. They have a vital role in determining who gets what, where, when, and how. Thus, they have a crucial role in making public policy.

Most state judges are white males, but this imbalance is changing rapidly. Nationwide there are about 5,000 female state court judges, about one in five, and by 2000 they were represented on all but one state supreme court (Indiana).[2]

State judges have the final say—most of the time. Through **writs of habeas corpus**—petitions to federal courts alleging that petitioners are

being held by a state as the result of a proceeding that denies them due process of law in violation of the U.S. Constitution—criminal defendants may occasionally get federal district judges to review the actions of state courts. Also, if state judges have to interpret the meaning of the U.S. Constitution, a national law, or a national treaty—that is, if the case raises a *federal question*—the losing party may request that the U.S. Supreme Court review the decision of the highest state court to which it may be taken under state law. Of the hundreds of thousands of decisions by state judges each year, very few are reviewed by the U.S. Supreme Court.

In recent decades, state courts have become more prominent in the political life of their state. In many states, a **new judicial federalism** has emerged, with judges interpreting the bill of rights in their state constitutions more broadly than the U.S. Supreme Court has in applying the national Bill of Rights, in such areas as the right of privacy, public school financing, and equal protection of the law.[3] There has also been a revolution in **tort law**—law relating to compensation for injuries to person, reputation, or property. This "tort revolution" has flooded state courts as more people sue more often about more disputes. For example, *product liability suits* are brought by people who believe they have been injured as the result of faulty products, and *malpractice suits* are brought by people who believe they have been injured as the result of mistakes by doctors, hospitals, lawyers, and other professionals. And there have been notable increases in cases relating to

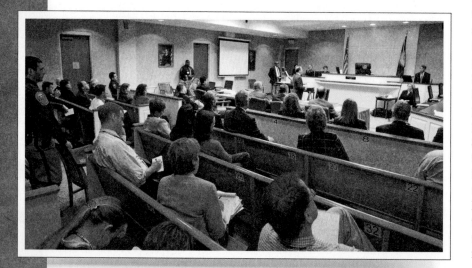

"The prospect that voters might be persuaded by party endorsements is not a corruption of the democratic political process; it is the democratic political process."

JUSTICE THURGOOD MARSHALL

713

property rights and breaches of contract. However, this has triggered a backlash against the explosion of tort filings, and many states have instituted legislative tort reforms that make it more difficult to bring lawsuits or that limit damage payments.

There has also been a significant increase in criminal cases as people press for tougher action against criminals. About half of the states have passed so-called three-strikes-and-you're-out laws, which prescribe a mandatory life sentence after three felony convictions.[4] These felony cases have increased caseloads in our courts and caused crowding in our prisons.

As state courts have become more active in our political life, state judges have become embroiled in controversial issues. And as the public has grown more sophisticated about the importance of judges as policy makers, judicial politics in the states is becoming a significant feature of the political landscape.

The Structure of State Courts

Each state has its own court system. Because the 50 systems vary, it is difficult to generalize about them. For convenience, we categorize and discuss state courts as (1) minor courts of limited jurisdiction, (2) trial courts of general jurisdiction, and (3) appellate courts (see Figure 26–1).

Minor Courts

In most states, minor courts handle **misdemeanors**—relatively minor violations of state and local laws—as well as traffic cases and civil suits involving small amounts of money. In some places, they also hold preliminary hearings and set bail for more serious charges. **Felonies** are serious crimes tried in trial courts; the penalty for a felony can range from imprisonment in a penitentiary for more than a year, to death. Decisions of the minor courts may be appealed and in most instances tried *de novo*—that is, tried all over again without reference to what happened in the minor courts. In most places, these courts are financed and administered by the local unit of government—the township, city, or county. In cities, these minor courts are known as *municipal courts* and are often divided into traffic courts, family courts, small claims courts, and police courts. Paid *magistrates* trained in the law preside over most of these courts.

Although traditional justice of peace courts are being phased out, the *justice of the peace* system survives in some states (Arizona, Arkansas, Delaware, Louisiana,

---

writ of *habeas corpus*
Court order requiring explanation to a judge why a prisoner is being held.

new judicial federalism
The practice of some state courts using the bill of rights in their state constitutions to provide more protection for some rights than is provided by the Supreme Court's interpretation of the Bill of Rights in the U.S. Constitution.

tort law
Law relating to injuries to person, reputation, or property.

misdemeanor
A minor crime; the penalty is a fine or imprisonment for a short time, usually less than a year, in a local jail.

felony
A serious crime, the penalty for which can range from imprisonment in a penitentiary for more than a year to death.

CALIFORNIA SUPREME COURT
Highest state court; seven justices

COURTS OF APPEAL
Intermediate court; reviews decisions of Superior Courts; divided into six districts

SUPERIOR COURT One in each county; 58 in the state. Each court may have many departments. Decide questions of fact and law			
SMALL CLAIMS Claims of $2,500 or less.	**CRIMINAL** Felonies: crimes punishable by imprisonment in state facilities.	**CIVIL** Disputes where the claim is over $2,500 and cases involving wills, land titles, divorce, child custody, etc.	**JUVENILE** Correction of offenders under age 18. Protection of abused and neglected minors.

FIGURE 26–1 The California State Courts.
SOURCE: Guide to California Courts, at www.courtinfo.ca.gov/reference/guide.

Montana, Texas, and Wyoming) and in rural areas; in New York, these civil authorities are called *town justices*. Justices of the peace are elected for short terms, usually two to six years. They need not be trained in the law, and their authority is limited to performing marriages, notarizing papers, handling traffic violations, and hearing misdemeanors, usually those involving fines of less than $200. They also hear minor civil disputes. Because plaintiffs can often choose among several justices of the peace in a county, they may pick the one most likely to decide in their favor. Thus, it has been said that the initials for *justice of the peace*, JP, stand for "judgment for the plaintiff."

Courts handling minor crimes are often so crowded that cases are "processed" with little time for individual attention. While many critics of the legal system contend that judges are too lenient and criminals are back on the streets too quickly, others charge that poor and ignorant defendants often spend days in jail waiting for their cases to go to trial. A new and apparently effective reform is the establishment of *court-watching groups*. In some cities, these groups are sponsored by organizations concerned with seeing that the courts treat fairly those charged with crimes. In other cities, groups are sponsored by organizations concerned that judges are too easy on defendants. Prosecutors, public defenders, and judges, it is alleged, become a comfortable work group, with little or no public scrutiny. Court watchers make these professionals more sensitive to the views of the general public.

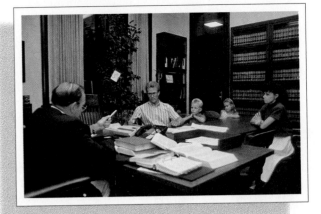

Family court judges deal with the legal issues of minors—children under the age of 18.

Trial Courts of General Jurisdiction

Trial courts where cases first appear (**original jurisdiction**) are called county courts, circuit courts, superior courts, district courts, and common pleas courts. They administer common, criminal, equity, and statutory law. Some states maintain separate courts for criminal and civil matters. States generally also have special *probate courts* to administer estates and handle related matters. These courts are all *courts of record* in which trials take place, witnesses are heard, and juries render verdicts, although most cases are heard and decided by a judge. *Appellate courts* may review decisions of trial courts; however, most decisions of trial judges are not reviewed and are final. There is a growing recognition that these courts do more than apply the law; they also participate in the never-ending process of shaping the law and public policy.[5]

Appellate Courts

In a few states—Delaware, Montana, New Hampshire, Nevada, North Dakota, Rhode Island, West Virginia, and Vermont—trial court decisions are appealed directly to the state supreme court. (In North Dakota, the supreme court can assign cases to a court of appeals composed of three judges chosen from among the trial judges.) Most states, however, have intermediate appeals courts that fit into the system in much the same way that the United States courts of appeals fit into the federal structure.

All states have a *court of last resort*, usually called the supreme court. In Maine and Massachusetts, the court of last resort is called the supreme judicial court; in Maryland and New York, this court is called the court of appeals; in West Virginia, it is the supreme court of appeals. And if that is not confusing enough, in New York, the trial courts are called supreme courts. Texas and Oklahoma have two courts of last resort— a supreme court that handles civil matters and a court of criminal appeals.

Unless a federal question is involved, state supreme courts are the highest tribunal to which a case may be appealed. State courts of last resort have five to nine judges; most have seven. Each state court has developed its own method of operating, with the pattern and practices varying widely among the states. Of the more than 60,000 decisions by state supreme courts, only 2 percent are appealed to the U.S. Supreme Court, which reviews less than 1 percent of all appeals.[6]

original jurisdiction
The authority of a court to hear a case "in the first instance."

History Makers

Judith S. Kaye

Judith S. Kaye

Chief Judge Judith S. Kaye is the first woman to serve as chief judge on New York's highest court, the New York State Court of Appeals. Chief Judge Kaye graduated from Barnard College and earned her law degree from the New York University School of Law. After practicing commercial law for 15 years, she was appointed to the court of appeals by Democratic Governor Mario Cuomo in 1983. In 1993, Governor Cuomo elevated her to chief judge.

Chief Judge Kaye is a leading advocate of judicial reforms—of re-engineering the court system in New York to make it more effective in meeting the legitimate needs of all parties and earning the public's confidence. For example, she has lightened the burdens of jury duty and spread its obligations among more citizens; she has eased access to the courts by allowing e-filing and opening court records to the public on the Web; she has worked to improve legal assistance to the

poor in both civil and criminal cases; and she has advocated initiatives to improve the integrity of judicial elections by financing them with public funds and by screening the professional qualifications of potential candidates.

Chief Judge Kaye has been particularly active in reorganizing the courts to make them effective in solving specific social and economic problems. Special drug courts have been created to focus on changing drug offenders' behavior through treatment, counseling, and training—all of which are enforced through intensive monitoring of drug usage. Courts have also been established to address the many legal issues facing families involved with domestic violence, so that a family deals with a single judge who has the jurisdiction, training, and resources to help end the violence. In the past, the problems of victims have fallen between the cracks of multiple courts, each dealing with only one facet of the domestic situation.

Some of Chief Judge Kaye's opinions are producing changes in other branches of New York State government; in particular, her majority opinion in the case in which the court of appeals directed the governor and legislature to ensure that every school in New York City have the resources necessary to provide the opportunity for a "sound basic education"; that is, "a meaningful high school education, one which prepares [students] to function productively as civic participants." Even her dissents have drawn widespread public interest, such as her sharp disagreement with the court of appeals' majority when it decided that a state law defining marriage as between a man and a woman was consistent with the state's constitution.

Chief Judge Kaye has lectured and written widely on the legal process, state constitutional law, women in the law, professional ethics, and judicial reform.* ∎

*See, e.g., Judith S. Kaye, "State Courts at the Dawn of a New Century: Common Law Courts Reading Statutes and Constitutions," in David M. O'Brien, ed., *Judges on Judging: Views from the Bench* (CQ Press, 2004), pp. 295–304. For an overview of reforms under Chief Judge Kaye, see Jonathan Lippman, "Court Reform in New York State," *Rockefeller Institute Public Policy Forum,* at www.rockinst.org/weinberg/pdf/LippmanTranscript.pdf.

judicial review

The power of a court to refuse to enforce a law or a government regulation that in the opinion of the judges conflicts with the U.S. Constitution or, in a state court, the state constitution.

All state judges of all state courts take an oath to uphold the supremacy of the U.S. Constitution, and all state judges have the power of **judicial review**. That is, they may refuse to enforce, and may restrain state and local officials from enforcing, state laws, regulations, or actions if they conclude that these conflict with the state constitution or the U.S. Constitution. State judges may also declare actions of federal officials or federal laws or regulations to be in conflict with the U.S. Constitution, subject to final review by the U.S. Supreme Court.

State supreme courts have also led the way in making judicial decisions available on the Internet. All have Web sites, and about 98 percent provide access to written opinions and decisions, along with other information, and 10 percent make oral arguments available.[7] The Web site of the National Center for State Courts (www.ncsconline .org) provides links to state court Web sites.

State Courts and State Politics

Judges are a much more prominent part of the American political scene, at both the national and state levels, than in other countries. But state courts differ from federal courts in several ways:

1. State judges are more likely to decide cases involving their legislative and executive branches than the U.S. Supreme Court is with respect to congressional and presidential matters.[8] State judges are likely to be part of the state's legal culture, since most of them have been educated in the state's law schools.[9]

2. State judges are unconstrained by the doctrine of federalism in dealing with local units of government.

3. State judges are much less constrained than federal courts from hearing cases brought by taxpayers. In federal courts, persons lack *standing to sue*—the legal right to sue—unless they show some immediate personal injury. Furthermore, in nine states, the state supreme court can give advisory opinions at the request of the governor or state legislature. An **advisory opinion** is an opinion unrelated to a particular case that gives a court's view about a constitutional or legal issue.

4. Unlike federal judges, most state judges serve for limited terms and stand for election, so they can claim to be representatives of the people. "As elected representatives, like legislators, they feel less hesitant to offer their policy views than do appointed judges."[10] In addition, if there is dissatisfaction with a decision of a state supreme court, it can be more readily set aside than can a decision of the U.S. Supreme Court.[11]

How Judges Are Chosen

Judges are selected in four different ways (see Figure 26–2): appointment by the governor, election by the legislature, popular election, or a modified appointment plan known as the Missouri Plan.

advisory opinion
An opinion unrelated to a particular case that gives a court's view about a constitutional or legal issue.

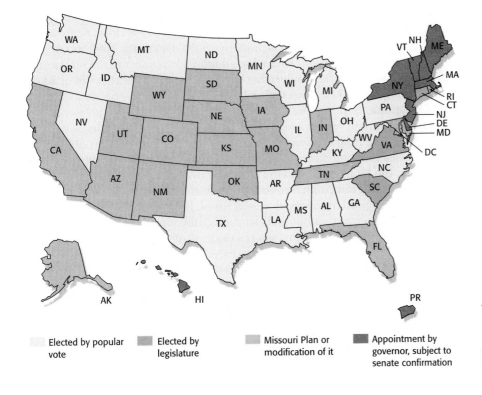

FIGURE 26–2 **Method for Selection of Judges of the Court of Last Resort.**

SOURCE: *The Book of the States, 2005* (Council of State Governments, 2005), pp. 318–321.

Legend:
- Elected by popular vote
- Elected by legislature
- Missouri Plan or modification of it
- Appointment by governor, subject to senate confirmation

Appointment by the Governor and Election by the Legislature

In Delaware, Hawaii, Maine, New Jersey, New York, and Vermont, judges are appointed by the governor and confirmed by the state senate. In Delaware and Massachusetts, governors select appointees from names submitted by judicial nominating commissions. Election by the legislature is the constitutional practice in Connecticut, Rhode Island, South Carolina, and Virginia. However, we need to look beyond the formal election procedures. "A majority of the judges serving in states utilizing an elective judiciary . . . are in fact initially appointed by the governor to fill mid-term vacancies, usually occasioned by the retirement or death of sitting judges . . . and these appointed judges are overwhelmingly favored in their first electoral bids following appointment."[12]

In addition to the formal process of nomination and selection, there are several informal processes. Lawyers interested in becoming judges may make their interest known either directly or indirectly to party officials; leaders of the local bar associations may promote favored members; various members of the bar may seek out candidates and recruit them. Political leaders and interest groups also participate. Following such suggestions, the names go through the formal appointment process.[13]

Popular Election

In nearly half the states, judges are chosen in elections. Over 85 percent of all state and local judges face elections, far more than the number of elected state legislators and executive officials. Appellate court judges in eight states face partisan elections, 13 states hold nonpartisan elections, and another 19 states have retention elections for state judges.[14]

Some states, mostly in the West and upper Midwest, hold *nonpartisan* primaries for nominating judicial candidates and elect them on nonpartisan ballots. However, nonpartisan judicial elections do not necessarily mean that political parties are not involved. In at least half of the states with nonpartisan judicial elections, parties actively campaign on behalf of candidates. Some states try to isolate judicial elections from partisanship by holding them separately from other elections.

In 1986, California amended its constitution to forbid political parties from endorsing candidates for judicial office. However, federal courts declared the proposition unconstitutional, and California political parties are once again endorsing judicial candidates. Apparently the prevailing view, as Justice Thurgood Marshall observed, is that "the prospect that voters might be persuaded by party endorsements is not a *corruption* of the democratic political process; it *is* the democratic political process."[15]

In recent years, most states have adopted provisions similar to the American Bar Association's code of judicial conduct that bar judicial candidates from telling the electorate anything about their views on legal and political matters—whether they are in favor, for example, of punishing criminals harshly or of expanding privacy rights. A "chief justices' summit" was convened in 2000 by the chief justices of the 17 most populous states with judicial elections; it recommended reforms, including public funding for judicial elections and closer monitoring of judicial campaigns. Some states have gone further; the Minnesota Supreme Court, for instance, prohibited judicial candidates from soliciting campaign contributions, declaring their party affiliation, or publicly voicing their positions on controversial issues. However, the U.S. Supreme Court struck down Minnesota's ban on judicial candidates' announcing their position on controversial legal and political matters as a violation of the First Amendment guarantee of free speech.[16] State and federal courts in Alabama, Georgia, Michigan, Ohio, and other states have also handed down decisions that are "a roadblock for efforts to curb the increasingly raucous nature of judicial politics."[17]

Until recently, there was little interest in judicial elections, and voter turnout tended to be low. But judicial elections are becoming increasingly costly and spirited. In the 2000 elections, candidates for state supreme courts raised an unprecedented $45 million, over 60 percent more than in 1998 and double that spent in 1994. Interest groups in five states with the most hotly contested judicial races raised an additional

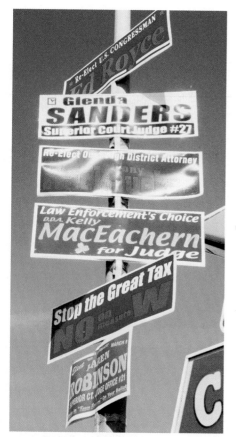

In states with elected judges, campaigns can become very competitive.

$16 million.[18] Special-interest groups focus attention on judges whose decisions they find objectionable. The issues vary from election to election and from state to state. In some states, the issue has been the death penalty. In Texas and California, efforts to limit liability lawsuits and damage awards have led to campaign clashes over judicial candidates, with trial lawyers, consumers, and union groups on one side and business interests on the other. In Idaho, one candidate for the supreme court campaigned on a platform that the theory of evolution could not be true—and won. In Wisconsin, the chief justice won reelection, although she had to fight for her seat and felt compelled to explain why she had once allowed an aerobics class in the court's hearing room. An Illinois judge was unseated because of his decisions in abortion cases. Judges now have to act like politicians and "feel they are under increasing pressure to be accountable to public opinion."[19] The image of impartial courts may well become a casualty of the increasingly heated politics of judicial campaigns and elections.

The costs of judicial elections are escalating. Critics charge that the need to raise large sums for their campaigns compromises the impartiality of judges and judicial candidates. In the 2004 elections, candidate spending was up to $47 million.[20] In 2006, $2.7 million was spent through the end of the primary election for Alabama supreme court, and the races in Georgia, Kentucky, Michigan, Ohio, and Washington state were also attracting a great deal of money.[21] In many states that elect judges, it is increasingly clear that judicial candidates are dependent on a small number of law firms, businesses, or special-interest groups, such as the U.S. Chamber of Commerce and the Business Roundtable, for their campaign funds.[22]

In response to the growing cost of state judicial elections, the American Bar Association, the American Judicature Society, and other organizations are promoting the public financing of state judicial campaigns and elections.[23] Two states, Wisconsin and North Carolina, provide public financing for some judicial elections. Wisconsin has had publicly financed elections for state supreme court justices since the 1970s; candidates are eligible for $97,000 in state money if they agree to a $215,000 spending limit. The system is paid for through a one dollar check-off contribution on income tax returns, and has been historically underfinanced. In 2004, North Carolina's Judicial Campaign Reform Act went into effect. Under it, all appellate-level judicial races are nonpartisan, and candidates who agree to fund-raising and spending limits receive public financing in the general election. The public financing of judicial elections is also under consideration in a number of other states, including Idaho, Illinois, New York, and Texas.

MINORITY REPRESENTATION The one-person, one-vote rule that applies to legislative elections does not apply to judicial elections.[24] States may create judicial districts so that one judge "represents" many more voters than another judge. However, although there is no requirement that states elect judges, if they choose to do so, the federal Voting Rights Act of 1965 applies to these judicial elections.[25]

Because the Voting Rights Act of 1965 forbids any practice or procedure that dilutes the voting power of minorities, it raises a question about the constitutionality of at-large judicial elections. When judges are elected at large for a city or a state, African American and Hispanic candidates sometimes find it difficult to get elected. African American and Hispanic voters tend to be concentrated in the inner cities or in certain geographical areas; thus their impact is diluted in citywide or statewide elections. For example, in a state in which the population consists of 20 percent African American voters, 20 percent Hispanic voters, and 60 percent Anglo voters, with five judges to be elected on a statewide basis, few if any African American judges or Hispanic judges will be elected. Some Hispanics and African Americans argue that the solution is to divide such a state into five districts, with one judge elected in each district, and draw district lines in such a way that African Americans and Hispanics make up a majority of voters in as many districts as possible, giving them a chance to elect at least one of their own.

Minorities now have greater opportunities to be elected judges, but are still underrepresented on the bench.

The Changing Face of American Politics

Women and Minorities on State Supreme Courts

State supreme courts were once composed overwhelmingly of white males. But women and minorities now constitute more than 30 percent of the judges on state supreme courts. In 2005–2006, there were 91 women on state courts of highest resort, and in three states—New York, Washington, and Wisconsin—they made up more than 50 percent of the bench. The New Mexico state supreme court has the largest number of Hispanic judges (60 percent of the bench). African American judges now sit in more than 20 percent of state high courts in Florida, Georgia, Indiana, Tennessee, and Texas. Asian and Pacific Islander judges sit on two state supreme courts, in California and Hawaii. ■

SOURCE: American Judicature Society at www.ajs.org/js/select.htm; American Bar Association, *The Directory of Minority Judges of the United States*, 3d ed. (American Bar Association, 2001).

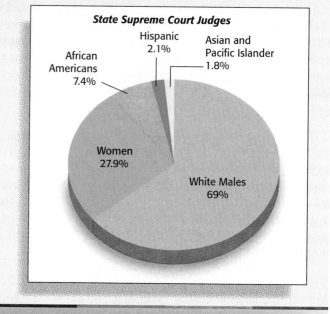

State Supreme Court Judges

- Hispanic 2.1%
- Asian and Pacific Islander 1.8%
- African Americans 7.4%
- Women 27.9%
- White Males 69%

Merit Selection: The Missouri Plan

Many lawyers and political scientists have argued in favor of some kind of selection procedure in which there is a screening process before judges are appointed or elected to ensure that only candidates of merit will be considered. Merit systems are used in 16 states.

One of the oldest merit plans is the Missouri Plan.[26] The **Missouri Plan**, as used in most states, provides that when a judicial vacancy occurs, a special *nominating commission* (usually composed of three lawyers elected by the bar, three citizens appointed by the governor, and the chief justice) nominates three candidates.[27] The governor selects one, who then serves as a judge for at least a year. At the next general election, the voters are asked, "Shall Judge X be retained in office?" If a majority of the voters agree, the judge serves a new full term (typically six to 12 years); if not, another person is selected by the same procedure. At the end of his or her term, the judge may ask to have his or her name placed on the ballot, and the voters are again asked whether they want to retain that judge in office.[28] These uncontested elections, in which judges run against their own record, are called *retention elections,* and some require a supermajority vote.

California has a slightly different form of merit selection. The governor appoints judges to the supreme court and the appellate court for 12-year terms, with the approval of the Commission on Judicial Appointments. The commission consists of the attorney general, chief justice, and senior appellate presiding justice for supreme court appointments or the senior presiding justice in the appellate district for appellate court appointments. In the next statewide election, the judge runs against his or her own record. The governor appoints trial judges to six-year terms; they may be challenged when seeking reelection, but their names do not appear on the ballot if they are running unopposed.

Even more of a hybrid is the system used in New Mexico, where a judicial nominating commission sends names to the governor, who selects a judge. At the next gen-

Missouri Plan

A system for selecting judges that combines features of the appointive and elective methods. The governor selects judges from lists presented by panels of lawyers and laypersons, and at the end of their term, the judges may run against their own record in retention elections.

eral election, an opponent nominated in the other party's primary may challenge the judge in a partisan election. If no opponent is nominated, the incumbent gets a "free ride." Whoever wins that election then serves one term and thereafter runs against his or her own record in a retention election.

Until recently, retention elections generated little interest and low voter turnout.[29] In all, of the almost 4,600 judicial retention elections since 1960, fewer than 60 judges have been removed by voters, although a few judges have decided not to run when they realized they might fail to be retained.[30] Recently, some state supreme court justices have been vigorously challenged in retention elections, especially when their decisions differed appreciably from the mainstream of public opinion and aroused the hostility of significant special interests. Frequently, the charge was that the judge was "soft on crime." Interest groups have learned that it is relatively easy to target incumbents, but because of constraints on the way judicial candidates are expected to campaign, it is "difficult for targeted judges to defend themselves."[31] One Pennsylvania supreme court justice lost a retention race in 2005, and another nearly lost, after the state legislature's adoption of a pay raise for itself and for other state officials including judges sparked a huge voter backlash.

Most voters know little about judges, and what information they get comes from interested parties and persons, especially those who dislike what the judges have done. To provide a more balanced picture, a few states—Alaska, Utah, Colorado, Arizona, Tennessee—have tried to supply more neutral information about judicial performance. In Colorado, an *evaluation committee* in each judicial district—jointly appointed by the chief justice, governor, president of the senate, and speaker of the house—disseminates information through newspaper supplements, including a final recommendation of "retain" or "do not retain."[32] In Alaska, a judicial council composed of three lawyers, three nonlawyers, and the chief justice provides evaluations that are widely publicized.[33] In Utah, the Judicial Council—consisting of the chief justice, another justice, an appellate court judge, five district court judges, two juvenile court judges, three other lower court judges, a state bar representative, and the state court administration—certifies incumbents, and this certification, or lack of it, is indicated on the ballot.

Even though contested retention elections are the exception, sitting judges are aware that if they make decisions that offend organized interest groups, they may face opposition the next time their names are placed on the ballot. Whether these pressures threaten the independence of the courts or are necessary to ensure judicial accountability within our political system in which judges play such an important role remains a matter of the political debate.[34]

The Appointive Versus the Elective System

For more than 200 years, people have debated the merits of an appointive versus an elective system for the selection of judges. Those who favor the appointive method contend that voters are generally uninformed about candidates and are not competent to assess legal learning and judicial abilities. Popular election, they claim, puts a premium on personality, requires judges to enter the political arena, and discourages many able lawyers from running for office. They also contend that the elective process conceals what is really going on. Absent name recognition, voters go for party labels, which are increasingly less significant as indicators of ideology.[35] In addition, because retirement and death create many vacancies, it is often the governor who selects the judges. The governor makes an interim appointment until the next election, and the temporary appointee usually wins the election.

Those who favor judicial elections counter that judges should be directly accountable to the people. When judges are appointed, they may lose touch with the general currents of opinion of the electorate. Moreover, the appointive process gives governors too much power over judges. And even if judicial elections do not result in the defeat of many sitting judges, elections serve to foster accountability because judges do not want to be defeated and will try to maintain popular support. In general, bar associations, corporate law firms, and judges themselves tend to favor some kind of merit selection system; plaintiffs, attorneys, women's associations, minority associations, and labor groups are skeptical or opposed.

How Judges Are Judged

While federal judges hold office during "good behavior"—essentially for life—among the states only Rhode Island's judges have life appointments. In Massachusetts and New Hampshire, judges serve to age 70. In all of the other states, judges serve for fixed terms of from six to 14 years.[36] Thirty-seven states and the District of Columbia mandate the retirement of judges at a certain age, usually 70.[37]

The states, rather than the national government, have taken the lead in establishing procedures to judge judges. Because impeachment has proved to be an ineffective means to remove judges, today each of the 50 states has a board, commission, or court to handle allegations of judicial misbehavior. Despite the objections of many judges, these commissions are most often composed of both nonlawyers and lawyers. They investigate complaints and hold hearings for judges who have been charged with improper performance of their duties or unethical or unfair conduct. Establishment of these commissions appears to have helped restore public confidence in the state judicial systems.[38]

For developments in the states and efforts to establish standards of conduct for judicial candidates, go to www.constitutionproject.org, the Web site of a nonpartisan group dedicated to protecting the independence of courts from partisan political attacks. See also the site of the Brennan Center's Project on Judicial Independence at the New York University Law School, www.brennancenter.org. You can also subscribe to its biweekly e-mail list to get summaries of news stories relating to judicial independence, judicial elections, and judicial appointments. Another valuable site for information about courts is that of the American Judicature Society, at www.ajs.org.

The Judicial Reform Movement

Many reforms—court unification, centralized management, state financing, and merit selection—have been adopted, but waste and delay continue to plague our courts. We are, many charge, a "litigious society." Dockets are crowded, relief is costly, and inordinate delays are common.[39]

Proposed reforms for improving the administration of justice include the following:

- Judges should be selected by some kind of merit system that screens candidates in terms of their qualifications.

- Judges should be paid adequately so that they have the financial independence to concentrate on their work and so that successful lawyers will be willing to serve on the bench. In most states, judges' salaries are considerably less than the average incomes of practicing attorneys of the same age and experience. Judges are unable to earn anything beyond their salaries, and they must be cautious about investments in order to avoid conflicts of interest.

- Judges should serve for long terms so that they can make decisions without fear of losing their jobs.

- Rule-making powers should be given to the state supreme court or its chief justice. States are permitting judges to adopt procedural rules and codes of professional conduct. Most require lawyers to continue their education by taking refresher courses.

■ Although no person should be appointed or elected to a court solely because of race, sex, or ethnic background, our courts need to become more representative of the communities they serve.[40]

■ States should provide for alternative dispute resolution.

Alternative dispute resolution (ADR) refers to procedures that serve as alternatives to formal trials. These procedures include mediation, arbitration, conciliation, private judging, and advisory settlement conferences. From time to time, Congress has made grants to encourage states and localities to develop alternative dispute resolution mechanisms, especially for domestic relations issues. ADRs can be part of the established court system or separate from it in neighborhood justice centers or arbitration and mediation forums. Half the states operate arbitration programs as part of their court system.

Despite the trendy nickname "rent-a-judge," the rather old practice of hiring private decision makers has been revived. These decision makers, often retired judges and lawyers, are paid by the parties to the dispute, who agree in advance to abide by the outcome. In some states, appeals courts can review these decisions. There is some concern that these alternative practices are drawing the best lawyers into the private system, resulting perhaps in one system for the rich, a private one, and one for the poor, a public one.

The judicial reform movement has been successful, but like most reform movements, it has its critics and skeptics. Some observers maintain that court delay is not as serious a problem as has been charged and that the remedies may undercut our system of checks and balances. Delay, for example, often works to the advantage of defendants and their attorneys, who wish to postpone trials. At other times, prosecutors want delays in order to put pressure on defendants to accept guilty pleas. Lawyers may seek delays so that they can accept more clients.

No matter how "modernized" the management of court business, the flow of legal business grows continuously. Some people have proposed that traffic violations, automobile injury cases, and so-called victimless crimes be handled by some procedure other than a court trial. New York has led the way in removing from the courts minor traffic offenses that do not involve serious moving violations; other states are following its lead. No-fault insurance programs could reduce the large number of cases stemming from automobile accidents. Because half the people in prison, as well as half the trials that are held, involve victimless crimes such as using marijuana, *decriminalization* could substantially reduce the load on the courts. Six states, for example, have already repealed statutes on public drunkenness and now consider alcoholism a disease rather than a crime.

The reform of state judicial systems is enmeshed in partisan, ideological, and issue politics. Judges are but one part of the total justice system, and their operations are best studied in the context of the entire justice system.

The Justice System

Justice is handled in the United States by a series of institutions that are only loosely connected to each other. In addition to judges, there are juries, prosecutors, defense counsels, public defenders, victims, and defendants. Parole, probation, and prison officials are also part of the justice system.

The Jury

Although most of us will never be judges or serve as professionals in the administration of justice, all adult citizens have an opportunity—even an obligation—to be jurors. Trial by jury in civil disputes is used less often these days; people make settlements

All citizens have an obligation to serve on juries, and lawyers develop skills in selecting people they think may be sympathetic to their client.

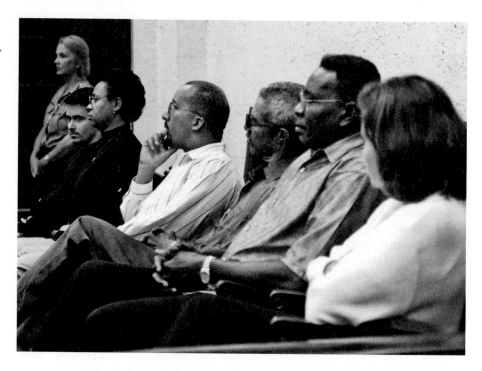

before a trial, elect to have their cases decided by a judge alone, or have their cases referred to a mediator or arbitrator. Furthermore, only a small fraction of criminal cases are actually disposed of by a trial before a jury. Still, jury trials, or the threat of them, remain a key feature of our justice system.

We have moved from a jury system in which service was restricted to white male property owners to one in which jury duty is the responsibility of *all* adult citizens. Today more time and energy are spent in trying to persuade (or coerce) people to serve on juries than in trying to exclude them. Because jury service may be time-consuming and burdensome, many busy people do their best to avoid serving. In the past, judges were often willing to excuse doctors, nurses, teachers, executives, and other highly skilled persons who pleaded that their services were essential outside the jury room. As a result, juries were often selected from panels consisting in large part of older people, those who were unemployed or employed in relatively low-paying jobs, single people, and others who were unable to be excused from jury service. Most states have reacted to these problems by making it more difficult to be excused. In addition, many states have adopted a "one-day, one-trial" policy, which makes jury service less frequent and less onerous. Because jury trials take more time than bench trials (trials before judges) and cost more, some states use juries of fewer than 12 people for some criminal trials. A few states also permit verdicts by less than a unanimous vote. The U.S. Supreme Court has approved these practices, provided the juries consist of at least six persons.[41]

Only a handful of those accused of committing a crime actually stand trial, and only 5 to 10 percent of those who are convicted are declared guilty as the result of a formal trial before either a judge or a jury. Most people who go to prison, or who have to pay a criminal fine, do so because they plead guilty.[42]

The Prosecutor

The prosecutor is largely an American invention, one of the few governmental positions we did not inherit from England. The 2,341 chief prosecutors in the United States (often called county attorneys or district attorneys) are usually county officials; most are locally elected and subject to little supervision by state authorities. In Connecticut, however, they are appointed by judges, in the Virgin Islands by the attorney general, and in New Jersey by the governor with the consent of the state senate. There are also about 27,000 assistant prosecutors.[43] A prosecutor has "more control over life, liberty, and reputation than any other person in America."[44]

When presented with a case by the police, the prosecutor must decide first whether to file formal charges. He or she may (1) divert the matter out of the criminal justice system and turn it over to a social welfare agency; (2) dismiss the charges; (3) take the matter before a grand jury, which almost always follows the prosecutor's recommendation; or (4) in most jurisdictions, file an **information affidavit**, which serves the same function as a grand jury **indictment**.

A prosecutor who decides not to charge a person accused of some notorious crime is often subject to political pressure and public criticism. But for routine crimes, the prosecutor is politically in a better position to dismiss a charge than the police are. Police are supposed to enforce every law all the time. Of course, it is impossible for them to do so, and they must exercise discretion.[45] But officers who fail to arrest a person alleged to have committed a crime could well be charged with failing in their duty. The prosecutor, however, has more leeway. In fact, the prosecutor is less likely to be criticized for dropping a case because of insufficient evidence than for filing a charge and failing to get a conviction.

Defense Counsel, Public Defenders, and Others

Many defendants cannot afford the legal counsel to which they are constitutionally entitled. The **assigned counsel system** is the oldest system to provide such defendants with an attorney, and it continues to be used, especially in rural areas. Judges appoint attorneys to represent defendants who cannot afford them. Most such attorneys are paid from the public treasury, but sometimes they are expected to do the work **pro bono**—for the public good. Seldom are they given funds to do any investigatory work on behalf of their clients. Often judges pick young lawyers just beginning their careers or old ones about to retire. Some less scrupulous lawyers make their living as assigned counsel; because it is often to their financial advantage to do so, they are quick to plead their clients guilty. They are known contemptuously as members of the "cop-out bar."[46]

Dissatisfaction with the assigned counsel system led to the creation of the **public defender system**, first started in Los Angeles in 1914 and now used in most big cities. Under this system, the government provides a staff of lawyers whose full-time job is to defend individuals who cannot pay. This system provides experienced counsel and relieves the bar of an onerous duty. Critics—including some defendants—protest that because public defenders are paid employees of the state, they are not likely to work as diligently on behalf of their clients as they would if they were specifically assigned to those clients. But most observers consider the defender system superior to the assigned counsel system. Steps are being taken to increase the pay of public defenders, protect their independence, and see that they win the confidence of the defendants they represent.

Victims and Defendants

When we talk about our criminal justice system, we sometimes forget the two most important parties in any criminal case—the victim of the crime and the person accused of it.

> The rights of victims or potential victims are not of the same order as the rights of the accused; the rights of the accused are constitutional rights spelled out in amendments, but nowhere in the Constitution is there any mention of the rights of victims or the public. The framers of the Constitution apparently were much more worried about protecting citizens against the government than about protecting citizens from each other.[47]

In general, terms, defendants are likely to be "younger, predominantly male, disproportionately black, less educated, seldom fully employed, and typically unmarried.

information affidavit
Certification by a public prosecutor that there is evidence to justify bringing named individuals to trial.

indictment
A formal written statement from a grand jury charging an individual with an offense; also called a *true bill.*

assigned counsel system
Arrangement whereby attorneys are provided for persons accused of crimes who are unable to hire their own attorneys. The judge assigns a member of the bar to provide counsel to a particular defendant.

pro bono
To serve the public good; term used to describe work that lawyers (or other professionals) do for which they receive no fees.

public defender system
Arrangement whereby public officials are hired to provide legal assistance to those persons accused of crimes who are unable to hire their own attorneys.

A disproportionate number of prisoners tend to be young, poorly educated, black males.

By the time the sorting process has ended, those sent to prison will consist of an even higher proportion of young, illiterate, black males."[48] Victims, too—compared with the rest of the population—tend to be young, black or another minority, and uneducated. A substantial number of victims—either because of lack of knowledge of what to do or fear of doing it, or because, as in the case of rape victims, they believe they have little chance of proving their attackers to be guilty—never report crimes to police and prosecutors.

Our system puts the responsibility for prosecuting criminals on the government. In most instances, victims have no role other than as witnesses. They are not consulted about what the charge should be or asked what they think might be an appropriate penalty. The matter is strictly between the state, represented by the prosecutor, and the accused, represented by an attorney.

As a result, in recent decades a victims' rights movement has emerged. The movement originated with liberals (chiefly feminists concerned about the difficulty of winning prosecutions for rape and about the harsh treatment of female witnesses), but has gained the support of conservatives who consider the judicial system unfair to victims. In the 1984 Victims of Crime Act, Congress authorized federal funds, which are distributed by the Office of Crime Victims in the Department of Justice, to support state programs compensating victims and providing funds to some victims of federal crimes as well.

About 30 states have amended their constitutions to provide for a "victims' bill of rights," which makes it easier for victims to recover stolen property held in police custody, among other things. Many also give victims a chance to be heard when prosecutors file formal charges, when judges set bail and impose sentences, and when parole boards consider releasing prisoners. These victims' bills of rights are not without constitutional problems. The introduction of "victim-impact statements" by prosecutors seeking the death penalty, for instance, has been controversial. The U.S. Supreme Court, after first holding to the contrary, has upheld the right of prosecutors to make "victim-impact statements" to a jury in murder trials about the personal qualities of the victim and to allow the jury to consider evidence relating to the murder victim's personal characteristics and the emotional impact of the crime on the victim's family.[49]

Plea Bargaining

Although most criminal cases end with a guilty plea, common practice is for the prosecution to offer to reduce the seriousness of the charge and sentence if a defendant will enter a plea of guilty to a lesser crime. This practice is called a **plea bargain**. At one time, this practice was universally condemned. Many people still consider there is something improper about it, like bartering away justice.

Critics say that plea bargaining forces people to give up their rights; moreover, defendants often do not get off much more leniently by pleading guilty to lesser offenses than if they had stood trial.[50] Defenders of plea bargaining contend it works, producing "a result approximating closely, but informally and more swiftly, the results which ought to ensue from a trial, while avoiding most of the undesirable aspects of that ordeal."[51] Many experts and investigators who have looked into the matter have endorsed plea bargaining.

Plea bargaining offers something to all involved. Prosecutors are able to dispose of cases quickly, avoid long and drawn-out trials, eliminate the risk of losing cases, and build up better "election-worthy" conviction records. The accused avoid the danger of being sentenced for more serious charges by pleading guilty to lesser offenses. Defense attorneys avoid "the dilemma of either incurring the expense of going to trial with a losing case or appearing to provide no service whatever to their clients."[52] By being able to handle more clients, they can also make more money. Judges are able to dispose of cases on their dockets more rapidly. In fact, were every case tried, it would overwhelm the judicial system.

plea bargain
Agreement between a prosecutor and a defendant that the defendant will plead guilty to a lesser offense to avoid having to stand trial for a more serious offense.

Once the bargain between the prosecutor and the defendant's attorney has been accepted, the matter is taken before a judge. The judge goes through a series of questions to the defendant: "Are you pleading guilty because you are guilty? Are you aware of the maximum sentence for the crime to which you are entering a guilty plea? Were you coerced into pleading guilty or offered anything in return for it? Are you satisfied with the representation afforded by your attorney?" Following appropriate responses, the plea is accepted.[53] As long as defendants know what they are doing and enter into the bargain intelligently, they waive their constitutional rights to trial by pleading guilty and may not subsequently back out of the arrangement. Prosecutors must also live up to their side of the bargain.[54]

Sentencing

Due process must be observed in sentencing, which takes place in open court. The prisoner must be present and represented by counsel. In many places, social workers are assigned to help the judge determine the proper sentence. The judge also receives recommendations from the prosecution (and in some jurisdictions from the victim as well), hears the arguments of the defense, and then sets the sentence within the limits prescribed by the state.

The judge sets the sentence, but concerns about sentencing permeate the judicial system. One writer has put it this way:

> Because police and prosecutors screen out a large proportion of the doubtful cases, most left to be dealt with by the courts are those in which there is no serious dispute over the guilt or innocence of the defendant. This fact sets the tone for the process. Everyone concerned—the defense lawyers, the prosecutor, the judge, the probation officer—becomes aware of the fact that he or she is involved in a process where the primary focus is on deciding what to do with the people who are in fact guilty.[55]

Early in our national history, retribution, deterrence, and protection of society were the primary purposes of sentencing. Then rehabilitation became the major goal, and many people thought it was a more humane approach. The indefinite sentence became popular, motivated by the idea that each prisoner should be considered an individual suffering from an "illness." Each prisoner should be diagnosed, a course of treatment should be prescribed, and if and when such experts as psychologists and social workers could certify a "cure," the prisoner should be released.

Most political leaders and many scholars have become disillusioned about our ability to bring about "cures."[56] Others are disillusioned about the deterrent effect of imprisonment. A comprehensive study of rehabilitative efforts inside prisons, although rejecting the conclusion that "nothing works," nonetheless stated: "We do not know of any program or method of rehabilitation that could be guaranteed to reduce the criminal activity of released offenders."[57]

Moreover, judges may enjoy considerable discretion in sentencing, and they frequently give different sentences to defendants convicted of the same crime.[58] To reduce such disparities in sentencing, several reforms have been suggested, including establishing more precise legislative standards, creating advisory sentencing councils, and adopting the British practice of allowing appellate courts to modify sentences.

Disillusionment with rehabilitation and disparate sentencing by judges, combined with growing concerns about crime and mounting criticism about alleged judicial leniency, has fueled legislative action for mandatory minimum sentencing requirements and for narrowing judicial discretion.[59] State after state has adopted mandatory prison terms—also known as *determinate sentencing*—for more and more crimes. As noted earlier, a three-strikes-and-you're-out requirement has been adopted by many states.

Probation and Prisons

Prison populations in the United States are skyrocketing. Including juvenile facilities, the United States has almost 2.3 million people behind bars, over 1.4 million in state and federal prisons, 714,000 in local jails, and more than 100,000 in juvenile facilities[60] (see Table 26–1). (*Prisons* are for committed criminals serving long sentences; *jails* are for short-term stays for persons awaiting trial and those with sentences of a year or less.) More people are imprisoned in the United States than in any other country. "The American inmate population has grown so large that it is difficult to fathom: imagine the combined population of Atlanta, St. Louis, Pittsburgh, Des Moines, and Miami behind bars."[61]

TABLE 26–1 Prisoners under the Jurisdiction of State and Federal Correctional Authorities	
State and federal prisons	1,421,911
Local jails	713,990
Juvenile facilities	102,338
Territorial prisons	15,757
Immigration and Naturalization Service facilities	9,788
Military facilities	2,117
Indian country jails	1,826

SOURCE: U.S. Department of Justice, Bureau of Justice Statistics, "The Nation's Prison Population Continues its Slow Growth," press release, October 23, 2005.

In addition to those in prison or jails, there are almost 4.9 million adult men and women on probation or parole. (*Probationers* are offenders courts have placed in community supervision rather than putting them in prison; *parolees* are people released after serving a prison term who are under supervision and are subject to being returned to prison for rule violations or other offenses.)

State and federal prison populations in the United States actually declined during the 1960s, but public demands for tougher sentences caused them to climb after 1969. The prison population has more than tripled since 1980 (see Figure 26–3), though the rate of increase slowed considerably after 1999.

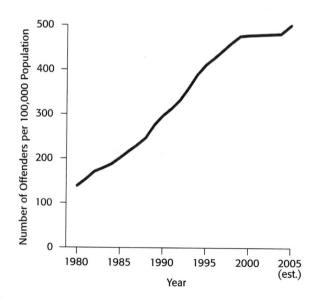

FIGURE 26–3 Incarceration Rates in Federal and State Jurisdictions.

SOURCE: U.S. Department of Justice, Bureau of Justice Statistics, at www.ojp.usdoj.gov/bjs/glance/incrt.htm.

The increase in the prison population has resulted in serious overcrowding. In some states, conditions were so bad that in the 1990s federal judges issued orders calling for either immediate improvement or the release of persons being held in conditions that violate the Eighth Amendment prohibition against cruel and unusual punishment. Most states responded to judicial intervention by spending millions to build new prisons and renovate old ones. It costs over $60,000 to build each cell, and an average of almost $23,000 a year must be spent for each prisoner.

Relatively few people commit most violent crimes. One out of every three persons let out of prison returns in three years. If we could identify these "career criminals" (**recidivists**) and keep them in prison, while at the same time releasing offenders who are not likely to commit other crimes, we might be able to cut down on the overcrowding in the prisons and better protect the public. The trouble with this idea is that it is not easy to determine in advance who is a career criminal and who is not. For this reason, some people argue that requiring every criminal convicted of a second offense to stay in prison for five years would cut the crime rate significantly.

Some cities and counties have even resorted to **privatization**, turning over the responsibility for operating jails to private firms on a contractual basis. Prison facilities have been privatized in New Jersey, Ohio, and Vermont, as well as in many southern and western states. Texas has the largest number of inmates in private facilities, and New Mexico has the largest proportion of its inmate population privatized, over 42 percent.[62] Correctional peace officers strongly oppose privatization and have become a potent interest group making major contributions to gubernatorial elections.

The high cost of correction is leading some states to rethink the wisdom of mandatory sentencing and to reconsider the need to create such alternatives for non-violent offenders as halfway houses, intensive probation, work release programs, and other community corrections facilities—even home confinement, first pioneered in New Mexico in 1983, whereby prisoners are observed by a variety of monitoring devices.[63] The problem is that these alternative solutions are subject to political attack for being "soft on criminals." Even so, pressure to find places to hold prisoners is so great that corrections officials believe that these alternatives, including home confinement, will become an increasingly important part of the criminal justice system.[64]

> *"The justice system is no longer a 'court of last resort'... but is becoming an emergency room for every social trauma."*
>
> **THE AMERICAN BAR ASSOCIATION**

Courts in Crisis

Crime is a national issue, confronting everyone. The public's attention has been focused on terrorist attacks, drive-by shootings, random killings—especially in schools—and other forms of violence. Yet courts are already overwhelmed by a huge volume of cases. As the American Bar Association observed, "Justice in the United States takes too long, costs too much and is virtually inaccessible and unaffordable for too many Americans.... Our courts are grossly overburdened ... and woefully underfunded.... The justice system is no longer a 'court of last resort' ... but is becoming an emergency room for every social trauma."[65]

There is widespread agreement that our justice system, on both the civil and the criminal side, is in recurring crisis. There is less agreement on what to do about it. The problems are complex, and the issues are political in the best sense of the word: each suggested reform—alternative dispute resolution, mandatory sentencing, or decriminalization, for instance—has costs and benefits. Change and reform are likely to come slowly, and perhaps this is as it should be, for our justice system has been created over the centuries, built on the accumulated wisdom of the past. How best to administer justice is a question likely to remain on our political agenda.

recidivist
A repeat offender.

privatization
Contracting public services to private organizations.

Summary

1. State and local courts are important forums for the making and carrying out of public policy. As they have become more active in political life, state judges have become embroiled in controversial issues, and the public has recognized their importance as policy makers. A new judicial federalism has emerged with state courts interpreting their state bills of rights more broadly than the U.S. Supreme Court applies the national Bill of Rights.

2. Each state has its own court system. Although the systems vary, they generally include minor courts of limited jurisdiction, trial courts of general jurisdiction, and appellate courts.

3. Judges are selected in four different ways: through appointment by the governor, election by the legislatures, popular election, or a merit system modeled along the lines of the modified appointment plan known as the Missouri Plan. Most legal reformers and political scientists appear to favor either the Missouri Plan or some merit selection system over judicial elections.

4. Judicial reforms are aimed at eliminating the waste and delay that plague courts. Among those suggested are alternative dispute resolution mechanisms, mandatory sentencing, and the decriminalization of some nonviolent crimes. Other reforms include merit systems that screen candidates for judgeships, higher pay and longer terms for judges to increase their judicial independence, rule-making powers for state supreme courts, and the appointment of judges more representative of the communities they serve.

5. Judges, together with jurors, prosecutors, defense counsel, public defenders, and correction officials, make up a loosely interrelated justice system. Many observers believe that this system is not properly dispensing justice to individual defendants or protecting the public from career criminals.

6. In recent years, more attention has been paid to the rights of victims at both the national and state levels, including amendments to state constitutions giving victims and their families the right to participate in the trial and providing for compensation to victims and their families.

7. There are more than 2 million persons in our prisons. Prisons are overcrowded. Imprisonment has been justified as retribution, deterrence, protection of society, and rehabilitation. Disillusionment with rehabilitation and the disparate sentencing by judges has led to the enactment of mandatory minimum sentencing requirements, including three-strikes-and-you're-out legislation.

Further Reading

STEPHEN J. ADLER, *The Jury: Trial and Error in the American Courtroom* (Times Books, 1994).

LAURENCE BAUM, *American Courts: Process and Policy,* 5th ed. (Houghton Mifflin, 2001).

MATTHEW BOSWORTH, *Courts as Catalysts: State Supreme Courts and Public School Finance Equity* (State University of New York Press, 2001).

DAVID COLE, *No Equal Justice: Race and Class in the American Criminal Justice System* (New Press, 1999).

GEORGE F. COLE AND **CHRISTOPHER E. SMITH,** *Criminal Justice in America,* 4th ed. (Wadsworth, 2004).

NORMAN J. FINKEL, *Commonsense Justice: Jurors' Notions of the Law* (Harvard University Press, 1995).

SUSAN P. FINO, *The Role of State Supreme Courts in the New Judicial Federalism* (Greenwood Press, 1987).

JULIA FIONDA, *Public Prosecutors and Discretion* (Oxford University Press, 1995).

JOHN B. GATES AND **CHARLES A. JOHNSON,** *The American Courts: A Critical Assessment* (CQ Press, 1991).

JOSEPH R. GRODIN, *In Pursuit of Justice: Reflections of a State Supreme Court Justice* (University of California Press, 1989).

DAVID HEILBRONE, *Rough Justice: Days and Nights of a Young D.A.* (Pantheon Books, 1990).

RANDOLPH JONAKAIT, *The American Jury System* (Yale University Press, 2003).

LAURA LANGER, *Judicial Review in State Supreme Courts: A Comparative Study* (State University of New York Press, 2002).

CHARLES LOPEMAN, *The Activist Advocate: Policymaking in State Supreme Courts* (Praeger, 1999).

MARILYN D. MCSHANE AND **FRANK P. WILLIAMS III,** EDS., *Encyclopedia of American Prisons* (Garland Press, 1996).

DANIEL JOHN MEADOR, *American Courts,* 2d ed. (West Publishing Co., 2000).

DAVID W. NEUBAUER, *America's Courts and Criminal Justice System,* 8th ed. (Wadsworth, 2004).

DAVID M. O'BRIEN, ED., *Judges on Judging: Views from the Bench* (CQ Press, 2004).

ELLIOT E. SLOTNICK, ED., *Judicial Politics: Readings from Judicature,* 3d ed. (American Judicature Society, 2005).

MICHAEL SOLIMINE AND **JAMES WALKER,** *Respecting State Courts: The Inevitability of Judicial Federalism* (Greenwood Press, 2000).

HARRY P. STUMPF AND **JOHN H. CULVER,** *The Politics of State Courts* (Longman, 1992).

G. ALAN TARR AND **MARY CORNELIA ALDIS PORTER,** *State Supreme Courts in State and Nation* (Yale University Press, 1988).

PAUL B. WICE, *Court Reform and Judicial Leadership* (Praeger, 1995).

See also *Judicature, The Journal of the American Judicature Society,* published bimonthly, and its Web site at www.ajs.org. The National Center for State Courts does not publish a regular journal but is an independent, nonprofit organization dedicated to the improvement of justice. Its materials can be obtained from its headquarters at 300 Newport Avenue, Williamsburg, Va. 23185; its home page is www.ncsconline.org.

Key Terms

writ of *habeas corpus,* p. 714

new judicial federalism, p. 714

tort law, p. 714

misdemeanor, p. 714

felony, p. 714

original jurisdiction, p. 715

judicial review, p. 716

advisory opinion, p. 717

Missouri Plan, p. 720

information affidavit, p. 725

indictment, p. 725

assigned counsel system, p. 725

pro bono, p. 725

public defender system, p. 725

plea bargain, p. 726

recidivist, p. 729

privatization, p. 729

Chapter 27

Local Governments and Metropolitics

★

LOCAL GOVERNMENT IS BIG, COSTLY, AND OVERLAPPING, AND IT AFFECTS EVERY ONE OF US EVERY DAY. COUNTIES, CITIES, SUBURBAN COMMUNITIES, SCHOOL DISTRICTS, TOWNSHIPS, METROPOLITAN PLANNING AGENCIES, WATER CONTROL DISTRICTS—ALL ARE CROWDED TOGETHER AND PILED ON TOP OF ONE ANOTHER. WE TYPICALLY LIVE UNDER SEVERAL LAYERS OF GOVERNMENT, PAY TAXES TO NEARLY ALL OF THEM, AND ALSO ELECT MOST OF THEIR LEADERS. THE COMPLEX AND FRAGMENTED ARRANGEMENTS OF METROPOLISES ALSO EXACERBATE

the ills of inner cities and limit the options for addressing urban problems. In short, "where we live has a powerful effect on the choices we have and our capacity to achieve a high quality life."[1]

Local governments in the United States employ about 11.7 million people in almost 88,000 different jurisdictions (see Table 27–1). Illinois has 6,903 units of local government, the largest number for any state, made up of 102 counties, 1,291 municipalities, 1,431 townships, 3,145 special districts, and 934 school districts. Hawaii has only 19 local government units: 3 counties, 1 municipality, and 15 special districts; all schools are run directly by the state.[2]

Why is there such a labyrinth of government in this country? The basic pattern was imported from England, as were many of our governmental forms. Over time, new governments were created to take on new jobs when existing units proved either too small or unequal to the task. Also, people kept moving into, or at least near, the large cities. The past three generations have seen millions of Americans moving from the cities to the suburbs, and a steady migration to urban and suburban areas continues from rural areas as well. Decades of compromise and struggle among conflicting groups have given us our present system. It creaks and groans. It costs a lot of money. People claim it is inefficient. But these local governments are democratically accountable and encourage experimentation in making public policy.

The Nature of State and Local Relations

Local governments vary in structure, size, power, and relation to one another. But in a *constitutional* sense, they all rely on power "borrowed" from the state. Most state constitutions create a **unitary system** in which power is vested in the *state* government, and local units exist only as agents of the state.[3] Local government is not mentioned in the U.S. Constitution. Local units exercise only those powers expressly given to them by their respective state governments. Most local units of government, unlike states, do not have constitutional status. State–local relations are generally unitary in nature, in contrast to the federal nature of nation–state relations.

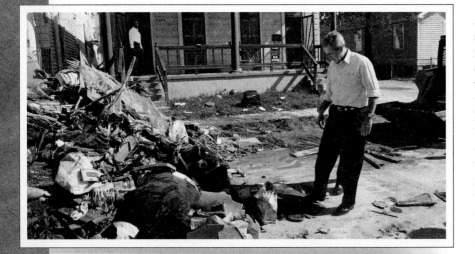

"*Where we live has a powerful effect on the choices we have and our capacity to achieve a high quality life.*"

DEIER, MOLLENKOPF, AND SWANSTROM,
PLACE MATTERS: METROPOLITICS FOR THE TWENTY-FIRST CENTURY

OUTLINE

733

TABLE 27–1 Growth of Governments in the United States

Type of Government	1972	1982	1992	2002
U.S. government	1	1	1	1
State governments	50	50	50	50
Local governments	78,218	81,780	84,955	87,525
County	3,044	3,041	3,043	3,034
Municipal	18,517	19,076	19,297	19,429
Township	16,991	16,734	16,656	16,504
School district	15,781	14,851	14,422	13,506
Special district	23,885	25,078	33,555	35,052
Total	**78,269**	**81,831**	**85,006**	**87,576**

SOURCE: U.S. Bureau of the Census, *Statistical Abstract of the United States: 2006*, available at www.census.gov/compendia/statab.

Because local governments are typically created by the state legislatures and usually have no constitutional authority in their own right, there are fewer obstacles to state interference in local matters than there are to national interference in state matters. State officers participate in local government to a much greater extent than federal officers do in state politics. When doubts arise about the authority of local governments, courts generally decide against them.

Initially, state legislatures had almost unlimited authority over their local governments and ran them pretty much at will. They granted, amended, and repealed city charters; established counties; determined city and county structure; set debt limits; and passed laws for the local units.

But by the end of the nineteenth century, voters amended or adopted state constitutions that curtailed the power of state legislatures. Many state constitutions forbade state legislatures from passing laws dealing with local governments, and constitutional provisions determined the structure, and in some cases even the process, of local governments.

Constitutional home rule granted constitutional independence to some local units, primarily larger cities, giving them constitutional authority over their form of government and a wide range of other matters. With the protection of constitutional home rule, state legislatures no longer determined the structure and powers of local units.

The extent of state control over local units today varies from state to state and also among the different kinds of local government within each state. At one extreme, local officials merely have to file reports with specified state officials. At the other extreme, state officials have the authority to appoint and remove some local officials, thus exerting considerable control over local affairs. When local governments prove ineffective, state officials may offer them financial assistance with certain strings attached or may even take over responsibilities previously handled locally. Pennsylvania, for instance, decided in 2002 to privatize 45 of the city of Philadelphia's worst-performing schools, the largest experiment yet in the privatization of public schools.[4] By contrast, after the September 11, 2001, terrorist attacks, governments took responsibility from private companies for screening airline passengers.

State officials are genuinely conscious of local problems. That is in part because problems once thought to be local have come to be viewed as involving the entire state, especially problems relating to law enforcement, the environment, finance, and welfare. This heightened concern is acknowledged by mayors and city managers, who regularly work with both state and federal officials. In recent years, the direct ties between national and local officials, especially in the larger urban areas—ties that used to ally them against state officials—have weakened as federal assistance has been

unitary system
Constitutional arrangement in which power is concentrated in a central government.

constitutional home rule
State constitutional authorization for local governments to conduct their own affairs.

cut back. Municipalities have also become more outspoken in opposing policies of the federal government. New York City and more than 390 other municipalities and counties, for instance, have enacted resolutions formally opposing the expanded investigatory powers granted to law enforcement agencies under the USA Patriot Act.[5]

Counties in the United States

Counties are the largest jurisdictions within a state. Yet they get a lot less attention from citizens and the media than do cities or school districts. There are three major types of counties: large urban ones, growing suburban ones, and more traditional rural ones. Urban and suburban counties have many of the same structures as their rural counterparts, but they are more intertwined with their urban centers. Some of the suburban counties are better known than any of the cities or municipalities within them: for example, Westchester County, New York; Montgomery County, Maryland; Marin and Orange Counties, California; and Bucks County, Pennsylvania. Some cities, such as Boston, Denver, Baltimore, Philadelphia, San Francisco, and Honolulu, are simultaneously cities and counties; New York City consists of five counties—New York, Kings, Queens, the Bronx, and Richmond.

States are divided into counties (in Louisiana they are called *parishes,* and in Alaska they are known as *boroughs*). With a few exceptions (such as Connecticut, Rhode Island, and much of Massachusetts, where counties have lost their governmental function), county governments exist everywhere in the United States. There are 3,034 of them, and they vary in size, population, and functions. Loving County, Texas, for example, has fewer than 70 inhabitants; Los Angeles County, California, has nearly 10 million. Besides Los Angeles County, the most populated counties are Cook County, Illinois; Harris County, Texas; Maricopa County, Arizona; and Orange County, California.[6] (Table 27–2 lists the 15 largest counties.)

Counties were originally organized on the idea that a county seat would be no more than a day's journey for anyone within the county's borders. Farm families could pile into their wagons and head for the county seat, and while farmers were attending to business, their families could shop and pick up the local gossip. Then they could all get home in time to do the evening chores. Today, of course, we can drive across a whole state or several states in a day.

The traditional functions of counties are law enforcement, highway construction and maintenance, tax collection and property assessment, recording of legal papers, and welfare. Until recently, counties were convenient subdivisions that largely carried out policies established elsewhere. Over the past generation, however, counties have taken on more tasks than they have lost. Counties in a few states have given up some of their responsibilities, but in most other states, especially in the South, they are taking over from the states such urban functions as transportation, water and sewer operation, and land use planning.[7] Elsewhere, cities are contracting with counties to provide such joint services as personnel training, law enforcement, and correctional facilities. County governments are least active in the New England states, where the county is often little more than a judicial and law-enforcement district; county officials do some road building but not much else.

County Government

Most counties have limited legislative power. The typical county has a central governing body, variously titled but most frequently called the *county commission* or *board of supervisors.* Most boards have from three to seven members, with a median size of six. Boards in very large counties can sometimes have several dozen members. They administer state laws, levy taxes, appropriate money, issue bonds, sign contracts on behalf of the county, and handle whatever jobs the state laws and constitution assign to them (see Figure 27–1).

TABLE 27–2 The 15 Largest U.S. Counties by Population

1. Los Angeles Co., Calif.
2. Cook Co., Ill.
3. Harris Co., Tex.
4. Maricopa Co., Ariz.
5. Orange Co., Calif.
6. San Diego Co., Calif.
7. Kings Co., N.Y.
8. Miami-Dade Co., Fla.
9. Dallas Co., Tex.
10. Queens Co., N.Y
11. Wayne Co., Mich.
12. San Bernardino Co., Calif.
13. Riverside Co., Calif.
14. King Co., Wash.
15. Broward Co., Fla.

SOURCE: U.S. Bureau of the Census, *2005 Population Estimates,* at http://factfinder .census.gov.

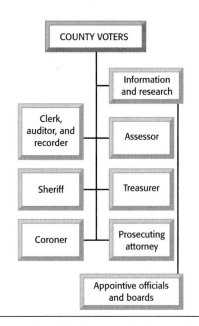

COUNTY VOTERS

FIGURE 27–1 **The Commission Form of County Government.**

Traditionally, many county boards were composed of the supervisors of townships or other township officials. Now, most of the boards in larger counties are elected from districts. The smaller boards are usually, though not always, elected in at-large elections. At-large elections make it difficult for minorities to be elected to office, especially when they are concentrated in a few areas. Minorities usually win more seats in a district election than in an at-large system.

The county board shares its powers with a number of other officials, most commonly the sheriff, the county prosecutor or district attorney, the county clerk, the coroner, and the auditor, who are generally elected rather than appointed. Sometimes county treasurers, health officers, and surveyors are also found on the ballot.

In general, counties are administered by an unwieldy collection of relatively independent agencies, and until recently, there was seldom a single executive responsible for coordinating such activities. However, today about 800 counties appoint a chief administrative officer who serves at the pleasure of the county commissioners. Approximately 400 counties now elect a *county executive* who is responsible for most administrative functions (see Figure 27–2).

County Performance

How well do counties perform? The picture is mixed. Counties can add to the fragmentation of authority and responsibility among a variety of elected officials, often producing needless jurisdictional conflicts, inefficiencies in purchasing, duplication of costs, and resistance to developing modern personnel systems.

Although counties have often been the forgotten government within the states, this is changing. Their jurisdictional boundaries give them great potential for solving complex problems that are difficult to address at the city level or have been decentralized to local levels of government by the states. The growing professionalization of county workforces and the trend of electing or appointing professional county executives are improving efficiency. "City-county functional consolidation in areas such as emergency medical services and natural-disaster planning is growing throughout the United States. . . . Increasing cooperation is likely to occur in the future as cities and counties struggle to provide more services to a tax-resistant public."[8]

Towns and Suburbs

Towns, also called townships, are the basic unit of government smaller than a county in 20 Northeastern and Midwestern states. The number of these towns has been declining slightly as they have been absorbed by growing municipalities (see Table 27–1). In most of the states that have towns, they are governed by elected officials including a supervisor, town board, clerk, and so on. However, in New England, the town meeting remains a celebrated institution. The New England town is sometimes pointed to as the one place in the United States where there is no elite and where participatory democracy really exists. The town meeting is our most obvious example of *direct democracy;* voters participate directly in making rules, passing new laws, levying taxes, and appropriating money. At least 1,000 New England towns, especially those with populations under 20,000, still hold annual town meetings. Maine has nearly 400 towns that use the town meeting system of democracy, and Vermont has about 200.

A group of active citizens that provides political and policy-making leadership usually dominates these town meetings. Also, officers elected at the town meeting perform most of the actual day-to-day governing of the town. Some New England towns have moved away from the town meeting process in recent years, and many of the large towns have adopted a modified *representative* town meeting, where 50 to 200 town residents are elected to represent their neighborhoods at the town meeting. Yet the open town meeting, at least in small towns in New England, still proves to be a vital way for people to participate in the policy making of their communities.

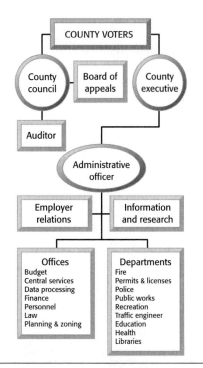

FIGURE 27–2 **The Council with Elected Executive Form of County Government.**

During the last half century, the areas around the cities have been the fastest-growing places in the United States (see Figure 27–3). At least 50 percent of Americans now live in suburban communities. Suburbs have grown up at the expense of cities for a variety of reasons: inexpensive land, lower taxes, cleaner air, more open space for recreational purposes, less crime, better highways, and the changing character of the inner cities. There is no one explanation for the exodus to the suburbs. In part, it was because people wanted to escape the deteriorating central cities. Resistance to mandatory busing to achieve integrated schools in the 1960s and 1970s also contributed to so-called white flight. But it was just as much a matter of class as of race, with middle- and upper-middle-income-level whites, Asians, and African Americans moving to the suburbs to escape urban crime and to seek more attractive environments in terms of class, religion, race, and lifestyle.[9]

In addition, suburbs have grown because industries have moved from the central cities in search of cheaper land, lower taxes, and less restrictive building and health codes. Other businesses followed the people and the industries, and a myriad of shopping centers grew in outlying communities. Much of this exodus was accelerated by federal policies promoting interstate highways and mortgages insured by the Federal Housing Administration. Most of the new jobs created in the United States continue to be located in the suburbs or newer cities on the fringes of the central cities.

The form of suburban government varies widely. Suburbs have grown in formerly rural townships, and in previously unincorporated areas of counties. Smaller municipalities located near larger central cities have also been swallowed up by the growth of suburbs and been absorbed by the larger metropolitan area composed of the central city and all of its suburban areas. The existing governments of these areas have had to adapt to the new, larger population and its different demands. The metropolitan areas around larger cities usually stretch across several counties and often into other states, presenting significant challenges when it comes to things like planning for land use and transportation.

The major tasks of suburban government are often bound together with those of the metropolis.[10] Larger cities usually maintain an elaborate police department with

The New England town meeting, like this one in Sandwich, New Hampshire, has long been a celebrated American institution.

Percentage of Americans Living in Suburbs and Central Cities at Each Census

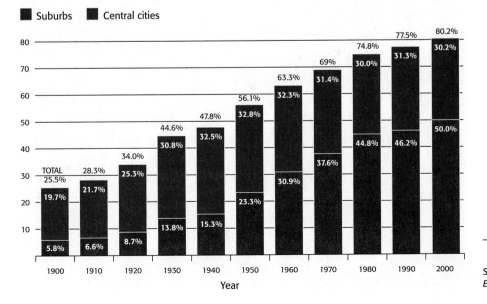

FIGURE **27–3 Moving to the Suburbs.**
SOURCE: U.S. Bureau of the Census, *Population Estimates* at http://factfinder.census.gov.

detective bureaus, crime detection laboratories, and communications networks, but its jurisdiction stops at the city line. Criminals, however, seldom stop at the city line. Suburbs have fewer police, and they are often untrained in criminology, so they call on urban police expertise. Highways, all of which have local access roads, also tie cities and suburbs together. In matters of health, too, there are often wide differences in services between city and suburb, but germs, pollution, and smog do not notice city signposts.

In Northeastern and Midwestern states, some of the larger suburban town governments have begun to resemble city governments, both in professionalization of the elected officials and bureaucracy, and in the services that the residents of the towns expect to receive. The town of Hempstead on Long Island in New York State, for instance, has a population of more than 750,000, and employs more than 2,000 people with a town budget of more than $370 million.

Older suburbs from Long Island to the San Francisco Bay Area are now experiencing some of the problems long associated with urban disinvestment and population decline. Some suburbs, too, are challenged by sprawling growth that creates crowded schools, traffic congestion, loss of open space, and a lack of affordable housing. Many people believe that there is a need for collaborative city–suburb strategies to address sprawl and the structural challenges facing older suburbs and inner cities. We will return to this topic later in this chapter.

The Rise of "Edge Cities"

In recent decades, cities have been built on the edges of metropolitan areas. Writer Joel Garreau calls these "edge cities" and suggests that virtually every expanding American city grows in the fashion of Los Angeles, with multiple urban cores.[11] Thus, we have Tysons Corner, Virginia, outside Washington, D.C.; the Perimeter Center at the northern tip of Atlanta's Beltway; the Galleria area west of downtown Houston; and the Schaumburg area northwest of Chicago.

Edge cities are defined as places with 5 million or more square feet of office space, 600,000 or more square feet of retail space, and more jobs than bedrooms. More often than not, these edge cities were empty spaces or farmland just 30 years ago. New freeways appeared first, then a shopping mall or two, and then industrial parks.

Some of the problems of the inner city have caught up with edge cities, just as they have with suburbs: traffic congestion, parking problems, crime, pollution, and urban blight. Political problems have cropped up as well. Most edge cities are in unincorpo-

Sixty miles outside Los Angeles, California, the town of Palmdale is in the midst of a housing construction boom as more people want to live near, but not in, the vast metropolis of L.A.

rated areas of counties and are subject in varying degrees to control by county governments. These edge cities are sometimes run by "shadow governments"—private owners who set the fees for policing, transportation, and various other services that are normally financed by taxes. There is not much room for government by the people in a community that is essentially a business.

City Government Today

What does the word "city" call to mind? Bright lights and crowded streets? A city is not merely improved real estate; it is also people—men and women living and working together. Aristotle observed that people came together in the cities for security, but they stayed there for the good life.

Different people define the "good life" differently, yet it often includes these attractions:

- Employment opportunities

- Cultural centers, museums, performing arts centers, theaters

- Diverse educational institutions

- Entertainment and nightlife

- Professional sports teams

- Wide variety of stores and specialty shops

- Good restaurants

- Diversity of people, architecture, and lifestyles

Although a few cities existed when the U.S. Constitution was written, the nation was overwhelmingly rural in 1787, and seven out of ten people worked on farms. People clustered mainly in the villages and small towns scattered throughout the 13 states and adjacent territories. The villages and towns were the indispensable workshops of democracy, the places where democratic skills were developed, where grand issues were debated, and above all, where the people resolved to fight the British to secure their fundamental rights.

The United States is now a nation of about 19,429 municipalities, and although some small cities or incorporated villages have just a few hundred people, the largest cities have millions. Three American supercities and their suburbs (New York, Los Angeles, and Chicago) each have populations larger than the total population of the Republic in the 1780s.

Every municipality has two major purposes. One is to provide government within its boundaries: to maintain law and order, keep streets clean, educate children, purify water, create and maintain parks, and make the area a good place in which to live.[12] As an instrument of the state, the city has a second major purpose: to carry out state functions.

A **charter** is to a city what a constitution is to a national or state government. It outlines the structure of the government, defines the authority of the various officials, and provides for their selection. Although charters are good sources of information on how the people in our cities are governed, they can be misleading. Different structures are not neutral in their impact, for different forms encourage different kinds of participation and responsiveness. In short, power and clout and who gets what, where, and how can definitely be shaped by a city's structural arrangements.

charter
City "constitution" that outlines the structure of city government, defines the authority of the various officials, and provides for their selection.

mayor-council charter
The oldest and most common form of city government, consisting of either a weak mayor and a city council or a strong mayor elected by voters and council.

The Mayor-Council Charter

The **mayor-council charter** is the oldest type of charter (see Figure 27–4). Under this type of charter, the city council is usually a single chamber. The size of the council

FIGURE 27–4 **The Mayor-Council Form of City Government.**

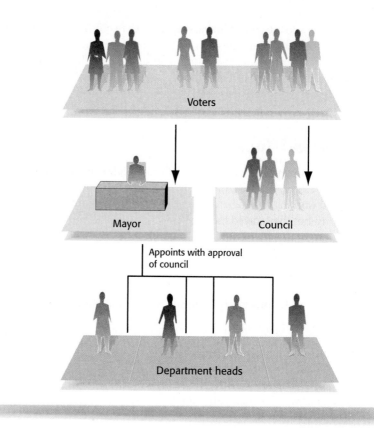

varies from as few as two members to as many as 50, though seven is the median size in cities with more than 5,000 people. Most small cities and municipalities use this type of charter. It is also still the most common type in the largest cities, and in medium-sized cities in the East and Midwest.

Many methods are used to select council members: nonpartisan and partisan elections, elections by large and small wards, or elections from the city at large. Large cities that elect members affiliated with political parties generally choose them by small districts or wards rather than at large. This arrangement tends to support strong party organizations. Nonpartisan at-large elections make party influence difficult. The larger the election districts, the more likely citywide considerations will affect the selection of council members, and the greater the influence of citywide institutions such as local newspapers.

The difference between at-large citywide elections and elections based on small, single-member districts within a city can be significant for racial and ethnic representation on the city council. The at-large system tends to produce councils made up of the city's elite and middle classes. The small district gives minorities and the less advantaged a somewhat better chance for representation where neighborhoods may have high concentrations of one minority.

The Voting Rights Act of 1965 forbids states and cities with a history of discrimination against minority voters from adopting the at-large system for electing council members if the effect would be to dilute the voting strength of these minorities. In fact, no local government in regions spelled out in this act can make a change in its voting system without the approval of the U.S. attorney general. But what of cities or counties that have long had at-large elections? Can they be forced to give them up because at-large elections virtually ensure that minorities will never be elected? The mere fact that no African American is elected under a certain system does not by itself constitute a violation of the Fourteenth or Fifteenth Amendment. The Supreme Court found that the Constitution forbids only practices adopted or maintained *with the intent to discriminate.*

When Congress debated the extension of the Voting Rights Act in 1982, civil rights advocates urged it to outlaw at-large systems. They contended that city officials are not so foolish as to admit that they want to keep minorities from being elected. Others argued that cities should be free to adopt whatever election system they wished; after all, the Constitution guarantees that no person will be denied the right to vote because of race, not that candidates of the voter's own race will win an election.

The Voting Rights Act as interpreted by the Supreme Court has made it easier to prove that at-large systems violate civil rights. Discriminatory intent need not be proved by direct evidence; it may be inferred if a city or county has a history of discrimination designed to keep minorities from voting, minorities make up a large majority of the population, and no member of a minority has ever been elected to office under an at-large system.[13]

Weak Mayor Councils and Strong Mayor Councils

The powers of the mayor-council form of government vary from charter to charter and even more widely from city to city and mayor to mayor. There are, however, two basic variations of the mayor-council form: the weak mayor council and the strong mayor council.

In cities with the **weak mayor-council form**, mayors are often chosen from members of the elected city council rather than elected directly by the people. The mayor's appointive powers are usually restricted, and the city council as a whole generally possesses both legislative and executive authority. The mayor must usually obtain the council's consent for all major decisions. Often weak mayor-council cities permit direct election by the voters of a number of department heads, such as police chief or controller. In weak mayor-council cities, there is no single administrative head for the city, and power is fragmented. The weak mayor-council plan was designed for an earlier era, when cities were smaller and government was simpler. It is ill-suited to large cities, where political and administrative leadership is vital.

Under the **strong mayor-council form**, the mayor is elected directly by the people and given fairly broad appointment powers. The mayor, often with the help of his or her staff, prepares and administers the budget, enjoys almost total administrative authority, and has the power to appoint and dismiss department heads. This system obviously calls for a mayor to be both a good political leader and an effective administrator—qualities not always found in the same person.

Many people believe the strong mayor-council system is the best form of government for large cities because it gives the cities strong political leaders and makes responsive administration possible. Further, by centering authority in the hands of a few individuals, it makes less likely the growth of "invisible government" by people who have power but are not publicly accountable for its use.

The Council-Manager Charter

Reformers in the early 1900s acclaimed the **council-manager plan** (also known as the *city-manager plan*), in which the city council hires a professional administrator to manage city affairs. It was indeed a significant governmental innovation. In 1908, the small city of Staunton, Virginia, appointed a general manager to oversee the city's work. Little note was taken of the step, but the council-manager plan soon became the darling of both reformers and the business elite. They liked the idea that the council would serve as a sort of "board of directors" in the business sense of setting broad policies, while a professional executive would see that these policies were carried out with businesslike efficiency (see Figure 27–5).

Under the council-manager charter, the council is usually elected in nonpartisan primaries and elections, either on a citywide basis or by election districts much larger than the wards in mayor-council cities. The council appoints a city manager and supervises the manager's activities. The council still makes the laws and approves the budget, and although it is not supposed to interfere in administration, the council often supervises city government through the manager. The mayor is expected to pre-

weak mayor-council form
Form of local government in which the members of the city council select the mayor, who then shares power with other elected or appointed boards and commissions.

strong mayor-council form
Form of local government in which the voters directly elect the city council and the mayor, who enjoys almost total administrative authority and appoints the department heads.

council-manager plan
Form of local government in which the city council hires a professional administrator to manage city affairs; also known as the *city-manager plan*.

FIGURE 27-5 The Council-Manager Form of City Government.

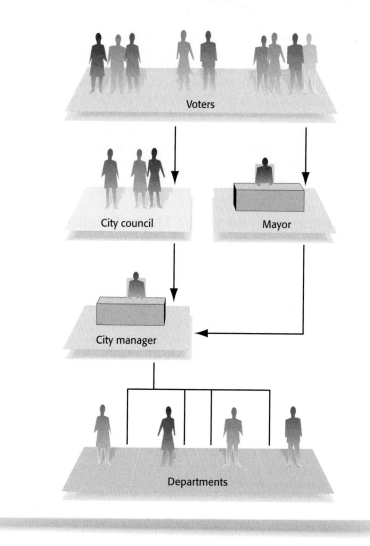

side over the council and represent the city on ceremonial occasions, but many mayors in fact do a good deal more than this. Contrary to what some textbooks imply, the mayor in council-manager cities can sometimes be a strong policy and political leader as well as a dominant influence in exercising political power.[14] This has surely been the case in cities as different as Cambridge, Massachusetts; San Antonio, Texas; and Colorado Springs, Colorado.

The city manager advises the council on policy and supervises the administration of city business. Because council-manager cities try to attract the best available persons, few of their charters require the councils to select managers from among local citizens, nor do they prescribe detailed qualifications. Although council-manager charters seem to call for a nonpolitical city manager who merely carries out policies adopted by the council and for council members who refrain from interfering with the administration of city affairs, it is often difficult to distinguish clearly between making and applying policy.

Today more than 3,100 cities, located in virtually every state, operate under a council-manager charter. In fact it has become the most popular form of local government in medium-sized cities of more than 10,000 citizens. It is especially popular in California, where about 98 percent of the cities use it, as well as in other western and Sun Belt cities. Some of the larger cities operating under a city manager are Dallas, San Antonio, San Jose, Kansas City, Cincinnati, Fresno, Colorado Springs, and Fort Worth.

How has the city-manager plan worked? In cities characterized by low social diversity and high consensus about community goals, the council-manager form has met

The Changing Face of American Politics

City Councils Are Becoming More Diverse

America's city councils are becoming more racially and ethnically diverse, with the number of people of color serving almost doubling in the last two decades, in all categories of cities (small, medium, and large), from 7 percent to 13 percent.

Over the last decade, Hispanic council membership has increased the most in medium cities, with populations of 70,000 to 199,999—jumping from 0 to 6 percent—and in large cities, with populations over 200,000, growing from 1 percent to 11 percent. During the same time, the percentage of Asian Americans declined from 3 percent to 1 percent.

The representation of women on city councils increased as well. The proportion of women grew from 21 percent to 25 percent in small cities, from 25 percent to 36 percent in medium-sized cities, and from 33 percent to 36 percent in large cities. ∎

Percentage of Council Members

Year	White	African American	Hispanic	Asian	Native American	Other
1979	92	5	1	–	–	–
1989	86	10	1	3	–	1
2001	87	8	3	1	1	1

SOURCE: National League of Cities, *Research Brief on America's Cities: The Faces of America's City Councils* (September 2003), available at www.nlc.org.

with success. Such cities have generally enjoyed improved standards of public employment, reduced costs, and better services. But some observers say this plan has also weakened political leadership in these cities and has confused citizens as to who really provides policy leadership.

In an effort to become more responsive, some council-manager cities have expanded the size of their councils and have abandoned at-large elections for district elections. More than 60 percent of the city-manager cities now also directly elect their mayors in an effort to provide greater political accountability and leadership.[15] Some cities, including Phoenix and San Diego, have recently moved from a council-manager form of government to a strong mayor form.

The Role of the Mayor

Two hundred years ago, the notion of a strong mayor providing vigorous leadership was nonexistent. The need for strong mayoral leadership developed in the late nineteenth century as a means to deal with the social revolution brought on by urbanization, massive waves of immigration, and mounting economic problems of growing cities. In the larger cities, gradually and often grudgingly, the office of mayor became a key position for political leadership.

The typical mayor is a college graduate, an experienced grassroots politician, a business or legal professional, and between 40 and 50 years old. Mayors in the largest cities earn $90,000 to $216,000 and in middle-sized cities between $40,000 and $80,000. City managers, chief city administrators, and top appointees sometimes make more than the mayors.

Although most mayors are male, several of the nation's largest cities have had female mayors, including Chicago, Pittsburgh, Houston, Dallas, San Diego, San Antonio, and Portland. In fact, about 17 percent of municipal governments in the United States with a population of 30,000 or more are headed by women, and the number is

Michael Bloomberg of New York City is one of the most well-known mayors in the country.

growing. Many of them worked their way up through service on school boards and city councils and in the League of Women Voters. An increasing number of African Americans also serve as mayors. More than 300 cities have had African American mayors, including Atlanta, Philadelphia, Denver, Detroit, Houston, San Francisco, Newark, Richmond, and Washington, D.C, as well as the three largest cities: New York, Chicago, and Los Angeles.

The main job of the mayor is administrative in the broadest sense of the term. Mayors supervise the line agencies—police, fire, public safety, traffic, health, sanitation—as well as a host of special agencies, such as the board of elections, the city planning agency, and commissions that regulate particular occupations and professions. Big-city mayors usually have staffs that carry out typical executive office functions such as personnel, management, budgeting, scheduling, and public relations. In this respect, mayors face the same tasks as corporate executives: coordinating a variety of activities, assigning responsibilities, checking that projects are carried out, finding the ablest people to take charge, and allocating money through control of the budget.

Usually mayors become involved with the private sector in an effort to promote economic opportunities. They try to secure additional jobs, increase the tax base, make the city more attractive to certain kinds of businesses, and coordinate public service expansion with private sector requirements. The private sector becomes involved in economic development because its success depends on having an educated labor base with appropriate skills, a constant consumer population, stable communities, and increasing property values.

Many mayors, such as those in New York, San Francisco, Seattle, Atlanta, Chicago, and Miami, have their own "foreign policies." That is, they play host to foreign dignitaries and business delegations and travel abroad seeking foreign investments as they sing the praises of local exportable goods.[16]

Sometimes a mayor must depend on the party organization to ensure support in the council, as in Chicago, where the huge city council consists of 50 members. Other mayors may have to deal with smaller councils, but they are likely to be weak unless they have enough political support to win cooperation.

Although partisan politics is waning as a feature of city government, mayors as party leaders still often dominate the party's city organizations. Mayors help recruit candidates for office, deal with revolts and opposition within their parties, and represent their parties in Washington or the state capitals. As chief legislators, mayors draw up proposed legislation and also make many specific policies. As chief fund-raisers, mayors bargain for more money for their cities before state and national legislatures. Mayors often climb the political ladder to run for governor, senator, or sometimes even president. For example, Ohio's former governor and now U.S. senator, George Voinovich, had previously been mayor of Cleveland, and former California governor Pete Wilson had been mayor of San Diego. U.S. Senator Richard Lugar of Indiana had been mayor of Indianapolis. Former mayor Rudolph Giuliani of New York City has been frequently mentioned as a possible candidate for president.

Mayors are expected to help revitalize the economy and attract investors, sports teams, tourists, and conventions. It takes courage and missionary zeal to overcome the pessimism and decay that beset most inner cities. But several recent mayors—including Rudolph Giuliani in New York City and both Richard J. Daley and his son Richard M. Daley in Chicago—succeeded in reducing crime, increasing economic opportunities, and revitalizing downtown businesses and residential areas.

In recent decades, mayors, like presidents and governors, have grown in power and importance. Most cities have altered their charters to give their mayors power to appoint and remove heads of departments, investigate departmental activities, send legislative messages to the city councils, prepare budgets, and veto council ordinances. In other words, mayors have been given a share in policy making, and city administration has been centralized under the mayor's direction.

History Makers

Harold Washington

Harold Washington was elected mayor of Chicago in 1983. He was not the first black mayor of a large city, but he won the election after a campaign that had become extremely racially polarized. Washington then went on to try to run a progressive, reform-minded administration in a city that had been one of the last and strongest bastions of corrupt politics.

Harold Washington began his political career as a regular Chicago Democrat in the era of longtime Mayor Richard J. Daley. He served for 15 years as a member of the Illinois legislature, and then was elected to Congress in 1980. There he achieved some notice for pressing for the renewal of the Voting Rights Act in 1981, and supporting the creation of a national holiday for Martin Luther King Jr. Meanwhile, black community leaders in Chicago were searching for a candidate for the 1983 elections. A voter registration drive had signed up about 180,000 new voters, expanding the registered black vote in the

city by 20 percent. Washington agreed to run, and managed to win in a three-way primary with incumbent Mayor Jane Byrne and Richard M. Daley, the son of the former mayor.

At this point, a significant segment of the Democratic party decided to support the Republican candidate, Barnard Epton, who had been seen as an insignificant candidate up to that point. This led to a very polarized outcome, with most blacks voting for Washington and more than 80 percent of whites voting for Epton. Washington's success with the growing Latino vote and with white progressives allowed him to achieve a narrow victory. The Democratic machine, led by chairman of the Cook County Democratic Party, Alderman Edward "Fast Eddie" Vrdolyak, continued to block Washington's agenda after the election. Only after court-ordered redistricting in 1986 was Washington able to get majority support on the council.

Harold Washington was re-elected in 1987 in a less polarized campaign, but died later

that same year. Since then many institutions in Chicago have been named or renamed for him, including a college, the main library building, and a cultural center.

For more on Harold Washington see: Alton Miller, *Harold Washington: The Mayor, The Man* (Bonus Books, 1989); and Pierre Clavel and Wim Wiewel, eds., *Harold Washington and the Neighborhoods: Progressive City Government in Chicago, 1983–1987* (Rutgers University Press, 1991). ■

Harold Washington

Washington . . . won the election after a campaign that had become extremely racially polarized.

Who Influences Local Policy Making?

Most Americans, most of the time, leave the responsibility of running the cities and counties to local officials and people willing to serve on boards and in local civic organizations. This does not mean that Americans rave about the quality of services received from local governments. Although they generally respond favorably to the services they get from city government and local public transportation agencies, they often rate them less favorably than they do the services provided by commercial organizations.

But if most people do not choose to be leaders in their communities, that does not mean they do not care about tax rates, the quality of schools in the community, and the availability of services. Hundreds of local people can be mobilized quickly if city hall mishandles local affairs or makes unpopular decisions. Indeed, activism has increased in recent years. It is now common for people to form groups to protect their communities from landfills, toxic dumps, shopping malls, and highways. With dogged perseverance and shoestring budgets, grassroots protest groups have often successfully taken on city hall or won victories for their neighborhoods in the courts.

A sure way to involve people in city government is to propose a policy that threatens the value or safety of the homes of middle- or upper-middle-class taxpayers. The slightest hint that a correctional facility, a freeway, a garbage dump, or a toxic disposal site is coming to their neighborhood will swiftly mobilize citizens who are otherwise happy to be passive spectators in local government. Similarly, the firing of a popular school principal, the closing of a neighborhood school, or a major increase in the property tax will produce a volley of citizen protests that can change the policy-making process at city hall.

Elected and appointed officials try to sense the mood of the local citizenry. They want to avert marches on city hall, recall elections, and citizen dissatisfaction. Their desire to be reelected and respected keeps them reasonably accountable.[17]

Interest Groups in Cities

The stakes and prizes in city politics are considerable: city jobs and commissioner posts, tax breaks, city contracts, regulations, licenses, and much more. Local politicians must deal with the kinds of interest groups found in any industrial society: organized workers, business leaders, neighborhood associations, professional associations, good government associations, homebuilders and developers, consumers, taxpayers, environmentalists, and various racial and ethnic groups.

The relative power and influence of these interest groups varies quite a bit from city to city. The most powerful groups in most cities are typically business groups. Employers provide the economic base for taxes and for jobs, and mayors know they will win or lose the next election based in large part on how well they promote the local economy.

Investors and businesses are free to locate wherever they please. Thus, they may move from a central city to a nearby suburb or from one city to another. City policy makers, therefore, must follow an "economic logic" that requires them to adopt policies that persuade businesses and investors to remain as participants in the local economy, either by keeping tax rates relatively low or by increasing the quality of service and amenities. If successful, this kind of growth politics enhances the prospects of city officials for reelection because economic growth, especially business investment, boosts the tax base and increases economic opportunities.[18]

But business groups have to share political power and influence with unions, environmentalists, ethnic groups, and many others. Most business officials learn that they can influence city political decision making by cultivating allies.[19] City politics generally involves informal alliances of public officials working together with private sector individuals and institutions.[20]

Police, firefighters, street cleaners, teachers, and other public employees are usually organized into unions, many of which are affiliated with national unions. Such unions are often a major influence in larger cities. They fight for improved pay, better working conditions, and job security. Although strikes by city employees providing vital services are prohibited by law in most states, enforcement is difficult. Teachers and municipal workers use the strike, or the threat of a strike, to force cities to increase wages and provide better benefits. Mayors complain that public employee unions are sometimes so powerful that they make the old-fashioned political machine look tame.

In addition, nonprofit groups such as the League of Women Voters, cultural foundations, local nonpartisan civic city clubs, independent local planning groups, and arts leagues exist in most urban areas, and they, too, want to be heard in the policy-making discussions of their cities.

Americans would like to believe that every citizen has a say in local government. Prominent families and local business leaders, however, often have more influence than the rest of us. Nursing home residents, the unemployed, migratory workers, young drifters, and the homeless are unlikely to have much influence. Participation in community affairs is often a middle-class and upper-middle-class practice. Low-income residents and the homeless are often ignored when mayors and business elites pursue aggressive economic development policies. "For renters and low-income residents, . . . a booming economy with rising land values may put affordable housing out of reach."[21] This is true in New York City as well as in places like Aspen, Colorado. There are costs as well as benefits to urban growth. Economic development can destroy neighborhoods and drive cities into debt.

The Central City and Its Politics

Today most Americans live in *metropolitan areas*, which include large cities and their suburbs, rather than in the small towns so beloved in American fact and fiction. A metropolitan area is, in the minds of most people, a big city and its suburbs. But the Census Bureau, which counts 280 metro areas, down from 284 in 1990, uses a more formal definition:

> A metro area is built around one or more central counties containing an urban area of at least 50,000 people. It also includes outlying counties with close ties—economic and social—to the central counties. To be considered part of the metro area, the outlying counties must meet certain criteria, including numbers of commuters, population density and growth, and urban population.[22]

About 80 percent of Americans (226 million) live in metropolitan areas, almost 55 percent live within 60 miles of a coastal shoreline (Atlantic, Pacific, Gulf of Mexico, Great Lakes, or St. Lawrence River), and 30 percent live in central cities. In the 1990s, the five fastest-growing metropolitan areas were in the South and the West: Las Vegas, Nevada; Naples, Florida; Yuma, Arizona; McAllen–Edinburg–Mission, Texas; and Austin–San Marcos, Texas.[23]

In the nineteenth century, masses of new immigrants arrived in the cities from Europe. In the twentieth century, migrants came from rural areas, especially from the South. More recently, this country experienced waves of newcomers from Cuba, Korea, Vietnam, the Philippines, Nicaragua, Haiti, Mexico, and other Latin American countries. Most newcomers settle first in the inner cities—usually in the poorest and most decayed sections—which inevitably puts great stress on the schools and sometimes on community safety as well. Overcrowding and substandard housing in these areas increases health and fire hazards.

The picture of central cities as composed exclusively of huddled, starving, homeless youth gangs and unemployed masses, however, is misleading. Nor is it fair to say simply that central cities have all the problems and suburbs have all the resources. Central cities do have more "high-cost citizens" (truly needy, handicapped, and senior citizens), and most aging cities have been losing population. They have lost businesses, too, because land, rents, utilities, and taxes are often less expensive in the outer suburbs, and businesses move to lower their operating costs. But their departure means that cities have smaller tax bases. Higher operating costs in the cities also result from aging public works.

The shrinking tax base has made it difficult for cities to raise sufficient revenue from sources like the property tax. However, the demand for services has not decreased. Many suburban dwellers commute into cities and use city services during the workday, but do not pay income taxes in the city. Most of the states have not permitted their cities to raise funds in any meaningful way with a local income tax, which means that cities cannot use the most direct method to make up the lost revenue.[24]

In an effort to recapture part of the tax base that escapes to the suburbs in the evenings, some cities have imposed local payroll or other types of *commuter taxes* to obtain revenue from people who work in the central cities and make frequent use of city facilities yet live in the suburbs. Some city officials say the payroll or commuter tax is an effective way to shift some of the burden to those who benefit from the city but live beyond its borders. But others say it is unlikely to provide significant long-term revenue growth, and they think it encourages even more businesses to leave the city.

Urban renewal has brought new life to the Inner Harbor in Baltimore, Maryland. Development and renewal projects such as this bring jobs and business to communities that were at one time ravaged by neglect and decay.

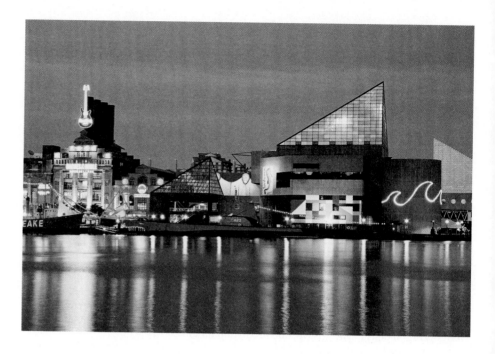

Recently, though, many of the once down-and-out central cities have shown signs of rejuvenation and gentrification. Cities such as Atlanta, Kansas City, and Newark, which were losing population a decade or two ago, are now gaining new residents. Gentrification and "yuppie" development have attracted some suburbanites to come back to central cities. The reasons for the rebound of many central cities varies from city to city, yet the sustained economic boom in the 1990s increased local tax revenues, which were then invested heavily in local infrastructure to make cities more appealing. The boom and investment in cities also helped create more jobs.[25]

However, there has also been a growing sentiment against trying to strengthen metropolitan structures and instead to move in the opposite direction. Perhaps the strongest movement in that direction is in Los Angeles, where there are serious attempts to have the San Fernando Valley withdraw from Los Angeles and create its own city. The issue is extremely controversial, especially among the large Hispanic population in the area, and even though the vote on secession failed in 2002, the matter will continue to be debated.

Meeting the Challenges of Growth and Economic Development

Until recently, almost everybody wanted to see his or her city grow. Everybody was a city booster. The local newspaper, television stations, radio stations, Chamber of Commerce, union leaders, business community, developers, teachers, and proud citizens worked together to attract new industries. Such industries would bring, they hoped, new jobs, more amenities, increased land values, and more opportunities for the young. The consensus was that a city with a growing population was a healthy one; one with a decreasing population was a sick one.

Local politicians found it risky to oppose economic development and economic growth; those who did feared that they would not be reelected. However, beginning two decades ago, an *antigrowth* movement developed in many cities. There had always been restraints in the wealthy suburbs outside of the central cities; in fact, many suburbs were created to escape the growth taking place in central cities. These suburbs adopted building and zoning codes and land use regulations to make it difficult, if not impossible, for industries to be located there and to keep out people who could not afford large houses on large lots. New suburbs were carefully planned to ensure that they would not become too crowded. These zoning regulations were attacked in the courts as strategies to keep the poor and minorities out, but as long as they were racially neutral on their face, the courts left them undisturbed.

In the last two decades, environmental awareness spread, and coalitions formed to fight unregulated growth. Disturbed by noise, pollution, and traffic jams and fearful that developers would build too many houses too close together and overload the infrastructure of roads, sewage disposal, and schools in the community, opponents of growth joined together.

Strategies to Govern Metro Regions

Divided executive authority, fragmented legislative power, splintered and noncompetitive political parties, the absence of strong central governments, and the necessity to bargain with national, state, and local officials—all these factors suggest that metro regions, where about 80 percent of Americans now live, are shapeless giants with nobody in charge. Metro regions, of course, encompass many cities, counties, towns, and suburbs, so they too are complicated and often splintered. The St. Louis metropolitan area, for instance, includes the city of St. Louis, 15 surrounding counties, 272 smaller cities, 107 townships, 136 school districts, and 411 special districts in two states.

At the turn of the twentieth century, reformers were afraid of domination by political bosses. But in the modern metropolis, political machines do not run the central city. Urban bureaucracies may wield a lot of power, but they do not offer metropolitan leadership. Special interests seldom really control the metropolis, nor does a business elite. Who, then, governs the metropolis? It's typically a "nobody's in charge" arrangement.

Growing fragmentation of government in large metropolitan areas has brought about a variety of reform movements and structural innovations aimed at improving efficiency, effectiveness, and performance. Political scientists and public administration specialists have never been bashful about proposing remedies. Here are the better-known ideas, all of which have been tried somewhere, yet none of which has been adopted nationwide.

ANNEXATION   In the South, West, and Southwest, large central cities have absorbed adjacent territories. Oklahoma City, for example, added almost 600 square miles. Houston; Phoenix; San Antonio; El Paso; Colorado Springs; and Kansas City, Missouri, also expanded their boundaries. The now-extended cities serve almost as regional governments.[26]

But annexation has not proved helpful to cities in the Northeast and Midwest because these cities are ringed by entrenched suburban communities that seldom want to be annexed, and state laws make it difficult for the central city to do so against the wishes of the suburbs. Even in such places as the Houston metropolitan area, the annexation option is plagued by legal obstacles and political jealousies.

AGREEMENTS TO FURNISH SERVICES   The most common solution to the problems of overlapping and duplicating jurisdictions is for the units of government to contract for services. This reform is applauded by many economists, who say it comes close to providing a market that operates according to laws of supply and demand. Most of these agreements involve a few cities sharing a single activity. For example, a city may provide hospital services to its neighbors or contract with the county for law enforcement. Especially popular in the Los Angeles area, the contract system is used with increasing success in many parts of the country.

PUBLIC AUTHORITIES   Public authorities such as the Port Authority in the New York City area or the Tennessee Valley Authority in the South were established to undertake specialized functions in their regions. They have a legal mandate granted to them by

This concept design shows what a new World Trade Center in New York might look like.

the state (or states) to raise money, hire experts, and take over some city services, such as transportation, water, and housing. The Port Authority of New York and New Jersey built the Twin Towers of the World Trade Center, which were destroyed by the terrorist attacks. It is now responsible for redeveloping the area and for overseeing the operation and security of the bridges and tunnels connecting New York and New Jersey. For more information, go to the Web site at www.panynj.gov.

Why public authorities? In part because state legislatures are sometimes hostile to mayors and prefer to place important functions outside the reach of mayors and political machines and in part because such authorities have financial flexibility (for example, they might be able to incur debt outside the limits imposed on the city by the state). But most important, many problems are simply too big or cover too wide a geographical area to be handled properly by a city or a group of cities.

Public authorities pose a special problem for mayors. Not only are many of the vital functions of metropolitan government removed from the mayors' direct control, but even worse, public authorities and special districts constantly come into conflict with local agencies dealing with the same problems in the city.

But if public authorities are a problem for mayors, they are also a temptation. By sponsoring these independent agencies, mayors can sometimes cut down on their administrative load. They can tap other sources of funds and keep city tax rates lower than they would otherwise be. If things go wrong, mayors can say they did not have authority over a certain function and hence cannot be held responsible.

SPECIAL DISTRICTS Special districts are units of government typically established to provide one or more specific services, such as sewage disposal, fire protection, water supply, or pollution control for a local or regional area. They are often created to enable an existing unit of government to evade tax and debt limits and to spread the tax burden over a wider area than individual municipalities or counties. Many smaller special districts are formed in suburban areas to obtain urban services without having to create a city government or be annexed by one.

Special districts usually have governing boards appointed by officials of other governments or elected by the general public. Special districts are useful for dealing with urgent problems that overlap boundaries of existing governmental units. Many urban and regional problems defy city and county boundaries, and special districts offer economies of scale that make sense. But critics charge that the rapid increase in the number of special districts over the last 30 years has prevented comprehensive planning. They also lament that few citizens know who runs these special districts, and even fewer know how these officials make decisions.

REGIONAL COORDINATING AND PLANNING COUNCILS   Almost all metro regions have some kind of *council of government* (COG). COGs began in the 1950s and were encouraged by the national government. Congress, in fact, mandated that certain federal grants be reviewed by regional planning groups. In essence, these councils bring locally elected officials together. They devote most of their time and resources to physical planning; rarely do they tackle problems of race, poverty, and financial inequities in metro regions. Councils are set up, moreover, in such a way as to give suburbs a veto over virtually any project that would threaten their autonomy. In a few regions, the councils assume operating responsibilities over such regional activities as garbage collection, transportation, and water supply. Critics say these councils rarely provide for creative areawide governance, yet they serve as an important common ground for elected officials to talk about mutual problems, and they help solve some problems in many of the regions.

CITY-COUNTY CONSOLIDATIONS   One traditional means of overcoming the fragmentation of metro regions is to merge the city with the county. This is a pet reform of business elites, the League of Women Voters, and Chambers of Commerce. It is viewed as a rational, efficient way to simplify administration, cut costs for taxpayers, and eliminate duplication.

More than 30 city-county mergers have taken place. In addition, one city occasionally joins with another, as Sacramento and North Sacramento did in the 1960s. Such mergers can usually be brought about only by a referendum approved by the citizens of the region. Most of the successful consolidations have take place in smaller urban areas. Indianapolis, Jacksonville, and Nashville are some of the larger consolidations that have occurred in recent decades. One recent successful regional merger is the 2000 consolidation of the City of Louisville and Jefferson County, Kentucky.[27]

The experience of Indianapolis is typical of these consolidations, most of which are in the South and West. In 1970, Indianapolis combined with Marion County to create UNIGOV. This merger required special permission from the legislature. UNIGOV provides many services, but the school systems remain separate, as do the police and sheriff departments.

Many proposed mergers have been rejected by county voters. But it is no longer unusual to find counties running what used to be city jails, zoos, libraries, and similar services. Formal and informal agreements abound as cities and counties remedy overlap and fragmentation by shifting responsibilities for providing specific services among themselves.

FEDERATED GOVERNMENT   This strategy attempts to take political realities into account by building on existing governments but assigning some crucial functions to an areawide metro government.[28] One of the few attempts—and there have been only a few—to create a federated government is the Twin Cities Metropolitan Council for the Minneapolis–St. Paul region. This regional organization, established by the legislature in 1967, consists of a 17-member council. Sixteen members are appointed by the governor to represent equal-population districts, and the seventeenth is a full-time executive who serves at the pleasure of the governor.

Today the Metropolitan Council, in essence a new layer of government superimposed on top of existing units, serves as a metropolitan planning and policy-making as well as policy-coordinating agency. It reviews applications for federal funds from the region. It guides regional planning and development and opposes local actions that would endanger the overall welfare of the region. It also has taxing authority for the region. The Twin Cities model appears to be a ready candidate for transfer elsewhere, yet this has happened only in Portland, Oregon.

Portland adopted a bold new charter for the Portland Metropolitan Services District. It is a directly elected regional government serving three counties and 24 cities. Its nonpartisan commission members and elected executive officer have an impressive budget and more than 1,200 employees. They oversee waste collection, a zoo, recycling, waste disposal, transportation planning, and regional air and water quality programs, and they constructed Portland's new Convention Center. They have also created a greenbelt around the metro area that preserves extensive open areas.

COMMUNITY SELF-HELP   The problems of governing urban and metro regions have also been addressed by community self-help organizations. Countless people are coming together in their own neighborhoods to tackle common problems or to form neighborhood cooperatives. Some of these self-help groups simply handle baby-sitting arrangements or organize charity events or golf tournaments; others are involved in neighborhood crime watches or Little League field construction. Local nonprofit groups in New York have built award-winning apartment complexes amid burned-out inner-city tenements. Other groups have mobilized to bring about storefront revitalization, street improvement, and area beautification programs by initiating farmers' markets, miniparks, and gardens.[29]

The contemporary self-help movement is rooted in an American past that has long been marked by volunteerism and local associations. In former times, the whole community often rallied when a neighbor's barn burned down; volunteer fire departments emerged out of this tradition. But as the nation has become more mobile and impersonal, we have drifted away from these traditions. Today, most Americans shop at shopping malls rather than on Main Street or in the old downtown area. At the same time, they resent the fact that public institutions have become remote and overly professionalized. Thus people across the country are joining together to do in an informal and decentralized way what extended families or small villages of the past used to do. Simply, they come together to lend a hand.

Many local groups seeking help from city hall or from county officialdom give up after running into a maze of building codes, zoning rules, and countless regulations that inhibit innovation in local government. The alternative to despair is to do it yourself. And this is exactly what is happening at the grassroots level right now. The more successful experiments are watched carefully by the professionals at city hall, and some of the innovations are copied by those in office.

Sometimes progress or justice comes about because some activists take issues to court. Such was the case in bringing in alternative housing for lower-income residents in Mount Laurel, New Jersey. And it was also the case in addressing the fatal effects of toxic dumping by businesses in Woburn, Massachusetts.[30]

Eminent Domain

Since the founding of the United States, governments have had the power to take private land for public purposes, even without the consent of the landowner. The power, called *eminent domain*, comes from English common law. In most cases state and local governments have tempered this power by recognizing a right to just compensation for the landowner, usually paying the market rate for the land. Normally this power has been used in cases of clear public need, for instance the construction of a road or bridge.

This power has recently become the source of some controversy. The city of New London, Connecticut, wished to redevelop an older residential neighborhood, and when some of the homeowners refused to sell, it used the power of eminent domain. The homeowners then sued the city, claiming that this redevelopment, which would have turned over the land to a private development company to build commercial and residential properties, was not lawful. The case was eventually appealed to the U.S. Supreme Court, which found that New London's redevelopment plan did constitute a public use for the land, and therefore the city was justified in using eminent domain to take the land.[31]

The Politics of Metropolitan Reorganization

In most metropolitan regions, to combine city and suburbs would be to shift political power to the suburbs. In most northern centers, this would give suburban Republicans more control of city affairs. In other cases, it would enable Democrats to threaten the one-party Republican systems in the suburbs. Under these circumstances, neither Democratic leaders in the central cities nor Republicans in the suburbs show much enthusiasm for metropolitan schemes. African Americans and Hispanics often oppose area consolidation or similar reform proposals that would invariably dilute their political power, often severely.

Some people believe that solutions to metropolitan problems are beyond the capacity of the metropolis itself. They favor a strengthened role for the national government, with special emphasis on ensuring "equity" or on relating services directly to needs. Some advocate reviving federal revenue sharing. Others believe that the job must be done by the states, which hold the fundamental constitutional power. Still others put forward bold proposals to establish regional planning and governance arrangements that would embrace "citistate" areas that include two or more metropolitan clusters, like Baltimore and Washington, D.C.[32]

Today's aging central cities unquestionably face problems: congestion, smog, tension, loss of community, drugs, unsafe streets, neglected children, and visual pollution. They live with racial and ethnic tensions, not just white–black rivalry but rivalry among Latinos, Koreans, and a host of other racial and ethnic groups. Gangs, poverty, broken families, drive-by shootings, and drug-related crimes make life miserable for many who live in the inner cities. Yet is this new? Writers and critics since Thomas Jefferson have projected an unflattering image of the city as a cold, impersonal, and often brutal environment in which crime flourishes and people lose their dignity.

Supporters contend, however, that the big city is not just a place of smog and sprawl; it is the center of innovation, excitement, and vitality. In the last couple of decades, many major cities, including Boston, New York, and Washington, have promoted the redevelopment of run-down areas. In this view, the city offers social diversity and puts less community pressure on the individual to conform. The large community is a meeting place for talent from all over the nation and the world: dancers, musicians, writers, scholars, actors, and business leaders. On the other hand, some critics have charged that redevelopment is *gentrification*, with the original lower-income

The historic Faneuil Hall Marketplace in Boston is an example of how a community can revive a declining urban area into a vibrant community landmark.

inhabitants displaced by the new wealthier residents. The displaced poor then just concentrate even more in other blighted neighborhoods.

Some observers dismiss the notion of an "urban crisis." They contend that most city dwellers live more comfortably than ever before, with more and better housing, schools, and transportation. By any conceivable measure of material welfare, the present generation of urban Americans is better off than other large groups of people anywhere at any time. Most cities, especially in the West and South, are thriving, and older cities such as Boston, Pittsburgh, and Indianapolis are generally viewed as revived and vital, not decaying.

Throughout history, cities have been threatened by political, social, and environmental catastrophes. Urban decay, in one form or another, has always been with us.[33] Cities thrive because over time they respond to crises and because they are an economic necessity. The economy, transportation systems, past investments, and cultural contributions all make cities inevitable. How well cities survive, and with what mix of people, will depend on the tides of the national economy, the way our regions are organized, the way our social and economic policies are designed, the vision and leadership individual cities muster to build their future, and the degree to which our national leaders promote policies that can help our central cities.[34]

Summary

1. Local government is big, costly, and overlapping. Local governments in the United States come in a variety of shapes and structures and perform various functions. However, since constitutional power is vested in the states, most counties, cities, towns, and special districts are agents of the state.

2. The most common governmental form at the county level is a board of county commissioners, although larger urban counties are moving to council-administrator or council-elected executive plans.

3. There is no typical suburb. Although many suburbs are homogeneous, the suburban United States is highly heterogeneous. Suburbs are confronting the same problems as the urban areas they surround. In fact, big cities and their suburbs are now referred to as metropolitan areas and are growing fastest in the South and West.

4. The most common governmental forms at the city level are the mayor-council and the council-manager (city-manager) plans. Mayor-council governments generally have a strong mayor elected by voters, though some plans have a weak mayor elected by the council. Council-manager plans appoint a professional administrator. In general, council-manager plans are found in medium-sized to large cities and in cities in the West, especially in the Sun Belt. Mayors and managers are key political leaders.

5. Although local governments are run by officials, business interests and interest group activism also influence policy.

6. The standard of living in the central cities of the United States may be much better than it was 50 years ago, but the inequalities between many central cities and their middle and outer rings of affluent suburbs are increasing. Central cities often struggle with economic hardships, racism, and drug-related gangs and criminals. Fragmentation and dis-

persal of political authority in the metropolitan areas and even in many of the central cities themselves often make it difficult not only to govern the big cities but also to respond with adequate policies and funds to treat the problems of the metropolis.

7. Cities, suburbs, and metro areas all face problems related to growth, uneven tax bases, environmental concerns, and fragmented authority. A variety of strategies have been used in an effort to solve these problems—annexation, agreements to furnish services, public authorities, special districts, regional coordinating and planning councils, city–county consolidations, federated government, and community self-help programs. Almost all of the strategies for meeting the challenges of growth and economic development involve shifts in political power.

Further Reading

BARBARA ACKERMANN, *"You the Mayor?" The Education of a City Politician* (Auburn House, 1989).

ROGER BILES, *Richard J. Daley: Politics, Race, and the Governing of Chicago* (Northern Illinois University Press, 1996).

BUZZ BISSINGER, *A Prayer for the City* (Random House, 1997).

MICHAEL BRIAND, *Practiced Politics: Five Principles for a Community That Works* (University of Illinois Press, 1999).

FRANK M. BYRAN, *Real Democracy: The New England Town Meeting and How It Works* (Cambridge University Press, 2004).

PETER DREIER, JOHN MOLLENKOPF, AND **TODD SWANSTROM,** *Place Matters: Metropolitics for the Twenty-first Century* (University Press of Kansas, 2001).

ALAN EHRENHALT, *The Lost City: Discovering the Forgotten Virtues of Community in the Chicago of the 1950s* (Basic Books, 1995).

JOEL GARREAU, *Edge City: Life on the New Frontier* (Doubleday, 1991).

STEPHEN GOLDSMITH, *The Twenty-First Century City: Resurrecting Urban America* (University Press of America, 1999).

DENNIS R. JUDD AND **TODD SWANSTROM,** *City Politics: Private Power and Public Policy,* 5th ed. (Longman, 2006).

DAVID L. KIRP ET AL., *Our Town: Race, Housing, and the Soul of Suburbia* (Rutgers University Press, 1997).

SUZANNE M. LELAND AND **KURT THURMAIER,** EDS., *Case Studies of City-County Consolidation* (M. E. Sharpe, 2004).

PAUL G. LEWIS, *Shaping Suburbia: How Political Institutions Organize Urban Development* (University of Pittsburgh Press, 1996).

DONALD C. MENZEL, ED., *The American County: Frontiers of Knowledge* (University of Alabama Press, 1996).

JOHN O. NORQUEST, *The Wealth of Cities: Revitalizing the Centers of American Life* (Addison-Wesley, 1998).

MYRON ORFIELD, *Metropolitics: A Regional Agenda for Community and Stability* (Brookings Institution Press, 1997).

DAVID RUSK, *Inside Game/Outside Game: Winning Strategies for Saving Urban America* (Brookings Institution Press, 1999).

MICHAEL H. SHUMAN, *Going Local: Creating Self-Reliant Communities in a Global Age* (Routledge, 2000).

DICK SIMPSON, *Inside Urban Politics: Voices from America's Cities and Suburbs* (Longman, 2004).

CLARENCE N. STONE, *Regime Politics: Governing Atlanta, 1946–1988* (University Press of Kansas, 1989).

JON C. TEAFORD, *Post-Suburbia: Government and Politics in the Edge Cities* (Johns Hopkins University Press, 1996).

HEATHER ANN THOMPSON, *Whose Detroit? Politics, Labor, and Race in a Modern American City* (Cornell University Press, 2002).

ROGER VOGEL AND **JOHN J. HARRIGAN,** *Political Change in the Metropolis,* 8th ed. (Longman, 2007).

ROBERT J. WASTE, *Independent Cities: Rethinking U.S. Urban Policy* (Oxford University Press, 1998).

WILLIAM JULIUS WILSON, *When Work Disappears: The World of the New Urban Poor* (Harvard University Press, 1996).

See also *Governing: The Magazine of States and Localities*, published monthly by Congressional Quarterly, Inc.; *The National Civic Review*, published by the National Civic League; *The Municipal Yearbook*, published annually by the International City Management Association; and the Web site of the U.S. Conference of Mayors at www.usmayors.org/uscm/home.asp.

KeyTerms

unitary system, p. 734

constitutional home rule, p. 734

charter, p. 739

mayor-council charter, p. 739

weak mayor-council form, p. 741

strong mayor-council form, p. 741

council-manager plan, p. 741

Chapter 28

Making State and Local Policy

⭐

STATE AND LOCAL OFFICIALS CONSTANTLY WRESTLE WITH POLICY DECISIONS AND CONTROVERSIES. WHAT IS THE BEST WAY TO ATTRACT BUSINESS AND INCREASE THE NUMBER OF JOBS YET ENCOURAGE ENVIRONMENTAL QUALITY? HOW SHOULD THE STATE DEAL WITH THE SOARING COSTS OF PROVIDING MEDICAID? WHAT CAN BE DONE ABOUT FRUS-TRATING PEAK-HOUR GRIDLOCK ON THE HIGHWAYS? SHOULD A COMMUNITY CLOSE ONE OF ITS HOSPITALS? WILL VOTERS APPROVE A BOND ISSUE TO CONSTRUCT A NEEDED NEW HIGH

school? Should states approve or ban marriage licensing or civil unions for same-sex couples? And what role should the states play in helping to reduce CO_2 emissions that are increasing global warming? State and local authorities also puzzle about how much they can do about terrorism threats.

Mayors, governors, state legislators, county commissioners, judges, union officials, developers, Chambers of Commerce, political party leaders, and many others strive to come up with public policy compromises to such dilemmas. These deliberations receive little media attention compared with the attention paid to decisions made in Washington, D.C., yet the effect of these choices on our day-to-day lives is often equally or perhaps even more important.

This chapter will examine some of the policy areas that consume much of the attention of state and local officials and the budgets of state and local governments. State and local governments spend most of their budgets on education, on welfare and health-related matters, on highway and transportation systems, and on safety and law enforcement. We will discuss them as well as the issues of planning and regulation.

Public Education

In ancient Greece, Plato and Aristotle saw education as a vital task of government. Thomas Jefferson, too, was convinced that an educated citizenry was essential to democratic government. But only in the twentieth century did the idea that government should provide tax-supported education for everyone become generally accepted.

For a long time, many people opposed "free" education. They feared it would lead to social unrest, undermine the family, give government control over the minds of the young, require huge bureaucracies, and result in a fatal mixture of education and politics. And was it fair, they asked, to make people who could afford to educate their own children in private schools pay taxes to educate other people's children? Despite these objections, today free public education for grades 1 through 12 is an established practice in the United States.

Education is now the number one policy priority for most states. State and local governments have the primary responsibility for education and provide most of the money to pay for it. Federal funding for education has been limited, never exceeding 10 percent of total spending on K–12 education. However, this small contribution has not deterred

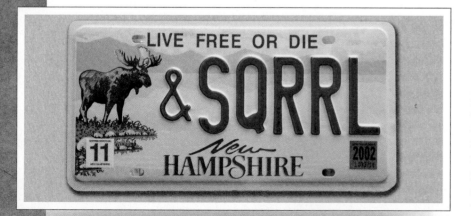

FREEWAY CONDITION
REDUCE POLLUTION CARPOOL

"The one thing you will always see on an economic development trip to Tokyo is another governor."

FORMER UTAH GOVERNOR NORMAN BANGERTER

OUTLINE

★

Public Education

★

Higher Education

★

Social Services

★

Law Enforcement

★

Planning the Urban Community

★

Regulation

★

The Importance of State and Local Policy

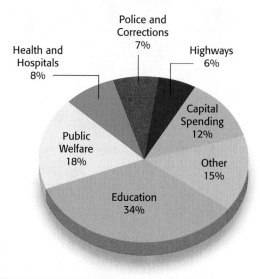

FIGURE 28–1 **State and Local Government Expenditures, 2004.**

SOURCE: U.S. Census Bureau, Governments Division, "State and Local Government Finances by Level of Government and by State: 2003–04," at www.census.gov/govs/estimate/0400ussl_1.html.

the federal government from pushing federal goals for education. An excellent example of this was the George W. Bush–sponsored No Child Left Behind Act of 2001, a reauthorization of an earlier law that required greater school district accountability, more testing, and increased emphasis on reading, especially for younger children. One of the most controversial educational reforms in decades, this national legislation used a combination of national standards and comprehensive testing to measure students' progress. If too many children in a public school fail to meet the desired standards, then parents have the right to move their children elsewhere. Yet many state and local officials have argued that the federal government has not adequately funded efforts to meet the new standards, and one state, Utah, even chose to opt out of the program.

Approximately one-third of all state and local government expenditures are for education—more than for any other function of government (see Figure 28–1). The federal government's contribution to education is fairly constant across states, but since 1979, overall state funding has surpassed that of local governments, with the exception of a few states in which revenues for education continue to come primarily from local government. The state role in financing education has increased over the last generation as a result, at least in part, of pressure from the courts to equalize expenditures on education across local school districts. There is also wide variation between states in the total amount of state and local spending per student, from a high of more than $12,000 in New Jersey to a low of under $5,000 in Utah, with an average of just over $8,000.[1]

Administration

Unlike most other democracies, which typically administer and fund education at the national level, the basic unit responsible for public elementary and secondary education in the United States is the local school district, and there are more than 14,000 of them. In almost all districts, voters elect a board of education that sets the school tax rate, appoints a superintendent of schools and other personnel, hires teachers, and runs the schools from kindergarten or grade 1 through grade 12. Each state has a state superintendent of public instruction or commissioner of education. In about a third of the states, this official is popularly elected; in almost all states, he or she shares authority with a state board of education.

Although actual operation of the public schools is the responsibility of the local community, state officers have important supervisory powers and distribute financial assistance to the communities. State money is distributed according to many formulas, but as noted, the trend is toward giving more money to poorer communities to equalize education spending. Many policies are established at the state level, and it is up to local authorities to enforce them. Local authorities must ensure that new school buildings meet the minimum specifications set by the state. In some states, officials have the authority to set the course of study in schools—that is, to determine what must be taught and what may not be taught. In several states, especially in the South and Southwest, state authorities determine which textbooks will be used as well.

The Role of the Federal Government

After the former Soviet Union's successful launch of *Sputnik,* the first satellite put into orbit, in 1957, Congress responded by increasing federal funding for education to strengthen math and science education. The federal government's share in financing local education rose from about 2 percent in 1940 to about 9 percent in 1980. The federal share of funding then declined to about 6 percent by the end of the 1980s and trended up again to more than 8 percent by 2003.

Through the Department of Education, created in 1979, and other agencies, the federal government makes grants to the states for facilities, equipment, scholarships, loans, research, model programs, and general aid at the elementary, secondary, and higher education levels. But federal control over how the money may be spent comes

The Changing Face of American Politics

Teachers in the Classroom

Lessons on diversity often start in the classroom with the number of minority and women teachers who work in the public schools. To the extent young Americans see the changing face of teaching, they may be more likely to embrace the changing face of diversity in the American economy more generally.

The changing face of America has not yet had a major impact on the gender of public school teachers, however. According to the most currently available statistics from the U.S. Census Bureau, the percentage of women in the classroom has increased somewhat over the past twenty years in both ele-

mentary, and junior- and senior-high schools.

The large percentage of women in the classroom dates back to the first public schools, but also reflects the lack of interest in teaching among men. Salaries for teachers are lower than comparable jobs elsewhere in the U.S. economy, in part because public schools are often a target for local budget cuts, and in part because women are generally underpaid regardless of their profession.

Minorities have made slightly more progress in becoming public school teachers, in part because colleges and universities are working harder to recruit minorities to the profession

and because public schools are under greater pressure to increase teacher diversity. Although the percentage of minority teachers has risen only slightly over the past two decades, the trend appears to be toward greater representation, especially in junior- and senior-high schools.

Although the U.S. Census Bureau has not followed the percentage of women and minority teachers in private schools as closely, its 2000 figures suggest no difference between the percentage of women teachers in public and private schools, but a significantly lower percentage of minority teachers. ■

Demographic Characteristics of Full-Time Public School Teachers, 2004–2005	
Men	26%
Women	74
White	84
African American	8
Other	2

SOURCE: U.S. Census Bureau, http://www.census.gov/compendia/statab/education/educ.pdf

with these federal dollars. Today federal regulations cover school lunch programs, employment practices, admissions, record keeping, care of experimental animals, and many other matters. Indeed, local school authorities regularly complain that there are more regulations than dollars.

Educational Issues

What shall be taught and who shall teach it are hotly contested matters. Schools are favorite targets for groups eager to have children taught the "right" things. Of course, little agreement exists on what the "right" things are. Religious groups want family values and morality emphasized, and some want constraints imposed on the teaching of evolution. Others want the schools to teach facts only, without regard for values, especially in areas like sex education. Labor leaders want students to get the right impression about labor and its role in society. Business leaders are eager for children to see the free enterprise system in a favorable light and want high school graduates who will be well prepared for increasingly technical jobs. Minorities and women's groups want textbooks to present issues from the perspective they consider correct. Professional educators and civil libertarians try to isolate schools from the pressures of all outside groups—or at least the ones with which they disagree. They say decisions regarding what textbooks should be assigned, what books should be placed in school libraries, and how curricula should be designed are best left to professionals.

It has long been an American tradition that education should be kept free from partisan political influences. The separation of schools from politics is strongly supported. Local school boards are usually nonpartisan and are often elected when no partisan races are on the ballot. Elaborate attempts have been made to isolate educational agencies from the rest of government. This separation is strongly supported by parent–teacher associations, the National Education Association, the American Federation of Teachers, and other educational groups. Most citizens also believe education should be kept out of the hands of mayors and city councils. However, education is of such concern to so many people, and there are so many different ideas about how schools should be run, that it cannot be divorced from politics.

PUBLIC SCHOOL INTEGRATION   During the 1970s and 1980s, battles were fought in many cities over how to overcome racial segregation in the public schools. In many places people lived in segregated neighborhoods, which meant that eliminating overt segregation at neighborhood-centered schools would not produce racially diverse schools. One method, which became contentious, was to bus students from one neighborhood to another to achieve racial balance in the schools and overcome the effects of past segregation. However, as more middle-class families—many of whom were white—moved out of the cities and into the suburbs, busing became an ineffective tool to achieve integration, since the courts declined in most cases to require states to integrate cities and suburbs. Racial segregation is still the pattern for the inner-city schools of most large cities in parts of the North, South, and West. Indeed, over the last 15 years there has been a substantial slippage toward segregation in most of the states that had experienced solid desegregation.[2]

EDUCATIONAL REFORM   Over the past two decades, a series of reports on education helped focus national attention on educational reform.[3] A 1990 meeting between President George H. W. Bush and many of the nation's governors laid the foundation for the Goals 2000: Educate America Act, which sought to achieve many of the goals identified as important since the 1960s. With the aid of federal money, states were encouraged to set educational standards in order to achieve a number of goals, including these:

■ All children will start school ready to learn.

■ The high school graduation rate will be at least 90 percent.

■ Students will have mastered a challenging curriculum by grades 4, 8, and 12.

■ Teachers will have access to professional development opportunities.

■ U.S. students will rank first in the world in science and math achievement.

■ All adults will be literate.

■ Schools will be free of drugs, violence, and firearms.

■ Every school will promote parental involvement in education.[4]

Several states initially objected to Washington's setting goals and standards for public education, which had traditionally been a local function. Further, some observers thought it unfair to "hold students to nationwide standards if they have not had the equal opportunity to learn" due to unequal resources among communities.[5] These concerns, however, did not deter states from setting goals and standards. The autonomy of local and state authorities is also protected, with the federal government's role defined in terms of general goals.

Education has been a key theme in recent elections, with candidates from both major parties and all ideologies insisting that we must improve the quality of public education. However, there are differences about how that should be done. Proposed reforms debated are vouchers, charter schools, national student testing, and more emphasis on reading. Some of these found their way into the Elementary and Secondary Education Act of 2001 (also called the "No Child Left Behind Act"). These conflicting reform proposals have become a regular part of the national political debate, affecting not only state and local elections but congressional and presidential elections as well.

VOUCHERS   Some reformers contend we will not see real progress in public education until we inject competition into the system by permitting parents to shop for schools the way they shop for goods and services in the economy. One way to do this would be to provide parents with a set amount of money—**vouchers**—that they could use to pay for part or all of their children's education in a public or private school of their choice. This reform has been labeled "choice in education" because it would give parents the freedom to choose where to send their children to school.[6]

This reform has proved divisive. Voucher advocates say it could help the neediest students escape failed schools and get the valuable academic preparation at private or religious schools. Yet opponents contend it will badly injure financially struggling public schools by diverting much-needed money.

Voucher programs have been tried since the mid-1980s in New York, Indianapolis, San Antonio, and Milwaukee. Some programs were directed at low-income students, a plan that, according to one observer, meant some poor families formed political alliances with conservative Republicans, not their more natural liberal Democratic allies. Political scientist and voucher advocate Terry Moe argues:

In many poorer communities, classes are conducted in overcrowded, poorly equipped buildings.

> In the new politics of education, the conservatives have become the progressives, pushing for major change, promoting the causes of the disadvantaged, and allying themselves with the poor. The progressives of yesteryear, meantime, have become the conservatives of today, resisting change, defending the status quo against threats from without, and opposing the poor constituents they claim to represent.[7]

Among the vigorous opponents of vouchers are teachers' unions, including the National Education Association (NEA) and the American Federation of Teachers (AFT), which, understandably, see vouchers as a threat to jobs and benefits because the use of vouchers could drain off financial support from the public schools.

Some proponents have proposed that voucher programs should include religious schools. Well over 80 percent of the students receiving vouchers in places like Milwaukee and San Antonio attend religious schools, most of them Catholic schools. Opponents of vouchers for religious schools argue that such an arrangement violates the constitutional separation of church and state. They fear too that in some parts of the country, vouchers would be used for schools that practice racial segregation.

Other people oppose the voucher system, even for public schools, on the grounds that such a system would have a negative impact on efforts to reform the public schools. Some argue that it would promote "skimming," meaning that the higher-achieving students would opt out of public schools, leaving behind the underachievers and the discipline problems and creating an increasingly negative atmosphere in public schools. In rural areas, where few private schools exist, some people fear that vouchers might encourage parents to keep the money under the guise of providing "private" home schooling.

Proposals for school vouchers that have been put before the voters have been defeated in Oregon, Colorado, and Washington. In recent years, California and Michigan voters have turned down initiatives that would have established vouchers, in spite of well-financed campaigns supporting their adoption. The political movement pushing vouchers lost some of its steam because of these defeats, the opposition of the teachers' unions, and court rulings that said poor families do not have the right to demand vouchers from state and local governments to allow their children to attend better schools.

In 2002, a divided U.S. Supreme Court ruled that poor children could be granted public money (vouchers) to attend religious schools without violating the separation of church and state provisions in the Bill of Rights. Chief Justice William Rehnquist

vouchers
Money provided by the government to parents for payment of their children's tuition in a public or private school of their choice.

wrote that his majority opinion was "not an endorsement of religious schooling" but merely a means "to assist poor children in failed schools."[8]

Colorado enacted a law in 2003 that provides for students in certain "low" or "unsatisfactory" performance schools to get out of public schools at the request of the parents. "Students qualify if they do badly on state tests and come from poor families living within one of the 11 desegregated districts."[9] A lawsuit was almost immediately filed to block this new Colorado law. The lawsuit claims this voucher program would force taxpayers in many instances to support religion, takes away funding from public schools, undermines our tradition of "full" public schools, and removes local control from school boards.

In 2004, a Florida appeals court ruled that a voucher program in that state violated Florida's constitution because it sent public money to religious institutions.[10]

CHARTER SCHOOLS   One educational reform that does not go as far as vouchers yet still provides publicly funded alternatives to standard public schools is the **charter school**. Some states now grant charters to individuals or groups to start schools and receive public funds if they can meet standards specified by law. Unlike vouchers, which provide funds to the parents, charter schools are under the direct authority of local school boards. There are more than 3,600 charter schools, with more than a million students. "The vast majority of the schools are operated by local nonprofit organizations, and the educational theories that guide them are as various as the communities they serve."[11]

As with privatization in other government services, charter schools are intended to interject the competition of the marketplace into elementary and secondary education. Charter schools generally have more flexibility to hire and fire teachers and are not subject to the collective bargaining arrangements that prevail in many public school systems. Proponents of charter schools want to remove these schools from state and local regulation as much as possible. Some of their teachers may not have extensive training as education majors, yet proponents of charter schools maintain that classroom performance is more important than the undergraduate major of the teacher.

This charter school in Jersey City, New Jersey, provides a computer lab for its science classes.

Teachers' unions are concerned about the charter movement, because they might lose their collective bargaining position with school boards if charter schools multiply. Other opponents contend that in school systems already strapped for money, it does not make sense to divert funds to such untested experiments. Concerns about what will be taught in charter schools and the level of teacher competence are often expressed. Also at issue is whether religious schools should qualify for public funds as charter schools.

Charter schools are the fastest-growing form of choice in K–12 education, and they got a big boost from the federally enacted "No Child Left Behind" law, which holds out conversion to charter schools as a possible solution for ineffective traditional public schools.

There is much to admire in the charter school movement. Two "Teach For America" alumni launched a series of charter schools under the name of Knowledge Is Power Programs or KIPP. With elementary schools in Houston, New York City, North Carolina, and elsewhere, they have demonstrated effective results. The key to their success is a strict and strong initial commitment by parents and pupils to a philosophy of hard work, longer hours of class time and homework, and no shortcuts. That, coupled with carefully recruited, dedicated teachers, has proved successful.[12]

Another success story is the Vaughn Street School, California's first charter school. Most of children at this school speak English as a second language and live in dangerous neighborhoods. In 1992, when the charter school was established, Vaughn Street's pupils ranked in the ninth percentile in reading (that is, 91 percent of public school students in America could read better than they) and the fourteenth percentile in math. Now their reading and math scores rank in the forty-seventh and fifty-ninth percentile, respectively. Principal Yvonne Chan attributes these changes to freedom from bureaucracy.

charter school

A publicly funded alternative to standard public schools in some states, initiated when individuals or groups receive charters; charter schools must meet state standards.

Yet charter schools vary widely in quality across the country. Indeed, initial test results in California and by the U.S. Department of Education find that economically disadvantaged students are making more rapid progress in traditional public schools than in the new charter schools.[13] This leads critics of the charter movement to say that there is no credible evidence that deregulating public education leads to higher student achievement. Supporters contend that the vast majority of charter schools serve students with academic and family problems who are poorly served by traditional public schools. Plainly, there are some excellent and some below-average charter schools. Opponents and supporters alike agree that quality schools must be constructed—one at a time.

NATIONAL STUDENT TESTING   Standardized testing is neither new nor controversial. What is new and controversial is *statewide* standardized testing. In 1990, only 14 states had standards for their core curriculum, but now almost every state has adopted standards for subjects such as math, reading, and science. After adopting standardized testing for students, Oregon rejected a ballot initiative that would have amended the state constitution to require annual testing of math and verbal skills of public school students in grades 4 through 12.

Even more controversial are *national* tests and *national* norms or goals. Such tests would be administered to students periodically to permit parents, administrators, and legislators to assess how individual students, classes, schools, school districts, and states compare with one another. Moreover, once such testing is established, it could be expanded to include year-to-year measurement of individual students as they progress through the public schools.

Some critics of standardized national tests contend that it is unfair and misleading to use such tests to measure learning. Minority students and students in districts in impoverished areas may not do well on these tests, and their low scores will reinforce cultural bias. Other critics worry that the use of such tests will force teachers to "teach to the test." Sensitive to the fact that their students will be compared with students in other classes, teachers will attempt to "beat the test" by emphasizing certain topics and ignoring others. This strategy might work for some students but would limit the learning of others. The main contention of the opponents of national testing, however, is that such measurement will not produce positive changes in education.

State and local policymakers continue to wrestle with how best to fund and implement the standardized testing that is mandated by the federal "No Child Left Behind" Act. While the general goals have been embraced, policymakers and educators hate to have their local schools labeled as "in need of improvement." And local authorities complain that state and national standards often measure factors that are beyond the control of a particular school and its staff. "It's really not fair to judge a school whose kids come without having ever read a book, and compare it to a school where kids go to the library and have libraries in their home," says Lynn Stockleg, a middle school teacher in Tulsa, Oklahoma. "It's rather discouraging when you're one of those schools. You know you're working very, very hard and yet your scores are consistently low."[14]

State and local officials have certainly discovered as well that complying with the "No Child Left Behind" Act is proving far more expensive than anyone had expected. One study suggests that fully implementing the requirements of the act could cost more than $140 billion dollars, while the federal government has appropriated only $4.6 billion, the remaining costs falling on state and local governments.[15]

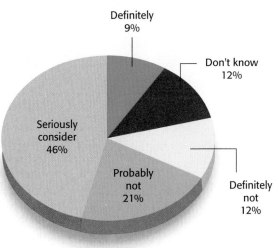

FIGURE 28–2 Would Parents Choose Charter Schools?

SOURCE: Public Agenda, reported in "Issues 2000: Education," *The Economist*, September 30, 2000, p. 20.

> *"It's really not fair to judge a school whose kids come without having ever read a book, and compare it to a school where kids go to the library and have libraries in their home."*
>
> LYNN STOCKLEG,
> TULSA, OKLAHOMA, MIDDLE SCHOOL TEACHER

Higher Education

Public higher education has generally been provided by states. States support many kinds of universities and colleges, including land-grant universities such as Michigan State University, which were created by the Morrill Act of 1862. In addition, since the end of World War II there has been a major expansion in the number and size of public *community colleges*, which typically receive funds from local as well as state governments, and which allow students to attend the first two years of college or receive a technical education in their own communities.

Administration

State colleges and universities are governed by boards appointed by the governor in some states and elected by the voters in others. These boards are designed to give public institutions of higher education some independence from state politics, even though many public universities rely heavily on their state legislatures and governors for funding.

With about 80 percent of our more than 15 million college students now attending publicly supported institutions, the control and support of higher education have become significant political issues. States spend between 8 and 15 percent of their budgets on higher education, thus making it the third largest allocation of state funds after K–12 spending and Medicaid. States have created boards with varying degrees of control over operations and budgets. In addition, governors have tried to impose controls on universities and colleges that many university administrators insist are inappropriate. Yet institutions of higher education have greater independence from political oversight than other tax-supported institutions. Publicly funded colleges and universities usually can control teaching loads, internal procedures, areas of teaching emphasis, hiring and promotion, and the allocation of funds among internal units.

Funding Higher Education

In the twenty-first century, we face questions of access and funding for our colleges and universities due to increasing enrollments. Who should go? Only those who can afford it? What about minorities who are underrepresented in our colleges and universities? Access to colleges and universities for all students who wish to go has long been the declared goal in many states, but is this goal realistic? Should students be required to pay higher tuition to cover the cost of their education? And should illegal immigrants be allowed to attend state colleges at in-state tuition rates?

Tuition at state universities has gone up, often at two or three times the rate of inflation. Professors' salaries have not kept pace with tuition increases and have grown only slightly more than the rate of inflation. Although many people agree we need an infusion of new money to update college laboratories, improve libraries, and recruit and keep first-rate college professors, there is little consensus about who should pay for these efforts. The federal government is the chief supplier of student financial aid, and many states are now making major efforts to expand their programs of student aid. Many states, such as Georgia, California, Washington, and Alaska, are investing in programs aimed at keeping top students in their states at state-run as well as independent colleges.

Most institutions of higher education—both independent and state-run—receive some kind of government subsidy, through a variety of devices, so that students do not pay the full cost of their education. The federal government and most states provide need-based financial assistance in the form of loans and grants, with students in the greatest financial need at the higher-cost institutions eligible for the most aid. Thus higher education has what is in effect a limited voucher system; students receive funds and can choose the kind of college or university that best serves their needs. It also means that in the United States, we have avoided a *two-track system*—one set of colleges and universities for the poor and another for the rich. Poor students can be found in most high-cost independent colleges and universities along with students from higher-income families.

Funding for the public universities must compete with the rising costs of other state services, notably Medicaid, transportation, elementary and secondary education, and the criminal justice system—and in most states, funding for higher education has been a lower priority than these other functions. One consequence of its lower priority is that state funding of public colleges and universities is unstable, rising when state revenues are growing but declining sharply during economic downturns.[16] Many states are therefore experimenting with new ways to fund higher education. As state funds for higher education have gone down in many states, public colleges and universities have been allowed to raise tuition levels. Gradually the burden of paying for college is being shifted from the state to students and their parents, a change that may further reduce access to public higher education for low- and moderate-income families.[17]

Colorado passed a law in 2004 that creates a voucher system for paying for higher education. If this plan survives current court challenges, Colorado will become the first state to fund undergraduate education primarily through grants to individual students. The state's three independent colleges are also entitled to these funds as the law currently stands. Other states will watch whether Colorado has found a better way to fund higher education or whether this mainly masks continued state investments in its higher education institutions.[18]

Social Services

What role should state and local governments play in making sure all citizens have their basic housing, health, and nutritional needs met? How important are these social services compared with government's obligation to provide police and fire protection, education, parks and recreation, and other services? For much of our history, human service needs were left to private charities that ran orphanages, old-age homes, hospitals, and other institutions. Philosophically, this reliance on private charity fit well with American notions of limited government and self-reliance. That view changed dramatically during the Great Depression of the 1930s, when poverty, unemployment, and homelessness affected such large numbers of people that the government could no longer act as if these were private matters. Then in the mid-1960s, with President Lyndon Johnson's Great Society agenda, the nation embarked on a second major wave of social service programs, which Johnson called the War on Poverty. Today we continue to debate whether such programs accomplish their goals and whether alternatives would prove more successful.

Public Assistance

No single program in the United States provides cash benefits to all poor people. Yet programs that provide payments to poor families with children are typically what people mean by the term "welfare." Pressure to reform the welfare system increased among both Democrats and Republicans in the last decades of the twentieth century. The number of American families on welfare soared from about 600,000 households in 1950 to more than 5 million in the early 1990s, growing 13 times faster than the general population.[19] Why such growth? Some said that this country had finally recognized its obligation to care for the truly poor. Others charged that "government handouts" robbed recipients of the self-confidence they need to go to work and succeed; in this sense, dependence on welfare is viewed as a curse.

In 1996, fundamental changes were made in welfare policy, including the roles of the federal and state governments. Landmark legislation called **Temporary Assistance for Needy Families (TANF)** replaced the 60-year-old program known as Aid to Families with Dependent Children (AFDC).[20] Under AFDC, states provided monthly cash payments to poor families, largely to help children receive the care they needed in their own homes. States set different benefit levels, which varied enormously, and states determined whether a smaller or larger proportion of poor families were eligible. The federal government picked up most of the costs of welfare, since it matched state spending at rates ranging from one federal dollar for every state dollar spent (in

Temporary Assistance for Needy Families (TANF)
Federal welfare reform law that replaced the 60-year-old assistance program for poor families with children, Aid to Families with Dependent Children. This 1996 law strengthened work requirements for recipients, limited the time that families can receive benefits, and gave states flexibility to develop service programs supporting work, marriage, and self-sufficiency.

wealthy states like Connecticut) to about three federal dollars for every state dollar (in low-income states like Mississippi).

Most of the administrative burdens, however, fell on state and local governments. Every state had a department of human services or welfare that either administered welfare programs directly or, in 13 states, supervised county officials who administered these programs. Administration of AFDC was strictly regulated by federal rules, which were designed to minimize errors and fraud and to ensure that families got the benefits they were entitled to receive given their financial circumstances.

TANF differs from AFDC in several ways. First, TANF imposes new restrictions on families receiving cash assistance. Welfare is no longer an entitlement for families in financial need. Under most circumstances, adults in the family must work soon after they begin getting benefits, and families may no longer receive benefits indefinitely—most must leave welfare after five years. Also, teen parents receiving cash benefits are required to attend school and live at home with their parents.

Second, TANF expanded the goals of welfare policy. In addition to helping poor children, the program was intended to help families find work and become self-sufficient and to promote marriage and reduce out-of-wedlock births.

Third, states were given greater flexibility in designing and administering welfare policies. States now receive block grants from the federal government and may use these grants to support a wide variety of programs; they need not spend most of their welfare dollars on monthly cash payments to families, as they did under AFDC. Rather, states may spend the grant dollars on services, such as child care for working families, transportation assistance, help in getting and keeping jobs, or programs that promote sexual abstinence among unmarried teens. States are also freed from many of the federal rules they followed when administering AFDC. For instance, they no longer need to use public bureaucracies to administer welfare but may instead use private agencies, even including for-profit corporations and religious institutions.

In exchange for this flexibility, each state must report to the federal government that a large proportion of its welfare cases (that is, families with able-bodied adults that are receiving cash assistance) are either working at jobs or engaged in some other work-related activity (such as job search). Each state also files a plan with the secretary of health and human services every two years that describes its TANF program, such as how the state will ensure that recipients engage in work activities within two months of receiving benefits, and the state's goals in preventing and reducing out-of-wedlock pregnancies. Money is distributed to states based on the highest amount of federal funding they received in the years just before TANF was passed. To continue receiving federal funds, states must spend at least 75 percent of the amount they spent in 1994. Grants to states may also be cut if the states fail to engage enough of their adult cases in work activities. Additional federal funds are available to states as incentives for high performance and as loans if states experience financial hardship.

After TANF was enacted, many states used their flexibility to make major changes in their welfare programs. Some states adopted policies that imposed even stronger restrictions on cash benefits than did the federal law. For example, most states require families with able-bodied adults to participate immediately in work-related activities, not just after two years as required by federal law. Also, 20 states provide no additional benefits to families in which children were born while the family was receiving welfare; eight states have stricter time limits than the federal law on how long families may receive cash assistance in their lifetimes; and 20 states withdraw all benefits to a family not complying with work requirements even after just one violation.[21]

However, many states have also adopted policies and administrative practices that provide positive assistance to family heads who seek employment. Nearly all states, with federal help, have greatly increased their spending on child care for low-income working families. Nearly all states also allow families to keep a larger share of the income they receive from jobs than was the case under AFDC.

This welfare-to-work trainee is learning skills that will enable her to find employment at a steady, well-paid job.

History Makers

Jane Addams

Jane Addams not only contributed to major reforms in laws governing juvenile justice, working conditions, and education; she also influenced the ways in which government policies were advocated. She was born in Cedarville, Illinois, in 1860, to an affluent and politically prominent family. Her father was a state senator and a friend of President Lincoln. During a European trip after graduation from college, she and a friend, Ellen Gates Starr, were struck by a "social settlement" they saw in the London slums, a house where young college men, typically from well-to-do families, lived and worked to improve the conditions of the poor, often through cultural education.

Addams and Starr were inspired by their trip to buy, in 1889, an old mansion in a working-class, immigrant-dominated neighborhood in Chicago and establish a secular version of a social settlement, which they called "Hull House." Hull House was essentially an educational institution designed to provide people with an escape from the terrible conditions produced by chronic poverty and the city's inadequate services. It sponsored dietetic instruction, athletic programs, and social clubs. Hull House also offered a children's day care; a kindergarten; a playground; classes and lectures in literature, theater, and art for all ages; and an employment bureau.

Hull House also became a policy research and advocacy organization. Addams eventually rejected the original settlement house idea of a "top-down" charity, in which educated middle- and upper-class people acted on their own vision of what the poor really needed. Instead, Hull House residents worked closely with neighbors to grasp their own views of their needs, and the residents then studied neighborhood conditions to learn more about the scope and causes of the problems. Addams's democratic, empirically based approach to serving the poor led her to conduct investigations into narcotics, milk supplies, sanitary conditions, and garbage collection—even to the point of following garbage trucks to determine whether they actually picked up refuse from the huge bins on Chicago's streets.

Hull House residents also drew from their extensive experiences to lobby the Illinois state legislature for a wide variety of policy reforms, including regulations to improve the working conditions of factory workers, the creation of special courts for juvenile offenders, restrictions on child labor, protective legislation for women and children, and a compulsory education law. These state reforms eventually influenced reforms at the national level, including the establishment of the federal Children's Bureau in 1912 and

Jane Addams

the enactment of a federal child labor law in 1916.

Addams also played major roles in establishing several important organizations with reform agendas, including the National Association for the Advancement of Colored People in 1909. In her later years, she played an important part in American peace movements. Largely for her work as a pacifist and internationalist, she was awarded the Nobel Peace Prize in 1931, not long before her death in 1935.

For more on Jane Addams, see her autobiography, *Twenty Years at Hull-House* (Macmillan, 1910) and a recent biography, *Citizen: Jane Addams and the Struggle for Democracy*, by Louis W. Knight (University of Chicago Press, 2006). ∎

> *Addams's democratic, empirically based approach to serving the poor led her to conduct investigations into narcotics, milk supplies, sanitary conditions, and garbage collection.*

Most states have also increased their provision of employment services to welfare families and those who recently left welfare, including programs that help parents to prepare themselves for jobs, find jobs, train for better jobs, and pay for some of the expenses that go along with work, such as transportation and clothing. Some states have experimented with **workfare** programs designed to help welfare recipients

workfare
A welfare strategy adopted by some states that gives able-bodied adults who do not have preschool-aged children the opportunity to learn job skills that can lead to employment.

"The main lesson of the 1996 law is that having a job and earning a livable income are two different things."

PETER EDELMAN, GEORGETOWN UNIVERSITY

develop the self-confidence, skills, and habits necessary for regular employment; and many states have developed **responsibility contracts**, requiring recipients to sign a written agreement specifying their responsibilities and outlining a plan for them to obtain work and achieve self-sufficiency.[22]

Partly as a result of the 1996 welfare reform, the number of families on welfare has been reduced by more than 60 percent since its peak in the 1990s—from about 5 million families in 1994 to under 2 million in 2005. Much evidence also suggests that welfare reform has greatly increased employment rates among low-income single mothers with children, the most common heads of families on welfare. It is also widely accepted that welfare reforms have contributed to changes in the sources of income among poor families with children: public cash assistance has declined substantially, while earnings from jobs have grown. However, not all of these developments were caused by federal and state welfare reforms. They were doubtless helped by the booming economy of the late 1990s, which created many new jobs.[23]

In some ways, then, the 1996 welfare reform seemed a very successful policy. However, the program has had its shortcomings. One critic who worked in the Clinton administration when federal welfare reform was passed, Georgetown University's Peter Edelman, says: "The main lesson of the 1996 law is that having a job and earning a livable income are two different things."[24] While many people worked themselves out of poverty, many others remained poor despite their jobs. While poverty rates fell in the 1990s, they have since risen, especially among children. A much larger proportion of the families living in poverty are now not receiving welfare benefits.[25] Also, the reforms did not seem to help the hardest cases—typically people with little education, no work experience, and tenuous personal backgrounds. Although in most states, 60 to 70 percent of families who leave welfare are working, even a year or so afterward, it is also true that 30 to 40 percent are not, and some of these families have few or no significant sources of financial support.

In early 2006, TANF was reauthorized by Congress, which adopted even more stringent work requirements for persons on cash assistance. But it is clear that states are now the prime laboratories for making and implementing social policy.[26] The federal government originally became involved in welfare programs because states had been unwilling or unable to tackle these problems on their own. Yet now the states will determine whether the needs of poor people will be given a higher or lower priority, and how poor families will be treated in bad as well as good economic times.

Health

During the hot summer of 1794, a yellow fever epidemic ravaged Philadelphia, then the nation's capital. The streets were deserted. All who could afford to do so had fled with their families to the country. Every night, the sounds of the death cart echoed through the nearly empty city. Most families that remained behind lost a child, a father, or a mother. Only when cool weather returned did the city resume normal activity.

Yellow fever, dysentery, malaria, and other diseases periodically swept American cities in the eighteenth and nineteenth centuries. As late as 1879, yellow fever struck hard in the South. Memphis was nearly depopulated. Following the lead of Louisiana and Massachusetts, state after state established a board of health to deal with such epidemics. Spurred by the medical discoveries of Louis Pasteur and other scientists, authorities undertook additional efforts to protect public health. Open sewers were covered, and hygienic measures were instituted.

Prevention and disease control are still major public health activities today. Doctors are required to report cases of communicable disease. Health department officials then investigate to discover the source of the infection, isolate the afflicted, and take whatever action is called for. Most state health departments give doctors free vaccine and serum, and many local departments give free vaccinations to those who cannot afford private physicians. Mobile units take free x-rays of schoolchildren, teachers, and the general public; county health departments provide free or low-cost inoculations,

responsibility contract
A welfare strategy adopted by some states in which recipients sign a written agreement specifying their responsibilities and outlining a plan for obtaining work and achieving self-sufficiency.

vision tests, and hearing tests. Public health officials also try to protect water supplies and ensure the safe disposal of waste and sewage. They protect the community's food supply by inspecting hotels, restaurants, and food markets.

Today the overwhelming public health issues are pollution, AIDS, smoking, drug abuse, depression, and obesity. Issues such as "mad cow" disease and the West Nile virus also demand state as well as national attention. Like the contagious and infectious disease issues of earlier times, they require concerted efforts and public health policies. Thousands of local governments—counties, cities, townships, and special health districts—have some kind of public health program. Every state has an agency, usually called a department of health, which administers the state program and supervises local health officials. At the national level, the U.S. Public Health Service conducts research, assists state and local authorities, and administers federal grants to encourage local agencies to expand their programs. Every state also administers various federally funded medical benefit programs for the needy, such as Medicaid, not to be confused with Medicare—the Social Security health care program for people over 65. Medicaid is now the largest item in overall state budgets.

The current health care crisis in the United States involves access and cost. Wealthy people may be able to afford the costs and gain access. But poor people have less access to health care, and the quality of their care is often lower. Also, an increasing number of people in the working and middle classes work at jobs that do not provide affordable health care plans, and even when they do have health insurance, many people worry about whether their insurance will be adequate to cover their health care needs.

Medicaid was originally created in 1965 to fill the health insurance gaps for low-income persons. But since then, Medicaid has come to serve many one-time working and middle class people—especially elderly and disabled people—who have low incomes largely because of their medical problems. Today, only a minority of Medicaid recipients is on welfare, and two out of three live in families in the workforce. More than half of the recipients have family income above the poverty level.[27]

Medicaid is a huge concern for state governments nationwide. The program is enormous, covering the health care needs for more than 40 million Americans and taking an average of at least 13 percent of annual state funds. The increasing number of Medicaid-eligible citizens, coupled with the rising cost of prescription drugs, long-term health care, and other health services—all growing beyond the rate of inflation—

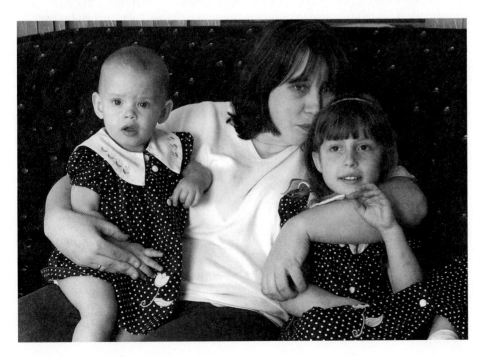

Social services programs help needy citizens survive. Often families with young children need assistance the most.

> *"That's the irony of Medicaid: The program has a difficult time doing its job when its services are most needed."*

WRITER TRINITY TOMSIE

add up to a Medicaid program whose expenditures grow much faster than the rest of the typical state budget. Further, the program was expanded during strong financial times, often to include low-income parents as well as children, but when state fiscal conditions are less than perfect, and more people are in financial need, Medicaid is in danger.[28] "That's the irony of Medicaid: The program has a difficult time doing its job when its services are most needed. A sour economy increases demand for coverage and spending, at the same time revenues are eroding and putting heavy pressure on state budgets," notes Trinity Tomsie, who covers Medicaid issues for the National Conference on State Legislator's Fiscal Affairs Program.[29]

State policy makers now face tough questions about whether or not to maintain coverage and if so, whose coverage and how. The most expensive Medicaid recipients to serve are elderly and disabled people, who often need long-term care. Should states cut benefits to such vulnerable populations? Children and parents in poor families are typically healthy and cheaper to serve. They constitute the largest share of Medicaid recipients, and cuts in Medicaid may have to include them. Yet health problems that are not treated among these younger people may have long-run consequences—and may be more expensive to treat in later years. If spending is to be restrained, states may have to decide whose health care must be cut or constrained, and such decisions are very hard for our political system to make.

Most states have tried to find Medicaid savings in administration and antifraud measures. But Medicaid's administrative costs are fairly low, and though fraud exists among both service providers and recipients, it is not easy to eliminate, nor does it seem large enough to greatly reduce costs even if it were eliminated. States have also tried to use various means to cut the costs of services. Can managed care organizations provide services at lower costs? Can drug manufacturers be leaned on for rebates? Should a preferred-drug list, based on cost and efficacy, be established?

Governors around the country pressed President George W. Bush and Congress to increase the federal share of Medicaid's costs, to no avail. Many were frustrated when the president advocated a large farm bill appropriating money for farm subsidies, seemingly ignoring what many think a more pressing financial issue, Medicaid funding. State officials acknowledge nowadays that soaring Medicaid spending threatens recent state goals such as reducing public school class size, increasing public transportation infrastructure, and funding innovative environmental programs. Some states "have reached into the funds received in settling their suits with tobacco companies, or tapped public employee pension funds, or drained their rainy day reserves in order to meet the requirement in state constitutions that they balance their budgets."[30]

In early 2006, the Congress passed the Deficit Reduction Act of 2005, which includes many new options for states trying to reduce the growth of Medicaid spending. Among other things, the act allows states to develop different benefit packages for different types of Medicaid recipients, and to require some recipients to pay for part of their health care. Because these choices affect the daily lives of so many people, as well as affect important and politically powerful health care institutions, the debates in state capitals over the next few years regarding how to use this new flexibility to reform the Medicaid program will certainly be intense.[31]

Law Enforcement

Many state and local government powers stem from their **police powers**, the inherent power of states to use physical force if necessary to protect the health, safety, and welfare of their citizens. This power is among those not delegated to the federal government by the Constitution and reserved to the states. It is on this basis that mayors or governors impose curfews, as they have in some urban riots. But the police power extends to other activities of government, such as regulating public health, safety, and morals. Most law enforcement takes place at the local level, but states also have a significant role.

police powers
Inherent powers of state governments to pass laws to protect public health, safety, and welfare; the national government has no directly granted police powers but accomplishes the same goals through other delegated powers.

The State Police

In 1835, the famous Texas Rangers were organized as a small border patrol. In 1865, Massachusetts appointed a few state constables to suppress gambling, a job the local police had proved unable or, more probably, unwilling to do. But not until 1905, with the organization of the Pennsylvania State Constabulary, did a state police system come into being. It was so successful that other states soon followed.

The establishment of the Pennsylvania State Constabulary marked a sharp break with traditional police methods. This was a mounted and uniformed body organized on a military basis; centralized control was given to a superintendent directly responsible to the governor. The Pennsylvania pattern was followed by other states.

State police became a part of our law enforcement system for a variety of reasons. The growth of urban and metropolitan areas, the coming of the automobile (and the resulting demand for greater protection on the highways and the creation of a mobile force for catching fleeing criminals), and the need for a trained force to maintain order during strikes, fires, floods, and other emergencies all promoted the creation of state police.

Other Police Forces

State police are not the only law enforcement agencies maintained by state governments. There are liquor law enforcement officials, fish and game wardens, fire wardens, detective bureaus, and special motor vehicle police. This dispersion of functions has been criticized, yet each department insists it needs its own law enforcement agency to handle its special problems.

At the local level, almost every municipality maintains its own police force; the county has a sheriff and deputies, and some townships have their own police officers. In fact, there are almost 18,000 separate state and local law enforcement agencies in the United States, employing more than 700,000 officers.

With crime continuing to be an important issue to many voters, crime control is always on the minds of elected officials. State and local governments spend more than $125 billion on police protection and correctional or prison institutions. Local governments pay for almost 70 percent of all police protection costs, including such routine activities as controlling traffic and patrolling neighborhoods but also maintaining court security and preventing juvenile crime. From 1987 to 2003, the number of full-time local officers increased by 30 percent or nearly 100,000.

Federal–State Action

The federal government has gradually moved into law enforcement, a field traditionally reserved for state and local governments, although the main cost of local law enforcement is still borne by local governments. Today, for example, it is a federal offense to transport kidnapped individuals or stolen goods across state lines. Taking firearms, explosives, or even information across state lines for illegal purposes is also a federal offense. Federal law enforcement agencies include the Federal Bureau of Investigation (FBI), the Bureau of Alcohol, Tobacco, and Firearms (ATF), and the Drug Enforcement Administration (DEA).

Crime rates have been declining. Despite positive trends, politicians in both parties continue to press for government to do more about crime. Some advocate stricter laws regulating guns, while others favor more police on the street or more prisons. Because politicians fear appearing "soft on crime," taking action on crime is almost always a high priority at all levels of government.

In some cases, attempts to reduce crime can lead to unwanted side effects. In the 1980s, the DEA enlisted local police forces to catch smugglers who were bringing drugs to major American cities on the highways. The New Jersey State Police participated in this program with considerable success. However, black and Hispanic drivers were subjected to frequent and unjustified traffic stops and searches. Even though the state officially banned racial profiling, there were reports that state troopers were singling out drivers by race or ethnicity. The issue came to a head when troopers shot and wounded three unarmed black and Hispanic men on the New Jersey Turnpike in 1998. Eventually the state acknowledged that it had been using racial profiling, and agreed to change its procedures and accept monitoring by a federal judge.[32]

Since the September 11, 2001, terrorist attacks on New York City and the Pentagon, every state has designated a homeland security coordinator. These state officials are working with the new federal Department of Homeland Security to beef up preparedness and training efforts aimed at preventing and dealing with future terrorist attacks. The federal government approved funds in 2002 that were to be used to train and equip "so-called first responders, along with grants to prevent bioterrorism, which have increasingly become the focus of many state officers."[33] While there is a clear need for new and expanded homeland security efforts, few states have the resources to support this. Many local and state officials have complained that most new federal funds are being redirected toward new homeland security concerns such as bioterrorism preparedness while ignoring many of the traditional and basic public safety systems. This has added to budget shortfalls in most states and has led state and local officials to insist on more federal funds and greater flexibility in how states and localities decide what their priorities are.[34]

Planning the Urban Community

Are our cities good places in which to live and work? Crime, pollution, garbage, crowded shopping areas, dented fenders, slums and blighted areas, inadequate parks, challenging traffic patterns, and shattered nerves—are these the inevitable costs of urban life?

For at least the first century of the United States' existence, American cities were allowed to grow unchecked. Industrialists were permitted to erect factories wherever they wished; developers were allowed to construct towering buildings that prevented sunlight from reaching the streets below; commuters, bicyclists, and pedestrians ended up with transportation systems that rarely met their needs.

Zoning Laws

The most common method of ensuring orderly growth is *zoning*—creating specific areas and limiting property usage in each area. A community may be divided into designated areas for single-family, two-family, or multifamily dwellings; for commercial purposes; and for light or heavy industry. Regulations restrict the height of buildings or require that buildings be located a certain distance apart or a certain distance from the boundaries of the lot.

Zoning regulations attempt to enable the city or county government to coordinate services with land use and to stabilize property values by preventing, for example, garbage dumps from being located next to residential areas. Day-to-day enforcement is usually the responsibility of a building inspector, who ensures that a projected construction project is consistent with building, zoning, fire, and sanitary regulations before granting a building permit. A zoning ordinance, however, is no better than its enforcement. In most cases, a zoning or planning commission or the city council can amend ordinances and make exceptions to regulations, and these officials are often under tremendous pressure to grant exceptions. But if they go too far in permitting special cases, the whole purpose of zoning is defeated.

Zoning is only one kind of community planning. Until recently, city planners were primarily concerned with streets and buildings. Today most are also concerned with the quality of life. Consequently, planning covers a broad range of activities, including methods to avoid air pollution, improve water quality, and provide for better parks. Planners collect all the information they can about a city and then prepare long-range plans. Can smaller-scale communities be devised within urban centers? Can downtown areas be revitalized, and if so, how? Where should main highways or mass-transit facilities be constructed to meet future needs? Will the water supply be adequate for the population 10, 20, or 50 years from now? Are hospitals and parks accessible to all? Does the design of public buildings encourage crime or energy waste?

Controlling Growth

Critics of urban and state planning are skeptical whether governors, mayors, or state and local legislators can prevent what they sometimes call the "Los Angelization" of the United States, by which they mean urban growth without much planning for transportation, environmental protection, or management of water and other resources. Unregulated market forces can cause severe harm to residents, and "politics as usual" does not ensure sensible growth patterns or protect the air, water, and beauty of most states and communities.

Seattle and San Francisco residents voted to limit the height and bulk of downtown buildings in an effort to protect these cities from excessive growth. Maryland and many other states have passed "smart growth" laws aimed at preserving large blocks of contiguous land and ensuring that the necessary roads, sewers, and schools are in place before development proceeds. This legislation is implemented in two ways. The state gives priority funding to development in areas designated by counties as having the proper infrastructure and meeting other guidelines; state funds are also allocated to local governments and private land trusts to purchase the development rights to land "rich in agricultural, forestry, natural, and cultural resources."[35]

The population of the United States will soar by over 80 million between 2000 and 2030. A few urban planners recommend looking at European cities such as Paris, where choice neighborhoods in the heart of the city combine elegant six- and seven-story apartment buildings above neighborhood retail stores. Most Americans would reject this dense, crowded lifestyle devoid of driveways, grassy front lawns, and backyard pools. But a closer look at European cities often finds a great number of interior gardens within apartments and meticulously groomed neighborhood parks. Columnist Neal Peirce writes that "density and mixed use aren't bad; they're just different—and sometimes better" and notes the discussion and advocacy of a U.S. version of Parisian greenery in a group called Community Greens: Shared Parks in Urban Blocks (www.communitygreens.org).[36]

Repair of deteriorating infrastructure, although a nuisance to residents, is necessary to maintain the quality of life in cities and also to attract businesses and consumers.

Obviously, planning and sensible growth depend on public support. They also depend on market forces. No plan will be effective, however, unless it reflects the interests and values of major groups within the community. Planning is clearly a political activity. Different groups view the ends and means of planning differently, and agreements on tough policy options are often hard to reach. Moreover, one of the barriers to successful planning is the general fear of government power. Effective planning therefore requires imaginative collaboration among planners, community leaders, and the popularly elected officials who must bear the responsibility for implementing the plans.[37]

Environmental Regulation

State and local governments have long been concerned about managing land use and protecting the environment. In such heavily polluted places as Pittsburgh, smoke abatement ordinances were enacted as early as 1860, but aggressive action on air pollution did not come until after World War II.[38] By the 1950s, states had established agencies to deal with resource management issues, but it was the federal legislation of the early 1970s that pushed environmental protection onto their agendas.[39] One important reason for the expanded federal role is the reality that pollution does not recognize state boundaries. Air and water pollution are particular examples of the interstate nature of environmental problems.

In the 1950s and 1960s, the federal government provided grants to state and local governments for research and assistance in developing and implementing their own environmental standards. The key piece of legislation in the transition to a greater role for the federal government was the Federal Environmental Protection Act, passed in 1970, which created the Environmental Protection.Agency (EPA). Other acts dealing with specific environmental problems followed: the Clean Air Act of 1970, the Clean Water Act of 1972, the Safe Drinking Water Act of 1974, the Toxic Substances Control Act of 1976, and Superfund (the federal Comprehensive Environmental Response, Compensation and Liability Act) of 1980. Most of these acts have been amended one or more times. Subsequent to the passage of the Superfund Act in 1980, which was created in response to public outcry regarding the most contaminated toxic dump sites across the United States, several state and local policies have been established to cover the toxic sites that do not qualify as Superfund sites but still warrant cleanup action.[40]

These wind turbines near Palm Springs, California, constitute an alternative source of energy.

As states became more involved in toxic waste regulation and air pollution in the 1960s and 1970s, pressure on the federal government to develop national environmental standards increased. Part of the pressure was due to the inconsistent state policies being considered and enacted. Not surprisingly, states tend to have different environmental concerns. For example, swine and poultry regulations are more important in the Midwest and Plains states, whereas nuclear cleanup is important in the West and Southwest, and timber regulation is of concern to the Pacific Northwest. Not only did environmental activists want a single national approach to the overarching problems of air and water pollution, but so did many of those who were being regulated. Automobile manufacturers, for instance, preferred one national standard for automobile emissions rather than dozens of differing state standards. Businesses operating in several states also pressed for uniform federal environmental standards.[41]

The basic model of environmental regulation has been for the federal government to set national standards for water and air quality. State and local governments are typically put in charge of both implementing standards and monitoring compliance. Typically, too, states complain that federal regulations and unfunded mandates impose a heavy financial burden on them.

Another area in which states are increasingly responsible for environmental policy is waste management. Not unexpectedly, states where the economy is growing have regulated waste management more aggressively than states where this is not the case. Economically hard-pressed states fear driving industries away. Fears about nuclear waste, acid rain, and hazardous wastes have sparked extensive efforts at regulation within states, as well as court battles with nearby states over the export of unwanted byproducts of energy development.

Although the EPA receives most of the headlines, state and local governments have more people working to control pollution. States can and do experiment with ways to improve air quality. California, for instance, has been a leader in testing automobile emissions. One innovation being considered is *remote sensing,* which uses roadside devices that shoot an infrared beam across a road to detect the emissions of passing cars. This device also has a video camera that records the license plates of vehicles in violation of emission standards. Such a system could replace the periodic state inspections now required for all vehicles.

Many states have been using alternative renewable energy both to cut down on energy costs and to rejuvenate dwindling rural economies. Large-scale wind-energy projects, for example, have been started in New York, Pennsylvania, Colorado, Iowa, Kansas, Texas, and Washington, among other states. Most of these were begun in the 1990s or more recently. As fossil fuel costs became increasingly unpredictable, states started to diversify their approach by investing in biomass, wind, hydroelectric, solar, and geothermal projects. Some states have even implemented innovative tax incentives and "net metering" programs (a practice allowing customers who have solar panels or other personal energy-generating capital to sell their energy back to the overall grid) in order to encourage more individual responsibility. Although none of these tactics have yet become widely accepted, nor is renewable energy expected to soon replace traditional energy sources, they are evidence of active state and local environmental efforts (Figure 28–3). Many states have also taken the lead in regulating coal-fired power plants, unsafe mercury pollution levels, and greenhouse gas emissions.[42]

Environmental interest groups continue to press for stronger state and local environmental regulation, "smart" hybrid cars, and cars with better gas mileage, and they continue to demand stiff penalties for violations of environmental laws. Further, some of the effort has shifted to individual action—recycling, conservation, saving and planting trees, and using public transportation. As the need for environmental regulation becomes more and more pressing, many state and local governments continue to react by expanding existing legislation and appropriating money for research and regulatory agency staff.[43] Indeed, since federal environmental grants to states have not increased since the early 1990s, despite the growth of state responsibilities and environmental problems, states have come to absorb an increasingly large share of the costs of environmental programs. States now pay about 80 percent of the costs of federal environmental programs.[44]

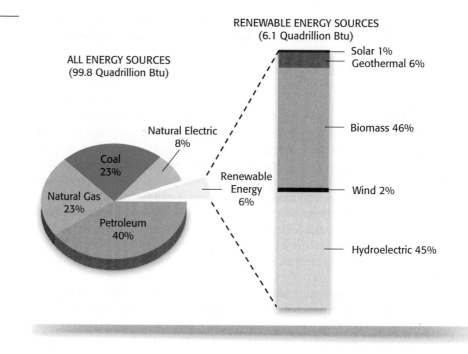

FIGURE 28–3 **U.S. Energy Consumption by Source, 2005.**

From 2000 to 2005, electricity generated from wind power increased 350 percent and geothermal use increased 11 percent.

SOURCE: Energy Information Administration. http://www.eia.doe.gov/.

ALL ENERGY SOURCES
(99.8 Quadrillion Btu)

Natural Electric
8%

Coal
23%

Natural Gas
23%

Petroleum
40%

Renewable
Energy
6%

RENEWABLE ENERGY SOURCES
(6.1 Quadrillion Btu)

Solar 1%
Geothermal 6%

Biomass 46%

Wind 2%

Hydroelectric 45%

Transportation

Before the automobile, long-distance commercial travel was mainly by canal and railroad. Local roads were built and repaired under the direction of city, township, and county officials. Able-bodied male citizens were required either to put in a certain number of days working on the public roads or to pay taxes for that purpose. By the 1890s, bicycle clubs began to urge the building of hard-surfaced roads, but it was not until the early 1900s and the growing popularity of the automobile that road building became a major industry. This function was gradually transferred from local governments to state governments and the federal government, but counties and townships still have important building and maintenance functions.

Although much of the money comes from the federal government, it is the state and local governments that build the highways, public buildings, airports, parks, and recreational facilities. State and local governments, in fact, spend more money on transportation than on anything else except education and welfare. Because highways and bridges around the nation are aging, a federal tax on gasoline was levied to help rebuild these public facilities.

The federal government has supported state highway construction since 1916, and through legislation passed since then, federal aid has increased. States do the planning, estimate the costs, and arrange for the construction work, even when they receive federal assistance. In order to receive support, however, states must submit their plans to, and have their work inspected by, the U.S. Department of Transportation (DOT). All federally funded highways must meet DOT standards governing the engineering of the roadbed, employment conditions for construction workers, and weight and load conditions for trucks.

Under the Federal Highway Act of 1956, states planned and built the National System of Interstate and Defense Highways. The Eisenhower Interstate System consists of more than 46,000 miles of superhighways linking almost all cities with a population of 50,000 or more. The federal government paid 90 percent of the cost of this system, with most of the money coming from taxes on gasoline, tires, and trucks that are placed in a trust fund designated for that purpose.

In 1998, Congress passed a $216 billion, six-year surface transportation bill that included $173 billion in funding for highways as well as $2 billion for highway safety. This legislation funds repairing cracked asphalt, increasing safety reinforcements on bridges, and expanding the network of highways. One billion dollars is dedicated to state programs to increase the percentage of drivers who use safety belts and to prevent drunk driving. The legislation also provided $41 billion for mass transit.[45] This massive federal investment is funded by continuing the 18.3 cents-per-gallon tax on gas. In 2005, Congress passed a $244 billion, five-year extension of the 1998 bill.

Traffic has become a major problem in recent years—especially in older cities such as Boston; Denver; Los Angeles; Seattle; San Francisco; Washington, D.C.; and New York. In addition to a growing population and an increasing number of car owners, drivers are driving more each year. As a result, traffic and congestion have become pressing issues for state governments. Increasing road space, building public transportation systems, or establishing staggered work hours should help; however, transportation policy makers have not found it that simple. Adding roads or lanes often leads more people to use them and may ultimately result in new traffic patterns that are no better than the old ones. Public transportation is an option, but Americans love their vehicles, illustrated by the fact that cities with public transportation often have more traffic problems than those without. Staggering work hours is also difficult because businesses work most effectively through collaboration—both with other businesses and within a firm—so it is most efficient for workers to be on the job at the same time each day. Consequently, as population and car ownership continue to rise and the traffic solution remains elusive, automobile congestion will continue to be a pressing state public policy issue.[46]

To encourage residents to purchase vehicles that use clean-burning fuel, Utah has issued these special license plates that allow people to drive in the carpool lane of I-15 without a passenger. Those with energy-efficient vehicles are also eligible to receive tax credits.

Economic Development

Another central priority for governors and mayors, as well as other state and local officials, is providing jobs for their citizens. Governors commonly spend a significant amount of time encouraging companies to relocate within their borders, courting corporate officials, going on trade missions to other countries to promote their state's products, and negotiating favorable tax and other incentives with new businesses. This interest is not new. What is new is the international scope of these activities. Former Utah Governor Norman Bangerter was fond of saying, "The one thing you will always see on an economic development trip to Tokyo is another governor."

States compete with one another because economic development is the key to increasing the tax base that funds government services. But states face a dilemma, because satisfying the demands of new businesses can be expensive, and tax incentives can reduce the tax return the new companies will generate. Competition among states has intensified to the point that localities are worried about keeping the jobs they have, not just persuading new companies to move to their area. New York City has offered billions of dollars in incentives to influence several companies not to leave. Critics of these "bidding wars" believe that states should spend tax money on rebuilding infrastructure and strengthening education rather than offering public funds to selected large private companies.

Regulation

States and local communities adopt safety regulations on the assumption (sometimes mistaken) that the benefits to the general public will outweigh the costs to the individuals and groups being regulated. Thus laws requiring drivers' licenses, compelling motorists to stop at red lights, mandating seat-belt use, or imposing severe penalties on people caught driving under the influence of alcohol or drugs are intended to protect the safety and freedom of innocent pedestrians or occupants of other motor vehicles. Most such laws are accepted as both necessary and legitimate. States have raised the drinking age and stiffened the punishments for drunk driving, in

Traffic congestion is a common concern in U.S. cities. Residents of Los Angeles have the worst problem, spending an average of 56 hours per year in traffic jams.

most cases because the federal government tied federal funds to the passage of such legislation. An interest group, Mothers Against Drunk Driving (MADD), also lobbied effectively to force the issue.

Public Utilities

Corporations receive their charters from the states. Banks, insurance companies, securities dealers, doctors, lawyers, teachers, barbers, and various other businesses and professions are licensed by the states, and their activities are supervised by state officials. Farmers and industrial and service workers are also regulated. But of all businesses, public utilities are the most closely monitored.

It is easier to list than to define public utilities. They include water plants, electric power and natural gas distribution companies, telephone companies, railroads, and bus lines. Public utilities are distinguished from other businesses because government gives them special privileges, such as the power of **eminent domain** (the right to take private property for public use), the right to use public streets, and a certain amount of protection from competition (monopoly). In return, utilities are required to give the public adequate service at reasonable rates.

Public utilities supply essential services in fields in which market competition may be counterproductive. In the United States, private enterprise—subject to public regulation rather than public ownership—has been the usual method of providing essential services. Nevertheless, more than two-thirds of our cities own their own waterworks, about 100 operate their own gas utilities, and many are taking over the operation of their transit systems. But other services—intercity transportation, airlines, telephone, and the supply of natural gas—are almost everywhere provided by private enterprises subject to government regulation.

Every state has a utilities commission (usually called the Public Utilities Commission, or PUC) to ensure that utilities operate in the interest of the public. In 36 states, utility commissioners are appointed by the governor, usually with the consent of the state senate. In Florida and Virginia, they are chosen by the legislature, and in 12 other states, they are elected by the voters.[47] PUC posts were once considered political plums, and commissioners used them as stepping-stones to higher elective office. This is less true these days.

PUCs must strike a balance between fair rates for consumers and adequate profits for the utility companies. "The tremendous work load on these commissions," writes

eminent domain
Power of a government to take private property for public use; the U.S. Constitution gives national and state governments this power and requires them to provide just compensation for property so taken.

one observer, "finds commissioners constantly walking a tightrope between helping a regulated industry get a decent return on investment, and making sure consumers get good service at a fair price."[48] Utility commissioners raise or lower utility rates—perhaps the most visible part of their job—but they are also involved in toxic waste disposal, nuclear power, and truck regulation, as well as telephone, cable television, and other energy-related disputes. The average tenure for commissioners is only about three and a half years, a statistic that suggests the burnout involved in the job.

Utility commissioners operate under the assumption that their decisions are not political, yet nearly every decision they make comes under political attack or stirs political reaction. Several states have enacted laws prohibiting conflicts of interest, limiting commissioners' affiliations with the utilities they regulate and, for at least a year after they resign from the PUC, prohibiting them from accepting employment with any company that was under their regulation. Other states have established a separate office of consumer advocate to encourage even greater responsiveness to consumer needs.

Technology and innovation are driving the deregulation of utilities across the nation. The deregulation of utilities is a controversial topic in virtually every state legislature, as telephone and power companies seek to influence the new rules for competition. Telephone communication is no longer limited to transmissions over telephone lines but now includes cellular and satellite communications. Gas turbines now make it possible for some consumers to generate their own electricity rather than depend on power from public utility companies. Much of the political pressure for deregulation of utilities comes from businesses as well as from consumers.[49]

State legislatures and utility regulators are adopting a marketplace model in which competition between providers is encouraged rather than restricted. In the past, state utility regulators structured rate systems to provide a subsidy to rural and low-income consumers of telephone and electricity services. It is likely that these subsidies will continue, but it is more difficult to identify who pays the subsidy with so many firms now providing telephone and electricity services.

The politics of regulation, especially regulation of public utilities, is of growing interest to citizens and consumers. In many areas, citizens' groups make presentations to the PUC and regularly monitor PUC operations. There has been an increasing interest in PUC activity all across the country, especially in regulating nuclear power and monitoring the cost of energy. For example, after many years of citizen concern over the environmental impact of the San Onofre Nuclear Generating Station, the California Coastal Commission adopted a plan that would mitigate, but not prevent, the destruction of fish and kelp.[50] In the winter of 2005/2006, PUCs in several states took steps to inform customers that natural gas prices would be much higher, and to urge conservation.

Employers and Employees

Despite expanded federal regulation, state and local governments still have much to say about working conditions.

- *Health and safety legislation:* States require proper heating, lighting, ventilation, fire escapes, and sanitary facilities in work areas. Machinery must be equipped with safety guards. Some standards have also been established to reduce occupation-related diseases. Health, building, and labor inspectors tour industrial plants to ensure compliance with the laws.

- *Workers' compensation:* Today all states have workers' compensation programs based on the belief that employees should not have to bear the cost of accidents or illnesses incurred because of their jobs. The costs of accidents and occupational diseases are borne by employers and passed on to consumers in the form of higher prices. In the past, employees had to prove that their employers were at fault if they suffered an accident on the job. Today if people are injured or con-

The San Onofre nuclear plant at San Onofre Beach, approximately 60 miles south of Los Angeles, California.

tract a disease in the ordinary course of employment, they are entitled to compensation set by a prearranged schedule. Workers' compensation is a controversial issue, with employers arguing that employee claims of workplace stress are excessive and will make American firms uncompetitive.

■ *Child labor:* All states forbid child labor, yet state laws vary widely in their coverage and in their definition of child labor. Many states set the minimum age for employment at 14. Higher age requirements are normal for employment in hazardous occupations and during school hours. Many of these regulations have been superseded by stricter federal laws.

■ *Consumer protection:* This movement, which became prominent in the 1960s and 1970s, believes that consumers should be provided with adequate safety information and should have their complaints heard. Most states have offices to hear consumer complaints, including lawyers working in the offices of the state attorney general. State governments often establish professional standards and handle complaints about legal and medical services or insurance practices.

Recent state activity to protect consumers has focused on fraud, especially "guaranteed prize schemes," which are mailed to more than 50 million Americans and to which millions respond. When the prize is not exactly what was promised or the method for selecting winners is deceptive, people often complain to their state government. Other areas in which state governments have been active in attempting to protect consumers include charitable solicitations by telephone, long-distance phone service promotions, credit and promotions, and auditing irregularities and fraud in corporations.

The Importance of State and Local Policy

All 50 state governments and more than 86,000 local governments are on the front lines of trying to solve community and regional social problems. They must often work closely with one another and the national government, and this is a frequent source of frustration.[51]

Divided government in Washington in recent years has meant that neither political party could have its way with domestic policy. Bill Clinton and George W. Bush had different priorities, and the generally divided U.S. Senate in recent years has usually taken a cautious approach on such issues as health care and environmental regulation.

State officials continue to be frustrated with national legislation such as the "No Child Left Behind" and homeland security legislation in recent years that mandate extensive federal requirements into core areas of state and local policy responsibilities yet provide inadequate federal funds to assist in the achievement of these goals.

Innovative governors and state legislators have sponsored important changes in welfare reform, educational testing, transportation, urban planning, and insurance regulation. But the challenges facing state and local officials never let up.

Summary

1. We ask our state and local governments to do many things for us, and what we request in the areas of education, public welfare, health and hospitals, public safety, and transportation are the most costly, accounting for most state and local expenditures.

2. In addition, we ask states and communities to keep our streets safe, protect our natural resources, provide parks and recreation, encourage job opportunities, and protect consumers. There are, of course, great differences in how states and communities set their priorities in these areas. Some communities are so concerned about environmental quality that they are settling for selective growth at the expense of job opportunities. Other communities favor attracting jobs and industry despite environmental costs.

3. Education has been a major area of state and local government activity and concern. It moved to center stage because of a growing concern that our system was not keeping pace with our needs or our global competitors. Several reform efforts have sought to improve our system.

4. Concern about the U.S. system of higher education has also grown as states attempt to balance budgets and meet pressing demands in corrections, health, welfare, and other areas. Few people question the need for a major investment in laboratories, computer instruction, and libraries at colleges and universities, yet the federal government has not offered to pay for these things, and most states do not have the resources to do more than stay afloat in this policy area.

5. The huge national welfare overhaul legislation in 1996 imposed new work requirements and time limits on families receiving cash assistance, and it gave states much greater flexibility in designing and administering programs that serve low-income families with children. The new law established block grants of federal money, money the states could use to provide employment services, child care, and other forms of noncash services and supports. The law was prompted by a desire to trim the federal budget, reverse the rapid growth of welfare caseloads, and eliminate disincentives for self-sufficiency and responsibility that the former welfare system seemed to create. Before the national legislation was passed, many states had experimented with limiting their caseload, placing time limits on welfare, implementing a work requirement, and placing special requirements on teenage mothers. Most of these ideas were then included in the 1996 federal law.

6. States play an important role in setting policies relating to public health. States have long sought to eradicate disease and foster practices conducive to a healthy population. The challenges for states today include the administration of federal outlay programs such as Medicaid, reforming health care services, and controlling the AIDS epidemic. Soaring Medicaid costs have posed an additional challenge to state governments.

7. Law enforcement is a traditional responsibility of state and local governments. After several decades of rising crime rates, that trend has recently been reversed, in part because of increased national and state expenditures.

8. Some state and local governments have taken the lead in protecting the environment, but more generally it has been the federal government that sets the policy standard in environmental matters. Businesses operating in several states are often most involved in pressing for national standards of air and water quality and policies on toxic wastes. The federal

government typically sets environmental standards; the states enforce them.

9. Transportation is a major area of state and local government activity. Although the federal government provides some financial assistance with the construction of roads and highways as well as urban mass transit, the responsibility of planning, building, and maintaining these transportation systems lies with the states. Federal and local fuel taxes have been used to help pay for transportation.

10. States openly compete with one another in the area of economic development by offering tax incentives, waiving environmental regulations, and giving other enticements to businesses to locate or stay within their boundaries.

11. The primary purpose of regulation is to protect the health and safety of individuals and to promote fairness in the marketplace. Among the most regulated industries are public utilities because they enjoy a monopoly. Government usually gives these companies special privileges, specifically eminent domain—the power to take private property for public use. Public utilities, like other industries, are being deregulated as state and federal governments permit competition in these areas. States regulate other economic activities by conducting inspections, granting licenses, and limiting land uses.

Further **Reading**

REBECCA BLANK AND **RON HASKINS,** EDS., *The New World of Welfare* (Brookings Institution Press, 2001).

JASON DEPARLE, *American Dream: Three Women, Ten Kids, and a Nation's Drive to End Welfare* (Viking Penguin, 2004).

JOHN D. DONAHUE, *Disunited States* (Basic Books, 1997).

DENNIS DRESANG AND **JAMES GOSLING,** *Politics and Policy in American States and Communities,* 3d ed. (Prentice Hall, 2001).

R. KENNETH GODWIN AND **FRANK KEMERER,** *School Choice and Tradeoffs: Liberty, Equity, and Diversity* (University of Texas Press, 2002).

VIRGINIA GRAY AND **RUSSELL HANSON,** *Politics in the American States: A Comparative Analysis,* 8th ed. (CQ Press, 2003).

JOHN J. HARRIGAN AND **DAVID NICE,** *Politics and Policy in States and Communities,* 9th ed. (Longman, 2005).

RICHARD D. KAHLENBERG, ED., *Public School Choice vs. Private School Vouchers* (Century Foundation Press, 2003).

NORMAN R. LUTTBEG, *The Grassroots of Democracy: A Comparative Study of Competition and Its Impact in American Cities in the 1990s* (Lexington Books, 1999).

DAVID C. NICE, *Policy Innovation in State Government* (Iowa State University Press, 1994).

GARY ORFIELD AND **CHUNGMEI LEE,** *Brown at 50: King's Dream or Plessy's Nightmare* (Harvard Civil Rights Project, 2004).

MICHAEL A. PAGANO AND **ANN O. M. BOWMAN,** *Cityscape and Capital: The Politics of Urban Development* (Johns Hopkins University Press, 1997).

PAUL E. PETERSON AND **MARTIN R. WEST,** EDS., *No Child Left Behind? The Politics and Practice of School Accountability* (Brookings Institution Press, 2003).

BARRY G. RABE, *Statehouse and Greenhouse: The Emerging Politics of American Climate Change Policy* (Brookings Institution Press, 2004).

ISABEL V. SAWHILL, R. KENT WEAVER, RON HASKINS, AND **ANDREA KANE,** EDS., *Welfare Reform and Beyond: The Future of the Safety Net* (Brookings Institution Press, 2002).

DENISE SCHEBERLE, *Federalism and Environmental Policy,* 2d ed. (Georgetown University Press, 2004).

MARK SCHNEIDER, PAUL TESKE, AND **MELISSA MARSHALL,** *Choosing Schools: Consumer Choice and the Quality of American Schools* (Princeton University Press, 2002).

C. EUGENE STEUERLE, VAN DOORN OOMS, GEORGE PETERSON, AND **ROBERT D. REISCHAUER,** EDS., *Vouchers and the Provision of Public Services* (Brookings Institution Press, 2000).

SANDRA VERGARI, ED., *The Charter School Landscape* (University of Pittsburgh Press, 2002).

JOHN F. WITTE, *The Market Approach to Education: An Analysis of America's First Voucher Program* (Princeton University Press, 1999).

See also *Governing: The Magazine of States and Localities,* published monthly by Congressional Quarterly, Inc., and the series of excellent books on state government public policy making published by the University of Nebraska Press.

Chapter 29

Staffing and Financing State and Local Governments

★

S TATE AND LOCAL GOVERNMENT WORKERS ARE AMERICAN GOVERNMENT'S FIRST RESPONDERS. NEW YORK CITY POLICE AND FIREFIGHTERS WERE THE FIRST TO ARRIVE AT THE WORLD TRADE CENTER ON SEPTEMBER 11, 2001; CITY PARAMEDICS WERE THE FIRST TO TREAT THE VICTIMS; CITY SOCIAL WORKERS WERE ON THE SCENE ALMOST IMMEDIATELY TO DEAL WITH THE GRIEF AND SHOCK; AND VIRTUALLY EVERY CITY WORKER WAS INVOLVED IN SOME WAY IN THE RECOVERY. THERE WAS A LESS POSITIVE RESULT WHEN HURRICANE

Katrina hit New Orleans. The police and other local responders were overwhelmed by the storm and flooding, which often prevented them from even reaching the worst-hit areas. The inability of local authorities to deal adequately with the immediate aftermath of the hurricane meant that the scope of the disaster built for several days until outside aid could arrive.

The nation's state and local employees are more than first responders to disaster, however. More than 5 million are public school teachers;

1 million work as police officers and fire-fighters; 700,000 work as prison guards and corrections officers; 500,000 work in public welfare; 900,000 work in state, county, and city hospitals; and almost 300,000 work in parks and recreation.

State and local employees have some of the most challenging jobs in the nation. They help families move from welfare to work; provide shelter for the homeless; keep the streets and sidewalks clean; drive the subways and buses; provide vaccinations for poor children; pave the streets and purify the water; build and run affordable housing; enroll families and children for Medicaid coverage; provide unemployment insurance and counseling; and even take the tickets at National League Baseball games. The federal government may design economic and social policy, but state and local government employees are the ones who often deliver on the promises.

This chapter will examine the role of state and local employees in more detail, while asking how states and localities raise the money to pay for such a large workforce. The chapter will also review the increasing financial pressure states and local governments face as needs increase and funding gets tighter.

The Role of Public Employees

S tate and local governments are responsible for many policy goals, including greater accountability in public education, greater access to

"[Property tax is] the worst tax known
in the civilized world."

EDWIN SELIGMAN

785

health care for uninsured children, and economic development for poor communities; but they do most of that work by hiring state and local government employees to actually deliver the goods and services. Unlike the federal government workforce, which actually has relatively few employees who work directly with citizens, almost all state and local employees have contact with the citizens.

As of 2005, roughly 19 million people worked for state and local governments, roughly seven times the number that worked for the federal government. And according to the U.S. Bureau of Labor Statistics, state and local governments will continue growing well into the next decade—by 2014, more than 21 million Americans will work in the nation's roughly 87,000 state and local governments, a growth rate of about 11 percent. During the same period, the federal government is expected to stay the same size.[1]

Merit Systems

More than one-third of the cost of state and local government is for people. How are these people chosen? A few of them are elected. The rest are generally hired through some kind of **merit system** in which selection and promotion depend on demonstrated performance (merit) rather than on political patronage. Although in many jurisdictions it still helps to know the right people and belong to the right party, patronage is not as prevalent as it once was. Affirmative action requirements call for recruitment through open procedures. The fact that many public employees now belong to unions has also reduced patronage.

Throughout much of the nineteenth century, governments at all levels were dominated by political patronage, a political **spoils system** in which employment was a reward for partisan loyalty and active political support in campaigns and elections. In 1883, the Pendleton Civil Service Reform Act was passed by Congress, which began to move the federal government from the spoils system to the merit system. This act did not directly affect state and local government. Though many state and local governments began to institute the merit system, there was still quite a bit of political patronage well into the twentieth century. However, in 1939, Democratic Senator Carl Hatch of Arizona pushed through Congress the first Hatch Act, which further promoted the merit principle and limited the political activities of federal, state, and local employees whose salaries were supported with federal funds. Subsequently, state and local governments enacted "little Hatch Acts" that enforced merit principles and restricted the political activities of their employees. Merit testing is now used in 30 states for hiring or promoting employees. Moreover, under a 1976 Supreme Court decision, states cannot dismiss civil servants for political reasons.[2]

Merit systems are generally administered by an office of state personnel, which prepares and administers examinations, provides lists of job openings, establishes job classifications, and determines salary schedules. It also serves as a board of appeal for employees who are discharged. State personnel offices are concerned with training the already employed, bargaining with labor unions, administering affirmative action programs, and filling top-level executive positions.

Critics complain that state personnel offices take too much time to fill job vacancies, in part because they are hampered by red tape and clumsy rules, and in part because job lists are not kept up-to-date. Some critics also complain that hiring and firing rules deprive responsible officials of authority over their subordinates. It is argued that there is so much emphasis on insulating public employees from political coercion that employees enjoy too much job security. Administrators cannot get rid of incompetents; sometimes it takes months and several elaborate hearings to dismiss public employees unwilling or unable to do their jobs. Although merit systems are supposed to emphasize ability and minimize political favoritism, they sometimes discourage able people from seeking public-sector jobs.

merit system
A system of public employment in which selection and promotion depend on demonstrated performance rather than on political patronage.

spoils system
A system of public employment based on rewarding party loyalists and friends.

Public Employee Unions

Public employee unions grew rapidly over the past generation as government workers organized to demand better wages, hours, working conditions, and pensions. These

The Changing Face of American Politics

The State and Local Workforce

Like the federal government, state and local governments have become more diverse over the past two decades and will become even more diverse as they add new jobs. Excluding school teachers, who are overwhelmingly white and female, the U.S. Census Bureau reports that the state and local workforce is becoming an employer of choice for both women and minorities. The increasing percentage of Hispanics is largely due to population growth in states such as California, Florida, and Texas, where Hispanic workers are moving into state and local government jobs at high rates.*

Although the percentages of women and minority workers have increased over the past two decades, both groups remain underpaid relative to males and whites. In 2003, males made an average of $42,200 a year, compared with $34,700 for females, $33,600 for African Americans, and $36,600 for Hispanics. Among high-paid professional jobs, men made more than $7,000 a year more than females, in part because men tend to concentrate in the higher-paying professions such as law, finance, and health administration, while women tend to concentrate in historically underpaid professions in human services such as child welfare. ■

	1983	2003
Male	60%	55%
Female	40	45
White, Non-Hispanic	76	68
African American	17	19
Hispanic	5	9

*See U.S. Census Bureau, *Statistical Abstract of the United States,* 2006 (U.S. Census Bureau, 2005), table no. 454.

unions now wield considerable political clout in most states and cities. In places such as New York City, they are viewed as one of the most powerful forces in political life. In dealing with unions, state and local governments participate in **collective bargaining**—negotiating disputes between unions and management—and **binding arbitration**—settling disputes by agreeing to adhere to the decision of an arbitrator.

Thirty-five percent of state employees and 46 percent of local employees are represented by unions, compared with less than 9 percent of private-sector employees.[3] Indeed, national employee unions see state and local government as a significant growth area.

The American Federation of State, County, and Municipal Employees (AFSCME), is the largest state and local government union, representing more than 1.4 million members, followed by the Service Employees International Union (SEIU), with more than 600,000 state and local government members. In addition, the National Education Association (NEA) represents roughly 2.5 million of the nation's 6 million public-school teachers, followed by the American Federation of Teachers (AFT), which represents another 1 million.

Many police officers and firefighters are also union members. The firefighters' union is often considered one of the most effective political organizations among public employee unions, and the union sometimes engages in door-to-door and telephone campaigning to elect city officials. Unions often raise funds for candidates and sponsor letter-writing campaigns to influence local and national elections. Union pressure in the 1970s and 1980s was a major reason the average pay of public employees, including benefits, rose faster than that of workers in private industry. However, since 1995, employees in private businesses have done better than public employees.

The failure of the merit system to meet many of the needs of public employees encouraged the growth of public sector unions. Growth was also spurred by the example of the success of collective bargaining in the private sector (see Table 29–1). But much of the success of public employee unions has come about because government workers learned how to become a political force in government. Most public employees are educated, intelligent people who can deliver two of the most valuable components of campaigns: money and labor (not to mention the votes of their members, members' families, and friends).

collective bargaining
Method whereby representatives of the union and the employer determine wages, hours, and conditions of employment through direct negotiation.

binding arbitration
A collective bargaining agreement in which both parties agree, in case of dispute over the terms of the union contract, to adhere to the decision of an arbitrator.

TABLE 29–1 Comparison of Merit and Collective Bargaining Systems

	Merit System	Collective Bargaining
Management rights	Extensive	Minimal
Employee participation and rights	Union membership not required	Union membership required
Recruitment and selection	Open competitive exam; open at any level	Union membership and/or occupational license
Promotion	Competitive on basis of merit (often including seniority)	On basis of seniority
Classification of position	Based on objective analysis	Classification negotiable
Pay	Based on balanced pay plan or subject to prevailing rates	Negotiable and subject to bargaining power of union
Hours, leave, conditions of work	Based on public interest as determined by legislature and management	Negotiable
Grievances	Appeal through management with recourse to civil service agency	Appeal by union representation to impartial arbitrators

SOURCE: From *Democracy and the Public Service*, 2d ed. by Frederick C. Mosher, © 1982. Used by permission of Oxford University Press, Inc.

Many people think that public workers have more job security and better wages and fringe benefits than people working in the private sector. Critics point out that public employees seem to have the best of both worlds: job protection coupled with the bargaining power of a labor union. Although collective bargaining and unionization have been generally accepted in the private sector, these rights were not as widely accepted in the public sector.

Because the public sector provides services almost everyone wants and perceives as necessities, demand is relatively constant. Also, public employee unions are an effective political force, so they can influence crucial decisions that affect taxation and the allocation of revenue. Some analysts believe these two factors may result in policies that favor public employees. Awareness of unions' political clout has stiffened the spines of some city and state officials. Today it is not uncommon for mayors in large cities to fight the unions and win support from taxpayers and business groups who think the unions have overstepped their bounds.

Should Public Services Make a Profit?

To make government more efficient and curb the growing influence of public employee unions, many communities have "contracted out" certain public services to the private sector. This practice, called **outsourcing**, can mean that governments save money while the private sector providers still make a profit.[4] Because state and local governments retain the power to raise the revenue for outsourced activities, they maintain control of how the private firms perform through very precise contracts. Today virtually every community service is contracted out somewhere in the United States, and this trend is expected to continue.[5]

In Texas, for example, any citizen who seeks public assistance can call a toll-free help number answered by private employees who have instant computer access to an

outsourcing
Contracting of government services to private firms.

array of state and local government benefits, as well as the caller's own financial information. Using the information, these telephone operators can tell each caller whether he or she qualifies for a variety of programs, from food stamps to health insurance for their children.

Texas is also poised to outsource its entire human service bureaucracy. In 2004, the state consolidated 12 separate human services agencies into four, then asked private contractors to run the entire operation. Although state employees will still make the final decision about who actually gets the benefits, private firms will actually run the administrative side of the new departments, from hiring employees to buying computers.[6]

Many state and local governments have also given private companies complete control of certain activities such as garbage collection through full **privatization**. Privatization involves the complete severance of a function from government—private firms are responsible for both performing a service and also for collecting the revenues through regular billing. Although states and localities vary widely in the extent to which they privatize, public–private partnerships have grown during the past two decades in order to reduce the costs of government services and to improve economic development. One frequently cited example of privatization is Indianapolis; under the leadership of former Mayor Stephen Goldsmith, the city claimed to have saved $230 million over a decade through outsourcing and full privatization.[7] In New York City, the administration of former Mayor Rudolph Giuliani privatized many functions of the government, achieving an estimated $42 million in savings each year.[8]

As cities and states have become pressed for cash, efforts to encourage entrepreneurs to provide public services at a profit have increased. Delegation of emergency and police powers to profit-making corporations, however, raises questions of liability and protection of individual rights. It also raises fears that private contractors will hire transient help at less pay, undermining merit systems and public employee morale.

For successful privatization to occur, the contract between the government and the private company providing the service must define that service to the satisfaction of both parties. On one hand, because of the wide range of services provided by local police departments or health departments, it may be difficult to word such a contract. On the other hand, garbage collection and snow removal can easily be defined and specified in a contract, making these services attractive for privatization, so the trend toward outsourcing municipal services like these will continue.[9]

Paying for State and Local Government

John Shannon, an authority in the field of public finance, has written that there were three "R's" that shocked state and local governments from the late 1970s to the early 1990s. The first "R" was the *revolt* of the taxpayers, which started with California's Proposition 13 and quickly became a national phenomenon. The second "R" was the *recession* of the late 1980s and early 1990s, which placed demands on state and local governments to care for the unemployed and needy. And the third "R" was the *reduction* in federal grants, which meant state and local governments were on their own.[10] States had to search for ways to make ends meet and to live within their revenue projections.

The three "R's" returned with a vengeance in the late 1990s and early 2000s. Taxpayers continued to protest against tax increases, especially property and income taxes; recession returned in 2001 with a devastating impact on state budget revenues; and the federal government continued to tighten grants. Although federal grants to the states did go up from $285 billion in 2000 to nearly $400 billion in 2004, three-quarters of the increase was due to increased spending for health care under the Medicaid program for poor citizens and for food stamps. With revenues declining and demand for services increasing, most states found themselves with little or no leeway to meet their budget needs. As of 2003, the 50 states found themselves with a combined $21.5 billion

privatization
Full release of government functions to private firms, including the power to collect revenues.

budget shortage, which they closed through budget cuts, and some tax increases. The impact of the recession lingered much longer for state governments than for the general economy, but did finally begin to dissipate by 2004.

While states were seeing strong revenue growth in 2005 and 2006, they still face challenges. Medicaid and other health care programs are taking up more and more resources. As energy costs soar, states must also dedicate more funding to energy assistance programs. There is also little hope that the federal government will give states more aid, and in fact there are constant warnings that federal spending on programs that affect the states will be cut.

Mississippi Governor Haley Barbour unveils "Operation: Streamline," a plan designed to eliminate the state's $709 million budget deficit in a year's time. Some of the efficiency measures outlined in the plan include removing civil service protection from some state jobs, which would allow several hundred state employees to be fired, and changing the health insurance plan for state employees and teachers by possibly making them pay for some of their own coverage.

Sources of Revenue

State and local governments get most of their money from taxes.[11] Yet unlike the federal government, they are more likely to share control of the process of raising taxes with the voters through referendums, which are sometimes required before they can levy new or higher taxes. In addition, state and local governments frequently have to meet responsibilities mandated by higher levels of government, which do not always provide the funding for those mandates.

The politics of reducing the federal budget deficit and the antitax mood of the public in recent decades have meant that Congress and the president often enacted policies and expected state and local governments to pick up the tab. At the same time, citizens had high expectations for services provided by their state and local governments—and wanted even more services. This combination of increasing demand and decreasing federal funding made state and local governments the fiscal "stress joints" of American government. When the economy is thriving, states often have surplus revenue and enact tax cuts, but when times are not as good, they have to raise taxes and cut spending. Because most states are constitutionally forbidden to use deficit spending for general government programs, they have to balance their budgets and respond to shortfalls by strengthening and diversifying their revenue bases.[12] Most states try to design their tax systems with broad bases and low rates. A broad base means that most economic activity is covered by taxes like the income tax and sales tax. Therefore the rate of taxation does not have to be very high to achieve sufficient revenue to run the state government. Local governments are usually more constrained in their ability to tax, often limited to property taxes and various fees.

The overlapping layers of government in the United States complicate the tax picture. Tax policies at different levels of government often conflict. While the federal government is reducing taxes, states may be raising them. Indeed, when the federal government cuts both taxes and federal grants, state and local governments have little choice but to raise taxes or cut spending. This is precisely what happened in the late 1970s and early 1980s, and in the economic slowdown of 2002.[13] But the ability of states to respond to changing economic circumstances has been hampered by the tax revolt of the late 1970s, which lowered taxes and brought forth constitutional amendments that make it harder to raise them. Many states also enacted spending limits, which reduced the discretion of state and local elected officials.

The ability of different levels and units of government to make their own tax policy has made tax collection more complicated and expensive. For example, national officials, state officials, and some local officials collect taxes on gasoline, and each level of government maintains its own tax-collecting office. Taxpayers are allowed to deduct certain business expenses and state income taxes from their federal income tax. Alaska, Florida, Nevada, New Hampshire, South Dakota, Tennessee, Texas, Washington, and Wyoming have no personal income tax, and most of these states rely primarily on sales taxes. In those states, taxpayers lose the deduction for state income taxes on their federal tax returns. By contrast, in Alabama, Iowa, Louisiana, Missouri, Montana, Oklahoma, Oregon, and Utah, taxpayers may deduct their federal income tax from their state taxes.[14] Thus changes in state laws can affect the amount of federal and state taxes a person must pay. Although there is little coordination in setting tax policy, there is cooperation between state and federal tax administrators.

No matter who collects the taxes, all the money comes out of a single economy. Although each level of government has a different tax base and each tax hits some groups rather than others, all taxes ultimately depend on the productivity of the American people. And that productivity is affected by many of the activities of government.

Who Pays the Taxes?

Who bears the cost of state and local services is decided in the United States by politics. State and local governments are free to extract whatever taxes they wish from whomever they wish, as long as their taxing practices meet the stipulations of the U.S. Constitution and, in most cases, unless the tax is in conflict with federal laws. The Constitution has been interpreted to prohibit states from taking the following actions:

1. Taxing exports or imports or levying tonnage duties without the consent of Congress

2. Using their taxing power to interfere with federal operations

3. Discriminating against interstate commerce, unduly burdening it, or taxing it directly

4. Using their taxing power to deprive persons of equal protection of the law

5. Depriving individuals of their property without due process

Constitutional lawyers and judges spend much of their time applying these principles to concrete situations. Out of hundreds of disputes, courts have decided that states may collect sales taxes from interstate sales and income taxes from persons and corporations within the states, even if the income was earned from interstate business. However, states may not tax the privilege of engaging in interstate commerce or the profits made through interstate transactions that cannot be apportioned to a single state. Congress has placed a moratorium on state sales taxes on Internet sales, to the anguish of most state officials and traditional firms competing with Internet commerce.

State constitutions also restrict state legislatures' taxing power. Certain kinds of property, such as that used for educational, charitable, and religious purposes, are exempt from taxation. State constitutions frequently list the kinds of taxes that may be collected and stipulate the amount of tax that may be collected from various sources.[15]

Funding Local Government: The Property Tax

In 1890, economist Edwin Seligman called the property tax, "the worst tax known in the civilized world." However, the **general property tax** is still a major revenue source for local governments. The property tax is difficult to administer, leads to favoritism and inequities, and takes little account of ability to pay.[16] Forty years ago, it provided 45 percent of the revenues for state governments and an even higher percentage of the revenues for local governments. In recent decades, most states have eliminated their property taxes, though it is still a major source of local government revenue. If we look at state and local governments together, property taxes still provide more than 30 percent of tax revenues, more than 95 percent of which is collected at the local level. The state that is still the most dependent on property taxes is New Hampshire, where more

general property tax
Tax levied by local and some state governments on real property or personal, tangible property, the major portion of which is on the estimated value of one's home and land.

than 60 percent of state and local tax revenue is from the property tax. At the other end of the scale, Hawaii and Delaware get under 15 percent of state and local taxes from the property tax.[17]

ADMINISTRATION OF THE PROPERTY TAX   A hundred years ago, wealth was primarily *real property*—land and buildings—that was relatively easy to value. Assessors could guess the value of the property a person owned, and that assessment was a good indicator of his or her ability to pay taxes. Today wealth takes many forms. People own varying amounts of personal property—both *tangible* (furniture, jewels, washing machines, rugs, paintings) and *intangible* (stocks, bonds, money in the bank). It is possible to concentrate a large amount of wealth in a small rented apartment. The nature of real property has also changed. It no longer consists mainly of barns, houses, and land but rather of large industrial plants, huge retail stores, and office buildings whose values are hard to measure. In addition, property ownership is less likely these days to reflect the ability to pay taxes. An elderly couple with a large house valued at $300,000 may be living on Social Security payments and a small allowance provided by their children. But they have to pay higher property taxes than a young couple with two healthy incomes who live in a rented apartment.

Although many communities stipulate that the general property tax be imposed on all property, this is not what actually happens. Significant amounts of real property are exempted from property taxes because they are owned by tax-exempt groups, such as churches and charitable organizations. Local governments often waive the tax as an economic development inducement or for other reasons. As a result, two taxpayers may own similar property, but one is assessed at a higher rate. This violates the principle of horizontal equity, that equals should be taxed equally. Intangible personal property is also seldom taxed. Some communities deliberately impose a lower rate on intangible property to induce owners to declare ownership. In addition, tangible personal property such as watches, rings, and other jewelry often escapes taxation or is grossly undervalued.

The general property tax is hard to adjust to changing circumstances. This tax is typically administered by an assessor, who attempts to place a value on property—an **assessment**. The assessment may or may not reflect the real market value of the property. In some states, the assessment is legally required to be a percentage of market value—say, 25 percent. The property tax rate is usually a tax per $100 or $1,000 of assessed valuation or some other such measure. Local and state governments can do very little to change the assessment, but they can raise or lower the tax rates. In the past it was also difficult to revise assessment because it involved a very time-consuming process of checking individual properties and keeping records. Modern advances in computer record-keeping and the use of sophisticated geographic information services have made it easier to keep assessments current.

During times of rising prices, assessed values increase much more slowly than the general price level does. So when governments need more money, the lagging tax bases fail to provide it. When prices fall, valuations do not drop at the same rate. When people cannot pay taxes, property may be sold on the market to cover tax delinquency, but such occurrences are rare. In some areas, property taxes are already so high that to increase them may discourage businesses and lower-income families from moving into the locality.

A property tax bill typically includes fees or taxes charged by three, four, or more governmental units, such as the city, county, school board, water utility, and other special districts. The lump-sum payment aspect of the property tax is one reason for its widespread unpopularity and has prompted some places to permit taxpayers to pay their taxes in installments, often collected with their mortgage payments.

PROPERTY TAXES AND PUBLIC EDUCATION   Local reliance on the property tax to support public schools has generated increasing controversy in recent years. The amount of money available to finance education varies tremendously from area to area; rich suburban areas with a high property valuation per pupil are able to spend much more

assessment
The valuation a government places on property for the purposes of taxation.

than poor areas like the central cities, which need the money most. Reformers have urged the states to take over the financing of public education, or at least to assume a greater share of the burden, in order to equalize differences from community to community. Although this is not a popular idea, most states do distribute funds to local districts in an attempt to ensure more equitable expenditures.

Those hoping for greater state support for the public schools have often turned to the courts. Several state courts have ruled that wide differences between school districts in per-pupil expenditures are inconsistent with the equal protection clause of the Fourteenth Amendment.[18] The California Supreme Court, for example, saw such differences as violating the California constitution.[19] However, in 1973, the U.S. Supreme Court held that there is no federal constitutional requirement that the amount spent per pupil in each school district must be the same.[20] The Court's 1973 decision temporarily slowed the push toward equalization of school expenditures, but the controversy and the issues remain. School funding cases have been brought in 45 of 50 states, some cases focusing on equity between school districts, and some cases focusing on a right to an "adequate" education. State courts in more than half the states have now handed down rulings that have required the states to take action to remedy either the equity or adequacy of their education systems.[21]

Third-grade students at Green Bay Elementary School in North Chicago, Illinois, which has the highest poverty level in its district. There is a continuing debate as to whether funding for such schools should come primarily from local property taxes.

Despite its weaknesses, the general property tax remains an important source of revenue for local government. Supporters of the tax say it is a practical and suitable tax because real rather than personal property is the chief beneficiary of many local services, such as fire protection. Alternatives are few, and each has disadvantages. Moreover, some of the bad features of the general property tax can be corrected by improving assessment and administration methods.

One effort to reform the general property tax is the *circuit-breaker exemption* (sometimes called a *negative income tax*) by which most states and certain cities give a form of tax relief to lower-income families and the elderly. The idea is to protect family income from property tax overload in the same way an electrical circuit breaker protects a family home from an electrical current overload: "When the property tax burden of an individual exceeds a predetermined percentage of personal income, the circuit breaker goes into effect to relieve the excess financial pressure."[22] The circuit-breaker property tax exemption seems to be most popular in the Great Lakes and Plains states and least popular in the Southeast, where property tax burdens are low.

THE PROPERTY TAX REVOLT Hostility to the property tax spawned the tax revolts of the last three decades of the twentieth century. The watershed event in the politics of tax cutting was the passage in 1978 of California's Proposition 13, which limits increases in property taxes to a maximum 2 percent each year. Throughout the 1970s, California property taxes had risen dramatically, spurring voters to pass this initiative to cut them. The passage of Proposition 13 led to similar property tax limitations in other states.

However, local governments still get a large majority of their tax revenue from the property tax. In states like California that have the most stringent limits on the growth of property taxes, the effect has been to shift more of the spending to the state level, where revenues are usually provided by taxes like the income and sales tax. Since states usually attach conditions to their aid, this means that local governments lose control over local programs, such as education. The property tax is also more stable than most other taxes, and when it is limited as a revenue source, the whole state and local tax system becomes more prone to big declines during recessions. Lastly, people tend to be more directly involved in the politics of their local governments, so as key spending and policy decisions move up to the state level, people have less of a chance to participate.

Direct citizen involvement in making fiscal policy is not uncommon in the United States, and there has been a resurgence of initiative and referendum activity in recent decades.[23] Passage of Proposition 13 made tax reduction an important issue nationwide. Heralded as the start of a modern tax revolt, it triggered taxing and spending limits in more than a dozen states and helped launch movements for constitutional

Rising local taxes often cause taxpayers to take to the streets in protest. Taxes are an important source of funding for local governments.

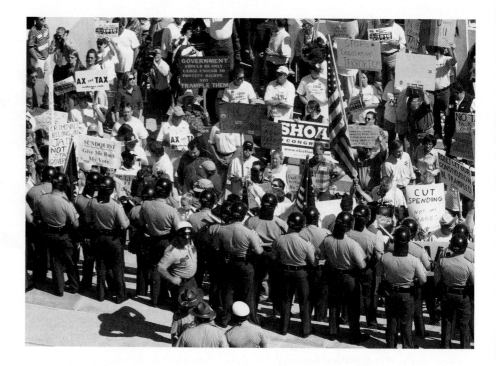

amendments setting federal spending limits, requiring a balanced federal budget, and **indexing** income tax brackets (automatically adjusting income tax rates to rise with inflation so that, in effect, they remain constant). Tax reduction was not limited to ballot initiatives but spread to state legislatures, most of which reduced income, sales, or property taxes.

State and local tax cuts are only one way of attempting to limit government spending. States and localities have also adopted various limits on spending. In their simplest form, such limits restrict future spending to current levels; more typically, they provide for an annual increase in spending that is either limited to a fixed percentage or tied to increases in personal income or inflation. Spending limits can be enacted without tax cuts and, unlike tax cuts, can incur few political costs since no services are being reduced in the short run. New Jersey was the first state to enact spending limits that applied to both state and local governments. Passed in 1976, the New Jersey law limited the growth in state expenditures to the annual percentage increase in per capita personal income and restricted localities to increases of no more than 5 percent without voter approval. Nearly half of the states have followed New Jersey's example and imposed limits on state expenditures.[24]

Funding State Government

While the property tax is the main source of local revenue, state governments raise revenues through a wide range of taxes. In some cases, local governments use these taxes also. Many of these taxes have been used for many decades, but they have become a larger part of total state and local tax collections since the property tax revolts of the 1970s and 1980s (see Figure 29–1). States and localities seek to diversify their taxes to "spread the pain" of taxes as much as possible.

SALES TAXES   Born during the Great Depression, the **sales tax** is the most important source of revenue for states, which annually collect more than $240 billion. Almost all states impose some kind of general sales tax, normally on retail sales, with Washington State and Tennessee (61 percent of all tax revenues come from the sales tax), Florida (56 percent), South Dakota (55 percent), and Texas (50 percent) all well above the national average of 33 percent.

Local sales taxes were uncommon until after World War II, but now 34 states also

indexing
Providing automatic increases to compensate for inflation.

sales tax
General tax on sales transactions, sometimes exempting food and drugs.

allow cities to impose sales taxes. Sales taxes are unpopular with local merchants, who fear they drive business away. In most cases, this is a minor issue that arises only along state borders where consumers can drive into another state with a lower sales tax to make purchases. Most consumers do not pay that much attention to the sales tax on most items.

Sales taxes are easy to administer and produce large amounts of revenue. Many consumers consider sales taxes relatively painless because paying a small amount every day avoids having to pay a large tax bill all at one time. But labor groups and low-income consumers remain opposed to sales taxes, favoring wider use of the income tax instead. They argue that people with small incomes spend a larger percentage of their budgets on food and clothing than the wealthy do, so sales taxes fall heaviest on those least able to pay. That is why many states exempt necessities—primarily food and drugs—from the sales tax.

States continue to search for ways to tax services, both because the states are under acute pressure to find new revenues and because the service sector of the economy continues to expand. All states tax some services, but none has a broad-based tax on services. Among the kinds of services taxed are cable television, landscaping, income tax preparation, pest control, videotape rental, laundry and dry cleaning, and photocopying.

State and local officials listen with concern to talk about the federal government's imposing a **value-added tax (VAT)** like that used in many western European countries. This tax is imposed on the value added to a product at *each stage* of production and distribution. Should the federal government impose such a tax, state and local officials fear that their ability to use the sales tax will be reduced.

There is a running battle about whether states can tax mail-order catalog and Internet sales. Opponents contend that taxing such sales violates the constitutional provisions governing interstate commerce. The Supreme Court has generally left the issue to Congress, and Congress has imposed a moratorium on all Internet taxes until 2007 while it sorts out the pros and cons. Under the moratorium, nine states are allowed to tax Internet sales, while another six allow local governments to tax Internet sales as well.[25]

Although Internet taxes only account for $80 to 120 million today, the future stakes are high. Online retail sales were expected to reach $170 billion in 2006 and are growing by more than 20 percent a year.[26] This is still a small proportion of total retail sales, but is growing much faster. Billions in revenues could go to states and localities if they taxed these purchases at the same rate they tax merchants operating within their states.

But there is a question of fairness. Local merchants who have to collect sales taxes are at a disadvantage if mail-order and Internet firms can escape these taxes. Mail-order merchants and their lobbyists claim it would be an administrative nightmare to collect and reimburse all the sales taxes, and they argue that they should not be obligated to collect taxes for a state in which they do not have a physical presence. But this position does not reduce complexity. It means if there is an Eddie Bauer store in your state and you buy a shirt from the Eddie Bauer catalog, you are charged sales tax, while a similar shirt from a Lands' End catalog would escape the tax in every state where it has no stores.

States are trying to resolve some of the legal obstacles that prevent them from collecting taxes on these online and mail-order sales. Beyond the federal moratorium on Internet taxes, there is the problem of the extreme diversity of state and local sales tax systems. This did not matter so much when sales taxes were collected locally, but if they were to be collected on a national basis, it would be a very great burden on the retailers to even discover what tax rate they would be required to pay in different localities. Forty-two states are participating in the Streamlined Sales Tax Project, which is supposed to simplify sales tax systems, and reduce the compliance costs for retailers.

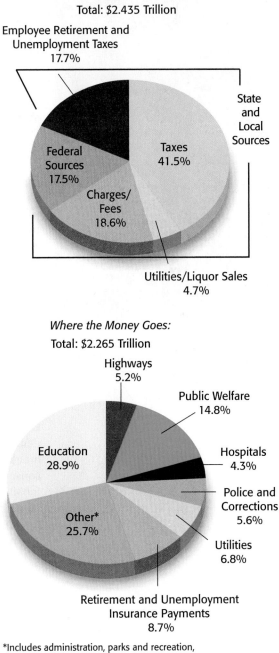

Where the Money Comes From:

Total: $2.435 Trillion

Employee Retirement and Unemployment Taxes 17.7%

State and Local Sources

Taxes 41.5%

Federal Sources 17.5%

Charges/Fees 18.6%

Utilities/Liquor Sales 4.7%

Where the Money Goes:

Total: $2.265 Trillion

Highways 5.2%

Public Welfare 14.8%

Education 28.9%

Hospitals 4.3%

Police and Corrections 5.6%

Other* 25.7%

Utilities 6.8%

Retirement and Unemployment Insurance Payments 8.7%

*Includes administration, parks and recreation, housing, transportation, etc.

FIGURE 29–1 State and Local Revenues and Expenditures, 2004.

SOURCE: U.S. Bureau of the Census, *State and Local Government Finances: 2003–04* at www.census.gov/govs/www/estimate04.html.

value-added tax (VAT)
A tax on increased value of a product at each stage of production and distribution rather than just at the point of sale.

Governments impose an excise tax on cigarettes to generate revenue but also to discourage smoking and to fund the cost of treating smokers.

INDIVIDUAL INCOME TAXES   The state individual, or personal, income tax has been one of the fastest-growing revenue sources for most states in recent decades. It is, with the sales tax, one of the two largest revenue sources for state government. The individual income tax accounts for about 33 percent of all state tax collections, with Oregon (individual income taxes account for 70 percent of its revenues), New York (54 percent), Massachusetts (52 percent), and Virginia (52 percent) well above the national average.

Individual income taxes are generally mildly **progressive taxes**; that is, the rate goes up with the size of the income. State income tax rates, however, do not rise as sharply as the federal income tax and seldom go above 8 percent of taxable income. In the 1990s, many states reduced their highest individual income tax rates. States usually start with federal taxable income and apply their own rates to it.

States generally do not allow local governments to levy income taxes. However, some cities—following the lead of Philadelphia and Toledo—now collect a *wage tax*, and most cities in Ohio, and cities, towns, and school districts in Pennsylvania, levy a similar *payroll tax* on all persons. For instance, visiting professional athletes who compete in Philadelphia are subject to the city's earned-income tax. The Toledo tax also applies to corporate profits. A municipal income tax enables hard-pressed cities to collect money from citizens who use city facilities but live in the suburbs. Similar taxes are collected by New York City, Detroit, and Louisville.

CORPORATE INCOME AND OTHER BUSINESS TAXES   Most states also impose a corporate income tax, usually imposed at a flat rate. These taxes account for about 5 percent of state taxes. Many states have cut corporate income tax rates or granted generous exemptions as a way to try to attract businesses to their state. States also collect a variety of other kinds of taxes on business activity. These can include taxes on business assets, corporate franchise taxes, licensing taxes and fees, and taxes imposed when new business are formed.

EXCISE TAXES   Almost all states tax gasoline, alcohol, and cigarettes; taxes on specific items are known as **excise taxes**. Because many cities also tax these items, the combined local, state, and federal levies often double the cost of these items for the consumer. Gasoline taxes are sometimes combined with the funds collected for automobile and driver's licenses and are earmarked for highway construction and maintenance. Liquor taxes often consist of both license fees to manufacture or sell alcoholic beverages and levies on their sale or consumption; they are often used for general government spending.

Some states own liquor stores, with the profits going to the state treasury. High taxation of liquor is justified on the grounds that it reduces the amount of alcohol consumed, falls on an item that is not a necessity of life, and eases the task of law enforcement. Some states, like North Carolina, set aside part of their alcohol taxes for mental health programs and the rehabilitation of alcoholics. If the tax is raised too high, however, liquor purchases tend to be diverted into illegal channels, and tax revenues fall off.

The rationale for taxing cigarettes is similar. High tobacco taxes in states like Alaska, New Jersey, and Hawaii, which do not grow tobacco, and low tobacco taxes in tobacco-growing states like Virginia and the Carolinas, have led to interstate smuggling. Some states levy a general sales tax on top of the excise tax, especially on tobacco products.

SEVERANCE TAXES   In several states, **severance taxes** have been a key source of revenue. These are taxes on the privilege of "severing" or removing such natural resources as coal, oil, timber, and gas from the land. Severance taxes are the main tax source in Alaska (with 50 percent of tax collections from severance taxes) and Wyoming (46 percent). New Mexico, North Dakota, and Oklahoma also get more than 10 percent of their tax revenue from the severance tax. Although 35 states have some type of severance tax, significant revenues from this tax are not available to most states, since they do not produce significant amounts of natural resources. Tax revenues from severance taxes go up and down with the price of oil, gas, and coal.

progressive tax
A tax graduated so that people with higher incomes pay a larger fraction of their income than people with lower incomes.

excise tax
Consumer tax on a specific kind of merchandise, such as tobacco.

severance tax
A tax on the privilege of "severing" such natural resources as coal, oil, timber, and gas from the land.

History Makers

Robert Moses

While he never held elective office, Robert Moses was one of the most powerful people in the government of New York City from the 1930s to the 1950s. If judged by his long-term impact on the physical reality of the city and the surrounding suburbs, his impact was second-to-none. Moses held many appointive positions in the New York City and New York State governments, many of them simultaneously. Moses was extremely aggressive in his highway and bridge planning, sweeping aside the objections of residents, land owners, and many elected politicians. Moses also was responsible for the building of most of the public housing projects in New York City. In addition, Moses was in many ways essential to the decision of the United Nations to locate its headquarters in New York.

Robert Moses was born in 1888 in New London, Connecticut. After attending Yale University and getting a Ph.D. from Columbia University, Moses became involved in reform politics in New York City, and soon fell into the orbit of Al Smith, then governor of New York. It was as Smith's aide that Moses began to get involved in public development, helping to build up the New York State park system. Moses also began to build a series of parkways on Long Island. When the New Deal came in the 1930s, Moses used the federal aid that became available to build numerous projects in New York, including the Triborough Bridge, the tolls from which allowed him to fund even more projects.

Eventually a backlash built up against Robert Moses's style of development. In particular, many people felt that the building of expressways and bridge access roads through the middle of neighborhoods was not only contributing to urban decay, it was doing little to make access to the city easier. The neighborhoods were divided and destroyed, and many of the residents moved out to the suburbs, soon adding to the traffic on those same expressways. Eventually getting into and out of the city was so difficult that businesses began to move out of the city also.

It was when Robert Moses proposed an expressway through lower Manhattan, one that would have cut through the neighborhoods of Greenwich Village and what is now SoHo, that his power and influence finally met its match. Public protest forced the cancellation of the project in 1964. Moses's power waned from that point on, and he was to complete no more major projects. In fact, the backlash against the building of expressways through the middle of urban areas extended beyond New York City. Most urban planners after the 1960s tended to stress the importance of keeping neighborhoods intact. Still, hundred of parks, highways, buildings, and bridges exist now because of the vision and drive that Robert Moses brought to urban planning in New York.

The most famous and controversial book on Robert Moses is Robert A. Caro, *The Power Broker: Robert Moses and the Fall of New York* (Alfred A. Knopf, 1974). ■

Robert Moses

Moses was extremely aggressive in his highway and bridge planning, sweeping aside the objections of residents, land owners, and many elected politicians.

The state and local taxes described here do not begin to exhaust the kinds of taxes collected by state and local governments. Admission taxes, stock transfer taxes, inheritance taxes, parimutuel taxes, and taxes on utilities and insurance are common.

Other Revenues

"The Bible Belt might as well be renamed the Blackjack Belt, with floating and land-based casinos."

JAMES POPKIN AND KATIA HETTER,
"AMERICA'S GAMBLING CRAZE"

In addition to taxation, states derive revenue from fees and special service charges. At least 10 percent of the money collected by state and local governments comes from inspecting buildings, recording titles, operating courts, licensing professions, disposing of garbage, and other services. Parking meters have become an important revenue source for some cities. Municipal governments frequently operate water supply and local transit systems. City-operated liquor stores are administered by, and turn a profit in, certain cities in Alaska, Minnesota, North Carolina, and South Dakota. The city of Dallas owns and operates an FM radio station (WRR), which plays classical music. Some states and cities run other business enterprises, such as cable television services, from which they make money (and sometimes lose it, too). North Dakota, for example, operates a state-owned bank. Municipally owned gas and power companies often contribute to city treasuries. In some cases, utility profits are large enough to make other city taxes unnecessary.

LEGALIZED GAMBLING Recent years have seen a dramatic increase in legalized gambling in the United States. Only Hawaii and Utah do not permit some form of legalized gambling. For many years, only Nevada permitted legalized casino gambling, but now 37 states, the District of Columbia, and Puerto Rico have legalized gambling, including lotteries, and 20 states allow casinos. This increase occurred to a great degree because Native American tribes asserted their right to self-rule on reservations and brought casinos to states like California, Michigan, Connecticut, and South Dakota. In addition, gambling companies asserted that prohibitions against land-based casinos did not apply to floating ones, and they promoted gambling on riverboats and dockside casinos. A casino is estimated to be within a four-hour drive for 95 percent of all Americans. "The Bible Belt might as well be renamed the Blackjack Belt, with floating and land-based casinos."[27]

Video poker and other forms of gambling have been spreading to more states. As improvements have been made in data encryption, it is now technologically possible for people to engage in virtual gambling in the privacy of their homes. What does this technology do to state laws limiting or banning gambling? The possibility of betting online also raises the issue of whether those who take bets can be prosecuted for permitting underage gambling.

The federal government has tried to play a role in restricting gambling in various forms, such as betting on college or high school sports and underage gambling. Many coaches of college sports have requested that limitations be placed on betting on their games. The American Gaming Association (www.americangaming.org) provides media updates on government efforts to restrict gambling. Or you can refer to the links and resources provided by the North American Gaming Regulators Association at www.nagra.org.[28]

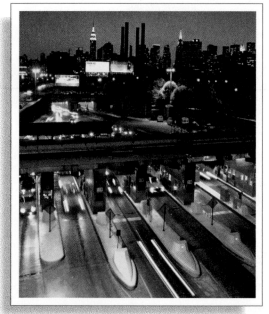

User fees, like the tolls collected at this tunnel entrance in New York City, contribute to the maintenance of such facilities.

LOTTERIES Lotteries are a special form of state-sponsored and state-administered gambling that are used to raise money for public purposes. Along with the District of Columbia and Puerto Rico, 40 states operate lotteries to generate revenue without raising taxes. Lotteries are not entirely new; the Continental Congress ran a lottery to help finance the Revolutionary War. Indeed, all 13 original states used lotteries as a form of voluntary taxation in the 1780s. Lotteries also helped establish some of the nation's earliest colleges, notably Princeton, Harvard, and Yale. In 1964, New Hampshire was the first state to revive the practice in modern times to help balance its budget.

In recent decades, state lotteries have increased in popularity, in part because they increase revenues without raising taxes. Although state-run lotteries provide less than 3 percent of all state revenues, they provide essential revenues that would have to be replaced by other sources, all of which are less politically popular. States pay out between 50 and 70 percent of their gross receipts from lotteries in prizes and roughly 6 percent to cover administration costs. The remaining revenues are used for public purposes.

Lotteries generate net profits in excess of $16 billion. Many of the state lotteries were adopted as a result of statewide referendums, and the revenues from lotteries are used for a variety of purposes. About half of the states with lotteries earmark most or all of their proceeds for education; a significant number of the remaining states commit their proceeds to the state general fund. Some states, like Kansas and Oregon, designate lottery profits for economic development; Minnesota commits part of what it makes through the lottery to the environment; Pennsylvania and West Virginia designate senior citizens' programs to receive lottery profits.

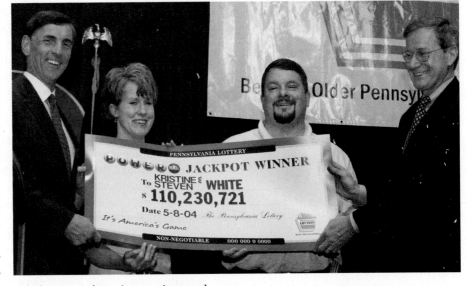

These Pennsylvania lottery winners collected over $110 million dollars. States rely on lotteries, among other methods, to raise revenue for various state functions.

Proponents of lotteries identify a popular cause like education, the environment, or senior citizens as the beneficiaries of lottery profits in hopes of getting popular support for passage of the lottery. Opposition to the lottery often comes from church groups, which contend that state lotteries are immoral because they are a form of legalized gambling. Proponents counter that churches often raise funds through raffles, bingo, and other games of chance. Opponents also argue that lotteries are a bad investment because they yield a poor rate of return. Proponents respond that tickets are purchased more for their entertainment value than as an investment.

GRANTS Grants from states to local governments have become increasingly important during the past several decades. The federal government once allocated large sums to cities, but has largely stopped providing such direct support. Local governments received about $380 billion in aid from the states in 2004, almost a third of their total revenue. State officials return revenues collected from certain taxes to local governments, often without specifying the purposes for which the money should be used. Local governments receive state and federal grants in a wide range of areas, including education, transportation, corrections, law enforcement, housing, welfare, community development, and health care. One reason local governments receive so much money in the form of grants is that they are the unit of government closest to the people and most experienced at providing services.

Local governments often see state and federal grants as enhancing the services they provide. In return for a modest investment of local tax revenue, local governments can get grant money from state or federal governments. But grant money may not be available for some pressing local priorities, or the strings attached to the money may permit state and federal governments to set local priorities. In such cases, are local governments wise to pursue the grants, or should they put their money into their most pressing priorities? Local governments also worry about depending on grant money if state or federal money should dry up in the future.

Borrowing Money

State and local governments collect large sums of money to pay for current operating expenses—garbage collection, police protection, and social services. To fund long-term projects—so-called *capital expenditures*—cities and states often have to borrow money. This long-term borrowing is necessary for building schools, constructing roads, and clearing slums—projects whose costs are so large that it is not feasible to pay for them out of current revenue. Moreover, because these improvements have long lives and add to the wealth of the community, it is reasonable to pay for them over time. For this purpose, governments issue bonds, most often with voter approval.

During the early years of the nineteenth century, states and cities subsidized railroad and canal builders. The money for these and other public improvements came from bonds issued by the cities or states and purchased by investors. Provision for payment of these debts was inadequate, and citizens were burdened with debts long after the improvements had lost their value. As a result, default on obligations was frequent. Aroused by the legislatures' abuse of their authority, voters insisted on constitutional amendments restricting legislative discretion to borrow money. The power to borrow money for the long term now routinely requires voter approval.

Increasingly important over the last few decades are special-purpose governments or special districts: airport authorities, bridge and highway authorities, water and wastewater districts, public transit authorities, and community college districts. Their creation has resulted in turning more and more to *revenue bonds* to help finance their operations. The repayment and dividends due investors come from tolls and fees charged by the facility. In most cases, revenue bonds do not require voter approval, making it much easier to issue this kind of debt and also to spend more on services like public transportation.[29]

State and local bonds are attractive to investors because the interest is exempt from federal income tax. State and local governments can borrow money at a lower interest rate than private businesses can, and although credit ratings differ sharply according to economic health, the credit of most cities and states is good. Hence they can easily find buyers for their bonds. Because governments are often permitted to issue bonds beyond the limitations on their general indebtedness, they use them whenever possible. However, as New York City learned in the 1970s, excessive reliance on bonds can be detrimental to the fiscal health of a state or city.

Intergovernmental Competition

State and local governments exist in a competitive environment in which they seek to enhance their own economy and overall reputation. They have become more competitive in courting business and economic growth because of the increasing mobility of business and the stagnant growth in some sectors of the economy and in some regions of the country. One way governments compete in this marketplace is through the use of *tax incentives* that offer reduced tax rates to promote business investment in the local community. Government officials assume that a pro-growth policy is good politics because voter confidence increases when new jobs and businesses move into a community or state.

Local governments that are successful in luring businesses to locate within their boundaries also assume that in the long run these new businesses will add to the tax base by stimulating sales taxes and property taxes. In the case of large shopping malls that attract shoppers from surrounding communities, the revenues from the sales tax may actually lower the tax burden for residents of the city because of sales taxes paid by nonresidents.

Developers of shopping malls or office complexes who are thinking about relocating often play one local government against another in an effort to drive down their tax burden. Established businesses in the community then cry foul about the tax incentives offered to attract new businesses or keep those who threaten to leave. Economists are skeptical about how important these incentives really are. Some believe that such factors as space availability, cost of land, cost of labor, and quality of life are at least as important in decisions about where businesses locate.[30]

Sports teams, stadiums, and arenas provide another example of intergovernmental

Safeco Field in Seattle, Washington, home to the Seattle Mariners, is one of the country's new sports stadiums built with a combination of state, local, and private funding.

competition for tax incentives. In recent years, competition between cities, especially larger cities, has drawn them into funding the construction of major sports facilities for professional football, basketball, hockey, or baseball teams. Because the teams are identified with the city or state and are perceived to enhance the community's reputation, local and state governments have been responsive to the demands of team owners. Some cities have offered team owners "sweetheart deals" to keep the team or build them a new stadium.[31] The New York Yankees threatened to leave their historic location in the Bronx for New Jersey's Meadowlands but agreed to stay put after winning concessions from local government. Often the building of new facilities requires a referendum, but other arrangements, such as the proceeds from parking and vendors, are open to negotiations between the owners and government officials.[32]

Finally, local governments are also competing to build prisons and other correctional facilities. As the number of people in prison has soared from 218,000 in 1974 to 1.5 million in 2004, the number of prisons has grown from 600 to more than 1,000. In small counties and poor areas of the country, a new prison can provide a variety of economic benefits, from jobs to construction income. In Texas, which has the largest number of state prisons in the country, the number of counties with a prison increased from just 3 percent in 1979 to 28 percent in 2000; in Florida, which has the second-largest number, the number surged from 45 percent to 78 percent.[33]

Competing for businesses, baseball teams, and prisons can have negative impacts on a state or local government, not the least of which is the uneven distribution of income on the basis of bidding wars. A dollar spent on prison construction and employment in one county means a dollar not spent in another—some experts estimate that Cook County, Illinois, will lose $88 million in federal benefits from 2000 to 2010 because thousands of its residents were counted in the county in which they were imprisoned rather than the county in which they originally lived.

Assessing State and Local Performance

As the old saying goes, states and localities are where the rubber meets the road. They are often responsible for delivering on the promises that the federal government makes, whether in health care, homeland security, economic development, or welfare reform. As the federal budget deficit continues to grow, and Social Security and Medicare spending grows, states can expect even greater pressure to fill the gap created by dwindling federal spending for discretionary programs.

Unfortunately, state and local governments vary greatly in their administrative capabilities. According to *Governing* magazine, which rates states, counties, and cities on overall management, only five states won an A or A– grade for their financial management in 2005, just three got an A or A– for managing their employees effectively, four received an A or A– for their management of state infrastructure, and five earned an A or A– for information technology. Alabama and California got C–, the worst report cards in 2005, with California getting a D in financial management, and Alabama getting a D in infrastructure management; while Utah and Virginia came out on top with A– overall.[34]

Although many state and local governments try to get better every year, most still have a long way to go to meet public expectations. It can also be difficult to sustain progress since they tend to cut budgets for management improvement during the lean years, which contributes to future performance problems.

Summary

1. Wages for public employees constitute more than one-third the cost of state and local government. These public employees, who are the first point of contact for many Americans, are hired through merit systems.

2. One of the most controversial aspects of state and local government in recent years has been the unionization of more than 50 percent of public employees at the state and local levels. Public employee unions have been increasingly successful in recruiting new members and bargaining for better wages, hours, working conditions, and pensions. Their success has caused some public backlash.

3. One response to growing costs has been the outsourcing of public services to the private sector. Garbage collection, recreation, and even emergency services are now contracted out in some cities. Arguments in favor of privatization include lower cost and better services. But others argue that this movement reduces government accountability and may lead to corruption in the awarding of contracts.

4. State and local governments get most of their money from taxes. Decreasing federal funding has made state and local governments the "stress joints" of American government.

5. The general property tax, despite its unpopularity, remains the most important source of revenue for many local governments. Property is generally thought of as real estate but can include other personal property like automobiles or boats. Administration of the tax is generally handled at the local level, but several states provide oversight. The property tax is a major revenue source for public schools.

6. Tax revolts in the 1970s and 1980s resulted in limits on property taxes in several states and often made it more difficult to raise property taxes. The property tax is now a less significant part of the tax base of local governments.

7. State and local governments have traditionally received revenues primarily from property taxes but also from sales taxes, income taxes, excise taxes, and severance taxes. Recently, they have diversified their revenue sources by turning to such devices as lotteries, legalized gambling, user fees, other fees and special service charges, and taxes not previously used at the state and local levels. This diversification was made necessary by economic downturns and by cutbacks in federal support. Intergovernmental grants from states to cities and school districts have increased in importance as local governments have had to deal with rising costs and expectations but limited revenues. In addition, the growth in special-district governments has led to greater reliance on revenue bonds to finance local services.

8. States and local governments have also become more competitive in courting business and economic growth, especially through tax incentives and subsidies.

Further **Reading**

J. RICHARD ARONSON AND **ELI SCHWARTZ,** EDS., *Management Policies in Local Government Finance,* 5th ed. (International City/County Management Association, 2004).

GLENN BEAMER, *Creative Politics: Taxes and Public Good in a Federal System* (University of Michigan Press, 1999).

DAVID BRUNORI, *State Tax Policy: A Political Perspective* (Urban Institute Press, 2006).

TERRY N. CLARK AND **LORNA C. FERGUSON,** *City Money: Political Processes, Fiscal Strain, and Retrenchment* (Columbia University Press, 1983).

RONALD C. FISHER, *Intergovernmental Fiscal Relations* (Kluwer, 1997).

KATHRYN A. FOSTER, *The Political Economy of Special-Purpose Government* (Georgetown University Press, 1997).

M. DAVID GELFAND, ED., *State and Local Taxation and Finance in a Nutshell,* 2d ed. (West, 2000).

STEVEN D. GOLD, ED., *The Fiscal Crisis of the States: Lessons for the Future* (Georgetown University Press, 1995).

CHARLES T. GOODSELL, *The Case for Bureaucracy,* 4th ed. (Chatham House, 2003).

ROY T. MEYERS, ED., *Handbook of Government Budgeting* (Jossey-Bass, 1999).

National Conference of State Legislatures, Legislative Budget Procedures in the 50 States (National Conference of State Legislatures, 1998).

DAVID ALAN NIBERT, *Hitting the Lottery Jackpot: State Governments and the Taxing of Dreams* (Monthly Review Press, 2000).

MICHAEL PAGANO AND **RICHARD MOORE,** *Cities and Fiscal Choices* (Duke University Press, 1985).

B. GUY PETERS, *The Politics of Taxation: A Comparative Perspective* (Blackwell, 1991).

JOHN E. PETERSEN AND **DENNIS R. STRACHOTA,** EDS., *Local Government Finance: Concepts and Practices* (Government Finance Officers Association, 1991).

HENRY J. RAIMONDO, *Economics of State and Local Government* (Praeger, 1992).

HARVEY S. ROSEN, *Public Finance,* 7th ed. (McGraw-Hill, 2004).

E. S. SAVAS, *Privatization in the City: Successes, Failures, Lessons* (CQ Press, 2005).

RONALD SNELL, *New Realities in State Finance* (National Conference of State Legislatures, 2004).

THOMAS R. SWARTZ AND **JOHN E. PECK,** EDS., *The Changing Face of Fiscal Federalism* (Sharpe, 1990).

Also, the U.S. Bureau of the Census regularly publishes reports on state and municipal finances.

KeyTerms

merit system, p. 786

spoils system, p. 786

collective bargaining, p. 787

binding arbitration, p. 787

outsourcing, p. 788

privatization, p. 789

general property tax, p. 791

assessment, p. 792

indexing, p. 794

sales tax, p. 794

value-added tax (VAT), p. 795

progressive tax, p. 796

excise tax, p. 796

severance tax, p. 796

Sustaining Constitutional Democracy

⭐

AMERICA'S FOUNDING GENERATION FOUGHT AN EIGHT-
YEAR REVOLUTION TO SECURE ITS RIGHTS AND LIBERTY.
FIRST AT THE CONSTITUTIONAL CONVENTION IN 1787
AND LATER IN THE FIRST CONGRESS, THEY CONFRONTED THE
CHALLENGES OF CREATING A GOVERNMENT, WRITING A CON-
STITUTION, AND DRAFTING A BILL OF RIGHTS THAT WOULD
PROTECT RIGHTS TO LIFE, LIBERTY, AND SELF-GOVERNMENT
FOR THEMSELVES AND SUBSEQUENT GENERATIONS. BUT THEY
KNEW, AS WE ALSO KNOW, THAT PASSIVE ALLEGIANCE TO IDEALS
and rights is never enough. Every generation must see itself as respon-
sible for nurturing these ideals by actively renewing the community
and nation of which it is a part.

The framers knew about the rise and decline of ancient Athens.
They were familiar with Pericles's funeral oration, which states that the
person who takes no part in public affairs is a useless person, a good-
for-nothing.[1] According to Pericles and many Athenians, the city's business was everyone's business. Athens had flourished as an example of
what a civilized city might be, but it collapsed when greed, self-
centeredness, and complacency set in. As time went on, the Athenians wanted security more than they wanted liberty, comfort more
than freedom. In the end they lost it all—
security, comfort, and freedom. "Responsibility was the price every man must
pay for freedom. It was to be had on no
other terms."[2]

If we are to be responsible citizens of
the United States in the truest meaning
of the term, our dreams must transcend
personal ambition and the accumulation of material goods. Our responsibilities as citizens include speaking up for
what we believe, such as support for or
opposition to particular policies like the
war in Iraq, same-sex marriages, health
care reform, or less regulation of the
economy. Such a discourse of opinion
helps produce more representative policy and informed citizens. Our country
needs citizens who understand that our
well-being is tied to the well-being of our
neighbors, community, and country.
This spirit was evident in the days and
weeks following the September 11, 2001,
terrorist attacks on New York City and
Washington, D.C. All across the country,
people contributed to relief efforts. In an
address to the nation in the evening of
the day of the attacks, President Bush
said, "Terrorist attacks can shake the
foundations of our biggest buildings, but
they cannot touch the foundation of
America. These acts shatter steel, but
they cannot dent the steel of American
resolve."[3] There was also a tremendous
response to requests for financial and
other assistance to charitable groups like
the Red Cross in the days and weeks after
Hurricane Katrina in 2005. As the war on
terrorism was waged, what also became
clear was the tremendous contrast
between the freedom of citizens in the
United States and the repression that

"Terrorist attacks can shake the foundations of
our biggest buildings, but they cannot touch
the foundation of America. These acts shatter
steel, but they cannot dent the steel of
American resolve."

PRESIDENT GEORGE W. BUSH

had been part of the Taliban regime in Afghanistan and the reign of Saddam Hussein in Iraq.

More people today live under conditions of political freedom than under authoritarian governments than at any previous time. The transition from living under authoritarian rule to political freedom is often difficult, as evidenced by the efforts to form democratic governments and defeat insurgencies in Afghanistan and Iraq. Throughout history, most people have lived in societies in which a small group at the top imposed its will on others. Authoritarian governments justify their actions by saying that people are too weak to govern themselves; they need to be ruled. Thus neither in Castro's Cuba nor in the military regime of North Korea, neither in the People's Republic of China nor in Saudi Arabia, do ordinary people have a voice in the type of decisions we Americans routinely make: Who should be admitted into college or serve in the military? Who should be allowed to immigrate into the country? How much money should be spent for schools, economic development initiatives, health care, or environmental protection? In America, we take the freedom to make such decisions for granted.

The theme in this last chapter is simple: Elected leadership and constitutional structures and protections are important, but an active, committed citizenry is equally important. Freedom and obligation go together. Liberty and duty go together. The answer to a nation's problems lies not in producing a perfect constitution or a few larger-than-life leaders. The answer lies in encouraging a nation of attentive and active citizens who will, above and beyond their professional and private ambitions, care about the common concerns of the Republic and strive to make democracy work.

The Case for Government by the People

The essence of our Constitution is that it both grants power to government and withholds power from it. Fearing a weak national government and popular disorder, the framers wanted to strengthen the powers of the national government so that it could carry out its responsibilities, such as ensuring domestic order and maintaining national defense. They also wanted to limit state governments in order to keep them from interfering with interstate commerce and property rights. Valuing above all the principle of individual liberty, the framers wanted to protect the people from too much government. They wanted a limited government—yet one that would work. The solution was to divide up the power of the national government, to make it ultimately responsive, if only indirectly, to the voters.

Most Americans want a government that is efficient and effective but that also promotes social justice. We want to maintain our commitment to liberty and freedom. We want a government that acts for the majority yet also protects minorities. We want to safeguard our nation and our streets in a world full of change and violence. We want to protect the rights of the poor, the elderly, and minorities. Do we expect too much from our elected officials and public servants? Of course we do!

Constitutional democracy is a system of checks and balances. It balances values against competing values. Government must balance individual liberties against the collective security and needs of society. The question always is, which rights of which people are to be protected by what means and at what price to individuals and to the whole society? These questions arose again and again in the war on terrorism following the terrorist attacks of September 2001. Following these attacks, the USA PATRIOT Act became law, allowing greater government surveillance. Both conservatives and liberals have criticized the USA PATRIOT Act, which was only renewed with the narrowest of majorities in 2006. The Supreme Court also rebuffed the Bush administration's position that it could hold "enemy combatants" indefinitely and without access to the courts.

Participation and Representation

No political problem is more complicated than working out the proper relationship between voters and elected officials. It is not just a simple issue of being sure that elected officials do what the voters want them to do. Every

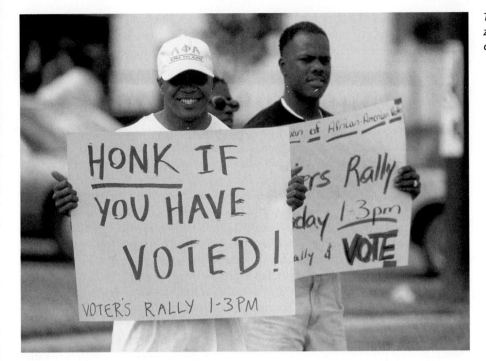

These participants in a voter's rally urge citizens to accept responsibility for perpetuating democracy.

individual has a host of conflicting desires, fears, hopes, and expectations, and no government can represent them all. But even if millions of voters could be represented in their many interests, the question of how they would be represented would remain. Through direct representation, such as a traditional New England town meeting or ballot initiatives and referendums? Through economic or professional associations, such as labor unions or political action committees? Through a coalition of minority groups? All of these and other alternatives can be defended as proper forms of representation in a constitutional democracy. Yet all also have limitations.

Some propose to bypass this thorny problem of representation by vastly increasing the role of direct popular participation in decision making.[4] An example of an expanded direct popular participation in governmental decision making is the recall, a process that removes office holders from office based on a petition process and election. The 2003 recall of California Governor Gray Davis and election of Arnold Schwarzenegger is an example of the recall in action. The use of the recall has been relatively rare at the statewide level, but the process has the potential to alter the relationship between voters and representatives. If the process were to become a means for people who disagree with policy positions of office holders to remove those persons from office between elections, representatives might hesitate to say or do much.

What many people regard as the most perfect form of democracy would exist when every person has a full and equal opportunity to participate in all decisions and in all processes of influence, persuasion, and discussion that bear on those decisions. Direct participation in decision making, its advocates contend, will serve two major purposes. First, it will enhance the dignity, self-respect, and understanding of individuals by giving them responsibility for the decisions that shape their lives. Second, direct participation will act as a safeguard against undemocratic and antidemocratic forms of government and prevent the replacement of democracy by dictatorship or tyranny. This idea rests on a theory of self-protection that says interests can be represented, furthered, and defended best by the people they concern directly.

New technologies as well as new uses of old technologies present ways in which governments can appeal directly to voters and voters can speak directly to public officials. We now have voting by mail in Oregon and other places, and some people advocate voting on the Internet. Digital town halls may be next. Some applaud these developments; others are appalled by them.

But we still need institutions such as elected legislatures, which can take the time to digest complicated information and conduct impartial hearings to air competing points of view. The average citizen rarely has the time or experience to evaluate all the available information. Experience with many forms of participatory democracy also suggests its limitations as a form of decision making. In an age of rapidly growing population, increasingly complex economic and social systems, and enormously wide-ranging decision-making units of government, direct participation works best in small communities or at the neighborhood level. As a practical matter, people simply cannot spend endless hours taking part in every decision that affects their lives.

Participatory democracy can still play an important role in smaller units—in neighborhood associations, local party committees, and the like. But much of the work of government at all levels requires elected representatives. Since we must have representatives, who shall represent whom? By electing representatives in a multitude of districts, it is possible to build into representative institutions—the U.S. Congress, for example—most minority interests and attitudes. In the United States, we generally have election processes in which only the candidate receiving the greatest number of votes wins. But there are other ways. For example, one way widely used in European nations like Austria and Denmark is proportional representation—a system in which each party running receives the proportion of legislative seats corresponding to its proportion of votes.[5]

Representation can also be influenced by whether there is only one party, two, or several. Ours is generally a strong two-party system that knits local constituencies into coalitions that can elect and sustain national majorities. A major factor in maintaining our two-party system is that single-member legislative districts such as those for the U.S. Congress and state legislatures tend to lead to two-party systems. This regularity, called *Duverger's law*, is generally seen as helping moderate our politics.[6] In contrast, when countries adopt proportional representation, minor parties have greater influence.

Which is better, elected officials who represent coalitions of minorities or officials who represent a relatively clear-cut majority and have little or no obligation to the minority? The answer depends on what you expect from government. A system that represents coalitions of minorities usually reflects the trading, competition, and compromising that must take place in order to reach agreement among the various groups. Such a government has been called *broker rule:* Elected officials act essentially as a go-between or mediator among organized groups that have definite policy goals. Under broker rule, leaders cannot get too far ahead of the groups; they must talk back and forth, shifting in response to changing group pressures. Instead of acting for a united popular majority with a fairly definite program, either liberal or conservative, the government tries to satisfy all major interests by giving them a voice in decisions and sometimes a veto over actions. In the pushing and hauling of political groups, the government is continually involved in delicate balancing acts, and no one wins all the time.

Some critics argue that fair representation has not been achieved in the American system. In the U.S. Congress and many state legislatures, for example, there are still relatively few women and minorities. Critics also point to the extent of nonvoting and other forms of nonparticipation in politics; the fact that low-income persons are less well organized than upper-income persons; the bias of strong organized groups toward the status quo; the domination of television and the press by a few corporations; and the virtual monopoly of party politics by the two major parties, which do not always offer the voters meaningful alternatives. Critics are concerned that our system of government builds in procedures designed to curtail legislative majorities—for example, the filibuster in the Senate or the power of the Supreme Court to declare laws unconstitutional. The use of the filibuster to block some judicial nominees from President George W. Bush and the threat to use the filibuster against Supreme Court nominees has renewed debate about procedures that empower the legislative minority. Examples of antimajoritarian rulings by the Supreme Court include declaring the Texas sodomy law unconstitutional in *Lawrence* v. *Texas.*[7]

Such charges may be exaggerated, but they cannot be denied. Those who believe that governments should be more directly responsive to political majorities can point to steady improvement in recent years. Election laws have been changed to simplify voter registration, expand and improve voting procedures, and enforce one-person, one-vote standards. Efforts to limit the ability of rich people and well-financed interests to influence elections were cited by Congress as a motivation for passage of campaign finance reform in 2002 and by the Supreme Court in upholding that legislation in 2003.[8] Pressure has also been building to streamline voting systems and simplify voter registration processes.

Over the course of U.S. history, there has been a shift toward greater direct democracy, and this trend is likely to continue. The founders designed a system with direct representation limited to the House of Representatives. Today both the House and Senate are directly elected. Moreover, with the advent of direct primaries, voters decide the nominees for federal office. The initiative and referendum process provides a direct way for citizens to enact or overturn laws, or even recall those in government. Who may vote in our elections has also been dramatically expanded from white male property owners to all citizens over 18 years of age.

In the age of the Internet, pressures to expand the role of citizens in making laws and voting on candidates or recalling officeholders via petition are examples of how direct democracy may be further expanded. Some states in recent elections have allowed voters to cast their ballots via the Internet. Arizona did so in the 2000 Democratic presidential primary, and Michigan did the same in 2004. The Internet also has become a means to help organize and inform volunteers, raise funds, and learn about current events.[9]

By this point, you undoubtedly appreciate that democracy has to mean much more than popular government and unchecked majority rule. A democracy needs competing politicians with differing views about the public interest. A vital democracy, living and growing, places its faith in the participation of citizens as voters, faith that they will elect not just people who will mirror their views but leaders who will exercise their best judgment—"faith that the people will not condemn those whose devotion to principle leads them to unpopular courses, but will reward courage, respect honor, and ultimately recognize right."[10]

The Role of the Politician

Americans today have decidedly mixed views about elected officials. They realize that at their best, politicians are skillful at compromising, mediating, negotiating, and brokering—and that governing often requires these qualities. But they also suspect politicians of being ambitious, conniving, unprincipled, opportunistic, and corrupt. Americans hold politicians in low esteem compared with people in other professions.

Still, we often find that individual officeholders are bright, hardworking, and friendly (even though we may suspect they are simply trying to win our vote). And our liking sometimes turns into reverence after these same politicians die. George Washington, Abraham Lincoln, Dwight D. Eisenhower, and John F. Kennedy are acclaimed today. Harry Truman liked to joke that "a statesman is a politician who has been dead for about ten or fifteen years."[11] Of course, we must put the problem in perspective. In all democracies, the public probably expects too much from politicians. Further, people naturally distrust those who wield power. Public officeholders, after all, tax us, regulate us, and conscript us. We dislike political compromisers and ambitious opportunists—even though we may need such people to get things done.[12]

Yet as we have demonstrated with numerous examples in this book, individuals can and do make a difference in public life. Individuals can make a difference in shaping policy on the local, state, national, and international levels, whether the policy be drunk driving, early childhood medical care, land mines, or using the courts to influence a policy agenda.

Politics is a necessity. Politics is a vital and at times a noble leadership activity. Politicians are essential for running the American Republic, whose fragmented powers require them to mediate among factions, build coalitions, and compromise among and within branches of government to produce policy and action.

"A statesman is a politician who has been dead for about ten or fifteen years."

PRESIDENT HARRY TRUMAN

Leadership in a Constitutional Democracy

While the need for leadership in government is easily recognized, defining what leadership is and how it operates in a constitutional democracy is more challenging. Leadership can be understood only in the context of both leaders and followers. A leader without followers is a contradiction in terms. Leadership is also situational and contextual; a person is often effective in only one kind of situation. Leadership is not necessarily transferable. James Madison, for example, was a brilliant political and constitutional theorist; he was also a superb politician. Yet he was not a brilliant president.[13] The leadership required to lead a marine platoon up a hill in battle is different from the leadership needed to change racist or sexist attitudes in city governments. The leadership required of a campaign manager differs from that required of a candidate.

Although leaders are often skilled managers, they need more than just managerial skills. Managers are concerned with doing things the right way; leaders are concerned with doing the right thing. Managers are concerned with efficiency and process, especially routines and standard operating procedures. Leaders, by contrast, concentrate on goals, purposes, and a vision of the future. Some leaders have indispensable qualities of contagious self-confidence, unwarranted optimism, and dogged idealism that attract and mobilize others to undertake tasks they never dreamed they could accomplish. In short, they empower others and enable many of their followers to become leaders in their own right. Most of the significant breakthroughs in our nation, as well as in our communities, have been made or shaped by people who, while seeing all the complexities and obstacles ahead of them, believed in themselves and in their purposes so much that they refused to be overwhelmed and paralyzed by self-doubts. They were willing to gamble, to take risks, to look at things in a fresh way, and often to invent new rules.

Must a politician gain public office by denouncing the profession of politics? From the tone of many recent congressional and presidential races, it would appear that this may be so. Presidential candidates who have denounced Washington politics include Jimmy Carter, Ronald Reagan, Bill Clinton, and Howard Dean. In 2004 Dean said that if he was elected, members of Congress were "going to be scurrying for shelter, just like a giant flashlight on a bunch of cockroaches."[14] Political scientist Richard Fenno's landmark study of congressional candidates found that incumbents often run against Washington in general and Congress in particular when at home in their districts.[15] Journalist Charles McDowell of the *Richmond Times-Dispatch* noted this trend in the PBS series *The Lawmakers* and suggested that such a tactic "demeans an honorable and essential profession—that of the politician." McDowell proposed that every member of Congress be required to take the following oath:

> I affirm that I am a politician. That I am willing to associate with other known politicians. That I have no moral reservations about committing acts of politics. Under the Constitution, I insist that politicians have as much right to indulge in politics as preachers, single-issue zealots, generals, bird-watchers, labor leaders, big business lobbyists, and all other truth-givers.
>
> I confess that, as a politician, I participate in negotiation, compromise, and trade-offs in order to achieve something that seems reasonable to a majority. And although I try to be guided by principle, I confess that I often find people of principle on the other side, too.
>
> So help me God.

Politics and politicians, including those who work in Washington, are necessary and important to our freedom, security, and prosperity. While people will disagree about particular policies and processes, there is no disputing the need for government. It is also the case that the vast majority of politicians are smart, honorable, and deserve our respect and admiration. Political leaders recognize the fundamental—unexpressed as well as expressed—wants and needs of potential followers. By bringing followers to a fuller consciousness of their needs, they help convert their hopes and aspirations into practical demands on other leaders, especially leaders in government. A leader in a democracy consults and listens while educating followers and attempting to renew the goals of an organization.

Reconciling Democracy and Leadership

Americans are fond of saying, "It is all politics, you know." This greatly oversimplified insight is offered as profound. More important, it is intended as a negative judgment, as if things somehow would be improved if we did not have politics and politicians.

But politics is the lifeblood of democracy, and without politics, there is no freedom. To conclude that politicians are interested in winning elections is about as profound as to conclude that businesspeople are interested in profits. Of course they are! We do not expect our economy to operate because the shoe store owner is motivated only by a desire to see that people have dry, warm feet. Rather, we harness the store owner's desire to make a living as a way to see to it that the largest number of people get the shoes they want at the lowest possible price. Similarly, we harness the elected official's desire for reelection as the way to ensure that elected officials do what most of the voters want them to do. It is the politician's need to serve and please the voters that is the indispensable link in making democracy work.[16]

One of our major political challenges is to reconcile democracy and leadership. In the past, we often have held a view of leaders as all-powerful. Yet a nation of subservient followers can never be a democratic one. A democratic nation requires educated, skeptical, caring, engaged, and conscientious citizens. It also requires citizens who will recognize when change is needed and have the courage to bring about necessary reforms and progress.[17] Such citizens provide the leaders that enable constitutional democracy to survive and thrive. Constitutional democracy requires citizens who are willing to run for office and then serve with integrity. It is understandable that good people shy away from seeking office, with the ensuing loss of privacy and other burdens of public office. But no matter how brilliant our Constitution or strong our economy, ultimately our system depends on individuals willing to compete for office.

Experience teaches that power wielded justly today may be wielded corruptly tomorrow. It is right and necessary to protest when a policy is wrong or when the rights of other citizens are diminished. Democracy rests solidly on a realistic view of human nature. Criticism of official error is not unpatriotic. Our capacity for justice, as theologian and philosopher Reinhold Niebuhr observed, makes democracy possible. But our "inclination to injustice makes democracy necessary."[18] Democratic politics is the forum where, by acting together, citizens become and remain free.[19]

Leadership thought of as an engagement among equals can empower people and enlarge their opinions, choices, and freedoms. The answer for our republic lies not in producing a handful of great, charismatic, Mount Rushmore-type leaders but in educating a citizenry who can boast that we are no longer in need of superheroes because we have become a nation of citizens who believe that each of us can make a difference and that all of us should regularly try to do so.[20]

Leaders will always be needed. However, our system of government is, in many ways, designed to prevent strong and decisive action, lest too much political power be placed in the hands of too few people. Thus, although we have emphasized the role of leadership in constitutional democracies in these last few pages, the potential for abuse is checked not only by an involved citizenry but also by the very structure of our constitutional system—separation of powers, checks and balances, federalism, bicameral legislatures, and the rule of law.

The ultimate test of a democratic system is the legal existence of an officially recognized opposition. A cardinal characteristic of a constitutional democracy is that it not only recognizes the need for the free organization of opposing views but also positively encourages this organization. Freedom for political expression and dissent is basic—even freedom for nonsense to be spoken so that good sense not yet recognized gets a chance to be heard.[21]

"Rulers always have and always will find it dangerous to their security to permit people to think, believe, talk, write, assemble, and particularly to criticize the government as they please."

FORMER SUPREME COURT JUSTICE WILLIAM J. BRENNAN

Lieutenant Governor Tim Kaine of Virginia speaks at a rally held in Woodbridge, Virginia. Kaine was elected governor to replace Mark Warner (left) who was barred from serving consecutive terms by the state's constitution.

The Democratic Faith

Crucial to the democratic faith is the belief that a constitutional democracy cherishes the free play of ideas. Only where the safety valve of public discussion is available and where almost any policy is subject to perpetual questioning and challenge can there be the assurance that both minority and majority rights will be served. To be afraid of public debate is to be afraid of self-government. "Rulers always have and always will find it dangerous to their security to permit people to think, believe, talk, write, assemble, and particularly to criticize the government as they please," said former Supreme Court Justice William J. Brennan, "but the language of the First Amendment indicates the framers weighed the risk involved in such freedoms and deliberately chose to stake this government's security and life upon preserving liberty to discuss public affairs intact and untouched by government."[22]

Thomas Jefferson once said, "Were it left to me to decide whether we should have a government without newspapers or newspapers without a government, I should not hesitate for a moment to prefer the latter." This is reflective of the high importance he placed on informing the citizenry. Jefferson also had boundless faith in education. He believed that people are rationally endowed by nature with an innate sense of justice; the average person has only to be informed to act wisely. In the long run, said Jefferson, only an educated and enlightened democracy can hope to endure.

Education is one of the best predictors of voting, participation in politics, and knowledge of public affairs. People may not be equally involved or equally willing to invest in democracy, but the attentive public—frequently people like yourself who have gone to college—has the willingness and self-confidence to see government and politics as necessary and important. An educated public has an understanding of how government works, how individuals can influence decision makers, and how to elect like-minded people.

As college students who are studying American government, you have knowledge of ways to influence public policy and the political process. You have gained an appreciation for the ways individuals and groups can both push and block an agenda. You also know that many people choose not to participate in elections or politics, enhancing the power of those who do. Finally, you should also have an appreciation that when knowledge is combined with political activity, the influence of the individual participant is expanded.

Does political participation by committed individuals bring about constructive change? It is important to recall that in the last half-century, restaurants, motels, and landlords once openly discriminated against individuals on the basis of race. Racial segregation in education was commonplace in several states; segregated neighborhoods were a fact of life in others and in some places remains so. Finally, in some sections of the country, discriminatory practices denied blacks and poor whites access to voting. Women were discriminated against in the workplace and in government. The significant changes toward more freedom and equality that have resulted from civil rights legislation and court cases are remarkable. This is not to say that we have erased the legacies of racism and other kinds of discrimination from our national life. But as historian Arthur M. Schlesinger Jr. writes, "The genius of America lies in its capacity to forge a single nation from peoples of remarkably diverse racial, religious, and ethnic origins." Schlesinger acknowledges that our government and society have been more open to some than to others, "but it is more open to all today than it was yesterday and it is likely to be even more open tomorrow than today."[23]

"Were it left to me to decide whether we should have a government without newspapers or newspapers without a government, I should not hesitate for a moment to prefer the latter."

THOMAS JEFFERSON

We are a restless, dissatisfied, and searching people. We are often our own toughest critics. Our political system is far from perfect, but it still is an open system and one that has become more and more democratic over time. People *can* fight city hall. People who disagree with policies in the nation can band together and be heard. We know only too well that the American dream is never fully attained. It must always be pursued.

Millions of Americans visit the great monuments in our nation's capital each year. They are always impressed by the memorials to Washington, Jefferson, Lincoln, Franklin D. Roosevelt, and the Vietnam, Korean, and World War II veterans. They are awed by the beauty of the Capitol, the Supreme Court, and the White House. The strength of the nation, however, resides not in these official buildings and monuments but in the hearts, minds, and behavior of citizens. If we lose faith, stop caring, stop participating, and stop believing in the possibilities of self-government, the monuments "will be meaningless piles of stone, and the venture that began with the Declaration of Independence, the venture familiarly known as America will be as lifeless as the stone."[24]

The future of democracy in America will be shaped by citizens who care about preserving and extending our political rights and freedoms. Our individual liberties will never be ensured unless there are people willing to take responsibility for the progress of the whole community, people willing to exercise their determination and democratic faith. Carved in granite on one of the long corridors in a building on the Harvard University campus are these words of American poet Archibald MacLeish: "How shall freedom be defended? By arms when it is attacked by arms, by truth when it is attacked by lies, by democratic faith when it is attacked by authoritarian dogma. Always, in the final act, by determination and faith."

Education fosters self-confidence in dealing with bureaucracy, is a strong predictor of voting, and provides a knowledge base important to political influence.

Further Reading

DEREK BOK, *The Trouble with Government* (Harvard University Press, 2001).

RICHARD D. BROWN, *The Strength of a People: The Idea of an Informed Citizenry in America, 1650–1870* (University of North Carolina Press, 1996).

JAMES MACGREGOR BURNS, *Leadership* (Harper & Row, 1978).

ROBERT COLES, *Lives of Moral Leadership: Men and Women Who Have Made a Difference* (Random House, 2000).

ROBERT A. DAHL, *On Democracy* (Yale University Press, 1998).

AMY GUTMANN AND **DENNIS THOMSON,** *Democracy and Discontent: Why Moral Conflict Cannot Be Avoided in Politics, and What Should Be Done About It* (Belknap Press, 1996).

Appendix

The Declaration of Independence

DRAFTED MAINLY BY THOMAS JEFFERSON, THIS DOCUMENT ADOPTED BY THE SECOND CONTINENTAL CONGRESS, AND SIGNED BY JOHN HANCOCK AND FIFTY-FIVE OTHERS, OUTLINED THE RIGHTS OF MAN AND THE RIGHTS TO REBELLION AND SELF-GOVERNMENT. IT DECLARED THE INDEPENDENCE OF THE COLONIES FROM GREAT BRITAIN, JUSTIFIED REBELLION, AND LISTED THE GRIEVANCES AGAINST GEORGE THE III AND HIS GOVERNMENT. WHAT IS MEMORABLE ABOUT THIS FAMOUS DOCUMENT IS NOT ONLY THAT IT DECLARED THE BIRTH OF A NEW NATION, BUT THAT IT SET FORTH, WITH ELOQUENCE, OUR BASIC PHILOSOPHY OF LIBERTY AND REPRESENTATIVE DEMOCRACY.

IN CONGRESS, JULY 4, 1776

(The unanimous Declaration of the Thirteen United States of America)

PREAMBLE

When, in the course of human events, it becomes necessary for one people to dissolve the political bands which have connected them with another, and to assume, among the powers of the earth, the separate and equal station to which the laws of nature and of nature's God entitle them, a decent respect to the opinions of mankind requires that they should declare the causes which impel them to the separation.

New Principles of Government

We hold these truths to be self-evident; that all men are created equal, that they are endowed by their Creator with certain unalienable rights, that among these are life, liberty, and the pursuit of happiness.

That, to secure these rights, governments are instituted among men, deriving their just powers from the consent of the governed.

That whenever any form of government becomes destructive of these ends, it is the right of the people to alter or to abolish it, and to institute new government, laying its foundation on such principles, and organizing its powers in such form, as to them shall seem most likely to effect their safety and happiness. Prudence, indeed will dictate that governments long established should not be changed for light and transient causes; and accordingly all experience hath shown that mankind are more disposed to suffer while evils are sufferable, than to right themselves by abolishing the forms to which they are accustomed. But when a long train of abuses and usurpations, pursuing invariably the same object, evinces a design to reduce them under absolute despotism, it is their right, it is their duty, to throw off such government, and to provide new guards for their future security.

Reasons for Separation

Such has been the patient sufferance of these colonies; and such is now the necessity which constrains them to alter their former systems of government. The history of the present king of Great Britain is a history of repeated injuries and usurpations, all having in direct object the establishment of an absolute tyranny over these states. To prove this, let facts be submitted to a candid world.

He has refused his assent to laws, the most wholesome and necessary for the public good.

He has forbidden his governors to pass laws of immediate and pressing importance unless suspended in their operation till his assent should be obtained; and when so suspended, he has utterly neglected to attend to them.

He has refused to pass other laws for the accommodation of large districts of people, unless those people would relinquish the right of representation in the legislature, a right inestimable to them, and formidable to tyrants only.

He has called together legislative bodies at places unusual, uncomfortable, and distant for the depository of their public records, for the sole purpose of fatiguing them into compliance with his measures.

He has dissolved representative houses repeatedly, for opposing, with manly firmness, his invasions on the rights of people.

He has refused, for a long time after such dissolutions, to cause others to be elected; whereby the legislative powers incapable of annihilation, have returned to the people at large for their exercise; the state remaining, in the meantime, exposed to all the dangers of invasion from without and convulsions within.

He has endeavored to prevent the population of these states; for that purpose obstructing the laws of naturalization of foreigners, refusing to pass others to encourage their migration hither, and raising the conditions of new appropriations of lands.

He has obstructed the administration of justice, by refusing his assent to laws for establishing judiciary powers.

He has made judges dependent on his will alone for the tenure of their offices, and the amount and payment of their salaries.

He has erected a multitude of new offices, and sent hither swarms of officers to harass our people and eat out their substance.

He has kept among us, in times of peace, standing armies, without the consent of our legislature.

He has affected to render the military independent of, and superior to, the civil power.

He has combined with others to subject us to jurisdiction foreign to our constitution and unacknowledged by our laws, giving his assent to their acts of pretended legislation:

For quartering large bodies of armed troops among us;

For protecting them, by a mock trial, from punishment for any murders which they should commit on the inhabitants of these states;

For cutting off our trade with all parts of the world;

For imposing taxes on us without our consent;

For depriving us, in many cases, of the benefits of trial by jury;

For transporting us beyond seas, to be tried for pretended offenses;

For abolishing the free system of English laws in a neighboring province, establishing therein an arbitrary government, and enlarging its boundaries, so as to render it at once an example and fit instrument for introducing the same absolute rule into these colonies;

For taking away our charters, abolishing our most valuable laws, and altering, fundamentally, the forms of our governments;

For suspending our own legislatures, and declaring themselves invented with power to legislate for us in all cases whatsoever.

He has abdicated government here, by declaring us out of his protection and waging war against us.

He has plundered our seas, ravaged our coasts, burned our towns, and destroyed the lives of our people.

He is at this time transporting large armies of foreign mercenaries to complete the works of death, desolation, and tyranny already begun with circumstances of cruelty and perfidy scarcely paralleled in the most barbarous ages and totally unworthy of the head of a civilized nation.

He has constrained our fellow-citizens, taken captive on the high seas, to bear arms against their country, to become the executioners of their friends and brethren, or to fall themselves by their hands.

He has excited domestic insurrections among us, and has endeavored to bring on the inhabitants of our frontiers the merciless Indian savages, whose known rule of warfare is an undistinguished destruction of all ages, sexes, and conditions.

In every stage of these oppressions we have petitioned for redress in the most humble terms; our repeated petitions have been answered only by repeated injury. A prince whose character is thus marked by every act which may define a tyrant is unfit to be the ruler of a free people.

Nor have we been wanting in attention to our British brethren. We have warned them, from time to time, of attempts by their legislature to extend an unwarrantable jurisdiction over us. We have reminded them of the circumstances of our emigration and settlement here. We have appealed to their native justice and magnanimity; and we have conjured them, by the ties of our common kindred, to disavow these usurpations, which would inevitably interrupt our connections and correspondence. They, too, have been deaf to the voice of justice and of consanguinity. We must, therefore, acquiesce in the necessity which denounces our separation, and hold them, as we hold the rest of mankind, enemies in war, in peace, friends.

We, therefore, the representatives of the United States of America, in General Congress assembled, appealing to the Supreme Judge of the world for the rectitude of our intentions, do, in the name and by authority of the good people of these colonies, solemnly publish and declare, that these united colonies are, and of right ought to be, free and independent states; that they are absolved from all allegiance to the British crown, and that all political connection between them and the state of Great Britain is, and ought to be, totally dissolved; and that, as free and independent states, they have full power to levy war, conclude peace, contract alliances, establish commerce, and do all other acts and things which independent states may of a right do. And, for the support of this declaration, with a firm reliance on the protection of Divine Providence, we mutually pledge to each other our lives, our fortunes, and our sacred honor.

The Federalist, No. 10, James Madison

THE FEDERALIST, NO. 10, WRITTEN BY JAMES MADISON SOON AFTER THE CONSTITUTIONAL CONVENTION, WAS PREPARED AS ONE OF SEVERAL DOZEN NEWSPAPER ESSAYS AIMED AT PERSUADING NEW YORKERS TO RATIFY THE PROPOSED CONSTITUTION. ONE OF THE MOST IMPORTANT BASIC DOCUMENTS IN AMERICAN POLITICAL HISTORY, IT OUTLINES THE NEED FOR AND THE GENERAL PRINCIPLES OF A DEMOCRATIC REPUBLIC. IT ALSO PROVIDES A POLITICAL AND ECONOMIC ANALYSIS OF THE REALITIES OF INTEREST GROUP OR FACTION POLITICS.

To the People of the State of New York: Among the numerous advantages promised by a well-constructed union, none deserves to be more accurately developed than its tendency to break and control the violence of faction. The friend of popular governments, never finds himself so much alarmed for their character and fate, as when he contemplates their propensity of this dangerous vice. He will not fail, therefore, to set a due value on any plan which, without violating the principles to which he is attached, provides a proper cure for it. The instability, injustice, and confusion introduced into the public councils, have, in truth, been the mortal diseases under which popular governments have everywhere perished; as they continue to be the favorite and fruitful topics from which the adversaries to liberty derive their most specious declamations. The valuable improvements made by the American constitutions on the popular models, both ancient and modern, cannot certainly be too much admired; but it would be an unwarrantable partiality, to contend that they have as effectually obviated the danger on this side, as was wished and expected. Complaints are everywhere heard from our most considerate and virtuous citizens, equally the friends of public and private faith, and of public and personal liberty, that our governments are too unstable; that the public good is disregarded in the conflicts of rival parties; and that measures are too often decided, not according to the rules of justice, and the rights of the minor party, but by the superior force of an interested and overbearing majority. However anxiously we may wish that these complaints had no foundation, the evidence of known facts will not permit us to deny that they are in some degree true. It will be found, indeed, on a candid review of our situation, that some of the distresses under which we labor have been erroneously charged on the operations of our governments; but it will be found, at the same time, that other causes will not alone account for many of our heaviest misfortunes; and, particularly, for that prevailing and increasing distrust of public engagements, and alarm for private rights, which are echoed from one end of the continent to the other. These must be chiefly, if not wholly, effects of the unsteadiness and injustice, with which a factious spirit has tainted our public administrations.

By a faction, I understand a number of citizens, whether amounting to a majority of the whole, who are united and actuated by some common impulse of passion, or of interest, adverse to the rights of other citizens, or to the permanent and aggregate interests of the community.

There are two methods of curing the mischiefs of faction: the one, by removing its causes; the other, by controlling its effects.

There are again two methods of removing the causes of faction: the one, by destroying the liberty which is essential to its existence; the other, by giving to every citizen the same opinions, the same passions, and the same interests.

It could never be more truly said, than of the first remedy, that it was worse than the disease. Liberty is to faction what air is to fire, an aliment without which it instantly expires. But it could not be a less folly to abolish liberty, which is essential to political life, because it nourishes faction, than it would be to wish the annihilation of air, which is essential to animal life, because it imparts to fire its destructive agency.

The second expedient is as impracticable, as the first would be unwise. As long as the reason of man continues fallible, and he is at liberty to exercise it, different opinions will be formed. As long as the connection subsists between his reason and his self-love, his opinions and his passions will have a reciprocal influence on each other; and the former will be objects to which the latter will attach themselves. The diversity in the faculties of men, from which the rights of property originate, is not less an insuperable obstacle to an uniformity of interests. The protection of these faculties is the first object of government. From the protection of different and unequal faculties of acquiring property, the possession of different degrees and kinds of property immediately results; and from the influence of these on the sentiments and views of the respective proprietors, ensues a division of the society into different interests and parties.

The latent causes of faction are thus sown in the nature of man; and we see them everywhere brought into different degrees of activity, according to the different circumstances of civil society. A zeal for different opinions concerning religion, concerning government, and many other points, as well of speculation as of practice; an attachment to different leaders ambitiously contending for preeminence and power; or to persons of other descriptions whose fortunes have been interesting to the human passions, have, in turn, divided mankind into parties, inflamed them with mutual animosity, and rendered them much more disposed to vex and oppress each other, than to cooperate for their common good. So strong is this propensity of mankind, to fall into mutual animosities, that where no substantial occasion presents itself, the most frivolous and fanciful distinctions have been sufficient to kindle their unfriendly passions and ex-cite their most violent conflicts. But the most common and durable source of factions, has been the various and unequal distribution of property. Those who hold, and those who are without property, have ever formed distinct interests in society. Those who are creditors, and those who are debtors, fall under a like discrimination. A landed interest, a manufacturing interest, a mercantile interest, a moneyed interest, with many lesser interests, grow up of necessity in civilized nations, and divide them into different classes, actuated by different sentiments and views. The regulation of these various and interfering interests forms the principal task of modern legislation, and involves the spirit of the party and faction in the necessary and ordinary operations of the government.

No man is allowed to be a judge in his own cause; because his interest will certainly bias his judgment, and, not improbably, corrupt his integrity. With equal, nay, with greater reason, a body of men are unfit to be both judges and parties at the same time; yet what are many of the most important acts of legislation, but so many judicial determinations, not indeed concerning the right of single persons, but concerning the rights of large bodies of citizens? And what are the different classes of legislators, but advocates and parties to the causes which they determine? Is a law proposed concerning private debts? It is a questions to which the creditors are parties on one side, and the debtors on the other. Justice ought to hold the balance between them. Yet the parties are, and must be, themselves the judges; and the most numerous party, or, in other words, the most powerful faction, must be expected to prevail. Shall domestic manufacturers be encouraged, and in what degree, by restrictions on foreign manufacturers? Are questions which would be differently decided by the landed and the manufacturing classes; and probably by neither with a sole regard to justice and the public good. The apportionment of taxes, on the various descriptions of property, is an act which seems to require the most exact impartiality; yet there is, perhaps, no legislative act, in which greater opportunity and temptation are given to a predominant party to trample on the rules of justice. Every shilling, with which they overburden the inferior number, is a shilling saved to their own pockets.

It is in vain to say, that enlightened statesmen will be able to adjust these clashing interests, and render them all subservient to the public good. Enlightened statesmen will not always be at the helm, nor, in many cases, can such an adjustment be made at all, without taking into view indirect and remote considerations, which will rarely prevail over the immediate interest which one party may find in disregarding the rights of another, or the good of the whole.

The inference to which we are brought is, that the causes of faction cannot be removed; and that relief is only to be sought in the means of controlling its effects.

If a faction consists of less than a majority, relief is supplied by the republican principle, which enables the majority to defeat its sinister views, by regular vote. It may clog the administration, it may convulse the society; but it will be unable to execute and mask its violence under the forms of the Constitution. When a majority is included in a faction, the form of popular government, on the other hand, enables it to sacrifice to its ruling passion or interest, both the public good and the rights of other citizens. To secure the public good, and private rights, against the danger of such a faction, and at the same time to preserve the spirit and the form of popular government, is then the great object to which our inquiries are directed. Let me add, that it is the great desideratum, by which alone this form of government can be rescued from the opprobrium under which it has so long laboured, and be recommended to the esteem and adoption of mankind.

By what means is this object attainable? Evidently by one of two only. Either the existence of the same passion or interest in a majority, at the same time, must be prevented; or the majority, having such coexistent passion or interest, must be rendered, by their number and local situation, unable to concert and carry into effect schemes of oppression. If the impulse and the opportunity be suffered to coincide, we well know that neither moral nor religious motives can be relied on as an adequate control. They are not found to be such on the injustice and violence of individuals, and lose their efficacy in proportion to the number combined together; that is, in proportion as their efficacy becomes needful.

From this view of the subject, it may be concluded, that a pure democracy, by which I mean a society consisting of a small number of citizens, who assemble and administer the government in person, can admit of no cure for the mischiefs of faction. A common passion or interest will, in almost every case, be felt by a majority of the whole; a communication and concert, results from the form of government itself; and there is nothing to check the inducements to sacrifice the weaker party, or an obnoxious individual. Hence, it is, that such democracies have ever been spectacles of turbulence and contention; have ever been found incompatible with personal security, or the rights of property; and have in general been as short in their lives, as they have been violent in their deaths. Theoretic politicians, who have patronized this species of government, have erroneously supposed, that by reducing mankind to a perfect equality in their political rights, they would, at the same time be perfectly equalized and assimilated in their possessions, their opinions, and their passions.

A republic, by which I mean a government in which the scheme of representation takes place, opens a different prospect, and promises the cure for which we are seeking. Let us examine the points in which it varies from pure democracy, and we shall comprehend both the nature of the cure and the efficacy which it must derive from the union.

The two great points of difference, between a democracy and a republic, are, first, the delegation of the government, in the latter, to a small number of citizens, elected by the rest; secondly, the greater number of citizens, and greater sphere of country, over which the latter may be extended.

The effect of the first difference is, on the one hand, to refine and enlarge the public views, by passing them through the medium of a chosen body of citizens, whose wisdom may best discern the true interest of their country, and whose patriotism and love of justice, will be least likely to sacrifice it to temporary or partial considerations. Under such a regulation, it may well happen, that the public voice, pronounced by the representatives of the people, will be more consonant to the public good, than if pronounced by the people themselves, convened for the purpose. On the other hand the effect may be inverted. Men of factious tempers, of local prejudices, or of sinister designs, may by intrigue, by corruption, or by other means, first obtain the suffrages, and then betray the interest of the people. The question resulting is, whether small or extensive republics are most favourable to the election of proper guardians of the public weal; and it is clearly decided in favour of the latter by two obvious considerations.

In the first place, it is to be remarked that, however small the republic may be, the representatives must be raised to a certain number, in order to guard against the cabals of a few; and that however large it may be, they must be limited to a certain number, in order to guard against the confusion of a multitude. Hence, the number of representatives in the two cases not being in proportion to that of the constituents, and being proportionally greatest in the small republic, it follows, that if the proportion of fit characters be not less in the large than in the small republic, the former will present a greater option, and consequently a greater probability of a fit choice.

In the next place, as each representative will be chosen by a greater number of citizens in the large than in the small republic, it will be more difficult for unworthy candidates to practice with success the vicious arts, by which elections are too often carried; and the suffrages of the people being more free, will be more likely to centre in men who possess the most attractive merit, and the most diffusive and established characters.

It must be confessed, that in this, as in most other cases, there is a mean, on both sides of which inconveniences will be found to lie. By enlarging too much the number of electors, you render the representatives too little acquainted with all their local circumstances and lesser interests; as by reducing it too much, you render him unduly attached to these, and too little fit to comprehend and pursue great and national objects. The federal constitution forms a happy combination in this respect; the great and aggregate interests being referred to the national, the local and particular to the state legislatures.

The other point of difference is, the greater number of citizens, and extent of territory, which may be brought within the compass of republican, than of democratic government; and it is this circumstance principally which renders factious combinations less to be dreaded in the former, than in the latter. The smaller the society, the fewer probably will be the distinct parties and interests composing it; the fewer the distinct parties and interests, the more frequently will a majority be found of the same party; and the smaller the number of individuals composing a majority, and the smaller the compass within which they are placed, the more easily will they concert and execute their plans of oppression. Extend the sphere, and you take in a greater variety of parties and interests; you make it less probable that a majority of the whole will have a common motive to invade the rights of other citizens; or if such a common motive exists, it will be more diffi-

cult for all who feel it to discover their own strength, and to act in unison with each other. Besides other impediments, it may be remarked, that where there is a consciousness of unjust or dishonourable purposes, communication is always checked by distrust, in proportion to the number whose concurrence is necessary.

Hence, it clearly appears, that the same advantage, which a republic has over a democracy, in controlling the effects of faction, is enjoyed by a large over a small republic—is enjoyed by the union over the states composing it. Does this advantage consist in the substitution of representatives, whose enlightened views and virtuous sentiments render them superior to local prejudices, and to schemes of injustice? It will not be denied that the representation of the union will be most likely to possess these requisite endowments. Does it consist in the greater security afforded by a greater variety of parties, against the event of any one party being able to outnumber and oppress the rest? In an equal degree does the increased variety of parties, comprised within the union, increase the security? Does it, in fine, consist in the greater obstacles opposed to the concert and accomplishment of the secret wishes of an

unjust and interested majority? Here, again, the extent of the union gives it the most palpable advantage.

The influence of factious leaders may kindle a flame within their particular states, but will be unable to spread a general conflagration through the other states; a religious sect may degenerate into a political faction in a part of the confederacy; but the variety of sects dispersed over the entire face of it, must secure the national councils against any danger from that source: a rage for paper money, for an abolition of debts, for an equal division of property, or for any other improper or wicked project, will be less apt to pervade the whole body of the union than a particular member of it; in the same proportion as such a malady is more likely to taint a particular county or district, than an entire state.

In the extent and proper structure of the union, therefore, we behold a republican remedy for the diseases most incident to republican government. And according to the degree of pleasure and pride we feel in being republicans, ought to be our zeal in cherishing the spirit, and supporting the character of federalists.

The Federalist, No. 51, James Madison

THE FEDERALIST, NO. 51, ALSO WRITTEN BY MADISON, IS A CLASSIC STATEMENT IN DEFENSE OF SEPARATION OF POWERS AND REPUBLICAN PROCESSES. ITS FOURTH PARAGRAPH IS ESPECIALLY FAMOUS AND IS FREQUENTLY QUOTED BY STUDENTS OF GOVERNMENT.

To what expedient, then, shall we finally resort, for maintaining in practice the necessary partition of power among the several departments as laid down in the Constitution? The only answer that can be given is that as all these exterior provisions are found to be inadequate the defect must be supplied, by so contriving the interior structure of the government as that its several constituent parts may, by their mutual relations, be the means of keeping each other in their proper places. Without presuming to undertake a full development of this important idea I will hazard a few general observations which may perhaps place it in a clearer light, and enable us to form a more cor-

rect judgment of the principles and structure of the government planned by the convention.

In order to lay a due foundation for that separate and distinct exercise of the different powers of government, which to a certain extent is admitted on all hands to be essential to the preservation of liberty, it is evident that each department should have a will of its own; and consequently should be so constituted that the members of each should have as little agency as possible in the appointment of the members of the others. Were this principle rigorously adhered to, it would require that all the appointments for the supreme executive, legislative, and judi-

ciary magistracies should be drawn from the same fountain of authority, the people, through channels having no communication whatever with one another. Perhaps such a plan of constructing the several departments would be less difficult in practice than it may in contemplation appear. Some difficulties, however, and some additional expense would attend the execution of it. Some deviations, therefore, from the principle must be admitted. In the constitution of the judiciary department in particular, it might be inexpedient to insist rigorously on the principle: first, because peculiar qualifications being essential in the members, the primary consideration ought to be to select that mode of choice which best secures these qualifications; second, because the permanent tenure by which the appointments are held in that department must soon destroy all sense of dependence on the authority conferring them.

It is equally evident that the members of each department should be as little dependent as possible on those of the others for the emoluments annexed to their offices. Were the executive magistrate, or the judges, not independent of the legislature in this particular, their independence in every other would be merely nominal.

But the great security against a gradual concentration of the several powers in the same department consists in giving to those who administer each department the necessary constitutional means and personal motives to resist encroachments of the others. The provision for defense must in this, as in all other cases, be made commensurate to the danger of attack. Ambition must be made to counteract ambition. The interest of the man must be connected with the constitutional rights of the place. It may be a reflection on human nature that such devices should be necessary to control the abuses of government. But what is government itself but the greatest of all reflections on human nature? If men were angels, no government would be necessary. If angels were to govern men, neither external nor internal controls on government would be necessary. In framing a government which is to be administered by men over men, the great difficulty lies in this: you must first enable the government to control the governed; and in the next place oblige it to control itself. A dependence on the people is, no doubt, the primary control on the government; but experience has taught mankind the necessity of auxiliary precautions.

This policy of supplying, by opposite and rival interests, the defect of better motives, might be traced through the whole system of human affairs, private as well as public. We see it particularly displayed in all the subordinate distributions of power, where the constant aim is to divide and arrange the several offices in such a manner as that each may be

a check on the other—that the private interest of every individual may be a sentinel over the public rights. These inventions of prudence cannot be less requisite in the distribution of the supreme powers of the State.

But it is not possible to give to each department an equal power of self-defense. In republican government, the legislative authority necessarily predominates. The remedy for this inconveniency is to divide the legislature into different branches; and to render them, by modes of election and different principles of action, as little connected with each other as the nature of their common functions and their common dependence on the society will admit. It may even be necessary to guard against dangerous encroachments by still further precautions. As the weight of the legislative authority requires that it should be thus divided, the weakness of the executive may require, on the other hand, that it should be fortified. An absolute negative on the legislature appears, at first view, to be the natural defense with which the executive magistrate should be armed. But perhaps it would be neither altogether safe nor alone sufficient. On ordinary occasions it might not be exerted with the requisite firmness, and on extraordinary occasions it might be perfidiously abused. May not this defect of an absolute negative be supplied by some qualified connection between this weaker department and the weaker branch of the stronger department, by which the latter may be led to support the constitutional rights of the former, without being too much detached from the rights of its own department?

If the principles on which these observations are founded be just, as I persuade myself they are, and they be applied as a criterion to the several State constitutions, and to the federal Constitution, it will be found that if the latter does not perfectly correspond with them, the former are infinitely less able to bear such a test.

There are, moreover, two considerations particularly applicable to the federal system of America, which place that system in a very interesting point of view.

First. In a single republic, all the power surrendered by the people is sub-

mitted to the administration of a single government; and the usurpations are guarded against by a division of the government into distinct and separate departments. In the compound republic of America, the power surrendered by the people is first divided between two distinct governments, and then the portion allotted to each subdivided among distinct and separate departments. Hence a double security arises to the rights of the people. The different governments will control each other, at the same time that each will be controlled by itself.

Second. It is of great importance in a republic not only to guard the society against the oppression of its rulers, but to guard one part of the society against the injustice of the other part. Different interests necessarily exist in different classes of citizens. If a majority be united by a common interest, the rights of the minority will be insecure. There are but two methods of providing against this evil: the one by creating a will in the community independent of the majority—that is, of the society itself; the other, by comprehending in the society so many separate descriptions of citizens as will render an unjust combination of a majority of the whole very improbable, if not impracticable. The first method prevails in all governments possessing an hereditary or self-appointed authority. This, at best, is but a precarious security; because a power independent of the society may as well espouse the unjust views of the major as the rightful interests of the minor party, and may possibly be turned against both parties. The second method will be exemplified in the federal republic of the United States. Whilst all authority in it will be derived from and dependent on the society, the society itself will be broken into so many parts, interests and classes of citizens, that the rights of individuals, or of the minority, will be in little danger from interested combinations of the majority. In a free government the security for civil rights must be the same as that for religious rights. It consists in the one case in the multiplicity of interests, and in the other in the multiplicity of sects. The degree of security in both cases will depend on the number of interests and sects; and this may be presumed to depend on the extent of country and number of people comprehended under the same government. This view of the subject must particularly recommend a proper federal system to all the sincere and considerate friends of republican government, since it shows that in exact proportion as the territory of the Union may be formed into more circumscribed Confederacies, or States, oppressive combinations of a majority will be facilitated; the best security, under the republican forms, for the rights of every class of citizen, will be diminished; and consequently the stability and independence of some member of the government, the only other security, must be proportionally increased. Justice is the end of government. It is the end of civil society. It ever has been and ever will be pursued until it be obtained, or until liberty be lost in the pursuit. In a society under the forms of which the stronger faction can readily unite and oppress the weaker, anarchy may as truly be said to reign as in a state of nature, where the weaker individual is not secured against the violence of the stronger; and as, in the latter state, even the stronger individuals are prompted, by the uncertainty of their condition, to submit to a government which may protect the weak as well as themselves; so, in the former state, will the more powerful factions or parties be gradually induced, by a like motive, to wish for a government which will protect all parties, the weaker as well as the more powerful. It can be little doubted that if the State of Rhode Island was separated from the Confederacy and left to itself, the insecurity of rights under the popular form of government within such narrow limits would be displayed by such reiterated oppressions of factious majorities that some power altogether independent of the people would soon be called for by the voice of the very factions whose misrule had proved the necessity to it. In the extended republic of the United States, and among the great variety of interests, parties, and sects which it embraces, a coalition of a majority of the whole society could seldom take place on any other principles than those of justice and the general good; whilst there being thus less danger to a minor from the will of a major party, there must be less pretext, also, to provide for the security of the former, by introducing into the government a will not dependent on the latter, or, in other words, a will independent of the society itself. It is no less certain that it is important, notwithstanding the contrary opinions which have been entertained that the larger the society, provided it lie within a practicable sphere, the more duly capable it will be of self-government. And happily for the *republican cause,* the practicable sphere may be carried to a very great extent by a judicious modification and mixture of the *federal principle.*

The Federalist, No. 78, Alexander Hamilton

The Federalist, No. 78, written by Alexander Hamilton, explains and praises the provisions for the judiciary in the newly drafted Constitution. Notice especially how Hamilton asserts that the courts have a key responsibility in determining the meaning of the Constitution as fundamental law. Hamilton is outlining here the doctrine of judicial review as we now know it.

We proceed now to an examination of the judiciary department of the proposed government.

In unfolding the defects of the existing Confederation, the utility and necessity of a federal judicature have been clearly pointed out. It is the less necessary to recapitulate the considerations there urged as the propriety of the institution in the abstract is not disputed; the only questions which have been raised being relative to the manner of constituting it, and to its extent. To these points, therefore, our observations shall be confined.

The manner of constituting it seems to embrace these several objects: 1st. The mode of appointing the judges. 2nd. The tenure by which they are to hold their places. 3rd. The partition of the judiciary authority between different courts and their relations to each other.

First. As to the mode of appointing the judges: this is the same with that of appointing the officers of the Union in general and has been so fully discussed in the two last numbers that nothing can be said here which would not be useless repetition.

Second. As to the tenure by which the judges are to hold their places: this chiefly concerns their duration in office, the provisions for their support, the precautions for their responsibility.

According to the plan of the convention, all judges who may be appointed by the United States are to hold their offices *during good behavior;* which is conformable to the most approved of the State constitutions, and among the rest, to that of this State. Its propriety having been drawn into question by the adversaries of that plan is no light symptom of the rage for objection which disorders their imag-inations and judgments. The standard of good behavior for the continuance in office of the judicial magistracy is certainly one of the most valuable of the modern improvements in the practice of government. In a monarchy it is an excellent barrier to the despotism of the prince; in a republic it is a no less excellent barrier to the encroachments and oppressions of the representative body. And it is the best expedient which can be devised in any government to secure a steady, upright, and impartial administration of the laws.

Whoever attentively considers the different departments of power must perceive that, in a government in which they are separated from each other, the judiciary, from the nature of its functions, will always be the least dangerous to the political rights of the Constitution; because it will be least in a capacity to annoy or injure them. The executive not only dispenses the honors but holds the sword of the community. The legislature not only commands the purse but prescribes the rules by which the duties and rights of every citizen are to be regulated. The judiciary, on the contrary, has no influence over either the sword or the purse; no direction either of the strength or of the wealth of the society, and can take no active resolution whatever. It may truly be said to have neither FORCE NOR WILL but merely judgment; and must ultimately depend upon the aid of the executive arm even for the efficacy of its judgments.

This simple view of the matter suggests several important consequences. It proves incontestably that the judiciary is beyond comparison the weakest of the three departments of power; that it can never attack with success either of the other two; and that all possible care is requisite to enable it to defend itself against their attacks. It equally proves that though individual oppression may now and then proceed from the courts of justice, the general liberty of the people can never be endangered from that quarter; I mean so long as the judiciary remains truly distinct from both the legislature and the executive. For I agree that "there is no liberty if the power of judging be not separated from the legislative and executive powers." And it proves, in the last place, that as liberty can have nothing to fear from the judiciary alone, but would have everything to fear from its union with either of the other departments, that as all the effects of such a union must ensue from a dependence of the former on the latter, notwithstanding a nominal and apparent separation; that as, from the natural feebleness of the judiciary, it is in continual jeopardy of being overpowered, awed, or influenced by its co-ordinate branches; and that as nothing can contribute so much to its firmness and independence as permanency in office, this quality may therefore be justly regarded as an indispensable ingredient in its constitution, and, in a great measure, as the citadel for the public justice and the public security.

The complete independence of the courts of justice is peculiarly essential in a limited Constitution. By a limited Constitution, I understand one which contains certain specified exceptions to the legislative authority; such, for instance, as that it shall pass no bills of attainder, no *ex post facto laws*, and the like. Limitations of this kind can be preserved in practice no other way than through the medium of courts of justice, whose duty it must be to declare all acts contrary to the manifest tenor of the Constitution void. Without this, all the reservations of particular rights or privileges would amount to nothing.

Some perplexity respecting the rights of the courts to pronounce legislative acts void, because contrary to the Constitution, has arisen from an imagination that the doctrine would imply a superiority to the judiciary to the legislative power. It is urged that the authority which can declare the acts of another void must necessarily be superior to the one whose acts may be declared void. As this doctrine is of great importance in all the American constitutions, a brief discussion of the grounds on which it rests cannot be unacceptable.

There is no position which depends on clearer principles than that every act of a delegated authority, contrary to the tenor of the commission under which it is exercised, is void. No legislative act, therefore, contrary to the Constitution, can be valid. To deny this would be to affirm that the deputy is greater than his principal; that the servant is above his master; that the representatives of the people are superior to the people themselves; that men acting by virtue of powers do not authorize, but what they forbid.

If it be said that the legislative body are themselves the constitutional judges of their own powers and that the construction they put upon them is conclusive upon the other departments it may be answered that this cannot be the natural presumption where it is not to be collected from any particular provisions in the Constitution. It is not otherwise to be supposed that the Constitution could intend to enable the representatives of the people to substitute their *will* to that of their constituents. It is far more rational to suppose that the courts were designed to be an intermediate body between the people and the legislature in order, among other things, to keep the latter within the limits assigned to their authority. The interpretation of the laws is the proper and peculiar province of the courts. A constitution is, in fact, and must be regarded by the judges as, a fundamental law. It therefore belongs to them to ascertain its meaning as well as the meaning of any particular act proceeding from the legislative body. If there should happen to be an irreconcilable variance between the two, that which has the superior obligation and validity ought, of course, to be preferred; or, in other words, the Constitution ought to be preferred to the statute, the intention of the people to the intention of their agents.

Nor does this conclusion by any means suppose a superiority of the judicial to the legislative power. It only supposes that the power of the people is superior to both, and that where the will of the legislature, declared in its statutes, stands in opposition to that of the people, declared in the Constitution, the judges ought to be governed by the latter rather than the former. They ought to regulate their decisions by the fundamental laws rather than by those which are not fundamental.

This exercise of judicial discretion in determining between two contradictory laws is exemplified in a familiar instance. It not uncommonly happens that there are two statutes existing at one time, clashing in whole or in part with each other and neither of them containing any repealing clause or expression. In such a case, it is the province of the courts to liquidate and fix their meaning and operation. So far as they can, by any fair construction, be reconciled to each other, reason and law conspire to dictate that this should be done; where this is impracticable, it becomes a matter of necessity to give effect to one in exclusion of the other. The rule which has obtained in the courts for determining their relative validity is that the last in order of time shall be preferred to the first. But this is a mere rule of construction, not derived from any positive law but from the nature and reason of the thing. It is a rule not enjoined upon the courts by legislative provision but adopted by themselves, as consonant to truth and propriety, for the direction of their conduct as interpreters of the law. They thought it reasonable that between the interfering acts of an equal authority that which was the last indication of its will should have the preference.

But in regard to the interfering acts of a superior and subordinate authority of an original and derivative power, the nature and reason of the thing indicates the converse of that rule as proper to be followed. They teach us that the prior act of a superior ought to be preferred to the subsequent act of an inferior and subordinate authority; and that accordingly, whenever a particular statute contravenes the Constitution, it will be the duty of the judicial tribunals to adhere to the latter and disregard the former.

It can be of no weight to say that the courts, on the pretense of a repugnancy, may substitute their own pleasure to the constitutional intentions of the legislature. This might as well happen in the case of two contradictory statutes; or it might as well happen in every adjudication upon any single statute. The courts must declare the sense of the law; and if they should be disposed to exercise WILL instead of JUDGMENT, the consequence would equally be the substitution of their pleasure to that of the legislative body. The observation, if it prove anything, would prove that there ought to be no judges distinct from that body.

If, then, the courts of justice are to be considered as the bulwarks of a limited Constitution against legislative encroachments, this consideration will afford a strong argument for the permanent tenure of judicial offices, since nothing will contribute so much as this to that independent spirit in the judges which must be essential to the faithful performance of so arduous a duty.

This independence of the judges is equally requisite to guard the Constitution and the rights of individuals from the effects of those ill humors which the arts of designing men, or the influence of particular conjunctures, sometimes disseminate among the people themselves, and which, though they speedily give place to better information, and more deliberate reflection, have a tendency, in the meantime, to occasion dangerous innovations in the government, and serious oppressions of the minor party in the community. Though I trust the friends of

the proposed Constitution will never concur with its enemies in questioning that fundamental principal of Republican government which admits the right of the people to alter or abolish the established Constitution whenever they find it inconsistent with their happiness; yet it is not to be inferred from this principle that the representatives of the people, whenever a momentary inclination happens to lay hold of a majority of their constituents incompatible with the provisions in the existing Constitution would, on that account, be justifiable in a violation of those provisions; or that the courts would be under a greater obligation to connive at infractions in this shape than when they had proceeded wholly from the cabals of the representative body. Until the people have, by some solemn and authoritative act, annulled or changed the established form, it is binding upon themselves collectively, as well as individually; and no presumption, or even knowledge of their sentiments, can warrant their representatives in a departure from it prior to such an act. But it is easy to see that it would require an uncommon portion of fortitude in the judges to do their duty as faithful guardians of the Constitution, where legislative invasions of it had been instigated by the major voice of the community.

But it is not with a view to infractions of the Constitution only that the independence of the judges may be an essential safeguard against the effects of occasional ill humors in the society. These sometimes extend no farther than to the injury of the private rights of particular classes of citizens, by unjust and partial laws. Here also the firmness of the judicial magistracy is of vast importance in mitigating the severity and confining the operation of such laws. It not only serves to moderate the immediate mischiefs of those which may have been passed but it operates as a check upon the legislative body in passing them; who, perceiving that obstacles to the success of iniquitous intention are to be expected from the scruples of the courts, are in a manner compelled, by the very motives of the injustice they mediate, to qualify their attempts. This is a circumstance calculated to have more influence upon the character of our governments

than but a few may be aware of. The benefits of the integrity and moderation of the judiciary have already been felt in more States than one; and though they may have displeased those whose sinister expectations they may have disappointed, they must have commanded the esteem and applause of all the virtuous and disinterested. Considerate men of every description ought to prize whatever will tend to beget or fortify that temper in the courts; as no man can be sure that he may not be tomorrow the victim of a spirit of injustice, by which he may be a gainer today. And every man must now feel that the inevitable tendency of such a spirit is to sap the foundations of public and private confidence and to introduce in its stead universal distrust and distress.

That inflexible and uniform adherence to the rights of the Constitution, and of individuals, which we perceive to be indispensable in the courts of justice, can certainly not be expected from judges who hold their offices by a temporary commission. Periodical appointments, however regulated, or by whomsoever made, would, in some way or other, be fatal to their necessary independence. If the power of making them was committed either to the executive or legislature there would be danger of an improper complaisance to the branch which possessed it; if to both, there would be an unwillingness to hazard the displeasure of either; if to the people, or to persons chosen by them for the special purpose, there would be too great a disposition to consult popularity to justify a reliance that nothing would be consulted by the Constitution and the laws.

There is yet a further and a weighty reason for the permanency of the judicial offices which is deducible from the nature of the qualifications they require. It has been frequently remarked with great propriety that a voluminous code of laws is one of the inconveniences necessarily connected with the advantages of a free government. To avoid an arbitrary discretion in the courts, it is indispensable that they should be bound down by strict rules and precedents which serve to define and point out their duty in every particular case that comes before them; and it will readily be conceived from the variety of controversies which grow out of the folly and wickedness of mankind that the records of those precedents must unavoidably swell to a very considerable bulk and must demand long and laborious study to acquire a competent knowledge of them. Hence it is that there can be but few men in the society who will have sufficient skill in the laws to qualify them for the stations of judges. And making the proper deductions for the ordinary depravity of human nature, the number must be still smaller of those who unite the requisite integrity with the requisite knowledge. These considerations apprise us that the government can have no great option between fit characters; and that a temporary duration in office which would naturally discourage such characters from quitting a lucrative line of practice to accept a seat on the bench would have a tendency to throw the administration of justice into hands less able and less well qualified to conduct it with utility and dignity. In the present circumstances of this country and in those in which it is likely to be for a long time to come, the disadvantages on this score would be greater than they may at first sight appear; but it must be confessed that they are far inferior to those which present themselves under the other aspects of the subject.

Upon the whole, there can be no room to doubt that the convention acted wisely in copying from the models of those constitutions which have established *good behavior* as the tenure of their judicial offices in point of duration, and that so far from being blamable on this account, their plan would have been inexcusably defective if it had wanted this important feature of good government. The experience of Great Britain affords an illustrious comment on the excellence of the institution.

Presidential Election Results, 1789–2004

Year	Candidates	Party	Popular Vote	Electoral Vote
1789	George Washington			69
	John Adams			34
	Others			35
1793	George Washington			132
	John Adams			77
	George Clinton			50
	Others			5
1796	John Adams	Federalist		71
	Thomas Jefferson	Democratic-Republican		68
	Thomas Pinckney	Federalist		59
	Aaron Burr	Democratic-Republican		30
	Others			48
1800	Thomas Jefferson	Democratic-Republican		73
	Aaron Burr	Democratic-Republican		73
	John Adams	Federalist		65
	Charles C. Pinckney	Federalist		64
1804	Thomas Jefferson	Democratic-Republican		162
	Charles C. Pinckney	Federalist		14
1808	James Madison	Democratic-Republican		122
	Charles C. Pinckney	Federalist		47
	George Clinton	Independent-Republican		6
1812	James Madison	Democratic-Republican		128
	DeWitt Clinton	Federalist		89
1816	James Monroe	Democratic-Republican		183
	Rufus King	Federalist		34
1820	James Monroe	Democratic-Republican		231
	John Quincy Adams	Independent-Republican		1
1824	John Quincy Adams	Democratic-Republican	108,740(30.5%)	84
	Andrew Jackson	Democratic-Republican	153,544(43.1%)	99
	Henry Clay	Democratic-Republican	47,136(13.2%)	37
	William H. Crawford	Democratic-Republican	46,618(13.1%)	41
1828	Andrew Jackson	Democratic	647,231(56.0%)	178
	John Quincy Adams	National Republican	509,097(44.0%)	83
1832	Andrew Jackson	Democratic	687,502(55.0%)	219
	Henry Clay	National Republican	530,189(42.4%)	49
	William Wirt	Anti-Masonic		7
	John Floyd	National Republican	33,108(2.6%)	11
1836	Martin Van Buren	Democratic	761,549(50.9%)	170
	William H. Harrison	Whig	549,567(36.7%)	73
	Hugh L. White	Whig	145,396(9.7%)	26
	Daniel Webster	Whig	41,287(2.7%)	14
1840	William H. Harrison	Whig	1,275,017(53.1%)	234
	Martin Van Buren	Democratic	1,128,702(46.9%)	60
1844	James K. Polk	Democratic	1,337,243(49.6%)	170
	Henry Clay	Whig	1,299,068(48.1%)	105
	James G. Birney	Liberty	63,300(2.3%)	
1848	Zachary Taylor	Whig	1,360,101(47.4%)	163
	Lewis Cass	Democratic	1,220,544(42.5%)	127
	Martin Van Buren	Free Soil	291,163(10.1%)	
1852	Franklin Pierce	Democratic	1,601,474(50.9%)	254
	Winfield Scott	Whig	1,386,578(44.1%)	42
1856	James Buchanan	Democratic	1,838,169(45.4%)	174
	John C. Fremont	Republican	1,335,264(33.0%)	114
	Millard Fillmore	American	874,534(21.6%)	8
1860	Abraham Lincoln	Republican	1,865,593(39.8%)	180
	Stephen A. Douglas	Democratic	1,381,713(29.5%)	12
	John C. Breckinridge	Democratic	848,356(18.1%)	72
	John Bell	Constitutional Union	592,906(12.6%)	79
1864	Abraham Lincoln	Republican	2,206,938(55.0%)	212
	George B. McClellan	Democratic	1,803,787(45.0%)	21
1868	Ulysses S. Grant	Republican	3,013,421(52.7%)	214
	Horatio Seymour	Democratic	2,706,829(47.3%)	80
1872	Ulysses S. Grant	Republican	3,596,745(55.6%)	286
	Horace Greeley	Democratic	2,843,446(43.9%)	66
1876	Rutherford B. Hayes	Republican	4,036,571(48.0%)	185
	Samuel J. Tilden	Democratic	4,284,020(51.0%)	184
1880	James A. Garfield	Republican	4,449,053(48.3%)	214
	Winfield S. Hancock	Democratic	4,442,035(48.2%)	155
	James B. Weaver	Greenback-Labor	308,578(3.4%)	
1884	Grover Cleveland	Democratic	4,874,986(48.5%)	219
	James G. Blaine	Republican	4,851,931(48.2%)	182
	Benjamin F. Butler	Greenback-Labor	175,370(1.8%)	
1888	Benjamin Harrison	Republican	5,444,337(47.8%)	233
	Grover Cleveland	Democratic	5,540,050(48.6%)	168

Presidential Election Results, 1789–2004

Year	Candidates	Party	Popular Vote	Electoral Vote
1892	Grover Cleveland	Democratic	5,554,414(46.0%)	277
	Benjamin Harrison	Republican	5,190,802(43.0%)	145
	James B. Weaver	Peoples	1,027,329(8.5%)	22
1896	William McKinley	Republican	7,035,638(50.8%)	271
	William J. Bryan	Democratic; Populist	6,467,946(46.7%)	176
1900	William McKinley	Republican	7,219,530(51.7%)	292
	William J. Bryan	Democratic; Populist	6,356,734(45.5%)	155
1904	Theodore Roosevelt	Republican	7,628,834(56.4%)	336
	Alton B. Parker	Democratic	5,084,401(37.6%)	140
	Eugene V. Debs	Socialist	402,460(3.0%)	0
1908	William H. Taft	Republican	7,679,006(51.6%)	321
	William J. Bryan	Democratic	6,409,106(43.1%)	162
	Eugene V. Debs	Socialist	420,820(2.8%)	0
1912	Woodrow Wilson	Democratic	6,286,820(41.8%)	435
	Theodore Roosevelt	Progressive	4,126,020(27.4%)	88
	William H. Taft	Republican	3,483,922(23.2%)	8
	Eugene V. Debs	Socialist	897,011(6.0%)	0
1916	Woodrow Wilson	Democratic	9,129,606(49.3%)	277
	Charles E. Hughes	Republican	8,538,211(46.1%)	254
1920	Warren G. Harding	Republican	16,152,200(61.0%)	404
	James M. Cox	Democratic	9,147,353(34.6%)	127
	Eugene V. Debs	Socialist	919,799(3.5%)	0
1924	Calvin Coolidge	Republican	15,725,016(54.1%)	382
	John W. Davis	Democratic	8,385,586(28.8%)	136
	Robert M. La Follette	Progressive	4,822,856(16.6%)	13
1928	Herbert C. Hoover	Republican	21,392,190(58.2%)	444
	Alfred E. Smith	Democratic	15,016,443(40.8%)	87
1932	Franklin D. Roosevelt	Democratic	22,809,638(57.3%)	472
	Herbert C. Hoover	Republican	15,758,901(39.6%)	59
	Norman Thomas	Socialist	881,951(2.2%)	0
1936	Franklin D. Roosevelt	Democratic	27,751,612(60.7%)	523
	Alfred M. Landon	Republican	16,681,913(36.4%)	8
	William Lemke	Union	891,858(1.9%)	0
1940	Franklin D. Roosevelt	Democratic	27,243,466(54.7%)	449
	Wendell L. Willkie	Republican	22,304,755(44.8%)	82
1944	Franklin D. Roosevelt	Democratic	25,602,505(52.8%)	432
	Thomas E. Dewey	Republican	22,006,278(44.5%)	99
1948	Harry S Truman	Democratic	24,105,812(49.5%)	303
	Thomas E. Dewey	Republican	21,970,065(45.1%)	189
	J. Strom Thurmond	States' Rights	1,169,063(2.4%)	39
	Henry A. Wallace	Progressive	1,157,172(2.4%)	0
1952	Dwight D. Eisenhower	Republican	33,936,234(55.2%)	442
	Adlai E. Stevenson	Democratic	27,314,992(44.5%)	89
1956	Dwight D. Eisenhower	Republican	35,590,472(57.4%)	457
	Adlai E. Stevenson	Democratic	26,022,752(42.0%)	73
1960	John F. Kennedy	Democratic	34,227,096(49.9%)	303
	Richard M. Nixon	Republican	34,108,546(49.6%)	219
1964	Lyndon B. Johnson	Democratic	43,126,233(61.1%)	486
	Barry Goldwater	Republican	27,174,989(38.5%)	52
1968	Richard M. Nixon	Republican	31,783,783(43.4%)	301
	Hubert H. Humphrey	Democratic	31,271,839(42.7%)	191
	George C. Wallace	American Independent	9,899,557(13.5%)	46
1972	Richard M. Nixon	Republican	46,632,189(61.3%)	520
	George McGovern	Democratic	28,422,015(37.3%)	17
1976	Jimmy Carter	Democratic	40,828,587(50.1%)	297
	Gerald R. Ford	Republican	39,147,613(48.0%)	240
1980	Ronald Reagan	Republican	42,941,145(51.0%)	489
	Jimmy Carter	Democratic	34,663,037(41.0%)	49
	John B. Anderson	Independent	5,551,551(6.6%)	0
1984	Ronald Reagan	Republican	53,428,357(59%)	525
	Walter F. Mondale	Democratic	36,930,923(41%)	13
1988	George Bush	Republican	48,881,011(53%)	426
	Michael Dukakis	Democratic	41,828,350(46%)	111
1992	Bill Clinton	Democratic	38,394,210(43%)	370
	George Bush	Republican	33,974,386(38%)	168
	H. Ross Perot	Independent	16,573,465(19%)	0
1996	Bill Clinton	Democratic	45,628,667(49%)	379
	Bob Dole	Republican	37,869,435(41%)	159
	H. Ross Perot	Reform	7,874,283(8%)	0
2000	George W. Bush	Republican	50,456,169(48%)	271
	Al Gore	Democratic	50,996,116(48%)	266
	Ralph Nader	Green	2,767,176(3%)	0
2004	George W. Bush	Republican	60,608,582(51%)	286
	John Kerry	Democratic	57,288,974(48%)	252
	Ralph Nader	Independent	400,924(.35%)	0

Presidents and Vice Presidents

1. George Washington (1789)
   John Adams (1789)

2. John Adams (1797)
   Thomas Jefferson (1797)

3. Thomas Jefferson (1801)
   Aaron Burr (1801)
   George Clinton (1805)

4. James Madison (1809)
   George Clinton (1809)
   Elbridge Gerry (1813)

5. James Monroe (1817)
   Daniel D. Tompkins (1817)

6. John Quincy Adams (1825)
   John C. Calhoun (1825)

7. Andrew Jackson (1829)
   John C. Calhoun (1829)
   Martin Van Buren (1833)

8. Martin Van Buren (1837)
   Richard M. Johnson (1837)

9. William H. Harrison (1841)
   John Tyler (1841)

10. John Tyler (1841)

11. James K. Polk (1845)
    George M. Dallas (1845)

12. Zachary Taylor (1849)
    Millard Fillmore (1849)

13. Millard Fillmore (1850)

14. Franklin Pierce (1853)
    William R. King (1853)

15. James Buchanan (1857)
    John C. Breckinridge (1857)

16. Abraham Lincoln (1861)
    Hannibal Hamlin (1861)
    Andrew Johnson (1865)

17. Andrew Johnson (1865)

18. Ulysses S. Grant (1869)
    Schuyler Colfax (1869)
    Henry Wilson (1873)

19. Rutherford B. Hayes (1877)
    William A. Wheeler (1877)

20. James A. Garfield (1881)
    Chester A. Arthur (1881)

21. Chester A. Arthur (1881)

22. Grover Cleveland (1885)
    T. A. Hendricks (1885)

23. Benjamin Harrison (1889)
    Levi P. Morton (1889)

24. Grover Cleveland (1893)
    Adlai E. Stevenson (1893)

25. William McKinley (1897)
    Garret A. Hobart (1897)
    Theodore Roosevelt (1901)

26. Theodore Roosevelt (1901)
    Charles Fairbanks (1905)

27. William H. Taft (1909)
    James S. Sherman (1909)

28. Woodrow Wilson (1913)
    Thomas R. Marshall (1913)

29. Warren G. Harding (1921)
    Calvin Coolidge (1921)

30. Calvin Coolidge (1923)
    Charles G. Dawes (1925)

31. Herbert C. Hoover (1929)
    Charles Curtis (1929)

32. Franklin D. Roosevelt (1933)
    John Nance Garner (1933)
    Henry A. Wallace (1941)
    Harry S Truman (1945)

33. Harry S Truman (1945)
    Alben W. Barkley (1949)

34. Dwight D. Eisenhower (1953)
    Richard M. Nixon (1953)

35. John F. Kennedy (1961)
    Lyndon B. Johnson (1961)

36. Lyndon B. Johnson (1963)
    Hubert H. Humphrey (1965)

37. Richard M. Nixon (1969)
    Spiro T. Agnew (1969)
    Gerald R. Ford (1973)

38. Gerald R. Ford (1974)
    Nelson A. Rockefeller (1974)

39. James E. Carter Jr. (1977)
    Walter F. Mondale (1977)

40. Ronald W. Reagan (1981)
    George H. W. Bush (1981)

41. George H. W. Bush (1989)
    James D. Quayle III (1989)

42. William J. B. Clinton (1993)
    Albert Gore (1993)

43. George W. Bush (2001)
    Richard Cheney (2001)

Glossary

527 organization A political group organized under section 527 of the IRS Code that may accept and spend unlimited amounts of money on election activities so long as they are not spent on broadcast ads run in the last 30 days before a primary or 60 days before a general election where a clearly identified candidate is referred to and a relevant electorate is targeted.

administrative discretion Authority given by Congress to the federal bureaucracy to use reasonable judgment in implementing the laws.

adversary system A judicial system in which the court of law is a neutral arena where two parties argue their differences.

advisory opinion An opinion unrelated to a particular case that gives a court's view about a constitutional or legal issue.

affirmative action Remedial action designed to overcome the effects of discrimination against minorities and women.

amendatory veto The power of governors in a few states to return a bill to the legislature with suggested language changes, conditions, or amendments. Legislators then decide either to accept the governor's recommendations or to pass the bill in its original form over the veto.

American dream The widespread belief that the United States is a land of opportunity and that individual initiative and hard work can bring economic success.

***amicus curiae* brief** Literally, a "friend of the court" brief, filed by an individual or organization to present arguments in addition to those presented by the immediate parties to a case.

Annapolis Convention A convention held in September 1786 to consider problems of trade and navigation, attended by five states and important because it issued the call to Congress and the states for what became the Constitutional Convention.

Antifederalists Opponents of ratification of the Constitution and of a strong central government generally.

antitrust legislation Federal laws (starting with the Sherman Act of 1890) that try to prevent a monopoly from dominating an industry and restraining trade.

appellate jurisdiction The authority of a court to review decisions made by lower courts.

Articles of Confederation The first governing document of the confederated states, drafted in 1777, ratified in 1781, and replaced by the present Constitution in 1789.

assessment The valuation a government places on property for the purposes of taxation.

assigned counsel system Arrangement whereby attorneys are provided for persons accused of crimes who are unable to hire their own attorneys. The judge assigns a member of the bar to provide counsel to a particular defendant.

attentive public Those citizens who follow public affairs carefully.

Australian ballot A secret ballot printed by the state.

bad tendency test Interpretation of the First Amendment that would permit legislatures to forbid speech encouraging people to engage in illegal action.

bicameral legislature A two-house legislature.

bicameralism The principle of a two-house legislature.

bill of attainder Legislative act inflicting punishment, including deprivation of property, without a trial, on named individuals or members of a specific group.

binding arbitration A collective bargaining agreement in which both parties agree, in case of dispute over the terms of the union contract, to adhere to the decision of an arbitrator.

Bipartisan Campaign Reform Act (BCRA) Largely banned party soft money, restored longstanding prohibition on corporations and labor unions for using general treasury funds for electoral purposes, and narrowed the definition of issue advocacy.

bipartisanship A policy that emphasizes a united front and cooperation between the major political parties, especially on sensitive foreign policy issues.

blanket primary Primary election open to all voters, who may vote for a candidate from any party for each office.

bundling A tactic in which PACs collect contributions from like-minded individuals (each limited to $2,000) and present them to a candidate or political party as a "bundle," thus increasing the PAC's influence.

bureaucracy A form of organization that operates through impersonal, uniform rules and procedures.

bureaucrat A career government employee.

Bush Doctrine A policy adopted by the Bush administration in 2001 that asserts America's right to attack any nation that has weapons of mass destruction that might be used against U.S. interests at home or abroad.

cabinet Advisory council for the president, consisting of the heads of the executive departments, the vice president, and a few other officials selected by the president.

candidate appeal How voters feel about a candidate's background, personality, leadership ability, and other personal qualities.

capitalism An economic system characterized by private property, competitive markets, economic incentives, and limited government involvement in the production, distribution, and pricing of goods and services.

caucus A meeting of local party members to choose party officials or candidates for public office and to decide the platform.

central clearance Review of all executive branch testimony, reports, and draft legislation by the Office of Management and Budget to en-sure that each communication to Congress is in accordance with the president's program.

centralists People who favor national action over action at the state and local levels.

charter school A publicly funded alternative to standard public schools in some states, initiated when individuals or groups receive charters; charter schools must meet state standards.

charter City "constitution" that outlines the structure of city government, defines the authority of the various officials, and provides for their selection.

checks and balances Constitutional grant of powers that enables each of the three branches of government to check some acts of the others and therefore ensure that no branch can dominate.

chief of staff The head of the White House staff.

civil disobedience Deliberate refusal to obey a law or comply with the orders of public officials as a means of expressing opposition.

civil law A law that governs relationships between individuals and defines their legal rights.

class action suit Lawsuit brought by an individual or a group of people on behalf of all those similarly situated.

clear and present danger test Interpretation of the First Amendment that holds that the government cannot interfere with speech unless the speech presents a clear and present danger that it will lead to evil or illegal acts.

closed primary Primary election in which only persons registered in the party holding the primary may vote.

closed rule A procedural rule in the House of Representatives that prohibits any amendments to bills or provides that only members of the committee reporting the bill may offer amendments.

closed shop A company with a labor agreement under which union membership can be a condition of employment.

cloture A procedure for terminating debate, especially filibusters, in the Senate.

coattail effect The boost that candidates may get in an election because of the popularity of candidates above them on the ballot, especially the president.

collective action How groups form and organize to pursue their goals or objectives, including how to get individuals and groups to participate and cooperate. The term has many applications in the various social sciences such as political science, sociology, and economics.

collective bargaining Method whereby representatives of the union and employer determine wages, hours, and other conditions of employment through direct negotiation.

commerce clause The clause in the Constitution (Article I, Section 8, Clause 1) that gives Congress the power to regulate all business activities that cross state lines or affect more than one state or other nations.

commercial speech Advertisements and commercials for products and services; they receive less First Amendment protection, primarily to discourage false and misleading ads.

community policing Assigning police to neighborhoods where they walk the beat and work with churches and other community groups to reduce crime and improve relations with minorities.

concurrent powers Powers that the Constitution gives to both the national and state governments, such as the power to levy taxes.

concurring opinion An opinion that agrees with the majority in a Supreme Court ruling but differs on the reasoning.

confederation Constitutional arrangement in which sovereign nations or states, by compact, create a central government but carefully limit its power and do not give it direct authority over individuals.

conference committee Committee appointed by the presiding officers of each chamber to adjust differences on a particular bill passed by each in different form.

Congressional Budget Office (CBO) An agency of Congress that analyzes presidential budget recommendations and estimates the costs of proposed legislation.

congressional–executive agreement A formal agreement between the U.S. president and the leaders of other nations that requires approval by both houses of Congress.

Connecticut Compromise Compromise agreement by states at the Constitutional Convention for a bicameral legislature with a lower house in which representation would be based on population and an upper house in which each state would have two senators.

conservatism A belief that limited government ensures order, competitive markets, and personal opportunity.

constituents The residents of a congressional district or state.

Constitutional Convention The convention in Philadelphia, May 25 to September 17, 1787, that framed the Constitution of the United States.

constitutional democracy A government that enforces recognized limits on those who govern and allows the voice of the people to be heard through free, fair, and relatively frequent elections.

constitutional home rule State constitutional authorization for local governments to conduct their own affairs.

constitutional initiative petition A device that permits voters to place specific amendments to a state constitution on the ballot by petition.

constitutionalism The set of arrangements, including checks and balances, federalism, separation of powers, rule of law, due process, and a bill of rights, that requires our leaders to listen, think, bargain, and explain before they act or make laws. We then hold them politically and legally accountable for how they exercise their powers.

contract clause Clause of the Constitution (Article I, Section 10) originally intended to prohibit state governments from modifying contracts made between individuals; for a while interpreted as prohibiting state governments from taking actions that adversely affect property

rights; no longer interpreted so broadly and no longer constrains state governments from exercising their police powers.

council-manager plan Form of local government in which the city council hires a professional administrator to manage city affairs; also known as the city-manager plan.

court of appeals A court with appellate jurisdiction that hears appeals from the decisions of lower courts.

criminal law A law that defines crimes against the public order.

cross-cutting cleavages Divisions within society that cut across demographic categories to produce groups that are more heterogeneous or different.

crossover voting Voting by a member of one party for a candidate of another party.

cycle of decreasing influence The tendency of presidents to lose support over time.

cycle of increasing effectiveness The tendency of presidents to learn more about doing their jobs over time.

de facto segregation Segregation resulting from economic or social conditions or personal choice.

de jure segregation Segregation imposed by law.

dealignment Weakening of partisan preferences that points to a rejection of both major parties and a rise in the number of Independents.

decentralists People who favor state or local action rather than national action.

defendant In a criminal action, the person or party accused of an offense.

deficit The difference between the revenues raised annually from sources of income other than borrowing and the expenditures of government, including paying the interest on past borrowing.

delegate An official who is expected to represent the views of his or her constituents even when personally holding different views; one interpretation of the role of the legislator.

democracy Government by the people, both directly or indirectly, with free and frequent elections.

democratic consensus Widespread agreement on fundamental principles of democratic governance and the values that undergird them.

demographics The study of the characteristics of populations.

department Usually the largest organization in government; also the highest rank in federal hierarchy.

deregulation A policy promoting cutbacks in the amount of federal regulation in specific areas of economic activity.

devolution revolution The effort to slow the growth of the federal government by returning many functions to the states.

direct democracy Government in which citizens vote on laws and select officials directly.

direct primary Election in which voters choose party nominees.

discharge petition Petition that, if signed by a majority of the House members of Representa-

tives, will pry a bill from committee and bring it to the floor for consideration.

disclosure A requirement that candidates specify where the money came from to finance their campaign.

dissenting opinion An opinion disagreeing with the majority in a Supreme Court ruling.

distributive policy A type of policy that provides benefits to all Americans.

divided government Governance divided between the parties, especially when one holds the presidency and the other controls one or both houses of Congress.

docket The list of potential cases that reach the Supreme Court.

double jeopardy Trial or punishment for the same crime by the same government; forbidden by the Constitution.

dual citizenship Citizenship in more than one nation.

due process clause Clause in the Fifth Amendment limiting the power of the national government; similar clause in the Fourteenth Amendment prohibiting state governments from depriving any person of life, liberty, or property without due process of law.

due process Established rules and regulations that restrain government officials.

earmarks Special spending projects that are set aside on behalf of individual members of Congress for their constituents.

economic sanctions Denial of export, import, or financial relations with a target country in an effort to change that nation's policies.

electoral college The electoral system used in electing the president and vice president, in which voters vote for electors pledged to cast their ballots for a particular party's candidates.

eminent domain Power of a government to take private property for public use; the U.S. Constitution gives national and state governments this power and requires them to provide just compensation for property so taken.

entitlement program Programs such as unemployment insurance, disaster relief, or disability payments that provide benefits to all eligible citizens.

enumerated powers The powers explicitly given to Congress in the Constitution.

environmental impact statement A statement required by federal law from all agencies for any project using federal funds to assess the potential effect of the new construction or development on the environment.

equal protection clause Clause in the Fourteenth Amendment that forbids any state to deny to any person within its jurisdiction the equal protection of the laws. By interpretation, the Fifth Amendment imposes the same limitation on the national government. This clause is the major constitutional restraint on the power of governments to discriminate against persons because of race, national origin, or sex.

establishment clause Clause in the First Amendment that states that Congress shall make no law respecting an establishment of religion. The Supreme Court has interpreted this to forbid governmental support to any or all religions.

ethnicity A social division based on national origin, religion, language, and often race.

ethnocentrism Belief in the superiority of one's nation or ethnic group.

ex post facto law Retroactive criminal law that works to the disadvantage of a person.

excise tax Consumer tax on a specific kind of merchandise, such as tobacco.

exclusionary rule Requirement that evidence unconstitutionally or illegally obtained be excluded from a criminal trial.

executive agreement A formal agreement between the U.S. president and the leaders of other nations that does not require Senate approval.

Executive Office of the President The cluster of presidential staff agencies that help the president carry out his responsibilities. Currently the office includes the Office of Management and Budget, the Council of Economic Advisers, and several other units.

executive order Directive issued by a president or governor that has the force of law.

executive orders Formal orders issued by the president to direct action by the federal bureaucracy.

executive privilege The power to keep executive communications confidential, especially if they relate to national security.

express powers Powers the Constitution specifically grants to one of the branches of the national government.

extradition Legal process whereby an alleged criminal offender is surrendered by the officials of one state to officials of the state in which the crime is alleged to have been committed.

faction A term the founders used to refer to political parties and special interests or interest groups.

Federal Election Commission (FEC) A commission created by the 1974 amendments to the Federal Election Campaign Act to administer election reform laws. It consists of six commissioners appointed by the president and confirmed by the Senate. Its duties include overseeing disclosure of campaign finance information and public funding of presidential elections, and enforcing contribution limits.

federal mandate A requirement the federal government imposes as a condition for receiving federal funds.

Federal Register An official document, published every weekday, which lists the new and proposed regulations of executive departments and regulatory agencies.

Federal Reserve System The system created by Congress in 1913 to establish banking practices and regulate currency in circulation and the amount of credit available. It consists of 12 regional banks supervised by the Board of Governors. Often called simply the Fed.

federalism Constitutional arrangement in which power is distributed between a central government and subdivisional governments, called states in the United States. The national and the subdivisional governments both exercise direct authority over individuals.

Federalists Supporters of ratification of the Constitution and of a strong central government.

felony A serious crime, the penalty for which can range from imprisonment in a penitentiary for more than a year to death.

fighting words Words that by their very nature inflict injury on those to whom they are addressed or incite them to acts of violence.

filibuster A procedural practice in the Senate whereby a senator refuses to relinquish the floor and thereby delays proceedings and prevents a vote on a controversial issue.

fiscal policy Government policy that attempts to manage the economy by controlling taxing and spending.

free exercise clause Clause in the First Amendment that states that Congress shall make no law prohibiting the free exercise of religion.

free rider An individual who does not join a group representing his or her interests yet receives the benefit of the group's influence.

full faith and credit clause Clause in the Constitution (Article IV, Section 1) requiring each state to recognize the civil judgments rendered by the courts of the other states and to accept their public records and acts as valid.

fundamentalists Conservative Christians who as a group have become more active in politics in the last two decades and were especially influential in the 2000 presidential election.

gender gap The difference between the political opinions or political behavior of men and of women.

General Agreement on Tariffs and Trade (GATT) An international trade organization with more than 130 members, including the United States and the People's Republic of China, that seeks to encourage free trade by lowering tariffs and other trade restrictions.

general election Elections in which voters elect officeholders.

general property tax Tax levied by local and some state governments on real property or personal, tangible property, the major portion of which is on the estimated value of one's home and land.

gerrymandering The drawing of legislative district boundaries to benefit a party, group, or incumbent.

government corporation A government agency that operates like a business corporation, created to secure greater freedom of action and flexibility for a particular program.

grand jury A jury of 12 to 23 persons who, in private, hear evidence presented by the government to determine whether persons shall be required to stand trial. If the jury believes there is sufficient evidence that a crime was committed, it issues an indictment.

Green party A minor party dedicated to the environment, social justice, nonviolence, and a foreign policy of nonintervention. Ralph Nader ran as the Green party's nominee in 2000.

gross domestic product (GDP) The total output of all economic activity in the nation, including goods and services.

hard money Political contributions given to a party, candidate, or interest group that are limited in amount and fully disclosed. Raising such limited funds is harder than raising unlimited funds, hence the term "hard money."

hard power The reliance on economic and military strength to solve international problems.

Hatch Act Federal statute barring federal employees from active participation in certain kinds of politics and protecting them from being fired on partisan grounds.

Health Maintenance Organization (HMO) Alternative means of health care in which people or their employers are charged a set amount and the HMO provides health care and covers hospital costs.

hold A procedural practice in the Senate whereby a senator temporarily blocks the consideration of a bill or nomination.

honeymoon Period at the beginning of a new president's term during which the president enjoys generally positive relations with the press and Congress, usually lasting about six months.

horse race A close contest; by extension, any contest in which the focus is on who is ahead and by how much rather than on substantive differences between the candidates.

idealism A theory of international relations that focuses on the hope that nations will act together to solve international problems and promote peace.

immunity Exemption from prosecution for a particular crime in return for testimony pertaining to the case.

impeachment Formal accusation by the lower house of a legislature against a public official, the first step in removal from office.

implementation The process of putting a law into practice through bureaucratic rules or spending.

implied powers Powers inferred from the express powers that allow Congress to carry out its functions.

impoundment Presidential refusal to allow an agency to spend funds that Congress authorized and appropriated.

incumbent The current holder of elected office.

independent agency A government entity that is independent of the legislative, executive, and judicial branches.

independent expenditure The Supreme Court has ruled that individuals, groups, and parties can spend unlimited amounts in campaigns for or against candidates as long as they operate independently from the candidates. When an individual, group, or party does so, they are making an independent expenditure.

independent regulatory commission A government agency or commission with regulatory power whose independence is protected by Congress.

indexing Providing automatic increases to compensate for inflation.

indictment A formal written statement from a grand jury charging an individual with an offense; also called a true bill.

inflation A rise in the general price level (and decrease in dollar value) owing to an increase in the volume of money and credit in relation to available goods.

information affidavit Certification by a public prosecutor that there is evidence to justify bringing named individuals to trial.

inherent powers The powers of the national government in foreign affairs that the Supreme Court has declared do not depend on constitutional grants but rather grow out of the very existence of the national government.

initiative Procedure whereby a certain number of voters may, by petition, propose a law or constitutional amendment and have it submitted to the voters.

interest group A collection of people who share a common interest or attitude and seek to influence government for specific ends. Interest groups usually work within the framework of government and try to achieve their goals through tactics such as lobbying.

interested money Financial contributions by individuals or groups in the hope of influencing the outcome of an election and subsequently influencing policy.

internationalism The belief that nations must engage in international problem solving.

interstate compact An agreement among two or more states. Congress must approve most such agreements.

iron triangle A policy-making alliance that involves very strong ties among a congressional committee, an interest group, and a federal department or agency.

isolationism The desire to avoid international engagement altogether.

issue advocacy Promoting a particular position or an issue paid for by interest groups or individuals but not candidates. Much issue advocacy is often electioneering for or against a candidate, and until 2004 had not been subject to any regulation.

issue network Relationships among interest groups, congressional committees and subcommittees, and the government agencies that share a common policy concern.

Jim Crow laws State laws formerly pervasive throughout the South requiring public facilities and accommodations to be segregated by race; ruled unconstitutional.

joint committee A committee composed of members of both the House of Representatives and the Senate; such committees oversee the Library of Congress and conduct investigations.

judicial activism Philosophy proposing that judges should interpret the Constitution to reflect current conditions and values.

judicial interpretation A method by which judges modify the force of a constitutional provision by reinterpreting its meaning.

judicial restraint Philosophy proposing that judges should interpret the Constitution to reflect what the framers intended and what its words literally say.

judicial review The power of a court to refuse to enforce a law or a government regulation that in the opinion of the judges conflicts with the U.S. Constitution or, in a state court, the state constitution.

justiciable dispute A dispute growing out of an actual case or controversy and that is capable of settlement by legal methods.

Keynesian economics Theory based on the principles of John Maynard Keynes, stating that government spending should increase during business slumps and be curbed during booms.

labor injunction A court order forbidding specific individuals or groups from performing certain acts (such as striking) that the court considers harmful to the rights and property of an employer or a community.

laissez-faire economics Theory that opposes governmental interference in economic affairs beyond what is necessary to protect life and property.

leadership PAC A PAC formed by an office holder that collects contributions from individuals and other PACs and then makes contributions to other candidates and political parties.

libel Written defamation of another person. For public officials and public figures, the constitutional tests designed to restrict libel actions are especially rigid.

liberalism A belief that government can and should achieve justice and equality of opportunity.

Libertarian party A minor party that believes in extremely limited government. Libertarians call for a free market system, expanded individual liberties such as drug legalization, and a foreign policy of nonintervention, free trade, and open immigration.

libertarianism An ideology that cherishes individual liberty and insists on minimal government, promoting a free market economy, a noninterventionist foreign policy, and an absence of regulation in moral, economic, and social life.

line item veto Presidential power to strike, or remove, specific items from a spending bill without vetoing the entire package; declared unconstitutional by the Supreme Court.

literacy test Literacy requirement some states imposed as a condition of voting, generally used to disqualify black voters in the South; now illegal.

lobbying Engaging in activities aimed at influencing public officials, especially legislators, and the policies they enact.

lobbyist A person who is employed by and acts for an organized interest group or corporation to influence policy decisions and positions in the executive and legislative branches.

logrolling Mutual aid and vote trading among legislators.

majority leader The legislative leader selected by the majority party who helps plan party strategy, confers with other party leaders, and tries to keep members of the party in line.

majority rule Governance according to the expressed preferences of the majority.

majority The candidate or party that wins more than half the votes cast in an election.

majority-minority district A legislative district created to include a majority of minority voters; ruled constitutional so long as race is not the main factor in redistricting.

malapportionment Having legislative districts with unequal populations.

mandate A president's claim of broad public support.

manifest destiny A notion held by nineteenth-century Americans that the United States was destined to rule the continent, from the Atlantic to the Pacific.

manifest opinion A widely shared and consciously held view, like support for homeland security.

mass media Means of communication that reach the public, including newspapers and magazines, radio, television (broadcast, cable, and satellite), films, recordings, books, and electronic communication.

mayor-council charter The oldest and most common form of city government, consisting of either a weak mayor and a city council or a strong mayor elected by voters and council.

means-tested entitlements Programs such as Medicaid and welfare under which applicants must meet eligibility requirements based on need.

Medicaid Federal program that provides medical benefits for low-income persons.

medical savings account Alternative means of health care in which individuals make tax-deductible contributions to a special account that can be used to pay medical expenses.

Medicare National health insurance program for the elderly and disabled.

merit system A system of public employment in which selection and promotion depend on demonstrated performance rather than on political patronage.

midterm election Elections held midway between presidential elections.

minor party A small political party that rises and falls with a charismatic candidate or, if composed of ideologies on the right or left, usually persists over time; also called a third party.

minority leader The legislative leader selected by the minority party as spokesperson for the opposition.

misdemeanor A minor crime; the penalty is a fine or imprisonment for a short time, usually less than a year, in a local jail.

Missouri Plan A system for selecting judges that combines features of the appointive and elective methods. The governor selects judges from lists presented by panels of lawyers and laypersons, and at the end of their term, the judges may run against their own record in retention elections.

monetarism A theory that government should control the money supply to encourage economic growth and restrain inflation.

monetary policy Government policy that attempts to manage the economy by controlling the money supply and thus interest rates.

monopoly Domination of an industry by a single company that fixes prices and discourages competition; also, the company that dominates the industry by these means.

movement A large body of people interested in a common issue, idea, or concern that is of continuing significance and who are willing to take action. Movements seek to change attitudes or institutions, not just policies.

multilateralism A philosophy that encourages individual nations to act together to solve international problems.

name recognition Incumbents have an advantage over challengers in election campaigns because voters are more familiar with them, and incumbents are more recognizable.

national debt The total amount of money the federal government has borrowed to finance deficit spending over the years.

national intelligence director The federal government's primary intelligence officer, responsible for overseeing all national intelligence agencies and providing advice to the president on terrorist threats.

national party convention A national meeting of delegates elected in primaries, caucuses, or state conventions who assemble once every four years to nominate candidates for president and vice president, ratify the party platform, elect officers, and adopt rules.

national supremacy Constitutional doctrine that whenever conflict occurs between the constitutionally authorized actions of the national government and those of a state or local government, the actions of the federal government prevail.

national tide The inclination to focus on national issues, rather than local issues, in an election campaign. The impact of a national tide can be reduced by the nature of the candidates on the ballot who might have differentiated themselves from their party or its leader if the tide is negative, as well as competition in the election.

natural law God's or nature's law that defines right from wrong and is higher than human law.

natural rights The rights of all people to dignity and worth; also called human rights.

naturalization A legal action conferring citizenship on an alien.

necessary and proper clause Clause of the Constitution (Article I, Section 8, Clause 3) setting forth the implied powers of Congress. It states that Congress, in addition to its express powers, has the right to make all laws necessary and proper to carry out all powers the Constitution vests in the national government.

New Jersey Plan Proposal at the Constitutional Convention made by William Paterson of New Jersey for a central government with a single-house legislature in which each state would be represented equally.

new judicial federalism The practice of some state courts using the bill of rights in their state constitutions to provide more protection for some rights than is provided by the Supreme Court's interpretation of the Bill of Rights in the U.S. Constitution.

news media Media that emphasize the news.

nongovernmental organization (NGO) A nonprofit association or group operating outside of government that advocates and pursues policy objectives.

nonpartisan election A local or judicial election in which candidates are not selected or endorsed by political parties and party affiliation is not listed on ballots.

nonprotected speech Libel, obscenity, fighting words, and commercial speech, which are not entitled to constitutional protection in all circumstances.

normal trade relations Trade status granted as part of an international trade policy that gives a nation the same favorable trade concessions and tariffs that the best trading partners receive.

North American Free Trade Agreement (NAFTA) Agreement signed by the United States, Canada, and Mexico in 1992 to form the largest free trade zone in the world.

obscenity Quality or state of a work that taken as a whole appeals to a prurient interest in sex by depicting sexual conduct in a patently offensive way and that lacks serious literary, artistic, political, or scientific value.

office block ballot Ballot on which all candidates are listed under the office for which they are running.

Office of Management and Budget (OMB) Presidential staff agency that serves as a clearinghouse for budgetary requests and management improvements for government agencies.

Office of Personnel Management (OPM) Agency that administers civil service laws, rules, and regulations.

offshoring The practice of exporting U.S. jobs to lower-paid employees in other nations.

one-party state A state in which one party wins all or nearly all the offices and the other party receives only a small proportion of the popular vote.

open primary Primary election in which any voter, regardless of party, may vote.

open rule A procedural rule in the House of Representatives that permits floor amendments within the overall time allocated to the bill.

open shop A company with a labor agreement under which union membership cannot be required as a condition of employment.

opinion of the court An explanation of a decision of the Supreme Court or any other appellate court.

original jurisdiction The authority of a court to hear a case "in the first instance."

outsourcing Contracting of government services to private firms.

override An action taken by Congress to reverse a presidential veto, requiring a two-thirds majority in each chamber.

oversight Legislative or executive review of a particular government program or organization. Can be in response to a crisis of some kind or part of routine review.

parliamentary system A system of government in which the legislature selects the prime minister or president.

party caucus A meeting of the members of a party in a legislative chamber to select party leaders and develop party policy. Called a conference by the Republicans.

party column ballot Type of ballot that encourages party-line voting by listing all of a party's candidates in a column under the party name.

party convention A meeting of party delegates to vote on matters of policy and in some cases to select party candidates for public office.

party identification An informal and subjective affiliation with a political party that most people acquire in childhood.

party registration The act of declaring party affiliation; required by some states when one registers to vote.

patronage The dispensing of government jobs to persons who belong to the winning political party.

petit jury A jury of six to 12 persons that determines guilt or innocence in a civil or criminal action.

plea bargain Agreement between a prosecutor and a defendant that the defendant will plead guilty to a lesser offense to avoid having to stand trial for a more serious offense.

pluralism A theory of government that holds that open, multiple, and competing groups can check the asserted power by any one group.

plurality Candidate or party with the most votes cast in an election, not necessarily more than half.

pocket veto A veto exercised by the president after Congress has adjourned; if the president takes no action for ten days, the bill does not become law and is not returned to Congress for a possible override.

police powers Inherent powers of state governments to pass laws to protect the public health, safety, and welfare; the national government has no directly granted police powers but accomplishes the same goals through other delegated powers.

policy agenda The informal list of issues that Congress and the president consider most important for action.

political action committee (PAC) The political arm of an interest group that is legally entitled to raise funds on a voluntary basis from members, stockholders, or employees to contribute funds to candidates or political parties.

political culture The widely shared beliefs, values, and norms about how citizens relate to government and to one another.

political ideology A consistent pattern of beliefs about political values and the role of government.

political party An organization that seeks political power by electing people to office so that its positions and philosophy become public policy.

political predisposition A characteristic of individuals that is predictive of political behavior.

political socialization The process—most notably in families and schools—by which we develop our political attitudes, values, and beliefs.

poll tax Tax required to vote; prohibited for national elections by the Twenty-Fourth Amendment (1964) and ruled unconstitutional for all elections in Harper v. Virginia Board of Elections (1966).

popular consent The idea that a just government must derive its powers from the consent of the people it governs.

popular sovereignty A belief that ultimate power resides in the people.

precedent A decision made by a higher court such as a circuit court of appeals or the Supreme Court that is binding on all other federal courts.

preemption The right of a federal law or regulation to preclude enforcement of a state or local law or regulation.

preferred position doctrine Interpretation of the First Amendment that holds that freedom of expression is so essential to democracy that governments should not punish persons for what they say, only for what they do.

president pro tempore Officer of the Senate selected by the majority party to act as chair in the absence of the vice president.

presidential election Elections held in years when the president is on the ballot.

presidential ticket The joint listing of the presidential and vice presidential candidates on the same ballot as required by the Twelfth Amendment.

primary election Elections in which voters determine party nominees.

prior restraint Censorship imposed before a speech is made or a newspaper is published; usually presumed to be unconstitutional.

privatization Contracting public services to private organizations.

pro bono To serve the public good; term used to describe work that lawyers (or other professionals) do for which they receive no fees.

procedural due process Constitutional requirement that governments proceed by proper methods; limits how government may be exercise power.

progressive tax A tax graduated so that people with higher incomes pay a larger fraction of their income than people with lower incomes.

property rights The rights of an individual to own, use, rent, invest in, buy, and sell property.

proportional representation An election system in which each party running receives the proportion of legislative seats corresponding to its proportion of the vote.

prospective issue voting Voting based on what a candidate pledges to do in the future about an issue if elected.

protectionism Policy of erecting trade barriers to protect domestic industry.

public assistance Aid to the poor; "welfare."

public choice Synonymous with "collective action," it specifically studies how government officials, politicians, and voters respond to positive and negative incentives.

public defender system Arrangement whereby public officials are hired to provide legal assistance to people accused of crimes who are unable to hire their own attorneys.

public opinion The distribution of individual preferences for or evaluations of a given issue, candidate, or institution within a specific population.

public policy A specific course of action taken by government to achieve a public goal.

quid pro quo Something given with the expectation of receiving something in return.

race A grouping of human beings with distinctive characteristics determined by genetic inheritance.

racial gerrymandering The drawing of election districts so as to ensure that members of a certain race are a minority in the district; ruled unconstitutional in *Gomillion* v. *Lightfoot* (1960).

racial profiling Police targeting of racial minorities as potential suspects of criminal activities.

rally point A rise in public approval of the president that follows a crisis as Americans "rally 'round the flag" and the chief executive.

random sample In this type of sample, every individual has a known and random chance of being selected.

realigning election An election during periods of expanded suffrage and change in the economy and society that proves to be a turning point, redefining the agenda of politics and the alignment of voters within parties.

realism A theory of international relations that focuses on the tendency of nations to operate from self-interest.

reapportionment The assigning by Congress of congressional seats after each census. State legislatures reapportion state legislative districts.

recall Procedure for submitting to popular vote the removal of officials from office before the end of their term.

recidivist A repeat offender.

redistributive policy A type of policy that takes benefits (usually through taxes) from one group of Americans and gives them to another (usually through spending).

redistricting The redrawing of congressional and other legislative district lines following the census, to accommodate population shifts and keep districts as equal as possible in population.

reduction veto The power of governors in a few states to reduce a particular appropriation.

referendum Procedure for submitting to popular vote measures passed by the legislature or proposed amendments to a state constitution.

Reform party A minor party founded by Ross Perot in 1995. It focuses on national government reform, fiscal responsibility, and political accountability. It has recently struggled with internal strife and criticism that it lacks an identity.

regressive tax A tax whereby people with lower incomes pay a higher fraction of their income than people with higher incomes.

regulation Efforts by government to alter the free operation of the market to achieve social goals such as protecting workers and the environment.

regulations The formal instructions that government issues for implementing laws.

regulatory taking Government regulation of property so extensive that government is deemed to have taken the property by the power of eminent domain, for which it must compensate the property owners.

reinforcing cleavages Divisions within society that reinforce one another, making groups more homogeneous or similar.

representative democracy Government in which the people elect those who govern and pass laws; also called a republic.

responsibility contract A welfare strategy adopted by some states in which recipients sign a written agreement specifying their responsibilities and outlining a plan for obtaining work and achieving self-sufficiency.

restrictive covenant A provision in a deed to real property prohibiting its sale to a person of a particular race or religion. Judicial enforcement of such deeds is unconstitutional.

retrospective issue voting Holding incumbents, usually the president's party, responsible for their records on issues, such as the economy or foreign policy.

revision commission A state commission that recommends changes in the state constitution for action by the legislature and vote by the voters.

revolving door Employment cycle in which individuals who work for governmental agencies that regulate interests eventually end up working for interest groups or businesses with the same policy concern.

rider A provision attached to a bill—to which it may or may not be related—in order to secure its passage.

right of expatriation The right to renounce one's citizenship.

rule A precise legal definition of how government will implement a policy.

rule-making process The formal process for making regulations.

safe seat An elected office that is predictably won by one party or the other, so the success of that party's candidate is almost taken for granted.

sales tax General tax on sales transactions, sometimes exempting food and drugs.

search warrant A writ issued by a magistrate that authorizes the police to search a particular place or person, specifying the place to be searched and the objects to be seized.

sedition Attempting to overthrow the government by force or use violence to interrupt its activities.

selective exposure The process by which individuals screen out messages that do not conform to their own biases.

selective incorporation The process by which provisions of the Bill of Rights are brought within the scope of the Fourteenth Amendment and so applied to state and local governments.

selective perception The process by which individuals perceive what they want to in media messages.

senatorial courtesy Presidential custom of submitting the names of prospective appointees for approval to senators from the states in which the appointees are to work.

Senior Executive Service Established by Congress in 1978 as a flexible, mobile corps of senior career executives who work closely with presidential appointees to manage government.

seniority rule A legislative practice that assigns the chair of a committee or subcommittee to the member of the majority party with the longest continuous service on the committee.

separation of powers Constitutional division of powers among the legislative, executive, and judicial branches, with the legislative branch making law, the executive applying and enforcing the law, and the judiciary interpreting the law.

severance tax A tax on the privilege of "severing" such natural resources as coal, oil, timber, and gas from the land.

Shays's Rebellion Rebellion led by Daniel Shays of farmers in western Massachusetts in 1786–1787, protesting mortgage foreclosures. It highlighted the need for a strong national government just as the call for the Constitutional Convention went out.

single-member district An electoral district in which voters choose one representative or official.

social capital Democratic and civic habits of discussion, compromise, and respect for differences, which grow out of participation in voluntary organizations.

social insurance Programs in which eligibility is based on prior contributions to government, usually in the form of payroll taxes.

Social Security A combination of entitlement programs, paid for by employer and employee taxes, that includes retirement benefits, health insurance, and support for disabled workers and the children of deceased or disabled workers.

social stratification Divisions in a community among socioeconomic groups or classes.

socialism An economic and governmental system based on public ownership of the means of production and exchange.

socioeconomic status (SES) A division of population based on occupation, income, and education.

soft money Unlimited amounts of money that political parties previously could raise for party-building purposes. Now largely illegal except for limited contributions to state and local parties for voter registration and get-out-the-vote efforts.

soft power The reliance on diplomacy and negotiation to solve international problems.

Speaker The presiding officer in the House of Representatives, formally elected by the House but actually selected by the majority party.

special or select committee A congressional committee created for a specific purpose, sometimes to conduct an investigation.

split ticket A vote for some of one party's candidates and some of another party's.

spoils system A system of public employment based on rewarding party loyalists and friends.

standing committee A permanent committee established in a legislature, usually focusing on a policy area.

stare decisis The rule of precedent, whereby a rule or law contained in a judicial decision is commonly viewed as binding on judges whenever the same question is presented.

State of the Union Address The president's annual statement to Congress and the nation.

states' rights Powers expressly or implicitly reserved to the states and emphasized by decentralists.

statism The idea that the rights of the nation are supreme over the rights of the individuals who make up the nation.

straight ticket A vote for all of one party's candidates.

strong mayor-council form Form of local government in which the voters directly elect the city council and the mayor, who enjoys almost total administrative authority and appoints the department heads.

substantive due process Constitutional requirement that governments act reasonably and that the substance of the laws themselves be fair and reasonable; limits what a government may do.

suffrage The right to vote.

take care clause The constitutional requirement (in Article II, Section 3) that presidents take care that the laws are faithfully executed, even if they disagree with the purpose of those laws.

tariff Tax levied on imports to help protect a nation's industries, labor, or farmers from foreign competition. It can also be used to raise additional revenue.

tax expenditure Loss of tax revenue due to federal laws that provide special tax incentives or benefits to individuals or businesses.

Temporary Assistance for Needy Families (TANF) Federal welfare reform law that replaced the 60-year-old assistance program for poor families with children, Aid to Families with Dependent Children. This 1996 law strengthened work requirements for recipients, limited the time that families can receive benefits, and gave states flexibility to develop service programs supporting work, marriage, and self-sufficiency.

The Federalist Essays promoting ratification of the Constitution, published anonymously by Alexander Hamilton, John Jay, and James Madison in 1787 and 1788.

theocracy Government by religious leaders, who claim divine guidance.

theory of deterrence A theory that is based on creating enough military strength to convince other nations not to attack first.

three-fifths compromise Compromise between northern and southern states at the Constitutional Convention that three-fifths of the slave population would be counted for determining direct taxation and representation in the House of Representatives.

tort law Law relating to injuries to person, reputation, or property.

trade deficit An imbalance in international trade in which the value of imports exceeds the value of exports.

treaty A formal, public agreement between the United States and one or more nations that must be approved by two-thirds of the Senate.

trust A monopoly that controls goods and services, often in combinations that reduce competition.

trustee An official who is expected to vote independently based on his or her judgment of the circumstances; one interpretation of the role of the legislator.

turnout The proportion of the voting-age public that votes, sometimes defined as the number of registered voters that vote.

two-party state A state in which the two major parties alternate in winning majorities.

uncontrollable spending The portion of the federal budget that is spent on programs, such as Social Security, that the president and Congress are unwilling to cut.

unemployment The number of Americans who are out of work but actively looking for a job. The number does not usually include those who are not looking.

unfunded mandates Programs that the federal government requires states to implement without federal funding.

unicameral legislature A one-house legislature.

unilateralism A philosophy that encourages individual nations to act on their own when facing threats from other nations.

union shop A company in which new employees must join a union within a stated time period.

unitary system Constitutional arrangement that concentrates power in a central government.

value-added tax (VAT) A tax on increased value of a product at each stage of production and distribution rather than just at the point of sale.

veto A formal decision to reject a bill passed by Congress.

Virginia Plan Initial proposal at the Constitutional Convention made by the Virginia delegation for a strong central government with a bicameral legislature dominated by the big states.

voter registration System designed to reduce voter fraud by limiting voting to those who have established eligibility to vote by submitting the proper documents.

vouchers Money government provides to parents to pay their children's tuition in a public or private school of their choice.

weak mayor-council form Form of local government in which the members of the city council select the mayor, who then shares power with other elected or appointed boards and commissions.

weapons of mass destruction Biological, chemical, or nuclear weapons that can cause a massive number of deaths in a single use.

whip Party leader who is the liaison between the leadership and the rank-and-file in the legislature.

white primary Democratic party primary in the old "one-party South" that was limited to white people and essentially constituted an election; ruled unconstitutional in Smith v. Allwright (1944).

winner-take-all system An election system in which the candidate with the most votes wins.

women's suffrage The right of women to vote.

workfare A welfare strategy adopted by some states that gives able-bodied adults who do not have preschool-aged children the opportunity to learn job skills that can lead to employment.

World Trade Organization (WTO) International organization derived from the General Agreement on Tariffs and Trade (GATT) that promotes free trade around the world.

writ of certiorari A formal writ used to bring a case before the Supreme Court.

writ of habeas corpus Court order requiring explanation to a judge why a prisoner is being held in custody.

writ of mandamus Court order directing an official to perform an official duty.

Notes

Chapter 1

1. Dan Balz, "Rove Offers Republicans a Battle Plan For Elections," *Washington Post*, January 21, 2006, p. A01.
2. The Federation of American Scientists, "Foreign Intelligence Surveillance Act," February 5, 2006. At www.fas.org/irp/agency/doj/fisa, February 8, 2006.
3. Charlie Savage, "Bush Bypassed Compliant Court on Wiretapping: Warrants Rarely Denied," *Boston Globe*, December 20, 2006.
4. Thomas Friedman, "The New 'Sputnik' Challenges: They All Run on Oil," *New York Times*, January 20, 2006, p. A17.
5. Peter Nicholas, "Gov.'s New Proposition: Cooperation," *Los Angeles Times*, November 11, 2005, p. A01.
6. Ibid.
7. Aristotle, *Politics* (New York: Oxford University Press, 1998); and George Huxley, "On Aristotle's Best State," *History of Political Thought* 6 (Summer 1985), pp. 139–149.
8. John Locke, *Two Treatises of Government and a Letter Concerning Toleration* (Yale University Press, 2003); and Virginia McDonald, "A Guide to the Interpretation of Locke the Political Theorist," *Canadian Journal of Political Science* 6 (December 1973), pp. 602–623.
9. Thomas Hobbes, *Leviathan* (Oxford University Press, 1998); and Frank M. Coleman, "The Hobbesian Basis of American Constitutionalism," *Polity* 7 (Autumn 1974), pp. 57–89.
10. Charles de Montesquieu, *The Spirit of the Laws* (Cambridge University Press, 1989); and E. P. Panagopoulos, *Essays on the History and Meaning of Checks and Balances* (University Press of America, 1986).
11. David B. Magleby, *Direct Legislation: Voting on Ballot Propositions in the United States* (Johns Hopkins University Press, 1984), p. 119.
12. Seymour Martin Lipset, "The Social Requisites of Democracy Revisited," *American Sociological Review* 59 (1994), pp. 1–22.
13. For a discussion of the importance for democracy of such overlapping group memberships, see David Truman's seminal work, *The Governmental Process*, 2d ed. (Knopf, 1971).
14. Robert A. Dahl, *On Democracy* (Yale University Press, 1998), p. 145.
15. Harold Stanley and Richard Niemi, *Vital Statistics on American Politics, 2001–2002* (CQ Press, 2001), pp. 25–29.
16. For a major theoretical work on the principle of majority rule, see Robert A. Dahl, *Democracy and Its Critics* (Yale University Press, 1989).
17. *Reitman* v. *Mulkey*, 387 U.S. 369 (1967).
18. Lesli J. Favor, "The Iroquois Constitution: A Primary Source Investigation of the Law of the Iroquois," (Rosen Publishing, 2003), p. 60.
19. Joyce Appleby, "The American Heritage: The Heirs and the Disinherited," *Journal of American History* 74 (December 1987), p. 808.
20. Kevin Butterfield, "What You Should Know About the Declaration of Independence," *St. Louis Post-Dispatch*, July 4, 2000, p. F1.
21. Richard L. Hillard, "Liberalism, Civic Humanism and the American Revolutionary Bill of Rights, 1775–1790," paper presented at the annual meeting of the Organization of American Historians, Reno, Nevada, March 26, 1988.
22. Quoted in Charles L. Mee Jr., *The Genius of the People* (Harper & Row, 1987), p. 51.
23. Charles A. Beard, *An Economic Interpretation of the Constitution of the United States* (Macmillan, 1913).
24. Robert Brown, *Charles Beard and the Constitution: A Critical Analysis of 'An Economic Interpretation of the Constitution'* (Princeton University Press, 1956).
25. Seymour Martin Lipset, "George Washington and the Founding of Democracy," *Journal of Democracy* 9 (October 1998), p. 31.
26. See the essays in Thomas E. Cronin, ed., *Inventing the American Presidency* (University Press of Kansas, 1989). See also Richard J. Ellis, ed., *Founding the American Presidency* (Rowman & Littlefield, 1999).
27. Charles A. Beard and Mary R. Beard, *A Basic History of the United States* (New Home Library, 1944), p. 136.
28. See Herbert J. Storing, ed., abridgment by Murray Dry, *The Anti-Federalist: Writings by the Opponents of the Constitution* (University of Chicago Press, 1985).
29. W. B. Allen and Gordon Lloyd, eds., *The Essential Antifederalist* (University Press of America, 1985), pp. xi–xiii.
30. On the role of the promised Bill of Rights amendments in the ratification of the Constitution, see Leonard W. Levy, *Constitutional Opinions* (Oxford University Press, 1986), chap. 6.

Chapter 2

1. Based on www.nationmaster.com.
2. Max Lerner, *Ideas for the Ice Age* (Viking, 1941), pp. 241–242.
3. Sanford Levinson, *Constitutional Faith* (Princeton University Press, 1988), pp. 9–52.
4. Richard Morin, "We Love It—What We Know of It," *Washington Post National Weekly Edition*, September 22, 1997, p. 35.
5. Thomas Jefferson, quoted in Alpheus T. Mason, *The Supreme Court: Palladium of Freedom* (University of Michigan Press, 1962), p. 10.
6. Alexander Hamilton, James Madison, and John Jay, *The Federalist Papers*, ed. Clinton Rossiter (New American Library, 1961), p. 301.
7. Justice Brandeis dissenting in *Myers* v. *United States*, 272 U.S. 52 (1926).
8. Charles O. Jones, "The Separate Presidency," in Anthony King, ed., *The New American Political System*, 2d ed. (AEI Press, 1990), p. 3.
9. Morris P. Fiorina, "An Era of Divided Government," *Political Science Quarterly* 107 (1992), p. 407.
10. David R. Mayhew, *Divided We Govern: Party Control, Lawmaking, and Investigations, 1946–1990* (Yale University Press, 1991), p. 4. See also James A. Thurber, ed., *Divided Democracy: Presidents and Congress in Cooperation and Conflict* (CQ Press, 1991).
11. Charles O. Jones, *Separate but Equal Branches: Congress and the Presidency* (Chatham House, 1995).
12. Judith A. Best, *The Choice of the People? Debating the Electoral College* (Rowman & Littlefield, 1996).
13. See Alec Stone Sweet, Wayne Sandholtz, and Neil Fligstein, *The Institutionalization of Europe* (Oxford University Press, 2001); Alec Stone Sweet, *Governing with Judges: Constitutional Politics in Europe* (Oxford University Press, 2000); and Anne-Marie Slaughter, Alec Stone Sweet, and J. H. H. Weiler, *The European Court and National Courts—Doctrine, Jurisprudence: Legal Change in Its Social Context* (Hart, 1998).
14. *Marbury* v. *Madison*, 1 Cranch 137 (1803).
15. Dumas Malone, *Jefferson the President: First Term, 1801–1805* (Little, Brown, 1970), p. 145.
16. J. W. Peltason, *Federal Courts in the Political Process* (Random House, 1955).
17. See Eleanore Bushnell, *Crimes, Follies, and Misfortunes: The Federal Impeachment Trials* (University of Illinois Press, 1992), and Michael J. Gerhardt, *The Federal Impeachment Process: A Constitutional and Historical Analysis* (Princeton University Press, 1996).
18. Richard E. Neustadt, *Presidential Power* (Free Press, 1990), pp. 180–181.
19. Antonin Scalia, "Originalism: The Lesser Evil," *University of Cincinnati Law Review* 55 (1989), p. 894.
20. William J. Brennan Jr., "The Constitution of the United States: Contemporary Ratification," lecture delivered at Georgetown University, October 12, 1985, and reprinted in David M. O'Brien, ed., *Judges on Judging* 2d ed. (CQ Press, 2004), pp. 183–193.
21. See Ruth Bader Ginsburg, "Speaking in a Judicial Voice: Reflections on *Roe* v. *Wade*," in O'Brien, *Judges on Judging*, pp. 194–200; Stephen Breyer, "Our Democratic Constitution," in *Judges on Judging*, pp. 201–215; and Stephen Breyer, *Active Liberty: Interpreting our Democratic Constitution* (Knopf, 2005).
22. Ann Stuart Diamond, "A Convention for Proposing Amendments: The Constitution's Other Method," *Publius* 11 (Summer 1981), pp. 113–146; Wilbur Edel, "Amending the Constitution by Convention: Myths and Realities," *State Government* 55 (1982), pp. 51–56.
23. Russell L. Caplan, *Constitutional Brinksmanship: Amending the Constitution by National Convention* (Oxford University Press, 1988), p. x. See also David E. Kyvig, *Explicit and Authentic Acts: Amending the U.S. Constitution, 1776–1995* (University Press of Kansas, 1996), p. 440.
24. Samuel S. Freedman and Pamela J. Naughton, *ERA: May a State Change Its Vote?* (Wayne State University Press, 1979).
25. Kyvig, *Explicit and Authentic Acts*, p. 286; *Dillon* v. *Gloss*, 256 U.S. 368 (1921).
26. Mark R. Daniels, Robert Darcy, and Joseph W. Westphal, "The ERA Won—at Least in the Opinion Polls," *P.S.: Political Science and Politics* (Fall 1982), p. 583.

27. Janet K. Boles, *The Politics of the Equal Rights Amendment: Conflict and Decision-Making Powers* (Longman, 1979), p. 4.

28. Gilbert Y. Steiner, *Constitutional Inequality: The Political Fortunes of the Equal Rights Amendment* (Brookings Institution Press, 1985), p. 64. See also Mary Frances Berry, *Why the ERA Failed: Politics, Women's Rights, and the Amending Process of the Constitution* (Indiana University Press, 1986).

Chapter 3

1. See Deil S. Wright, "How Did Intergovernmental Relations Fail in the USA after Hurricane Katrina?" *Federations* 5 (2005), pp. 11–12; and Louise K. Comfort, "Fragility in Disaster Response: Hurricane Katrina," *The Forum* 3 (The Berkeley Electronic Press, 2005), Article 1, available at www.bepress.com/forum.

2. For background, see Samuel H. Beer, *To Make a Nation: The Rediscovery of American Federalism* (Harvard University Press, 1993).

3. The term "devolution revolution" was coined by Richard P. Nathan in testimony before the Senate Finance Committee, quoted in Daniel Patrick Moynihan, "The Devolution Revolution," *The New York Times*, August 6, 1995, p. B15.

4. See Kalypso Nicolaidis and Robert Howse, eds., *The Federal Vision: Legitimacy and Levels of Governance in the United States and the European Union* (Oxford University Press, 2001); and Ann L. Griffiths, ed., *Handbook of Federal Countries, 2005* (McGill-Queens University Press, 2005).

5. *United States* v. *Lopez*, 514 U.S. 549 (1995).

6. *Alden* v. *Maine*, 527 U.S. 706 (1999); *Kimel* v. *Florida Board of Regents*, 528 U.S. 62 (2000); *Vermont Agency of Natural Resources* v. *United States ex rel. Stevens*, 529 U.S. 765 (2000).

7. *Saenz* v. *Roe*, 526 U.S. 489 (1999).

8. *Reno* v. *Condon*, 528 U.S. 141 (2000).

9. Martha Derthick, "American Federalism: Half-Full or Half-Empty?" *Brookings Review* (Winter 2000), pp. 24–27.

10. William H. Stewart, *Concepts of Federalism* (Center for the Study of Federalism/University Press of America, 1984). See also Preston King, *Federalism and Federation*, 2d ed. (Cass, 2001).

11. Ronald L. Watts, *Comparing Federal Systems* 2d ed. (McGill-Queen's University Press, 1999), p. 6. See also David M. O'Brien, "Federalism as a Metaphor in the Constitutional Politics of Public Administration," *Public Administration Review* 49 (1989), p. 411.

12. Morton Grodzins, "The Federal System," in *Goals for Americans: The Report of the President's Commission on National Goals* (Columbia University Press, 1960).

13. Thomas R. Dye, *American Federalism: Competition Among Governments* (Lexington Books, 1990), pp. 13–17.

14. Michael D. Reagan and John G. Sanzone, *The New Federalism* (Oxford University Press, 1981), p. 175.

15. Gregory S. Mahler, *Comparative Politics: An Institutional and Cross-National Approach* (Prentice Hall, 2000), p. 31.

16. Frederick K. Lister, *The European Union, the United Nations, and the Revival of Confederal Governance* (Greenwood Press, 1996); Daniel J. Elazar, "The United States and the European Union: Models for their Epochs," in Nicolaidis and Howse, *The Federal Vision*, pp. 31–52.

17. William H. Riker, *The Development of American Federalism* (Academic, 1987), pp. 14–15. Riker contends not only that federalism does not guarantee freedom but also that the framers of our federal system, as well as those of other nations, were animated not by considerations of safeguarding freedom but by practical considerations of preserving unity.

18. Charles Evans Hughes, "War Powers Under the Constitution," *ABA Reports*, 62 (1917), p. 238.

19. *Gibbons* v. *Ogden*, 9 Wheaton (22 U.S.) 1 (1824).

20. *Reno* v. *Condon*, 528 U.S. 141 (2000).

21. *Champion* v. *Ames*, 188 U.S. 321 (1907).

22. *Caminetti* v. *United States*, 242 U.S. 470 (1917).

23. *Federal Radio Commission* v. *Nelson Brothers*, 289 U.S. 266 (1933).

24. *Heart of Atlanta Motel* v. *United States*, 379 U.S. 241 (1964).

25. *United States* v. *Lopez*, 514 U.S. 549 (1995). See also *United States* v. *Morrison*, 529 U.S. 598 (2000), striking down the Violence Against Women Act.

26. *Gonzales* v. *Raich*, 125 S.Ct. 2195 (2005), reaffirming *Wickard* v. *Filburn*, 317 U.S. 111 (1942).

27. *Printz* v. *United States*, 521 U.S. 898 (1997). See also *New York* v. *United States*, 505 U.S. 144 (1992).

28. See Jesse Choper, *Judicial Review and the National Political Process* (University of Chicago Press, 1980); and John T. Noonan, Jr., *Narrowing the Nation's Power: The Supreme Court Sides with the States* (University of California Press, 2002).

29. See Michael S. Greve, *Real Federalism: Why It Matters, How It Could Happen* (American Enterprise Institute, 1999).

30. Ibid.

31. *Seminole Tribe of Florida* v. *Florida*, 517 U.S. 44 (1996); *Alden* v. *Maine*, 527 U.S. 706 (1999); *Kimel* v. *Florida Board of Regents*, 528 U.S. 62 (2000).

32. See *Franchise Tax Board of California* v. *Hyatt*, 538 U.S. 488 (2003).

33. See Nicol C. Rae, "A Right Too Far? The Congressional Politics of DOMA and ENDA," in Colton C. Campbell and John Stack, Jr., eds., *Congress and the Politics of Emerging Rights* (Rowman & Littlefield, 2002), p. 62.

34. *Lawrence* v. *Texas*, 539 U.S. 558 (2003).

35. *California* v. *Superior Courts of California*, 482 U.S. 400 (1987).

36. David C. Nice, "State Participation in Interstate Compacts," *Publius* 17 (Spring 1987), p. 70. See also Council of State Governments, *Interstate Compacts and Agencies* (1995), for a list of compacts by subject and by state with brief descriptions.

37. *McCulloch* v. *Maryland*, 4 Wheaton 316 (1819).

38. Joseph F. Zimmerman, "Federal Preemption Under Reagan's New Federalism," *Publius* 21 (Winter 1991), pp. 7–28.

39. Oliver Wendell Holmes Jr., *Collected Legal Papers* (Harcourt, 1920), pp. 295–296.

40. See, for example, *United States* v. *Lopez*, 514 U.S. 549 (1995).

41. *U.S. Term Limits, Inc.* v. *Thornton*, 514 U.S. 779 (1995)

42. *Seminole Tribe of Florida* v. *Florida*, 517 U.S. 44 (1996).

43. *Alden* v. *Maine*, 527 U.S. 706 (1999); *Kimel* v. *Florida Board of Regents*, 528 U.S. 62 (2000); *Vermont Agency of Natural Resources* v. *United States ex rel. Stevens*, 529 U.S. 765 (2000).

44. George Will, "A Revival of Federalism?" *Newsweek*, May 29, 2000, p. 78.

45. *United States* v. *Morrison*, 529 U.S. 598 (2000).

46. John E. Chubb, "The Political Economy of Federalism," *American Political Science Review* 79 (December 1985), p. 1005.

47. Paul E. Peterson, *The Price of Federalism* (Brookings Institution Press, 1995), p. 127.

48. Donald F. Kettl, *The Regulation of American Federalism* (Johns Hopkins University Press, 1987), pp. 154–155.

49. National Council of State and Local Governments Budgets and Revenue Committee, *Mandate Monitor*, August 12, 2005.

50. See Paul J. Posner, *The Politics of Unfunded Mandates: Whither Federalism?* (Georgetown University Press, 1998).

51. Joseph Zimmerman, "Congressional Regulation of Subnational Governments," *PS: Political Science and Politics* 26 (June 1993), p. 179.

52. See Jerome J. Hanus, ed., *The Nationalization of State Government* (Heath, 1981).

53. Advisory Commission on Intergovernmental Relations, *Restoring Confidence and Competence* (Author, 1981), p. 30.

54. Cynthia Cates Colella, "The Creation, Care and Feeding of the Leviathan: Who and What Makes Government Grow," *Intergovernmental Perspective* (Fall 1979), p. 9.

55. Aaron Wildavsky, "Bare Bones: Putting Flesh on the Skeleton of American Federalism," in *The Future of Federalism in the 1980s* (Advisory Commission on Intergovernmental Relations, 1981), p. 79.

56. Peterson, *Price of Federalism*, p. 182.

57. Amanda Ripley and Sonia Steptoe, "Inside the Revolt Over Bush's School Rules," *Time* (May 9, 2005), p. 30.

58. Nick Anderson, "Bush Administration Grants Leeway on 'No Child' Rules," *Washington Post*, November 22, 2005, p. A1.

59. John Kinkaid, "Devolution in the United States: Rhetoric and Reality," in Nicolaidis and Howse, *The Federal Vision*, p. 144.

60. Eliza Newlin Carney, "Power Grab," *National Journal*, April 11, 1998, p. 798.

61. Luther Gulick, "Reorganization of the States," *Civil Engineering* (August 1933), pp. 420–421.

62. David E. Osborne, *Laboratories of Democracy* (Harvard Business School Press, 1988), p. 363.

63. Dye, *American Federalism*, p. 199.

64. Richard A. Oppel and Christopher Drew, "States Planning Their Own Suits on Power Plants: Battle that E.P.A. Quit," *The New York Times*, November 9, 2003, p. A1; and Scott Richards and Yvette Hurt, "States Sue the Federal Environmental Agency," *Federations* 11 (November, 2003).

65. Edward Felsenthal, "Firms Ask Congress to Pass Uniform Rules," *Wall Street Journal*, May 10, 1993, p. B4.

66. John J. DiIulio, Jr. and Donald F. Kettl, *Fine Print: The Contract with America, Devolution, and the Administrative Realities of American Federalism* (Brookings Institution Press, 1995), p. 60.

67. Kincaid, "Devolution in the United States," p. 148.

Chapter 4

1. Robert D. Putnam, "Bowling Together," *American Prospect* 13, 3 (February 2002), www .prospect.org/print-friendly/print/V13/3/

putnam-r.html, April 17, 2006; Gary Rotstein, "Donations Are Outpacing 9/11: Donations for New Orleans Coming Faster than those for 9/11," *Pittsburgh Post-Gazette*, September 18, 2005.

2. Office of New York State Attorney General, "September 11th Charitable Relief," www.oag.state.ny.us/charities/september11_charitable_report/sept11_report.html, April 18, 2006.

3. American Association of Fundraising Council, "Charitable Giving Reaches $212 Billion (Giving USA 2002)," press release June 20, 2002, www.aafrc.org/press_releases/trustreleases/charitablegiving.html, April 18, 2006.

4. CNN, "Still Charitable? Eventful Year Raises Concerns over Donor Fatigue," www.cnn.com/2005/US/11/17/still.charitable/index.html?section=cnn_latest, April 18, 2006.

5. Stephanie Strom, "Accountability: New Equation for Charities: More Money, Less Oversight" *New York Times*, November 17, 2003, p. F1.

6. Ibid.; Simone A. Glynn, "Effect of a National Disaster on Blood Supply and Safety: The September 11 Experience," *Journal of the American Medical Association* 289, 2246–2253.

7. FEMA, "FEMA and Voluntary Agencies: Partners in Mississippi Recovery," Press Release August 17, 2006, http://www.fema.gov/news/newsrelease.fema?id=29040.

8. Oxford Analytica, "U.S. Giving Routinely Underestimated." Forbes.com, www.forbes.com/2005/11/11/government-private-aid-cx, May 1, 2006.

9. Margaret Thatcher, "The Moral Challenges For the Next Generation," *Brigham Young Magazine* 50, 3 (August 1996), p. 21; also available at magazine.byu.edu/?curiss=19, May 3, 2006.

10. Putnam, "Bowling Together."

11. Robert D. Putnam, "Bowling Alone: America's Declining Social Capital," *Journal of Democracy* 6 (January 1995), pp. 65–78. See also Robert D. Putnam, *Bowling Alone: The Collapse and Revival of American Community* (Simon & Schuster, 2000), and Robert D. Putnam, "Bowling Together."

12. See Pippa Norris, "Does Television Erode Social Capital? A Reply to Putnam," *PS: Political Science and Politics* 29 (September 1996), pp. 474–479. See also Everett Carl Ladd, *The Ladd Report* (Free Press, 1999), and Michael Schudson, *The Good Citizen: A History of American Civic Life* (Harvard University Press, 1998).

13. Putnam, "Bowling Together."

14. Dan Morgan, "An End to the Day of High Cotton? GOP Constituents Caught in Battle Over Subsidies," *Washington Post*, March 8, 2005, p. A1.

15. Clinton Rossiter, *Conservatism in America* (Vintage, 1962), p. 72.

16. Bernard Bailyn, *The Ideological Origins of the American Revolution* (Belknap Press, 1967); Gordon S. Wood, *The Creation of the American Republic, 1776–1787* (University of North Carolina Press, 1969).

17. See Ronald Dworkin, *Taking Rights Seriously* (Harvard University Press, 1977).

18. *Marbury* v. *Madison*, 1 Cranch 137 (1803).

19. "A Nation Challenged: Excerpts from President's Speech: 'We Will Prevail' in War on Terrorism," *The New York Times*, November 9, 2001, p. B1.

20. Robert Coles, *The Political Life of Children* (Atlantic Monthly Press, 1986).

21. Fred I. Greenstein, *Children and Politics* (Yale University Press, 1965).

22. Raymond E. Wolfinger and Steven Rosenstone, *Who Votes?* (Yale University Press, 1980).

23. Franklin Boudotte, "Education for Citizenship," *Public Opinion Quarterly* (Summer 1942): 269–279.

24. Rachel X. Weissman, "The Kids Are All Right—They're Just a Little Converged," *American Demographics* 20, no. 12 (December 1998), pp. 30–32.

25. Jeremy Rifkin, *The European Dream* (Penguin Group, 2005).

26. Alberto Alesina and Edward Glaeser, *Fighting Poverty in the U.S. and Europe: A World of Difference* (Oxford University Press, 2004).

27. www.commoncause.org/laundromat/stat/top50.htm.

28. Floyd Norris and Joseph Kahn, "Enron's Many Strands: The Overview; Rule Makers Take On Loopholes That Enron Used in Hiding Debt," *The New York Times*, February 14, 2002, p. A1.

29. OpenSecret.org, www.opensecrets.org/races/summary.asp?ID=NJSI&Cycle=2000; Chris Cillizza, "Corzine Defeats Forrester to Become Governor," *Washington Post*, November 9, 2005, p. A18.

30. Glen Justice, "Advocacy Groups Reflect on Their Role in the Election," *The New York Times*, November 5, 2004, p. A1.

31. When adjusted using the consumer price index (CPI1), the percentage of households earning over $75,000 a year has risen from 10.1 percent in 1970 to 22.6 percent in 1999. U.S. Bureau of the Census, *Statistical Abstracts of the United States, 2001* (Government Printing Office, 2001), tab. 661.

32. See Michael B. Katz, *The "Underclass" Debate* (Princeton University Press, 1993); Theodore Dalrymple, *Life at the Bottom: The Worldview That Makes the Underclass* (Dee, 2001); and Charles A. Murray, *The Underclass Revisited* (AEI Press, 1999).

33. The Pew Research Center for the People and The Press, Release, October 31, 2005, p. 1.

34. Bailyn, *Ideological Origins*.

35. Robert A. Dahl, "Liberal Democracy in the United States," in William Livingston, ed., *A Prospect of Liberal Democracy* (University of Texas Press, 1979), p. 64.

36. Ibid., pp. 59–60.

37. Franklin D. Roosevelt, State of the Union Address, January 11, 1944, in *The Public Papers of the President of the United States, 1944* (Government Printing Office, 1962), pp. 371–394.

38. Harry S Truman, State of the Union Address, 1949, in *The Public Papers of the President of the United States, 1949* (Government Printing Office, 1964), pp. 1–7.

39. E. J. Dionne Jr., *They Only Look Dead: Why Progressives Will Dominate the Next Political Era* (Simon & Schuster, 1996), p. 13.

40. Quoted in David Brooks, "Need a Map? The Right," *The Washington Post*, October 31, 1999, p. B1.

41. David B. Magleby, *The Outside Campaign* (Rowman & Littlefield, 2001).

42. David B. Magleby, J. Quin Monson, and Kelly D. Patterson, *Dancing Without Partners: How Candidates, Parties, and Interest Groups Interact in the Presidential Campaign* (Rowman & Littlefield, forthcoming).

43. Warren B. Rudman, *Combat: Twelve Years in the U.S. Senate* (Random House, 1996), p. 270.

44. David B. Magleby, "Issue Advocacy in the 2000 Presidential Primaries," in David B. Magleby, ed., *Getting Inside the Outside Campaign* (Center for the Study of Elections and Democracy, Brigham Young University, 2000), p. 13. Also at www.byu.edu/outsidemoney.

45. Jonathan Rauch, "The Accidental Radical," *National Journal*, July 26, 2003, 2404–2410.

46. Kathleen Day, *S&L Hell: The People and the Politics Behind the $1 Trillion Savings and Loan Scandal* (Norton, 1993).

47. James L. Sweeney, *The California Electricity Crisis*, (Hoover Institution Press, 2002).

48. Loren Fox, *Enron: The Rise and Fall*, (John Wiley & Sons, Inc., 2003).

49. Sylvia Nasar, "Even Among the Well-Off, the Rich Get Richer," *The New York Times*, March 5, 1992, p. A1.

50. Irving Howe, *Socialism and America* (Harcourt, 1985); Michael Harrington, *Socialism: Past and Future* (Arcade, 1989).

51. Daniel Yergin and Joseph Stainslaw, *The Commanding Heights: The Battle Between Government and the Marketplace That Is Remaking the Modern World* (Simon & Schuster, 1998).

52. Charles Murray, *What It Means to Be a Libertarian* (Broadway Books, 1997).

53. Brian Faler, "A Polling Sight: Record Turnout," *The Washington Post*, November 5, 2004, p. A7.

54. Center for Political Studies, University of Michigan, *American National Election Study, 1990: Post-Election Survey*, April 1991.

55. Michael Kranish, "Discord Replaced by Desire to Win," *The Boston Globe*, July 31, 2000, p. A10.

56. Steven S. Smith and Gerald Gamm, "The Dynamics of Party Government in Congress," in *Congress Reconsidered*, 7th ed. Lawrence C. Dodd and Bruce I. Oppenheimer, eds. (CQ Press, 2001), p. 259.

57. Earl Black and Merle Black, *The Rise of Southern Republicans* (Belknap Press, 2002).

58. Herbert McClosky and Alida Brill, *Dimensions of Tolerance: What Americans Believe About Civil Liberties* (Russel Sage Foundation, 1983).

59. Nat Hentoff, "Liberal Trimmers of the First Amendment," *The Washington Post*, January 17, 1998, p. A25.

60. Dinesh D'Sousa, *Illiberal Education: The Politics of Race and Sex on Campus* (Free Press, 1991), p. 313.

Chapter 5

1. *Border Protection, Antiterrorism, and Illegal Immigration Control Act of 2005*, 109th Cong., 1st sess., H.R. 4437; see also, Dan Balz, "Political Splits on Immigration Reflect Voter's Ambivalence; Americans Favor Tighter Border but Divide on Entrants' Fate," *The Washington Post*, January 3, 2006, p. A07.

2. Robert D. McFadden, "Across the U.S., Protests for Immigrants Draw Thousands," *New York Times*, April 10, 2006, p. A14; Anna Gorman and J. Michael Kennedy, "The Immigration Debate," *Los Angeles Times*, April 11, 2006, p. A11.

3. Judy Keen and Martin Kasindorf, "From Coast to Coast, 'We Need to Be Heard'," *USA Today*, May 2, 2006, p. 3A.

4. Franklin Delano Roosevelt, quoted in William Safire, *Lend Me Your Ears: Great Speeches in History* (Norton, 1997), p. 646.

5. Mark Hyman, "Sure, He's Latino. But Don't Expect Salsa at the Park," *BusinessWeek* 3835 (June 2, 2003), p. 85.

6. Rachel L. Swarns, "Senator Introduces Bill Creating Guest Worker Program," *The New York Times*, February 24, 2006, p. A10.

7. Albert Einstein, quoted in Laurence J. Peter, *Peter's Quotations* (Morrow, 1977), p. 358.

8. Alexis de Tocqueville, *Democracy in America*, ed. J. P. Mayer, trans. George Lawrence (Doubleday, 1969), p. 278. Originally published 1835 (*Volume 1*) and 1840 (*Volume 2*).

9. Food and Agriculture Organization of the United Nations, "Trade," *Food Outlook* 1 (February, 2003), at <http://www.fao.org/docrep/005/y8525e/y8525e06.htm>, August 31, 2006.

10. de Tocqueville, *Democracy in America*, trans. Henry Reeve, eBook at www.netlibrary.com, p. 153.

11. Harold Hongju Koh, "On American Exceptionalism," *Stanford Law Review* 55 (May, 2003): 1481.

12. Seymour Martin Lipset, *American Exceptionalism: A Double-Edged Sword* (W. W. Norton, 1997).

13. U.S. Bureau of the Census, *Statistical Abstract of the United States, 2006* (Government Printing Office, 2006), p. 263.

14. V. O. Key Jr., *Politics, Parties, and Pressure Groups*, 5th ed. (Crowell, 1964), p. 232.

15. Earl Black and Merle Black, *The Vital South: How Presidents Are Elected* (Harvard University Press, 1992), p. 4.

16. Arthur C. Paulson, *Realignment and Party Revival: Understanding American Electoral Politics at the Turn of the Twenty-First Century* (Westport, 2000), p. 46.

17. Joseph A. Pika and Richard A. Watson, *The Presidential Contest*, 5th ed. (CQ Press, 1996), pp. 80–81.

18. Colbert I. King, "Dean's Faith-Based Folly," *The Washington Post*, January 10, 2004, p. A19.

19. Dan Balz, "Rove Offers Republicans a Battle Plan For Elections," *The Washington Post*, January 21, 2006, p. A01.

20. National Governor's Association, *Governor's Political Affiliations*, at www.nga.org/cda/files/GOVLIST2004.PDF, March 3, 2006.

21. U.S. Bureau of the Census, at www.census.gov/population/cen2000/tab01.pdf, March 3, 2006.

22. www.polstate.com/archives/004713.html, March 3, 2006

23. Justices Affirm GOP Map for Texas, <http://www.washingtonpost.com/wp-dyn/content/article/2006/06/28/AR2006062800660.html> September 5, 2006. See also: *League of United Latin American Citizens et al. v. Perry, Governor of Texas, et al.*, http://caselaw.lp.findlaw.com/cgi-bin/getcase.pl?court=US&navby=case&vol=000&invol=05-204> September 8, 2006

24. Robert S. Erikson, Gerald C. Wright, and John P. McIver, *Statehouse Democracy: Public Opinion and Policy in the American States* (Cambridge University Press, 1993).

25. U.S. Bureau of the Census, *Statistical Abstract of the United States, 2006* (Government Printing Office, 2006), p. 21.

26. Holly Idelson, "Count Adds Seats in Eight States," *Congressional Quarterly Weekly Report* 48 (December 29, 1999), p. 4240.

27. John M. Broder, "Term Waning, Gov. Davis Reflects on the Battle Lost," *The New York Times*, November 12, 2003, p. A12.

28. *Statistical Abstract, 2006*, p. 31.

29. *Statistical Abstract, 2006*, p. 31

30. U.S. Census Bureau, Current Population Survey, March 2002, Racial Statistics Branch, Population Division. From www.census.gov/population/socdemo/race/black/ppl-164/tab21.pdf.

31. Ibid.

32. *Statistical Abstract, 2003*, pp. 38–39.

33. David R. Harris and Jeremiah Joseph Sim, "Who is Multiracial? Assessing the Complexity of Lived Race," *American Sociological Review*, August 2002, p. 615.

34. *Statistical Abstract of the United States, 2006*, p. 18.

35. Ibid.

36. Ibid.

37. William N. Evans and Julie H. Topoleski, *The Social and Economic Impact of Native American Casinos*, (National Bureau of Economic Research, 2002), at http://www.nber.org/papers/w9198.pdf, September 1, 2006.

38. See James Meader and John Bart, "The More You Spend, the Less They Listen: The South Dakota U.S. Senate Race," in *The Last Hurrah?: Soft Money and Issue Advocacy in the 2002 Congressional Elections*, David B. Magleby and J. Quin Monson, eds. (Brookings Institution Press, 2004), p. 173; see also Elizabeth Theiss Smith and Richard Braunstein, "The Nationalization of Local Politics in South Dakota," in *Dancing Without Partners: How Candidates, Parties, and Interest Groups Interact in the New Campaign Finance Environment*, David B. Magleby and J. Quin Monson, eds. (Center for the Study of Elections and Democracy, 2005), pp. 241–242.

39. Robert D. Ballard, "Introduction: Lure of the New South," in *In Search of the New South: The Black Urban Experience in the 1970s and 1980s*, Robert D. Ballard, ed. (University of Alabama Press, 1989), p. 5; *Statistical Abstract, 2006*, p. 28.

40. Ibid., p. 463.

41. Ibid., p. 475.

42. *Statistical Abstract, 2003*, p. 463.

43. *Statistical Abstract of the United States, 2006*, p. 463.

44. Pew Hispanic Center, "Wealth Gap Widens Between Whites and Hispanics," October 18, 2004, at <http://pewhispanic.org/newsroom/releases/release.php?ReleaseID=15>, May 8, 2006.

45. Statistical Abstract, 2006, p. 147.

46. Ibid., p. 174.

47. Ibid., p. 16.

48. Jeremy D. Mayer, *Running on Race* (Random House, 2002), pp. 4, 297. See also Mark R. Levy and Michael S. Kramer, *The Ethnic Factor: How America's Minorities Decide Elections* (Simon & Schuster, 1973). See also Mark Stern, "Democratic Presidency and Voting Rights," in *Blacks in Southern Politics*, Lawrence W. Mooreland, Robert P. Steed, and Todd A. Baker, eds. (Praeger, 1987), pp. 50–51.

49. For 1984–2000 see Harold W. Stanley and Richard G. Niemi, *Vital Statistics on American Politics, 2000–2001* (CQ Press, 2001), p. 122; for 2004 see Harold W. Stanley and Richard G. Niemi, *Vital Statistics on American Politics, 2005–2006* (CQ Press, 2006), p. 124.

50. Stanley and Niemi, *Vital Statistics on American Politics, 2005–2006*, p. 124.

51. *Statistical Abstract, 2006*, p. 27.

52. See Earl Black, "Presidential Address: The Newest Southern Politics," *The Journal of Politics*, August 1998, pp. 595–607.

53. Stanley and Niemi, *Vital Statistics on American Politics, 2005–2006*, pp. 63–64.

54. Ibid.

55. Rodolfo O. de la Garza, Louis De Sipio, F. Chris Garcia, John Garcia, and Angelo Falcon, *Latino Voices: Mexican, Puerto Rican, and Cuban Perspectives on American Politics* (Westview Press, 1992), p. 14. See also Richard E. Cohen, "Hispanic Hopes Fade," *National Journal* (February 2, 2002).

56. *Statistical Abstract, 2006*, p. 27.

57. Ibid, p. 43.

58. Rodney Hero, F. Chris Garcia, John Garcia, and Harry Pachon, "Latino Participation, Partisanship, and Office Holding," *P.S.: Political Science and Politics* 33 (September 2000), p. 529. See also de la Garza et al., *Latino Voices*, p. 14.

59. Betsy Guzmán, "The Hispanic Population," U.S. Bureau of the Census, at <http://www.census.gov/prod/2001pubs/c2kbr01-3.pdf>, September 1, 2006. Tom Squitieri, "Redistricting Falls Short of Hispanics' Hopes," *USA Today*, August 27, 2002, p. 11A

60. Wendy K. Tam, "Asians—A Monolithic Voting Bloc?" *Political Behavior* 17 (June 1995)

61. Andrew L. Aoki and Don T. Nakanishi, "Asian Pacific Americans and the New Minority Politics," *PS: Political Science and Politics* (September 2001), p. 605.

62. *Statistical Abstract, 2006*, p. 27.

63. U.S. Bureau of the Census, *Profile of the Foreign-Born Population in the United States, 2000* (Government Printing Office, 2001) at <http://www.census.gov/prod/2002pubs/p23-206.pdf>, March 3, 2006.

64. *Statistical Abstract, 2006*, p. 147.

65. *Statistical Abstract, 2006*, p. 9.

66. Ibid., p. 44.

67. U.S. Census, "Historical Census Statistics on Foreign-born Population of the United States," at www.census.gov/population/www/documentation/twps0029/twps0029.html.

68. James West Davidson, William E. Gienapp, Christine Leigh Heyrman, Mark H. Lytle, and Michael B. Stoff, *Nation of Nations* (McGraw-Hill, 1990), pp. 833–834.

69. G. Thomas Edwards, *Sowing Good Seeds: The Northwest Suffrage Campaigns of Susan B. Anthony* (Oregon Historical Society Press, 1990), p. 136.

70. Paul Kleppner, *Continuity and Change in Electoral Politics, 1893–1928* (Greenwood Press, 1987), p. 172.

71. Margaret C. Trevor, "Political Socialization, Party Identification, and the Gender Gap," *Public Opinion Quarterly* 63 (Spring 1999), p. 62.

72. *Statistical Abstract, 2006*, p. 263; Sue Tolleson-Rinehard and Jyl J. Josephson, eds., *Gender and American Politics* (Sharpe, 2000), pp. 77–78.

73. U.S. Census Bureau, "U.S. Voter Turnout Up in 2004," www.census.gov/Press-Release/www/releases/archives/voting/004986.html, September 1, 2006.

74. Tolleson-Rinehard and Josephson, *Gender and American Politics*, pp. 232–233. See also Cindy Simon Rosenthal, ed., *Women Transforming Congress* (University of Oklahoma Press, 2002), pp. 138–139.

75. Barbara C. Burrell, *A Woman's Place Is in the House: Campaigning for Congress in the Feminist Era* (University of Michigan Press, 1994).

76. Marjorie Connelly, "The Election; Who Voted: A Portrait of American Politics, 1976–2000," *The New York Times*, November 12, 2000, p. D4.

77. *Statistical Abstract, 2006*, p. 247.

78. Diane L. Fowlkes, "Feminist Theory: Reconstructing Research and Teaching About American Politics and Government," *News for Teachers of Political Science* (Winter 1987), pp. 6–9. See also Sally Helgesen, *Everyday Revolutionaries: Working Women and the Transformation of American Life* (Doubleday, 1998); Karen Lehrman, *The Lipstick Proviso: Women, Sex, and Power in the Real World* (Anchor/Doubleday, 1997); Tanya Melich, *The Republican War Against Women: An Insider's Report from Behind the Lines* (Bantam Books, 1998); and Virginia

Valian, *Why So Slow? The Advancement of Women* (MIT Press, 1998).

79. Arlie Russell Hochschild, "There's No Place like Work," *The New York Times*, April 20, 1997, p. 51.

80. The Pew Research Center, *Gay Marriage a Voting Issue, but Mostly for Opponents*, February 27, 2004, at www.people-press.org/reports/display.php3?ReportID=204; and Alexis Simendinger, "Why Issues Matter," *National Journal*, April 1, 2000, based on data from a Pew Center Poll conducted March 15–19, 2000.

81. *Statistical Abstract, 2006*, p. 466.

82. *Statistical Abstract, 2006*, p. 467.

83. Carmen DeNavas-Walt, Bernadette D. Proctor, and Cheryl Hill Lee, U.S. Census Bureau, Current Population Reports, P60-229, *Income, Poverty, and Health Insurance Coverage in the United States: 2004* (U.S. Government Printing Office, 2005), www.census.gov/prod/2005pubs/p60-229.pdf, March 14, 2006.

84. Wendy Margolis, Bonnie Gordon, Joe Puskarz, and David Rosenlieb, eds., *ABA LSAC Official Guide to ABA-Approved Law Schools, 2005 Edition* (Law School Admissions Council and the American Bar Association, 2004).

85. The University of Virginia Law School, "Gender Influences Law Firm Hiring, Promotion, Sociology Professor Says," at <www.law.virginia.edu/home2002/html/news/2006_spr/Gorman.htm>, September 1, 2006.

86. Study of Women MBA's, at <http://www.princetonreview.com/mba/research/articles/decide/women.asp>, September 5, 2006.

87. U.S. Small Business Administration, *Women in Business*, at <http://www.sba.gov/advo/stats/wib01.pdf#search=%22women%20percentage%20in%20business%20management%22>, September 5, 2006.

88. Anna Quindlen, "Some Struggles Never Seem to End," *The New York Times*, November 14, 2001, p. H24.

89. Elsa Brenner, "The Invisible Population," *The New York Times*, November 14, 1999. See also www.census.gov/population/www/documentation/twps0034.html.

90. Erica Goode. "Sunday Q & A," *The New York Times*, September 2, 2001, p. 16.

91. Rose Arce, "Massachusetts Court Upheld Same-Sex Marriage," at www.cnn.com/2004/LAW/02/04/gay.marriage/, September 1, 2006.

92. Rachel Gordon, "Newsom's Plan for Same-Sex Marriages; Mayor Wants to License Gay and Lesbian Couples," *The San Francisco Chronicle*, February 11, 2004, p. A1.

93. *Hebel v. West*, 803 N.Y.S. 2d (2005); *Lockyer v. City of San Francisco*, S122923 (2004).

94. "One Down, One to Go," *New York Times Editorial*, June 8, 2006, p. A24.

95. Adam Clymer, "Senate Expands Hate Crimes Law to Include Gays," *The New York Times*, June 21, 2000, p. A1.

96. *Boy Scouts of America v. Dale*, 120 S. Ct. 2446 (2000).

97. *Lawrence v. Texas*, 123 S. Ct. 2472 (2003).

98. David Masci, "The Future of Marriage," *The CQ Researcher Online*, Vol. 14, No. 17 (May 7, 2004), pp. 397–420.

99. *Statistical Abstract, 2006*, p. 68.

100. U.S. Census Bureau, "Table MS-2. Estimated Median Age at First Marriage, by Sex: 1890 to the Present," June 29, 2005, at http://www.census.gov/population/socdemo/hh-fam/ms2.pdf, March 14, 2006.

101. *Statistical Abstract, 2003*, p. 100.

102. *Statistical Abstract, 2006*, p. 67.

103. United Nations Statistics Division, "Social Indicators," unstats.un.org/unsd/demographic/products/socind/childbr.htm, April 17, 2006.

104. *General Social Survey (GSS) 1972–2000 Cumulative Codebook*, at www.icpsr.umich.edu/GSS/index.html, September 1, 2006.

105. Leni Yahil, *The Holocaust: The Fate of European Jewry* (Oxford University Press, 1990).

106. Stephen C. LeSuer, *The 1838 Mormon War in Missouri* (University of Missouri Press, 1987), pp. 151–153.

107. John Conway, "An Adapted Organic Tradition," *Daedalus* 117 (Fall 1988), p. 382. For an extended comparison of the impact of religion on politics in the United States and Canada, see Seymour Martin Lipset, *Continental Divide: The Values and Institutions of the United States and Canada* (Routledge, 1990), pp. 74–89.

108. www.whitehouse.gov/news/releases/2004/01/20040120-7.html.

109. Charles Wesley, "A Charge to Keep I Have," Text, 1778. Music by Lowell Mason, 1832.

110. "Address of Senator John F. Kennedy to the Greater Houston Ministerial Association," September 12, 1960. See <http://millercenter.virginia.edu/scripps/diglibrary/prezspeeches/kennedy/index.html>, September 1, 2006.

111. Jodi Wilgoren, "Dean Attacks Bush on Research," *The New York Times*, January 10, 2004, p. A9.

112. Taylor Branch, *Parting the Waters: America in the King Years, 1954–63* (Simon & Schuster, 1988), p. 3.

113. Douglas Usher, "Strategy, Rules and Participation: Issue Activists in Republican National Convention Delegations 1976–1996," *Political Research Quarterly*, Vol. 53, No. 4. (December, 2000), p. 888.

114. Ronald Inglehart and Wayne E. Baker, "Looking Forward, Looking Back: Continuity and Change at the Turn of the Millennium," *American Sociological Review* (February 2000), pp. 29, 31.

115. Gallup Brain, "Religion," at http://institution.gallup.com/content/?ci=1690.

116. William H. Flanigan and Nancy H. Zingale, *Political Behavior of the American Electorate*, 11th ed. (CQ Press, 2006), p. 141.

117. *Statistical Abstract, 2006*, p. 59.

118. Ibid.

119. *Statistical Abstract, 2006*, p. 58.

120. *Statistical Abstract, 2006*, pp. 21, 67; American Religion Data Archive, State Membership, at www.thearda.com/mapsReports/reports/selectState.asp, March 8, 2006.

121. Statistical Abstract, 2006, pp. 21, 59; see also www.thearda.com/mapsReports/reports/selectState.asp, March 8, 2006.

122. Ibid.

123. American Religion Data Archive, Jewish Estimate–Number of Adherents, at www.thearda.com/mapsReports/maps/map.asp?state=101&variable=20, March 8, 2006; ARDA, Metro Area Membership Report, at www.thearda.com/mapsReports/reports/metro/5602_2000.asp, March 8, 2006.

124. CNN, "Exit Polls: Results," at www.cnn.com/ELECTION/2000/results, September 1, 2006.

125. *2000 American National Election Study* (Center for Political Studies, 2000); *2004 American National Election Study* (Center for Political Studies, 2004). Post-election surveys often overestimate the vote and that appeared to be

especially the case in the 2004 National Election Study. See Morris Fiorina and Jon Krosnick, "*Economist/YouGov Internet Presidential Poll*," at www.economist.com/media/pdf/Paper.pdf; Michael P. McDonald and Samuel Popkin, "The Myth of the Vanishing Voter," *American Political Science Review* 95 (2001), pp. 963–974.

126. Data provided by John C. Green from the Fourth National Survey of Religion and Politics, May 6, 2006.

127. Ibid.

128. CNN, "Exit Polls: Results," at www.cnn.com/ELECTION/2000/results, March 21, 2006.

129. American National Election Studies, *1960 ANES* and *2004 ANES* at www.umich.edu/~nes/studypages/2004prepost/2004prepost.htm and www.umich.edu/~nes/studypages/1956to1960merged/1956to1960merged.htm. Note: Southern defined by census region, party ID includes leaners as partisans.

130. Raymond E. Wolfinger, Fred I. Greenstein, and Martin Shapiro, *Dynamics of American Politics*, 2d ed. (Prentice Hall, 1980), p. 19.

131. Thomas Jefferson, "Autobiography," in *The Life and Selected Writings of Thomas Jefferson*, Adrienne Koch and William Peden, eds. (Modern Library, 1944), p. 38.

132. Laura D'Andrea Tyson, "Needed: Affirmative Action for the Poor," *BusinessWeek*, July 7, 2003, p. 24.

133. *Statistical Abstract, 2006*, p. 184.

134. "Plans to Tackle College Costs Risk Tripping Up Students," *USA Today*, January 5, 2004, p. 12A.

135. Harold W. Stanley and Richard G. Niemi, *Vital Statistics on American Politics, 2005–2006* (CQ Press, 2006), p. 366–367.

136. Stanley Fischer, "Symposium on the Slowdown in Productivity Growth," *Journal of Economic Perspectives* 2 (Fall 1988), pp. 3–7.

137. Robert Gavin, "Q&A Boston Fed Chief Cathy Minehan, On Soaring Productivity Rate," *The Boston Globe*, December 21, 2003, p. E2.

138. *Statistical Abstract, 2006*, p. 473

139. U.S. Bureau of the Census, at www.census.gov/hhes/www/poverty/threshold/thresh05.html, March 15, 2006.

140. U.S. Bureau of the Census, at www.census.gov/prod/2003pubs/p60-222.pdf, September 1, 2006.

141. *Statistical Abstract, 2006*, p. 473.

142. Ibid.

143. Ibid., p. 464.

144. Ibid.

145. Ibid., p. 443. "Real" means that inflation has already been taken into account.

146. Daniel Bell, *The Coming of Post-Industrial Society: A Venture in Social Forecasting* (Basic Books, 1973), p. xviii.

147. *Statistical Abstract, 2006*, p. 407.

148. Ibid., p. 443.

149. Ibid., p. 407.

150. Mattei Dogan and Dominique Pelassy, *How to Compare Nations: Strategies in Comparative Politics*, 2d ed. (Chatham House, 1990), p. 47.

151. *Index to International Public Opinion, 1996–97* (Greenwood Press, 1997), p. 397.

152. Seymour Martin Lipset, *Continental Divide: The Values and Institutions of the United States and Canada* (Routledge, 1990), p. 170.

153. *Statistical Abstract, 2006*, p. 25, 103.

154. United Nations, "Expert Group Meeting on Policy Responses to Population Ageing and Population Decline," www.un.org/esa/population/

publications/popdecline/Chesnais.pdf, April 17, 2006.

155. Susan A. MacManus, *Young v. Old: Generational Combat in the 21ˢᵗ Century* (Westview Press 1996), pp. 48–49, 174–176, 245.

156. *Statistical Abstract, 2001*, p. 433; *Statistical Abstract, 2006*, p. 473.

157. Ceci Connolly and Mike Allen, "Medicare Drug Benefit May Cost $1.2 Trillion: Estimate Dwarfs Bush's Original Price Tag," *The Washington Post* February 9, 2005, p. A01; See also, Editorial, "A Good but Puzzling Drug Benefit" *The New York Times*, November 27, 2005, Section 4, page 9.

158. Editorial, "A Good but Puzzling Drug Benefit" *The New York Times*, November 27, 2005, Section 4, page 9.

159. Jose Antonio Vargas, "Vote or Die? Well, They Did Vote," *The Washington Post*, November 9, 2004, p. C1.

160. CNN, "Exit Polls: Results," at www.cnn.com/ ELECTION/2000/results, September 1, 2006.

161. Thomas Jefferson to P. S. du Pont de Nemours, April 24, 1816, in *The Writings of Thomas Jefferson*, Paul L. Ford, ed. (Putnam, 1899), vol. 10, p. 25.

162. *Statistical Abstract, 2006*, p. 145.

163. Ibid., p. 148.

164. Ibid.

165. Herbert McClosky and John Zaller, *The American Ethos: Public Attitudes Toward Capitalism and Democracy* (Harvard University Press, 1984), p. 261.

166. John Gunther, *Inside U.S.A.* (Harper, 1947), p. 911.

167. Carl N. Degler, *Out of Our Past: The Forces That Shaped Modern America*, 3d ed. (Harper & Row, 1984), p. 322.

Chapter 6

1. Karen Tumulty, "The Man Who Bought Washington," *Time*, January 16, 2006, at www.time.com/ time/archive/preview/0,10987,1147156,00.html, accessed July 7, 2006.

2. Dan Balz and Jeffrey H. Birnbaum, "Case Bringing New Scrutiny to a System and a Profession," *The Washington Post*, January 4, 2006, p. A1.

3. Susan Schmidt and James V. Grimaldi, "Abramoff Pleads Guilty to 3 Counts," *The Washington Post*, January 4, 2006. p. A1.

4. Ibid.

5. Thomas B. Edsall and Dan Balz, "From a Conservative, a Lack Of Compassion for Ralph Reed," *The Washington Post*, March 26, 2006, p. A5.

6. "Abramoff Pleads Guilty, Will Help in Corruption Probe" *Bloomberg News Service*, January 3, 2006, at *bloomberg.com/apps/news?pid_10000087& sid=aDq6Gy_iOshA&refr+top_world_news*, accessed July 6, 2006.

7. "Abramoff May Strike Deal with Prosecutors," *Associated Press*, December 22, 2005, at www. msnbc.msn.com/id/10553782/, accessed July 6, 2006.

8. Elizabeth White, "A Look at Abramoff-Related Donations," *The Associated Press*, January 6, 2006.

9. James Madison, *Federalist Papers*, No. 10, November 23, 1787, in Isaac Kramnick, ed., *The Federalist Papers* (Penguin Books, 1987), pp. 122-128.

10. See Robert Dahl, *Who Governs?* (Yale University Press, 1961).

11. Center for Responsive Politics, "Wal-Mart Stores Soft Money Donations," at http://www.open secrets.org/softmoney/softcomp2.asp?txtName =Wal%2DMart+Stores&txtUltOrg=y&txtSort= name&txtCycle=2000, accessed September 25, 2006. See also Center for Responsive Politics, "Retail Sales: Top Contributors to Federal Candidates and Parties," at http://www.opensecrets .org/industries/contrib.asp?Ind=N03&Cycle= 2004m, accessed June 30, 2006.

12. Center for Responsive Politics, "Microsoft Corp: Donor Profile," at http://opensecrets.org/orgs/ summary.asp?ID=D000000115&Name= Microsoft+Corp, accessed September 25, 2006.

13. www.changetowin.org/members.html.

14. Steven Greenhouse, "4th Union Quits AFL-CIO in Dispute Over Organizing," *New York Times*, September 15, 2005, p. A14; Steven Greenhouse, "2 Major Construction Unions to Leave AFL-CIO Unit," *New York Times*, February 15, 2006, p. A16.

15. U.S. Bureau of Labor Statistics, "Union Members in 2005," press release, January 20, 2006, at www .bls.gov/news.release/pdf/union2.pdf, accessed May 18, 2006.

16. U.S. Bureau of Labor Statistics, at www.bls.gov/ cps/cpsaat40.pdf.

17. Michael Podhorzer, Department of Political Research, AFL-CIO, personal communication, June 14, 2002.

18. Brian C. Mooney, "Nation's Two Biggest Unions to Wait on Presidential Endorsement," *The Boston Globe*, September 11, 2003, p. A3.

19. Herbert B. Asher et al., *American Labor Unions in the Electoral Arena* (Rowman & Littlefield, 2001).

20. James MacGregor Burns and Stewart Burns, *A People's Charter: The Pursuit of Rights in America* (Knopf, 1991).

21. William R. Donohue, *The Politics of the American Civil Liberties Union* (Transaction Books, 1985).

22. www.concordcoalition.org/about.html.

23. Internal Revenue Service, "Exemption Requirements," at www.irs.gov/charities/charitable/ article/0,,id=96099,00.html. accessed July 7, 2006.

24. National Education Association, at www.nea .org/aboutnea.

25. Sam Dillon and Diana Jean Schemo, "Union Urges Bush to Replace Education Chief Over Remark," *The New York Times*, February 25, 2004, p. A15.

26. See Mancur Olson, *The Logic of Collective Action* (Harvard University Press, 1971).

27. Robert Salisbury, "Interest Representation: The Dominance of Institutions," *American Political Science Review* 78 (March 1984), p. 66.

28. Ceci Connelly, "Democratic Candidates Criticize AARP," *The Washington Post*, November 19, 2003, p. A12.

29. Amy Goldstein, "AARP to Seek a Better Drug Benefit," *The Washington Post*, January 28, 2006, p. A7.

30. V. O. Key Jr., *Public Opinion and American Democracy* (Knopf, 1961), pp. 504–507.

31. www.bipac.org/home.asp.

32. R. Kenneth Godwin, *One Billion Dollars of Influence: The Direct Marketing of Politics* (Chatham House, 1988).

33. David B. Magleby and J. Quin Monson, eds., *The Last Hurrah? Soft Money and Issue Advocacy in the 2002 Congressional Elections* (Brookings Institution Press, 2004) p. 107; and David B. Magleby, J. Quin Monson, and Kelly Patterson, eds., *Electing Congress: New Rules for an Old Game* (Prentice Hall, 2006).

34. Lucius J. Barker, "Third Parties in Litigation: A Systemic View of the Judicial Function," *Journal of Politics* 29 (February 1967), pp. 41–69; Jethro K. Lieberman, *Litigious Society*, rev. ed. (Basic Books, 1983).

35. Gregory A. Caldeira and John R. Wright, "Organized Interests and Agenda Setting in the U.S. Supreme Court," *American Political Science Review* 82 (December 1988), pp. 1109–1127. See also Gregory A. Caldeira and John R. Wright, "*Amici Curiae* Before the Supreme Court: Who Participates, When, and How Much?" *Journal of Politics* 52 (August 1990), pp. 782–806.

36. Karen O'Connor, *Women's Organizations' Use of the Courts* (Lexington Books, 1980).

37. Steven P. Brown, *Trumping Religion: The New Christian Right, Religious Liberty, and the Courts* (University of Alabama Press, October 2002), Ph.D. dissertation.

38. Lee Epstein and C. K. Rowland, "Debunking the Myth of Interest Group Invincibility in the Courts," *American Political Science Review* 85 (March 1991), pp. 205–217.

39. Robert D. McFadden, "Across the U.S., Protests for Immigrants Draw Thousands," *The New York Times*, April 10, 2006, p. A14; Anna Gorman and J. Michael Kennedy, "The Immigration Debate," *Los Angeles Times*, April 11, 2006, p. A11.

40. Judy Keen and Martin Kasindorf, "From Coast to Coast, 'We Need to Be Heard'," *USA Today*, May 2, 2006, p. 3A.

41. See Kenneth Klee, "The Siege of Seattle," *Newsweek*, December 13, 1999, p. 30.

42. League of Conservation Voters, "Key Races of the 2004 Congressional Election Cycle," at www.lcv. org/campaigns/2004-congressional.

43. For a discussion of the 1998 New Mexico race, see Lonna Rae Atkeson and Anthony C. Coveny, "The 1998 New Mexico Third Congressional District Race," in Magleby, *Outside Money*, pp. 135–152.

44. Joshua Weinstein, "Angry Ralph Nader: Scorn, Anger, and Resolve Sustain Nader," *Portland Press Herald*, October 6, 2004.

45. Ethan Bronner, *Battle for Justice: How the Bork Nomination Shook America* (Norton, 1989), pp. 50–55.

46. Hugh Heclo, "Issue Networks and the Executive Establishment," in *The New American Political System*, Anthony King, ed. (American Enterprise Institute, 1978).

47. David Mayhew, *Congress: The Electoral Connection* (Yale University Press, 1974), p. 45.

48. John R. Wright, "Contributions, Lobbying, and Committee Voting in the U.S. House of Representatives," *American Political Science Review* 84 (June 1990), pp. 417–438.

49. www.opensecrets.org/softmoney/softcomp1 .asp?txtName=wal-mart.

50. www.clubforgrowth.org/what.php.

51. David B. Magleby and Jonathan W. Tanner, "Interest Group Electioneering in the 2002 Congressional Elections," in *The Last Hurrah*, David B. Magleby and J. Quin Monson, eds. (Brookings Institution Press, 2004), p. 81. See also Thomas B. Edsall, "Drug Industry Financing Fuels Pro-GOP TV Spots; Spending Swamps Donations for Liberal Ads by 3–1 Margin," *The Washington Post*, October 23, 2002, p. A11.

52. Christopher Rowland, "That Spoonful of Sugar Medicare Bids Mollify Makers on a Key Point: No Price Controls," *The Boston Globe*, June 29, 2003, p. H1.

53. Dana Milbank, "Conservatives Criticize Bush on Spending; Medicare Bill Angers Some Allies," *The Washington Post*, December 6, 2003, p. A1.

54. Dana Milbank and Claudia Deane, "President Signs Medicare Drug Bill; Supporters, Opponents Jockey for 2004 Edge," *The Washington Post*, December 9, 2003, p. A1.

55. *McConnell v. Federal Elections Commission*, 124 S.Ct. 621 (2003).

56. For evidence of the impact of PAC expenditures on legislative committee behavior and legislative involvement generally, see Richard L. Hall and Frank W. Wayman, "Buying Time: Moneyed Interests and the Mobilization of Bias in Congressional Committees," *American Political Science Review* 84 (September 1990), pp. 797–820.

57. Federal Election Commission, "FEC Issues Semi-Annual Federal PAC Count," press release, February 23, 2006, at www.fec.gov/press/press2006/20060223paccount.html, accessed May 24, 2006.

58. Ibid.

59. Edwin M. Epstein, "Business and Labor Under the Federal Election Campaign Act of 1971," in *Parties, Interest Groups, and Campaign Finance Laws*, Michael J. Malbin, ed. (American Enterprise Institute for Public Policy Research, 1980), p. 112. See also Gary Jacobson, *Money in Congressional Elections* (Yale University Press, 1980).

60. Open Secrets, at opensecrets.org/pacs/industry .asp?txt=N00&cycle=2004.

61. Amy Keller, "Leadership PACs 'Not Sinister,' FEC Told," *Roll Call*, February 27, 2003.

62. Political Money Line, at www.fecinfo.com/cgi-win/x_polpaclead.exe?DoFn=06.

63. Federal Election Commission, at www.fec.gov.

64. Gary C. Jacobson, *Money in Congressional Elections* (Yale University Press, 1980), p. 77.

65. Paul Krugman, "Toward One-Party Rule," *The New York Times*, June 27, 2003, p. A27.

66. J. Quin Monson, "Get On TeleVision vs. Get On The Van: GOTV and the Ground War in 2002," in *The Last Hurrah*, David B. Magleby and J. Quin Monson, eds. (Brookings Institution Press, 2004), p. 108.

67. David B. Magleby and Nicole Carlisle Smith, "Party Money in the 2002 Congressional Elections" in *The Last Hurrah*, David B. Magleby and J. Quin Monson, eds. (Brookings Institution Press, 2004), p.54; David B. Magleby and Eric A. Smith, "Party Soft Money in the 2000 Congressional Elections," in *The Other Campaign*, David B. Magleby, ed. (Rowman & Littlefield, 2003), pp. 34–35; Mariane Holt, "The Surge in Party Money," in *Outside Money*, David B. Magleby, ed. (Rowman & Littlefield, 2000), p. 36; and David B. Magleby, "Conclusions and Implications," in *Outside Money*, David B. Magleby, ed. (Rowman & Littlefield, 2000), p. 214.

68. Ruth Marcus, "Labor Spent $119 Million For '96 Politics, Study Says; Almost All Contributions Went to Democrats," *The Washington Post*, September 10, 1997, p. A19.

69. David B. Magleby, "Party and Interest Group Electioneering in Federal Elections," in *Inside the Campaign Finance Battle: Court Testimony on the New Reforms*, Anthony Corrado, Thomas E. Mann, and Trevor Potter, eds. (Brookings Institution Press, 2003); and Sandra Anglund and Clyde McKee, "The 1998 Connecticut Fifth Congressional District Race," in Magleby, *Outside Money*, pp. 164, 166.

70. John Mintz, "Texan Aired 'Clean Air' Ads; Bush's Campaign Not Involved, Billionaire Says," *The Washington Post*, March 4, 2000, p. A6.

71. *FEC v. Mass. Citizen's for Life, Inc.*, 479 U.S. 238; 107 S.Ct. 616 (1986).

72. Kate Zernike, "Kerry Pressing Swift Boat Case Long After Loss," *The New York Times*, May 28, 2006, p. A1.

73. Allan J. Cigler, "Interest Groups and Financing the 2004 Elections," in David B. Magleby, Anthony Corrado, and Kelly D. Patterson, eds., *Financing the 2004 Election* (Brookings Institution Press, 2006), p. 229-230.

74. America Coming Together, at http://actfor victory.org/.

75. Internal Revenue Code, Title 26, at frwebgate .access.gpo.gov/cgi-bin/getdoc.cgi?dbname= browse_usc&docid=Cite:+26USC501, accessed July 10, 2006.

76. Nicholas Confessore, "Bush's Secret Stash," *Washington Monthly* 36 (May 2004), pp. 17–23.

77. E. J. Dionne Jr., "Fear of McCain-Feingold," *The Washington Post*, December 3, 2002, p. A25.

78. The Campaign Legal Center, "Interveners Urge Supreme Court to Sustain BCRA in its Entirety," at www.campaignlegalcenter.org/press-814 .html, accessed September 26, 2006.

79. Hall and Wayman, "Buying Time," p. 814. A different study of the House Ways and Means Committee found campaign contributions to be part of the representatives' policy decisions, but even more important was the number of lobbying contacts; see Wright, "Contributions, Lobbying, and Committee Voting."

80. David B. Magleby and Kelly D. Patterson, "Campaign Consultants and Direct Democracy: Politics of Citizen Control," in *Campaign Warriors: The Role of Political Consultants in Elections*, James E. Thurber and Candice J. Nelson, eds. (Brookings Institution Press, 2000).

81. Ronald Reagan, "Remarks to Administration Officials on Domestic Policy," December 13, 1988, *Weekly Compilation of Presidential Documents*, vol. 24 (December 1988), pp. 1615–1620.

82. Sylvia Tesh, "In Support of Single-Interest Politics," *Political Science Quarterly* 99 (Spring 1984), pp. 27–44.

83. Adam Clymer, "Congress Sends Lobbying Overhaul to Clinton," *The New York Times*, December 16, 1995, p. A36.

84. Legislative Resource Center's Lobbying Section, telephone interview, April 7, 2004.

Chapter 7

1. John E. Mueller, "Choosing Among 133 Candidates," *Public Opinion Quarterly* 34 (Fall 1970), pp. 395–402.

2. E. E. Schattschneider, *Party Government* (Holt, Rinehart and Winston, 1942), p. 1.

3. See Scott Mainwaring, "Party Systems in the Third Wave," *Journal of Democracy* (July 1998), pp. 67–81.

4. Joseph A. Schlesinger, *Political Parties and the Winning of Office* (University of Michigan Press, 1994).

5. James A. Thurber and Candice J. Nelson, eds., *Campaign Warriors: The Role of Political Consultants in Elections* (Brookings Institution Press, 2000).

6. David Kocieniewski, "From Capitol to State House," *New York Times*, November 9, 2005, p. B5.

7. Robert R. Alford and Eugene C. Lee, "Voting Turnout in American Cities," *American Political Science Review* 62 (September), pp. 809–810.

8. Nick Anderson and Jonathan Peterson, "China Trade Vote: House OK's China Trade Bill," *The Los Angeles Times*, May 25, 2000, p. A1.

9. Elizabeth A. Palmer, "Bill to Extend Residency Program Passes House After Six-Month Wait," *Congressional Quarterly*, March 16, 2002, p. 706.

10. Gary W. Cox and Mathew D. McCubbins, *Legislative Leviathan: Party Government in the House* (University of California Press, 1993).

11. David B. Magleby and J. Quin Monson, eds. *The Last Hurrah? Soft Money and Issue Advocacy in the 2002 Congressional Elections* (Brookings Institution Press, 2004).

12. John Bart and James Meader, "The More You Spend, the Less They Listen: The South Dakota U.S. Senate Race," in *The Last Hurrah*, Magleby and Monson, eds., pp. 159–179.

13. See three books edited by David B. Magleby: *Outside Money: Soft Money and Issue Advocacy in the 1998 Congressional Elections* (Rowman & Littlefield, 2000); *The Other Campaign: Soft Money and Issue Advocacy in the 2000 Congressional Elections* (Rowman & Littlefield, 2002); and *Financing the 2000 Election* (Brookings Institution Press, 2002).

14. Amy Keller, "FEC Offers Post-BCRA Legislative Ideas," *Roll Call*, April 29, 2004.

15. Federal Election Commission, "The Biennial Contribution Limit," at www.fec.gov/pages/brochures/biennial.htm#Biennial%20Limit, February 2004; and Paul S. Herrnson, *Congressional Elections: Campaigning at Home and in Washington* (CQ Press, 2004), p. 16.

16. *Federal Election Commission v. Colorado Republican Federal Campaign Committee*, 116 S.Ct. 2309 (1996).

17. Federal Election Commission, ftp://ftp.fec.gov/FEC/, accessed July 27, 2004.

18. David W. Brady and Craig Volden, *Revolving Gridlock: Politics and Policy from Carter to Clinton* (Westview Press, 1998); James A. Thurber, ed., *Divided Democracy: Cooperation and Conflict Between the President and Congress* (CQ Press, 1991); James A. Thurber, ed., *Rivals for Power: Presidential-Congressional Relations* (CQ Press, 1996); Charles O. Jones, *Separate but Equal Branches: Congress and the Presidency* (Chatham House, 1995), chaps. 5 and 6; and Jon R. Bond and Richard Fleisher, *The President in the Legislative Arena* (University of Chicago Press, 1990).

19. *California Democratic Party et al. v. Jones*, 120 S.Ct. 2402 (2000).

20. Bruce E. Cain and Elisabeth R. Gerber, eds., *Voting at the Political Fault Line: California's Experiment with the Blanket Primary* (University of California Press, 2002), pp. 341–342.

21. "Iowans Flock to Caucuses," *The Associated Press State & Local Wire*, January 20, 2004, Section: "Political News."

22. Arthur Sanders and David Redlawsk, "Money and the Iowa Caucuses," in *Getting Inside the Outside Campaign*, David Magleby, ed. (Center for the Study of Elections and Democracy, 2000), pp. 20–29.

23. *The Book of the States, 2000–2001* (Council of State Governments, 2000), pp. 164–165.

24. For an analysis of the potential effects of different electoral rules in the United States see Todd Donovan and Shawn Bowler, *Reforming the Republic: Democratic Institutions for the New America* (Prentice Hall, 2004).

25. William H. Riker, "The Two-Party System and Duverger's Law: An Essay on the History of Political Science," *American Political Science Review*

76 (December 1982), pp. 753–766. For a classic analysis, see Schattschneider, *Party Government*.

26. Robin Toner, "The 1992 Elections: The World–News Analysis; At Dawn of New Politics, Challenges for Both Parties," *The New York Times*, November 5, 1992, p. B1.

27. See Paul S. Herrnson and John C. Green, eds., *Multiparty Politics in America*, 2d ed. (Rowman & Littlefield, 2002); and J. David Gillespie, *Politics at the Periphery: Third Parties in Two-Party America* (University of South Carolina Press, 1993).

28. L. Sandy Maisel and John F. Bibby, *Two Parties— or More? The American Party System* (Westview Press, 1998).

29. Ted G. Jelen, ed., *Ross for Boss* (State University of New York Press, 2001), p. 88.

30. Steven J. Rosenstone, Roy L. Behr, and Edward H. Lazarus, *Third Parties in America: Citizen Response to Major Party Failure*, 2d ed. (Princeton University Press, 1996). See also Xandra Kayden and Eddie Mahe Jr., *The Party Goes On: The Persistence of the Two-Party System in the United States* (Basic Books, 1985), pp. 143–144. The Republican Party, which started as a third party, was one of the two major parties by 1860, the year Republican Abraham Lincoln won the Presidency; see Lewis L. Gould, *Grand Old Party: A History of the Republicans* (Random House, 2003) pp. 3–17.

31. Dean Lacy and Quin Monson, "The Origins and Impact of Voter Support for Third-Party Candidates: A Case Study of the 1998 Minnesota Gubernatorial Election," *Political Research Quarterly* 55(2), pp. 409–437.

32. On the impact of third parties, see Howard R. Penniman, "Presidential Third Parties and the Modern American Two-Party System," in *The Party Symbol*, William J. Crotty, ed. (Freeman, 1980), pp. 101–117. See also Frank Smallwood, *The Other Candidates: Third Parties in Presidential Elections* (University Press of New England, 1983).

33. Interview with Steve Gordan, National Libertarian Party Communications Director, October 2, 2006.

34. Benjamin Franklin, George Washington, and Thomas Jefferson, quoted in Richard Hofstadter, *The Idea of a Party System* (University of California Press, 1969), pp. 2, 123.

35. For concise histories of the two parties, see Jules Witcover, *Party of the People: A History of the Democrats* (Random House, 2003); and Lewis L. Gould, *Grand Old Party: A History of the Republicans* (Random House, 2003).

36. See V. O. Key Jr., "A Theory of Critical Elections," *Journal of Politics* 17 (February 1955), pp. 3–18; Walter Dean Burnham, *Critical Elections and the Mainsprings of American Politics* (Norton, 1970), pp. 1–10; and E. E. Schattschneider, *The Semisovereign People: A Realist's View of Democracy in America* (Holt, Rinehart and Winston, 1975), pp. 78–80.

37. William E. Gienapp, *The Origins of the Republican Party, 1852–1856* (Oxford University Press, 1987).

38. Gould, *Grand Old Party*, p. 88.

39. Ibid.

40. David W. Brady, "Election, Congress, and Public Policy Changes, 1886–1960," in *Realignment in American Politics: Toward a Theory*, Bruce A. Campbell and Richard Trilling, eds. (Texas University Press, 1980), p. 188.

41. L. Sandy Maisel, *Parties and Elections in America: The Electoral Process* (Rowman & Littlefield, 2002), pp. 48–49.

42. Gerald Pomper, "Classification of Presidential Elections," *Journal of Politics* 29 (August 1967), p. 538.

43. Earl Black and Merle Black, *The Rise of Southern Republicans* (Belknap Press, 2003).

44. V. O. Key Jr., *Political Parties and Pressure Groups*, 5th ed. (International Publishing, 1964). See also Marjorie Randon Hershey, *Party Politics in America*, 12th ed. (Longman, 2006).

45. Federal Election Commission, "Party Activity Summarized for the 2004 Election Cycle," press release, March 14, 2005, at www.fec.gov/press/ press2005/20050302party/Party2004final.htm, accessed May 25, 2006.

46. Hershey, *Party Politics in America*.

47. Virginia Sapiro, "It's the Context, Situation, and Question, Stupid: The Gender Basis of Public Opinion," in *Understanding Public Opinion*, 2d ed., Barbara Norrander and Clyde Wilcox, eds. (CQ Press, 2001), p. 41.

48. At "Ten Years of Leadership," www.house.gov/ cardoza/BlueDogs/history.htm, accessed May 23, 2006.

49. Zell Miller, "George Bush vs. the Naïve Nine," *The Wall Street Journal*, November 3, 2003, p. A14.

50. GOP.com, "RNC Chairman Ken Mehlman," at www.gop.com/About/Bio.aspx?id=3, accessed May 25, 2006.

51. See L. Sandy Maisel, *From Obscurity to Oblivion: Running in the Congressional Primary*, rev. ed. (University of Tennessee Press, 1986).

52. The early Republican efforts and advantages over the Democrats are well documented in Thomas B. Edsall, *The New Politics of Inequality* (Norton, 1984); and Gary C. Jacobson, "The Republican Advantage in Campaign Finances," in *New Direction in American Politics*, John E. Chubb and Paul E. Peterson, eds. (Brookings Institution Press, 1985), p. 6.

53. David C. King, "The Polarization of American Political Parties and Mistrust of Government," in *Why People Don't Trust Government*, Joseph S. Nye, Philip Zelikow, and David C. King, eds. (Harvard University Press, 1997); and National Election Study, "Important Difference in What Democratic and Republican Parties Stand For, 1952–2000," at www.umich.edu/~nes/nesguide/ toptable/tab2b_4.htm, accessed July 2004.

54. Tom Shales, "Bush, Bringing the Party to Life; From the New Nominee, a Splendid Acceptance Speech," *The Washinton Post*, August 19, 1988, p. C1.

55. Kelly D. Patterson, *Political Parties and the Maintenance of Liberal Democracy* (Columbia University Press, 1996), pp. 30–31.

56. John F. Bibby, *Politics, Parties, and Elections in America*, 5th ed. (Wadsworth, 2002). For further data on these roles, see Cornelius P. Cotter, James L. Gibson, John F. Bibby, and Robert J. Huckshorn, *Party Organizations in American Politics* (Praeger, 1984).

57. See James L. Gibson, Cornelius P. Cotter, John F. Bibby, and Robert J. Huckshorn, "Assessing Party Organizational Strength," *American Journal of Political Science* 27 (May 1983), pp. 193–222. See also Cotter et al., *Party Organizations in American Politics*.

58. Paul S. Herrnson, *Party Campaigning in the 1980s: Have the National Parties Made a Comeback as Key Players in Congressional Elections?* (Harvard University Press, 1988), p. 122.

59. A list of many of these positions appears in *Policy and Supporting Positions* (Government Printing Office, November 9, 1988). For a general discussion of presidential appointments, see G. Calvin Mackenzie, "Partisan Presidential Leadership: The President's Appointees," in L. Sandy Maisel, ed., *Parties Respond: Changes in American Parties and Campaigns*, 4th ed. (Westview Press, 2002), pp. 267–289.

60. *Marbury* v. *Madison*, I Cranch 137 (1803).

61. Michael A. Fletcher and Charles Babington, "Miers, Under Fire From Right, Withdrawn as Court Nominee," *The Washington Post*, October 28, 2005, final edition.

62. Henry J. Abraham, *Justices, Presidents, and Senators* (Rowman & Littlefield, 2001) describes the role of political parties in judicial appointments.

63. See Angus Campbell, Philip E. Converse, Warren E. Miller, and Donald E. Stokes, *The American Voter* (University of Chicago Press, 1960); Norman A. Nie, Sidney Verba, and John R. Petrocik, *The Changing American Voter*, enlarged ed. (Harvard University Press, 1979); and Warren E. Miller and J. Merrill Shanks, *The New American Voter* (Harvard University Press, 1996).

64. Angus Campbell et al., *The American Voter*, pp. 121–128.

65. Ibid.

66. Bruce E. Keith et al., *The Myth of the Independent Voter* (University of California Press, 1992).

67. Earl Black and Merle Black, *The Rise of Southern Republicans* (Harvard University Press, 2002).

68. See Byron E. Shafer, *The End of Realignment: Interpreting American Electoral Eras* (University of Wisconsin Press, 1991).

69. Michael F. Meffert, Helmut Norpoth, and Anirudh V. S. Ruhil, "Realignment and Macropartisanship," *American Political Science Review* 95 (December 2001), pp. 953–962.

70. Hedrick Smith, *The Power Game: How Washington Works* (Random House, 1988), p. 671.

71. Nine percent of all voters were Pure Independents in 1956 and 1960; Keith et al., *The Myth of the Independent Voter*, p. 51. In 1992, the figure was also 9 percent; *1992 National Election Study* (Center for Political Studies, University of Michigan, 1992).

72. Earl Black and Merle Black, *The Rise of Southern Republicans* (Harvard University Press, 2002).

73. Ibid.

74. David B. Magleby and Candice J. Nelson, *The Money Chase: Congressional Campaign Finance Reform* (The Brookings Institution, 1990), p. 16.

75. See Magleby, *Outside Money* and *The Other Campaign*.

76. Jonathan S. Krasno and Daniel E. Seltz, *Buying Time: Television Advertising in the 1998 Congressional Elections*, report of a grant funded by the Pew Charitable Trusts (1998).

77. *McConnell* v. *FEC*, 124 S.Ct. 516 (2003).

78. See David B. Magleby and Nicole Carlisle Squires, "Party Money in the 2002 Congressional Elections," *The Last Hurrah?* Magleby and Monson, eds., p. 41.

79. Sidney M. Milkis, "Parties versus Interest Groups," *Inside the Campaign Finance Battle*, Anthony Corrado, Thomas E. Mann, and Trevor Potter, eds. (Brookings Institution Press, 2003), p. 40.

80. Michael J. Malbin, ed., *Life After Reform: When the Bipartisan Campaign Reform Act . . . Meets Politics* (Rowman & Littlefield, 2003), p. 11.

81. Kelly D. Patterson, "Spending in the 2004 Election," *Financing the 2004 Election*, David B. Magleby, Kelly Patterson, and Anthony J. Corrado, eds. (Brookings Institution Press, 2006), pp. 80–81.

82. *Colorado Republican Federal Campaign Committee* v. *Federal Election Commission*, 518 U.S. 604 (1996).

83. Kelly D. Patterson, "Spending in the 2004 Election," *Financing the 2004 Election*, Magleby, Patterson, and Corrado, eds., pp. 76–77.

84. Magleby, Patterson, and Corrado, eds., *Financing the 2004 Election*, p. 170.

85. Martin Kady II, "Party Unity: Learning to Stick Together," *CQ Weekly* 64, no. 2 (January 9, 2006), p. 93.

86. Barbara Sinclair, "Congressional Parties and the Policy Process," in Maisel, *Parties Respond*, pp. 209–229.

87. Paul S. Herrnson, *Party Campaigning in the 1980s* (Harvard University Press, 1988), pp. 80–81.

Chapter 8

1. Jim Siegel, "Thousands of New-Voter Cards in Ohio Undeliverable," *The Cincinnati Enquirer*, October 20, 2004 at www.enquirer.com/editions/2004/10/20/loc_fraud20.html.

2. Peverill Squire, "Why The 1936 *Literary Digest* Poll Failed," *Public Opinion Quarterly* 52 (Spring 1988), 125–133.

3. Ibid., 128.

4. Robert Coles, *The Political Life of Children* (Atlantic Monthly Press, 2000), pp. 24–25. See also Stephen M. Caliendo, *Teachers Matter: The Trouble with Leaving Political Education to the Coaches* (Greenwood, 2000).

5. Coles, *The Political Life of Children*, pp. 59–60.

6. Pamela Johnston Conover, "The Influence of Group Identifications on Political Perception and Evaluation," *Journal of Politics* 46 (August 1984), pp. 760–785; and Henry E. Brady and Paul M. Sniderman, "Attitude Attribution: A Group Basis for Political Reasoning," *American Political Science Review* 79 (December 1985), pp. 1061–1078.

7. Caliendo, *Teachers Matter*, pp. 16–17.

8. James Garbarino, *Raising Children in a Socially Toxic Environment* (Jossey-Bass, 1995).

9. Russell J. Dalton, "Reassessing Parental Socialization: Indicator Unreliability Versus Generational Transfer," *American Political Science Review* 74 (June 1980), pp. 421–431.

10. Suzanne Koprince Sebert, M. Kent Jennings, and Richard G. Niemi, "The Political Texture of Peer Groups," in *The Political Character of Adolescence*, M. Kent Jennings and Richard G. Niemi (Princeton University Press, 1974), p. 246. See also Richard G. Niemi and M. Kent Jennings, "Issues and Inheritance in the Formation of Party Identification," *American Journal of Political Science* 35 (November 1991), pp. 970–988.

11. Paul Nieuwbeerta and Karin Witterbrood, "Intergenerational Transmission of Political Party Preference in the Netherlands," *Social Science Research* 24 (September 1995), pp. 243–261.

12. Lee H. Ehman, "The American School in the Political Socialization Process," *Review of Educational Research* 50 (Spring 1980), pp. 99–119; and J. L. Glanville, "Political Socialization or Selection? Adolescent Extracurricular Participation and Political Activity in Early Adulthood," *Social Science Quarterly* 80 (1999), p. 279.

13. National Association of Secretaries of State, *New Millennium Project, Part I: American Youth Attitudes on Policies, Citizenship, Government and Voting* (Author, 1999). "Political Interest on the Rebound Among the Nation's Freshmen," Higher Education Research Institute, Fall 2003. Accessed October 23, 2006 at www.gseis.ucla.edu/heri/03_press_release.pdf

14. Margaret Stimmann Branson, "Making the Case for Civic Education: Educating Young People for Responsible Citizenship," paper presented at the Conference for Professional Development for Program Trainers, Manhattan Beach, Calif., February 25, 2001.

15. Kenneth Feldman and Theodore M. Newcomb, *The Impact of College on Students*, vol. 2 (Jossey-Bass, 1969), pp. 16–24, 49–56. See also David O. Sears and Nicholas A. Valentino, "Politics Matters: Political Events as Catalysts for Preadult Socialization," *American Political Science Review* 91 (March 1997), pp. 45–65.

16. Daniel B. German, "The Role of the Media in Political Socialization and Attitude Formation toward Racial/Ethnic Minorities in the US," in *Nationalism, Ethnicity, and Identity: Cross National and Comparative Perspectives*, Robert F. Farnen, ed. (Transaction Publishers, 2004) p. 287.

17. James G. Gimpel, J. Celeste Lay, Jason E. Schuknecht, *Cultivating Democracy: Civic Environments and Political Socialization in America* (Brookings, 2003), p. 127 (see chap. 5).

18. Robert D. Putnam, "Bowling Together," *American Prospect* 13 (February 11, 2002), pp. 20–22.

19. Robert D. Putnam, "Bowling Together," in *United We Serve*, E. J. Dionne Jr., Kayla Meltzer Drogosz, and Robert E. Litan, eds. (Brookings Institution Press, 2003), p. 19. The Putnam data is available at www.ksg.harvard.edu/saguaro/.

20. Benjamin I. Page and Robert Y. Shapiro, *The Rational Public* (University of Chicago Press, 1992), p. 267.

21. Quoted in Hadley Cantril, *Gauging Public Opinion* (Princeton University Press, 1944), p. viii.

22. John G. Geer, *From Tea Leaves to Opinion Polls: A Theory of Democratic Leadership* (Columbia University Press, 1996).

23. Everett C. Ladd and John Benson, "The Growth of News Polls in American Politics," in *Media Polls in American Politics*, Thomas Mann and Gary Orren, eds. (Brookings Institution Press, 1992), pp. 19–31.

24. Benjamin I. Page and Robert Y. Shapiro, *The Rational Public: Fifty Years of Trends in Americans' Policy Preferences* (University of Chicago Press, 1992), p. 237.

25. George J. Church, "What in the World Are We Doing?" *Time*, October 18, 1993, p. 42.

26. "Do you approve or disapprove of the way George W. Bush is handling the situation with Iraq?" CBS News/*New York Times* Poll, May 3, 2003, and May 20, 2004, at www.pollingreport.com/iraq2.htm.

27. Lawrence R. Jacobs and Robert R. Shapiro, *Politicians Don't Pander* (University of Chicago Press, 2000), p. 3.

28. Robert S. Erikson and Kent L. Tedin, *American Public Opinion: Its Origins, Content and Impact*, 6th ed. (Longman, 2001), pp. 272–273; on the centrality of the reelection motive see David R. Mayhew, *Congress: The Electoral Connection* (Yale University Press, 1974).

29. For a general discussion of political knowledge, see Michael Delli Carpini and Scott Keeter, *What Americans Know About Politics and Why it Matters* (Yale University Press, 1996).

30. The 2000 National Election Study, Center for Political Studies, University of Michigan. See the NES Guide to Public Opinion and Electoral Behavior at www.umich.edu/~nes/nesguide/nesguide.htm.

31. Robert S. Erikson and Kent L. Tedin, *American Public Opinion: Its Origins, Content and Impact*, 6th ed. (Longman, 2001), p. 304.

32. Neil S. Newhouse and Christine L. Matthews, "NAFTA Revisited: Most Americans Just Weren't Deeply Engaged," *Public Perspective* 5 (January–February, 1994), pp. 31–32.

33. *2002 National Election Study* (Center for Political Studies, University of Michigan, 2002).

34. BBC, "Timeline: Battle for Ukraine." Accessed October 23, 2005 at http://news.bbc.co.uk/2/hi/europe/4061253.stm

35. *2042 National Election Study* (Center for Political Studies, University of Michigan, 2004).

36. Federal Election Commission, "Presidential Election Campaign Fund," at www.fec.gov.

37. For a discussion of the relationship between civic skills and participation, see Sidney Verba, Kay Lehman Schlozman, and Henry E. Brady, *Voice and Equality: Civic Voluntarism in American Politics* (Harvard University Press, 1995).

38. Frank R. Parker, *Black Votes Count: Political Empowerment in Mississippi After 1965* (University of North Carolina Press, 1990), p. 3.

39. Bernard Grofman and Lisa Handley, "The Impact of the Voting Rights Act on Black Representation in Southern State Legislatures," *Legislative Studies Quarterly* 16 (February 1991), pp. 111–128.

40. Charles Babington, "Voting Rights Act Extension Passes In Senate, 98 to 0," *The Washington Post*, July 21, 2006, p. A1.

41. International Institute for Democracy and Electoral Assistance, "Voter Turnout from 1945 to Date: A Global Report on Political Participation," at www.idea.int/voter_turnout/index.html.

42. Raymond E. Wolfinger and Steven J. Rosenstrone, "The Effect of Registration Laws on Voter Turnout," *American Political Science Review* 72 (March 1978), p. 41.

43. Raymond E. Wolfinger and Steven J. Rosenstone, "The Effect of Registration Laws on Voter Turnout," *American Political Science Review* 72 (March 1978), p. 24.

44. Raymond E. Wolfinger and Steven J. Rosenstone, *Who Votes?* (Yale University Press, 1980), pp. 78, 88.

45. Federal Election Commission, "The Impact of the National Voter Registration Act on Federal Elections 1999–2000," at www.fec.gov.

46. See Raymond E. Wolfinger and Ben Highton, "Estimating the Effects of the National Voter Registration Act of 1993," *Political Behavior* (June 1998), pp. 79–104; and Raymond E. Wolfinger and Jonathan Hoffman, "Registering and Voting with Motor Voter," *PS: Political Science and Politics* (March 2001), pp. 85–92.

47. Al Baker, "New York Risking the Loss of Ballot Equipment Money," *The New York Times*, April 29, 2004, p. B05.

48. Ibid.

49. Maha Al-Azar, "Broad Election Reforms Are Urged; Education Called As Crucial As Machines," *The Washington Post*, July 17, 2003, p. T04; Harris N. Miller, "Electronic Voting Is a Solution," *USA Today*, February 4, 2004, p. 14A.

50. The Associated Press, "Ruling Party Candidate Wins Mexico Vote," July 6, 2006.

51. Hector Tobar, "Judges Name Calderon Winner of Vote," Los Angeles Times, September 6, 2006. Pg 1.

52. Stevenson, Mark. 2006. "Mexican leftists push for vote recount." *The Washington Post.* July 24.

53. Obrador, Andrés Manuel López. qtd. in James C. McKinley, Jr. 2006. "Mexico's losing leftist defiantly awaits election ruling." *The New York Times.* July 23.

54. Adam Thomson, "Mexico's leftwing candidate proclaims himself president-elect of 'new republic.'" *Financial Times,* September 18, 2006, p. 8.

55. James C. McKinley, Jr. "Mexican Leftist Suffers Setback in Local Race." *The New York Times,* October 16, 2006. A4.

56. For a discussion of the differences in the turnout between presidential and midterm elections, see James E. Campbell, "The Presidential Surge and Its Midterm Decline in Congressional Elections, 1868–1988," *Journal of Politics* 53 (May 1991), pp. 477–487.

57. David E. Rosenbaum, "Democrats Keep Solid Hold on Congress," *The New York Times,* November 9, 1988, p. A24; Louis V. Gerstner, "Next Time, Let Us Boldly Vote as No Democracy Has Before," *USA Today,* November 16, 1998, p. A15; and Michael McDonald, "2004 Voting-Age and Voting-Eligible Population Estimates and Voter Turnout" at http://elections.gmu.edu/Voter_Turnout_2004.htm.

58. Data from Curtis Gans, "President Bush, Mobilization Drives Propel Turnout to Post-1968 High; Kerry, Democratic Weakness Shown," *Center for Voting and Democracy,* November 4, 2004 at www.fairvote.org/reports/csae2004election report.pdf.

59. Raymond E. Wolfinger and Steven J. Rosenstone, *Who Votes?* (Yale University Press, 1980), p. 102.

60. For a discussion of mobilization efforts and race see Jan Leighley, *Strength in Numbers? The Political Mobilization of Racial and Ethnic Minorities* (Princeton University Press, 2001).

61. Howard W. Stanley and Richard G. Niemi, *Vital Statistics on Politics, 1999–2000* (CQ Press, 2000), pp. 120–121; and Harold W. Stanley and Richard G. Niemi, *Vital Statistics on Politics, 2005–2006* (CQ Press, 2006), pp. 124–125.

62. The Vanishing Voter, "Election Interest Among Young Adults Is Up Sharply From 2000," March 12, 2004, available at www.vanishingvoter.org/Releases/release031104.shtml.

63. See the classic book on this topic, Angus Campbell, Philip E. Converse, Warren E. Miller, and Donald E. Stokes, *The American Voter* (Wiley, 1960). This volume is a foundation of modern voting analysis despite much new evidence and reinterpretation. See also Warren E. Miller and J. Merrill Shanks, *The New American Voter* (Harvard University Press, 1996); and Eric R.A.N. Smith, *The Unchanging American Voter* (University of California Press, 1989).

64. David B. Magleby, J. Quin Monson, and Kelly D. Patterson, "Mail Communications in Political Campaigns: The 2004 Campaign Communications Survey," paper presented at the Midwest Political Science Association, April 20–23, 2006.

65. U.S. Census Bureau, "Voting and Registration in the Election of November 2000." Accessed on October 23, 2006 at www.census.gov/prod/2002pubs/p20-542.pdf.

66. Austin Ranney, "Nonvoting Is Not a Social Disease," *Public Opinion,* October–November 1983, pp. 16–19.

67. Thomas Byrne Edsall, *The New Politics of Inequality* (Norton, 1984), p. 181.

68. Steven J. Rosenstone and John Mark Hansen, *Mobilization, Participation, and Democracy in America* (Longman, 2003).

69. Frances Fox Piven and Richard A. Cloward, "Prospects for Voter Registration Reform: A Report on the Experiences of the Human SERVE Campaign," *PS: Political Science and Politics* 18 (Summer 1985), p. 589.

70. Ibid., p. 589.

71. Raymond E. Wolfinger and Steven J. Rosenstone, *Who Votes?* (Yale University Press, 1980), p. 109.

72. E. E. Schattschneider, *The Semisovereign People* (Dryden Press, 1975), p. 96.

73. Stephen Earl Bennett and David Resnick, "The Implications of Nonvoting for Democracy in the United States," *American Journal of Political Science* 84 (August 1990), pp. 771–802.

74. Bruce E. Keith, David B. Magleby, Candice J. Nelson, Elizabeth Orr, Mark C. Westlye, and Raymond E. Wolfinger, *The Myth of the Independent Voter* (University of California Press, 1992), pp. 60–75; and 2004 National Election Study, Center for Political Studies, University of Michigan, Ann Arbor.

75. David Menefee-Libey, *The Triumph of Campaign-Centered Politics* (Chatham House/Seven Bridges Press, 2000).

76. Barry Goldwater, quoted in Theodore H. White, *The Making of the President, 1964* (Athenaeum, 1965), p. 217.

77. William H. Flanigan and Nancy H. Zingale, *Political Behavior of the American Electorate,* 8th ed. (CQ Press, 1994), p. 173.

78. Tim Graham, "Media-Powered Howard," *National Review Online,* January 30, 2004.

79. CNN. "Exit Polls Election 2000." Accessed on October 23, 2006. at http://www.cnn.com/ELECTION/2000/results/index.epolls.html.

80. J. Merrill Shanks and Warren E. Miller, "Policy Direction and Performance Evaluation: Complementary Explanations of the Reagan Elections," *British Journal of Political Science* 20 (1990), pp. 143–235; and Warren E. Miller and J. Merrill Shanks, "Policy Direction and Performance Evaluation: Comparing George Bush's Victory with Those of Ronald Reagan in 1980 and 1984," paper presented at the annual meeting of the American Political Science Association, Atlanta, August 31–September 2, 1989.

81. Amihai Glazer, "The Strategy of Candidate Ambiguity," *American Political Science Review* 84 (March 1990), pp. 237–241.

82. Robert S. Erikson and David W. Romero, "Candidate Equilibrium and the Behavioral Model of the Vote," *American Political Science Review* 84 (December 1990), p. 1122.

83. Morris p. Fiorina, *Retrospective Voting in American National Elections* (Yale University Press, 1981).

84. CNN. "Exit Polls Election 2000." Accessed on October 23, 2006. at http://www.cnn.com/ELECTION/2000/results/index.epolls.html.

85. Gerald H. Kramer, "Short-Term Fluctuations in U.S. Voting Behavior, 1896–1964," *American Political Science Review* 65 (March 1971), pp. 131–143. See also Edward R. Tufte, "Determinants of the Outcomes of Midterm Congressional Elections," *American Political Science Review* 69 (September 1975), pp. 812–826; and Andrew E. Busch, *Horses in Midstream: U.S. Midterm Elections and Their Consequences* (University of Pittsburgh Press, 1999).

86. John R. Hibbing and John R. Alford, "The Educational Impact of Economic Conditions: Who Is Held Responsible?" *American Journal of Political Science* 25 (August 1981), pp. 423–439; and Morris P. Fiorina, "Who Is Held Responsible? Further Evidence on the Hibbing-Alford Thesis," *American Journal of Political Science* (February 1983), pp. 158–164.

87. Robert M. Stein, "Economic Voting for Governor and U.S. Senator: The Electoral Consequences of Federalism," *Journal of Politics* 52 (February 1990), pp. 29–53.

88. www.cnn.com/ELECTION/2004/pages/results/states/US/P/OO/epolls.O.html.

Chapter 9

1. United States Census Bureau, "Number of Elected Officials Exceeds Half Million—Almost All Are With Local Governments," press release, January 30, 1995.

2. United States Senate, at www.senate.gov/general/contact_information/senators_cfm.cfm.

3. See U.S. Term Limits, at www.termlimits.org.

4. In the 1992 and 1994 National Election Studies, approximately 78 percent of Americans favored term limits. Center for Political Studies, *1992 National Election Study and 1994 National Election Study* (University of Michigan, 1992, 1994).

5. *U.S. Term Limits Inc.* v. *Thornton,* 514 U.S. 799 (1995).

6. For an insightful examination of electoral rules, see Bernard Grofman and Arend Lijphart, eds., *Electoral Laws and Their Political Consequences* (Agathon Press, 1986).

7. National Archives and Records Administration, *Historical Election Results Electoral College Box Scores 1789–1996,* at September 25, 2006.

8. Arend Lijphart, "The Political Consequences of Electoral Laws, 1945-85," *American Political Science Review* 84 (June 1990), pp. 481–495. See also David M. Farrell, *Electoral Systems: A Comparative Introduction* (Macmillan, 2001).

9. www.fairvote.org/e_college/faithless.htm.

10. As noted, one of Gore's electors abstained, reducing his vote from 267 to 266; CNN, at www.cnn.com/2001/ALLPOLITICS/stories/01/06/electoral.vote/index.html.

11. Paul D. Schumaker and Burdett A. Loomis, *Choosing a President: The Electoral College and Beyond* (Seven Bridges Press, 2002), p. 60. See also George Rabinowitz and Stuart Elaine MacDonald, "The Power of the States in U.S. Presidential Elections," *American Political Science Review* 80 (March 1986), pp. 65–87; and Dany M. Adkison and Christopher Elliott, "The Electoral College: A Misunderstood Institution," *PS: Political Science and Politics* 30 (March 1997), pp. 77–80.

12. See, for example, David R. Mayhew, *Congress: The Electoral Connection* (Yale University Press, 1974); Richard F. Fenno Jr., *Home Style: House Members in Their Districts* (Little, Brown, 1978); and James E. Campbell, "The Return of Incumbents: The Nature of Incumbency Advantage," *Western Political Quarterly* 36 (September 1983), pp. 434–444.

13. Gary King and Andrew Gelman, "Systemic Consequences of Incumbency Advantage in U.S. House Elections," *American Journal of Political Science* 35 (February 1991), pp. 110–137.

14. Alan I. Abramowitz, "Economic Conditions, Presidential Popularity, and Voting Behavior in Midterm Congressional Elections," *Journal of Politics* 47 (February 1985), pp. 31–43. See also Gary C. Jacobson, *The Politics of Congressional Elections,* 5th ed. (Addison-Wesley, 2001), pp. 146–153.

15. See Edward R. Tufte, *Political Control of the Economy* (Princeton University Press, 1978); see also his "Determinants of the Outcomes of Midterm Congressional Elections," *American Political Science Review* 69 (September 1975), pp. 812–826. For a more recent discussion of the same subject, see Jacobson, *Politics of Congressional Elections*, pp. 123–178.

16. Alan I. Abramowitz and Jeffrey A. Segal, "Determinants of the Outcomes of U.S. Senate Elections," *Journal of Politics* 48 (1986), pp. 433–439.

17. This includes the postelection switch of Alabama Senator Richard Shelby to the Republican Party.

18. Campaign Tracker 2006. http://election.nationaljournal.com/2006/house, accessed October 2, 2006

19. Campaign Tracker 2006. http://election.nationaljournal.com/2006/senate, accessed October 2, 2006.

20. Linda L. Fowler and Robert D. McClure, *Political Ambition: Who Decides to Run for Congress* (Yale University Press, 1989); Herrnson, *Congressional Elections*, p. 45.

21. Kathleen Hall Jamieson, *Everything You Think You Know About Politics . . . and Why You're Wrong* (Basic Books, 2000), p. 38.

22. For a discussion of different explanations of the impact of incumbency, see Keith Krehbiel and John R. Wright, "The Incumbency Effect in Congressional Elections: A Test of Two Explanations," *American Journal of Political Science* 27 (February 1983), p. 140.

23. Harold W. Stanley and Richard G. Niemi, *Vital Statistics on American Politics 2005–2006* (CQ Press 2006), pp. 53–55.

24. Albert D. Cover, "One Good Term Deserves Another: The Advantages of Incumbency in Congressional Elections," *American Journal of Political Science* 21 (August 1977), pp. 523–542; Morris P. Fiorina, *Congress: Keystone of the Washington Establishment* (Yale University Press, 1978); and David Mayhew, *Congress: The Electoral Connection* (Yale University Press, 1974), pp. 52–53.

25. Mayhew, *Congress*, p. 61; Richard F. Fenno Jr., *Congressmen in Committees* (Little, Brown, 1973); and Steven S. Smith and Christopher J. Deering, *Committees in Congress*, 3d ed. (CQ Press, 1997).

26. "Financial Activity of Senate and House General Election Campaigns," Federal Election Commission at http://www.fec.gov/press/sen%5Fhse20pre.htm, accessed September 25, 2006.

27. Candice J. Nelson, "Spending in the 2000 Elections," in *Financing the 2000 Election*, David B. Magleby, ed. (Brookings Institution Press, 2002), pp. 28–30.

28. Jonathan S. Krasno, *Challengers, Competition, and Reelection: Comparing Senate and House Elections* (Yale University Press, 1994), p. 2.

29. Alan I. Abramowitz, "Explaining Senate Election Outcomes," *American Political Science Review* 82 (June 1988), pp. 385–403.

30. David B. Magleby, "The Importance of Outside Money in the 2002 Congressional Elections," in *The Last Hurrah? Soft Money and Issue Advocacy in the 2002 Congressional Elections*, David B. Magleby, ed. (Brookings Institution Press, 2004), p. 18.

31. Ted Barrett, John Mercurio and John Bisney, "Ryan Drops Out of Senate Race in Illinois," *CNN*, at www.cnn.com/2004/ALLPOLITICS/06/25/il.ryan/, accessed September 25, 2006.

32. David B. Magleby, "More Bang for the Buck: Campaign Spending in Small State U.S. Senate Elections," paper presented at the annual meeting of the Western Political Science Association, Salt Lake City, March 30–April 1, 1989.

33. Associated Press, "Edwards Actions Doing Talking Over Possible Presidential Run," *Associated Press State and Local Wire* for North Carolina, June 18, 2001; and Christopher Graff, "Vermont Governor Takes First Step Toward Presidential Campaign," *The Associated Press State & Local Wire* of Vermont, November 19, 2001.

34. Arthur Hadley, *Invisible Primary* (Prentice-Hall, 1976).

35. "State by State Summary 2004 Presidential Primaries, Caucuses, and Conventions," at www.thegreenpapers.com/P04/tally.phtml, accessed September 25, 2006.

36. Ibid.

37. "Republican Delegate Selection and Voter Eligibility," at www.thegreenpapers.com/P04/R-DSVE.phtml, accessed September 25, 2006.

38. The descriptions of these types of primaries are drawn from James W. Davis, *Presidential Primaries*, rev. ed. (Greenwood Press, 1984), chap. 3. See pp. 56–63 for specifics on each state (and Puerto Rico). This material is used with the permission of the publisher.

39. Paul T. David and James W. Caesar, *Proportional Representation in Presidential Nominating Politics* (University Press of Virginia, 1980), pp. 9–11.

40. See Rhodes Cook, *Race for the Presidency: Winning the 2004 Nomination* (CQ Press, 2004), p. 5. See also the Republican National Committee, at www.rnc.org.

41. Nelson W. Polsby and Aaron Wildavsky, *Presidential Elections: Strategies and Structures of American Politics*, 11th ed. (Rowman & Littlefield, 2004), p. 110.

42. The Green Papers, *The Green Papers, 2004 Presidential Primaries, Caucuses, and Conventions: New York Republican*, www.thegreenpapers.com/P04/NY-R.phtml.

43. Costas Panagopoulos, "Election Issues 2004 in Depth," *Campaigns & Elections,* May 2004, p. 48.

44. Jonathan Finer, "No Tea, but Democrats Get the Party Started," *The Washington Post*, July 29, 2003, p. A4.

45. National Association of Secretaries of State, at www.nass.org/issues.html#primaryplan, accessed September 25, 2006.

46. Federal Elections Commission, "2004 Presidential Primary Dates and Candidates Filing Deadlines for Ballot Access," May 26, 2004, at www.fec.gov.

47. David Redlawsk and Arthur Sanders, "Groups and Grassroots in the Iowa Caucuses," in *Outside Money in the 2000 Presidential Primaries and Congressional Elections*, David B. Magleby, ed., in *PS: Political Science and Politics* (June 2001), pp. 270; see also Iowa Caucus Project 2004, at www.iowacaucus.org/.

48. Blake Morrison, "Dean Scream Gaining Cult-Like Status on Web," *USA TODAY*, January 22, 2004, p. 4A.

49. "A Useful Piece of Scream Therapy," *The Economist*, February 14, 2004, United States Section.

50. The viewership of conventions has declined as the amount of time devoted to conventions dropped. In 1988, Democrats averaged 27.1 million viewers and Republicans 24.5 million. By 1996, viewership for the Democrats was 18 million viewers on average and for the Republicans, 16.6 million. See John Carmody, "The TV Column," *The Washington Post*, September 2, 1996, p. D4. Viewership figures improved somewhat in 2000: Democrats averaged 20.6 million viewers and Republicans 19.2 million. See Don Aucoin, "Democrats Hold TV Ratings Edge," *Boston Globe*, August 19, 2000, p. F3.

51. Barry Goldwater, Speech to the Republican National Convention accepting the Republican nomination for president, July 16, 1964, at www.washingtonpost.com/wp-srv/politics/daily/may98/goldwaterspeech.htm.

52. Acceptance Speech at the 1980 Convention, July 17, 1980, at http://www.nationalcenter.org/ReaganConvention1980.html Accessed September 25, 2006.

53. Text of John Kerry's speech to the Democratic National Convention accepting the Democratic nomination for president, July 29, 2004, at www.washingtonpost.com/ac2/wp-dyn/A25678-2004Jul29?language=printer.

54. Jeff Fishel, *Presidents and Promises* (CQ Press, 1984), pp. 26–28.

55. See White House, Education Reform: No Child Left Behind Act, at www.whitehouse.gov/infocus/education.

56. Adam Nagourney, "Kerry Camp Sees Edwards Helping with Rural Vote," *The New York Times*, July 9, 2004, p. 1.

57. John M. Glionna, "The Race to the White House; Nader Bid for Spot on Oregon's Ballot Fails; The State was the First Stop in the Populist Candidate's Quest to Qualify in all 50 States," *Los Angeles Times*, April 6, 2004, p. 14.

58. Arthur Kane, "Reform Party Endorsement Boosts Nader: The Liberal Activist is Now Eligible to Ease onto the Presidential Ballot in Seven States, Including Colorado," *The Denver Post,* May 13, 2004, p. A1.

59. Election Reform.org, at www.ballot-access.org.

60. Time, "Burden of Proof," August 9, 2000; at http://www.time.com/time/magazine/article/0,9171,641158,00.html, accessed September 25, 2006.

61. CNN, The Nader Factor, at www.cnn.com/ELECTION/2004/special/president/candidates/nader.ballot.html, accessed September 25, 2006.

62. Charles Babington, "Staggering Sum-Raising," *The Washington Post*, June 19, 2004, p. A6.

63. Lisa Getter, "GOP Can't Beat '3rd Party' Groups, So It Forms Them," *Los Angeles Times*, June 6, 2004, p. A20.

64. Stephen Koff, "VP Debate to Have Free-Flowing Exchange," *Plain Dealer* (Cleveland, Ohio), June 18, 2004, p. A21.

65. Sidney Kraus, *The Great Debates: Kennedy vs. Nixon, 1960* (Indiana University Press, 1962). See also Myles Martel, *Political Campaign Debates* (Longman, 1983).

66. "Televised Debate History, 1960–1996," at www.museum.tv/debateweb/html/history/1976/video.htm.

67. Commission on Presidential Debates, at www.debates.org/pages/news_040617_p.html.

68. *The New York Times*, "The Great Ad Wars of 2004," November 11, 2004, at www.polisci.wisc.edu/tvadvertising/Press_Clippings/Press_Clipping_PDFs/110104%20NYTIMES_AD_GRAPHIC.pdf.

69. University of Wisconsin-Madison and the Brennan Center for Justice at NYU School of Law, "Political Advertising Nearly Tripled in 2000 With Half-a-Million More TV Ads," press release, March 14, 2001.

70. Mark Memmot and Jim Drinkard, "Election Ad Battle Smashes Record in 2004," *USA Today*, November 26, 2004, p. 6A.

71. Nielsen Monitor-Plus and the University of Wisconsin Advertising Project, "Presidential TV Advertising battle Narrows to Just Ten Battleground States," press release, October 12, 2004.

72. Robert S. Erikson, "Economic Conditions and the Presidential Vote," *American Political Science Review* 83 (June 1989), pp. 567–575. Class-based voting has also become more important. See Robert S. Erikson, Thomas O. Lancaster, and David W. Romers, "Group Components of the Presidential Vote, 1952–1984," *Journal of Politics* 51 (May 1989), pp. 337–346.

73. John C. Fortier and Norman J. Ornstein, "The Absentee Ballot and the Secret Ballot: Challenges for Election Reform," *University of Michigan Journal of Law Reform* 36 (Spring 2003), pp. 483–517.

74. Jerrold G. Rusk, "The Effect of the Australian Ballot Reform on Split Ticket Voting: 1876–1908," *The American Political Science Review* 64 (December 1970), pp. 1220–1238.

75. John C. Fortier and Norman J. Ornstein, "The Absentee Ballot and the Secret Ballot: Challenges for Election Reform," *University of Michigan Journal of Law Reform* 36 (Spring 2003), pp. 483–517.

76. Ibid.

77. L. E. Fredman, "The Introduction of the Australian Ballot in the United States," *Australian Journal of Politics and History* 13 (June 1967), pp. 204–220.

78. Lewis L. Gould, *Grand Old Party*, (Random House, 2003), p. 236.

79. David B. Magleby and Candice J. Nelson, *The Money Chase: Congressional Campaign Finance Reform* (Brookings Institution Press, 1990), pp. 13–14.

80. Lewis L. Gould, *Grand Old Party: A History of the Republicans* (Random House 2003), pp. 389–391, and Jules Witcover, *Party of the People: A History of the Democrats* (Random House 2003), pp. 589–590.

81. Anthony Corrado, "Money and Politics: A History of Campaign Finance Law," *Campaign Finance Reform: A Sourcebook* (Brookings Institution Press, 1997), p. 32.

82. Ibid.

83. *Buckley* v. *Valeo*, 424 U.S. 1 (1976).

84. See Herbert E. Alexander and Monica Bauer, *Financing the 1988 Election* (Westview Press, 1991); Frank J. Sorauf, *Inside Campaign Finance: Myths and Realities* (Yale University Press, 1992); and Herbert E. Alexander, *Financing Politics: Money, Elections, and Political Reform* (CQ Press, 1992).

85. Anthony Corrado, Thomas E. Mann, Daniel R. Ortiz, and Trevor Potter, eds., *The New Campaign Finance Sourcebook* (Brookings Institution Press, 2005).

86. Elizabeth Drew, The Corruption of American Politics: What Went Wrong and Why (Carol Publishing Group, 1999), pp. 7–8.

87. See Senate Committee on Governmental Affairs, "1997 Special Investigation in Connection with the 1996 Federal Election Campaigns," www.senate.gov/~gov_affairs/sireport.htm.

88. David B. Magleby, *Dictum Without Data: The Myth of Issue Advocacy and Party Building* (Center for the Study of Elections and Democracy, Brigham Young University, 2001), pp. 1, 12; David B. Magleby, ed., *Outside Money: Soft Money and Issue Advocacy in the 1998 Congressional Elections* (Rowman & Littlefield, 2000), p. 17; David B. Magleby and J. Quin Monson, eds., *The Last Hurrah? Soft Money and Issue Advocacy in the 2002 Congressional Elections* (Brookings Institution Press, 2004), p. 1; and David B. Magleby, ed., *The Other Campaign: Soft Money and Issue Advocacy in the 2000 Congressional Elections.* (Rowman & Littlefield, 2003), p. 1.

89. David B. Magleby, ed. *Financing the 2004 Election* (The Brookings Institution, 2006) p. 103.

90. *McConnell* v. *Federal Election Commission*, 540 U.S. 93 (2003).

91. Corrado, Mann, Ortiz, and Potter, *The New Campaign Finance Sourcebook*, p. 79.

92. Beth Donovan, "Parties Turned Soft Money Law into Hard and Fast Spending," *Congressional Quarterly Weekly*, May 15, 1993, pp. 1196–1197; David E. Rosenbaum, "In Political Money Game, the Year of Big Loopholes," *The New York Times*, December 26, 1996, p. A1; and "Party Fundraising Escalates," at www.fec.gov.

93. David B. Magleby, ed. *The Last Hurrah* (Brookings Institution Press, 2004), pp. 44–45.

94. Ibid., p. 46.

95. *McConnell* v. *Federal Election Commission*, 540 U.S. 93 (2003).

96. *Buckley* v. *Valeo*, 424 U.S. 1 (1976), footnote 52.

97. See Joseph A. Pika, "Campaign Spending and Activity in the 2000 Delaware U.S. Senate Race," in *Election Advocacy: Soft Money and Issue Advocacy in the 2000 Congressional Elections*, David B. Magleby, ed. (Center for the Study of Elections and Democracy, Brigham Young University, 2001), pp. 51–61.

98. John C. Green and Nathan S. Bigelow, "The 2000 Presidential Nominations: The Costs of Innovation," in *Financing the 2000 Election*, David B. Magleby, ed. (Brookings Institution Press, 2002), p. 68.

99. Magleby, *Dictum Without Data*, p. 12.

100. *Bipartisan Campaign Reform Act of 2002*, 107th Cong., 1st sess., H.R. 2356.

101. David B. Magleby, "Change and Continuity in the Financing of Federal Elections," in *Financing the 2004 Elections*, David B. Magleby, Anthony J. Corrado, and Kelly D. Patterson, eds. (Brookings Institution Press, 2006), p. 15.

102. Corrado, Mann, Ortiz, and Potter, *The New Campaign Finance Sourcebook*, pp. 74–76.

103. David B. Magleby, ed. *Dancing Without Partners Monograph*, at http://csed.byu.edu/Publications/DancingwithoutPartners.pdf, p. 53. accessed September 25, 2006.

104. Kate Zernike, "Kerry Pressing Swift Boat Case Long After Loss," *New York Times*, May 28, 2006, p. A1.

105. Federal Election Commission, "Disclosure Data Base: PAS200.ZIP," at www.fec.gov. See also David B. Magleby and Jason Richard Beal, "Independent Expenditures and Internal Communications," in *The Other Campaign*, David B. Magleby, ed. (Rowman & Littlefield, 2003), p. 83.

106. *Colorado Republican Federal Campaign Committee* v. *Federal Election Commission*, 518 U.S. 604 (1996).

107. BCRA does allow candidates to pay themselves out of their campaign funds, something that helps less affluent candidates run. But given the high cost of campaigns, such a strategy is often not going to be helpful to winning election.

108. Federal Election Commission, "2000–2001 Financial Activity of Senate and House General Election Campaigns," at www.fec.gov; Federal Election Commission, "1999–2000 Financial Activity of Senate and House General Election Campaigns," at www.fec.gov.

109. U.S. Census Bureau, *Statistical Abstract of the United States: 2006* (Government Printing Office, 2006), p. 267.

110. Morton M. Kondracke, "McCain to Lead New Reform Fight for Free TV Time," *Roll Call*, May 30, 2002, at www.rollcall.com/pages/columns/kondracke/00/2002/kond0530.html.

111. Federal Elections Commission, at herndon1.sdrdc.com/fecimg/srssea.html. See also FEC, "Congressional Candidates Spend $1.16 Billion During 2003–2004," press release, June 9, 2005, at www.fec.gov/press/press2005/20050609candidate/20050609candidate.html.

112. Rick Hampson, "Former Banker Was Big Spender," *USA Today*, November 9, 2000, p. A9.

113. Charlie Cook, "Win, Lose, or Draw," at www.cookpolitical.com/column/2004/110805.php, accessed November 8, 2005.

114. See Todd Donovan and Shawn Bowler, *Reforming the Republic: Democratic Institutions for a New America* (Prentice Hall, 2004).

115. Curtis B. Gans, Director, Committee for the Study of the American Electorate, facsimile to author, September 22, 2004.

116. The President's Commission for a National Agenda for the Eighties, *A National Agenda for the Eighties* (U.S. Government Printing Office, 1980), p. 97, proposed holding four presidential primaries, scheduled about one month apart.

117. Nelson W. Polsby, *Consequences of Party Reform* (Oxford University Press, 1983), p. 118.

118. Thomas E. Cronin and Robert Loevy, "The Case for a National Primary Convention Plan," *Public Opinion*, December 1982–January 1983, pp. 50–53.

119. Barbara Norrander and Greg W. Smith, "Type of Contest, Candidate Strategy, and Turnout in Presidential Primaries," *American Politics Quarterly* 13 (January 1985), p. 28.

120. Neal R. Peirce and Lawrence Longley, *The Electoral College Primer 2000* (Yale University Press, 1999).

121. Nelson W. Polsby and Aaron B. Wildavsky, *Presidential Elections: Contemporary Strategies of American Politics*, 11th ed. (Rowman & Littlefield, 2004).

Chapter 10

1. Neil Sheehan, Fox Butterfield, Hedrick Smith, and E.W. Kenworthy, *The Pentagon Papers As Published by the New York Times: The Secret History of the Vietnam War* (Times Books, 1971).

2. Pete Yost, "Rove Testifies Again in CIA Leak Case," *Associated Press*, April 26, 2006; see also David Johnston and Jim Rutenberg, "No Rove Charges in Testimony over C.I.A. Leak Case," *New York Times*, June 14, 2006, p. A1.

3. Joseph Wilson, "What I Didn't Find in Africa," *New York Times*, July 6, 2003, A9.

4. Robert D. Novak, "Mission to Niger," *Washington Post*, July 14, 2003, p. A21.

5. Michael Isikoff, "Matt Cooper's Source: What Karl Rove Told *Time* Magazine's Reporter," *Newsweek* (July 18, 2005) p. 44.

6. Michael Isikoff, "The Rove Factor? *Time* Magazine Talked to Bush's Guru for Plame Story," *Newsweek* (July 11, 2005) p. 54.

7. Robert D. Novak, "Armitage's Liak," *The Washington Post*, September 14, 2006, p. A21; see also, Jeffrey Smith, "Novak Accuses Plame Source of Distortion," *The Washington Post*, September 14, 2006, p. A12.

8. William Rivers, *The Other Government* (Universe Books, 1982); Douglas Cater, *The Fourth Branch of Government* (Houghton Mifflin, 1959); Dom

Bonafede, "The Washington Press: An Interpreter or a Participant in Policy Making?" *National Journal*, April 24, 1982, pp. 716–721; Michael Ledeen, "Learning to Say 'No' to the Press," *Public Interest* 73 (Fall 1983), p. 113.

9. Leslie G. Moeller, "The Big Four: Mass Media Actualities and Expectations," in *Beyond Media: New Approaches to Mass Communication*, Richard W. Budd and Brent D. Ruben, eds. (Transaction Books, 1988), p. 15.

10. Pew Research Center for the People and the Press, "Far More Voters Believe Election Outcome Matters," questionnaire, http://people-press.org/reports/print.php3?PageID=802, May 9, 2006. One service that e-mails customized news and reminders to subscribers is infobeat.com.

11. See Doris A. Graber, "Say It with Pictures: The Impact of Audiovisual News on Public Opinion Formation," paper presented at the annual meeting of the Midwest Political Science Association, Chicago, April 1987; and Benjamin I. Page, Robert Y. Shapiro, and Glenn R. Dempsey, "What Moves Public Opinion?" *American Political Science Review* 76 (March 1987), pp. 23–43.

12. U.S. Bureau of the Census, *Statistical Abstract of the United States, 2006* (Government Printing Office, 2006), pp. 736–737.

13. Journalism.org, "The State of the News Media 2006," at www.stateofthenewsmedia.org/2006/narrative_networktv_audience.asp, May 2, 2006.

14. Ibid.

15. David B. Magleby and J. Quin Monson, eds., *The Last Hurrah?* (Brookings Institution Press, 2004); David B. Magleby, ed., *The Other Campaign* (Rowman & Littlefield, 2003); David B. Magleby, ed., *Outside Money* (Rowman & Littlefield, 2000); David B. Magleby, J. Quin Monson, Kelly D. Patterson, *Dancing Without Partners: How Candidates, Parties, and Interest Groups Interact in the Presidential Campaign* (Rowman & Littlefield, 2007); David B. Magleby, J. Quin Monson, and Kelly D. Patterson, *Electing Congress: New Rules for an Old Game* (Prentice Hall, 2006).

16. David B. Magleby, ed., *Dictum Without Data: The Myth of Issue Advocacy and Party Building* (Center for the Study of Elections and Democracy, 2000); David B. Magleby, "Party and Interest Group Electioneering in Federal Elections," in *Inside the Campaign Finance Battle*, Anthony Corrado, Thomas E. Mann, and Trevor Potter, eds. (Brookings Institution Press, 2003), p. 147.

17. Magleby and Monson, eds., *The Last Hurrah?*; Magleby, ed., *The Other Campaign;* Magleby, ed., *Outside Money.*

18. David D. Kirkpatrick, "One Nominee, Two Very Different Portraits in a New Round of Ads," *New York Times*, November 18, 2005, p. A26; Thomas B. Edsall, "Vacancy Starts a Fundraising Race: Court Nomination Battle Could Rival 2004 Election's Totals," *Washington Post*, July 5, 2005, p. A4.

19. Journalism.org, "Local TV," at www.stateofthenewsmedia.org/narrative_loyalty_content analysis.asp?cat=2&media=6, March 15, 2004. See also, Marc Fisher, "TV Stations Offer a Clear Picture of Indifference," *The Washington Post*, September 26, 2000, p. B1.

20. Alliance for Better Campaigns, *Political Standard* 4 (March 2001), p. 6.

21. www.localnewsarchive.org/pdf/LocalTV2002.pdf.

22. The Lear Center, Local News Archive, "Final Report: Local TV Coverage of the 2004 Elections," at www.localnewsarchive.org/pdf/LCLNAFinal2004.pdf, May 2, 2006.

23. David B. Magleby, "Direct Legislation in the American States," in *Referendums Around the World: The Growing Use of Direct Democracy*, David Butler and Austin Ranney, eds. (AEI Press, 1994), pp. 218–257.

24. *Statistical Abstract of the United States, 2006*, p. 737

25. Leonard Wiener, "Radio's Future Shock," *U.S. News & World Report*, December 2, 2002, p. 40.

26. Robert E. Crew, Terri Susan Fine, and Susan A. MacManus, "The 2004 Florida U.S. Presidential Race," in *Dancing Without Partners: How Candidates, Parties, and Interest Groups Interact in the Presidential Campaign*, David B. Magleby, J. Quin Monson, Kelly D. Patterson, eds. (Rowman & Littlefield, 2007) pp. 70–71.

27. National Public Radio at www.npr.org/about/, May 10, 2006.

28. Tim Feran, "Airing the Issues; Chairman of NPR Board Considers All Things Facing His Organization," *Columbus Dispatch*, January 26, 2006, p. B1.

29. *Statistical Abstract of the United States, 2006*, p. 738.

30. Newspaper Association of America, "Readership Statistics," at www.naa.org/CirculationPages/Circulation-Statistics-and-Trends/Readership-Statistics.aspx, May 2, 2006.

31. Audit Bureau of Circulations, at http://www.accessabc.com/reader/top150.htm.

32. Ibid.

33. Annys Shin, "Newspaper Circulation Continues to Decline," *Washington Post*, May 3, 2005, p. E3. Rachel Smolkin, "Reversing the Slide," *American Journalism Review*, April/May 2005, at www.ajr.org/Article.asp?id=3853, June 8, 2006.

34. Arthur L. Norberg and Judy E. O'Neill, *Transforming Computer Technology: Information Processing for the Pentagon, 1962–1986* (Johns Hopkins University Press, 1996).

35. John Markoff, "In Silicon Valley, a Debate Over the Size of the Web," *The New York Times*, August 15, 2005, p. C6.

36. VeriSign, *The Domain Name Industry Brief* Vol. 2, No. 4, November 2005, at www.verisign.com/static/036316.pdf, May 3, 2006.

37. John B. Horrigan, "For Many Home Broadband Users, the Internet is a Primary News Source," Pew Internet & American Life Project, March 22, 2006, at www.pewinternet.org/pdfs/PIP_News.and.Broadband.pdf; May 3, 2006.

38. Pew Internet & American Life Project, *Teens and Technology*, July 27, 2005, at www.pewinternet.org/pdfs/PIP_Teens_Tech_July2005web.pdf, May 12, 2006.

39. Henry J. Kaiser Foundation, *Generation M: Media in the Lives of 8-18 Year-olds*, at www.kff.org/entmedia/upload/Executive-Summary-Generation-M-Media-in-the-Lives-of-8-18-Year-olds.pdf, May 8, 2006.

40. "Inside the 2004 Campaign Tool Chest: Blogs and Online Voting," *Los Angeles Times*, January 5, 2004, p. A10.

41. Mark Singer, "Running on Instinct. Howard Dean's Critics Say He Is Winging It. Can That Get Him to the White House?" *New Yorker*, January 12, 2004, p. 43.

42. Cass Sunstein, *Republic.com* (Princeton University Press, 2002), pp. 73–75.

43. Pew Research Center for the People and the Press, "Web News Takes Off," press release, June 8, 1998, p. 1; Pew Research Center for the People and the Press, Survey Reports, "Public's News

Habits Little Changed by September 11," June 9, 2002. See people-press.org/reports.

44. James Fallows, *Breaking the News: How the Media Undermine American Democracy* (Pantheon Books, 1996), p. 3.

45. Pew Research Center for the People and Press, Survey Reports, "Bottom-Line Pressures Now Hurting Coverage, Say Journalists" May 23, 2004. See http://people-press.org/reports/display.php3?PageID=826.

46. Howard Kurtz, "Jayson Blair, Continued; With a Story of Lies, The Fallen Writer Hopes to Turn a Page," *The Washington Post*, March 7, 2004, p. D01.

47. Jacques Steinburg, "Editor of USA Today Resigns; Cites Failure Over Fabrications," *The New York Times*, April 21, 2004, p. A1.

48. See Robert A. Rutland, *Newsmongers: Journalism in the Life of the Nation, 1690–1972* (Dial Press, 1973).

49. David Paul Nord, *Communities of Journalism* (University of Illinois Press, 2001), pp. 80–89.

50. Quoted in Frank Luther Mott, *American Journalism*, 3d ed. (Macmillan, 1962), p. 412.

51. During the 1930s, more than 1,000 speeches were made by members of Congress on one network alone. See Edward W. Chester, *Radio, Television, and American Politics* (Sheed & Ward, 1969), p. 62.

52. Frances Perkins, quoted in James MacGregor Burns, *Roosevelt: The Lion and the Fox* (Harcourt, 1956), p. 205.

53. Fred Emery, *Watergate: The Corruption of American Politics and the Fall of Richard Nixon* (Touchstone, 1995).

54. Bob Woodward and Carl Bernstein, *All the President's Men,* (Simon & Schuster, 1994).

55. Mark Felt, John D. O'Connor, and W. Mark Felt, *A G-Man's Life: The FBI, Being 'Deep Throat' and The Struggle for Honor in Washington* (Public Affairs Press, 2006).

56. "Media Giants," at www.pbs.org/wgbh/pages/frontline/shows/cool/giants, September 5, 2006.

57. Ibid.

58. Gannett Corporation, "Company Profile," at www.gannett.com/about/company_profile.htm, May 4, 2006.

59. "Tribune at a Glance," at http://www.tribune.com/media/pdf/glance_06.pdf, May 6, 2006.

60. See Robert W. McChesney, "The New Global Media," *The Nation* 269, no. 18, pp. 11–15.

61. Katharine Q. Seelye, "Players Big and Small Are Sifting Through Pieces of Knight Ridder," *The New York Times*, March 27, 2006, p. C1.

62. Seth Schiesel, "FCC Rules on Ownership Under Review," *The New York Times*, April 3, 2002, p. C1.

63. Paul Davidson, "Spending Bill Settles Two Key Issues," *USA Today*, January 23, 2004, p. B3.

64. Stephen Labaton, "Court Orders FCC to Rethink New Rules on Growth of Media," *The New York Times*, June 25, 2004, p. 1.

65. Annys Shin, "Limits on Media Ownership Stand; Supreme Court Declines to Hear Appeal," *Washington Post*, June 14, 2005, p. D1

66. Shanto Iyengar and Donald R. Kinder, *News That Matters* (University of Chicago Press, 1987).

67. Federal Communications Commission, "FCC Issues 12th Annual Report to Congress on Video Competition," press release, February 10, 2006, at hraunfoss.fcc.gov/edocs_public/attachmatch/DOC-263763A1.pdf, May 11, 2006.

68. Donna Britt, "Janet's 'Reveal' Lays Bare an Insidious Trend," *The Washington Post*, February 4, 2004, p. B1.

69. www.pewinternet.org/reports/chart/asp?, April 13, 2004.

70. Harvey G. Zeidenstein, "News Media Perception of White House News Management," *Presidential Studies Quarterly* 24 (Summer 1984), pp. 391–398.

71. See, for example, Jack Dennis, "Preadult Learning of Political Independence: Media and Family Communications Effects," *Communication Research* 13 (July 1987), pp. 401–433; and Olive Stevens, *Children Talking Politics* (Robertson, 1982).

72. Elihu Katz and Paul Lazarsfeld, *Personal Influence: The Part Played by People in the Flow of Mass Communications* (Free Press, 1955).

73. See Angus Campbell, Philip E. Converse, Warren E. Miller, and Donald E. Stokes, *The American Voter* (Wiley, 1960).

74. Pew Research Center for the People and Press, Survey Reports, "News Audiences Increasingly Politicized" June 8, 2004, at http://people-press.org/reports/display.php3?ReportID=215.

75. Paul Lazarsfeld, Bernard Berelson, and Hazel Gaudet, *The People's Choice: How the Voter Makes Up His Mind in a Presidential Campaign*, 3d ed. (Columbia University Press, 1968); Bernard Berelson, Paul Lazarsfeld, and William McPhee, *Voting: A Study of Opinion Formation in a Presidential Campaign* (University of Chicago Press, 1954).

76. Pew Research Center for the People and the Press, "Scandal Reporting Faulted for Bias and Inaccuracy: Popular Policies and Unpopular Press Lift Clinton Ratings," press release, February 6, 1998, p. 6.

77. Gallup Organization, "Americans Agree With House Contention That Clinton Committed Perjury and Obstructed Justice," at http://www.galluppoll.com/content/?ci=4099&pg=1, September 6, 2006.

78. Stuart Oskamp, ed., *Television as a Social Issue* (Sage, 1988); James W. Carey, ed., *Media, Myths, and Narratives: Television and the Press* (Sage, 1988).

79. Times Mirror Center for the People and the Press, "Times Mirror News Interest Index," press releases, January 16 and February 28, 1992.

80. Tides Center, "Internet and American Life," at www.pewinternet.org/reports/reports.asp, April 13, 2004.

81. Rush Limbaugh, *See, I Told You So* (Pocket Books, 1993), p. 326.

82. Michael Parenti, *Inventing Reality: The Politics of the Mass Media* (St. Martin's Press, 1986), p. 35.

83. Rick Lyman, "Multimedia Deal: The History; 2 Commanding Publishers, 2 Powerful Empires," *The New York Times*, March 14, 2000, p. C16.

84. David Broder, "Beware of the 'Insider' Syndrome: Why Newsmakers and News Reporters Shouldn't Get Too Cozy," *The Washington Post*, December 4, 1988, p. A21; see also Broder, "Thin-Skinned Journalists," *The Washington Post*, January 11, 1989, p. A21.

85. See Nelson Polsby, *Consequences of Party Reform* (Oxford University Press, 1983), pp. 142–146. See also Stanley Rothman and S. Robert Lichter, "Media and Business Elites: Two Classes in Conflict!" *Public Interest* 69 (Fall 1982), pp. 119–125.

86. Bernard Goldberg, *Bias: A CBS Insider Exposes How the Media Distort the News* (Regnery Publishing, Inc., 2002).

87. Eric Alterman, *What Liberal Media? The Truth About Bias and the News* (Basic Books, 2003).

88. Daniel p. Moynihan, "The Presidency and the Press," *Commentary* 51 (March 1971), p. 43.

89. S. Robert Lichter, Stanley Rothman, and Linda S. Lichter, *The Media Elite* (Adler & Adler, 1986).

90. Larry J. Sabato, *Feeding Frenzy: How Attack Journalism Has Transformed American Politics* (Free Press, 1991).

91. See Thomas Patterson, *Out of Order* (Knopf, 1993); Paul Weaver, *News and the Culture of Lying* (Free Press, 1993); and Anthony Munro, "Yet Another Conspiracy Theory," *Columbia Journalism Review* 33 (November 1994), p. 71.

92. Maxwell McCombs and Donald Shaw, "The Agenda-setting Function of Mass Media," *Public Opinion Quarterly* 36 (1972), pp. 176–185.

93. Shanto Iyengar, Mark D. Peters, and Donald R. Kinder, "Experimental Demonstrations of the 'Not-So-Minimal' Consequences of Television News Programs," *American Political Science Review* 76 (December 1982), pp. 848–858.

94. Ibid.; Maxwell E. McCombs and Donald L. Shaw, "The Agenda-Setting Function of the Mass Media," *Public Opinion Quarterly* 36 (1972), pp. 176–187; Maxwell E. McCombs and Sheldon Gilbert, "News Influence on Our Pictures of the World," in *Perspectives on Media Effects*, Jennings Bryant and Dolf Gillman, eds. (Erlbaum, 1986), pp. 1–15; and Iyengar and Kinder, *News That Matters*.

95. Quoted in Michael J. Robinson and Margaret A. Sheehan, *Over the Wire and on TV: CBS and UPI in Campaign '80* (Russell Sage Foundation, 1983), p. xiii.

96. ABC News, at abcnews.go.com/sections/us/DailyNews/WTC_MAIN010914.html.

97. David B. Magleby, *Direct Legislation: Voting on Ballot Propositions in the United States* (Johns Hopkins University Press, 1984).

98. CNN, "Election Results: Exit Poll," at www.cnn.com/ELECTION/2004/pages/results/states/US/P/00/epolls.0.html, May 4, 2006.

99. Randal C. Archibold, "Edwards Tries Personal Touch to Gain in Iowa," *The New York Times*, December 3, 2003, p. A29; and Kathy Kiely, "Clark Catching On With Voters as Contests Near," *USA Today*, January 9, 2004, p. 4A.

100. Maureen Dowd, "Whence the Wince?" *The New York Times*, March 11, 2004, p. A29.

101. Larry J. Sabato, "Gerald Ford's 'Free Poland' Gaffe—1976," *The Washington Post*, at www.washingtonpost.com/wp-srv/politics/special/clinton/frenzy/ford.htm, May 9, 2006.

102. Dana Milbank, "Steak Raises Stakes for Kerry in Philly," *The Washington Post*, August 13, 2003, p. A3.

103. Larry J. Sabato, "George Romney's 'Brainwashing'—1967," *The Washington Post*, at www.washingtonpost.com/wp-srv/politics/special/clinton/frenzy/romney.htm, May 9, 2006.

104. opensecrets.org, "Swift Boat Veterans for Truth, 2004 Election Cycle," at www.opensecrets.org/527s/527events.asp?orgid=61, May 9, 2006.

105. David B. Magleby, J. Quin Monson, and Kelly D. Patterson, *Dancing Without Partners: How Parties, Candidates, and Interest Groups Interact in the 2004 Presidential Campaign* (Rowman & Littlefield, 2007), pp. 24–25.

106. Mike Allen, "Ship Carrying Bush Delayed Return," *The Washington Post*, May 8, 2003, p. A29.

107. Paul T. David, Ralph M. Goldman, and Richard C. Bain, *The Politics of the National Party Conventions* (Brookings Institution Press, 1960), pp. 300–301.

108. Richard Davis, *The Press and American Politics: The New Mediator*, 2d ed. (Prentice Hall, 1996), p. 279.

109. Frank I. Lutz, *Candidates, Consultants, and Campaigns* (Blackwell, 1988), chap. 7.

110. www.pewinternet.org/reports/chart.asp?, April 13, 2004.

111. Larry J. Sabato, *The Rise of Political Consultants* (Basic Books, 1981).

112. See Sabato, *Rise of Political Consultants*; James David Barber, *The Pulse of Politics: Electing Presidents in the Media Age* (Norton, 1980); and Fred Barnes, "The Myth of Political Consultants," *New Republic*, June 16, 1986, p. 16.

113. Quoted in Sabato, *Rise of Political Consultants*, p. 144.

114. Alliance for Better Campaigns, "Lawmakers Unveil Free Air Time Proposal," press release, June 19, 2002, at www.campaignlegalcenter.org/press-145.html, May 12, 2006.

115. John R. Zaller, *The Nature and Origins of Mass Opinion* (Cambridge University Press, 1992).

116. Shanto Iyengar and Donald R. Kinder, *News that Matters: Television and American Opinion* (University of Chicago Press, 1987), p. 2.

117. Thomas E. Patterson, *The Mass Media Election: How Americans Choose Their President* (Praeger, 1980), chap. 12.

118. John H. Aldrich, *Before the Convention* (University of Chicago Press, 1980), p. 65. See also Patterson, *Mass Media Election*.

119. John Foley et al., *Nominating a President: The Process and the Press* (Praeger, 1980), p. 39. For the press's treatment of incumbents, see James Glen Stovall, "Incumbency and News Coverage of the 1980 Presidential Election Campaign," *Western Political Quarterly* 37 (December 1984), p. 621.

120. Priscilla Southwell, "Voter Turnout in the 1986 Congressional Elections: The Media as Demobilizer?" *American Politics Quarterly* 19 (January 1991), pp. 96–108.

121. William Glaberson, "A New Press Role: Solving Problems," *The New York Times*, October 3, 1994, p. D6.

122. Patterson, *Mass Media Election*, pp. 115–117.

123. Raymond Wolfinger and Peter Linguiti, "Tuning In and Tuning Out," *Public Opinion* 4 (February–March 1981), pp. 56–60.

124. Marvin Kalb, "Financial Pressure Doomed Networks on Election Night," *Deseret News*, December 3, 2000, p. AA7.

125. Michael Traugott, Benjamin Highton, and Henry E. Brady, *A Review of Recent Controversies Concerning the 2004 Presidential Election Exit Polls*, March 10, 2005 at http://elections.ssrc.org/research/ExitPollReport031005.pdf. See also Michael Traugott, "The Accuracy of the National Preelection Polls in the 2004 Presidential Election," *Public Opinion Quarterly*, 69 (Special Issue 2005) pp. 642–654.

126. Lewis Wolfson, *The Untapped Power of the Press* (Praeger, 1985), p. 79.

127. Lloyd Cutler, "Foreign Policy on Deadline," *Foreign Policy* 56 (Fall 1984), p. 114.

128. Michael B. Grossman and Martha Joynt Kumar, *Portraying the President* (Johns Hopkins University Press, 1981), pp. 255–263; and Fredric T. Smoller, *The Six o'Clock Presidency: A Theory of Presidential Press Relations in the Age of Television* (Praeger, 1990), pp. 31–49.

129. Stephen Hess, *Live From Capitol Hill!* (Brookings Institution, 1991), pp. 62–76; Timothy E. Cook, *Making Laws and Making News* (Brookings Institution, 1989), pp. 81–86.

130. Susan Heilmann Miller, "News Coverage of Congress: The Search for the Ultimate Spokesperson," *Journalism Quarterly* 54 (Autumn 1977), pp. 459–465.

131. See Stephen Hess, *Live from Capitol Hill: Studies of Congress and the Media* (Brookings Institution Press, 1991), pp. 102–110.

132. Richard Davis, "Whither the Congress and the Supreme Court? The Television News Portrayal of American National Government," *Television Quarterly* 22 (1987), pp. 55–63.

133. For a discussion of the Supreme Court and public opinion, see Thomas R. Marshall, *Public Opinion and the Supreme Court* (Unwin Hyman, 1989); and Gregory Caldiera, "Neither the Purse nor the Sword: Dynamics of Public Confidence in the Supreme Court," *American Political Science Review* 80 (December 1986), pp. 1209–1228.

134. For a discussion of the relationship between the Supreme Court and the press, see Richard Davis, "Lifting the Shroud: News Media Portrayal of the U.S. Supreme Court," *Communications and the Law* 9 (October 1987), pp. 43–58; and Elliot E. Slotnick, "Media Coverage of Supreme Court Decision Making: Problems and Prospects," *Judicature* (October–November 1991), pp. 128–142.

135. Todd S. Purdum, "TV Political News in California Is Shrinking, Study Confirms," *The New York Times*, January, 13, 1999, p. A11.

136. Times Mirror Center, "Campaign '92," *Times Mirror*, January 16, 1992.

137. Quoted in Herbert Schmertz, "The Making of the Presidency," *Presidential Studies Quarterly* 16 (Winter 1986), p. 25.

Chapter 11

1. Charles Warren, *The Making of the Constitution* (Little, Brown, 1928), p. 195.

2. Richard F. Fenno Jr., *Home Style: House Members in Their Districts* (Little, Brown, 1978), p. 168.

3. *Bush v. Vera*, 517 U.S. 952 (1996).

4. See David M. Magleby, *Last Hurrah? Soft Money and Issue Advocacy in the 2002 Elections* (Brookings Institution Press, 2004).

5. For a discussion of how members have evaded federal legislation against bulk e-mails, or spam, see Jennifer S. Lee, "We Hate Spam, Congress Says (Except When It's Sent by Us)," *The New York Times*, December 18, 2003, p. A1.

6. R. P. Fairfield, *The Federalist Papers* (Doubleday, 1961), p. 160.

7. See Roger H. Davidson and Walter J. Oleszek, *Congress and Its Members*, 10th ed. (CQ Press, 2005).

8. Richard F. Fenno Jr., *The United States Senate: A Bicameral Perspective* (American Enterprise Institute, 1982), p. 1.

9. For discussion of the modern Speakership, see Barbara Sinclair, "House Majority Party Leadership in an Era of Legislative Constraint," in *The Postreform Congress*, Roger H. Davidson, ed. (St. Martin's Press, 1992), pp. 91–111; and Ronald M. Peters Jr., ed., *The Speaker: Leadership in the U.S. House of Representatives* (CQ Press, 1995).

10. See Keith Krehbiel, and Alan E. Wiseman, "Joe Cannon and the Minority Party: Tyranny or Bipartisanship," research paper no. 1858, Stanford University Graduate School of Business, July 2004.

11. Newt Gingrich, *To Renew America* (HarperCollins, 1995) and *Lessons Learned the Hard Way* (HarperCollins, 1998).

12. Dennis Hastert, quoted in Greg Hitt, "Hastert Is Tapped as House Speaker to Fill Vacuum Created by Livingston," *Wall Street Journal*, December 21, 1998, p. A20.

13. Richard E. Cohen and David Baumann, "Speaking Up for Hastert," *National Journal*, November 13, 1999, pp. 3298–3303.

14. For insightful memoirs by three recently retired U.S. senators, see Bill Bradley, *Time Present, Time Past: A Memoir* (Knopf, 1996); Warren B. Rudman, *Combat: Twelve Years in the U.S. Senate* (Random House, 1996); and Alan K. Simpson, *Right in the Old Kazoo: A Lifetime of Scrapping with the Press* (Morrow, 1997). See also the reflections of Joseph I. Lieberman, *In Praise of Public Life* (Simon & Schuster, 2000); and Adam Clymer, *Edward M. Kennedy: A Biography* (Morrow, 1999).

15. For an insightful set of essays on Senate leadership, see Richard A. Baker and Roger H. Davidson, eds., *First Among Equals: Outstanding Senate Leaders of the Twentieth Century* (CQ Press, 1991).

16. Barbara Sinclair, "Unorthodox Lawmaking in the Individualist Senate," *Extensions: A Journal of the Carl Albert Congressional Research and Studies Center*, vol. 3, no. 2 (Fall 1997), p. 11. See also Sinclair, *Unorthodox Lawmaking: New Legislative Processes in the U.S. Congress*, 2d ed. (CQ Press, 2000), chap. 3.

17. Nicol Rae and Colton Campbell, "The Changing Role of Political Parties in the U.S. Senate in the 104th and 105th Congresses," paper presented at the annual meeting of the American Political Science Association, Boston, September 3–6, 1998, p. 21.

18. Sarah A. Binder and Steven S. Smith, *Politics or Principles? Filibustering in the United States Senate* (Brookings Institution Press, 1997).

19. See David Nather, "Feud with Democrats over Judicial Nominees Keeps Frist's Cloture Score Down," *Congressional Quarterly Weekly*, November 29, 2003, p. 2949.

20. For a criticism of recent confirmation hearings and various reform proposals, see Stephen L. Carter, *The Confirmation Mess: Cleaning Up the Federal Appointments Process* (Basic Books, 1994). See also G. Calvin Mackenzie and Robert Shogan, eds., *Obstacle Course: The Report of the Twentieth Century Fund Task Force on the Presidential Appointment Process* (Twentieth Century Fund Press, 1996); and Michael Comiskey, *Seeking Justice: The Judging of Supreme Court Nominees* (University of Kansas, 2004).

21. Helen Dewar, "Senate Filibuster Ends with Talk of Next Stage in Fight," *The Washington Post*, November 15, 2003, p. A9.

22. Woodrow Wilson, *Congressional Government* (Houghton Mifflin, 1885; reprint, Johns Hopkins University Press, 1981), p. 69.

23. Christopher J. Deering and Steven S. Smith, *Committees in Congress*, 3d ed. (CQ Press, 1997).

24. Joel D. Aberbach, *Keeping a Watchful Eye: The Politics of Congressional Oversight* (Brookings Institution Press, 1990), p. 33. Aberbach's data exclude hearings by Appropriations, Administration, and Rules but do include Budget and the revenue committees.

25. The figures come from Citizens Against Government Waste, and can be found at www.cagw.org/site/News2?page=NewsArticle&id=9528, accessed on February 9, 2006.

26. Karen Foerstel, "Chairman's Term Limits Already Shaking Up House," *Congressional Quarterly Weekly*, March 24, 2000, p. 628.

27. Aberbach, *Keeping a Watchful Eye*.

28. "Résumé of Congressional Activity, 105th Congress," *Congressional Record*, Daily Digest, January 19, 1999, p. D29.

29. Ronald Reagan, quoted in Lawrence Longley and Walter Oleszek, *Bicameral Politics* (Yale University Press, 1989), p. 1.

30. For an example of intense bargaining on a major defense appropriation bill, see Pat Towell, "Camouflage-Green Defense Bill Poised for President's Signature," *Congressional Quarterly Weekly*, July 22, 2000, pp. 1819–1822.

31. Davidson and Oleszek, *Congress and Its Members*, p. 307.

32. For a history of the early Congresses, see James Sterling Young, *The Washington Community, 1800–1828* (Columbia University Press, 1966).

33. Davidson and Oleszek, *Congress and Its Members*, p. 30.

34. Nelson Polsby, "The Institutionalization of the U.S. House of Representatives," *American Political Science Association* (March 1968), pp. 144–168.

35. Norman J. Ornstein, Thomas Mann, and Michael Malbin, *Vital Statistics on Congress, 1999–2000* (AEI Press, 2000), p. 170.

36. Pew Research Center for the People and the Press, *Washington Leaders Wary of Public Opinion* (Author, 1998), p. 30.

37. Herbert Asher, "The Learning of Legislative Norms," *American Political Science Review* 67 (June 1973), pp. 499–513.

38. See the case studies in Richard F. Fenno Jr., *Senators on the Campaign Trail: The Politics of Representation* (University of Oklahoma Press, 1996), p. 331. See also Benjamin Bishin, "Constituency Influence in Congress: Does Subconstituency Matter?" *Legislative Studies Quarterly* (August 2000), pp. 389–415.

39. Statistics from congressional Web sites (www.senate.gov; www.house.gov). See also the Library of Congress Web site (thomas.loc.gov).

40. Bradley, *Time Present, Time Past*, chap. 4.

41. See Richard Morrin, "Tuned Out, Turned Off: Millions of Americans Know Little About How Their Government Works," *The Washington Post National Weekly Edition*, February 5, 1996, pp. 6–7.

42. A 1999 CBS survey reported in "Poll Readings," *National Journal*, October 9, 1999, p. 2917.

43. For a fascinating comparison of two Rhodes scholars, one liberal from Maryland and the other a conservative from Indiana, and what has shaped their votes over several terms in the U.S. Senate, see Karl A. Lamb, *Reasonable Disagreement: Two U.S. Senators and the Choices They Make* (Garland, 1998).

44. Richard E. Cohen, "Vote Ratings," *National Journal*, February 21, 2005, p. 426.

45. Quoted at http://www.house.gov/israel/biography/index.htm.

46. Lieberman, *In Praise of Public Life*, p. 109.

47. Constance Ewing Cook, *Lobbying for Higher Education* (Vanderbilt University Press, 1998). See also Ken Kolman, *Outside Lobbying* (Princeton University Press, 1998).

48. Martin Kady II, "Party Unity: Learning to Stick Together," *Congressional Quarterly Weekly*, January 9, 2006, p. 92.

49. Jill Barshay, "Bush Starts a Strong Record of Success with the Hill," *Congressional Quarterly Weekly*, January 12, 2002, p. 110.

50. Dennis Thompson, *Ethics in Congress: From Individual to Institutional Corruption* (Brookings Institution, 1995).

51. Joseph p. Kennedy II, quoted in Clifford Krauss, "How Personal Tragedy Can Shape Public Policy," *The New York Times*, May 16, 1993, p. A16.

52. See David Baumann, "The Heavy Reliance on Riders to the Must-Pass Appropriations Bills as a Crutch to Act on Significant Policy Issues," *National Journal*, January 10, 2004, p. 97.

Chapter 12

1. George W. Bush, "President's Radio Address," December 17, 2005.

2. Sheryl Gay Solberg and David E. Sanger, "Facing Pressure, White House Seeks Approval for Spying," *New York Times*, February 20, 2006, p. A1.

3. Alexander Hamilton, James Madison, and John Jay, *The Federalist Papers* (Bantam Classic, 2003), pp. 426–427.

4. Richard Pious, *The American Presidency* (Basic Books, 1978).

5. This history of presidential powers draws heavily on Sidney M. Milkis and Michael Nelson, *The American Presidency: Origins and Development, 1976–2000*, 4th ed. (CQ Press, 2003).

6. Letter from Abraham Lincoln to his Illinois law partner W. H. Herndon, February 15, 1848, in *Abraham Lincoln, Speeches and Writings, 1832–1858* (Library of America, 1989), p. 175.

7. Miles A. Pomper, "Bush Hopes to Avoid Battle with Congress over Iraq," *Congressional Quarterly Weekly*, August 31, 2002, p. 2251.

8. Leonard C. Meeker, "The Legality of U.S. Participation in the Defense of Vietnam," *Department of State Bulletin*, March 28, 1966, pp. 448–455.

9. Louis Fisher, *Congressional Abdication on War and Spending* (Texas A&M Press, 2000), p. 184.

10. Raoul Berger, *Executive Privilege: A Constitutional Myth* (Harvard University Press, 1974).

11. Mark J. Rozell, "The Law: Executive Privilege—Definition and Standards of Application," *Presidential Studies Quarterly* (December 1999), p. 924.

12. *United States* v. *Nixon*, 418 U.S. 683 (1974).

13. The president's executive orders can be reviewed on the White House Web site at www.whitehouse.gov.

14. *Clinton, et al.,* v. *New York City, et al.*, 524 U.S. 417 (1998).

15. See William G. Howell, "Unilateral Powers: A Brief Overview," *Presidential Studies Quarterly*, vol. 35, no. 3, (September 2005), pp. 417–439, for a review of these and other tools of presidential influence.

16. See Phillip J. Cooper, "George W. Bush, Edgar Allan Poe, and the Use and Abuse of Presidential Signing Statements," *Presidential Studies Quarterly*, vol. 35, no. 3, (September 2005), pp. 515–532.

17. For a recent biography of Washington, see Richard Brookhiser, *Founding Father: Rediscovering George Washington* (New York: Free Press, 1996).

18. See Paul Starobin, "Long Live the King!" *National Journal*, February 17, 2006, pp. 16–20.

19. See Bradley H. Patterson Jr., *The White House Staff: Inside the West Wing and Beyond* (Brookings Institution Press, 2000).

20. For the views on presidents and the White House staff of a highly placed White House aide in several administrations, see David Gergen, *Eyewitness to Power: The Essence of Leadership, Nixon to Clinton* (Touchstone, 2000).

21. See Irving Janis, *Groupthink* (Houghton Mifflin, 1982).

22. See Shelley Lynne Tomkins, *Inside OMB: Politics and Process in the President's Budget Office* (Sharpe, 1998).

23. See Thomas Cronin and Michael Genovese, *Paradoxes of the American Presidency*, 2d ed. (Oxford University Press, 2004), chap. 9.

24. Alexis Simendinger, James Kitfield, Peter H. Stone, and Kirk Victor, "Just the Ticket?" *National Journal*, February 14, 2004, p. 27.

25. See Paul C. Light, *The President's Agenda: Domestic Policy Choice from Kennedy Through Clinton* (Johns Hopkins University Press, 1999).

26. *United States* v. *Curtiss-Wright Export Corp.*, 299 U.S. 304 (1936).

27. For commentary by analysts who believe the *Curtiss-Wright* ruling was too sweeping, see Harold H. Koh, *The National Security Constitution* (Yale University Press, 1990); Louis Fisher, *Presidential War Power* (University Press of Kansas, 1995); and David Gray Adler and Larry N. George, eds., *The Constitution and the Conduct of American Foreign Policy: Essays on Law and History* (University Press of Kansas, 1996).

28. Richard E. Neustadt, *Presidential Power and the Modern Presidents* (Free Press, 1991).

29. Samuel Kernell, *Going Public: New Strategies of Presidential Leadership*, 3d ed., (Congressional Quarterly, 1997).

30. James David Barber, *The Presidential Character: Predicting Performance in the White House*, 4th ed. (Prentice Hall, 1992).

31. See, *The President's Agenda* for a discussion of the agenda-setting process.

32. The phrase "power to persuade" is from Richard Neustadt, *Presidential Power and the Modern Presidents: The Politics of Leadership from Roosevelt to Reagan* (The Free Press, 1990), p. 7.

33. See Paul Light, "The Focusing Skill and Presidential Influence in Congress," in C. Deering, ed., *Congressional Politics* (Dorsey Press, 1989), p. 256.

Chapter 13

1. U.S. House of Representatives, Committee on Government Reform, *A Failure of Initiative: Final Report of the Select Bipartisan Committee to Investigate the Preparation for and Response to Hurricane Katrina* (Government Printing Office, 2006).

2. Alexander Hamilton, James Madison, and John Jay, *The Federalist Papers* (Bantam Classic, 2003), p. 427.

3. See Stanley Elkins and Eric McKitrick, *The Age of Federalism* (Oxford University Press, 1993), pp. 50–51.

4. See John A. Rohr, *To Run a Constitution: The Legitimacy of the Administrative State* (University of Kansas Press, 1986).

5. Donald Kettl, *Leadership at the Fed* (Yale University Press, 1986).

6. James Fesler and Donald Kettl, *The Politics of the Administrative Process* (Chatham House, 1991).

7. See Paul C. Light, *Thickening Government* (Brookings Institution Press, 1995).

8. See Terry M. Moe, "The Politics of Structural Choice: Toward a Theory of Public Bureaucracy," in *Organization Theory: From Chester Barnard to the Present and Beyond*, Oliver E. Williamson, ed. (Oxford University Press, 1990), pp. 140–162.

9. Leonard White, *The Federalists* (Macmillan, 1956), p. 1.

10. For an analysis of the use and abuse of the civil service system in the early twentieth century,

see Stephen Skowronek, *Building a New American State* (Cambridge University Press, 1982).

11. Andrew Kohut, *Deconstructing Distrust: How Americans View Government* (Pew Research Center for the People and the Press, 1998), p. 124.

12. See Paul C. Light, "To Give or Not to Give," *Reform Watch #7*, (Brookings Institution Press, 2003).

13. An exception is a book of essays in praise of innovations by federal agencies, John D. Donahue, ed., *Making Washington Work: Tales of Innovation in the Federal Government* (Brookings Institution Press, 1999).

14. These attitudes were discovered in surveys conducted by the Brookings Institution's Presidential Appointee Initiative in May, 2002.

15. See Paul C. Light, *The New Public Service*, Washington, D.C.: The Brookings Institution, 1999.

16. See Paul C. Light, *The New Public Service*, Washington, DC: Brookings Institution Press, 1999.

17. See James Eccles, *The Hatch Act and the American Bureaucracy* (Vantage Press, 1981).

18. See Jeanne Ponessa, "The Hatch Act Rewrite," *Congressional Quarterly Weekly*, November 13, 1993, pp. 3146–3147.

19. Theodore J. Lowi Jr., *The End of Liberalism*, 2d ed. (Norton, 1979).

20. Eric Pianin, "EPA Aims to Change Pollution Rules," *Washington Post*, December 5, 2003, p. A2.

21. Kent Weaver, *Automatic Government: The Politics of Indexation* (Brookings Institution Press, 1988), p. 1; updated estimate provided by Paul C. Light.

22. James Q. Wilson, *Bureaucracy: What Government Agencies Do and Why They Do It* (Basic Books, 1989), p. 257.

23. See David E. Lewis, "The Presidential Advantage in the Design of Bureaucratic Agencies," paper presented at the annual meeting of the American Political Science Association, Boston, September 3–6, 1998.

24. Morris P. Fiorina, "Flagellating the Federal Bureaucracy," *Society* (March–April 1983), p. 73.

25. See Steven S. Smith, *The American Congress* (Houghton Mifflin, 1995); see also Joel D. Aberbach, *Keeping a Watchful Eye: The Politics of Congressional Oversight* (Brookings Institution Press, 1990).

26. See Matthew McCubbins and Thomas Schwartz, "Congressional Oversight Overlooked: Police Patrols Versus Fire Alarms," *American Journal of Political Science* 2 (February 1984), pp. 165–179.

Chapter 14

1. For a discussion of the new generation of cases, see Kenneth Jost, "Fitting the Nine in a New Docket," *Congressional Quarterly Weekly*, June 27, 2005, p. 1704.

2. Roy p. Fairfield, ed., *The Federalist Papers* (Johns Hopkins University Press, 1981), p. 227.

3. Jerome Frank, *Courts on Trial: Myth and Reality in American Justice* (Princeton University Press, 1949), pp. 80–103. See also Martin Shapiro, *Courts* (University of Chicago Press, 1981), and Robert P. Burns, *A Theory of the Trial* (Princeton University Press, 1999).

4. *Flast* v. *Cohen*, 392 U.S. 83 (1968); *Lujan* v. *Defenders of Wildlife*, 504 U.S. 555 (1992).

5. Many of these workload statistics can be found in the Supreme Court's *2005 Year-End Report on* *the Federal Judiciary*, Washington, D.C.: U.S. Supreme Court, January 1, 2006.

6. Fairfield, *The Federalist Papers*, p. 228.

7. Harold W. Chase, *Federal Judges: The Appointing Process* (University of Minnesota Press, 1972); Sheldon Goldman, *Picking Federal Judges: Lower Court Selection from Roosevelt Through Reagan* (Yale University Press, 1997).

8. See David M. O'Brien, "Ironies and Disappointments: Bush and Federal Judgeships," in Colin Campbell and Bert A. Rockman, eds., *The George W. Bush Presidency* (CQ Press, 2004), pp. 133–157; and Brannon p. Denning, "The Judicial Confirmation Process and the Blue Slip," *Judicature* (March–April 2002), pp. 218–226.

9. Lisa M. Holmes and Roger E. Hartley, "Increasing Senate Scrutiny of Lower Federal Court Nominees," *Judicature* (May–June 1997), p. 275.

10. George Watson and John Stookey, "Supreme Court Confirmation Hearings: A View from the Senate," *Judicature* (December 1987–January 1988), p. 193. See also John Massaro, *Supremely Political: The Role of Ideology and Presidential Management in Unsuccessful Supreme Court Nominations* (State University of New York Press, 1990).

11. Barbara A. Perry and Henry J. Abraham, "A 'Representative' Supreme Court? The Thomas, Ginsburg, and Breyer Appointments," *Judicature* (January–February 1998), pp. 158–165.

12. Goldman, *Picking Federal Judges*, pp. 161, 327–336.

13. Sheldon Goldman, "Bush's Judicial Legacy: The Final Imprint," *Judicature* (April–May 1993), p. 291.

14. Eleanor Dean Acheson, quoted in David M. O'Brien, "Judicial Legacies: The Clinton Presidency and the Courts," in *The Clinton Legacy*, Colin Campbell and Burt A. Rockman, eds. (Chatham House, 2000), p. 101.

15. Robert A. Carp and C. K. Rowland, *Politics and Judgment in Federal District Courts* (University Press of Kansas, 1996).

16. Sheldon Goldman, "Reagan's Judicial Legacy: Completing the Puzzle and Summing Up," *Judicature* (April–May 1989), pp. 318–330.

17. Robert A. Carp, Donald Songer, C. K. Rowland, Ronald Stidham, and Lisa Richey-Tracey, "The Voting Behavior of Judges Appointed by President Bush," *Judicature* (April–May 1993), pp. 298–302.

18. David G. Savage, *Turning Right: The Making of the Rehnquist Supreme Court* (Wiley, 1992).

19. Naftali Bendavid, "Diversity Marks Clinton Judiciary," *Recorder* (December 30, 1993), p. 11.

20. David M. O'Brien, *Judicial Roulette: Report of the Twentieth Century Fund Task Force on Judicial Selection* (Priority Press Publications, 1988), pp. 10–11.

21. See Citizens for Independent Courts Task Force on Federal Judicial Selection, *Justice Held Hostage: Politics and Selecting Federal Judges* (Century Foundation, 2000).

22. Donald Santarelli, quoted in Jerry Landauer, "Shaping the Bench," *The Wall Street Journal*, December 10, 1970, p. 1.

23. Michael A. Kahn, "The Appointment of a Supreme Court Justice: A Political Process from Beginning to End," *Presidential Studies Quarterly* 25 (Winter 1995), pp. 26, 39.

24. See Benjamin N. Cardozo, *The Nature of the Judicial Process* (Yale University Press, 1921)—a classic.

25. William O. Douglas, quoted in David M. O'Brien,

Storm Center: The Supreme Court in American Politics, 7th ed. (Norton, 2005), p. 184.

26. Ibid., p. 30 (figures as of the end of the 2003–2004 term).

27. See Keith Perine, "Precedent Heeded, But Not Revered on High Court," *Congressional Quarterly Weekly*, November 28, 2005, pp. 3180–3184.

28. Ex parte *McCardle*, 74 U.S. 506 (1869).

29. Barry Friedman, "Attacks on Judges: Why They Fail," *Judicature* (January–February 1998), p. 152.

30. Quoted in Walter Murphy and C. Herman Pritchert, *Courts, Judges, and Politics: An Introduction to the Judicial Process* (Random House, 1979), p. 37.

31. Felix Frankfurter, letter to Justice Hugo Black, December 15, 1939, quoted in David M. O'Brien, *Constitutional Law and Politics*, 6th ed. (Norton, 2005), p. 74.

32. William H. Rehnquist, quoted in John R. Vile, "The Selection and Tenure of Chief Justices," *Judicature* (September–October 1994), p. 98.

33. David Danelski, "The Influence of the Chief Justice in the Decisional Process of the Supreme Court," in *The Federal Judicial System: Readings in Process and Behavior*, Thomas P. Jahnige and Sheldon Goldman, eds. (Holt, Rinehart and Winston, 1968), p. 148.

34. David M. O'Brien, "The Rehnquist Court's Shrinking Plenary Docket," *Judicature* (September–October 1997).

35. H. W. Perry Jr., *Deciding to Decide: Agenda Setting in the United States Supreme Court* (Cambridge, 1991), p. 278.

36. O'Brien, *Storm Center*, p. 63.

37. See Perry, *Deciding to*, p. 258.

38. Edward Lazarus, *Closed Chambers: The First Eyewitness Account of the Epic Struggles Inside the Supreme Court* (Times Books/Random House, 1998).

39. O'Brien, *Storm Center*, chap. 3.

40. Lincoln Caplan, *The Tenth Justice: The Solicitor General and the Rule of Law* (Knopf, 1987); and Rebecca Mae Salokar, *The Solicitor General: The Politics of Law* (Temple University Press, 1992).

41. Charles Fried, *Order and Law: Arguing the Reagan Revolution—A Firsthand Account* (Simon & Schuster, 1991). See also Rebecca Dean, Joseph Ignagni, and James Meernik, "The Solicitor General as Amicus, 1950–2000: How Influential?" *Judicature* 87 (September–October, 2003), p. 60.

42. Jeffrey A. Segal and Robert M. Howard, "How Supreme Court Justices Respond to Litigant Requests to Overturn Precedent," *Judicature* (November–December 2001), pp. 148–157.

43. Gregory A. Caldeira and John R. Wright, "Organized Interest and Agenda Setting in the U.S. Supreme Court," *American Political Science Review* 82 (December 1988), p. 1110; and Donald R. Songer and Reginald S. Sheehan, "Interest Groups' Success in the Courts: *Amicus* Participation in the Supreme Court," *Political Research Quarterly* 46 (June 1993), pp. 339–354.

44. *Webster* v. *Reproductive Health Services*, 492 U.S. 490 (1989); *Roe* v. *Wade*, 410 U.S. 113 (1973); and Susan Behuniak-Long, "Friendly Fire: *Amici Curiae* and *Webster* v. *Reproductive Health Services*," *Judicature* (February–March 1991), pp. 261–270.

45. *United States* v. *Lopez*, 514 U.S. 549 (1951).

46. Caldeira and Wright, "Organized Interest and Agenda Setting"; Songer and Sheehan, "Interest Groups' Success in the Courts," *American Political Science Review* 82 (December 1988), p. 1118.

47. Tony Mauro, "The Supreme Court as Quiz Show," *Recorder* (December 8, 1993), p. 10.

48. Joyce O'Connor, "Selections from Notes Kept on an Internship at the U.S. Supreme Court, Fall 1988," *Law, Courts, and Judicial Process* 6 (Spring 1989), p. 44.

49. William H. Rehnquist, *The Supreme Court: A New Edition of the Chief Justice's Classic History* (Knopf, 2001), pp. 289–290.

50. Forrest Maltzman, James F. Spriggs III, and Paul Wahlbeck, *Crafting Law on the Supreme Court: The Collegial Game* (Cambridge University Press, 2000).

51. Daniel M. Berman, *It Is So Ordered: The Supreme Court Rules on School Segregation* (Norton, 1986), p. 114; and O'Brien, *Storm Center*, pp. 262–272.

52. Charles Evans Hughes, quoted in Donald E. Lively, *Foreshadows of the Law: Supreme Court Dissents and Constitutional Development* (Praeger, 1992), p. xx.

53. *Brown* v. *Board of Education of Topeka*, 347 U.S. 483 (1954).

54. Gerald N. Rosenberg, *Hollow Hope: Can Courts Bring About Sound Change?* (University of Chicago Press, 1991).

55. J. W. Peltason, *Fifty-Eight Lonely Men: Southern Federal Judges and School Desegregation* (University of Illinois Press, 1971); and Gary Orfield and Chungmei Lee, *Brown at 50: King's Dream or Plessy's Nightmare* (The Civil Rights Project, Harvard University, 2004).

56. See Shawn Francis Peters, *Judging the Jehovah's Witnesses* (University of Kansas Press, 2002); Clyde Wilcox, *Onward, Christian Soldiers? The Religious Right in American Politics* (Westview Press, 1996); Mark Tushnet, *The NAACP's Legal Strategy Against Segregated Education, 1925–1950* (University of North Carolina Press, 1987); and Karen O'Connor, *Women's Organizations' Use of the Court* (Lexington Books, 1980).

57. Philip J. Cooper, *Hard Judicial Choices: Federal District Court Judges and State and Local Officials* (Oxford University Press, 1988), pp. 347–350.

58. Arthur S. Miller, "In Defense of Judicial Activism," in *Supreme Court Activism and Restraint*, Stephen C. Halpern and Charles M. Lamb, eds. (Heath, 1982), p. 177.

59. *United States* v. *Carolene Products*, 304 U.S. 144 (1938). Variations on this basic position have been restated in dozens of books. Halpern and Lamb, *Supreme Court Activism and Restraint*, and Mark Tushnet, *Red, White, and Blue: A Critical Analysis of Constitutional Law* (Harvard University Press, 1988) provide analysis from all perspectives. See also Terri Jennings Peretti, *In Defense of a Political Court* (Princeton University Press, 1999).

60. J. W. Peltason, "The Supreme Court: Transactional or Transformational Leadership," in *Essays in Honor of James MacGregor Burns*, Michael R. Beschloss and Thomas E. Cronin, eds. (Prentice Hall, 1988), pp. 165–180; and Valerie Hoeksta, *Public Reactions to Supreme Court Decisions* (Cambridge University Press, 2003).

61. *Planned Parenthood* v. *Casey*, 505 U.S. 833 (1992).

62. Thomas R. Marshall, *Public Opinion and the Supreme Court* (Unwin Hyman, 1989), p. 193. See also William Mishler and Reginald S. Sheehan, "The Supreme Court as a Counter-Majoritarian Institution: The Impact of Public Opinion on Supreme Court Decisions," *American Political Science Review* 87 (January 1993), pp. 87–101;

and Helmut Norpoth and Jeffrey A. Segal, "Popular Influence on Supreme Court Decisions," *American Political Science Review* 88 (September 1994), pp. 711–724.

63. See John B. Gates, *The Supreme Court and Partisan Realignment* (Westview Press, 1992).

64. Rosenberg, *Hollow Hope*, p. 343.

65. Rehnquist, *Supreme Court*, p. 98.

66. Gallup Organization, "Confidence in Institutions," June 8–10, 2001, at www.gallup.com; and Herbert Kritzer, "The Impact of *Bush* v. *Gore* on Public Perceptions and Knowledge of the Supreme Court," *Judicature* (July–August 2001), pp. 32–38.

67. Edward White, "The Supreme Court of the United States," *American Bar Association Journal* 7 (1921), p. 341.

Chapter 15

1. Jeffrey Smith, *War and Press Freedom* (Oxford University Press, 1999); and David Cole, *Enemy Aliens: Double Standards and Constitutional Freedoms in the War on Terrorism* (The New Press, 2003).

2. *Felker* v. *Turpin*, 518 U.S. 651 (1996); *Winthrow* v. *Williams*, 507 U.S. 680 (1993); *McCleskey* v. *Zant*, 499 U.S. 467 (1991); and *Stone* v. *Powell*, 428 U.S. 465 (1976).

3. *Rasul* v. *Bush*, 542 U.S. 466 (2004); and *Hamdi* v. *Rumsfeld*, 542 U.S. 507 (2004).

4. *Hamdan* v. *Rumsfeld*, 126 S.Ct.2749 (2006).

5. *Stogner* v. *California*, 539 U.S. 607 (2003).

6. *United States* v. *Lovett*, 328 U.S. 303 (1946).

7. Neil H. Cogan, ed., *The Complete Bill of Rights: The Drafts, Debates, Sources, and Origins* (Oxford University Press, 1997); Robert A. Rutland, *The Birth of the Bill of Rights, 1776–1791* (University of North Carolina Press, 1955).

8. *Barron* v. *Baltimore*, 7 Peters 243 (1833).

9. *Gitlow* v. *New York*, 268 U.S. 652 (1925).

10. Richard C. Cortner, *The Supreme Court and the Second Bill of Rights: The Fourteenth Amendment and the Nationalization of Civil Liberties* (University of Wisconsin Press, 1981).

11. Dorothy Toth Beasley, "Federalism and the Protection of Individual Rights: The American State Constitutional Perspective," in *Federalism and Rights*, Ellis Katz and G. Alan Tarr, eds. (Rowman & Littlefield, 1996); and Charles Lopeman, *The Activist Advocate: Policymaking in State Supreme Courts* (Praeger, 1999).

12. *Witters* v. *Washington Department of Services for the Blind*, 474 U.S. 481 (1986); and *Locke* v. *Davey*, 540 U.S. 712 (2004).

13. *Everson* v. *Board of Education of Ewing Township*, 333 U.S. 203 (1947).

14. *Lemon* v. *Kurtzman*, 403 U.S. 602 (1971).

15. *Capital Square Review Board* v. *Pinette*, 515 U.S. 753 (1995).

16. *Lynch* v. *Donnelly*, 465 U.S. 669 (1984).

17. *Allegheny County* v. *Greater Pittsburgh ACLU*, 492 U.S. 573 (1989).

18. *Bowen* v. *Kendrick*, 487 U.S. 589 (1988); *Lee* v. *Weisman*, 505 U.S. 577 (1992); *Board of Education of Kiryas Joel Village School District* v. *Grumet*, 512 U.S. 687 (1994); and *Zelman* v. *Simmons-Harris*, 536 U.S. 629 (2002).

19. *Mitchell* v. *Helms*, 530 U.S. 793 (2000).

20. *Agostini* v. *Felton*, 521 U.S. 74 (1997).

21. *Lee* v. *Weisman*, 505 U.S. 577 (1992); and *Santa Fe Independent School District* v. *Doe*, 530 U.S. 290 (2000).

22. *Engel* v. *Vitale*, 370 U.S. 421 (1962).

23. *Edwards* v. *Aguillard*, 482 U.S. 578 (1987).

24. *Marsh* v. *Chambers*, 463 U.S. 783 (1983).

25. *Stone* v. *Graham*, 449 U.S. 39 (1980).

26. *Van Orden* v. *Perry*, 125 S.Ct. 2854 (2005).

27. *McCreary* v. *American Civil Liberties Union of Kentucky*, 125 S.Ct 2722 (2005).

28. *Elk Grove Unified School District* v. *Newdow*, 124 S.Ct. 2301 (2004).

29. *Witters* v. *Washington Department of Services for the Blind*, 474 U.S. 481 (1986).

30. *Mueller* v. *Allen*, 463 U.S. 388 (1983); and *Zelman* v. *Simmons-Harris*, 536 U.S. 639 (2002).

31. *Zobrest* v. *Catalina Foothills School District*, 515 U.S. 1 (1993); *Agostini* v. *Felton*, 521 U.S. 74 (1997); *Mitchell* v. *Helms*, 530 U.S. 793 (2000).

32. *Zelman* v. *Simmons-Harris*, 536 U.S. 639 (2002).

33. See V. Dion Haynes, "Vouchers Breathe New Life into D.C. Catholic Schools," *The Washington Post*, June 13, 2005, p. A1.

34. *Employment Division of Human Resources of Oregon* v. *Smith*, 494 U.S. 872 (1990).

35. *Church of Lukumi Babalu Aye* v. *City of Hialeah*, 508 U.S. 520 (1993).

36. *City of Boerne* v. *Flores*, 521 U.S. 507 (1997).

37. *Cutter* v. *Wilkinson*, 544 U.S. 709 (2005).

38. *Rosenberger* v. *University of Virginia*, 515 U.S. 819 (1995).

39. *Board of Regents of the University of Wisconsin System* v. *Southworth*, 529 U.S. 217 (2000).

40. *Locek* v. *Davey*, 540 U.S. 712 (2004).

41. Oliver Wendell Holmes Jr., in *Abrams* v. *United States*, 250 U.S. 616 (1919).

42. John Stuart Mill, *Essay on Liberty*, in *The English Philosophers from Bacon to Mill*, Arthur Burtt, ed. (Random House, 1939), p. 961.

43. Robert Jackson, in *West Virginia State Board of Education* v. *Barnette*, 319 U.S. 624 (1943).

44. *Brown* v. *Hartlage*, 456 U.S. 45 (1982), reversing a decision of the Kentucky Court of Appeals based on the bad tendency test.

45. Oliver Wendell Holmes Jr., in *Schenck* v. *United States*, 249 U.S. 47 (1919).

46. *Dennis* v. *United States*, 341 U.S. 494 (1951).

47. *New York Times* v. *Sullivan*, 376 U.S. 254 (1964).

48. *Yates* v. *United States*, 354 U.S. 298 (1957).

49. *Brandenburg* v. *Ohio*, 395 U.S. 444 (1969).

50. *New York Times* v. *Sullivan*, 376 U.S. 254 (1964).

51. *Hustler Magazine* v. *Falwell*, 485 U.S. 46 (1988).

52. *Masson* v. *New York Magazine, Inc.*, 501 U.S. 496 (1991).

53. *Gertz* v. *Robert Welch, Inc.*, 418 U.S. 323 (1974).

54. Potter Stewart, concurring in *Jacobellis* v. *Ohio*, 378 U.S. 184 (1964).

55. John Marshall Harlan, in *Cohen* v. *California*, 403 U.S. 15 (1971).

56. *Miller* v. *California*, 413 U.S. 15 (1973).

57. *Young* v. *American Mini Theatres*, 427 U.S. 51 (1976); *Renton* v. *Playtime Theatres, Inc.*, 475 U.S. 41 (1986); and *City of Los Angeles* v. *Alameda Books, Inc.*, 535 U.S. 425 (2002).

58. *Barnes* v. *Glen Theatre, Inc.*, 501 U.S. 560 (1991); and *City of Erie* v. *Pap's A.M.*, 529 U.S. 277 (2000).

59. *New York* v. *Ferber*, 458 U.S. 747 (1982); and *Ashcroft* v. *Free Speech Coalition*, 535 U.S. 234 (2002).

60. *General Media Communications* v. *Cohen*, 524 U.S. 951 (1998).

61. See Catharine A. MacKinnon, *Only Words* (Harvard University Press, 1993); and compare another feminist, Nadine Strossen, *Defending Pornography: Free Speech, Sex, and the Fight for Women's Rights* (Scribner, 1995).

62. *Butler* v. *Her Majesty the Queen*, 1 S.C.R. 452 (1992).

63. *Chaplinsky* v. *New Hampshire*, 315 U.S. 568 (1942).

64. *Cohen* v. *California*, 403 U.S. 115 (1971).

65. *R.A.V.* v. *St. Paul*, 505 U.S. 377 (1992). See also *Wisconsin* v. *Mitchell*, 508 U.S. 476 (1993); and *Apprendi* v. *New Jersey*, 530 U.S. 466 (2000).

66. *Virginia* v. *Black*, 538 U.S. 343 (2003).

67. *44 Liquormart, Inc.*, v. *Rhode Island*, 517 U.S. 484 (1996); and *Thompson* v. *Western States Medical Center*, 535 U.S. 357 (2002).

68. *New York Times Company* v. *United States*, 403 U.S. 670 (1971).

69. *Near* v. *Minnesota*, 283 U.S. 697 (1930); ibid.

70. *Hazelwood School District* v. *Kuhlmeier*, 484 U.S. 260 (1988).

71. *R.A.V.* v. *St. Paul*, 505 U.S. 377 (1992). See also *Wisconsin* v. *Mitchell*, 508 U.S. 476 (1993).

72. *Branzburg* v. *Hayes*, 408 U.S. 665 (1972).

73. *Richmond Newspapers, Inc.*, v. *Virginia*, 448 U.S. 555 (1980). See also David M. O'Brien, *The Public's Right to Know: The Supreme Court and the First Amendment* (Praeger, 1981).

74. Oliver Wendell Holmes Jr., dissenting in *Milwaukee Publishing Co.* v. *Burleson*, 255 U.S. 407 (1921).

75. *Lamont* v. *Postmaster General*, 381 U.S. 301 (1965).

76. *Rowan* v. *Post Office Department*, 397 U.S. 728 (1970).

77. *McIntyre* v. *Ohio Election Commission*, 514 U.S. 334 (1995).

78. *Southeastern Promotions, Ltd.*, v. *Conrad*, 420 U.S. 546 (1975).

79. *Federal Communications Commission* v. *Pacifica Foundation*, 438 U.S. 726 (1978).

80. *Turner Broadcasting System* v. *Federal Communications Commission*, 518 U.S. 180 (1997).

81. *United States* v. *Playboy Entertainment Group*, 529 U.S. 803 (2000); and *Denver Area Educational Television* v. *Federal Communications Commission*, 518 U.S. 727 (1996).

82. See and compare *Federal Communications Commission* v. *Pacifica Foundation*, 438 U.S. 726 (1978); and *Sable Communications* v. *Federal Communications Commission*, 492 U.S. 115 (1989).

83. *Reno* v. *American Civil Liberties Union*, 521 U.S. 844 (1997).

84. *Ashcroft* v. *ACLU*, 542 U.S. 656 (2004).

85. *Ashcroft* v. *Free Speech Coalition*, 535 U.S. 234 (2002).

86. Eric Lichtblau, "F.B.I. Watched Activist Groups, New Files Show," *The New York Times*, December 20, 2005, p. A1.

87. See Congressional Research Service, *Presidential Authority to Conduct Warrantless Electronic Surveillance to Gather Foreign Intelligence Information* (Author, January 5, 2006).

88. *Walker* v. *Birmingham*, 388 U.S. 307 (1967).

89. *Madsen* v. *Women's Health Center*, 512 U.S. 753 (1994); *Schenck* v. *Pro-Choice Network*, 519 U.S. 357 (1997); and *Hill* v. *Colorado*, 530 U.S. 703 (2000).

90. *West Virginia State Board of Education* v. *Barnette*, 319 U.S. 624 (1943).

Chapter 16

1. Rick Weiss, "Vast DNA Bank Pits Policing Va. Privacy," *The Washington Post*, June 3, 2006, p. A1.

2. See Congressional Research Service, "Presidential Authority to Conduct Warrantless Electronic Surveillance to Gather Foreign Intelligence Information" (Author, 2006).

3. *Vance* v. *Terrazas*, 444 U.S. 252 (1980).

4. G. Pascal Zachary, "Dual Citizenship Is Double-Edged Sword," *The Wall Street Journal*, March 25, 1998, pp. B1, B15, quoting T. Alexander Aleinikoff of the Carnegie Endowment for International Peace.
5. *Slaughter-House Cases*, 83 U.S. 36 (1873).
6. *Ex Parte Milligan*, 71 U.S. 2 (1866).
7. *Korematsu v. United States*, 323 U.S. 214 (1944).
8. *Ex Parte Quirin*, 317 U.S. 1 (1942).
9. *Reid v. Covert*, 354 U.S. 1 (1957).
10. *Hamdi v. Rumsfeld*, 542 U.S. 466 (2004); and *Rasul v. Bush*, 542 U.S. 507 (2004).
11. *Hamdan v. Rumsfeld*, 126 S.Ct. 2749 (2006).
12. *Mathews v. Diaz*, 426 U.S. 67 (1976); *Shaughnessy v. United States ex rel Mezei*, 345 U.S. 206 (1953).
13. *Demore v. Kim*, 538 U.S. 510 (2003).
14. *Zadvydas v. Davis*, 533 U.S. 678 (2001).
15. *Yick Wo v. Hopkins*, 118 U.S. 356 (1886); *Kwong Hai Chew v. Colding*, 344 U.S. 590 (1953); *Zadvydas v. Davis*, 533 U.S. 678 (2001); *Rasul v. Bush*, 542 U.S. 466 (2004); and *Hamdi v. Rumsfeld*, 542 U.S. 507 (2004).
16. *Foley v. Connelie*, 435 U.S. 291 (1978); *Ambach v. Norwick*, 441 U.S. 68 (1979); and *Cabell v. Chavez-Salido*, 454 U.S. 432 (1982).
17. *Plyler v. Doe*, 457 U.S. 202 (1982).
18. Editorial, "Latest Immigration 'Crisis' Defies Simplistic Solutions," *USA Today*, March 30, 2006, p. 10A; and Robert Pear, "Racial and Ethnic Minorities Gaining in Nation as a Whole," *The New York Times*, August 12, 2005, p. A1.
19. Karen De Young, "Bush Lowers Refugee Quota to 70,000," *The Washington Post*, November 22, 2001, p. A45.
20. *Sale v. Haitian Centers Council, Inc.*, 509 U.S. 155 (1993).
21. Francis X. Clines, "Harsh Civics Lesson for Immigrants," *The New York Times*, November 11, 2001, p. B7.
22. *Chicago Home Building & Loan Association v. Blaisdell*, 290 U.S. 398 (1934).
23. *Chicago, Burlington & Quincy Railway Co. v. Chicago*, 166 U.S. 226 (1897).
24. *First English Evangelical v. Los Angeles County*, 482 U.S. 304 (1987). See Richard A. Epstein, *Taking: Private Property and the Power of Eminent Domain* (Harvard University Press, 1985).
25. *Lucas v. South Carolina Coastal Commission*, 505 U.S. 647 (1992).
26. *Tahoe-Sierra Council, Inc., v. Tahoe Regional Planning Agency*, 535 U.S. 302 (2002).
27. *Kelo v. City of New London*, 125 S.Ct. 2655 (2005).
28. *United States v. 564.54 Acres of Land*, 441 U.S. 506 (1979).
29. *Mathews v. Eldridge*, 424 U.S. 319 (1976), restated in *Connecticut v. Doeher*, 501 U.S. 1 (1991).
30. *Meyer v. Nebraska*, 262 U.S. 390 (1923).
31. *Lochner v. New York*, 198 U.S. 45 (1905).
32. *Griswold v. Connecticut*, 381 U.S. 479 (1965).
33. Philip B. Kurland, *Some Reflections on Privacy and the Constitution* (University of Chicago Center for Policy Study, 1976), p. 9. A classic and influential article about privacy is Samuel D. Warren and Louis D. Brandeis, "The Right to Privacy," *Harvard Law Review*, December 15, 1890, pp. 193–220.
34. *Roe v. Wade*, 410 U.S. 113 (1973).
35. *Planned Parenthood of Southeastern Pennsylvania v. Casey*, 505 U.S. 833 (1992).
36. *Stenberg v. Carhart*, 530 U.S. 914 (2000).
37. *Bowers v. Hardwick*, 478 U.S. 186 (1986).
38. *Boy Scouts of America v. Dale*, 530 U.S. 640 (2000).
39. *Lawrence v. Texas*, 539 U.S. 558 (2003).
40. *Romer v. Evans*, 517 U.S. 620 (1996).
41. But see *Washington v. Chrisman*, 455 U.S. 1 (1982), and compare *Georgia v. Randolph*, 126 S.Ct. 1515 (2006).
42. *Katz v. United States*, 389 U.S. 347 (1967).
43. *County of Riverside v. McLaughlin*, 500 U.S. 44 (1991).
44. *California v. Hodari D.*, 499 U.S. 621 (1991).
45. *Bond v. United States*, 529 U.S. 334 (2000).
46. *Terry v. Ohio*, 392 U.S. 1 (1968).
47. *Hiibel v. Sixth Judicial District of Nevada*, 542 U.S. 177 (2004).
48. *Minnesota v. Dickerson*, 508 U.S. 366 (1993).
49. *Almeida-Sanchez v. United States*, 413 U.S. 266 (1973); *United States v. Ortiz*, 422 U.S. 891 (1975); *United States v. Arvizu*, 534 U.S. 161 (2002); and *United States v. Flores-Montano*, 541 U.S. 149 (2004).
50. *United States v. Ramsey*, 431 U.S. 606 (1977).
51. *Coolidge v. New Hampshire*, 403 U.S. 443 (1971); and *Arizona v. Hicks*, 480 U.S. 321 (1987).
52. *Brigham City, Utah v. Stuart*, 126 S.Ct. 1943 (2006).
53. *United States v. Ross*, 456 U.S. 798 (1982).
54. *Pennsylvania v. Mimms*, 434 U.S. 110 (1977); and *Ohio v. Robinette*, 519 U.S. 33 (1997).
55. *Illinois v. Caballes*, 543 U.S. 405 (2005).
56. *Thorton v. United States*, 541 U.S. 615 (2004).
57. See and compare U.S. Department of Justice, "Legal Authorities Supporting the Activities of the National Security Agency Described by the President" (Author, 2006), and Congressional Research Service, "Presidential Authority to Conduct Warrantless Electronic Surveillance to Gather Foreign Intelligence Information (Author, 2006).
58. *Chandler v. Miller*, 520 U.S. 305 (1997).
59. Randall Kennedy, *Race, Crime, and the Law* (Pantheon Books, 1997), pp. 136–168; and David Cole, *No Equal Justice: Race and Class in the American Criminal Justice System* (New Press, 1999).
60. Quoted in Eric Lichtblau, "Bush Limits Use of Race in Federal Investigations," *International Herald Tribune*, June 19, 2003, p. 5.
61. *Treasury Employees v. Von Raab*, 489 U.S. 656 (1989); *Skinner v. Railway Labor Executives' Association*, 489 U.S. 602 (1989); *Vernonia School District 47J v. Acton*, 515 U.S. 646 (1995); and *Chandler v. Miller*, 520 U.S. 305 (1997).
62. *Board of Education of Independent School District No. 2 of Pottawatomie City v. Earls*, 536 U.S. 822 (2002).
63. *Mapp v. Ohio*, 367 U.S. 643 (1961).
64. Senate Committee on the Judiciary, *The Jury and the Search for Truth: The Case Against Excluding Relevant Evidence at Trial: Hearing Before the Committee, 104th Cong., 1st sess.* (U.S. Government Printing Office, 1997).
65. *United States v. Leon*, 468 U.S. 897 (1984); and *Arizona v. Evans*, 514 U.S. 1 (1995).
66. *Miranda v. Arizona*, 384 U.S. 436 (1966), but see *Yarborough v. Alvardo*, 541 U.S. 652 (2004).
67. *Dickerson v. United States*, 530 U.S. 428 (2000).
68. Justice Felix Frankfurter, dissenting in *United States v. Rabinowitz*, 339 U.S. 56 (1950).
69. *United States v. Enterprises, Inc.*, 498 U.S. 292 (1991).
70. *Williams v. Florida*, 399 U.S. 78 (1970); and *Burch v. Louisiana*, 441 U.S. 130 (1979).
71. *J.E.B. v. Alabama ex rel T.B.*, 511 U.S. 127 (1994); *Batson v. Kentucky*, 476 U.S. 79 (1986); *Powers v.* *Ohio*, 499 U.S. 400 (1991); *Hernandez v. New York*, 500 U.S. 352 (1991); and *Georgia v. McCollum*, 505 U.S. 42 (1990).
72. *Ewing v. California*, 538 U.S. 11 (2003).
73. *Benton v. Maryland*, 395 U.S. 784 (1969). See also *Kansas v. Hendricks*, 521 U.S. 346 (1997).
74. *Graham v. Collins*, 506 U.S. 461 (1993).
75. Barry Scheck, Peter Neufeld, and Jim Dwyer, *Actual Innocence: Five Days to Execution and Other Dispatches from the Wrongly Convicted* (Doubleday, 2000); and Timothy Kaufman-Osborn, *From Noose to Needle: Capital Punishment and the Late Liberal State* (University of Michigan Press, 2002).
76. *Penry v. Lynaugh*, 492 U.S. 302 (1989).
77. *Atkins v. Virginia*, 536 U.S. 304 (2002).
78. Jerome Frank, *Courts on Trial* (Princeton University Press, 1949), p. 122. See also Steven Brill, *Trial by Jury* (American Lawyer Books/Touchstone, 1989).
79. Harry Kalven Jr. and Hans Zeisel, *The American Jury* (University of Chicago Press, 1971), p. 57. See also Jeffrey Abramson, *We, the Jury: The Jury System and the Ideal of Democracy* (Harvard University Press, 2000).
80. George Edwards, *The Police on the Urban Frontier* (Institute of Human Relations Press, 1968), p. 28. See also Jerome G. Miller, *African-American Males and the Criminal Justice System* (Cambridge University Press, 1996).
81. Sandra Bass, "Blacks, Browns, and the Blues: Police and Minorities in California," *Public Affairs Report* 38 (November 1997), p. 10.
82. See David Cole, *No Equal Justice: Race and Class in the American Criminal Justice System* (New Press, 1999); and Randall Kennedy, *Race, Crime, and the Law* (Pantheon, 1997).
83. See Community Policing Consortium, U.S. Department of Justice, at http://www.community-policing.org/
84. Robert H. Jackson, *The Supreme Court in the American System of Government* (Harvard University Press, 1955), pp. 81–82.

Chapter 17

1. Andrew Hacker, *Two Nations: Black and White, Separate, Hostile, Unequal* (Scribner, 1992).
2. *Slaughter-House Cases*, 83 U.S. 36 (1873); and *Civil Rights Cases*, 109 U.S. 3 (1883).
3. *Plessy v. Ferguson*, 163 U.S. 537 (1896).
4. *Brown v. Board of Education of Topeka*, 347 U.S. 483 (1954); and *Brown v. Board of Education of Topeka*, 349 U.S. 294 (1955).
5. *Gomillion v. Lightfoot*, 364 U.S. 339 (1960).
6. Michael R. Belknap, *Federal Law and Southern Order: Racial Violence and Constitutional Conflict in the Post-Brown South* (University of Georgia Press, 1987), pp. 128–204.
7. Taylor Branch, *Parting the Waters: America in the King Years, 1954–1963* (Simon & Schuster, 1988). See also Harris Wofford, *Of Kennedys and Kings: Making Sense of the Sixties* (Farrar, Straus & Giroux, 1980).
8. See Charles Whalen and Barbara Whalen, *The Longest Debate: A Legislative History of the 1964 Civil Rights Act* (Mentor, 1985); and Hugh Davis Graham, *The Civil Rights Era* (Oxford University Press, 1990).
9. Aldon D. Morris, *The Origins of the Civil Rights Movement: Black Communities Organizing for Change* (Free Press/Macmillan, 1985); James Farmer, *Lay Bare the Heart: An Autobiography of the Civil Rights Movement* (Arbor House, 1985).

10. National Advisory Commission on Civil Disorders, *The Kerner Report* (U.S. Government Printing Office, 1968), p. 1.

11. Ellen Carol Du Bois, *Feminism and Suffrage: The Emergence of an Independent Women's Movement in America, 1848–1869* (Cornell University Press, 1978); Joan Hoff-Wilson, "Women and the Constitution," *News for Teachers of Political Science* (Summer 1985), pp. 10–15.

12. Susan M. Hartmann, *From Margin to Mainstream: American Women and Politics Since 1960* (Temple University Press, 1989); and Susan Gluck Mezey, *In Pursuit of Equality: Women, Public Policy, and the Federal Courts* (St. Martin's Press, 1992).

13. *United States* v. *Virginia,* 518 U.S. 515 (1996). See also Philippa Strum, *Women in the Barracks: The VMI Case and Equal Rights* (University Press of Kansas, 2002).

14. David M. O'Brien, "Ironies and Unanticipated Consequences of Legislation: Title VII of the 1964 Civil Rights Act and Sexual Harassment," in *Congress and the Politics of Emerging Rights*, Colton C. Campbell and John F. Stack Jr.. eds. (Rowman & Littlefield, 2002), pp. 27–44.

15. *Meritor Savings Bank, FBD* v. *Vinson,* 477 U.S. 57 (1986).

16. *Oncale* v. *Sundowner Offshore Services,* 523 U.S. 75 (1998); and *Faragher* v. *City of Boca Raton,* 524 U.S. 775 (1998); and *Burlington Industries* v. *Ellerth,* 524 U.S. 742 (1998).

17. Gregory Rodriguez, "The Nation: Where Minorities Rule," *The New York Times,* February 10, 2002, p. WK6.

18. Celia W. Dugger, "U.S. Study Says Asian-Americans Face Widespread Discrimination," *The New York Times,* February 29, 1992, p. 1, reporting on U.S. Civil Rights Commission, *Civil Rights Issues Facing Asian Americans in the 1990s* (U.S. Government Printing Office, 1992).

19. Won Moo Hurh, *Korean Immigrants in America* (Fairleigh Dickinson University Press, 1984).

20. Antonio J. A. Pido, *The Filipinos in America: Macro/Micro Dimensions of Immigration and Integration* (Center for Migration Studies of New York, 1986).

21. Harold L. Hodgkinson, *The Demographics of American Indians: One Percent of the People, Fifty Percent of the Diversity* (Institute for Educational Leadership/Center for Demographic Policy, 1990), pp. 1–5.

22. Charles F. Wilkinson, *American Indians, Times, and the Law* (Yale University Press, 1987); and Vine Deloria Jr. and Clifford M. Lytle, *The Nations Within: The Past and Future of American Indian Sovereignty* (Pantheon Books, 1984).

23. *County of Yakima* v. *Yakima Indian Nation,* 502 U.S. 251 (1992).

24. Theodora Lurie, "Shattering the Myth of the Vanishing American," *Ford Foundation Letter* 22 (Winter 1991), p. 5.

25. Spencer Rich, "Native Americans: They Can Still Get Free Health Care If They're Indian Enough," *The Washington Post National Weekly Edition,* July 14, 1986, p. 34, quoting the Office of Technology Assessment.

26. *Morey* v. *Doud,* 354 U.S. 459 (1957); *Allegheny Pittsburgh Coal Co.* v. *County Commission,* 488 U.S. 336 (1989).

27. *City of Cleburne, Texas* v. *Cleburne Living Center,* 473 U.S. 432 (1985); *Heller* v. *Doe,* 509 U.S. 312 (1993); and *Roemer* v. *Evans,* 517 U.S. 620 (1996).

28. *Roemer* v. *Evans,* 517 U.S. 620 (1996).

29. *San Antonio School District* v. *Rodriguez,* 411 U.S. 1 (1973).

30. *Frontiero* v. *Richardson,* 411 U.S. 677 (1973).

31. *Califano* v. *Webster,* 430 U.S. 313 (1977).

32. *Mississippi University for Woman* v. *Hogan,* 458 U.S. 718 (1982); and *United States* v. *Virginia,* 518 U.S. 515 (1996).

33. *San Antonio School District* v. *Rodriguez,* 411 U.S. 1 (1973); Douglas Reed, *On Equal Terms: The Constitutional Politics of Educational Opportunity* (Princeton University Press, 2001).

34. Matthew Bosworth, *Courts as Catalysts: State Supreme Courts and Public School Finance Equity* (State University of New York Press, 2001).

35. Sandra Day O'Connor, in *Kimel* v. *Florida Board of Regents,* 528 U.S. 62 (2000).

36. Ibid.

37. *Washington* v. *Davis,* 426 U.S. 229 (1976). See also *Hunter* v. *Underwood,* 471 U.S. 522 (1985).

38. Sandra Day O'Connor, concurring in *Hernandez* v. *New York,* 500 U.S. 352 (1991).

39. *Personnel Administrator of Massachusetts* v. *Feeney,* 442 U.S. 256 (1979).

40. *Smith* v. *Allwright,* 321 U.S. 649 (1944).

41. *Gomillion* v. *Lightfoot,* 364 U.S. 339 (1960).

42. *Harper* v. *Virginia Board of Elections,* 383 U.S. 663 (1966).

43. *Report of the United States Commission on Civil Rights* (U.S. Government Printing Office, 1959), pp. 103–104.

44. Harold W. Stanley, *Voter Mobilization and the Politics of Race: The South and Universal Suffrage, 1952–1984* (Praeger, 1987).

45. Abigail M. Thernstrom, *Whose Votes Count? Affirmative Action and Minority Voting Rights* (Harvard University Press, 1987), p. 15.

46. Thernstrom, *Whose Votes Count?* For a contrary view, see Bernard Grofman, Lisa Handley, and Richard G. Niemi, *Minority Representation and the Quest for Voting Equality* (Cambridge University Press, 1992).

47. *Morse* v. *Republican Party of Virginia,* 517 U.S. 116 (1996).

48. *Shaw* v. *Reno,* 509 U.S. 630 (1993).

49. *Hunt* v. *Cromartie,* 532 U.S. 234 (2001); and *League of United Latin American Citizens* v. *Perry,* 126 S.Ct. 2594 (2006).

50. Orlando Patterson, *The Ordeal of Integration: Progress and Resentment in America's "Racial" Crisis* (Civitas/Counterpoint, 1997), p. 67.

51. *Plessy* v. *Ferguson,* 163 U.S. 537 (1896).

52. *Brown* v. *Board of Education of Topeka,* 347 U.S. 483 (1954). See also J. W. Peltason, *Fifty-Eight Lonely Men: Southern Federal Judges and School Desegregation* (University of Illinois Press, 1971), p. 248.

53. *Brown* v. *Board of Education of Topeka,* 349 U.S. 294 (1955).

54. *Freeman* v. *Pitts,* 503 U.S. 467 (1992); and *Missouri* v. *Jenkins,* 515 U.S. 70 (1995).

55. See Gary Orfield, Susan E. Eaton, and the Harvard Project on School Desegregation, *Dismantling Desegregation: The Quiet Reversal of Brown v. Board of Education* (New Press, 1996).

56. Raymond Hernandez, "NAACP Suspends Yonkers Leader After Criticism of Usefulness of School Busing," *The New York Times,* November 1, 1995, p. A13.

57. Gary Orfield and Chungmei Lee, *Brown at 50: King's Dream or Plessy's Nightmare?* (The Civil Rights Project, Harvard University, 2004), available at www.civilrightsproject.harvard.edu. See also Charles Clotfelter, *After Brown: The Rise and Retreat of School Desegregation* (Princeton University Press, 2004).

58. See Reed, *On Equal Terms,* pp. 21–22.

59. William O. Douglas, dissenting in *Moose Lodge No. 107* v. *Irvis,* 407 U.S. 163 (1972).

60. *New York State Club Association* v. *New York City,* 487 U.S. 1 (1988).

61. *Boy Scouts of America* v. *Dale,* 530 U.S. 640 (2000).

62. *Civil Rights Cases,* 109 U.S. 3 (1883).

63. *Heart of Atlanta Motel* v. *United States,* 379 U.S. 421 (1964).

64. Darryl Van Duch, "Plagued by Politics, EEOC Backlog Grows," *Recorder,* August 18, 1998, p. 1; David Rovella, "EEOC Chairman Casellas: 'We Are Being Selective,'" *National Law Journal,* November 20, 1995, p. 1.

65. Charles M. Lamb, "Housing Discrimination and Segregation," *Catholic University Law Review* (Spring 1981), p. 370.

66. *Shelley* v. *Kraemer,* 334 U.S. 1 (1948).

67. Daniel Mitchell, quoted in CQ Researcher, *Housing Discrimination* 5 (February 24, 1995), p. 174.

68. John Marshall Harlan, dissenting in *Plessy* v. *Ferguson,* 163 U.S. 537 (1896).

69. *University of California Regents* v. *Bakke,* 438 U.S. 265 (1978). See Howard Ball, *The Bakke Case* (University Press of Kansas, 2000).

70. Sandra Day O'Connor, in *Richmond* v. *Croson,* 488 U.S. 469 (1989).

71. See *Adarand Constructors, Inc.,* v. *Pena,* 515 U.S. 2000 (1995).

72. *Shaw* v. *Reno,* 509 U.S. 630 (1993); *Miller* v. *Johnson,* 515 U.S. 900 (1995).

73. "Affirmative Action in California Passed," *The Economist,* April 8, 2000, p. 29.

74. "Affirmative Action," *The Economist,* April 20, 2002, p. 30; "Affirmative Action: Moving on, but Very Slowly," *The Economist,* October 4, 2003, p. 29.

75. *Hopwood* v. *Texas,* 518 U.S. 1016 (1996).

76. *Gratz* v. *Bollinger,* 539 U.S. 244 (2003).

77. *Grutter* v. *Bollinger,* 539 U.S. 306 (2003).

78. Carol M. Swain et al., "When Whites and Blacks Agree: Fairness in Educational Opportunities," Institute of Governmental Studies, University of California at Berkeley, Working Paper 98–11, 1998, p. 6.

79. James Farmer, quoted in Rochelle L. Stanfield, "Black Complaints Haven't Translated into Political Organization and Power," *National Journal,* June 14, 1980, p. 465.

80. Gary Orfield and Chungmei Lee, *Brown at 50;* Clotfeler, *After Brown.*

81. D'Vera Cohn, "Hispanic Growth Surges Fueled by Births in the U.S.," *The Washington Post,* June 9, 2005, p. A1.

82. Gary Orfield, "Separate Societies: Have the Kerner Warnings Come True?" in *Quiet Riots: Race and Poverty in the United States—The Kerner Report Twenty Years Later,* Fred R. Harris and Roger W. Wilkins, eds. (Pantheon, 1988), p. 103. See also Nicholas Lehmann, *The Promised Land* (Knopf, 1991).

83. Patterson, *The Ordeal of Integration,* p. 54.

84. Gary Orfield and Carole Ashkinaze, *The Closing Door: Conservative Policy and Black Opportunity* (University of Chicago Press, 1991), p. 26.

85. William J. Wilson, *The Truly Disadvantaged: The Inner City, the Underclass, and Public Policy* (University of Chicago Press, 1987), esp. chap. 5; and Kevin Phillips, *The Politics of Rich and Poor* (Random House, 1995).

86. Orfield and Ashkinaze, *Closing Door,* pp. 221–234; and A. Leon Higginbotham Jr., *Shades of Freedom* (Oxford University Press, 1996).

Chapter 18

1. Joseph J. Schatz, "The Power of the Status Quo on Taxes," *Congressional Quarterly Weekly*, February 6, 2006, p. 332.
2. See John Kingdon, *Agendas, Alternatives, and Public Policies* (Little, Brown, 1984), for a description of the policy-making process.
3. Kingdon, *Agendas, Alternatives, and Public Policies*, p. 3.
4. Anthony Downs, "The 'Issue-Attention Cycle,'" *The Public Interest* 28 (Summer 1972), p. 38.
5. Lester Salamon and Michael Lund, "The Tools Approach: Basic Analytics," in L. Salamon, ed., *Beyond Privatization: The Tools of Government Action* (Urban Institute Press, 1989).
6. Hugh Heclo, "Issue Networks and the Executive Establishment," in A. King, ed., *The New American Political System* (American Enterprise Institute, 1978), pp. 87–124.
7. See "National Debt," at www.jeffords.senate.gov/debt.html.
8. For a discussion of the budgetary cycle, see Allen Schick, *The Federal Budget: Politics, Policy, Process*, rev. ed. (Brookings Institution Press, 2000).
9. Efforts at past tax reform are described in Jeffrey H. Birnbaum and Alan S. Murray, *Showdown at Gucci Gulch: Lawmakers, Lobbyists, and the Unlikely Triumph of Tax Reform* (Vintage, 1988). See also Timothy J. Conlan, Margaret T. Wrightson, and David R. Beam, *Taxing Choices: The Politics of Tax Reform* (CQ Press, 1990).
10. Quoted in Frederick Lewis Allen, *Since Yesterday* (Harper, 1940), p. 64.
11. The debate over Keynes and his economic theories is still alive in the United States. See Donald E. Moggridge, *Maynard Keynes: An Economist's Biography* (Routledge, 1992).
12. Gary Burtless, Robert J. Lawrence, Robert E. Litan, and Robert J. Shapiro, *Globaphobia: Confronting Fears About Open Trade* (Brookings Institution Press, 1998), p. 29. For more information about GATT and the World Trade Organization, go to www.wto.org.
13. Mary Jordan, "Mexican Workers Pay for Success," *The Washington Post*, June 20, 2002, p. A1.
14. Burtless et al., *Globaphobia*, p. 126.
15. Jyoti Thottam, "Is Your Job Going Abroad?" *Time*, March 1, 2004, pp. 26–30.
16. See Robert W. Crandall et al., *An Agenda for Federal Regulatory Reform* (American Enterprise Institute/Brookings Institution, 1997), for a discussion of reasons for the increased activity.
17. Harold W. Stanley and Richard G. Niemi, *Vital Statistics in American Politics, 1999* (CQ Press, 1999), p. 258.
18. Stephen Moore, ed., *Restoring the Dream: The Bold New Plan by House Republicans* (Times Books, 1995), p. 156.
19. *United States* v. *E. C. Knight Co.*, 156 U.S. 1 (1895).
20. On the origins of the Federal Trade Commission and the role of Louis D. Brandeis, see Thomas K. McCraw, *Prophets of Regulation* (Belknap Press, 1984), chap. 3.
21. For a useful history of airline deregulation, see Steven A. Morrison and Clifford Winston, *The Evolution of the Airline Industry* (Brookings Institution Press, 1995).
22. On Southwest Airlines and its longtime chief executive Herb Kelleher, see Kevin Freiberg and Jackie Freiberg, *Nuts!* (Bard Press, 1996).
23. *Reno* v. *American Civil Liberties Union*, 521 U.S. 844 (1997).
24. See Robert W. Crandall and Harold Furchtgott-Roth, *Cable TV: Regulation or Competition?* (Brookings Institution Press, 1996); Richard Klinger, *The New Information Industry: Regulatory Challenges and the First Amendment* (Brookings Institution Press, 1996); and Lawrence Lessig, *Code and Other Laws of Cyberspace* (Basic Books, 2000).

Chapter 19

1. Mary Agnes Carey, "Reining in Medicare Costs," *Congressional Quarterly Weekly*, January 30, 2006, p. 417.
2. Quoted in Janet Hook, "Medicare Drug Program May Harm, Not Help, GOP," *Los Angeles Times*, January 21, 2006, p. 1.
3. The Pew Research Center for The People & The Press, *Katrina Relief Effort Raises Concern over Excessive Spending, Waste* (Pew Research Center, 2005), p. 1.
4. Michael B. Katz, *In the Shadow of the Poorhouse: A Social History of Welfare in America* (Basic Books, 1986).
5. This history draws heavily on Theda Skocpol's research on the subject, starting with "America's First Social Security System: The Expansion of Benefits for Civil War Veterans," *Political Science Quarterly* 108 (Winter 1993), pp. 64–87.
6. Ibid., pp. 85–86.
7. Joel F. Handler, *The Poverty of Welfare Reform* (Yale University Press, 1995), p. 21.
8. The 2006 guidelines can be found at http://aspe.hhs.gov/poverty/06fedreg.htm.
9. See U.S. Census Bureau, "Poverty Highlights, 2004," www.census.gov/hhes/www/poverty/poverty04/pov04hi.html.
10. Gertrude Schaffner Goldberg and Eleanor Kremen, eds., *The Feminization of Poverty: Only in America?* (Greenwood Press, 1990).
11. See, for example, Margaret Weir, "Political Parties and Social Policymaking," in *The Social Divide: Political Parties and the Future of Activist Government*, Margaret Weir, ed. (Brookings Institution Press, 1998).
12. Self-employed workers must cover both amounts, and many state and local government workers are not required to participate.
13. These and other simple facts about Social Security can be found at www.ssa.gov/policy.
14. Martha Derthick, "No More Easy Votes for Social Security," *Brookings Review* 10 (Fall 1992), pp. 50–53.
15. For a pessimistic view of the viability of Social Security, see Neil Howe and Richard Jackson, "The Myth of the 2.2 Percent Solution," at http://www.cato.org/dailys/7-21-98.html. Robert D. Reischauer of the Brookings Institution testified before the House Committee on Ways and Means on November 19, 1998, that Social Security will start running deficits by 2021 and that by 2032, "reserves will be depleted."
16. See Theda Skocpol, *Protecting Soldiers and Mothers: The Political Origins of Social Policy in the United States* (Belknap Press, 1992), chap. 9, for a history of the act.
17. Lyndon Johnson, speech at the University of Michigan, May 1964, in *Congress and the Nation, 1965–1968: A Review of Government and Politics During the Johnson Years* (CQ Press, 1969), vol. 2, p. 650.
18. For a history of Medicare and other Great Society programs, see James L. Sundquist, *Politics and Policy: The Eisenhower, Kennedy, and Johnson Years* (Brookings Institution Press, 1968).
19. William J. Clinton, acceptance speech, Democratic National Convention, Chicago, July 6, 1992.
20. Robert Pear, "Judge Rules States Can't Cut Welfare," *The New York Times*, October 14, 1997, p. A1.
21. Isabel V. Sawhill, R. Kent Weaver, Ron Haskins, and Andrea Kane, eds., *Welfare Reform and Beyond: The Future of the Safety Net* (Brookings Institution Press, 2002), p. 19.
22. See for example, Ron Haskins and Isabel V. Sawhill, *Work and Marriage: The Way to End Poverty and Welfare*, Welfare Reform & Beyond Brief No. 28, Washington, D.C.: The Brookings Institution, 2003.
23. Centers for Medicare and Medicaid Services, "Health Accounts," at www.cms.hhs.gov/statistics/nhe.
24. Ibid., p. 93.
25. Laurene A. Graig, *Health of Nations: An International Perspective on U.S. Health Care Reform* (CQ Press, 1993), p. 20.
26. Michael D. Lemonick, "Doctors' Deadly Mistakes," *Time*, December 13, 1999, p. 74.
27. Jennifer Steinhauer, "At Beth Israel, Lapses in Care Mar Gains in Technology," *The New York Times*, February 15, 2000, p. B1.
28. "Medicare Funds Going Up in Smoke," *Deseret News*, May 17, 1994, p. 1.
29. Congressional Budget Office, *How Many People Lack Health Insurance and for How Long?* (Author, 2003).
30. U.S. Bureau of the Census, at www.census.gov.
31. "Measuring the HMOs," *Los Angeles Times*, October 3, 1998, p. B7.
32. Mary Agnes Carey and Rebecca Adams, "Managed-Care Conferees Agree on Appeals Principles; Key Details Remain Unresolved," *Congressional Quarterly Weekly*, April 15, 2000, p. 903.
33. Congressional Budget Office, *How Many People Lack Health Insurance and for How Long?* Issue Summary, Washington, D.C.: Congressional Budget Office, May 12, 2003.
34. Institute of Medicine, Committee on Employer-Based Health Benefits, *Employment and Health Benefits: A Connection at Risk*, Marilyn J. Field and Harold T. Shapiro, eds. (National Academy Press, 1993), p. 5.
35. The amount permitted for a medical savings account is 75 percent of the maximum total deduction for medical expenses for an individual or couple.
36. Martin Kady II, "America's Uneasy Mandate for Domestic Security," *Congressional Quarterly Weekly*, April 24, 2004, p. 950.

Chapter 20

1. Quoted in Daniel Boorstin, ed., *An American Primer*, vol. 1 (University of Chicago Press, 1966), pp. 192–210; emphasis in the original.
2. See Joseph Nye, *Soft Power: The Means to Success in World Politics* (Public Affairs, 2005).
3. See John Gershman, "Is Southeast Asia the Second Front," *Foreign Affairs*, July/August 2002, for a discussion of the roots of Islamic terrorism.
4. For more information, visit the Peace Corps Web site at www.peacecorps.gov. For a useful study of the Peace Corps, see Elizabeth Cobbs Hoffman, *All You Need Is Love: The Peace Corps and the Spirit of the 1960s* (Harvard University Press, 1998).
5. See Glenn Kessler, "U.S. Decision On Iraq Has Puzzling Past Opponents of War Wonder When,

How Policy Was Set," *The Washington Post*, January 12, 2003, p. A1, for a detailed history of the increasing interest in Iraq.

6. Condoleezza Rice, quoted in Glenn Kessler, "Rice Lays Out Case for War in Iraq," *The Washington Post*, August 16, 2002, p. A1.

7. Remarks to the United Nations, September 12, 2003

8. United States Senate Select Committee on Intelligence, *Report on the U.S. Intelligence Community's Prewar Intelligence Assessments on Iraq*, Committee print, reported July 7, 2004, Committee summary p. 1, available at www.intelligence .senate.gov/conclusions.pdf.

9. The "slam dunk case" story is reported in Bob Woodward's *Plan of Attack* (Simon & Schuster, 2004).

10. U.S. Department of Defense, at www.defense link.mil; U.S. Department of State, at www.state .gov.

11. For a fascinating history of U.S. intelligence operations, see Christopher Andrew, *For the President's Eyes Only: Secret Intelligence and the American Presidency from Washington to Bush* (HarperCollins, 1995). See also Rhodri Jeffreys-Jones, *The CIA and American Democracy*, 2d ed. (Yale University Press, 1998).

12. National Commission on Terrorist Attacks on the United States, *The 9/11 Commission Report*, p. 12.

13. See George C. Wilson, *This War Really Matters: Inside the Fight for Defense Dollars* (CQ Press, 2000).

14. Thomas L. Friedman, "India, Pakistan, and G.E.," *New York Times*, August 11, 2002, sec. 4, p. 13.

15. For an examination of how Japanese companies try to influence foreign policy and trade officials in Washington, see Pat Choate, *Agents of Influence* (Knopf, 1990).

16. "G.O.P. Returns $100,000 Gift," *The New York Times*, January 20, 2001, p. A8.

17. For a useful review of how Congress has occasionally challenged and even more often failed to challenge the White House when it comes to the war power, see Louis Fisher, *Presidential War Power* (University Press of Kansas, 1995).

18. For an analysis that asserts U.S. foreign policy is almost entirely shaped by self-appointed elites, see Eric Alterman, *Who Speaks for America? Why Democracy Matters* (Cornell University Press, 1998). More generally, see Ole Holsti, *Public Opinion and American Foreign Policy* (University of Michigan Press, 1996).

19. Dennis C. Jett, "The U.N.'s Failures Are Everyone's Fault," *The New York Times*, May 22, 2000, p. A23. See also Christopher S. Wren, "Era Waning: Holbrooke Takes Stock," *The New York Times*, January 14, 2001, p. 8.

20. "U.S. Foreign Aid Spending Since World War II," *Public Perspective* 8 (August–September 1997), p. 11.

21. Gallup Poll, May 2000, www.gallup.com.

22. See Sebastian Mallaby, "Why So Stingy on Foreign Aid?" *Washington Post National Weekly Edition*, July 3, 2000, p. 27.

23. Ibid. But see Doug Bandow, "The Case Against Foreign Aid," *Christian Science Monitor*, September 29, 1999, p. 9; and Eric Schmitt, "Helms Urges Foreign Aid Be Handled by Charities," *The New York Times*, January 12, 2001, p. A4.

24. Richard Lugar, in Gerald F. Seib, "Capital Journal," *The Wall Street Journal*, June 17, 1998, p. A18.

25. Gary Hufbauer, "Foreign Policy on the Cheap," *Washington Post National Weekly Edition*, July 20, 1998, p. 22.

26. See Robert Kagan, "The Kerry Doctrine," *The Washington Post*, August 1, 2004, p. B7, for this argument.

27. Gary Hufbauer and Jeffrey J. Schott, "Economic Sanctions and Foreign Policy," *PS: Political Science and Politics* 18 (Fall 1985), p. 278.

28. John Prados, *The President's Secret Wars: CIA and Pentagon Covert Operations Since World War II* (Morrow, 1986); Daniel Patrick Moynihan, *Secrecy: The American Experience* (Yale University Press, 1998).

29. p. W. Singer, "Winning the War of Words: Information Warfare in Afghanistan," *Brookings Analysis Paper No. 5*, October 2001.

30. Norman A. Graebner, "The President as Commander in Chief: A Study in Power," in *Commander-in-Chief: Presidential Leadership in Modern Wars*, Joseph G. Dawson III, ed. (University Press of Kansas, 1993), p. 31.

31. Eric Schmitt and Thom Shanker, "Army to Call Up Recruits Earlier," *The New York Times*, July 22, 2004, p. A1.

32. Evan Thomas and Gregory L. Vistica, "Falling Out of the Sky," *Newsweek*, March 17, 1997, p. 26.

33. Office of Management and Budget, *Budget of the United States, Fiscal Year 2007* (U.S. Government Printing Office, 2007D).

34. John Spratt and Hugh Brady, "National Security v. Social Security," *Brookings Review*, vol. 20, no. 3 (Summer 2002), p. 12.

35. See, for example, James Kitfield, "Ships Galore!" *National Journal*, February 10, 1996, pp. 298–302.

36. *Public Papers of the Presidents*, Dwight D. Eisenhower, 1957, pp. 1035–1040.

37. See Renae Merle, "Contract Workers Are War's Forgotten," *The Washington Post*, July 31, 2004, p. A1.

38. Michael Rich, John Birkler, and Mark Lorell, "Defense Industry Goliaths," *The Atlantic Monthly*, July/August, 2003, p. 89.

Chapter 21

1. Donald Boyd, "State Finances: Solid Recovery but Challenges Ahead," in *The Book of the States, 2006* (The Council of State Governments, 2006).

2. For a discussion of what factors improve economic performance and state policy effectiveness, see Paul Brace, *State Government and Economic Performance* (Johns Hopkins University Press, 1993); and Susan E. Clarke and Martin R. Saiz, "Economic Development and Infrastructure Policy," in *Politics in the American States*, eds. Virginia Gray, Russell Hanson, and Herbert Jacob, 7th ed. (CQ Press, 1999), pp. 540–543.

3. U.S. Bureau of the Census, *Statistical Abstract of the United States*, available at www.census.gov/ compendia/statab/.

4. Robert S. Lynd and Helen M. Lynd, *Middletown* (Harcourt, 1929). See also their analysis of Muncie ten years later in *Middletown in Transition* (Harcourt, 1937).

5. Floyd Hunter, *Community Power Structure* (University of North Carolina Press, 1953). For a reassessment and rebuttal of Hunter's findings, see M. Kent Jennings, *Community Influentials: The Elites of Atlanta* (Free Press, 1964).

6. Robert A. Dahl, *Who Governs? Democracy and Power in an American City* (Yale University Press, 1961).

7. See the interesting study of San Jose, California, by Phillip J. Troustine and Terry Christensen, *Movers and Shakers: The Study of Community Power* (St. Martin's Press, 1982). See also Clarence N. Stone, *Regime Politics: Governing Atlanta, 1946–1988* (University Press of Kansas, 1989).

8. See, for example, Peter Bachrach and Morton S. Baratz, *Power and Poverty: Theory and Practice* (Oxford University Press, 1970); Matthew A. Crenson, *The Unpolitics of Air Pollution: A Study of Non-Decision Making in Two Cities* (Johns Hopkins University Press, 1971); and John Gaventa, *Power and Powerlessness: Quiescence and Rebellion in an Appalachian Valley* (University of Illinois Press, 1980).

9. Bryan D. Jones and Lynn W. Bachelor, *The Sustaining Hand: Community Leadership and Corporate Power*, 2d ed. (University Press of Kansas, 1993), p. 254. See also Stone, *Regime Politics*.

10. U.S. Census, Governments Division, "2005 Public Employment Data, State and Local Governments, United States Total" (July 2005) at http:// ftp2.census.gov/govs/apes/05stlus.txt; and "Federal Government Civilian Employment" (December 2005) at http://ftp2.census.gov/ govs/apes/05fedfun.pdf.

11. U.S. Census, Governments Division, "2005 Public Employment Data, State and Local Governments, United States Total" (July 2005) at http:// ftp2.census.gov/govs/apes/05stlus.txt.

12. Stone, *Regime Politics*, p. 232.

13. For a detailed analysis of how the W. R. Grace Company and Beatrice Foods Company had to rely on law firms to fight legal actions surrounding their operations in Woburn, Massachusetts, see Jonathan Harr, *A Civil Action* (Vintage Books, 1996). See also Alan Rosenthal, *The Third House: Lobbyists and Lobbying in the States*, 2d ed. (CQ Press, 2001).

14. See Clive S. Thomas and Ronald J. Hrebenar, "Interest Groups in the States," in *Politics in the American States*, Gray et al., eds., pp. 122–158.

15. For a general discussion of ethics reform and enforcement efforts, see *Spectrum: The Journal of State Government* (Winter 1993).

16. On various efforts to improve ethical practices and professionalism in the state legislatures and the limits of these efforts, see Alan Rosenthal, *Drawing the Line: Legislative Ethics in the States* (University of Nebraska Press, 1996).

17. Jimmy Carter, *Why Not the Best?* (Bantam Books, 1976), p. 101. See also the memoir by Tom Loftus, a former speaker of the Wisconsin State Assembly, *The Art of Legislative Politics* (CQ Press, 1994), chap. 3.

18. Diane D. Blair, *Arkansas Politics and Government* (University of Nebraska Press, 1988), p. 118.

19. William p. Browne and Kenneth VerBurg, *Michigan Politics and Government* (University of Nebraska Press, 1995), pp. 241–245.

20. *The Book of the States, 2005* (Council of State Governments, 2005), p. 384.

21. Paul Peterson, *City Limits* (University of Chicago Press, 1981), p. 124. See also the useful discussion of the challenge of covering state legislative politics in Browne and VerBurg, *Michigan Politics and Government*, pp. 242–245.

22. Joseph F. Zimmerman, *The New England Town Meeting: Democracy in Action* (Praeger, 1999).

23. See for example, Daniel Kemmis, *The Good City and the Good Life* (Houghton Mifflin, 1995); and David L. Kirp, John p. Dwyer, and Larry A. Rosenthal, *Our Town: Race, Housing, and the*

Soul of Suburbia (Rutgers University Press, 1997).

24. Eugene F. Rivers III, "High-Octane Faith," in *Community Works: The Revival of Civil Society in America*, E. J. Dionne Jr., ed. (Brookings Institution Press, 1998), p. 61.

25. For the efforts of a big-city mayor and his team of advisers, see Buzz Bissinger, *A Prayer for the City* (Random House, 1997). See also the example of Milwaukee's mayor, John O. Norquist, *Wealth of Cities* (Addison-Wesley, 1998).

26. Jonathan Weisman, "2006 Cuts In Domestic Spending On Table," *Washington Post* (May 27, 2004); Kavan Peterson, "Bush Budget Cuts Education," www.stateline.org, accessed on February 6, 2006.

Chapter 22

1. http://www.iandrinstitute.org/BW%202006-5%20(Election%20results).pdf

2. Temporary New York State Commission on Constitutional Revision, *Effective Government Now for the New Century* (Nelson A. Rockefeller Institute of Government, 1995).

3. Mario M. Cuomo, "Real Reform: It's Time for a People's State Constitutional Convention," *Rockefeller Institute Bulletin* (1993), pp. 41–46.

4. Richard Perez-Pena, "Voters Reject Constitutional Convention: Last-Minute Campaign Appears to Sway Ballot," *The New York Times*, November 5, 1997, p. B1.

5. Michigan Department of State, Bureau of Elections, at www.sos.state.mi.us/law; and Arkansas Government Relations, at www.uark.edu/~govinfo/PAGES/History/del.html.

6. Gerald Benjamin, "The Functions of State Constitutions in a Federal System," paper presented at the American Political Science Association Round Table, Washington, D.C., 1984.

7. John Adams, quoted in Judith S. Kaye, "Federalism's Other Tier," *Constitution* 3 (Winter 1991), p. 50.

8. G. Alan Tarr, *Understanding State Constitutions* (Princeton University Press, 2000), p. 47.

9. Donald S. Lutz, "Toward a Theory of Constitutional Amendment," in *Responding to Imperfection: The Theory and Practice of Constitutional Amendment*, Sanford Levinson, ed. (Princeton University Press, 1995), pp. 237–274.

10. *The Book of the States, 2005* (Council of State Governments, 2005), pp. 10–11; John Kincaid, "State Constitutions in the Federal System," *Annals of the American Academy of Political and Social Science* 496 (March 1988), p. 14.

11. *The Book of the States, 2005*, pp. 10–11.

12. *The Book of the States, 2005*, p. 10.

13. Steve Geissinger, "Changing the Constitution Is a Powerful Government-Reform Tool Avoided by Officials," *Alameda Times-Star*, November 9, 2003, p. C1.

14. Jack W. Strain, *An Outline of Oklahoma Government*, Leroy Crozier and Carl F. Reherman, eds. (Bureau of Local Government Services, Department of Political Science, Central State University, 1984), p. 21.

15. South Dakota Constitution, Article XI, Section 8.

16. Alabama Constitution, Amendment 383 (1901).

17. Christopher W. Hammons, "State Constitutional Reform: Is It Necessary?" *Albany Law Review* 64 (2001), pp. 1328–1334.

18. Christopher W. Hammons, "Was James Madison Wrong? Rethinking the American Preference for

Short, Framework-Oriented Constitutions," *American Political Science Review* 93 (December 1999), p. 838. See also ibid.

19. *Indiana* v. *Gerschoffer*, 763 N.E.2d 960 (2002).

20. *Anchorage Police Department Employees Association* v. *Anchorage*, 24 P.3d 547 (2001).

21. *American Academy of Pediatrics* v. *Lungren*, 490 P.2d 797 (1997).

22. Kaye, "Federalism's Other Tier," p. 54.

23. See, e.g., Matthew Bosworth, *Courts as Catalysts: State Supreme Courts and Public School Finances Equity* (State University of New York Press, 2001); and Charles Lopeman, *The Activist Advocate: Policy Making in State Supreme Courts* (Praeger, 1999).

24. *Michigan* v. *Long*, 463 U.S. 1032 (1983); "Our Judicial Federalism," *Intergovernmental Perspective* 15 (Summer 1989), pp. 8–15; William M. Wiecek, "Some Protection of Personal Liberty: Remembering the Future," and Kermit L. Hall, "Mostly Anchor and Little Sail: The Evolution of American State Constitutions," in *Toward a Usable Past: Liberty Under State Constitutions*, Paul Finkelman and Stephen E. Gottlieb, eds. (University of Georgia Press, 1991), pp. 371–417.

25. Deborah Baker, "Canvassing Board Certifies Amendment Election," *Santa Fe New Mexican* (October 14, 2003), p. A1.

26. *The Book of the States, 2005*, pp. 12–13, 18.

27. Fred Keeley, "Calfornia Dreamin': An On-time Budget," *The Sacramento Bee* (July 17, 2005).

28. *The Book of the States, 2005*, p. 17.

29. Tip H. Allen Jr., "The Enduring Traditions of the State Constitutions," in *Mississippi Government and Politics: Modernizers Versus Traditionalists*, Dale Krane and Stephen D. Shaffer, eds. (University of Nebraska Press, 1992), pp. xx–xxv.

30. *The Book of the States, 2002–2003*, p. 14.

31. David B. Magleby, "Direct Legislation in the American States," in *Referendums Around the World: The Growing Use of Direct Democracy*, David Butler and Austin Ranney, eds. (American Enterprise Institute Press, 1994), p. 225.

32. California Commission on Campaign Financing, *Democracy by Initiative: A Summary of the Report and Recommendations of the California Commission on Campaign Financing* (Center for Responsive Government, 1992), p. 25.

33. *Amador Valley Joint Union High School District* v. *State Board of Equalization*, 22 Cal. 3d 208 (1978), quoted in Eugene C. Lee, "The Revision of California's Constitution," *CPS Brief: A Publication of the California Policy Seminar* 3 (April 1991), p. 1.

34. *The Book of the States, 2002–2003*, p. 11. See also Magleby, "Direct Legislation," p. 251.

35. Tarr, *Understanding State Constitutions*, p. 158; and Thomas Gais and Gerald Benjamin, "Public Discontent and the Decline of Deliberation: A Dilemma in State Constitutional Reform, *Temple Law Review*, vol. 68, no. 3 (1995), pp. 1292–1300.

36. Ibid., pp. 160–161.

37. Gerald Benjamin and Thomas Gais, "Constitutional Conventionphobia," in *State Constitutions: Competing Perspectives*, Burton C. Agata and Eric Lane, eds. (Hofstra Law and Policy Symposium, 1996), vol. 1, p. 69; Tarr, *Understanding State Constitutions*, p. 25; and *The Book of the States 2005*, p. 17.

38. Caleb Nelson, "A Re-evaluation of Scholarly Explanations for the Rise of the Elective Judiciary in Antebellum America," 37 Am. J. Legal Hist. 221 (1993).

39. Elder Witt, "State Supreme Courts: Tilting the Balance Toward Change," *Governing*, August 1988, p. 33.

40. G. Alan Tarr, *Keynote Address*, Conference on State Constitutional Reform, May 4, 2000, at www.camlaw.rugers.edu/statecon/keynote.html.

41. Lee, "Revision of California's Constitution," p. 7. See also Lutz, "Toward a Theory of Constitutional Amendment," pp. 355–370.

42. "State of Rhode Island General Assembly," http://www.rilin.state.ri.us/studteaguide/RhodeIslandHistory/chapt9.html, Accessed October 24, 2006.

43. Re Jan Ruggiero, Director of Elections, Elections Division, Office of the Secretary of State, Providence, R.I., at www.state.ri.us.

44. Common Cause of Rhode Island, "Separation of Powers," at www.commoncauseri.org/news.

45. Cecil Morgan, "A New Constitution for Louisiana," *National Civic Review*, July 1974, pp. 343–356.

46. Tarr, *Understanding State Constitutions*, p. 143.

47. Beryl E. Pettus and Randall W. Bland, *Texas Government Today* (Dorsey Press, 1979), pp. 34–36. See also Janice C. May, "Texas Constitutional Revision and Laments," *National Civic Review*, February 1977, pp. 64–69.

48. Andre Henderson, "Selling a Constitution: California Desperately Needs a New Charter, That Doesn't Mean It Will Get One," *Governance*, December 1995, pp. 30–31.

49. B. Drummond Ayres Jr., "Alabama Governor Set for Tough Race," *The New York Times*, February 27, 2002, p. A16.

50. Albert E. McKinley, "Two New Southern Constitutions," *Political Science Quarterly* 18 (September 1903), pp. 480–511.

51. For more information go to the Web site of the Alabama Citizens for Constitutional Reform at www.constitutionalreform.org.

52. *Montgomery Advertiser*, December 11, 2002, the Associated Press, "Constitution Work May Come in 2003," at www.montgomeryadvertiser.com.

53. Editorial, "Constitutional Count, House Sending Clear Message: People Can't Be Trusted," *The Birmingham News*, March 21, 2002, p. A20.

54. David White, "Constitution Could Lose Segregation Provisions," *The Birmingham News*, April 16, 2003, p. A1.

55. See, for instance, the Web site of Alabama Citizens for Constitutional Reform, www.constitutionalreform.org/.

56. *The Book of the States, 2005*, pp. 3–9.

Chapter 23

1. John Mintz, "It's Not as Easy as 1-2-3; Problems Exist with Both Hand, Machine Counts," *The Washington Post*, November 19, 2000, p. A1.

2. www.electionline.org, *Election Reform Since November 2000: What's Changed, What Hasn't and Why, 2000–2006* (www.electionline.org, 2006), p. 11. The Election Reform Information project started in the wake of the election administration problems in the 2000 presidential election. Funded by the Pew Charitable Trusts, the project is a nonpartisan clearinghouse on election reform.

3. Katharine Q. Seelye, "Panel Suggests Election Changes That Let States Keep Control," *The New York Times*, February 5, 2001, p. A16.

4. Mark Crispin Miller, "None Dare Call it Stolen," *Harper's Magazine*, August 2005.

5. John F. Bibby, *Politics, Parties, and Elections in America*, 5th ed. (Wadsworth, 2003).

6. Florida Department of State, www.election.dos .state.fl.us.

7. www.electionline.org.

8. According to Todd Taylor, executive director, Utah Democratic party, these requirements are intended to promote gender equity; personal communication, November 18, 1998.

9. See Cornelius P. Cotter, James L. Gibson, John F. Bibby, and Robert J. Huckshorn, *Party Organizations in America* (Praeger, 1984).

10. Ronald E. Weber, ed., *American State and Local Politics: Directions for the 21st Century* (Chatham House, 1999), p. 174.

11. United States Election Assistance Commission, "The Impact of the National Voter Registration Act, 2003—2004," www.eac.gov/NVRA-2004-Survey.htm#nvra11, accessed October 18, 2006.

12. Benjamin Highton and Raymond E. Wolfinger, *Political Behavior*, vol. 20, no. 2. (June 1998), pp. 94–97.

13. California Secretary of State, www.ss.ca.gov/ elections/ror/15day_06/hist_reg_stats.pdf, accessed October 18, 2006.

14. Mary Clare Jalonick, "Utah GOP Floats a Salt Lake Split-Up," *Congressional Quarterly Weekly*, May 5, 2001, p. 1032.

15. United States Election Assistance Commission, "Voter Registration and Turnout 2000," www .eac.gov/, accessed June 16, 2006.

16. United State Department of Commerce, *Statistical Abstract of the United States 2006*, (October 2005), p. 264; and Greg McDonald, "Primary Turnout May Prolong Downtrend," *Stateline.org* (September 17, 2002).

17. For a discussion of coordinated campaigns, see Paul Herrnson, "National Party Organizations and the Postreform Congress," in *The Postreform Congress*, Roger Davidson, ed. (St. Martin's Press, 1992), pp. 65–67.

18. See Cotter et al., Party Organizations in America.

19. Richard Perez-Pena, "A Federal Soft-Money Ban Could Benefit State Parties," *The New York Times*, March 22, 2002, p. B6.

20. Richard A. Oppel Jr., "Election Panel Rebuffs Effort to Weaken 'Issue Ad' Limits," *The New York Times*, June 20, 2002, p. A1.

21. David B. Magleby, ed., *Financing the 2000 Elections* (Brookings Institution Press, 2002), p. 223.

22. Ibid., p. 203.

23. David B. Magleby and J. Quin Monson, *The Last Hurrah* (Brookings Institution Press, 2004), p. 5.

24. Eric Kelderman, "Colorado Is Hot Spot for Politicking by 527s," *Stateline.org*, April 4, 2006.

25. See Bruce E. Keith, David B. Magleby, Candice J. Nelson, Elizabeth Orr, Mark C. Westlye, and Raymond E. Wolfinger, *The Myth of the Independent Voter* (University of California Press, 1992), p. 52.

26. The Field Poll, "Voters Very Dissatisfied with State Budget Negotiations. Blame Davis and Both Parties in the Legislature. Three in Four Fear the State Is Seriously Off on the Wrong Track," at www.field.com/fieldpollonline/subscribers/ RLS2074.pdf, accessed July 15, 2003.

27. The Field Poll, "How Schwarzenegger's History and Characteristics Helps and Hurts Him in His Bid to Become Governor," at www.field.com/ fieldpollonline/subscribers/RLS2083.pdf, accessed August 17, 2003.

28. William H. Flanigan and Nancy H. Zingale, *Political Behavior of the American Electorate*, 8th ed. (CQ Press, 1994), p. 171.

29. See BetterCampaigns.org at www.better campaigns.org/standard/display.php?StoryID= 10. Michigan Democratic Party. "Where Are My Judges." Videocassette, thirty seconds, 2000. In possession of author.

30. William Glaberson, "Fierce Campaigns Signal a New Era for State Courts," *The New York Times*, June 5, 2000, p. A1.

31. Deborah Goldberg, Sarah Samis, Edwin Bender, and Rachel Weiss, *The New Politics of Judicial Elections, 2004* (Justice at Stake Campaign, 2004).

32. Willis D. Hawley, *Nonpartisan Elections and the Case for Party Politics* (Wiley, 1973), pp. 81–82. See also Brian F. Schaffner, Matthew Streb, and Gerald Wright, "Teams Without Uniforms: The Nonpartisan Ballot in State and Local Elections," *Political Research Quarterly* 54 (March 2001), pp. 7–30.

33. Susan Welch and Timothy Bledsoe, "The Partisan Consequences of Non-Partisan Elections and the Changing Nature of Urban Politics," *American Journal of Political Science*, vol. 30, no. 1 (February 1986), pp. 128–139.

34. National Conference of State Legislatures, "2006 Partisan Composition of State Legislatures," www.ncsl.org/ncsldb/elect98/partcomp.cfm? yearsel=2006, accessed April 17, 2006.

35. Bill Mears, "Texas Redistricting Reaches High Court," *CNN*, February 28, 2006, www.cnn.com/ 2006/LAW/02/28/scotus.texas/. The Supreme Court decision was *League of United Latin American Citizens, et al.* v. *Perry, Governor of Texas, et al.*, No. 05-204 (2006).

36. Kevin Duggan, "GOP Map Cast Aside," *The Fort Collins Coloradoan*, December 2, 2003, http:// coloradoan.com/news/coloradoanpublishing/ Legislature2004/redistricting/120203_ruling. html, accessed October 17 2006.

37. Terrel L. Rhodes, *Republicans in the South: Voting for the State House, Voting for the White House* (Praeger, 2000), p. 88.

38. Harvey L. Schantz, "Sectionalism in Presidential Elections," in *American Presidential Elections: Process, Policy, and Political Change*, Harvey L. Schantz, ed. (SUNY Press, 1996), pp. 106–107. See also Zell Miller, "The Democratic Party's Southern Problem," *The New York Times*, June 4, 2001, p. A17.

39. U.S. Bureau of the Census, *Statistical Abstract of the United States, 2001* (U.S. Government Printing Office, 2001), p. 26.

40. Raymond E. Wolfinger and Steven J. Rosenstone, *Who Votes?* (Yale University Press, 1980), p. 130.

41. Election Data Service, "Voting Equipment Study," at www.electiondataservices.com/home. htm, accessed February 6, 2006.

42. Ibid.

43. Ibid.

44. Brennan Center Task Force on Voting System Security, *The Machinery of Democracy: Protecting Elections in an Electronic World* (Brennan Center for Justice, New York University School of Law, 2006).

45. David B. Magleby, "Participation in Mail Ballot Elections," *Western Political Quarterly* 40 (March 1987), pp. 79–91.

46. Priscilla Southwell, "Five Years Later: A Reassessment of Oregon's Vote by Mail Electoral Process," (2003); Paul Gronke, "Ballot Integrity and Voting by Mail: The Oregon Experience," (2005), both available at www.sos.state.or.us/ executive/policy-initiatives/vbm/execvbm.htm, accessed October 17 2006.

47. Absentee ballots for all states are available from www.justvote.org.

48. Amber Cervantes, "Absentee Ballots," presentation of Washington Secretary of State's office, May 2006, available at www.secstate.wa.gov/ elections/auditorsCTP/ppt/Mail_Ballots_files/ frame.htm.

49. Bruce E. Cain and Elisabeth R. Gerber, eds., *Voting at the Political Fault Line: California's Experiment with the Blanket Primary* (University of California Press, 2002), p. 341.

50. *California Democratic Party et al.* v. *Jones, Secretary of State of California, et al.*, 530 U.S. 567 (2000); and Linda Greenhouse, "Split Decisions: The Court Rules, America Changes," *The New York Times*, July 2, 2000, sec. 4, p. 1.

51. Malcolm E. Jewell and David M. Olson, *Political Parties and Elections in American States*, 3d ed. (Dorsey Press, 1988), p. 121; Flanigan and Zingale, *Political Behavior of the American Electorate*, p. 195.

52. James I. Lengle, Representation and Presidential Primaries: The Democratic Party in the Postreform Era (Greenwood Press, 1981). For more on primary elections, see Larry M. Bartels, Presidential Primaries and the Dynamics of Public Choice (Princeton University Press, 1988); Jeane J. Kirkpatrick, The New Presidential Elite: Men and Women in National Politics (Basic Books, 1976); and Barbara Norander, "Ideological Representativeness of Presidential Primary Voters," Journal of Politics 51 (November 1989), pp. 977–992.

53. Edward D. Feigenbaum and James A. Palmer, *Campaign Finance Law 2002* (U.S. Federal Election Commission, 2002), chart 2-A. For more information on campaign finance laws, see www.fec.gov.

54. Other "clean money" states include Arizona, Connecticut, and Vermont. See www .publicampaign.org/where. For an assessment of the effects of two of these programs, see U.S. Government Accountability Office, *Campaign Finance Reform: Early Experiences of Two States That Offer Full Public Funding for Political Candidates*, GAO-03-453 (Washington, DC: U.S. Government Accountability Office, 2003).

55. Michael Malbin and Thomas Gais, *The Day After Reform: Sobering Campaign Finance Lessons from the American States* (Rockefeller Institute Press, 1998), pp. 65–70.

56. See Maine Citizens for Clean Elections, "Clean Election Supporters Call for Full Restoration of Clean Election Fund," at www.maineclean elections.org/, accessed July 11, 2006.

57. The Supreme Court decision is *Randall et al.* vs. *Sorrell et al.*, No. 04-1528 (2006).

58. David B. Magleby, "Campaign Spending and Referendum Voting," paper presented at the annual meeting of the Western Political Science Association, Albuquerque, N.M., March 1994.

59. Financing California's Statewide Ballot Measures: Receipts and Expenditures Through December 31, 1998 (California Secretary of State, 1998), p. 2.

60. David B. Magleby, *Direct Legislation: Voting on Ballot Propositions in the United States* (Johns Hopkins University Press, 1984), chaps. 7–9.

61. California Secretary of State Kevin Shelly, at www.ss.ca.gov/elections/elections_recall_faqs .htm#20, accessed June 15, 2006.

62. U.S. Department of State, "Schwarzenegger Wins California Gubernatorial Vote," at usinfo. state.gov/dhr/Archive/2003/Oct/09-562246. html, accessed June 15, 2006.

63. See Larry Gerston and Terry Christensen, *Recall: California's Political Earthquake* (M. E. Sharpe, 2004).

64. California Voter Foundation, at www.calvoter .org/voter/elections/archive/recall/index.html, accessed June 15, 2006.

Chapter 24

1. For a useful look at Nebraska's unique legislature, see Jack Rodgers, Robert Sittig, and Susan Welch, "The Legislature," in *Nebraska Government and Politics*, Robert D. Miewald, ed. (University of Nebraska Press, 1984), pp. 57–86.

2. Richard A. Clucas, "Exercising Control: The Power of State House Speakers," paper presented at the annual meeting of the Western Political Science Association, Los Angeles, March 1998. See also Malcolm E. Jewell and Marcia Lynn Whicker, *Legislative Leadership in the American States* (University of Michigan Press, 1997).

3. *The Book of the States, 2005* (Council of State Governments, 2005), pp. 136–137.

4. National Conference of State Legislatures, "Size of State Legislative Staff, 2003," www.ncsl.org/ programs/legman/about/staffcount2003.htm, updated May 6, 2004.

5. Alan Rosenthal, *Legislative Life: People, Process, and Performance in the States* (Harper & Row, 1981), pp. 112–113.

6. Tom Birmingham, quoted in Karen Hansen, "Legislator Pay: Baseball It Ain't," *State Legislatures* (July–August 1997), p. 20.

7. See Peverill Squire, "Uncontested Seats in State Legislative Elections," *Legislative Studies Quarterly* 35 (February 2000), pp. 131–146.

8. Alan Rosenthal, "The Legislative Unraveling of Institutional Fabric," in *The State of the States*, 3d ed., Carl E. Van Horn, ed. (CQ Press, 1996), p. 118.

9. Gary F. Moncrief, Peverill Squire, and Malcolm E. Jewell, *Who Runs for the Legislature?* (Prentice Hall, 2000).

10. Frank Smallwood, *Free and Independent: The Initiation of a College Professor into State Politics* (Stephen Greene Press, 1976), p. 223.

11. National Conference of State Legislatures, "2006 Partisan Composition of State Legislatures" www.ncsl.org/ncsldb/elect98/partcomp.cfm? yearsel=2006, accessed April 17, 2006.

12. See Sue Thomas, *How Women Legislate* (Oxford University Press, 1994). See also Lesley Dahlkemper, "Growing Accustomed to Her Face," *State Legislatures*, July–August 1996, pp. 37–45, and Kathleen Dolan and Lynne Ford, "Change and Continuity Among Women State Legislators," *Political Research Quarterly*, vol. 50 (March 1997), pp. 137–151.

13. Alexander Russo, "Switching Hallowed Halls," *State Legislatures*, July/August 2005, p. 60.

14. For fascinating comparative data, see *Inside the Legislative Process: A Comprehensive Survey by the American Society of Legislative Clerks and Secretaries* (National Council of State Legislatures, 1998).

15. Keith E. Hamm and Gary F. Moncrief, "Legislative Politics in the States," in Virginia Gray et al., *Politics in the American States*, 7th ed. (CQ Press, 1999), p. 184.

16. Lobbying strategies are outlined in Jay Michael and Dan Walters, *The Third House: Lobbyists, Power, and Money in Sacramento* (Berkeley Public Policy Press, 2001). Other lobbying realities are discussed in Loftus, *Art of Legislative Politics*, chap. 10, and Alan Rosenthal, *Drawing the Line: Legislative Ethics in the States* (University of Nebraska Press, 1996).

17. Thomas Frank, "Ex-Legislators Use Contacts," *The Denver Post*, July 5, 1996, p. 16A. See also Loftus, *Art of Legislative Politics*.

18. Samuel K. Gove and James D. Nowlan, *Illinois Politics and Government* (University of Nebraska Press, 1996), p. 53.

19. Joel A. Thompson and Gary F. Moncrief, eds., *Campaign Finance in State Legislative Elections* (CQ Press, 1998).

20. Frank Smallwood, *Free and Independent* (S. Greene Press, 1976), p. 165. See also Alan Rosenthal, *The Third House: Lobbyists and Lobbying in the States*, 2d ed. (CQ Press, 2001); but also "State Legislators Mix Public and Private Business, Study Says," *The New York Times*, May 21, 2000, p. 26.

21. Winnie Hu, "Lobbying Code Puts an End to Lawmakers' Gravy Train," *The New York Times*, April 11, 2000, pp. A1, A27. See also Christopher Swope, "Winning Without Food and Cigars," *Governing*, November 2000, pp. 40–46.

22. Charles Mahtesian, "The Ethics Backlash," *Governing*, October 1999, pp. 39–41.

23. John E. Brandl, *Money and Good Intentions Are Not Enough: Or, Why a Liberal Democrat Thinks States Need Both Competition and Community* (Brookings Institution Press, 1998), p. 58.

24. Karl T. Kurtz, "The Old Statehouse, She Ain't What She Used to Be," *State Legislatures*, January 1994, pp. 20–23. See also Alan Rosenthal, *The Decline of Representative Democracy* (CQ Press, 1998).

25. Alan Rosenthal, "The Legislative Institution: In Transition and at Risk," in *The State of the States*, 2d ed., Carl E. Van Horn, ed. (CQ Press, 1993), pp. 136–137. See also Alan Ehrenhalt, "An Embattled Institution," *Governing*, January 1992, pp. 28–33; and Karen Hansen, "Our Beleaguered Institution," *State Legislatures*, January 1994, pp. 12–17.

26. Rosenthal, "The Legislative Institution," p. 144.

27. See, for example, Christopher Conte, "Laptop Legislatures," *Governing*, November 1999, p. 36.

28. Carrie Koch, "A Room for a View," *State Legislatures*, May 1997, pp. 32–34.

29. Bette H. Dillehay, "E-Government as Virginia's Vision," in *Spectrum: The Journal of State Government* (Winter 2002), pp. 24–25.

30. Rich Jones, "The State Legislatures," in *The Book of the States, 1992–1993* (Council of State Governments, 1992), p. 125.

31. National Conference of State Legislatures, "Florida Voters to Reconsider Term Limits," April 20, 2005, at www.ncsl.org/programs/legman/ about/floridanews.htm, accessed July 7, 2006.

32. Michael Janofsky, "Idaho Legislature Repeals Term Limit Law, Undoing Voter Approved Measure," *The New York Times*, February 2, 2002, p. A11. See also Wayne Hoffman, "The Battle over Term Limits," *State Legislatures*, May 2002, pp. 25–29.

33. Janofsky, "Idaho Legislature," p. A11.

34. See Daniel B. Wood, "The Term-Limit Movement of the '90s Stalls," *Christian Science Monitor*, April 27, 2004, p. A1.

35. See John M. Carey, Richard G. Niemi, and Lynda W. Powell, *Term Limits in the State Legislatures* (University of Michigan Press, 2000).

36. Jack Quinn et al., "Redrawing the Districts, Changing the Rules," *Washington Post National Weekly Edition*, April 1, 1991, p. 23.

37. Gordon E. Baker, *The Reapportionment Revolution* (Random House, 1966), p. 47.

38. *Baker v. Carr*, 369 U.S. 186 (1962).

39. *Wesberry v. Sanders*, 376 U.S. 1 (1964).

40. *Reynolds v. Sims*, 377 U.S. 533 (1964).

41. *Brown v. Thomson*, 103 S.Ct. 2690 (1983).

42. *Shaw v. Reno*, 509 U.S. 630 (1993); *Abrams v. Johnson*, 138 L.Ed. 2d 285 (1997). For a summary of state and federal judicial cases on drawing legislative district lines, see *Redistricting Case Summaries from the '90s* (National Conference of State Legislatures, 1998); see also Ronald E. Weber, "Emerging Trends in State Legislative Redistricting," *Spectrum: The Journal of State Government*, Vol. 75 (Winter 2002), pp. 13–15; additional updates can be found at the National Conference of State Legislature Web site, www .ncsl.org.

43. *League of United Latin American Citizens v. Perry*, 399 F. Supp. 2d 756 (2006); *Davis v. Bandemer*, 478 U.S. 109 (1986).

44. Samuel Issacharoff, "In Real Elections, There Ought to Be Competition," *The New York Times*, February 16, 2002, p. A31.

45. Ibid.

46. See Spencer C. Olin, *California's Prodigal Sons: Hiram Johnson and the Progressives, 1911–1917* (University of California Press, 1968).

47. Teri Renner, "Local Initiative and Referendum in the United States," at www.iandrinstitute.org/ Local%20I&R.htm.

48. Alan Greenblatt, "Total Recall," *Governing*, September 2003, p. 21.

49. See, for example, Eugene C. Lee, "The Initiative Boom: An Excess of Democracy," in *Governing California*, Gerald C. Lubenow and Bruce E. Cain, eds. (Institute of Governmental Studies, University of California, 1997), pp. 113–136. See also David S. Broder, *Democracy Derailed: Initiative Campaigns and the Power of Money* (Harcourt, 2000). But see Zolton L. Hajnul, Elisabeth R. Gerber, and Hugh Louch, "Minorities and Direct Legislation: Evidence from California Ballot Proposition Elections," paper presented at the annual meeting of the American Political Science Association, Washington, D.C., September 1–3, 2000. See also Elisabeth Gerber, *The Populist Paradox* (Princeton University Press, 1999).

50. See Peter Schrag, *Paradise Lost: California's Experience, America's Future* (New Press, 1998). See also the decidedly negative appraisal offered by Richard Ellis, *Democratic Delusions: The Initiative Process in America* (University Press of Kansas, 2002).

51. David B. Magleby and Kelly D. Paterson, "Consultants and Direct Democracy," *PS: Political Science and Politics* 31 (June 1998), pp. 160–161. See also Broder, *Democracy Derailed*.

52. David B. Magleby, "Ballot Initiatives and Intergovernmental Relations," paper presented at the annual meeting of the Western Political Science Association, Los Angeles, March 1998, p. 2.

53. Ibid., p. 13.

54. Thomas E. Cronin, *Direct Democracy: The Politics of the Initiative, Referendum, and Recall* (Harvard University Press, 1989).

55. Michael G. Hagen and Edward L. Lascher Jr., "Public Opinion About Ballot Initiatives," paper presented at the annual meeting of the American Political Science Association, Boston, September 3–6, 1998.

Chapter 25

1. See Thad L. Beyle, "Enhancing Executive Leadership in the States," *State and Local Government Review* (Winter 1995), pp. 18–35, and Thad L. Beyle, "The Governors," in *Politics in the American States: A Comparative Analysis*, 7th ed., Virginia Gray, Russell Hanson, and Herbert Jacob, eds. (CQ Press, 1999), pp. 191–231.

2. Lamar Alexander, *Steps Along the Way: A Governor's Scrapbook* (Nelson, 1986), p. 112. Similar views can be found in former Vermont Governor Madeleine M. Kunin's memoir, *Living a Political Life* (Vintage, 1995).

3. See Earl H. Fry, *The Expanding Role of State and Local Governments in U.S. Foreign Policy* (Council on Foreign Relations Press, 1998). See also, for example, Alan Johnson, "Taft Shows He's Up to the Job on Foreign Grounds," *Columbia Dispatch*, February 14, 2000.

4. *The Book of the States, 1998–1999* (Council of State Governments, 1998), p. xxiii.

5. *The Book of the States, 2005* (Council of State Governments, 2005) p. 217.

6. Ibid., p. 218.

7. This story is adapted from Robert S. McElvaine, *Mario Cuomo: A Biography* (Scribner, 1988), pp. 337–338. See also the assessment of Governor Pete Wilson's turbulent first years as governor of California in Robert Reinhold, "The Curse of the Statehouse," *New York Times Magazine*, May 3, 1992, pp. 27–28, 54, 58–59.

8. Paul Foy, "Utah Governor Defies No Child Left Behind Act," *Associated Press*, May 2, 2005.

9. Thad L. Beyle, "Governors," *The Book of the States, 2005* (Council of State Governments, 2005), p. 192.

10. Charlie LeDuff, "The California Recall: The Governor-Elect," *The New York Times*, October 9, 2003, p. A33.

11. James M. Perry, "Virginia's New Governor Joins a GOP Trend," *The Wall Street Journal*, February 11, 1998, p. A24.

12. Richard F. Winters, "The Politics of Taxing and Spending," in *Politics in the American States*, Gray et al., eds., p. 329.

13. Kathleen Gallagher, "Doyle Will Give Keynote Speech at Stem Cell Summit," *Milwaukee Journal Sentinel*, June 6, 2006.

14. In some cases, a governor's style and strategy alienate legislators. See, for example, Charles Mahtesian's analysis of Minnesota's Jesse Ventura, "Can He Govern?" *Governing*, May 2000, pp. 36–42. In contrast, Governor Bruce Babbitt worked effectively even with a legislature controlled by the opposition party. See David R. Berman, *Arizona Politics and Government* (University of Nebraska Press, 1998), pp. 116–117.

15. For a lighthearted commentary by a member of Governor Pete Wilson's Electronic Commerce Advisory Council, see Stewart Alsop, "Helping the Governor Figure Out E-Commerce," *Fortune*, June 8, 1998, p. 269.

16. *2004 State Expenditure Report* (National Association of State Budget Officers, 2005).

17. National Conference of State Legislatures, news release, April 7, 2004, www.ncsl.org/programs/press/2004/pr040407.htm, accessed on April 27, 2004.

18. Kathleen Gray, "Granholm Stars in Her Own 'Kill Bill,'" *Detroit Free Press*, April 26, 2004, p. A1.

19. John Kennedy and Jason Garcia, "Governor's Veto Pen Leaves Heavy Mark," *Orlando Sentinel*, May 26, 2006.

20. Cited in a profile of New York in *Governing*, February 1999, p. 66.

21. Thad L. Beyle, "Being Governor," in *The State of the States*, 3d ed., Carl E. Van Horn, ed. (CQ Press, 1996), p. 89. See also Beyle, "The Governors."

22. But see Governor Tommy Thompson's defense of using frequent vetoes, *Power to the People: An American State at Work* (HarperCollins, 1996), and the view of one of his main critics in the Wisconsin legislature, Tom Loftus, *The Art of Legislative Politics* (CQ Press, 1994), chap. 5. On the varied effectiveness of the line item veto as a tool for fiscal responsibility, see Glenn Abney and Thomas p. Lauth, "The Item Veto and Fiscal Responsibility," *Journal of Politics* 59 (August 1997), pp. 882–892. On how a governor's rash use of the line item veto can infuriate legislators, see Mahtesian, "Can He Govern?" p. 40.

23. Katie Zezima, "Obey Same-Sex Marriage Law, Officials Told," *The New York Times*, April 25, 2004, p. A15.

24. *Perpich et al.* v. *Department of Defense*, 110 L.Ed. 312 (1990).

25. Mark Sappenfield, "Katrina Poses Key Test for Stretched National Guard," *Christian Science Monitor*, September 2, 2005.

26. Peter Baker, "Bush Set to Send Guard to Border," *Washington Post*, May 15, 2006, p. A1.

27. Ryan Alessi and Jack Brammer, "Fletcher Pardons 9," *Lexington Herald-Leader*, August 30, 2005.

28. For background on this controversy, see Jonathan Alter, "The Death Penalty on Trial," *Newsweek*, June 12, 2000, pp. 26–34.

29. For a scholarly analysis of the role political parties play in nominating and assisting governors, see Sarah McCally, *The Governor as Party Leader: Campaigning and Governing* (University of Michigan Press, 1998).

30. Beyle, "The Governors," p. 230.

31. Sarah F. Liebschutz et al., *New York Politics and Government* (University of Nebraska Press, 1998), p. 93.

32. Thomas Hardy, "The 'Weak' Governor," in *Mississippi Government and Politics*, Dale Krane and Stephen Shaffer, eds. (University of Nebraska Press, 1992), p. 152.

33. See, for example, how hard it is for a governor to control the economic fortunes of a state, especially during a recession, in Paul Brace, *State Government and Economic Performance* (Johns Hopkins University Press, 1993).

34. *State Legislatures*, June 2000, p. 7.

35. Kunin, *Living a Political Life*, p. 382.

36. Beyle, "The Governors," pp. 224–226.

37. Thomas H. Kean, quoted in Barbara Salmore and Stephen Salmore, *New Jersey Politics and Government* (University of Nebraska Press, 1998), p. 136.

38. Jesse Ventura, *I Ain't Got Time to Bleed* (Signet Press, 2000), pp. 296–297.

39. Beyle, "The Governors," pp. 224–226.

40. Alan Ehrenhalt, "Reinventing Government in the Unlikeliest Place," *Governing*, August 1993, pp. 7–8.

41. "Two New Agencies Launch under Reorganization," *Associated Press*, August 31, 2004.

42. Richard C. Elling, "Bureaucracy: Maligned Yet Essential," in *Politics in the American States: A Comparative Analysis*, 6th ed., Virginia Gray and Herbert Jacob, eds. (CQ Press, 1996), p. 308.

43. Jonathan Walters, "Fad Mad," *Governing* 9, September 1996, p. 49.

44. Beyle, "Being Governor," p. 106.

45. See the discussion of Governor George W. Bush and his relationship with his lieutenant governor in Jonathan Walters, "The Taming of Texas," *Governing*, July 1998, p. 20. See also "The Future of the Texas Lieutenant Governor," *Comparative State Politics*, October 1995, pp. 21–24.

46. But see Charles N. Wheeler III, "Why Illinois Still Needs Lieutenant Governor's Position," *Illinois Issues*, September 1994, pp. 6–7.

47. For additional information on the office of the Attorney General, State of California, visit www.caag.state.ca.us\.

48. Professor Thad L. Beyle at the University of North Carolina at Chapel Hill tracks state polls on governors' job performances and finds that Democratic, Republican, and Independent governors alike all averaged about 60 percent public approval in the 1990s.

49. Alexander, *Steps Along the Way*, p. 141.

50. Thomas H. Kean, *The Politics of Inclusion* (Free Press, 1988), p. 248.

51. Scott Matheson with James Edwin Kee, *Out of Balance* (Peregrine Smith Books, 1986), p. 186. See also the reflections of another popular western governor in Cecil Andrus and Joel Connelly, *Cecil Andrus: Politics Western Style* (Sasquatch Books, 1998).

Chapter 26

1. National Center for State Courts, *Examining the Work of State Courts, 2004* (National Center for State Courts, 2005), p. 14.

2. See Mark S. Hurwitz and Drew Noble Lanier, "Women and Minorities on State and Federal Appellate Benches," *Judicature* 85 (September–October 2001), p. 84; and Chris W. Bonneau, "The Composition of State Supreme Courts," *Judicature* 85 (July–August 2001), p. 26.

3. See Michael Solimine and James Walker, Respecting State Courts: The Inevitability of Judicial Federalism (Greenwood Press, 2000); and Matthew Bosworth, Courts as Catalysts: State Supreme Courts and Public School Finance Equity (State University of New York Press, 2001).

4. The Supreme Court upheld these laws in *Ewing* v. *California*, 538 U.S. 11 (2003).

5. Lynn Mather, "Policy Making in State Trial Courts," in *The American Courts: A Critical Assessment*, John B. Gates and Charles A. Johnson, eds. (CQ Press, 1991), pp. 119–157.

6. Henry R. Glick, "Policy Making and State Supreme Courts," in ibid., pp. 87–88.

7. Patrick Schmidt and Paul Martin, "To the Internet and Beyond: State Supreme Courts on the World Wide Web," *Judicature* 84 (May–June 2001), pp. 314–325.

8. Robert F. Williams, "In the Supreme Court's Shadow: Legitimacy of State Rejection of Supreme Court Reasoning and Results," *South Carolina Law Review* 56 (Spring 1984), p. 353.

9. Harry P. Stumpf and John H. Culver, *The Politics of State Courts* (Longman, 1992), pp. 8–11.

10. Hans A. Linde, "Observations of a State Court Judge," in *Judges and Legislators: Toward Institutional Comity*, Robert A. Katzmann, ed. (Brookings Institution Press, 1988), p. 118.

11. Peter J. Galie, "The Other Supreme Courts: Judicial Activism Among State Supreme Courts," *Syracuse Law Review* 33 (1982), pp. 731–793.

12. Philip L. Dubois, "State Trial Court Appointments: Does the Governor Make a Difference?" *Judicature* 68 (June–July 1985), pp. 20–21.

13. Charles H. Sheldon and Nicholas p. Lovrich Jr., "State Judicial Recruitment," in *The American Courts*, pp. 172–173.

14. See American Judicature Society at www.ajs.org/js/judicialselectioncharts.pdf.

15. Thurgood Marshall, in *Renne* v. *Geary*, 501 U.S. 312 (1991).

16. *Republican Party of Minnesota* v. *White*, 536 U.S. 765 (2002).

17. William Glaberson, "Court Rulings Curb Efforts to Rein in Judicial Races," *The New York Times*, October 7, 2000, p. A8.

18. Roy A. Schotland, "Financing Judicial Elections," in *Financing the 2000 Elections*, David B. Magleby, ed. (Brookings Institution Press, 2002), p. 103.

19. "Judges Say Political Influence Threatens Independence of Judiciary," *Press and Dakotan*, at www.pressandakotan.com/stories/101797/judges.html.

20. Scott Michels, "Judicial Elections Turn Expensive, Polarized, and Nasty," *U.S News and World Report*, June 16, 2006.

21. Ibid.

22. Michael Scherer, "The Making of the Corporate Judiciary," *Mother Jones*, November 2003, p. 72.

23. See Justice at Stake Campaign, the Brennan Center for Justice at New York University Law School and the National Institute on Money in State Politics, *The New Politics of Judicial Elections* (Justice at Stake Campaign, 2001); and American Bar Association, Standing Committee on Judicial Independence, *Public Financing of Judicial Campaigns: Report of the Commission on Public Financing of Judicial Campaigns* (American Bar Association, 2002).

24. *Wells* v. *Edwards*, 409 U.S. 1095 (1973).

25. *Chisom* v. *Roemer*, 501 U.S. 400 (1991); *Houston Lawyers' Association* v. *Texas Attorney General*, 501 U.S. 419 (1991). See also Tracy Thompson, "The New Front in the Battle for Civil Rights: Judgeships," *Washington Post National Weekly Edition*, December 18, 1989, p. 34.

26. J. W. Peltason, *The Missouri Plan for the Selection of Judges* (University of Missouri Studies, 1945). The plan was previously known as the Nonpartisan Plan for the Selection of Judges or the Kales Plan until called the Missouri Plan by this monograph.

27. Beth M. Henschen, Robert Moog, and Steven Davis, "Judicial Nominating Commissioners: A National Profile," *Judicature* 73 (April–May 1990), pp. 328–334.

28. Philip L. Dubois, "The Politics of Innovation in State Courts: The Merit Plan of Judicial Selection," *Publius* 20 (Winter 1990), p. 40.

29. Warren K. Hall and Larry T. Aspin, "What Twenty Years of Judicial Retention Elections Have Told Us," *Judicature* 70 (April–May 1987), pp. 340–347; Susan B. Caron and Larry C. Berkson, *Judicial Retention Elections in the United States* (American Judicature Society, 1980).

30. Larry T. Aspin, "Trends in Judicial Retention Elections, 1964–1968," *Judicature* 83 (September–October 1999), p. 79; "Evaluating the Performance of Judges Standing for Retention," *Judicature* 79 (January– February 1996), pp. 190–195.

31. Traciel Reid, "The Politicization of Retention Elections," *Judicature* 83 (September–October 1999), p. 68.

32. Thomas E. Cronin and Robert D. Loevy, *Colorado Politics and Government* (University of Nebraska Press, 1993), pp. 251–253.

33. "The Need for Judicial Performance Evaluations for Retention Elections," *Judicature* 75 (October–November 1991), p. 124.

34. Henry Weinstein, "Forum Airs Questions of Jurist Independence," *The Los Angeles Times*, November 22, 1998, p. A18.

35. Anthony Champagne and Greta Thielemann, "Awareness of Trial Court Judges," *Judicature* 74 (February–March 1991), p. 276.

36. *The Book of the States, 2005* (The Council of State Governments, 2005), pp. 309–312.

37. Jeffrey Shaman, Steven Lubet, and James Alfini, *Judicial Conduct and Ethics*, 3d ed. (Lexis, 2000), sec. 15.07.

38. Jolanta Juskiewicz Perlstein and Nathan Goldman, "Judicial Disciplinary Commissions: A New Approach to the Discipline and Removal of State Judges," in *The Analysis of Judicial Reform*, Phil Dubois, ed. (Lexington Books, 1982), pp. 93–106.

39. Franklin M. Zweig et al., "Securing the Future for America's State Courts," *Judicature* 73 (April–May 1990), pp. 297–298.

40. Beverly Blair Cook, "Women Judges in the Opportunity Structure," in *Women, the Courts, and Equality*, Laura L. Crites and Winfred L. Hepperle, eds. (Sage, 1987), pp. 143–171.

41. *Burch* v. *Louisiana*, 441 U.S. 130 (1979); *Ballew* v. *Georgia*, 435 U.S. 223 (1978). See Reid Hastie, Steven D. Penrod, and Nancy Pennington, *Inside the Jury* (Harvard University Press, 1983), for a study showing that nonunanimous verdicts are more likely to bring convictions than those requiring unanimity. Federal courts often use juries of fewer than 12 for civil cases. For federal criminal trials, the Supreme Court still requires both the common law jury of 12 and unanimous verdicts.

42. *Felony Sentences in State Courts, 2002* (United State Department of Justice, Bureau of Justice Statistics, 2004).

43. *Prosecutors in State Courts, 2001* (United State Department of Justice, Bureau of Justice Statistics, 2002).

44. Robert H. Jackson, quoted in Jack M. Kress, "Progress and Prosecution," *Annals of the American Academy of Political and Social Science* (January 1976), p. 100.

45. William K. Muir, *Police: Streetcorner Politicians* (University of Chicago Press, 1977).

46. Charles E. Silberman, *Criminal Violence, Criminal Justice* (Random House, 1978), p. 303.

47. Jay Livingston, *Crime and Criminology* (Prentice Hall, 1992), p. 474.

48. Silberman, *Criminal Violence*, p. 218. See also David Cole, *No Equal Justice: Race and Class in the American Criminal Justice System* (New Press, 1999).

49. *South Carolina* v. *Gathers*, 490 U.S. 805 (1989); *Payne* v. *Tennessee*, 501 U.S. 808 (1991).

50. Thomas M. Uhlman and N. Darlene Walker, "A Plea Is No Bargain: The Impact of Case Disposition on Sentencing," *Social Science Quarterly* 60 (September 1979), pp. 218–234. See also Malcolm M. Feeley, *The Process Is the Punishment* (Russell Sage, 1979).

51. Thomas Church Jr., "Plea Bargains, Concessions and the Courts: Analysis of a Quasi-Experiment," *Law and Society Review* 14 (Spring 1976), p. 400. For a contrary view, see National Advisory Commission on Criminal Justice Standards and Goals, *Report of the Task Force* (U.S. Government Printing Office, 1979).

52. Church, "Plea Bargains," p. 400.

53. Jonathan D. Casper, *American Criminal Justice: The Defendant's Perspective* (Prentice Hall, 1972), pp. 52–53. Abraham S. Goldstein, *The Passive Judiciary: Prosecutorial Discretion and the Guilty Plea* (Louisiana State University Press, 1981), is critical of judges for not supervising plea bargains more actively.

54. *Santobello* v. *New York*, 404 U.S. 257 (1971).

55. Edward Barrett, "The Adversary Proceeding and the Judicial Process," lectures to the National College of State Trial Judges, quoted in Lynn M. Mather, "Some Determinants of the Method of Case Disposition: Decision-Making by Public Defenders in Los Angeles," *Law and Society Review* 12 (Winter 1974), pp. 187–188.

56. Henry N. Pontell, *A Capacity to Punish* (Indiana University Press, 1985).

57. Lee Sechrest, Susan O. White, and Elizabeth D. Brown, eds., *The Rehabilitation of Criminal Offenders: Problems and Prospects* (National Academy of Sciences, 1979), pp. 3–6.

58. John Hagan and Kristin Bumiler, "Making Sense of Sentencing: A Review and Critique of Sentencing Research," in *Research on Sentencing*, Alfred Blumstein et al., eds. (National Academy Press, 1983), vol. 2; Susan Welch, Michael Combs, and John Gruhl, "Do Black Judges Make a Difference?" *American Journal of Political Science* 32 (February 1988), pp. 126–135.

59. William B. Eldridge, "Shifting Views of the Sentencing Functions," *Annals of the American Academy of Political and Social Science* (July 1982), pp. 104–111.

60. Bureau of Justice Statistics, "The Nation's Prison Population Continues its Slow Growth," press release, October 23,2005.

61. Eric Schlosser, "The Prison-Industrial Complex," *Atlantic*, December 1998, p. 52.

62. Paige M. Harrison and Allen J. Beck, *Prisoners in 2004* (Bureau of Justice Statistics, 2005).

63. Barbara Fink, "Opening the Door on Community Corrections," *State Legislatures*, September 1984, pp. 24–31.

64. Gary Enos, "Despite New Technology, Home Confinement Faces Risks, Public Opposition," *City and State*, May 21, 1990, p. 14.

65. Quoted in Associated Press, "ABA 'Public Jurist' Considers Reforms in Legal System," December 1993.

Chapter 27

1. Peter Dreier, John Mollenkopf, and Todd Swanstrom, *Place Matters: Metropolitics for the Twenty-first Century* (University Press of Kansas, 2001), p. 21.

2. *2002 Census of Governments, Volume 1, Number 1, Government Organization* (United States Census Bureau, December 2002).

3. *Hunter* v. *City of Pittsburgh*, 208 U.S. 161 (1907).

4. See Jacques Steinberg, "42 Failing Schools in Philadelphia to Be Privatized," *The New York Times*, April 18, 2002, p. A1; Raven Tyler, "School Reform in Philadelphia," *OnLine News Hour*, www.pbs.org/newshour/bb/education/reform/schools.html.

5. Michelle Garcia, "N.Y. City Council Passes Anti-Patriot Act Measure," *The Washington Post*, February 5, 2004, p. A11; The Bill of Rights Defense Committee keeps a list of governments passing resolutions opposing USA Patriot Act and related federal laws at www.bordc.org.

6. U.S. Bureau of the Census, *Statistical Abstract of the United States, 2001* (U.S. Government Printing Office, 2001).

7. An excellent overview of counties is Donald C. Menzel, ed., *The American County: Frontiers of Knowledge* (University of Alabama Press, 1996).

8. Ellen Perlman, "Polite Tenacity," *Governing*, November 2000, pp. 34, 214.

9. For a history of suburban development, see Rosalyn Baxandall and Elizabeth Ewen, *Picture Windows: How the Suburbs Happened* (Basic Books, 2000).

10. See Paul G. Lewis, *Shaping Suburbia: How Political Institutions Organize Urban Development* (University of Pittsburgh Press, 1996).

11. Joel Garreau, *Edge City* (Doubleday, 1991).

12. For the views of three mayors on the good city, see Stephen Goldsmith, *The Twenty-First Century City* (Regnery, 1997); Daniel Kemmis, *The Good City and the Good Life* (Houghton Mifflin, 1995); and John O. Norquist, *The Wealth of Cities: Revitalizing the Centers of American Life* (Addison-Wesley, 1998).

13. *Rogers v. Lodge*, 458 U.S. 613 (1982); *Thornburg v. Gingles*, 478 U.S. 30 (1986).

14. For the experience of one mayor in a council-manager city, see the memoir by Cambridge, Massachusetts, Mayor Barbara Ackermann, *"You the Mayor?" The Education of a City Politician* (Auburn House, 1989).

15. See James II. Svara and Associates, *Facilitative Leadership in Local Government: Lessons from Successful Mayors and Chairpersons in the Council-Manager Form* (Jossey-Bass, 1994).

16. See Earl H. Fry, *The Expanding Role of State and Local Governments in U.S. Foreign Affairs* (Council on Foreign Relations, 1998), esp. chap. 4.

17. It is fascinating to examine how mayors of different cities view their roles and responsibilities. Excellent books about important mayors are Roger Biles, *Richard J. Daley: Politics, Race, and the Governing of Chicago* (Northern Illinois University Press, 1995); Adam Cohen and Elizabeth Taylor, *American Pharaoh: Mayor Richard J. Daley: His Battle for Chicago and the Nation* (Little, Brown, 2000); and Robert A. Dahl, *Who Governs? Democracy and Power in an American City* (Yale University Press, 1961), a classic study of Mayor Richard Lee of New Haven. See also two reflective books by mayors in medium-sized or smaller cities: Kemmis, *The Good City and the Good Life*; and Ackermann, *"You the Mayor?"*

18. Dennis R. Judd and Todd Swanstrom, *City Politics: Private Power and Public Policy*, 2d ed. (Longman, 1998), p. 7.

19. See, for example, the analysis of other groups such as the African Americans in Atlanta in Clarence N. Stone, *Regime Politics: Governing Atlanta, 1946–1988* (University Press of Kansas, 1989). See also Bryan D. Jones and Lynn W. Bachelor, *The Sustaining Hand: Community Leadership and Corporate Power*, 2d ed. (University Press of Kansas, 1993).

20. For suggestions on how to form community groups and effective alliances seeking progress in cities, see Michael Briand, *Practical Politics: Five Principles for a Community That Works* (University of Illinois Press, 1999).

21. Judd and Swanstrom, *City Politics*, p. 7.

22. For greater detail, see U.S. Bureau of the Census, "Standards for Defining Metropolitan Areas," at www.census.gov.

23. U.S. Bureau of the Census, *Statistical Abstract of the United States, 2000* (U.S. Government Printing Office, 2000).

24. The legal constraints on Baltimore, for example, are outlined in David Rusk, *Baltimore Unbound: A Strategy for Regional Renewal* (Abell Foundation/Johns Hopkins University Press, 1996).

25. D'Vera Cohn, "A New Millennium for America's Cities," *Washington Post National Weekly Edition*, October 30, 2000, p. 34.

26. David Rusk, former mayor of Albuquerque, makes this case well in *Baltimore Unbound* and in *Cities Without Suburbs*, 2d ed. (Woodrow Wilson Center Press/Johns Hopkins University Press, 1995).

27. See Suzanne M. Leland and Kurt Thurmaier, eds., *Case Studies of City-County Consolidation* (M. E. Sharpe, 2004); and Jered B. Carr and Richard C. Feiock, eds., *City-County Consolidation and Its Alternatives* (M. E. Sharpe, 2004).

28. See Myron Orfield, *Metropolitics: A Regional Agenda for Community and Stability* (Brookings Institution Press, 1997); and Manuel Pastor, ed., *Regions That Work: How Cities and Suburbs Can Grow Together* (University of Minnesota Press, 2000).

29. See E. J. Dionne Jr., ed., *Community Works: The Revival of Civil Society in America* (Brookings Institution Press, 1998).

30. See David L. Kirp, et al., *Our Town: Race, Housing, and the Soul of Suburbia* (Rutgers University Press, 1997); and Jonathan Harr, *A Civil Action* (Vintage, 1996).

31. *Kelo v. City of New London*, 125 S. Ct. 2655 (2005).

32. See the recommendation often prescribed by a major proponent of regionalism, Neal R. Peirce, in Charles Mahtesian, "The Civic Therapist," *Governing*, September 1995, pp. 24–27. See also Dreier, Mollenkopf, and Swanstrom, *Place Matters*, chap. 7.

33. "The End of Urban Man? Care to Bet?" *The Economist*, December 31, 1999, pp. 25–26.

34. See the thoughtful recommendations in Robert J. Waste, *Independent Cities: Rethinking U.S. Urban Policy* (Oxford University Press, 1998). But also see Clarissa Rile Hayward, "The Difference States Make: Democracy, Identity, and the American City," *American Political Science Review* 97 (November 2003), p. 501.

Chapter 28

1. *Digest of Education Statistics Tables and Figures, 2005*, National Center for Education Statistics, available at: http://nces.ed.gov/programs/digest/d05/tables/dt05_164.asp.

2. See Gary Oldfield and Chungmei Lee, *Brown at 50: King's Dream or Plessy's Nightmare* (The Harvard Civil Rights Project, 2004). Also see Gary Orfield, Susan E. Eaton, and the Harvard Project on School Desegregation, *Dismantling Desegregation: The Quiet Reversal of Brown v. Board of Education* (New Press, 1996).

3. National Commission on Excellence in Education, *A Nation at Risk: The Imperative for Educational Reform—An Open Letter to the American People* (U.S. Government Printing Office, 1983). Ernest L. Boyer, *High School: A Report on Secondary Education in America* (Harper & Row, 1983), based on observations of high schools, contains a detailed series of recommendations. See also the National Science Board Commission on Precollege Education, *Mathematics, Science, and Technology: Educating Americans for the 21st Century* (U.S. Government Printing Office, 1983), and Carnegie Forum on Education and the Economy, *A Nation Prepared: Teachers for the 21st Century* (Carnegie Forum, 1986).

4. James B. Steman and Wayne C. Riddle, *Goals 2000: Educate America Act Implementation Status and Issues* (Congressional Research Service, 1996), pp. 2–4.

5. Rochelle L. Stanfield, "Learning Curve," *National Journal*, July 3, 1993, pp. 1688–1691.

6. C. Eugene Steuerle, Van Doorn Ooms, George Peterson, and Robert D. Reischauer, eds., *Vouchers and the Provision of Public Services* (Brookings Institution Press, 2000). See also "Colorado Adopts Statewide School Vouchers," *State Legislatures*, July–August 2003, p. 7.

7. Terry M. Moe, "Private Vouchers," in *Private Vouchers*, Terry M. Moe, ed. (Hoover Institution Press, 1996), p. 35. Yet see also John F. Witte, *The Market Approach to Education: An Analysis of America's First Voucher Program* (Princeton University Press, 1999).

8. William H. Rehnquist, quoted in Richard Rothstein, "Failed Schools? The Meaning Is Unclear," *The New York Times*, July 3, 2002, p. A14.

9. "Colorado Adopts Statewide School Vouchers," *State Legislatures*, July–August 2003, p. 7.

10. Greg Winter, "Florida Court Rules Against Religious School Vouchers," *The New York Times*, August 17, 2004, p. A15.

11. Elizabeth Kolbert, "Unchartered Territory," *New Yorker*, October 9, 2000, p. 36. For an example of charter schools being initiated in Rhode Island, see Maureen Moakley and Elmer Cornwell, *Rhode Island Politics and Government* (University of Nebraska Press, 2001), pp. 189–190.

12. See, for example, Lynn Rosellini, "Closing the Gap," *U.S. News*, March 22–29, 2004, pp. 87–88.

13. See Diana Jean Schemo, "Charter Schools Lagging Behind, U.S. Data Reveal," *The New York Times*, August 17, 2004, pp. A1, A16. See also Richard Lee Colvin, "What's Wrong With Our Schools?," *State Legislatures*, September 2003, pp. 12–15.

14. Quoted in "Statewide Student Tests," *State Legislatures*, February 2004, p. 33. See also Dewayne Matthews, "No Child Left Behind: The Challenge of Implementation," *The Book of States* (Council of State Governments, 2004), pp. 493–496. See also, June Kronholz, "Bush's Education Law Gets an Incomplete," *The Wall Street Journal*, September 1, 2004, p. A6.

15. William J. Mathis, "The Cost of Implementing the Federal No Child Left Behind Act: Different Assumptions, Different Answers," *Peabody Journal of Education* Vol. 80, No. 2 (2005) pp. 90–119.

16. Michael S. McPherson and Morton Owen Schapiro, "Funding Roller Coaster for Public Higher Education," *Science*, November 14, 2003, p. 1157.

17. See Christine Walton and Julie Davis Bell, "New Ways to Fund Higher Ed," *State Legislatures*, December 2003, pp. 28–31. See also John Buntin, "Setting Colleges Free," *Governing*, September 2003, pp. 18–22.

18. See Alexander Russo, "Varsity Vouchers," *State Legislatures*, June 2004, p. 27.

19. Administration for Children and Families, "Recipients and Families 1936-2001," available at www.acf.hhs.gov/news/stats/3697.htm.

20. R. Kent Weaver, *Ending Welfare as We Know It* (Brookings Institution Press, 2000).

21. On state policies, see Office of Family Assistance, Administration for Children and Families, U.S. Department of Health and Human Services, *Temporary Assistance to Needy Families: Sixth Annual Report to Congress* (Office of Family Assistance, 2004), chap. 12.

22. See Rebecca Blank and Ron Haskins, eds., *The New World of Welfare* (Brookings Institution Press, 2001); Isabel V. Sawhill et al. *Welfare Reform and Beyond: The Future of the Safety Net* (Brookings Institution Press, 2002); and Carol W. Weissert, ed., *Learning from Leaders: Welfare Reform Politics and Policy in Five Midwestern States* (Rockefeller Institute Press, 2000).

23. For an extensive review of studies on the effects of welfare reform, see Rebecca Blank, "Evaluating Welfare Reform in the U.S.," *Journal of Economic Literature*, December 2002, pp. 1105–1166.

24. Peter Edelman, "The True Purpose of Welfare Reform," *The New York Times*, May 29, 2002, p. A21.

25. "Testimony Of Sharon Parrott, Director Of Welfare Reform And Income Support Policy, Center On Budget And Policy Priorities Before the Committee on Ways and Means, United States House of Representatives" (Center for Budget and Policy Priorities, July, 19, 2006).

26. See, for example, David Hage, *Reforming Welfare by Rewarding Work, One State's Successful Experiment* (University of Minnesota Press, 2004), and Courtney Jarchow and Jack Tweedie, "Welfare and Wedding Vows," *State Legislatures*, April 2003, pp. 24–28.

27. Dennis G. Smith, Janet G. Freeze, Susan N. Hill, and Lyn R. Killman, "The Future of Medicaid," in *The Book of the States*, 2006 Edition (The Council of State Governments, 2006), p. 491.

28. See Katherine Barrett, Richard Greene, and Michele Mariani, "A Case of Neglect: Why Health Care Is Getting Worse, Even Though Medicine Is Getting Better," *Governing*, February 2004, pp. 22–24. See also other articles in this edition of *Governing*.

29. Trinity D. Tomsie, "Managing Medicaid in Tough Times," *State Legislators*, June 2002, p. 13.

30. David S. Broder, "States in Fiscal Crises," *Washington Post National Weekly Edition*, May 27, 2002, p. 4

31. For a brief overview of the changes in Medicaid produced by the Deficit Reduction Act, see the Kaiser Commission on Medicaid and the Uninsured, "Deficit Reduction Act of 2005: Implications for Medicaid" (Henry J. Kaiser Foundation, 2006), at www.kff.org/medicaid/upload/7465.pdf.

32. David Kocieniewski and Robert Hanley, "An Inside Story of Racial Bias and Denial," *The New York Times*, December 3, 2000, pp. 53, 56.

33. Jodi Wilgoren, "New Terror Alert Brings No Change in States' Security," *The New York Times*, May 25, 2002, p. A11.

34. See Amy C. Hughes, "State Emergency Management: New Realities in a Homeland Security World," *The Book of States* (Council of State Governments, 2004), pp. 485–488.

35. Larry Morandi, "Growing Pains," *State Legislatures*, October–November 1998, pp. 24–28.

36. Neal Peirce, "Parisian Green: A Hint for Us," Washington Post Writers Group, at www.npeirce@citistates.com, June 2, 2002, p. 1.

37. See Robert B. Albritton, "Subsidies: Welfare and Transportation," in *Politics in the American States: A Comparative Analysis*, 7th ed., Virginia Gray, Herbert Jacob, and Kenneth Vines, eds. (C.Q. Press, 1999), and E. J. Dionne Jr., ed., *Community Works: The Revival of Civil Society in America* (Brookings Institution Press, 2000).

38. For a discussion of the evolution of environmental policy in a particularly interesting place, see Charles O. Jones, *Clean Air: The Policies and Politics of Pollution Control* (University of Pittsburgh Press, 1973).

39. Jacqueline Vaughn Switzer and Gary Bryner, *Environmental Politics*, 2d ed. (St. Martin's Press, 1998), pp. 64–66.

40. Jeff Dale, "Realistic Redevelopment," *State Legislatures*, February 1999, pp. 28–31.

41. Bruce A. Williams, "Economic Regulation and Environmental Protection," in *Politics in the American States*, Gray et al., eds. (C.Q. Press, 1996), pp. 478–515.

42. See Larry Morandi, "Clearing the Air," *State Legislatures*, February 2004, pp. 30–31. Also see Barry George Rabe, *Statehouse and Greenhouse: The Emerging Politics of American Climate Change Policy* (The Brookings Institution, 2004).

43. See Garry Boulard, "The Great Hydrogen Hope," *State Legislatures*, February 2004, pp. 12–15.

44. R. Steven Brown, "Trends in State Environmental Spending," in *The Book of the States*, 2004 Edition (The Council of State Governments, 2004), pp. 240–243.

45. Alan K. Ota, "Congress Clears Huge Transportation Bill, Restoring Cut-Off Funding to States," *Congressional Quarterly Weekly*, May 23, 1998, pp. 1385–1386.

46. But see Michele Mariani, "Transit's High-Tech Route," *Governing*, May, 2004, pp. 60–67; and Rob Gurwitt, "Connecting the Suburban Dots," *Governing*, October 2003, pp. 36–40.

47. *The Book of the States, 2005* (Council of State Governments, 2005), p. 237.

48. Nancy M. Davis, "Politics and the Public Utilities Commissioner," *State Legislatures*, May 1985, p. 20. See also William T. Gormley Jr., "Policy, Politics, and Public Utility Regulation," *American Journal of Political Science* 27 (February 1983), pp. 86–105.

49. See, for example, Rebecca Smith, "States Face Fights as Caps Expire on Electric Rates," *The Wall Street Journal*, August 17, 2004, p. 1 and p. 12.

50. Amy Wallace, "San Onofre Mitigation Plan Wins Approval," *The Los Angeles Times*, July 17, 1991, p. A3.

51. See Donald F. Kettl, "Federalism, Anyone?" *Governing*, February 2004, p. 14.

Chapter 29

1. U.S. Bureau of Labor Statistics, "Table 1: Employment by Major Industry Division, 1994, 2004, and Projected 2014 Employment," www.bls/gov/news.release/ecopro.t01.htm, modified on December 7, 2005.

2. *Elrod v. Burns*, 427 U.S. 347 (1976).

3. Barry T. Hirsch and David A. Macpherson, *Union Membership and Coverage Database from the Current Population Survey*, available at www.unionstats.com.

4. Werner Z. Hirsch, "Factors Important in Local Government's Privatization Decisions," *Urban Affairs Review*, 31 (November 1995), pp. 226–243.

5. Edwin Blackstone and Simon Hakim, "Private Ayes: A Tale of Four Cities: New York, Philadelphia, Indianapolis, and Phoenix," *American City and County* 112 (February 1997), pp. 4–8.

6. See Jonathan Walters, "Going Outside," *Governing*, May 2004, pp. 7–15.

7. Stephen Goldsmith, *The Twenty-First Century City* (Regnery, 1997), p. 10.

8. E. S. Savas, "Privatization Initiatives," (National Council for Public Private Partnerships, 2001), at: http://ncppp.org/resources/papers/savas_privatization.pdf.

9. See Reason Public Policy Institute, a pro-privatization think tank, at www.privatization.org.

10. John Shannon, "The Deregulation of Fiscal Federalism," in *The Changing Face of Fiscal Federalism*, Thomas R. Swartz and John E. Peck, eds. (Sharpe, 1990), p. 31.

11. See Henry S. Wulf, "Trends in State Government Finances," in *Book of the States, 2002*, (The Council of State Governments, 2002) pp. 269–277.

12. John Shannon, "The Deregulation of the American Federal System, 1789–1989," in *The Changing Face of Fiscal Federalism*, Swartz and Peck, eds., pp. 17–34.

13. Roy W. Bahl Jr., "Changing Federalism: Trends and Interstate Variations," in ibid., p. 59.

14. *Book of the States, 2005*, (The Council of State Governments, 2005), p. 448.

15. For a recent discussion of state and local tax issues, see Katherine Barrett, Richard Greene, Michele Mariani, and Anya Sostek, "The Way We Tax: A 50-state Report," *Governing*, February 2003, pp. 11–40.

16. For a brief history of the property tax, see Dennis Hale, "The Evaluation of the Property Tax: A Study of the Relation Between Public Finance and Political Theory," *Journal of Politics* 47 (May 1985), pp. 382–404. See also C. Lowell Harris, ed., *The Property Tax and Local Finance* (Academy of Political Science, 1983).

17. *Statistical Abstract of the United States, 2006* (U.S. Government Printing Office, 2005), Table 430.

18. See Roy Bahl, David L. Sjoquist, and W. Loren Williams, "School Finance Reform and Impact on Property Taxes," *Proceedings of the Eighty-Third Annual National Tax Association Conference, 1990* (National Tax Association, Tax Institute of America, 1991), pp. 163–171.

19. *Serrano v. Priest*, 5 Cal.3d 487, 96 Cal. Rptr. 601 (1971).

20. *San Antonio Independent School District v. Rodriquez*, 411 U.S. 1 (1973).

21. Michael A. Rebell, "Educational Adequacy, Democracy, and the Courts," in *Achieving High Educational Standards for All: Conference Summary*, Timothy Ready, Christopher Edley, Jr., and Catherine E. Snow, eds. (National Academies Press, 2002) pp. 218–268; for more information, see: www.schoolfunding.info/index.php3.

22. J. Richard Aronson and John L. Hilley, *Financing State and Local Governments*, 4th ed. (Brookings Institution, 1986), p. 138. See also U.S. Advisory Commission on Intergovernmental Relations, *Property Tax Circuit-Breakers: Current Status and Policy Issues* (U.S. Government Printing Office, 1975), and Steven D. Gold, "Circuit Breakers and Other Relief Measures," in *Property Tax and Local Finance*, Harris, ed., pp. 119–132.

23. David B. Magleby, *Direct Legislation: Voting on Ballot Propositions in the United States* (Johns Hopkins University Press, 1984), pp. 61–76.

24. *Survey of Legislative Fiscal Officers* (National Conference of State Legislatures, 1996); Mandy Rafool, NCSL tax specialist, personal communication, September 15, 1998.

25. Carl Hulse, "Senate Extends until 2007 Ban on Internet Access Tax," *The New York Times*, April 30, 2004, p. A12.

26. "comScore Forecasts Total E-Commerce Spending by Consumers Will Reach Approximately $170 Billion in 2006," comScore Networks, at www.comscore.com/press/release.asp?press=959, accessed June 10, 2006.

27. James Popkin and Katia Hetter, "America's Gambling Craze," *U.S. News and World Report*, March 14, 1994, p. 43.

28. To find out more about lotteries go to the Web site of the Multi-State Lottery Association at www.musl.com or the North American Association of State and Provincial Lotteries at www.naspl.org. You may find more about the history of lotteries at www.scigames.com.

29. Kathryn A. Foster, *The Political Economy of Special-Purpose Government* (Georgetown University Press, 1997); Robert L. Bland and Wes Clarke, "Budgeting for Capital Improvements," in *Handbook of Government Budgeting*, Roy T. Meyers, ed. (Jossey-Bass, 1999), pp. 653–677.

30. For a thorough discussion of issues related to intergovernmental competition in attracting business and related tax issues, see Robert L. Bland, *A Revenue Guide for Local Government* (International City Managers Association, 1989), chap. 9.

31. Charles Mahtesian, "The Stadium Trap," *Governing*, May 1998, p. 22.

32. See Mark Rosentraub, *Major League Losers: The Real Cost of Sports and Who's Paying for It* (Basic Books, 1997).

33. Sarah Lawrence and Jeremy Travis, *The New Landscape of Imprisonment: Mapping America's Prison Expansion* (Urban Institute, 2004), p. 14; Bureau of Justice Statistics, "The Nations Prison Population Continues its Slow Growth," *Press Release*, October 25, 2005.

34. See "Grading the States, 2001," *Governing*, February 2001.

Epilogue

1. Thucydides, *History of the Peloponnesian War*, trans. Benjamin Jowett (Prometheus Books, 1998).

2. Edith Hamilton, *The Echo of Greece* (Norton, 1957), p. 47.

3. The White House, at www.whitehouse.gov/news/releases/2001/09/20010911-16.html.

4. For a book advocating more direct democracy, see Ted Becker and Christa Daryl Slaton, *The Future of Teledemocracy* (Praeger, 2000); for a contrary view, see Richard J. Ellis, *Democratic Delusions: The Initiative Process in America* (University Press of Kansas, 2002).

5. For an extensive list of countries that use some form of proportional representation, see debianista.org/pr.html.

6. For more on the relationship between electoral institutions and party systems, see Maurice Duverger, *Political Parties: Their Organization and Activity in the Modern State* (Wiley, 1954).

7. *Lawrence* v. *Texas*, 539 U.S. 558 (2003).

8. The Campaign Legal Center, at www.campaignlegalcenter.org/BCRA.html; *McConnell* v. *FEC*, 124 S.CT. 619 (2003).

9. Bruce Bimber and Richard Davis, *Campaigning Online: The Internet in U.S. Elections* (Oxford University Press, 2003).

10. John F. Kennedy, *Profiles in Courage* (Pocket Books, 1956), p. 108.

11. Harry S Truman, impromptu remarks before the Reciprocity Club, Washington, D.C., April 11, 1958, as reported by the *New York World-Telegram*, April 12, 1958, p. 4. Found at www.bartleby.com/73/1405.html.

12. These three books will give you insight into the life of a politician: Bill Bradley, *Time Present, Time Past: A Memoir* (Knopf 1996); Warren B. Rudman, *Combat: Twelve Years in the U.S. Senate* (Random House, 1996); Mark Hatfield, *Against the Grain: Reflections of a Rebel Republican* (White Cloud Press, 2001).

13. For a contrary view of Madison's presidency, see Gary Rosen, *American Compact: James Madison and the Problem of the Founding* (University Press of Kansas, 1999).

14. Judy Wilgoren, "Dean Spares No Opponent as He Sprints Across Iowa," *The New York Times*, October 15, 2003, p. A17.

15. Richard F. Fenno Jr., *Home Style: House Members in Their Districts* (Little, Brown and Company, 1978), pp. 162–169.

16. See Lawrence R. Jacobs and Robert Y. Shapiro, *Politicians Don't Pander* (University of Chicago Press, 2000); Christopher Beem, *The Necessity of Politics* (University of Chicago Press, 1999); and John E. McDonough, *Experiencing Politics* (University of California Press, 2000).

17. See Kareem Abdul-Jabar and Alan Steinberg, *Black Profiles in Courage* (Morrow, 1996).

18. Reinhold Niebuhr, *The Children of Light and the Children of Darkness* (Scribner, 1944), p. xi.

19. See Bernard Crick, *In Defense of Politics*, rev. ed. (Pelican Books, 1983); and Stimson Bullitt, *To Be a Politician*, rev. ed. (Yale University Press, 1977).

20. See Benjamin R. Barber, *A Passion for Democracy* (Princeton University Press, 1998).

21. See Nat Hentoff, *Free Speech for Me—but Not for Thee: How the American Left and Right Relentlessly Censor Each Other* (Harper Perennial, 1993).

22. William J. Brennan, commencement address, Brandeis University, May 18, 1986.

23. Arthur M. Schlesinger Jr., *The Disuniting of America* (Norton, 1993), p. 134.

24. John W. Gardner, *Self-Renewal*, rev. ed. (Norton, 1981), p. xiv.

Photo Credits

Index

About the Authors

David B. Magleby

David B. Magleby is nationally recognized for his expertise on direct democracy, voting behavior, and campaign finance. He is dean as well as Professor of Political Science at Brigham Young University and has taught at the University of California, Santa Cruz, and the University of Virginia. His writings include *Direct Legislation* (1984), *The Money Chase* (1990), and *Myth of the Independent Voter* (1992), and he is editor of *Financing the 2000 Election* (2002) and co-editor of *The Last Hurrah? Soft Money and Issue Advocacy in the 2002 Congressional Elections* (2004). He was president of Pi Sigma Alpha, the national political science honor society, has received numerous teaching awards, and was a Fulbright Scholar at Nuffield College, Oxford University.

David M. O'Brien

David M. O'Brien is the Leone Reaves and George W. Spicer Professor at the University of Virginia. He was a Judicial Fellow and Research Associate at the Supreme Court of the United States, a Fulbright Lecturer at Oxford University, held the Fulbright Chair for Senior Scholars at the University of Bologna, and a Fulbright Researcher in Japan, as well as a Visiting Fellow at the Russell Sage Foundation. Among his publications are *Storm Center: The Supreme Court in American Politics*, 6th ed. (2005); a two volume casebook, *Constitutional Law and Politics*, 5th ed. (2005); an annual *Supreme Court Watch;* and *Animal Sacrifice and Religious Freedom: Church of Lukumi Babablu Aye* v. *City of Hialeah* (2004). He received the American Bar Association's Silver Gavel Award for contributing to the public's understanding of the law.

Paul C. Light

Paul C. Light is currently the Paulette Goddard Professor of Public Service at New York University's Wagner School of Public Service and Douglas Dillon Senior Fellow at the Brookings Institution. Professor Light has a wide-ranging career in both academia and government. He has worked on Capitol Hill as a senior committee staffer in the U.S. Senate and as an American Political Science Association Congressional Fellow in the U.S. House. He has taught at the University of Virginia, University of Pennsylvania, and Harvard University's John F. Kennedy School of Government. He has also served as a senior adviser to several national commissions on federal, state, and local public service. He is the author of 15 books on government, public service, and public policy.

J.W. Peltason

J.W. Peltason is a leading scholar on the judicial process and public law. He is Professor Emeritus of Political Science at the University of California, Irvine. As past president of the American Council on Education, Peltason has represented higher education before Congress and state legislatures. His writings include *Federal Courts in the Political Process* (1955), *Fifty-Eight Lonely Men: Southern Federal Judges and School Desegregation* (1961), and with Sue Davis, *Understanding the Constitution* (2000). Among his awards are the James Madison Medal from Princeton University, the Irvine Medal from the University of California, Irvine, and the American Political Science Association's Charles E. Merriam Award.

Thomas E. Cronin

Thomas E. Cronin is a leading student of the American presidency, leadership, and policy-making processes. He was a White House Fellow and a White House aide and has served as president of the Western Political Science Association. His writings include *The State of the Presidency* (1980), *U.S. v. Crime in the Streets* (1981), *Direct Democracy: The Politics of Initiative, Referendum, and Recall* (1989), *Colorado Politics and Government* (1993), and *The Paradoxes of the American Presidency* (1998). Cronin is a past recipient of the American Political Science Association's Charles E. Merriam Award.